The Cambridge History of
Literary Criticism

VOLUME 2

The Middle Ages

This is the first-ever history of the literary theory and criticism produced during the Middle Ages that covers all the main traditions in Latin, the major European vernaculars, and Byzantine Greek. Starting with sections on the rich array of materials found within the study of grammar and the formal 'arts' of poetry, letter-writing and preaching, it proceeds to offer a full description of the Latin commentary tradition on classical and classicising literature, followed by explanations of medieval views on literary imagination and memory, and the ways in which certain texts were believed to achieve moral profit through pleasure. The remainder of the volume, and its largest part, is taken up with accounts of the diverse theoretical and critical traditions which developed in the vernacular languages, ranging from Medieval Irish to Old Norse, Occitan to Middle High German. Since many of the most significant developments occurred in Italy, a series of chapters is devoted to the contributions made by Dante and the commentators on his *Commedia*, the debates on Latin versus vernacular, and humanist views on poetry and prose. Finally the volume moves from the Latin West to Greek Byzantium, to review the attitudes held there concerning literature and its various uses.

The Cambridge History of
Literary Criticism

FOUNDING EDITORS
Professor H. B. Nisbet
University of Cambridge
Professor Claude Rawson
Yale University

The Cambridge History of Literary Criticism provides a comprehensive historical account of Western literary criticism from classical Antiquity to the present day, dealing with both literary theory and critical practice. The *History* is intended as an authoritative work of reference and exposition, but more than a mere chronicle of facts. While remaining broadly non-partisan it will, where appropriate, address controversial issues of current critical debate without evasion or false pretences of neutrality. Each volume is a self-contained unit designed to be used independently as well as in conjunction with the others in the series. Substantial bibliographical material in each volume provides a foundation for further study of the subjects in question.

VOLUMES PUBLISHED
Volume 1: *Classical Criticism*, edited by George A. Kennedy
Volume 2: *The Middle Ages*, edited by Alastair Minnis and Ian Johnson
Volume 3: *The Renaissance*, edited by Glyn P. Norton
Volume 4: *The Eighteenth Century*, edited by H. B. Nisbet and Claude Rawson
Volume 5: *Romanticism*, edited by Marshall Brown
Volume 7: *Modernism and the New Criticism*, edited by A. Walton Litz, Louis Menand and Lawrence Rainey
Volume 8: *From Formalism to Post-Structuralism*, edited by Raman Selden
Volume 9: *Twentieth-Century Historical, Philosophical and Psychological Perspectives*, edited by Christa Knellwolf and Christopher Norris

VOLUMES IN PREPARATION
Volume 6: *The Nineteenth Century*, edited by M. A. R. Habib

The Cambridge History of
Literary Criticism

VOLUME 2
The Middle Ages

Edited by

ALASTAIR MINNIS AND IAN JOHNSON

CAMBRIDGE
UNIVERSITY PRESS

CAMBRIDGE UNIVERSITY PRESS
Cambridge, New York, Melbourne, Madrid, Cape Town, Singapore, São Paulo

Cambridge University Press
The Edinburgh Building, Cambridge CB2 2RU, UK

Published in the United States of America by Cambridge University Press, New York

www.cambridge.org
Information on this title: www.cambridge.org/9780521300070

© Cambridge University Press 2005

First published 2005

Printed in the United Kingdom at the University Press, Cambridge

A catalogue record for this book is available from the British Library

Library of Congress Cataloguing in Publication data

ISBN-13 978-0-521-30007-0 hardback
ISBN-10 0-521-30007-X hardback

Contents

Contributors

Zygmunt Barański, Serena Professor of Italian in the University of Cambridge and Fellow of New Hall, has published extensively on Dante, medieval poetics, fourteenth-century Italian literature, and modern Italian literature and culture. He is editor of the interdisciplinary journal *The Italianist*.

Steven Botterill is Associate Professor of Italian Studies and Associate Dean of the Undergraduate Division at the University of California, Berkeley. He is the author of *Dante and the Mystical Tradition: Bernard of Clairvaux in the 'Commedia'* (1994), of an edition and translation of Dante's *De vulgari eloquentia* (1996), and of numerous articles on Dante and other medieval topics. Appointed editor-in-chief of *Dante Studies* in 2003, he is currently working on a book to be called *Dante and the Language of Community*.

Kevin Brownlee is Professor of Romance Languages at the University of Pennsylvania, where he teaches medieval French and Italian literature, and is Graduate Chair of Italian. He is the author of *Poetic Identity in Guillaume de Machaut* (1984) and *Discourses of the Self in Christine de Pizan* (forthcoming), as well as numerous articles on Dante; currently he is working on a study of Jean de Meun's *Roman de la Rose*. His most recent co-edited volume is *Generation and Regeneration: Tropes of Reproduction* (2001).

Margaret Clunies Ross is McCaughey Professor of English Language and Early English Literature at the University of Sydney. Among her most recent publications are *Prolonged Echoes: Old Norse Myths in Medieval Northern Society* (2 vols., 1994 and 1998), *The Norse Muse in Britain, 1750–1820* (1998), and *Old Icelandic Literature and Society* (2000). She is one of five general editors of a new edition of the corpus of Old Norse skaldic poetry and has a new book, *A History of Old Norse Poetry and Poetics* (Boydell & Brewer, forthcoming).

Thomas M. Conley, Professor of Speech Communication, the Classics, and Medieval Studies at The University of Illinois, Urbana-Champaign, is the author of numerous studies on Byzantine rhetoric and culture, including 'Practice to Theory: Byzantine "Poetrics"' and *Byzantine Culture in Renaissance and Baroque Poland* (1994).

John L. Flood is Emeritus Professor of German in the University of London. He has published widely in such fields as the history of the German language, medieval and early modern German literature, the history of the book, and the history of medicine. His books include *Die Historie von Herzog Ernst* (1991), *The German Book 1450–1750* (1995), *Johannes Sinapius (1505–1560), Hellenist and Physician in Germany and Italy* (1997), and he is currently preparing a bio-bibliographical handbook on Poets Laureate in the Holy Roman Empire.

Simon Gaunt is Professor of French Language and Literature at King's College London, is the author of *Troubadours and Irony* (1989), *Gender and Genre in Medieval French Literature* (1995) and *Retelling the Tale: An Introduction to Medieval French Literature* (2001). He is also co-editor of *The Troubadours: An Introduction* (1999, with Sarah Kay) and of *Marcabru: A Critical Edition* (2000, with Ruth Harvey and Linda Paterson). Currently he is working on a study of love and death in medieval literature.

Vincent Gillespie is J. R. R. Tolkien Professor of Medieval English Literature and Language at the University of Oxford and a Fellow of Lady Margaret Hall. His publications include an edition of the late-medieval library catalogue of Syon Abbey (2001), studies of devotional writing in England, essays on the problems of mystical language, and explorations of the history of the book in medieval England.

Ralph Hanna is Professor of Palaeography in the University of Oxford, and Tutorial Fellow in English at Keble College. He has published widely on Middle English texts and their manuscripts, especially on the relation of Latinate and vernacular cultures in the fourteenth century.

Marged Haycock, Reader in Welsh Language and Literature in the University of Wales, Aberystwyth, is the author of *Blodeugerdd Barddas o Ganu Crefyddol Cynnar* (1994) and co-editor of *Cyfoeth y Testun* (2003), a volume of textual criticism in memory of J. E. Caerwyn Williams. She is preparing a study and edition of the poems in the Book of Taliesin.

Tony Hunt, a Fellow of the British Academy and Besse Fellow in French, St Peter's College, Oxford, was formerly a British Academy Research Reader and Visiting Professor of Mediaeval Studies at Westfield College, London. He has published widely on Chrétien de Troyes, Medieval Latin, Anglo-Norman and vernacular medicine, as well as a monograph on Villon.

Martin Irvine is the Founding Director of the Communication, Culture, and Technology Program at Georgetown University, where he is also an Associate Professor. He has published on medieval literary theory and *grammatica*, semiotics, Abelard and Heloise and gender theory, and on the Internet and Web technology in higher education. Current interests include media theory and contemporary visual culture.

Ian Johnson is Senior Lecturer in English at the University of St Andrews, where he has taught since 1985, and General Editor of *Forum for Modern Language Studies*. He has published widely on medieval literary thought and translation, versions of Boethius, and gender. Currently, he is working on academic literary discourse in relation to the Middle English Lives of Christ.

Ananya Jahanara Kabir is a Lecturer in the School of English, University of Leeds. Her publications include a monograph, *Paradise, Death and Doomsday in Anglo-Saxon Literature* (2001), a co-edited collection of essays, *Postcolonial Approaches to the European Middle Ages* (2004), and articles on textuality, transmission and reception of medieval culture. Current research involves the overlap between the medieval, the postmodern and the postcolonial, and the relationship between medievalism and British imperialism.

Ron Keightley was Professor of Spanish at Monash University (Melbourne), 1972–92. He has published several articles on medieval and Renaissance narrative, and on translations of and commentaries on Boethius and Eusebius, in Spanish and Catalan, in addition to material on Latin American Literature. Currently he is working on a database for the Benedictine monastery at New Norcia (Western Australia), covering the period from 1855 to 1880.

John Marshall is Emeritus Professor of Romance Philology in the University of London (Westfield College). His publications include editions such as *The Razos de trobar of Rainan Vidal and Associated Texts* (1972) and *The Donatz Proensals of Uc Faidit* (1969) as well as numerous articles on medieval Occitan poetics, grammar and literature and on Old French literature.

Martin McLaughlin, Fiat-Serena Professor of Italian Studies and Fellow of Magdalen College, Oxford, is the author of *Literary Imitation in the Italian Renaissance* (1995), *Italo Calvino* (1998), has edited *Britain and Italy from Romanticism to Modernism* (2000), and translated Italo Calvino's essays, *Why Read the Classics?* (1999). He was General Editor of *The Modern Language Review* (2002–3), and is currently working on a study of Leon Battista Alberti.

Alastair Minnis is a Humanities Distinguished Professor at Ohio State University, having previously taught at the Universities of York and Bristol and at Queen's University, Belfast. He is the author of, among other works, *Medieval Theory of Authorship: Scholastic Literary Attitudes in the Later Middle Ages* (1984), editor, with A. B. Scott, of *Medieval Literary Theory and Criticism c. 1100–c. 1375: The Commentary Tradition* (1988), and General Editor of *Cambridge Studies in Medieval Literature*.

James J. Murphy, Professor Emeritus of English and Professor Emeritus of Rhetoric and Communications at the University of California at Davis, is the author or editor of eighteen books, including *Rhetoric in the Middle Ages* (1974, 2001), *Medieval Eloquence* (1978), *Renaissance Eloquence* (1983), *A Synoptic History of Classical Rhetoric* (1995) and *A Short History of Writing Instruction* (2001). He is currently working on a history of rhetoric in the fifteenth century, with emphasis on the movement from manuscript to print.

Glending Olson is Professor Emeritus and former Chair of the Department of English at Cleveland State University. He has published *Literature as Recreation in the Later Middle Ages* (1982) and co-edited, with V. A. Kolve, *The Canterbury Tales: Nine Tales and the General Prologue* (1989). He has held fellowships from the National Endowment for the Humanities and the Guggenheim Foundation.

Nigel F. Palmer is Professor of Medieval German Studies at the University of Oxford. He is the author of numerous studies on Medieval German literature and culture, and has a particular interest in the fields of codicology, late-medieval prose, and the literature of the Cistercian order. His most recent books are a study of the library of the abbey of Eberbach, Rheingau (1998) and an edition of the Fifteen Signs before the Last Judgement in German (2002).

Erich Poppe is Professor of Celtic Studies and General Linguistics at the Philipps-Universität Marburg. He is the author of *The Irish Aeneid: The Classical Epic from an Irish Perspective* (1995) and articles on Medieval Irish and Welsh literature and language, as well as co-editor of *The Legend of Mary of Egypt in Medieval Insular Hagiography* (1996) and *Übersetzung, Adaptation und Akkultiration im insularen Mittelalter* (1999).

David Robey is Professor of Italian at the University of Reading and Emeritus Fellow of Wolfson College, Oxford. He has published on fifteenth-century humanism (educational and poetic theory), language and style in Dante and Renaissance narrative poetry, the computer analysis of literature, and modern critical theory, and was joint editor of The *Oxford Companion to Italian Literature*. He is author of a computer-based study on Sound and Structure in Dante's *Divine Comedy*, and is currently extending this work to include the major narrative poems of the Italian Renaissance.

Patrick Sims-Williams is Professor of Celtic Studies in the University of Wales, Aberystwyth. His publications include *Religion and Literature in Western England, 600–800* (1990), *Britain and Early Christian Europe* (1995), and *The Celtic Inscriptions of Britain: Phonology and Chronology, c. 400–1200* (2003), and he is the editor of *Cambrian Medieval Celtic Studies*. Currently he is working on ancient Celtic place- and personal names and on medieval literary connections between Ireland and Britain.

David Thomson is Archdeacon of Carlisle. His publications include *A Descriptive Catalogue of Middle English Grammatical Texts* (1979) and *An Edition of the Middle English Grammatical Texts* (1984).

Julian Weiss is Reader in Medieval and Early Modern Spanish Literature in the Department of Spanish and Spanish American Studies, King's College London. His publications include *The Poet's Art: Literary Theory in Castile, c. 1400–60* (1990) and *Poetry at Court in Trastamaran Spain: From the 'Cancionero de Baena' to the 'Cancionero general'* (1998, co-edited with E. M. Gerli).

Siegfried Wenzel, Professor Emeritus of English at the University of Pennsylvania, has published *The Sin of Sloth: Acedia in Medieval Thought and Literature* (1967), *Verses in Sermons: 'Fasciculus Morum' and its Middle English Poems* (1978), *Summa virtutum de remediis anime* (1984), *Preachers, Poets, and the Early English Lyric* (1986), *'Fasciculus Morum':*

A Fourteenth-Century Preacher's Handbook (1989) and *Macaronic Sermons: Bilingualism and Preaching in Late Medieval England* (1994). Currently he is completing a survey and study of Latin sermon collections from England, 1350–1450.

Winthrop Wetherbee is Avalon Foundation Professor in the Humanities at Cornell University. His publications include a translation of Bernard Silvester's *Cosmographia* (1973, 1990), an edition and translation of Johannes de Hauvilla's *Architrenius*, a monograph on Chaucer's *Troilus and Criseyde* (1984), and an introduction to the *Canterbury Tales* (1989).

Gruffydd Aled Williams is Professor of Welsh at the University of Wales, Aberystwyth. He is the author of *Ymryson Edmwnd Prys a Wiliam Cynwal* (1986), has contributed to published editions of twelfth- and thirteenth-century Welsh poetry, and has published many articles on medieval and Renaissance Welsh literature. He is Editor of *Llên Cymru*.

Ronald G. Witt is William B. Hamilton Professor of History at Duke University. He is the author of *Coluccio Salutati and his Public Letters* (1976), *Hercules at the Crossroads: The Life, Work, and Thought of Coluccio Salutati* (1983), and *'In the Footsteps of the Ancients': The Origins of Italian Humanism from Lovato to Bruni* (2000). He has just completed a book on Latin culture in Italy from 800 to 1250 entitled *The Italian Difference: The Two Cultures of Medieval Italy*.

Abbreviations

AGr	*Anecdota graeca,* ed. J. Boissonade (4 vols., Paris, 1829–32).
AGrO	*Anecdota graeca oxoniensia,* ed. J. Cramer (4 vols., Oxford, 1835–7).
AHDLMA	*Archives d'histoire doctrinale et littéraire du Moyen Âge*
ANTS	Anglo-Norman Texts Society
BGPM	Beiträge zur Geschichte der Philosophie des Mittelalters
CCCM	Corpus Christianorum, continuatio medievalis
CCSL	Corpus Christianorum, series latina
CFHB	*Corpus fontium historiae Byzantinae*
CHLMP	*The Cambridge History of Later Medieval Philosophy*
ChR	*The Chaucer Review*
CIBN	Bibliothèque nationale, *Catalogue des incunables* 1– (Paris 1981–)
CIMAGL	*Cahiers de l'Institut du moyen âge grec et latin*
CP	*Classical Philology*
CSEL	Corpus scriptorum ecclesiasticorum latinorum
EETS ES	Early English Text Society, Extra Series
EETS OS	Early English Text Society, Original Series
EETS SS	Early English Text Society, Supplementary Series
FRB	*Fontes rerum byzantinarum,* ed. V. Regel and N. Novasadskij (1892–1917; rpt. Leipzig, 1982).
GL	*Grammatici latini,* ed. H. Keil (8 vols, Leipzig, 1857–80)
GW	*Gesamtkatalog der Wiegendrucke* (7 vols., Leipzig 1925–38); 8– (Stuttgart, 1978–).
Hist. ling.	*Historiographia linguistica*
HTR	*Harvard Theological Review*
JEGP	*Journal of English and Germanic Philology*
MÆ	*Medium Ævum*

MB	*Mesaiônikê bibliothekê*, ed. K. Sathas (7 vols., Venice, 1872–94).
MF	*Des Minnesangs Frühling, I: Texte*, 38th rev. edn., ed. H. Moser and H. Tervooren (Stuttgart, 1988).
MGH	Monumenta germaniae historica
MGH AA	Monumenta germaniae historica, auctores antiquissimi
M&H	*Medievalia et humanistica*
MLN	*Modern Language Notes*
MLQ	*Modern Language Quarterly*
MLR	*Modern Language Review*
MP	*Modern Philology*
MS	*Mediaeval Studies*
Notices et extraits	*Notices et extraits des manuscrits de la Bibliothèque nationale*
PBB	*Beiträge zur Geschichte der deutschen Sprache und Literatur* (Tübingen).
PG	*Patrologia cursus completus, series graeca*, ed. J.-P. Migne (161 vols., Paris, 1844–66).
PL	*Patrologia cursus completus, series latina*, ed. J.-P. Migne (217 vols. and 4 vols. of tables, Paris, 1841–64).
PMLA	*Publications of the Modern Language Association of America*
PS	*Prolegomenôn syllogê*, ed. H. Rabe (Leipzig, 1935).
Reg. patr.	*Les regestes des actes du patriarchat de Constantinople*, vol. 1: *Les actes des patriarches*, ed. V. Grumel (Paris, 1932–47).
RG	*Rhetores graeci*, ed. C. Walz (9 vols., 1832–6; rpt. Osnabrück, 1968).
RP	*Romance Philology*
RR	*Romanic Review*
RTAM	*Recherches de théologie ancienne et médiévale*
SAC	*Studies in the Age of Chaucer*
SATF	Société des anciens textes français
SMC	*Studies in Medieval Culture*
SP	*Studies in Philology*
StLV	*Bibliothek des Litterarischen Vereins in Stuttgart*
TAPA	*Transactions of the American Philological Association*
TSL	*Tennessee Studies in Literature*

Acknowledgements

On the completion of the present book, which has taken many years to grow into its state of completion, the editors wish to extend their warmest thanks both to those longstanding contributors who in the early stages laid its foundation by producing chapters and materials for comment and compilation, and to those who joined the team of contributors quite recently and filled in major gaps in its coverage. Winthrop Wetherbee, the author of Chapter 5, wishes to acknowledge the original contribution of the late Judson Boyce Allen, who was to have been his collaborator in chronicling the medieval study of classical authors. We can only regret that Professor Allen was unable to set his own hand to a task for which he was so uniquely qualified.

The editors are grateful to Oxford University Press for permission to publish extracts from A. J. Minnis and A. B. Scott with D. Wallace (eds.), *Medieval Literary Theory and Criticism, c. 1100–c. 1375: The Commentary-Tradition* (1988; rev. edn, 1991, rpt. 2001), and to Indiana University Press for permission to publish a passage from Guido delle Colonne, *Historia destructionis Troiae*, translated by M. E. Meek (1974). We owe a special debt to James Simpson for early work, material and suggestions concerning Chapter 15. David Robey's chapter (Chapter 24) is a revised version of an earlier article, 'Humanist Views on the Study of Poetry in the Early Italian Renaissance', *History of Education*, 13 (1984), 7–25. It is reprinted here by kind permission of the journal's editor. The contribution of the founding editors of the *Cambridge History of Literary Criticism*, H. B. Nisbet and Claude Rawson, in helping to specify and approve the shape of this volume, and in advising on preliminary synopses of the contributions, is warmly acknowledged.

Alastair Minnis
Ian Johnson

Introduction

Alastair Minnis and Ian Johnson

This is the first general history of medieval literary theory and criticism.
It has been achieved through a long process of selection and compromise.
When the project originally was conceived, we did not know (we could
not have known then) what quantity and quality of materials awaited
us, what would happen when scholars from a wide range of disciplines,
segregated within the modern academy, would come together and pool
their expertise – and, indeed, be encouraged to work on materials which
had hitherto been ignored, or unexplored from the perspective of literary
theory and criticism.

For a long time this subject has suffered from a refusal to believe in its
very existence. George Saintsbury, in his *History of Criticism and Literary
Taste in Europe* (1900–4), declared that 'the Middle Ages were . . . certainly not Ages of Criticism'; 'their very essence was opposed to criticism
in any prevalence' (I, p. 373). Writing some forty years later, in his *English
Literary Criticism: The Medieval Phase*, J. W. H. Atkins challenged Saintsbury's claim, yet supposed that the period was 'one of confused thinking
in literary matters' (p. 3). The 1957 short history of literary criticism by
W. K. Wimsatt and Cleanth Brooks felt obliged to seek aesthetic, rather
than distinctively literary, theory in the Middle Ages, and came away disappointed that 'no new theory of beauty, of fine art in general, or of poetry'
is offered by St Thomas Aquinas or 'other theologians of the high Middle
Ages' (p. 126). Giovanni Boccaccio's account of poetics in his *Genealogy of the Gentile Gods* is, however, given honourable mention. Charles
Osgood had performed a major service to the history of literary criticism
by publishing in 1930 a translation of substantial extracts from that
treatise; this challenged the tendency to see Dante as the single oasis of theoretical sophistication in a cultural desert (Saintsbury had characterised
him as the 'one mighty figure' who passes on 'the torch from Aristotle
and Longinus, through unknowing ages, to Coleridge and Sainte-Beuve';
p. 3). Hazard Adams' attractive anthology of critical texts, *Critical Theory
since Plato* (1971), includes extracts from Aquinas, Dante and Boccaccio.
Far more radically, the 1974 collection *Classical and Medieval Literary
Criticism: Translations and Interpretations*, which O. B. Hardison compiled in collaboration with A. Preminger and K. Kerrane, attempted to

lay to rest the myth that the Middle Ages were ignorant of Aristotle's
Poetics by including the first modern English translation of Hermann the
German's Latin rendering of Averroes' Arabic commentated version. This
was the dominant interpretation of the *Poetics* for over four centuries,
Hardison asserted, until Ludovico Castelvetro published his treatise in
1570. (Subsequently, the extent of the influence of the Averroistic *Poetics*
has been questioned, but there is no doubt that it found a readership in the
thirteenth-century University of Paris, and it stands as a striking example
of the medieval acculturation of a classical text.)

The seminal articles by G. Przychocki (1911), E. A. Quain (1945) and
R. W. Hunt (1948) on the *accessus ad auctores*, school prolegomena to
the prescribed trivium texts wherein major critical issues are raised, did
not impinge significantly, if at all, on the writers of general histories or the
anthologists; the same was largely true of R. B. C. Huygens' editions of a
selection of *accessus* (1954) and Conrad of Hirsau's *Dialogus super auctores* (1955). But substantial work was being done on medieval rhetoric;
R. McKeon's inspirational 1952 article is a foundation stone of the subject, while in the 1970s J. J. Murphy published a landmark history of
medieval rhetoric, a translation of three rhetorical arts (representing the
arts of poetry, preaching and letter-writing), and a collection of essays
on medieval eloquence. Brian Stock and Winthrop Wetherbee anticipated
later approaches to the subject with their studies (both published in 1972)
of the Neoplatonic literary theory associated with the so-called 'School
of Chartres'. However, vestiges of the 'Saintsbury view' persisted, and
continue to persist. 'The Middle Ages . . . were not in fact ages of literary theory or criticism . . . It was an age of theological thinking in
a theologically oriented and theocratic society. Such a society does not
characteristically promote the essentially humanistic activity of literary
criticism . . .'. Thus wrote Wimsatt and Brooks in 1957 (p. 154). As
late as 1995, Peter Barry managed to avoid any mention of the Middle
Ages, leaping from the *Poetics* of Aristotle – deemed to be 'the earliest
work of theory' – to *The Apology for Poetry* of Sir Philip Sidney, who
is termed 'the first prestigious name in English writing about literature'
(pp. 21–2).[1] All kinds of questions are begged here. How transhistorical
are terms like 'literature', 'theory' and 'criticism', and is 'literary criticism'
(whatever that means) really an 'essentially humanistic' (whatever that
means) activity? Furthermore, is 'theological thinking' essentially antithetical to 'literary criticism'?

---

[1] The chapter on 'Literary Theory in the Middle Ages' in Richard Harland's *Literary Theory
from Plato to Barthes* (1999) occupies a mere seven pages, and contains the assertion that
'drama disappeared from the scene until the very last phase of the Middle Ages' (p. 23).
The thriving vernacular traditions of mystery and miracle plays are thereby ignored, not
to mention the transformation of classical notions of drama at the hands of Aristotle's
Arabic interpreters.

An initial, and narrowly pragmatic, answer to most of these questions may be ventured with reference to the Cambridge University Press guidelines for the *History of Literary Criticism* of which this volume forms part. These require that attention should be paid to the 'evolution of the concept of literature', the growth of literary study within institutions, the formation and re-formation of the literary canon, the emergence and development of genres, the relationship between theory and practice, and 'continuities and relationships between different historical periods'. Given that in the Middle Ages 'literature' did not occupy a privileged space in contrast with other texts, what we have offered is, inevitably, a compromise, which seeks to address issues of a kind which other volumes in this *History* have deemed to be 'literary', while respecting the otherness of medieval textuality and the types of institution – elementary school, monastery, university, court, etc. – which provided the economic and intellectual frameworks for textual production.

Fuller answers have been offered, and are still in the process of being offered, in what has been a 'golden age' for the study of medieval literary theory and criticism, beginning in the 1980s and continuing to the present day. Substantial contributions have been made by, *inter alia*, Judson B. Allen (friars as critics, the 'ethical poetic'); Karl-Heinz Bareiss (discussions of comedy); Christopher Baswell (the interpretation and influence of Virgil in medieval England); Robert Black (Italian schooling and commentaries); Rosalind Brown-Grant (the *querelle de la Rose*); Martin Camargo (rhetorics of prose composition); Mary Carruthers (imagination and memory); Thomas Conley (Byzantine rhetoric); Rita Copeland (the relations between rhetoric and exegesis within medieval translation); John Dagenais (Juan Ruiz and the ethics of reading); Gilbert Dahan (scholastic poetics at the University of Paris); Paule Demats (*fabula* in Latin theory and French literature); Peter Dronke (twelfth-century theory of integumental fiction); Kantik Ghosh (hermeneutic theory and practice in Wycliffite and anti-Wycliffite texts); Fernando Gómez Redondo (Iberian poetics); Walter Haug (the emergence of a semi-autonomous poetics in Middle High German); Ralph Hexter (Ovid in the medieval schools); Tony Hunt (the Latin grammar textbooks used in England); Martin Irvine (*grammatica* as the central discipline concerned with literacy, language and literary interpretation); H. A. Kelly (theory of tragedy); Udo Kindermann (theory of satire); Alastair Minnis (theory of authorship; traditions of commentary on sacred and secular texts); Glending Olson (literature as recreation); Suzanne Reynolds (satire and scholastic linguistics); Bruno Sandkühler (Dante commentary); John O. Ward (Ciceronian rhetoric); Julian Weiss (Castilian literary theory); Edward Wheatley (Aesop commentary and reception); and Jocelyn Wogan-Browne with her fellow-contributors to *The Idea of the Vernacular* (Middle English literary theory). Many significant treatises and commentaries have now been edited; helpful finding-lists of texts in manuscript have been provided by such scholars as Frank T. Coulson, Birger Munk Olsen and Bruno Roy, and the ongoing *Catalogus translationum et commentariorum* (originated by Paul Kristeller in 1960) serves as a spur to continuing work on the medieval reception of classical literature.

As editors we have suffered from an embarrassment of riches, and have been obliged to be selective, particularly in view of the guidelines set by Cambridge University Press which required a single volume for the entire period from Late Antiquity until the fifteenth century. The general brief for the *History* was to produce an account of Western literary criticism which would deal with both literary theory and critical practice; such fields of knowledge as history of ideas, linguistics, philosophy and theology were deemed 'related' but not essential, to be drawn upon when necessary but not forming part of the central core of the enterprise. The main consequence of this remit has been the omission of any substantial treatment of medieval exposition of the sacred text – the Old and New Testaments and certain patristic materials – but this should not be seen as any lack of respect for the importance of scriptural commentary within medieval textual culture, and we would vigorously contest O. B. Hardison's exclusion of biblical exegesis from medieval literary criticism. No book was more assiduously studied during the Middle Ages than the Bible; no text received more careful exegesis. Indeed, certain theoretical issues achieved initial definition within medieval exposition of the sacred page, whence they passed into secular poetics (good examples being afforded in Italian theoretical discussions of the fourteenth and fifteenth centuries). Far from 'theological thinking' being essentially antithetical to 'literary criticism', on many occasions it served as a major stimulus. In any case, theologians received an educational grounding in the liberal arts (though the extent and depth varied according to time and place), and many of the analytical techniques they applied in interpreting Scripture had been acquired as their schoolteachers led them through such 'set texts' as Priscian, Ovid and Juvenal; some distinguished *artistae* went on to produce important biblical scholarship, Peter Abelard and Robert Kilwardby being two notable examples among many.

It is simply incorrect to claim, as some have supposed, that every single scriptural passage had assigned to it four distinct 'senses' or levels of meaning, i.e. the literal, the allegorical, the tropological (or moral) and the anagogical (whereby the mind is lifted up to the celestial goals of the Christian life). Some passages certainly received that treatment, but not all, and St Gregory the Great memorably warned against trying so hard to find profound meaning hidden deep in a passage that one neglected its literal sense, thereby losing that which can be apprehended without difficulty on the surface (*Moralia in Job*, dedicatory letter; PL 75, 5-16).

St Augustine, who famously took great delight in extravagant allegorisation of the Song of Song's beautiful woman with teeth 'like flocks of sheep' (4:2), nevertheless warned against taking 'literal expressions as though they were figurative', lest sound moral doctrine be set at naught (*De doctrina christiana* 2.6.7–8; 3.10.14). Furthermore, the ancient rhetorical idea that one should suit style to audience functioned powerfully in late-medieval uses of scriptural texts; a commentator could engage in rigorous literal/historical analysis of some textual crux, while a preacher (perhaps the commentator himself, performing a different function) could subject that same passage to virtuoso allegorising which moved far beyond 'the letter' – a common justification being that preaching sought to move rather than prove. The existence of various fads and fashions within exegesis should also be acknowledged. In the late thirteenth and fourteenth centuries certain textual features (metaphor, parable, fable, etc.) which hitherto had been assigned to the *sensus allegoricus sive mysticus* were deemed to be types of literal sense or in some way comprised within it; indeed, the paradoxical notion of 'double literal sense' features in the exegesis of, for example, Nicholas of Lyre, William of Nottingham and the fifteenth-century Spanish polymath Alfonso de Madrigal. Given all these relativities, it would be highly reductive to view the history of medieval biblical exegesis in terms of a perpetual confrontation between the 'allegorical' and the 'literal' senses of Scripture. In a manner of speaking, both Henri de Lubac (whose monumental *Exégèse médiévale* emphasises the continuity and continued importance of allegorical interpretation) and Beryl Smalley (in whose 'grand narrative' the literal sense triumphs as the spiritual exposition declines) were right – or, better, they saw disparate aspects of a complicated cultural situation which does not easily (if at all) lend itself to positivistic solution. The senses of Scripture were subjected to the requirements (whether real or supposed) of different audiences, and the demands of the different professionals who had to cater for those audiences. Bible scholars were fully prepared to offer one type of exegesis in one place and another type in another, bending one and the same text to take on different meanings. In many cases what mattered crucially was not whether the Bible *should* be interpreted in one way or another but rather such pragmatic considerations as the specific didactic purpose of the given interpretation and the perceived nature and needs of its target-audience. In sum, medieval exegesis was a lot more flexible and context-specific than has sometimes been allowed.

It is also incorrect to claim that at an early stage the 'fourfold' system of scriptural exegesis was applied extensively to the ancient 'fables of the poets'. On the contrary, many scholars sought to spell out the distance between the two kinds of text, as when the Martianus Capella commentary which may be the work of Bernard Silvester explains that 'allegory is a mode of discourse [*oratio*] which covers under a historical narrative a true meaning which is different from its surface meaning, as in the case of Jacob wrestling with an angel. An *integumentum*, however, is a mode of discourse which covers a true meaning under a fictitious narrative, as in the case of Orpheus' (ed. Westra, p. 24). A different hermeneutic system developed in respect of secular literature, which may be illustrated from the elaborate version found in the *Ovidius moralizatus* of Pierre Bersuire (d. 1362). The 'literal' reading is an astrological one: for instance, Mars is the hot and dry planet which governs a choleric disposition in man. Naturally, the pagan gods can be seen in terms of natural elements and processes, as when Saturn, who eats his young, is said to be all-devouring time. Historically, the gods are interpreted euhemeristically as men who, through gentile error, came to be worshipped as gods. A wide range of spiritual interpretations, in both positive and negative senses, is on offer: hence Diana may be interpreted either as the Virgin Mary or as Avarice. Bersuire justified such an array of possibilities on the grounds that they would be useful in sermons; more austere minds condemned the use of such distracting frivolities by preachers of the Word of God.

All that having been said, it must be admitted that there was some inter-action and cross-influence between the two hermeneutic systems. After all, theologians had been trained in the liberal arts, and commentary on secu-lar texts was part of their intellectual formation (as already noted), and – even more fundamentally – both secular and sacred allegorisation had roots in ancient interpretation of Homer. In the later Middle Ages there may indeed be found certain intriguing applications of one or more of the four scriptural senses to secular poetry, as in some passages of the *Ovide moralisé* and occasionally in Boccaccio's *Genealogia* and Dante-commentary. In his *Convivio* – a ground-breaking 'self-commentary' – Dante himself famously compared and contrasted the 'allegory of the poets' and the 'allegory of the theologians'. But there is scant evidence to support D. W. Robertson's claim, as made in his *Preface to Chaucer* of 1962, that the four senses of scriptural exegesis are to be sought and found in a wide range of medieval texts. Particularly telling is the fact that the early-fifteenth-century defenders of Jean de Meun's *Roman de la Rose* do not resort to it. However, for Robertson 'medieval literary theory' licenses a reading method which inevitably and invariably discloses textual skir-mishes in the age-old war between charity and cupidity. This method-ology represents a powerful appropriation of medieval exegesis for the modern interpretation of vernacular literature, but many of Robertson's readers have been unconvinced or even repelled by what they see as a kind of interpretative determinism that impoverishes the possible range of meanings available to authors of literary texts. Antipathy towards what Lee Patterson has termed the critical formation of 'Exegetics' is hardly conducive to new (much-needed) scholarship on the theological contribution to medieval literary theory and criticism.

Then again, dubious distinctions between 'humanism' and 'scholasticism' have bedevilled the subject, not least because of the assumption (as illustrated above) that 'literary criticism' requires humanistic soil in which to thrive, while by its very nature scholasticism is inimical to the 'critical spirit' (Atkins, p. 2). According to a still-tenacious grand narrative, an early flowering of humanism in the 'twelfth-century Renaissance' was stunted by the advent of thirteenth-century scholasticism, the rediscovered Aristotle having banished the poets; in the fifteenth and sixteenth centuries humanism revived, this time putting down stronger roots, and scholasticism – mocked by such innovative thinkers as Erasmus, Ramus, Vives and Valla – died away. This view is untenable for many reasons. For a start, commentaries on the Latin *auctores* continued to be produced in the thirteenth and fourteenth centuries; indeed, some of the most impressive examples date from this later period, including three major thirteenth-century commentaries on Ovid (William of Orléans' *Bursarii Ovidianorum*, John of Garland's *Integumenta Ovidii*, and the anonymous 'Vulgate' commentary on the *Metamorphoses*), the commentaries on Boethius and Seneca which Nicholas Trevet produced in the early fourteenth century, and of course the commentaries on Dante's *Commedia*, written in both Latin and Italian. The thirteenth century also saw a burgeoning of massive compilations, which collected together *auctoritates* (i.e. extracts, sententious passages) culled from the experts on every subject. Furthermore, at a time when the study of grammar had developed, in one of its main branches, into speculative analysis of the theoretical structures of language itself, theologians and scriptural exegetes were devising a comprehensive interpretative programme for examining the richly varied styles and modes to be found in the different books of the Bible, together with the diverse roles and functions, both literary and moral, believed to have been performed by the inspired but human authors of Scripture. All these arguments lend support to R. W. Southern's provocative assertion that, 'far from the humanism of the twelfth century running into the sand after about 1150 to re-emerge two centuries later, it has its fulfilment in the thirteenth and early fourteenth centuries – in the period which the humanists of the Renaissance most despised' (*Medieval Humanism*, p. 31). If it is indeed true, as Southern contends, that 'the period from about 1100 to about 1320' was 'one of the greatest ages of humanism in the history of Europe: perhaps the greatest of all', then the literary theory produced in that period may be deemed a product of humanism of a high order.

Last but certainly not least, the 'scholastic' period saw an extraordinary flourishing of vernacular literature (the *Roman de la Rose*, Dante, Juan Ruiz, Chaucer . . .), though of course the relationship between the schools and the milieux in which those works were produced is complicated and contested. It would certainly be naïve to assume that 'humanism' is essentially and invariably supportive of vernacular literature: several of the Italian humanists took Dante to task for having written in the vernacular rather than in Latin.

It may also be argued that, in respect of Latin textual culture in particular, the process of transition and change from 'medieval' to 'Renaissance' has been oversimplified and distorted. Even the most 'original' literary theory produced in late-medieval Italy takes its points of departure and many of its categories and concepts from scholastic literary theory: witness the way in which scholars like Albertino Mussato, Francesco da Fiano and Leonardo Bruni set about discussing the 'usefulness' of poetry, its place within the hierarchy of the sciences, its spiritual and moral senses, the ancient poet-theologians (or 'myth-lovers'), the styles common to both classical and scriptural writers, and so forth. To focus on one major chronological strand: the thirteenth-century Franciscan Alexander of Hales discussed theology as poetry; Albertino Mussato discussed poetry as theology; Pico della Mirandola constructed a poetic theology. We cannot appreciate the significance of any single one of these positions without some awareness of the intellectual continuum of which they formed part.

Such an approach finds ample justification in the research of modern scholars like Walter Ullmann, Paul Kristeller and Charles Trinkaus, from which it may be concluded that aspects of the Aristotelian tradition of learning continued long into the Renaissance, and in Italy scholasticism developed alongside humanism. Concetta C. Greenfield has argued that 'their relationship was dialectical, so that rather than simply opposing each other, they stimulated persistently each other's revival and growth'. The implications for poetic theory were considerable: 'Practically every scholastic statement on poetics is countered by a belligerent humanist answer and vice versa. The investigation of humanist poetics in relation to scholastic poetics casts a new light on many humanist beliefs, and it changes a number of notions traditionally held by scholars who have examined humanist poetics as an isolated growth' (pp. 11–12). We would endorse these views, while entering the caveat that such binary thinking cannot do full justice to the intellectual common ground which was shared by many thinkers who can all too easily be located on one or other side of the divide. Very often they relied on the same authorities and the same theoretical concepts, even in the act of constructing different hierarchies of the sciences and affording poetics different degrees of prestige within those intellectual structures. Neither should the foundational contribution of scholastic culture to post-medieval Europe be undervalued. As R. W. Southern said, 'a large part of the teaching of the medieval schools continued to influence the thoughts and conduct of the majority of people in western Europe on both sides of the great divide between Roman Catholic and Protestant until the twentieth century, when the long-lasting tincture of scholastic principles which had survived among the great mass of the population of western Europe began to disappear altogether' (*Scholastic Humanism*, p. 1). Here Southern is speaking of 'schools' in the most inclusive sense, rather than designating the schools of philosophy and theology in particular, though they certainly are included in his vision. His enthusiastic *apologia* affords powerful encouragement for careful consideration of 'scholastic' poetics in each and every sense of that adjective. The term 'scholastic poetics' is certainly not an oxymoron; rather it bespeaks a textual culture in which poetry both sacred and profane was frequently described as pertaining to ethics or some higher branch of science, and many schoolmen believed that theology itself was in some sense poetic, particularly in view of the fact that its procedures were different from, and transcended, those of ratiocinative logic and philosophy. Here, then, is an intellectual deposit of major substance and significance, a broad and commodious basis on which later literary thought inevitably, and creatively, built.

These are large issues, and a single-volumed history can only go so far. The present book is essentially a selective history of the literary theory and criticism relating mainly to Western secular literature in the Middle Ages, though we have drawn on religious texts at crucial moments. Beginning with the fundamental institution of the grammar school, in which children were taught the basics of Latin and introduced to the canon of classical authors (augmented with medieval 'classicising' texts of a kind believed to be suitable for young minds), we proceed to the prescriptive rhetorical arts – those 'recipe books' of textuality which showed the reader how to produce a poem, sermon or formal letter. We then focus on the medieval reception of major *auctores*, as manifest in commentary, compilation and appropriation. The volume then takes a synchronic turn, in chapters on those 'textual psychologies' which involved imagination and memory and were conducive to decorous textual pleasure and profitable entertainment. The next two sections return to a basically diachronic approach, grouping together 'early-medieval' and 'late-medieval' traditions of vernacular literary theory and criticism, whilst recognising that at least some of the 'early' traditions continued well into the 'late' period (the Irish/Gaelic and Old Norse/Icelandic traditions provide ample illustration of this); no single historicising template fits all.

The relationship between vernacular literary theory and *Latinitas* is highly complicated. Certain traditions basically transmit Latin terms and values, while others transform them; some use Latin along with their vernacular to express theoretical interests and values which had little if anything to do with Latin literary theory, while within others vernacular theoretical discourse seems to enjoy a remarkable amount of intellectual autonomy (the Occitan material being particularly rich and strange). Our ambition has been to allow vernacular discourses to speak for themselves, far more loudly than in any previous overview of the medieval contribution to the history of literary criticism. Thus we have sought to respect the diversity and distinctiveness of the respective textual cultures, while being aware of the common ground which many of them inevitably share. Treating every major national/regional unit separately would have resulted in repetitiveness and redundancy, with the same (or at least similar) literary conditions and conventions being discussed with reference to one language after another. Hence our compromise: two chapters (14 and 15) track parallel manifestations of crucial concepts in different countries, whereas others focus on particular places and times, allowing detailed investigation of their specific theoretical contributions. An entire section, comprising six chapters, has been devoted to Italian literary theory, in recognition of its exceptional contribution. Even more space could be assigned in a future history: the commentary traditions on Petrarch and on Ariosto's *Orlando furioso*, and the influence of Aristotle's Arab commentators on scholastic and humanistic poetics, await full scholarly investigation (compare p. 254 below). And finally: we travel to Byzantium, entering a world which is markedly different, but in at least some respects intriguingly familiar. If 'criticism' was understood by Byzantine readers or writers 'to have its feet in grammar, its head in rhetoric, and its eyes on moral utility' (as Thomas Conley says; p. 670 below), then most Western European readers and writers would have found little if anything to quibble with in such a claim. Furthermore, in the efforts of Byzantine scholars to preserve the Hellenic heritage in face of threats posed by the barbarous 'Latins' may be found counterpoints to the (far less precarious) hegemony of Latin over the European vernaculars in the medieval West.

Conley's chapter affords a trenchant refutation of the widespread assumption that Byzantine textual culture is marked by 'slavish imitation', 'millennial stasis, abstract judgements devoid of any individuality, and predictable homogeneity' (see p. 691 below). At the beginning of a volume which (quite rightly) affords considerable space to vernacular textual theorising, a similar caveat may be ventured against holding similar assumptions concerning the allegedly stultifying dominance of Latin within Western European textual culture, a dominance which could be escaped only through the subversive resources of some vernacular or other. Medieval Latin was not inevitably hegemonic, patriarchal, misogynistic and repressive of the local, the provincial, or the personal, though in certain contexts it could be any or all of those things – as indeed, could the vernacular. In fact, there was an abundance of 'Medieval Latins'. The Latin of the schools of philosophy and theology was markedly different from that of the neoclassical epic, satire or drama, and different again from the language of the will or of the charter, of the *historia* or of the chronicle. Canon lawyers had idioms all of their own, as did the grammarians, rhetoricians, logicians, astrologers/astronomers, medical doctors and speculative theologians, while the experts on such secular 'arts' as warfare and hunting purveyed a jargon which is bewildering to the outsider. Even within a given subject-area the amount of variation can be remarkable – familiarity with the logical schema of the theological *quaestio* is of little help in approaching, for example, the prosimetric elegance of Thomas Bradwardine's *De causa Dei* (written in proud imitation of Augustine's *De civitate Dei*) or the pellucid, image-laden style of Gertrude of Helfta, and of no help whatever in seeking to comprehend the vigorous grammar-abuse (or rhetorical innovation, if one prefers) of Richard Rolle's *Melos amoris*. Turning to the secular literary genre of the neoclassical epic, the standards of Latinity and intellectual ambitions of, say, Walter of Châtillon's *Alexandreis* and Petrarch's *Africa* are light-years apart (and had Petrarch known the relative 'audience figures' for the two texts, no doubt his own poor showing would have confirmed – if further confirmation were needed – his sense of alienation from the common herd). Then again, heresy expressed in Latin was far more potent than anything found in any vernacular – it could travel right across Europe, and infect a far greater number of people. Hence it is at once unhelpful and inaccurate to claim the vernacular as the natural repository of heresy. As one of John Wyclif's followers tartly remarked, 'there is much heresy in books of Latin, more than in English books' (cit. Hudson, *Lollards and their Books*, p. 158). In short: Latin could be seen as *the* great medieval European vernacular, with part of the secret of the language's success being its receptivity to a wide range of appropriations and idiolects.

Such a peroration in defence of the rich plurality of Latin literary culture may be forgiven, we hope, in the introduction to a volume which has treated vernacular literary theory with the seriousness it deserves. But the limits of what we have achieved must be acknowledged. With world enough and time – and a more capacious *Cambridge History of Literary Criticism*, more multicultural in orientation and less emphatically 'Western'– we could have included chapters on Islamic and Jewish traditions, and explored the relatively unknown literary-theoretical territories of the major Slavonic languages (including the forerunners of modern-day Russian, Czech and Polish), together with relevant materials produced during the 'medieval' epochs of (for instance) Egypt and South Asia. However, the present book has taken far too long to produce as it stands, and the difficulties in its production have afforded sufficient penance for its editors.

Suffice it to conclude with the frank admission that much is still to be done, including further research on the traditions that *are* represented in the chapters that follow. If the study of medieval literary theory and criticism has developed beyond its infancy (thanks largely to the efforts of those scholars listed above), it is still some way from full maturity. It may be hoped that this volume will assist the maturation process, and that future histories of literary criticism will find the medieval contribution harder to ignore or trivialise.

Part I

The liberal arts and the arts of Latin textuality

Grammatica and literary theory

Martin Irvine with David Thomson

No single medieval discipline embraced all that we call literary criticism
or theory today, but the discipline closest to literary criticism – in the
sense of the interpretation of a traditional literary canon and the description of literary language – was *grammatica*. The scope and cultural effects
of *grammatica* are large topics, embracing literacy, linguistic theory, traditions of commentary and exegesis, and the development of a literary
canon, but here we must limit the field to those aspects of *grammatica* that had a direct bearing on the practice of literary criticism and
interpretation.

 Grammatica was traditionally defined as having two main methodological divisions and subject-areas: 'the science of interpreting the poets and
other writers and the systematic principles [*ratio*] for speaking and writing
correctly',[1] that is, the methods for reading, interpreting and evaluating
literary works, especially the canon of classical poets, and the rules or
principles for speaking and writing according to normative Latin conventions. The literary division of the discipline, *scientia interpretandi*, was
understood to have four main parts or methodological divisions – *lectio*,
the principles for reading a text aloud from a manuscript, including the
rules of prosody; *enarratio*, exposition of content and the principles for
interpretation, including the analysis of figurative language; *emendatio*,
the rules for establishing textual authenticity and linguistic correctness,
and *iudicium*, criticism or evaluation of writings. In the linguistic division, the object of analysis was the language of classical literary texts, the
auctores, not ordinary speech. From its beginnings, then, *grammatica* was
a science of the text, embracing a systematic description of the authoritative textual language (Greek or Latin) and the methods for reading and
interpreting an established literary canon.

 Furthermore, *grammatica* was practised at various levels, and although
students were introduced to the discipline as children in the grammar school, the methods of reading and interpreting that were learned
through *grammatica* became the mainstay of adult literate life. Therefore

---

[1] See, *inter alia*, Diomedes, *GL* 1, 426; Maximus Victorinus, *GL* 6, 188; Alcuin, PL 101,
857; Rabanus Maurus, PL 107, 395; John of Garland, *Compendium grammatice*.

grammatica, in the medieval sense, is not to be reduced to what is found in a primer text like Donatus' *Ars grammatica*, but should be understood to include a range of literate and literary practices shared by the grammatically educated. Because of the wider range of subject-matter associated with the medieval discipline, the Latin word *grammatica*, rather than the modern term 'grammar', will be used here to designate the body of discourse and methodology practised in the Middle Ages.

The following diagram illustrates a traditional division of subject-matter and methodology of *grammatica* within the trivium or arts of discourse. Following the main divisions we have also indicated some of the products of grammatical methodology in medieval literary culture:

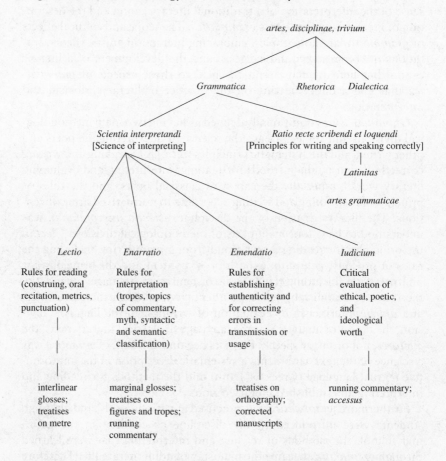

The linguistic division is exemplified by the many *artes* (handbooks or systematic guides to the discipline), chief of which were Donatus' *Ars grammatica* and Priscian's *Institutiones grammaticae*, and the literary or interpretative division by commentaries like Servius' *Commentarius in Virgilium* and the large body of glosses on the standard *auctores*. This model (and the methodology that it entailed) was perpetuated from the late-classical era to the mid-twelfth century, at which time it underwent a reconfiguration that endured to the Renaissance.

1. The history and development of *grammatica*

The history of *grammatica* from the classical era to the Renaissance can be divided into three main stages: late Roman (to the early fifth century or the age of Augustine), early medieval (to around 1150–1200), and later medieval (the era of the dominance of the universities, *c.* 1200–*c.* 1450). Throughout this long stretch of time, the kind of cultural work performed by *grammatica* remained stable in the elementary and intermediate levels of the discipline – namely that of initiating new members of *literati* into textual culture – but the aims and methods of the discipline articulated at the advanced levels of scholarly debate changed in the light of new cultural developments. The schools and intellectual capitals of the late-Roman world were succeeded by episcopal capitals and monastic and cathedral schools where the methods of the Roman discipline were applied to a revised Christian canon of texts. The late-Roman era saw the codification of an imperial *grammatica* based on a normative literary Latin and a literary canon of both classical and late-Roman *auctores*. At the close of the classical Roman era in Christian centres of textual culture, a hybrid Latinity and literary canon were formed, constructed on the foundations of imperial *grammatica* with additions from Christian texts, vocabulary and idioms. This hybridisation of *grammatica* – the late-classical base with its Christian reception and reinterpretation – provided the foundations for textual culture in the early-medieval period, when *grammatica* was defined and institutionalised in the cathedral and monastic schools, libraries and scriptoria, and major court centres of the Anglo-Saxon and Carolingian era. During this period (*c.* 700–*c.* 1100), *grammatica* was codified as a discipline defining broad cultural practices like reading, writing, literary study, poetics, biblical exegesis, and the scribal arts. *Grammatica* would retain this cultural function in many grammatical schools up to the time of its further reinterpretation during the humanist movement of the fifteenth and sixteenth centuries.

The main authorities for the development of the early-medieval model of *grammatica* were Augustine, Cassiodorus, and Isidore of Seville. Augustine (354–430) taught *grammatica* in North Africa before moving on to Rome, where he taught rhetoric, and then to Milan, where he was appointed to an official chair of rhetoric. Many of his works utilise Roman grammatical methodology, and his *De ordine, De dialectica, De magistro* and *De doctrina christiana* provided the outlines for a Christian *grammatica* that would endure to the twelfth century and beyond. Following a movement that was already underway among educated Roman Christians, Augustine transferred the whole methodology of Roman *grammatica* – the study of imperial, textual Latin and the knowledge of a set group of *auctores* – to a new canon of Christian writings. The Scriptures and Christian literature became objects of interpretation, constructed as authoritative and canonical through grammatical discourse. Augustine's *De doctrina christiana* attempts to produce a Christian encyclopaedic grammarian, equipped with knowledge of languages and rules for interpretation that would allow readers to resolve problems of interpretation in the Scriptures. Books 1–3 are an attempt at writing a Christian manual for *lectio* and *enarratio* and presuppose elementary grammatical schooling.

Cassiodorus (490–*c*. 583) had all the benefits of late-Roman education and served as an administrator and minister of culture under the Ostrogothic kings who controlled Italy in the sixth century. Later in life he founded the monastery of Vivarium, which included a major library and scriptorium, and devoted his later years to promoting Christian literary culture. His main works, the *Expositio psalmorum* and the *Institutiones divinarum et humanarum lectionum*, are thoroughly indebted to Roman imperial *grammatica* and continue to promote the model for a Christian *grammatica* which Augustine had authorised. Cassiodorus' last work, a *De orthographia*, was written for the scribes and readers in his monastery.

The writings of Isidore of Seville (602–36) represent a synthesis of Christian and Roman grammatical traditions. His *magnum opus*, the *Origines sive etymologiae* (commonly known as the *Etymologiae*), is a thoroughly grammatical work in the tradition of the late-classical polymath and encyclopaedic grammarian. In Isidore's model, *grammatica* consists of the following subject-matter:

Etymologiae 1: 'De grammatica'

1. On discipline and art.	12. On the conjunction.
2. On the seven liberal disciplines.	13. On the preposition.
3. On letters commonly used.	14. On the interjection.
4. On Latin letters.	15. On letters according to grammarians.
5. On *grammatica*.	16. On syllables.
6. On the *partes orationis*.	17. On metrical feet.
7. On the noun.	18. On accents.
8. On the pronoun.	19. On figures of accent.
9. On the verb.	20. On punctuation.
10. On the adverb.	21–6. On signs and abbreviations.
11. On the participle.	27. On orthography.

28. On analogy.	37. On tropes.
29. On etymology.	38. On prose.
30. On glosses.	39. On metres.
31. On *differentiae*.	40. On fables/fiction.
32. On barbarisms.	41. On history.
33. On solecisms.	42. On the first authors of histories.
34. On faults.	43. On the usefulness of history.
35. On metaplasms.	44. On the genres of history.
36. On schemes (figures)	

This part of the *Etymologiae* was frequently extracted for compilations of grammatical *artes*. Isidore's definitions and outline of methodology, written for use in monastic and cathedral communities, were widely disseminated in the eighth to twelfth centuries and became the core of Anglo-Saxon and Carolingian grammatical education.[2]

Grammatica came into its own institutionally in the schools, libraries and scriptoria of the Carolingian and Anglo-Saxon era. In this period, hundreds of grammatical manuscripts, compilations of both grammatical *artes* and literary *auctores*, were copied and transmitted. Schools and book production enjoyed royal patronage and support, and in the age of Charlemagne grammatical culture actually became the law of the land, enforced by mandates from Charlemagne himself. In the Anglo-Saxon world, the work of Aldhelm, Boniface, Bede, Alcuin, and Ælfric formed a Christian *grammatica* devoted to exegesis, reading, and knowledge of some of the liberal arts. Alcuin brought the broadly conceived model of *grammatica* to Charlemagne's court, and the ninth and tenth centuries are characterised by a new interest in the classical *auctores* and in further systematising grammatical doctrine. Scholars like Remigius of Auxerre (*c.* 841–*c.* 908), who wrote commentaries and glosses on a wide range of texts used in the grammar curriculum, and Abbo of Fleury (*c.* 945–1004), author of an *Ars grammatica* and leader in the monastic reform movement, consolidated the learning of the ninth-century schools and re-established the model for grammatical education that endured until the rise of the universities.

---

[2] Exactly how the classical grammatical heritage was transmitted to the monasteries of Ireland and England remains a matter of debate. It seems likely, however, that even before the death of Gregory the Great in 604, the *Ars asporii* (a Christianised edition of Donatus) was in circulation in the Columban mission. Holtz ('Irish Grammarians') would also locate the *Anonymus ad Cuimnanum*, Malsachanus, the *Ars Ambrosiana* and the mysterious Virgilius Maro Grammaticus in seventh-century Ireland or Irish centres on the Continent. The study of grammar in England had significant roots in the Irish tradition, but this is certainly not to say that it was either late or merely dependent. Well before Theodore and Hadrian arrived in Kent and gave a new impetus to Anglo-Saxon scholarship, Aldhelm (born *c.* 639 within a few years of Isidore's death), had mastered his grammar, and appears to have been familiar with, *inter alia*, Donatus, Priscian, Servius and Isidore.

In the later twelfth to fourteenth centuries, the traditional conception of the discipline was modified by the rise of logic and metaphysics in the universities, which followed the introduction of the newly translated corpus of Aristotle's works.[3] According to a commonly held but highly reductive grand narrative, the 'Battle of the Liberal Arts' (as characterised in Henri d'Andeli's oft-quoted poem) was won by dialectic: traditional, 'literary' *grammatica* lost out to Aristotelian logic and metaphysics in the schools, and the Latin authors and the form of *grammatica* based on them were dropped from university curricula. The object language, Latin, was retained but its systematic description became separated from the activity of interpreting texts. *Grammatica* was reconceived and redefined as a speculative or theoretical science and became a part of logic, the science of language and reasoning. In the universities, *grammatica* came to mean the study of the abstract features of Latin, especially syntax and semantics, as a preparation for studying logic and metaphysics. A specialised movement known as 'speculative' or modistic grammar, named from the terms of study introduced by these grammarians, emerged from the new impetus to isolate syntax and semantics as a subject of enquiry.

In the context of university study, the traditional unified divisions of the discipline split apart into three nearly independent spheres of activity: theoretical grammar, like Peter Helias' influential *Summa* on Priscian's *Institutiones* (written *c.* 1140) and works by the speculative grammarians; poetics, exemplified by works like Geoffrey of Vinsauf's *Poetria nova* (see Chapter 2 below), and commentary on the *auctores*, as practised by scholars who continued the exegetical methodology of *grammatica* like Alexander Nequam, Nicholas Trevet, and the many anonymous glossators of classical texts. Some twelfth- and thirteenth-century scholars, including Ralph of Beauvais, John of Salisbury and John of Garland, resisted the trend towards specialisation and fragmentation in the subject-areas traditionally associated with *grammatica*. Furthermore, an abundance of evidence suggests that many grammarians continued to teach and comment on the traditional *auctores* both in the grammar schools and in their own writings, even after the focus of grammatical instruction had shifted in the universities. In any case, 'speculative grammar' was a short-lived phenomenon, and most of its vestiges were swept away by the humanists, who installed what may be seen as a version of the earlier-medieval model of literary *grammatica*.

Later-medieval sources also indicate that most authorities who defined the scope of *grammatica*, or at least provided a rationale for the aims and ends of the discipline, continued to think in terms of the two complementary divisions: one linguistic and pedagogical, the other interpretative

---

[3] See Kretzmann, Kenny and Pinborg (eds.), *CHLMP*, part 2.

and literary. Honorius 'of Autun' (*fl.* 1106–35), in his treatise on the liberal arts, *De anima exsilio et patria*, likens *grammatica* and the other *artes* to cities along a highway to the lost spiritual homeland (*patria*) which is wisdom (*sapientia*). Honorius maintains the two divisions of *grammatica* in his allegory of the student-pilgrim's progress. In the city of *grammatica*, 'Donatus and Priscian teach the travellers the new language and lead the wanderers along the road to the homeland by certain rules', and this city has various dwellings – the works of the poets (*libri poetarum*), which are divided into the four main genres (tragedy, comedy, satire, lyric; PL 172, 1243). In his *De grammatica*, Hugh of St Victor (d. 1142) defines *grammatica* as 'the science of discoursing correctly [*recte loquendi*] according to the principles of liberal letters', and he presupposes the literary divisions of study in his treatise, which is largely based on Isidore and Donatus (*Opera propaedeutica, De grammatica*, ed. Baron, p. 76).

Hugh's *Didascalicon*, a guide to learning written in the late 1120s, appears to reduce *grammatica* to its linguistic division as a part of logic, but the traditional literary and interpretative methodology of the discipline is dispersed and redistributed throughout the whole work (e.g. 1.11, 2.28–9, 3.4–9, and 6). Hugh's work discloses that the impetus to classify the arts of discourse according to their abstract functions was in conflict with the need to preserve the textual methodology of *grammatica*. At the moment when the literary and interpretative divisions of *grammatica* appeared to be defined out of existence, the literary methodology was simply relabelled and repositioned within the overall model of the disciplines. For Hugh, writing under the influence of the new logic, the literary division of *grammatica* was either simply presupposed as needing no further treatment (2.29) or merged with larger questions of reading and interpretation (3.4, 8–9).

Ralph of Beauvais (*fl. c.* 1140–80), who was born in England and studied with Peter Abelard in Paris, also offers an interesting blend of the old and the new. He wrote a work in the tradition of literary-exegetical grammar, the *Liber Tytan*, and a commentary on Donatus, *Glose super Donatum*, that reflects the new interest in speculative grammar.[4] *Grammatica* is classified under logic but the function (*intentio*) of *grammatica* is defined as, 'to teach writing correctly and reciting what is written correctly' (*docere recte scribere et scripta recte pronunciare*), this being a version of the old definition of *lectio* (ed. Kneepkens, p. 2).

A much stronger case for keeping the literary *auctores* and poetics within the province of *grammatica* was made in the *Metalogicon* of John

---

[4] See Hunt, 'Studies on Priscian, II', and Ralph of Beauvais, *Glose super Donatum*, ed. Kneepkens, pp. xvii–xxxi.

of Salisbury (*c.* 1115–80). This may be considered here in some detail, as one of the most powerful twelfth-century defences of the arts of discourse. In John's view, the stakes were high: either *grammatica* retained the study of poetry, or poetics would be eliminated from the course of the liberal arts.

John of Salisbury's model for grammatical studies

John promoted a model of the trivium based on a synthesis of traditional and new methodology: he renewed the conception of *grammatica* as an adult discipline embracing skill in Latin and knowledge of the literary *auctores*, the model he learned from William of Conches (*c.* 1080–*c.* 1154) and Bernard of Chartres (d. *c.* 1130), and he also promoted the new interest in logic and disputation, which he learned from Abelard and other Parisian teachers. Book 1 of the *Metalogicon* provides the rationale for grammatical studies and Books 2–4 concern logic and dialectic. The title of the work means 'a discourse on logic', 'logic' here having the broad sense of matters pertaining to 'logos' – the arts of discourse, the fusion of reason and eloquence – and John argues for renewing the ideal union of reason and words, logic and poetry (*coniugatio rationis et verbi*; *Metalogicon*, ed. Webb, pp. 3, 6–7, 27). John invokes Martianus Capella's allegory of the marriage between Mercury (eloquence) and Philology (learning, philosophy) for the model he is defending (1.1, 4.29). Since it pertains to *logos* in the broad sense, *grammatica* is a branch of *logica* or the trivium. The system of the trivium discloses the force or meaning of all discourse ('ratio trivii omnium vim sermonum . . . exponebat'; p. 30).

For the chapters on *grammatica*, John's basic sources are Isidore of Seville, Augustine, Quintilian, Cicero, and the standard corpus of *artes grammaticae*. For John, *grammatica* is not only the starting-point for a sequence of disciplines, it is foundational and constitutive of the others, especially philosophy and the disciplines dependent on texts and reading: '*grammatica* is the cradle of all philosophy, and, it can be said, the first nourisher of the whole of literary studies [*totius litteratorii studii*]' (p. 31). *Grammatica* is 'not occupied with one subject' but rather 'prepares the mind for everything that can be taught in words'. Hence, it is 'the key of everything written', the *clavis . . . omnium scripturarum* (1.21; ed. Webb, p. 51). Citing Quintilian, John asserts that *grammatica* is not simply a discipline for the young, but rather accompanies the love of reading to the end of one's life.[5] John asserts that without skill in language (here Latin is understood), no one can become a philosopher (1.13, 1.21). While

---

[5] See Quintilian, *Institutio oratoria* 1.8.12.

many disciplines may contribute to literary studies (*ad litteraturam*) only *grammatica* has the unique privilege of making one 'lettered', *litteratus* (1.25). It is this form of 'letteredness' or literary competence which is presupposed by the other disciplines.

John argues that grammatical rules are arbitrary and follow human conventions but that they imitate the underlying rational principles in nature (1.14–16). Poetry also belongs to *grammatica* because it follows the kind of rules recognised by *grammatica* alone (1.17). The purpose of learning the system of *grammatica* is to avoid mistakes and 'to imitate the graceful style of the authors' (1.18). Learning to discriminate between literal and figurative language is necessary for reading any kind of text, and *grammatica* especially concerns itself with mapping out the *modi locutionum*, the tropes and figures which must be learned for accurate reading (1.18–19). Following a brief survey of Isidore's division of grammatical subject-matter, John asserts that these subjects are essential for interpreting what is read (*ad instructionem legendorum*; p. 49).

The core of John's discussion of *grammatica* is his account of reading and commenting on the *auctores* according to the method he learned from Bernard of Chartres (1.24), who updated the traditional methods of *lectio* and *enarratio*. John appropriates Quintilian's term *prelegens/prelectio* for the teacher's preliminary 'lectures', a practice that meant explanations of grammar, metre, tropes and other stylistic devices, and various kinds of narrative. The poets are read as guides to philosophy, especially ethics: 'examine Virgil or Lucan, and whatever philosophy you may profess, there you will find its foundation' (1.24). Bernard of Chartres used the following method for teaching the reading of authors (*lectio auctorum*). He would point out what was simple and according to rule, the grammatical figures, the 'colours of rhetoric', sophistic quibbles, and the connection of the reading to other disciplines. Students were required to carry out imitation of the authors and to commit passages to memory daily. Bernard also emphasised philosophical and ethical interpretation of the *auctores*, a practice consistent with the positioning of the study of poetry within ethics.[6]

For John of Salisbury, then, there was no separation between the linguistic and literary divisions of *grammatica*: the whole point of the *Metalogicon* is that the abstract system of logic and grammar should not be cut off from the study of the *auctores* and poetry. Logic and grammar have complementary but distinct functions in an overall model of the arts of discourse.

[6] See Delhaye, ' "Grammatica" et "Ethica" '; Allen, *Ethical Poetic*.

From ars grammatica *to* sermocinalis scientia

The world of the thirteenth-century scholar Robert Kilwardby (a Parisian master of arts who returned to England and became archbishop of Canterbury in 1273) was a very different one. In his *De ortu scienciarum*, *grammatica* embraces the art of letter-writing (*ars dictandi*) and poetics (*poemata fingendi*; ed. Judy, pp. 165–6, 212–13). However, the influence of the new learning is marked by Robert's description of *grammatica* as the first part of *scientia sermocinalis*, the science of discourse and reasoning, which treats significative discourse (*sermo significativus*) in itself (pp. 162, 165, 167).

The impact of Aristotle's logical works had been largely absorbed by grammar by the mid-twelfth century, but the rediscovery of the *libri naturales* during the next seventy years which brought new and stricter definitions and methodological requirements to the sciences also caused a major reorientation for grammar as a discipline, from *ars grammatica* to *sermocinalis scientia*. The insistence of William of Conches on the *causae inventionis* was a harbinger of this fresh approach, and as early as 1150 Dominicus Gundissalinus, in Toledo and close to Arabic influence, had explored the idea of a universal grammar. In a commentary on *Priscian minor* by a 'Master Jordan' this reorientation is fully reflected, the change being apparent even in its opening words: 'Linguistic science [*sermocinalis sciencia*], since it treats of language, is subdivided in the same way as language; for as Aristotle says in the second part of his *De anima*, sciences are to be divided after the manner of the things [of which they treat]' (Grabmann, 'Jordanus', p. 234).

Within linguistic science, grammar is divided from rhetoric and logic as treating language in respect of its manner of signification (*modus significandi*), and within grammar *orthographia*, *prosodia*, *ethymologia* and *diasynthetica* are distinguished as corresponding to *littera*, *syllaba*, *dictio* and *oratio*, so providing a systematic justification for what became a standard framework for grammars outside the modistic tradition (which itself has its point of departure in the 'Jordan' commentary's *modus significandi*). Once established as autonomous, it was also necessary to demonstrate that grammar was theoretical, i.e. it treats of universal and immutable reality. 'Jordan' meets the immediate objection that grammar cannot be a science because the *voces* it treats of are *sensibilia* and neither universal nor immutable by responding that 'a physical sensation [*sensibile*] can be considered in two ways: according to its common essence', i.e. 'according to what one abstracts from this or that sensation', or 'according to its significatory essence', i.e. 'according to what this or that sensation has to do with'. Taken in the first way, 'Jordan' explains, 'it is universal, and a science can treat of it'. True, 'sounds as sounds are not the same everywhere, but they are the same everywhere according to their manner of ordering and according to the understanding which they form'. There are tantalising hints here of phoneme theory, and these are further developed in a commentary on *Priscian minor* of *c.* 1250 which has falsely been attributed to Kilwardby, wherein a theory of signs and metalanguages is also developed. In the period of Kilwardby Oxford was rapidly establishing itself as a centre for study, and for a half century he, his predecessor Robert Grosseteste (d. 1253), and his successor Roger Bacon (d. *c.* 1292), carried through many exciting developments in scientific or speculative grammar, though with very different characteristics. Bacon was *sui generis*, 'radically conservative' inasmuch as he provides a standard definition of speculative grammar as 'one and the same according to substance in every language, though it is allowed that it varies in accidents', yet he also writes a practical grammar of Greek and insists on the functional, performative and contextual aspects of language and meaning.[7]

As a group of grammarians, those Oxford scholars deserve further study. Developments in Paris during the period, between about 1220 and 1270, have also received less attention than those which immediately followed them. Papal attempts to ban the study of the *libri naturales* before they were finally accepted as part of the curriculum in 1255 may have played some part in the apparent lull which seems to have taken place in speculative grammar in these years, but further examination of the manuscript tradition will probably show that such study was continuous if less public. Far more prominent at this time was the growth in popularity of new pedagogic grammars such as the *Doctrinale* and *Graecismus* (more on which later), and the conflict between 'literary' and 'scientific' grammar which is so graphically represented in the *Bataille du VII arts* of Henri d'Andeli. The works of John of Garland, who was a student at Oxford in the time of Grosseteste and subsequently taught at Paris until *c.* 1272, illustrate the tensions of this period and, like d'Andeli's poem, show the submergence of any serious attempts to relate grammar to the study of literature, squeezed as it now was between speculative treatises and versified pedagogic tracts. Not surprisingly, his most popular works were his practical *Dictionarius* (he may be the coiner of this term), *Synonyma* and *Equivoca*, which link him with Alexander Nequam in England and with the school of the Petit Pont in Paris.

Around 1270, however, a new theoretical framework for grammatical study becomes established in Paris which remained dominant for some thirty years. Its first representatives seem to have been Danes (Boethius

---

7 Bacon, *Grammatica Graeca*, p. 278; Rosier, 'Roger Bacon', pp. 21–2; Pinborg, 'Speculative Grammar', pp. 266–7.

and Martin of Dacia, followed by John and Simon), and in the next generation a whole school of grammarians comment on and develop the new
approach – Gentilis de Cingulo, Albertus Swebelinus, Siger of Courtrai,
Pseudo-Albert the Great, Radulphus Brito, Michel of Marbais and, giving
as it were the classic presentation of the theory, Thomas of Erfurt. The
works of these *modistae* can be seen as the culmination of the attempt
to present grammar as a theoretical science with distinct and explicit
principles, complete coherence and universal application. To achieve this,
grammar was conceived as the study of those semantic components (called
modi significandi) which constitute word classes and their congruous construction in syntactic structures, which components were then taken to
be universals derived from features of objects themselves (*modi essendi*)
which are 'co-understood' by the mind (*modi intelligendi*) along with the
concept of the object itself.[8] In this way not only is there a direct relationship between real-world objects, mental concepts and verbal signs,
but also between the properties of those objects, thought and linguistic
structure. In the short term this epistemology provided a launching pad
for a subtle and many-layered analysis of the semantic structures of sentences, much of which – if disentangled from its scholastic terminology –
can seem very modern. But with Thomas of Erfurt's *Grammatica speculativa*, however, the ferment of development came to an end, and 'after
1300 no original contribution to modistic theory was made',[9] although
treatises such as those by John Josse (written in verse in 1322) and John
of Stobniczy for a Prague gentleman in the sixteenth century show that
lack of originality did not always mean lack of use.[10] Nevertheless it is
clear that speculative grammar fell out of favour as quickly as it gained
it. If its sudden popularity was due to the appeal of its synthesis and
addictive terminology, together with the prospect it offered of a grammar
rehabilitated in scholastic thought and an unveiling of the mental world,
its demise was the result of a pincer movement between nominalism and
realism. For nominalists like Walter Burley (*c.* 1275–*c.* 1344), William
of Ockham (*c.* 1285–1347) and Jean Buridan (*c.* 1292–*c.* 1358), the epistemological presuppositions which had so excitingly launched modistic
theory also entangled it in unacceptable ontological confusions between
linguistic forms, mental concepts and objective entities. For thoroughgoing 'Averroistic realists' like John of Jandun at Paris and his pupil John
Aurifaber at Erfurt (who undertook a public demonstration *c.* 1330 of the
non-existence of the *modi significandi*), language mirrored all the distinctions of reality so perfectly that intermediate analyses were pointless.[11]

---

[8] See Covington, *Syntactic Theory*, pp. 31–2.
[9] Pinborg, 'Speculative Grammar', p. 256.
[10] Covington, *Syntactic Theory*, pp. 25, 138.
[11] Pinborg, 'Speculative Grammar', pp. 268ff.

From such very different starting-points both groups pushed grammar back towards the straightforward description of linguistic usage and the teaching of its rules. And it is to the continuing pedagogic tradition that we must therefore turn once again.

Just as speculative grammar freed itself from Priscian in the early thirteenth century and developed new methodological concerns, so in preceptive grammar we see the emergence of new textbooks and a growing awareness of method. Mnemonic verse tags on grammatical subjects were common enough in Peter Helias' time for him to attack them as 'tyrannical',[12] but it is Alexander of Villa Dei's *Doctrinale*, written *c.* 1199, which in 2,645 hexameters offers in verse a definitive description of the Latinity of the day. Although Chapters 8 and 9 of Alexander's poem treat of *regimen* (the inflectional cases 'governed' by certain parts of speech), adverbs and a miscellany of constructions, its substance is a concise but exhaustive listing of noun and verb forms, and especially those which are exceptional. That the similar poem composed perhaps twenty-five years later by Évrard of Béthune should have become known as the *Graecismus* on the basis of a short section *de nominibus exortis a Graeco* shows the market value of such an approach. In order to illustrate his achievement, Alexander needs to be quoted in Latin as well as in English translation:

> Rectis as es a dat declinatio prima,
> atque per am propria quaedam ponuntur Hebraea,
> dans ae diphthongon genetivis atque dativis.
> am servat quartus; tamen en aut an reperimus,
> cum rectus fit in es vel in as, vel cum dat a Graecus.

(29–33)

[The first declension gives -*as*, -*es* and -*a* to its nominatives, and certain Hebrew proper names with -*am*, giving the diphthong -*ae* to genitives and datives. The accusative keeps -*am*, although we also find -*en* or -*an* when the nominative is made with -*es* or -*as*, or when a Greek word gives -*a*.]

The *Doctrinale* was enormously popular for some three centuries. Like Priscian it attracted glosses and commentaries, and it was eventually apotheosised into the Paris curriculum in place of Priscian in 1366.

For serious thirteenth-century teaching grammars in prose we must, however, turn to the more pragmatically oriented Italian universities. Papias had already written his much-used dictionary called the *Elementarium* as well as an *Ars grammatica* around 1050, but there are few grammatical texts surviving from Italy between then and the time of the thirteenth-century treatises of Bene of Florence (d. 1239?) and Peter of

---

[12] Hunt, 'Studies on Priscian, II', p. 69.

Isolella (which had an Italian circulation) and, more importantly, those of Hugutio and John Balbus of Genoa (which had a wide European circulation). Hugutio's *Magnae derivationes* is an alphabetically organised compilation of simple definitions and longer articles of obvious practical value (despite its grandiloquent prologue), while John Balbus of Genoa's *Catholicon*, completed in 1286, offers a dictionary prefaced by an extensive account of the divisions and subject-matter of *grammatica*.

John discusses *orthographia*, *etymologia*, *diasyntastica* (or *diasynthetica*) and *prosodia*, using the terms in newly specialised senses. *Orthographia* is defined as the treatment of 'correct writing' and embraces the traditional material on letters and syllables in Donatus and in Priscian's *Institutiones* (the 'Priscianus maior'). A treatment of accent and word endings is inserted into this section, maintaining John's focus on prosody. *Etymologia*, based on the terms 'etymon' (true) and 'logos' (discourse), is defined as the treatment of 'the truth of all parts of speech absolutely' (pp. 1, 33), and embraces the study of the word classes or 'parts of speech', also the traditional material in Donatus and Priscian. To this section John appends a treatment of *constructio* or syntax and that innovation of later-medieval grammar teaching, *regimen*. He explains that *diasyntastica*, or syntax in the broadest sense, is mixed in with the other sections and does not have a separate treatment (*tractatus*). The last part of the opening section is a treatment of figures and tropes, both the faults (*vitia*) of construction and the traditional poetical figures (p. 107), and concludes with the 'colours of rhetoric'. This section is a compilation of Donatus' *Barbarismus*, the corresponding chapters of Isidore of Seville's *Etymologiae* 1, and Bede's *De schematibus et tropis*, together with John's own commentary. John's focus on *prosodia*, writing, and encyclopaedic definitions in the tradition of Isidore reveals that *grammatica* retained its primary textual function for a broad base of readers and writers who had no practical use for speculative grammar.

A similar redefinition of the traditional subject-areas of *grammatica* can be seen in other thirteenth- and fourteenth-century works. The *Speculum doctrinale* of Vincent of Beauvais (part of the vast *Speculum maius* which he composed in the mid-thirteenth century) contains a book devoted to *grammatica*. His account is a compilation of Isidore of Seville, Peter Helias, Priscian and other standard *artes*, but Vincent rearranges the material from Isidore to correspond to the division of the arts and sciences found in Al-Fārābī and Gundissalinus. Book 2 is an outline of *grammatica* much like that in the *Catholicon*, and Book 3 combines logic, rhetoric, poetics, the genres of poetry and prose writing, and other literary subjects included at the end of Isidore's *Etymologiae* 1: 'De grammatica'. Here yet again, the literary functions of *grammatica* have been preserved but rearranged within a different model of the trivium.

The *Catholicon* and *Speculum doctrinale* certainly circulated in England in the fourteenth century, and it is at Oxford once more, this time in the developing grammar schools on the fringe of the university rather than in the faculty of arts proper, that we can see the continuing tradition of practical grammars stretching from the thirteenth century – from Richard of Hambury, who was teaching *c.* 1288 (before Bacon's death), through Adam Nidyard, Thomas of Hanney, John of Cornwall and John Leylond, to Stanbridge, Whittinton, the Renaissance grammarians and beyond.[13] It was a time of considerable development in pedagogy and literacy. Following on from Alexander of Villa Dei's 'new grammar', teachers composed their own treatises to suit their own needs. Around the major *summae*, such as Thomas of Hanney's *Memoriale iuniorum* (completed in 1313) and John of Cornwall's *Speculum grammaticale* (1346), cluster a host of shorter, often anonymous, texts on particular points of grammar, and from these grow an increasingly systematic curriculum of graded treatises. In John of Cornwall's *Speculum* we see a snatch of schoolroom dialogue in English: by the end of the century we have in the works of John Leylond actual vernacular treatises on the more elementary aspects of Latin grammar (accidence, comparison and simple construction), followed up by Latin works on more difficult subjects.

In how mony maner of wyse shall þu bygyn to mak Latten and to construe by ry3twyse ordyr of construccion? In v [i.e. in five ways]. In whych v? By a vocatif case, by a nominatif or by sumwhat set yn þe stytt of a nominatif case and a verbe of certayn person, by an ablatif case absolute, and a verbe inpersonell. How bygynne 3e by a vocatif case to mak your Latten? As 'Willam make fyre', *Willelme fac ignem. . . .* (Thomson, *Middle English Grammatical Texts*, p. 82)

Texts such as these proliferate in the fifteenth century as paper makes manuscripts cheaper and new school foundations make education more accessible.

Not surprisingly, grammars in the vernacular can be seen emerging in mainland Europe at this same time. Scarcer are grammars *of* the vernacular, although in any vernacular grammar there will be a certain transference of application, which is well marked, for instance, in the Middle English treatises. A much earlier Irish grammar which develops terminology to cover initial mutations, the twelfth-century Icelandic *First Grammatical Treatise* (primarily concerned with spelling reform but offering a remarkable phonemic analysis based on minimal pair contrastive analysis), a thirteenth-century grammar of Welsh: all of these provide fascinating glimpses of what was possible on the fringes of the *orbs Latina*. The first grammars of Provençal, Catalan and Spanish are written in the later-medieval period, and Dante both urges the study of the vernacular and

---

[13] Hunt, 'Oxford Masters'; Thomson, 'Oxford Masters Revisited'.

consolidates its use in Italy as a major literary vehicle. Such an empowering interest in the vernacular crosses the somewhat artificial barrier between medieval and Renaissance, and the linguistic awareness thereby produced proved a fertile seed-bed for the irony of a Geoffrey Chaucer or the technical achievements of the Wycliffite Bible translators, as much as for the divine 'high style' of a Dante.

2. Linguistic theory: speech and writing

Medieval *grammatica* was not merely a pedagogical programme or a body of descriptive linguistic doctrine. The *artes grammaticae* transmitted a philosophy of language, indeed, a whole ideology of language with explicit links to centres of institutional authority. In general, medieval grammatical theory privileged writing over speech, universal features – as embodied in Latin, a 'fixed', written language – over individual spoken languages, and the classical literary models, the *auctores*, over recent writings. Much of the philosophy of language underlying grammatical theory had a connection with literature, although later speculative grammar attempted to sever this connection to work out a universal science of language. A sense of how *grammatica* provided the basic assumptions about language, writing, speech and literary texts can be gained by considering the theories of *vox* (utterance, vocal expression) and *littera* ('letter'; pl. 'writing').

In medieval theories of writing and texts, the act of reading (*lectio*) was understood to be a repetition of discourse in the mouth and mind of the reader, the text constituted as such by a reader's production of what the grammarians called *vox articulata litterata*, 'articulated [i.e. conjoined] utterance' which is also *litterata*, 'scriptible', or representable in written characters.[14] In medieval grammatical theory, language is unthinkable outside writing, and even the theory of speech was modelled on the properties of writing.

The model for articulate speech is writing, not spoken utterances. The vocal utterance considered the *materia* of the grammatical art was written, and, conversely, articulate speech was understood to bear the marks of writing. Peter Helias states that the *materia* of *grammatica* is *vox*, although not as sound but as an expression of an animate being; the *litteratus* is the person who forms letters, words and sentences, that is, expression

---

[14] Donatus, *De littera*: 'Vox est aer ictus sensibilis auditu, quantum in ipso est. Omnis vox aut articulata est aut confusa. Articulata est quae litteris comprehendi potest, confusa quae scribi non potest' ['Speech/spoken utterance is struck air perceptible to hearing, inasmuch as it is in itself. Every *vox* is either articulate or confused. Articulate is what can be comprehended in letters; confused is what cannot be written']. (*GL* 4, 367; ed. Holtz, *Donat*, p. 603.)

representable in writing or best exemplified in writing (ed. Reilly, p. 2). Earlier in the tradition Diomedes asserted that articulate utterance is the 'expression [*explanata*] of rational human discourse' and that speech derives its rationality from being 'letterable' or 'scriptible', that which can be 'comprehended in letters/writing' (*De voce*; *GL* 1, 420).

The form of writing that provided the model for articulated, scriptible expression was the authoritative literary text. The definition in Priscian's *Institutiones grammaticae*, the central text for higher grammatical theory in the medieval schools, provides the key:

'Vox' has four *differentiae* – articulated [*articulata*], non-articulated [*inarticulata*], resolvable into discrete units [*litterata*], not resolvable into discrete units [*illiterata*]. Articulate spoken utterance is compressed [*coartata*], that is, what is produced when joined with some meaning in the mind of the one speaking. Non-articulate spoken utterance is the opposite of this, that which originates in no mental experience. *Vox literata* is what can be written; *vox illiterata* is that which cannot be written. Therefore, certain articulate spoken utterances which can be both written and understood are under investigation, like 'Arms and the man I sing' (*Aeneid* 1.1).   (*GL* 2, 5)

These assumptions are the necessary starting-point for any understanding of medieval literary theory. Since grammatical discourse privileged writing over speech, it also contained the metaphors for the convertibility of writing and articulate speech. Articulate speech is what can be written, and, conversely, whatever is read is, therefore, articulate discourse:

Articulate speech is what can be written, that which is subject to joints [*articulis*], that is, the fingers which write, or because it carries out an art [*artem*] or acts as a model. . . . Moreover, whatever is read is *vox articulata*. If you unravel that which is joined together in reading, you produce discourse [*sermo*]. (*GL* 4, 519)

Whatever is read is, by this fact alone, articulate speech. Speech bears the imprint of writing; indeed, speech is considered meaningful only as it manifests the distinctive features of writing – externality, mediation, a sequential string of parts tied together (*conligatum*). In grammatical discourse, the Platonic sense of the secondariness of writing has been erased; speech and writing become dual manifestations of a single activity – signifying or the production of meaning.[15]

The theory of 'letters' (*litterae*) distinguished the minimal unit of sound or distinct phonic value marked by a written character (*elementum*) from the written character itself (*figura, nota*). The phonetic theory of writing thus extends the conceptual and discursive link between articulate speech and writing. A 'letter' was termed an atom or element, an indivisible and irreducible part of scriptible speech. The written character or mark of an

---

[15] See Derrida, 'Plato's Pharmacy'.

element had the status of a mould, form or model (*forma*) of letterable speech. Priscian's definition underlies all subsequent theory:

> A letter is the smallest part of composite speech sound [*vox*], that is, what exists by the composition of letters; it is the smallest with respect to the whole comprehension of scriptible speech sound – in this also are found the briefest parts of emitted utterances – or because it is the briefest of all divisible things, it being indivisible itself. We can define it this way: a letter is a speech sound that can be written as an indivisible particle.
>
> It is called 'letter' from 'legitera', as it were, because it shows the way for reading [*legens + iter*], or from 'litural' (erasure), as some have it, because the ancients used to write often in wax tablets. But they call 'letters' by the term 'elements' from a similarity to the elements of the world: as the elements conjoin and make each corporeal thing, likewise conjoined elements make scriptible speech sound [*literalis vox*] as if they compose some corporeal entity.
>
> (GL 2, 6–7)

The etymological interpretation of the term *littera* reveals the important connection between linguistic theory and the practice of reading and exegesis. The three main etymologies, with varying amounts of commentary, are found in a wide range of sources and became standard topics for explanation in commentaries on Donatus' and Priscian's chapter on letters.[16] According to the well-worn (bogus) etymologies, a letter takes its name from 'reading-way' (*lege + iter*) or from the fact that it is repeated in reading (*lege + iteratur*), or because it was frequently erased (*litura*, 'erasure') in wax tablets. Letters show the way for reading and allow the repetition of discourse in reading (*lectio*). The explanatory pun on 'erasure' (*litura*) exposes the temporality and impermanence of recorded utterance. Wax tablets were rubbed or smeared over to allow new writing. Writing is thus subject to loss and oblivion without its repetition in reading and in further writing.

Grammatical theory thus places writing at the centre of its discourse through its own network of explanatory metaphors: articulate speech is 'scriptible' or 'letterable', and letters, as minimal written/spoken units, are the 'elements' or 'atoms' of speech. The term *vox articulata literata* means that the temporal succession of discrete units (in speech) and the sequence of spatially separable units (in script) were considered mutually convertible forms of signifying. Articulate utterance is always already inscribed or imprinted with the primary characteristics of writing – temporality,

---

[16] See Servius, *In Donatum*, GL 4, 421; Sergius, *De littera*, GL 4, 475; Anon., *Explanatio litterae*, GL 4, 518; Marius Victorinus, GL 6, 5; Sergius (?), GL 7, 538; Isidore of Seville, *Etymologiae* 1.3.1–2; Remigius of Auxerre, *In Donatum*, GL 8, 221; Sedulius Scottus, *In Donati artem maiorem*, ed. Löfstedt, p. 6; Murethac, *In Donati artem maiorem*, ed. Holtz, p. 8.

externality, and endless deferral seemingly held off by repetition in reading. The theory of speech and writing has important implications for medieval notions of textuality. Letters 'are that which remain' (Priscian, *De accentu*; GL 3, 519); speech vanishes. Writing is thus a memory system that attempts to resist the frail temporality of human utterances. Isidore of Seville provides a summary of the traditional view:

Letters are the indices of things, the signs of words, in which there is such great force that they speak to us without vocal utterance the things said by those absent. The practice of letters was invented for the memory of things. Things would vanish into oblivion unless they were bound in letters. In such a great variety of things, everything can neither be learned nor retained in the memory. 'Letters' [*litterae*] are so called from '*legiterae*', as it were, because they show the way for readers [*legens* + *iter*], or because they are repeated in reading [*legens* + *itero*].   (*Etymologiae* 1.3.1–2)

Important assumptions here are the iterability of things written in the process of reading and the notion that writing was invented for the memory of things. Writing 'binds' things absent in an externalised memory system that defers meaning until read. History for Isidore is to be subsumed under *grammatica* since letters preserve the memory of past and absent experience:

History is the narration of things done, through which those things which happened in the past are distinguished. This discipline pertains to *grammatica* because whatever is worthy of memory is committed to letters. Histories, then, are called monuments because they bestow the memory of things done.

(*Etymologiae* 1.41.1–2)

History, therefore, is intimately connected with textuality; what is past and absent must always be represented in narrative form, that is, follow discursive rules. The theory in Isidore's grammatical encyclopaedia became the common stock of later-medieval encyclopaedias and commentaries.[17]

3. Theories of metaphor and allegory

In the *artes grammaticae*, the core curriculum of linguistic categories was completed by the treatment of metre and accent, barbarisms, solecisms, metaplasms and figurative language (schemes and tropes).[18] The theory of

[17] See Papias, *Vocabulista*, s.v. 'littera'; the anonymous gloss on Priscian known as *Promisimus*, in Oxford, Bodleian Library, MS Laud Lat. 67, fol. 24va; Vincent of Beauvais, *Speculum doctrinale* 1.4, 'De littera'.

[18] See Donatus, *Ars maior* 3; Diomedes, *Ars grammatica* 3; Isidore of Seville, *Etymologiae* 1.17–19, 32–7; John Balbus, *Catholicon*, 'De figuris', pp. 107–27; Vincent of Beauvais, *Speculum doctrinale* 2: 'De grammatica'.

tropes and figures in the *artes* results from a synthesis of Aristotelian and Stoic rhetoric and dialectic filtered through the late-classical grammatical schools. As a result, grammatical theory carried over certain philosophical agendas that posed problems for the valuation of poetic language.

In the classical tradition, the model statement for philosophical analysis was the proposition, the statement bearing a truth-value. A rift was thus imposed between dialectic and poetics by the criteria established for the serious, semantically normative kind of statement that could be reduced to logical rules, that is, the kind of statement with which philosophy was supposed primarily to be concerned. For Aristotle, philosophy and clear writing use words in their ordinary, 'dominant' (*kyrion*) meaning; a metaphor or trope (from *tropos*, 'a turn') is a deviation or turning away from ordinary and propositional meaning (*Poetics* 21–2, *Rhetoric* 3, *De interpretatione* 4). In this model, the virtues of poetry – unusual diction, metaphor, stylistic effects of all kinds – become the vices of prose discourse. In Aristotle's definition, metaphor is a word used not in its own, customary or dominant meaning, which is produced through a transfer 'from the genus to the species, from the species to the genus, from one species to another, or by analogy' (*Poetics* 21.7). Poetry remained problematic because its kind of statement was excluded from philosophy and admitted in rhetoric only if kept under control (*Rhetoric* 3.2.1–3).

Medieval *grammatica* thus inherited a discourse in which tropes were not discussed as part of *oratio* (the statement or discourse in general), but as deviant forms of expression – the *vitia* or 'faults' of style – requiring a separate analysis following the treatment of grammatical deviations from normative Latinity (barbarisms and solecisms). *Grammatica* was left with the internal contradiction of having to treat seriously forms of expression which had been systematically excluded from the philosophical discourse from which it developed. In short, grammatical theory merged rhetorical discourse on style and trope with dialectic discourse on the kinds of statement, producing a hybrid doctrine that attempted to explain poetical language.

Let us consider a few examples from Donatus' *Ars maior*, the main source book on tropes and figures right up to the time of the Renaissance.[19]

On tropes. A trope is a word [*dictio*] transferred from its own signification to a likeness not its own for the sake of ornament or need. There are thirteen tropes: metaphor, catachresis, metalepsis, metonymy, antonomasia, epitheton, synecdoche, onomatopoeia, periphrasis, hyperbaton, hyperbole, allegory, homoesis.

[19] In *GL* 4, 392–402, and ed. Holtz, *Donat*, pp. 653–74.

A metaphor is a transfer [*translatio*] of things and words. This transfer occurs in four ways: from animate to animate, from inanimate to inanimate, from animate to inanimate, from inanimate to animate. For example, from animate to animate, as in: 'they made Tiphys charioteer of the swift ship',[20] for both a charioteer and a pilot are animate. From inanimate to animate, as in: 'when the rafts gained the sea' (*Aeneid* 5.8), for both ships and rafts are inanimate. From animate to inanimate, as in: 'Atlas, whose pine-wreathed head [is] continually girt with black clouds', for while these things are animate, a mountain, to which human parts are attributed, is not. From inanimate to animate, as in: 'if you foster such strength [*robur*, lit. 'oak'] in your breast' (*Aeneid* 11.368), for while oak is inanimate, Turnus, about whom this is said, is animate. We should also know that some metaphors are reciprocal, and others hold in one direction only.

Donatus thus preserves the classical notion of figure as transfer (*translatio*), based on the Greek term *metaphora*, which means literally 'a carrying across, a transfer', and the Aristotelian notion of classes of transferred meaning. Rather than seeing metaphor as part of the basic semantic structure of language, grammatical theory posits two zones or fields of meaning: one, the semantic field 'proper' (*proprius*) to a word, that is, 'its own' meaning, and the other, a field not belonging to the word but of some other, to which the word shifts in its 'transfer' of semantic field. These semantic fields were then broken down into two simple categories, animate and inanimate (literally, that which has, or does not have, an *anima*), thus yielding the four possible kinds of transfer. The theory relies almost exclusively on nouns and adjectives as words capable of forming metaphors and neglects the figurative use of verbs and other parts of speech. Even with these limitations, the conception of metaphor and figure found in the *artes grammaticae* provided a foundation for literary theory for over a thousand years.

The definition of the trope *allegoria* was universally used to explain allegorical interpretation, and Donatus' definition became the point of departure for later discussions of allegory:[21]

Allegory is a trope in which something other than what is said is signified, such as: 'and now it's time to loosen the necks of our foaming horses' (Virgil, *Georgics* 2.542), that is, 'to end the poem'. This trope has many species, of which seven are prominent: irony, antiphrasis, enigma, charientismos, paroemia, sarcasm, astismos.

The grammatical definition of enigma, or riddle, was also frequently cited to account for difficulties in the Scriptures and for interpreting riddles like those by Aldhem:

[20] Source unknown. Tiphys was the pilot of the Argonaut. The quotation was also used by Charisius (*GL* 1, 272) and Diomedes (*GL* 1, 457).
[21] See Rollinson, *Classical Theories*, and Irvine, 'Interpretation'.

Enigma is a hidden meaning through a secret likeness of things, such as: 'a
mother gave me birth, and then the same one was born from me', when it
signifies that water grows together/hardens in ice and then again flows out from
the same.

Isidore of Seville's treatment of allegory and enigma is also closely
connected to exegesis:

Allegory is 'other-speaking' [*alieniloquium*]. For it sounds one way, but is
understood in another; for example, 'he observes three stags wandering on the
shore' (*Aeneid* 1.184), which signifies the three leaders of the Punic Wars or the
three Punic Wars. Also, in the *Eclogues*: 'I have sent ten golden apples' (3.71),
which means the ten pastoral eclogues sent to Augustus. There are many species
of this trope, of which seven are prominent – irony, antiphrasis, aenigma,
charientismus, paroemia, sarcasm, astismus. . . . An enigma is an obscure
problem which is difficult to understand unless it is revealed; for example, 'out
of the eater came forth meat, and out of the strong came forth sweetness'
(Judges 14:14), which signifies that honeycomb was drawn from the mouth of a
lion. Between allegory and enigma there is this difference: the force of allegory is
double and indicates something figuratively under other things; but an enigma is
an obscure meaning, and is represented through certain semblances.

(*Etymologiae* 1.37.22, 26)

The pressure exerted by dialectic on the theory of figurative language
was resisted by writers of *artes* who placed the question of tropes and
figures squarely within exegetical practices. Augustine's *De doctrina
christiana*, Books 1–3 of which form an *ars grammatica* for Christian literature, treats tropes, figures and allegory as forms of 'transferred signs'
requiring interpretation by the reader:

Those trained in letters should know that in all those modes of expression which
the grammarians call by the Greek name 'tropes' were used by our authors in
many places and more copiously than those who do not know them or have
learned them elsewhere are able to suppose or believe. But those who know the
tropes recognise them in the sacred writings, and the knowledge of the tropes is
of considerable assistance in the understanding of these writings. But it is not
appropriate to teach them to the ignorant here, lest we seem to be teaching *ars
grammatica*. . . . Moreover, not only examples of all these tropes are read in the
sacred books, but also the names of some of them, like allegory, enigma and
parable, are read. However, almost all these tropes, which are said to be learned
by the liberal art, are found in the speech of those who have attended to no
grammarian and are content with the usage of common speech. For who does
not say, 'so may you flourish'? This trope is called a metaphor. Who does not say
'piscina' ('basin'), which takes its name from 'pisces' ('fish')? This trope is called
catachresis. . . . Therefore, knowledge of them is necessary for solving the
ambiguities in Scripture, for when the meaning is absurd if taken according to

the proper signification of the words, it is to be enquired whether what we do not understand is said in this or that trope; and in this way, many things are discovered which are hidden. (3.29.40–1)

The Augustinian perspective is made more explicit in Bede's handbook, *De schematibus et tropis*, which is modelled on Donatus' *Ars grammatica* 3. Bede combines the definitions of *allegoria* in grammar and exegesis, using the structure of the grammatical trope as a foundation. Working from a Donatan template that had already been filled in with examples from the Scriptures and Christian Latin literature, Bede went beyond Donatus to explain how tropic language is used in the Scriptures. His lengthy treatment of the trope allegory distinguishes between allegory in words (*allegoria verbia*, the trope proper) and allegory in events and actions (*allegoria factis/operis*, typology) and also contains one of the earliest statements of the so-called 'four levels' of allegorical meaning. Bede's work was used throughout the Middle Ages, and formed a core of theory that was continually extracted for compilations like John Balbus of Genoa's *Catholicon*.

4. Curriculum and reading

The elementary grammar-school curriculum was remarkably consistent throughout the Middle Ages. Students would be expected to learn Donatus' *Ars minor* and parts of the *Ars maior*, supplemented with other texts used in various regions, and after the Carolingian era, Priscian's *Institutiones grammaticae* completed the study of *Latinitas*. In the thirteenth century, verse versions of such basic grammatical doctrine, Alexander of Villa Dei's *Doctrinale* and Évrard of Béthune's *Graecismus*, were produced as aids to memorising the rules, and (as intimated above) these texts seem to have superseded Donatus as teaching manuals in the later thirteenth and fourteenth centuries.

For an accurate picture of the range of texts used and of the content of the grammatical curriculum we must consider the main primary sources – surviving manuscript compilations, booklists, library catalogues, and references to schooling in medieval texts. Library catalogues and compiled manuscripts show that two kinds of books belonged to *grammatica* – collections of grammatical *artes* and collections of *auctores*, often combined in the same volume.[22] Important sources for understanding what texts were used in *grammatica* in the early Middle Ages include the

[22] See Glauche, *Schullektüre*.

ninth-century library catalogues from St Gall, Reichenau and Lorsch, major centres of Carolingian literary culture. These library records, together with actual surviving manuscripts from Carolingian and Anglo-Saxon centres, show that there were established patterns of compilation for grammatical books that disclose the scope and subject-matter of *grammatica*. For example, the St Gall library contained several compilations of texts, two of which provided introductions to studying poetry:[23]

Donatus, *Ars minor et maior*	Asporius, 'Partes' [= *Ars Asporii*]
Bede, *De arte metrica*	Donatus, 'Partes' [= *Ars minor*]
Alcuin, *De grammatica*	Servius, 'Ars' [= *In Donatum commentarium*]
Isidore, *Etymologiae* 1	Diomedes, 'De metro' [= *Ars grammatica* 3]
Juvencus, *Evangelia*	Bede, *De arte metrica*
Sedulius, *Carmen paschale*	Donatus, *Ars minor et maior*
Disticha Catonis	Pompeius, *Commentum artis Donati*
Misc.	Misc.

These two volumes of texts reveal a rationale for compilation dictated by the grammatical programme. Basic primer texts led the way to a study of metrics, beginning poetry, and the standard Christian Latin biblical epics. Many compiled manuscripts like these have survived from both before and after the twelfth century. Some compilations of *artes* were designed to be encyclopaedic reference works covering the entire range of subject-matter from elementary grammar to poetics and metrics.[24]

The manuscripts and library records reveal that a basic reading curriculum was established in schools throughout Europe and Britain from the ninth to the twelfth century. In an 'ideal' form, the literary canon formed by *grammatica* included the following:

The *Disticha Catonis* (proverbial lore in couplets)
Avianus, *Fabulae* (beast fables)
Theodulus, *Ecloga*
Bede, *De die iudicii* (poem on Judgement Day) ⎰ beginning texts
Prosper, *Epigramata* (epigrams drawn from Augustine)
Ilias Latina (Latin poem on the Trojan War)

---

[23] Based on Lehmann, *Mittelalterliche Bibliothekskataloge*, 1, no. 16, pp. 71–82. The texts have been designated with titles conventionally used today.

[24] The groups of texts that formed the foundation of grammatical instruction can be seen clearly in Holtz's descriptions of manuscripts containing Donatus' *Ars* and in Passalacqua's catalogue of Priscian manuscripts.

Juvencus, *Evangelia*
Sedulius, *Carmen paschale*
Arator, *De actibus apostolorum* } corpus of Latin biblical
Avitus, *Carmen de spiritualis* epic poetry
   historiae gestis
Prudentius, *Psychomachia*

Symphosius, *Aenigmata*
Aldhelm, *Aenigmata* } a group of literary riddles
Boniface, *Aenigmata*

Boethius, *De consolatione philosophiae*

Virgil, *Eclogues, Georgics, Aeneid*
Lucan, *De bello civili* } the main hexameter and
Statius, *Thebaid, Achilleid* epic poems

Juvenal, *Satirae* } satires
Persius, *Satirae*

All these texts were not necessarily available to every student who went through the grammar curriculum, but the surviving manuscripts reveal a pattern of compiling texts for use in the schoolroom or for reading in the *grammatica* section of the library. Students would be introduced to reading Latin texts, especially poetry, early on. Depending on the kind of grammar school a student began with, the first Latin texts encountered would be primers like Pseudo-Cato's *Distichs*, the Psalter, prayers and other liturgical texts, followed by hexameter poems. These beginning texts helped fix Latin syntax and vocabulary in the students' memories.

Other works were added to the basic reading list after the twelfth century. Ovid became popular, for instance, while interest in the Latin biblical epics seems to have declined (though Prudentius was still read). *Florilegia* of extracts from classical writers became widely used. However, the standard list of authors that took shape before the rise of the universities endured in various forms to the fourteenth century. True, they had to jostle for place with such medieval works as the *Liber floretus* (or *facetus*), *Cartula* (*De contemptu mundi*), *Thobiadis* and the *Liber parabolarum* attributed to Alan of Lille, which featured in the grammar-school compendia known as the 'six authors' and the 'eight authors' (on which see Chapter 6 below). But reports of the death of the classical author under scholasticism are much exaggerated. The evidence from late-medieval manuscript collections is highly revealing. London, British Library, MS Add. 16380 (thirteenth century) is a compilation of grammatical texts by Ralph of Beauvais with commentaries on Virgil, Juvenal, Ovid, Lucan, Statius and Priscian. London, British Library, MS Add. 10093 (fourteenth century) contains the *Disticha Catonis*, an anonymous grammatical text, Prosper's *Epigrams*, Boethius' *De consolatione philosophiae* (Books 1–2), and the fables of 'Aesop'. Another fourteenth-century manuscript, Oxford, Bodleian Library, MS Auct. F. 1. 17, brings together long-established texts and newer additions to the curriculum: the *Liber parabolarum*, *Thobiadis* and Geoffrey of Vinsauf's *Poetria nova*, together with Virgil's works, an anthology of Ovid's poetry, Sedulius' *Carmen paschale* and Prudentius' *Psychomachia*.

The traditional methodology of *grammatica* also proved resistant. If additional proof be needed, we need look no further than the poetry of Geoffrey Chaucer. The Eagle's discourse on speech in the *House of Fame* was lifted from standard glosses on Priscian's treatment of *vox* in the *Institutiones*,[25] and the *Nun's Priest's Tale* has been read as a parody of grammar-school texts and exercises.[26] When Chaucer says that John the carpenter in the *Miller's Tale* did not know Cato 'for his wit was rude' (*Canterbury Tales*, I(A), 3227), or when Chaucer assigns a string of quotations from the *Disticha Catonis* to the Manciple (IX(H), 318ff.), he was signalling that the Manciple had, but John had not, been to grammar school.

A term for grammar-school learning in Middle English is 'lettrure', derived from *litteratura*, the Latin term used as a synonym for the Greek-based *grammatica*. In Chaucer it connotes basic competence in reading Latin and familiarity with the textbooks used in the grammar curriculum (see *Canterbury Tales*, VII, 2296, 2496; VIII(G), 846). The seven-year-old student described in the *Prioress's Tale* seems typical of the late-medieval choir-school grammar student. He was in school 'to syngen and to rede' (VII, 500), i.e. to learn to sing the liturgy and acquire basic reading skills. He begins by learning some hymns by rote from a primer and asks a fellow student to 'expounden' a hymn in his own language (l. 526), construing the Latin and explaining its meaning. This evokes the standard procedures of elementary *lectio* and *enarratio*. Chaucer's familiarity with the methods and texts of *grammatica* doubtless began in his own school, which, one may suppose, was well endowed with both *artes* and *auctores*.[27]

*

Knowledge of *grammatica* defined one's position in literate culture. From the time of Bede to the age of Dante, Chaucer and Gower, it was the precondition for having a literate culture at all. It gave readers and writers what we now call a 'literate subjectivity', a position in a network of texts and language that defined how to read and what could be written.

---

[25] See Irvine, 'Medieval Grammatical Theory'.
[26] See Travis, '*Nun's Priest's Tale*' and 'Chaucer's Trivial Fox Chase'.
[27] See Rickert, 'Chaucer at School'.

It provided the cultural category of the literary as such, which meant an available network of writings and a textual genealogy extending back to the early *auctores*. It provided the first assumptions, the main presuppositions, of any understanding of language, writing and texts. *Grammatica* meant literacy, but literacy in a specific kind of language and with a specific canon of texts.

We are used to having multiple paths and teaching methods for literacy and multiple literary canons taught in schools and universities and embraced by different cultural groups. From the eighth to fifteenth centuries, Europe really only had one gateway and methodology. There were, of course, variations in emphases, new philosophical traditions about language that got folded into the tradition, local limitations of access to literary works, and other modifications to what was very much a living tradition.

Today we also talk about 'digital literacy' or 'computer literacy', and educators around the world are redefining literature, theory and criticism in a radically decentred multimedia communications environment. People today know multiple literacies, multiple objects that we call literature, and multiple methods for criticism and analysis. Studying the foundational assumptions expressed in medieval *grammatica* discloses the way cultural literacy of any kind works. Roland Barthes once said that literature is what gets taught: a culture determines the literary canon through official instruction. This ongoing cultural practice represents a continuity in education since Chaucer's day. The legacy of *grammatica* remains inscribed in all our contemporary literacies and literatures as these are expected and assumed of educated people regardless of language or culture.

2

The arts of poetry and prose

J. J. Murphy

In medieval terminology the Latin word *ars* (plural: *artes*) denoted a body of principles relating to a specific activity such as painting, music, preaching or writing. By extension the term was also used for a written treatise on the subject of a particular art. For example the *Ars nova* of Philippe de Vitry, written at Paris about 1320, lays out the principles for musical notation which were dominant during the fourteenth century. The term 'art' or *ars* when applied to such a treatise indicates a discussion of what the ancient Greeks would have called *techné* – 'technique' or 'craft' – rather than an abstract or theoretical discussion of a subject.

Medieval writers had access to three major types of such *artes* dealing with separate kinds of literary composition. The first type was the school art, usually called an *Ars poetriae* but teaching how to compose both poetry and prose regardless of genre. The second was the *Ars dictaminis*, or art of letter-writing (on which see Chapter 3 below), while the third was the *Ars praedicandi*, or the art of preaching (see Chapter 4). All three types deal with specific techniques for finding ideas, arranging them, and putting them into verbal language for transmission to an audience of readers or hearers.

At the outset it may be recalled that medieval language-use involved a much greater oral element than is common nowadays. Poems were written to be read aloud, just as letters were often written to be heard and therefore involved careful attention to aural rhythms in their prose; the audience's experience of the sermon was of course primarily aural. Since even private reading generally was vocalised – that is, accompanied by lip movement and sound production – there is an oral element to be considered in virtually every sort of medieval writing, whether in poetry or prose. The architecture of the medieval monastery often reflected this fact, with study cells facing outward into a courtyard rather than inward to a hallway, so as to minimise the vocal interference between readers; the carrell system was another solution to this problem in large libraries. This fact of vocalisation helps to explain the constant concern for the aural which runs through all three types of medieval composition manuals.

The manuals in each of these three areas of composition belong to a 'genre' in the literal sense of the word, sharing common characteristics of purpose and method. At the same time there is a remarkable similarity among these genres in their concern to provide opportunity for individual creativity within a specified form. Taken together they are an index to medieval habits of composition.

The present chapter will confine itself to the school 'arts' of poetry and prose. These treatises grew out of the practical teaching situation which coordinated a set of teaching methods inherited from ancient times and refined over many centuries of experience. They were not composed in isolation, being written by the masters who taught in the schools. We have seen that the number of schools was large, and that instruction in grammar went on universally throughout Europe during the period. Therefore it may be surprising at first glance to note that the schools produced only a small number of writing treatises – six Latin works in all – over a period of about ninety years beginning in 1175. (The later, vernacular 'arts' are a different story – for example, see Chapter 16 on the rich Occitan tradition.) This can be compared with over 200 *artes praedicandi* and some 300 separate works of the *ars dictaminis*.

This apparent anomaly proves in fact to be another proof of the homogeneity of instruction in the art of writing. What occurred was that one of the six books – the *Poetria nova* of the Englishman Geoffrey of Vinsauf – proved to be so well suited to the core curriculum of the schools that it dominated all the others and became, by medieval standards, a runaway best-seller. Nearly 200 manuscripts of the *Poetria nova* have survived, many with commentaries. To place this number in perspective (there are only eighty-two surviving manuscripts of Chaucer's *Canterbury Tales*),[1] it may be noted that there are only 213 medieval manuscripts of Alexander of Villa Dei's *Doctrinale*, the advanced grammar which was so successful that it continued in use in some places (e.g. Vienna) into the eighteenth century. Furthermore, there are more manuscripts of the *Poetria nova* surviving from the Middle Ages than there are of Ciceronian rhetorical works like the *De inventione* or the Pseudo-Ciceronian *Rhetorica ad Herennium*. Clearly the *Poetria nova* was one of the most popular non-religious books of its time.

To understand the reasons for this success it is useful to review the nature of these various manuals, their relation to the school curriculum, and the ways in which Geoffrey of Vinsauf's surpasses the others in meeting the needs of that curriculum. The six Latin works are: Matthew of Vendôme's *Ars versificatoria* (*c.* 1175); Geoffrey of Vinsauf's *Poetria nova* (*c.* 1200–15) and *Documentum de modo de arte dictandi et versificandi* (after 1213); Gervase of Melkley's *Ars versificaria* (*c.* 1215); John of Garland's *Parisiana poetria de arte prosayca, metrica, et rithmica* (*c.* 1220;

---

[1] See Pearsall, *Life of Chaucer*, p. 231.

revised *c.* 1231–5); and Eberhard the German's *Laborintus* (after 1213, before 1280). All these authors were teachers of the *ars grammatica*, as described in the previous chapter. Consequently their concerns are for composition based both on precept and on example or imitation. They have been described as 'rhetoricians' because they look to Cicero as well as to Horace for some of their concepts of invention, arrangement and style.[2] Nevertheless these masters are firmly rooted in the typical curriculum of the medieval school; their treatises clearly indicate the type of classroom instruction that lay behind much of medieval language use.

1. The six 'arts'

Matthew of Vendôme

Matthew of Vendôme was a teacher who had studied under Bernard Silvester at Tours and then taught grammar himself at Orléans before departing angrily for Paris after a dispute with another teacher, Arnulf (whose literary scholarship is discussed in Chapters 5 and 6 below). It was at Paris, shortly before 1175, that he composed his *Ars versificatoria*.[3] The book is in prose with numerous verse examples. It is divided into four main parts, with sections numbered consecutively within each part: 'elegance of interior meaning' (118 sections); 'elegance of words' (forty-six sections); 'the quality or mode of expression' (fifty-two sections); and 'the execution of the material' (fifty-one sections). A brief summary follows.

The *Ars versificatoria* of Matthew of Vendôme
Prologue

Since many writers are called *versificatores*, without being truly qualified as such, this work is offered to present elementary instruction in the art.

I

Verse is metrical discourse, proceeding through *clausula*, provided with embroidery through the marriage of beautiful words and flowers of sense, containing neither anything too mean nor anything useless. Neither the connecting of words, the counting of feet, nor the marking of quantities makes verse, but rather the elegant joining of words, the expression of the proper qualities and the provision of the proper epithet for each and every thing.

Epithet attributes a certain accident to a substantive. Thus an epithet pertains either to the good, the bad or the indifferent.

---

[2] By Faral, *Les arts poétiques.*   [3] Text in Faral, pp. 109–93.

A beginning may be made in one of four ways: *zeugma*, *ypozeusis*, *methonomia*, sententia or *proverbium*.

The discourse should avoid incongruities of disposition of parts, as well as incongruities of word position (e.g. *cacosyntheton*).

In giving descriptions, a person other than the person described should give it. Words will be better if they proceed from the manliness of the person, the flexibility of his mind, his desire for honour, and his distaste for servitude. The properties of persons ought to be observed: for instance, age, duty or position, sex, place of birth, and other properties which Cicero calls *personae attributa*. Horace agrees, and uses these methods. [Then follow thirteen pages of examples, supplying complete descriptions of a Pope, Caesar, Ulysses, a glutton (Davus), two beautiful women (Marcia, Helen) and a hag (Beroe).] These examples may also be applied to disparaging descriptions, but it is better to teach by good examples, because of the natural tendency to incline towards vice. Proper names of particular persons may be employed as epithets descriptive of general qualities; for example, Caesar's name may convey the idea of a certain age, condition, or some other attribute. Many epithets ought to be assigned to the description of one person, in order that he may be described better. Some attributes are proper to link with either men or women. Description should follow what is true or what is like the truth.

Description may be of two kinds, both suited to either praise or vituperation. The first kind is of the exterior (*superficialis*), dealing with the beauty of the body or external appearance. The second kind (*intrinseca*) deals with internal attributes of a person.

There are eleven attributes of persons: Name, Nature (which includes body, spirit, and others such as nation, age or sex), Social relations, Fortune, Deportment, Zeal, Disposition, Counsel, Calamity (*casus*), Deeds and Speech.

Next to be considered is the description of affairs, either of deeds or words. There are nine *attributa negotio*: name or definition, cause (impulsive or reasoned), circumstances before the fact, circumstances during the fact, circumstances after the fact, opportunity for acting, quality of the act, time and place. Just as a house is more secure that sits on many columns, so will a description be more valued that supplies many examples. It is also useful to employ *zeugma*, *ypozeusis* and the other schemes and tropes.

II

There are three sources of beauty or elegance in poetry: the beauty of internal thought, the ornament of words and the manner of speaking. [Following this statement there is a lengthy treatment of individual words which are beautiful in themselves – for instance, adjectives ending in *-alis*, in -*osus*, or in -*autus* – as well as treatment of comparatives and of words not in plebeian use.]

III

The quality or mode of expression (*qualitas sive modus dicendi*) depends upon polished words, colours of speaking and interior intricacy. The mode of expression produces beauty more often than the substance or material does. Just as in a statue, where the material itself is not beautiful and art must be employed to produce beauty, so in a poem the material of words is not of itself beautiful but is made so by the artistic use of schemes, tropes and colours of rhetoric.

There are seventeen schemes, of which thirteen are useful in the exercise of composing verses: *zeugma, ypozeusis, anaphora, epynalensis, anadiplo-sis, epyzeusis, paranomasia, paranomeon, scesisonomaton, omoetholeu-ton, poliptoton, polissinteton, dialiton* or *assinteton*.

There are thirteen tropes of which nine are most useful in versifying: *metaphora, antithetus, methonomia, sidonoche, peryfrasis, epithetum, methalemsis sive climax, allegoria, aenigma*.

There is a certain correspondence or parallelism between certain schemes and certain tropes, on the one hand, and certain *coloures rhetorici* on the other: *contentio* and *antithetus, anaphora* and *duplicatio, parono-masia* and *annominatio, epanalempsis* and *repetitio, scesisonomaton* and *membrum orationis* sive *articulus, dialiton* and *dissolutus, polissyne-theton* and *conjunctum, methalempsis* or *climax* and *gradatio*. Moreover, several tropes or schemes may be found in one line of verse, as in Statius (*Theb.* 2.446), 'A short-lived kingship spares not the populace', where *sententia, metaphora* and *methonomia* may be identified.

It will be sufficient here merely to name the colours of rhetoric,[4] since the reader can find them treated elsewhere: *repetitio, conversio, com-plexio,* t*raductio, contentio, exclamatio, ratiocinato, sententia, contrar-ium, membrum orationis* or *articulus, similiter cadens, similiter desinens,*

---

[4] Matthew's use of the term 'colour' introduces us to a complex set of terminological dif-ficulties. The most commonly used ancient Latin term for an ornamenting device (as in the *Rhetorica ad Herennium*) was *exornatio*, typically Englished as 'figure'. But by Quintilian's time ten of the so-called 'figures of speech' had acquired the name of 'trope' (*tropus*). In late Antiquity the term 'scheme' (*scema*) was applied to certain other figures of speech, especially by grammarians. Onulf of Speyer's *Colores rhetorici* (*c.* 1050) seems to have been the earliest text to use the term 'colours', and thereafter the word seems to be in common use – generally, though not always, applied to a designated set of figures of speech. Geoffrey of Vinsauf's *Summa de coloribus* (ed. Faral, pp. 321–7) lists twenty figures of speech; Matthew lists twenty-nine; Évrard of Béthune's *Graecismus* limits the list to twenty-five – but John of Garland uses the term generically as if to apply to every figure. By the fourteenth century (as in Chaucer) the word 'colour' had become a petrified term which denoted ornamentation in general.

commixtio, annominato, subjectio, gradatio, diffinitio, transitio, correptio, occupatio, disjunctio, conjunctum, adjunctum, conduplicatio, commutatio, dubitatio, dissolutio, praecisio, conclusio.

Finally, we must point out that three sources of beauty ought to be present (as was said in part II above) whenever poetry is written.

IV

The execution of material is one area in which the poorly instructed, when writing their school exercises (retelling poetic stories), merely produce word-for-word paraphrases as if they wanted to write a verse commentary. But I feel that I have to go deeper into the subject, and discuss the methods which the students should emulate. It is not enough to render word for word, in order to achieve a faithful imitation or a true interpretation of a work. Therefore I shall now discuss the subjects treated in Antiquity, and also shall discuss new subjects.

The ancients have rightly pointed out that certain words should be avoided in verse, and that barbarisms, prolixity and multiplication of new genres should be avoided. Moderns however should avoid some things – such as digression and improper word usage – that were allowed to the ancients.

Modern writers have given us directions for the proper use of the attributes of persons and deeds for description and for renovating old texts. There are two methods of permutation: changing the words but not the sense, and changing both the words and the sense.

The master or teacher has two primary duties: to note the vices in (student) verse, and to offer remedies for these vices. The student, on the other hand, has three duties: the admission of faults, the removal of written faults and avoidance of future faults.

Methods of conclusion are as varied as their authors. Some methods used by the ancients are recapitulation, petition for indulgence, pleas for glory, or presentation of thanks. I end with a praise of God.

Matthew of Vendôme's *Ars versificatoria*, as this summary shows, is something like Horace's *Ars poetica* in that it rather loosely organises bits of advice to verse-makers. A great deal of prior knowledge is assumed. Despite his frequent assaults on false versifiers and poor teachers, Matthew seems to be concerned primarily with students rather than with other teachers. 'This little book instructs boys about verses', he says at the end (2.51, v. 29). He calls upon students to try to understand the general principles behind his examples, lest they be misled into mistaking the intentions of the authors they read. It is interesting to note that Matthew customarily refers to his 'hearers' (*auditores*) rather than 'readers'. This may mean that what we have here are published lectures, or that Matthew is merely using a convention of his time to indicate that verse is to be heard, not to be read silently.

Geoffrey of Vinsauf

Very little is known of Geoffrey of Vinsauf's career. He seems to have been an Englishman, and may have taught at Northampton. There are also connections to Paris. The Preface to his *Poetria nova* says he visited Rome, and the poem is dedicated to Pope Innocent III.[5] Perhaps he also taught at a studio or lower school in Bologna, a possibility reinforced by the fact that he may have composed an *ars dictaminis* in the Italian mode.[6] He is also the author of a *Documentum de modo et arte dictandi et versificandi*, and of a treatise on figures titled *Summa de coloribus rhetoricis*. Summaries of his *Poetria nova* and *Documentum* follow.

THE *POETRIA NOVA* OF GEOFFREY OF VINSAUF

General observations. Just as a person building a house first plans what he is to do, so a poet must plan his poem in advance of the writing. The poet must first find things to say, either in his mind or from material things. Then he must consider the order in which he says these things, the language in which he says them, and finally the use of voice, facial expression and action.

Disposition. There are two forms of orders, the natural and the artificial. There is only one kind of natural order (that is, beginning at the beginning), but there are eight forms of artificial order: beginning at the end, beginning in the middle, *sententia* at the beginning, *sententia* in the middle, *sententia* at the end, *exemplum* in the beginning, *exemplum* in the middle, *exemplum* at the end.

Amplification and abbreviation. In the beginning, art lays out the general plan; you must carry it out, either by shortening or lengthening. If you wish to amplify, you may use the following methods: *interpretatio, circumlocutio, collatio, apostrophe, prosopopeia, digressio, descriptio, oppositio*. If you wish to abbreviate, you may use the following methods: *emphasis, articulus, ablativus, prudentia dicti, sensus multarum clausus in una* and *asyndeton*.

Ornaments of style. Whether short or long, let the discourse colour itself inside and out, but with the proper class of colours. One kind of colour (*tropus*) is achieved by the changing the form of words (*transsumptio*) to make new ones (*homo ad rem similem, re ad hominem similem*); or the replacement of a word by a more effective word having the same metrical

---

[5] Text in Faral, *Les arts poétiques*, pp. 197–262.   [6] Ed. Licitra, 'La "Summa"'.

usefulness; or the movement of words for emphasis or clarity; opposition of sense, or the joining of all meanings in one expression or word. No matter which of these methods is used, grammatical rules must be followed. When the following are used, the sound of the voice will bring joy to the ear and will touch the mind with new delight: *translatio, permutatio, pronominatio, nominatio, denominatio, yperbolicus, intellectio, abusio, transgressio*. You must be careful that the use of these colours does not make your expression obscure. Consider not your own ability but that of your listener, for though you speak yourself, you speak among others who must hear you.

There are two other types of colours: the first is Figures of Speech (*flores verborum*), which are: *repetitio, conversio, complexio, traductio, contentio, exclamatio, interrogatio, ratiocinatio, sententia, contrarium, membrum, articulus, continuatio in sententia (in contrario* and *in occlusione), compar, similiter cadens, similiter desinens, subjectio, gradatio, diffinitio, transitio, correctio, occupatio, disjunctio, conjunctio, adjunctio, conduplicatio, interpretatio, commutatio, permissio, dubitatio, expeditio, dissolutio, praecisio, conclusio*.

The second type is Figures of Thought (*flores sententiarum*): *distributio, licentia, diminutio, descriptio, disjunctio, frequentatio, expolitio per sermocinationem*, and *expolitio per exsuscitationem, commoratio, contentio, similitudo, exemplum, imago, effictio, notatio, sermocinatio, conformatio, significatio, brevitas, demonstratio*.

Other effects may be gained by conversions, that is, by changing verbs into nouns, or adjectives into nouns. Moreover, the simple style can be aided by collecting clauses or words together appositively.

Finally, in respect to style, there are some general observations to be made: choose words appropriate to persons and circumstances; choose words appropriate to poetry. The plain style is appropriate to comedy. Everything in comedy should be light (*levis*): spirit, things or words. These faults should be avoided: hiatus, repetition of the same ending, overly long periods, forced metaphors. Finally, the writer should submit his work to a triple judgement of mind, ear and usage.

Memory and delivery. Memory is best served by repetition and rehearsal of what is new or novel; the system outlined by Cicero is too difficult. No one praises an inept recitation, so we must study this subject. There are three languages in reciting: the voice, the countenance and movement. All should be moderate, and suited to the matter of the recitation. Everything should concur at once – the invented matter, the smooth discourse, the polished sequences, the ready memory. An inept recitation of good material is as bad as a beautiful recitation of poor material.

THE *DOCUMENTUM* OF GEOFFREY OF VINSAUF

The *Documentum*, which Geoffrey apparently composed shortly after the *Poetria nova*, survives in two versions, one short and one longer. So far only the short version has been edited.[7] The longer version includes materials not printed by Faral, notably a section on *dictamen*; the short version is in most respects a repetition of the ideas found in the *Poetria nova*, though often in a different order. The *Documentum* employs a somewhat different technical vocabulary, one notable instance being the use of the terms *ornata facilitas* and *ornata difficultas* for sets of figures which appear in the *Poetria nova* without that designation. Virtually every item in the short *Documentum* appears in the *Poetria nova*. Geoffrey's own summary from the end of the short *Documentum* gives a clear idea of its contents:

In summation let us draw together those things which were treated extensively above. This has been said concerning the beginning and the transition. Concerning the beginning what has been said? How a natural beginning is made one way and an artistic beginning in eight ways. Concerning the transition, first, how it is to be continued in the beginning. For the continuation is easy if the beginning is natural. But if it is artistic it is to be continued in three ways: one way, if the beginning is taken near the middle or end; another way if the beginning is taken from a proverb; a third way, if the beginning is taken from an *exemplum*. Afterwards it was stated how it happens that shorter matter can be enlarged, and extensive matter made shorter: we treated fitting and sufficient theory for amplifying brevity and for abbreviating extended matter. Third, we treated how in the continuation of the matter there are two methods of expressing something well: one method is using ornamented facility, the other method is using ornamented difficulty. We taught clearly those things to which ornamented facility and difficulty are compared, subjecting general rules to an end, by which every meaning which anyone has in mind or on his tongue can be said ornately. There are three ways to handle the ending of material: from the body of the matter, from a proverb, or from an exemplum.

It is interesting to note one important feature of the *Documentum* which illustrates once again the extent to which Geoffrey, like the other masters, conceives of a basic 'art' underlying all forms and species of composition. That is, Geoffrey takes it for granted that his precepts apply to both prose and verse. The very title of the work, of course, indicates that both prose and verse are to be considered. His summary here clearly could apply to any kind of discourse. Moreover, the most complete manuscripts (e.g. London, British Library, MS Cleopatra B.6) reveal that Geoffrey applies to letter-writing the same principles of amplification and abbreviation recommended for verse in the *Poetria nova*. He does point out special

---

[7] In Faral, *Les arts poétiques*, pp. 265–319.

features of a letter, such as the need for a salutation and the arrangement of the body into four parts, but he also cites Horace (*Antiqua poetica*) and Aristotle (*Poetica*) in a way that no professional Italian dictator would have done in his century. The specialised letter-writing manuals of the *dictatores* regarded letter-writing as a self-contained and unique art, but here Geoffrey places letters within a much broader tradition of composition based on precepts applying to both verse and prose.

Gervase of Melkley

Nothing at all is known of the life of Gervase of Melkley except that most contemporary references in his *Ars versificaria* are to English persons or places and that these references as well as his sources date his work to the period 1213–16. He cites Geoffrey of Vinsauf as well as Matthew of Vendôme, Horace, Cicero, Seneca, Ovid and John of Hanville (author of the twelfth-century allegorical satire *Architrenius*). Gervase restates, though in a different order, basically the same ideas found earlier in Matthew and Geoffrey.

THE *ARS VERSIFICARIA* OF GERVASE OF MELKLEY

Teaching consists in the prevention of faults, in the provision for permitted faults (i.e. figures), and in precepts derived from grammar and rhetoric. But theory alone is not enough: the reading of ancient and modern authors should be coupled with ample practice in composition. There are three sources of ornaments of style: identity, similitude and contrariety.

Identity consists of Consonance and Mutation. Consonance includes: (1) simple narration using *annominatio, paronomasia, leonitas, homeoptoton, homoioteleuton, repetitio, conversio, complexio, traductio* and *gradatio*; (2) vehement language using *correctio, exclamatio* and *dubitatio*; and (3) question-and-answer using *sermocinatio, subiectio* and *ratiocinatio*.

Mutation includes: (1) subtractions using *praecisio* and *prolempsis*; (2) additions using *occupatio, coadunatio* (with *coniunctio, disiunctio* and *reiteratio*, its species being *repetitio, conduplicatio, interpretatio*) and *determinatio*; and (3) changes using *aequalitas, digressio, transversio* (*inversio* and *transmutatio*) and *transcensus* (*hyperbaton, litotes* and *hyperbole*).

Similitude derives from *assumptio* and *omyosis*.

Contrariety includes: (1) allegory (*ironia, antifrasis, carientismos, sarcasmos*); (2) enthimema (*contrarium, conversio, adversitas, metathesis, contentus* and *antithetum*); and (3) *paroemia*.

Disposition consists of either natural order or artistic order. There are three levels of style: plain, moderate and sublime.

Study of language includes both the rules of metrics and the rules of prose (*dictamen*). The versificator needs to know all kinds of literature. *Dictamen* uses three kinds of language: metric, rhythmic and prosaic. Grammar supplies the rules for *accentus* so it can be known whether a given syllable is long or short.

While the *Ars versificaria* of Gervase is valuable more for its reinforcement of standard precepts than for any uniqueness of concept, it does state the basic doctrines clearly.

John of Garland

Perhaps the most ambitious work in this whole series is the *Parisiana poetria de arte prosayca, metrica, et rithmica* of John of Garland (*c.* 1195–1272), an Englishman who had studied at Oxford but spent most of his teaching career in Paris. His name in fact derives from the *clos de Garlande* on the left bank of the Seine in what became known as 'The Latin Quarter' because so many students flocked there during the twelfth and thirteenth centuries. John was so well regarded as a teacher that the Count of Toulouse brought him to that city in 1229 as one of two grammar masters for a new university; when financial support failed to materialise, however, John returned to Paris and spent the rest of his life there. He was a prolific writer, composing Latin hymns in addition to grammatical and religious works.

The title of his major work is significant – a single 'art' deals with all three types of composition (i.e. prose, verse, rhythmics). He says 'The Art' (*de arte*) rather than 'The Arts' (*de artis*), believing that a single set of ideas governs all discourse. As a matter of fact he includes oral language as well as writing, treating oral Memory as well as the *oratio* or persuasive speech. (The 'Parisiana poetria' of the title, as the *accessus* or literary-theoretical overview[8] which introduces the work [probably the work of John himself] points out, simply comes from the first words of the treatise, which should not be thought of as focusing exclusively on poetry.) The book's purpose is to impart a technique 'for treating any subject whatever'. John's ambition, then, is to lay out the basic principles which in his view underlie any

---

[8] On the *accessus*, which had a variety of forms (depending on the choice of headings under which a given text was discussed), see especially the relevant discussion in Chapters 5, 6, 14 and 21 below. The one used to introduce the *Parisiana poetria* follows a well-established model, which was popular during the twelfth century. During the second decade of the thirteenth century, a new model rapidly gained popularity, which took its terms of reference from the 'four causes' associated with Aristotle (and hence in modern scholarship it is sometimes termed the 'Aristotelian Prologue'; see particularly Minnis, *Authorship*, pp. 28–9). The efficient cause was the author, the material cause his subject-matter, the formal cause his style and/or textual structure, and the final cause his purpose or ultimate objective in writing.

communicative effort. If the *modistae* (discussed in the previous chapter) went beyond Latin to seek a metalanguage that would explicate all human utterance, John sought a meta-art, beyond genre, which would enable any species of future discourse to be well organised and effective.

The opening words of the *accessus* provide the best index to John's intention to make a whole out of many apparently different parts:

Five things about this short work should be examined at the start: the subject-matter [*materia*], the author's purpose [*intentio*], its usefulness for its audience [*utilitas audientis*], what field of knowledge it belongs to [*cui parti philosophie supponatur*], the method [*modus agendi*]. The subject-matter is the art of writing letters, of quantitative verse and of rhymed syllabic verse; but behind these three lie five others, which are: the art of invention, of selection, of memory, of arrangement and of embellishment. The author's purpose is to publish a manual of style. Its usefulness is that it imparts a technique for treating any subject whatever in prose, quantitative verse or rhymed syllabic verse. This book belongs to three particular fields of knowledge: grammar, since it teaches how to speak properly; rhetoric, since it teaches how to speak elegantly, and ethics, since it teaches or instils a sense of what is right, and from this according to Cicero every virtue springs. This is the approach: the author teaches how to invent, according to the categories of invention, words, that is, substantives, adjectives and verbs used both literally and metaphorically, in any kind of composition, whether it be a legal or academic letter, or an elegiac poem, or a comedy, or satire, or a history. For he heals sometimes with the art of prose, sometimes with that of poetry, back and forth from one to the other; sometimes with rhymed syllabic verse, but this towards the end; and at the very end he deals in a special way with quantitative verse, where nineteen poems, each in a different metre, are created in imitation of Horace, who assembled nineteen different metres in his odes, to one or another of which any other metrical poem or hymn is reducible. Thus he treats now of this matter, now of that, in part and by turns; for there are some who might cut the art of prose out of the book for his own sake, and others who might cut out the art of quantitative verse, or of rhymed syllabic verse, or of poetry in general, as they wish, and thus the poor book would be torn up into rags. Insofar as anyone wishes to have a part, then, it is necessary to take the whole.   (tr. Lawler, p. 3, with minor changes)

The concept of wholeness should be understood, otherwise one might think John's *Parisiana poetria* to be merely a jumble of miscellaneous precepts. John does not in fact succeed always in demonstrating how all the parts fit together, but it is abundantly clear throughout that he regards his hundreds of examples as 'modes' based on fundamental principles of composition. Proliferation is for John not tedium but proof. There is little which is unique about his particular ideas – for example the eight methods of artificial beginning in his third chapter prove to be precisely those of Geoffrey of Vinsauf's *Documentum* – but it is this very sharing of contemporary doctrine which enables him to make the claim that all these compositional precepts do form an identifiable whole. The following summary will indicate his method.

THE *PARISIANA POETRIA DE ARTE PROSAYCA, METRICA, ET RITHMICA* OF JOHN OF GARLAND

I

This book is divided into seven parts: the doctrine of invention, the method of selecting material, disposition or ordering of material, parts of letters and vices in any kind of writing rhetorical ornament (amplification and abbreviation including figures), examples of letters, metrical and rhythmical composition.

Whoever treats an art should define its terms. Prose is ornate and sententious discourse written without metre and distinguished by appropriate sequences of clausulae. [Then follow two letters as examples.] Verse is a regular ordering of feet, a foot being a certain measure of syllables and quantities.

As Horace says in the *Poetria* (i.e. the *Ars poetica*), we ought to find material before selecting any of it, and should select before we arrange in any order. Therefore invention or finding of material is our first concern. As Cicero says in the *Secunda rethorica* (i.e. the *Rhetorica ad Herennium*), invention is the devising of matter, true or probable, that would make the case convincing. There are five species of invention: Where, What, What Kind, How and Why. The first of these (*ubi invenitor*) includes three types of persons (courtiers, city dwellers and rustics), examples and etymology. Example (*exemplum*), which can also be used for 'What', is a saying or deed of some esteemed person (*autentice persone*) worthy of imitation; a proverb is a brief moral statement useful as an example, and can be invented through praise or blame, from the subject, or from the character of persons involved. The third species of 'What Kind' deals with the honourable or the dishonourable. The fourth species of 'How' uses seven figures: *annominatio, traductio, repetitio, gradatio, interpretatio, diffinitio* and *sermocinatio*. The final species of 'Why' deals with the final cause of the invention.

Care should be taken to choose words – nouns, verbs and adjectives – which are appropriate to their subjects, as Virgil has done. The boy (or student) should know how to convert nouns into verbs to use them metaphorically, and be familiar with the method of circumlocution.

II

Following invention comes the selection of material. Cicero places disposition after invention, then adds style, memory and delivery. But in poetical and epistolary writing it is useful for selection of material to follow invention. We ought to choose material for three reasons: because it is useful or profitable, offers pleasure to our minds, and offers delight or beauty to our sight. The material should be easy to write, clearly understandable, and either brief (as in letters) or prolix (as in poems). If some of the material is difficult to understand, we should select things that make it light. There are nine ways to make slight material grave and authoritative: property of a thing to stand for the thing, matter for what is made from it, consequent for antecedent, part for whole, whole for part, cause for the caused, container for the thing contained, genus for species, species for genus.

As to the problem of memory, it is best to follow Cicero's method of imagining mental 'areas' in which to place the things we wish to remember. But I also propose that you make three columns within each area, corresponding to the three types of persons and the three appropriate styles. [This is, to imagine each area divided by persons and styles; see section V below.]

If you wish to abbreviate difficult material, you may do it by avoiding the nine methods listed above, or by changing verbs into nouns, nouns into adjectives, etc.

III

After invention and selection of material come the beginning and disposition. It is important that the parts of a discourse be in the mind of the writer before they are in his mouth. Any discourse has three parts to consider: beginning, progression, and end or conclusion. There are two kinds of beginnings, natural and artificial. The natural method relates things in the order in which they occur. The artificial method begins at the end or in the middle, and either with or without a proverb.

IV

In letters, however, there are eight ways to devise an exordium: with a proverb, with an example, with a comparison, with a similitude, with a condition using 'if', with the adverb 'since', with 'while', or with an ablative absolute.

There are six parts to a discourse (*oratio*) whenever we wish to persuade or dissuade. [Then follows an eighty-one-line hexameter poem as an example.]

There are five ways to abbreviate material: emphasis, conversion of a verb to a participle, asyndeton, ablative absolute, and choice of expressive words. There are five ways to amplify material: *digressio, descriptio, circumlocutio, prosopopeia* and *apostrophe* (which includes five colours of rhetoric: *exclamatio, subjectio, duplicatio, dubitatio* and *interpretatio*).

V

There are six vices of composition which must be avoided in poetry even more than in prose: the mixing of comedy and tragedy in the same work; unsuitable digressions; obscure brevity; unsuitable mixing of styles; improper mixing of subjects; and the use of endings not suitable for the type of writing. For instance, recapitulation is suitable at the end for orators or preachers; exemplum or proverb is suitable to end a poem; and letters usually end with a clause beginning *ut*, *ne* or *quia*. There are three styles, according to the three states of men. Accordingly, Virgil has written three types of works for the three states: the *Bucolics*, in the lowest style, for pastoral men; the *Georgics*, in the middle style, for husbandmen; and the *Aeneid*, in the highest style, for the most important men. [Then follows a long digression on the acceptability of certain names and appellatives to be used in letters to dignitaries, especially in *salutationes*.]

Since narration is common to both prose and poetry, I shall discuss it here. As Cicero says, narrative is of three kinds: fable, or what is neither true nor like the truth; history, or deeds from the distant past; and argument, or fictitious events of the type found in comedy. There are three kinds of poetry: dramatic, narrative and mixed. All the following kinds of poems are historical (except comedy, which is argumentative): epithalamium, epitaph, bucolic, georgic and lyric poetry, epodon, hymn, invective, satire, tragedy and elegy.

Besides the three styles named by the ancients, there are four styles used by the modern writers: the Gregorian, Tullian, Hilarian and Isidorian. Each style follows the example of the writer named.

VI

Embellishment of poetry. Word order in prose. Both prose and poetry may be ornamented by changes in word position, especially if the change results in a better sound or a more emphatic meaning. [Following this, without any transition or explanation, John begins a long list of figures with examples.]

Colours of words are *repetitio, complexio, traductio, contentio, exclamatio, interrogatio, ratiocinatio, sententia, contrarium, membrum, articulus, compar, similiter cadens, similiter desinens, annominatio* (in thirteen mutations), *conduplicatio, subjectio, gradatio, diffinitio, transitio, correctio, occupatio, disjunctio, conjunctio, adjunctio, interpretatio, commutatio permissio, dubitatio, expeditio, dissolutio, precisio, nominatio, prenominatio, denominatio, circuitio, transgressio, superlatio, intellectio, translatio, abusio, permutatio, conclusio.*

Colours of thought are *distribucio, licentia, diminucio, descriptio, divisio, frequentatio, explicatio, commoratio, contentio, similitudo, exemplum, imago, effectio, notatio, sermocinatio, conformatio, significatio, demonstratio.*

The author may choose colours to be used either for amplification or abbreviation.

The eleven attributes of persons from rhetoric are also essential: name, nature, social position, wealth, character, motives, disposition, occupation, circumstances, actions and speech.

VII

The characteristics of a tragedy are that it is written in the high style; it deals with shameful and criminal actions; it begins in joy and ends in tears. [Then follows a 126-verse account of a jealous woman who admits the enemy to a besieged castle to cover up her murder of her rival and her lover when she finds them together, even though her own brother is killed in the assault.[9] This example of a tragedy written in high style is followed by examples of various kinds of epistles.]

The art of rithmus (*rithmica*): Rithmus is a species of art like music. Music is divided into mundane, which consists of due proportion of elements; into human, which consists of the proportion and concord of humours; and into instrumental, which consists of the concord of instruments. These species are lyrical, metrical and rhythmical. *Rithmica* is the art which teaches the making of *rithmus*. *Rithmus* is a consonance of clause-endings ordered with a certain measure but without metrical feet. Consonance of *rithmus*, as is music, is a consonance of tones and of things, of *concordia discors* or *discordia concors*. The term 'clause endings' is used to distinguish *rithmus* from lyrical composition, just as the term 'certain measure' signifies that it may consist of more or fewer syllables. Also, it is said to be 'without metrical feet' to distinguish it from metrical composition. The term 'ordered' means that the clauses should fall into a rhythmical pattern. *Rithmus*, some say, takes its origin from the rhetorical colour which is called *similiter desinens*. In a sense *rithmus* proceeds like iambic metre or like spondaic. By iambus in this connection is meant an expression whose penultimate term is shortened, for an iambus is made from short and long. A spondeus in this sense is an expression in the spondaic mode. [Then follows an eighty-eight-line poem as an example of the two metres.] Colours of rhetoric are necessary in *rithmus* as in metrics, and especially the following: *similiter desinens* or *homoteleuton*, *compar in numero sillibarum*, *annominatio*, *traductio*, *exclamatio* and *repetitio*.

There are various ways to apply *rithmus* to the writing of religious hymns. [Then follows a seventy-nine-line hymn in four- and six-line

[9] For further discussion of this tragedy see below, pp. 210, 403.

stanzas, *De beata virgine rithmus diversimode coloratus*. The treatise concludes with a discussion of various rhythmical modes, including nineteen types of Horace's odes.

It must be observed that John's efforts to describe a single art are not always successful. Sometimes he offers simply a set of examples, or – as in the case of the *oratio* – simply patches in a pre-existing set of notions from an author like Cicero. The *Parisiana poetria* is so clearly a school-related text that John may have expected its users to make their own oral connections and summaries for their young students. His efforts in any case provide another interesting insight into the concerns of thirteenth-century grammar masters – especially the concerns for systematic invention of ideas, for order and arrangement, and for *amplificatio* (and *abbreviatio*). While these three areas correspond of course to the ancient Ciceronian rhetorical canons of invention, arrangement and style, it is clear that John sees them equally as Horatian, or perhaps simply as natural steps in any creative process. They are true for John not because they are Ciceronian or Horatian but because they work.

The *Parisiana poetria de arte prosayca, metrica, et rithmica* thus stands at the apogee of the movement begun by Matthew of Vendôme in the preceding century. The medieval use of Geoffrey's *Poetria nova* was much greater, but it could well be that John's treatise furnishes for us a more revealing look at what the schoolmasters thought they were about.

Eberhard the German

If John of Garland's *Parisiana poetria* marks a high point in the movement of the *artes poetriae*, then the final work in that series seems to indicate a drying-up of enthusiasm about the craft. Evrardus Allemanus (not to be confused with Evrard de Béthune, author of the *Graecismus*) studied at Orléans then at Paris, but taught in Bremen or possibly Cologne. The title of his major work, *Laborintus*, is a double play on words: on *labyrinthus* or labyrinth, and on *laborem habens intus*, 'having labour in it'.[10] It was written sometime between *c.* 1225 and 1280.

The compositional doctrines of the *Laborintus* are those already familiar from the works of Vendôme, Vinsauf, Melkley and Garland, but the interesting thing is that only half of its 1,005 lines are devoted to versification and style. The subjects are by now routine – ways to commence a poem, amplification and abbreviation, ornaments of style, and rhythmical verse – and so a further summary seems unnecessary here. Eberhard devotes 238 of the 1,005 lines to complaints about the plight

---

[10] In Faral, *Les arts poétiques*, pp. 338–77.

of schoolteachers, another 169 to a list of the Seven Liberal Arts, and another eighty-seven to a list of authors for study.

What sets the *Laborintus* off from similar works is the tone of cynicism, almost despair, with which the author approaches the task of educating the young in the lore of composition. He says that grammar and rhetoric suffocate him, and he has qualms of conscience about teaching the young to disguise things with flowers of language: 'When the word flowers', he says, 'the mind dries up' ('Cum verbum floret, mens aret'). Eberhard is a good journeyman, dispensing examples of figures and tropes and concluding with brief samples of rhythmical verse. He is clearly an experienced teacher – perhaps too experienced, and too weary of his labours. The innovative has now become ordinary, and the ordinary tiresome.

In any case the *Laborintus* is the last of the six Latin 'arts of poetry' that have come down to us. The movement flickered out less than a century after it had begun with Matthew of Vendôme's *Ars versificatoria*. Paradoxically, as we know, the schools which had given rise to the arts of poetry continued to proliferate, and their teaching masters with them. Why then do we not have 300-odd arts of poetry to match what happened with preaching and letter-writing? All three fields deal with compositional creativity in one way or another – they are what one modern scholar has called 'medieval rhetorical genres'[11] – but the grammar masters tired of producing preceptive manuals while their colleagues in other arts did not. The answer may lie in the overwhelming success of one of those works, the *Poetria nova* of Geoffrey of Vinsauf. Nearly 200 manuscripts survive, for example, compared to six for Garland's *Parisiana poetria* and five for Vendôme's *Ars versificatoria*. The *Poetria nova* was still being copied in the seventeenth century. More than a dozen whole and distinct commentaries on it have been identified, further proof of extensive use in the schools.

There are several reasons for this ascendancy. First of all, Geoffrey is a poet in his own right, presenting his ideas in fine hexameters and devising his own adroit examples. He has a gift for analogy and metaphor, as can be seen from the famous opening verses of his text:

If a man has a house to build, his hand does not rush, hasty, into the very doing; the work is first measured out with his heart's inward plumb line, and the inner man works out a series of steps beforehand according to a definite plan; his heart's hand shapes the whole before his body's hand does so, and his building is a plan before it is an actuality.   (tr. Kopp in Murphy, *Rhetorical Arts*, p. 34)

Thus it is with poetry, he continues, so that the poet's thought must precede his writing. Geoffrey's pedagogy is clear. When he comes to the

[11] Murphy, *Rhetoric*, pp. 362–3.

figures and tropes, for example, he offers a *tour de force* – two sustained sermon-like compositions which are connected discourses yet illustrate these rhetorical devices in exactly the order in which they appear in his source, the *Rhetorica ad Herennium*. The student is thus shown that the figures are not to be used as isolated flashes but as parts of a whole. Moreover, his deployment of examples is intended to indicate that many genres can be served by the central ideas he purveys. For Geoffrey the faculty of composition is clearly antecedent to any genre. The *Poetria nova* has clear transitions, is easy to follow, and in fact has often been given new headings in modern times (e.g. by Faral) to show recent readers how well organised it is. His use of everyday experience, and his reference to proverbial wisdom are other strengths. For example he says of lazy learners that they are like a cat: a cat wants a fish but does not want to go fishing. And he recounts personal experience – how he himself remembers, not just what Cicero says about memory. All in all the *Poetria nova* seems to have been well suited to the needs of the schools, offering clear doctrine presented in an intriguing manner.

Thus the composition of the *artes* stops with Eberhard before the end of the thirteenth century, though obviously their use did not stop. This continuing use, together with the continuity of school curriculum which gave rise to them, therefore makes it important that modern readers understand the literary implications of this movement.

2. Literary implications of the arts of poetry

One immediate distinction must be made about the intended audience of the Latin medieval arts of poetry which have come down to us. While the medieval *artes praedicandi* were written for use by adults who already possessed a certain level of education, and while the *artes dictaminis* sometimes served in the schools and sometimes served as guides to adults, the medieval *artes poetriae* just discussed are inextricably bound to the school environment. They are part – not the whole – of an instructional programme for the young which was designed not just to impart ideas (*doctrina*) but to instil habits of mind. These habits include the capacity to choose from among many ideas, to choose from among several modes of organisation, and to choose for the given occasion from among an almost unlimited number of modes of development amplification of the language itself. All these capacities depend on knowing many alternatives, so that choices may be made among them – hence these manuals, with their sets of possibilities. Choice is not possible without knowledge of alternatives, but effective compositional choice is not possible without practice in the effects of this or that choice – hence the actual classroom compositions for which the manuals are guides.

The manuals themselves have survived, but as far as we know very few of the practice compositions have survived. Yet we know that some later authors like Ben Jonson and John Milton actually did publish their school-boy exercises (*Timber* and *Prolusions* respectively).[12] Did some medieval authors do the same without acknowledgement? We do not always know, for instance, the origins of items in medieval 'teaching anthologies' or in other *florilegia* of the period. At the same time we do know that Alexander Nequam's *Corregationes Promethei* (c. 1187) was written to purpose, as a job-seeker's demonstration that he could compose rapidly and well enough to be a grammar teacher, and it has been suggested that the anonymous Middle English poem *The Owl and the Nightingale* (about the same period) may have had a similar purpose. One of Chaucer's earliest poems, 'The ABC', has the relentless quality of a writing-exercise, whether self-imposed or mandated by some master. In any case, it seems reasonable to assume that at least some medieval students preserved their early efforts in the usual medieval manner – by copying them and/or circulating them among friends. Surely, many thousands of practice-compositions must have been written down. Note that John of Garland ends his *Parisiana poetria* with a seventy-nine-line hymn which provides examples of various rhythmical patterns; if a reader found that hymn by itself in a manuscript, would it immediately be evident that it was once part of a schoolbook? Perhaps we have seen some medieval school compositions and have not known it.

The school-centredness of these Latin arts of poetry also marks them off from the several vernacular treatises of the fourteenth and fifteenth centuries which at first glance seem to be similar. The fourteenth-century Provençal *Las leys d'Amors* was composed by a committee of the Consistoire du Gai Savoir at Toulouse under the chairmanship of Guilhem Molinier: this was an art of poetry in the vernacular, composed for use by the adult members of a literary society (see further Chapter 16 below). It is not the language of composition which makes this Provençal art different from one by Geoffrey of Vinsauf or Matthew of Vendôme, then, but its intended use by practising poets rather than by young learners of language. The same can be said about Eustace Deschamps' *L'art de dictier*, along with the various 'arts' of the 'Seconde rhétorique' like those of Baudet Hérenc and Jean Molinet (on which see Chapter 15).[13] The brilliantly illuminated *Les Douze dames du rhétorique* (1444) which survives in Paris, Bibliothèque nationale de France, MS fr. 1174, is more of

---

[12] See Clark, *Milton at St Paul's School*.   [13] See Kelly, *Arts*, pp. 146–79.

an artistic encomium than it is an instructional manual.[14] These are all adult pieces. They usually presume prior knowledge. Moreover, they focus on poetry, and poetry alone. On the other hand the school manuals teach both poetry and prose, they start from the beginnings, and they encourage a catholicity of genre.

It is important to remember that the grammar masters regard themselves as custodians of language – not just Latin or French or any other single language, and not just verse or prose. The *habitus*, or learned capacity to compose, which made creativity possible in Latin could surely make it possible in Catalan, Tuscan or German. The *habitus* belongs to the person, not the nationality. For these masters there is a meta-literary principle, a meta-genre of composition, which must be absorbed before turning to a specific form like a *canzone* or a *lai*. 'The language of the great poets', Dante says in his *De vulgari eloquentia*, 'was regulated by art' (2.4). To inculcate this art into the young was the great ambition of these masters. And if they had been accused of seeking literacy rather than *ingenium* (personal ingenuity, not to be confused with the later sense of 'genius'), they probably would have replied that literacy is a prelude to literary *ingenium* – and, moreover, that literacy may be planned even if *ingenium* may not. Matthew of Vendôme claims that bad poets are those badly disciplined people who are wont to stray off the track of what they learned in school.

Another crucial characteristic of these works is that they are practical rather than theoretical. Geoffrey, Matthew and John are little concerned with matters which are treated in other branches of medieval literary theory and which have received recent scholarly attention – whether poetry relates more to ethics than to logic, or whether for medieval poets, Horace is a better source of ideas than Cicero, or whether (with Giovanni Boccaccio, 1313–75) poetry 'proceeds from the bosom of God' (*Genealogia deorum gentilium* 14.7). In his seventh chapter John of Garland uses 125 lines of verse as an example of tragedy, but provides only one sentence on the characteristics of tragedy. The fact that these writers did not even limit themselves to verse is once again an indication that they considered themselves as dealing with language-use at its most basic – a language-use prior to genre, applicable to all forms and subjects. Hence prose-verse-rhythmics are simply variant forms, just as the lyric is a form of verse, *cursus* a form of prose, and the hymn a form of rhythmics. But human invention, disposition and style are common to all forms. Even Geoffrey, so well known for his one work on verse-writing,

---

[14] Ed. by Brown, 'De nouveau', pp. 203–25. Elsewhere she has identified other fragments and related manuscripts.

also applied the concepts of that book to his own *ars dictaminis* in the so-called 'long version' of his prose *Documentum*, and included as well a treatment of *cursus* not printed in Faral's edition. In relation to verse these writers looked to 'the future poem' – the potential poem resident in the capacities (*habitus*) of the writer – and it seems fair to conclude also that they all looked to the 'future discourse' no matter what its form.

In Aristotelian terms[15] the writers of the arts of poetry worked in the realm of efficient causality. The very heterogeneity of examples proves that they were not concerned with final, formal or even material causes. The 'why', 'how' or 'what' of the particular discourse were less important to them than the 'way-in-which' the human mind conceives ideas and presents them in language. In Ciceronian terms they were 'rhetorical' in the sense that they argued for a systematic ordering of the creative process. In Horatian terms they were ready, like that Roman writer, to provide practical advice to the would-be writer.

3. Creativity through form: the modes of amplification

The arts of poetry embody a basic idea which has been common in Europe for two millennia – the idea that literary 'creativity' stems from plan and order. Geoffrey's famous analogy of the house – that a poem like a house needs to be blue-printed in the mind before it is built by the hand – is simply a striking statement of this principle, not an extreme or radical view of it. The schoolmasters take it for granted that whatever is written (or spoken or read aloud) will be composed in some particular format; we might attach the term 'genre' to a particular format like epic, elegy or lyric, but the masters are clearly less concerned with such particularities than they are with ways-to-say-things. What doth it profit a writer, John of Garland might ask, who knows what 'tragedy' is but cannot describe people, cannot recount events, cannot set up oppositions, cannot praise the virtuous and blame the vicious, cannot use epithets, cannot transsume verbs into nouns and vice versa, cannot 'colour' language with figures and tropes – who cannot, in short, express himself in any way?

Just as the overall structure of the composition needs to be planned, so also the basic building-blocks of language need to be plotted out in the writer's mind. 'Be it brief or long', Geoffrey says in his *Poetria nova*, 'let your discourse always "colour" itself [i.e. by figures of speech] within and without, the colour being chosen by a careful plan'. But this kind of planning can only proceed when there is knowledge of what is available.

[15] See n. 8 above.

The medieval teachers of the young worked hard at showing their charges how to discover what is available. The lengthy lists of modes of amplification (which may seem somewhat tedious nowadays) are evidence of that hard work. The schools sought to make them familiar, and therefore useable. He who has fashioned an apostrophe or devised a zeugma while young will then better be able to choose to use one of these modes later in his career if he wishes; it is knowledge-plus-practice which underlies those seemingly endless descriptions of the modes of amplification. The emphasis is always on the multiplication of choices – on various options for beginnings, for endings, and for middles. What is sought is an arsenal of possibilities.

Amplificatio, which may be translated as 'development', is therefore at the heart of their enterprise. It is clear that all these writers regard each discourse as operating within some kind of frame – some form of beginning-middle-end – in which the most important element is the middle. A literary genre could provide a frame, for instance, specifying the usual way in which such things were to be written; the same could be said of a sermon; the entry and the departure are for the sake of audience attention, but what is actually said is the crux of the matter. Matthew, and even John of Garland for that matter, take this so much for granted that they do not even bother to mention it, but proceed directly to modes of amplification. Note that Geoffrey's advice on beginnings (e.g. use of *exemplum*) is borrowed from what he says elsewhere about middles. This common stock of modes of amplification is shared as well by writers of medieval preaching manuals and of letter-writing manuals – evidence that it is in fact truly cultural in scope. The cross-fertilisation of the arts of discourse had begun to produce at least by Bede's time what was to become a common, shared European heritage of linguistic capacity. Medieval practitioners cared far less than we do whether their ideas came from grammar, rhetoric or dialectic, or whether they had obtained their knowledge from this or that teacher, or from one specific textbook as opposed to some other. They all partook of the linguistic heritage which made *amplificatio* available to any literate person. (The same is true of the basic modes of *abbreviatio* usually discussed along with amplification.) This concept is so central to medieval language use that the term *amplificatio* acquired a widely used set of synonyms – such as *executio, progressio, prosecutio, dilatio* – each of which denotes the same principle of building on a planned base of language.

A reading of the arts of poetry and prose, together with a consideration of the ways in which composition was practised in schools, will also remind us that in the Middle Ages *amplificatio* applied not only to what the ancients called *elocutio* (style) but also to matters of invention and ordering of parts. The tropes and figures play an important role in this accepted infrastructure, though they are not the only elements to be considered. Their full history has yet to be written.[16]

The handiest ancient codification of these devices occurs in the fourth book of the *Rhetorica ad Herennium*, which includes sixty-four of them grouped under figures of speech (or diction) and figures of thought. (The devices, and their order, can be seen in Geoffrey's *Poetria nova*.) It is not a comprehensive set, nor is it organised in a rigorously logical fashion. Yet it achieved almost canonical status during the Middle Ages, frequently being copied by itself. Numerous independent sets of figures appeared in the period; Geoffrey himself produced one under the title *Summa de coloribus rhetoricis*. 'Schemes' and 'tropes' were also the subject of the brief *Barbarismus* of Donatus, the third part of his *Ars maior*, which circulated as a separate treatise. Preachers recommended and used them, letter-writers used them, grammarians taught them. Meanwhile the grammarians themselves added hundreds more to the stock.

The schools systematised and reinforced the various modes of amplification, including the figures, which were already a part of the warp and woof of medieval culture. They permeated that culture, regardless of nationality and of period. That is why the modes of amplification can be identified in literary works and sermons in the eleventh and twelfth centuries, long before Matthew or Geoffrey ever put pen to parchment. It is important to recognise, therefore, that they do not stem from the school manuals, which merely employ them as part of the pre-existing general culture of the times. The schools were broadcasters, not founders, of these modes. Yet, because the schools did reflect the norms of their day, the manuals which come out of them can provide us with an index to medieval expectations of literacy. The fact that Geoffrey of Vinsauf's *Poetria nova* was copied (and commented on) so frequently over the centuries demonstrates among other things that what Geoffrey writes is at the core of these expectations.

One medieval commentary on Geoffrey provides a useful insight into these expectations. It begins with the statement that the purpose of the *Poetria nova* is 'to teach the reader what he should know of speaking rhetorically, whether in verse or in prose, so what is noted there serves prose as well as verse'.[17] For this purpose, the commentator says, Geoffrey's text offers both the precepts of the art of composition and his own examples of how the precepts are carried out in practice:

---

[16] Lausberg's *Handbuch* is a useful catalogue of ancient rhetorical terms, including the figures, but it does not deal with their medieval history. See Murphy, *Rhetoric*, pp. 182–91.

[17] *Early Commentary*, ed. Woods, p. 9. While this particular commentary dates from the early thirteenth century, it was copied well into the fourteenth. The survival of nine manuscripts into modern times is probable evidence of a substantial medieval reception.

To speak about an art is to give the precepts of the art. To speak artfully is to imitate the precepts, which is more difficult, just as it is more difficult to write verse than to give the precepts of verse. This author does both: he says about his art what he demonstrates from it.[18]

The way in which the commentator then proceeds to analyse the treatise line-by-line reveals a great deal about what a medieval reader would see as blameworthy or praiseworthy. At every stage there is an awareness of choices made by the author, an assumption of multiple possibilities for expression. For example the commentator's remarks on l. 1302 point to the use of dialogue by Geoffrey, following the *Rhetorica ad Herennium* in noting that 'by easy rhetoric the figure is developed in multiple ways'. And he applauds Geoffrey's treatment of the method of conversion (*modus commutandi*) in ll. 1603–1735, by which one part of speech may be changed into another, such as changing verbs into nouns, or adjectives into nouns. His basic principle is interesting: 'in whatever case the idea is better expressed [*sententia melior*], that is the way it should be set down'. 'Better expressed' is of course a comparative, and again assumes the existence of alternatives from which to choose. It is this choice-making imperative that leads both Vinsauf and his commentator to argue for the 'conversion' of adverbs in particular, since an adverb has only one form it is invariable and therefore artistically unexciting.

   A medieval reader/hearer, then, would not only be alert to the ways in which a text was actually developed, but would also be sensitive to the writer's mastery of options from which he made his final choices. What the commentators tell us is that the medieval writer (and, therefore, his readers) looked for a richness of textual development based on a broad range of available modes of expression. Such expectations raise another question. These arts of poetry are written in Latin. What is the relation between them and the vernacular literatures of the Middle Ages? In our previous chapter we have noted how, for example, English vernacular grammar treatises followed Latin grammar textbooks like Donatus. Yet we do not have vernacular Vinsaufs or Garlands, even though the French grammarian Alexander of Villa Dei's acknowledges that readers of his own Latin *Doctrinale* must be prepared to deal with boys speaking the vernacular (*laica lingua*). Any Latinate person of the Middle Ages was bilingual, if not trilingual. Yet the vernacularisation of education is a phenomenon of the very late Middle Ages, and later than that in some countries. Is the lore of the school, then, limited to Latin?

   It is not difficult to imagine the answer which would be received if the question were posed to one of the schoolmasters discussed here. Since the intent of the school is to teach language-use, he would point out,

[18] *Early Commentary*, ed. Woods, p. 7.

the *habitus* resides in the learner and not in the species of language he employs. Therefore a Picard student who learns how to 'transsume' Latin nouns into Latin verbs can just as well perform the same function in his vernacular or any other dialectal variation. Garland notes, for instance, that one of the rhythmical modes he discusses in Book 7 of the *Parisiana poetria* is 'common in French lyrics' (7.1342). The function once learned is transferable. Hence the inference is that vernacular facility may derive from Latin training. The school arts of poetry and prose, then, help us to understand what truly may be called the literary infrastructure of the Middle Ages.

3

The arts of letter-writing

Ronald G. Witt

Beginning in the late eleventh century and ending in the mid-fifteenth century, *ars dictaminis* consisted of a highly formalised code of rules governing the composition of prose letters in Latin and, sometimes towards the end of the period, in the vernacular.[1] While acknowledging that letters could also be composed in verse or in *prosametron*, a mixture of prose and poetry, the manuals of the *ars* focused solely on prose communication. If they emphasised eloquent expression, the goal of the instruction was eminently practical: to attain the purpose for which the letter was being sent.

The ancients never developed a theoretical approach to letter-writing, claiming as they did that the letter needed the flexibility of conversation. In practice, in the case of letters having the status of official or public communications, however, they seem to have followed the rules governing oratory for which textbooks like Cicero's *De inventione* and the Pseudo-Ciceronian *Ad Herennium* abounded. By the twelfth century, especially in Italy, the word *dictamen* came to be intimately associated with the rules of letter-writing while the professional writer of letters or teacher of the art became known as the *dictator*. Whereas in practice the ancients distinguished between public and private letters, medieval *ars dictaminis* tended to ignore any distinction and assimilated all letters to the oratorical model. In Italy the generation of Peter Damian (d. 1073) and Pope Gregory VII (d. 1085) was the last until the advent of humanism in the fourteenth century to give a personal tone to correspondence. More than a century later the death of Peter of Blois (*c.* 1212) marked the eclipse of the ancient conception of the letter as conversation north of the Alps as well.

---

[1] The most complete bibliography on *ars dictaminis* and formularies of letters from 1100–1700 is Emil Polak's census of medieval and Renaissance letter treatises and form letters, two volumes of which have been published, with a third forthcoming. Two other important bibliographical guides are Murphy, *Select Bibliography*, pp. 76–103, and Camargo, *Ars dictaminis, ars dictandi*.

1. The early Italian development of *ars dictaminis* textbooks

Cathedral, not monastic, schools had been the guiding force for education in northern and central Italy in the Carolingian and Ottonian periods. Despite the rapid growth of the economy and the increasing political integration at the regional level by the eleventh century, these schools remained loyal to the traditional book culture of grammatical and rhetorical studies designed to prepare students for careers in the imperial chancery and for ecclesiastical preferment. These educational institutions, flourishing like their northern counterparts by 1050, fell victims within decades to the divisive struggle between pope and emperor regarding lay interference in the church, commonly labelled the Investiture Conflict. A number of cathedral schools simply disappeared from the documents. With the exception of Bologna, Italian cathedral schools in the twelfth century had only local importance.

This disarray of traditional book culture encouraged the burgeoning documentary culture centred on law and *ars notaria*. Throughout the ninth and tenth centuries notarial documents had played an enormous role in the lives of individuals at all levels of Italian society. A significant number of laymen and clerics, if unable to read Virgil, had sufficient literacy to make out a sales contract of a lease. Notaries, the largest group of semi-literates, were very often laymen by 1000 and in the course of the eleventh century most bishops came to rely on the local town notary to do the work done north of the Alps by clerics.

The tremendous impetus given to the documentary culture by the economic and political revival led to an improvement and enrichment of legal formulas and to a deeper understanding of law. While this more mature approach to the law was sometimes taught in cathedral schools, the legal renaissance of the eleventh century was accomplished on the whole by practising lawyers, a new group of legal practitioners who gradually distinguished themselves from the notaries. The criticism of reformers like Peter Damian indicated that clerics like laymen were attracted to legal education which made accessible new opportunities for employment. In ever-increasing numbers the semi-literate also became aware of letter-writing as a key to participating in the evolving society. Responding to this demand, the manuals of *ars dictaminis* endeavoured to democratise the art of composition. They promised to teach letter-writing skills without demanding of students an extensive background in classical prose and poetry. This kind of instruction did not require a large library; a single manual would do. In effect, the rise of *ars dictaminis* in Italy represents the victory of a mature practical culture over a book culture centring on ancient Latin literary texts.

There are indications that theories associated with *dictamen* had been circulating in Italy for centuries before the 1070s when Alberic of Monte-cassino authored the first surviving manual of *ars dictaminis*.[2] Writing for his students in the monastic school of Montecassino, the cultural centre of southern Italy in the eleventh century, he considered letter-writing to be a branch of rhetoric. The rules for letter-composition in his *Brevarium de dictamine* form only a part of a much longer treatise on rhetorical topics, while in the *Flores rhetorici* they are almost buried by a discussion of *colores*.

Because Alberic offered a wide conception of rhetoric, his claim to have initiated *ars dictaminis* has been questioned. Scholars who espouse this position attribute the title of founder to Adalbert of Samaria, who devoted his *Praecepta dictaminum* (written in Bologna between 1111 and 1118) solely to letter-composition. While Alberic's pioneering role in inte-grating the rules in written form has subsequently been reaffirmed, the gulf between Alberic and Adalbert cannot be ignored. The former saw letter-writing against the backdrop of a literary tradition grounded in the classics and as one among a number of areas of rhetorical training, while the latter treated it as equivalent to rhetoric and as presupposing little more preparation than elementary Latin.

The forty years or so that separated the two authors and the geograph-ical shift from a monastery in southern Italy to Bologna in the north serve to explain the resulting impoverishment of rhetorical teaching. That Adalbert's simplified instruction better fitted the needs of an urban society is shown by the appearance within a few years of at least two manuals using his approach: the *Rationes dictandi prosaice* (1119–24) of Hugh, canon of Bologna, and the *Aurea gemma* (1119), by Henry of Francigena, probably written in Pavia. Other manuals followed over the next three decades, but by mid-century the pioneering age of *ars dictaminis* in Italy was about over. Only a handful of Italian rhetoricians in the succeeding two generations appear to have tried to improve on their predecessors' work.

2. The twelfth-century Italian letter

Since the major impetus behind the growing demand for letter-writing came from the increasing organisation of political and economic power, *ars dictaminis* from the outset was orientated towards oral presentation of the message within a formal setting. Official communications, partic-ularly important letters, were usually read aloud by recipients or in the

---

[2] Adalbert, *Praecepta dictaminum*, pp. 1–17.

recipient's presence, thus taking on the appearance of a speech at the moment of communication. Because of the difficulty in separating private from public personalities and individuals from office, letter-writers were encouraged to make no distinction between official and what other ages might consider personal correspondence.

The letter-models offered for imitation by *ars dictaminis* manuals have a ritualistic quality due to their formulaic character and obsessive caution in utilising proper terminology. The attraction of the legal document is particularly evident in these respects. Just as the oration had six parts, so the letter was strictly divided into distinct sections. The five divisions of the letter, consisting of *salutatio, exordium, narratio, petitio* and *conclusio*, become almost standard by 1150. Frequently the manuals supplied a choice of words or phrases appropriate for introducing the last four parts. Like the speech the letter normally had an *exordium* designed to render the listener compliant. This use of an *exordium* best exemplifies the oratorical character of the letter. The tone of the letters, even when they were supposedly personal communications, was formal and consciously crafted to evoke the desired response. These letters were geared to efficiency with no allowance made for digressions that did not serve to advance the central object of the composition.

A large portion of every manual was usually devoted to discussing the formulas in the *salutatio* and *exordium* cast to please and convince the addressee. In contrast very little space was given to treating the *narratio*, or the narrative part of the letter, which was the most unstructurable element of the letter. As if intentionally aiming to constrict the writer's freedom of invention, the *dictatores* stressed that the *narratio* should be reduced to the briefest statement of facts. Of course, in practice the situation described in the *narratio* could be too complicated to be expressed in a few lines and some letters are in fact quite long. However, Horace's dictum on brevity (*Ars poetica* 25–6) constituted the guiding principle for the *narratio*. Although *brevitas* could be justified as appropriate in official letters, the appeal was enhanced by the obvious aesthetic pleasure offered by a message condensed into a few highly crafted lines. Such pleasure would be further heightened by the regular use of prose metre or *cursus*, which became fashionable from the last decade of the twelfth century.

Letters conceived on such impersonal lines suited official purposes very well. Indeed, *ars dictaminis* provided the contemporary language for diplomatic communication, a genre which by its very nature uses generally recognised verbal formulas as codes to transmit messages beyond the literal meaning of the words to the addressee. A subtle change in the *salutatio*, for example, was sufficient for this purpose. At the same time *dictamen*'s tyranny of stylistic prescriptions discouraged that spontaneity and direct expression of thought and feeling which give the personal letter its character. Furthermore, the demands of *brevitas* meant that *dictatores* had little space for the philosophical ruminations and anecdotal meanderings found in the personal letters of other ages.

Although not uncommonly *dictamen* manuals recognised the three-style theory inherited from Antiquity (*humilis, medius* and *altus*), the Italian masters of the twelfth century reflected in their examples a preference for the *stilus humilis*, a style using simple vocabulary and straightforward syntax with a minimum of *colores rhetorici*. A sample letter found in the collection of Hugh of Bologna's *Rationes dictandi prosaice* (1119–24) provides an example of this style:

> P reuerendo ac diligendo patri ac domino M quicquid uere
> est. [*salutatio*]
> Dilectionem quam erga uos – pater – habeo, lingua
> dicere et stilo scribere nequeo, michi namque nunc
> quoque gratum ut aliis pluribus sepe numero affectum
> uestre caritatis nouiter exhibuistis. [I]uste quidem,
> quia desolatos consolari, pauperibus erogare,
> necessitatem patientibus uiscera non claudere eos
> qui possunt decet. [Q]uin immo ex precepto
> domini – sicut scitis – debent. [*exordium*]
>
>   Idcirco largitatem uestre caritatis suppliciter
> exposco, quatinus adhuc mihi diuine lectioni uacanti
> et necessitatibus ingruentibus unde emam non
> habenti, et ideo non equum proficienti, [*narratio*]
> per presentium latorem psalterium siue eius pretium
> si placet mittatis, [*petitio*]
> ut sic me uobis in uita debitorem asciscatis. [*conclusio*]

> (Rockinger, *Briefsteller und Formelbücher*, II, p. 85)

[To P. reverend and loving father and lord M. whatever truly is:
I am unable, O father, to say with my tongue nor write with my pen what love
I have towards you, for now again you have recently exhibited to me the proof
of your love as I reckon you have often done to many others. Indeed you do
this rightly because it becomes those who can to counsel the bereft, aid
paupers, and not close their hearts to those suffering under necessity. Nay
rather they ought to do it, as you know, according to the command of the lord.
For this reason I humbly beg the generosity of your love to send by the bearer
of the present letters a psalter or its cost to me, lacking holy reading and
pressed by necessities, not having the means to purchase one and for this
reason not profiting as is right. Thus you will know that I am your debtor for
life.]

It is vital to emphasise, however, that the fate of *dictamen* in northern Europe and later in Italy itself shows there to be no necessary connection between the rules of *dictamen* and the humble style common in twelfth-century Italy.

3. Early *dictamen* in France and the Italian golden age, 1190–1250

Already by the 1130s Italian theories of *dictamen* were known in France and in the second half of the century they were undergoing a transformation in a very different cultural setting. Because of the struggle over investiture had had far less impact on the church in France, the elite institutions of education there had evolved without much disturbance. Moreover, whereas in Italy the intensification of communication due to political and economic development primarily encouraged an expansion in the number of lay notaries, the French responded by increasing the number of chanceries operating at different levels of political authority and of the clerical personnel to staff them. Products of the traditional cathedral school, French *dictatores* put their own stamp on *ars dictaminis* imported in its *stilus humilis* dress.

As the French began to produce their own manuals in the last decades of the century, the tension between the demand for a spare, efficient means of communication able to be mastered by large numbers of people and the literary orientation of French education based on an extensive training in ancient literature became obvious. Typically the anonymous *Libellus de arte dictandi* (1181–5), attributed to Peter of Blois, presented *dictamen* theory, heavily borrowed from an Italian source, as part of a general course in rhetoric, itself presupposing intensive training in syntax and literature. At the same time the self-conscious ornateness of French *ars dictaminis* was formulaic enough to be accessible to a broad strata of literate men who could not meet the rigorous demands of traditional French Latin epistolography with its emphasis on a rich, learned, but personal style. With the deaths of John of Salisbury (d. 1180) and Peter of Blois, masters of the older epistolography, *ars dictaminis* triumphed in France over its rival.

By the late twelfth century, France was also beginning to export its own theories to Italy. Two contemporary Italian *dictatores*, Bene da Firenze (d. 1240) and Boncompagno da Signa (d. 1248), agreed in distinguishing the French import from native Italian *dictamen* on the grounds that the French, specifically the *dictatores* of Orléans, varied from Italians in some of their forms of salutation and in showing preference for placing proverbs in the *exordium*. For Boncompagno this latter practice proved reprehensible because the proverb generated obscurity. He chiefly criticised the French, however, for treating the letter as a work of literature, expending great effort on its composition. In the practical world the notary or chancellor needed a *stilus humilis* permitting rapid composition.

A further characteristic difference between French and Italian *dictatores*, which is mentioned by Bene but not Boncompagno, was their

approach to the *cursus*. In his *Candelabrum* (1222–6) Bene defines the
Italian *cursus*, the *cursus romanus*, as based on three patterns of alternating accented and unaccented syllables (*planus* ['␣␣'␣], *tardus* ['␣␣␣'␣]
and *velox* ['␣␣␣␣'␣]) used by the Roman Curia in its correspondence for
terminating clauses and periods. For example:

planus retributi (ónem merétur)
tardus commodit (átis intúitu)
velox iu (dícium ultiónis)

On the other hand, Bene described the French *cursus*, the *cursus aureliensis*, as more complicated. Not only did the French demand the use of
prose metre at the end of clauses and periods but also at the beginning
of both. Moreover, the French recognised a greater variety of metric patterns basing them on blocks of accented and unaccented syllables called
dactyls and *spondees*, terms borrowed from ancient metric feet calculated
on the succession of long and short syllables. By definition every bisyl-
labic word was a *spondee*, while a three-syllabic word accented on the
antepenultimate (*dóminum*) was a dactyl and a three-syllabic accented
on the penultimate (*vocále*) was a *spondee*-and-a-half. The metres of
the *cursus romanus* above would be counted in the French system as
follows: (ónem merétur) a *spondee* and a *spondee*-and-a-half; (átis intúitu)
a *spondee*-and-a-half and a *dactyl*; (dícium ultiónis) a *dactyl* and two
spondees.

Preliminary research would suggest that what Bene referred to as the
cursus aureliensis was very likely a French adaptation of what had been an
experimental theory of *cursus* used at the papal Curia in the last decades
of the twelfth century. That the theory took on vigour in France in the
first half of the thirteenth century means, of course, that Bene was right
to consider it a competitor with the more traditional *cursus romanus*.
However, in actual practice, the difference in the *cursus* found in letters
produced on both sides of the Alps appears minimal. While the French
occasionally used *cursus* in the first words of clauses and periods, they
were reluctant to create the long rhythmic patterns found in their manuals.
Translated into the language of the *cursus romanus*, their metres,
described in terms of *dactyls* and *spondees*, were reducible to two, *velox*
and *planus*. What brought the French and Italian *cursus* closer on this
point was that beginning in 1178 and for decades thereafter the *tardus* of
the *cursus romanus* almost disappeared form the papal registers.

It should be added that, if still restricted to final metres, the *cursus
romanus* itself continued to change and at least by the first quarter of the
fourteenth century Italian *dictatores* employed four metres for final words
of clauses and periods: besides the traditional *velox*, *tardus* and *planus*,
there was a second *planus* ('␣␣␣'␣␣).

If different theories of the *cursus* were of negligible importance in distinguishing between letters written in France and Italy in the early thirteenth century, the elaborate approach of the French to *dictamen* clearly set off the French from the Italian product. Marked by complicated sentence structure, frequent resort to allegory, metaphor and obscure vocabulary, model French letters seem more a creation of the schoolroom and study than the busy chancery. Here is an example of a letter taken from John of Garland's *Parisiana poetria* (already discussed in the previous chapter), probably written in the 1220s:

Reverendo Patri ac Domino W., Dei gratia Archiepiscopo Remensi; R., Scolaris Parisiensis in cliuum arduitatis Aristotilice nitens: salutem, et ad eterni Veris pascua pervenire.
    Si Dedalus alis caruisset, numquam pelagus transuolando desiderate portum patrie tetigisset. Cum per pelagus profundum rationis Aristotilice sit ausa paruitatis mee fragilis nauicula decurrere, mihi paupertatis abyssum hyare prospicio, nisi dextera vestra prudens, iusta, fortis, moderata, uela studii mei quam cicius sumat et dirigat et deducat.

[To the Reverend Father and Lord W., by the grace of God archbishop of Reims; R., Scholar at Paris, struggling up the hill of Aristotelian difficulty: greeting, and may he arrive at the pastures of the eternal Spring.
    If Dedalus lacked wings he would never have touched the port of the land he sought by flying across the sea. The fragile bark of my insignificance has dared to run a course through the deep sea of Aristotelian reasoning; and now I see the abyss of poverty opening before me, unless your right hand, prudent, just, strong, moderate, should as quickly as possible raise and trim and spread full the sails of my study.]   (Ed. and tr. Lawler, pp. 42–5)

The inclusion of *dictamen* instruction in a wide-ranging rhetorical work like the *Poetria* devoted to prose and poetic composition in general contributes to the impression of a literary emphasis in the French letter.

The invasion of Italy by the French dictaminal theories was only one element in a much wider intellectual onslaught from beyond the Alps. Doubtless, while teaching at Bologna in 1188–90, Geoffrey of Vinsauf was expounding literary doctrines which were integrated into his *Poetria nova* (compare the discussion in our previous chapter). French Latin poetry by authors like Matthew of Vendôme and Walter of Châtillon profoundly affected Henry of Settimella's *Elegia* (1193), the only noteworthy poetic work written in the twelfth century in northern and central Italy. Henry, moreover, already reflected the influence of French poetry in imitation of the poets of Provence. By at least 1200 Italian grammarians were championing new French grammatical theories and in the course of the next decade, manuals of *ars predicandi*, a French innovation designed to aid the composition of sermons, began circulating in the peninsula.

Indeed, even the revival of preaching itself in Italy, vigorously sponsored by Pope Innocent III (1196–1216), probably had its origin in an immediate inspiration from France.

While the effect of the French *dictamen* in its homeland was to destroy a great epistolographic tradition, in Italy, already dominated by a native *stilus humilis* school of *dictamen*, its influence was very different. From the mixing of the native Italian tradition with important French literary and religious elements emerged what modern scholars refer to as the *stilus rhetoricus*, the most impressive creation of Italian *ars dictaminis*. Beginning in 1217 the papal, and after 1221 the imperial, *dictatores* preferred this style for the most important letters. Conceived frankly as an oration, the letter in *stilus rhetoricus* was marked by frequent interjections and interrogatives designed to create the impression of deep feeling. The masters of the style displayed an attraction to rhymed prose, strongly reminiscent of the Psalms, while echoes and actual quotations of biblical passages were frequent.

A section of a letter of Pope Honorius III to Emperor Frederick II in 1226 provides a good instance of this style:

Quia scriptum est: 'Ego sum Deus celi qui vindico peccata patrum in filios usque in quartam et terciam generationem'. Nam Fredericus [I] ipse volens sepulcrum Domini personaliter visitare, Isrealitis non immerito potuit comparari, qui propter peccata sua repromissionis terram nequaquam ingredi meruerunt; qui antequam Jerusalem intraret, morte fuit repentina in quodam flumine suffocatus, cujus animam optamus ad celestis Jerusalem consorcuim pervenisse. Postea sicut totus orbis manifeste novit, divina ultio filios ejus, Henricum videlicet et Philippum, tetigit et punivit. Quid ergo in malitia gloriaris? Quid in iniquitate desideras esse potens? Quid invadere niteris aliena, cum latissime sufficiant tibi tua et cum ipsa non sis longo tempore possessurus?

(*Honorii III opera omnia*, V, p. 98)

[Because it is written: 'I am the God of heaven who punishes the sins of the father in the sons down to the fourth and third generation'. For Frederick [I] himself, wanting to visit personally the sepulchre of the Lord, has been rightly compared to the Israelites, who in no way merited the right to enter the promised land because of their sins; and in his case, before he could enter Jerusalem, he met a sudden death by drowning in a certain river. We hope that his soul reached the fellowship of the heavenly Jerusalem. Afterwards as the whole world plainly knows, divine revenge touched his sons, that is, Henry and Philip, with punishment. Why therefore do you glory in evil doing? Why do you desire to be great in iniquity? Why do you strive to invade the lands of others when your own are on all sides sufficient for you and when you are not going to possess them for very long?]

The most probable source of inspiration for this style came from the revival of preaching in Italy. Given the close link between speech and letter, the rules of *ars dictaminis* were flexible enough to allow for the adaptation of certain aspects of the sermon to the letter. Indeed, the *stilus rhetoricus* developed to the fullest the aural potential of the letter. Initially drawing force for their compositions from biblical associations, by mid-century the *dictatores* using this style were beginning to introduce references to and quotations from ancient pagan authors to reinforce their arguments and appeals while the biblical presence receded.

A second new style and one closely associated with the *stilus rhetoricus* was the *stilus obscurus*, a term used by modern scholars to describe the highly allusive and figurative style of Pietro della Vigna, imperial chancellor. Pietro's tendency to use *stilus rhetoricus* in his official capacity in the imperial chancery and the *obscurus* in his private writings suggests his awareness, contrary to *dictamen* tradition, of a difference between the two genres of letters. Whereas the *rhetoricus* made wide use of *colores rhetorici*, the message was generally communicated in a simple vocabulary without complicated syntax. In his private letters, however, Pietro often limited oratorical effects while indulging in very complex sentence structure and rich figurative language replete with neologisms. Authors in this style relied heavily on echoes of the Psalms and the Song of Solomon both in their vocabulary and imagery. Perhaps the high point in obscurity for productions in this style was reached in the correspondence between two papal notaries, Giordano di Terracino and Giovanni di Capua, in 1260. The letters are so laden with pretentious use of biblical allegory as to require heroic efforts on the part of the modern editor to make sense of the exchange.[3]

If less spectacularly, the Bolognese *dictatores* were doubtless the first to be affected by the transalpine doctrines. Despite his vigorous defence of the *stilus humilis*, already in the *Palma* (1198), Boncompagno manifested the effects of French sermon and dictaminal literary influence by employing figurative language strongly echoing the Psalms in the preface to the work. This style reappeared in some of his private letters, the *Rota Veneris* and in the introduction to his law treatises like the *Cedrus*. With its focus on composing Latin prose love-letters, the *Rota*, purportedly written because requested by friends, seems to have combined a new Italian penchant for biblical language with themes reminiscent of French and Occitan love-poetry and the *De amore* of Andreas Capellanus.

Like Boncompagno, Bene of Florence relied on biblical language and associations in his preface to the *Candelabrum* as did Guido Faba, the third in the trio of great Bolognese *dictatores* of the period, in the beginning of his *Summa dictaminis*. Significantly, although they demonstrate in their model letters how to exploit the new styles, Faba and

Boncompagno – nothing survives of Bene's models – urged their students to cultivate a simple style in their future careers as professional
dictatores. While they permitted themselves restricted indulgence in the
literary approach of the French, the two teachers apparently saw no place
for it in the practical realm which was the principal focus of eloquent
prose in Italian society.

The early thirteenth century witnessed the extension of the manual of
ars dictaminis into the area of oratory. Given the conception of the letter
as a written speech, the step seems natural but only the Italians appear
to have taken it. The major difference between the speech manuals and
those of letter-writing was that usually the former lacked a treatment
of the salutation found in the latter. The speaker usually had no need
to identify himself to his audience. Beginning with the *Oculus pastoralis*
and a series of works by Guido Faba, the production of these manuals
referred to as the *ars arengandi* or the art of speech-making continued into
the early fourteenth century before it more or less ceased. The decrease
in communal liberty and the use of the vernacular for speeches on formal
occasions help explain its demise.

Understandably, the *ars arengandi* manuals were almost from the outset translated into the vernacular so they could be utilised in the political life of thirteenth-century communal Italy. The *Rettorica* of Brunetto
Latini, an uncompleted commentary on Cicero's *De inventione* written
in Tuscan in the 1260s, represents the first effort to furnish guidance
in composing letters as well as speeches in any vernacular. While the
Rettorica tends to confuse letter-writing and oration in its instructions,
the contemporary *Sommetta ad amaestramento di componere volgar-
mente lettere*, probably by Latini as well, is expressly composed for teaching vernacular letter-writing. It remains the only surviving Italian work of
its kind down into the last half of the fifteenth century. Italian translations
of Latin manuals also began to appear in the fourteenth century, but not in
great numbers. Apparently down to the mid-fifteenth century, Italian vernacular letter-writing remained for the most part relatively idiosyncratic
and independent of restrictive formulas.

4. *Ars dictaminis* outside Italy after 1200

The first quarter of the thirteenth century marked the high point of French
influence on Italian *dictamen*, but very quickly, with the production of the
great *summae* of Boncompagno, Bene and Faba, the current of influence
reversed and the new Italian manuals began to move across the Alps. The
period of dictaminal creativity in France had actually been brief, about
forty years. Significantly, France had no great chancery where inventive

efforts by *dictatores* could be focused. The royal chancery, while improving its style over the twelfth century, showed little interest in *ars dictaminis*. It never accepted, for example, the use of *cursus* for its documents. Consequently, study of *ars dictaminis* would have received no reinforcement as royal power expanded. The introduction of French for official correspondence in the middle decades of the thirteenth century also had a negative effect on Latin creativity in *dictamen*. Despite the frequent use of the letter for artistic purposes in French vernacular literature, at least manual instruction in writing letters in French seems to have been negligible for the next two centuries and teaching was based largely on the use of formularies. Nonetheless, the presence in modern French libraries of scores of Italian manuals of Latin *ars dictaminis* by the great Bolognese *dictatores* of the early thirteenth century indicates that there was still a market for Latin dictaminal instruction and that the Italians set the standard for epistolary excellence.

Several German letter-collections testify to the circulation of Italian manuals of *ars dictaminis* from the middle decades of the twelfth century. The *Liber dictaminum* of Baldwin of Viktring, composed in the last third of the century, constitutes an example of a German manual inspired by Italian influence. Down to the fifteenth century this dependency continued: apart from a few locally written manuals borrowing heavily from Italian theories, like Conrad von Mure's *Summa de arte prosandi* (1275), the Germans concentrated mainly on the production of collections of letters and legal documents like the *Summa dictaminum* of Master Ludolfo (*c.* 1250), intended to be used for teaching purposes and as guides to professional writers. In Bohemia, however, the exiled Henry of Isernia left behind him a number of disciples whose relationship with *dictamen* and nascent humanism at the court of Charles IV still needs definition. As opposed to Italy and like France, the collections suggest that the *ars notaria* and *dictamen* were taught in the same course.

As for the development of *ars dictaminis* in Spain, Castile has so far been the primary area investigated. The results suggest that Castile like Germany was largely under Italian influence. The two thirteenth-century manuals identified as written there, the *Ars epistolaris ornatus* by the Englishman Geoffrey of Eversley (*c.* 1270) and the anonymous *Dictamen epithelamium* (1277–81), both owe their greatest debt to the Bolognese *dictatores* earlier in the century.

As for England, although some of the leading northern *dictatores* like Geoffrey of Vinsauf and John of Garland were of English origin, they did their important work in France. A manual written in the Oxford area in the early part of the reign of Henry III included a brief treatise on letter-writing together with examples and discussion of legal procedure and tracts on accounting and conveyance. There is strong evidence of the influence of Pietro della Vigna on English royal correspondence in the 1230s. Yet only with Edward I (1272–1307) did the royal chancery begin utilising *cursus* with any consistency and then almost exclusively in letters written to foreign princes.

Of the manuals authored by Englishmen in the fourteenth and fifteenth centuries almost all appear to have been composed at Oxford for teaching in grammar courses, and all, with the possible exception of Thomas Merke's *De moderno dictamine* (1401–4), were slavishly dependent on Italian manuals. Some of the work of Thomas Sampson (*fl.* 1350–1400) indicates that formal instruction in French *dictamen* was also available at Oxford in the last half of the fourteenth century, but the increasing use of English for correspondence in the next century had a negative effect on *dictamen* instruction in French as well as in Latin.

On the other hand, the creation of English letter-models based on French and Latin precedents had positive consequences for the evolution of English prose. *Dictamen* with its set phrases and tight structure enabled English writers to express themselves with a degree of syntactical correctness, clarity and precision not found earlier. Furthermore, because the major reason for utilising *dictamen* came from the royal administration and those who shaped the administrative language of the country did so in London, *dictamen* gave England not only a stylistic model for prose but also a linguistic one. In part by means of royal correspondence the East Midland dialect of the London area came to be the standard for written English.

5. The letter as literary form

The effect of *ars dictaminis* on letters written primarily as literary works or included in literary works was negligible. Even Boncompagno, in the love-letters written for the *Rota Veneris*, found it necessary to modify the form to fit the character of the communication. Not only is the *salutatio* omitted because of the secret nature of the message, but, set out as a dialogue between man and woman, the other formal divisions of the letter flow together in each of the responses of the interlocutors. Indeed, of all the medieval literary examples of the letter only a few like the Latin poetic letters of Matthew of Vendôme (*fl.* 1180) and the 1206 Latin translation of a letter found in the Middle High German *Udo von Magdeburg* adhere to such rules of the *ars* as the clear division into the standard parts.

Independently of *dictamen* theory, members of the cathedral school of Angers beginning with Marbod of Rennes (*fl.* 1100) and including Hilarius (*fl. c.* 1125) and Baudri of Bourgueil (d. 1130) produced poetic love-letters in Latin. The influence of Ovid's *Heroides* was particularly strong on Baudri. In the second half of the twelfth century, while Matthew of Vendôme at Orléans composed his poetic letters in elegaic metre using dictaminal patterns, Raimbaut d'Aurenga and Arnaud de Mareuil created the *salut* in Provençal with its emphasis on salutation of the lady.[4] Flexible in structure, the poem in letter form normally consisted of paired rhyming lines (aabbcc) of eight syllables each. Only by the middle years of the next century would northern France have its equivalent in the *salut d'amour* imitative of Provençal. It is noteworthy that by the fourteenth century poems of this northern variety were surely being authored by women. Finally, from the last part of the thirteenth century with Philippe de Remi, the *salut d'amour* extended its influence by incorporation into the *dit*.

By *c.* 1160, moreover, also in northern France, the *Roman d'Eneas* utilised the summary of a letter as the turning-point in the plot, while, beginning with the prose *Roman de Tristan* (1225–30),[5] letters directly included in the text served as important means for connecting the many scenes and subplots together. Similarly epistolary exchanges were central to subsequent *romans* of the thirteenth century like the *Roman du Châtelain de Couci et de la dame Fayel* and the *Roman de la Poire*.[6]

Influenced by the French, Germans began utilising the letter for literary purposes at about the same time as the French. Basing himself on the French *Roman d'Eneas*, Heinrich von Veldeke, in his *Eneide* (*c.* 1170–85), provided the actual love-letter from Lavinia to Aeneas whose contents had merely been described in his model. Belonging to that part of the epic written by 1174, the letter lacked the salutation formula which, inspired by the Provençal *salutz*, became a key element in the German *Minnebrief* within a few decades. In fact, by *c.* 1210 Wolfram von Eschenbach's *Parzival* fixed the form of the *Minnebrief* as including (1) the salutation, (2) assurances of service at one or more points in the letter, (3) the praise of the woman's qualities, and finally (4) the petition. 'Epics' like *Parzival* and the contemporary *Wigalios* (1204–10) together with Ulrich von Lichtenstein's *Frauendienst* (completed in 1255) provided models for Middle High German poetic love-letters down to the next century when the courtly variety became gradually mixed with popular elements, often drawn from the *lied*.

Italy stands in contrast with France and Germany as far as literary use of the letter is concerned. There were, of course, Boncompagno's *Rota* and occasional prose Latin love-letters found in manuals or isolated in various manuscripts. Furthermore, a significant portion of the writings of the first two generations of humanism, the new classicising anti-dictaminal

---

4 For the argument that a *salut d'amour* of disputed attribution is by Raimbaut (and hence antedates Arnaud's *saluts*) see Raimbaut d'Aurenga, ed. Pattisson, pp. 149–50.
5 See Vinaver, *Études*, p. 23.
6 Much of this discussion is based on Ruhe, *De amasio ad amasiam*.

movement, consisted of Latin poetic letters which the authors clearly thought of as literary creations. However, the form played almost no role in the rich Italian production of poetry in Provençal and native dialects in the thirteenth and fourteenth centuries. The one glaring exception was the *Filostrato* of Boccaccio (d. 1375), whose brilliant use of the letter inspired Aeneas Silvius Piccolomini's *Historia de duobus amantibus* (1444).

The rich tradition of English love-letters began only in the last quarter of the fourteenth century with Chaucer's *Troilus and Criseyde*, who was himself inspired by Boccaccio's *Filostrato*. By developing the letter's potential in the ritual of courtly love, Chaucer created a genre of verse love epistle new in England. But the emergence of a genre of verse letter independent of a larger text occurred only in the second quarter of the fifteenth century in the circle of the hostage French prince, Charles d'Orléans, and the English court nobility. The genre reached the height of popularity around 1500 but by the middle decades of sixteenth century was in senescence.[7]

6. *Ars dictaminis* and humanism in Italy

By the last decades of the thirteenth century the golden age of *ars dictaminis* in Italy itself was past. Few *dictatores* had the skill to utilise the more difficult styles. The *stilus rhetoricus* had been almost the private preserve of the imperial and papal chanceries, and the destruction of the Hohenstaufen chancery by the 1260s removed the papacy's need for stylistic competition. Only Henry of Isernia (d. 1301) in far-off Bohemia remained from the brilliant group of writers at the imperial court and his last years were devoted to pleasing new patrons. Apart from a few exceptional cases like those of Brunetto Latini, Dante and, late in the fourteenth century, Coluccio Salutati, the *stilus humilis* resumed its quasi-monopolistic position in *ars dictaminis*. Its simplicity and clarity made it the obvious vehicle for commercial and official correspondence. In the course of the fourteenth century, however, the revival of the ancient conception of the letter began to threaten the hold of *ars dictaminis* itself over the private letter, but until the beginning of the next century *ars dictaminis* remained dominant in both private as well as public spheres of communication.

Although Lovato's poetic letters in the 1260s constituted some of the first classicising Latin poetry and his major disciple, Albertino Mussato, utilised the classicising style in poetic letters to express a wide variety of ideas, prose letter style remained unaffected until Geri d'Arezzo in the late 1320s. With Geri, heavily influenced by Seneca, the conception of the

---

[7] This passage is based on Camargo, *Middle English Verse Love Epistle*.

letter as a conversation returned, but it fell to Petrarch in his introductory letter to the *Rerum familiarium* to make it explicit. Rejecting the approach of the orator to letter-writing, he expressed his commitment to a 'plain, domestic and friendly style' in personal correspondence.

Although the manuals of the great thirteenth-century *dictatores* continued to circulate in the next two centuries, classicising scholars like Giovanni del Virgilio (d. after 1327) and Domenico Bandini (d. 1417) along with others kept up a flow of new manuals in Italy. Despite their own scholarly interests in classical learning, the manuals of both del Virgilio and Bandini continued to repeat the by-now traditional rules of the *ars dictaminis* with few variations. Only in the 1420s did a different species of letter manual endorsing classical letter-models begin to make its appearance, thus signalling the sapping of the vitality of the medieval form. Even then, so thoroughly did *ars dictaminis* dominate official language that, until the mid-decades of the fifteenth century, the humanists themselves were reluctant, when writing such correspondence, to introduce reforms.

The domain of Latin letter-writing over which humanism eventually came to preside was a vastly diminished one compared to that previously governed by *ars dictaminis*. The great virtue of *ars dictaminis* had been its accessibility: the relative ease by which its techniques could be learned had enabled a population which was, in the main, semi-literate in Latin to communicate effectively over great distances despite myriad dialects. Nonetheless, from the thirteenth century the various vernaculars had increasingly been encroaching on Latin's control of epistolography. The triumph of the humanists, with their high standards for Latin letter-writing, only reinforced the trend towards the vernacular.

From the last quarter of the fifteenth century, Italians such as Cristoforo Landino and Francesco Negri, themselves humanists, began to create Italian vernacular manuals which in their stylistic prescriptions were analogues of the Latin humanist ones. After the turn of the century northern European authors with humanist tendencies followed suit for their own vernaculars. While the Latin letter became the preserve of a narrow, scholarly elite, these new manuals legitimised the vernacular letter for most educated men and women by endowing the genre with the potential for attaining eloquence.

4

The arts of preaching

Siegfried Wenzel

In Christian society, preaching is a formal response to the injunction the risen Christ had given to his apostles to 'go out to the whole world and proclaim [*praedicate*] the Good News to all creation' (Mark 16:15; cf. Matthew 10:16–17). Whatever form it has taken through history, its content or subject (the Good News, i.e. the word of God as revealed and deposited in Scripture) and its purpose (instruction and emotional appeal aiming at conversion and moral perfection) have remained constant elements. Preaching thus is an essential ministry that has been carried out since the beginnings of Christian history. From early times on, it was naturally accompanied by reflections and instructions on its nature and form. Thus, in his treatise on how to understand and explain Scripture, *De doctrina christiana*, Augustine devoted the last of four books to such questions as the relation between wisdom and eloquence, the various functions the latter might have, and the use of rhetorical art in preaching. In a more practical vein, Gregory the Great in his *Cura pastoralis* provided specific advice on what the spiritual shepherd (called *praedicator* in 3.19ff.) should say to various social and moral groups and types in his attempt to foster virtue and eradicate vice. And for many centuries church authorities collected homilies preached by the Fathers and made them available for official use in the liturgy. Yet in spite of such longstanding practice and concomitant instructions on how to carry it out, it was not until the late twelfth century that the conception of preaching as a rhetorical art gained its full realisation in the proclamation of the sermon as an art form which obeyed rules that could be taught to, and followed by, individual preachers. This development evidently stemmed from the teaching and pastoral concerns of theologians at Paris and other schools and the inclusion of preaching as one of the three main activities pursued by students of theology. Specifically, practical concerns with preaching were directly linked to the study of Scripture in the university milieu. After the 1220s such concerns gained a renewed and stronger impetus with the missionary activities of the mendicant orders, primarily the Dominicans and Franciscans.

Raising preaching to an *ars* – a rational method or technique employed to carry out a practical task – was accompanied, and perhaps caused, by profound innovations and changes in the form of the sermons themselves. The older form used in pulpit oratory, for which, following medieval examples (for instance Waleys, *De modo*, p. 344) one may use the technical name 'homily', obeyed very few structural constraints. It was essentially an exposition of a scriptural text, most often the pericope (the prescribed passage) of the day. After reading the biblical text, the preacher would explain it and then add some moral lessons drawn from it. In its most developed form the homily would have three parts: biblical text, literal exposition and spiritual (moral or allegorical) exegesis. This structure appears in such collections as the Lambeth Homilies, the 'Kentish Sermons', the French homilies of Maurice de Sully, and the 'Wycliffite Sermons'. In contrast, the new or 'scholastic' sermon[1] has a much tighter structure of several parts whose nature, function and execution are neatly regulated and which are verbally and logically derived from a relatively short scriptural passage called the sermon's *thema*, which may be as brief as a single word. Though the precise steps that led to this innovation are not yet entirely clear, it would seem that at some point during the twelfth century highly trained preachers – perhaps, as some scholars claim, under the influence of a renewed interest in classical rhetoric[2] – found it desirable to replace the older 'inorganic form',[3] which essentially followed the narrative order of a Gospel passage, with a more logical and 'organic' one that would allow much greater concentration on a single subject, deeper exploration of a given scriptural text, and more artistic development of the proposed subject by means of well-established rhetorical techniques. In the rhetorical development of the *thema*, dividing a key term into a number of related parts or aspects played a predominant role, and hence the formal 'division of the *thema*' (*divisio thematis*) became the crucial initial step in logically and verbally building a long prose discourse from a relatively short verbal string. Throughout the later Middle Ages, and in both theoretical treatises and actual sermons, the *divisio thematis* was considered the essential feature of the scholastic sermon, frequently called its 'root', whose declared purpose was to help the preacher invent or generate material for his work (see Waleys, *De modo*, p. 370). This is exemplified in the sermons of Oxford, Bodleian Library, MS Bodley 649, where the divisions are frequently marked 'radix sermonis' in the margins.

The division could proceed strictly from the actual words of the *thema* (*divisio intra*), or it could be drawn from a related idea or image suggested by the *thema* (*divisio extra*; see for example Pseudo-Bonaventure,

---

[1] For alternate names see Wenzel, *Preachers*, pp. 61–2.
[2] See Caplan, *Of Eloquence*, pp. 79–92, 105–34; Murphy, *Rhetoric*, pp. 315–16, 321–5; Jennings, 'Rhetor redivivus?'; but see Morenzoni in Thomas of Chobham, *Summa*, pp. lxii–lxiii.
[3] Caplan, *Of Eloquence*, p. 43

Ars concionandi, p. 9). The meanings thus extracted from the *thema* then had to be confirmed with supporting biblical authorities (*confirmatio*). This basic outline of the sermon would then be developed, one principal part at a time.[4] For the development (*prosecutio* or *processus*) medieval preachers could use a wide variety of modes and devices of amplification, including a second division of the respective member of the original division (*subdivisio*), quotation of biblical and classical authorities, 'etymologising' names, and illustrating points with similes, biblical stories, and all kinds of tales (*exempla*) with or without moralisation. The resulting composition, thus, could easily be compared to a tree whose trunk, branches and top not only grew all from the root of the original *thema* and its division but were, in actual delivery, audibly linked to it because the respective parts of the verbal *thema* would be repeated at the beginning and often at the end of their development, and the confirming authorities were expected to share an element with the *thema* that was similar in either verbal form (*concordantia vocalis*) or at least meaning (*concordantia realis*). This main body of the sermon could be introduced by one or more additional sections, which again had clear and precise features and functions. Thus, in its most developed form, the entire sermon could be preceded by a *prothema* or *antethema*, a section designed to lead up to a prayer in which the preacher invited his audience to invoke divine help for his task. The *prothema* might even have its own biblical *thema*, different from the main one though ideally related to it in some fashion. This section often dealt with the function of preaching or the moral characteristics required of a preacher, and besides its main function of leading to prayer it also served to allow some time for latecomers. A second introductory section, between *prothema* and the main part of the sermon, was the *introductio thematis*, which often explained the literal meaning of the *thema* or the meaning of the feast day on which the sermon was being preached.

According to this plan, therefore, a full scholastic sermon consisted of the *thema*, quoted and properly identified; the *prothema*, beginning with its own biblical or other text; an invitation to pray; the repetition of the *thema*; the *introductio thematis*; the *divisio* (also called *partitio*), with confirmation of its members; the development of the principal parts of the sermon as established in the *divisio*; and the conclusion. The two sections before the division (*prothema* and *introductio thematis*) could be omitted or could take special forms. Essential, however, were the *thema* and its division; their central importance is clearly affirmed in the following definition of preaching given in the *Ars praedicandi* by the

---

[4] For more complicated processes of multiple divisions and their weaving together, see Wenzel, *Preachers*, pp. 95–9.

late-thirteenth-century Franciscan John of Wales: 'Preaching is the clear
and devout expounding of the announced *thema* by means of dividing and
confirming it with fitting authorities after God's help has been invoked,
for the purpose of enlightening the mind in the faith and kindle the heart
in love'.[5] This importance is further shown by the fact that the opening part of medieval sermons is often developed with great care, usually
including the use of syntactic parallelism and end rhyme, in both Latin
and the vernacular languages.

The application of such principles led to a work of verbal art distinguished by 'a beauty of its own',[6] whose major qualities are structural
control, verbal concordance (created by the repetition of structural mark-
ers and of etymologically related words, that is, the classical figure of
adnominatio), variation and decoration, the last feature including the use
of rhyme and of verses, especially in the *divisio*.

The principles and rules for this sermon form were expounded and
illustrated in technical treatises referred to as *artes praedicandi*, 'arts of
preaching'. Over 200 such treatises, written in the period from shortly
after 1200 until the early sixteenth century, have been identified, of which
only very few have so far been edited and even fewer translated into
English. They have been surveyed topically[7] and historically,[8] and their
doctrine has often been summarised.[9] These works vary considerably, not
only in their degree of intelligibility and comprehensiveness, but more
importantly with respect to their basic orientation. Some *artes* treat, in a
systematic and comprehensive way, the entire structure of the scholastic
sermon with all its parts, to which they may add some discussion of the
preacher's intellectual and moral qualifications as well as aspects of sermon delivery. Perhaps the fullest and most systematic expositions of this
type are the *artes* by John of Wales (end of the thirteenth century)[10] and
by Thomas Waleys (*fl.* 1340s), though similar treatments can be found
in several other works of varying length by such writers as Thomas of
Chobham, Alexander of Ashby, Pseudo-Aquinas, Geraldus de Piscario,
Eiximenis, Thomas of Tuderto, Henry of Hesse and the writer of the treatise which begins 'Predicacio est'. On the other hand, however, a number

---

5 'Predicacio est, invocato Dei auxilio, propo[s]iti thematis dividendo et concordando
congrue clara et devota exposicio, ad intellectus catholicam illustracionem et affectus
caritativam inflammacionem' (John of Wales, *Ars praedicandi*, cit. by Ross, 'Brief
Forma', p. 340, n. 18). I have regularised the spelling and introduced one necessary
emendation.
6 'Une beauté sui generis'; Gilson, 'Michel Menot', p. 119.
7 Charland, *Artes praedicandi*.
8 Roth, *Mittelalterliche Predigttheorie*; Murphy, *Rhetoric*.
9 E.g. various articles in Caplan, *Of Eloquence*; Gilson, 'Michel Menot'; *Middle English
Sermons*, ed. Ross, pp. xliii–lv; Wenzel, *Preachers*, pp. 66ff.
10 See Roth, *Mittelalterliche Predigttheorie*, pp. 76–86.

of relevant treatises deal with only one aspect of sermon-making, the 'modes of amplification', which list and illustrate a variable number of ways (eight in Richard of Thetford, forty-five in Simon Alcok) of developing or 'dilating' the announced *thema* and its parts. This concentration on *amplificatio* highlights the practical purposes of the *artes praedicandi*; it also reminds us that technical instructions for preachers were but a part of the same cultural and educational milieu that included the teaching of rhetoric and poetry and even letter-writing (see above, Chapters 2 and 3). It should be added that in their suggesting ways of amplification, the *artes praedicandi* do not merely follow traditions that stem from classical rhetoric but add procedures current in scholastic logic and in biblical exegesis, such as various ways of drawing distinctions and invoking the four senses of Scripture. The orientation of this second type of *artes praedicandi* may occasionally confuse the reader because terms that usually refer to structural parts of the scholastic sermon (especially the division) are here considered devices of amplification; Basevorn's *Forma praedicandi* particularly, which has received prominent exposure in modern studies, discusses such topics as *thema* (Chs. 15–19 and beyond), *antethema* (Ch. 23), and *divisio thematis* (Chs. 20–2) on a par with eight modes of dilation (Ch. 39), gestures, and *cursus* (Ch. 50), thus furnishing twenty-two sermon 'ornaments' with subdivisions. But Basevorn, as well as writers of shorter treatises that limit themselves more strictly to modes of amplification (Alcok, 'Ad habendam materiam', Richard of Thetford, William of Auvergne; similarly John de la Rochelle), nonetheless assume their audiences' familiarity with the basic structure and parts of the scholastic sermon outlined above.

Most *artes praedicandi* also show an awareness that the new sermon form they describe is fundamentally different from the older homily, and Robert of Basevorn in particular gives evidence that the new form issued from the universities of Paris and Oxford, where it was practised with differences he duly notes (*Forma praedicandi*, pp. 244, 264, 271, 279–90, 319). At the same time, the *artes* make it clear that in the period from the thirteenth to the fifteenth centuries the old homily or *postillatio* remained in use, in Italy as well as elsewhere (see Waleys, *De modo*, p. 344). In fact, the more complete *artes praedicandi* commonly speak of three or four major different sermon patterns, one of which is the old-fashioned homily 'without distinction and concordance'.[11] Besides recognising such major structural differences, the *artes* acknowledge variations in minor aspects, so that Robert of Basevorn can say: 'There are almost as many different

---

[11] 'Absque distinctione et concordantia'; John of Wales, cit. Zafarana, 'La predicazione francescana', p. 230.

ways of preaching as there are able preachers',[12] and Thomas Waleys echoes him by declaring that, 'in our present undertaking it is not possible to embrace every way of preaching under clear examples and rules', for 'one can hardly find two preachers composing their own sermons who in every respect agree in their sermon form'.[13] The major section where such differences are recognised by the *artes* is the sermon beginning before the division of the *thema*, especially the *prothema* and *introductio thematis*. But such variation notwithstanding, it must be emphasised that all *artes praedicandi* that have been studied and are available in modern editions agree on the nature and function of *thema* and *divisio thematis* as the two basic parts that are essential to the 'modern' or 'university' or 'scholastic' sermon.

Gauging the extent to which this formal art of sermon-making influenced actual preaching during the last three medieval centuries is made complicated by a number of factors. The just-noted variation in some parts of the scholastic sermon is indeed found in surviving sermons. Thus, the group of Middle English sermons edited by W. O. Ross contains items of very different structural patterns, ranging from the full scholastic sermon to the simple homily; and the same is true of some Latin sermon collections (e.g. Worcester, Worcester Cathedral, MS F.126). Furthermore, it has been shown that the nature and purpose of preaching demanded by certain occasions caused even the most 'scholastic' preachers to adopt a more homily-like style, which instead of dividing its *thema* into logical sections would simply follow the order of the Gospel narrative, as did the *sermo historialis* used on Good Friday.[14]

Another complicating factor concerns the form in which actual sermons have been preserved. The relation between their oral delivery and the written record can vary rather significantly. It may be assumed that some sermons were written out before delivery, or were preached from written texts that may or may not have been committed to memory; conversely, others took written form at the hand of a *reportator* or of the preacher himself only after their delivery. Hence the surviving texts yield a picture that is at best two or three steps removed from their actual delivery, and they usually lack any direct indication as to the exact way by which they came into being. Thus, the remaining documents of medieval preaching are essentially literary works, and to varying degrees self-consciously so.

[12] 'Fere quot sunt praedicatores valentes, tot sunt modi distincti praedicandi'; Robert of Basevorn, *Forma praedicandi*, p. 243.

[13] 'Non est possibile in presenti negotio omnem modum praedicandi sub certis exemplis aut regulis comprehendi'; and 'Vix inveniantur duo, sermones a seipsis compositos praedicantes, qui in forma praedicandi quoad omnia sint conformes' (Waleys, *De modo*, pp. 355, 329).

[14] See Wenzel, *Preachers*, pp. 149–51.

They range from polished sermon cycles intended to serve as models of what good and complete sermons should be like and hence provided with all kinds of visual aids, such as rubrics and marginalia, underscoring, use of red ink, etc., to hastily scribbled notes on flyleaves or otherwise blank spaces which the preacher happened to have at hand. The result is a remarkable variation in the degree of fullness, so that next to fully worked-out sermons, in which all principal parts are completely developed, one may find mere schemata outlining *thema*, division, and perhaps some confirming authorities, or else a carefully worked-out introductory section leading to the division and then followed by only a few notes suggesting authorities and stories with which to develop the sermon's main body.[15] In consequence, while there is plentiful evidence that composers or compilers of individual sermons and larger collections were indeed aware of the structure taught by the *artes praedicandi*, we can never be sure how much of such a complete structure a given audience heard from a given pulpit on a given Sunday. Furthermore, many records preserve only bits and pieces: occasionally a scribe might write down only a *prothema* that attracted his attention, whether the piece is so marked or not, a situation that may apply to the famous 'sermon' on 'Atte wrastlinge'.[16]

Finally, the audience of a particular sermon, too, affected the chosen sermon form. Historians of medieval preaching emphasise that authors of *artes praedicandi* as well as sermon writers distinguished carefully between learned audiences and common people, and that this distinction led directly to different patterns recommended for the sermon division; as one *ars praedicandi* says: 'We must divide our thema in one way [i.e. using the division from within] when we preach before the clergy, in the other way [i.e. by using the division from without] when we preach to the people'.[17] Not surprisingly, a similar distinction was maintained in the employment of proper modes of amplification – Aristotle and scholastic definitions for the learned, common proverbs and marvellous or blood-curdling tales for the populace. Hence modern students speak of 'two mighty streams' in medieval preaching, learned and popular.[18] But closer analysis of sermon collections that give us some hint about their intended audience, both from the thirteenth century and from later times, has shown that this distinction was not observed in practice,[19] or else that many sermons were written with both audiences or even a single but mixed audience in mind.[20] The difference in audience also affects the

---

[15] For an example see Wenzel, p. 83.   [16] Wenzel, pp. 213–14.

[17] 'Aliter enim dividendum est, cum clero, aliter, cum populo praedicatur'; Pseudo-Bonaventure, *Ars concionandi*, p. 9.

[18] 'Zwei mächtige Ströme'; Schneyer, 'Eine Sermonesliste', pp. 5–6. See also Schneyer, *Geschichte*, pp. 131–2, 186.

[19] Davy, *Les Sermons*, p. 36; Lerner, 'Collection of Sermons', p. 475.

[20] Wenzel, *Preachers*, pp. 70–2; Wenzel, *Macaronic Sermons*, pp. 31–64, 71–3.

vexed question of what language was used in the actual delivery, since the majority of written sermons have been preserved in Latin. Presumably Latin was used for clerics and the vernacular for the common people, but as the principles articulated in the *artes praedicandi* were applied in sermons preserved in either language, this question is of no concern here.

Despite these cautions and qualifications, however, the reader of late-medieval sermons will find that the artistic structure proposed by the *artes praedicandi* did not remain in the schoolroom or the university pulpit but found expression in sermons for all kinds of audiences. The formal *artes* themselves indicate that their doctrine is based on the practice of contemporary preachers, and they frequently name the universities of Paris and Oxford as focal points of diverging patterns. Conversely, extant sermon collections indicate beyond doubt that individual preachers practised what the *artes praedicandi* taught. Not only are numerous sermons of the thirteenth, fourteenth and fifteenth centuries, in Latin and vernacular languages, constructed along the principles outlined above, but the technical terms used in the *artes* appear in the sermons as well, either marginally or in the body of the text. A good example is furnished by the Worcester Cathedral sermons in Middle English, whose major parts are clearly labelled in the manuscript.[21] Striving for such art and elegance, especially where the use of divisions, of learned authorities, and of erudite lore went beyond reasonable limits, caused adverse criticism and sharp denunciation on the part of moralists and most authors of *artes praedicandi* themselves. Yet it is clear that theorists, from St Augustine on, found good reasons to reconcile 'eloquence' and 'wisdom' by pointing to the usefulness of rhetorical devices in giving sacred oratory persuasive power. There is also evidence that medieval sermon audiences included at least some connoisseurs, clerical and lay, who paid keen attention to the structural skills displayed by individual preachers. Thus the biographer of the late-fifteenth-century bishop and archbishop Hernando de Talavera, after praising his simple style that was immediately accessible to the common people, adds: 'This, so some elegant courtiers would say, was not preaching but giving counsel'.[22] And from earlier times comes Peter of Cornwall's enthusiastic response to the verbal art used by Gilbert Foliot[23] as well as the charming note left by a student at Paris who, in the 1270s, collected sermons and, after jotting down the plan for a sermon as it had been announced by a Franciscan preacher, added: 'But he got it all mixed up!'[24]

---

[21] *Three Middle English Sermons*, ed. Grisdale, pp. 1–21.
[22] 'Esto decian algunos curiosos y palacianos que no era predicar, sino decir consejas'; cit. Deyermond, 'The Sermon', p. 130.
[23] Spearing, 'The Art of Preaching', p. 113.
[24] 'Sed totum confundebat simul'; Bériou, 'La prédication', p. 113.

Can one find evidence that this formal art had a similar influence on contemporary poets? The question has some urgency because, while technical treatises on how to make a poem – *artes poetriae, artes versificandi, artes grammaticae* and the like – give much advice on rhetoric and figures of speech, they fairly neglect concerns with structure and formal composition. In contrast, the major thrust of the *artes praedicandi* is their interest in, and prescription of, structural rules. One treatise tellingly identifies preaching itself with the formal steps analysed above: 'Preaching means to take a *thema*, divide it, subdivide its divisions, quote confirming authorities that concord with these, and explain the quoted authorities clearly and devoutly'.[25] It is therefore plausible that secular writers and poets would have taken some interest in this structural concern and perhaps even learned from it. To become familiar with these principles would of course not have required lengthy study of technical treatises, since their precepts could have been experienced by listening to the Sunday sermon. Hence it is not surprising that a number of modern studies should have argued for a more or less precise influence of medieval sermon art on a variety of poems, which include, for example, *Patience* and *Cleanness*, several of Chaucer's *Canterbury Tales*, Langland's *Piers Plowman*, and, outside English literature, Juan Ruiz's *Libro de buen amor*.

The *Libro*, for instance, begins with a prose prologue in which the author quotes Psalm 31:8 in Latin, identifies the quotation, and offers a division which he introduces with a clause that is exactly like a standard formula in sermons: 'In this verse I understand three things'.[26] (Middle English sermons use similar formulas to introduce divisions: 'I vndirstonde', 'I see', 'I conceyve', 'ye shall yndyrstond'.[27]) The three members of the division are neatly linked to individual parts of the psalm verse and further 'confirmed' with other scriptural quotations that accord with the *thema* in either sound or sense, thus producing *concordantia verbalis* or *realis*. All this is indeed very much like the formal beginning of a scholastic sermon, though without *prothema* and *introductio thematis*, and some further elements may be found in this text which, though they are not exclusive features of sermon language, also occur frequently in sermons.[28] However, despite its striking resemblance to sermon style, this text is not a sermon – neither a serious one nor a parody – but a carefully crafted prologue (see further Chapters 14 and 17 below). Late-medieval literary prologues or introductions to longer treatises, such as works on

[25] 'Predicacio est thematis assumpcio, eiusdem thematis diuisio, thematis diuisi sub-diuisio, concordanciarum congrua cotacio, et auctoritatum adductarum clara et devota explanacio'; Ross, 'Brief *Forma*', pp. 340–1.
[26] 'En el qual verso entiendo yo tres cosas'; Juan Ruiz, *Libro*, p. 73.
[27] *Middle English Sermons*, ed. Ross, pp. 77, 165, 201, 271, 73–4, etc.
[28] Chapman, 'Juan Ruiz's "Learned Sermon"'.

penance, including Chaucer's *Parson's Tale*,[29] very often begin exactly as the *Libro* does, with a scriptural quotation and a division (and less often, confirming authorities); yet they certainly do not introduce a sermon. It is of course possible that in these cases their authors imitated part of the scholastic sermon structure.[30] The question of which of the two, scholastic sermon or prologue, developed first, must remain in abeyance until we know more about the genesis and early history of the scholastic sermon form, especially its relation to twelfth-century rhetorical studies. Until then, it is safe to conclude that similar techniques, such as initial scriptural quotation and division, were used in a variety of literary genres by scholastic authors, and that, specifically, a scriptural quotation, such as Psalm 31:8 in the *Libro de buen amor*, could fulfil the function of a sermon *thema* as well as, conversely, that of a *sententia* or *proverbium* (i.e. an 'authoritative quotation' or 'general truth') which was recommended by medieval *artes poeticae* as one way of starting a literary composition or poem.[31]

In contrast to the *Libro*, the Middle English *Patience* has been claimed to utilise sermon structure not merely in its opening but in its totality. The poem retells the story of Jonah, but it goes beyond merely following the biblical account, as a simple biblical narrative or epic in verse would, by opening with a sixty-line disquisition on the virtue of patience, of which the main part of the poem may function as an illustration, and by ending with a brief moralisation. Such a structure invites detailed comparison with the sermon pattern described by the *artes praedicandi*, though several scholars have been less than willing to equate the poem's parts with standard components and structures of the scholastic sermon.[32] In fact, *Patience* does not follow these. The poem lacks the division altogether, which we have seen to be an essential element of the sermon. More crucially, the claimed equation founders on the putative 'theme' of the poem. *Patience*'s opening line, 'Pacience is a poynt þaȝ hit displese ofte' is not a *thema* in the sense understood by the *artes praedicandi*,[33] which without exception demand that the *thema* of a sermon must be a scriptural passage (see for example Waleys, *De modo*, p. 341). *Thema*, the word or string of words on which the entire sermon is built, normally a biblical passage, and 'theme' in the sense of topic or subject must not be confused. Line 1 of *Patience* indeed announces the poem's 'theme' in the latter sense of

---

[29] Wenzel, 'Notes on the *Parson's Tale*', pp. 248–51.
[30] Scholastic sermon structure was also imitated in academic speeches by arts masters, philosophers and lawyers: see Wenzel, 'Academic Sermons' and 'A Sermon'.
[31] Faral, *Les arts poétiques*, p. 58.
[32] For an analysis in favour of the influence of the *ars praedicandi*, see *Pearl Poems*, ed. Vantuono, II, p. x. For disagreement, see Bloomfield, '*Patience*', p. 41.
[33] See Vantuono, 'Structure and Sources', p. 403.

the word; its *thema*, however, it is not. This confusion is unfortunately common in modern critical analyses of the influence of sermon structure on poetry.

Such influence, however, seems more unquestionably present in Chaucer's *Pardoner's Tale*. Not only does its fictional speaker belong to a professional group that relied on preaching for its avowed purpose of raising money, but he also explicitly gives the Canterbury pilgrims an account of his pulpit activity, in which the tale of the three rioters evidently functions as a sample sermon (*Canterbury Tales*, VI(C), 329, 915). Moreover, the Pardoner refers to the constant 'theme' of his preaching, a biblical phrase he quotes twice in Latin (*Radix malorum est cupiditas*; ll. 333–4, 426); his tale includes a moralising discourse that is neatly divided into three marked sections (at ll. 589–90, 629, 660) and contains a welter of authoritative quotations, references to biblical and other illustrative stories, and images that certainly were current in fourteenth-century sermons. Even his 'confessional' prologue, though directed to his fellow pilgrims, may be seen as an analogue to the *prothema* (though surely a parodic one). The Dominican Humbert of Romans recommended: 'Sometimes the *prothema* is based on the person of the preacher, so that, when an acceptable Dominican or Franciscan preacher wants to preach in a church where he himself and the profession of his order is unknown, he begins by explaining his own profession and that of his order, lest he be thought to be a preaching pardoner, saying the words of Paul in 2 Cor. 12:14, "I do not seek what belongs to you but yourselves".'[34] Hence it is only natural for certain critics to argue that what the Pardoner gives the pilgrims, including his self-revealing prologue, '*is* a sermon, carefully unified, and quite similar structurally to the university or "modern" sermons'.[35] However, others have voiced strong demurrals and pointed at notable discrepancies between the ideal form of a scholastic sermon and the *Pardoner's Tale*.[36] In reply, one may indeed point out, as Robert P. Merrix does, that there was no 'ideal' form of a scholastic sermon, and that the irreconcilable variations in the several patterns for the *Pardoner's Tale* that have been proposed by pro-sermon critics can in fact be blamed on medieval *artes praedicandi* and extant sermons themselves.[37] As noticed earlier, such variations

---

[34] 'Prothema quandoque sumitur a persona praedicatoris, ut quando aliquis gratus Praedicator de Ordine Praedicatorum vel Minorum vult praedicare in aliqua, in qua est ignotus ipse, et status Ordinis sui: exponit a principio statum suum, et Ordinis sui, ne forte credatur esse quaestuarius Praedicator, dicens illud Pauli 2 Corinthiorum 12: "Non quaero quae vestra sunt, sed vos"'; *De eruditione religiosorum praedicatorum*, 1.6.44, p. 76.

[35] Merrix, 'Sermon Structure', p. 247.

[36] See the summaries in Merrix, 'Sermon Structure', p. 235 and notes, and in C. R. Hilary's notes in *The Riverside Chaucer*, p. 905.

[37] See Merrix, 'Sermon Structure', and Fletcher, 'The Preaching of the Pardoner'.

concern especially the *prothema* and the *introductio thematis*, introductory parts which were defined variously and confusingly by the *artes*, and which were employed with great freedom in actual sermons, a freedom allowing even complete omission. However, extensive study of *artes* and sermons suggests that while such 'introductory matter'[38] was indeed held to be variable, in both theory and practice, other elements were definitely considered essential constituents of the scholastic sermon: the *thema* and its formal division. While the Pardoner quotes a biblical phrase and actually calls it his 'theme', this string of words in either its totality or its parts does not recur in his tale in any way reminiscent of the practice current in scholastic sermons: the words *radix*, *mala* and *cupiditas*, in either Latin or English, are not repeated in the tale itself. Moreover, the *Pardoner's Tale* contains no formal division of the *thema* that would even approximate to what one finds in the *artes praedicandi* and scholastic sermons, and the connection between the *thema* and the putative members of the division – gluttony and lechery, 'hasardrye', and swearing – lacks the clarity and explicitness that are ever present in contemporary sermons. Nor is there a discrete *introductio thematis*, for Chaucer's text is explicitly marked as one and the same 'tale' to which the narrator returns at ll. 660–1. It would seem therefore that with respect to its most basic features, the *Pardoner's Tale* diverges significantly from the model of the scholastic sermon as embodied in *artes praedicandi* and employed in extant sermons.

This review of different but paradigmatic cases suggests that the putative influence of *artes praedicandi* on poets should be met with scepticism. Yet this is not to deny that medieval poets were thoroughly familiar with sermon techniques, the language used by contemporary preachers, and even technical terms specific to the art of preaching, as several scholars have demonstrated.[39] Keeping in mind the wide variety of sermon structures used by fourteenth-century preachers that was noticed earlier, one will readily grant that in structuring *Patience* or *Cleanness* or the discourse of Holy Church in *Piers Plowman*, B-text, 1,[40] the poets may well have drawn on some compositional features they had observed, or that in creating the Pardoner and Fra Cipolla Chaucer and Boccaccio may well have followed the model furnished by an actual historical character. But with respect to the central features of formal sermon construction found in the *artes praedicandi*, the case for clear influence seems to be unproven, despite their saliency as a general context or even as a gauge of writers'

---

[38] Wenzel, *Preachers*, pp. 68–9.
[39] E.g. Shain, 'Pulpit Rhetoric'; Mroczkowski, '*The Friar's Tale*'; Pratt, 'Chaucer and the Hand that Fed Him'; and Wenzel, 'Chaucer and Contemporary Preaching'.
[40] See Wenzel, 'Medieval Sermons'.

invention. Even so, our appreciation of what late-medieval poets were actually about when they dealt creatively with preachers and preaching can only be enhanced by an awareness of the norms and nuances of that most elegant and subtle, articulate and authoritative tradition witnessed in the arts of preaching.

Part II

The study of classical authors

5

From late Antiquity to the twelfth century

Winthrop Wetherbee

The history of medieval literary studies properly begins in the early fourth century, and is heralded by a renewal of interest in the study of the great Latin writers of the past. With the exception of Horace's *Ars poetica*, the major texts of ancient literary criticism seem to have been little known during this period, and critical activity is largely confined to commentaries directed to teachers and students of grammar and rhetoric. It was in the classroom that the emergent Christian culture came to terms with its pagan heritage, and the negotiations this involved largely determined the shape of education and literary criticism throughout the medieval period.

The role of the great Latin authors of the republic and early empire in preserving the authority of ancient culture during the third and fourth centuries is hard to overestimate. The study of literature had always been an important part of the imperial system of education, and the prestige of literary culture seems to have grown during this period. In the face of the growing influence of Christian apologists sceptical of all pagan institutions, education became an important preserve of national culture, and literature was increasingly valued as a repository of ancient traditions of all kinds. The later fourth century is an important time in the history of commentary on classical texts and of textual criticism, and Virgil, Livy and other major figures seem to have enjoyed in some circles a virtual cult status.

Christian culture in this period also owes a great deal to its long and uneasy involvement with the pagan classics. Tertullian, whose famous query 'What has Athens to do with Jerusalem?' has gained him the reputation of one who wholly repudiated the classical world, had in fact been one of the most learned men of his day, thoroughly grounded in classical poetry, history and philosophy, and master of a full range of literary styles and genres. The apologist Minucius Felix, and Lactantius, the 'Christian Cicero', though largely concerned to expose the errors and absurdities of pagan thought and belief, frequently quote passages consonant with the truths of Christian theology, and acknowledge the 'cleverness' of poets whose commitment to the vanities of mythology does not prevent their speaking at times with 'distinctness, accuracy, and truth' (Lactantius, *Inst.* 1.5, 2.1; Minucius Felix, *Octavius* 19, 23). Both Tertullian and

Lactantius, as well as Cyprian and Augustine, were teachers of rhetoric, and the writings of Ambrose, Jerome, Sulpicius Severus and their literate contemporaries display their classical training.

Virgil had of course been the canonical author *par excellence* from the beginning of the imperial period, and he enjoys this status in Christian literary culture as well, quite apart from his importance as author of the supposedly prophetic fourth *Eclogue*. From the outset the new, classicising Latin poetry on Christian themes is simultaneously and inevitably a contribution to the cult of Virgil. The tradition begins with Juvencus, who embarks on his rendering of the Gospels into Virgilian hexameters with a jaunty 'Ergo age' ('Let's go') which is revealed as a genial humility when we recognise the hinted comparison between his task and that of the humble *juvenci* whose labour prepares the earth for the sowing of seed in the first *Georgic* (*Evangelorium libri*, Praef. 25). The finest of the Christian poets, Prudentius, whose *Psychomachia* begins with the quick and horrible death of the 'Cult-of-the-Ancient-Gods' at the hands of Faith, and whose treatment of pagan culture in the *Contra Symmachum* ranges from burlesque to harsh criticism, alludes continually and with great sensitivity to the *Aeneid*, and much of the effect of his work depends on that intimate familiarity with the Virgilian corpus which the education of the period ensured. Even the hymns of Ambrose set off their spiritual themes by allusion to familiar contexts in the *Aeneid*, and Sedulius, seeking a standard of comparison for the joys of Paradise, can only cite the idyllic landscape of the *Eclogues*, the 'happy crops' of the *Georgics*, and the Elysium of *Aeneid* 6 (*Paschale carmen* 1, 49–59).[1]

There is probably no better illustration of the status of Virgil as a cultural symbol than the famous chapter of the *Confessions* in which Augustine seeks to exorcise the memory of his early love of the *Aeneid* (*Conf.* 1.13). The passage has been seen as a uniquely violent expression of 'deep-seated hostility to the old cultural tradition' (Hagendahl, *Augustine*, p. 715), yet the reminiscences of Virgil's poem are deployed with care and feeling: Dido is recalled as 'she who made death by the sword a last resort', the words of Aeneas on meeting her shade in the underworld (*Aen.* 6.457). The echo combines with the evocation of 'the very shade of Creusa' (*Aen.* 2.772) to show us a hero who, like Augustine himself, is suspended between commitment to a new, higher mission and desire for a remembered past. Virgilian shades and Virgilian rhythms seem to come unbidden to Augustine's mind, and perhaps the most powerful effect of the passage is in demonstrating their persistent hold on his imagination.

This pervading awareness of the great poet of Rome reflects most obviously the respect for literary tradition and verbal form which the standard

[1] See Fontaine, 'L'apport', pp. 318–55.

literary education of the period sought to instil. The academic equivalent of such *pietas* is the long-standing tradition of Neoplatonising commentary which had explicated literary texts by reading them as allegorical expressions of a physics and psychology derived, like the theory of language on which their allegorising depends, from Stoicism.[2] The verbal surface meaning of the text was treated as a 'veil', designed to protect its inner significance from vulgar misunderstanding and to stimulate the initiate to an appreciation of the mysteries it concealed. Mystification of this sort is a frequent target of Christian polemic against pagan culture (Augustine complains about the pretensions of teachers of literature in the passage just discussed), but its pervasive influence appears clearly in the common habit of using Virgilian phrases and motifs to illustrate theological or homiletic arguments. The habit is deeply ingrained, and shows Christian writers reading Virgil with a sense of the essential ethical and philosophical character of his work which reflects the assumptions of the *grammatici* and their Neoplatonist forebears. Jerome, commenting on Ezechiel, naturally compares the difficulties of his text to the 'inextricable error' of the Daedalian labyrinth (*Aen.* 6.27); Ambrose sees in Daedalus' escape from his creation an image of the inherent capacity of the soul; and for both Ambrose and Lactantius the task of penitence calls to mind the challenge of escaping the underworld as posed to Aeneas by the Sibyl ('this is the task, this the labour'; *Aen.* 6.129). Many patristic authors discover in Anchises' great metaphysical discourse (*Aen.* 6.724–51) ideas consonant with Christian orthodoxy regarding the nature and destiny of the soul (see Jerome, *In Ezech.* 14, *Praef.*; Ambrose, *De excessu Satyri* 2.128.5; Lactantius, *Inst.* 6.24.9; Ambrose, *De Caïn et Abel* 2.9.35). Such quasi-allegorical allusions, no doubt almost unconscious, are incidental to the authors' purposes; but as Pierre Courcelle has shown, it is possible to piece together a Neoplatonic allegorisation of the Virgilian underworld, and to a lesser extent the *Aeneid* as a whole, from such reminiscences.[3]

What is harder to discern in the writers of the fourth century is a systematic approach to the interpretation of literature. The assumptions of Neoplatonist commentary about the function and significance of classical texts, though undoubtedly taken for granted in the world of the grammarians, do not generate a synthetic treatment of the *Aeneid* or any other ancient text by a fourth-century pagan or Christian writer. Jerome, the pupil of the famous grammarian Aelius Donatus, and Augustine, whose own labours in the schools are well attested, take it for granted that poetry will be studied, and that this study will be aided by the use of standard commentaries, which they compare to their own commentaries on

---

[2] See Coulter, *The Literary Microcosm*; Holtz, *Donat*, pp. 7–11.
[3] See Courcelle, 'Les Pères', pp. 5–69; *Lecteurs*.

Scripture (Jerome, *Contra Rufinum* 1.16; Augustine, *De utilitate credendi* 7.17). But the similarities seem to be limited to a common concern with the glossing of difficult passages and the supplying of necessary historical information. These are the essential functions of the surviving scholia on ancient works, and to the extent that Christian exegesis affirms a deeper meaning beneath the surface of the text, it seems to be set apart. If we except the often brilliant use of classical models in Christian Latin poetry, nowhere in fourth-century Christian writing do we find any sustained reflection on the literary character of the pagan classics. The only direct attempts to appropriate Virgil to Christian purposes are compilations like the *cento* of Proba, which depend less on interpretation than on a fortuitous correspondence of word and idea, and so were viewed with scepticism (see for example Jerome, *Epist.* 53, 7). And with the exception of Donatus' commentaries on Virgil and Terence, no work produced by a non-Christian commentator before the end of the fourth century can be said to have exerted a shaping influence on medieval approaches to the interpretation of literature.

We do however have good evidence for the continuing importance of a more coherent conception of the literary text in the work of the early-fifth-century writers Servius and Macrobius,[4] the first authors whose work anticipates medieval literary criticism in any significant way. Servius was the disciple and perhaps, like Jerome, the student of Donatus,[5] and before considering his treatment of Virgil it is necessary to say something about the work of this extremely influential figure. Donatus' own lost Virgil commentary seems to have survived at least until the ninth century, and can be largely reconstructed from the evidence of borrowing in early-medieval compilations.[6] It cannot really be called literary criticism in that its glosses seem to have been concerned, not with the interpretation of Virgil's poems, but with extracting from them illustrations of points of rhetoric and grammar. As such his work fundamentally influenced the character of instruction in the early-medieval schools, and set the pattern for medieval commentary on classical texts down to the late-Carolingian period. Aside from this, Donatus' chief contribution to medieval literary criticism was his still-surviving *vita* of the poet, largely borrowed from Suetonius, which reports in anecdotal fashion the known facts and traditions of Virgil's life, and relates them to the *causa* and *intentio* of his poems. Such *vitae*, borrowed or assembled from the scholiasts, were to become a standard feature of medieval commentary and of the prologues or *accessus* to curriculum authors which are one of the most characteristic

---

[4] On their dates see Cameron, 'Macrobius', pp. 30–3.
[5] But see Holtz, *Donat*, pp. 224–5.
[6] See Schindel, *Figurenlehren*, pp. 96–183; Holtz, 'A l'école', pp. 529–30; Brugnoli, 'Donato, Elio'.

forms of criticism in the medieval period. Evidence of a more synthetic view of the corpus of Virgil is provided by a passage in the introduction to the *Eclogues* that concludes the *vita*, which correlates the sequence of *Eclogues, Georgics* and *Aeneid* with the evolution of human activity from its pastoral origins to the arts of agriculture and war (Brummer, *Vitae Vergilianae*, p. 14).

Beyond this we can only speculate about Donatus' approach to interpretation, but it is reasonable to assume that it is reflected to some extent in the commentaries of Servius. These too are concerned primarily with figures of speech and peculiarities of syntax, but Servius also shows himself to be a versatile and learned mythographer, and his explanations of the religious, philosophical and scientific meanings conveyed by Virgil's use of myth or *fabula* provided perhaps the single most influential model for the work of medieval mythographers. He is responsive to the strain of physical and psychological allegory already present in Virgil's treatment of the gods and their activities as well as to the Stoic and Neoplatonic tradition which treats myth as representing natural and spiritual processes; he has an extensive knowledge of ancient religious rites and mythological traditions, and he offers humbler euhemeristic, moralising and etymological glosses which smack of the classroom.[7]

Like the work of earlier scholiasts, Servius' commentary has no consistent theme, and offers only brief and general suggestions about the larger meaning of Virgil's enterprise. Writing at the end of a century of polemic between pagan and Christian over the religious and philosophical significance of myth, he is content to compile different views, and places euhemeristic, naturalistic and semi-mystical interpretations side-by-side without acknowledging their inconsistency or relative importance. At times he even seems impatient with Virgil's recourse to *fabula*, and dismisses his mythic imagery as no more than poetic licence, arbitrarily and superfluously juxtaposed with more meaningful utterance.[8] But the range of information he brings to bear on Virgil's text gives a sense of the kind of lore the grammarian was responsible for providing, and could serve as the basis for more sustained exercises in various kinds of interpretation. The commentary abounds in historical glosses which discover in the events of Virgil's narrative foreshadowings of later Roman history, or compare Aeneas' actions with those of Augustus and the great leaders of the Republic, in ways that at times suggest the typological use of the Old Testament in patristic exegesis. Virgil's gods and goddesses are aligned with natural forces in a way that implies a coherent cosmological reading of the traditional pantheon, and the sixth book of the *Aeneid*, in which

---

[7] Demats, *Fabula*, pp. 26–30; Murrin, *Epic*, pp. 3–50.
[8] See Demats, *Fabula*, pp. 30–6, and compare Lactantius, *Inst.* 1.11.19–24.

Servius finds the 'deep learning' of philosophers and theologians, leads him to depart from his normal practice of *ad verbum* glossing to provide more extended discussions of the structure of the universe and the life of the soul (*In Aen. VI, Praef.*; ed. Thilo-Hagen, II, p. 1).[9]

The philosophical view of literature tentatively suggested by Servius' treatment of Virgil is emphatically present in Macrobius. His chief works are the *Saturnalia*, a long imaginary dialogue set in the Rome of the 380s and bringing together a number of the leading figures of the pagan revival of that time; and a commentary on the *Somnium Scipionis* or *Dream of Scipio*, the visionary episode which, in imitation of Plato's vision of Er in *Republic* 10, formed the climax of Cicero's now largely lost *De re publica*. Both works are encyclopaedic in character, the commentary tending to reduce Cicero's dream-vision to a framing device for the discussion of a number of scientific and psychological topics, the *Saturnalia* being largely concerned with philology, the history of religion, and Roman antiquities. Both works treat imaginative literature as a vehicle of philosophy, and both elevate the authors with whom they are principally concerned, Cicero and Virgil, to the status of sages, authorities on any and all topics, and (most important of all) thoroughgoing Platonists.

While the commentary deals at length with cosmological topics, and provided the Middle Ages with an authoritative model of the physical universe, its primary purpose (a purpose that Macrobius imputes, somewhat anachronistically, to Cicero himself; *Comm.* 1.4.1), is to expound the Neoplatonic view of the nature and life of the human soul. As preparation for dealing with such matters, the commentary begins by discussing the role of *fabula* in philosophical discourse.[10] First, merely entertaining stories are distinguished from instructive ones, then the latter are subdivided into the wholly fictive, such as the fables of Aesop, and those 'fabulous narratives' which we might call myths, in which fiction provides a decorous covering for truths about the gods or the life of the spirit. Here, as well, distinctions must be made: philosophers reject myths which show gods engaging in violence or immorality; and in dealing with the 'supreme' god (*to agathon*, or *summus deus*) they abandon myth altogether in favour of simile, as when Plato uses the sun to exemplify the Good (*Comm.* 1.2.6–21). In using myth to discuss the gods and the soul, Macrobius says, we emulate nature herself, whose mysteries are veiled by the variety of created life, accessible only to the wise, and only through the rites and mysteries of religion.

The implicit analogy between the natural world and the literary text, and the sense that an element of inner mystery is common to both,

---

[9] See also *In Aen.* VI, 404, 724, 730–48; pp. 63, 99–102, 103–6; and the discussion by Gersh, *Middle Platonism*, II, pp. 747–55, and Setaioli, 'Evidence et évidenciation'.

[10] For earlier discussion in Latin writers, see Trimpi, *Muses*, pp. 287–95.

pervades Macrobius' writings. The text of a great author contains all knowledge: Plato is the repository of truth itself ('ipsius veritatis arcanum'; 1.6.23), and Cicero's little vision, too, unfolds to reveal a complete philosophy ('universa philosophiae integritas'; 2.17.17) in the light of Macrobius' assumption that its conciseness must conceal profound knowledge (2.12.7). At its centre is a rich and thoroughly Neoplatonic understanding of the life of the soul: its divine origin; its descent into the world, where it is incarcerated for a time in the 'hell' or 'prison' or 'death' of bodily existence; and its return to the realm of the undying at the death of the body (1.7–14).

If Cicero takes us to 'the heights of philosophy' (*Comm.* 2.17.17), Virgil is even more highly praised in the *Saturnalia*: not only is he supremely learned ('omnium disciplinarum peritus'; *Sat.* 1.16.12), but the richness of his style, embracing the 'copiousness' of Cicero and much besides, seems divinely inspired (5.1.7, 18). The *Aeneid* is a sacred text, and must be approached with the reverence owed to the shrine of a religious mystery (1.24.13). In Virgil the analogy between nature and literary language implicit in the theoretical discussion of the commentary is fully realised: the rich variety of his eloquence is comparable to that of the *natura rerum*, his poetry linked by deep affinities to the divine work of creation (5.1.19–20). There is some evidence that the religious element in Macrobius' veneration for Virgil is reinforced by a body of Neoplatonic commentary on the *Aeneid*, no longer extant, but Macrobius himself does little to substantiate his lofty claims by analysis of particular passages. We can only speculate about the promised discourse of Eustathius on Virgil's mastery of 'astrology and the whole of philosophy' (1.24.18), which was apparently one of the now-missing portions of Book 3. In its absence the *Saturnalia* treat Virgil more as rhetorician and a man of learning than as philosopher, and in fact the Commentary on Cicero has more to say about the underlying meaning of the *Aeneid*, though here Macrobius tends, as in dealing with the *Somnium Scipionis* itself, to reserve philosophical and religious treatment for passages like Anchises' discourse on the soul, where the religious orientation of the text is already clear, and the demonstration of an inner spiritual meaning is largely a matter of expansion.

Despite his professed reverence for Virgil, and a manifest sensitivity to the stylistic qualities of his poetry, Macrobius seems to consider the philosophical significance of the *Aeneid* as something all but independent of the particulars of the text. In the few cases in which Virgil's mythological references are explained (usually as embodying hints of an underlying monotheism, in keeping with one of the main themes of Macrobius' dialogue), what is in question is the 'fabulous narrative' itself, the myth in its essential outlines, irrespective of its specific literary context. The overriding concern is to show that the use of myth in Virgil's poetry is one expression of a broad and ongoing cultural tradition in which Virgil and the *personae* of Macrobius' dialogue are understood to participate together. Text and author are important only to the extent that they provide the commentator with the opportunity to set forth a view of history and national traditions, a set of cosmological and philosophical ideas, and ultimately a Neoplatonic view of spiritual experience.

A work of the later fifth century, the *De nuptiis Philologiae et Mercurii* of Martianus Capella, provides a counterpart to this conception of the function of literature in the form of an original *fabula*. The *De nuptiis*, a manual of the Seven Liberal Arts, is prefaced by an elaborate narrative of the quest of Mercury, or eloquence, for a bride, the election of Philology, or earthly knowledge, as his mate, and her preparation for marriage through an initiation into divine wisdom. As announced in an opening hymn to Hymen, the overarching theme of this fable is marriage, understood as including the interaction of the principles of cosmic order and a host of correspondences between the paradigms and symbolic languages of earthly knowledge and the universal principles they seek to express. In the course of the story a broad range of classical deities is encountered and described in terms of their various attributes and cosmic functions. The lengthy process by which Philology is enabled to rise to a knowledge of the causes of things, and ultimately to a visionary awareness of 'that truth which exists by virtue of powers beyond existence' (*De nupt.* 2.206), is made the occasion for a thorough review of the organisation of knowledge and its relation to the order of the universe.

Like the writings of Macrobius, the *De nuptiis* is pervaded by a sense of the affinity between literature and religious ritual, and it is modelled in certain respects on actual initiatory rites. At the same time it is written in a self-consciously learned style, and pervaded by a kind of pedantic humour which reminds us of its essentially didactic character and, without excluding moments of real beauty and religious feeling, prevents our taking its mystical aspect too seriously. It is finally the work of a teacher, and in its didactic function it can be seen to develop tendencies already present in Macrobius' treatment of classical poetry.

In effect, the *De nuptiis* is commentary turned inside-out. As we have seen, the theme of human life as an intellectual and spiritual journey constituted for Macrobius the latent content of classic literature. In Martianus' allegory this theme emerges to the surface, wholly displacing the traditional 'fabulous narrative', and the same schematising tendency is evident in the treatment of the gods. In the universe of the *De nuptiis* cosmology and mythology are precisely integrated, and mythographical analysis involves no more than a translation from one set of terms to the other. Both developments were to prove extremely important for the literary criticism of the early Middle Ages, and both are carried a step further by the early-sixth-century Christian writer Fulgentius, whose work can be said to mark the transition from late-antique to medieval literary studies.

Fulgentius' 'Exposition of the Content of Virgil' promises to clarify the 'elusive wanderings' of the *Aeneid* by proceeding 'in accordance with the moral philosophers'. Written in a style which constitutes a debasement of the facetiously pedantic manner of Martianus, it takes the form of a dialogue between the shade of Virgil and the narrator, a self-important *homunculus* for whom the poet grudgingly condescends to explain how the *Aeneid* expresses 'the entire condition of human life'. The moral purpose of the *Aeneid* is expressed by the opening juxtaposition of 'arms' (manhood) and 'man' (wisdom). From this point 'Virgil' proceeds to read the first five books of the poem as a progression from birth (the shipwreck of Book 1) to the burning, in Book 5, of the ships in which youth had pursued its stormy course, which marks the point at which one is ready to assume the responsibility of mature understanding. Book 6 dramatises the attainment of learning, through which one conquers pride and superstition and comes at last to a knowledge of God and human destiny. The final six books of the poem are then reviewed in a hasty and random way as dramatising the wise man's alliance with goodness (Evander) and his conquest of impiety, defiance and madness (Mezentius, Messapus, Turnus).

Rome is never mentioned in the commentary, and no hint is given of the historical context or purpose of the *Aeneid*. At the outset the narrator asks Virgil to expound, not the deeper meanings of his poem, but such 'easy' matters as a grammarian might present to boys, and it is obvious that the commentator has neither the learning nor the seriousness of purpose of Macrobius. But the *Expositio*, together with the more sophisticated counterpart to its pedagogical plot embodied in Martianus' *De nuptiis*, largely determined the basic form in which, after an interval during which literary studies were necessarily in abeyance, the legacy of the ancient commentary tradition would be recovered. For literary criticism from the Carolingian period forward, major poetry tends to be seen as expressing one great theme, the formation of the human spirit through learning and the pursuit of wisdom. The emphasis can be religious, as for Macrobius and Martianus Capella, or pedagogical, as in Fulgentius and later critics of Virgil, but the basic pattern remains the same, and will provide a frame for discussions of classical poetry throughout the Middle Ages.

The tendency to treat meaning as something independent of authorial intention, already well developed in Macrobius, has obviously become still more pronounced in the less sophisticated pedagogical circumstances implied by Fulgentius' work. In his *Mitologiae*, which were to prove a fundamental contribution to the resources of the medieval commentator, the split between meaning and intention is taken to its logical extreme.

The *Mitologiae* present a series of allegorical readings of mythological figures and episodes in which the doctrinal content of myth is expounded *in vacuo*, without reference to any ancient text. In a prefatory vision, the Muses appear to the author and promise to make him immortal, 'not, like Nero, by mere poetic praises, but like Plato, through mystical knowledge' (*Expositio*, ed. Agozzino-Zanlucchi, p. 44; ed. Helm, p. 87). In the event, the knowledge vouchsafed is a repertoire of possible allegorisings of the stories and figures treated, in which moralisation, euhemerism and vestiges of Stoic and Neoplatonic mythography are presented simply as alternative and occasionally contradictory possibilities, in no clear order and with no perceptible emphasis. Myth has finally been reduced to an occasion for exercises in allegory, or at best a kind of adornment to the teachings of philosophy; in either case its rationale has become wholly independent of its function in a particular literary context.

Fulgentius remarks on the great renown enjoyed by Ovid and Lucan among the grammarians (*Mitologiae* 1.21; ed. Helm, p. 32), suggesting that his own work was not an isolated phenomenon in sixth-century Africa, but there is every indication of decline after his day. The implications that Macrobius, Martianus and Fulgentius were to have for literary theory and criticism began to be realised only in the later Carolingian period. In the early medieval centuries the primary task was to keep alive a rudimentary knowledge of ancient culture and a minimum standard of Latinity, tasks to which the scholiasts and grammarians were better suited than the purveyors of philosophical allegory. Servius remained in wide circulation, together with a body of commentary, probably somewhat later, associated with the name of Junius 'Philargyrius' (or 'Philagrius'), which, while primarily grammatical, offered interpretations of the *personae* and allusions in the *Eclogues* and *Georgics* in terms of biographical, political and religious allegory.[11]

In general, after Fulgentius, the sixth century has little to tell us about the critical study of literature. Cassiodorus in several works notes the importance of a knowledge of secular authors to the study of the Bible, but he makes remarkably little use of them in his own writings, and there is no suggestion of a canon of ancient texts in the programme of study outlined in his *Institutiones*. (Indeed the library at Vivarium may not have possessed a copy of Virgil.) Boethius, too, justly praised by Cassiodorus for his work in preserving and commenting on ancient authors in several fields, seems not to have given literature an important role in his view of education, though the example of his *De consolatione philosophiae* is more than sufficient compensation. Not only does the *Consolatio* bespeak a high degree of literary culture, but it has marked structural and thematic

[11] See Funaioli, *Esegesi*, pp. 332–401; Geymonat, 'Filargirio'; Irvine, *Making*, pp. 148–55.

affinities with the work of Martianus and Fulgentius, and its brilliant distillation of Platonic and Stoic themes into a narrative of intellectual and
spiritual evolution provided authoritative reinforcement for the Neoplatonic view of the ideal function of literature inherited by the Middle Ages
from late Antiquity.

The great encyclopaedist Isidore of Seville, whose *Etymologiae* or
Origines appeared early in the seventh century, provided the Middle Ages
with a compact and comprehensive survey of literature and literary studies
which was to prove widely influential. His opening book traces the evolution of formal language from the first written representations of speech to
the development of the major poetic forms, which he follows Jerome and
Cassiodorus in assigning to the Jews (*Etym.* 1.3.39). The *carmen heroicum* is first realised in the climactic 'Song of Moses' in Deuteronomy,
while the first hymns are owed to David, the epithalamium to Solomon,
the lament to Jeremiah. History begins with Moses, *fabula* with the trees'
search for a king in Judges 9 (1:40–2). But Isidore also notes the employment of these and other lesser modes and genres in Greece and Rome,
and later provides a simplified mythographical analysis of the ancient
pantheon which combines the Christian euhemerism of Lactantius and
Augustine with material from the scholiasts (8.11).

Brief quotations from Virgil and other poets abound in the *Etymologiae*,
and Isidore reveals a broad familiarity with the commentary tradition as
well as a special predilection for Servius. But rather than providing the
basis for study of literary texts, the grammarians and commentators are
probably the chief, if not the sole, source of Isidore's knowledge of Horace,
Statius and the other Latin poets he cites. These authors are duly recalled,
along with Ovid, Lucan and Persius, in Isidore's *Versus in bibliotheca*,
but in words that leave it unclear whether his library actually included
them;[12] and his works provide scant evidence of a first-hand knowledge
even of Virgil.

The primary function of the poetry deployed in the *Etymologiae*, then, is
to provide an occasion for the work of the glossator. But it is important to
note Isidore's concern to inventory the forms and techniques employed by
classical poets, and the clear evidence of his appreciation of the scattered
membra poetarum with which he deals reminds us that he encountered
them not only through the grammarians, but in Tertullian, Minucius Felix,
Lactantius and Jerome.[13] Thus survived the classical tradition which was
to produce such late and isolated flowerings as the poems of the seventh-
century bishop Eugenius of Toledo.[14]

[12] See Fontaine, *Isidore*, II, pp. 735–62; Holtz, 'La survie', pp. 217–18.
[13] See Fontaine, 'Isidoro'.
[14] See Fontaine, *Isidore*, II, p. 744; Riou, 'Quelques aspects', pp. 11–15; Codoñer, 'Poetry
of Eugenius'.

As important for our purposes as the substance of Isidore's learning is his use of etymology to reveal an inner meaning, often illustrative of some scientific principle or historical fact, in the names and terms with which he deals. The principle that one can discover the 'origins' of words and concepts by breaking them up and revealing their supposed roots in simpler Latin words or in Greek is already present in Servius and Fulgentius, and Cassiodorus had stressed the importance of etymology for biblical exegesis (*Expositio psalmorum*, In Ps. I.1). From early on it had been recognised that its procedures were arbitrary, and Augustine compares them sceptically to the methods of dream-interpretation (*Principia dialecticae*, PL 32, 1411; also *Conf.* 4.3), but in Isidore they become a tool for systematising knowledge, a way of linking words to ideas which makes philosophy in all its aspects largely an extension of grammar, enabling him, and those succeeding centuries when the tools and concepts of philosophy were largely absent, to practise a kind of 'grammatical Platonism'. For Isidore etymology is a way of engaging the world itself, rather than particular texts, but his lexical approach deeply influenced the study of literature, and etymology remained an essential means of access to the truth of literary language throughout the Middle Ages.

During the early medieval centuries the study of the classics is random and for the most part superficial. The tradition of classicising Christian Latin poetry that survives in Eugenius is interrupted in Italy and Gaul after Venantius Fortunatus. In the forward-looking schools of seventh-century Ireland and England, where Latin was a painfully acquired second language, the grammarians were probably the only secular writers studied in a systematic way, and there is nothing in the surviving poetry of the period to indicate a critical interest in ancient authors. The supposed classical culture of Columbanus has been shown to be a matter of false attribution, and the often-cited contribution of Irish teachers to the tradition of Virgil commentary consisted almost entirely of compilation from ancient sources.[15] The *Hisperica Famina* and related writings reveal some knowledge of Virgil, but no real evidence of wider reading in the poets. Virgil himself seems to have served the Irish writers chiefly as a source of rhetorical formulas to be imitated in inflated 'Hisperic' diction, an exercise for which the quotations in the grammarians would be at least as useful as the text of the poet himself (*Hisperica Famina*, ed. Herren, pp. 24–6).

In England, though 'Hisperic' influences are less pervasive, the situation in other respects is similar. Aldhelm gave a prominent place to metrics in his scheme of education, and his own hexameter verse, perhaps the first

[15] See Lapidge, 'Authorship'; Holtz, 'Redécouverte', pp. 11–12, and 'La Survie', pp. 219–20; Herren, 'Classical and Secular Learning', pp. 136–8; Irvine, *Making*, pp. 148–55.

we possess by a poet for whom Latin was a wholly learned language, is a remarkable achievement (*De metris, Opera*, pp. 77–96, 150–201; *Poetic Works*, pp. 191–211). His letters contain seemingly appreciative allusions to Virgil together with frequent mythological references, but he can also express a harsh scorn for classical studies (*Epistola* 3, in *Opera*, pp. 479–80; *Prose Works*, pp. 139–40). Bede, writing at the height of the eighth-century Northumbrian renaissance, and in a style of discriminating purity in both prose and verse, rarely alludes to classical authors. His treatise on metre draws most of its examples from Christian Latin poetry, and it has been argued that this seeming avoidance of the classics reflects a lack of first-hand knowledge that may have been a matter of deliberate choice.[16] But whereas in the case of Isidore, and perhaps Aldhelm, it is possible to account for nearly every classical allusion by reference to the grammarians or earlier Christian authors, Bede's sensitivity and allusiveness almost certainly indicate at the least a thorough knowledge of Virgil.

In general, however, it seems clear that ancient literature had relatively little importance in the British Isles during this period, apart from its fundamental role in the grammatical tradition, though it is also clear that classical studies were reviving over the course of the eighth century. The essentials of the classical culture of Alcuin must have been acquired before he left England, and even where the curriculum remained confined to Christian authors, the Anglo-Saxon schools were remarkable in the range and sophistication of the techniques they developed for dealing with the metrics, syntax, figures of speech and often largely classical vocabulary of Christian Latin poetry.

For Europe generally, the decisive impetus to renewal was to come from the educational reforms introduced by Alcuin in the name of Charlemagne, but already in the 780s Charlemagne could summon to France a number of scholars who had acquired considerable general learning and some knowledge of classical literature in the schools of their own countries. In addition to Alcuin himself, master at the school of York with its famous library, these include the Irishman Dungal, scientist and 'corrector' of Lucretius; the Italians Paul the Deacon, historian of the Lombards, and the grammarian Peter of Pisa; and Theodulf, later bishop of Orléans, from Visigothic Spain.[17] With the partial exception of Lombard Italy, the Latin culture of these countries was centred very largely in the monasteries, and we cannot easily trace the immediate sources of the classical culture which appears so strikingly in the often graceful and richly allusive imitations of classical Latin poetry produced by Alcuin, Paul, Theodulf and other poets

[16] See Hunter Blair, *World of Bede*, pp. 288–9.
[17] See Fichtenau, *Carolingian Empire*, pp. 79–103; Laistner, *Thought and Letters*, pp. 191–202; Brunhölzl, 'Bildungsauftrag'.

of the Carolingian 'renaissance', but it plainly bespeaks a new interest in literary studies. Alcuin names Virgil, Horace, Ovid, Lucan and Statius in describing the library at York, though he is likely to have known some of these only through the grammarians, and Theodulf gives an indication of how poetry was studied in eighth-century Spain, in a poem on his early reading (Alcuin, *Bishops, Kings and Saints*, pp. 1554–5; and Theodulph, in Godman, *Poetry*, pp. 168–71). This reading encompassed the Fathers, the Christian poets, and finally Virgil and Ovid, whose words are outwardly deceitful and frivolous, but conceal many truths which it is the task of the wise to uncover. Theodulf illustrates these truths by a series of brief moral glosses on mythological figures, suggesting the survival of something of the tradition of Fulgentius and the grammarians of the late empire.

In Charlemagne Alcuin and his colleagues found a patron anxious to identify himself with the promotion of education and culture, and whose programme of *renovatio* encompassed the founding of schools and libraries, aiming at a complete reform of the organs and institutions of Christian learning. The higher objectives of late-antique pedagogy are recalled in Alcuin's treatises on rhetoric and grammar, which firmly establish the study of the ancient authors as the starting-point, and the Seven Liberal Arts as the essential pattern of advancement, in the orderly pursuit of a wisdom which is finally divine. For Alcuin the programmatic role of literature as an introduction to philosophy is no mere pedagogical contrivance. His intellectual programme, though inevitably hampered by a lack of philosophical and scientific resources, owes more to Boethius than to Fulgentius, and his assertion that the Arts are the seven pillars of the temple of Wisdom defines an ideal which will remain central to educational thinking through the twelfth century.[18] His own role in the renewal of education, though it included the compilation of influential school-books and the emendation of texts essential to the work of the clergy, was largely administrative. The strongest surviving evidence of his appreciation for ancient literature are his essays in the adaptation of Virgilian pastoral to Christian themes, easily the finest poems of the Carolingian era. But the reforms he effected were to lead to a newly ambitious programme of study which gave a new significance to the study of literature.

The early symptoms of this renewal are random. The establishment of lines of communication with libraries and centres of learning across Western Europe enabled the court library to accumulate a rich collection of important manuscripts of classical literature, a source from which other centres were to be greatly enriched in the course of the ninth century. The

[18] See Courcelle, *Consolation*, pp. 32–47.

teaching of the palace school at this early stage was probably conducted more by way of text-books compiled from earlier works on the several arts than by direct study of a curriculum of ancient texts; knowledge of many authors was narrowly localised, and a number of the works that reappear at this time, such as Lucretius' *De rerum natura* and the Virgil commentary of the fourth-century rhetorician Tiberius Claudius Donatus, became lost again in the course of the ninth century. But it was the work of this period in recovering and emending ancient texts that led to the gradual emergence of a canon of school authors. The great teacher and compiler Rabanus Maurus, the most eminent of the pupils of Alcuin, seems to have held very conservative views on the value of classical studies, but his own pupil and friend Lupus of Ferrières was a remarkable textual critic, whose many surviving letters show him combining the life of a busy churchman with an amazingly active concern to acquire new texts, pagan as well as Christian, and to collate his own manuscripts with those possessed by friends in other parts of France and Germany.[19] There is also good evidence for an increased circulation of anthologies, copied in many cases from earlier models but including also contemporary compilations like the *Collectanea* of Heiric of Auxerre and Sedulius Scottus. Their contents varied widely but they typically included pagan as well as Christian authors, and Sedulius in particular seems to have taken pains to bring together a wider range of texts than any single Carolingian library was likely to possess. His collection includes selections from seven different works of Cicero and Macrobius' commentary on the *Somnium Scipionis*, and indicates an interest in philosophy as well as the concern of all teachers of his time for style and moral *sententiae*. A compilation by Walafrid Strabo contains a thoughtful selection from the letters of Seneca. From this period, too, date the earliest *florilegia* devoted to such specific subjects as metrics, secular and biblical history, and the rudiments of moral philosophy.[20]

Recovery of classical texts meant in many cases a rediscovery of accompanying *vitae* and scholia, and already in the early ninth century (if the *Commentum Brunsianum* on Terence can be dated this early)[21] there is evidence of a renewed concern with commentary. But the full flowering of Carolingian commentary did not to occur until after the mid-century, and was stimulated by the teaching of such figures as Martin of Laon and Heiric of Auxerre.[22] Its first important manifestation is a body of glosses

[19] See Severus, *Lupus*, pp. 41–131; Pellegrin, 'Les manuscrits'; Bischoff, 'Paläographie'.
[20] See Glauche, *Schullektüre*, pp. 31–6; Contreni, *Cathedral School*, pp. 146–9; Reynolds and Wilson, *Scribes and Scholars*, p. 91; Irvine, *Making*, pp. 334–64; Munk Olsen, 'Les classiques latins'.
[21] See Rand, 'Commentaries', pp. 387–8; Riou, 'Essai', pp. 79–80; Zetzel, 'History'.
[22] See Contreni, *Cathedral School*, pp. 95–151; Mariani, 'Persio', pp. 145–52; Quadri, *Collectanea*, pp. 11–28.

on the *De nuptiis* of Martianus Capella which evidently reflect the teaching of Irish masters at Laon and at the palace school of Charles the Bald.[23] These include at least two versions of a commentary by John Scotus Eriugena, the greatest scholar of his day, and collectively they represent the first really original literary criticism produced in medieval Europe. The encyclopaedic character of the *De nuptiis* and its educational theme, the richness and density of its mythological apparatus, and the religious Neoplatonism which informs its allegory all served to make it an especially challenging and valuable text for study in an age concerned to rediscover the intellectual universe, and the Carolingian scholars assimilated it to their needs and interests with an impressive boldness. Martianus' allegory seemed to confirm the role of the liberal arts in the attainment of religious understanding, and indeed provided the basis for the view of a number of ninth-century educators that the arts are themselves divine. Philosophy is the sum of the arts for Eriugena, and the true philosophy is at the same time the true religion (Eriugena, *De divina praedestinatione liber*, PL 122, 358a; also *Annotationes*, p. 64). In the same spirit an anonymous contemporary of Eriugena observes that a knowledge of the Arts is inherent in human nature, though it has been clouded by sin and must be 'recalled into the presence of understanding' through study (*Dunchad glossae*, p. 23).

Within this religious-pedagogical framework the allegorical *mythos* of the *De nuptiis* could be explored with a new confidence, and Eriugena and his fellow commentators readily discover a spiritual significance in its already half-allegorical use of mythology. Thus when Martianus, describing the gifts bestowed by the gods on Psyche, the human soul, speaks of Sophia-Minerva's gift of the 'speculum Aniae', Eriugena, with the help of a dubious Greek etymology and a sensitive appreciation of Martianus' own purpose, discovers in the mirror a reflection of 'the natural dignity and primordial fountain' of the human soul (*Annotationes*, p. 12). Vulcan, whose gift of 'unquenchably enduring figures' is juxtaposed with Venus' infusion of the pleasurable itch of lust, becomes, in the light of what Eriugena calls 'higher natural theory' (*Annotationes*, p. 13), a figure of the *ingenium* or natural orientation present in all rational natures which keeps alive the memory of their original dignity and its divine source. Pallas, who, in her *solivaga virginitas* refuses to participate in the nuptial rites of Mercury and Philology, is for one commentator, possibly Martin of Laon, a symbol of the incorruptibility of the supreme wisdom, and her 'crown of seven radiant lights' is that ideal synthesis of the liberal arts which human language cannot fully comprehend.[24]

---

[23] See Leonardi, 'Commenti', 483–98; Préaux, 'Jean Scot'.
[24] See Préaux, 'Jean Scot', pp. 168–70.

For our purposes, the importance of these commentaries is not in the profundity of meaning they discover but in the attitude they imply towards Martianus' text. They neither adapt the *mythos* arbitrarily to a Neoplatonic paradigm in the manner of Macrobius nor moralise it like Fulgentius, and they exhibit none of the anxiety of the pioneering ninth-century commentary on Boethius' *Consolatio* associated with the 'Anonymous of St Gall', whose conviction that Boethius was a Catholic enables him to find straightforward Christian meanings in much of Philosophy's message, but leaves him helpless in the face of the blatant Platonism of certain passages.[25] Instead they seek to discover the intrinsic character of Martianus' pagan poetic language, and the similarity of purpose and idea which link his pursuit of the liberal arts to their own. Eriugena offers the most striking insights: traces of Martianus' language and imagery inform his account of the psychology of fallen man in the *Periphyseon*, and even affect his treatment of the mystery of the Incarnation;[26] it is not surprising that his engagement with the *De nuptiis* should have been regarded with suspicion by less adventurous contemporaries. The 'higher theory' that Eriugena discerns in Martianus' mythological imagery has real affinities with the 'high' or 'gnostic' character of theological speculation as he conceives it, and it is complemented by a lofty conception of the value of poetry. Eriugena made serious efforts to gain a sense of Homeric Greek from passages quoted in Priscian and elsewhere, and he can speak of 'a kind of theological poetry' which uses biblical imagery to elevate our minds just as literary study uses the fables and images of heroic poems (Eriugena, *Super ierarchiam* 2.142–51; ed. Barbet, p. 24).

Not all ninth-century scholars were up to the challenge of analysing Martianus' complex allegory, and the Martianus commentaries themselves are for the most part devoted to brief glosses on points of grammar and the meanings of individual words. But these commentaries are part of a more general adaptation of the ancient authors to the purposes of the schools which advanced rapidly over the course of the ninth century. As we might suppose, Virgil is the author for whom the evidence is richest. Virgil manuscripts are regularly prefaced by a version of one or more of the ancient *vitae* and equipped with mnemonic verses which introduce the poet's several works and summarise the individual books of the *Georgics* and the *Aeneid*. The text itself is typically accompanied by glosses drawn largely from Servius and other ancient commentators, and in the case of a compilation like Laon MS 468 we are given a window on the broader context of classical studies at the mid-century (*Codex Laudunensis 468*, ed. Contreni). It is a sort of companion to the study of Virgil and

---

[25] See Courcelle, *Consolation*, pp. 275–8; Troncarelli, 'Ricerca', pp. 367–8.
[26] Leonardi, 'Nuove voci', pp. 165–6; 'I commenti', pp. 487–94.

the liberal arts, and includes, in addition to extensive glosses on Virgil, a *vita* of the poet, excerpts from Servius' prologues, mythographical information from Isidore, Fulgentius and other mythographers, and further material from Isidore on the arts and on ancient culture and religion. Few surviving codices are this elaborate, but the fact that the *vitae* and summarising verses are found even in Virgil manuscripts which contain no other gloss is evidence that the poetry itself was becoming the primary object of study, rather than simply providing an occasion for grammatical commentary. The same conclusion has been drawn from those cases where a text of one of the commentators has survived accompanied by only a fragmentary text of Virgil, or no text at all: whereas the commentary was a reference work, to be consulted when necessary, the poems themselves were classroom texts, to be handled and annotated until they simply wore out.

A similar literary emphasis is found in commentaries on Terence, largely compiled from the scholiasts and grammarians, but often augmenting these sources in ways which demonstrate both a concern with complexities of language, and a new interest in the character and structure of the poetry itself. Terence's place in the medieval curriculum was assured by the traditional pairing of his comedies with the tragic poem of Virgil, and their association with the name of Donatus (though the evidence for first-hand knowledge of his commentary in the early-medieval period is minimal).[27] In the case of Terence we possess a series of related commentaries which seem to reflect roughly definable stages in the development of a Carolingian commentary tradition.[28] The first, the so-called *Commentum Brunsianum*, probably a work of the early ninth century, draws on very limited sources: its brief *vita* is evidently based wholly on Orosius' passing reference to Terence as having been brought from Carthage to Rome as a captive and subsequently elevated by Scipio Africanus (*Historiae adv. paganos* 4.19). Horace's *Ars poetica* is cited on the nature of comedy, and the metrical character of Terence's dialogue is affirmed on the authority of Priscian. The occasionally 'turgid and inflated' style is explained as a function of comic characterisation, and the commentator excuses the relative simplicity of the *fabulae* on which Terence's plots are based by noting that he inserts many moral observations (*honesta*). The running commentary on the plays includes summaries of the scenes, carefully explaining the relations of the speakers, and extensive glosses on words and action, and it is typical of Carolingian commentary in providing explanations of individual words both simpler and more numerous than those in the ancient scholia, and in the freedom with which the glossator invents explanations of names, customs and historical details.

---

[27] See Reeve and Rouse, 'New Light', pp. 246–9; Riou, 'Les commentaires', pp. 38–9.
[28] On these see Rand, 'Commentaries'; Riou, 'Essai', pp. 79–80, and 'Les commentaires', pp. 33–9; Villa, *La 'lectura Terentii'*, I, 1–42.

The second commentary, the *Commentum Monacense*, based on the *Brunsianum* and assigned by Rand to the circle of Heiric of Auxerre, differs from the earlier work chiefly in the addition of material from ancient scholia and in replacing false glosses with more accurate ones from these sources.[29] The commentator knows some Greek, and alludes to a wider range of Latin authors. The third, identified in manuscripts as the *Expositio*, and tentatively attributed to Remigius of Auxerre, the student of Heiric, is distinguished by the range of its critical vocabulary and the orderliness of its procedure. After a brief *vita* close to that of the *Brunsianum*, it proceeds to Terence's motives for writing comic drama, a spurious etymological glossing of *comedia* as 'peasant song', and some notes on the character of comedy. Low comedy (*togata*, plays of Roman origin dealing with ordinary people) and high (*palliata*, plays based on Greek models) are distinguished, the subject-matter of comedy (people of all kinds, a *materia magna*) is defined, and its purpose and ethical value reviewed before the commentator proceeds to the individual plays (*Scholia Terentiana*, ed. Schlee, pp. 163–74).[30]

In this sequence we can see both the steady recovery of ancient material which is one of the important achievements of this period, and the taking shape of the characteristic concerns of Carolingian commentary. Texts are referred to clearly defined generic categories; the author's intention is explained historically and thematically; and an ethical rationale or *utilitas* is discovered in his work.

The more typical activity of the period is displayed in the work of Remigius of Auxerre, the most authoritative figure of the late-Carolingian era, whose glosses on an extraordinary range of texts, religious and secular, can be seen as a summarial illustration of the achievement of Carolingian literary culture. In addition to many sets of glosses on the poets and grammarians who were coming to comprise the standard curriculum of the schools, Remigius produced lengthy and extremely influential commentaries on both Martianus Capella and Boethius. In his dealings with the classical past he shows himself to be primarily a teacher, whose mission is accomplished through commentaries aimed at nothing more or less than a coherent sense of the verbal meaning and thematic development of the texts he engages. His commentary on Persius, like the *Expositio* on Terence tentatively assigned to him, adapts earlier Carolingian commentary, and give a good sense of his methods. Remigius simplifies and clarifies the earlier material, at times glossing the commentary itself or providing synonyms for his own words; often he will reorder Persius'

[29] Rand, 'Commentaries', pp. 362–3, 369–72. See further Mariani, 'Persio', pp. 155–6; Elder, 'Cornutus', pp. 244–5; Anderson, 'Marston Ms.', pp. 410–14.
[30] See further Rand, 'Commentaries', pp. 380–6; Sabbadini, 'Biografi', pp. 322–7.

words to clarify a difficult phrase, and at times when confronted with an unfamiliar word he will seek recourse to spurious etymologies to devise a meaning in keeping with his sense of the continuity of Persius' argument.[31] He provides long summaries of the myths to which the satirist alludes, keeps careful track of the implicit dramatic situation, and places very little reliance on his reader's ability to appreciate the frequent irony with which the poet's *reprehensio* is conveyed.

In commenting on Martianus, Remigius draws frequently on Eriugena and others, and while certain of Eriugena's speculations exceed his grasp, his commentary is both better balanced and more thorough. He is neither interested in the speculative aspects of Eriugena's work nor content, as the other commentators often are, to provide disconnected glosses on individual words. He discusses alternate readings of corrupted passages in the light of their context, and introduces only such comments of his own as will sustain the reader's awareness of the theme of Martianus' allegory of education.[32] The commentary on Boethius' *Consolatio* associated with his name (though isolating his work amid the mass of late-Carolingian commentary on Boethius presents formidable difficulties) reveals the same basic traits. In general he is a clear if often simplistic expositor of Boethius' ideas, capable of clarifying or correcting earlier commentators, and firmly maintaining a middle ground between speculation and mere annotation. At times his refusal to lose himself in an *O altitudo* seems almost eccentric: glossing the climactic phrase of Boethius' great cosmic hymn, 'to behold You is our end' (*te cernere finis*; *Cons.* 3, met. 9.27), he devotes himself to a discussion of the senses of the word *finis*, carefully distinguishing its sense of 'perfection' from the 'finishing' of a job of work or a piece of bread (in *Saeculi noni auctoris*, ed. Silk, pp. 310, 339). Many details of Boethius' text are rather arbitrarily Christianised: the ancient philosophers who died for their beliefs (*De cons. phil.* 2 pr. 4) become Christian martyrs; Philosophy's reference to 'the laws of your city' (1 pr. 5) alludes to the heavenly Jerusalem; and her 'wings' (4 met. 1.1) are glossed by reference to the figure described by John in Revelation 12:1 (Stewart, 'Commmentary', pp. 28, 29, 36). At the same time Remigius shows a certain willingness to explain away Boethius' occasional divergences from Christian orthodoxy, and to adopt uncritically arguments concerning the creation which had been strongly censured when put forward by Eriugena. This may reflect simple ignorance of the complexities with which he is dealing, but it may also reveal a conscious strategy, aimed at rendering the *Consolatio* accessible to the purposes of Christian scholars while

---

[31] See Marchesi, 'Gli scoliasti', p. 2; Elder, 'Medieval Cornutus', p. 245; Mariani, 'Persio', p. 155; Robathan and Cranz, 'Persius', pp. 237–9.
[32] See Leonardi, 'I Commenti', pp. 479–508.

preserving as much as possible of the rich classical culture contained in it (*Saeculi noni auctoris*, ed. Silk, pp. 305–8).

An important feature of the presentation of texts for study in this period, and one for which the practice of Remigius was influential, is the use of a standard prologue or *accessus*. This provided certain basic information about the author and his work, and aimed, in the words of one practitioner, 'to make the authors' beginnings, their subject-matter and intentions, the basis for determinations regarding the content and end of their work' ('ex principio eorum, id est materia vel intentione, colligere medietatem et finem'; Conrad of Hirsau, *Dialogus*, p. 15; *Accessus, etc.* [1970], p. 74). Various types of *accessus* appear, all of them traceable to ancient models. Servius had prefaced his commentary on the *Aeneid* by reviewing the life of Virgil and then considering in succession the title and 'quality' (form and style) of the poem, the intention of the author, the number and order of the books, and finally the 'explanation' which is the substance of his commentary. A second scheme, based on the *circumstantiae* by which ancient rhetoricians defined the issue or *quaestio* of a speech, and associated in its medieval form with the name of Eriugena, defines the circumstances as 'who, what, why, in what manner, when, where, by what means', a sequence later reduced to a mnemonic hexameter, 'Quis, quid, ubi, quibus auxiliis, cur, quomodo, quondam'. A simpler version of this scheme, which seems to have entered the Carolingian schools by way of Irish biblical commentary, considered the *persona* (author), *locus* (place of composition) and *tempus* (date or occasion) of the work, and sometimes the author's motive or *causa* for writing. A third type of prologue, sometimes called the scheme of the *moderni* and apparently derived from Boethius' introductions to his commentaries on Porphyry and Aristotle, gradually emerged as the most common. With many variations this scheme considered the intention, usefulness (or 'fruit for the reader'), and order (structure or disposition) of the work, the name of the author, the title, and the 'part of philosophy' (usually physics, logic or ethics) to which the work could be referred.

In the Carolingian period the purpose served by the *accessus* was elementary but essential. However fanciful the information it provided, and contrived and reductive as its analyses often prove to be, it had the important effect of providing a starting-point for approaching sophisticated texts. The *vita* of an author could be the basis for a circumstantial account of his motive for writing (the *causa operis*) and might reveal a social and political context to account for his *materia*, explain his rhetorical *modus*, or shed light on the *intentio* of his work. The *utilitas* of nearly all ancient literature was understood to consist in the inculcation of moral awareness, and the branch of philosophy to which it was assigned was *ethica*. Adapting a text to these seemingly restrictive norms could involve a certain amount of special pleading, but it could also provide the basis for a discussion of such useful topics as the various ways in which poets use language, whether 'mystically', like the philosopher-poet Virgil, whose words are always potentially a means of access to philosophical truth, or with the 'naked' directness of the satirists, who deliberately repudiate the elaborate exordia and decorous language of the high style in order to lay bare the objects of their scorn (Conrad, *Dialogus*, pp. 54–5; *Accessus, etc.* [1970], pp. 118–19; William of Conches, *Glosae in Iuvenalem*, ed. Wilson, pp. 89–91). A clear grasp of the author's *intentio* can help one deal with such problems as the irony of a Juvenal, who, *more romano*, 'praises what should be vituperated, vituperates that which should be praised' (Bernard of Utrecht, in *Accessus, etc.* [1970], p. 62). Consideration of the 'cause' and 'order' of a work can give rise to suggestive contrasts: the difference between the elaborate *figmenta* and complex narrative sequence of the *Aeneid* and the straightforward narration of real historical events in Lucan's *Pharsalia* (*De bello civili*) is in one sense so vast that Servius could declare Lucan no poet, since to deal 'openly' with historical reality is against 'the law of the art of poetry' (Servius, *In Aen.* 1.382; ed. Thilo-Hagen, I, p. 129. Compare Isidore, *Etym.* 8.7.10). Yet the characters and events in both poems are *exempla* of moral and political truth. And the goals of the *accessus* method were not limited to the control of literal meaning and rhetorical strategy. In principle, recognition of the literary character and purpose of a particular work would dictate a particular application of the verbal arts and prepare the way towards the discovery of an underlying philosophical meaning. Practice in this period was of course more tentative. Eriugena seems to have been unique in making the glossing of a school-text an occasion for original scientific and theological speculation. But the paradigms of the Carolingian commentators proved durable and versatile, and came to serve more sophisticated purposes in the schools of the twelfth century.

The tenth century saw a falling-off in education, but the achievements of the Carolingian period were to prove lasting, and it is possible henceforth to speak of a standard school curriculum based on a canon of authors. In addition to the proliferation of glossed manuscripts of individual texts, a number of manuscripts of the ninth and tenth centuries mingle the works of the Christian Latin poets with selections from ancient writers and material from the grammarians or Isidore to produce what amount to compendia of liberal culture. Christian authors predominate, and the ancient texts are typically the *Disticha Catonis* or the Fables of Avianus, but Terence, Horace, Lucan, Juvenal and Persius also appear (Remigius, *In Martianum*, ed. Lutz, pp. 11–16). For all of these authors there exist glosses or *accessus* attributed to Remigius, and his importance in establishing the classical curriculum was clearly very great. His methods as commentator were refined, but not essentially altered, by twelfth-century scholars, and his commentaries remained authoritative well into the later Middle Ages.

Remigius was an important source as well for the first of the three 'Vatican Mythographers' (so named by their first editor, the Vatican librarian Cardinal Angelo Mai), whose treatise must be dated between the early tenth century and the mid-eleventh, though a case has been made for assigning it to the later Merovingian period.[33] Its terse, often awkward summaries are based on the scholiasts, Servius, and the *narrationes* of Ovidian legend attributed to Lactantius Placidus, as well as Fulgentius. They include occasional allegorisations, but there is no trace of a systematic design. The disorderly arrangement of the three books, together with the obscurity and inaccuracy of many references and the inclusion of figures from Roman history side-by-side with mythical ones, suggest a rather desperate attempt to preserve a minimum of classical culture, and it is important to remember that the compilation of a manual of ancient mythology was a pioneering venture. The fabulist did not know Hyginus, and his only models were Isidore's overview of the pagan gods and the *Mitologiae* of Fulgentius, which did not pretend to be a systematic repertoire of myth.

Mythographus Primus was used by the pseudonymous author of the *Eclogue* of 'Theodulus', a skilful exercise in amoebaean pastoral which provides an impressive illustration of the advance of classical studies between Remigius' death in 908 and the mid-eleventh century. The *Eclogue* cannot be assigned an author, date or place of origin, but it attained the status of a standard primer-text. The bulk of the poem consists of alternating quatrains which play off the views of Pseustis (Falsehood), who presents a pagan version of religion and world history, and Alithia (Truth), spokeswoman for the biblical and Christian view, in a debate overseen by Fronesis (Prudence). Mythological versions of the major issues and events of human experience are capped, one after another, by biblical and theological authority, and at the end, inevitably, Pseustis gives up in frustration. But the most interesting feature of the poem is the good-humoured detachment with which it balances the points of view of the two protagonists, and hints at their complementarity by suggesting analogies between their cosmologies and legendary traditions. Fronesis is greeted by Alithia as 'nostra' in the poem's opening lines, but when Pseustis appeals to her to end the debate, he reminds her that it was the pagan Martianus Capella who had proclaimed her the sister of truth and the mother of human knowledge. Fronesis herself, intervening to award the victory to Alithia, urges her to show compassion for Pseustis,

[33] See Elliott and Elder, 'A Critical Edition', pp. 193–9.

comparing his sorrows to the tears of Orpheus. The superiority of Alithia is beyond question, but it is clear that Fronesis is also capable of expressing a kind of truth in the language of Pseustis.

'Theodulus' is an impressively learned writer, capable of resonant allusion to Claudian, Statius and a range of classical and Christian Latin poets, and the sense he gives of a thriving classical culture is borne out by other evidence. This consists chiefly of the contents of manuscripts and the inventories of libraries containing classical texts, which indicate a steady increase in the circulation of the ancient authors, and a growing emphasis on their place in the curriculum. Reims, where Remigius had spent much of his career as a teacher, remained an important centre of manuscript production and the study of the liberal arts, attaining a new prominence at the end of the tenth century under Gerbert, who among various contributions to the study of the arts required that his students be 'steeped' in the works and style of the classical poets.[34] The monastery of Fleury, under Gerbert's contemporary Abbo, was also an active centre. The influence of the French schools soon spread. We know from Notker Labeo's account of his work as teacher and translator that at St Gall in the same period students were prepared for theological studies through a curriculum which included Virgil, Terence, Martianus and Boethius (*Schriften*, ed. Piper, I, pp. 859–61). At Tergernsee the monk Froumond laboured to assemble a large library of well-annotated classical texts.[35] And the *Libellus scholasticus* of Walter of Speyer provides deft characterisations of the series of classical poets to whose study the Speyer curriculum apparently devoted four years (*Libellus* 91–113; ed. Vossen, pp. 39–40). Perhaps most striking of all is the evidence provided by manuscripts of a broad range of classical and early Christian authors which include glosses in Old High German.[36]

By the later eleventh century a literary canon has been established which includes traditional beginners' texts like the *Disticha Catonis* and the Fables of Avianus, now often augmented by the *Ilias latina* and the elegies of Maximian, together with a higher group commonly consisting of Virgil, Lucan, Statius, the Horace of the Satires and Epistles, Persius, Juvenal, Terence, and finally Ovid, who had been little studied in earlier centuries, but is now frequently represented by the *Metamorphoses* and *Ars amatoria*. The curious *Ars lectoria* (1086) of the French scholar, Aimeric, in which first biblical and Christian authors and then secular ones are ranked as golden, silver, tin or lead, names these eight poets together with the historian Sallust as the nine 'golden' authors, followed by a group including Plautus, Ennius, Boethius and others, and finally 'Catunculus'

---

[34] See Glauche, *Schullektüre*, pp. 62–6.   [35] See Glauche, pp. 91–2.
[36] On which see Siewert, 'Vernacular Glosses'.

and the other primer-texts (*Ars lectoria*, V, p. 170). Aimeric's categories
and criteria are somewhat obscure, but the implicit analogy between his
Christian and secular canons is significant of the established status of
classical studies.

A valuable source of information for this period is a commentary on the
Eclogue of 'Theodulus' by Bernard of Utrecht which is remarkable both
in the range of critical techniques it brings to bear and in its mirroring
of the subtlety of the poem. The purpose of the *Eclogue* for Bernard is
to provide moral and spiritual edification through a sustained comparison of pagan error with sacred truth (*Accessus, etc.* [1970], pp. 63–4,
67), but he acknowledges that poetic fable, as well as biblical history,
is capable of harbouring an underlying meaning, a 'mystery'. Hence
he applies two different methods to the two principal actors, viewing
Alithia's words and descriptions in the light of patristic exegesis, while
treating those of Pseustis in the spirit of Macrobius and Fulgentius, not
simply as manifestations of pagan blindness, but as endowed with a
moral and philosophical content of their own. Thus at one point he
can compare the Ark, whose literal dimensions and structural principles
are symbolic of spiritual attributes, to the mere child's play of the Arts
(*auctorum neniis*), yet he asserts elsewhere that it is the writings of the
pagans which equip us to understand celestial things (*Commentum*, ed.
Huygens, p. 43, 335–7; p. 27, 187–9). Without evading the implications of
human folly that are inseparable from the doctrinal content of Pseustis'
mythological exempla, he recognises that the victory of Alithia is not
the sole point of the poem, and concludes his commentary by remarking that Theodulus, like Fronesis, prudently ends on a reconciliatory
note.

The commentary is introduced by an unusually full *accessus*, which
takes us all the way from a definition of 'book' as physical object to
subtle comments on the poem and its purpose. This document is worth
considering in some detail, since it seems intended as a comprehensive
illustration of the proper concerns of the teacher of literature, and was
to prove extremely influential. From 'book' we pass to prose, metre and
the varieties of metre, and a fourfold classification of those who compose
books: 'authors' (*auctores*, glossed etymologically as those who 'augment'
the Latin language or who write of the *acta* of history); poets, whose work
is marked by the mingling of truth and falsehood; *vates*, seers or prophets,
whose name derives from their powers of mind (*vi mentis*) and winding
incantations (*viendis carminibus*), and commentators or expositors. Then,
after noting that ancient commentators introduced their commentaries by
considering seven questions, while the *moderni* have reduced these to four,
Bernard elects the former course and proceeds through Servius' scheme
of *vita auctoris, titulus operis, qualitas* and the rest.

The biography of the pseudonymous 'Theodulus' is in all likelihood Bernard's invention, and may thus be seen as a contrived illustration of the kind of grist such *vitae* were supposed to provide for the mill of the critic. The son of no mean parents, Theodulus grew up in Italy, then studied in Athens, where he heard debates between Christians and pagans of the sort which he later incorporated into his poem. The title, *Ecloga*, is explained in ways which emphasise the diversity of the materials of which the poem is composed ('collection' is one of the glosses provided), and the function of titles in general is explained by the derivation of *titulus* from *Titan*, the sun, which illuminates the world as a title illuminates the ensuing work. The etymology is itself a commonplace, traceable via Remigius to the ancient grammarians (Servius, *In Aen.* 6.580; ed. Thilo and Hagen, II, p. 81), but Bernard enhances it mythographically, noting that the 'singular' significance of sun and title are expressed by Titan's refusal to join the other giants in their attack on the gods (*Accessus, etc.* [1970], p. 61).

The *qualitas* of the work is defined as 'bucolic song', leading to a discussion of the varieties of *carmen* in terms of subject-matter (comic, tragic, satiric, lyric) and occasion (epithalamium, lament, elegy). The *Eclogue* mingles fable and history; these are duly defined, along with the *argumentum*, the plot or dramatic structure which renders their interplay plausible, and related to Theodulus' *intentio* of setting off the superiority of Christian belief by comparison with pagan falsehood. Theodulus' *ordo artificialis* is contrasted with 'natural' or chronological development like that of Lucan, and it is noted that the poem provides matter for *explanatio* of several kinds, moral and allegorical as well as literal. Its 'mode of expression' (*modus dicendi*) is the humble style, as in Virgil's *Bucolica*. Its 'character' is neither narrative (like Solomon's Proverbs or Lucretius' *De rerum natura*) nor dramatic (like Terence's comedies or the Song of Songs) but mixed, like the *Aeneid*. Proceeding to the questions asked of a work by 'modern' critics, Bernard defines the *materia* of the poem (its source or 'mother', *mater rei*) as the persons and actions (in this case the *sententiae* put forward by the debaters) with which it deals. Theodulus' *intentio*, that which his eloquence aims to persuade, is the superiority of the truth of Scripture to pagan foolishness; inasmuch as it proffers a knowledge of truth its *utilitas* is ethical.

As suggested above, the sheer comprehensiveness of this *accessus* is largely an end in itself, and Bernard acknowledges that some of the categories to which he refers in passing are so rarely applied in his day as to have become scarcely intelligible (*Accessus, etc.* [1970], p. 66). But the contrivances by which he incorporates the discussion of topics like *vita* and *titulus* into his exposition, and the endless series of comparisons with other authors and texts for which the structure of his *accessus* provides an occasion, illustrate clearly how a literary text could be grounded in a context of scriptural and classical authority and become part of a larger course of study. Bernard's *accessus* is one of the major texts of what might be called the literary theory of the early Middle Ages. It was imitated by other compilers of *accessus*, and came to constitute the framework for a whole course of study when most of it was incorporated into the introduction of the *Dialogus super auctores* of Conrad of Hirsau.

The *Dialogus*, produced at the beginning of the twelfth century, is a humbler counterpart to Bernard's commentary, and provides what amounts to a comprehensive *accessus* to the principal curriculum authors in the form of a discussion between Master and Disciple. It begins with general definitions of the terms the *accessus* employs, taken for the most part from Bernard, proceeds to introduce the standard Latin authors, pagan and Christian, and ends with a brief survey of the liberal arts. It was presumably written for the monastery school at Hirsau, and its most memorable feature is probably the gingerly way in which the Master approaches the problem of teaching Ovid to boys, an issue he may have been the first medieval writer to confront directly. He does nothing to counter the indignation of his rather toadyish Disciple at being exposed to the *Metamorphoses* and *Amores*, but he does point to the suggestions of monotheism in Ovid's account of the creation, and makes this the occasion for a general discussion of the wisdom Christian authors have found in pagan literature. Often this has taken the form of weapons which a Paul or Augustine could turn against their inventors, but Jerome's frequent use of Juvenal elicits some approving remarks on the moral force of Roman satire, in which language is deployed with a deliberate disregard for decorum and lays bare the objects of its censure (*Dialogus*, ed. Huygens, pp. 51–5; *Accessus, etc.* [1970], pp. 114–19). Elsewhere Conrad discovers a similar purpose and force in Lucan's 'sudden intrusion' (*subita invectio*) on his Roman audience in the opening lines of the *Pharsalia* (*De bello civili*), and he praises unstintingly the devastating use of a high style (*palliata littera*) in Lucan's ironic praise of Nero (*Dialogus*, pp. 47–8; *Accessus, etc.* [1970], p. 110). At times his knowledge of the texts he cites is minimal, as when he asserts that Statius' *Thebaid* exemplifies virtue in the conquest and destruction of Thebes by Adrastus (*Dialogus*, p. 56; *Accessus, etc.* [1970], p. 120), but in his remarks on Lucan and Juvenal the conventional judgements of the *accessus* tradition are informed by real appreciation. For the purposes of monastic education, as the Disciple reminds his Master, one does not need a complete inventory of the contents of an author's house, only the keys to a few doors (*Dialogus*, p. 15; *Accessus, etc.* [1970], pp. 73–4), but Conrad, working always at this rudimentary level, manages nonetheless to communicate something of the appeal, as well as the necessity, of classical studies.

While the work of Bernard and Conrad attests to an active programme of literary study in the schools of the eleventh century, it does not reflect any significant advance in the scope or methods of commentary on the ancient authors. From the end of the Carolingian period to the later eleventh century there is little evidence of anything but the passing along of existing material on Virgil, Terence, Horace and the satirists. There are signs of a renewal of interest in Lucan and Statius, but commentary seems to have been confined largely to the transmission and incidental augmentation of ancient scholia. During the later eleventh century, the picture changes significantly. The work begun by Carolingian commentators is taken up again, and by the mid-twelfth century the study of ancient literature has been transformed. Important testimony to this renewal is a Berlin manuscript of the early twelfth century containing glosses on Lucan, Statius' *Thebaid*, and the *Eclogues*, *Georgics* and *Aeneid* of Virgil. The Virgil and Statius glosses are certainly by the same author, and it is likely that those on Lucan are his as well. On the basis of a reference to 'magister ansellus uel anselmus' among the *Aeneid* glosses, this material has been attributed to Anselm of Laon or his school.[37] For our purposes what is most important is the originality and sophistication of the Berlin glossator's treatment of the ancient texts.

From Servius onward, Lucan had been viewed as a hybrid, at once poet and historian. Though his use of poetic language and techniques was acknowledged *ad hoc*, and admired, the emphasis of the scholia was largely on the rhetorical aspects of his style.[38] The *accessus* to the Berlin glosses directly engages this view, acknowledging that *poesis* properly speaking involves *fictio*, but noting that it can also consist in imaginative description. The glossator goes on to call attention to the full range of Lucan's poetic qualities, and credits him with a measure of poetic 'inspiration',[39] thus anticipating twelfth-century criticism, which will place an increasing emphasis on the exemplary and philosophical aspect of the *Pharsalia* (*De bello civili*).

Interest in Statius seems to have been renewed in the tenth century, and the *Achilleid* soon began the long career as a school-book which would lead to Statius' installation as one of the standard authors in the *Liber Catonianus*.[40] The *Thebaid*, too, circulated widely, but the glosses in the Berlin manuscript are our earliest evidence of a serious medieval reassessment of that text. They rapidly became the standard commentary, wholly replacing the late-antique scholia attributed to Lactantius Placidus,

[37] Berlin, Staatsbibl., MS lat. 2.34. See Bischoff, 'Living with the Satirists', pp. 81–92; *Mitt. St.* III, pp. 260–1; de Angelis, 'I commenti', pp. 112–36; Baswell, *Virgil*, p. 339, n. 98.
[38] See Moos, '*Poeta* und *historicus*'; Malcovati, *Lucano*, pp. 123–6.
[39] See Marti, 'Literary Criticism', pp. 247–50.
[40] See Boas, 'Librorum Catonianorum'; Clogan, *Medieval Achilleid*, pp. 1–11.

while showing abundant evidence of a careful and appreciative reading
of Lactantius' comments on lexical and syntactical matters, and the evidence he provides for the text of the poem.[41] The commentator brings to
the *Thebaid* a sound knowledge of earlier Roman poetry, and a feeling
for the style and allusiveness of Statius' poem which enables him to pronounce on the authenticity of doubtful lines and words, and even at times
to reject the views of Lactantius on points of interpretation or textual
criticism.

The commentary on Virgil, too, enjoyed wide circulation, and soon
established itself as the most influential medieval (i.e. post-Servian) treatment of the *Aeneid*. It follows Servius closely, but freely edits and adapts
Servius' glosses and augments his comments on metre and rhetoric. In a
few striking instances the commentator departs from his source to draw
comparisons between Virgilian and biblical narrative, and offers suggestions towards a providential reading of the stories of Aeneas and Rome
which anticipates their role in the historical vision of Dante.

It is again to the late eleventh and early twelfth centuries that we must
assign the first really innovative commentaries on Horace. Whereas Persius and Juvenal are well attested in the early Middle Ages, and both were
equipped with largely new commentaries by Remigius,[42] Horace seems to
have been less studied, and though he gained steadily in popularity in the
post-Carolingian period, earlier commentary is confined to the transmission of the scholia of the Pseudo-Acro.[43] But Bischoff has noted a number
of late-eleventh-century commentaries in which the *Satires* and *Epistles*
are read in relation to contemporary situations, often awkwardly but with
a clear appreciation of their character as poetry.[44] A commentary from
the same period on Horace's *Ars poetica* combines the dogmatic view of
poetry as the mirror of philosophy and the Liberal Arts with an unusually articulate response to the nuances of Horace's epistolary style.[45] In the
course of arguing that Horace's 'knowledge' (*sapere*; *Ars poetica* 309), the
'beginning and fount' of good writing, signifies a grounding in the liberal
arts, and providing clear glosses on mythology and critical dicta (including a full and genealogically precise explanation of what Horace means
in forbidding a poet of the Trojan War to begin *ab ovo*), the commentator
becomes caught up in the argument at several points and abandons the
'id est' and 'quasi dicat' of the glossator in favour of his own first-person

---

[41] Reeve, 'Statius', p. 396; De Angelis, 'I commenti', pp. 92–106.
[42] See Robathan, 'Persius', pp. 205, 237–9; Sanford, 'Juvenal', pp. 176–7.
[43] See Siewert, 'Vernacular Glosses', pp. 144–7; Glauche, *Schullektüre*, pp. 89–97;
Reynolds, *Medieval Reading*, pp. 13–14.
[44] Bischoff, 'Living with the Satirists', pp. 85–92 (*Mitt. St.* III, pp. 262–9).
[45] See Zechmeister, *Scholia Vindobonensia*; Mancini, 'Commento oraziano'; de Bruyne,
Esthétique médiévale, I, pp. 223–38. On the dating of this commentary, see Friis-Jensen,
'Medieval Commentaries', pp. 53–4.

version of Horace's point of view. His unobtrusively learned style and the coherence of his tracing of Horace's argument suggest an excellent classroom teacher, and show a marked willingness to place commentary at the service of the author's own intended meaning.

It is commonly claimed that the medieval Horace was the poet of the *Satires* and *Epistles*, a moralist known largely from excerpts in *florilegia*, but as the recent work of Karsten Friis-Jensen has made strikingly clear, his lyric poetry was also widely read, and formed an essential part of the image of Horace that emerges in the *accessus*. These explain the sequence of his work in terms of a progression from the concerns of youth, as illustrated by the subject-matter of the *Odes*, to the ripe moral wisdom of the *Epistles*.[46] This chronological paradigm, undoubtedly inspired by the time-honoured critical tradition which recognised a similar progression in the *œuvre* of Virgil, was also a way of putting Horace's lyric poems in a more or less moral perspective. Citing Horace's own *dictum* that poets aim to provide either profit or pleasure (*Ars poetica* 333), a number of commentators place the *Odes* under the rubric of *delectatio*, on the grounds of their themes, their metrical variety, their obligation to flatter and amuse a patron, and their close alliance with the pleasure-giving art of music. But there is a perceptible tension in the commentary tradition between this tolerant view and the traditional critical dogma that what justified the study of ancient literature was its ethical value. One late-eleventh-century commentary which offers exegesis of the occasions, tone and arguments of the *Odes* which is often astute and appreciative, strains to assign morals to them. Thus 1.20, inviting Maecenas to the Sabine farm, is an indirect comment on those *rustici* who refuse hospitality to their lords; the reflections on the powers of wine in 3.21 are aimed at the excessive drinking of Corvinus; and several glosses compare the Horace who looks back on his youthful amours from the vantage point of middle age to a monk or canon recalling the world he has renounced (*Scholia in Horatium*, ed. Botschuyver, pp. 35, 126, 132–3).[47] Other commentators deal more pragmatically with the challenge of reading the *Odes* in moral terms, acknowledging that Horace does not always censure the vices he depicts, or taking his very degeneracy as a lesson in itself (see Conrad, *Dialogus*, p. 50; *Accessus, etc.* [1970], p. 113).

The most striking new departure in classical studies in this period is the widespread interest in Ovid, who by the mid-twelfth century will have assumed a stature greater than that of Virgil himself. As early as the tenth century extended glosses had been added to a ninth-century text of the *Ars amatoria*, in the famous 'Classbook of St Dunstan'.[48] But the new

---

[46] See Friis-Jensen, 'The Medieval Horace', pp. 257–69.
[47] On date and attribution, see Bischoff, 'Living with the Satirists', pp. 88–9.
[48] See Hexter, *Ovid*, pp. 23–41.

status of Ovid from the later eleventh century forward reflects a larger development, the emergence of an aristocratic and ecclesiastical audience capable of appreciating the urbanity of his epistles and love-poetry. On the grounds that his advice on gaining and retaining the love of young women and his illustrations of immoral love were offered as examples of what was to be avoided in loving, these poems found their way into the schools, and introductions to most of Ovid's works appear in *accessus* collections from the later eleventh century onward (*Accessus, etc.* [1970], pp. 1–6, 28–38). Symptomatic of the 'Ovidianism' that is a striking feature of the new, urban-courtly culture of the period are many skilful imitations of the *Amores, Heroides* and epistles *Ex Ponto*, which appear in a variety of contexts, not excluding the convent.

Baudri of Bourgueil (1046–1130), who produced a number of such poems, also produced several longer works with broad implications for our subject. In one verse epistle he deploys an elaborate repertoire of mythological exempla to advise a noble lady about the need for prudent conduct. The lustful gods are figures of the many young men who seek to emulate the sexual exploits of a Jove or Mars; Baudri by contrast offers himself as a champion of chastity, one who seeks to imitate the virtues 'mystically' expressed in the feats of Hercules and Perseus (Baudri, *Carmen* 200, 89–136; ed. Hilbert, pp. 268–70). Like Theodulph's poem on his early reading, Baudri's letter seems to imply a school tradition of allegorising classical story, and this is suggested again by a long poem on the interpretation of ancient myth which is essentially a verse paraphrase of Fulgentius' *Mitologiae*. Baudri follows his author closely for the most part, but develops his own interesting readings of Apollo as a model for the aspiring philosopher, and of Prometheus as a type of divine wisdom and creativity. In justification he offers the attractive argument that it is by such creative reading that we keep the ancient *fabulae* alive ('Credo, vivit adhuc nobiscum fabula lecta, / Vivit enim quicquid fabula significat'), thus anticipating by nearly a century the programme for vernacular poetry announced in the prologue to the *Lais* of Marie de France (Baudri, *Carmen* 154, 165–71, 599–614, 651–2; pp. 209, 220, 222). Baudri's Ovidian borrowings are for the most part confined to imitation of the form and style of his epistles, but in one remarkable instance he adopts the stance of the cosmic and mythical-historical poet of the *Metamorphoses*. This occurs in a long poem in which the bed-chamber of the Countess Adela of Blois, with its tapestries, painted ceiling and intricately paved floor surrounding the elaborately carved bed, become a collective image of the universe, world history and the arts which comprise philosophy (*Carmen* 134; pp. 149–85). The extravagant compliment is introduced by the posturings of the Ovidian lover in his reverent mode, and ends with a fulsome appeal to the Countess' largesse, but the very scope and grandeur of the project suggest a new sense, inspired by Ovid, of larger possibilities for poetry. It marks perhaps the first stirring of the desire to integrate the role of the poet as celebrant of urban culture with the traditional ideal of the universally learned *poeta platonicus*, an ambition which will be central to the literary activity of the twelfth century, and which will require coming to terms for the first time since late Antiquity with the *Metamorphoses*.

The *Metamorphoses* seem to have been transmitted to the Middle Ages unaccompanied by any tradition of ancient scholia, and even their potential role as a source for mythographers was to some extent pre-empted by the prose *narrationes* or *argumenta* associated with the name of Lactantius Placidus.[49] Isidore names Ovid in quoting *Metamorphoses* 1.84–6 as part of his account of the nature of man (*Etym.* 11.1.5), but explicit citation is random and infrequent in the early-medieval period. It is only around the beginning of the twelfth century that we find clear evidence of the assimilation of the *Metamorphoses* into the curriculum, largely on the grounds of their ethical and religious content.

An anonymous commentary, probably of the early twelfth century and evidently based on the teaching of Manegold of Lautenbach,[50] develops the notion of a monotheistic Ovid already grudgingly conceded as a possibility by Conrad of Hirsau, explaining the outward polytheism of the *Metamorphoses* as a political necessity for Ovid under the emperors, and that such metamorphoses as the reduction of Jove to a lustful beast in the tale of Europa (for the patristic tradition a manifestation of Ovid's impiety) show his true scorn for the classical gods. The commentator imputes a kind of religious Platonism to Ovid, professing to find in his cosmogony the workings of the Platonist 'trinity' of 'Good', 'Mind' and 'World Soul' (*togaton, nous* and *anima mundi*), interpreting the 'better nature' of *Metamorphoses* 1.21 as 'the will of god, the son of god', and glossing Pythagoras' reference to the instability of the elements (*Met.* 15.237) by distinguishing the elements as they inhere in created things from the pure form in which they exist in the divine mind.[51]

As will be true of even the most sophisticated twelfth-century commentators on the *Metamorphoses*, the commentator makes no attempt to engage Ovid on the level of his elaborate irony; the *intentio* of Ovid's poem is to instruct by pleasing ('delectare et delectando tamen mores instruere'), and its *utilitas* consists in making readily accessible a wide range of fables, gracefully told. A very different critique of Ovid appears in an anonymous work of the same period as the 'Manegold' commentary, a mock-sermon in leonine hexameters found in a single Tegernsee

49 See Otis, '*Argumenta*'; Tarrant, 'Ovid'.
50 See Villa, 'Tra *fabula* e *historia*', pp. 247–8.
51 See Meiser, 'Commentar', pp. 50–2; Demats, *Fabula*, pp. 113–15; Bischoff, 'Ovid-Legende'.

manuscript in which the irony of the *Metamorphoses* is brought to the fore.[52] Professedly a clerk's carefully anonymous discourse to a group of nuns, it reviews the pros and cons of reading poetry which treats the loves of the gods, with special reference to the poet who employs 'the metaphor of changing forms'. Throughout the speaker oscillates between straightforward moralisation of Ovid's subject-matter and a recourse to allegory which enables him to find positive meanings in it. Taken literally, the loves of the gods are wanton, violent, often incestuous, an example to be shunned. But as *mystica fabula* they are a great example: nuns are goddesses, clerics are gods. Subject, like Ovid's deities, to desire, they can commingle on their own exalted plane, or descend in earthly form and bestow their love upon the laity, informing the world with heroic passion as Jove begot Hercules on a human mother.

Ovid's cosmic setting provides a foil to the twofold significance of his mythology. Even as its harmony stands in contrast to the erratic and violent events of divine and human legend, inspiring us to thoughts of purity and transcendence, the divine vitality that sustains it infuses our wills with lustful energy. And yet, it is finally that same harmony, the commingling of the elements, the influences of the stars, the orderly cycles of growth and decay, that men have sought to express by their myths: all the forces of life, 'whatever you know and feel, whatever is begotten and exists by virtue of the elements – all this men have declared to be the loves of the gods'.

Mythography, the poem suggests, is all too easy to manipulate; the more complex the poem, the greater the opportunity it presents to the virtuosity of the adventurous commentator. There can clearly be no facile reducing of the *Metamorphoses* to a Neoplatonic *Bildungsroman*, and this curious poem points the way forward to the subversion of the twelfth-century project of reading classical myth 'integumentally' by Jean de Meun in the *Roman de la Rose*.

The markedly philosophical emphasis of the glosses attributed to Manegold and the concern with cosmological allegory in the poem just discussed suggest that both writers were aware of the renewal of interest in Plato and in cosmological questions which was taking place in the early years of the twelfth century. 'Plato' for the Middle Ages meant the cosmological portions of the *Timaeus* (17–53c), with Calcidius' commentary, and his vision of the order of the universe exercised great authority even during long centuries when the *Timaeus* was virtually unstudied. Since the Carolingian period a tradition of commentary on the 'O qui perpetua', the cosmic hymn which is the highlight of the third book of Boethius' *Consolatio*, had grounded Boethius' own status as *auctor* in his vivid

---

[52] See Dronke, *Medieval Latin*, I, pp. 232–8, and II, pp. 452–63; Demats, *Fabula*, p. 147.

distillation of the cosmology and theology of the *Timaeus*. Similar emphasis was placed on the Platonic-Stoic vision of the life of the universe in *Aeneid* 6, and the cosmological portions of the first *Georgic* (1.233–58).

The great teacher Bernard of Chartres seems to have been the pioneer of a movement which made the Timaean cosmology the framework for a new, philosophically ambitious, exploration of the relationship of God and the eternal ideas to the created universe. This project is important for our purposes because it gave rise to a way of reading Plato which was eventually extended to other texts, introducing a new philosophical dimension into the study of classical authors. The *Timaeus* was by its own account a literary text, a highly imaginative 'likely story' of the nature of things. Even its elaborate mathematical formulations are largely metaphorical in function, and there is no way of engaging its philosophical content without first penetrating its outer surface of myth. Since the *Timaeus* was universally regarded as providing the authoritative model of the universe, its study generated reflection on the role of mythic or figurative elements in the language of philosophy in general, and led to a new and more rigorous application of Macrobius' conception of the role of *fabula* and metaphor in conveying the deepest intuitions of philosophy.

Bernard himself, in his seminal commentary on the *Timaeus*, was apparently the first to use the term *integumentum* to characterise such figurative devices,[53] and his student and follower William of Conches extended its application in commentaries on Plato, Macrobius, Boethius and other authors. For Bernard, according to John of Salisbury's reverent account of his teaching, the text of a great author, rightly understood, was an *opus consummatum*, 'an image of all the Arts' (*Metalogicon* 1.24; ed. Webb, p. 54), and in William's glosses the concept of the *integumentum* is a means to integrating the application of the different arts to the study of a particular text, encompassing everything from the scientific metaphors of the *Timaeus* and technical treatises like Boethius' *opuscula sacra* and *De arithmetica* to rudimentary etymologies in the fashion of Isidore and Fulgentius. Exploring the potential scope of the *integumentum* led William to ponder the affinities between pagan and Christian uses of imagery, and at times his view of philosophical imagery suggests the treatment of symbols by religious Neoplatonists like Pseudo-Dionysius. The most striking results of his method, however, occur in the treatment of classical myth in literary contexts. For William, as for many Neoplatonists, 'thinking through myth' is a fundamental resource of philosophy, and thus, glossing Macrobius, he meets head-on what seems to him arbitrary in that author's strictures on the use of myth in philosophy. Even fables of divine violence or sexual intrigue, he declares, can harbour a 'beautiful and

---

53 See Dutton, 'Uncovering', p. 218; Jeauneau, 'La notion d'*integumentum*'.

honourable' meaning,[54] and he illustrates his thesis by developing original and compelling readings of classical myth as a way of illustrating the kind of speculation invited by mythic allusion in the works of the great authors.

Commenting on Macrobius' association of 'fabulous narrative' with religious ceremony he imagines a pagan priest preaching on the significance of the winnowing-fan in the temple of Bacchus: as Bacchus, dismembered by the Giants and placed in the winnowing-fan, reappeared wholly restored on the third day, so the soul, beset by earthly temptations, is subjected to a winnowing which purges it of fleshly contamination.[55] William has developed suggestions in Servius' gloss on the 'mystic fan of Iacchus' in *Georgic* 1.166 and Calcidius' on the fan image in *Timaeus* 52e, and it is significant that his reading totally ignores the obvious Christian associations of the violation and resurrection he describes. His concern is to show the potential range of meaning inherent in the mythic imagery of non-Christian thinkers. The same development of earlier mythography appears in the treatment of Erichthonius in William's gloss on *Timaeus* 23e, where Fulgentius, Servius and the Carolingian commentators on Martianus provide William with the materials for a new synthesis. Erichthonius was born of the discharge of Vulcan's seed on to the earth after he had failed to unite himself to Pallas. Vulcan's thwarted love represents the impulse of human imagination to attain divine wisdom, an attempt which the burden of corporeal existence renders impossible, but which nonetheless reveals a certain affinity of human *ingenium* with the divine. Erichthonius, half-man, half-dragon, represents the dual condition of humanity, rationally and spiritually drawn towards heavenly things, yet inescapably involved with the earthly by our lower nature. As inventor of the chariot he showed the office of reason, intellect and virtue, vehicles by which we rise towards an understanding of reality, and which help us conceal or disguise the bestial aspect of our nature (William, *Glosae super Platonem*, pp. 93–4).

We might dismiss all of this as yet another instance of the tendency of so much medieval criticism to appropriate ancient literature to its own purposes. Like most sophisticated allegory, William's unfolding of the meanings of his *integumenta* rarely allows us to establish a clear or consistent demarcation between the strategy of the author-philosopher and the ingenuity of the reader-interpreter. He insists repeatedly that the *integumentum* constitutes a *modus loquendi* for the philosophers themselves (*Glosae*, pp. 153, 201, 211–15), but his interpretations typically involve the translation into cosmological or philosophical terms of a mythic narrative which, though based on a more or less explicit allusion in the text

---

[54] See Dronke, *Fabula*, pp. 25–30.   [55] See Dronke, pp. 21–3.

being glossed, is itself wholly his own. In this respect his revelations of underlying *veritas* may appear as little dependent on the specific details of the texts they are ostensibly intended to illuminate as the wholly free-standing moralisations of myth in Fulgentius' *Mitologiae*. Moreover, his implicit assumption that the cosmology and theology of the *Timaeus* are part of the essential context of all serious literature is hardly less arbitrary than the Neoplatonist rationalisations of Macrobius.

But while it cannot be denied that William inherits many of the limitations of his predecessors, his more original mythographic essays are set apart by his confidence in the underlying integrity and coherence of the corpus of what he considers authentic myth, a confidence which enables him to practise a kind of archetypal criticism, circumscribed in its findings only by the limited philosophical resources he brings to bear on the fables he examines. If the pertinence of his integumental readings to the text under discussion is sometimes questionable, they are nonetheless serious attempts to demonstrate how myth could plausibly be used to generate philosophical meaning, a 'creative' mode of criticism which seeks to illustrate the potential depth and range of meaning embodied in the *auctores*. A gloss on the god Hymenaeus, in a fragmentary commentary on Martianus Capella which almost certainly reproduces William's teaching,[56] provides an unusually full illustration of the potential scope of the *integumentum*, and the faith in the integrity of myth that this mode of criticism requires.

Proposing to treat in succession the 'historical', 'fabulous', 'scientific' and 'philosophical' aspects of Hymenaeus, the commentator begins with a plausible euhemeristic narrative, summarises Hymenaeus' role in traditional myth, then explains the physical hymen as that which admits and retains together the elements which unite to form the human embryo. The mythic and the physiological are then brought together in an account of how Hymenaeus prepares for the procreative union of the bridal chamber, and his parents, Bacchus and either 'Camena' (as in Martianus' proem) or Venus, are glossed as figures of the desire and 'proportionate commingling' necessary to ensure procreation. A comparison of this proportionality to that of the elements which constitute the universe at large introduces an extended gloss *secundum philosophiam*. Here Hymenaeus stands for the larger force that encompasses and informs all mutual loves, identified first as the Boethian love that rules the earth, sea and heavens, then as the effect of 'the holy spirit which infuses a certain ardour of charity into all things', and finally as the activity of the World Soul.[57]

Theologically, the crowning 'philosophical' reading of Hymenaeus reflects the tendency of William and other cosmologists of the early twelfth century to associate the World Soul, viewed as an expression

[56] See Dronke, pp. 101–6, 167–83.   [57] See Dronke, pp. 102–4.

of God's benevolence, with the third person of the Trinity, a tendency which evoked strong reactions from more conservative thinkers, accompanied by suspicion about the legitimacy of the 'integumental' approach to pagan authors. But whatever implications of Christian pantheism or sexual mysticism such a passage may harbour, its importance for the development of literary criticism – and, I would argue, its primary importance for William himself – is in the plausibility of the chain of associations it forms between Martianus' mythic imagery and what William sees as the intellectual substance of the narrative of the *De nuptiis*. In this expansion of the scope of mythography William's commentaries provided an influential example, inspiring new and more adventurous interpretations of other texts.

Both the strengths and the limitations of William's criticism are reflected in two commentaries clearly written under his influence, and clearly by a single author, on Virgil and Martianus Capella. The earlier of the two, on the first six books of the *Aeneid*, is ascribed in one late manuscript to Bernard Silvester, but it may be of English origin, and seems indeed to show the full flowering of an English tradition of Virgil commentary which departs from the traditions of Servius and ninth-century humanism to deal allegorically with the deeper significance of the *Aeneid*. It takes Virgil's narrative as an allegory of 'what the human soul, placed for a time in a human body, achieves and undergoes', emphasising Aeneas' growth in philosophical and spiritual understanding, and in effect reworking Fulgentius' rudimentary tracing of the hero's passage from youth to maturity in the light of Macrobius' conception of the poet as a Neoplatonist sage. The possibility of such a reading of Virgil had been adumbrated in Eriugena's comparison of the work of the 'heroic poet', who traces his hero's progress from a 'puerile' involvement with the sensible world towards a mature understanding of intelligible reality, and by so doing stimulates the mind to moral reflection, with that 'theological poetry' which applies the imagery of Scripture to the needs of the spirit (Eriugena, *Super ierarchiam* 2.142–51; ed. Barbet, p. 24). But the commentary does not develop the theme, instead breaking off as Aeneas and the Sibyl approach the gates of Elysium, the point at which 'the visible universe having been traversed, it remains to explore the invisible' (*Commentum*, ed. Jones and Jones, p. 114). Hence it is not clear how the commentator would have approached such a tour de force as the discourse of Anchises, but it seems unlikely that he would have broken new ground. He is capable of vivid and original interpretations, and a number of digressions on psychological and philosophical topics reveal his awareness of the advanced thought of his day, but the reading of the *Aeneid* itself, when not simply a translation of Virgil's imagery into the terms of twelfth-century pedagogy, is almost entirely a compilation from William and earlier commentators and mythographers, harmonised and occasionally elaborated to conform to the allegory of education which it is the author's main business to expound.

The Martianus commentary, by contrast, explores Martianus' mythic imagery with an intuitive boldness as striking as William's own, and conveys a sense like William's of dealing with the genuinely archetypal aspect of literature. The *accessus* includes an unusually precise, if somewhat simplistic distinction between *allegoria*, the mode of figuration proper to Scripture, and *integumentum*, the mode employed by philosophy, each of which harbours a hidden meaning (*misterium occultum*). Bernard of Utrecht had juxtaposed pagan and Christian *mysteria*, but the Martianus commentator emphasises their complementarity, and follows William in asserting that they are two ways of expressing one essential truth (ed. Westra, pp. 45–6). Thus in Martianus' opening paean to Hymenaeus, the 'sacred bond' of cosmic marriage, whereby the divine joins itself to mortal life 'just as mortal is united with divine in eternity', is compared to the bond which caused Pollux to accept mortal existence in order to confer a share of his immortality upon his brother Castor, and the commentator concludes: 'the god underwent mortal death that he might confer his godhead upon mortality; for spirit dies temporally that flesh may live eternally' (p. 69). Glossing Martianus' Vulcan as a figure of human *ingenium*, the commentator expands on William's treatment of Vulcan's abortive pursuit of Pallas in virtually Pauline terms, making him an image of fallen man, powerless to realise his aspirations or control his desires. The commentary breaks off at the entrance of Mercury and Apollo into the court of Jove, and Martianus' presiding deities, Jove, Pallas and Juno are equated, with a directness which recalls the earlier pairing of *allegoria* and *integumentum*, to the Persons of the Christian Trinity (pp. 245–6).

Perhaps the most significant feature of the commentary for our purposes is a comment in the *accessus* on Martianus' intention. Martianus' purpose is 'imitation', in that he follows Virgil. For as Aeneas and the Sibyl pass through the underworld to meet Anchises, so Mercury and Virtue must traverse the universe to reach the court of Jove; so too Boethius and Philosophy rise through false goods to the *summum bonum*. Thus, says the commentator, 'these three *figurae* express virtually the same thing' (p. 47). Here, with the spare lucidity typical of this commentator, the archetypal tendency of criticism in the Neoplatonic tradition is made explicit.

The same tendency is present in the highly sophisticated treatise of the third of the Vatican Mythographers, the so-called *Poetria*, commonly attributed to Alberic of London, and perhaps reworked by him into its present form in the later twelfth century, though large portions seem to have originated somewhat earlier in Germany, and may have been known to William and the author of the 'Bernard Silvester' commentaries. Far more selective and coherent than earlier treatises of its kind, it brings together the myths associated with each of the major classical deities and the heroes Hercules and Perseus. A prologue found in some manuscripts hints that the treatise may be of use in philosophical studies, and its review of the classical underworld includes what amounts to a treatise on the soul in the form of a commentary on several passages from Virgil (*Myth. tertius* 3.6, 8–20; ed. Bode, I, pp. 178–86), but the focus of the work is almost exclusively literary. It quotes continually from the poets, and reviews and compares the views of earlier commentators. More than any work of criticism of the period, it gives the impression of having been conceived as a companion to the study of poetry, but poetry considered in terms of its intellectual content. The author ends his prologue by noting his divergence from Augustine's *De civitate Dei* on certain points of mythography, but asserts that the sort of collaboration between ancient wisdom and modern ingenuity that his work both illustrates and encourages has a legitimacy of its own ('Prologus', ed. Jacobs and Ukert, p. 204).

The new departures in the allegorical criticism of poetry represented by the *Poetria* and 'Bernard Silvester' seem to have remained largely confined to commentary on Virgil, Martianus and Boethius, but there are stirrings of interest in other poets as the twelfth century progresses. Juvenal would seem an unpromising subject for the would-be allegorist, but a fragmentary commentary evidently based on lectures of William of Conches augments its running historical and mythographical gloss with detailed and often strikingly apposite explanations of sexuality, psychology and other natural phenomena (*Glosae in Iuvenalem*, ed. Wilson, pp. 64–74). Occasionally unwieldy, the commentary nonetheless represents a notably successful integration of widely varied learning with a coherent critical purpose. The evident appreciation of the force of Juvenal's concrete imagery will appear again in the *Architrenius* of John of Hanville (1184), a vast satirical assault on the vices of church, court and schools.

A brief commentary on Statius' *Thebaid*, ascribed in the unique manuscript to 'St Fulgentius the Bishop', is almost certainly a work of the twelfth century (*Super Thebaiden*, in Fulgentius, *Opera*, ed. Helm, pp. 180–6). Its introductory discussion of the fictive 'teguments' of poetry strongly suggests the influence of William, and it resembles the commentaries attributed to Bernard Silvester in the pedagogical emphasis of its allegorising, in which Thebes, the human soul, is besieged by Philosophy and the Liberal Arts (the Argive champions), resisting them through pride (Creon) and avarice (Eteocles) until brought by divine power (Theseus) to a state of humility.

Lucan was becoming the subject of increasing critical attention in the mid-twelfth century, though he remains largely the historian among poets, distinguished by the straightforwardness and factual truth of his narrative of civil war. As such he provided a model for Joseph of Exeter, whose *Iliad*

(1188–90), based on the 'historical' account of the Trojan War by Dares Phrygius, is professedly a truthful substitute for the elaborate fictions of Virgil. But twelfth-century criticism places an increasing emphasis on the exemplary and philosophical aspect of his poetry. The author of the early-twelfth-century *Sacerdos ad altare* notes that the war Lucan describes is internal as well as civil,[58] and Arnulf of Orléans, discussing Lucan's *intentio* in the *accessus* to his very full commentary (*c.* 1180), stresses not only the dissuasive power of his representation of the horrors of civil war but also his positive exemplification of the cardinal virtues in Cato and other good citizens (*Glosule*, ed. Marti, p. 3). In the course of the commentary he notes Lucan's allusions to the traditional *fabulae* of the poets, offering frequent allegorisations, and he deploys a wealth of philosophical and cosmological material from William of Conches and Macrobius to explain Lucan's views on death and his treatment of such episodes as the posthumous experience of the soul of Pompey (pp. 431–4). In effect the barrier between history and poetic fiction becomes almost non-existent, as it seems to have been for Arnulf's contemporary, the historian Otto of Freising, who quotes Lucan and Virgil together as containing 'certain intimate secrets of philosophy'.[59]

Evidence for the critical study of Ovid is still largely confined to widespread and increasingly ambitious imitation in Latin and vernacular poetry, but over the course of the twelfth century new commentaries appeared on all of Ovid's works, and the *Metamorphoses* finally assumed an established position in the curriculum. The glosses in the 'Liber Titan' of Ralph of Beauvais, which seems to have appeared in the middle years of the century, are concerned entirely with grammar in the strict sense,[60] but during the 1170s Arnulf of Orléans produced, along with a series of traditional glosses on other works of Ovid, a compendium of *allegoriae* devoted to the legends of the *Metamorphoses* which effectively domesticated that work for the purposes of the schools and inaugurated a tradition of moralisations of Ovid which is perhaps the chief legacy of medieval mythography to the Renaissance. Arnulf's *accessus* explains Ovid's focus on physical metamorphosis as intended to help us understand inward, psychological change. As in the universe at large the erratic movements of the planets are balanced by the regular countermovement of the firmament, so our will responds to both spiritual and carnal impulses, and it is these opposed tendencies that Ovid illustrates through fables of outward transformation (*Allegoriae*, ed. Ghisalberti, p. 181). By thus adapting to the *Metamorphoses* the cosmic analogy of the *Timaeus*, Arnulf provides himself with a rationale for allegorising Ovid's stories as figures of spiritual

---

[58] See Sanford, 'Lucan', p. 237.   [59] Sanford, p. 237.
[60] See Alton and Wormell, 'Ovid', pp. 67–80; Hunt, 'Studies on Priscian', pp. 49–52.

elevation or degeneration, expressive of 'the stability of heavenly things and the changeableness of things on earth', and places himself squarely in the tradition of William of Conches. In practice, however, his allegorisation of Ovid is less coherent than the *accessus* would imply: he goes on to define other types of metamorphosis, the natural (involving the combining and dissolution of elements), spiritual (the loss or recovery of sanity) and magical; and stories read in these terms, together with the many stories treated euhemeristically, far outnumber those read as images of moral transformation. His interpretations, moreover, are largely drawn from the mythographers and commentary on other authors, rather than based on Ovid's text. They soon became a standard feature of manuscripts of the *Metamorphoses*, comparable in this respect to Servius on the *Aeneid*, but as criticism they represent a turning away from the largely philosophical concerns of William and 'Bernard'. The Platonic tradition does not inform Arnulf's work as commentator sufficiently to generate a coherent interpretation of the work as a whole.

Two anonymous commentators of the late twelfth century seek to engage Ovid's text more directly. The commentary of Copenhagen, Køngelige Bibliotek, MS Hafn. 2008 contains an elaborate *accessus* which includes a classification of the types of metamorphosis and a cosmological rationale close to Arnulf's, along with a defence of Ovid's monotheism borrowed from the commentary associated with Manegold.[61] Here the philosophical emphasis extends into the commentary proper, which begins with a technical discussion of certain points in Ovid's opening cosmogony, but as in the case of Arnulf it is not sustained, and the discussions of individual legends are for the most part mere summaries. Oxford, Bodleian Library, MS Bodley 807 contains a curious text, possibly fragmentary, which begins by arguing for the compatibility of the opening lines of the *Metamorphoses* with Christian thought regarding the soul and world history, then shifts rather abruptly to a discussion of human nature and the Fall based on copious borrowings from a sermon of Alan of Lille on the Virgilian text 'facilis descensus Averno'.[62]

In one sense, of course, the tentative character of these approaches to the *Metamorphoses* is itself an authentic response, an acknowledgement of the many-layered irony of Ovid's masterpiece. The refusal to engage the poem as a whole receives its most authoritative formulation in the *Integumenta Ovidii* of John of Garland (*c.* 1234), a work written, as its author elsewhere declares, 'lest fable should deceive the would-be philosopher', and offering 'keys' to Ovidian myth in the form of terse elegiac couplets (*Integumenta Ovidii* 5–6; ed. Ghisalberti, p. 35). John's

---

[61] See Demats, *Fabula*, pp. 151–6.
[62] Ganz, '*Archani celestis*'; d'Alverny, 'Variations'.

claves soon became a standard feature of *Metamorphoses* manuscripts, but they are as little concerned as Arnulf's *allegoriae* with the particulars of Ovid's text, and the *Integumenta* were commonly treated as a free-standing, moralised mythography in their own right. Like so much in the history of Ovid commentary, they suggest that the segmentation of Ovid's text and the compartmentalising of his *fabulae* as individual allegories are not just a pedagogical convenience, but a way of neutralising the complex and potentially subversive power of his poetry.

In a sense this failure fully to assimilate the *Metamorphoses* marks the end of the critical project of the early Middle Ages. From Fulgentius to Alberic, criticism above the level of elementary pedagogy had been firmly in the grasp of hermeneutics. Poetry was assumed to aspire to the condition implied by the dictum attributed to Bernard of Chartres, that a great work of literature is 'an image of all the arts'. The *Metamorphoses* conform to this ideal in the encyclopaedic range and variety of their subject-matter, but their structural complexity cannot be reduced to an allegory of intellectual or spiritual pilgrimage. In commentary on Ovid we may detect a faltering of the confidence of the *grammatici* of the earlier twelfth century in their power to bring to light the true, archetypal character of myths and poetic texts, and a new tendency to reduce literary materials to tools within a larger and more highly compartmentalised scholastic enterprise.

A more actively critical perspective on this failure of synthesis appears in the work of two twelfth-century Latin poets who sought to emulate the character of the great poetic *auctores* in new literary forms, Bernard Silvester and Alan of Lille. If Bernard can not be assigned the authorship of the commentary on Martianus discussed above, he is unquestionably the author of a work very close to it in spirit, the *Cosmographia* (c. 1147), a philosophical allegory which is also an experiment in the creative use of *integumenta*, an attempt to produce a new mythic cosmology in the tradition of the *Timaeus* (*Cosmographia*, ed. Dronke, pp. 16–24; tr. Wetherbee, pp. 49–55). The first of the two books of this work begins with Nature's appeal to Noys, or Providence, on behalf of *Silva*, primal matter, which yearns for translation into a nobler form. Noys responds by creating the greater universe, or Megacosmus. The second book describes Nature's enlisting of Urania, celestial reason, and Physis, the principle of physical life, to create a soul and body which Nature then joins together to form the human Microcosmus.

Written in the prosimetrum form employed by Martianus and Boethius and echoing them repeatedly, the *Cosmographia* is similarly concerned with the problem of human self-realisation and the search for God. Though Bernard's cosmogony makes due acknowledgement of the beauties of the creation in its pristine state, his universe is pervaded by hints of the complexity and uncertainty of the status of humanity within it. The universe at large is a continuum, balanced and self-sustaining, but the human constitution is a precarious synthesis, liable to the disrupting effects of passion and violence. The conflict of order and violence in human history is foretold in the newly created stars, and both the challenge of destiny and the burden of experience seem to be inseminated into human life from the beginning. From Nature's first appeal to God the *Cosmographia* is an image of the tension between the will to order and enlightenment and the menace of chaos and the irrational; man's attempt to maintain order within himself and right relations with the larger cosmic order becomes a heroic and potentially tragic theme. Like Boethius' prisoner or the hero of the Neoplatonised *Aeneid*, the human protagonist of Bernard's cosmic drama must withstand the storms of confusion and rise above the clouds of ignorance in order to attain that knowledge of the self and of the order of things which Martianus' Urania promises to Mercury and Philology, and thereby prepare himself to ascend 'per creaturas ad creatorem'.

If the *Cosmographia* is an attempt to recover the archetypal character of ancient literature, the *De planctu naturae* of Alan of Lille (1160–70) may be viewed as a critique of this undertaking, a serious questioning of the possibility of realising truth by human means, or expressing it in human language, in the absence of revelation. In this Boethian dialogue the goddess Nature manifests herself to the poet-narrator and in a series of elaborate sexual, linguistic and political metaphors seeks to explain the proper relation of humanity to the natural order and the human failings which have led to a 'divorce' between them. At one point the poet interrupts her harangue to ask why human conduct alone should be censured, when poetry shows the gods to have engaged in similar misdeeds. Nature's answer is careful and doctrinaire. It is the nature of poetry to present a surface of falsehood, though this may conceal an inner truth. Mankind has violated Venus' rules, but poems which show a multiplicity of gods revelling in Venus' *gymnasia* are wholly false, and should not be discussed. But this Macrobian dismissal of the problem is unsatisfying, and the poet returns to it later, demanding an explanation of the nature of Cupid, whom the poets have treated in deeply ambiguous ways. Nature responds with a poem which begins as a string of oxymora, and ends by advising a total avoidance of Cupid and Venus, but then explains that what the poem condemns is not Cupid's 'original nature', which is intimately linked with her own, but a new, perverse form of cupidinous behaviour which she proceeds in spite of herself to describe in mythological terms. Though the poem makes it clear that the problem is a fundamental dislocation beyond Nature's power to explain or resolve, Nature herself never realises this, and instead seeks to 'explain the inexplicable' (as she herself admits) by ignoring the contradictions of poetic mythology and trafficking in the very deceitful figments she urges the poet to repudiate. In the end she can only inveigh against the seeming incorrigibility of human nature.

Theologian as well as poet, Alan approaches his literary task with a radical sense of the division between the natural and spiritual realms and the consequent inadequacy of the mythic archetypes of traditional poetry as adumbrations of divine realities. By giving the problems of mythographic analysis a thematic function within the economy of a particular poem, he exposes the arbitrariness of traditional mythography once and for all, creating a situation in which the contradictory associations of particular mythic figures cannot be allowed to sit in unresolved coexistence, or their unsavoury aspects be simply ignored. Alan's other major allegory, the verse-epic *Anticlaudianus* (1182), offers a hypothetical resolution of these problems. Here Nature undertakes the creation of a 'new man', who will be endowed with all the virtues. The poem is largely the narrative of the heavenly journey of *Prudentia*, the human capacity for wisdom, who appeals to God to create a soul for this new being, and it ends, after he has led an army of Virtues to victory over the Vices, with his installation as the ruler of a new Golden Age. The reconstitution of human nature in the new man is at the same time a revalorisation of poetry, for in him 'nature triumphs', and the traditional mythic figures of harmony, goodness and wisdom find a new realisation. Taken on its own terms, the *Anticlaudianus* is thus a new kind of writing, of a wholly different order (as Alan's allusions clearly imply) from such merely imitative 'epics' as the *Alexandreis* of Walter of Châtillon (1182), whose author had sought presumptuously to rival the ancients on their own ground (*Anticlaudianus* 1.1–17; ed. Bossuat, p. 57). In his prose prologue Alan boldly declares that he has aspired to a new kind of epic, a new extension of the classical tradition in which poetry will become capable of transcending the mere 'dreams of imagination' and emulating the range of meaning of religious allegory (p. 56).

Whether Alan succeeded in realising these lofty aims is of course open to question; clearly he seemed to his contemporaries to have achieved something remarkable, a *summa* of secular wisdom which was at the same time a work of lofty spirituality, and on both grounds a realisation of the ideal of twelfth-century criticism, fittingly honoured by the full-scale encyclopaedic commentary of Ralph of Longchamp. But if in one sense the *Anticlaudianus* represents a kind of consummation of the relationship of medieval Latin poetry with the classical tradition, it also places that tradition in a wholly new perspective. Like the commentary of Alexander Nequam on Martianus Capella, in which Mercury and Philology are revealed as ultimately symbolic of Christ and the soul, the divine bridegroom and bride of the Song of Songs,[63] Alan's epic takes us well beyond any *intentio auctoris* of which the classical authors or their earlier commentators could have dreamed. In the freedom with which they appropriate traditional material, and their spiritualising of traditional themes, such projects may be compared to vernacular works like the *Queste del Saint Graal*, and they point the way forward to the radically Christianising mythography of Pierre Bersuire and the *Ovide moralisé* (discussed in the following chapter).

The influence of the ambitious poetry of Bernard and Alan is clear in the *artes poeticae* of the later twelfth and thirteenth centuries. Matthew of Vendôme, whose pride it was to have been Bernard's student, couches practical maxims on disposition and imitation in a diction which emulates the Platonic-mythological richness of the *Cosmographia* and *De planctu naturae*, and Geoffrey of Vinsauf evokes Noys' taming of the unruly elements in dealing with the relations of form and matter.[64] Chrétien de Troyes, the finest vernacular writer of the period, was clearly preoccupied with the affinities between courtly ideals and the Platonist poetics of the schools; the coronation robes of his Erec, adorned with learned imagery professedly borrowed from 'Macrobe', culminate a sustained pattern of allusion to the philosophical *Aeneid* of mythographic tradition, and the characteristic pattern of his romances recalls the cosmic themes of Bernard and Alan in many respects.[65]

The writings of these poets and teachers were recognised as a significant extension of the classical tradition, and became an established part of the grammar curriculum. As late as the 1280s Hugo von Trimberg will include four great *moderni*, Alan of Lille, Matthew of Vendôme, Geoffrey of Vinsauf and Walter of Châtillon, among the *auctores* in this field, with John of Garland occupying a somewhat lower position (*Registrum* 283–365; ed. Langosch, pp. 171–4). But despite the tribute this implies, the preponderance of writers of *artes poeticae* reflects a diffusion of literary studies into new and more specialised channels which had taken place over the course of the thirteenth century, and an accompanying diminution of the prestige of the classical tradition.

John of Garland, writing on the art of poetry in the 1230s, gives us a sense of the new situation. Matthew of Vendôme and Geoffrey of Vinsauf had composed their *artes poeticae* under the stimulating influence of a new wave of creativity in Latin poetry. Challenged by the work of Bernard and Alan, they had sought to convey some sense of what poetry *is*. In contrast, John's *Parisiana poetria* is marked by an absence of quotations from or

---

[63] See Wilson, 'Pastoral and Epithalamium', pp. 44–5.
[64] See Wetherbee, *Platonism*, pp. 146–51.
[65] See Wetherbee, pp. 236–41; Uitti, 'Philologie'; Hunt, 'Chrestien and Macrobius'.

allusions to other medieval poets, and a predominant concern with fine points of rhetoric, which seem to reflect the growing influence of the practically orientated *ars dictaminis* in the schools and (his own ambitious poems notwithstanding) a lack of involvement with the active concerns of contemporary poetic practice. John, too, knew and admired the poetry of Bernard and Alan, and his writings lament the dissolution of the liberal arts curriculum of the twelfth-century schools (see *Morale scolarium*, ed. Paetow, pp. 82–106). But he views this tradition from a distance, and when in one of the specimen *rithmi* of his *Parisiana poetria* he recalls the motif of the threefold *speculum rationis* from the *Anticlaudianus*, he adds that such 'Platonic' thinking, though it leads to truth, will seem outmoded to his audience (*Parisiana poetria* 7.690–3; ed. Lawler, pp. 168–9). Implicit in this admission is the recognition of a new scholastic environment where poetry, which had enjoyed a special status by virtue of its traditional relation to Platonism, has been relegated to a smaller role in a far larger plan of study.

6

From the twelfth century to *c.* 1450

Vincent Gillespie

. . . Parisius dispensat in artibus illos
Panes unde cibat robustos. Aurelianis
Educat in cunis auctorum lacte tenellos.

(Geoffrey of Vinsauf, *Poetria nova*
[*c.* 1200–15], ll. 1010–12)[1]

In the course of the thirteenth century, the intellectual initiative passed from Orléans to Paris, from school to university, from the *antiqui* to the *moderni*. This changed topography of learning had important implications for the ways in which texts were transmitted and read. The continuing ramification of higher education into ever more vocational areas of study and training was a response to the rediscovery of Aristotelian learning and to the pastoral effects of the Fourth Lateran Council of 1215. The technologising of preaching and the development of more sophisticated analyses in applied pastoral theology went hand-in-hand with refinements in logical terminology. When scholastic *lectio* replaced monastic *lectio* as the dominant style of academic reading, new questions were asked about *how* books meant. The modistic analysis of the written word, developed from the practices prevailing in the exposition of secular classical texts, acquired new subtleties in its application to the literary strategies of the Bible and was again in turn reapplied to secular texts with some added emphases drawn from scriptural commentary. Throughout the thirteenth century a fruitfully symbiotic relationship existed between exegesis of the sacred page and of the secular text, mediated through a common interest in the affective force of all literature. These developments depended for their success on a continuing and reliable supply of literate and competent students.

Although the logic of language came to be studied with new rigour, it would be wrong to suggest that the old ways of learning decayed. The interplay between disciplines and institutions was always more subtle and profound than medieval satirists and modern social historians care

[1] 'At Paris arts are taught and bread dispensed to feed the strong. At Orléans the young are gently weaned on ancient authors' milk'; ed. Faral, p. 228 and tr. Rigg, *Anglo-Latin*, p. 68.

to allow: even logicians must learn to read, and must sit at the knee of Dame Grammar. So, although the Paris schools became the centre of the new learning, the influence of the older liberal arts schools, particularly Chartres and Orléans, never disappeared, despite their transmutation into centres for vocational training. The basic hermeneutical skills of students, their awareness of the impact and effect of the power of words, were acquired, as they had been in previous centuries, through their exposure to the analysis of Latin literature in grammar and liberal arts schools and within the ambit of institutions of cultural privilege and social power.

The gift of the library of the Orléans-trained Richard de Fournival to become the backbone of the Sorbonne collection is perhaps emblematic of the shift of geographical focus and intellectual emphasis. But the eagerness with which thirteenth-century friars like John of Wales and Roger Bacon, both Paris schoolmen, fell on the new books reflects the continuing and even deepening classicism and humanism of such men. Bacon's reverence for Seneca and his respect for the intellectual challenges of Aristotle, for example, produced a commitment to the ethical force of literature that was certainly no less absolute than in previous centuries but was explored in his writing with more psychological depth and rigour than before.

Most medieval literary theory is found in the surviving *accessus* and commentaries on secular and classical authors. The *accessus* was the most significant locus for abstract thinking about literary texts and their effect on a reader or audience. Yet an *accessus* is only a small part of the hermeneutic exercise. In the classroom, the teacher's linear exposition and enarration of the text must often have quickly swamped the memory of the broader themes touched on in the *accessus*, and it is frequently the case that the linear exposition does not carry though the presuppositions, ambitions or literary ideology of the *accessus*. 'Ultimately, the central conflict around which the *expositio auctorum* is played out is not one of Ciceronianism versus Christianity, but one of linguistic difficulty versus various degrees of illiteracy' (Reynolds, *Medieval Reading*, p. 154). But the disjunction between *accessus* and commentary does not devalue their reflections on texts and authors. The broad and common taxonomy of literary analysis found in most medieval *accessus* encoded a way of thinking about a text (and not just the one under immediate study) that was transferable to other texts and other contexts. The literary prospectus provided by such introductions usually offers a more reflective and theoretical perspective on the text under discussion and on its relationship to the metatextual and archetypal literary issues of intention, utility and philosophical orientation. The *accessus* was a means of placing a text in the literary continuum of history, in the narrative continuum of an author's work, or in the ethical and hermeneutic continuum of the textual community of its original and medieval readers. It taught a way of looking at and thinking about literature that was formative as well as summative. In other words, it sought to create the taste by which it was to be appreciated. For the humanists, that role was to be performed by the familiar letter, the public disputation or the defence of poetry. Such broad discussions helped to shape the literary consciousness of readers when they applied their literacy to reading (or indeed writing) other texts.

Underpinning the commentaries and analyses that survive from the medieval period, therefore, are larger assumptions about the nature of literature, the psychology of literary response and the role of the poet. Those assumptions change, even when the language used to express them remains the same. Reflected and refracted over successive generations of readers, the commentaries on classical authors in this period illustrate the remarkable textual continuity between those generated in the twelfth-century French schools and those produced by proto-humanists in the Italian schools of the fourteenth. But they also demonstrate how each generation of readers appropriated their interpretative inheritance by artfully realigning the waxen noses of their critical authorities. A humanist use of twelfth-century ideas is as much an act of cultural translation as a thirteenth-century reading of the Averroistic *Poetics* or a fourteenth-century euhemerist reading of the *Metamorphoses*. The commentary tradition is thus both more protean and more stable than it appears on the surface.

In his *Dialogue on the Authors*, written before 1150, Conrad of Hirsau's fictional pupil asks his grammar master 'to insert the keys in the closed doors' of the world of classical literature. By the end of the medieval period, students were still brought to the threshold of understanding by similar methods and similar texts to those found in late Antiquity. But once through the door, the routes taken by readers changed somewhat in the thirteenth and fourteenth centuries. In particular, between 1150 and 1450 increasing numbers of commentators showed a heightened interest in the *effects* of reading poetry on its audience. This interest was not just in the ways those effects were created verbally (which had always been a concern of the rhetorical tradition and became the concern of the new medieval Arts of Poetry), but also in the impact that poetic effects had on the affections, imagination and moral understanding of readers and listeners. The theoretical and practical aspects of the study of poetry were considered to be parts of moral philosophy:

To define ethics in medieval terms is to define poetry, and to define poetry is to define ethics, because medieval ethics was so much under the influence of the literary paideia as to be enacted poetry.   (Allen, *Ethical Poetic*, p. 12)

Beginning in the twelfth century with commentaries on Horace's *Ars poetica*, expanding in the thirteenth to encompass the Averroistic version of Aristotle's *Poetics*, and reaching its apotheosis in the full-blown humanist poetics of the fourteenth and fifteenth centuries, this strand of commentary placed increasing emphasis on the responsibilities of readers to respond appropriately and alertly to the challenges and strategies of the texts they read. Though never as formal or as systematised as modern reception theory, this new emphasis in the commentary tradition emancipated the reader's response as a legitimate and central part of the hermeneutic process. Readers could now be recognised as active participators in the generation of meaning, not just passive consumers of an encoded truth. This required them to be ethically engaged and imaginatively involved in the reading process. The desire for such active reading lies behind Chaucer's repeated exhortations to his readers to *assay* his texts and read with *avisement*.

This interest in the affective force of poetry is latent in all levels of the commentary tradition, from the simple expositions of liturgical hymns in the song school through to the elaborate and sophisticated 'moralised' retellings of Ovid's *Metamorphoses* largely undertaken outside of the academy. It can also often be glimpsed in discussions of the key *accessus* category of *intentio*, 'the hermeneutic forum in which all other manoeuvres of the glossators are played out. Intention is what guarantees the moral value which allows the text to be read at all' (Reynolds, *Medieval Reading*, p. 148). Although medieval commentators showed a great appetite for inductive biographies of their *auctores*, and the *accessus* category of *intentio auctoris* remained as part of the taxonomy of literary analysis, there are signs that the category was being used by commentators to collapse the distinction between the intention of the author and the perception of the reader. As a result, 'the medieval *accessus* . . . is always a preview of the exegete's intentions disguised as a preview of the author's achievement' (Copeland and Melville, p. 176). So moral worth increasingly emerges from the reader's engagement with the text rather than from the author's imputed or perceived intention. In fact, 'the category of intention allows the reader . . . to appropriate for him or herself the place and authority of the author by claiming to have "grasped" the originating thought behind the discourse' (Reynolds, *Medieval Reading*, p. 148).

'*Auctoritas* is not a cultural monolith . . .; it is forged in practice out of the interaction of texts and readers and is, therefore, reinvented for each of the various purposes it is made to serve' (Reynolds, 'Inventing Authority', p. 16). The medieval passion for compilations and anthologies, with their tendency to extract maxims and *sententiae* out of their original contexts, in theory argued that the *auctoritas* of the extracts remained that of their *originalia*. In practice, the new context (by juxtaposition or selection) generated potential new meanings and facilitated potential new uses and readings. Similar shifts of perception in relation to classical texts can be observed in discussions of the major narrative forms and genres. Medieval attempts to make sense of classical thinking about tragedy and epic, for example, allowed a fruitful elision between those two genres that complicated and enriched their interaction in ways that produced from medieval authors sophisticated and profound rereadings and rewritings of epic narratives. Writers of medieval satire and comedy similarly extrapolated from the period's patchy knowledge and partial understandings of the classical genres to produce their own distinctive and idiosyncratic versions.

If commentators were placing new emphasis on the *effects* of a text, and compilers were contriving new contexts, and writers new generic syntheses, what implications did this have for the interpretative status accorded to the (presumed) intentions of the classical author? One answer to this question, an answer given by many commentaries in this period, is to impute all discoverable responses to the farsightedness of the original author, either allowing a wide range of diverse intentions to have been part of his narrative masterplan or taking refuge in the Horatian precept that poets write 'to instruct . . . or delight' (*Ars poetica* 333–4). But another answer, developed especially in commentaries on the difficult and elusive works of Ovid but soon applied elsewhere as well, was to recognise that the intentions of the author were historically determined and specific to the period in which he lived, and that it was legitimate to distinguish between the immediate intention of an author and the long-term effects of his text. This led to a 'growing exegetical independence from the historical situation of the author, a tendency to register but then ignore authorial intention' (Baswell, *Virgil*, p. 165). Such a separation between historical intent and contemporary effect had a (perhaps unintended) liberating effect on the kinds of commentaries that might be produced:

By expressing meanings that were previously implicit, ignored or repressed, commentaries transform the representational powers of texts and make them work in new ways. They canonize texts, authorize specific understandings of textual meaning as official or legitimate, and ordain their reproduction or replacement according to the needs of the present.

(Kennedy, *Authorizing Petrarch*, pp. 27–8)

'The gloss's role is somehow to negotiate between what is actually there in the text, linguistically speaking, and what the audience needs from it' (Reynolds, 'Inventing Authority', p. 11). The needs of schoolchildren and of university scholars, of clerics and of laymen, of readers and of writers changed over time and over an individual lifetime, and were often incompatible with each other. In recognising the powerful role of the imagination in the workings of poetry, medieval commentators also recognised how important it was to train their readers to read openly and responsively as well as wisely and ethically. Classical poetry was nearly always difficult, often morally dangerous, and frequently obscure in its imagery and figurative language. No wonder Giovanni Boccaccio (1313–75) advised the opponents of poetry to 'go back to the grammar-schools, bow to the ferule, study and learn what licence ancient authority granted the poets'. But, as Boccaccio knew full well, the process did not stop at the grammar school. 'You must read, you must persevere, you must sit up nights, you must enquire, and exert the utmost power of your mind' (*Genealogia deorum gentilium* 14.12; tr. Minnis and Scott, pp. 430–1). Learning to read was the vocation of a lifetime.

1. Learning to read wisely: the grammar-school curriculum

As a religion of the book, Christianity is necessarily also a religion of interpretation. In the twelfth and thirteenth centuries, academic scriptural exegesis placed renewed emphasis on the *modus agendi* of the human authors of the Bible and the affective force of the many literary modes used there. This manner of reading Scripture was produced by, and in its turn required, readers and commentators of peculiar acuteness and sensitivity to the literary strategies at work in Scripture. But such advanced commentary stood at the apex of a pyramid of hermeneutical endeavour, which relied for much of its technical vocabulary and many of its critical concepts on modes of analysis passed on from classical Antiquity: the *enarratio poetarum*, consisting of a magisterial exposition or 'reading' of a text, preceded by an introduction or *accessus* structured either according to a Servian model, or, more commonly from the twelfth century onwards, according to a more technically analytical format deriving from Greek commentary on philosophical texts. At the base of the textual pyramid, on the nursery slopes of interpretation, was a loose and evolving collection of classical, neo-classical and (increasingly in the thirteenth and fourteenth centuries) Christian verse texts which introduced the student to the disciplines of textual exegesis alongside the stylistic and linguistic decorums of secular and Christian Latin poetry.

The aim of the late-medieval grammar school was to produce Christian readers. Since classical times, training in grammar had always involved not only the art of writing and speaking well, but also the ability to understand the meaning of a text (see Chapter 1 above). The principles of Quintilian's *enarratio poetarum* live on in the *accessus ad auctores*, as reflected in a note in a fifteenth-century Oxford University book: 'grammatica quid

est: ars recte scribendi recteque loquendi, poetarum enaracionem con-
tinens' (*Register of Congregation*, p. 408). But reading poetry blurs the
boundaries of grammar and rhetoric, creating a procedural overlap which
required students (or at least allowed masters) to think about the ways
such texts worked on the responses of their readers or listeners, and, given
that these poems used rhetoric to affect their audiences, how such works
should be read by Christians. The aim of Christian grammar, therefore,
was not only the acquisition of technical expertise in vocabulary, metre,
tropes and generic form, but also the ability to read figuratively and with
discrimination in a wide range of different kinds of texts. The glosses
and commentaries on those reading-texts studied in the later-medieval
grammar schools taught the student how to construe the literal difficulties of the text's language and form. But the *accessus* show that there was
also an emphasis on a hermeneutics of cultural engagement that fostered
awareness of an interpretative system based on the ethical foundations of
Christian thought. Students acquired technical expertise and, more importantly, the active and searching application of a cultural and ideological
perspective. By 1200 that cultural perspective was developed by means
of the teacher's interpretations of a mixed anthology of genuine classical
and later classicising poetry, with little explicit Christian content. By 1300
the poems most commonly found in such collections of grammar-school
texts much more openly invite and indeed require sententious and ethical
reading.

Broad grammatical and interpretative competence was an essential
qualification for entry into the textual and clerical elites of the Christian community in either the monastery, the cathedral school or, increasingly, the university. Especially before 1300, the grammar-school texts
exposed students to a rudimentary notion of fictiveness grounded in an
understanding of the profoundly ethical nature of all literary experience.
Signification was never allowed to be an end in itself, and not all signification was considered worthwhile. Discrimination was necessary between
worthless fiction, seductive ornament and useful narrative, and such discrimination was applicable to life as well as to art. Christian grammar
taught how to decode the Book of the World as well as the world of
books.

For many pupils in song schools and cathedral grammar schools, their
first exposure to the Latin language and its literary devices was through
the medium of Latin hymns. Commentaries and glosses on liturgical and
paraliturgical poems, usually tied to a particular liturgical Use, survive
from the twelfth century until their appearance in print. Using the headings of the secular *accessus ad auctores*, the authors of Christian hymns
are discussed and their literary strategies analysed. The hymns themselves
are construed and glossed lexically. The *Expositiones hymnorum* occupy

a distinctive place in school commentary on verse. Although the Latinity of their students may have been limited, these commentaries and glosses blended lexical and linguistic instruction with ethical and spiritual interpretation. They applied secular techniques of verbal analysis and critical reading to morally unproblematic and overtly religious short poems, whose *materia* was the doctrines and history of the church, whose *modus agendi* employed literary skill to praise God, and whose *intentio* was to encourage understanding and contemplation of the deity. Above all, they encouraged the exercise of interpretative skills in an ethically secure arena. In addition, they reflect and refract the exegetical vocabulary of the more advanced commentators on Scripture, acting as *prima facie* evidence of and facilitators for the spread of interest in the affective force of Scripture and, by extension, of all religious verse.

The *Expositiones* have much in common with the experimental and critically sophisticated Psalter commentaries of the period, which were fundamental to the emergence of the new affective exegesis. Indeed, the Psalter was often referred to as a *liber hymnorum*, and commentaries on it often treated the individual psalms as lyric or elegiac verse. Gilbert of Poitiers (*c.* 1080–1154), chancellor of Chartres and a product of the liberal arts schools, could write of the affective force and intent of the Psalter and relate it to its metrical form: 'unde metrice scripsit'. Gilbert's 'unde' rests on a raft of *a priori* literary assumptions about the impact of verse and the nature of the psychological response it generated in its readers. These assumptions owe something to the emergent theoretical distinctions between the psychological force of rhetoric and poetic, but they also owe something to the nature of the analytical training given to readers of Latin verse in the early stages of grammar training.

School-texts produced and consumed within the penumbra of the Faith posed only limited problems for their readers, since their *auctoritas* was self-validating. But many of the texts that had survived from classical Antiquity posed more serious intellectual and interpretative challenges. Some of the shorter of these secular texts were also confronted by students as part of their training in grammar, a discipline which Rabanus Maurus had memorably described as 'scientia interpretandi poetas' (PL 107, 395).

Commentators on these texts were acutely aware of the partial classical inheritance they had received and the imperfect knowledge they possessed of it, as Conrad of Hirsau makes clear:

I cannot give you precise information . . . concerning the amount each author has written, or when he wrote, especially since most of them wrote a great deal which has not been transmitted to our times or to our part of the world. But it will not be difficult for me to rely on the paths others have blazed and bring you . . . as it were to the threshold of a door.   (tr. Minnis and Scott, p. 42)

This liminal imagery is appropriate for the ancillary functions performed by these verse reading-texts. The minor authors or shorter texts usually studied in grammar schools provided poetic gateways that could lead later to the study of Ovid and Virgil and probably to the study of the sacred page. 'The nourishing milk you draw from the poets', says the monastic Conrad, 'may provide you with an opportunity for taking solid food in the form of more serious reading' (tr. Minnis and Scott, p. 54).

These shorter texts usually circulated in compilations or collections of booklets containing several poems. Collections could be specially designed for glossing (with wide margins and double spacing of the main text), or might consist of separate copies of individual poems brought together in an *ad hoc* fashion. Although surviving manuscripts suggest that certain texts habitually travelled together in such school collections, medieval descriptive and prescriptive accounts of the texts read in the schools necessarily reflect availability, preference and individual and geographical emphasis. The list of approved authors in the *Sacerdos ad altare* attributed to Alexander Nequam reflects the classical bias of late-twelfth-century France. Conrad's list, from a monastic milieu, includes more advanced and difficult authors as well as a selection of Christian writers using classical motifs and techniques, and may be seeking a deliberate contrast with the syllabus and tastes of the liberal arts schools. Hugo von Trimberg's late-thirteenth-century German *Registrum multorum auctorum* shows signs of the later augmentation of the genuine classical repertoire by a moralistic new wave of contemporary compositions geared to changing tastes and shifting pedagogic priorities. In addition, the *post hoc* label 'school author' does not preclude the reading of such texts outside the schools or at higher levels of the educational system (Ovid's *Remedia amoris*, for example, seems to have floated freely in different educational environments, and is sometimes left unglossed in collections that otherwise show heavy school use). Nevertheless, the large numbers of copies designed specifically to accommodate glosses (and the regular presence of glosses in manuscripts not so designed) indicate that an evolving canon of texts was systematically read and expounded as part of elementary training in grammar. Indeed medieval grammatical works by the likes of Alexander de Villa Dei and John of Garland are often found in company with thirteenth-century collections of reading-texts, and are often glossed in a similar manner.

The most common grouping of texts in the thirteenth century is now often known as the *Liber Catonianus* or the *Sex auctores*. Invariably headed by the *Disticha Catonis*, such collections often included the *Ecloga* of 'Theodulus', the *Elegies* of Maximian, the *Fables* of Avianus (or sometimes 'Aesop', often the elegiac *Romulus* attributed to 'Walter of England' [Galterius Anglicus]), Claudian's *De raptu Proserpinae* and the *Achilleid* of Statius. Common thirteenth-century substitutions are of the *Remedia amoris* (which acquired its own commentary, perhaps by a Parisian master) or contemporary poems like the *Pamphilus* or *Geta*, whose virtuoso deployment of secular love tropes made them attractive, if morally challenging, subjects for exposition. The ethical imperative is evident throughout the commentaries on these texts. The tone of the collection was set by the text that invariably came first and often gave the collection its name, the *Disticha Catonis*, a third-century collection of maxims and precepts. Hugo von Trimberg praises 'Cato' as a fitting leader of the minor authors and texts represented in the *Liber Catonianus*:

> Virtutum expositor regulator morum
> Catho prior sedeat in ordine minorum.
>
> (*Registrum multorum auctorum*
> 3.563-4, p. 184)
>
> [The expositor of virtues and regulator of morals,
> Cato sits first in the rank of minor authors.]

The *Disticha Catonis* offered few interpretative challenges: the moral credentials of 'Cato' were impeccable. In an age committed to the gathering of *flores*, the *Disticha* were a readily exploited resource: the twelfth-century *Florilegium morale Oxoniense* manages to appropriate nearly the whole work. The sententiousness of the couplets appealed to the contemporary taste for memorable aphorisms. Moreover its couplet format made it ripe for textual augmentation and it grew incrementally and steadily in its passage through the medieval period and into most European vernaculars. Many of the medieval additions to the *Disticha* reflect contemporary concerns and moral issues (such as the behaviour appropriate towards clergy). As proverbs and *sententiae* were widely used in compositional exercises for training in versification, imitation and augmentation, some of these additions may themselves be scholastic exercises or magisterial elaborations in the aphoristic style of the original.

For Dante, Cato's status and function in the *Purgatorio* (1.31-75; 2.118-34) mark him out as a type of pagan wisdom, and the standard *accessus* on the *Disticha* etymologises his name as *catus*: wise. Particular impetus was given to the ethical status of the text by the perceived similarity of its *modus agendi* to the sapiential books of the Old Testament. Commentaries and glosses came to see the *Disticha* as dealing with the four cardinal virtues, though such a way of reading is in fact alien to the work's actual structure. As is so often the case in medieval readings of 'classical' texts, what might be called the *intentio commentatoris* is projected on to the *intentio auctoris*. Even the early *accessus* are already clear that the work pertains to ethics 'for its aim is to make a useful contribution to men's morals' (tr. Minnis and Scott, p. 16). This systematising of Cato's 'intentions' was a gradual but relentless process, culminating in some very detailed early humanist Italian commentaries which sought to rediscover the third-century Roman civil philosophy submerged under the layers of later Christian moralising. After the morsel-sized moral maxims of the *Disticha*, the fables of 'Aesop' (a collection of sixty stories in elegiacs) or, more commonly, of Avianus, provided what must have been the first contact many pupils would have had with figurative language, allegorical interpretation and the relation between fiction and truth. The opposition between shell and kernel, still an interpretative model of real power in this period, locates true pleasure in the 'correct' decoding of the moral meaning or *sententia*. Medieval commentators, usually following the lead of William of Conches (*c*. 1080–*c*. 1154; see above, Chapter 5), distinguished between fables that were mere entertainment and morally worthless (a category to which Aesopic fables were often assigned) and those more useful fables which could be proved to have a philosophical integument or hidden moral truth to be uncovered by the reader (usually more sophisticated poetic works like the *Aeneid* or the *Metamorphoses*). Even if Aesop and Avianus were minimally integumental, such fables could offer easy exegetical exercises for trainee fabulists. However, even at the level of elementary school commentary, there is a clear recognition that the highly schematised and symbolic model of signification found in fables with integuments is not universal to all fables, let alone to all poetry. Indeed, with many fable texts, the moral of the story could become so explicit as to be included as a *moralitas* at the end of the story.

Avianus' fables are repositories of reminiscences of Virgil and other authors, especially Ovid. Hence, though few of the borrowings are well integrated, there might be said to be some integumental potential in them. It was, therefore, a pedagogically versatile text, offering rudimentary allegorical exegesis, a verse-form easy to scan and to imitate, and an anthologising taste for classical citation. This allowed appreciation of classical style without the difficulties and dangers of confronting the more morally demanding *originalia*. It was just the sort of text to appeal to thirteenth-century taste. Alexander Nequam's *Novus Avianus*, a rendering of the first six fables into elegiac couplets, illustrates the sort of scholastic exercise likely to be perpetrated on such collections of fabular material.

The *Ecloga* of 'Theodulus', another persistent part of the textual repertoire, combined many of the advantages of Cato and the fables in a slightly more challenging format, offering controlled but genuine opportunities for interpretation (compare pp. 121–2, 123–5 above). The poem is a debate between Pseustis (Falsehood) and Alithia (Truth) on the pagan and Christian views of history and the world, refereed by Fronesis (Prudence).

It had an easily managed verse-form (quatrains alternating between the protagonists); *ex persona* dramatic action (the mode of narration where fictional characters speak, but not the author); exposure to the generic disciplines of the pastoral eclogue; skilful and allusive blending of facets of classical culture; and allusions to and quotations from classical authors, with the added bonus of balancing material from authoritative Christian writers like Sedulius and Prudentius (themselves prized for their eloquence and utility as stylistic models). It was an almost perfect text for the early stages of the curriculum. It facilitated mythographical analysis in inviting comparison between the partial mythologies of the pagans and the plenitude of revelation offered by Christianity. In comparing and contrasting aphorisms, attitudes and *sententiae* drawn from pagan and Christian writers, it further encouraged the primacy of the aphoristic 'sentence' as the basic unit of ethical teaching in works of this kind, a sort of portable piety.

New commentaries augmented the earlier detailed exposition of the *Ecloga* by Bernard of Utrecht (discussed above in Chapter 5), most notably that by Alexander Nequam, which was widely quarried later and became known as the 'common gloss' on the poem. The pagan myths receive an euhemerist interpretation, sensitive to the fact that 'Theodulus' nowhere invites allegorisation of his pagan stories. But later commentators, in line with the trend towards increasingly explicit interpretation, exploited the mythographic potential. The anonymous German commentary (ed. Orban) fully exploits the latent Christian allegory and offers little in the way of grammatical help or textual exposition, though the shadow of the schoolroom never disappears: Hercules is (*moraliter*) the scholar seeking the golden apple of knowledge and (*allegorice*) Christ fighting and killing the dragon/devil. Orpheus is a good teacher soothing his pupils (*moraliter*) and a good preacher rescuing a soul from the shadow of death and ignorance (*allegorice*). In the early fifteenth century, Odo of Picardy broadened the commentary tradition still further by adding mirror-for-princes material, and this commentary, written in 1406–7 for the son of Charles VI of France, accompanied the *Ecloga* into print alone (Paris, between 1488 and 1489; *CIBN* T-105, etc.) and as part of the augmented late-medieval syllabus in editions from 1490 onwards (Lyon, *c.* 1490; *GW* 2776, etc.).

Some of the commonly recurring verse reading-texts in pre-1300 collections required more substantial and ingenious interpretative reorientation to bring out their latent ethical force. The *Elegies* of Maximian, for example, with their laments for old age and lusts for young flesh, are not the most obviously appropriate subjects for study by impressionable schoolboys. Claudian's *De raptu Proserpinae* offers similar hermeneutic challenges. Vincent of Beauvais worried about this: while recognising that knowing the metrical rules was valuable, he fretted that the content was unprofitable, indeed even calamitous for young readers to be exposed to 'the teaching of the poets' (*De eruditione filiorum nobilium*, written 1246–9; 5.57–60). Hugo von Trimberg, recognising the profanity of Maximian, nevertheless praised the skill of his verse and his technical innovations. Searching for the ethical core of texts of this kind developed skills of perspicacity and balance in a reader that were readily transferred to other texts of moral ambiguity and sophistication (the longer works of Ovid, for example) and by extension to the complexities of moral decisions to be found in the real world. It encouraged *analytical* comparison between the two-dimensional moral universe of the text and the more complicated moral universe of real life. Commentaries on Claudian speak of the multiple intentions in the author's mind; commentaries on Maximian say that the *materia* of the text is 'gloria mundi' (e.g. Oxford, Bodleian Library, MS Auct. F. 5. 6, fol. 17v; late thirteenth century). Clearly an ethical reading of such texts required the application of moral principles already formed by instruction. To be able to read the fables of Avianus as 'reprehending vice' or 'correcting our morals' required a simultaneous understanding of the workings of fabular narrative, the mechanics of figural interpretation and an awareness of the complexity and dangers of free will and moral choice. In other words, it required a morally engaged as well as a critically competent reader. The *accessus* claim that 'almost all authors treat of ethics' was a challenge to medieval readers: the hermeneutical imperative of ethical commentary was always to facilitate the proper discernment of the hidden sentential wheat from the fictive chaff.

In the school-texts, this process was often (and unsurprisingly) rather mechanical, but it was capable of extension into longer texts and harder moral worlds outside the classroom. In the thirteenth century, commentators and readers in universities and beyond began, as we shall see below, to explore the implications of an emerging interest in 'affective poetics' (with its emphasis on the power of poetry to move and manipulate the imagination of the audience) to inform their own critical and creative engagement with the more morally challenging poems of the classical inheritance. Many of these discussions grow organically out of the kinds of issues that might be covered in school expositions of the verse reading-texts. Perhaps paradoxically, at the very same time the loose syllabus of school reading-texts was evolving into a more thoroughly sentential and less critically ambitious repertoire.

In the thirteenth century, classical authors 'came to be read rather for the information they contained than as models to imitate' (Hunt, 'English Learning', p. 113). This is emphatically true of the school-texts. At the end of the twelfth century the syllabus was dominated by minor but genuinely antique texts. The thirteenth-century collections sometimes supplemented the repertoire with contemporary love-poems (like the Pseudo-Ovidian *Facetus*; incipit: 'Moribus et vita') or the mini-epic of Statius' *Achilleid* or the modern epic *Alexandreis* written in the late twelfth-century by Walter of Châtillon. By the 1280s, however, Hugo von Trimberg's list of minor poets currently being studied makes no mention of Claudian or Maximian. Whereas Nequam's list offered a judicious assessment of the ethical worth of the deposit of the past, Hugo's list, though still containing much contemporary pastiche-classicism, reflects an increasing shift to a more overtly moralistic emphasis. The *De commendatione cleri* (1347–65) recommends the study of 'texts of a moral character and of poetical deduction . . . in which is acquired both fruit of virtues and fertility of good morals, while traces of rhetorical polish are found in the same' (cap. 1; ed. Thorndike, *University Records*, p. 211). While the universities discarded or redeployed classical authors in the light of new academic and pastoral priorities (e.g. Oxford's early-fourteenth-century proscription of 'the book of Ovid, *De arte amandi*' and *Pamphilus*, while allowing 'poesias honestas'; *Statuta antiqua*, ed. Gibson, p. 173), the grammar schools and the primary readers underwent a similar ethical sea change in favour of moral poems, often of recent composition. The common theme of these new texts is unequivocally that of *contemptus mundi*, supplanting and effacing the *gloria mundi* ostensibly celebrated by some of the earlier texts. As the *Cartula* (*De contemptu mundi*) puts it:

> Si quis amat Christum mundum non diligit istum.
>
> (PL 184, 892)
>
> [Whoever loves Christ does not love this world.]

The pan-European popularity of this new collection was so substantial that they survived together to enjoy a substantial and lengthy circulation in print under the title *Auctores* (*or Actores*) *octo*, accompanied by full commentaries blending moral exposition and literary analysis. (The usual eight are: the *Disticha Catonis*, *Ecloga* of 'Theodulus', *Cartula* [*De contemptu mundi*], *Thobiadis*, *Liber parabolarum* by Alan of Lille(?), Fables of 'Aesop' [i.e. the elegiac *Romulus* attributed to 'Walter of England'], and the *Liber floretus* or *facetus*.)

The *Liber facetus* (incipit: 'Cum nihil utilius'), for example, was probably composed in France, perhaps in Paris around the turn of the thirteenth century, and was popular almost immediately. Proverbially sententious, it combines commonplace wisdom with some degree of metrical and lexicographical discipline. Like the still-ubiquitous *Disticha Catonis*, whose form it imitates, the hexameter couplets of the *Facetus* proved easy to expand and interpolate, and many copies subsumed extra couplets that may originally have been glosses. For the poem soon generated a scholarly apparatus: lexical issues were addressed in interlinear glosses; proverbs and mnemonics bristled in the margins. A key early copy (Paris, Bibliothèque nationale de France, MS Lat. 8207) contains references to Cato, Solomon, Virgil, Prudentius, Claudian, Martial, Paul, Geoffrey of Vinsauf, Statius, Walter of Châtillon and Alan of Lille – a representative sample of the authors read in the schools, but reduced to dicta and aphorisms supporting an essentially banal text.

Morals stand at the heart of these new texts, and that heart is worn firmly on the textual sleeve. The morally upright life is never represented as a matter of difficulty or complexity, or open to interpretation or personal responsibility. Little ingenuity is required to uncover their ethical imperative. Hortatory and forthright, these texts address the catechetic fundamentals of Christian doctrine with muscular relish. In a text like the *Liber floretus*, the attributes of a good sermon and the necessities for a good death jostle with the rules for a good life. Only the occasional gloss on metrical form or some stylistic feature recall that they purport to assist in grammatical training, and it is unsurprising to find texts of an avowedly pastoral or penitential nature, like the *Paeniteas cito* of William de Montibus, as fellow travellers in such collections, fitted out with their own glosses and commentaries. The *Thobiadis* or metrical life of Thobit, composed by the rhetorician Matthew of Vendôme towards the end of the twelfth century, admittedly has more literary pretensions. But much of this is vulgar display, a sort of theme-park classicism, which culminates in a lengthy and self-regarding discussion of metrical form, polemically justifying Matthew's choice of elegiac distichs in preference to the hexameters of his near contemporary and rival Walter of Châtillon. Matthew's self-conscious stylistic games display more ingenuity than good taste and more conceit than decorum:

> Odit, amat, reprobat, probat, execratur, adorat
> Crimina, iura, nefas, fas, simulacra, Deum.
>
> (89–90)

[He hates crimes, loves laws, reproves unlawful things, approves of divine law, curses idols and adores God.]

More typical is the *Liber parabolarum* or *Parvum doctrinale*, attributed to Alan of Lille, which combined exposure to metrical discipline and sententiously enigmatic wisdom: each of the six books uses a verse unit two lines longer than the preceding book, so that Book 1 is in couplets and Book 6 in twelve-line stanzas.

The moral credentials of the *Actores octo* collection were unimpeachable, their metrical virtuosity only marginally reduced from that of the *Liber Catonianus*. But the nature of the commentary reveals the real shift. The new commentary reinforces, expands and illustrates the moral mnemonics of the text. It reinforces and supplements what is already explicit, where the older commentary had sought to develop habits of active and engaged reading, to reveal what was implicit in the text or could be figuratively deduced from it or projected on to it. With the exception of the surprisingly persistent *Ecloga* of 'Theodulus', the new syllabus texts are almost entirely devoid of irony, personification, mythography and allegory. The old texts were recognisably 'poetic' in that they required their readers to engage with and understand the complexity of the moral positions portrayed and the shifting voices of their narrative *personae*. The new texts tell rather than show. They are genuinely didactic in that they expect no moral engagement or philosophical assessment from their readers, only a passive consumption and reinforcement of unproblematic moral paradigms.

The verse reading-text, on this evidence, becomes a delivery system for largely pre-digested and pre-selected classical and moral lore. The educational experience of a pupil exposed to texts like the *Facetus* was very different from that of a reader of Claudian's *De raptu Proserpinae*, Statius' *Achilleid* or Maximian's *Elegies*. At the very least it deferred his exposure to the interpretative complexities of classical literature to a later stage in the curriculum. The protean and elliptical strategies of Ovid's *Metamorphoses* are nowhere prepared for in this later moral collection, whereas in the earlier collection the *Pamphilus* or the *Remedia amoris* might have offered some foretaste of the Ovidian textual agenda. Perhaps the often reductive but frequently ingenious fourteenth-century moralisations of Pierre Bersuire (d. 1362) and the *Ovide moralisé* have their ideological origins in these new sanitised grammar-school texts. Equally, perhaps the removal of Ovidian material from these collections liberated fourteenth-century writers such as Chaucer in their reactions to these works. In the later Middle Ages, the moral challenges and ethical dilemmas of classical literature had to be confronted elsewhere in the academic curriculum, and, increasingly often, outside of the curriculum altogether. Learning how to read these more challenging texts increasingly meant thinking freshly about how those texts worked on their readers. Medieval poetic theory is as much about reading as it is about writing.

2. Reading minds: medieval poetic theory

'But if passage of time improves poems as it does wine, I have a question: how many years will give value to a book?' (Horace, *Epistola* 2.1). By the fifteenth century Horace's question was answered by the dominant status enjoyed by the *Ars poetica* (*Ad Pisonem*) in humanist thinking about the nature and effects of poetry. But that eminence was not achieved overnight. Although the renewed study of Ciceronian rhetoric in the fourteenth and fifteenth centuries added a new dimension to the preceptive reading of the *Ars poetica*, the foundations of Horace's influence lay in its early assimilation into the educational syllabus of the Western schools, in defiance of Horace's own light-hearted dread at the prospect ('You're not, I take it, insane enough to want your poems dictated in the elementary schools? I am not'; *Satires* 1.4).

In his *Dialogue*, Conrad had explained to his young student of grammar how the study of philosophy is habitually divided into logical, physical and ethical branches. When applied to literary texts the standard *accessus* question 'to which part of philosophy does it pertain' invariably produces the answer 'Ethicae subponitur'. This is because, as Conrad argues in his introduction to Cato, 'almost all authors concern themselves with morality' (ed. Huygens [1970], p. 83). Literary texts are thus studied under two distinct but interrelated disciplines: insofar as the mechanics of signification and the disciplines of writing follow certain conventions, literature falls under the aegis of logic. But what authors actually say falls under the gaze of ethics, because the precepts of the text must be tested against the principles of moral philosophy. This division is reflected in a twelfth-century commentary on Horace's *Ars poetica*. The work pertains to logic 'because it guides us to a knowledge of correct and elegant style and to habitual reading of authors who may serve as models'. It also pertains to ethics 'since it shows what behaviour is appropriate for a poet' (tr. Minnis and Scott, p. 33). In the thirteenth century, Roger Bacon, discussing more precisely the rules and effects of poetry, makes the same distinction between 'docens componere argumentum poeticum' which is a part of logic, and 'utens eo' which is a part of moral philosophy (*Opus tertium*, cap. 75; ed. Brewer, p. 308). Implicit in this attempt to integrate ethics into the teaching of the liberal arts was a renewed emphasis on the effects of a poetical text on its readers. When, in the late twelfth and early thirteenth centuries, commentators and readers became more explicitly aware of the affective force of language and its ethical impact, this raised moral issues that were distinct from the rules for composition and theories in prescriptive handbooks. Moreover, the perceived ethical indirectness of much of the classical poetry that had survived argued for a warier exegetical approach than was applied to the rhetorical moralists like Cato and Seneca. The affective force of such texts acted on the imagination of its readers or hearers in powerful and unpredictable ways. Different criteria for analysis and assessment were needed because poetry was essentially a private experience, in contrast to the originally public nature of classical forensic rhetoric and its medieval sibling preaching. Sharpened by academic interest in pulpit rhetoric and biblical poetics, some thirteenth-century thinking about the nature and effect of poetic discourse explored the symbiosis between the dicta in Horace's *Ars poetica* and the more extensive and penetrating analysis of the same issues in the newly available Latin versions of Arab commentary on Aristotle's *Poetics*. The predominantly Parisian study of the *Poetics* in the thirteenth century should probably be seen as a symptom of the already burgeoning interest in the affective power of literature rather than as a direct cause of it. But from 1250 onwards, secular poetic theory was an arena where Aristotelian readings of Horace complemented and supplemented Horatian readings of Aristotle.

Perhaps by the end of the fifth century CE, the miscellaneous *scholia* later pseudonymously attributed to Acro had begun the trend of seeing the *Ars poetica* as a collection of precepts and *sententiae* on the writing of poetry and on the need for poetry to have an ethical impact. Commenting on *Ars poetica* 99 ('It is not enough for poetry to be beautiful, it must also be pleasing [*dulcia*]'), Pseudo-Acro glosses *dulcia* as *ethica* (ed. Keller, p. 246). The twelfth-century *accessus* reinforce this idea, focusing primarily on Horace's prescriptive teachings about decorum, appropriate form and the necessary blending of innate talent and acquired skill in the disposition of the material. One commentary speaks of it teaching what ought to be done and criticising what ought to be avoided ('docendo que sunt facienda et reprehendendo que sunt respuenda'; Paris, Bibliothèque nationale de France, MS Lat. 8223). According to the hugely influential 'Materia' commentary (1125–75), which begins, 'Materia huius auctoris in hoc opere est ars poetica. Intentio vere est dare precepta de arte poetica', the *Ars poetica* teaches 'what is to be shunned and afterwards what is to be embraced' (ed. Friis-Jensen, '*Ars poetica* in Twelfth-Century France', p. 336). In commentaries on the *Ars poetica* phrases such as these are more commonly applied to the rules of composition than to the rules of moral behaviour (as in *accessus* to other literary texts): 'non de morum formatione sed de verborum compositione'.[2] The emphasis throughout the commentary tradition is on the impact of the poetic composition on its intended audience, and this view of Horace is reflected in the newly composed Arts of Poetry of the late twelfth and early thirteenth centuries. The influence of the 'Materia' commentary, for example, can be seen on the prescriptive writings of Matthew of Vendôme, Geoffrey of Vinsauf and John of Garland.

There is no quantum leap in the study of Horace in the thirteenth century. Materials from the twelfth and earlier centuries continued to be circulated and copied throughout the thirteenth and fourteenth centuries. They

---

[2] Paris, Bibliothèque nationale de France, MS Lat. 350, fol. 40r. The same comment is made in an *accessus* to the *Ars* in Oxford, Magdalen College, MS Lat. 15, fol. 63v; ed. Friis-Jensen, '*Horatius liricus*', p. 137.

were, however, read somewhat differently after 1250 – initially from a perspective that uses Aristotelian and Averroistic terminology to describe the poetic response, and eventually in the light of the Italian humanist synthesis of Ciceronian rhetoric and medieval poetic. But common to all these readings of Horace is the increasingly explicit valuation of his focus on the impact and effect of a poem on the responses of its hearers and readers. Horace's *Ars poetica* is the backbone of medieval poetic theory.

The aphoristic nature of *Ars poetica* meant that, like the much less widely available *Poetics* of Aristotle, its influence was greater than its readership. Horatian dicta, especially *ut pictura poesis* (*Ars poetica* 361–3) and the deprecation of the *fidus interpres* (131–7), were explored, appropriated and colonised by writers and commentators. *Aut prodesse volunt, aut delectare poete* (333–4) enjoyed similar popular application, and this psychological paradox disguised as a moral dichotomy also had, as we shall see, an emphatic influence on medieval thinking about poetry. Horace provided the core vocabulary for thinking about the special force of poetry, even when that thinking was undertaken in terms increasingly coloured by Aristotelian precept and methodology. His technical prescriptions also underpinned the prescriptive arts of poetry composed in the late twelfth and early thirteenth centuries, some of which, like Matthew of Vendôme's *Ars versificatoria* (*c.* 1175), may have started life as school lectures on Horace's art. Geoffrey of Vinsauf's *Poetria nova* (*c.* 1200–15) explicitly sets out to augment and elucidate the precepts of the *Poetria vetus* (as the *Ars poetica* was sometimes known) by applying the lessons of the rhetorical tradition to the writing of poetry, and his prose *Documentum de arte versificandi* (written with or shortly after the *Poetria nova*) uses material from the 'Materia' commentary on Horace's *Ars*. By its popularity and the number of commentaries it generated, especially in the fourteenth century in Italy, the *Poetria nova* is an important witness to the assimilation and appropriation of Horatian ideas and is an obvious bridge between medieval poetic theory and practice (see further the discussion in Chapter 2 above).

One of the key precepts of the *Ars poetica* asserts that poetic 'truth' differs from historical 'truth' because the disposition of material by the poet is governed by the imaginative and affective needs of his audience, even if his style and subject-matter must pay a debt to real life. On occasion the demands of poetic decorum require the poet to depart from or vary his subject-matter (*Ars poetica* 42), like Virgil, who chooses to allow Aeneas to come to Dido. The poet's skill makes the audience believe that this is really in the sequence of events and part of the story, and only poets characteristically vary their *materia* in this way. This precept of Horace's allowed his commentators to develop a distinct narrative decorum for poetry which contributed to the emerging theoretical separation between poetic and rhetoric. Borrowing a rhetorical distinction from the *Ad Herennium*'s discussion of *dispositio* or structure of a discourse, literary commentators distinguished between the natural order of events (which they ascribed to the genre of history or historiography) and the artificial order of events which is distinctive of poetry, encouraged by Horace's instruction to start the poem *in medias res*. (This distinction also occurs in comments on the generic status of Lucan's *Pharsalia* [*De bello civili*] and in some discussions of epic narrative.) The distinction was even applied to the *Ars poetica* itself. In that poem Horace presents himself as both a poet and a poetic theorist, and this virtuoso double *modus agendi* is reflected in some commentaries on the *Ars* and in medieval imitations like Geoffrey of Vinsauf's *Poetria nova* and the many later commentaries on that new text. Contrary to this view, other commentaries argued that Horace should not be seen as a poet (using imagination) in the *Ars poetica*, but rather as a maker of verses (as a kind of historian or *preceptor* of the art), because he is writing about things that actually exist. In general, the commentary tradition follows the standard philosophical distinction in classifying the *Ars poetica* as belonging either to logic (because it expounds the rules of the art) or to ethics (because it explains the behaviour appropriate for a poet, though surely this refers not to his own moral behaviour but rather to his ethical and stylistic responsibilities – 'function and duty'– as a maker of fictions). This second categorisation reflects the widespread medieval description of the poet as a shaper of fictions, a definition repeated in many early commentaries on the *Ars poetica*: 'Poetica vero ars sive poesis est fictio sive figmentum, quod suum est poetarum' (the *Anonymus Turicensis* commentary in Zurich, Zentralbibliothek, MS Rheinau 76, fol. 15r; similar comments are found in the 'Materia' commentary).

Fictiveness and figural language were seen as the distinctive features of poetry, as Lactantius had argued in his early-fourth-century definition of the *officium poetae*: elegantly and with oblique figures, poets turned and transferred things that had really happened into other representations (PL 6, 111–822). This commonplace definition of the function of poets, repeated by Isidore, Vincent of Beauvais and Pierre Bersuire, while in one direction giving 'a license to poets'[3] in other ways put commentators on their guard for the slipperiness of poetic meaning. A careful and productive reading of pagan texts such as Horace's, for example, always required sensitivity to their literary strategies. In Conrad's colloquy, Horace's teachings on the need for decorum of poetic form and in the conduct of poetic argument trigger a lengthy and detailed discussion about the utility of reading pagan poems and the value of the *sententiae* that may be extracted from them. Rhetoric relied on the Ciceronian

---

[3] See Zeeman, 'Schools Give a License to Poets'.

emphasis on the orator as a 'vir bonus dicendi peritus' ('a good man skilled in speech'), where the presence of a *vir bonus* offered some guarantee of the morality of the discourse. Theorists grappling with the literary works of long-dead writers of uncertain morality and puzzlingly protean moral stances soon realised that poets like Ovid could not confidently, easily or consistently be described as 'good men'. Similarly, one apparent omission in Horace's teachings in the *Ars poetica* was his lack of emphasis on the importance of the good character of the poet. So a separation between the poet and his voices became desirable and indeed necessary. Equally, because of Horace's importance as a poetic *preceptor*, it was important to develop an appropriately ethical reading of his own literary output, especially given the apparent indirection of his poetic voice in the *Satires* and *Odes*. Many of the early *accessus*, including Conrad's, stress that when Horace's poems address or describe vices, 'it is rather the case that individual examples of vice are recorded rather than that the author himself is subject to those vices' (tr. Minnis and Scott, p. 56). Thus the medieval commentary tradition, in characterising Horace as a possibly ventriloquial recorder of human folly, switches the emphasis away from the poet towards the manner in which the strategy of an individual poem may be targeted at the moral needs of a particular audience.

So it became possible to justify the *materia* and *modus agendi* used by the Horace of the *Odes* and *Satires* by constructing an image of Horace as a strategic moralist and a master of narrative and structural decorum. This was achieved by combining the medieval notion of *poetria* as an indirect and figurative mode of discourse with an application of the Servian rules of *ex persona* narration (where the characters speak without an authorial or editorial voice), and by placing these alongside the medieval definition of satire as an ethically engaged genre where, even if the poet's moral intention is only indirectly manifested, satire follows rhetoric in its desire to praise or blame. Because, according to the definition of poetry in the *Ysagoge in theologiam*, all poetry commonly offers examples of the brave and moral and the cowardly and immoral (Landgraf, p. 72), the moral intention of any author in any text, no matter how elliptical, can thus be deduced by the ability of medieval commentators to generate a moral reading of his text. Such acts of interpretative deduction privileged the effect of the poem on its medieval readers, collapsing the (largely fictitious) gap between the hermeneutic category of *intentio auctoris* and the contemporary audience's reception of, and response to, the text. They also encouraged the development and application of ways of interpreting 'difficult' poetic texts, like those of Ovid, and the development and application of these interpretative assumptions in vernacular works of similarly uncertain or elusive moral valency.

Horace's most famous aphorism, on the balance and blend of instruction and delight to be striven for in poetry, also made a significant contribution to the emergent ethical poetic of the period from the twelfth century onwards, and to the debate about the psychological impact and affective force of poetry – what the thirteenth-century Aristotelians came to call its 'imaginative syllogisms'. In the prevailing twelfth-century literary mode of integumental allegory (discussed in the previous chapter), it is unsurprising that Horace's teachings on instruction and delight were assimilated to the model of fictional signifying that saw the pleasant shell concealing a kernel of instruction or truth. Often the attainment of the kernel was seen as the source of the delight and sweetness, in contrast to the seductively fictive shell which should be discarded. This interpretative model fitted well with Neoplatonic and Augustinian modes of reading, and the Horatian dictum was often repeated in vernacular texts – both religious and secular – of the thirteenth century. It was also used to negotiate the moral complexities of challenging texts like Ovid's *Heroides*, where the *utilitas* is seen as '*delectatio* as well as the calling back from all illicit loves' because 'the intention of all poets is *aut delectare aut prodesse*' (*Accessus* to Ovid in University of California, Berkeley, MS Bancroft 95, fol. 60r). But some commentators sought instead to explain Horace's precept with reference to the distinctive features of particular kinds of writing:

> Some poets write with a useful purpose in view, like the satirists, while others, such as the writers of comedies, write to give pleasure, and yet others, for example the historians, write to a useful end and to give pleasure.

> ('Bernard Silvester', *Commentary on the Aeneid, Books I–VI*, Prologue;
> tr. Minnis and Scott, p. 152)

The commentary now known as the *Anonymus Turicensis* similarly allowed different effects to different kinds of poem 'quia poete diversa scribunt': 'some write solely for utility, in order to instruct us in morals. Others solely write pleasurable trifles, such as fables. Yet others write on both playful *and* morally fitting subjects which treat of morality and of pleasure' (Zurich, Zentralbibliothek, MS Rheinau 76, fol. 19r). Other theorists preferred to see Horace's teaching as alluding to the more complex psychological response distinctively generated by the form and style of poetry, where instruction and delight form part of an indissoluble matrix of moral assessment and aesthetic pleasure. This increasingly permitted a procedural distinction to be opened up between the *modus agendi* of rhetoric and that of poetic. Dominicus Gundissalinus' definition of the purpose of poetry in his *De divisione philosophiae* (after 1150, but often attributed in manuscripts to the thirteenth-century Oxford scholar Robert Grosseteste), for example, is overtly Horatian ('aut ludicris delectare, aut seriis edificare'; ed. Baur, p. 56; compare Dahan, p. 190).

But, as one of the earliest translators of the Arabic versions of Aristotle into Latin, Gundissalinus uses the Horatian phrase in parallel with Al-Fārābī's mid-tenth-century definition, which is markedly more affective and Aristotelian: 'The proper function of poetic words is to make us imagine beautiful or foul things which are not real so that the hearer may believe in them and finally abhor or desire them' (ed. Baur, p. 74; compare Dahan, p. 190). Gundissalinus and Al-Fārābī tellingly continue: 'Imagination is always more powerfully at work in mankind than knowledge or thought'.

This early synthesis of Horace and Aristotle was prophetic of the liveliest thinking about the impact of poetry to be undertaken in the more overtly Aristotelian schools of the thirteenth century. For the increasing subtlety and sophistication of thirteenth-century faculty psychology led to a growing recognition of the Aristotelian basis to Horace's thought. Already implicitly recognised by Gundissalinus, it was explicitly signalled by Hermann the German (d. 1272) in the preface to his version of the *Poetics* (made in Spain *c.* 1256) and by Roger Bacon (d. 1294). Hermann's version was in fact a translation from the Arabic of Averroes' (1126–98) Middle Commentary on the *Poetics* of Aristotle, and Averroes, a Muslim from Cordoba in Moorish Spain, shared some cultural and literary assumptions with Al-Fārābī. Averroes, unaware that Aristotle's primary focus in the *Poetics* was tragedy and comedy as dramatic genres, had interpreted his teaching as applying to poetry, and this emphasis was carried over by Hermann's translation. So there was scope and encouragement for medieval readers to see its precepts as contributing to an already lively contemporary discussion about the nature and force of secular poetry.

In this discussion, Horace was seen to share with Aristotle an emphasis on the engagement of the audience's imaginative faculty: 'What comes in through the ear is less effective in stirring the mind than what is put before our faithful eyes and told by the spectator to himself' (*Ars poetica* 180). In one of his most well-known aphorisms, Aristotle had stated that man naturally delights in representations. Therefore the process of what the Latin *Poetics* call poetic *assimilatio* ('likening') can produce pleasure, 'for the mind will more perfectly assimilate teachings as a result of the pleasure which it takes in examples' (tr. Minnis and Scott, p. 293; compare Chapter 7 below). This is because the nature of the *assimilatio* or 'imaginative likening' constructed by the skilful poet invites the audience to test or assay the comparison and to validate it against his own knowledge and experience of real life: this is a key element in the distinctive power of poetic discourse. There is in this a potential parallel with Horace's advice to 'the skilled imitator' to 'keep his eye on the model of life and manners and draw his speech living from there' (*Ars poetica* 319), and with his canonical assertion that poetry can both teach and delight. Art must imitate nature: outlandish and incredible stories must be avoided for this reason. The need for credibility (*credulitas* in Averroistic terms) is a function of the status of art as a stimulus to the initial apprehension and subsequent ordered assessment and analysis of the workings of the audience's imagination. Medical discussions of the so-called 'hygienic justification' of literature emphasised the therapeutic effects of such processes of ordered imaginative engagement with *confabulatio*.[4] But such confabulations should not stimulate the imagination by outlandish or un-natural images which might lead to an ever more morally degenerate process of fantastical free-association. For both Aristotle and Horace, pleasure and instruction can both derive from the process of arriving at a moral judgement as a result of an ethical assessment of the sense-data and stimuli encoded in the poetic text, reinforced by man's natural delight in rhythm and metre. Literary theorists from the thirteenth century onwards, in their attempts to define the distinctive nature and effect of poetic discourse, found fertile common ground in Horatian and Aristotelian interest in the affective force of poetic discourse.

In the thirteenth century, this incipient reception theory was developed under the impetus and mental taxonomies of the new Aristotelianism by the recognition that poetry constituted a special branch of logic which possessed rules and procedures that were different from those addressed in the study of rhetoric. Al-Fārābī's tenth-century listing of the constituent parts of Aristotle's logical corpus – the *Organon* – soon became widely accepted in the new university schools. In the *Organon*, the *Rhetoric* was the eighth book and the *Poetics* the ninth and last. Poetry's place as the last and lowest form of logic provided a convenient schema within which its distinctive features could be discerned and defined. The twelfth-century Latin versions of Al-Fārābī's *De scientiis* had described logic as the search for, and implementation of, rules by which the truth of a saying might be ascertained. The rules and procedures are different for different kinds of discourse. While rhetoric inclines the hearer to acquiesce in what is being said and to persuade him of its credibility (*credulitas*), poetic discourse works by appealing to the imagination to produce an emotional response. The appeal to the imagination by means of similitude is what distinguishes poetry from rhetoric. In the twelfth century Gundissalinus, incorporating Al-Fārābī's comments with Horace's dicta, argued, as we have seen, that poetry creates something beautiful or hateful by imagination and, believing it, the hearer or reader longs for it or is repelled from it. Imagination, it was argued, was a more powerful force in man than discursive thought or *scientia*. Although this often unpredictable potency

4 See Olson, *Literature as Recreation*, pp. 70–1, 80–5, and Chapter 8 below.

was usually a source of moral concern (see Chapter 7 below), some literary commentators came to feel that, properly controlled and assessed, the
affective potential of the imagination might explain the peculiar potency
of poetry when compared to other kinds of discourse. Thus poetry generates an image that provokes an instinctive moral judgement from the
estimative faculty by the force of its impact on the affections of its audience. This affective response is more powerful as an instrument of morality than argument or demonstration because it involves the psyche of
the audience in a simulation of the processes of choice and assessment
found in real life. (Of course powerful imaginative engagement with a
poetic text might provoke bad behaviour as well as good, and so this line
of argument could equally serve to reinforce the traditional distrust of
poetry.)

In the early fourteenth century, John Buridan (*c.* 1292–*c.* 1358), a
philosopher at Paris University, classified both rhetoric and poetic as
'moral logic', but was able to distinguish between them. Rhetoric desires
clear knowledge and deploys words in their proper significations. Poetry,
by contrast, proceeds by a delightful obscuring of knowledge, 'per verbum
transumptionem' (the characteristic use of figurative language). However,
they both differ from the other branches of logic because in them understanding is arrived at by the manipulation or engagement of the passions.
But already in the thirteenth century, Roger Bacon (*c.* 1220–*c.* 1292), in
a sophisticated and ambitious analysis of the utility of poetic language,
had recognised that speculative logic could have only a limited impact on
moral behaviour because of its abstraction and difficulty, and because of
the defects of perception in man's fallen nature. Bacon, a scholar at Paris
and probably at Oxford, was one of the first academics to lecture on
some of Aristotle's physical and metaphysical works. His thinking was
deeply influenced by the classicism and early Aristotelianism of Robert
Grosseteste (d. 1253), first *lector* of the Oxford Franciscans, whom Bacon
joined during his time in Oxford, and perhaps by Grosseteste's comments
on affectivity in his *Introitus* originally given at the beginning of the liberal
arts course at Oxford.[5]

Bacon's attitude to the study of literary texts reflects the explicit influence of the Averroistic *Poetics* and the writings of Avicenna and Al-Fārābī.
He is driven by the importance of exploring and properly interpreting the
riches of pagan writings, many of which were becoming available for
the first time to his generation of Parisian scholars. This endeavour was
sanctioned by his passionate belief in the overriding importance of moral
philosophy which, he says, 'claims as its right whatever it finds written
elsewhere pertaining to it'. In its totalising and ambitious view of the

[5] See Callus, 'Robert Grosseteste', and McEvoy, *Philosophy*, pp. 13–19, 346–9, 448–9.

field of moral enquiry, this is an important extension of the range and intellectual scope of the common *accessus* claim that 'almost all authors direct themselves towards ethics'. The principles of moral philosophy are gathered from other sciences; hence any relevant findings fall under the remit of moral philosophy 'since in substance they relate to morals' (*Opus maius*, ed. Bridges, pp. 636–7). This is the perfect justification for the exploration of all pagan writings and for the engagement with the more slippery moral world of pagan secular literature. The 'unclouded glory' of pagan writers makes them essential reading for all Christian philosophers.

According to Bacon in part five of his *Moralis philosophia*, the speculative procedures of dialectic and demonstration are unsuitable for moral philosophy because, as Aristotle says in the *Ethics*, its end is not that we should contemplate grace, but that we should become good (pars V, cap. 2.3, citing *Nichomachean Ethics* 2.2; 1103b, 26–8). Bacon therefore recommends instead the use of 'sermo potens ad inclinandum mentem' (pars V, cap. 2.1). Although much moral argument and persuasion can properly be called rhetoric, he maintains that there is another kind of persuasive language which deals with subjects that move us to work for worship, laws and virtues ('que nos flectunt ad opus in cultu divino, legibus et virtutibis'; pars V, cap. 3.6). This kind of rhetoric, he says, is called poetic by Aristotle and other philosophers, 'quia poete veraces usi sunt eo in flectendo homines ad virtutis honestatem' (pars V, cap. 3.7; the argument is capped by a citation of 'prodesse volunt aut delectare poete' from Horace's *Ars poetica*). While the speculative sciences delight in argument, opinion and knowledge for its own sake ('nuda'), the 'practical sciences' (for him, theology and moral philosophy) consider arguments *ad praxim*. Their aim is to stir up the audience to good works. Likewise, poetical argument pursues vice and honours virtue in order that men may be attracted to honour and moved to hatred of sin.

Bacon's psychology of poetic response places great emphasis on the importance of the moving of the audience's soul to good ('flectere animum ad bonum') as a distinctive difference between the nature of an audience's response to rhetoric and poetic. He stresses the engagement of the will and affections of the reader in a process of assessment and moral classification. *Moralis sciencia*, Bacon argues, operates by literary methods to influence the emotions of the audience. Poetry, in particular, aims to move the soul unexpectedly ('sine praevisione'). Repeatedly drawing parallels between the poetical modes of Scripture and those used by human writers, he defends the beauty of metrical and rhythmical texts, citing in his support the Averroistic Aristotle, Avicenna and Al-Fārābī. Sublime and decorous words have the power to carry away the soul to love the good and detest the bad. In this respect, he says,

Scripture and moral philosophy rely on the same kind of poetical argument. It is the ability of literature to move the soul unexpectedly that gives it its peculiar power as an instrument of ethical teaching and moral exploration. The *sermo potens* is the essential partner of the study of wisdom. Wisdom without eloquence is like a sharp sword in a paralysed hand; eloquence without wisdom is like a sharp sword in an enraged hand (*Opus tertium*, ed. Brewer, pp. 4, 266–7). Literary criticism is, by implication, an essential and indispensable weapon in the armoury of the moral philosopher.

For Roger Bacon the books of Aristotle were the 'fundamenta totius sapientiae', and the *Rhetoric* and *Poetics* were 'the two best books of logic' (*Compendium studii*, ed. Brewer, p. 469; Massa, '*Poetica*', pp. 459, 472). For Bacon, and for others who thought about the power of literary language, the renewed study of Aristotle in the thirteenth century was decisive in focusing attention on the moral logic of poetry. The importance he attached to these works is apparent, not least in the extraordinary rudeness of his attacks on the Philosopher's translators, whom he accuses of lacking the scientific, logical and the linguistic skills to do him justice. He laments that on the subject of poetry 'we do not have the full thinking ['mentem . . . plenam'] of Aristotle in Latin' (*Moralis philosophia*, pars VI, 4). Bacon knew the work of both William of Moerbeke and Hermann the German, and Hermann's version of the *Poetics*, undertaken in 1256 after he had completed his version of the *Rhetoric*, has much in common with Bacon's own views on poetry. Hermann's translation of the 'Middle Commentary' of Averroes on the Arabic version of the Aristotelian text works in a coherent and systematic way to present poetry as a didactic instrument, operating on the psychological responses of its audience through its use of what Avicenna (980–1037) and Averroes (1120–98) had called 'the imaginative syllogism' leading to the imaginative representation that is distinctive of poetic discourse. Avicenna, at the start of his shorter commentary on the *Poetics*, had carefully distinguished between assent (the end of rhetoric) and imagination (the end of poetic):

Poetic premises are premises whose role is to cause acts of imagination, and not assent, to befall the soul, whenever they are accepted. . . . And it is not one of the conditions of these premises that they be true or false, or widely accepted or repugnant, but rather that they be imaginative.

(tr. Black, 'Imaginative Syllogism', p. 245)

The newly available Arabic interpretation of Aristotle's views on the psychology of literary response buttressed the thirteenth century's developing interest in faculty psychology. The Averroistic revamping of the original *Poetics* made its annexation in support of the ethical basis of medieval literary theory a relative formality. The famous opening claim of the Averroistic *Poetics* – that all poetry consists of either praise or blame – chimed with contemporary interests in moral philosophy and reinforced interpretative trends already apparent in the commentaries produced in the liberal arts schools on classical reading-texts. Averroes, however inadvertently, brings out more prominently aspects of the moral potential of poetry implicit in the Greek.[6] Aristotle says that the tragic poet, presenting individually characterised people in specific circumstances, makes us aware of moral facts and moral possibilities relevant to more than the situation he envisages (*Poetics* 1451b–1452a). *Mimesis* is a means of acquiring knowledge not otherwise available, by engaging in a process of 'likening'. In Hermann this key term is rendered as *imaginatio* or *assimilatio* (tr. Minnis and Scott, pp. 289, 291, etc.). Thus it was in the mid-thirteenth century that the Arabic perception of the characteristic Aristotelian link between imagination, desire and action was assimilated into, and made intelligible, for the mainstream of medieval psychological theory and for wider thinking about the force of poetry.

According to Aristotle-Averroes, man naturally delights in representations, one of the aphorisms from the *Poetics* that achieved the widest circulation in the Latin West. The link between delight and utility was already familiar to medieval readers from their knowledge of Horace's *Ars poetica* and its accumulated scholia. The Averroistic *Poetics* allowed Horace's elliptical reference to be regrounded in a psychology of literary response: poetry appeals to the instinct of delight by its use of the imaginative syllogism. The process of *assimilatio* involves relating the imaginative syllogism to our knowledge of the world and deducing from that an appropriate moral response. Examples are used in teaching, therefore, because they move the imagination. The pleasure which man takes in the representation facilitates understanding, and the process is enhanced by the use of metre, rhythm and harmony. Hermann calls this pleasure *delectatio*, perhaps deliberately aligning it with Horace's dictum (tr. Minnis and Scott, p. 294). In the Averroistic model, therefore, *assimilatio* emerges as the crucial psychological process in literary response: a quasi-allegorical matrix whereby the imagination is stimulated to work out the kinds of association and similarity that exist between the world of the text and the world of moral choice inhabited by the reader or hearer.

It follows, however, that for the process of likening to succeed, the material of the poem must not be too outlandish or lack credibility (*credulitas*). Averroes stresses that 'poems of praise have as their purpose the

[6] See Halliwell, 'Aristotle's *Poetics*'.

encouragement of acts of the will. When such acts are possible and seem real they have greater power to persuade, in other words to promote poetic belief which moves the mind to pursue something or reject it' (tr. Minnis and Scott, p. 300). By contrast, proverbs and fables are not really poems. Although they convey 'a kind of instruction in prudence' (p. 299), they achieve their effect by the stories themselves and not by any stimulation of the imagination and judgement of the readers. By Averroistic criteria, the very didactic openness that recommended school-texts like the proverbs of Cato and the fables of Aesop and Avianus to their commentators disqualifies them from the more complex moral world of true poetic because they require little hermeneutical engagement on the part of the reader. As we have seen, by the end of the thirteenth century, the syllabus of grammar-school texts had begun to drop most of the morally difficult poems earlier studied at this stage of the curriculum in favour of more explicitly didactic and religious texts. This trend away from 'poetic' texts at lower levels of hermeneutical training may help to explain why the texts that most closely approximated to the Averroistic model of literary reception – the morally complex and ethically difficult writings of Ovid, for example, which required discrimination and imaginative engagement from their audience in deciding which characters were to be 'praised' and which 'blamed'– increasingly came to be read, assessed, contested and rewritten by readers, commentators and imitators outside the conventional venues and frameworks of academic training.

The technical discipline and psychological credibility of the genuine poetic experience had its reward in the Averroistic version of *katharsis* (very different from the Greek), 'which arouses in the soul certain passions which move it to pity or fear or to other like passions which the representation arouses and stimulates by what it makes virtuous men imagine about virtue and corruption' (ed. Minio-Paluello, p. 47; tr. Hardison, *Classical and Medieval Literary Criticism*, p. 354). The different kinds of representation explored by Hermann/Averroes are different strategies of affective engagement. In texts which operate by means of poetic affectivity and the 'imaginative syllogism', the reader is involved in a proactive response of appraisal as opposed to the reactive response of acquiescence usually sought by a rhetorical discourse. The nature of the moral experience being presented in poetry will be more complicated and in need of interpretation against personal moral and ethical values and principles already encoded in the estimative faculties of the audience. Thus the relationship between poetry and real life is indirect. Poetry operates by similitude. The success of poetry depends on the degree to which it achieves a plausible likeness of human issues, situations and moral dilemmas. But the process of assimilating the similitudes, of decoding the issues at work in a particular text requires deep psychological engagement from the moral being of the reader or hearer. This is the essence of thirteenth-century poetic theory. Such ideas found their ready echo in contemporary faculty psychology and in the moral poetics of philosophers like Roger Bacon. Considered together, the thirteenth-century reception of the *Poetics* and other contemporary developments in literary theory and practice offer initially parallel and ultimately converging traces of a new psychological subtlety in examining the force and impact of 'powerful words'.

The Parisian interest in the Averroistic *Poetics*, evinced by Bacon and by references in Aquinas, is confirmed by the existence of a major recension of the text probably undertaken there late in the thirteenth century. The recension sought to distinguish the supposedly authentic Aristotelian material from the Averroistic gloss, and omitted the largely grammatical section towards the end. It is the source of most of the aphorisms and *sententiae* from the *Poetics* which survive in miscellanies and *florilegia* after this date. The survival of a set of glosses, of extra-curricular lectures given by Bartholomew of Bruges in 1307, and of an anonymous *quaestio* on the nature of poetry also testify that Paris was a centre – perhaps the only one – of interest in the *Poetics*. The fact that Bartholomew's lectures were additional and extra-curricular shows that the text was not part of any formal syllabus. Nevertheless, when taken in parallel with the sustained thirteenth-century study of the psychology of man's response to imaginative stimuli found in exegetical, mystical and pastoral writing, the evidence for study of the *Poetics* reinforces the sense of an increasingly sophisticated understanding of the repertoires of literary persuasion, particularly in the French intellectual circles that educated Europe's academic elite.

This later Parisian study of the *Poetics* continues to focus on the ethical force and imaginative stimulus of poetic texts. *Delectatio*, the ambiguous partner of Horace's *utilitas*, is shown to be an appropriate part of the literary experience because it engages the imagination and estimative faculty. Bartholomew assembles examples from elsewhere in the Aristotelian corpus to explore the workings of the rational soul and its susceptibility to imaginative manipulation (ed. Dahan, 'Notes et textes', pp. 220–39). Rhetoric persuades while poetry teaches by imagination or supposition (*existimatio*). Rhetoric is a communal form; poetry, which is private, is philosophically a lesser activity but potentially more powerful. The imagination is provoked or invited to assessment or moral judgement by the images or similitudes used in the representation, and by the riddling element of the indirect and metaphorical modes of expression typically used by poetry.

The anonymous *quaestio* is even more explicit on the distinctions between rhetoric and poetic. Poetry constitutes a special part of logic and operates on a more personal and intuitive level than rhetoric:

Because everyone has most trust in his own instinctive estimations and relies particularly on his own imaginings, poetic discourse or poetic syllogism is therefore called by the Philosopher 'imaginative'.   (tr. Minnis and Scott, p. 309)

Rhetoric lays down guidelines in relation to actions which are subject to justice, and to compulsion, but poetry [does so] in relation to acts that are of a more voluntary nature. . . . The purpose of rhetoric is to make the opposing side abandon vice by vanquishing it. But the purpose of poetry is to win its listeners to the practice of virtue through praise and encouragement.

(tr. Minnis and Scott, pp. 311–12)

Rhetoric aims at the common good and because this is more important than the individual good it preceded poetry in the classification of the logical sciences (i.e. the *Organon*). Poetry is a special kind of logic because it 'produces a certain weak attraction which merely inclines someone to desire something or to avoid something'. Nevertheless it has particular merit because it is 'more applicable to moral realities' (tr. Minnis and Scott, pp. 313, 311). The affective force of poetry justifies its use for the exploration of moral issues, therefore, but only if the fundamental principles of ethics are already encoded in the intellect of its audience. It is not a mode of instruction; it is a mode of catalysis.

These turn-of-the-century Parisian texts, and the widespread circulation of aphorisms and commonplaces from the recension in *florilegia* throughout Europe in the fourteenth century, suggest that, although the *Poetics* did not change the way the thirteenth century thought about poetry, it was sufficiently consonant with emergent patterns of thought about poetic discourse for it to be quarried and commented on: *ars poetica est ars logicalis* (see Boggess, '*Poetics*', pp. 285, 291, 292, 293). It is indeed questionable whether the later fourteenth- and fifteenth-century pre-eminence of Horace's *Ars poetica* as *the* benchmark art of poetry for the humanists could have been achieved without the implicit recognition in earlier thirteenth-century commentaries that Horace's teachings were developments of an essentially affective and ultimately Aristotelian view of poetry.

Copying of manuscripts of Horace's *Ars poetica* increased dramatically after 1300. At this time there are signs of scholarly attempts to blend the poetic precepts of Horace and Aristotle. The treatise on poetry by the Swede Matthew of Linköping (now Uppsala University, MS C.521, fols. 169r–172r), who was to become one of the supporters of St Bridget of Sweden, was composed in Paris between 1318 and 1332.

Matthew attempted an artful synthesis of the prescriptive portions of the medieval *artes poetriae* (themselves often Horatian in scope and style) and the theoretical sections of the *Poetics* and Horace's *Ars poetica*. Starting from the Horatian analogy between the skill of a painter and that of a poet, who delights the soul by making us imagine a thing according to its (recognisable and true) characteristics (*proprietates*; ed. and tr. Bergh, pp. 46–7), he focuses in particular on three Aristotelian terms, *representacio*, *tonus* and *metrum*, which, he argues, distinguish poetry from other modes of discourse. Rhetoric uses prosaic words in persuasion and enthymemes. Poetry is characterised by visualisation (*representacionem*) in verse (ed. and tr. Bergh, pp. 54–5). Matthew's modest gift for summary and encapsulation rests on an informing sense of the ethical basis of all poetry: poetic eulogy is something said in verse that incited to virtues ('Est igitur laus poetica sermo metricus incitativus ad virtutes'; ed. and tr. Bergh, pp. 54–5).

The Horatian bias in Matthew's reading of poetic theory is apparent in his selection for particular attention of those sections of the Latin version of the Averroistic text that deal with the plausibility of the poetic experience: *consuetudo*, *credulitas* and *consideracio*. *Consideracio* resolves moral doubt in the audience, not by reason or persuasion, but by certain and credible representations so that the subject-matter does not seem to have been made up ('ut non credatur res ficta esse'; ed. and tr. Bergh, pp. 64–5). Harking back to earlier rhetorical theories, he says that belief (*credulitas*) can be ensured by the paying careful attention to the circumstances (the rhetorical *circumstantiae*) of both the events and characters of his poem and, almost more importantly, of those who read or hear the poem. In this Matthew is reflecting the awareness in medieval commentaries on the *Ars poetica* that Horace focused on the need to target specific audiences in order to capture and hold their attention and goodwill. In his discussion of *tonus* Matthew includes irony and a range of different poetic moods and passions, all of which intensify the poem's impact on the soul of the audience. Intonation, according to Averroes, prepares the mind to a fitter reception of versified visualisation ('Tonus secundum Auerroym preparat animam, ut apcius recipiat representacionem in metro factam'; ed. and tr. Bergh, pp. 68–9). Under metre, he addresses the double narrative order (natural and artificial) traditionally discussed in Horatian commentary and in other poetic commentaries. His prescriptive rules for genre, style, augmentation and abbreviation come mainly from that fourteenth-century bestseller the *Poetria nova*, with examples mainly from Virgil and, less often, Ovid. But his regular and extensive appeal to Horace in the more rhetorical sections dealing with narrative decorum and the needs of audiences adds a valuably pragmatic slant to his theoretical discussion. Such synthetic and sympathetic medieval readings of Horace and Aristotle finally make accessible and explicit much of the original intention of both writers that had been clouded by the circumstances of their transmission.

However, it was in Italy in the fourteenth and fifteenth centuries that the most significant reassessment and realignment of poetic theory was to take place. The precepts of Cicero and Horace were allowed to resonate with and against those of the *Poetics* as Italian theorists hammered out their syncretist views of the role of the poet. Particularly striking is the evidence of extensive Italian interest in the *Poetria nova*. The commentary on Geoffrey of Vinsauf by the Paduan Pace of Ferrara (Assisi, Biblioteca Communale, MS 309, fols. 1r–74v) blends many of the precepts of the *Ars poetica* with many of the categories and ideas of the Averroist *Poetics* in its analysis of Geoffrey's poem. According to Pace, the end of poetry is 'to delight by trifles and fictions [*ludicris et fictionibus*], or to edify by morality or to do both at the same' (fol. 1v). In support he cites both Horace on *prodesse et delectare* and the key Averroistic description of the end of poetry as to praise or blame (*laudare vel vituperare*). He is similarly synthetic in his discussion of the triple *utilitas* of the *Poetria nova*. First it teaches the art of poetry. Secondly it teaches *artificiosa eloquentia*. Thirdly, its utility is *delectatio*, which may be had from the ornateness of the words and the music or harmony (*simphonia*) of the poetry as well as from the beauty of the teaching (*ex sententiarum pulcritudine*; fol. 2r). This eclectically subtle handling of critical terminology is characteristic of many humanist treatises on poetics and poetic theory. The blending of rhetoric and poetic, the reapplication of Cicero's oratorical dicta to poetry and the creative synthesis of different strands of theoretical discourse (not least the Neoplatonic and Augustinian) characterise the theoretical writings of Boccaccio, Petrarch and Salutati. But it might be argued that much of it was already there in embryo in the earlier tradition of commentary on and imitation of Horace's *Ars poetica*. Boccaccio's blending of the inspirational frenzy of Plato with the rhetorical training and exercise of Horace, for example, resonates throughout the rest of the Italian Renaissance, surfacing emphatically in the Neoplatonic realignments of Cristoforo Landino's Ciceronian poetics. Humanist attitudes look back to the rhetorical readings of Horace developed in the twelfth and thirteenth centuries: indeed the plausible attribution of the 'Materia' commentary on the *Ars poetica* to Paul of Perugia (d. 1348), a friend of Boccaccio, was only seriously challenged by the recent discovery of twelfth-century copies of that long-lived and influential work, which Boccaccio may have used in his own defence of poetry.[7]

---

[7] See Friis-Jensen, '*Ars poetica*: Addenda', and 'Horace and Early Writers'; Anderson, *Before 'The Knight's Tale'*, p. 7.

Salutati's knowledge of the *Poetics* is reflected in his concern to harmonise his view of the poet as a good man skilled in speech ('vir bonus dicendi peritus'), reclaiming the Ciceronian definition from the rhetor, with his almost twelfth-century sense of poetic allegory: 'Thus the poet is a good man skilled in the art of praise and blame, who by means of a material and figurative speech, hides truths under the mysterious narration of some event' (*De laboribus Herculis* 1.63; cit. Greenfield, *Poetics*, pp. 140–1). The linking of Aristotelian praise and blame with the Horatian ideals of delight and instruction brings out explicitly in a humanist context the potential of poetry for ethical exploration and engagement which had been implicitly present in earlier discussions of some of the most challenging texts to confront medieval commentators and theorists. Cicero's *Brutus* (49.185, 188) remarks that the *orator* teaches, delights and moves an audience. The medieval cross-fertilisation of Horace and Aristotle arrived at the same conclusion in its attempts to define and refine the distinctions between poetry and rhetoric.

3. Reading for the sense: Florilegia, friars and the rise of the compiler

To answer the question 'How were Ovid and Virgil read?' requires a knowledge of how medieval readers were trained and of the kinds of literary competence they acquired, and an understanding of contemporary thinking about poetic theory. But it also needs an appreciation of the forms and formats in which they would have been exposed to those texts. The medieval perception and understanding of classical texts and authors depends crucially on the cultural and material circumstances of their transmission and dissemination. The history of literary criticism is thus not just a history of literary attitudes and literary theory. It must also be, at least in part, a history of literary reception. Where readers encounter a text affects how they read it. The formal procedures and ethical assumptions of the medieval *florilegia* and compilations, which sheltered and transmitted so many fragments of classical literature and learning, had a formative impact on how their contents were understood.

The thirteenth century marks the beginning of the age of the compilers and a watershed in the developing technologies of information-retrieval and hermeneutics. The systematisation of knowledge, and the development of more sophisticated aids to study, which had begun in the twelfth century with the production of copies of Gratian's *Decretum* and the *Sentences* of Peter Lombard, gained renewed impetus in the thirteenth century with the emergence of scholastic *lectio* as the dominant academic mode of confronting a text. It also had a significant impact on the transmission and reception of classical literature.

The eclipse of Chartres, Orléans and the other liberal arts schools as sites of innovation and scholarship has been overstated. Many of the scholars labouring at the thirteenth-century frontiers of knowledge in the Paris schools still relied, wittingly or unwittingly, on the fruits of Orléans' earlier intellectual pre-eminence and continuing intellectual innovation and refinement. Nowhere is this more apparent than in the field of *florilegia* and compilations, whether in codifying the accumulated wisdom of the Orléans masters commenting on Ovid into the great Vulgate commentary on the *Metamorphoses*, or in preserving and transmitting precious fragments of the classical heritage to a wider readership through literary *florilegia*. By the end of the twelfth century, there are already signs of increasing specialisation in the production of Orléans *florilegia*. The *Florilegium angelicum*, for example, moves away from the typical *modus agendi* of a monastic *florilegium* (the collection and presentation of moral sentences and precepts) towards an anthology of extracts from ancient and patristic letters and speeches, chosen for their eloquence and geared for use in dictaminal training. The important dictaminal schools in Orléans could have provided both the sources for such a compilation and a ready market and readership among the students being trained for careers in episcopal chancelleries. Vocational training in eloquence offered an important stimulus to the circulation and anthologising of some rare and unusual texts in the twelfth and thirteenth centuries, just as it would do later in the Italian schools and chancelleries of the Trecento.

The *Florilegium gallicum*, another Orléans collection, combines short moralising or aphoristic quotations of a kind familiar from the texts in the developing grammar-school curriculum. Substantial guidance for the budding writer is provided by generous extracts from Horace's *Ars poetica* and by more theoretical discussion drawn from the *Rhetorica ad Herennium*, Quintilian's *Institutio oratoria* and Cicero's *De oratore*. The emergent popularity of Claudian is reflected in generous quotations from his works, while interest in specific genres such as *planctus* and panegyric are also catered for. The set-piece descriptions of epic poetry illustrate and exemplify some of the genre's technical demands and stylistic decorums, while the sustained interest in personification found in many of the longer extracts probably also reflects contemporary taste and emphases. Perhaps surprisingly, mythology does not play a significant part in the extracts; less surprisingly, careful editing removes morally exceptionable material from writers such as Tibullus.

In these early Orléans anthologies, the *ordinatio* of the material is less fully articulated by headings and finding aids than it will become in later thirteenth-century collections. Although works are grouped together by genre, works by a single author are also usually gathered together and this blurring of category distinctions reduces the ease of casual consultation. But the *Florilegium gallicum* is significant less for its scientific and formal excellence than for its vital role in transmitting rare classical texts: Valerius Flaccus; Ovid's Epistle of Sappho in the *Heroides*; Tibullus and Petronius; and the *Laus Pisonis* of which it preserves the only surviving text. Later copies of the *Florilegium gallicum* or of selections from it are augmented by the addition of extracts from the elegies of Propertius and material drawn from contemporary verse like the *Pamphilus*, *Geta* and *Tobias*. Compilers of later *florilegia* turned to it as a rich resource rather than as a role model, and it was used extensively to supplement the exposure to the genres of classical poetry offered by the verse reading-texts of the grammar-school syllabus. At least eleven thirteenth-century manuscripts containing permutations of the syllabus of school-texts also contain borrowings from the *Florilegium gallicum*.

This dual process of remodelling and penetration into the school curriculum suggests that the *Florilegium gallicum* was a continuously evolving source of teaching material for composition, imitation and secular literary analysis. The existence of condensed versions offering shorter and simpler extracts and explanatory glosses of a linguistic kind suggest its use at elementary stages of the arts curriculum. Other manuscripts suggest that the resources of the *Florilegium gallicum* might offer wider literary horizons for those outgrowing the restrictions of the syllabus. Similarly, later restructurings of the *Florilegium angelicum* supplied it with explicitly moral subject-headings or indices, or highlighted its moral potential, or enhanced its comprehensiveness by the addition of new extracts from school authors and their more advanced colleagues Horace, Virgil, Persius, Juvenal and Prudentius.

Whatever level of sophistication pupils brought to these kinds of anthologies, their influence (and perhaps the books themselves) remained with them throughout their own writing careers. Many of Gerald of Wales' Latin prose quotations come from the *Florilegium angelicum*; John of Salisbury's prose is studded with florilegial quotations and allusions; Peter of Blois seems to have used the *Florilegium gallicum*; Peter Cantor's *Verbum abbreviatum* relies heavily on the *Florilegium gallicum* or a related or adapted version. This influence continued into the Renaissance: Petrarch's Tibullus allusions may derive from the *Florilegium gallicum*; Boccaccio's first-hand textual knowledge in the *Genealogia deorum gentilium* seems to have extended only to Virgil, Ovid, Cicero and Seneca, and some of this may itself be florilegial.

Florilegia 'play a role in the process by which favourite quotations come to be detached from their context and then even from their author's name, to pass into common currency as pieces of proverbial wisdom' (Burton, *Classical Poets*, p. 41). For many thirteenth-century readers and writers, they were probably the primary context in which they encountered the aphoristic wisdom, stylistic virtuosity and generic range of the large number of classical authors whose works were not otherwise read or taught as part of the arts syllabus. Such exposure left an indelible mark on the literary tastes and compositional procedures of the period. It also affected the perception of classical writers. The systematic deprivation of context, inherent in the florilegial process and more rigorously applied in more systematic forms of compilatory activity, sustained and encouraged the multifarious characterisations attributed in this period to classical authors as diverse as Ovid and Seneca. Deprived of the tone and texture of their original literary context, dicta and *proverbia* could be massaged into outlandish and contradictory significations or else, stripped of their originally satiric and subversive force, could be safely deployed as part of a carefully spiked battery of moral *sententiae*. When Christine de Pizan complained of 'the glosses of Orléans which destroyed the texts' (*Le Débat*, ed. Hicks, p. 144; tr. Baird and Kane, p. 140), she had in mind a way of approaching texts typified by the *florilegia*, compilations and integumental allegorisations that came to typify that city's schools.

In a parallel development, driven by the theological priorities of the new orders of friars, the increasing academic study of preaching and the pastoral care in the thirteenth-century universities encouraged the absorption of earlier literary materials into preaching manuals or more sophisticated compilations. The Cistercian *Flores paradysii*, for example, originally contained mainly patristic precepts, but its subsequent recensions included material from both the *Florilegium angelicum* and the *Florilegium gallicum* and from the *Disticha Catonis*. Their aphoristic and moral resources, conveniently detached from their original pagan contexts, were readily redeployed as *materia predicabilis*, easily accessed by means of a detailed subject index. The resultant mixture of pagan and Christian wisdom harks back to the *florilegia* of the twelfth century in content but is resolutely of its period in the sophistication and complexity of its referencing and retrieval apparatus.

The intellectual architecture of the schools of Orléans was remodelled in the lecture halls and pulpits of Paris in a modern and more amicable version of the *spoliatio Egyptorum*. John of Wales, a classicising friar of the thirteenth century, was able finally to quote from a complete text of Aulus Gellius only once Richard de Fournival's copy had arrived at the Sorbonne from Orléans in 1272. Working in the early fourteenth century, the Franciscan Thomas of Ireland compiled his *Manipulus florum* using the resources of the Sorbonne library (its quotations often occur in the same order as the source works were found on the library shelves). It is indebted to the older Orléanais learning directly (in that Thomas used Richard de Fournival's copy of the *Florilegium angelicum*) and indirectly (in that Thomas also used the *Flores paradysii*, which itself draws on the *Florilegium angelicum*).

The snapshot of classical literary values and culture offered by such anthologies was inevitably clouded and distorted. Authority lies in the worth of the aphorism rather than the status or worth of its author. *Auctoritas: id est sententia digna imitatione* (Hugutio of Pisa, *Magnae derivationes*, s.v. *augeo*). In contexts such as these, *intentio auctoris*, despite its resilience as an *accessus* heading, is in hermeneutic terms increasingly defined, supplemented and supplanted by *arbitrium lectoris* (the free choice of the reader) or even more remotely by what we might term the *intentio compilatoris*. For in the land of the compiler, *ordinatio* is king. No matter how much deference is paid to the authority of the sources; no matter how many topoi defer authority away from the compiler to the texts, the *a priori* ordering of material under topical or moral headings imposes an external interpretative context on the collected materials. When this process of selection operates under an implicit ethical imperative, as it invariably does at this period, such compilations have a material impact on the period's perceptions of pagan Antiquity and its literature.

It is no accident, therefore, that the king of the compilers, Vincent of Beauvais (*c.* 1194–1264), an early member of the new preaching order of the Dominicans, is also the king of the ordinators. Vincent was appointed lector to the Cistercian abbey of Royaumont near Paris in 1246, where he came into close contact with Louis IX who supported him financially and may have facilitated his visits to French libraries in search of texts. He also received help in collecting material from the Cistercians and employed a body of research assistants. His major work, the hugely ambitious *Speculum maius*, draws widely and deeply on the known writings of over 450 authors and consists of a *Speculum naturale* (extant in two versions from *c.* 1245–6 and 1256–7), a *Speculum doctrinale* and a *Speculum historiale* (extant in five recensions produced from *c.* 1244–5 until after 1254). The project was further augmented at the end of the thirteenth century by an apocryphal *Speculum morale*.

The clarity of Vincent's exposition of the theoretical assumptions behind his *modus agendi* in the *Speculum maius* meant that he contributed more than any other individual to the elevation of *compilatio* into a prestigious literary genre. The traditional florilegial justification – the facilitating of learning by gathering flowers from the garden of scholarship – is toughened by a new emphasis that the *auctoritas* of the works included in the *Speculum* is not vested in Vincent himself but remains with the original works. His role, he modestly claims, is limited to the ordering of the parts. His sophisticated prologue (known as the *Apologia actoris* or *Liber apologeticus*, which passed through several recensions to match the development of the book it introduced) seeks to define the stance and strategy of the compiler by contrast with those characteristic of the *auctor*. Whereas an *auctor* bears the responsibility for what he has written Vincent the compiler roundly disclaims responsibility for the veracity of what he has merely reported or repeated (the verb used is *recitare*) from his sources, even when those sources may be apocryphal. The *auctoritas* (and the moral responsibility) is the authors'; the compiler's task is to extract and organise the *auctoritates*.

> For this work is new, and yet at the same time old, short and at the same time long. It is old in terms of its subject-matter and authority [*auctoritas*], but new in its compilation [*compilatio*] and the way in which it puts together the various parts [*partium aggregatio*]. It is short in that it condenses many words into a narrow compass, but yet long because of the vastness of the material treated. . . . [T]his work is not in the true sense of the word mine, but is the work of those authors from whose writings I have put together almost the whole book. For I have added little or nothing that is my own. So the authority [*auctoritas*] is theirs, while only the ordering of the various parts [*partium ordinatio*] is ours.

> (*Apologia*, cap. 4; ed. von den Brincken, pp. 469–70)

This is unproblematic in relation to scriptural and patristic sources, which have a clearly accepted authority. But the position is more complicated in regard to apocryphal, anonymous and secular pagan texts of dubious and shifting moral authority, where Vincent's disavowal of responsibility is frankly disingenuous. Although there can be little doubt that many classical authors were deemed to merit and possess independent moral authority in this period, the most common hermeneutical posture attributed this authority only after considerable cosmetic surgery to their works, and required a certain economy with the truth in relation to their lives and careers. The deemed ethical intent of most classical writings is a direct reflection or mirror image of a set of prior moral expectations and conventional interpretative gestures on the part of their medieval readership. To adapt Walter Ong's dictum, the (medieval) audience's (classical) writer is always a fiction, the function of a desire to create a synthetic ethical discourse from the available resources and in line with prevailing moral and spiritual criteria.

While subscribing to the ethical fiction, Vincent is equally aware of, and anxious to facilitate, the processes of assessment and probation that reading such material necessarily and properly entails. To do so, he drew on recent scholastic developments in *ordinatio* and layout that were designed to preserve textual integrity, to assist navigation and information retrieval, and to signpost layers of text and commentary in complicated authoritative texts, such as the increasingly sophisticated contemporary collections of canon law. Vincent states that, rather than placing the names of his authors in the margins (as habitually done in copies of the glossed Psalter, the Pauline Epistles and the *Sentences* of Peter Lombard), he has decided to follow the mise-en-page of copies of Gratian. He has placed the names within the body of the text (*inter lineas ipsas*: *Apologia*, cap. 3; ed. von den Brincken, p. 468) so that they will not be easily displaced in scribal copying as they often are in cases of marginal citation. Many surviving copies of the *Speculum* also regularly rubricate authors' names, enabling the reader to identify and assess the authority of the extract. In addition, views, comments and interpretations added by Vincent to the extracts (and for which he is prepared to take responsibility) are headed *actor* to distinguish them from reported material. This is a technique also developed from copies of Gratian, where Gratian's personal comments – the so-called *dicta Gratiani* – are distinguished from the rest of the text by paraph marks, and from the Cistercian Helinand of Froidmont's *Chronicon*, perhaps Vincent's major theoretical and practical source, where the compiler's own comments are headed *auctor*.

The compiler, declared St Bonaventure in his famous account of the *quadruplex modus faciendi librum*, 'writes the materials of others, adding, but nothing of his own' (*In primum librum sententiarum*, proem, qu. 1; *Bonaventurae opera*, 1, p. 14). Vincent was careful about giving credit to the 'others' when it was due, and, when he did add something 'of his own', he carefully labelled it as such. Anticipating the charge that he was over-presumptuous in daring to include all the separate branches of knowledge and of the arts in his work, Vincent declared his method (*modus*) was not that of a teacher or one who treats a subject fully (*tractator*) but of an anthologist (*excerptor*) (*Apologia*, cap. 8; ed. von den Brincken, p. 477). He explicitly points out that he has made no attempt to harmonise the conflicting views expressed by many of his *auctoritates*. Therefore he leaves it to the judgement of the reader which *sententia* should be adhered to in any conflict of authorities. Echoing St Paul, he exhorts: 'Omnia probate; quod bonum est tenete' (I Thess. 5:21: *Apologia*, cap. 9; ed. von den Brincken, p. 479).

But, while recognising that the onus on responsible literary consumption rests with the reader, Vincent's classical authorities have, of course, already served their probation in his own assessment and ordering of them. His ostensibly non-authoritative arrangement operates according to a powerful submerged agenda about the worth and utility of classical literature. Vincent is a 'strong' reader, albeit a self-effacing one. In his pedagogical treatise *De eruditione filiorum nobilium*, composed between 1246 and 1249 for the young Prince Philip of France (and significant for the whole tradition of 'Mirrors for Princes' through its influence on Giles of Rome's *De regimine principum*), he reveals his attitude to the riches of pagan Antiquity. His work is compiled from the writings of saints and 'men of prudence', and he argues that Christians may properly read all kinds of books, citing Jerome's dictum: 'if we find something useful in them, we convert it to our doctrine' (cap. 16; ed. Steiner, p. 58). However, Vincent deploys the weighty dogma of Gratian against those who read secular books 'ad voluptatem', delighting in the figments of poets and their verbal ornaments. But those same books may still be read, so long as the reader's intent is to despise the errors of the gentiles. Provided that such texts can be converted for the use of 'sacred learning', their study may be praiseworthy. Indeed, going beyond Gratian, Vincent argues that many writings of the gentiles are consonant with Christian dogma (cap. 16; ed. Steiner, pp. 59–62). Vincent's principles of reading classical texts seem, on the face of it, to drive a wedge between the twin Horatian ideals of delight and utility, but he emphasises the reader's responsibility to convert the old texts to the new doctrine through the kind of probing ethical engagement which was consonant with medieval understanding of Horace's teaching.

The *Speculum maius* reveals the same principles at work in its selection of classical texts for inclusion. Subsuming almost all the *Florilegium gallicum*, Vincent and his team of research assistants assimilated other classical texts in excerpts apparently drawn from copies of their *originalia* ('extat apud nos' is his usual formulation); yet more come via another literary intermediary (such as Aulus Gellius, Seneca, Augustine, Jerome and Helinand of Froidmont) and so have already been partly predigested. In selecting from the *originalia*, he is swayed by the pithy and the memorable, praising Cato, for example, for his usefully brief and sententious couplets (*Speculum historiale* 5.107). When confronted with ten works by Ovid, he selects 'especially those in which morality may be seen' (*Speculum historiale* 6.106–22). Vincent's readers, therefore, have an inevitably highly coloured perception of such writers and of their works. Given the enormous influence of this compilation, it is perhaps hardly surprising that the art of imaginative and inductive biography of classical writers continued to flourish in the following centuries. The sanitised and predigested view of, for example, Ovid presented in such works offered little preparation for the hermeneutical challenges facing a reader of the original texts.

Like his Cistercian predecessors and sources, and in a gesture imitated and repeated by many later compilers, Vincent describes the *Speculum* as an aid to preachers, putting that at the head of an ambitious list of intended functions, which includes most of the newer scholastic modes of academic discourse: reading, disputation, explanation and explication (*Apologia*, cap. 4; ed. von den Brincken, p. 469). His work reveals or acknowledges the ideological influence of previous compilers and theorists of learning: Isidore of Seville's *Etymologiae*; Hugh of St Victor's *Didascalicon*; Richard of St Victor's *Liber exceptionum*; and the work of Hugh of Fleury. The new compendium has been ordered to accumulate proof of the dogmas of faith; to instruct morals; to excite the will to devotion; or to expound the mysteries of Holy Scriptures. It is emphatically not a classicising compilation in the intention of its creator.

But at least one fourteenth-century reader found a different and less pragmatic use for the *Speculum historiale*, the most successful part of the whole work: Jean de Hautfuney, the King's Procurator at the papal Curia and subsequently bishop of Avranches from 1331 to 1358 (*Tabula* to the *Speculum historiale*, ed. Paulmier[-Foucart]). The work's chronological format allowed relatively easy access to its information about the ancient gods and the *vitae* of classical authors. But the sophisticated apparatus of the *Speculum* was topic- and doctrine-centred. Jean's interest was more literary: he wanted to identify the sayings of particular authors and the authors of particular sayings. So he added a further table identifying *sententiae* by author and vice versa.

By allowing systematic access to the writings of a particular author, Jean facilitates the subversion of Vincent's topical framework, reaching back beyond his *ordinatio partium* to permit the reassembly of the scattered shards of those fragmentary and unique witnesses preserved in the *Florilegium gallicum*. Jean has taken to heart Vincent's use of the Pauline dictum 'Omnia probate: quod bonum est tenete' and applied it in a gesture of readerly emancipation. Even so, his liberated classical *sententiae* inevitably retain the colouring of the compilation's ethical filter. While this may represent another example of the classicising tastes of the fourteenth century, it could equally well illustrate a mode of reading such compilations for their literary content that may have been an important, if usually unacknowledged, part of their utility and delight. He is unlikely to have been alone in so doing. The *arbitrium lectoris* remains a powerful and unpredictable force in the medieval appropriation of classical literature. Nowhere is this more apparent than in responses to the writings of Ovid.

4. Reading under the covers: Ovid

The subtlety and elusiveness of Ovid's literary *personae* posed perhaps the most significant challenge to the hermeneutical systems of the medieval commentary tradition. Disapproval and a desire to control the perceived wilfulness and immorality of the Ovidian text by masterful moralisation were common responses. But his writings did provoke some commentators to a more flexible and innovative approach to problems of authorial intent, utility and philosophical justification, particularly in their responses to Ovid's major work, the *Metamorphoses*. Along the way this led to a sustained and often fanciful attempt to explicate the circum-stances of the composition of the different texts and the order of their writing. This was partly out of a desire to account for the existence of conflicting narrative tones and inconsistent narrative *personae* within the corpus. The task was in one sense complicated but in another sense sim-plified by the absence of ancient scholia on Ovid. This allowed him to be subjected to a wholesale inductive biography more extensive than that for any other author. Despite this sustained exegetical activity, 'Ovidian poetics remained obstinately resistant to closure, refused to be reducible to neat critical aphorism. This was of course, a wonderfully creative space for a writer to inhabit' (Minnis, *Magister amoris*, p. 12). The medieval Ovid spawned fertile subcultures of imitation and appropriation, leading the fourteenth-century backlash in the *Antiovidianus* to complain that Ovid wrote nothing that was not false and that his works separated the pious from piety.

Such protests at the manifestly unsuitable nature of many of the poems for study by young people had been recurrent from the twelfth century onwards. Despite this, omnibus editions of Ovid's collected works began to appear and circulate in the twelfth and thirteenth centuries. Some of these collections included the *Metamorphoses* and represented the final stage in Ovid's apotheosis as a canonical poet. His literary influence was enormous. It may even have been greater than that of Virgil, who was deferred to, respected, cited and emulated, but who generated much less new criticism in this period. Until the proto-humanist revival, Virgil was 'un dieu, main un dieu crépusculaire' (Bourgain, 'Virgile', p. 187), described by Dante as 'one grown faint from too much silence' (*Inferno* 1.1, 62–3). By contrast, inside and outside the curriculum, Ovid was read, studied, expounded and, above all, imitated. Love him or loathe him, Ovid was not a writer who could be ignored.

Part of the attraction was his generic virtuosity. The spasmodic and occasional incorporation of the *Ars amatoria* or the *Remedia amoris* into the canon of school reading-texts, for example, suggests that Ovid's provi-sion of precepts and *sententiae*, however ironically intended by the writer who styled himself the 'preceptor amoris' (*Ars* 1.17), was welcomed and appropriated by preceptors who may not always have been less subtle and self-aware than Ovid himself. Hugo von Trimberg described Ovid as joyful and elegant or well made, filled in various ways with the flowers of meaning ('letus et facetus / sentenciarum floribus / multimodis repletus'; *Registrum multorum auctorum* 1.124–5; ed. Langosch, p. 164). *Accessus* on the *Remedia amoris* commonly assert that it originated from Ovid's repentance at the effects of the *Ars amatoria* and that it could have a prophylactic as well as curative function: 'He prescribes just like a doctor. For a good doctor gives medicine to the sick to heal them, and to the healthy so that they may escape illness' (tr. Minnis and Scott, p. 25). Commentaries variously recommend the *Remedia* because it 'gives precepts whereby it may remove unlawful love' (tr. Minnis and Scott, p. 25) or praise its utility in restraining the immoderate ardour of our minds by remembering its teachings (ed. Przychocki, '*Accessus Ovidiani*', p. 101). With no apparent sense of incongruity, Nicholas Trevet quotes the *Remedia* in his commentary on Boethius' *De consolatione philosophiae* as part of his discussion of sloth and *luxuria*, clearly valuing the epigrammatic directness of his source.

Arnulf of Orléans (*fl.* 1175), whose teachings cast a long shadow across the Middle Ages through a sequence of genetically related Orléanais commentaries on Ovid, saw the *Ars amatoria* as teaching rules and precepts, the knowledge of things that should and should not be adhered to in love, while, he argued, the *Remedia* teaches precepts and shows things that both instruct and woo away from love. The ambiguity of supplied intention shows the thinness of the ethical ice on which the commentators were skating, but it also shows how easily and readily Ovid could be assimilated both to contemporary discourses on love (in Latin and in the vernacular) and to contemporary preceptive attitudes in schools. French vernacular poetry relished the playfulness and elusiveness of the love epistles, while they could be presented more cautiously for the schoolroom. The early-thirteenth-century *Bursarii Ovidianorum* of William of Orléans, a commentator much influenced by Arnulf, seeks to explain *cruces* in the text of Ovid for the sake of the purse (*bursa*) of his students' memory. Avoiding allegory or sophisticated Christianisation, this initiation into the world of Ovid deploys William's philological skill and historical knowledge in an unsophisticated and simple way. The modest intellectual ambitions of the *Bursarii* probably reflect their position in the curriculum. Certainly his citations from Statius, 'Theodulus', Juvenal, Claudian and the *Disticha Catonis* suggest a text where grammar-school interests are uppermost. The most popular school-commentary on the *Remedia* is similarly indebted to the accumulated wisdom of several generations of Orléans commentaries.

One thirteenth-century commentator emphatically denies that the *Ars amatoria* is scurrilous in purpose (a manual of pickup and courtship techniques, as it is sometimes described). It is, rather, a prescriptive art 'de amore ad artis compositionem', presumably by analogy with Horace's *Ars poetria* (Paris, Bibliothèque nationale de France, MS Lat. 7994; ed. Ghisalberti, 'Medieval Biographies', pp. 45–8). According to this perspective, the intention of the *Remedia* is technical rather than ethical: its utility derives from its collection of skilful precepts on the art of love. This somewhat sophistical justification illustrates the way some of the moral dilemmas surrounding these texts could be resolved. The *materia* of the text is not the behaviour it describes (and the effect it may have on its young and impressionable readers), argues a later commentary on the *Ars*, but rather the precepts it collects: a gap is being opened up between the treatment of the material by Ovid and the effect it has on its audience, which is itself beginning to be separated from Ovid's responsibility. Just as masters of grammar and rhetoric have those subjects as their *materia*, not the pupils they teach, so Ovid's aim in giving precepts is to encourage us to love wisely, but only in the sense of giving rules (Naples, Biblioteca Nazionale, MS V.D.52; ed. Ghisalberti, 'Medieval Biographies', pp. 58–9). This perception of Ovid is reflected in contemporary productions like the *De amore* of Andreas Capellanus and the *Liber facetus* (incipit: 'Moribus et vita'), which offer an intelligent, perceptive and often deeply ironic imitation of the sentential mode of the *Ars* and the *Remedia amoris* and often add to this a subtle awareness of the play of *personae* and voices in the Ovidian source. This awareness of ironic distance should not be underestimated when considering the products of contemporary vernacular or Latin Ovidianism such as the *Roman de la Rose*, *Pamphilus* or *Geta*. Indeed, the late-eleventh-century 'Ovidian sub-culture' among the lower ranks of monastic and cathedral schools, typified by the poems of Baudri of Bourgueil, suggests that Ovid was being read and imitated outside of the grammatical tradition in ways that liberated him from the moral and allegorical straitjacket of schoolroom reading and responded playfully and immediately to his literary techniques and to his amatory teasings.

A commentary found in several thirteenth-century manuscripts goes to the nub of the problem by explicitly identifying the tone of the *Amores*: 'in hoc opere ludicra tractat et iocosa' (ed. Hexter, *Medieval Schooling*, p. 224). And indeed the *Amores* did provoke a puzzled and ingenious set of responses from its medieval readers. 'In his *On the Art of Love* Ovid gives certain precepts to lovers to put them on their guard. But here, in the *Amores*, he puts these precepts into practice in his own case' (tr. Minnis and Scott, p. 28). The medieval title (or non-title), *Sine titulo*, is explained as resulting from his fear of provoking the anger of the Romans in general and the Emperor in particular. The subject is his mistress Corinna and his attempts to woo her. (The influence of this view of the *Amores* can be seen in Boccaccio's description of *Il Filostrato* – a poem to woo his own mistress – as 'senza titulo'.) In expounding his own love, Ovid displays a Horatian double intention: either to delight or to instruct. A later recension of this commentary effaces the Horatian balance: 'either to delight, as Horace says, or to commend himself to Corinna' (ed. Ghisalberti, 'Medieval Biographies', p. 46). The effect is interestingly to reinforce the pleasure at the expense of the useful instruction (the *utilitas* in both recensions is described as *delectatio*).

But then pleasure, like sex, is never far from the minds of medieval readers of Ovid: even some twelfth-century *accessus* see *delectatio* as the author's sole intention without the usual Horatian reflex. There may be something about the playfulness of the *Amores* in particular that encouraged commentators to see them in less narrowly ethical terms. 'Because love in Ovid is always a textual affair, [it] makes us see that ethical abstinence is itself a species of desire' (Ginsberg, p. 69). Indeed, the usual and commonplace ascription to ethics is quite commonly omitted in discussions of this text, while some introductions point to a more narrowly literary and rhetorical *utilitas*: that we should recognise in it verbal embellishments ('ornatus verborum') and an attractive word order ('pulchras positiones'); moreover the *Amores* was considered to offer a pleasurable introduction to the technique of *prosopopoeia* (tr. Minnis and Scott, p. 28).

The popularity of the exile elegies in the thirteenth-century – no doubt encouraged by their ready availability in the 'Vulgate' corpus of Ovidian texts – led to an increased interest in the *Tristia* and continuing attention to the *Epistulae ex Ponto*. The circumstances of Ovid's exile and his reactions to it are widely addressed in commentaries, many of which reveal a vivid capacity for authorial characterisation and inductive biography. The political motivations adduced for their composition allowed an element of cultural history and political theory to creep into the expositions (such as accounts of the four different kinds of banishment: inscription, proscription, exile and relegation). Furthermore the *Epistulae* contained a range of different stylistic techniques that could usefully be assimilated and imitated by readers interested in acquiring or enlarging dictaminal skills. Ovid's attempts at political persuasion offered object lessons of political rhetoric. Moral science or ethics feature only because each letter 'discusses behaviour': the real focus of attention often lies elsewhere. Occasionally a double *utilitas* can be drawn: the immediate use to which Ovid put the letters and the contemporary value of reading them, not least the lesson to other poets not to tempt fate in the same way (Munich, Bayerische Staatsbibliothek, MS Clm 14753; ed. Hexter, *Medieval Schooling*, p. 220). The *Ibis*, recognised as an imitation of Callimachus, was seen as a deeply personal exercise in cathartic invective whose utility lay in Ovid's need to let off steam, while the modern reader might benefit from knowledge of the *fabulae* compiled in the work and, presumably, from contact with an emergent but under-represented quasi-satirical sub-genre of invective.

The *Heroides* offered a more complicated challenge, partly because, as Ovid himself acknowledged, they were formally innovative. Some commentators suggested that he was imitating a Greek form of epistle, citing Hesiod as his exemplar. But more substantially they were of interest to medieval readers because they used the so-called 'dramatic' mode of speech, where the author speaks only in the *personae* of his characters. Moreover, like the more unwieldy *Metamorphoses*, they required the explication of a substantial body of mythological material. It is in commentaries on the *Heroides* that one finds the clearest evidence of medieval awareness of Ovid's narrative subtlety. Some *Heroides* commentaries draw distinctions between the intention of the speaking *persona* and that of Ovid, complicating the exegesis of the texts and demanding a reader who could engage with a narrative that was layered and split between different voices and purposes. The overarching moral purpose attributed to the author is balanced against and mediated through the strong sense of local intention and purpose ascribed to the individual *personae* locked into the circumstances of their particular emotional crises. The twelfth-century Tegernsee *accessus* draws together a striking range of possible intentions, culminating in a Horatian general intention for Ovid and recognising the differing motivations of the fictional authors:

His intention is to write about three kinds of love: foolish love, unchaste love, and demented love. . . . Another interpretation is that the intention of this book is to commend chaste love . . . or to attack unchaste love. . . . Another interpretation is that the intention is to praise some of those who write letters for their chastity, and to blame some for their unchaste love. According to another interpretation, Ovid's intention is that since, in his manual on the art of love, he does not explain how someone might be courted by letter, he completes this part of his teaching here. According to another interpretation, his intention in this book is to encourage the pursuit of virtue and to reject vice. . . . It must be understood also that although throughout the whole book he has this intention, and those mentioned above, there are two further intentions in this book, one general and one particular. The general intention is to give pleasure and to give profitable advice to all his readers. But he has a particular intention in individual letters . . . And different letters have different intentions, because he had different purposes in mind in setting out <to commend> some for their chastity and blame others for their unchaste love.   (tr. Minnis and Scott, pp. 22–3)

Here, perhaps, is the closest recognition of the structural irony and narrative discrimination of the *Heroides*. The use of *ex personae* or 'dramatic' narration creates exactly the kind of matrix of moral complexity that the theorists of poetics saw to be its distinctive feature and its ethical justification. The impact of this Ovidian ellipsis of intention on vernacular poetics is hard to overstate. Moreover, it is only in the medieval Ovid that commentators and imitators could find a substantial body of speaking women who could be shown using the arts of oratory and forensic rhetoric in a purposeful, if ultimately hopeless, manner. The medieval popularity of the complaint or lament as the genre of disempowerment for both male and female speakers may derive some of its impetus from contemporary readings of the *Heroides* and some of the *Metamorphoses*, creating a feminine space for male readers to think through and in. If it is true that 'for the all-male students of the medieval *studium* or university the feminine is not only good to think with, but is also presented as a model good to "speak with"' (McKinley, p. 89), then the representation of thoughtful and aspiringly autonomous women in such Ovidian imitations as the *Pamphilus* and in the carefully gendered voices of Chaucerian narration, for example, may derive some of their impetus from this strand of Ovidian commentary. Indeed the specifying influence of the *Heroides* on the Chaucer's *Legend of Good Women* could be extended much further to encompass many of his other narrative *personae*. Ovid, or perhaps the *accessus* on him, taught Chaucer how to 'do the police in different voices', leading Deschamps to hail him as 'Ovides grans en ta poëterie' (*Autre Balade*, cit. Calabrese, p. 1).

However, the potential for hermeneutic subtlety identified in these introductions and *accessus* is rarely if ever fulfilled in the detailed commentaries on individual letters that follow. Usually the double intention of character and author is unequivocally stated: Ariadne seeks to conquer the infidelity of Theseus, for example, but Ovid's aim is 'to reprehend foolish love'. Only in the sense that the reader must identify whether each letter represents an example of foolish love or demented love does the ambiguity of the initial analyses survive. And many remained unconvinced that medieval readers of Ovid would exercise the necessary discrimination: Jean Gerson, in his early-fifteenth-century contribution to *la querelle de la Rose*, warned that the usual admonition to take the good and leave the evil might not work with Ovid and his imitators, who will 'take the evil and leave the good' (*Le Débat*, ed. Hicks, p. 110; tr. Baird and Kane, p. 163).

In the later Middle Ages, commentary on *Ovidius minor* (as the non-*Metamorphoses* texts were known) remained under the influence of the work produced in the schools of the Orléanais, later criticised by Christine de Pizan as 'the glosses of Orléans which destroyed the texts' (see p. 181 above). The major twelfth-century commentaries, particularly those of Arnulf of Orléans, display an almost glacial capacity to move slowly through the following centuries accumulating a moraine of new details but revealing only subtle changes of emphasis. Arnulf's work informs thirteenth-century codifications of the Ovidian corpus and proved a priceless resource for the early humanists in their search for the 'authentic'

Ovid. Only in commentary on the *Ovidius maior* – the *Metamorphoses* –
does there seem to have been a sea change in interpretative attitudes.

The *Metamorphoses*, Ovid's distinctive and unusual contribution to
epic narration, offered red meat to the exegete. None of the surviving school collections of *accessus* from the twelfth and thirteenth centuries treats the *Metamorphoses*. Although Arnulf of Orléans and John of
Garland had already begun to reveal the moral integuments of the text,
others felt strongly that this was not a suitable work to put into the hands
or minds of impressionable students. Conrad of Hirsau's prissy *magister* characterises Ovid as 'the inventor of a large part of idol-worship'
(tr. Minnis and Scott, p. 56), while Alexander de Villa Dei thought that
Arnulf's commentary was irreligious. Roger Bacon contrasted Ovid with
his beloved Seneca and criticised the vogue for instructing others 'in
the fables and nonsenses ('in fabulis et insaniis') of Ovid . . . where all
errors of faith and morals are put forward' (*Opus tertium*, ed. Brewer,
pp. 54–5). But Alexander Nequam found the *Metamorphoses* a valuable source of mythological lore for his *De naturis rerum*, and agreed
with other moralising critics that 'moral instruction is sometimes
[*nonnumquam*] hidden under the fables of the poets' (*De naturis rerum*
2.107; ed. Wright, p. 189). It is that 'sometimes' that caused the problem
and led commentators to devise increasingly rigorous and exhaustive systems of moral recuperation, culminating in the fourteenth century with
the *Ovide moralisé* and the *Ovidius moralizatus*.

The narrative framework of the *Metamorphoses* – simpler than that
of the *Heroides* – allowed commentators to apply Horatian criteria to
the text: the intention of Ovid and of all writers of fables is above all to
delight and by delighting to instruct in morals. This somewhat predictable
defence is parodically invoked in the (probably tongue-in-cheek) account
of Ovid in the *Carmina Burana* 105:

> ab errore studuit mundum revocare
> Qui sibi notus erat, docuit sapienter amare.

[He (i.e. Ovid) studied to call the world back from error; who was known to
him he taught to love wisely.]

(The second line alludes to the *Ars amatoria* 2.501.)

Ovid moved away from the narrative linearity and single-hero focus
usually found in epic, preferring a cyclic narrative of linked episodes, a
sort of 'collective' poem in imitation of the *Aetia* of Callimachus. He
also showed an intense interest in the psychology of his characters, and,
as in the *Heroides*, allowed some of his women characters to emerge as
prominent figures in the narrative and as powerful advocates for their
cause. Medieval commentators dealt with these deviations from epic

norms by seeking to consider the poem as a source of mythological lore and as a collection of fables, though some also show interest in the rhetorical tropes used by the women. By considering the *Metamorphoses* to be fables, commentators were making a strategic decision to bring a wayward and challenging text under the control of the branch of commentary that could most effectively subdue it. Fables and their integuments can be decoded in a variety of different ways and on a variety of different levels from the simply schematic to the subtly allegorical.

The sense of an almost mechanical decoding of the fabular narrative is already present in early commentaries on the *Metamorphoses*. John of Garland's *Integumenta* claims to untie knotty secrets, to open closed matters, to clarify cloudy matters and to proclaim hidden things (ed. Ghisalberti, ll. 6–7). The process is almost the opposite of that appeal to the engaged affections required by the Averroistic imaginative syllogism. But Averroes had warned against proverbs and fables: 'For when a fictional account is untrustworthy and clearly made up on the basis of doubtful material, it will not produce the effect it was intended to produce. For a statement that someone has not really believed will not move him to fear or pity' (tr. Minnis and Scott, p. 306). The Averroistic tradition did not consider fables to be genuinely poetic, because in many cases the moral engagement was of a simple and mechanical order. But while many commentaries struggle to constrain the *Metamorphoses* within the fabular model of exegesis, others, while still moralising in their approach to the text, saw it as a treasure house of learning and cultural history. And as a text that was often studied outside of the formal curriculum or as a supplement to it, mythographic and allegorical readings of increasing ingenuity and subjectivity might readily be generated by its readers.

The prologue of Arnulf's influential *Metamorphoses* commentary sees Ovid's intention as clearly moral: to call us back from immoderate love of temporal things and to urge us to sole worship of the creator by showing the stability of heavenly things and the mutability of earthly things. Alternatively he sees Ovid's use of physical mutation as a strategy to illuminate internal changes 'to lead us back from error to the knowledge of the true creator' (*Allegoriae*, tr. Elliott, 'Accessus', p. 15). In discussing the work's utility he suggests two possible modes of reception which in fact characterise the two main streams of interpretation in the thirteenth and fourteenth centuries. The first approach saw the utility of the *Metamorphoses* as deriving from the reader's ability to acquire knowledge of the various fables, assembled together in this collection as a convenient (but not structurally coherent or significant) basis for a variety of modern interpretations. (Arnulf suggests in passing that Ovid's purpose might have merely been the compilation of a collection of scattered fables, but this intention, significant in decentring the author in later moralisations, is not a dominant consideration in his integumental view of the text.) This integumental model of reading allows a reader to unlock the meaning of the fable untrammelled by the supposed mythographic intentions of the author himself or by the need to supply a complexly structured moral metamorphosis. Such a reading-model was always likely to be popular with readers trained on proverbs and the fables of Aesop and Avianus.

The second approach sees the *utilitas* as 'the instruction in divine matters gathered from the transformation of temporal things' (tr. Elliott, p. 17). In this 'mutation' model, Arnulf explores the text in terms of its natural, magical and spiritual transformations, and has a consistently implied but not explicitly articulated interest in moral change. This approach, which was perhaps more demanding for both commentator and reader, offered the opportunity to generate allegorical, historical and moral readings of each metamorphosis. In practice both approaches often existed in parallel in the transmitted commentaries: Giovanni del Virgilio, the great proto-humanist commentator who lectured on Ovid and Virgil at the University of Bologna in 1322–3, happily used the integumental model of John of Garland alongside the mutation model of Arnulf.

A distinction between the private and common *causa intentionis* was a frequent feature of commentaries from the twelfth century onwards, and once again much of this can be traced back to Orléans. An influential strand of commentary deployed a notion of implicit allegory which argued that the mythographical riches of the text could be unlocked by unravelling the sophisticated and complex intentions of Ovid in compiling the *Metamorphoses*. This strand wove together material from Arnulf and from some platonising texts from twelfth-century Chartres, such as the commentaries of William of Conches on Boethius and Plato's *Timaeus* (which also show interest in mutation theory). Glosses surviving in at least five copies cite Macrobius, Bernard Silvester and Lucretius and seem to preserve traces of older platonising approaches to the poem (e.g. Copenhagen, Køngelige Bibliotek, MS Gl. Kgl. S. 2008; ed. Demats, *Fabula*, pp. 179–84). The decentering of authorial intention involved in such approaches prepared the ground for the energetic mythography and allegoresis of the French moralised Ovids of the fourteenth century. In the early-thirteenth-century commentary by William of Orléans, a pragmatic view of the poem is already emerging: Ovid intended to praise Augustus to recoup ground lost after the debacle of the *Ars amatoria*, but this was the *utilitas auctoris* and can therefore now be disregarded: the *utilitas legentis* is simply knowledge of the fables contained in the collection, now available for the reader to interpret afresh (ed. Coulson, 'Unedited', pp. 172–7). The ambitious Arnulfian aspiration to an elaborate scheme of multi-layered exegesis based on various kinds of transformation and mutation is here focused instead on a single level of reading: by describing transformations, the text considers morals. In other words: *Ethice subponitur*. William's comments on the *Metamorphoses* enjoyed extensive transmission and were later incorporated into the commentary of Guillelmus de Thiegiis and, much later, into Sozomeno da Pistoia's 1431 Florence commentary. William's *accessus* to the *Metamorphoses* joins those of Lactantius Placidus and Arnulf as the commonplace points of entry to the poem in the late Middle Ages. Other commentaries suggest that some readers might have been able to distinguish between the historical circumstances of the *Metamorphoses*' composition and the contemporary value that was being attached to them: 'there is minimal utility for the author but maximum utility for the hearer' is a frequently repeated comment.[8]

Many of these commentaries use Ovid's fables as convenient structural metaphors for cultural and intellectual features of their own society. In his prologue Arnulf offers the possibility of allegorical, historical, spiritual and moral expositions. In practice he finds in the fables tractable patterns which allow him to expound on the structure of knowledge, or to build metaphorical models which schematise the workings of the world. The serpent's teeth in the fable of Cadmus allow an ingenious exposition that briefly characterises the acuity of the Greeks, the skilfulness (or tricksiness) of poets compared to 'layci', the mordancy of satirists and the belligerence of rhetoricians (*Allegoriae*, ed. Ghisalberti, pp. 207–8). John of Garland similarly likens the seven pips of the golden apple in the Atlas story to the liberal arts (*Integumenta*, ed. Ghisalberti, p. 54). An anonymous commentary from around 1200 creates a parallel between the *trivium* and the Trinity, arguing that Ovid was not ignorant of the *archana celestis* and offering learned expositions of the secret meanings attached to the letter Y (ed. Ganz, '*Archani celestis*', p. 202). This markedly Christian commentary is counterpointed by the increasing citation of the *Metamorphoses* in contemporary theological writings, contingent on the attribution to Ovid of Christian sympathies and prophetic insights.

The construction and application of this kind of external structural and cultural matrix allows Ovid to be seen as a moralist, a natural theologian (prefiguring the humanist defence of poets as theologians) and a scientist in his work in the *Metamorphoses*. The responsiveness of his mythology to new mythographic systems of classifying knowledge and of analysing natural phenomena was buttressed by the longest of the pseudonymous compositions attributed to him, the *De vetula* (*c.* 1260?), which was

---

[8] E.g. Paris, Bibliothèque nationale de France, MS Lat. 8253; ed. Ghisalberti, 'Medieval Biographies', p. 52. See also Sozomeno of Pistoia, ed. Coulson, 'Unedited', p. 187, and Sozomeno's probable source (Berlin, Staatsbibliothek, MS Preussischer Kulturbesitz Diez B Sant 2, ed. Coulson, 'Unedited', p. 207).

reputedly found in his grave and purported to show a deathbed conversion to Christianity. Probably the work of the Orléans-trained Richard de Fournival, the thirteenth-century benefactor of the Sorbonne, the *De vetula* is a transparent exercise in cultural syncretism. The evidence it provided of Ovid's final metamorphosis – the mutation of his life into a better spiritual form – suggests the interest there was in framing, contextualising and appropriating this most protean of classical writers. Roger Bacon accepted the authenticity of the *De vetula* because it helped to justify the ethical value attributed by some to Ovid's poetry, and the poem soon acquired its own *accessus* and commentary, claiming that in it the author sought through his own example to recall us from profane love (ed. Robathan, p. 43). But it is significant that in the fourteenth century, when doubts were expressed about its authenticity, more elaborately moralised versions of the *Metamorphoses* saw no need to appropriate Ovid as a Christian fellow-traveller in this way. It is the slipperiness of the authentic Ovid, and the implicit recognition that the mythographical mode is only one culturally convenient trajectory across a shifting and threatening literary landscape, that make some thirteenth-century readers so keen to anchor him into the presuppositions of Christian moral philosophy.

Around the middle of the thirteenth century, somewhere in central France, probably in the region of Orléans, there appeared a commentary on the *Metamorphoses* which was 'perhaps the most influential commentary on the poem in circulation during the later Middle Ages' (Coulson, 'Unedited', p. 158). This so-called Vulgate Commentary synthesises the medieval scholarship on Ovid from the late-eleventh to the mid-thirteenth centuries. Its wide and impressively uniform circulation attest to the respect in which it was held. At its head is one of the fullest critical biographies produced in the period. It supplements the conventional biographical accounts and comments on the size of Ovid's nose (because of his cognomen *Nasonis*) with an elaborate allegory of the name *Ovidius*, deriving it from *ovum dividens* (an etymology ultimately descended from Martianus Capella). It creates a fantastic similitude between the four concentric layers of the world and the structure of an egg. Ovid's skill, it suggests, lies in his ability to encompass and divide the structure of the world in the colossal achievement of his writings (ed. Coulson, 'Unedited', pp. 177–82). By making explicit Arnulf's implied fourth category of moral mutation alongside the existing three (natural, magical and spiritual), the *accessus* can describe Ovid as *phisicus* ('assignando generacionem elementorum') and *ethicus* ('in assignacione mutacionem que faciunt ad mores'). The utility relates to the benefit derived by the reader from this array of codified wisdom ('Vtilitas siquidem est magna, non actoris sed legencium'; ed. Coulson, 'Unedited',

p. 182). The *Metamorphoses* are presented as texts to be engaged with proactively rather than consumed reactively by a reader. As a result of that engagement, the reader first gains 'knowledge of the fables', and can then proceed to an exposition of them (if he chooses that matrix), or, if he prefers, he can treat the collection as a kind of cultural history of different times.

In response to the widely acknowledged literary sophistication of the *Metamorphoses*, the Vulgate Commentary demonstrates an augmented interest in literary precepts (some of which reflect the explicit influence of Horace's *Ars poetica*). The commentary remarks on the intertextuality between Ovid's poems and other classical texts, the tendency to self-referentiality and self-quotation within Ovid's different works, and their intertextuality with contemporary medieval writings. It also reveals how a careful reading of the *Metamorphoses* requires an energetic sense of stylistic decorum and intellectual sprightliness. Ovid is seen as a natural physician, a moralist, and a skilled poet. Recognition of the virtuosity of Ovid's narrative procedures in the *Metamorphoses*, for example, produces a discussion of the four main modes of storytelling used, which relates each of them to a common medieval taxonomy of narrative: *historia*, which speaks of truth under the species of truth; *argumentum*, which speaks of the truth under the species of falsehood; *fabula*, which speaks of falsehood under the species of falsehood, and *comedia* (often linked to *argumentum*), which speaks of falsehood under the species of truth. The *Metamorphoses* becomes, therefore, a showcase of narrative and literary techniques. In an elaboration of the usual checklist of commentary concerns, the Vulgate Commentary also shows some interest in characterisation and motivation, and in the responses of fictional individuals both within the *Metamorphoses* and in other poems, notably those of Virgil and Lucan, suggesting that the *Metamorphoses* were correctly coming to be considered in relation to the mythography and narrative procedures of classical epic. Ovid's characterisations are necessarily fuller here than in his epistolary works, and his heroines present a more complex subjectivity than in earlier epics. The Vulgate Commentary is noticeably sensitive to such literary nuance and complexity. Through these deliberative speeches, 'Ovid contributes a real advance in the representation of feminine subjectivity and agency in western narrative literature . . . the Ovidian heroine gave voice to the perplexities and ambiguities of selfhood that led to a profound resonance for many generations of readers' (McKinley, pp. 173–4, 178).

The modes of interpretation open to Ovid's readers steadily diversified throughout the Middle Ages. Twelfth-century commentaries had already recognised the range of narrative styles and approaches used by Ovid in the *Metamorphoses*. The material of poetry could be sometimes false and sometimes true; the mode of narration could be moral or historical (Anonymous *Accessus* C [twelfth century], ed. Coulson, 'Unedited', pp. 202–4). This sense of Ovid's capacity for stylistic and narrative metamorphosis resonates through most later commentaries:

He is sometimes a poet; sometimes a historian; sometimes a philosopher. He is a poet where he makes fictions; a historian where he follows history; a philosopher when he is philosophical. Therefore we can say the material cause of this work is *fabula, argumentum* and *historia*.

(Wolfenbuttel, Herzog August Bibliothek, MS Guelf 4.5 Aug. 40., ed. Demats, *Fabula*, p. 191)

The very diversity and richness of the text encourages the proliferation of approaches to it:

Consider the diverse intentions according to the diverse *materia*. . . . Consider the various utilities according to the various intentions.

(Anonymous *Accessus* C, ed. Coulson, 'Unedited', p. 203)

It was this diversity that ultimately preserved the *Metamorphoses* from the pedagogic fate and poetic scorn heaped on other collections of fables. It typified 'an œuvre which is marked by inherent instability of meaning [and which] was interpreted and augmented by medieval scholars and writers in ways which often accentuated that instability' (Minnis, *Magister amoris*, p. 12). The poem remained a rich resource for later readers, especially those like Thomas Walsingham, chronicler and monk of St Albans, who positioned themselves outside of the academy. His *Arcana deorum* (*c.* 1400–10) offers a powerful defence of studying Ovid against 'our grammarians' who argue that 'poetry consists of frivolous and empty fictions'. Walsingham, whose *Proehmia poetarum* offers late examples of *accessus* to classical authors,[9] uses Arnulf, Bersuire and the Third Vatican Mythographer in his historical and naturalistic readings of the *Metamorphoses* and he is alert both to Ovid's irony and to his interest in psychology. He largely avoids Christian allegorisations, seeking explanations of the mutations 'as reasonable as they are useful. . . . Let them indeed see fruit which they previously had no inkling existed in poetry' (Oxford, St John's College MS 124, fol. 9v; tr. McKinley, p. 115). Apparently denied a formal place in the curriculum of thirteenth century schools, both lower and higher, the *Metamorphoses* bathed itself promiscuously in the techniques and approaches of its framing academic contexts, while being constrained by neither. It occupied a textual no-man's-land. No wonder it was a source

---

9 Extant in a single MS, London, British Library, MS Harley 2693.

of moral concern to many, and a fountain of delight to the early humanists like Giovanni del Virgilio.

Just as the classical *florilegia* of the schools of Orléans came to be redeployed in the more explicitly Christian contexts of preaching manuals and encyclopaedias in the thirteenth century, so the medieval commentary tradition on Ovid was itself subjected in the fourteenth century to a final mutation into its most explicitly moralised and most overtly Christian form. As in the thirteenth century, the impetus came from France. As in the thirteenth century, it came from members of the orders of friars. But unlike the thirteenth century, it was not part of a shift in the structure of literary knowledge: by then the hermeneutical initiative had already passed to the universities and schools of Italy, and, most decisively, to the Italian scholar-poets. In these moralised *Metamorphoses*, produced outside the formally author-centred intentionalism of the *accessus* tradition, the poet Ovid disappears and his collection of fables is subjected to an unrelenting process of narrative reconstruction that reconfigures the pagan stories as vehicles for (rather dull) surface morality, mythographic display on all manner of subjects (like earthly kingship), and (often spectacular) allegorical ingenuity.

The anonymous Franciscan responsible for the composition between 1316 and 1328 of the *Ovide moralisé* approached Ovid's *Metamorphoses* with the zeal of a compiler. He is explicitly working under the syncretist Pauline mandate that fuelled, justified and protected much later medieval interpretation of difficult secular texts: 'All that is written is written for our doctrine' (Romans 15:4):

> Si l'escripture ne me ment,
> Tout est pour nostre enseignement
> Quanqu'il a es livres escript,
> Soient bon ou mal li escript

(I. 1–4)

[Unless Scripture is lying to me, all was intended for our instruction, everything that is written in books, whether they were written well or badly.]

Good is presented for imitation, evil so that it can be guarded against. He finesses the traditional academic prologues to the Ovidian corpus in a way which suggests the compiler's familiarity with the range of interpretative postures and ethical gestures found in the commentary tradition. But, in a break with this tradition, inductive biography is omitted. *Intentio* in this prologue rests with the compiler/translator rather than the original author. This is allegoresis rather than allegory. His purpose is to translate the fables of ancient times 'selonc ce qu'Ovides les baille' (1. 19), thus aligning his text with that strand of earlier commentary which saw Ovid himself as a collector of fables from a variety of sources, who transmitted them without being aware of their full signification or true meaning. Truth is to be discerned from the fable and emphatically not from the intentions of their original compiler, who is denied the hermeneutical purchase and insight of his modern counterpart. Ovid's intention, which is not addressed until Book 15, is seen merely as an example of misguided paganism, with his interest in mutation nothing but a pragmatic and short-term strategy for political ingratiation (15.7141). None of this impinges on the self-referential world of the modern compiler's prologue. Although the fables may appear to be 'mençoignables', the truth covered in them will be 'aperte' to whomever has the know-how to read them (1.41–5):

> Mes sous la fable gist couverte
> la sentence plus profitable (15.2536–7)

[But beneath the fable/story, there lies hidden a more profitable truth.]

The *Ovide moralisé* never attributes moral intention to Ovid. This is superfluous when the emphasis is unequivocally on the virtuoso (and often self-regarding) Christian interpretation provided by the modern author. There is no need for the sophistical political correctness of many earlier accounts of the *intentio auctoris*. Instead, the author exercises the combined exegetical and rhetorical roles of *compilator*, *translator* and *expositor* in a series of inventive and elaborate retellings. This is transformation through translation, an explicit act of ethical and verbal appropriation. The fables have keys which the new text supplies. Indeed, the literal meaning of the text must invariably be discarded as 'contraire a droite creance' (15.2524):

> Voirs est, qui Ovide prendroit
> a la letre, et n'i entendroit
> autre sen, autre entendement
> que tel com l'auctors grossement
> I met en racontant la fable,
> tout seroit chose mençognable,
> poi profitable et trop obscure . . .
> Mes sous la fable gist couverte
> la sentence plus profitable (15.2525-31, 2536–7).

[Indeed, whoever takes Ovid at his word and will not see any other meaning or intention in him than the one that the author has crudely put into telling the story, then all would be misleading or mendacious (to him), of little profit and too obscure. . . . But under the fable lies covered a more useful moral message.]

The interpretative world is little different from John of Garland's *Integumenta Ovidii*, except that the truths emerging from the fables are more assertively moralistic. However, once the mode of allegoresis is established, the *Ovide moralisé* interprets Paul's dictum in a properly inclusive way. Readers must be alienated from the 'letter' of the narrative which Ovid has 'grossement' recorded in the fable. But once the *Metamorphoses* and their readers have been 'translated' away from the pagan world and into the world of Christian discourse, they are allowed to inhabit an intertextually mythographic environment. Scripture is allowed to illuminate Ovidian myth and vice versa, because they contain similarly polysemous layers of signification, which, with the strong guidance and firm editing of the author, the reader should be competent to decode. Other classical legends and narratives can be adduced as evidence: episodes from the *Heroides*; versions of Hero and Leander; the Danäides, and Jason and the Golden Fleece (this latter using the Troy narratives of Benoît de Sainte-Maure and the *De excidio Troiae*). Even the *Roman de la Rose* and perhaps Jean de Meun's French version of *De consolatione philosophiae* are brought to bear on the explication of the mythical narratives, while euhemerist readings of legends sometimes include discussion of motivation and character. The order and disposition of the narrative reorders stories and links them into cycles or 'gestes'.

But none of this is motivated by interest in poetic effect or rhetorical force. The author deploys these structural and interpretative refigurings 'pour mieux accomplir ma matire' (2.4583; compare 'Pour plus comprendre de matire', 4.3155). The possessive is revealing. *All* that is written is grist to the exegetical mill of the author's *materia*, which is Christian truth, 'la sentence plus profitable' (15.2537). The *Ovide moralisé* is an exercise in otherness: 'autre sen, autre entendement' (15.2527), 'a move to recover the sign that has become alien' (Copeland and Melville, p. 164). The dominant integumental approach leaves no room for the subtle psychological challenges of mutation-theory offered by other commentators. The *involucrum* of the original narrative is radically cut and remade to suit a new fashion; the letter is killed so that the spirit can be given life. This is allegoresis as closure: there is no free play of the signifier in the world of the *Ovide moralisé*.

Like the *Ovide moralisé*, its cousin the *Ovidius moralizatus* is a witness to an explicit expropriation of the textual resources of the medieval Ovid. Neither work treats the *Metamorphoses* as the object of literary study. Both reject the exegesis of the grammarians, preferring to see the poem as a resource-text in the making of a new work. The author of the *Ovidius moralizatus*, Pierre Bersuire, was a Franciscan who became a Benedictine and served as part of the *familia* of the vice-chancellor of the papal

Curia in Avignon in the 1330s. Like its author, the *Ovidius moralizatus* grew from humble beginnings to a position of power and prestige. It forms Book 15 of Bersuire's ambitious *Reductorium morale*, a grandly moralised key to the storehouse of human knowledge which includes thirteen books on the properties of created things (using Bartholomew the Englishman), one book on the wonders of the world and one on biblical characters. Integral to this scheme was a section on the fables of the poets, although the *Ovidius moralizatus* circulated separately from the main work, and its first chapter 'De formis figurisque deorum', containing influential and concise descriptions of the pagan gods, also broke away and enjoyed independent circulation, sometimes in a truncated form. Two early recensions of Book 15 were made in Avignon around 1340, using the mythographical resources of Fulgentius, the Third Vatican Mythographer, some Rabanus Maurus and an extract from Petrarch's *Africa*. This unusual and uncharacteristic release of Petrarch's text to an outsider may suggest his esteem for the Frenchman's enterprise and should encourage us to see Bersuire's work in the context of early humanist defences of poetry and of the mythographic study of classical poetry, such as Boccaccio's *Genealogia deorum gentilium*. A third recension, made in Paris between 1350 and 1362, supplements these sources by reference to the *Ovide moralisé* and the *Fulgentius metaforalis* of the English 'classicising friar' John Ridevall (d. after 1340).

Bersuire's defence of fables rests partly on a sophistical reading of St Paul and St Augustine, and on the example of fables used in the Old Testament. Operating within the standard *accessus* claim that 'almost all authors deal with ethics', Bersuire says that 'anyone reading the books of poets agrees that scarcely or never do they tell a tale which does not contain some truth, either natural or historical' (*Prologus*, tr. Reynolds, p. 63). In fact he deduces four layers of meaning in poetic fictions: literal, natural, historical and spiritual. The structural parallel with the four senses of Scripture is obvious, but potentially misleading, and Bersuire is actually closer to the four kinds of mutation discussed by Arnulf of Orléans. Unlike the *Ovide moralisé*, Bersuire is not working by implicit analogy with the *modus agendi* of scriptural commentators. Indeed, although he sees similarities in the use of fables in Scripture and in pagan poets, he does not equate their intention or end purpose:

For Sacred Scripture is accustomed to use these and similar fables and fictions so that from them some truth may be drawn out or demonstrated. The poets who first fabricated stories worked in similar fashion [*simili modo*], for through figments of this kind they always wished to communicate some truth.

(*Prologus*, tr. Reynolds, p. 63)

As Dante had already argued earlier in the fourteenth century, the allegory of poets is different from the allegory of Scripture, not least because
of the different status of metaphor and of the literal meaning of their
texts, but unlike Dante and other humanist apologists for poetic inspiration and the *poeta theologus*, Bersuire has no desire to blur or fudge
the distinction between them. Bersuire's exegesis of fables, like that of
the *Ovide moralisé*, places no store by any *intentio auctoris* that might
be imputed to Ovid: authoritative doctrine trumps authorial intention.
The truth-content of the fable is to be supplied for it by the ingenuity of
the Christian reader; the pagan narrative must be conscripted, however
unwillingly, to serve the cause of Christian truth:

Fables, enigmas and poems must for the most part be used so that some moral
sense may be drawn out [*extrahatur*] from them and so that even that very
falsity may be forced [*cogatur*] to serve truth.   (*Prologus*, tr. Reynolds, p. 63)

The kinetic verbs are revealing: Bersuire's moralisation of the fables is an
energetic mass-conversion of the pagans, spattered with verbs of bending,
gathering, drawing and binding:

so that through man-made fictions I may be able to confirm the mysteries of
morals and faith. For, if he be able, a man may collect grapes from thorns, suck
honey from the rocks, take oil from the hardest stone, and build a tabernacle of
the covenant from the treasures of the Egyptians. And Ovid says that it is proper
to be taught by an enemy.   (*Prologus*, tr. Reynolds, pp. 63–4)

This mode of recuperative reading or allegoresis allows no prophetic or
proto-Christian perception to the pagan author, however rich and fruitful his text may prove to be. This Ovid is no *ethicus*. Instead of the
fables covering truth, they are covered by it in a virtuoso deployment
of hermeneutic resourcefulness: 'by reading the text as allegory, allegoresis in effect *supplies* the *integumentum* or veil with which to cover the
text; it recuperates the text through concealment of it' (Copeland and
Melville, p. 171). Bersuire offers parallel strings of possible interpretation for application to the narratives and poetic images he collects, often
supplying reading *in bono* and *in malo*. His habit of concluding his moralisations with a proof text from Scripture 'rehearses hundreds of times, in
fact probably thousands of times, the reinscription of the Biblical and
Christian on the Ovidian and classical' (Hexter, '*Allegari*', p. 65). The
very fecundity of his moralisation confirms that what such an approach
to fabular narrative offered above all else was a way of structuring contemporary knowledge of the world and developing imaginative models
for retaining and retrieving that information: in effect a sophisticated
narrative memory-system. The allegorical edifices and tableaux he draws

from his mythographical predecessors are accessed by keys provided by Bersuire:

Because the ancients set up many gods and believed that certain properties of things were gods and called certain properties of things gods, as, for example, they perceived time through Saturn . . . they wished to call natural things or at least properties of natural things gods. Indeed they even wanted to attach certain gods to the properties of these gods.   (*Prologus*, tr. Reynolds, p. 67)

Fables handled in this way, and with Bersuire's degree of elaboration and sophistication, become kinds of poetic syllogisms, escaping from the Averroistic criticism of the simplicity and ethical thinness of fabular representation. Rabanus Maurus says that it is the poet's manner to retell actual events by indirect figures of speech with a degree of elegance. Unlike Lucan, whose direct manner of narration led to him being characterised as a historian rather than a poet, the indirectness of the poetic fictions of the ancients, when skilfully handled in this way, liberates them from any primary literal meaning. Thus the fables become a system of structural metaphors capable of multiple reinterpretation, where the Christian morality is only a further layer of interpretation, an integument with moral integrity.

Hence Bersuire concentrates on the moral and allegorical meanings, treating the literal sense only rarely. Astrology, natural science and euhemerism all appear, while the allegorical readings – where Bersuire is at his most inventive – often offer multiple readings, to stress that the material is capable of flexible treatment. Because, in the Fulgentian manner of the classicising friars, his pagan gods are frozen in the word-images of poets ('pingitur a poetis'), his stories 'may be understood' in a variety of ways. They lack a kernel of inherent truth; prior expositions may be discarded or superseded.

The treatise varies its mode of address between singular imperatives (aimed at the preacher preparing his sermon) and plural vocatives, introducing sections ready for wholesale incorporation into other discourses, many of which follow the structural rules of the *artes praedicandi*, concording on the key word of the exposition. The fables become mannequins in a fashion show of alternative interpretations. High-mindedness in the moral exposition of the text is achieved by high-handedness in its treatment of its original form and content. Indeed the inventiveness of the moralisations succeeds by mimicking rhetorical *inventio*. And the wide circulation enjoyed by the *Ovidius moralizatus* outside of the homiletic context of the *Reductorium morale* suggest that 'with increasing force from Bersuire's time on, the *Metamorphoses* was proving stronger (as a master text) than the Bible' (Hexter, '*Allegari*', p. 56), with the eventual result that Bersuire's text was banned by the Catholic church in 1559. In the sterner and more authoritarian intellectual world of the Counter-Reformation, its unpoliceable self-generating polysemousness began to look like free-thinking:

> To regard a classical fable as veiled truth, necessarily open to interpretation on different levels, and to keep simultaneously in one's head several equally valid but self-contradictory 'meanings' for a single text and make the equations between them, is an attitude of mind which remained with sixteenth-century writers and with their public long after the moralized Ovids themselves were forgotten.　　　　　(Moss, *Ovid in Renaissance France*, p. 26)

Bersuire's text is not just Ovid moralised: it is Ovid remade, and ultimately – most unexpectedly and perhaps unintendedly – Ovid liberated.

5. Reading between the lines: the blurring of the genres

At various points in *De triumphis ecclesiae* (c. 1250), an eight-book poem on the crusades, John of Garland invokes the epic spirit of Virgil. He begins with 'Arma crucemque cano' (*Prologus* 11), invites Melpomene to sing the 'tragica gesta' of the Tartars (3. 689–90), calls his work an elegy, and smugly celebrates his skill in blending together historical, satirical and tragic deeds (7.499–500).

For all his literary display and self-advertisement, John's gleeful generic promiscuity serves as a valuable reminder that medieval literary practice was rarely hampered by the rigours of what we would call genre-theory. Indeed, in looking back at the prescriptions and performances of their classical predecessors, it is doubtful whether these provided medieval readers and writers with much assistance in their attempts to annotate, emulate and appropriate their Latin heritage. The twelfth-century *Ysagoge in theologiam*, commenting that 'generally speaking a poem offers examples of the courageous and cowardly', distinguishes only between satire, which eliminates vice and encourages virtue, and tragedy, which teaches contempt for Fortune and tolerance of burdens (ed. Landgraf, *Écrits théologiques*, p. 72). More ambitiously, in the mid-thirteenth century Vincent of Beauvais could list the seven 'species' of poetry as comedy, tragedy, invective, satire, fable, history and argument (*Speculum doctrinale* 3.109), without apparently realising that in so doing he was collapsing together genres and modes of narration.[10] Despite the (largely stylistic) prescriptions of the arts of poetry, narrative commentary and narrative composition often blur stylistic boundaries and redraw generic

---

[10] Mehtonen, *Old Concepts*, p. 44.

maps. Most medieval discussions of classical literary form look like tightropes strung over chasms of bemusement. But the inductive and post-hoc understanding of classical narrative genres shown by medieval commentators, although the often puzzled outcome of their attempts to read the past, proved strangely empowering and liberating to those medieval authors who chose instead to rewrite it.

Tragedy and epic

When Dante makes his Virgil refer to the *Aeneid* as 'alta mia tragedia' (*Inferno* 20.112-3), it is a defining moment in the medieval critical history of tragedy and of epic. When Chaucer modestly echoes this phrase in his *envoi* to *The Book of Troilus* ('Go, litel bok, go, litel myn tragedye'; V.1786), he tells it to be subject to Virgil, Homer, Ovid, Lucan and Statius. For both writers, the generic expectations and narrative criteria encompassed by their understanding of the concept of tragedy extended to include much writing that would normally be described by classical and modern readers as epic or history. For tragedy was, for much of the Middle Ages, an empty genre. Dictionaries, glossaries and commentaries all sought to define its main features (though a consensus was rather slow to emerge), but they usually did so without knowledge of or access to actual examples of the form. Their understanding of conditions of performance was patchy, idiosyncratic and highly inferential. Many writers grappled to define the genre in ignorance of the efforts of others. The medieval literary concept of tragedy was, therefore, little more than a set of very loose generic parameters which could plausibly be applied to a wide range of narrative poems composed in the dramatic mode. The most substantial body of such poems known to the Middle Ages was the epic.

Medieval views of tragedy were formed by three main sources of information. The first was the discussion of tragedy in Books 8 and 18 of Isidore of Seville's *Etymologiae*. The second was commentary on Boethius' *De consolatione philosophiae*. Thirdly, medieval commentators acquired random, and sometimes conflicting, information from commentaries on classical dramatists or *scholia* on earlier discussions of dramatic theory and practice, such as the opaque and elliptical remarks on tragedy and comedy in Horace's *Ars poetica*. The Averroistic *Poetics* offered no help and reinforced the blending of tragedy and epic as they reflected the Arab appropriation of the *Poetics* to discuss narrative lyric poetry rather than the generics of drama (indeed the Greek *Poetics* remarks that epics differ from tragedies only in lacking staged presentation). Not surprisingly, the resultant blend of ideas, half-truths and inferences lacked clarity and consistency.

Isidore was himself hampered by imprecise and often second-hand information and a partial grasp of the texts and the critical issues. In Book 8 he derives *tragoedi* (tragic poets) from the Greek word for goat (*tragos*), citing Horace in support. Later tragedians received praise for the excellence with which their stories were made in the image of truth. In Book 18, following Lactantius, he gives a second definition: 'Tragedians are those who sang in poetry of the ancient deeds and sorrowful crimes of wicked kings while the people looked on' (tr. Kelly, *Ideas and Forms*, p. 46).[11] Thus in Isidore drama has already become recited or sung poetry (*carmina*). Despite Isidore's comments on miming actors, which later medieval commentators returned to and attempted to gloss, the emphasis is on the matter of the stories in tragedy rather than the manner of their presentation. And the matter of the story concerns the sad and sinful deeds of evil kings.

Isidore's views are refracted by many later commentators. Bernard of Utrecht's influential late-eleventh-century commentary on the *Eclogues* of 'Theodulus', for example, transmitted to a wider school audience the view that tragedy described public events and the crimes of powerful men. Papias, in his *Elementarium doctrinae rudimentum* (before 1045), blends together the discussions from Books 8 and 18 to produce a concise (and atextual) definition, adding to it, in a significant broadening of the genre's boundaries, the comment that tragedy (spoken of in the past tense as an obsolete genre) was what men of former times wrote about or described in sad poems. Thus any mournful poem could retrospectively be considered to be a tragedy. In particular, distinctions between elegy and tragedy could easily become blurred. As late as the fourteenth century, Nicholas Trevet used Book 18 of the *Etymologiae* as a specifying source for his discussion of Senecan tragedy and for his commentary on Boethius (which is how Chaucer came to know the definition).

Boethius' discussion of tragedy led to the creation of a different tragic paradigm. Philosophy asks Boethius:

What other thynge bywaylen the cryinges of tragedyes but oonly the dedes of Fortune, that with an unwar strook overturneth the realmes of greet nobleye?

(Chaucer's *Boece*, 2 pr. 2, 67–70)

Earlier Boethian commentaries, notably that by Remigius of Auxerre (d. 908), had repeated Isidore's discussion in elucidation of this part of the text. But in the commentary of William of Conches a new definition of tragedy emerges from the blending of the Boethian emphasis on the indiscriminate nature of Fortune's blows with the Isidorean stress on the

---

[11] 'Tragoedi sunt qui antiqua gesta atque facinora sceleratorum regum luctuosa carmine spectante populo concinebant' (18.45).

human iniquities that bring them about. This blending made it possible for some commentators to see the genre more in terms of the trajectory of its plot and the operation of the mutability of Fortune than the guilt of its participants: tragedy is a writing about great iniquities which begins in prosperity and ends in adversity. By contrast, comedy begins with some adversity and ends in prosperity. This paradigm was widely incorporated into subsequent medieval discussions of tragedy either directly or indirectly. Nicholas Trevet's commentary on Boethius follows the Conches version, and the glossed Boethius used by Chaucer (almost certainly the Trevet commentary) also contained it, providing him with his keynote definition of the genre:

Tragedye is to seyn a dite of a prosperite for a tyme, that endeth in wrechidnesse.

(*Boece*, 2 pr. 2, 70–2)

Chaucer elaborated this model in his fullest description of tragedy at the beginning of the *Monk's Tale*:

> Tragedie is to seyn a certeyn storie,
> As olde bookes maken us memorie,
> Of hym that stood in greet prosperitee
> And is yfallen out of heigh degree
> Into myserie, and endith wrecchedly.

(*Canterbury Tales*, VII, 1973–7)

Whereas Boethius stressed the indiscriminate blows of Fortune, William of Conches reintroduced the Isidorean notion of crime and sin precipitating the downfall. But it is interesting that, when employing Trevet's definition (which follows William's), Chaucer removed the reference to villainy, as did Trevet himself in his later commentary on Seneca's tragedies.

The emergence of this more 'positive' view of the tragic protagonist as merely a victim of circumstance rather than a criminal may have been reinforced by the diffusion through *florilegia* of aspects of the discussion of tragedy in the Averroistic *Poetics*. The definition of tragedy as the art of praise, one of the most widely circulating aphorisms from the *Poetics*, discouraged a sense of the tragic hero as someone brought low by his own faults, while reinforcing the Isidorean emphasis on sadness and misfortune and on the element of retributive justice in the bringing low of those guilty of crimes. The outstanding virtue required of the Averroistic protagonist further reinforced the possibility that most narrative poetry dealing with great men (i.e. epic) could be seen as tragedy. Indeed this assimilation is arguably already implicit in the Greek *Poetics*, where Aristotle's 'treatment of epic depends integrally on the principles already laid down for tragedy' (Halliwell, 'Aristotle's Poetics', p. 165).

Tragedy, according to the Averroistic *Poetics*, is 'not an art representing men as they strike us individually, but rather represents their honourable characteristics and praiseworthy actions and ennobling beliefs' (tr. Minnis and Scott, p. 294). Pity and compassion result from unjust misery and misfortune. 'The recounting of the death of relations and similar misfortunes, happening to brave and virtuous men, moves and arouses in men an intense desire for what is good' (tr. Minnis and Scott, p. 305). As the Averroistic *Poetics* broadens Aristotle's notions of tragedy to encompass non-dramatic Arabic poetry, its primary impact may have been on perceptions of the nature and effect of poetry in general. But this may also have contributed to the widening of the textual horizons of a genre that lacked defining representatives. Matthew of Linköping's early-fourteenth-century *Poetics* describes 'the exaltation of lofty matters ['magnarum rerum'] in tragedy in accordance with the high style' (56; ed. and tr. Bergh, pp. 60–1). A florilegial extract in the fourteenth-century *Tabula moralium* of Johannes de Fayt made the link explicit: 'tragedia est ars laudandi' ('tragedy is the art of praise'; cit. Boggess, '*Poetics*', p. 289).

But it is aspects of the 'Boethian' view of tragedy that are most widely reflected in medieval literary discussions. The mid-twelfth-century *Ysagoge in theologiam* argues that tragedy teaches contempt for Fortune and tolerance of labour and tribulation. Geoffrey of Vinsauf's early-thirteenth-century *Documentum de arte versificandi* (expanded version) offers an eclectic and synthetic definition of tragedy as a song or poem (*carmen*), dealing with the contempt of Fortune, showing the misfortunes of 'gravium personarum', which begins in joy and ends in mourning (ed. Lawler, *Parisiana poetria*, p. 332). Much of this is repeated by John of Garland in his *Parisiana poetria* (c. 1220; revised c. 1231–5), but he adds that tragedy is a high-style genre and that it deals with shameful and calamitous or criminal (*scelerata*) deeds. To illustrate the point he adds his own tragedy – a narrative poem about murder and treachery among washerwomen ending in the fall of a besieged town. Apart from his own effort, John thinks that the only other Latin tragedy is Ovid's lost *Medea*. Vincent of Beauvais defines tragedy as poetry which has a joyful beginning but a sad denouement. But elsewhere in his encyclopaedia he independently repeats Isidore's two definitions, so it is unlikely that he had any clear or consistent sense of the genre. (His citations from Seneca's plays were acquired from a florilegial collection.) Such encyclopaedic definitions probably lie behind the commonly repeated views of tragedy and comedy as governed by the different trajectories of their plot and the different levels of their style. In fourteenth-century England, both Pseudo-Walter Burley and Thomas Walsingham repeated simplified versions of these formulations in their works, but there seems to be little consistency or accuracy in many of the late-medieval non-Chaucerian English usages of the term 'tragedy'.

Earlier discussions of tragedy in *scholia* on Horace may have fed into the Horatian descriptions of the form found in Matthew of Vendôme's *Ars versificatoria* and the *Poetria nova* of Geoffrey of Vinsauf. Horatian influence is also likely in Hugutio of Pisa's lexical encyclopaedia, the *Magnae derivationes* (*c.* 1165), where, because of the composite etymology applied to them (goat song and food song), tragedy and comedy are discussed under the topic of *oda*. Tragedy is here defined by contrast with comedy: it deals with kings and magnates (comedy is of private persons); it is written in high style (comedy uses *sermo humilis*); comedy begins in sadness and ends in joy, whereas tragedy is the reverse. Tragedy deals, he says with 'crudelissimis rebus' such as the man who has killed his father and mother and eaten his child 'vel e contrario' (Oxford, Bodleian Library, MS Laud Misc. 626, fol. 124r–v; ed. Kelly, *Tragedy and Comedy*, pp. 6–7, n. 27). (One of Chaucer's monkish tragedies does, of course, deal explicitly with the father forced to eat his child in the story of Hugutio's fellow Pisan Ugolino.) Much of Hugutio's material was reused by John Balbus of Genoa in his even more influential *Catholicon* (1286), which survived as a primary reference-book well into the age of printing.

Passing references to tragedy in *accessus* and commentaries on school authors offer an even simpler paradigm. A twelfth-century accessus to Ovid's *Sine titulo* (i.e. the *Amores*), for example, describes tragedy as 'the goddess of poetry about the deeds of nobles and kings' (tr. Minnis and Scott, p. 28), while a fourteenth-century gloss on the *Laborintus* of Eberhard says it is 'the description of poems about the deeds of kings, like Alexander' (tr. Kelly, *Tragedy and Comedy*, p. 2). Indeed this may have been influenced by the neo-epic *Alexandreis*, composed by the prolific late-twelfth-century Walter of Châtillon in imitation of Statius. The twelfth-century Tegernsee *accessus* on Lucan says that tragedy dealt with royal persons and had a joyful beginning and a sad end (ed. Huygens [1970], pp. 42–3). Significantly for the assimilation of tragedy and epic, Lucan seems to be described as a tragedian rather than (as per usual) an historian.

What is consistently absent from these discussions of tragedy (and indeed of the parallel discussions of comedy) is any developed sense of the theatrical dimension of the genre, though there is some sense of performance through recitation and mime in some of the more sophisticated discussions. Instead, as the use of the term in connection with Ovid's *Amores* suggests, tragedy is seen as a kind of narrative poem with an elevated subject-matter and a comparably elevated style. Tragedy is dramatic only insofar as it employs one of the three *modi recitandi* used in narrative poems: exegematic or narrative, when the author speaks in his own person; dramatic or *ex personae*, when the author speaks only in the *personae* of others; and mixed, when both modes are used. (Significantly these modes of narration ultimately derive from Servian commentary on Virgil's epic.) 'Dramatic narration' would, of course, adequately describe surviving drama texts, but many other poems, such as the *Amores*, fell into the loose stylistic net as well. William of Saint-Thierry could describe the erotic narrative of the Song of Songs as 'written in the mode of a drama and in theatrical style [*stylus comicus*]', as if to be recited by characters and with action' (ed. Davy, pp. 80–2; tr. Minnis, *Theory of Authorship*, p. 57), an idea that goes back at least as far as Bede.

Early rhetorical commentaries had associated the high, middle and low styles of narration with the modes of discourse associated with tragedy, elegy and comedy respectively. (Satire sometimes features in this list, especially in the *Poetria nova* and its commentaries, whose popularity in Italy gave the idea a particular prominence there.) Tragedy's association with high style and its popular definition as dealing with the deeds of kings and nobles put it on a converging narrative trajectory with epic. The typical example of high style in rhetorical handbooks was Virgil's *Aeneid*, said to be written in the highest style for the most important men. Furthermore, the three kinds of storytelling described in Cicero's *De inventione* 1.27 (*historia*, *argumentum* and *fabula*) could be linked with the three Servian modes of narration (narrative, dramatic and mixed) and the three levels of style to create a loose taxonomy of discourse: history in dramatic mode using high style. Many 'historical' narratives could therefore be seen as tragedies and vice versa. Medieval discussions of 'tragedy' often include reference to the 'historical' deeds of Alexander or Arthur (probably perceived in terms of the Boethian Wheel of Fortune described in the same section of the *Consolatio* which contains the definition of tragedy); and Lucan, as we have seen, was sometimes also considered to be a tragic poet (though his exact status was often debated). The medieval French translations of Boethius sometimes equate tragedy with *chansons de geste*, probably because of the epic and Virgilian elements in the *romans antique*, which in poems like the *Roman d'Eneas* offer 'certainly the most completely achieved "Virgil" of the high Middle Ages' (Baswell, *Virgil*, p. 15).

Many medieval discussions of epic overlap with these loose criteria for tragic narrative. Epic writers are often referred to as historians: Alexander Nequam, for example, calls Virgil, Statius and Lucan 'ystoriographos' (ed. Hunt, *Teaching and Learning*, p. 269); Statius was known to the Middle Ages only as an epic poet, until the rediscovery of his *Sylvae* in 1416–17). One of the major medieval commentaries on Statius, the

late-twelfth-century 'In principio', begins with a generalisation about
'actoris historiographi' which draws on the authority of Servius (ed.
Anderson, *Before 'The Knight's Tale'*, p. 230). The Servian discussion of
the *Aeneid* had established two defining features of epic narration: heroic
verse (*metrum heroicum* or *carmen heroicum*) and mixed action. Heroic
verse 'consists of both human and divine characters, containing the true
with the false' (ed. Thilo and Hagen, I, p. 4; tr. Anderson, *Before 'The
Knight's Tale'*, p. 146). Mixed action involves the mode of narration where
both the characters and the author speak. Epic could be regarded as historical discourse provided that the characteristic intervention of the pagan
gods (the 'divine characters' of Servius) was regarded as poetic fiction
requiring allegorisation, while the reported action of the human characters was regarded as historical fact. Conrad of Hirsau, reflecting Isidore,
says that poets sometimes intermingle truth with falsehood and notes
that the *Aeneid* and the *Thebaid* offer a mixture of history and fiction.
Boccaccio, whose own response to the *Thebaid* is one of the major vernacular interventions in rewriting epic narration, comments that heroic poets
can appear to be writing history, 'yet their hidden meaning is far other than
appears on the surface' (*Genealogia deorum gentilium* 14.9; tr. Minnis and
Scott, p. 424).

This blurry distinction between epic and historical narration is echoed
and repeated in medieval commentaries on Statius, where the *Thebaid* is
said to be a kind of history embellished by poetic imagination for the purposes of moral and political instruction. The twelfth-century 'In principio'
commentary, for example, which was still being read and copied in the
sixteenth century, says that the *materia* receives tripartite treatment: historical, allegorical and by means of poetic fiction (ed. Anderson, *Before
'The Knight's Tale'*, p. 232). In addition, Statius is said to use high
style which was, of course, traditionally the style associated with epic
and tragedy. Similarly, the late-medieval 'Autor iste' Statius commentary asserts that Statius imitates Homer in the *Achilleid* and Virgil in
the *Thebaid*, and employs heroic song, high style and artificial order,
while noting that *Thebaydos* can be glossed as 'historia de Thebis' (ed.
Anderson, p. 245).

By contrast, Arnulf of Orléans describes the Lucan of the *Pharsalia* (*De
bello civili*) as both poet and historian ('non est iste poeta purus, sed poeta
et historiographicus'), and distinguishes him from normal epic procedures
because 'nichil fingit' (ed. Marti, p. 4): by omitting 'fictions' of the pagan
gods and by not employing artificial order in his narration he can be seen
to differ from other epic writers. Boccaccio, a thorough Arnulfian, says
of Lucan that many think of him as a 'metrical historian' rather than a
poet (*Genealogia deorum gentilium* 14.13; tr. Minnis and Scott, p. 435).
Nevertheless, Arnulf argues that Lucan uses poetic devices when he puts

forward three viewpoints without privileging or affirming any of them 'in the manner of a poet [*more poete*]', and when he writes in verse (*metrice scribit*, commenting on *Pharsalia* 1.412; ed. Marti, p. 55). Moreover, Arnulf notes that Lucan is ethical not because he offers moral precepts but because he presents noble and virtuous characters to be admired, making virtue attractive to his readers. Boccaccio reflects this in his comments on Virgil, arguing that one of his intentions 'concealed within the poetic veil, was to show with what passions human frailty is infested, and the strength with which a steady man subdues them' (*Genealogia deorum gentilium* 14.13; tr. Minnis and Scott, p. 435). A similar attitude is found in the anonymous fourteenth-century *Compendium* on the *Achilleid* of Statius, a text that received increased critical attention after 1100 as it began to be included as the epic exemplar among the texts studied as part of the grammar syllabus. The intention of Statius was 'that we should become great-spirited and strong by consideration of the actions of great-spirited and victorious men'. The book pertains to ethics, but only *mediate*: it does not treat of morals principally. Therefore 'judgement is required in our assessment of what is honest, useful and worthwhile' in the text (ed. Jeudy and Riou, p. 162). The emphasis in such readings is firmly placed on the engagement of the reader in a process of *consideratio* leading to *assimilatio* (to use the Averroistic terms) revolving around the assessment and application of praise or blame.

The link between epic and tragic narration is made explicit in the *Compendium* when it links the moral *modus agendi* of the *Achilleid* with that found 'in aliis tragoediis', and cites the standard Boethian definition of the tears and tumult of tragedy: 'the overthrow of happy realms by the random strokes of Fortune' (ed. Jeudy and Riou, p. 162). The praise of heroes; the beneficial effects of their example on the audience; and the indirect and challenging way they are required to make moral judgements: all these allow the *Achilleid* (and the *Thebaid*) to be seen as a tragedy, not only in a Boethian sense but in an Aristotelian (if not an Averroistic) sense. Yet we are told that the poet was writing in imitation of Homer and Virgil. When Dante reveals to Statius the identity of his guide, he describes him as 'that same Virgil from whom you derived the power to sing of men and of the gods' (*Purgatorio* 21.125–6), alluding to the distinctive Servian epic mode of *carmen heroicum*. Yet Dante, in making Virgil refer to the *Aeneid* as 'alta mia tragedia' (*Inferno* 20.112–13), implicitly accepts the blurring and blending of the genres characteristic of medieval discussion of both. The results of that process are apparent in the theoretical writings of Boccaccio and even more apparent in his own reworkings of the *Thebaid* in his *Teseida*.

Dante's own knowledge of tragedy and comedy was probably derived from handbooks and dictionaries rather than from any first-hand acquaintance with representative classical texts, though Boccaccio tells us that in Florence Dante 'heard lectures on the poetic authors [and] studied the historiographers' (*Esposizioni sopra la Comedia di Dante, accessus* 32; tr. Wallace in Minnis and Scott, p. 510). Dante repeats an older stylistic model that associated high, middle and low style with tragedy, elegy and comedy respectively. Tragic style involves the harmonious blending of gravity of *sententia*, excellence of vocabulary, superb verses and elevated construction, and should only be applied to the most dignified subjects, 'salus, amor et virtus' (*De vulgari eloquentia* 2.4.8). Virgil's epic clearly satisfies both the stylistic requirements and the subject-matter, so that the fountainhead of Latin epic can also be seen as the model for 'new' tragedy.

Dante's description of Virgil in the *Inferno* as 'one grown faint, perhaps from too much silence' (*Inferno* 1.1, 62–3) may reflect his perception of the relative critical neglect of the *Aeneid* and perhaps of other epics in the earlier Middle Ages (though in truth there seems to have been continued critical and imaginative interest), and this perception presumably lies behind Boccaccio's comment that Dante saw 'Virgil and the others to be as good as abandoned' (*Esposizioni sopra la Comedia di Dante, accessus* 76; tr. Wallace in Minnis and Scott, p. 519). But that perceived neglect was to be triumphantly reversed in Trecento Italy with new lectures and commentaries drawing on the riches of the earlier tradition (particularly the commentary attributed to Bernard Silvester). Giovanni del Virgilio, one of the new breed of classicists beginning to emerge in the generation after Dante, was hired in 1321 (the year of Dante's death) by the city authorities of Bologna, to offer extra-curricular lectures on classical literature: the 'set authors' were to be Virgil, Statius, Ovid and Lucan, the same Latin authors invoked by Chaucer at the end of *Troilus*, and traditionally associated with epic and tragedy. All the early commentators on the *Commedia* (who show a high degree of intertextual dependence) include Virgil as the outstanding tragic exemplar against which Dante is refining and measuring his own comic creation, and their commentaries constitute a significant and influential body on the generic labelling of narrative verse.

In his commentary on the *Commedia* (*c.* 1328), the Carmelite Guido da Pisa defines tragedy in terms which blend Isidore and Horace. He sees it as a *narratio* with a plot trajectory from pleasing to fearful or dreadful (*horribilis*), and says that Homer and Virgil are the best tragic poets, though he also cites Seneca (tr. Minnis and Scott, pp. 474–5). Guido also says that one of the objectives of the *Commedia* was to 'give men a fresh knowledge of the works of the poets which had been completely abandoned and consigned to oblivion, but in which there are many teachings useful and necessary for living a good life' (tr. Minnis and Scott, p. 473).

In addition to this typically ethical (and typically epic) view of poetry, he adds that another objective is to condemn by exemplary stories the wicked life of evil men and especially of prelates and princes, and to commend the life of good and virtuous men (tr. Minnis and Scott, p. 473), an intention that seems both to echo the wider view of poetry as praise of virtue and perhaps to mark the reinstatement of the Isidorean view of tragedy as dealing with 'villainous' rulers.

Jacopo della Lana, whose commentary on *Inferno* 20 was finished before 1328, distinguishes between comedy (which deals with daily events of lowly people) and tragedy (which deals with those initially of great estate who are brought low; cit. Kelly, *Tragedy and Comedy*, p. 23). Jacopo Alighieri (writing in the early fourteenth century) argues that tragic style deals with 'architettoniche magnificenze' (perhaps alluding to the structural analyses often included in epic commentary) and is illustrated by Lucan and Virgil (ed. Jarro, pp. 43–4). Andrea Lancia's *Ottimo commento* offers in its third recension (1337–40) a double definition that distinguishes between epic and tragedy proper: tragedy either treats great things (as in Lucan and Virgil), or begins in happiness and ends in misery.[12] The earliest version of Pietro Alighieri's commentary on Dante (*c.* 1340) is the first to link comedy and tragedy with theatrical performance, perhaps under the influence of Trevet's commentary on Seneca, though in other respects he depends on Hugutio's definition and through him on Isidore.[13] One version of Benvenuto da Imola's commentary (1375–6), which cites the Averroistic *Poetics*, though not to any effect in regard to tragedy, offers a stylistic view:

Tragedy is a high and proud style; for it deals with memorable and horrifying deeds, like changes of kingdoms, the uprooting of cities, conflicts in war, deaths of kings, the destruction and slaughter of men, and other great disasters.

(tr. Kelly, *Tragedy and Comedy*, p. 48)

Benvenuto links the high style of tragedy with epic, describing the works of Homer, Virgil, Euripides, Statius, Simonides, Ennius 'and many others' as tragedies. His list, and the fact that two versions of his commentary make reference to the tragedies of Seneca, reflect the broadening classical horizons and deepening textual knowledge of late-Trecento humanism.

Benvenuto's lectures on Dante were given in the same decade that Chaucer was commanding his 'tragedy' of *Troilus and Criseyde* to kiss the steps trodden by 'Virgile, Ovide, Omer, Lucan, and Stace'. Dante's definition of the *materia* of tragedy ('salus, amor, virtus') comfortably fits Chaucer's tragical-historical epic, the *materia* of Chaucer's acknowledged

---

[12] Kelly, *Tragedy and Comedy*, p. 25.   [13] Kelly, pp. 27–9.

'tragic' antecedents and what his unacknowledged antecedent Boccaccio had done with the epic *materia* of Statius in the *Teseida*. Indeed what is most striking about these largely inductive medieval definitions of tragedy is how dependent they are on the models of classical epic they possessed and how inadequate they are as descriptions of the formal and stylistic features of genuine classical tragedy (unsurprisingly given the paucity of such texts available to them).

The only body of authentically tragic verse to have survived intact to the later Middle Ages was, of course, the tragedies of Seneca. But although copies of the A-text of the plays were available in northern Europe in the late-twelfth and thirteenth centuries and were apparently widely copied, *Seneca tragicus* was much less influential than *Seneca ethicus*. They are referred to in Gervase of Melkley's *Ars versificaria* (*c.* 1215; described in Chapter 2 above). Nequam recommends them as a school-text though his grammatically curious comment that 'Tragediam ipsius et Declamationes legere non erit inutile' (ed. Hunt, *Teaching and Learning*, p. 270) does not inspire confidence in his knowledge of them. But the tragedies were most influential in a form that denied them the possibility of serious and sustained literary attention. They were systematically excerpted and anthologised, and at best reduced to mere plot-summaries. Helinand of Froidmont's *Chronicon* includes 'sententie egregie et morales' in its twelfth book, while another set of extracts, probably produced in Paris, was the source of the Senecan citation in the *Flores paradysii* and Vincent of Beauvais' *Speculum historiale* (9.113–14). Northern interest in the text seems to have waned in the later thirteenth century, just as it was beginning to flare up in pre-humanist Padua. Lovato Lovati discovered a copy of an alternative, and much less widely known and disseminated, text of the tragedies at Pomposa around 1290. This new Italian interest in the *Tragedies* motivates the only two substantial literary discussions of the plays in the later Middle Ages.[14]

In December 1315, the Paduan statesman, lawyer and poet Albertino Mussato (1262–1329) was crowned Poet Laureate for his Latin tragedy *Ecerinis*, the first since classical times to be written in classical metre. It is likely that Mussato intended his poem to be recited rather than performed, as in his critical writings he condemns dramatic fictions (*fictiones scenicae*; *Epistola* 7, cit. Greenfield, p. 85). Indeed the custom was established in Padua of publicly reciting the poem in the presence of the poet, during the Christmas celebrations. This followed the received wisdom on the performance of Senecan tragedy, and Mussato openly

---

[14] However, it should be noted that Thomas Walsingham's *Prohemia poetarum* (on which see p. 199 above) includes a series of *accessus* to Seneca's tragedies, apparently of his own making and consisting largely of plot-summaries; they exhibit no debt to Trevet's introductions to his commentaries on those texts.

imitates the style of *Hercules furens* in his own tragedy. This same received wisdom informs his thinking about the nature of tragic poetry, especially in one of his epistles written before the *Ecerinis*. The influence of Boethius is apparent: tragedy 'commemorates the acts of leaders and the names of generous kings, and the deep pall which overturns their fortunes and dwellings' (*Epistola* 1; cit. Greenfield, p. 86). Noble poems require noble characters. Whimsical Fortune provides the *materia* for the tragic writer. The lightning of tragedy strikes the high towers but does not reach the low huts. The instability of human events can be ethically useful by instilling fear in the audience. Tragedy 'teaches constancy in the face of the adversity of destiny and comforts the anxious soul of man' (*Epistola* 1; cit. Greenfield, p. 87). Tragedy is a moral form: the essence of Senecan moral stoicism as distilled by his medieval readers is blended with a reading of Boethius and a sprinkling of Virgilian moral nobility.

These generalised perceptions were applied by Mussato directly to the plays of Seneca. His *Evidentia tragediarum Senece*, written after his own tragedy, perhaps in 1315 or 1316, and addressed to Marsilius of Padua, addresses the proper *materia* of tragedy in the form of a fictional dialogue between Lovati, discoverer of the new E-text of the tragedies, and Mussato. Lovati had in fact died in 1309, and his role as *magister* in the debate is an act of literary homage on Mussato's part, allowing him to attribute extensive wisdom and knowledge to his friend. Explicitly citing Boethius, 'Lovati' offers a wholly conventional definition of tragedy: 'eversi regni cuiuspiam sub deploratione descriptio' (*Evidentia tragediarum Senece*, ed. Megas, p. 124). Mussato apparently did not have the benefit of William of Conches' glosses on Boethius or of other discussions of the genre in dictionaries such as Hugutio's *Magnae derivationes* or the *Catholicon*. But Lovati's E-text had been prefaced by brief extracts from Books 8 and 18 of Isidore. These may have been known to Mussato but would have been of little value to him in isolation. Instead Mussato seems to have generated his own extrapolation of Boethian tragedy in alliance with his sense of Seneca's moral agenda, and perhaps from his own sense of epic purpose.

The twin interests of the *Evidentia* are the appropriateness of the different metrical forms employed by Seneca and a concern to analyse the effect of the texts on their audience. This probably reflects the Horace of the *Ars poetica*, whose form and intention motivated many of Mussato's own epistles in defence of poetry. But his thinking may also be coloured by the Aristotelianism that was still influential in the Padua of his time. Indeed he cites the *Poetics* translation by William of Moerbeke both in the *Evidentia* and in his *Vita et Mores L. A. Senece*. Although it is unclear how extensive his knowledge of the *Poetics* was, his blending of Horace and Aristotle into an original synthesis underpins his various attempts to articulate his sense of the elevated status of poetry. His understanding of poetic worth was to be developed and augmented by later humanist writers like Boccaccio and Salutati, but it is significant that it should have been Seneca – the moral philosopher par excellence for medieval critics – who was the inspiration for him to apply his theories to actual texts.

According to the *Vita Senece*, the first poets were philosophers and theologians, who wrote about philosophical truths using allegory, enigma, similitudes and other figures in order to lead the awareness of their audience to the contemplation of the divine. In this they paralleled the *modus agendi* of Scripture. Mussato, extrapolating from the moral status enjoyed by Seneca throughout the medieval period, argues that insights in Seneca's letters (especially the spurious correspondence with St Paul) support the view of his Christian conversion. Seneca, in following the Greek lead of Sophocles and Aeschylus, assumed the tragic style, 'poetice artis supremum apicem et grandiloquum' (*Vita et mores*, ed. Megas, p. 159), which was appropriate to the high status as well as the downfall and death of kings and leaders (a plot structure supported by citation of Boethius). Many of these narrative features discerned by Mussato in Senecan tragedy had already been applied to epic writers.

Mussato argues that in the tragedies Seneca blended Christian revelation with Latin rhetoric to create 'poetic theology':

> Lest he might seem lacking something from what is knowable to human powers, he engaged in composing poetic theology after he had written almost all his other works so as to show himself clearly a theologian and a poet in the same work.
>
> (*Vita et mores*, ed. Megas, p. 157)

This blend of theology and poetics becomes a major hallmark of the poetic theorists of the early Renaissance, which in its generalised ethico-spiritual view of the role of the narrative poet further encouraged the gathering together of epic and tragic writers into a single fold.

Mussato, in this and other respects, must be seen as a transitional figure who adapts and refines inherited medieval attitudes to literature while analysing and synthesising with increasing rigour and breadth of literary vision. Because of his interest in verse-forms and stylistic decorum, for example, Mussato is able to make a highly significant distinction between two kinds of high style found in those classical texts he regards as tragedies, thereby creating a narrative taxonomy that allowed genuine tragedy and those poems usually described as epics to coexist within a loose generic framework but without collapsing and conflating them together. The first form of tragedy, written in iambics, is the conventional

Boethian model: the ruin and fall of great kings and princes.[15] This kind is exemplified by Sophocles and Seneca. The second, exemplified by Ennius, Lucan, Virgil and Statius, concerns epic victories of sublime lords and kings.[16] This kind of 'tragedy' uses the heroic metre. Thus although the process of assimilating epic to tragedy had been patchily underway for centuries, Mussato's framework allowed epic to retain a kind of narrative integrity while profiting from the accumulated wisdom of medieval thinking about high style narrative and its psychological and moral impact on an audience.

The *Ecerinis* was of sufficient interest and importance to generate two early Paduan commentaries. Guizzardo da Bologna's was finished in December 1317, perhaps to coincide with that year's performance of the text. Somewhat later came Pace of Ferrara's *Evidentia Ecerinis*. Both follow Mussato in relying on the (unglossed) Boethian description of tragedy; both rely heavily on Horace's *Ars poetica*. Both men also produced commentaries on Geoffrey of Vinsauf's *Poetria nova*. Horatian literary prescription and neo-Horatian literary production are increasingly combined to fill the textual void at the heart of medieval understanding of tragedy. Although the *Ecerinis* and its commentaries were the product of renewed interest in tragic form among the *literati* of Padua, an interest probably stimulated by Lovati, it would be misleading to see the play's performance as the dawn of a new understanding of tragedy: interest was local and limited, and the real work of excavating classical tragedy from its layers of medieval misunderstanding did not begin until later in the century. Earlyfourteenth-century readers of Seneca still viewed him from a medieval perspective.

When the Italian cardinal Nicholas of Prato encountered a text of Seneca's tragedies, he was struck by the difficulties of the text and felt the need of the sort of euhemerist and mythographical exposition traditionally applied to works like Ovid's *Metamorphoses* and, closer in form, the epic narratives of Virgil and Statius. He wrote to his fellow Dominican Nicholas Trevet, whose commentaries on Boethius and Seneca's *Declamationes* were already known to him, that,

the book . . . is full of such obscurities, tangled up in such deeply hidden meanings, and has interwoven into it such a jumble of mythological stories [*fabulae*].   (tr. Minnis and Scott, p. 341)

Between 1314 and 1317, Trevet obliged with a patient exposition of the mythography of the texts, occasionally pointing out moral implications or

---

[15] '. . . de ruinis et casibus magnorum regum et principum, quorum maxime exitia, clades, cedes, seditiones, et tristes actus describunt'; *Vita et mores*, ed. Megas, p. 160.

[16] '. . . regum et ducum sublimium aperte et campestria belle et triumphales victorias'; p. 160.

showing how the plays illustrate general ethical truisms. There was little in the way of earlier commentary to assist Trevet in his task, and the wide circulation achieved by his completed exposition must have contributed significantly to the fourteenth-century popularity of Seneca's plays. Some of that popularity was likely to have been an extension to the now more widely available *Tragedies* of the esteem already granted to Seneca as a moralist. In his reply to Nicholas of Prato, Trevet praises Seneca for his eminence in moral philosophy, and, more strikingly, for his ability to adapt his teachings to 'the varied capacities of men's minds' (tr. Minnis and Scott, p. 342). He varies simple precepts with familiar examples and brief and obscure epigrammatic sayings. Sententiousness had long been considered one of Seneca's great virtues, and this reputation was reinforced by the collections of *Proverbia* attributed to his authorship which achieved a wide circulation throughout the period. Furthermore, legends of his friendship with St Paul and secret conversion to Christianity, and the spiritual *spuria* attributed to him, enhanced his status as an almost neo-patristic figure (Mussato described him as a natural theologian). But the dominant view of Seneca saw him as a moralist.

Trevet, having already written on the *Declamationes*, was conscious that the *modus agendi* of the tragedies differed from that of the other works. His explanation echoes that of Mussato, without being influenced by it: Seneca was 'a mature scholar who had moved in the lofty realms of virtue', and he wrote the tragedies 'to instil into tender minds ethical teachings wrapped in pleasant stories [*fabulae*], while at the same time amusing them' (tr. Minnis and Scott, p. 342). Modern readers, however, are put off the texts because their innermost recesses are wrapped in a dark cloud of fabular narrative. Trevet's introduction to his commentary cites Augustine's Varronian division of theology into fabular or mythical (used by poets); natural (used by philosophers); and civil (used by priests and people). Mythical theology, he says, belongs to the theatre and can be divided into tragedy and comedy. Tragic writers excelled in the argument of myths, which they invented to conceal truth. Trevet has an almost Horatian sense of Seneca's blend of instruction and delight. In Trevet's analysis, for example, the final cause of *Hercules furens* is described as 'delectatio'. However, it can 'in a certain manner' be placed in the category of ethics, because it narrates actions deserving of praise and blame, and deals with the correction of behaviour by means of the examples. Trevet's careful modulation into ethics *by means of* 'delectatio' may be a conscious attempt to explain the integumental nature of Seneca's moral procedures in the tragedies, in contrast to the explicit morality of his popular *persona*. Selectively paraphrasing Isidore, Trevet shows that Seneca's 'book of tragedies' also respects the generic outlines of the form, 'for it contains sorrowful verses on the misfortunes of great men, in which the poet never speaks in his own person, but only the characters who have been introduced' (tr. Minnis and Scott, p. 344). This dramatic manner of representation is strictly appropriate to tragic and comic poets.

Like Mussato, Trevet recognises both the material similarities and the stylistic differences between epic and tragedy. He distinguishes the tragic or dramatic mode of expression from tragic *materia*. The result of this is that texts that use the mixed mode of narrative (where both the author and the characters speak) may be considered tragic by virtue of their subject-matter rather than their style. The examples he cites are by the keystone epic poets: Virgil in the *Aeneid*, Lucan, and Ovid's *Metamorphoses*. They can be called tragic poets because their *materia* was the misfortunes of kings and great men, and affairs of state. The generic boundaries are widened to include epic, history and mythology, while recognising the greater generic decorum of Seneca who writes about tragic material in the tragic (i.e. dramatic) mode of narration. Trevet's sense of the mythological force and mythographic potential of the plays may also have promoted an awareness that a common factor in the exegesis of epic and tragedy was the hermeneutics of myth.

While earlier commentators had supplied the absence of surviving classical tragedies by applying largely Boethian definitions of tragedy to epic narrative, readers like Mussato and Trevet showed greater sensitivity to the different literary decorums of epic and tragedy. But when Boccaccio came to emulate the epic gesture in poems like *Teseida*, he did so from a background of commentary on Virgil and Dante that allowed elements of tragic theory to enrich and embellish his reading of Virgil's achievement and his understanding of Statius' endeavours to flow into his own playful and purposeful development of epic narrative. With the humanist return to serious study of Virgil, the later Renaissance emancipation and generic separation of epic and tragedy was already in sight.

The empty genre of tragedy had, by the end of the fourteenth century, become the *locus* of a genuinely dramatic synthesis of genres, modes of reading and psychologies of poetic response. The term could now sometimes be used with purpose and edge. When the Benedictine Thomas Walsingham, himself a poetic commentator of wide reading and traditional training, wrote in his chronicle of the 1381 English rising that 'we have now written the tragic history of the lordship of the rustics [historiam tragicam ... de dominatione rusticorum] and the wild bacchae of the commons and the madness of the villeins' (*Historia anglicana* 2.13), he perhaps knew from his own earlier discussions of the Isidorean and Boethian definitions of tragedy that his carnivalesque sense of a world turned upside-down could best be signalled by allowing the *dramatis personae* of comedy (the rustics) to suffer a strategically parodic tragic overthrow from their false positions of eminence at the hands of Fortune. At about the same time in England, Chaucer was elaborating a concept of narrative tragedy that was initially as inductive as earlier attempts to understand the term. Chaucer seems to have differed from many commentators in believing that tragedy was a current and live genre rather than obsolete and historical. For him, '"Bewailing" rather than "advising" or "consoling" is the principal business of tragedy' (Kelly, *Chaucerian Tragedy*, p. 91). With more recent vernacular Italian materials on which to draw, especially the writings of Boccaccio (whose *De casibus virorum illustrium* Chaucer considered to be in the tragic mode even if Boccaccio himself did not), he eventually produced an idiosyncratically workable concept that had a surprisingly vigorous afterlife among fifteenth-century readers and imitators in Britain, and his influence perhaps survived as late as Shakespeare.

Satire and comedy

Satire was a serious business in the Middle Ages. If, as the Averroistic *Poetics* asserted, all poetry concerned itself with either praise or blame, then satire represented the vanguard of the medieval blame culture. In this respect satire is related to rhetoric in its explicit engagement with moral and social behaviour, and in terms of the Aristotelian ranking of the truth content of discourse in the *Organon* might be said to occupy a position between rhetoric and poetic. The *lex satire* of the Middle Ages ostensibly aspired to police the state with ethical rigour.[17] Not surprisingly, satire seems often to have been produced within clerical milieux and its aspirations and procedures increasingly came to overlap with those of preaching and moral theology, though in practice satire is often on the whimsical wing of moral righteousness.

Alexander Nequam's *Sacerdos ad altare* recommends that after due scholarly attention has been paid to rudimentary books (i.e. grammars and early reading-texts) the student should pass on to read 'satiricos et ystoriographos', so that the young may on the one hand learn that vices are to be fled and, on the other, might desire to imitate 'nobilia gesta' (ed. Hunt, *Teaching and Learning*, p. 269). This linking of satirists and historians (and implicitly of blame and praise) derives from the sense that both categories draw on non-fictional materials as their subject-matter, holding, as it were, a mirror up to nature. As one thirteenth-century poem puts it: 'Verum sub hac satira loquar-nichil fingam' (*Licet mundus varia*, cit. Kindermann, p. 44). Satire operated only at the literal level of signification and was therefore naked (*nuda*) and direct in its intentions and

---

[17] 'Lex satire est criminalia dampnare, venialia condonare' ('the law of satire is to condemn serious faults and to deliver up or condone venial faults'). Gloss on Horace, Vatican City, Biblioteca Apostolica Vaticana, MS Reg. lat. 1780, fol. 76r; cit. Reynolds, *Medieval Reading*, p. 146.

executions, avoiding the poetic fictions and coverings (*integumenta*) of other genres and other modes of writing. For this reason it was particularly suited to young readers who had yet to master more advanced interpretative manoeuvres, and this explains the popularity of Horace's *Satires* as a school-text, and the huge bulk of commentary generated by that text. The commentary on *Aeneid* Books 1–6 attributed to Bernard Silvester says that poets who write *cause utilitatis* are satirists, those who write 'causa delectationis' produce comedies, and those who write for both reasons are historians (*Prologus*, tr. Minnis and Scott, p. 152). Hence, Conrad of Hirsau is able to impute some satirical purpose to the 'historian' Lucan, whose works the Middle Ages had perennial difficulty in classifying.

For the medieval reader, classical satire was represented by Persius, Juvenal and, perhaps above all, Horace. According to Nequam, Juvenal's *moralia dicta* should be locked in the bosom of the student while Horace should be studied to avoid the vices he depicts. Over a century later, Hugo von Trimberg's *Registrum multorum auctorum* praises Horace as 'prudent and discreet, a steadfast tamer and drawer out of vices' ('prudens et discretus, Viciorum emulus / firmus et mansuetus'; 1.116–17, ed. Langosch, p. 164). Juvenal and Persius are erroneously grouped by the *Registrum* with the 'philosopher' Seneca and the 'historians' Lucan and Statius as poets of Neronian Rome. By implication they are seen to share a commitment to moral and political philosophy, nurtured in the unfavourable soil of a corrupt regime. Juvenal is 'biting, constant and true and no admirer of ills' ('mordax . . . Constans et veridicus non adulans malis'), while Persius is 'the encourager of honest living and the critic of vice, the rasping file of depravity' ('cultor honestatis / Reprehensor vicii lima pravitatis'; 1.158–9, 160–1, ed. Langosch, p. 166).

All three satirists reached the later Middle Ages with well-established bodies of Vulgate scholia, strengthened and reordered by Carolingian commentators, and still being copied and quarried in the fifteenth century. The relative stability of these commentary traditions, and the agreement among them about the generic and stylistic attributes of the form allow the emergence of what has been called a 'vocabulary of censure':

> the subject-matter of satire is vice [*vitium*]; the satirist is motivated by indignation [*indignatio*] or some such other passionate reaction which leads to his sudden [*ex abrupto*] outburst against human iniquity. The scholia present the satirist as a bold, just reformer who sees the need to counteract the moral degeneration of the community; a man who admits to his own failings while sparing no one from his censure; a poet who aims to correct with constructive criticism, not to defame with malicious slander. (Miller, 'Satiric Poet', p. 81)

Distinctions can be made, therefore, between satire and invective, and between complaint and satire. Satire is more constructive:

Intentio omnium satirarum communis esse dicitur virtutem persuadere et vitia
reprehendere spe correctionis et non spe malevolentiae.

(Commentary 2 on Juvenal, ed. Dürr, p. 27)

[The common intent of all satirists is said to be to persuade to virtue and to
reprehend vices in the expectation of correction and not in the expectation
(spirit?) of malevolence.]   (tr. Miller, 'Satiric Poet', p. 85)

From the end of the eleventh century, the salient features of the genre were
made more accessible by the collection and classification of information
dispersed throughout the scholia into collections known as *accessus ad
satiricos* which became, as it were, the case-law of the *lex satire*. As with
many *accessus*, they acted as a bridge between the praxis of past ages and
the praxis of the present by distilling the essential requirements of satiric
writing into a format that was easily detached from its host text and
equally easily served as a blueprint for new writing. An essential part of
this generalising process was the creation or elaboration of false etymologies for the word *satyra*. The two most popular link it with 'naked, mocking satyrs, because in this [kind of] poem depraved morals are stripped
of their clothing and mocked' (the stripping of the satyrs alluding to the
naked literalness of the satiric method) or with a great bowl or dish filled
with different morsels of food, 'for in a certain sense satire is full of the
vices which it reprehends'.[18] Horace himself encouraged (perhaps inadvertently) a probably spurious link between satyr plays and satire in his
elliptical comments on his own style 'as a satyr-writer' in the *Ars poetica*
(*AP* 234).

In addition to commentaries, generic descriptions in literary dictionaries and encyclopaedias necessarily separated the lineaments of the genre
from first-hand experience of its classical manifestations. Papias' *Elementarium doctrinae rudimentum* (before 1045), influenced by the definitions
in Isidore's *Etymologiae*, sees satirists as a subgroup of comic writers,
'quibus generaliter uitia carpuntur . . . Et nudi pinguntur, quia uitia
denudent' (ed. Kelly, *Tragedy and Comedy*, p. 8, n. 31). Similarly, prescriptive arts of poetry offered definitions as part of their treatment of
the four main compositional genres. Something of the paradoxical regard
in which satire was held emerges from the allusive description of her in
Matthew of Vendôme's *Ars versificatoria* (*c.* 1175):

Satire, fasting from silence; although her brow is filled with timidity, her
downcast eyes give testimony to the slyness of her mind. Even her lips are
widespread from constant chatter. She also makes a big show of her modesty
which has never blushed at the naked body.   (2.6; tr. Galyon, p. 64)

---

[18] Bernard of Utrecht, *Commentum in Theodolum*, ed. Huygens [1970], p. 62; Conrad of
Hirsau, tr. Minnis and Scott, p. 60; 'School of William of Conches', tr. Minnis and Scott,
p. 137, ed. Wilson, p. 90.

The common *materia* of satirists is vices, addressed either singly or as part of a survey of society. The common intent of the satirist is to reprehend vice and persuade or commend virtue either in a particular sub-group or in society at large. The utility of the poem is that it enhances morality, and it can thus comfortably be attributed to ethics. Satire generally uses *sermo humilis*, but should be in verse. But despite its use of the literal sense and naked expression, by no means all satire was open and clear. Indeed in many cases the endemic irony of the satiric mode introduces a certain interpretative responsibility on its readers to locate its moral centre of gravity. Bernard of Utrecht's influential commentary on 'Theodulus' says that satire commonly reprehends vices, and that satirists 'yronice laudant vituperandi et vituperant laudandi' (ed. Huygens [1970], p. 62). Thus although the *moralia dicta* of Persius and Juvenal could be accepted with reasonable comfort, the obliquity of Horace's *Satires*, or *Sermones* as they are usually known in the period, required more careful negotiation. A standard interpretative response was to analyse the satires in terms of dramatic or *ex persona* narration or in terms of a more mixed narrative style:

The discourse [*sermo*] is so called because it is distributed between the writer and at least two other persons, and is tailored to suit the character speaking. For this reason too, the preaching of bishops is rightly called 'a sermon' [*sermo*].

(Twelfth-century Tegernsee *accessus*; tr. Minnis and Scott, p. 34)

The mixed narrative style therefore requires a heightened rhetorical awareness on the part of audience to enable them to locate and identify the morality.

As this *accessus* makes clear, there was some common ground between the moral rhetoric of the satirist and that of the preaching office of the church. Perhaps for this reason, satire emerges as one of the sprightliest genres in the academic and ecclesiastical coteries of the twelfth and thirteenth century. In this world, 'highly respectful attitudes to poetic forms and rhetorical devices could coexist with mockeries of the follies of men and the alleged failings of women' (Minnis, *Magister amoris*, p. 194). The satiric schools of Golias, Primas and the Archpoet contained many stylistic innovators and imitators. These verse satires prove to be remarkably popular and consistent components in the many poetic anthologies of the thirteenth and fourteenth centuries, and were in some cases still being copied in the fifteenth. While such longevity, and their conventional subject-matter, significantly reduces their value as documents for social history, it also suggests that donnish humour is slow to change. Walter of Châtillon (*c.* 1134-*c.* 1204) finesses the commentary tradition in his self-proclaimed satires. He skilfully deploys the goliardic strophe *cum auctoritate* (a stanza ending in a hexameter line borrowed from a classical poem) as part of his often playful homage to the classical satirists. Many of these early *auctoritas*-poems seem to have been composed for institutional celebrations and competitions and are often associated with the Feast of Fools. Later poems look more like occasional satires or appeals for preferment produced in scholarly contexts. This kind of imitation often has its tongue firmly in its cheek and wears its learning prominently on its sleeve, displaying its virtuosity by, for example, restricting the *auctoritates* to one author. The insouciant antifeminism of many such texts, while reflecting the all-male atmosphere of most educational institutions, found echoes in some of Juvenal's writings, and encouraged the popularity of works like Walter Map's late-twelfth-century *Dissuasio Valerii ad Ruffinum philosophum ne uxorem ducat*, which follows most of the rules of the genre.

Medieval satiric practitioners often reveal in their self-reflexive comments the extent to which the precepts of classical satiric theory have been appropriated into their own poetic practice, even if in Latin that practice owes more to the Goliardic line and to the rhythmical strophic forms of liturgical and paraliturgical hymns and sequences than to classical models. In the dedicatory letter which serves as an *accessus* to his poem *De contemptu mundi*, Bernard of Cluny claims 'materia est mihi viciorum reprehensio, et a vitiis revocare intentio' (ed. Hoskier, p. xxxviii). By 1241, in the *Morale scolarium* (also known as the *Opus satiricum* or *Liber satiricum*) of John of Garland, the process of critical appropriation has extended to application to the new work of the interpretative apparatus which had been used in expounding the old satires. John's preamble deliberately invokes the traditional parameters of satiric commentary:

> Scribo novam satiram, set sic ne seminet iram,
> Iram deliram, letali vulnere diram,
> Nullus dente mali lacerabitur in speciali,
> Immo metro tali ludet stilus in generali.
>
> (1–4, ed. Paetow)

[I am writing a new satire, but in order not to spread anger, which is maddening, terrible, deadly and wounding, no one in particular will be lacerated by the sharp words, but rather in such a style will my pen amuse itself.]

The rules of this 'new satire', while drawing on the old *lex satire*, also reflect the decorums of medieval preaching, where individual sinners should not be singled out for comment in sermons, but where common failings of society should be identified and reproved. The (perhaps occasionally authorial) glosses and commentaries accruing to the text see it as a 'carmen morale' or 'sermo moralis', while one *accessus*, recognising that 'satirice loquitur in hoc libro', goes on to define the two elements in 'sermo reprehensorius' as praise of the good and blame of the bad (Oxford, Bodleian Library, MS Rawlinson, G. 96, fol. 155r; cit. Kindermann, p. 42). As with Horace's *Ars poetica*, or Geoffrey of Vinsauf's *Poetria nova*, the application of a commentary to the work means that the earnest *Morale scolarium* becomes the locus of study for both the theory and the praxis of satire:

> Hec est lex satire, vitiis ridere, salire,
> Mores excire, que feda latent aperire.
>
> (423–4, ed. Paetow; tr. Rigg,
> *Anglo-Latin*, p. 167)
>
> [For this is satire's law: mock vice and jump around,
> Encourage upright ways and hidden filth expound.]

Jean de Meun's *apologia* for the *Roman de la Rose* shows clear knowledge of the *accessus ad satiricos* and probably of the textual practice of others as well.[19] Later vernacular writers like John Gower, described by a contemporary as 'satirus poeta' (*Works*, ed. Macaulay, III, p. 479), and Geoffrey Chaucer reveal clear indebtedness to medieval communal and estates satire, even when they explore, expand or explode its imaginative horizons.

Despite the high proportion of genuinely Juvenalian and Horatian lines used in the concluding *auctoritates* of strophic medieval satires, and the extent to which those compositions reflect the *lex satira* generated in the *accessus ad satiricos* tradition, many of the new compositions wander into a peculiar and generically uncertain no-man's-land between satire and comedy. Narrative poems, usually in elegiac distichs, begin to appear in the schools of the Loire valley around the middle of the twelfth century. This sub-genre is now usually described as the elegiac comedy, where echoes of, and fragments from, the classical satirists and Ovid are woven into a new or reworked narrative frame. Ovid is the presiding genius, providing a linguistic, stylistic and metrical model as well as pervasively subtle erotic and didactic irony that positions such texts ambiguously between comedy and satire. Vitalis of Blois wrote the *Geta* (based on the *Amphitryo* of Plautus) and the *Aulalaria* (based on the comedy *Querolus* attributed to Plautus) in a form recalling ancient comedy. William of Blois produced the *Alda*, ostensibly based on an epitome of Menander. Matthew of Vendôme's *Milo* is referred to as a comedy in some manuscripts. English examples include the *Babio*, *Baucis et Thraso* along with the 'De clericis et rustico' often attributed to Geoffrey of Vinsauf. The *Pamphilus*,

---

[19] Minnis, *Magister amoris*, pp. 96–7.

a richly Ovidian story that achieved astonishingly wide circulation as a school curriculum text, is written *ex persona* in dialogue form. Commentaries on the *Pamphilus* and extracts from it in *florilegia* suggest that the official attitude expressed towards it by teachers was focused more on its rhetorical and intertextual exuberance and its richness as a source of *sententiae* and one-liners. Even the lament of the raped woman could be related to and defused by medieval interest in the rhetorical strategies of female complaint (widely studied in Ovidian commentary). 'Rape scenes function in this tradition as the paradigmatic site for working out issues of power and powerlessness' (Woods, 'Sexual Violence', p. 73). The presence of *Pamphilus* in twelfth- and thirteenth-century school collections, often after the equally unsettling hankerings after young flesh of the *Elegies* of Maximian, implies a young, male and crypto-clerical readership, though later readers (perhaps of the vernacular versions and spin-offs) may have found the dynamics of sexual abuse less comfortably concealed behind a veneer of sentential pastiche. In their heavy-handed humour, aggressively male sexual innuendo, and self-conscious delight in wordplay and grammatical jokes, such texts suggest that their origin and performance was close to the schoolroom and the cloister. They highlight aspects of comic style by display and exaggeration, though the 'happy ending' required by definitions of the plot trajectory of comedy usually involved the subordination of women and the fulfilment of male sexual desires and fantasies. Many of these texts seem more concerned with sexual power than moral censure, though their interest in virility 'may be, in every sense, academic' (Minnis, *Magister amoris*, p. 194).

But, in theory at least, comedy was not a laughing matter. In the *Ars versificatoria*, Matthew of Vendôme's description of comedy alludes to its distinctive features when he speaks of her 'bowed head and workaday garb' which 'give no hint of merriment' (2.7; tr. Galyon, p. 64). Comedy is defined by contrast to tragedy by its modest style and unelevated subject-matter. The conception of comedy revealed here owes much to the older textbook definitions of comic style and plot. Isidore says that 'the comic speaks out on the deeds of private men, the tragic on public affairs and the histories of kings. Moreover, the arguments of tragic poets come from sorrowful things, those of the comic from joyful' (Isidore, *Etymologiae* 8.7.6; tr. Kelly, *Ideas and Forms*, p. 39).[20] Isidore also deploys a definition of comedy (derived from Lactantius) that brings it closer to the world of medieval *fabliau*, either in Latin or the vernacular:

---

[20] By describing the comic mode of procedure as 'dramatic', Isidore and his later readers would, of course, have been thinking primarily of Servian *ex persona* narration rather than theatrical performance.

Comedians are those who sang of the affairs of private men, in their speech or gestures, and they set forth in their stories the defilements of virgins and the loves of whores.　　　　(*Etymologiae* 18.46; tr. Kelly, *Ideas and Forms*, p. 46)

Papias, influenced by Placidus and Donatus on Terence, defines comedy as dealing with private matters and humble people using a middle and sweet style. Later Hugutio offers a fuller account, which may owe something to an earlier commentary on Terence:

Comedia -e: id est uillanus cantus uel uillana laus, quia tractat de rebus uillanis, rusticanis, et affinis est cottidiane locucioni.

(ed. Kelly, *Tragedy and Comedy*, pp. 6–7, n. 27)[21]

[Comedy: that is, the song or praise of villeins or rustics, because it treats of rustic matters and is associated with everyday speech.]

The standard definition in medieval dictionaries and prescriptive arts stresses that the plot trajectory of comedy goes from sorrow to joy; that comedy deals with private men and that it is written in low style. These discussions, although regularly citing Terence and Plautus as exponents of classical comedy, show little knowledge of the original texts. As so often with medieval discussion of classical genres, terms were accumulated, appropriated, modified and reapplied to rather different kinds of writing. Though less devoid of examples than the label of 'tragedy', contemporary commentators were comfortable in discarding the illustrations provided by classical antecedents and substituting their own examples drawn from contemporary practice in elegiac comedy. Perhaps reflecting the form or plot of contemporary compositions, John of Garland says that every comedy is an elegy (*Parisiana poetria* 5.372; ed. Lawler, pp. 102–3). Geoffrey of Vinsauf's *Documentum*, while referring readers to Horace's *Ars poetica* on matters of comic theory and to the comedies of Terence on matters of praxis, considered Horace's teachings on comedy to be obsolete and he instead addressed himself explaining how contemporary writers should deal with *jocosa materia* (2.162–3; ed. Faral, p. 317). Several discussions see comedy as a style of writing rather than as a distinct poetic or dramatic form. Despite the playful innovations of goliardic verse and elegiac comedy, the genre was imperfectly understood and never established its ethical credibility in the medieval period.

　　Meanwhile the moral seriousness of satire was reinforced by a rewriting of literary history that allowed it to steal what little ethical thunder comedy still had. John Balbus, in his discussion of *comedia* in the *Catholicon*, uses Isidore to distinguish between the 'old' writers of comedy like

---

[21] Oxford, Bodleian Library, MS Laud Misc. 626, fol. 124r–v.

Terence and the new, who he says are also called satirists and are represented by Persius and Juvenal. The claim in the Averroistic *Poetics* that all poetry is either praise or blame also appeared to sanction the supplanting of comedy by satire. When Hermann the German's version of the *Poetics* describes 'reprehensio et vituperatio' as pertaining to satire rather than tragedy, Hermann is substituting the word 'satire' for Aristotle's original 'comedy' (tr. Minnis and Scott, p. 304; compare the Greek *Poetics* 1453a). Matthew of Linköping distinguishes between comedy and satire in characteristic terms that downgrade the ethical status of comedy:

[S]atira vero de correccione morum sollicita mediocri utitur stilo; comedia uero de rebus cotidianis non nisi humilem admittit stilum.

(101; ed. and tr. Bergh, pp. 74–5)

[Satire, concerned with the correction of morals, uses the middle style. Comedy, however, which deals with everyday matters, admits of the low style only]

Both praise and blame, according to Matthew, function 'for the stirring up of the virtues' (35). Matthew follows Hermann in replacing Aristotle's 'comedy' with 'satire' (56). And whereas Horace (*Ars poetica* 93–8) had argued that tragedy and comedy could borrow from each other's styles for local effect, Matthew cites but rewrites this to make the contrast between tragedy and satire: 'Horace has pointed out that insignificant matters are brought up in tragedy and important ones in satire' (103; ed. and tr. Bergh, pp. 76–7). Comedy, increasingly marginalised in medieval discussions of genre, had little left to cover its modesty except a distinctive plot trajectory (misfortune to good fortune) expressed in low style about low-class characters.

By the end of the Middle Ages the thoroughly baggy concept of comedy had been stretched to cover an eclectic multitude of narrative sins from the *delectatio* of 'Bernard Silvester' through the *jocosa materia* of Geoffrey of Vinsauf to the Vulgate *Metamorphoses*' description of comedy as 'falsehood under the species of truth',[22] which itself sounds like the deception plot from a medieval *fabliau*. Inevitably a link could and would be made between the 'low style' and 'everyday speech' prescribed for comedy and the use of the vernacular for poetic composition.

Indeed the most substantial discussion of the nature of comedy in the period is found not in relation to a classical author at all, but in connection with a poem in the vernacular: Dante's *Commedia*. Dante engaged with this issue of comic style and vernacular poetry in *De vulgari eloquentia*, and in the early-fourteenth-century *Epistle to Can Grande della Scala*

---

[22] On *Metamophoses* 6. 169, which lists the four narrative sub-genres as *argumentum*, *fabula*, *historia* and *comedia*; cit. Coulson, *Study*, p. 32.

(perhaps partly by him?)[23] the link between them is fully articulated: the style of language used in Dante's *Commedia* is described as 'unstudied and lowly, as being in the vulgar tongue, in which even womenfolk hold their talk' (tr. Minnis and Scott, p. 461). The incestuous and textually inter-related early commentaries on the *Commedia* struggle to make sense of the title and its generic implications. Their ruminations do not mark a turning-point in the fortunes of the genre. Given the low status that comedy had come to occupy in relation to tragedy and satire, Dante's title appeared to his first commentators to present an embarrassing paradox. Eager to make sense of his father's classification of his great poem (and less willing than Petrarch to admit to honest bafflement), Pietro Alighieri appeals to Horace's teaching on mixed styles (*Ars poetica* 93–8) to argue that comedians, tragedians and satirists were all allowed, on occasion, to reprehend the wicked (*Prologus*; tr. Minnis and Scott, pp. 480–1). Boccaccio's extensive analysis of the plot and style of comedy in his *lecturae Dantis* (1373–4) could only weakly oppose the argument that Dante's work had been misnamed, not least because his taxonomy of the genre shows how poorly the *Commedia* fulfils its formal stylistic require-ments. He argued that Dante's thinking was more influenced by the plot trajectory of classical comedy ('a comedy should have a turbulent begin-ning, full of uproar and discord, and then the final part should end in peace and tranquillity'; *Prologus* 25, tr. Wallace in Minnis and Scott, p. 509) than by its formal elements. (This recalls the way that Mussato and Trevet distinguished between tragic material and tragic style in their discussions of epic and tragedy.) Boccaccio shows no real commitment to the genre, and suggests that Dante had been 'speaking figuratively' in naming his poem a comedy.

Benvenuto da Imola, meanwhile, in the last redaction of his commen-tary, more audaciously suggests that Dante's poem is simultaneously a tragedy, comedy and satire. It is tragic in its elevated subject-matter, comic in plot trajectory (beginning with sad material and ending in joy), and satiric ('id est reprehensoria') because it criticises all vices and spares no dignity and power. Indeed Benvenuto argues that it might more properly be called *Satire* than either *Tragedy* or *Comedy* (1.19; ed. Kelly, *Tragedy and Comedy*, pp. 49–50). A sense of the high moral purpose and high lit-erary status of satire emerges from these attempts to manoeuvre Dante's work away from its self-definition as what was coming to be seen as a low-status vernacular genre into a more generically respectable and culturally elevated literary category. In the hands of his commentators, Dante's *Commedia* becomes, in effect, the apotheosis of medieval satire.

---

[23] On the authorship of this work see Chapter 21 below.

But then, in this and many other respects, 'what Dante's language enacts, other medieval books presume' (Allen, *Ethical Poetic*, p. 13).

*

Any history of the book . . . must be a history of misreadings. . . . Every society rewrites its past, every reader rewrites its texts.   (McKenzie, p. 25)

By 1450, the topography of the literary landscape had once again changed, and the centre of literary commentary had moved from France to Italy. Humanist poetics were redefining the role of the contemporary poet. Dante had been canonised as a *poeta theologus*; Petrarch, Boccaccio and Salutati had emphasised the poet as prophetic seer (*vates*) and Landini would soon definitively reinforce that view. Humanist educational treatises had praised and recommended the study of poetry as an enlightening and humanising force for good. The 'new learning' was winning its ideological battles with the 'obscure men' of scholasticism. The study of ancient literature was unquestionably an essential part of the training of a civilised man. Scholarly research by Petrarch and others had redrawn the literary map: new texts had been found, old forgeries discredited. The *fama* of classical authors was secure, but in some cases (especially that of Cicero) rather different from what it had been in 1300.

When the authorship of favoured texts suddenly became questioned (as they did with dizzying frequency in the heady textual discoveries of early Italian humanism), this raised in an acute form those ideological questions about the locus of textual authority that we have seen being tentatively explored in medieval commentary tradition. Petrarch, for example, cast doubt on the authenticity of *De vetula*, the poem (allegedly found in his tomb) that signalled Ovid's deathbed conversion to Christianity. By the time that Petrarch challenged the poem, it had become a popular and apparently valued text in poetic anthologies and had acquired its own glosses and commentaries. Was it now to be regarded as worthless because it was written not by Ovid but by a thirteenth-century Frenchman, Richard de Fournival? Or did the response and valuation of its readers over a century of transmission legitimate its ethical worth?

Authorial decentring could be threatening when authors followed through the implications of that process for themselves and their works. In Chaucer's *House of Fame*, the dreamer Geoffrey is shown an array of *auctores* – what is recognisably the canon of great writers in the fourteenth century – perched on columns in the Palace of Fame. But in what must be one of the earliest-recorded attempts at canon-busting, Geoffrey soon discovers that the *fama* of those apparently authoritative authors is neither reliable nor always deserved. In tracing the origin of all discourses back behind the façade of the House of Fame into the narrative sweatshop that is the House of Rumour, Chaucer chooses a word to describe

those discourses (*tydynges* = *novelle?*) that appears deliberately to avoid
the value-laden critical terminology of the author-centered commentary
tradition associated with most of the canonical texts and authors he has
seen in Fame's palace. The democracy of discourse implied by describing
all utterances as *tydynges* (rather than as, say, epic, or *geste*, or tragedy
and comedy, or *historia, argumentum* or *fabula*) throws attention on to
what has been said rather than *how* and *by whom*. When asked if he has
himself come seeking *fama*, the dreamy poet Geoffrey reacts with alarm
at the prospect:

> Sufficeth me, as I were ded,
> That no wight have my name in hond.
> I wot myself best how y stonde;
> For what I drye, or what I thynke,
> I wil myselven al hyt drynke,
> Certayn for the more part,
> As fer forth as I kan my art. (1876–82).

His unwillingness to allow his name to stand as guarantee for the authority
of his writings focuses attention instead on the process of engaged interpretation involved in reading those texts, and in particular on his own
role as reader of his art. His reading is not privileged, nor authoritative,
but likely to be partial and limited by his understanding of the text ('as
fer forth as I kan my art'). This is a radical moment in the history of reading and writing poetry, and Chaucer is positioning himself at the opposite
extreme from the humanist notion of the author as a divinely inspired and
authoritative *poeta theologus*. As his poems repeatedly demonstrate in
their borrowings from glossed copies of canonical classical texts, Chaucer
is every bit as much a product of medieval commentary tradition as
Dante, Petrarch or Boccaccio. Whereas they chose to configure themselves as *auctores*, Chaucer preferred instead to inscribe himself as a
reader or commentator. But this was never an insignificant role in the
Middle Ages, as Conrad of Hirsau knew: 'Commentators are those who
can work out many ideas, beginning with just a few facts, and illuminate
the obscure sayings of others' (*Dialogus*, tr. Minnis and Scott, p. 43).

Commentary is never a morally innocent activity. Reading is always
a critical act: to read is to interpret; to interpret is to judge; to judge is
invariably to use the prevailing values and criteria of the interpretative
community. Commentary on classical authors (and on secular authors,
for that matter) was never confined to the schoolroom or lecture hall. It
was part of the way that writers and readers shaped and expressed their
own cultural identity. Theory and practice melded together in the crucible
of new writing. The authors of the twelfth- and thirteenth-century arts
of poetry were Latin poets in their own right. In the fourteenth century,

Mussato, Dante, Petrarch and Boccaccio all struggled to define and artic-ulate a 'humanist' (and increasingly 'vernacular') conception of what it was to be a poet. Chaucer, Gower and Langland all reflect in their differ-ent ways on the theory and praxis of their art. Their reading and writing interpenetrated in their thinking about poetry. For all of them, poetic the-ory was a theology of real poetic experience. It may be, therefore, that many of the most subtle and sustained responses to the strategies and aspirations of classical writers came not in the academic commentary tradition – whose hermeneutic horizons were often circumscribed – but in the original compositions provoked and inspired by reading the texts made available through that tradition. *Imitatio* is, after all, the sincerest form of flattery.

Part III

Textual psychologies: imagination, memory, pleasure

7

Medieval imagination and memory

Alastair Minnis

In his *Biographia literaria* (written 1815, published 1817), Samuel Taylor Coleridge gave his theory of the literary imagination its fullest exposition. The ideal poet, he declares, 'brings the whole soul of man into activity, with the subordination of its faculties to each other, according to their relative worth and dignity. He diffuses a tone and spirit of unity that blends and (as it were) fuses, each into each, by that synthetic [i.e. synthesising] and magic power to which we have exclusively appropriated the name of imagination' (pp. 173–4). This connection between imagination and the value of creative genius persists in modern use of the term 'imagination' and especially in use of the adjectival form 'imaginative'. But it is the tradition which Coleridge was breaking away from, the empiricist-materialist view of literary imagination as memory images brought together by association, which has more in common with medieval views on the subject. Moreover, while Coleridge was interested in the psychology of composition, medieval thinkers were more interested in the psychology of audience-response, images being common property of author and audience, having a life beyond the psyches of their creators.

Standard late-medieval theory of imagination is cogently summarised in the encyclopaedic *De proprietatibus rerum* of Bartholomew the Englishman (compiled before 1250), which was translated into several European vernaculars. The brain, he explains (following a description which goes back to Galen), is divided into three small cells, the first being *ymaginatiua*, where things which the exterior senses perceive 'are ordered and put together'; the middle chamber is called *logica*, where the power of estimation is master; and the third and last is *memorativa*, the power of remembrance, by which things which are apprehended and known by imagination and reason are held and preserved in the treasury of memory (3.10).[1] Underlying this account is a psychological model which envisages objects perceived by the five exterior senses meeting in the 'common sense' (*sensus communis*), and the imagination, stimulated by these sensations, forming the mental pictures (*imagines* or *phantasmata*) necessary for thought. Images thus produced are handed over to the reason, which

---

[1] Following John Trevisa's English translation (1398), ed. Seymour, p. 98.

employs them in the formation of ideas. These ideas, with or without their related images, are then handed over to the memory for storage. The basic triad of *imaginatio–ratio–memoria* was widely accepted by Bartholomew's contemporaries, but their terminology could differ widely, as did the status which they afforded the faculty of *imaginatio* or *phantasia*. However, even those who afforded imagination a relatively high value evinced a definite suspicion of it, and the reasons for this suspicion are crucial for an understanding of the medieval literary theory of imagination.

'The word "imagining" [*phantasia*] itself', declares Thomas Aquinas in his commentary on Aristotle's *De anima* (1269–70), is taken from 'seeing' or 'appearing' (3.3.632 [lect. 4]; tr. Foster and Humphries, p. 383). That is, the Greek term φαντασία was derived from a verb meaning 'to make apparent', to 'cause to appear'. Plato spoke of *phantasmata* in describing the appearances or images which present themselves to the mind, imagination being conceived of as something quite passive and scarcely a distinct mental faculty at all. On the other hand, in a famous passage in the *Philebus* (39b–c) he does envisage a more active function, in describing an artist at work in the soul who paints likenesses of things perceived, which are then offered to the reason for its deliberation. However, this aspect of his thought is undeveloped, and in general Plato's terminology has derogatory implications, for he also uses the term *phantasma* to describe unreal appearances, hence creating the impression that the products of the 'phantasia' are deceptive and misleading, a theme found constantly in medieval thought. But for Aristotle, who rejected Plato's disjunction between the world of Forms and the world of sense, because knowledge arises from experience the soul must inevitably use 'phantasms' in its thinking. As Aquinas puts it, 'whenever the intellect actually regards anything there must at the same time be formed in us a phantasm, that is, a likeness of something sensible' (*In lib. de Anima comment.* 3.8.791 [lect. 13]; p. 456). Although he does use *phantasia* to describe the mere impression of sense-perceptions on the mind (which is common to man and beast), and although he echoes Plato's suspicion of imagery arising from sensory experience, Aristotle's thought allows for the emergence of a comprehensive theory of *phantasia* as a distinct mental faculty (not to be subsumed under either sense-perception or judgement) which represents objects as mental images and constructs further images from them.

Aristotle also explored the moral implications of imagination. In the sphere of practical reason it plays an important part in helping to regulate conduct, in large measure due to its ability to produce images of things past or absent and indeed images relating to future things. 'By means of the phantasms or concepts in the soul' one 'calculates as if seeing' and 'deliberates on future or present matters' (*De anima* 431b; Moerbeke text, tr. Foster and Humphries, p. 443). Our 'affective nature' is such that the vision of things brought about by imagining, along with opinion concerning what is, for example, disagreeable or frightening, immediately makes us feel hopeful or sad. The implications for ethics are enormous. We do not seek or avoid a course of action by thinking in abstract terms; rather we conjure up images which please or repel us, as when for instance shame prevents us from doing something because we can picture what we would be like if we lost our reputations (*Rhetorica* 1384a23; also 1371a9 and 19, 1382a21). Thus mental pictures help in moving the will to initiate courses of action. These ideas underlie many medieval manifestations of ethical poetics and 'affective piety', as we will see.

St Augustine seems to have been the thinker most responsible for the early establishment in Latin usage of *imaginatio* (the term not being current before the time of Quintilian and Cicero) in preference to *phantasia*. Moreover, he gave new emphasis to the notion that the imagination makes its own associations of sense-experiences, and connected this with the freedom of the will, with the result that the production of images became distinctly an operation of the 'eye of the mind' (*acies animi*).[2] This faculty of internal vision, he declares, when it is acted upon by the will, may become a faculty of 'diminution and addition'. 'If the image of a crow', for example, 'which is very familiar to the eye, be set before the eye of the mind', it 'may be brought, by the taking away of some features and the addition of others, to almost any image such as was never seen by the eye' (*Epistula* 7.3.6). Thus the imagination forms a construct which, in its totality, was never observed by any of the senses, though all its constituent parts had actually been observed, albeit 'found in a variety of different things: for example, when we were boys, born and brought up in an inland district, we could already form some idea of the sea'. In contrast, 'the flavour of strawberries and of cherries could in no wise enter our conceptions before we tasted these fruits in Italy'. Augustine's successors gave similar examples of such effects, though they argued about precisely which faculty produced them (the variety and confusion of terminology can be bewildering). Avicenna, whose views on the matter circulated widely in thirteenth-century Christendom (see for example Vincent of Beauvais, *Speculum naturale* 25.86), thought that it was

---

[2] Accounts of moral perception which mingle scientific/literal and metaphorical notions of 'sight' were to abound in the Middle Ages. A particularly elaborate example may be found in the *De oculo morali* which the Parisian Franciscan Peter of Limoges wrote (in the 1260s or 1270s) under the influence of Alhazen's *Perspectiva*. Here the process of moral perception is described as a movement from the 'carnal eye' (of sense) to the 'interior eye' (of imagination) to the 'mind's eye' (of reason) to the 'heart's eye' (of volitional consent to what the reason has approved).

the 'cogitative power' which feigns a golden mountain (by compounding the image of gold with the image of a mountain) or a chimera (by compounding the images of a lion's head, a goat's body and a serpent's tail). According to Albert the Great, however, it is *phantasia* which enables one to imagine a man with two heads or a being with a human body, the head of a lion and the tail of a horse (*Summa de creaturis*, pars 2, qu. 37 and 38). Here Aquinas disagreed with his master: since *phantasia* and *imaginatio* are one and the same faculty, it is the imaginative power (*vis imaginativa*) which creates the mental picture 'which we have never seen' of a golden mountain (*Summa theologica* 1a 78, art.4, resp.). 'Images can arise in us at will, for it is in our power to make things appear, as it were, before our eyes – golden mountains, for instance, or anything else we please, as people do when they recall past experiences and form them at will into imaginary pictures' (*In lib. de anima comment.* 3.3.633). Thus he also dispenses with Avicenna's category of the *vis cogitativa*. Furthermore, Aquinas rejects Avicenna's view that the *vis imaginativa* is merely passive: rather it has an active capacity of forming images of things which the senses either had not or could not perceive. This point of view was reiterated by Bartholomew the Englishman: by the imaginative power, we form likenesses and shapes of things which are based on apprehensions of the exterior sense, as when it seems that we see golden hills or the hill Mount Parnassus, on account of the resemblance to other hills and mountains (*De proprietatibus rerum* 3.11).

Clearly, this doctrine had the potential to develop into a theory of literary aesthetics. This is obvious from Augustine's famous statement that, thanks to the power of his own imagination, on reading the relevant texts he could picture to himself 'the appearance of Aeneas, or of Medea with her team of winged dragons, or of Chremes, or Parmeno' (*Epistula* 7.2.4). 'To this class belong also', he continues, 'those things which have been brought forward as true, either by wise men wrapping up some truth in the folds of such inventions, or by foolish men building up various kinds of superstition: for example, the Phlegethon of Tartarus, and the five caves of the nation of darkness, and the North Pole supporting the heavens, and a thousand other prodigies of poets and of heretics.' An unequivocally positive version of this approach – and one which, moreover, illustrates the often-exploited connection between mental images and images both textual and plastic – is found in the early-fourteenth-century *Bestiaires d'amours* of Richard de Fournival. The imagination, he declares, 'makes what is past seem as if it were present. And to this same end, one can come either by painting or by speech. For when one sees a story painted, whether a story of Troy or of some other thing, one sees the deeds of the brave men who were there in past times as if they were present. And so it is with speech', he continues. 'For when one hears a tale read, one perceives the wondrous deeds as if one were to see them taking place' (tr. Kolve, *Chaucer*, p. 25).

But the derogatory implications of much of the Augustine passage make perfectly clear why a full theory of imaginative aesthetics never did develop. Wise men who wrap up the truth in inventions are set beside foolish men who build up superstitions; poets and heretics are spoken of in the same breath. The imagination is, it would seem, as potentially misleading as it is wonderful. Phantasies can be so powerful that, far from prompting a man to perform good moral actions, they cause him to act against his better judgement; thus imagination can override reason. Similarly, in acts of practical or speculative intellection, the imagination can often hinder rather than help. Even when the empirical objects in question are right before our eyes, Aristotle warns, the imagination can be potentially deceptive – as when it tells us that the sun is only a foot in diameter. It is crucial, then, that the imagination should be controlled by the reason. Warnings against the unbridled imagination are ubiquitous in the Middle Ages – and beyond, for we find a particularly zealous one in the *De imaginatione* of Giovan Francesco Pico della Mirandola (1470–1533), nephew of Giovanni Pico della Mirandola and a follower of Savonarola. If the imagination is guided by the reason, it 'beatifies man', but if it is disobedient to reason, 'imagination dooms him'. 'We can without difficulty affirm that not only all the good, universally, but also all the bad, can be derived from the imagination' (p. 43). Gianfrancesco further deduces that 'the Christian life, which consists in both belief and action', can be 'ruined by false imagination' (p. 49).

Insufficient control of imagination occurs when one is gripped by some powerful emotion (such as anger or desire), hindered by some physical disease or impediment – or asleep. Dreams hold special dangers. Aristotle explains that at night, owing to the inactivity of the sense and the intellect, the imagination becomes particularly vivid (*De somniis* 3, 460b–61a). When its phantasms seem to refer to future events are they to be regarded as prophetic? This is not incredible, says Aristotle, but highly unlikely (*De divinatione per somnum* 1). Such suspicion was widely held throughout the Middle Ages, being neatly encapsulated in the *sententia* 'Take no account of dreams, for while asleep the human mind sees what it hopes and wishes for', as found in the *Disticha Catonis* (2.31). Do any dreams, then, have divine origin? The very idea is absurd, pronounces Aristotle, because in addition to its irrationality, one observes that these dreams do not come 'to the best and wisest, but to commonplace persons, all sorts of men' (462b). He proceeds to suggest rational explanations for such phenomena, concluding that most prophetic dreams are to be classed as mere coincidences (463a–b). By contrast, Plato did believe that divine powers can use the human imagination as a means of communicating with the human mind through the implanting of visions. In *Republic* 9 he argues that if a man manages to quieten the parts of his mind which are likely to produce hallucinations he can in sleep receive divine emanations: 'then he attains truth most nearly, and is least likely to be the sport of fantastic and lawless visions' (571d–72b; tr. Jowett, II, p. 442). In the *Timaeus* this vision is conceived of as a kind of disorder or madness: 'God has given the art of divination not to the wisdom, but to the foolishness of man. No man, when in his wits, attains prophetic truth and inspiration.' While he continues to be demented, 'he cannot judge of the visions which he sees or the words which he utters'; this can be done only after he recovers his wits (72a; III, p. 759). This doctrine was, quite clearly, regarded by Aristotle as subversive; hence his remark that so-called prophetic dreams do not come to 'the best and wisest' of men. But for Plato the expert in dialectic was not the highest type of the man of vision.

The phantasies of dreams, insanity and illness come about, according to the *Timaeus*, through 'the gentle inspiration of the understanding', a means whereby the empirical world and man's normal rational procedures are transcended and the world of Forms intimated. The imagination, informed by light from above, can produce a vision higher than anything the reason is able to attain. In the *Phaedrus* this power of vision, insight or intuition is described in terms of the madness of the lover. Only souls of the highest type, those of the philosopher, or artist, or some 'musical and loving nature', can attain the highest state of vision (248c–d). They alone have the highest insight, because they alone can remember in sufficient measure something of the eternal beauty of that real world in which their souls pre-existed before being imprisoned in the flesh. 'In this theory the prophet, the poet and the lover are as closely bound together in the bonds of imagination as ever Shakespeare's lunatic, lover, and poet' (Bundy, *Theory of Imagination*, p. 55). However, the *Phaedrus* was a closed book for much of the medieval period; instead part of the *Timaeus* (as translated by Calcidius) ruled the roost, supported by the Neoplatonic commentary on Cicero's *Somnium Scipionis* by Macrobius (*fl.* 400). Macrobius distinguishes between five main types of dreams (*In Somnium Scipionis* 1.3; tr. Stahl, pp. 87–92). These are: the enigmatic dream (*somnium*), the prophetic vision (*visio*), the oracular dream (*oraculum*), the nightmare (*insomnium*) and the apparition (*visum*, compare the Greek *phantasma*). The last two, declares Macrobius, are not worth interpreting since they have no prophetic significance. The apparition occurs when one is half-asleep, between wakefulness and slumber, in which condition a man, supposing he is fully awake, may imagine spectres rushing at him, or an incubus pressing upon him. Nightmares are caused by some sort of distress, whether mental (as when the lover dreams of having his mistress or of losing her) or physical (caused for example by an excess of food or drink), or by anxiety about the future, as when a man dreams that he is gaining or losing some important position. Virgil, Macrobius continues, holds nightmares to be deceitful; thus, the poet has the love-stricken Dido say to her sister Anna, 'what dreams [*insomnia*] thrill me with fears?' (*Aeneid* 4.9). The concerns of love 'are always accompanied by nightmares'. The other three types of dream, however, are of assistance in foretelling the future. Hence in the *oraculum* a pious or revered individual, or even a god, appears to reveal to the dreamer what will or will not transpire, and what should be done or not done about it. These dreams provide clear information, and actually come true. The enigmatic dream, however, 'requires an interpretation for its understanding', for it 'conceals with strange shapes and veils with ambiguity the true meaning of the information being offered'. Gone, then, is Plato's empowerment of the insightful madness of the lover; in its place is a distrust of the excesses of human love. And, even when certain dreams are deemed to be of value, their interpretation is often unclear and open to dispute.

Christian philosophers often drew on Macrobius as they sought to steer between the Scylla of Platonic enthusiasm and the Charybdis of Aristotelian scepticism. Another major source-text was the twelfth book of Augustine's *De Genesi ad litteram* (Ch. 6ff.). Here divine influence on the imagination is discussed within an account of 'spiritual' vision, this being seen as a sort of mean between the extremes of 'corporeal' vision and 'intellectual' vision. 'Corporeal' vision refers to normal sight; it can be deceptive, as when the navigator thinks that the stars are moving. 'Intellectual' vision occurs when God is seen in His own nature, as the rational and intellectual part of man is able to conceive of him. This never errs; it is beyond all likeness and every image. 'Spiritual' vision combines aspects of both these types, given that here one sees not a body but an image of a body. Here the imagination plays a crucial role, supplying either 'true images, representing the bodies that we have seen and still hold in memory, or fictitious images, fashioned by the power of thought' (tr. Taylor, II, p. 186).

This categorisation was highly popular in medieval biblical exegesis. It was summarised in an Apocalypse-prologue which may be the work of Gilbert of Poitiers, an introduction which enjoyed wide dissemination because it was incorporated into the 'Paris Bible' as one of the standard set of prefaces to the various scriptural books. In this account of the *triplex genus visionum* the *visio spiritualis seu imaginaria* is said to occur when, either when sleeping or awake, we see a likeness of something which betokens other things, as when the sleeping Pharaoh dreamed of ears of corn growing (Genesis 41:5) or the awake Moses beheld the bush burning but not being consumed (Exodus 3:2). By contrast, in the *visio intellectualis*, due to the revelation of the holy Spirit the human mind understands the truth of spiritual mysteries to the extent that it is capable of so doing. The obvious example of this occurred, as many medieval transmitters of the doctrine note, when St Paul was caught up to the third heaven (II Cor. 12:2–3). But Gilbert, rather surprisingly, declares that this happened in St John's Apocalypse, on the grounds that St John not only saw the images but also understood their significance. Not everyone agreed with him – after all, Augustine himself had classified the Apocalypse as a spiritual/imaginative vision (*De Gen. ad litt.* 12.27). However, one can understand Gilbert's desire to elevate a text which constituted the most extensive piece of oracular writing in the Bible. Here, then, we may note how vision-theory could be appropriated to bestow prestige on a 'visionary' work – together with the considerable room for confusion within a given system of classification, due to the inherent conflicts between the heterogeneous ideas which Christian thinkers were trying to yoke together.

The Augustinian *triplex genus visionum* was often drawn upon by medieval holy women, and their male sponsors, as they sought to authenticate their visionary experiences. Barred from entry into the priesthood, since the sacerdotal *character* or stamp could not be imprinted on the female body, women could be allowed the gift of prophecy – providing certain stringent requirements were met. A particularly full account of crucial questions to be asked in the 'discernment of spirits' (*discretio spirituum*) is provided in the *Epistola solitarii ad reges* which Alfonso of Jaén composed shortly after the death of Bridget of Sweden in 1373 as part of the dossier in support of her canonisation. Book 12 of *De Genesi ad litteram* is cited, and Alfonso is keen to emphasise that Bridget's visions often went far beyond the realm of *visio spiritualis seu imaginaria*. Sometimes she was rapt and out of her senses, as God aroused her soul to see or hear celestial matters; this experience meets exactly the criteria of intellectual vision. This may be compared with a passage in the *vita* by Bridget's two Swedish confessors, Prior Peter and Master Peter, which describes her first divine revelations: not asleep but whilst awake and at prayer, 'she was caught up from her bodily senses in ecstasy and in visions, either spiritual or imaginary, with the coming of a vision or a supernatural and divine illumination of her intellect, for she saw and heard spiritual things and felt them in spirit' (Ch. 27; tr. Kezel, p. 78). Jacques de Vitry recounts how, 'purged from the cloud of all corporeal images and from every fantasy and imagining', Marie d'Oignies (d. 1213) 'received in her soul simple and divine forms as if in a mirror' (tr. King, p. 106). The Umbrian holy woman Angela of Foligno (*c.* 1248–1309) saw before her, during a procession to St Francis' church at Assisi, an image of the crucified Christ 'held aloft before her eyes – and not by somebody carrying it' (tr. Lachance, p. 249). Elsewhere a higher level of visionary experience is claimed: 'I cannot tell whether while I was in that extremely lofty state I was standing or whether I was in the body or out of it' (p. 178).

One of the most interesting features of the late-medieval theory of *discretio spirituum* was its emphasis on the quality of the *mulier sancta* (i.e. her unimpeachable personal piety) as well as on the quality of the prophecy itself. In the extensive discussion of prophecy included in his *Quaestiones de veritate*, Thomas Aquinas had emphasised that moral goodness is not necessary for prophecy, for it can exist in a sinner (like Baalim, for instance; see qu. 12, art. 5). He also insists that prophecy which has the sight of understanding is more noble than that which involves the sight of imagination. The imagination is further put in its (inferior) place by Aquinas' statement that in prophecy it must be wrenched away from its normal operations: 'whenever prophecy takes place according to the sight of imagination, the prophet must be transported out of his senses' (qu. 12, art. 9; *Disputed Questions on Truth*, tr. Mulligan, II, p. 150). Such a transport is not necessary, however, when only the prophet's judgement is inspired – again, the hierarchy of the human faculties is affirmed. Furthermore, not all supernatural influence on the human imagination is benign. Both in prophecy and in more ordinary circumstances the devil, who strives to darken man's reason, can lead men to sin by stimulating the imagination and the sense appetite (*Summa theologica* 1a 2ae, 80, art. 2). Here Aquinas gives the example of enticement to sexual sin: Aristotle's statement in *De somniis* (460b) that 'even the faintest resemblance attracts the lover to the beloved' is cited in support of the view that the devil can stir up passions in the sense appetite which make one even more acutely aware of the imagined reality – hence even a 'faint resemblance' can produce a considerable temptation. Imagination may play a major part in much prophecy, but clearly it is a mixed blessing.

Aquinas *cum suis* were quite willing to accept that some prophecies had natural explanations, as when, for example, the imagination is influenced by heavenly bodies 'in which there pre-exist some signs of certain heavenly events' (*Quaestiones de veritate*, qu. 12, art. 3; tr. Mulligan, II, p. 119). It was the natural causes of dreams, including those supposed to signify future events, which were emphasised in the brief treatise *De somniis* written by the 'Latin Averroist' Boethius of Dacia, a major figure within the Arts Faculty at the University of Paris in the early 1270s. Some of our dreams have no connection whatever with future events, but are matters of coincidence: 'the event would have happened even if there had been no appearance similar to it in a dream'.

Bodily causes of dreams include the motions and combinations of fumes and vapours and the various rates at which they rise. Thus, black and earthly vapours may cause someone to dream of flames and fires, or of black monks (i.e. Benedictines), 'and certain foolish ones, having awakened, swear that they have seen devils while they were asleep'. On the other hand, the power of imagination may be moved by clear vapours, so that the sleepers 'dream that they are seeing brilliant places and angels singing and dancing. And when they have awakened they swear that they were carried away [*raptos*] and have in truth seen angels. And they are deceived because they are ignorant of the causes of things.' Illness may produce similar effects. But nonetheless, Boethius adds hastily, 'I do not deny that by divine will an angel or a devil can in truth appear to a person who is sleeping or to one who is ill'. Soon he moves to discuss dreams produced in us by causes in the soul. Clearly influenced by the second chapter of Aristotle's *De somniis*, he notes that 'when a sleeper is subject to a strong passion of fear or of love, his imaginative power forms images which correspond to these passions, such as a phantasm of an enemy or of his beloved'. The extent to which Boethius strives to arrive at a scientific explanation of dreams in terms of their causes is remarkable. But he was too naturalistic for some. The thirty-third article from the list of propositions condemned by Bishop Stephen Tempier in 1277, 'That raptures and visions do not take place except through nature', seems to refer to this treatise. Obviously, Boethius' protestation that he does not deny that the divine will can act on the imagination, as quoted above, was too little and too late.

The Parisian condemnations did not stop intellectual enquiry into the nature and significance of visionary experience, however, as may be illustrated from the *De causis mirabilium* (*c.* 1370) of Nicole Oresme, the most distinguished scholar among the translator-commentators commissioned by Charles V of France. Natural causes are offered for many apparent 'marvels', which tend to befall people who are in a frenzy, melancholic, or beset by some disease, and hence have abnormally active imaginations. 'Even many saints have too easily been able to believe many things; yes, even many thoughtful theologians' often form beliefs far too quickly about things which in fact have 'direct, natural causes and are deluded by many people by not attending to what is said in the Gospel [Matt.10:16], "You shall be as wise as serpents etc."'(ed. and tr. Hansen, p. 265). Oresme certainly does 'not wish to deny totally that miracles have often been done, and are done, and that demons sometimes have been permitted by our glorious God to do many things and to enter people's bodies', and the like. But nonetheless 'we should not too quickly believe that such things now occur, since miracles, and especially such marvels as seem not to be miracles, do not occur without a cause. . . .'. And strong imagination (*fors imaginatio*) can cause many natural effects. For example, it can make a person angry or afraid; one imagining fat perhaps vomits, and a man imagining a woman may have an erection (p. 345). But the power of imagination is limited, as Oresme makes clear in his rejection of Avicenna's belief in its power to move objects. The idea that 'your imagining would move me, when I am unwilling, or would move a stone, is directly contrary to Aristotle' (p. 315). Avicenna is criticised for supposing that imagining can make a mule fall down. The source of this remark is unclear. However, Algazel had told a similar story of a camel, and among the 1277 Parisian condemnations we find the proposition that a wizard could by sight alone make a camel fall into a pit (art. 112).

Given the strong suspicion of imagination which runs through all these accounts, it is little wonder that we have no fully articulated theory of literary dream-vision – i.e. a theory to describe and justify the fictions which were stimulated by the facts of visionary experience as recorded in the Bible and other works of unimpeachable authority. This is most evident in the most widely influential of all medieval dream-vision poems, the *Roman de la Rose*, which Guillaume de Lorris began in the period 1230–5 and Jean de Meun completed some forty years later. Far from providing a self-justifying genre theory this poem actually appears to undermine that human faculty which, according to the psychologists, was its very source and mechanism. In particular, Jean de Meun evinces a scepticism about the human powers of eyesight and imagination, and a disposition to seek natural causes for unusual phenomena, which remind us that he lived and wrote in that Parisian intellectual milieu which could produce a thinker like his contemporary Boethius of Dacia.

Jean's Dame Nature remarks that many people are so deceived by their dreams that they suffer extreme forms of sleep-walking, getting up and preparing themselves for work, even travelling considerable distances on horseback. Then, when they awake, they are lost in wonder and amazement, and tell people that devils took them from their homes and brought them there (ll. 18274–96). Sometimes sickness, or an excess of melancholy or fear, acting on the imagination can cause extraordinary effects. Then again, some contemplatives cause 'the objects of their meditations to appear in their thoughts', and 'truly believe that they see them clearly and objectively. But these are merely lies and deceits . . .' (ll. 18327–33). Such a person, Nature declares with heavy irony, has experiences similar to Scipio's, seeing 'hell and heaven, the sky and the air, the sea and the land, and all that you might find there' (ll. 18337–40). Alternatively, he may dream of wars and tournaments, balls (*baleries*) and dances, or indeed of feeling his sweetheart in his arms although she is not really there (ll. 18351–8). Similarly, those who are in a state of deadly hatred dream of anger and battles, and so forth.

These remarks place the opening statement (ll. 1–10) of the *Rose* in a fascinating light. There Guillaume de Lorris had cited Macrobius' commentary on the dream of Scipio as proof that dream-visions can be true and authentic, *pace* those who say there is nothing in dreams but lies and fables (*fables non et mençonges*). Jean de Meun seems to be agreeing with those doubters, holding that most dreams are indeed nothing but *fables* and *mençonges*. This undermines the authority – or, at least, brings out the ambivalence – of the foundational literary form in which the *Rose* is composed. And Jean is leaving open the possibility that the entire poem may be read as a passion-induced fancy on the part of the lover-narrator Amant, hardly one of 'the best and wisest' of men, who vividly illustrates that overthrow of rational judgement which commonly occurs during sleep. Yet the *Rose* stands as a work which contains 'the whole art of love', as Guillaume says – as a veritable medieval *Ars amatoria*. That certainly was how it was received, for better or worse (see our account of the *querelle de la Rose* in Chapter 14 below). Reductive readings should therefore be avoided, and the shifting ambivalence of the text respected. And that ambiguity is due in some measure to the contradictions inherent in medieval theory of vision and imagination.

The legions of vernacular poets who were influenced by the *Rose* were well aware of the role which imagination played in the psychology of their fictional lovers. For example, Guillaume de Machaut (*c.* 1300–77) can take the lady's image as a source of consolation and hope: 'There is still many a recourse: remembrance, imagination of the sweet pleasure of seeing, hearing his lady, her noble bearing, the recall of the good that springs from her conversation and from her sweet gaze' (*Remède de fortune*, ll. 445–54; tr. Kelly, p. 53). Elsewhere such imaginations are shown as being anything but joyful, as when in the *Knight's Tale* Chaucer describes how the unrequited lover Arcite suffers through imaginative delusion (I(A), 1358–79). His condition is a complicated one, but clearly involves the effects of melancholy on the front cell of the brain, where imagination resides ('his celle fantastik'). Then again, in the *Merchant's Tale* exaggerated fancy ('heigh fantasye') takes hold of the old man who is seeking to acquire a young wife (IV(E), 1577–87). It is as if he takes a mirror and sets it in the market-place, Chaucer declares; thus January's mind ranges over the various maidens who live nearby, imagining them in turn. In the *Tristan* of Gottfried von Strassburg (composed *c.* 1210) not a lover but the first-person narrator engages in exaggerated fancy as he evokes the wonders of the cave wherein Tristan and Isolde enjoy a long amatory interlude. 'I know this well', he exclaims, 'for I have been there'. But the narrator has been there only in his imagination – 'Diz weiz ich wol, wan ich was dâ' – since he never has visited Cornwall (ll. 17104, 17140–2). Quite what the reader is meant to make of this self-consciously fanciful account is a matter of contemporary critical controversy. Should we share the enthusiasm of the figure who imagines it, or reject it as a dangerous delusion?

Positive attitudes to imagination often appear in vernacular religious poetry. Guillaume de Deguileville's *Pèlerinage de la vie humaine* (first version, 1330–1) begins with a dream-vision which richly images the heavenly Jerusalem, seen from afar as if in a 'mirour' which is 'sanz mesure grans', large beyond measure (ll. 39–40). And in the medieval vision poem *par excellence*, Dante's narrator eulogises the imagination which is moved by divine agency rather than sense-perception:

> O imaginativa che ne rube
> talvolta sì di fuor, ch'om non s'accorge
> perché dintorno suonin mille tube,
> che move te, se 'l senso non ti porge?

> (*Purg.* 17.13–16)

[O imagination, that do sometimes so snatch us from outward things that we give no heed, though a thousand trumpets sound around us, who moves you if the sense affords you naught?]

At the climax of the *Commedia* this figure experiences a rapture which is described in terms evocative of St Paul's ascent to the third heaven. But Dante draws back from an unequivocal statement that he is describing a *visio spiritualis* of the highest kind, which involves full understanding rather than mere imagination; indeed, the poem ends by emphasising that his human mind was incapable of receiving (just as now it is incapable of communicating) his heavenly vision, for his high fantasy (*alta fantasia*) had reached its limit (*Par.* 33.142, compare ll. 55–7). More than literary decorum inhibited Deguileville and Dante from claiming something which implied a superlative gift of divine grace. Hence some ambivalence had to remain. Deguileville declares that, if he has not dreamed his dream well, it should be corrected by others who can dream better (ll. 13517–20). The very medium calls in question the authority of the message:

> Tant di aussi (que), se menconge
> I a aucune que a songe
> Soit repute, quar par songier
> Ne se fait pas tout voir noncier.

> (13521–4)

[I say, too, that if there is any falsehood here it may be attributed to the dream, for in dreams the complete truth may not indeed be revealed.]

> (tr. Clasby, pp. 185–6)

And Dante's medieval commentators could debate whether the vision described in the *Commedia* had really happened to their author or if it was fictional (see Chapter 22 below). A poem obviously written with the *Commedia* in mind, Chaucer's *House of Fame*, opens with a narrator who is frankly confused by all the technical jargon traditionally used to classify dreams (here he clearly has Macrobius in mind), and by the varying explanations of their causes – good luck, he declares, to the great clerks who deal with this puzzling matter! (1.1–65).

Interpretative problems of a different kind are raised by *Piers Plowman*, wherein the personification Ymaginatif takes the fictional Dreamer to task for meddling with 'makynges' (poetic compositions) rather than saying his Psalter and praying for others (B-text, Passus 12). It may seem odd that the *virtus imaginativa* should call into question such an imaginative activity – but the point may be that imagination itself is not being called in question but rather a use of it which some would regard as trivial. The Dreamer, embarrassed, offers a brief twofold defence of poetry. It has a recreational function, allowing holy men to 'play' in order that they may be more perfect (see our following chapter), and besides, the Dreamer wants to learn more about how to Do-Well, Do-Better and Do-Best – his poetry, it would seem, is conducive to such knowledge. The Passus (at least, on my reading) proceeds to illustrate how the imaginative power can help the human mind to formulate charitable possibilities in areas of enquiry wherein a mere mortal cannot expect to reach firm conclusions. That is the extent of Langland's empowerment of the imagination, in my view; I am unconvinced by the suggestion (as made by Kaulbach) that the poet was influenced by the Avicennan view of an imagination so strong that it could, *inter alia*, relocate a mule or a camel.

The vernacular poems here mentioned seem also innocent of the position afforded to imagination in the 'Middle Commentary' on Aristotle's *Poetics* produced by another Arab scholar, Averroes (Ibn Rushd) of Cordoba in Islamic Spain, who lived from 1126 until 1198. This was best known in Western Europe – though its main sphere of initial influence was dominantly Parisian – in the Latin translation made in 1256 by Hermann the German, a monk living in Toledo. Both in the original Arabic and in Hermann's version, this work should be read as a reconfiguration of the values of Aristotle's text, in the light of medieval cultural values (and the vaguest of notions of classical theatrics), rather than as a 'misunderstanding' of what Aristotle had meant (see the discussion in Chapter 6 above).The fact that it continued to be used in preference to the (impressively accurate) translation which William of Moerbeke made in 1278, is most telling; medieval thinkers found the Averroes/Hermann treatise more comprehensible within their hierarchies of the sciences and in respect of long-established notions concerning the rhetorical methods and ethical aims of poetry.

The crucial point to grasp is that the concept of imitation (*mimesis*) has largely been replaced with that of imagination (*imaginatio*) or imagistic 'likening' (*assimilatio*), representation of a kind which arouses the emotions of the audience in a way which encourages them to follow virtue and flee from vice; here Avicenna's definition of poetry as 'imaginative speech' has creatively been elaborated.[3] Averroes/Hermann declares that since all *assimilatio* involves what is either becoming or base, the art of poetry must have as its purpose 'the pursuit of what is becoming and the rejection of what is base' (tr. Minnis and Scott, p. 283). Good men are to be praised and evil men are to be blamed, whence tragedy is defined as 'the art of praise' and comedy, which is reduced to satire, is defined as 'the art of blame' or vituperation. (Here poetics is assimilated to epideictic rhetoric, the branch of that subject which is concerned with the praising or blaming of some particular person.) It would seem that poetry should imaginatively heighten certain natural qualities relating to what is fair and what is foul, thus ensuring that the audience is in no doubt concerning its correct response. This ethical impact must, of course, be continuous; for it to stop would mean that poetry had ceased to perform its proper function. Here we may find an explanation of the commentary's view of *katharsis*: pity, fear and other virtue-provoking feelings are to be aroused by tragedy, positively and constantly, rather than being over-stimulated and hence purged by it.

On this theoretical model, 'reversal' becomes 'indirect' or 'circular' imagination, while 'discovery' becomes 'direct' imagination or recognition. Moreover, 'simple plot' is replaced with 'simple imitation' (*imitatio simplex*) and 'complex plot' with 'compound imitation' (*imitatio composita*). What Aristotle had said was that a simple plot represents a simple dramatic action, i.e. one which is 'single and continuous' and in which 'the change of fortune comes about without a reversal or discovery' whereas 'a complex action is one in which the change is accompanied by a discovery or a reversal, or both' (*Poetics* 10, 1462a16–18; tr. Dorsch, p. 45). What Averroes/Hermann is saying is that indirect imagination is representation of what is to be blamed whereas direct imagination is of what is to be praised. Simple imitation occurs when one or the other, either indirect or direct imagination, is used, whereas compound imitation occurs when both are used, beginning with the blameworthy and ending with the praiseworthy, or vice versa. Compound imitation is preferable to simple imitation, and within compound imitation the kind which begins with indirect imagination and ends with direct imagination is deemed the better structure. Applying these ideas in his commentary on Dante's *Commedia*, Benvenuto da Imola describes how the poem begins with representation of blameworthy sinners in Hell, proceeds with representation of the inhabitants of purgatory (who have some redeeming qualities), and ends with those who, having received their heavenly reward,

---

[3] Compare Avicenna, *Commentary on the 'Poetics'*, pp. 31–58, 61–4, etc.

are unqualifiedly worthy of praise and emulation. In thus proceeding from tragedy to comedy, the entire work is an excellent example of compound imitation: 'no other poet knew how to praise or blame with more excellence'.[4]

Such an application of the doctrine of the 'Middle Commentary' is rare, however; it did not achieve deep cultural penetration, though it seems to have been known among Italian humanists and their scholastic opponents, including Giovannino of Mantua, Salutati, Savonarola, Robortello, Segni, Maggi and Lombardi. Peter Auriol O.F.M., who taught theology at Toulouse and Paris before being appointed archbishop of Aix (1321), found 'in primo Poeticae' – apparently the Averroes/Hermann version – material which enabled him to describe the first part of the Book of Isaiah as a tragedy because of its reproaching and threatening style (*exprobrativa ac comminativa*). The second part is identified as a comedy because of its exhortative and consolatory style (*exhortativa et consolatoria*; see *Compendium totius divinae scripturae*, p. 118). Furthermore, Matthew of Linköping, who was to become the confessor of St Bridget of Sweden, obviously drew on the Averroistic *Poetics* in composing his own *Poetria* (whilst studying at Paris, probably in the 1320s). Matthew explains that the *poeta* is rightly compared to the *pictor*. 'The skilful painter, by the appropriate arrangement [*conuenienciam disposicio*] of the different parts and colours of the picture', produces an agreeable representation of something that would not in itself be agreeable to look at'. 'In the same way' he continues, 'the perfect poet gives pleasure [*delectat animam*] by making us imagine a thing in accordance with its characteristics' (*faciendo rem secundum suas proprietates imaginari*; ed. Bergh, pp. 46–7). Poetic imagination is accomplished by three means, representation (*representatio*), intonation (*tonum*) and metre (*metrum*), but only *representatio* is of the very essence of poetry. Matthew defines *representatio* – which corresponds to Hermann's *assimilatio* – as a manifestation of something in words in such a way that it seems to appear immediately before our eyes.[5] 'Therefore, to my mind it is not so much Virgil's subtle style [*subtilitatem eloquii*] that has given him the first place among poets as his very representation, so skilfully accomplished [*representacionem conuenientissime factum*]'. Whereas other sciences attain their ends by means of rational arguments (*raciones*), poetry accomplishes its end by means of representation.

The Averroes/Hermann commentary has replaced an aesthetic poetic with a rhetorical-ethical one. This is a consequence of Averroes' belief

---

4 Cit. Preminger, Hardison and Kerrane, *Classical and Medieval Criticism*, pp. 346–7.
5 '. . . est igitur representacio ostensio rei per sermonem, tanquam iam ante oculos fieri videtur.'

that poetry is part of logic – a belief which Aristotle's Arab readers had inherited from the Greek commentators. The *Rhetoric* and the *Poetics* were classified as respectively the seventh and eighth parts of the *Organon*, preceded hierarchically by the six familiar treatises on logic proper. According to the highly influential *Catalogue of the Sciences* which Al-Fārābī had produced in the middle of the tenth century, rhetoric seeks to persuade and employs the enthymeme and the example, whereas poetics has imaginative representation as its purpose and the imaginative syllogism as its device (see Minnis and Scott, p. 280). In the same vein, Averroes/Hermann's 'Middle Commentary' makes clear how, in place of the intellectual assent demanded by scientific demonstration, poetic representation elicits psychological assent; its imaginative syllogisms seek to move rather than prove. According to an anonymous thirteenth-century Parisian *quaestio* on the nature of poetry (prompted by the 'Middle Commentary'), in poetry it is the individual's imagination and faculty of desire which is appealed to, and imaginative syllogism is appropriately used because everyone is especially fond of 'his own instinctive estimations and relies particularly on his own imaginings' (tr. Minnis and Scott, p. 309). Since, however, the good of the population as a whole is more important than the good of the individual, poetry must be placed after rhetoric. A similar statement is found in the prologue to Bartholomew of Bruges' Parisian commentary (dated 1307) on Hermann's Averroistic *Poetics*.

Here, then, is a quite paradoxical empowerment of poetry as 'imaginative' art: it is allowed considerable purchase within its own sphere of operation (personal ethical behaviour), but within the grand scheme of things that sphere occupies a lowly position, given the culture's prioritisation of community over individualism. A similar location of the imagination – as enjoying great importance only within a strictly subordinate situation – features in the medieval reception of the apophatic imagery of 'Pseudo-Dionysius', a Neoplatonic Monophysite of *c.* 500 who for centuries was believed to be the philosopher whose conversion by St Paul had been recorded in Acts 17:34. If, in the later Middle Ages, the authority of Aristotle had established the importance of imagination in epistemology and psychology, it was Pseudo-Dionysius who, more than any other, assured its position in theology.

The crucial doctrine of *The Celestial Hierarchy* is that sacred Scripture offers us figures, formations, forms, images, signs, symbols and veils (to use some of the terms employed by its medieval readers), whereby the heavenly orders are manifested. This is a mark of God's infinite condescension and goodness to his creatures. For our benefit visible beauties are made to reflect the invisible beauties of heaven, sweet sensory odours used as emblems of the intelligible teaching, and material lights serve as a likeness of the gift of immaterial enlightenment. According to the

Extractio on *The Celestial Hierarchy* by Thomas Gallus, who carried out his major work on Pseudo-Dionysius between 1232 and 1244, 'various material figures and figurative compositions' are used in the Bible 'so that we, as far as each is able', through these 'sensible forms' may be 'led back to the contemplation of the supernal virtues' which 'cannot be given any shape, and always remain the same'.

> For it is not possible for our mind to be uplifted to that immaterial imitation and contemplation of the heavenly hierarchies, unless that same mind, in line with its present blindness, employs the guidance of material figures. It then realises . . . that beauties which are accessible through the senses are images of invisible beauty, and that fragrances that please the senses are expressions of the distribution of fragrance which cannot be sensed, and that material lights are images of a light visible to the intellect . . .   (tr. Minnis and Scott, pp. 174–5)

Difficult doctrine – some of which is clarified, though also adulterated (on which process, more later), in a passage in the *Benjamin minor* of Richard of St Victor (d. 1173) which is obviously indebted to the Dionysian scholarship of Hugh of St Victor (d. 1142). Richard praises the imaginative style of the holy Scriptures, adding that they stimulate the imaginations of their readers:

> They describe unseen things by the forms of visible things and impress them upon our memories by the beauty of desirable forms. Thus they promise a land flowing with milk and honey; sometimes they name flowers or odours and describe the harmony of celestial joys either by human song or by the harmony of bird-song. Read John's Apocalypse and you will find that the heavenly Jerusalem is often described as being adorned with gold and silver, pearls, and other precious gems. Yet we know that none of these things is present in that place from which no good thing is absent. For none of these things is there in 'form' (reality) while all are present in 'likeness'. . . . And we can immediately imagine these things as we like. The imagination can never be more useful to the reason than when she ministers to it in this way.   (tr. Kirchberger, pp. 92–3)

But the limits of such *imagines* must be recognised: we should not remain at the level of symbols derived from the material world, or confuse them with the spiritual realities which they symbolise. To fail to make this transition is to run the risk of thinking, as the uneducated do, that the heavenly intellects actually have many feet and faces, and are formed with the brutishness of oxen, or the savagery of lions, the curved beaks of eagles, etc. A detailed explanation of such imagery is provided in the fifteenth chapter of *The Celestial Hierarchy*. Why are angels sometimes depicted as naked and unshod? To signify 'that they are free, and easily liberated, and indeed cannot be detained by any chance or preoccupation of the lower world' (tr. Minnis and Scott, pp. 186–7). But why, then, do they wear priestly garb on other occasions? To signify 'the power of bringing angels or men to fulfil the divine wishes'. In particular, why do they wear belts? Because belts indicate 'the power of preserving and firmly drawing together one's own virtues and spiritual graces'. Why are the heavenly realities sometimes imaged with horses? To signify 'that angels obey God and submit to His every wish, as the horse is managed by the use of the bridle'. And so forth.

The fact that all images must ultimately be left behind in the soul's journey to God, since heaven and heavenly intelligences have in reality nothing in common with them at all, does not, however, render them worthless. On the contrary, they work in an 'anagogic' and 'reductive' way (i.e. an elevating and transcending manner) to raise up the mind towards things which are simple (because uncompounded) and pure. Ultimately we may 'contemplate the divine and intellectual beings', explains Robert Grosseteste (d. 1253) in his commentary on *The Celestial Hierarchy*, 'yet we shall not be able to attain to this contemplation unless we first use both the uplifting forms and material figures' (ed. and tr. McQuade, p. 20). In sum, the reason and imagination, working together as mistress and handmaiden, are to be respected in the early stages in the soul's journey to God but rejected in the higher reaches of contemplation.

It was the supra-rational nature of the very highest type of contemplation which most interested Thomas Gallus. He firmly placed the will above the intellect, and affection or love above reasoning of however elevated a kind. In his *Explanatio* of *The Mystical Theology*, a superintellectual method of knowing God is elaborated. There is a power which exceeds that of the intellect, namely the 'principal affection', by which unique means the very highest point of the mind (*apex mentis*) may be united with God. By *principalis affectio* is meant the purest and most sublime activity of the affection, rising to its utmost limits with the aid of divine grace, leaving far behind any corporeal comparisons and earthly affections. Similarly, Grosseteste identified the superior function of the mind as love, *amor*.

The importance which the anonymous English author of *The Cloud of Unknowing* (late fourteenth century) afforded to love and affection places him firmly beside Gallus, whose glosses he had used (as he openly acknowledges) in translating *The Mystical Theology*. Moreover, the Dionysian tradition of 'anagogic' imagery provides the key to understanding the central paradox of the *Cloud*, the fact that it can at once attack the imagination (as a faculty which ties the mind down to the mundane) and also offer a rich abundance of figurative language, the most striking being that of the cloud of unknowing itself. Such is the way of the Dionysian imagination.

The *Cloud* is, however, quite unusual in the extent to which it is willing to promote the *via negativa* or 'negative way' of contemplative ascent, i.e. the idea that it is more appropriate to describe God in terms which do not signify what He is but rather what He is *not*, as when He is called *in*visible, *in*definable and *in*comprehensible. This is part and parcel of the Dionysian theory of 'similar' and 'dissimilar' similes, as explained in *The Celestial Hierarchy*. In the first case, God is described in terms of, for instance, light and life. Since these are immaterial qualities it seems fitting to refer to Him in this way; in the process we are implying that God does possess such qualities, albeit to a superlative degree. However, such imagery can be misleading, since we may lose sight of the great distance between each and every created thing, however noble, and its Creator. 'God's divinity far surpasses all substance and life', as Gallus puts it, and therefore 'no light can worthily represent it' (tr. Minnis and Scott, p. 178). The negative way is better than the positive way, denial better than assertion, anagogy better than analogy, and 'dissimilar' images better than 'similar' ones. When God is referred to as an ointment, a stone, a wild beast, or indeed a worm, this may seem quite shocking, but the mind is not allowed to rest with such images: rather it is provoked to disentangle all material qualities from its thinking about God, since the corporeal analogies used in these symbols are so obviously dissimilar and remote from Him. Even those who can easily believe that 'the heavenly beings have the glitter of gold, or shine with the splendour of the fire and sun', will baulk at the notion that 'other celestial beings are like horses or cattle or lions or some other such creatures', explains Grosseteste. 'By the evidence of their materiality and corruptibility [they] most manifestly cry out that they are not the divine beings, but very far removed from them and very unlike them' (ed. and tr. McQuade, pp. 70–1, 65). Such imagery may surprise by its ugliness but it will not deceive.

It was Pseudo-Dionysius' clear preference for dissimilar similes which his medieval readers found hardest to accept. The pull of the *via positiva* was too strong, the pressure of analogical thinking too great. A Paulist-Augustinian emphasis on the progression from creature to Creator tended to encroach, as summed up by the Apostle's words at Romans 1:20: 'For the invisible things of Him, from the creation of the world, are clearly seen, being understood by the things that are made.' For example, the prologue to the *De proprietatibus rerum* initially justifies Bartholomew's interest in the kinds and properties and things on the grounds that it is not possible for the human wit to ascend to the 'contemplacioun vnmaterial' of the heavenly hierarchies except through 'material ledynge'. The authority of *The Celestial Hierarchy* is here invoked. But Bartholomew proceeds to remark that we cannot ascend to the contemplation of unseen things unless we are led by contemplation of things that are seen – and at this point, of course, Romans 1:20 is cited. A similar dilution of the *via negativa* may even be found in the Richard of St Victor passage quoted above (on p. 256), in the nervous assurance that 'no good thing is absent' from heaven. That very passage (albeit misattributed to Hugh of St Victor) was used to justify the visions of Gertrude of Helfta (1256–1301/2), on the grounds that 'as invisible and spiritual things cannot be understood by the human intellect except in visible and corporeal images, it is necessary to clothe them in human and visible forms' (tr. Winkworth, pp. 54–5).[6] This may be true to the letter of Richard's text, but its Pauline implication deviates significantly from the spirit of Pseudo-Dionysius.

Moreover, the theory of *principalis affectio* which Gallus elicited from Pseudo-Dionsysius, wherein the *affectus* is treated as a noetic faculty, is light years away from the highly emotive form of late-medieval religiosity which nowadays is generally designated as 'affective piety'. When the *Cloud* author ordered his 'goostly freende in God' to put away all recollection of earthly things, no matter how good they may be (even thoughts of the benevolence or goodness of God, our Lady, and the saints and angels in heaven being ruled out), he was disassociating himself from that emotional empathy which is a major driving force in legions of meditational treatises, written both in Latin and *in vulgari*, which appeared throughout late-medieval and Counter-Reformation Europe. An excellent example is afforded by the Latin and vernacular versions of a Franciscan treatise of the early fourteenth century, the Pseudo-Bonaventuran *Meditationes vitae Christi* (maybe the work of Johannes de Caulibus, but this attribution is highly controversial). Originally addressed to an anonymous 'Poor Clare', it offers as a model of devotion St Cecilia, who meditated day and night on 'the most pious facts of the life of Jesus' (tr. Ragusa and Green, pp. 1–5). The continuous contemplation of the *vita Christi* fortifies the intellect against trivial and transient things, Pseudo-Bonaventure explains, going on to suggest that illiterate and simple people may gain a greater awareness of things divine – witness St Francis, who engaged in 'familiar conversation with and contemplation of his Lord Jesus'. In the following work he has recounted the events of Christ's life 'as they occurred or as they might have occurred according to the devout belief of the imagination and the varying interpretation of the mind'. Thus when the text says that such-and-such 'was said and done by Jesus Christ', if this cannot be demonstrated from Scripture it must be considered 'only as a requirement of devout contemplation'. Adapting this doctrine in his

---

[6] This citation is introduced with the careful statement that 'one must not suppose' that what Gertrude's book relates 'was simply the result of her natural qualities, or the liveliness of her intelligence, or what it pleased her to imagine'; rather 'it must be firmly and unhestatingly believed that all this proceeded from the fount of Divine wisdom and was a gift of infused grace from the [holy] Spirit . . .'.

Middle English translation, *The Mirror of the Blessed Life of Jesus Christ* (*c.* 1409), Nicholas Love suggests that simple souls should form in their imaginations principally the image of Christ's incarnation, passion and resurrection. 'A symple soule þat kan not þenke bot bodyes or bodily þinges mowe haue somwhat accordynge vnto is affecioun where wiþ he maye fede & stire his deuocion' (ed. Sargent, p. 10). The 'diuerse ymaginacions' provided by the text are written in a specific mode and with a specific intent: as 'devoute ymaginacions and likenessis styryng symple soules to þe loue of god & desire of heuenly þinges'. In similar vein, Bishop Reginald Pecock (writing *c.* 1449) claimed that every man needs to have 'gode affecciouns' concerning Christ, as if He were his best friend; and since this friend does not give to us His visible presence therefore it is 'profitable to ech man for to ymagine this freend be present to us bodili and in a maner visibili' (*Repressor*, ed. Babington, I, p. 269). And for this the image of Christ crucified serves well. Pecock claims ancient Christian precedent: 'the oolde practik of deuoute Cristen men was forto so ymagyne', although they knew full well that everything they 'deuoutli ymagineden' was 'not so in deede'. Here, then, is a defence of fictional writing in the service of devout arousal, and disposition, of the 'affeccioun'.

Material images – paintings, drawings, sculptures – could be just as efficacious as textual ones. Whenever Angela of Foligno 'saw the passion of Christ depicted', she could 'hardly bear it, and would come down with a fever and fall sick'. As a result, her companion 'hid paintings of the passion or did her best to keep them out of [Angela's] sight' (p. 131).[7] On pilgrimage to St Francis' Portiuncula church at Assisi, Angela sees a stained-glass window of the saint being held close by Christ, whereupon she begins to shout out and cry uncontrollably (p. 142). Marie d'Oignies could not gaze at an image of the cross without falling into ecstasy (tr. King, p. 50). Catching sight of 'a fayr ymage of owr Lady clepyd a pyte', Margery Kempe cries 'full loude' and weeps 'ful sor', as if she would die (*The Book of Margery Kempe*, ed. Meech and Allen, p. 148). John Lydgate responded more soberly to a *pietà* which he found 'sett out in picture' in a book: this 'ymage ful notable' of Mary 'with weepyng eyen, and cheer most lamentable' prompts him to write a series of ballades on the fifteen joys and sorrows of the Virgin (ed. MacCracken, pp. 268–9). In another poem on the same subject he has Christ urge the reader to 'Set this lyknesse in your remembraunce, / Enprenteth it in your Inward sight' (p. 250;

---

[7] Later in her *Memorial*, however, Angela is keen to emphasise that her revelations excel such paintings: 'Whenever I passed near a painting of the cross or the passion, it seemed to me that the representation was nothing in comparison with the extraordinary suffering which really took place and which had been shown to me and impressed in my heart. This is why I no longer wanted to look at these paintings . . .' (p. 162).

compare p. 290). Writing about the image of pity, Lydgate explains that portraiture and 'ymages of dyverse resemblaunce' were established so 'That holsom storyes thus swewyd in fygur / May rest with ws with dewe remembraunce' (p. 299).

St Gregory the Great's famous dictum that images in church serve as the books of the unlearned (*Epist*. 11.10)[8] was frequently quoted in defence of sacred painting and statuary. 'We have a threefold memorial [*triplex memoriale*] of the Lord's passion', explains Jacobus de Voragine in his popular *Legenda aurea* (*c.* 1260), and they appeal respectively to the senses of sight, hearing and taste (*ad visum, ad auditum, ad gustum*). The first memorial 'is in writing, i.e. depicted in the images of the passion of Christ, and this is directed to the eye. Thus the crucifix and the other images in the church are intended to awaken our memories and our devotion, and as a means of instruction; they are the laypeople's book.' The second memorial, Jacobus continues, is the 'spoken word, namely in the preaching of the passion of Christ, and this is addressed to the ear', while the third 'is in the sacrament, which so signally expresses the passion', this being 'directed to the sense of taste' (*Legenda aurea*, tr. Ryan, II, p. 385). However, not everyone was content to accept such a justification, fearing – in a manner akin to the concerns of Pseudo-Dionysius, as summarised above – that such imagery led to anthropomorphic views of deity and indeed to idolatry of a kind which had been rife among the heathen. Iconoclastic attitudes among the followers of John Wyclif prompted Walter Hilton (who died as an Augustinian Canon in 1396) to write the treatise *De adoracione ymaginum* in defence of the *status quo*. Citing St Gregory as authority for the view that what Scripture conveys to clerics *pictura* habitually displays to layfolk, Hilton argues that the institution of Christian images is perfectly rational. Just as clerics by 'inspection'[9] of Scripture can be instructed and stimulated to recollect all the benefits that God has bestowed upon mankind, so layfolk by 'inspection' of an image can be recalled to the memory of the incarnation of God and his passion. Images provide a useful focus for the imagination, recalling the wandering mind to spiritual things. Learned people, including pious laymen, know full well that the images are merely wood or stone, and worship before them with the correct 'explicit intention'. However, the church also contains 'imperfect' and simple layfolk, who have to be fed on the milk of corporeal signs. They worship rather with an 'implicit intention': while their attention is fixed on the images themselves and not on the divine realities which they represent, nevertheless such practice is not sinful because they

[8] Compare with this the notion of ecclesiastical imagery as 'mute preaching', discussed by Gougaud, 'Muta predicatio'.
[9] *Inspeccio*, meaning 'regarding', 'looking at/into'.

are worshipping in God's name, and in line with the custom and intention of the church. Ignorant men tend to judge of divine things from the analogy of corporeal things, imagining, for example, that God in His own nature has the body of a man like their own. But, properly used, images are a material means to a spiritual end, namely the worship of those holy realities of which they are images. Thus, the Middle English treatise *Dives et Pauper* exhorts the Christian to perform his worship *before* the image but not *to* the image, otherwise one is practising idolatry. The 'book of peynture and of ymagerye' is ordained 'to steryn mannys affeccioun and his herte to deuocioun, for often man is more steryd by syghte' than by 'heryng or redyngge' (I, pp. 82–7).

Indeed, some supposed that pagan imagery could serve Christian truth, and was not simply to be condemned as idolatry. John of Wales O.F.M. (*magister regens* in Oxford *c.* 1260) quoted with approval St Augustine's account of the pagan *pictura* of Pleasure on a throne like a delicate queen, with all the virtues about her, ready to do her commands. *Potest imaginari triplex pictura . . .* This threefold imagination is considered to be of assistance to one's understanding of ways in which the virtues may be abused (*Florilegium*, pars 1, cap. 10). These techniques were enthusiastically developed by the English 'classicising friars' of the early fourteenth century, who designate their allegorical images with such phrases as *poetica pictura*, *secundum poeticam imaginem* and *pingitur a poetis*. Fulgentius himself had used the verb *pingere* to describe depiction in painting; clearly, here the meaning has broadened to include verbal depiction. In such works as John Ridevall's *Fulgentius metaforalis*, Robert Holcot's *Moralitates*, and the anonymous *Imagines Fulgencii* all the 'fancy is verbal, not visual', as Beryl Smalley says; an artist would need 'a whole row of miniatures' to illustrate the conflicting details which are provided in abundance (Smalley, *English Friars*, p. 118). We are dealing, then, with 'aural aids to preaching' rather than accounts of actual paintings or sculptures. However, the *picturae* did have a visual dimension insofar as they were intended to stimulate the picture-making faculty of the mind.

This tradition of 'poetic painting' – which should not be confused with the Renaissance notion of *ut pictura poesis* – influenced several vernacular works, including the Middle High German *Ackermann aus Böhmen* which the Bohemian schoolmaster and notary Johannes von Tepl wrote shortly after 1400, and the Old Czech *Thadleček* (composed shortly after 1408). The former contains a description of Death as allegedly portrayed on a wall-painting in a Roman temple; this directly influenced the latter text, which also follows the *Imagines Fulgencii* and commends the Romans as wise people who 'painted us as they understood us and they knew us', i.e. with a fine sense of the vagaries of human behaviour (tr. Palmer, 'Antiquitus depingebatur', p. 222). At least some of the writers who utilised such imagery believed that they were imitating an ancient tradition of moral iconography, 'and it is taken for granted' that the constructs 'described in the Roman pictures are gods, even in those cases where this is not specified' (Palmer, p. 183). In the mythographic commentary on the *Eschez amoureux* which was composed by Charles V's physician, Evrart de Conty (*c.* 1330–1405), it is explained that ancient poet-philosophers assigned to the various gods and goddesses, according to the properties of their natures, certain *descripcions et figures diverses* in a manner similar to the way 'we [Christians] make images of Saints' (ed. Guichard-Tesson and Roy, p. 65). Evrart goes so far as to claim that 'there is no good thing imaginable to a reasonable man that the ancient poets, who were wise and great philosophers, have not meant to express by various gods and goddesses – neither maintaining nor believing that they were real deities[!]' (p. 63). Other writers stuck to the standard justification of 'despoiling the Egyptians'. Thus heathen *picturae* were pressed into the service of 'the true God who sits in the assembly of the gods but who is our God', to borrow a phrase from Pierre Bersuire's prologue to his *Ovidius moralizatus*, a thoroughgoing allegorisation of the *Metamorphoses* wherein, as Bersuire puts it, all the pagan fables 'seem to be collected together as it were in the manner of a register [*tabula*]' (tr. Minnis and Scott, pp. 367, 368).[10] Predictably enough, the Lollards objected to the use of pagan fables in sermons, just as they questioned the use of images in churches.

But if the deeds of Christ and the saints may be represented in painting, why may they not also be represented in theatrical representation, especially since a painting is a dead book while a play is a living one? That argument is set up in order to be refuted in the Lollard *Tretise of Miraclis Pleyinge* (written between 1380 and 1425), a work which has been described as the 'chief surviving antitheatrical document from the Middle Ages' (Barish, *Antitheatrical Prejudice*, p. 67). Its author grudgingly admits that painting, provided it is not over-elaborate and conducive to idolatry, can be 'as nakyd lettris to a clerk to riden the treuthe' (p. 104). But miracle plays cannot be justified on the same principle: they are made 'more to deliten men bodily than to ben bokis to lewid men' (Gregory's dictum yet again). Good men know that life is just too short, and occupy themselves with sound and earnest works, fleeing from such idleness (p. 104). What, then, of the obvious affective power of dramatic performance? After all, men and women, seeing the passion of Christ and His saints, are moved to compassion and devotion, 'wepinge bitere teris' (p. 98). The Lollard reply is that 'miraclis pleyinge' does not give

---

[10] From the Paris redaction, completed by 1362. Bersuire claims that a man may 'build and construct the ark of the covenant from the treasures of the Egyptians'.

any occasion for lamentation which is true and meritorious of reward; men and women are weeping not for their sins but merely on account of the outward show. Therefore, it is actually 'reprovable' to 'wepen for the pley of Cristis passioun' (p. 102). However, the *Tretise*'s claim that such performance is a kind of lying, since it presents only 'signis withoute dede', finds few echoes elsewhere. Angela of Foligno was impressed by a dramatic performance of the passion of Christ on the Piazza Santa Maria (in Foligno). But her story has a twist: 'the moment when it seemed to me one should weep was transformed for me into a very joyful one, and I was miraculously drawn into a state of such delight that when I began to feel the impact of this indescribable experience of God, I lost the power of speech and fell on the ground' (p. 176).

A more predictable response may be illustrated from John Lydgate's reaction to a Corpus Christi procession. Such an occasion, he explains, can stimulate one's imagination to consider spiritual things. The beholder is admonished to see and consider 'in youre ymaginatyf' how Christ was crucified for Adam's sin, in order that this feast may be more greatly magnified (ed. MacCracken, p. 36). Of course, the liturgy offered many opportunities for even the most humble parishioner to play a part in the symbolic drama of redemption. The practice of creeping to the cross on Good Friday was commended by Reginald Pecock as a means of engendering 'loue and good affeccioun'. When the people kiss the feet of the image that is not all they are doing, for they are fully aware of the spiritual significance of their action: 'thei ymagineden' Christ Himself 'to be there in bodili maner present' (*Repressor*, ed. Babington, I, p. 270).

Such devout imaginations had to be stored away in the treasury of memory, a well-stocked and effectively trained memory being deemed essential for correct moral behaviour and devout religious practice. It was in the trained, 'artificial' memory that 'one built character, judgment, citizenship, and piety' (Carruthers, *Book of Memory*, p. 9). In particular, *memoria* came to be regarded as an integral part of the virtue of prudence (on which more later), whereby one was enabled to make good decisions concerning future action. 'The ability of the memory to re-collect and re-present past perceptions' was therefore 'the foundation of all moral training and excellence of judgment' (Carruthers, p. 69). Of course, one could over-do it: the anonymous author of the *Chastising of God's Children* (1382–1408) worried about the way in which some men 'imagyne' things about predestination and divine foreknowledge, getting themselves into a state of despair (pp. 117–18). Guidance was therefore necessary, and preachers sought to provide it; the compilers of preachers' handbooks ensured that they were well-equipped with illustrative stories or *exempla* since, to quote Humbert of Romans O.P. (d. 1277), 'people find exemplary anecdotes more moving than mere words; they are also easier to grasp and make a deeper impression on the memory' (tr. Tugwell, p. 373). A more elaborate version of the same theory is provided in the preface to the *Tractatus de diversis materiis predicabilibus* which Stephen of Bourbon O.P. compiled not later than 1261. Examples are of the utmost usefulness in the instruction of the simple and 'rude' man, because they imprint themselves on his memory the more easily, and he retains them the longer (ed. Lecoy de la Marche, pp. 3–5). St Gregory is quoted as saying that things teach better than words and *exempla* teach better than preachings. This is why Jesus Christ, the sum of divine wisdom, first taught by deeds rather than by words (see Acts 1:1) and rendered the subtlety of his doctrine in a basic way, as it were in corporeal and visible fashion, equipping and clothing it with diverse similitudes, parables, miracles and examples. Thus His doctrine was the more firmly grasped, the more easily comprehended, the more strongly retained in the memory and the more efficaciously implemented.

Indeed, Stephen continues, although Christ was eternal wisdom, incorporeal and invisible, because of the limitations of men He became incarnate and clothed Himself in flesh. 'The Word was made flesh and dwelt among us' (John 1:14). Incarnational theology therefore provides the ultimate justification for our use of material likenesses and *exempla* in teaching the truth. The support of 'Saint Dionysius' is then enlisted for this populist, all-embracing ideal of education and edification (yet another instance of the elasticity of his doctrine): wise philosophers made their sayings corporeal by clothing them in similitudes and examples. And corporeal discourse moves more easily from the sense to the imagination and from the imagination to the memory.

Worries about the fragility and fallibility of human recollection were expressed with remarkable frequency, *memoria* being seen as engaged in mortal combat with the forces of oblivion. 'Memory is fragile and cannot cope with the whirling storm of things', Thomas of Ireland remarks at the beginning of his *Manipulus florum* (1306; preface ed. Rouse and Rouse, p. 236). This popular reference book is being offered as a major memory-aid. As Isidore of Seville had said over 600 years earlier, 'The practice of letters was invented for the memory of things. Things would vanish into oblivion unless they were bound by letters' (*Etymologiae* 1.3.12). John of Salisbury (writing between 1154 and 1159) was even more eloquent. The little which we can know in our brief human life 'is constantly banished and torn from the soul by forgetfulness which deceives knowledge through perpetual hostility and infidelity to its stepmother, memory. Who would know of Alexander or Caesar, or would respect the Stoics or the Peripatetics, unless they had been distinguished by the memorials of writers?' (*Policraticus*, tr. Nederman, p. 3). Introducing his *Historia destructionis Troiae* (completed by 1287), Guido delle Colonne remarks that, 'although every day past events are obliterated by more recent ones', nevertheless certain past events which happened a long time ago 'are so worthy of memory [*digna memoria*] on account of their enduring greatness that age does not succeed in destroying them by imperceptible corrosion'. Their survival is due to the efforts of writers.

> Writings of the ancients, faithful preservers of tradition, depict the past as if it were the present, and, by the attentive readings of books, endow valiant heroes with the courageous spirit they are imagined [*spiritum ymaginarie*] to have had, just as if they were alive – heroes whom the extensive age of the world long ago swallowed up by death. . . . To keep it alive in the minds of succeeding generations, by means of continuous records, the pen of many writers described it in a trustworthy account.
>
> (tr. Meek, p. 1)

Books, therefore, have their own voiceless speech, a speech which allows the absent or dead to speak, thereby conserving what time would otherwise destroy. As the English Benedictine Ralph Higden put it, God has helped us to redress the slippery nature of memory (*memorie labilitas*) through His gift of history. *Historia* (here bearing the sense of the written historical record) is 'the testimony of tymes' and 'the memory of life' (*memoria vitae*), 'renewenge as thro immortalite' things which are likely to perish, being in a manner of speaking 'a conseruatiue perpetualle to thynges mortalle' (*Polychronicon* [completed *c.* 1352], here quoted in the anonymous fifteenth-century translation; ed. Babington and Lumby, I, pp. 4–7).

But these acts of recuperation are neither bounded by an interest in 'fact' nor primarily motivated by a sentimental desire to encounter dear dead men and women. John of Salisbury brings out the crucial point well, in remarking that, without letters, 'things worth knowing' would not have been experienced; 'arts would have perished, laws would have disappeared, faith and all religious duties whatsoever should have shattered, and even the correct use of eloquence would have declined'. 'The examples of our ancestors', he continues, 'never would have encouraged and been heeded by anyone'. Medieval historians, then, provide exemplary history from the past which must be heeded by readers in their present and future – an objective which is particularly evident throughout the *Chroniques* of Jean Froissart (*c.* 1337– after 1404). In writing 'one finds the memory of good and valiant men of former time, like the Nine Worthies who made their way forward by their prowess, the twelve knight-companions who defended the pass against Saladin and his army, and the twelve peers of France who stayed behind at Roncevaux and so valiantly sold their lives'. These figures provide models of heroic conduct for their aristocratic successors. 'People talk about the exploits of such men', 'clerics write down and record their fortunes' – and the knights of today seek to emulate their achievements. Froissart encourages such readers to follow his lead in exercising the imagination in a review of the state of military prowess, how and where it has reigned and held sway, and moved from one country to another, because this information will be of practical use in their professional lives (ed. de Lettenhove, I, pp. 4–5).

The late-medieval histories and reference-books cited above may be regarded as products of an age of 'information overload' in which readers want to look specific things up, rather than spend hours meditating on the spiritual significance of a single page – this being an aspect of the cultural transition from monastic to scholastic *lectio*. Indexes, concordances and summaries (sometimes called *intentiones*) attained a remarkably high level of technical sophistication in the thirteenth century, and compilations became more rigorous and transparent in their structural layout, the *Speculum maius* of Vincent of Beauvais being one of the biggest and best (as already noted in our previous chapter). Vincent presents his tripartite work (a fourth part, the apocryphal *Speculum morale*, was added later) as an essential reference-book for an age when there are too many books to read and the human memory simply cannot cope. 'The large numbers of books, the lack of time in which to read them, and the slipperiness of the human memory [*memorie labilitas*] do not allow the mind to take in equally well everything which has been written' (*Apologia totius operis*, Ch. 1; p. 465). Therefore, 'having diligently perused and read attentively many authors over a long period', Vincent concluded that he should condense extracts (*flores*) from just about all the authors he had read 'into one volume by careful abbreviation and arrangement'. (He did not work alone, however; many fellow-Dominicans were at hand to help – this 'industrialisation' of book-production being another sign of the times.) The mise-en-page of the *Speculum maius* contrasts interestingly with that of the *Speculum universale* on which Raoul Ardent was still working at the time of his death around 1200. Here a series of diagrammatic images (termed *arbores*) are offered as guides to the contents of this large anthology. But they are woefully inadequate – the information provided by Raoul is simply too vast and complicated to be covered by such a device. It could be inferred that mnemonic images of a type favoured in the earlier Middle Ages receded as new technologies of the book emerged.

However, one should be wary of such a totalising conclusion. Mary Carruthers has argued persuasively that 'the valuing of *memoria* persisted long after book technology itself had changed'. The foundational thesis of her two magisterial studies of medieval memory is that 'medieval culture was fundamentally memorial, to the same profound degree that modern culture in the West is documentary' (*Book of Memory*, p. 8). And previously Frances Yates had contended that, while 'the age of scholasticism was one in which knowledge increased', it was 'also an age of Memory, and in the ages of Memory new imagery has to be created for remembering new knowledge . . . The moral man who wished to choose the path of virtue, whilst also remembering and avoiding vice, had more to imprint on memory than in earlier, simpler times' (*Art of Memory*, p. 95). Evidence of such continuity of technique is available in abundance. For a start, prodigious feats of memorisation of a type common in late Antiquity and the early Middle Ages – one may recall that Augustine's friend Simplicius could recite Virgil backwards – are not unknown in the later period. Thomas Aquinas, who has important things to say about the art of memory (see pp. 269–70 below), himself had an impressively trained memory. In the *vita* which Bernard Gui published during the period 1323–5, shortly after Aquinas' canonisation, we learn that 'his memory was extremely rich and retentive: whatever he had once read and grasped he never forgot'. For instance, Aquinas seems to have put together his *Catena aurea* (a 'chain' or sequence of patristic texts commenting on the four Gospels) 'for the most part . . . from texts that he had read and committed to memory from time to time while staying in various religious houses' (*Life of Aquinas*, ed. and tr. Foster, p. 51). According to the *vita* of Juliana of Mont-Cornillon which was written by a Canon of St Martin of Liège in the period 1261–4, this French holy woman learned her Psalter by heart while still a child, 'for God had given her both a capable understanding and a retentive memory' (p. 30). The Psalter was one of the most memorised texts of the Middle Ages, but Juliana's gender and youth help construct this as a considerable achievement, and clear proof of her holiness. In later life she 'learned by heart more than twenty sermons from the last part' of Bernard's commentary on the Song of Songs 'in which the blessed Saint seemed to transcend human knowledge. These she committed firmly to memory' (p. 33).

What psychological techniques were used to assist such procedures? Valuable clues are afforded by Hugh of St Victor's *De tribus maximis circumstantiis gestorum* (*c.* 1130). Specific passages are more easily remembered, it would seem, through recollection of their location on the manuscript page, with the assistance of such features of layout as rubrication, textual division and subdivision, marginalia and illuminations. Furthermore, Hugh advocates the use of a grid or structuring/locating-device for images of textual passages, the idea being that when one recalls the grid (whether whole or in part) along with it will come the images which have been organised within it. A simple numerical grid is offered, and the Psalter (predictably) chosen as an example of a text for memorisation:

First I consider how many psalms there are. There are 150. I learn them all in order so that I know which is first, which second, which third, and so on. I then place them all by order in my heart along my [mental] numerical grid, and one at a time I designate them to the seats where they are disposed in the grid . . .

(tr. Carruthers, Book of Memory, p. 262)

Once this entire structure has firmly been committed to memory, any desired part of it can be accessed:

. . . without hesitation I may answer, either in forward order, or by skipping one or several, or in reverse order and recited backwards according to my completely mastered scheme of places, what is first, what second, what indeed 27th, 48th, or whatever psalm it should be.   (tr. Carruthers, pp. 262–3)

These techniques are relatively simple – as befits a treatise which is directed at novices. But the principles which Hugh has followed may be identified as a (somewhat pale) reflection of the classical theory of *ars memorativa* which was transmitted, almost exclusively, to the Middle Ages by Book 3 of the Pseudo-Ciceronian *Rhetorica ad Herennium*, then known as the 'Second Rhetoric'. Behind Hugh's grid or 'scheme of places' lies the *Ad Herennium* author's recommendation of the location of specific images (*imagines*) within architectural structures (*locos*) which are easily grasped by the memory, such as 'a house, an intercolumnar space, a recess, an arch, or the like' (*Ad Herennium* 3.16.29; ed. and tr. Caplan, pp. 208–9). The images themselves, imaginative likenesses of what we wish to remember, fall into two categories, relating to words and to things (*verborum simil-itudines* and *rerum similitudines*; 3.20.33). 'Memory for words' involves finding images which prompt recall of every single word in a chosen text, whereas 'memory for things' means memorisation of the gist of a text, its argument or key concepts. According to the *Ad Herennium*, the more bizarre the images the better, because such likenesses will stay longest in the memory. To achieve this mnemonic effect, we should construct 'active images' (*imagines agentes*) of exceptional beauty or ugliness. For instance, we may ornament some of them, as with 'crowns or purple cloaks', so that 'the likeness may be more distinct to us', or we may 'dis-figure them' in some way, for example by presenting a figure 'stained with blood or soiled with mud or smeared with red paint, so that its form is more striking'; alternatively, certain 'comic effects' might be assigned to them: whatever is necessary to ensure our perpetual recollection (3.22.37; pp. 220–1).

When this theory was revived in the thirteenth century by Albert the Great and Thomas Aquinas, the Pseudo-Ciceronian theses were assim-ilated to Aristotelian faculty psychology (*De memoria et reminiscentia* being the crucial source), as when Aquinas remarked that one may invent mnemonic similitudes and images because spiritual intentions slip easily from the soul unless they are linked to corporeal similitudes (*Summa theologica* 2a 2ae, qu. 49, art.1, ad 2um). Albert the Great even relates the Pseudo-Ciceronian *sententia* that strange and wonderful images are to be used, because they move the memory better than the ordinary, to what Aristotle had said about the 'first philosophers' who expressed themselves in poetry; since a fable 'is composed of marvels it is more affecting' (*De bono*, tract. 4, qu. 2, art. 2; tr. Carruthers, *Book of Memory*, pp. 279–80).[11] Albert illustrates such imagery with a version of the *Ad Herennium*'s example (3.20.33) of how the details of a law-case featuring a charge of poisoning may be remembered through the image of the defendant standing by a man's sick-bed and 'holding in his right hand a cup, in his left hand tablets, and a physician standing upright holding the testicles of a ram': the cup is 'the memory-cue of the poison which he drank', while the tablets bring to mind 'the will which he signed' and 'in the physician may be figured the accuser and by the testicles the witnesses and accessories,[12] and by the ram the defence against the matter being adjudicated' (pp. 272–3). Looking further ahead, the legacy of the *Ad Herennium*'s advocacy of esoteric imagery may be found in those striking 'poetic paintings' of the kind beloved of the 'classicising friars' (and already discussed above); such *picturae*, which defy sourcing in material paintings or sculptures, may in fact be memory-images designed to help both author and audience remember the key features of important virtues, vices and other crucial didactic concepts. Returning to Albert and Aquinas, one of the most culturally significant aspects of their recuperation of the *Ad Herennium*'s relevant teaching is the relocation of *artificiosa memoria* (i.e. the 'artificial' or trained memory, developed 'through subtlety of mind')[13] from rhetoric to ethics: it is now firmly established as an integral part of the virtue of prudence, that which makes moral judgement possible. 'Memory takes in an event that is past as though it stayed ever-present in the soul as an idea and as an emotional effect on us', explains Albert, 'and so this event can be very effective for providing for the future' (*De bono*, tract. 4, qu.2, art.1; tr. Carruthers, p. 269). Aquinas agreed completely: 'Our calculations about the future should be based on what has happened in the past. Accordingly our memory of them is needed for being well-advised about the future' (*Summa* 2a 2ae, qu. 49, art. 1; p. 65).

But the mnemonic system of the 'Second Rhetoric' did not meet with widespread approval. John of Salisbury and Geoffrey of Vinsauf (in his

---

[11] Compare Aristotle, *Meta.* 1.2 (982b15–20) and 1.3 (983b 28–32).

[12] With *testiculi* ('testicles') compare *testis* ('a witness').

[13] To borrow a phrase from the thirteenth-century dictaminist Boncompagno da Signa; see Yates, *Art of Memory*, p. 69.

Poetria nova) seem to have found its methodology impractical and over-elaborate; Geoffrey and Hugh of St Victor were content with the practice of dividing up texts into small, easily memorised pieces – this perhaps being the same technique intimated by Thomas Waleys in his *De modo componendi sermones*, when he says that one should be mindful of the listener's memory in avoiding prolixity. Thomas of Chobham comments that in spite of what 'Tully' had said, 'memory works better from prac-tice and diligence' (*Summa de arte praedicandi*, p. 268). In yet another *ars praedicandi*, Francesc Eiximenis O.F.M. (*c.* 1327–1409) criticises the 'ancient method' of Cicero for remembering things, and recommends his own 'new mode'. Francesc, whose main problem seems to have been with the grand-scale 'architectural' model, offers a drastically simplified ver-sion of what the *Ad Herennium* had said concerning memory 'places'. Imagine a road from Rome to Santiago de Compostella, and think of, say, six other cities along the way – Florence, Genoa, Avignon, Barcelona, Saragossa and Toledo. They must be well known and hence easily remem-bered, but also distinct from each other, to avoid mental confusion. If we have eight subjects to memorise, each item may be assigned to the city which most closely corresponds to it. Material concerning clerics may best be recalled through association with Rome, since it is the city of clerics, and money matters through association with Florence, since that city is famous for finance, and so on.

Such an account is highly unusual in the *artes praedicandi*, for two major reasons. First, the formal aspect: most remarks concerning mem-orisation of sermons simply advocate good organisation (Thomas of Chobham) or the use of careful divisions and arresting images (Waleys). It may be inferred that such well-known structuring devices as the fifteen joys and sorrows of Mary, the fourteen articles of faith, the ten com-mandments, and the seven deadly sins, cardinal virtues, sacraments, gifts of the Holy Spirit, and works of mercy, would help a wide audience of layfolk to remember those things most needful to know for their sal-vation. Such structuring methods depended on the pedagogic training of the schools, and no doubt in that sphere the quite rigid form of the *quaestio* – with its arguments *pro* and *contra*, and its final *determinatio* – helped recall of the issues which were located within that structure. Pre-sumably images of poisoned cups and ram's testicles were not always necessary.

Secondly, Francesc's account is unusual because it aims to help preach-ers remember their sermons.[14] Other *ars praedicandi* authors are far

[14] The 'Pseudo-Aquinas' preaching treatise recommends the use of the image of a tree, with an elaborate branch-system, which would certainly help a preacher to memorise the

more interested in helping their listeners to remember their sermons. A well-structured sermon can be easily followed and better recalled by its audience, remarks Thomas of Chobham. The early-fourteenth-century *Summa de exemplis ac similitudinibus rerum* of Giovanni di San Gimignano O.P. provides unusual similitudes which, when used by the preacher, will facilitate the comprehension of his audience: 'preach to them in "unusual" similitudes for these will stick better in memory than the spiritual intentions will do, unless clothed in such similitudes' (Yates, *Art of Memory*, p. 96). Here, then, is a major shift in the history of *ars memorativa* – we have moved from the psyche of the speaker to the psychology of audience-response, from memorisation techniques which are private to the orator (who does not seek to divulge the tricks of his trade) to mnemonic devices recommended for use by the populace at large.

The desire to share and propagate such mnemonic devices was not, of course, limited to sermons. St Bonaventure's professed objective in producing his *Lignum vitae* is to enkindle the *affectus*, assist the mind and stamp the memory (*imprimatur memoria*). 'Since imagination aids understanding' he has arranged his selected passages 'in the form of an imaginary tree [*in imaginaria quidam arbore*]', disposing them 'in such a way that in the first or lower branches the Saviour's origin and life are described; in the middle, His passion; and in the top, His glorification'. But the reader is not to receive this image passively – rather he too has to exercise his imagination. 'Picture in the spirit of your mind [*in spiritu mentis*] a tree whose roots are watered by an ever-flowing fountain . . .' (pp. 119–20).

Neither was it limited to religious works. To take one example among many, at the beginning of *The Tree of Battles* which he addressed to King Charles VI of France, Honoré Bonet explains that he has

imagined the thing in such a wise that I make a Tree of Mourning at the beginning of my book, on which you may see, first, at the head, the governors of Holy Church in such sharp tribulation as never was before. . . . Next, you may see the great dissension which is today among Christian princes and kings, and afterwards you may see the great grief and discord which exist among the communities. And in accordance with this Tree, I shall arrange my book in four parts. The first shall treat of the tribulation of the Church . . . before the coming of Jesus Christ our Lord; the second part shall be of the destruction and

structural principles of his sermon; compare the *Libellus artis praedicationis* of Jacobus de Fusignano O.P., who flourished around the beginning of the fourteenth century, and the elaborate *arbor de arte siue modo praedicandi* found in Munich, Bayerische Staatsbibliothek, MS Clm 23865. All are discussed by Dieter, 'Arbor picta'. Crucially, Pseudo-Aquinas remarks that his *arbor* is 'as useful to intelligent preachers *as to hearers*', thereby affording further evidence of the cultural shift proposed above.

tribulation of the four kingdoms of old times; the third part shall be of wars in general; and the fourth part shall be of battles in particular.

(tr. Coopland, pp. 79–80)

This 'Tree of Mourning' may easily be remembered, and with it the foundational points of Bonet's treatise. Organisational principles for the material text and memory images for the reader's mind work hand in glove.

As Geoffrey Chaucer said so memorably, if we did not possess the 'olde bokes', the key of remembrance would be lost (*Legend of Good Women*, F and G Prol. 25–6). On the other hand, if we lacked the powers of imagination and memory, the books could hardly have been written, and certainly they would have had little if any effect on the human psyche. People cannot think without images; people cannot remember what they thought without images; people cannot plan for the future without images. Furthermore, images could operate in the mind or take on material form in painting and sculpture or textual form in a literary narrative; psychological theory was therefore the prime mover for the relevant spheres of literary theory and aesthetics. Above all else, *memoria* and *scriptura* were not seen as being in competition but rather as enjoying a mutually beneficial relationship. Texts could be remembered, with extraordinary visual accuracy. Indeed, texts could recommend ways in which their contents might be held in the treasury of memory, ready for application in the individual reader's intellectual and moral life. Memory could operate confidently in the absence of texts, with the gist (*res*) of each and every argument being recalled and conclusions being drawn through an orderly mental process which involved scanning a memory-bank and reordering significant ideas to maximum effect. But books too were a sort of memory-bank, affording a written reservoir of knowledge far greater than anything that a single human mind could contain or sustain: here, then, was a wonderful divine gift which enabled mankind to conserve information which otherwise would have perished, and this gift must have seemed even more wonderful when, in the 'information explosion' of the thirteenth century, there was more and more to remember.

Little wonder, then, that in metaphorical descriptions of imagination and memory which draw on images of writing and book-production the distinction between tenor and vehicle is often creatively blurred. Thomas Bradwardine – the 'Bisshop Bradwardyn' cited by Chaucer in the *Nun's Priest's Tale* (VII, 3242) – introduces his *De memoria artificiali* (*c*. 1335) with the statement that two things are necessary for memory-training, 'firm locations and also images for the material'. This is basically an updated version of what the *Ad Herennium* author had said in the first century CE (see 3.17.30). The locations are 'like tablets on which we write', explains Bradwardine, while the images are 'like the letters written on them'. Moreover, 'the locations are permanent and fixed, whereas the images are now inked on like letters and are then erased' (tr. Carruthers, *Book of Memory*, p. 281). Introducing a very different type of treatise, his mould-breaking *Vita Nova*, Dante talks in a similar if more personalised mode, of how, in the book of his memory, following the first pages which are almost blank, 'there is a section headed *Incipit vita nova*. Beneath this heading I find the words which it is my intention to copy into this smaller book, or if not all, at least their meaning' (tr. Reynolds, p. 29). That is to say, he looks into his memory and finds, as it were, the *incipit* or opening phrase to the 'book' of his new life; looking at the 'text' which then follows, he discovers the words which he proceeds to copy into the 'smaller book' which he is now writing, the material book entitled the *Vita Nova*.

Dante returns to confront the agency of *memoria* at the very end of a work which begins not with his boyhood but in the middle of 'the journey of our life' (*Inf.* 1.1). Here the narrator's soul eventually enjoys a superlative vision of deity: 'Thenceforward my vision was greater than speech can show, which fails at such a sight, and at such excess memory fails' (*Par.* 33.55–7). The poem then ends, there being nothing more which can be said, imaged, or held in the memory. When the *apex mentis* is reached the soul must leave behind the operations of those human faculties, no matter how elevated or inspired they may be. And herein lies the ultimate paradox of the psychologies of imagination and memory. Despite their perpetual battle with the forces of forgetfulness and oblivion, when they are working to the best of their ability they must collude in the realisation of their own redundancy. *Cede la memoria a tanto oltraggio.*

8

The profits of pleasure

Glending Olson

What we normally think of as medieval literary criticism – whether in the form of gloss, commentary, treatise on writing poetry, or defence of classical studies – predominantly concerns written composition. It presupposes texts or lettered traditions of enough heuristic value to warrant critical study or imitation. Such criticism dominates the available manuscript evidence, which obviously reflects learned, usually academic and clerical, interests. Yet throughout medieval Europe people not only studied literature but attended performances or read poems (aloud or silently) or told stories for their own enjoyment. In 734 Bede complained of bishops who support people 'addicted to laughter, jests, storytelling [*fabulis*], gluttony and drunkenness'. In 1119 the entertainment at a marriage feast in Iceland was reported as including 'many kinds of games, dancing as well as wrestling and saga entertainment'. Around 1300 a prioress complained about damage to her convent's property from Londoners trekking across it to see 'miracles and wrestling'.[1] One of the major lessons we have learned from contemporary theory is that no attitude towards literature is free of social or ideological influence and implication; some sort of interpretative context underlies even the most seemingly transparent descriptions of literary activity and reception. These three brief passages, the tiniest tip of a medieval iceberg of references to performance, signal as well medieval attitudes towards it: in every case forms of narration or representation that might in more modern contexts be treated as literary genres are linked with other types of amusement, recreational activity or social indulgence. Stories, sagas and enactments of some sort are conceptualised not as 'literature' but as part of a diverse group of activities that provide entertainment.

While Bede's complaint reminds us of the well-documented hostility of the medieval church and sometimes of secular authority towards rowdy festive pleasures, the complaint of the prioress – if in fact the 'miracles' she names are religious plays – reminds us that not all medieval literary entertainment was necessarily secular or morally suspect. Thomas of

---

[1] Ogilvy, '*Mimi*', p. 607; Lönnroth, *Njáls saga*, p. 171; Hassall, 'Plays at Clerkenwell', p. 565; Clopper, '*Miracula*'.

Chobham's differentiation of types of minstrels, made early in the thirteenth century, recognises that some *ioculatores* sing of noblemen's deeds and saints' lives rather than of subjects that incite lasciviousness (*Summa confessorum*, pp. 291–3). Yet his concern is the moral status of entertainers, not analysis of the purposes and genres of literature. The criticism of vernacular entertainment – songs, romances, spectacles, drama – developed chiefly in response not to whatever textual basis (if any) it had but to its presentation through public performance and to concerns about the effects of such performance on the audience. Much of the criticism explored in this chapter, then, is not principally literary or textual in focus. Nevertheless, it advances medievally compelling psychological and physiological arguments in order to understand, justify and even celebrate varied kinds of entertainment and the pleasure they generate. These arguments, more tolerant of the non-didactic than 'official' medieval culture is often thought to be, became sufficiently fixed in social thinking to furnish the basis for more self-consciously literary reflections by such writers as Boccaccio and Chaucer.

This sort of criticism and theorising is to be found in the writings of theologians, philosophers and physicians as they reflect on people's behaviour in social settings and what role entertainment should play in their lives. I delineate these ideas here in three sections, exploring first a medical and psychological theory that finds taking pleasure in the arts beneficial to health; second an ethical theory that treats proper play, including literary performance, as legitimate recreation; and finally some more purely literary theorising that incorporates these critical ideas while addressing the relationship of pleasure to the profit or usefulness of poems and stories.

I

Let us return to Thomas of Chobham. His discussion in the *Summa confessorum* of different types of entertainers is very well known, but his understanding of the function of the one type he considers legitimate has received much less attention. One might imagine, when Thomas indicates approval of jongleurs who recite worthwhile narratives, that he has in mind the standard medieval justification of such stories as exemplary – they offer models of behaviour for emulation or rejection. But Thomas points out psychological rather than didactic benefits: tellers of such tales 'bring solace to people in their illnesses or in their mental discomfort' ('faciunt solatia hominibus vel in egritudinibus suis vel in angustiis suis'). He might in part be thinking of spiritual consolation here, yet the wisdom offered by stories of princes and saints would surely be germane to a wider audience than only the ill or the depressed. When Thomas speaks of the ability of certain narrative songs to solace particularly those in discomfort, he seems to be thinking of a distinctive power that resides inherently in pleasurable performance.

His claim belongs to a substantial tradition that recognises music and storytelling as therapeutic. It is commonplace in the history of medicine to cite the Hippocratic corpus as the beginning of Western rational medicine and to stress its almost purely bodily orientation relative to non-Western medicine; nevertheless, at least to some extent the Western tradition has always recognised a complicated and often reciprocal relationship between mind and body. One aspect of that relationship includes the healing power of words and music. More generally, as embodied in traditional wisdom like 'Laughter is the best medicine' and in much recent holistic thought, Western culture has always acknowledged a relationship between positive mental outlook and good health. In the Middle Ages, from at least 1100 onwards, this relationship received explicit articulation in a number of regimens of health that drew on, ultimately, Galen's concept of the non-naturals, six factors that lead either to health or illness depending on whether they are used wisely or not: air, food and drink, exercise and rest, sleeping and waking, repletion and evacuation, and the accidents of the soul. The sixth non-natural, which refers in part to what we would call the passions or emotions, entails medieval understanding of how various mental affections or dispositions can affect the body. The regimens usually warn against fear, sorrow and anger as dangerous to one's health, and they recommend as the most desirable mental attitude the cultivation of a moderate cheerfulness (*gaudium temperatum*). This disposition is effective both hygienically in maintaining and therapeutically in restoring health, and the regimens usually offer a brief physiological explanation – the moderate expansion throughout all the body of heat and *spiritus* – to account for its beneficial effects.

Most of the regimens state principles rather than offer practical advice. But some, along with medieval medical *consilia* (case-histories of illnesses and physicians' treatments of them), indicate means of attaining cheerfulness or avoiding destructive passions; these include conversation with friends, walks in pleasant surroundings, listening to music, and enjoying stories. The fourteenth-century regimen of Barnabas of Reggio, *De conservanda sanitate*, in a chapter on remedies for disturbances of the accidents of the soul, offers this advice: 'Hearing agreeable songs and the delightful sounds of various instruments assuages not only anger but also sadness and anguish, as do reading and hearing delightful books' (fol. 10r). The popular *Secretum secretorum* similarly lists 'pleasaunt songis' and 'delectabil bookis' among the pleasures that work to better people's 'helth and digestion'. The *Tacuinum sanitatis* includes an entry on the *confabulator* in its inventory of items related to hygiene: a good conversationalist-storyteller (*recitator fabularum*) will know both the right material and the best strategies of presentation in order to bring pleasure to an audience, which in turn will purify people's blood, enhance digestion and promote untroubled sleep.[2]

There is, then, from a medical perspective, ample justification for enjoying works of art that please, and the physical/psychological reasoning behind this view appears not only in treatises on health but in texts more directly concerned with the nature and function of the arts. One example is the tradition of *theatrica*. In his *Didascalicon*, written in the 1120s, Hugh of St Victor enumerates seven mechanical arts, parallel to the liberal arts. The seventh, theatrics, he defines as a 'science of entertainment' (*scientia ludorum*), including within it a variety of ancient forms of play: sporting events, song, dance and various types of staged performance. Hugh says that the ancients legitimised these activities because 'natural heat is fostered in the body through moderate activity and the mind is reinvigorated through pleasure' (*laetitia animus reparatur*). This rationale for play and entertainment is essentially physiological and psychological and is based in part on the medical principle of the restorative power of *gaudium temperatum*. *Theatrica* appears in a number of medieval discussions influenced by the *Didascalicon*, and although there is variation in the activities subsumed within the categorisation, the theoretical justification remains. St Bonaventure, in *De reductione artium ad theologiam* (written in the 1250s), says that the goal of theatrics is *solatium*, and we have seen the therapeutic implications of that term in Thomas of Chobham. Bonaventure's view of theatrics is one of the most purely literary in the tradition: for him the science of entertainment includes songs, music, stories and pantomime. There is an equally arts-focused approach in the work of a Dominican friar, John of San Gimignano, writing early in the fourteenth century. He says that in contemporary society *theatrica* includes singing, instrumental music and *representationes*, although he does not specify any more precisely what kind of histrionic activity he has in mind. He perceives these artistic endeavours in the context of the mechanical arts and their ministrations to bodily demands; their goal is *solatium*, and John makes substantial claims for the physical and psychological value of good entertainers: 'they lighten the tediousness of this mortal life, reinvigorate the mind, delight the senses, strengthen the weak, console the sad, and confer many other benefits in life' (*Summa de exemplis*, fol. 343v).

This medical justification of entertainment becomes applied to a variety of compositions in the later Middle Ages. A few of the Old French *fabliaux* call attention to their powers to make people forget sickness or

---

[2] For the regimens and *consilia* see Olson, *Literature as Recreation*, pp. 39–64, 77–83.

grief. In some cases the claim appears to be that an entertaining story is distraction from pain, in others that the joy generated by a humorous tale has directly therapeutic benefits. The thirteenth-century chantefable, *Aucassin et Nicolette*, begins with a brief prologue that almost seems to parody by excess the medical ideas presented above: 'There is no one so perplexed, so grief-stricken, miserable, or beset with illness, who upon hearing it will not be improved in health and cheered up through joy – it is that pleasant'. But Jean de Condé, a fourteenth-century writer at the court of Hainaut, is probably serious when he defends minstrelsy because it brings 'joie' to 'chevaliers' who need such restorative pleasure in order to keep themselves ready to defend church and state; and so too Laurent de Premierfait when, in offering his translation of the *Decameron* to the Duke of Berry, he mentions that reading it strengthens one's spirits (i.e. the three bodily *spiritus*) and thus lengthens one's life.

The *Decameron* itself is obviously indebted to medieval theories of literary pleasure as hygienic. The framing story of ten young men and women who leave plague-ravaged Florence and partake of orderly pleasures in the surrounding countryside dramatises some of the very recommendations made by contemporary plague tracts in response to the Black Death. Physicians often advised leaving the infected area, and that is the first step taken by the *brigata*, the youthful company of storytellers. Physicians advised taking one's mind off the suffering of others, and that too is part of the *brigata*'s strategy, for one of the points most strongly made in Boccaccio's introduction is the psychological damage done by contemplating the many horrors of the pestilence. Finally, following the medical principles of the medieval regimens of health, the plague-tracts recommended cheerfulness as the best mental attitude for warding off the plague, and this of course is the goal of the *brigata*'s controlled recreations, which include not only storytelling but also music, dance and pleasant garden walks. At the end of their fortnight Panfilo, king of the tenth day, asserts that the purpose of their activities has been to escape from the melancholy visited on Florence and to 'take some entertainment in order to sustain our health and our lives'.

The motives of the *brigata* are not necessarily Boccaccio's own, but he embeds his plague-to-pleasure frame action in a preface and conclusion that point to a similar process of achieving mental well-being through literary enjoyment. His book, he says, is written for ladies suffering from the melancholy and anxiety of love, just as the ten Florentines suffered from the melancholy and anxiety of the plague. The analogy between the *brigata*'s movement from distress (*noia*) to a rationally controlled cheerfulness (*allegrezza*) and the intended change in Boccaccio's audience of idle ladies gives to the entire work a large element of the therapeutic. In the *Genealogia deorum gentilium* Boccaccio acknowledges from a theoretical position the restorative power of literature; the *Decameron*'s framing strategies put that principle into dramatised form (*Genealogia*, tr. Osgood, pp. 50–1).

Portions of the *Decameron*'s preface and conclusion belong to what today would be called reader-response theory. Boccaccio speculates on exactly what happens in the ladies' minds through reading that might lead to the alleviation of their distress. His vocabulary tends to be psychological and medical rather than aesthetic, and we can see a similar outlook in a number of Boccaccio's early readers, who in one way or another articulate mental refreshment as a major effect of the hundred tales. Laurent de Premierfait, whose preface to his French translation of the *Decameron* is a substantial piece of literary criticism, states that Boccaccio's immediate purpose was the 'confort et soulaz' of the survivors of the plague, deeply saddened by the loss of friends and relatives and still fearful of death. Franco Sacchetti, writing his *Trecentonovelle* with an explicit debt to the earlier collection, begins with a portrait of his wretched times, beset by pestilence, war and poverty. In such a world people are especially interested in reading books 'which give comfort by provoking laughter in the midst of so many sorrows' (*Italian Renaissance Tales*, tr. Smarr, p. 10). Other tale collections in the later Middle Ages and the Renaissance feature similar 'disaster cornices', framing stories in which some natural or personal misfortune prompts storytelling, which functions as relief. One plague tract from the fifteenth century even goes so far as to include the *Decameron* among those things which work to dispose the accidents of the soul most effectively to help resist catching the plague.[3]

As the tale collections testify, the medieval idea of literary or dramatic entertainment as medically beneficial continued well beyond the Middle Ages. Rabelais draws on it, and so do countless early modern jestbooks and collections of humorous material. Sophisticated critical thinking as well as popular belief in these centuries maintained that recreation, including literary recreation, promotes physical and psychological well-being.

II

A related tradition in medieval theorising about literature that provides entertainment also has classical roots. The most detailed treatment appears in Aristotle's *Nicomachean Ethics* 4.8, which defines and explains a virtue in connection with play and social joviality. *Eutrapelia*, which entails propriety in one's jesting and carefulness about its extent, is the

---

[3] For Laurent, see Hortis, *Studi*, p. 744; for the 'disaster cornice', Clements and Gibaldi, *Anatomy*, pp. 41–6; for the plague-tract, Olson, *Literature as Recreation*, p. 198.

virtuous mean between two extremes, an excessive interest in play and laughter and a defective boorishness that engages in no amusement whatsoever. With Robert Grosseteste's Latin translation of the complete text in 1246–7, Aristotle's full discussion of this virtue became available to the later Middle Ages, and commentaries on the *Ethics* by Albert the Great and Thomas Aquinas expanded on his ideas. Subsequent medieval commentaries and moral treatises relied heavily on Albert and Aquinas in both defending and delimiting acceptable play. Perhaps the most influential text within this tradition is Aquinas' discussion of play in *Summa theologica* 2a 2ae, qu. 168, in the context of modesty in one's actions. Relying principally on the *Ethics*, Aquinas explains that people need rest, that forms of play offer rest to the soul, and that there can be a virtue in regard to play since it is activity governable by reason. Virtuous play – decent, controlled and suitable to the circumstances – serves as recreation for the soul and enables one to return to serious endeavours more eagerly.

Within this context Aquinas mentions that entertainers (*histriones*) perform a legitimate function since their purpose is to bring people a necessary *solatium*. This remark, which was often incorporated into later discussions of Aristotle's ideas on play, extends into a philosophical treatment of virtue and vice the tolerance for certain kinds of performance that Thomas of Chobham had shown earlier in the century. Entertainment *per se* is not condemned; the moral focus shifts to a set of concerns about its decency and appropriateness. Thus John Buridan, in a question on *eutrapelia* in his *Ethics* commentary, notes that *histriones* would not go beyond the virtuous mean even if they played frequently, for that is their job; but they would exceed the mean if they used vulgar language (*turpiloquio*) or performed more than desired by those who hired them (*Questiones*, fol. 89r). The Aristotelian consideration of social wittiness becomes extended to the medieval social reality of minstrels and patrons. In Nicole Oresme's translation of the *Ethics* it is extended to religious plays. Glossing a reference to old and new comedy in Aristotle's discussion of *eutrapelia*, Oresme explains that by 'comedies' the author is thinking of 'gieux' such as those in which a person represents St Paul or Judas and speaks in character. Sometimes in such plays vulgar and 'deshonnestes' words are used (*Livre de éthiques*, p. 271). Oresme's comment here is surely not the only critical opinion he would have had about medieval religious theatre, but it serves to show the ease with which dramas and other kinds of performance were apprehended within the analytical framework applied to play as a social pastime.

The idea of decent entertainment as recreation was certainly not restricted to later medieval Aristotelianism. It appears in cautious form in Cicero's *De officiis* 1.29, known throughout the Middle Ages, and in one of the schoolbook distichs of 'Cato': 'Mix pleasures with your work at times, so that you may endure your labours more readily'. Such views of the psychological necessity of entertainment made their way into Christian thinking well before the scholastic assimilation of *eutrapelia* into discussions of the pleasures and problems of entertainment. For example, Baudri of Bourgueil (1046–1130), both an ecclesiastic and an author of various kinds of poetry, tends to discuss his secular Latin verse as a type of leisuretime play; he even echoes the *Disticha Catonis* in telling a duke to 'intersperse such poetic games [*ludos*] among your manifold concerns; the state will find you more productive because of it'.[4] But Baudri's assertions that the function of some poems is essentially playful and thus recreative was aimed at a select audience, and justifications such as his are relatively rare before the rise of vernacular literature in the twelfth century and the incorporation of Aristotelian ideas into literary thinking in the thirteenth.

While the connection between the medical and the recreational theories of literature is close, the two have different histories and different emphases. The medical theory is concerned with the benefits to one's health of being psychologically well-disposed. The recreational theory begins with an awareness of physiological and psychological necessity but emphasises more the moral demands surrounding that need: play is inferior to serious endeavour and is justified only insofar as it leads one to work more vigorously; play is legitimate only if it meets the standards of rational control demanded by ethical doctrine. Physicians themselves were aware that discussing the accidents of the soul brought medicine into an arena that was considered the province of moral philosophy; but as Bernard de Gordon explained, since disturbances of the soul harm not only the soul but also the body, they are legitimately the concern of the physician as well as the moral philosopher (*Lilium medicinae*, pp. 158–60). Many medieval justifications of literary pleasure draw on ideas from both medical and ethical traditions, and doubtless few writers paid attention to their separate lines of development. Yet frequently the defence of literary entertainment clearly relies on either one or the other line of reasoning. The distinctly recreational argument is obvious in a comment in a fourteenth-century letter from the abbot of St Augustine's Abbey asking a friend for a copy of the story of Godfrey de Bouillon and the conquest of the Holy Land. The letter makes reference to certain books that the friend is accustomed to read 'in order to mix entertainment with your duties'.[5] As in Baudri, the echo of the *Disticha Catonis* is clear; it establishes a certain kind of reading – even of a substantial narrative with a notable Christian theme – as recreational, a temporary indulgence in legitimate pleasures necessitated by the onerous chores of office.

---

4 See Bond, '*Iocus amoris*', p. 190.   5 See Pantin, 'Letters', pp. 216–17.

There is a strong recreational and hygienic dimension to late-medieval lyric theory, as one might expect in a culture where the composition of verses was perceived in a context of social entertainment and, often, courtly accomplishment. The Provençal *Leys d'Amors*, in its first version, maintains that the science of composing verse renders poetry more pleasurable, that such pleasure assuages distress, and that through 'solas' and 'deport' one sustains work better. The revised prose version alludes to the Latin distich cited above and expands on the medical value of pleasure (*Monumens*, 1, p. 10; *Leys d'Amors*, 1, pp. 7–8). Both versions argue that poems offer other benefits as well, but the recreational value of *trobar* is among the most prominent. Later in the fourteenth century Eustache Deschamps, in the *Art de dictier*, a short treatise on how to write verse in fixed forms, defines lyric poetry (whether sung or spoken) as a species of music and categorises music as the 'medicine' of the seven liberal arts. Its sweetness revives and recreates tired souls, making them more able subsequently to work at the other six arts. His treatise articulates in the terms of literary theory what other evidence (such as that of the fourteenth-century London *pui* and the later Parisian court of love) suggests from the standpoint of social history – that the performance or reading of poetry often functioned as public recreation and was thus conceptualised within systems of thought appropriate to all forms of entertainment perceived as social pastimes.

So too storytelling. The earliest major collection of Italian anecdotes and tales, *Il novellino*, defines itself as speech 'for our recreation' that is presented 'as honestly and courteously as possible' (*Italian Renaissance Tales*, tr. Smarr, p. 2). This self-definition as verbally proper pleasingness locates the *novelle* within the boundaries of that sort of amusing social discourse governed ethically by Aristotelian *eutrapelia* or related norms of proper play. A more intricate negotiation of those boundaries occurs at the end of Boccaccio's *Decameron*. As we have seen, his frame narrative of a tale-telling journey to escape from the plague depends on ideas of the therapeutic value of literature. The author's conclusion also relies on the ethical idea of proper recreation to help define and then fend off what he considers inappropriate criticism of his hundred tales, some of which he acknowledges might seem improper to some readers. Boccaccio explains that the tales were told in gardens, places for 'sollazzo', solace, rather than in church or school; that they were told by mature young people who were not likely to be seduced by the stories; and that they were told at a time of extreme license. This listing of appropriate or mitigating circumstances (where, by whom, when) belongs to a longstanding classical and medieval use of the *circumstantiae* in rhetorical and ethical analysis, and it is precisely what scholastic and earlier treatments of play consider necessary in determining the acceptability of any form of entertainment.

Boccaccio applies the idea to readers as well as to purveyors of literary recreation: the stories lay claim to usefulness only if they are read at the appropriate time and by those people (idle ladies) for whom they were written. The circumstantial constriction works to secure a kind of ethical space for the stories told by the *brigata* and as well a kind of artistic space for Boccaccio through his limitation of readership (which is really a strategic positing of a fictive ideal audience) to people ready for the kind of entertainment he offers.

Much less willing to grant the kind of ethical/artistic immunity that literary play-spaces (whether generated by Baudri or Boccaccio) try to create is the Middle English *Tretise of Miraclis Pleyinge*. Written around the turn of the fifteenth century, and espousing at least some attitudes associated with the Lollards, this text is a polemic against popular plays on religious subjects. It attacks several arguments advanced by people who approve of such plays, one of which is that the plays offer a nec-essary 'recreacioun' more conducive to piety than other entertainments. The *Tretise* rejects this argument not by disputing the premise of recre-ational necessity but by challenging whether the plays achieve the effects that scholastic moral philosophy says all recreation should: play is sup-posed to lead to more ardent pursuit of more important work, yet the actions of those who support such drama reveal no increased spiritual endeavour. In its appeal to the idea of recreational play, and in its use of the word 'play' throughout, the *Tretise* starts from the premise that the 'pleyinge' of 'miraclis' is fundamentally one of many kinds of ludic activity. Its comprehensive view is like that found in typologies of play in religious *distinctiones*, Aristotelian ethical categorisations and ency-clopaedic treatments of *ludus*. Since it grants no prior aesthetic status to the drama (even though it recognises that the drama does have certain distinctive features), it can condemn the playing of 'miraclis' by associ-ating that kind of play-action with various non-dramatic forms of play condemned in the Bible (ed. Davidson, pp. 39–40, 44–5).

Even a brief account of the incorporation of the recreational view of literature into literary criticism needs to mention Chaucer's *Canterbury Tales*. The stories are told as part of a contest explicitly defined through-out as 'pley' and 'game' and put forth initially as a source of 'confort' and 'mirth', i.e. as having psychological benefit by making the pilgrimage to Canterbury more enjoyable. The play frame contextualises storytelling as a form of social entertainment and, as in the *Decameron*, seems in part designed to foreground the author's elevation of vernacular tale and anecdote into the realm of more substantial literary achievement. Aris-totle's mean, excess and defect in regard to play may be epitomised in Chaucer's opening triad of narrators, the well-meaning Knight, mocking Miller and humourless Reeve. However, Chaucer seems ultimately less interested in justifying or illustrating recreational notions of fiction than in dramatising their limitations. Scholastic ideals of proper playing soon become subjected to the manipulations of various pilgrims, who often profess to tell their stories for the pleasure of the company while harbouring other intentions that are more private, mean-spirited or self-justifying. If the *Decameron* uses recreational theory to help isolate and insulate certain kinds of literary experience, and the *Tretise* uses the same theory to reject the possibility of such insulation, the *Canterbury Tales* offers the most detailed exploration of the middle ranges of that spectrum, where the recreational principle – not to mention other notions of literature – is subjected to the various appropriations of self-interested taletellers. Chaucer problematises 'solaas' as well as 'sentence' – but for the purposes of this chapter, what is important is that he, like Boccaccio, takes such 'solaas' as a given in the way one thinks about how stories affect audiences.

III

Although the theories defined above apply principally to literature presented in a context of public performance, clerical culture was not oblivious to the possibility that even some of its academic texts offered pleasure as well as (or possibly rather than) profit. Horace's discussion in the *Ars poetica* of the aims of poetry – to please or to profit or to do both – became, as E. D. Hirsch has said, 'the most influential statement about literary evaluation in the whole history of literary theory'. Certainly it was the most familiar dictum in the Middle Ages about what Hirsch would call the 'instrumental' or M. H. Abrams the 'pragmatic' values of literature.[6] A fourteenth-century commentary on Ovid, citing Horace, notes that some poetry pleases, some profits, and the best does both. Other *accessus* occasionally allow for the purely pleasurable: 'utilitas est delectatio', says one about the *Amores*; 'utilitas solum est delectatio' says another about the *Copa* attributed to Virgil.[7] We are now in a position to understand how, given medieval medical and psychological ideas, delight itself could be considered useful.

Even medieval criticism that finds both pleasure and profit in a single literary work usually treats the two functions separately rather than attempting to discuss how they are interconnected. The extensive late-fourteenth-century commentary on the *Eschez amoureux*, recently attributed to

---

[6] Hirsch, 'Two Traditions', p. 287; Abrams, *Mirror*, pp. 14–21.
[7] Olson, *Literature as Recreation*, pp. 24, 30; Allen, *Ethical Poetic*, p. 10 and n. 23. Suchomski cites a similar line in a Terence commentary; '*Delectatio*', p. 88.

Evrart de Conty, notes that the subject of the poem, love, is 'ioyeuse et plaisant' and that the author has mixed with it other material which will provide profit along with the delight that comes from reading about love. As in one's response to classical literature, says Evrart, delight improves the body, profits the soul. The poem's principal intention is to lead to virtue, but there is a separate therapeutic value simply to enjoying the poem (ed. Guichard-Tesson and Roy, pp. 2–3). Similarly, the prologue to a fifteenth-century prose narrative of Charlemagne begins by citing the didactic benefits of reading and remembering examples of noble behaviour. It then adds two sentences about the pleasures of the work as well, the first focusing on the ethical value of recreational activity rather than idleness, the second on the psychological benefits of the pleasure derived from agreeable reading (*Croniques et conquestes*, I, p. 12).

Pleasure and profit are more unified, though still conceptually separate, in the prologue to the *Fables* of Robert Henryson (*fl.* 1460–80). Henryson points out that people find the 'sweit rhetore' of fables 'richt plesand', while at the same time the tales reprove immoral behaviour through 'figure'. He expands on the 'morall sweit sentence' of poetry, using the traditional allegorical imagery of husk and kernel, and also on Horatian *dulce*, advancing the recreational argument that mixing 'merie sport' with 'ernist' gladdens the spirit and keeps the mind from becoming dull with too much 'studying' (ed. Fox, pp. 3–4, 189–91). Clearly there is a separation of form and content here (as Hirsch maintains is true throughout the history of literary criticism until Kant equated literary value with aesthetic value): the rhetoric offers pleasure, the kernel of meaning profit. But Henryson deliberately calls the 'sentence' as well as the rhetoric 'sweit'. Profit is pleasurable too: beyond the surface pleasure lies the pleasure of discovering the important truth hidden behind the veil. Or as Dante put it so categorically, 'the goodness and the beauty of any discourse are separate and distinct from each other, because the goodness lies in the meaning while the beauty lies in the adornment of the language; and while both the one and the other are accompanied by delight, it is the goodness which is to the greatest degree delightful' (Dante, *Literary Criticism*, tr. Haller, p. 71).[8]

Implicit here is the incorporation into literary theory of a medieval psychology of perception; like other sense-data, literary works have the power to activate one's mental faculties and move the listener/reader to desire (or reject) that which is presented. (On the role of the *affectus* in literary theory, see the previous chapter.) Of course, the ability of texts and performances to impel their audiences to desire what they portray could be a danger as well as a benefit, as repeated clerical condemnations of indecent

---

[8] On the pleasure of discovering allegorical meaning see Robertson, *Preface*, pp. 60–4.

entertainment testify. In considering only justifications of literary pleasure here I do not mean to deny the existence of substantial medieval criticism of works perceived to have no moral or spiritual value. I have focused rather on two important and closely related theories, ones reflected in a good deal of practical medieval criticism, that with due allowances find benefit in entertainment more or less independently of questions of moral profit. But that does not by any means exhaust medieval thinking about the role of literary pleasure, which imputed to *delectatio* many kinds of usefulness, *utilitas*, a broadly conceived category that could accommodate benefits beyond the morally or religiously instructive. Delight may function to sugar-coat a doctrinal pill, to enhance appreciation of ideas, to further sensitivity to style. The provision of psychological refreshment and the promoting of good health would in this view be further kinds of *utilitas*.

Recent employment of both music and poetry in therapeutic situations and recent interest in the psychological effects of exposure to certain kinds of films or television programmes suggest that medieval concern with the helpfulness or dangerousness of taking pleasure in tales and performances is no more inherently naïve than any other effort to consider the complicated question of what effects entertainment has on its audience. About that question medieval criticism developed its own considered opinions, including those outlined here that recognised the experience of enjoying works of art as recreational or therapeutic. Those ideas, as we have seen, played a particularly important role in the interpretative context within which much vernacular literature – *fabliaux*, romances, plays, lyric poetry, and works by sophisticated writers like Boccaccio and Chaucer – was experienced and understood. They constitute an important part of medieval literary criticism, and considered more diachronically they constitute an important part of the history of literary criticism that is concerned with instrumental or pragmatic questions. Their answers to those questions are probably neither more nor less historically limited than later efforts (such as post-Kantian aesthetics, post-Freudian psychologising, or postmodernist ideas of textual play) to think about what happens when human beings enjoy a tale, a song or a performance.

Part IV

Vernacular critical traditions: the early Middle Ages

9

Medieval Irish literary theory and criticism[1]

Patrick Sims-Williams and Erich Poppe

1. Poetic theory

Medieval Irish vernacular poetics were hierarchical, reflecting a prescriptive and idealised vision of Irish society. The various metres and poetic forms were held to correspond to the status and functions of various types of poets (*filid* and *baird*) and their appropriate patrons. Poetry with a social function – praise and satire – was of paramount importance, at the expense of the now much-anthologised informal lyrics. This emphasis no doubt reflects some degree of institutional continuity from the ancient Celtic world, for the old Celtic term for poet, *bardos*, pl. *bardi*, survived in Old Irish as *bard*, *baird* (and in Welsh as *bardd*, *beirdd*). Three Celtic learned classes held in exceptional honour were generally noted by the classical writers: bards who were singers and poets, given to singing praise and satire to the accompaniment of lyre-like instruments, *vates* (οὐάτεις) or diviners (μάντεις), and druids.[2] These correspond to Old Irish *bard* 'poet (of a lower grade)', *fáith* 'prophet (pagan or biblical)', and *druí* 'druid', although the fact that the Irish terms occur alongside a plethora of other terms and not as a discrete triad discourages speculation about the possible survival of a tripartite system.

The Old Irish laws, which were mostly written in the seventh and eighth centuries, give us a generalised and probably rather idealised picture of early Irish society, as seen by the writers of the laws, who were either professional lawyers or legally minded churchmen (or both). The laws are obsessed with rank and status and are careful to specify the exact rank of poets and other professional persons in a hierarchy ranging from the

---

[1] In the following chapter the question of how medieval Irish *literati* viewed their activities will be considered from two angles, their ideas about poetry and poetic inspiration and their perception of some major genres of narrative prose. Part 1 is by Patrick Sims-Williams and Part 2 by Erich Poppe. The term 'Irish', which is synonymous with 'Gaelic', is used here to cover the language and literature of the Irish-speaking population of both medieval Ireland and Scotland. The two were a linguistic unity at least until the thirteenth century, and professional poets from both areas continued to employ the same metres and the same highly standardised language until the seventeenth century. Evidence for links with literary criticism in Wales is slight (see Sims-Williams, 'Person-switching').

[2] Kidd, *Posidonius*, II.i, pp. 317–18.

'free/noble' (*sóer*) down to the 'unfree/base'(*dóer*). Poets appear at the top of the hierarchy, along with kings, lords and clerics, in the category called *nemed* 'sacred, holy, privileged'. They are the only 'craftsmen' (*áes dána*, lit. 'people of art/talent' or *áes cerdda* 'people of craft') to be placed so high up as the *sóernemed* or 'noble *nemed*' category; other craftsmen such as physicians, blacksmiths and harpists are grouped in a lower *dóernemed* or 'base *nemed*' category. The *nemed* class was a meritocracy as well as an aristocracy; a poet could be elevated to it on the basis of his art (*dán*) and the fraudulent poet who overcharged or composed inadequately could be degraded to a commoner. Normally, however, poetry was a hereditary profession passed down from father to son, and a poet whose father and grandfather were not poets could attain only the status of an *ánruth*, a step down from the *ollam*, the highest category.

From the point of view of the lawyers, the poet's principal public role was to enhance honour (*enech*, lit. 'face') through praise and, conversely, to shame the dishonourable through satire. The poet thus acted as an instrument of social control and public relations, no doubt usually on behalf of the king or lord (or churchman) who patronised him, although he reserved the right to bite the hand that fed him. A poet travelled freely and had rights outside his own community (*túath*); hence he could easily transfer his allegiance to the king of one of the hundred or more other *túatha* of early Ireland. The chief poet (*ollam*) could apparently be engaged by the *túath* itself or by its king. Every *túath* was expected to have its *fili*, according to *Bretha Nemed*:

A *túath* is not a *túath* without an ecclesiastical scholar, a churchman, a poet (*fili*), a king by whom contracts and treaties are extended to (other) *túatha*.

(*Uraicecht na Ríar*, p. 90)

Payments for various types of poems ranged from a chariot worth a *cumal* ('female slave', a standard unit of currency) down to a three-year-old dry heifer and a cauldron. The penalty for composing or repeating an unwarranted satire could range from death (commutable to a heavy fourteen-*cumal* fine) down to the composition of a praise poem, and a poem of exaggerated praise could itself be regarded as a form of satire by irony or sarcasm.

The Irish poet, as panegyrist and satirist, had the same function as the *bardos* of ancient Gaul and the *bardd* of medieval Wales. In the Irish sources, however, the cognate term *bard* (pl. *baird*) is used of inferior grades of poet, with a lower honour-price, and the higher-ranking poet is termed the *fili* (pl. *filid*) or *éces*. The term *fili* (later *file*) derives from a Celtic root meaning 'to see' (compare the Welsh *gwelaf* 'I see') and may originally have meant 'seer' (compare the name of the seeress *Veleda*, mentioned by Tacitus, *Histories* 4.61 and 66). The *fili* was indeed believed to derive his status from the three ancient skills – two of them allegedly banned by St Patrick – of *imbas forosna* 'encompassing knowledge which illuminates', *teinm láeda* 'breaking of marrow(?)', and *díchetal di chennaib* 'chanting from heads(?)'. Despite this, it is unlikely that the term *fili* was understood etymologically in early Ireland, since the root did not survive in Irish with the meaning 'to see'. There is therefore no reason to think that prophecy was regarded as the *fili*'s principal role in the historic period rather than just one of his possible roles, along with knowing legal precedents, stories (*scéla*) and other lore (*senchas*) and, above all, composing praise and satire. Despite the etymology of his title, it may be more helpful to see the *fili* as a 'professor of literature and man of letters'[3] than to compare him with the ancient druids. Why the terms *fili* and *bard* had come to be placed in the hierarchy in which they are found in Ireland cannot now be known, and may have nothing to do with their etymologies. It was almost inevitable, however, given the early Irish obsession with ranking, that they would be distinguished hierarchically in one order or another and not be treated as synonyms (unlike such terms as *dramatist* and *playwright* in English).

The laws divide the *filid* into seven grades (probably under the influence of the seventh-century church's seven ecclesiastical orders from bishop down to doorkeeper), of which the highest is the *ollam* or *ollam dána* ('highest of art'), with the same honour-price as the king of a *túath* and a retinue of twenty-four, and the lowest is the *fochloc* with his retinue of two. Legal divisions of the ranks of the *baird* range between six and sixteen types. The highest was the *rígbard* or *tigernbard* ('king/lord-bard'), originally meaning a king or lord who was also an amateur(?) poet, and the *baird* are only rarely stated to have retinues. The *bard*, unlike the *fili*, was not expected to have studied or undergone professional training, but had to rely on innate ability alone. While not necessarily illiterate, the *baird* evidently operated in an oral environment, without the benefit of formal study; according to *Bretha Nemed*, 'although knowledge of letters and metrics is not required of the bards, it is required of them to perceive and recognise their proper measure by ear and nature. It is thus that the free bards make their bardic poetry' ('Old-Irish Tract on Privileges and Responsibilities of Poets', pp. 43–4). In the modern world we could perhaps compare the distinction between musicians who play 'by ear' and those who can read music and have studied the theory of music. To some extent the *baird* may have acted as reciters in the employment of the *filid*.

The studies expected of the *filid* included grammar, knowledge of the vernacular *ogam* alphabets, and the reading of texts such as *Bretha Nemed* and *Auraicept na nÉces*, and thus overlapped with a regular ecclesiastical

---

[3] Bergin, *Irish Bardic Poetry*, p. 4.

education. This convergence is highlighted in *Míadshlechta* by the borrowing of the terms *ollam* and *ánruth* for, respectively, the first highest grade (alias *roshuí* or *suí littre*) and second highest grade of seven grades of ecclesiastical scholars.[4] Of course, it is difficult to know how far in practice the ecclesiastically orientated lawyers were successful in making lack of learning a bar to promotion through the ranks of the *filid* (any more than lack of 'theory' has ever thwarted a talented musician). Certainly there is an element of idealism in the legal stipulation that a king shall only accept an *ollam* whom another *ollam* declares to be innocent of adultery (*Uraicecht na Ríar* §6), and the same may apply to stipulations about ecclesiastical-style learning. Admittedly, the Irish Annals give particular prominence to *filid* with monastic connections, but Richter attributes this to 'the limited horizon of the annalists to whom apparently Christian scholars were of the greater interest' (pp. 203, 221). In practice (according to a sixteenth-century poem) appointment to the supreme position of *ollam flatha* or *ollam ríg* ('chief's/king's poet') could be secured without completing the full course of poetic training, and a fifteenth-century poet maintains that the title *ollam* is bestowed by the chief, rather than the head of a school (*aide*) as claimed in the Metrical Tracts discussed below.[5]

Below the status of the *filid* and *baird*, the Laws refer to the unruly satirist (*cáinte* or *rindile*), often with hostility, especially where female satirists are concerned – the Laws know nothing of the more exalted *banfhili* (female *fili*). There were also many entertainers, such as the *crossán*, and *drúth*, who occasionally composed satirical verses.

One eighth-century law tract, *Uraicecht na Ríar* ('The Primer of the Stipulations'), is devoted to stipulating the qualifications and privileges of the seven grades of *filid*, and three other tracts from the Old Irish period discuss these grades, or those of the *baird*, among other material concerning social status: *Bretha Nemed* ('Judgements of Privileged Persons' – in two main versions), *Míadshlechta* ('Passages on Rank') and *Uraicecht Becc* ('Short Primer/Introduction [to *Bretha Nemed*?]').[6] *Uraicecht na Ríar* and *Uraicecht Becc* draw on and refer to *Bretha Nemed*, whereas *Míadshlechta* is independent of it. In descending order, the hierarchy of *filid* in *Uraicecht na Ríar* and *Uraicecht Becc* are: *ollam*, *ánruth*, *clí*, *cano*, *dos*, *macfhuirmid* and *fochloc*, plus (in *Uraicecht na Ríar*) three sub-grades: *taman*, *drisiuc* ('briar-dog') and *oblaire*. The sub-grades are not true *filid* for even the first, the *taman*, 'does not have knowledge of letters' (*Uraicecht na Ríar*, §18). The seven grades are common to the various texts (although *Míadshlechta* uses the terms *ollam* and *éces* interchangeably and *Bretha Nemed* places the *suí* 'sage' even higher than the

---

4 MacNeill, 'Ancient Irish Law', p. 313.
5 Breatnach, 'Chief's Poet', pp. 37–9 and 67–8.
6 On all four see Breatnach's commentary on *Uraicecht na Ríar*.

ollam), but there is some variation in the details of the poets beneath the *fochloc*: *Míadshlechta* places the *bard*, *fer cerda* and *cáinte* here. As already mentioned, the ranks of the *baird* (who are excluded from consideration in *Uraicecht na Ríar*, apart from the three 'sub-grades' noted above) are enumerated much more inconsistently and number between six and sixteen.

Whereas generally there were limitations to upward social mobility, the lawyers envisage the seven grades of *filid* as stages through which the aspiring *ollam* would hope to pass through examination by an established *ollam*:

He may rise over each grade from *fochloc* to *ollam*, as Neire says: 'He may make a full ascent to the designated position of sage.' (*Uraicecht na Ríar*, p. 87 and §4)

By contrast, no *cursus honorum* is normally associated with the ranking of the various types of *baird*. There are traces in *Bretha Nemed*, however, of what may be an older state of affairs in which one could progress through *six* stages from *dul* through *drisiuc*, *bard*, *admall* and *lethcerd*, to the rank of *fili* or *deán*; here the *fili/bard* distinction is less rigidly drawn than usual.

Several treatises on metre survive from the later Old Irish and Middle Irish periods (edited by Thurneysen as 'Mittelirische Verslehren'), and some of these give additional information about the types of poets, in the course of prescribing the metres appropriate to each grade. The earliest tract ('Mittelirische Verslehren' i) seems to have been compiled in the tenth century on the basis of ninth-century materials. Although written from the point of view of the *filid*, this First Metrical Tract is devoted to the metres of *bairdne*, that is, the poetry of the *baird*, and in particular that of the *sóerbaird* or 'noble/free bards', rather than that of the *dóerbaird* or 'base bards'. It enumerates eight noble bards and eight base bards (§2), but there are in practice only seven grades among the former (from *rígbard* down to *bóbard*) since the eighth, the *bard áine*, is the son or grandson of a *bard* who does not himself compose. The grades of the *sóerbaird* are compared with those of the *filid* in that each one 'surpasses the other in abundance of knowledge and *ségda* [bardic composition] except for letters and verse-syllables [*dëich*] and declensions etc.', but the *bard* has a lower honour-price than the *fili* because he 'neither studies nor does one study under him' (§3). *Bairdne* ('bardic composition') is divided into various types, of which the 'four principal divisions' are *nathbairdne*, *ollbairdne*, *casbairdne* and *dúanbairdne*; these belong to the four highest grades of bard (§4). The body of the tract (§§5–56) gave (in its original form) forty-four examples of the various bardic metres (mostly eulogistic quatrains), beginning with *nathbairdne*, that is, the metres of the *rígbard* (here meaning the 'supreme'[7] rather than 'king' bard), also called the *ollam bairdne*; his metres comprise *dechnad mór* ('great *dechnad*') and six other types of *dechnad* (§§6–12) – the element *nath-/-nad* in these names is cognate with *nad* in Welsh (as in *marwnad* 'death-song, elegy'). The tract concludes by explaining that each grade of bards composes both in his own peculiar metres and in those of the grades inferior to himself (§67), and that the bardic metres are paid for *ad hoc* and do not have set rewards because they are *óig-rechta* (var. *núa-chrutha*), 'new forms', invented by *nue-thigthi*, 'newcomers' (var. *núa-litridi* 'recent authors'), unlike the established *prím-aisti* ('chief metres'), which had an agreed tariff of rewards and were peculiar to the *filid* (§68). It is implied that although the *filid* did not make any claim to the exclusive use of these 'new forms', they did use them and expect payment at a lower level for them. The idea that these rhyming and syllabic metres were 'new' seems to be already an old one by the time the First Metrical Tract was composed, when they were perhaps only 'new' by comparison with the more ancient and obsolescent metres peculiar to the *filid*. The latter tend to be marked by the presence of alliteration and by the absence of rhyme and stanza, and sometimes by the use of accentual and/or syllabic patterning either in the line as a whole or at least in its cadence. In the extant manuscripts (all post-1100) such old (or seemingly old) metres are sometimes labelled *retoiric* (< Latin *rhetorice*), frequently abbreviated '.r.' (which, however, could also stand for the native words *rosc, roscad*, etymologically 'great utterance'), but the extent to which they are indebted to Latin rhetorical models has been hotly debated. Similarly, the extent of the debt of the stanzaic, rhymed 'new forms' to Latin hymn-metres is contested. The First Metrical Tract analyses them in terms of syllable-count and cadence only, ignoring the additional presence of accentual patterns in some of them, notably the metres ascribed to the *tigernbard*. By contrast, *Bretha Nemed* makes a distinction between the syllabic poetry of the *filid* and non-syllabic *bairdne*, comparing *rhythmus* versus *metrum* in Latin.[8]

An interpolation near the end of the First Metrical Tract (§§57–8) adds two types of *sétnad* (later *sétrad*) metre to the repertoire of the *rígbard* (see below on Tract IV), and this interpolation is followed by an originally independent ninth-century account of *dëich* – a *dëach* (perhaps the first element of *dechnad* above) being a sort of metrical 'foot' of one to eight syllables (§§59–66). One manuscript of the Tract (the Book of Ballymote) includes a list of the metres of the eight base bards in §67.

[7] Ó hAodha, 'First Metrical Tract', pp. 221–2.
[8] Ó hAodha, pp. 223–4; Tranter, 'Divided and Scattered', p. 269, with review by McManus, pp. 180–1.

The Second Metrical Tract ('Mittelirische Verslehren' ii), in its original, probably early-tenth-century, form, described the curriculum of the aspiring *fili*, with seven years of study matching the seven grades of *filid* (§§2–31 = years I–VI and §§113–20 = year VII). In its extant, eleventh-century form, however, the seven years of study have been expanded to twelve years for twelve grades of poets, notably by including the contents of the First Metrical Tract as the curriculum for a new seventh year of study, namely *bairdne na mbard* (§§33–89). The extant version also includes discussion of the metres of the eight base bards and of the *taman*, *drisiuc* and *oblaire* (§§132–5). The original core of the tract, however, stressed the old non-syllabic metres, the *filid's* prerogative, although (according to Murphy, *Early Irish Metrics*, p. v, n. 1) the compilers 'do not really seem to have understood the principle on which those metres were built'. Presumably the *filid* by this time were accustomed to use the same 'new forms' as the *baird*, but kept up their interest in the older metres as part of the 'study' by which they differentiated themselves from the *baird* – rather as the modern academically qualified composer acquires a mastery of sixteenth-century harmony and counterpoint which he rarely has occasion to use.

By the time the Third Metrical Tract ('Mittelirische Verslehren' iii) was put together, about 1060, the explicit distinction between the metres of *filid* and *baird* had been abandoned. Its topic is the metres of the *filid*, but these are nearly all syllabic and are divided on a scale ranging from 'usual metres' (§§2–127) to 'uncommon metres' (§§167–205). It claims that there were 365 metres (§1), but this was a conventional 'large number' in Irish sources and in fact less than 60 per cent are exemplified. As in the other tracts, the examples are partly drawn from existing poems, and partly specially composed or at least adapted (e.g. §§6–7 and 8–9, where the order of lines is reversed to illustrate variant forms).

The so-called Fourth Metrical Tract ('Mittelirische Verslehren' iv) belongs to the same period. It is a poem by Cellach Úa Rúanada, who died in 1079 as 'ardollam Erenn' (pre-eminent *ollam* of Ireland), and illustrates by example the 'good metres of poetry' (*dagaisti in dána*), twelve in number and again all syllabic ones. Most of these were those assigned to *bairdne* in the First Metrical Tract, but Cellach does include some prestigious metres such as *sétrad* (*sétnad*) and *dían midsheng* (similar to *sétnad mór*) which had not been included by that Tract in its original form, before the expansion mentioned above.

The general impression given by the sources is that the *baird's* metres formed part of the repertoire of the *filid* already in the Old Irish period and that as time went by the older metres exclusive to the *filid* fell out of fashion, with the result that there came to be no clear formal distinction between the poetry of the *filid* and the *baird*, except perhaps in the level of learning that might be displayed. In cases when we have no external evidence of authorship, it is presumably impossible for us to distinguish between examples of *bairdne* composed by *baird* and examples of *bairdne* composed by *filid*.

The tracts all classify metres according to a terminological system referring to length of line, rhyme scheme and cadence. For instance, *rannaigecht cetarchubaid gairit dialtach* 'indicates a four-lined stanza based on a seven-syllable line and with *rimes croisées* [*rannaighecht*], with four rhyming words [*cetarchubaid*], a truncated (trisyllabic) first line [*gairit*] and monosyllabic cadences [*dialtach*]'.[9] Here is a typical example of how a metre is defined in the First Metrical Tract (§15):

Casbairdne ['intricate bardistry'?] comes now, which consists of four lines, each line being a seven-syllable unit. It resembles the *duan* in measure, in that there is a seven-syllable unit in each, that is twenty-eight syllables in each of them, but the *duan* concludes in a monosyllable, while the *casbairdne* concludes in a trisyllable, as follows:

> A *D*orchaidi *d*elbchathaig*,
>   a *d*eil *t*resa *t*romthoraig*,
> a *m*inn *m* a r c s h l ú a i g *m*unchoraig*,
>   a *m*aic *c* a r p r ú a i d *Ch*onchobair*.

[O Dorchaide of warlike appearance, O goad of battle involving mighty hosts, O diadem of the necklet-wearing cavalry, O strongbodied son of Conchobar.][10]

It will be noted that many of the metrical intricacies in the example are passed over in the prose; moreover, the metre is defined by comparison with the *dúan*, but the latter is not dealt with until later in the tract (§§18–23). Evidently much oral exposition and exemplification needed to go on alongside the metrical tracts; they were not 'teach yourself' manuals. Indeed, their tendency to classify the metres according to the status of the poets specialising in them rather than according to their inherent taxonomy makes them less practical than modern treatises such as Murphy's *Early Irish Metrics*. They would appear to have grown out of the social classifications of the Irish laws rather than the metrical analyses of classical Antiquity, such as Servius' *De centum metris* and Augustine's *De musica*.[11] Vernacular Irish scholars were certainly aware of Latin terminology, as we see from the discussion of 'rithim . . . artificialis et

---

[9] Tranter, 'Divided and Scattered', p. 264.
[10] Tranter, p. 264; Ó hAodha, 'First Metrical Tract', p. 229. For the system of editorial diacritics to denote rhyme, consonance and alliteration see Murphy, *Early Irish Metrics*, p. vi.
[11] For a different view, see Tranter, 'Divided and Scattered', p. 266, and his 'Metrikwandel' generally.

uulgaris' in the Irish preface to the Latin *Altus prosator* in the eleventh-century *Liber hymnorum*, but they rarely chose to apply it to poetry in Irish.

Besides the four Metrical Tracts ('Mittelirische Verslehren') discussed above, a great deal of similar material survives. *Trefhocul*, a prose tract on poetics, is as early as the tenth century, to judge by the terminus of the dates of its latest verse illustrations; this date is supported by its ascription to Cináed ua Con Mind, bishop of Lismore and Scattery Island, who died in 958.[12] It lists and exemplifies a dozen poetic faults (metrical, grammatical and stylistic) and then deals with twice as many poetic licences by which metrical faults may be avoided. Versification is also discussed in verse; for example, a poem on *Trefhocul* is appended to the Book of Ballymote copy of *Auraicept na nEces* (ll. 1962–2180), followed by another Middle Irish poem on varieties of *dúnad* 'conclusion', the device by which Irish poems were expected to begin and end in the same way – already in the ninth century an Old Irish glossator noted that Psalm 8 also shows *dúnad*, 'as the *filid* do among us', and *dúnad* is the very first branch of the *filid*'s art covered in the Second Metrical Tract ('Mittelirische Verslehren' ii).[13] In the Book of Ballymote, the poem on *dúnad* is in turn followed by a poem on the retinues of the seven grades of poet (ll. 2219–55). The duties and responsibilities of the *ollam* are covered in another Middle Irish poem, which states that he is fined in cattle if his poem is late.[14] The need for the Celtic bard to be punctual was already a theme in the time of the ancient Greek philosopher Posidonius.[15]

Besides tracts dealing with the technicalities of status and metrics, there are also more philosophical or mythological discussions of the nature of poetry. Thus *Bretha Nemed* includes an obscure Old Irish tract on *aí* 'inspiration' (cognate with Welsh *awen*) and its relation to *guth* 'voice', *anál* 'breath', *son* 'sound', and so on.[16] Another early tract discusses poetic ability in terms of three 'cauldrons' within a person, each of which may be inverted and empty, on its side, or upright and brimful. The first is innately upright in most people and includes basic grammatical knowledge, the second is on its side for the practitioner of *bairdne*, but upright for the *ánroth*, and the third and most important is the Cauldron of Knowledge. The second cauldron can be converted from its upside-down position

---

[12] Edited by Calder as an appendix to *Auraicept*, pp. 258–69, and discussed by Breatnach, 'Poets and Poetry', pp. 66–7, and Hollo, 'Metrical Irregularity'.

[13] Henry, 'Celtic-English Prosodic Feature'; Murphy, *Early Irish Metrics*, pp. 43–5; McManus, '*Úaim do rinn*'.

[14] 'Pflichten und Gebühren', ed. Meyer. See Breatnach, 'Chief's Poet', p. 53.

[15] Kidd, *Posidonius*, II.i, p. 314: a bard sang a song lamenting his late coming.

[16] 'Old-Irish Tract', ed. Gwynn, pp. 5, 35–40, and 227–8. Watkins, 'Indo-European Metrics', pp. 215–16 and 239–40, connects *aí/awen* with the root of Welsh *awel* 'breeze', but in *How to Kill a Dragon*, p. 117, he prefers a root 'to see'.

by the emotions of sorrow or joy, both divine and human. The latter, human joy, has four (successive) divisions: sexual longing; the carefree life of one who has not begun to practise *bairdne*; joy at the privileges of poetry, and joy at the mythological arrival of *imbas* upstream along the surface of the River Boyne every seventh year from the hazels of Segais. These ideas are contrasted by the tract itself with theories deriving poetic art from the soul, an ecclesiastical view, or from the body, which was probably the view of the families of hereditary poets (§3).[17] A number of Old Irish tales deal with the nature of poetry in mythical guise, through stories about archetypical early poets, and even include a character called the 'spirit of poetry' (*spiritus Poematis*).[18] The ninth-century 'Colloquy of the Two Sages', a dialogue between two legendary *filid*, alludes to the nature of poetry in obscure, riddling language; for instance, the reply to the question 'whence hast thou come?' is: 'Not hard [to say]: from the heel of a sage, from a confluence of wisdom, from perfections of goodness, from brightness of sunrise, from the hazels of poetic art [see above], from [bardic] circuits of splendour, out of which they measure truth according to excellence, in which righteousness is taught, in which falsehood sets, in which colours are seen, in which poems are freshened' (pp. 16–19).

While the earlier material on metrics discussed above continued to be copied in the later Middle Ages (which is how it survives), that period saw the production of newer, more relevant works. For example, a tract from the fourteenth century beginning 'Here are the faults which commonly occur in all verse compositions' exemplifies and names some fifty metres, some of them rare and unattested in the earlier tracts, as well as incorporating the traditional 'faults' from the *Trefhocul* tract; this tract's attention to metrical faults reflects the increasingly strict refinement of the *filid*'s art which set in during the twelfth century (under circumstances still unclear, but perhaps under the influence of the Ó Dálaigh family, according to Katharine Simms). This led to a break between the new 'strict art' (*dán díreach*) and the freer syllabic metres that were of high status when the earlier tracts were composed but which were now labelled *óglláchas*. The so-called 'Bardic Grammatical Tracts' and 'Bardic Syntactical Tracts', which originated in the later-medieval schools of the *filid*, include comments on metrical rules alongside grammatical and

---

[17] '"Caldron of Poesy"', ed. Breatnach. Compare the image of *scientia exterior* as 'a cauldron [*uassis*] from which all may drink' in the *Anonymus ad Cuimnanum* (Breatnach, 'Bernhard Bischoff', p. 10), and Virgilius Maro Grammaticus' image of memory which 'overflows with countless thoughts all poured into it as if it were a sturdy pot' (Law, *Wisdom*, p. 70).

[18] Ford, 'The Blind', and *Celtic Poets*, pp. 35–42.

syntactical ones, which is not surprising since their main aim was to maintain the standard of *dán díreach* by precept and example.[19] McManus has estimated that the 'database' used by the tracts' compilers included well over a thousand poems.[20] He argues that their basic doctrine, which goes back to the late twelfth century, may have been put in writing much earlier than the earliest manuscript, which is from the fourteenth century (and contains the above-mentioned metrical tract). It held its own down to the seventeenth century. The poets' aggressively elitist attitude to their 'science' (*aithne, foglaimm*) is well expressed in a poem on the technicalities of poetry by Gofraidh Fionn Ó Dálaigh (d. 1387):

> Ar na ceasdaibh ad-chluine
> dá n-urmaise énduine
> –an aithnesi ní haisgidh–
> ar mh'aithrisi urmaisdir.
>
> In fhoghluimsi an iongnadh libh
> dá mbeith a haithne ag éigsibh,
> 's iad leisin ndán druim ar druim,
> is gan iad dá rádh romhuinn. . . .
>
> Is mé Gofraidh mac meic Thaidhg
> a-ndeas ón Mhumhain mhíonaird;
> tearc trá ón lios i luighim
> gá dtá fios a bhfiafruighim.
>
> Tacmhang na héigse uile
> conntabhairt é ag énduine;
> tearc as ionchomhráidh orra
> friothghobhlain na foghloma.

[If a man would approach these questions I am telling you of let him approach them under my direction; this knowledge is not a gift [but requires work?].

Seeing that the poets have always been dealing with poetry, do you wonder that they should possess a knowledge of this science, even if they have not been telling of it up to this? . . .

I am Gofraidh, grandson of Tadhg, from smooth lofty Mumha in the south; few are they who can answer the questions I send forth from this fort where I dwell.

To grasp poetry is hard for any man; few are fitted to speak of the branches of this science.]

---

[19] For primary and secondary literature see Ó Macháin, 'Early Modern Irish Prosodic Tracts', Ó Cuív, 'Concepts', and McManus, 'Classical Modern Irish'.
[20] 'Classical Modern Irish', p. 172. See also Breatnach, 'Metres of Citations'.

2. The evidence of narrative prose

Medieval Irish textual culture embraces a wide variety of genres, including various religious text-types, secular law, functional prose (genealogy,
chronicles and historiography, didactic texts), secular poetry and secular
narrative. The oldest vernacular Irish texts appear to have been composed
during the seventh century, whereas the scribes of the oldest manuscript
to contain such texts (*Lebor na hUidre*) were active probably between
the middle of the eleventh and the middle of the twelfth century. Earlier
manuscripts, now lost, can be deduced as having existed as far back as the
eighth century. Textual remains from the Old Irish period, which lasted
from the beginning of the eighth century to the middle of the tenth century,
are scarce in contemporary manuscripts. Hiberno-Latin and vernacular
texts share the same cultural background; already by the ninth century
Irish begins to oust Latin. Until the twelfth century the transmission of
texts was the domain of ecclesiastical environments. The Anglo-Norman
conquest and the church reform of the twelfth century were important cultural watersheds, and one of their results was the emergence of learned
families as the dominant bearers of a secular tradition of learning and
literature.

One issue central to the investigation of medieval Irish literary theory
is the contemporary perception and function of secular narrative texts,
since these are traditionally equated with medieval Irish 'prose literature'. A substantial part of this corpus can be characterised as (pseudo-)
historical, that is, it is associated with characters and events in Irish history as well as with Irish places and traditions. A wide concept of what
constitutes 'history' for medieval Irish scholars is advocated here, which
includes narrowly historical as well as legendary events, insofar as the latter were integrated into explicit or implicit chronological or genealogical
systems. This discussion will focus on evidence for textual self-reflection
and for conceptions of such pseudo-historical narrative as *historia* and
as written memory, with relevance to authors and audiences in their
own time.

Medieval Irish narrators rarely, and obliquely, intrude in their narratives, and accordingly, there are very few explicit comments on their
perception of the texts they produced. The Latin colophon to *Táin Bó
Cúailnge* ('The Cattle-Raid of Cooley') in the Book of Leinster, produced
in the last quarter of the twelfth century, is therefore particularly significant. The conventional formal end of the narrative ('The account and
the story and the end of the *Táin* so far') and the request to transmit
it unchanged ('A blessing on every one who will learn the *Táin* faithfully in this form and who will not add another form to it'), are both
in Irish. The scribe, who was probably the scholar responsible for the

compilation and organisation of the manuscript, then switches to Latin and adds:

But I who have written this *historia*, or rather this *fabula*, do not trust certain things in this *historia*, or *fabula*. For some things there are delusions of demons, others poetic inventions, some resemble the truth, others do not, some are for the delectations of fools.[21]

Here the scribe as literary critic comments on the truth-value of his narrative and distances himself from its status as *historia* – defined by Isidore as 'a narrative of things done, by which these [things] which were done in the past are distinguished' (Isidore, *Etymologiae* 1.41).[22] At the same time he indicates that this was probably the normal and expected interpretation of its textual genre. The critical concepts *historia* and *fabula* were widely used from late-classical Antiquity; they are discussed by Hiberno-Latin scholars such as Sedulius Scottus (*In Donati artem maiorem*, p. 80), and in a note in a fifteenth-century manuscript the triad *scél* ('fabula'), *arramainte* ('argumentum') and *stair* ('historia') is briefly defined in the vernacular, with reference to Macrobius and to the acceptance or rejection of these different modes in theology and philosophy. A collocation of *fabula* with *delectatio* is also found, for example, in Augustine (*Solil.* 2.11.19), an author well known in early-medieval Ireland. It is tempting to think that at least for the scribe and scholar responsible for the colophon in the Book of Leinster, the enormous political and cultural changes of the twelfth century entailed a shift in his understanding of the narrative tradition and that its status as *historia* was no longer self-evident.

Another text, also of the late twelfth century, *Acallam na Senórach* ('The Tales [literally "conversation"] of the Elders'), contains an unusual number of comments on the functions of the embedded narratives by one of the characters of the frame narrative. That this character is in most instances Saint Patrick himself gives his literary evaluations special weight. He authorises the written transmission of secular topographical and historical lore in the combined interest of learning and entertainment, and thus privileges a written form of memory over an oral form. However, in the first instance his own fascination with this material is endorsed by angels:

'You [i.e. Caílte, one of the narrators of the embedded narratives] have lightened our spirits and our mind [*as gairdiugud menman 7 aicenta*], even though our religious life is being disrupted and our prayers neglected', [said Patrick]. They

---

[21] *Táin Bó Cúalnge*, ed. O'Rahilly, p. 136: 'Sed ego qui scripsi hanc historiam aut uerius fabulam quibusdam fidem in hac historia aut fabula non accommodo. Quaedam enim ibi sunt praestrigia demonum, quaedam autem figmenta poetica, quaedam similia uero, quaedam non, quaedam ad delectationem stultorum.'

[22] 'Narratio rei gestae, per quam ea, quae in praeterito facta sunt, dinoscuntur.'

were there until the following morning . . . Aibelán and Solusbrethach, his two
guardian angels, then came to Patrick and he asked them if it were the will of the
King of Heaven and Earth that he be listening to the tales of the *Fían* [*re scéla na
Féinne*]. They answered him with one voice. 'Dear holy cleric', they said, 'these
old warriors tell you no more than a third of their stories, because their
memories are faulty. Have these stories written down on poets' tables in refined
language, so that the hearing of them will provide entertainment [*gairdiugudh*]
for the lords and commons of later times'.

(tr. Dooley and Roe, *Tales*, pp. 11–12; *Acallamh*, ll. 286–302)

Accordingly, Patrick himself later says, again insisting on written
transmission:

Let the story be written out . . . , so that it may entertain [*gomba gairdiughadh*]
the chieftains of later times.

(tr. Dooley and Roe, *Tales*, p. 34; *Acallamh*, ll. 1062–3)[23]

A translation of *gairdiugud* (lit. 'a shortening [of time]') as 'entertainment'
in the modern sense, may, however, be misleading. In the course of its
authentication as an eyewitness report, *Immram Curaig Máele Dúin* ('The
Voyage of Máel Dúin') refers to Virgil for future uses of such tales ('it
will some day be a joy to recall . . .'). The scribe of one manuscript
version expands this with a comment on his intention of redacting it,
'for delighting the mind [*ar ghairdechad menman*] and for the people of
Ireland after him' (*Voyage of Máel Dúin*, ed. Oskamp, pp. 176–9).[24] Given
the tale's religious subtext, entertainment would appear to be too narrow
as its main function. Similarly, in an Irish saint's Life *gairdiugud* is used for
the beneficial and positive effects of preaching on an audience (*Bethada
Naém nErenn*, I, p. 168). *Gairdiugud* may therefore more appropriately
be defined as a useful as well as pleasant mental diversion. It is thus no
contradiction that in the *Acallam* Patrick's initial emphasis on *gairdiugud*
as the function of the embedded narratives is then replaced by an insistence
on their information-value and the necessity of their transformation and
further dissemination as written memory:

Where are the wise men and the historians of Ireland? Whatever Caílte and
Oisín have told us of their great deeds of valour and of prowess, as well as all
the knowledge, learning, and the place-name lore of Ireland, let it all be
preserved on the staffs of poets, in the texts of scholars, and in the tales of sages,
so that each might carry his share with him to his own native land.

(tr. Dooley and Roe, *Tales*, p. 79; *Acallamh*, ll. 2589–93)[25]

---

[23] See Dooley and Roe, *Tales*, pp. 16, 64, 216; *Acallamh*, ed. Stokes, ll. 467–8, 2094–5,
7758–9, 7792.
[24] See *Aeneid* 1.203: 'Haec olim meminisse iuuabit.'
[25] See Dooley and Roe, *Tales*, pp. 82, 88, 203; *Acallamh*, ll. 2702–3, 2876–7, 7253–8.

The perhaps late-fourteenth-century second recension of *Cath Muighe Rath* ('The Battle of Moira', about a historical event of 637 CE) contains a rather unusual introduction which includes discussion of the intention of the narrative and the duties of the *senchaid*, the bearer of historical tradition (*senchas*, recognisably connected with *sen*, 'old'):

> For the *senchaid* has to relate . . . the old knowledge [*seneolus*] and the noble descent of the nobility and of the monarchs through [their] illustrious noble ancestors, for there are two reasons for which it is fitting for us to relate the noble names of the well-born families of the nobility and of the monarchs thus, i.e. for commemoration first, and to consolidate their kinship through the reign of the lines of kings before them, and to remind the family-groups of a kindred of their blood relationship, by relating the famous stories about them after them.
>
> (*Banquet of Dun na nGedh*, p. 96)

Thus the primary functions of a narrative about past events are the written preservation of historical and genealogical information, the commemoration of ancestors and the forging of kinship identity, and thus the transmission of the history of an extended family for contemporary and future audiences.

The Battle of Moira can be dated by references in medieval Irish chronicles, and in one of these, the so-called 'Annals of Tigernach', the cattle-raid described in *Táin Bó Cúailnge* is assigned to the year 19 BCE and confidently synchronised with the death of Virgil. However, the Battle of Moira is recorded in post-Patrician, and possibly contemporary, sections of Irish chronicles, but the *Táin Bó Cúailnge* appears in pre-Patrician, legendary sections. Other narratives supply their own relative chronology; for example, 'the battle between them was three hundred years before the birth of Christ' or 'for the men of Ireland had been without a king's rule over them for seven years after the death of Conaire in Bruden Dá Derca until this assembly' (*Scéla Mucce*, p. 6; *Serglige Con Culainn*, p. 8). Conaire's death is dated to 30 BCE, and also alternatively to 44 CE, in the 'Annals of Tigernach'.

Some narratives were subordinated as background to other narratives, for example the so-called fore-tales (*remscéla*) to *Táin Bó Cúailnge*, to form minor chronological and thematic cycles. The personnel of the majority of medieval Irish narrative prose was part of a complex and highly organised, though not always consistent, chronological and genealogical system of Irish prehistory, and the notion of the narrative tradition's historicity is still reflected in the synthetic history *Forus feasa ar Éirinn* ('The Foundation of Knowledge about Ireland') of Geoffrey Keating (*c.* 1580–*c.* 1644), wherein he used many of these narratives as sources. Furthermore, frequent explanations of features of the Irish landscape (there is also a distinct learned sub-genre *dindshenchas*, the explanation of traditions about place-names, in both prose and verse), of the association of places with historical events, and of the origin of traditions, support the view that this corpus was part of a massive historical project, the creative appropriation and interpretation of Ireland in terms of both its chronological and geographical space. Internal inconsistencies or references to alternative accounts in many versions of narratives show that their redactors attempted to incorporate all available information about the events described. A comparison between the first and the second recensions of *Táin Bó Cúailnge* indicates the conceptual difference between the collection of information about an event in the past and the creation of a more unified narrative, and also the extent to which textual meaning has accrued to the second recension in this process.

Narratives perceived as *historia* serve as a textualisation in writing of the memory of the traditions about Ireland. Much earlier, Isidore had pointed out that one of the functions of *historia* was 'the instruction of the present' ('praeterita hominum gesta ad institutionem praesentium'; *Etymologiae* 1.43), and in the case of medieval Irish genealogy and hagiography it has been amply demonstrated that these works about the past met the needs of their present, and were adapted accordingly. In the case of (pseudo-)historical narratives a parallel transferred applicability is more difficult to prove, but such a reading is clearly authorised in *Airec menman Uraird maic Coise* ('The Stratagem of Urard mac Coise'), probably of the tenth century in its original form. The central characters in its narrative frame are a poet, Urard mac Coise (d. 990), and the contemporary king of Tara, Domnall mac Muirchertaig (d. 980). Urard is despoiled by kinsmen of the king, and therefore approaches him to seek compensation. For this occasion he devises the stratagem of the title, 'to compose the penetrating obscured [or allegorical] narrative [*scél*] through poetic arrangement, in order that they should give him satisfaction for the deed they had done against him' (*Airec menman*, p. 42).[26] At the court, he offers the king a narrative, by reciting his repertoire in the form of a tale-list (see below), and the king selects one which is new in the poet's canon, *Orgain Cathrach Maíl Milscothaigh* ('The Destruction of Máel Mílscothach's Fort'), 'since this [Máel Mílscothach] was the name Mac Coise had given himself in order to conceal his name' (*Airec Menman*, p. 47). This embedded narrative is an exact analogue to Mac Coise's present: a poet, Máel Mílscothach, complains to the unnamed king of Tara of his time about the plundering and destruction of his homestead, and is promised full reparation. The transition from the embedded

---

[26] In my translation from this text some of its stylistic ornamentations are reduced.

narrative to the frame is appropriately effected by an angel, who gives the judgement in Máel Mílscothach's case and at the same time establishes the equations between the characters of the two narrative strands, which then leads to the result desired by Urard:

[The angel said,] 'There was a king of Tara at this time, namely Domnall mac Muirchertaig. And Urard mac Coise is Máel Mílscothach who was mentioned here [i.e. in the embedded narrative]'. . . . When Domnall heard the words of evidence, he gave Máel Mílscothach witnesses that messengers would go from him [i.e. Domnall] to pursue what was taken from him [i.e. Máel Mílscothach = Urard].[27]   (*Airec menman*, p. 65)

The conventional role of an angel as legitimating agent is used by Urard to establish a specific reading of his text, namely its applicability to the author's present, and the embedded narrative is thus authorised to be understood as an *exemplum* for appropriate present conduct on the basis of a narrative precedent. Urard's precedent is clearly invented, and thus fictitious, and it is an interesting question whether this is also meant to legitimise the creative invention of a past. *Airec menman* does not teach conduct proper for a king, as its embedded narrative would do on its own; rather it teaches a proper way of understanding the meaning and implication of a performance of (pseudo-)historical narrative, and offers important, although admittedly limited, evidence for non-literal interpretations of texts of this genre. An isolated, and late, explicit reference to the possibility of non-literal readings of secular narratives is found in a sixteenth-century legal manuscript: 'the preachers apparently adapt secular fables [*na faidbhle daonna*] to theological morality [*maraltachta na díaachta*]', here with special reference to religious subtexts.[28] Possibilities of transferred meanings were, of course, well known from Hiberno-Latin grammatical and exegetical works, and the concepts of 'historical sense' and 'moral sense' are found in Irish as *stoir* and *morolus* respectively in ninth- and tenth-century discussions of the Psalter. Recent successful interpretations of a number of individual (pseudo-)historical texts have shown the extent to which their narrative re-creation of the past 'was shaped by the present, and . . . legitimised the aspirations of the present'.[29]

The one area of literary theory in which medieval Irish scholars developed an active but limited interest was the classification of narratives by event-types. Their system reflects 'a structuralist disposition among the early *literati*, which accords well with the legacy of patristic

---

[27] Compare also p. 73: 'Then Domnall pondered in his mind the injustice which had been inflicted formerly on Máel Mílscothach.'
[28] Quoted by Breatnach, 'The Religious Significance', p. 40.
[29] Herbert, '*Cathréim Cellaig*', p. 332.

exegesis and with medieval formalism in general'.[30] Two versions of a list of relevant event-types and of individual texts belonging to each category are transmitted; their common source is dated to the tenth century. List A was composed as a mnemonic; list B is part of *Airec menman Uraird maic Coise*, where it defines the narrative canon available to Urard. List A gives the following major event-types: 'destructions' (*togla*), 'cattle-raids' (*tána*), 'wooings' (*tochmarca*), 'battles' (*catha*), 'terrors' (*uatha*), 'voyages' (*imrama*), 'death-tales' (*oitte*)', 'feasts' (*fessa*), 'sieges' (*forbassa*), 'adventures' (*echtrada*), 'elopements' (*aithid*), 'plunderings' (*airggne*), with the additional categories 'bursting-forths [of lake/river]' (*tomadmann*), 'visions' (*físi*), 'loves' (*serca*), 'hostings' (*slúagid*) and 'proceedings' (*tochomlada*). Some of these terms are traditionally used in titles of narratives, whereas others seem to have been invented for the sake of this classification. Classification of a narrative as a 'fore-tale' cuts across this classification by event-types.

A small number of metatextual narratives indicate how medieval Irish *literati* perceived aspects of the intellectual background of their productions and of the compositional process itself. The fusion of Latin and vernacular learning (including literature) in written texts is given narrative expression in, for instance, the story about Cenn Fáelad's loss of his 'brain of forgetfulness'. During a time of convalescence he learns from the three schools of Latin learning, native law and literature, and by night commits his newly acquired learning to writing. The superiority of clerical information (even with regard to secular traditions associated with places) is maintained in a short narrative about the confrontation between Eochaid Rígéiges ('royal/pre-eminent sage/poet') and four young clerics, and it thus recommends the transmission of *senchas* by monastic scholars.[31] The narrative about the 'Finding of *Táin Bó Cúailnge*', *De Fhailsiugud Tána Bó Cúailnge*, authenticates the text as an eyewitness report and explains at the same time that prior to this eyewitness's recitation the knowledge of a complete version had been lost in Ireland and that the *Táin* was only known 'in fragments'.

Examples of aspects of the practice of medieval Irish literary criticism are provided by the tenth-century prefaces to the hymns in the *Liber hymnorum* and by the early-eleventh-century preface to the early, and difficult, poem *Amra Coluim Cille*, with their emphasis on four of the *circumstantiae*, namely *locus*, *tempus*, *persona* and *causa scribendi*. The prefaces, and the gloss-commentary on the *Amra*, are rooted in medieval

---

[30] Scowcroft, 'Abstract Narrative', p. 122.

[31] Ó Riain, 'Der Schein, der trügt', pp. 145–6, and, for some cautionary remarks, Sims-Williams, 'The Medieval World', pp. 84–5.

commentary tradition and the approach to the understanding of texts endorsed by *grammatica*. It has been noted that,

[o]f the *circumstantiae* set out in the prefaces [in the *Liber hymnorum*], that of *causa scribendi* generally receives most elaboration. Thus the preparatory material becomes largely narrative, rendering the works accessible not so much by association with *auctores* as by association with memorable events in the lives of saints or biblical personages.   (Herbert, 'The Preface', pp. 68–9)

An interest in the historical background of biblical stories is a characteristic trait of medieval Irish exegesis. It is tempting to see a parallel between the medieval Irish scholars' narrative approach to the understanding of the hymns and their narrative approach to the interpretation and appropriation of their own history in the pseudo-historical narratives.

10

Anglo-Saxon textual attitudes

Ananya Jahanara Kabir

Moððe word fræt.   Me þæt þuhte
wrætlicu wyrd,   þa ic þæt wundor gefrægn,
þæt se wyrm forswealg   wera gied sumes,
þeof in þystro,   þrymfæstne cwide
ond þæs strangan staþol.   Stælgiest ne wæs
wihte þy gleawra,   þe he þam wordum swealg.

(Riddle 47, *The Exeter Book*[1])

[A moth ate words. That seemed to me a curious occurrence when I heard that miracle, that this worm, thief in the dark, gulped down a certain man's utterance, his illustrious discourse and its strong foundation. The thieving visitor was not a whit the wiser because he had gulped in those words.]

In the fifth century CE, the erstwhile colony of the Roman Empire known as Britain became home to the Angles, Saxons and Jutes, Germanic tribes moving across continental Europe in what has been somewhat romantically characterised as the 'Age of Migrations'. Pushing the Romano-British and Celtic inhabitants of Britain westward and northward, these tribes rapidly consolidated their hold over the island, which they soon termed *engla-lond*, 'land of the Angles' (and hence 'England'). The Germanic dialects they brought with them developed into a language that they called *englisc*, 'English'. Modern scholarship terms this language 'Old English' (in distinction from 'Middle English', which developed after the Norman Conquest of 1066), or, sometimes, 'Anglo-Saxon', after the two major tribal groups, while 'Anglo-Saxon England' refers to England between the Saxon Advent and the Norman Conquest.[2]

---

[1] *Anglo-Saxon Poetic Records*, I, ed. Krapp and Dobbie, p. 205, and *Anglo-Saxon Poetry*, tr. Bradley, p. 380. All translations of Old English poetry are cited from this work. Old English prose translations are mine, unless otherwise noted.

[2] For an introduction to 'Anglo-Saxon England' and Old English, see Godden and Lapidge, *Old English Literature*. For the terms 'Anglo-Saxon', 'Anglo-Saxons' and 'English', see Reynolds, 'What Do We Mean?', and Wormald, 'Bede'. Following the conventions generally accepted within contemporary scholarship, I refer to the vernacular language and its literature as 'Old English' and apply the adjective 'Anglo-Saxon' to the overall literary culture (both Anglo-Latin and Old English) of the period, and to those who produced and consumed that culture before 1066.

Anglo-Saxon England was one of the earliest European cultures to produce a substantial corpus of vernacular prose, alongside a flourishing monastic literacy in Latin and a robust tradition of vernacular poetry in the alliterative Germanic style. Much of this writing has survived in the dialect of Old English that philologists distinguish as 'late West Saxon'.[3] Both prose and poetry were used for narrative, hagiographic, exegetical and hortatory purposes. Embedded within them are also numerous pronouncements on literary composition, interpretation, translation and genre, attesting to the multiple cultural affiliations that gave rise to this varied body of vernacular writing. If, by literary criticism, we understand discourse concerning the form, function and interpretation of texts, then from these statements, and notwithstanding the lack of a dedicated Anglo-Saxon *ars poetica*, we may extrapolate some broad trends in Old English 'literary criticism'.

Our epigraph enunciates the themes most persistently encountered within Anglo-Saxon discourse on the vernacular written word: an interest in its corporeality (i.e. the physical aspects of writing and manuscript production), its hermeneutics and its pleasures. Such preoccupations within Anglo-Saxon literary culture fed into a wider consciousness of the interplay between the technologies of textual production that we now separate into 'orality' and 'literacy', and the alignment of this interplay with a lively cultural politics of bilingualism in Latin and the vernacular.[4] These features are by no means unique to Anglo-Saxon England, being discernible within literary cultures spanning the chronological and geographical reach of the Middle Ages. What is particularly noteworthy about Anglo-Saxon writers is their acute, and from a later medieval perspective, precocious sensitivity to, in the well-known words of Paul Zumthor, 'la fait d'oralité' (*La Lettre*, p. 17), or, following a more recent characterisation by Joyce Coleman, 'la nostalgie de la bouche' (*Public Reading*, p. 47). The nostalgic association of orality with a mythopoeticised pre-Christian past coexists with the monastic and literate milieu of book production and textual reception, and competes with anxieties about authorship and the pleasures of new creative possibilities arising from that interface.

Possibly the best known descriptions of Anglo-Saxon poetry are given in the period's most famous text: the heroic poem *Beowulf*.[5] The *scop*

---

3 Other Old English dialects are Northumbrian, Mercian, Kentish and early West Saxon. Although the terminology derives from Anglo-Saxon political divisions, there is not enough evidence to map consistently dialect onto geography. See, in this context, Toon, 'Old English Dialects'.

4 The literary criticism and theory of certain Anglo-Latin writers from the period are treated elsewhere in this volume. More generally, see Lapidge's two volumes, *Anglo-Latin Literature*.

5 The bulk of Old English poetry is contained in three major manuscript codices, the Exeter Book (Exeter, Chapter Library, MS 3501, housed in Exeter Cathedral since the late eleventh

(poet, singer) appears in two accounts of feasting in Heorot, the hall of the Danes and the poem's social and emotional centre. The first passage celebrates the *scop*'s clear singing (*swutol sang*) about creation and the joyous sound of the harp (ll. 89–102); *scop* and harp reappear at the feast celebrating Beowulf's victory over the monster Grendel and his mother. Music and singing were gathered together, the harp (*gomenwudu*, 'glee-wood') was plucked and often a lay (*giedd*) recited, and it was time for Hrothgar's *scop* to beguile the hall with some entertainment (ll. 1063–8). These accounts present the *scop* as pivotal in heroic society. His traditional skills and subject-matter make him the repository of that society's memory of its shared past as well as the guarantor of its present conviviality. Critics have read this picture of the *scop* as a *mise-en-abîme* for not only the *Beowulf*-poet himself but of Anglo-Saxon poetic activity in general. During the eighteenth and nineteenth centuries, the combined influence of Percy's *Reliques* and Ossian romanticised the *scop* into an Anglo-Saxon counterpart of the Celtic 'bard'. From the 1950s onwards, the *scop* was marshalled into service of 'oral-formulaic' theory, which initiated a paradigm shift of sorts in Anglo-Saxon literary studies.

Developed in the context of Homeric epic and tested on contemporary Serbo-Croatian oral singers, this theory claimed oral composition for any text which exhibited a high percentage of formulas, or words or phrases expressive of a 'given essential idea' operating under pre-defined metrical conditions. Early oral-formulaicists equated oral composition with 'spontaneous' oral performance or song, distinguished from memorised recitation and the fixed-in-writing poem. This performative dimension of oral composition was seemingly validated by the descriptions of poetic activity given in *Beowulf*. Other statements from the Old English poetic corpus were similarly deployed to buttress oral-formulaic stylistic analyses. In *Deor* (an Exeter Book poem) a minstrel laments having lost favour with his lord, who now patronises another *scop*; this picture augmented

century); the Vercelli Book (Vercelli, Biblioteca Capitolare, MS 117, possibly left in Vercelli, northern Italy, by an Anglo-Saxon pilgrim monk); the Junius manuscript (Oxford, Bodleian Library, MS Junius 11), and the *Beowulf* manuscript (London, British Library, MS Cotton Vitellius, A xv). Poetic texts are also dispersed throughout the corpus of extant manuscripts. The titles of the manuscript collections (e.g. the Exeter Book) and texts (e.g. Riddle 47, *Beowulf*), and the standardised print format of Old English poetry – which was written out in manuscript like prose – are post-medieval conventions; for these issues, see Pasternack, *Textuality*, pp. 1–32. Dating the poetry and, indeed, much of the prose, or assigning them to specific regions of Anglo-Saxon England remain unsolved issues (and are possibly insoluble), the major stumbling-blocks being the normative anonymity of the literary text, the use of a poetic *koiné* studded with archaic spellings, and the survival of most texts in manuscripts copied during the tenth century, and in the late West Saxon dialect. The difficulties and ideological pitfalls encountered in the dating question are exemplified in the controversies surrounding the dating of *Beowulf*, for which see Chase, *Dating*.

the idea of the *scop* as performer and the aristocratic audience as patron. The opening statement of another Exeter Book poem, *Widsith* – 'Widsith spoke, he unlocked his wordhoard' (*Widsið maðolade, wordhord onleac*; l. 1) – likewise fitted nicely into the oral-formulaic vision of the *scop* creatively drawing on a traditional pool of resources, a wordhoard of formulas which were his building blocks on structural and thematic levels. The formulaic opening of most Anglo-Saxon poems also consolidated this view, as a comparison of *Beowulf* and the Vercelli Book poem *Andreas* demonstrates:

Listen [*hwæt*]! We have heard report [*gefrunon*] of the majesty of the people's kings of the spear-wielding Danes in days of old.   (*Beowulf*, ll. 1–2)

Listen [*hwæt*]! We have heard tell [*gefrunan*] in distant days of twelve famous heroes [the apostles] here beneath the constellations.   (*Andreas*, ll. 1–2)

The topos of a poet addressing his audience, narrating his song from traditional sources, whether biblical, hagiographical or mythical, served the oral-formulaic argument both stylistically and thematically. The poet as spontaneous composer of Christian and secular songs was extrapolated also from Bede's account in the *Historia ecclesiastica gentis anglorum* (completed 731) of Cædmon, the illiterate and unmusical monk who, in 680, was divinely inspired to begin composing Old English verse on biblical subject-matter (4.24).

The oral-formulaic approach, although enabling the evaluation of Anglo-Saxon poetry through terms other than New Critical views of authorship and originality, nevertheless presented Old English poetry somewhat reductively, as oral songs inadvertently trapped in manuscript culture. In the heroic world constructed by Anglo-Saxon poets, words were deeds, poetry was oral and the *scop* sang the *leoð* or the *giedd* in the meadhall. But the *scopas* of *Beowulf*, *Deor* and *Widsith* arguably represent an Anglo-Saxon view not of poetry *per se*, but of one kind of poetry, predicated on a particular cultural and aesthetic configuration that we now designate as 'heroic'. Anglo-Saxon authorial self-fashioning did assume other forms, even as the term *scop* was applied to poets who, to Anglo-Saxon writers, represented written rather than oral cultures. The *Old English Orosius* (late ninth century) an Anglo-Saxon transla-tion of Orosius' *Historiae adversum paganos*, refers (p. 31) to 'the *scop* Homer' ('psalm-*scop*' (*sealmscop*) is the Old English word for 'psalmist'), and *Aldhelm*, a short macaronic poem on that most arcane stylist among Anglo-Latin poets, Aldhelm, refers to him as 'that noble *scop*' (l. 3).

These complexities of Anglo-Saxon literary culture are now recognised in scholarship which increasingly engages the roles of the memory and of technologies of writing within the clearly formulaic style of Old English

poetry and, to a great extent, its prose. Initially rigid oral-formulaic positions have been modulated thereby into more complex concepts such
as 'oral tradition', 'transitional literacy', 'residual orality' and 'memorial transmission', and a more nuanced understanding of the vernacular
text as embedded within overlapping oral and written cultural matrices,
and within a bilingual monastic world. Bede's Latin ventriloquising of
Cædmon's English voice thus offers not an uncontested account of vernacular poetic inspiration but a parable of the interaction between Germanic
poetic tradition and Latin Christian learning, another response to which
was the famous complaint of Alcuin (*c.* 730/5–804), an Anglo-Saxon at
Charlemagne's court, 'what has Ingeld to do with Christ?' (*quid Hinieldus
cum Cristo?*). This rhetorical separation of the representatives of Germania and Christianity actually highlights their constant interaction within
the early-medieval monastery as a space wherein different cultures could
come into contact.

This revised picture captures better the wide range of Anglo-Saxon
responses to vernacular textuality. Consider, for instance, the juxtaposition of paradoxes played out within the Old English riddle cited in my epigraph. The bookworm's swallowing of words emphasises the corporeality
of the literary composition even when it has ceased to be a poetic utterance (*giedd, cwide*) released from the body of the poet-as-performer. The
'strong foundation' of the monastic book that contains the *giedd* ushers
in a new aesthetics of the 'illustrious' illuminated manuscript, but it does
not guarantee the poem a less protean life than does its oral circulation.
Neither does the bookworm's literalising of the monastic practice of
ruminatio ('chewing over', rumination) guarantee the successful understanding and dissemination of the wisdom within words. Rather, its
destructive encounter with textuality foregrounds the productive hermeneutic activities of the riddle's reader, and the riddle's own fragile status.
As a *giedd* preserved in the anthology of Old English poetic verse we
know as the Exeter Book, its survival through the ravages of time, book-
worms, Vikings and other 'thieving visitors' owes more to chance than
choice.

The 'Bookworm' riddle's treatment of the word as a sign to be deciphered rather than devoured is paralleled by the next riddle in the Exeter
Book (Riddle 48), which describes a sacred object, possibly a paten or
chalice. Despite its lack of tongue and loud voice, this object resembles
the written word in 'speaking out' in 'strong words'. An enigma to those
unable to 'read' its 'secret words' and decode its mystery (*ryne*, 'runes'),
it nevertheless shows the discerning person (*gleaw*) the route to salvation.
This privileging of the Christian as the ideal reader recalls the emphases
of the Old English poem *Daniel*, preserved in the Junius manuscript.
Its repeated description of Daniel as *gleaw* contrasts with the irrational

bestiality of Nebuchadnezzar, and culminates in Daniel's ability to interpret both the latter's dreams and the proverbial writing on the wall. Like Daniel, but unlike the bookworm who was not a whit the wiser (*gleawra*), the 'reader' of the liturgical vessel is the possessor of knowledge which releases the hermeneutic potential of a mute object and transforms it into a signifier of meaning.

The commentaries on literary creation and reception provided by the Exeter Book riddles often resonate startlingly with postmodern theorising on the ideal reader, the author-function, and the relationship between signifier and signified. Yet, their preoccupation with the body is a very medieval trait, closely connected with the physicality of manuscript production, the practice of reading aloud, and the talismanic and sacred nature of the book that was enhanced, as has been argued in a slightly different context, through prayer and liturgy (Clanchy, pp. 34–5). Indeed, these associations are borne by diverse objects metonymic of Anglo-Saxon literacy, as the various solutions posited for Riddle 60, 'reed-pen', 'rune-stave' or 'gospel book' suggest. This riddle wonders how the knife-point, the right hand and man's intention together transform a natural object into an instrument that, though 'lacking a mouth', can 'exchange words' and thereby further transform speech (*wordcwidas*), an oral and public means of communication, into the written message (*ærendspræc*) shared by 'us two alone' – the riddle and its reader. The intimacy of reading is reiterated by the poem that immediately follows this riddle, *The Husband's Message*. Here, a rune-stave bearing a message from one lover to another prosopopeically addresses the recipient with the declaration, 'now I will speak to you in secrecy' (l. 1). The secrecy is underscored by the actual incorporation of runes within the body of the poem, the meaning of which remains controversial among scholars.

Anglo-Saxon authors frequently allude to the currency of two systems of writing, the Roman and the runic, to comment on vernacular textuality. The hermetic nature of reading and interpretation, a common theme in Old English poetry, is often expressed through the trope of the rune as secret writing, as in a celebrated passage from the poem *Exodus* in the Junius manuscript:

If the intellect [*lifes wealhstod*, 'life's translator/ mediator'], bright within the breast, wishes to unlock [*onlucan wile*] ample benefits with the key of the spirit [*gastes cægon*], the mystery will be explained [*run bið gerecenod*], good counsel will go forth.   (ll. 523–6)

This passage may well describe, as critics claim, allegorical and typological interpretation derived from patristic exegesis. Certainly, Anglo-Saxon authors used and commented upon these methods. For example, the Exeter Book poem, *The Phoenix*, explicitly calls the phoenix a sign (*tacen*) that signifies (*beacnað*), among other things, the deeper Christian truth of the Resurrection (ll. 574–5). However, the tropes of hoarding, unlocking and decoding that evoke the processes of intellection tap also into an indigenous wellspring of literary criticism. For Anglo-Saxon authors, the chest, metaphorised as a treasure-hoard, was the location of all psychic faculties (Jager). Actively to utilise those faculties – in reading, thinking or poetic composition – was to unlock the hoard with the keys of methodology and skill. Widsith unlocking his formulaic wordhoard can be thus placed alongside the *Exodus*-poet's more arcane reference to the keys of the spirit, and the pragmatic comment by Ælfric, tenth-century Anglo-Saxon prose author and monastic reformer: 'grammar [*stæfcræft*] is the key that unlocks the meaning of books' (*Grammatik*, p. 2).

This cluster of tropes recurs in an account of poetic activity given by the single poet of Anglo-Saxon England, Cynewulf (*fl.* early ninth – late tenth century?) who has 'signed' his work. At the close of his poem *Elene* (ll. 1236–51), preserved in the Vercelli Book, he describes how through long nights he wove (*wæf*) and sifted (*læs*) 'word-craft' or poetry (*word-cræft*) – metaphors emphasising the corporeality of the word. The creative act was completed only when God, to instil divine grace, unshackled the poet's body (*bancofan onband*), opened up the heart (*breostlocan onwand*), and unlocked the craft of poetry (*leoðucræft onleac*), which the poet used joyously (*lustum breac*). A passage interspersed with runes spelling out 'Cynewulf' follows. The disjunction between the two alphabets invites decoding of the runes as well as the reason for their utilisation. Another poem 'signed' thus by Cynewulf, *The Fates of the Apostles*, declares that the discerning (*gleaw*) person who enjoys poetry (*lysteð leoðgiddunga*) can deduce the author's name through the runic passage (ll. 96–8).

Cynewulf's view of literary creativity differs considerably from both the image of the *scop* in heroic society, and from what has been called the 'anonymous polyphony' of Old English poetry (Pasternack, pp. 33–59). Creative agency is relocated in God, who supplants the poet as the unlocker of creative potential from its corporeal container before it can be converted to the written text. The tension between the authority of the named poet and the authority of God the creator is both diffused and aggravated by the runic signature that showcases while disguising the poet's name. Simultaneously, the runes privilege the reader's position in the hermeneutic process in a manner reminiscent of contemporary reception theory, but distinct from the relationship between reader-as-audience and poet-as-performer encountered in other Old English poems. As indicated by his manipulation of the traditional tropes of corporeality, runic decoding and unlocking, as well by as his general use of the oral traditional style, Cynewulf plays with the boundaries between that shared 'we' and the 'poetic I', fully aware of the new pleasures generated thereby in creativity and reception (Schaefer).

The repercussions of inscribing one's name within a predominantly anonymous literary culture are explored also by those Anglo-Saxon prose writers who stamped, albeit in less arcane ways than Cynewulf, their authorial identities on their work. These discussions are closely linked to the function of the prose vernacular translation as mediator between laity and learned culture, and are usually conducted within the preface that itself mediates between translator-as-author and the translated text. In his famous preface to the translation of Pope Gregory's *Cura pastoralis* by Werferth, bishop of Worcester, King Alfred (reigned 871–99) provides a firmly functional basis for his unprecedented programme of translating into the vernacular those Latin texts 'most necessary [*niebeðearfosta*] for all men to know' (p. 7). Educational resources in England have declined thanks to Viking depredations and English neglect of the Northumbrian legacy of learning, argues Alfred, and amelioration can only occur through a new prose vernacular culture. The utility of prose is thus aligned to the same interdependence of writing, reception and hermeneutics emphasised within Anglo-Saxon poetry. However, the difference lies in the authorial and regal self-assertion evident in Alfred's opening address to the translator Werferth, as well as to the other bishops asked to possess a copy of the work: 'King Alfred bids greet Bishop Werferth with his words lovingly and with friendship' (p. 2). This regal voice conflates authorial and social responsibilities, although subsuming, in the process, the identities of the translator and the author of the source text.

In the preface to his translation of St Augustine's *Soliloquies*, Alfred expresses through an elaborate metaphor the pleasures and anxieties arising from this conflation:

> Then I gathered for myself staves and posts and tie-beams [*kicglas, stuþansceaftas* and *lohsceaftas*], and handles for each of the tools I knew how to use, and building-timbers and beams and as much as I could carry of the most beautiful woods [*þa wlitegostan treowo*] for each of the structures I knew how to build. (*Anglo-Saxon Prose*, tr. Swanton, pp. 47–8)

Alfred instructs his readers to construct similarly a 'neat wall', 'excellent building' and 'fair town' to inhabit comfortably through winter and summer. The joyful, even vertiginous exuberance of literary creativity is shown as arising from the gathering, transformation and reception of a diverse range of sources. The metaphoric conversion of nature to culture does not privilege Latin patristic sources over their vernacular translations – rather, the former embodies one kind of beauty ('the most beautiful woods') and the latter, the marriage of aesthetics and utility. Through an approximation of translating and reading to earthly transience, Alfred nevertheless subordinates, as does Cynewulf, vernacular literary activity to divine authority. The heavenly home remains superior to the earthly one, which is only leased to us by God. Yet, adds Alfred somewhat whimsically, it remains a place to hunt and fish and fowl in after its construction has been laboured over. Through this evocation of bodily work and relaxation, a degree of agency is claimed for both author and reader.

For Ælfric (*c.* 945– *c.* 1015), a homilist associated with the Benedictine Reform in Anglo-Saxon monasticism during the second half of the tenth century, responsibility rather than shared pursuits defines the authorial position vis-à-vis his reader/audience. His substantial corpus includes two series of homilies and a series of saints' lives constructed to run through the different feasts of the liturgical calendar. In the Latin preface to the First Series of the *Catholic Homilies* (pp. 173–4), Ælfric insists that the author of homilies be a responsible translator of the cultural capital invested in patristic sources such as Augustine and Jerome, Bede, and various Carolingian writers. The translation of their Latin texts into homilies written in our ordinary discourse (*nostram consuetam sermocinationem*) edifies the non-learned (*simplicium*) through their reading or listening (*siue legendo siue audiendo*). Since the laity (*secularis*) cannot grasp everything they may hear from the mouths of doctors (*ex ore doctorum*), the homiletic text should benefit their souls (*ad utilitatem animarum suarum*) by penetrating the hearts of listeners and readers (*ad cor peruenire legentium uel audientium*), another typically corporeal metaphor. In the Latin preface to his Saints' Lives (pp. 3–4), Ælfric ascribes a similar hortatory function to his translations of hagiographic material into simple discourse (*usitatam Anglicam sermocinationem*).

These prefaces distinguish not between readers and listeners, both of whom are envisaged for the written text, but, rather, between the monolingual laity and the bilingual monastic author. The Latin prefaces are accompanied by Old English prefaces, whose contents diverge considerably from the former. It is clear therefore that Ælfric considered each language as commanding a separate but overlapping textual community, and performing different cultural work. Proficiency in Latin equals the ability to separate error (*gedwyld*) from truth, and the authorial duty of preventing heresy through circumspect translation (Preface to *Catholic Homilies*, I, pp. 174–5). The author thus mediates between worlds while occupying a superior pedagogical position to his readers and audience – and also to the anonymous homilists in contrast to whom Ælfric constructs his authorial persona.

This dual function of mediator and instructor dictates the style of Ælfric's prose – the eschewing of obscure words (*obscura verba*) in favour of simple English (*simplicem anglicam*) – as well as the method of translating not word-for-word but sense-for-sense. The latter dictum was an axiom of Anglo-Saxon 'translation theory'. In his Preface to the *Cura pastoralis* translation, Alfred describes his translation technique as 'sometimes word-for-word, and sometimes sense-for-sense' (p. 7). Bede assesses his own summary of Cædmon's first composition, through the literary critical corollary that 'it is not possible to translate verse, however well composed, literally from one language to another without some loss of beauty and dignity' (*Historia ecclesiastica* 4.24). For Ælfric, furthermore, this mode of translation encourages brevity, which lends stylistic charm to Old English and prevents boredom in his audience.

To translate, then, is to interpret: the two verbs *transferre* and *interpretari* are used interchangeably in Ælfric's Latin prefaces; Alfred, similarly, says in his Preface to the *Cura pastoralis* that he translated into English (*on Englisc awende*) only after he could most clearly interpret the Latin (*andgitfullicost areccean meahte*; p. 7). This attempt by the translator to claim some element of authorship brings its own caveats: the translator-as-author lays himself open to charges of misinterpretation of his sources, as well the danger of himself being misinterpreted. The possibility of thereby slipping into, rather than preventing, error is acknowledged, but somewhat defensively: in the *Catholic Homilies* preface, Ælfric declares that anyone dissatisfied with his interpretation should produce (*condat*) his own books. This anxiety of authorship is also evident in his frequent instructions to future scribes to preserve the overall structure and sequence of his collections. Like Cynewulf and Alfred, Ælfric balances such authorial self-assertion with deference to God: *ex dei gratia non causa iactantiae. nos studiose sicuti ualuimus interpretari* ('not through boasting, but by the grace of God, we are just as zealously capable of interpretation [as our detractors]'). In his Old English preface to his Saints' Lives (pp. 4–6), he describes his tasks as reaffirming God's authority through narratives of his saints, encouraging his readers in their faith and guaranteeing, through saintly intercession, his own security (*mannum to getrymminge and to munde us sylfum*). Patristic authorities are also acknowledged, more deferentially and expansively than in the Latin prefaces, where they are simply named. Devout fathers and holy doctors (*geleaffulle fæderas and halige lareowas*) have written Latin books which are a lasting memorial (*langum gemynde*) for future generations. Hence Ælfric has himself done nothing new in his authorial work.

We say nothing new in this book [*gesetnysse*], because it had stood written down long since in Latin books [*ledenbocum*], though lay-men [*læwedan men*] knew it not.   (*Lives of Saints*, ed. and tr. Skeat, p. 5)

Here self-assertion vis-à-vis his lay audience combines with self-abnegation in a strident assertion of unoriginality, a stance which we find being taken by some of the most independent-minded of medieval writers. Yet, for Ælfric at least, the insistence on lack of originality allows the author of vernacular prose to masquerade as mere translator of uncontested Latin authority, while staking new claims on the cultural terrain.

These authorial postures find exaggerated articulation in the bilingual *Enchiridion* or *Handbook* of Byrhtferth of Ramsey, who flourished towards the end of the Anglo-Saxon period (*fl.* 985–1011). Byrhtferth prostrates himself before divine authority and patristic writers with as much vigour as he castigates his readership of 'rustic priests' for their ignorance and provincialism. In the opening chapter (p. 17), he declares that, although himself trivial (*exigui sumus*), with the lord operating through him (*operante per nos Domino*), his trivial work (*hoc exiguo opere*) written with a hasty pen (*stilo festinante*) will expose the ignorant to 'the precious words of the fathers, that is, the mysteries of allegorical understanding' (*id est mysteria allegorica sensus*). Byrhtferth's obsessively pedagogical and subservient style is epitomised by his baroque conceits (often borrowed directly from Aldhelm), which, especially in his characteristic explication of them, present his authorial task in as flattering a light as possible. Comparing his writing on the calculations of the *computus* (the science of computation as it pertained to the ecclesiastical calendar), to valiant negotiation of stormy seas and impassable cliffs (p. 17), he remarks, 'the waves stand for this profound science and the mountains stand for the magnitude of this science' (*þa yðan getacniað þisne deopan cræft, and þa muntas getacniað eac þa mycelnyssa þises cræftes*). The explication bypasses the author as unimportant oarsman in favour of his more towering precedents, but the latter foreground his achievement as all the more remarkable.

Byrhtferth's rejection of secular Latin literature likewise affords further opportunities for self-promotion (p. 135). Through a technique similar to an Anglo-Saxon literary practice especially associated with the Benedictine Reform, the glossing of Latin manuscripts in the vernacular, he flaunts his familiarity with the subjects of 'the ancient idlers'. He commands to depart from him 'mermaids who are called Sirens', 'the Castalian nymphs (mountain elves – *dunylfa*) who dwelled on Mount Helicon' and 'Latona (the mother of the sun, Apollo and Diana) whom Delos brought forth', invoking instead the 'sublime cherub' whose 'golden tongs might bring to his dumb mouth sparks from the embers of the supreme altar'. That this disengagement with classical Latin literature is merely ostensible is apparent from the later inventory and discussion of classical rhetorical devices (pp. 164–71), which Byrhtferth derives largely from Bede's *De schematibus et tropis*.

Although this lineage testifies to the circulation of knowledge of classical rhetoric throughout the Anglo-Saxon period, it was not incorporated systematically into assessment of their vernacular prose and poetry. The rhetorical apparatus of that poetry in particular was largely alliterative and formulaic in inspiration, including the 'kenning' (compare the Old Norse *Kenningar*) or periphrastic expression, for example *banhus* ('bone-house', designating the body); the 'envelope pattern' or near-repetition of formulaic phrases to 'block off' sense-units; and the 'type-scene', such as accounts of the so-called 'hero on the beach' and the 'beasts of battle', which recurs throughout the poetic corpus to signal narrative turning-points. These terms are, however, coined by modern scholars; poetic terminology used within the Anglo-Saxon corpus tends to be less precise in application, a good example being *fitt*, which can mean either a poem or a section of a poem.[6]

In the absence of both vernacular rhetorical terminology and a consistent application of classical rhetorical figures to vernacular writing, Byrhtferth's view of rhetoric as the key to the secrets of other authors seems gratuitously self-congratulatory, as does his discussion of the three kinds of poetry (p. 163). He distinguishes between '*actiuum opus uel imitatiuum*', '*enarratiuum*' and '*commune*' or '*mixtum*', providing also their corresponding Greek terminologies: *drammatikon* or *mictikon*, *exegamatikon* or *apangeltikon*, and *koenon* or *micton*. Parading further his knowledge of classical literary criticism, he adds that 'the things [*þas þing*] called the *Iliad* and the *Odyssey* of Homer and the *Aeneid* of Virgil' were thus composed. However, these poetic categories correspond neither to other Anglo-Saxon discussions of vernacular literary genres, nor to any differences of style and function discernible within the vernacular corpus. Rather, as his elucidation of '*commune*' suggests – 'when the poet brings in other personae who speak with him as if to answer him' (*þonne se sceop in gebringð oðre hadas þe wið him wurdlion swylce hig him andswarion*) – Anglo-Saxon writers regularly employed their own literary critical vocabulary in order to understand texts and concepts inherited from other cultures.

A suggestive example of such lexical mapping is the frequent mention of 'lying tales' in different Old English texts. In the *Old English*

---

6 However, it is clear that the term *fitt* or *fitte* referred to the oral performance of poetry, associating it with song or chant which could be accompanied on the harp. Following his translation of Boethius' *De consolatione philosophiae* 3 met. 5, King Alfred speaks of Wisdom having 'sung this *fitt*'. Compare the Latin term *vitteas* in the preface to the Old Saxon *Heliand*: 'according to the custom of that kind of poetry [i.e. vernacular poetry with its own traditions], he [i.e. the *Heliand* poet] divided the whole work into *vitteas*, which we may call "lectiones" or "sententiae"'. Eamonn Ó Carragáin, whose ongoing research we draw on here, speculates that Germanic poetry was chanted in a way analogous to the way in which liturgical *lectiones* were intoned, rather than in the way hymns or psalms were modulated. He offers a tentative definition of *fitt* as 'a poem, or part of a poem, suitable for singing as a single unit'.

Orosius, these 'lies' are ascribed to various non-Christian societies, as in the statement: 'their poets sang in their poems and their "lying tales"'(*heora scopas on heora leoðum giddiende sindon and on heora leaspellengum*; p. 53). Ælfric asserts that his saints' lives do not feign (*liccetan*) with lies (*leasung*; p. 4); and the *Phoenix*-poet declares that his poem (*leoð*) does not contain lying words (*lygeword*, ll. 546–8). While these 'lies' could signal apocrypha as opposed to biblical and patristic truth, it is tempting to read them as references to fictional writing. Although the idea of *fabula* ('fable') as opposed to *historia* ('history') had passed down to early-medieval Europe via Isidore's *Etymologiae* (40.44), Franz Bäuml, among others, has argued (though perhaps somewhat sweepingly) that an awareness of the category of 'fiction' was reactivated only during the twelfth century flowering of vernacular literature in Europe. How aware Anglo-Saxon vernacular writers were of fictional possibilities is a question awaiting sustained research: the Orosian examples suggest that they at least recognised it as a genre of classical literature, although not one some Anglo-Saxon writers themselves wished to engage.

For Anglo-Saxon writers, the widest generic category seems to be 'narrative divested of lies', corresponding roughly to the semantic range of *historia* in the Middle Ages. In its *incipit*, the late Old English prose translation of the Latin romance of *Apollonius of Tyre* (mid-eleventh century) translates *historia* as *gerecednes* ('narrative'); the related verb *reccan* ('to narrate') appears, for example, in the *Andreas*-poet's declaration that he will narrate a bit more of his poetry (*leoðworda dæl furður reccan*; ll. 1488–9). A parallel verb-noun pair is *(ge)settan* (to set down, establish, compose) and *gesettnys* (composition, work, including narrative). Ælfric uses this word for his compilation of saints' lives, and Byrhtferth, for his own writing, as well as the works of Virgil and Jerome (pp. 38, 69, 138, 60, 38). Both prose and poetic narratives share broadly hortatory functions: the verb *getrymman* (to incite, exhort, inspire) describes in the Old English *Orosius* the impact of the songs of *scopas* (*scopleoð*; p. 35) and, in Ælfric's Old English preface to the Saints' Lives, of Latin hagiography. Speaking of his own prose, Byrhtferth declares, 'earthen vessels are the more useful the cheaper they are' (p. 37). Prose is cheap because, unlike poetry, it is not fairly adorned (*on leoðwisan fægre geglenged*). Ultimately, Anglo-Saxons distinguished poetry and prose on the basis not of content, function or manuscript layout, but of form, most crucially metrical and prosodic regularity, which rendered a text capable of being sung or chanted. As Byrhtferth says, Bede 'sang thus about the months in poetical metre' (*mid leoðlicum metre be þam monðum þus giddode*; p. 49).

While the Anglo-Saxons have not left any overt discussion about their alliterative half-line, recent research on metre[7] confirms their deep, almost instinctual understanding of its metrics and prosody. That this understanding went beyond the technicalities of the half-line to an appreciation of creative virtuosity is apparent in a highly revealing passage in *Beowulf* (ll. 867–74). Echoing his own activities, the poet describes how, 'from time to time, a thane of the king, a man laden with exultant words whose mind was full of songs [*gidda gemyndig*], and who had in memory a great multitude of tales of antiquity [*ealdgesegena*], found other words bound in truth[8] [*soðe gebunden*]'. This man 'cleverly set about reconstructing Beowulf's exploit, and successfully recited [*on sped wrecan*] a skilful narrative [*spel gerade*], achieving variety in words [*wordum wrixlan*]'. That final phrase, *wordum wrixlan*, communicates the essence of poetic performance and achievement within the parameters of oral traditional poetry that draws on the repertoire of a long-established wordhoard. A praiseworthy poet must have at his command the resources of memory and a store of inherited narratives; but equally important are the skills of correct alliteration and artful variation that are needed to embody these narratives anew in verse.

The *Exodus*-poet's designation of Pharaoh's *scopas* as 'laughter-smiths' (*hleatorsmiðas*; l. 43) undoubtedly drew on an imaginative construct of the role of poetry in traditional societies. But it signals, as does Ælfric's desire to avoid tedium in his readers or audience and Cynewulf's reference to readers who enjoy *leoð*, that, for the Anglo-Saxons, the literary text should generate pleasure. As the description of Alfred in the proem to *The Metres of Boethius* says, approvingly: 'Thus Alfred, king of the West Saxons, narrated to us an old story [*ealdspell reahte*], revealed his craft [*cræft meldode*], the skill of the poet [*leoðwyrhta list*]. He greatly desired to relate poems to this people, diverse stories for the pleasure of men [*mannum myrgen*; ll. 1–5].' Utility and deference to God notwithstanding, pleasure is the quality that Anglo-Saxon writers highlighted repeatedly in their assessment of vernacular textuality. Despite the discontinuities, occasioned particularly by the Norman Conquest, between Anglo-Saxon and later English traditions of literature and literary criticism, this emphasis on pleasure strikes a chord with anyone who, unlike the bookworm, consumes the literary text but also ruminates its mysteries.

---

[7] See especially Momma, *Old English Poetry*.
[8] I.e. correctly linked in an alliterative metre.

11

Literary theory and practice in early-medieval Germany

John L. Flood

Written transmission of German texts begins in the Old High German (= OHG) period.[1] The earliest texts of significance date from the last third of the eighth century, but the richest period of transmission is the ninth century. Though the OHG period witnesses the dawn of writing in German it was already a period of massive cultural transition. This was the time of the spread and consolidation of Christianity among the German tribes; consequently a few texts preserve tantalising traces of pagan thought. Virtually all the texts which survive do so thanks to the church. The church relied on Latin writing, while secular culture was orally transmitted in the vernacular. Some texts reflect the struggle to express the Latin culture of the church in German writing; others the attempt to record secular vernacular culture. And within the particular sphere of vernacular poetry we witness the giant leap from alliterative verse to rhyme.

The surviving OHG texts form a varied if not particularly extensive corpus. Doubtless many more texts were written than have come down to us, but the total written output of the period represents but the tip of the iceberg of the whole of OHG literary culture. That any secular literature has survived at all is remarkable given the church's monopoly of writing. As Alcuin declared in 797, there was not room for both: 'The Word of God should be read while the clergy are eating. They should listen to the reader, not to the harpist, to the sermons of the Fathers, not to the songs of the pagans. What has Ingeld to do with Christ? The house is small, and there is not room for both.'[2] The Latin-based texts include glosses, Latin–German conversation guides for travellers, translations of basic church texts (prayers, creeds, confessions, the Benedictine Rule, Tatian's gospel harmony, Ambrosian hymns), theological treatises (Isidore), Martianus Capella, Boethius, Aristotle, the *Physiologus*, and a great deal of biblical poetry. The relics of vernacular secular culture include inscriptions, charms and heroic poetry. Other texts – such as the *Muspilli*, *Ludwigslied* or the Old Saxon (Old Low German) *Heliand* – straddle

---

[1] 'Old High German' denotes the oldest period of development of the German language, from *c.* 600 to the second half of the eleventh century.
[2] MGH, *Epistolae Karolini aevi*, IV, no. 124.

the two cultural traditions. In many cases we have but a single instance of each type, so it is difficult to say how representative the texts are of particular genres. They are simply too various and mostly too short for us to be able to extrapolate much about any theory which underlay them.

For convenience the following account will attempt to distinguish traditional Germanic features from those of the Latin, Christian tradition. Such a distinction is, however, somewhat artificial, not only because the Germanic tradition was essentially oral and any relics of it have survived only thanks to transmission by the church, but also because many texts owe something to both the Germanic and the Latin, Christian traditions.

1. Native literary traditions

Literary terms in the vernacular

Such terms as are attested for literary genres are vague and ill-defined. Haubrichs (*Geschichte*, p. 92) has drawn attention to a mid-ninth-century document of canon law, perhaps from Mainz or the West Frankish Reims, which discourages the enjoyment of *fabulae*, *locutiones*, *cantationes* and *saltationes* in public places on holy days, terms which seem to indicate the existence of prose narratives, verse recitations, songs and dancing songs as distinct popular genres. *Cantatio* perhaps corresponds to OHG *leod*, *liod* 'song', a term which is common Germanic though in some Germanic languages it is attested only as a compound (Gothic *awi-liuþ*, Old English *leoþ*, Old Saxon *uuinilieth*, Old Norse *ljóð*). It was also borrowed into Latin as *leudus* 'war song'. In OHG it has a broad range of meanings. It occurs as a gloss for *carmen* and in compounds with *wini-*, *huor-*, *tod-* and *scipscof-*. It collocates with *singan* and thus implies a song, rather than a poem. *Lioth frono* (*Ludwigslied*, l. 46) is a song sung by the Franks in praise of God and their king. The compound *winiliod* is interesting. In Old Saxon *uuinilieth* renders Latin *psalmus*, but Charlemagne is on record as having forbidden abbesses to send or write *uuinileudos*, which earlier scholars imagined to be amorous verses but which more probably refers to little vernacular poems thanking relatives or friends for gifts received.[3]

Alliterative verse[4]

While more than 6,000 lines of alliterative verse have come down to us in the mid-ninth-century Old Saxon *Heliand* (*The Saviour*, a book

---

[3] De Smet, 'Winileod'.
[4] On Germanic versification generally see Bliss, *Metre*; Bostock, *Handbook*, pp. 303–26; Hoffmann, *Altdeutsche Metrik*; von See, *Germanische Verskunst* and 'Stabreim und Endreim'.

epic – of 5,983 lines – in the Anglo-Saxon mould) and *Genesis*, fewer than 200 lines survive in OHG. Apart from the *Lay of Hildebrand*, the sole relic of the once extensive body of heroic poetry we posit, they include the short religious poems the *Wessobrunn Creation and Prayer* and *Muspilli*, and some charms. Alliterative poetry tends to feature archaic lexis, formulaic language and 'variation' (i.e. the use of synonyms and near-synonyms to elaborate the discourse). On the other hand, poetry on contemporary events, on the evidence of the *Ludwigslied*, and most OHG biblical poetry lack the archaic vocabulary and were composed in rhyming verse. This might be held to indicate that the Germans had an appreciation of different genres and poetic styles, though it must be remembered that while the texts mentioned were all written down during the ninth century, they were composed at very different times: the *Lay of Hildebrand* probably goes back a very long way – it reflects events that took place in the late fifth century – while the *Ludwigslied* was composed within a year of a battle fought in August 881.

According to the testimony of Jordanes (*De origine actibusque Getarum*, Ch. 4), the Goths sang songs about events in their history. No Gothic poetry survives, but all other Germanic heroic poetry, whether in Norse, Old English or German, shares many features of action, forms and motifs, which point to a common Germanic sophisticated poetic style in the Migration Period. The consummate artistry of the *scop* is neatly described in *Beowulf* 867ff. (see Chapter 10 above).[5] The language of heroic poetry was rich in topoi, formulas and archaic vocabulary. This is well illustrated in the last six lines of the *Lay of Hildebrand*:

> Do lettun se aerist   asckim scritan
> scarpen scurim,   dat in dem sciltim stont.
> do stoptun to samane   staimbort chludun,
> heuwun harmlicco   hwitte scilti,
> unti im iro lintun   luttilo wurtun,
> giwigan miti wabnum.

[Then they first let fly with ash spears in fierce showers: these stuck in the shields. Then they clashed together their resounding battle-boards, struck fiercely at the white shields until their limewood shields became small, hacked with the weapons.]

These lines contain no fewer than seven items of battle terminology which are not attested elsewhere in OHG: *asck* 'spear', *scritan* 'to rush', *scur* 'shower', *stopian* 'to clash', *staimbort* 'battle-boards' (a kenning for shield), *harmlicco* 'fiercely', *lintun* 'lime-wood shields'. The technique of 'variation' is exemplified in the use of *scilti*, *staimbort* and *lintun*, all meaning 'shields', the rushing of the spears is intensified through the phrase 'in

---

5 On the *scop* see Werner, 'Leier und Harfe', pp. 9–15; Werlich, 'Der westgermanische Skop', pp. 352–75.

fierce showers', and a similar effect is achieved through the repetition of the idea of the hacking of the shields in the words *giwigan miti wabnum*. These lines also illustrate *Hakenstil*, the technique whereby the long lines are bound together by the syntactical structure with the clause or sentence ending at the caesura and, in this case also, by the alliterative patterning, with *scritan, stont, chludun* (= *hludun*) and *wurtun* linking up with *scarpen scurim* and *sciltim*; *stoptun* and *staimbort*; *heuwun, harmlicco* and *hwitte*, and *giwigan* and *wabnum* respectively in the following lines in each case.

Most Germanic alliterative verse is pathos-laden and solemn in tone. Klaus von See has sought to characterise it as a kind of highly stylised prose discourse, a description which helps to explain what others have generally regarded as liberties or irregularities in the alliterative patterns and the metre which are characteristic of most of the surviving relics of OHG alliterative verse. For whereas the basic pattern as would be required by the Icelander Snorri Sturluson (on whom see Chapter 13 below) – that the key alliteration should fall on the first accented syllable of the second half-line, and that the first half-line may have one or two alliterations – apply to Old English and Old Saxon verse (though the Old Saxon poet is innovative in some details), in OHG the technique is at any rate freer, a fact which may possibly derive from a weakening of the Germanic initial accent on which alliterative verse essentially depends for its effect.

2. The Latin Christian tradition

Charlemagne

It seems that no one gave greater encouragement to writing in German in the OHG period than the Frankish king and emperor Charlemagne (reigned 768–814). Though the monarch found it difficult to write himself, he was, according to Einhard (*Vita Caroli Magni*, Ch. 25) at least, an accomplished linguist, speaking Latin as fluently as German, and even understanding Greek well enough. He gathered grammarians such as Peter of Pisa, Paul the Deacon, Clemens Scottus, and above all Alcuin of York (*c*. 735–804) at his court.

Einhard (*Vita Caroli Magni*, Ch. 29) makes a tantalising reference to Charlemagne's wish to have a collection made of 'ancient vernacular songs [*barbara et antiquissima carmina*] in which the deeds and battles of the kings of old were recounted'. Whether heroic lays (like the *Lay of Hildebrand*) are meant or songs celebrating contemporary historical events (of the type represented later by the *Ludwigslied*), or indeed both kinds, is not clear. Heroic poetry is traditional, and tradition was seen as a guarantee of truth. When the *Lay of Hildebrand* begins 'I heard it said'

('Ik gihorta ðat seggen') there is an implication of truth (a truth sometimes challenged by the church as mendacious and dangerous). One recalls Tacitus' statement (*Germania*, Ch. 2) that songs were the only form of history known to the Germans. The context suggests that Charlemagne's aim was to collect such material as the basis for a written history such as the Franks needed if they were to be esteemed as the heirs of the Romans (Einhard specifically mentions that the initiative for this collection was taken after Charlemagne's assumption of the imperial title in 800).[6]

Einhard's epithet for the songs, *barbarus*, means 'non-Latin', 'vernacular'. Though the Greek βαρβαρος had pejorative connotations, the same does not apply to *barbarus* as used by Frankish writers. They were proud of their people. Einhard tells us Charlemagne also wished to promote a grammar of his native tongue and this too was clearly intended to help raise the Franks to the same cultural level as the Romans.

Charlemagne played a crucial role in the development of German as a medium for writing. Not only did he promote the translation of utilitarian church texts, there is good reason to believe that he was behind the preparation of a body of model translations – of Isidore's *De fide catholica contra Iudaeos*, of the Gospel of Matthew, of a sermon of Augustine – the aim of which was to demonstrate that German could be as sophisticated a linguistic medium as Latin. Though these translations are all fragmentary and the circumstances of their production are far from clear, there can be no doubt that they are linked with the court and the philological and grammatical endeavours of the group of intellectuals based there.[7] These translations exhibit clear indications of an attempt to systematise German orthography. All in all, Charlemagne's programme was a remarkable one which stretched the intellectual resources of the period to their limits and which collapsed after the emperor's death in 814.

Otfrid of Weißenburg and rhyming verse

The mid-ninth century witnessed a flowering of biblical poetry in Germany. Apart from the Old Saxon alliterative poems *Heliand* and *Genesis* the major work of the period was the *Evangelienbuch* ('Book of the Gospels') of Otfrid of Weißenburg (Wissembourg in Alsace), a life of Christ in 7,104 lines of rhyming verse, written *c.* 863. Otfrid, who claims to be writing in the tradition of Juvencus, Arator and Prudentius, is the first German poet known by name and was at least one of the first to compose in rhyming verse. He dedicated his work to Charlemagne's grandson Louis the German (reigned 840–76), and a Latin preface

---

[6] On Einhard's account see Meissburger, 'Heldenliederbuch', but also Haubrichs, *Geschichte*, pp. 142ff.

[7] On the translations produced under Charlemagne, see Haubrichs, *Geschichte*, pp. 305–11; Matzel, *Untersuchungen*. On Charlemagne's 'academy' see Langosch, *Profile*, pp. 83–133.

believed by some to refer to the *Heliand* (though not attested until the sixteenth century) implies that Louis encouraged the composition of this work too. All this points to a strengthening of German (East Frankish) cultural awareness. Indeed, the *Evangelienbuch* exhibits the patriotic fervour we have also seen in Charlemagne's endeavours. The first section of Book 1 is headed 'Why the writer composed this book in German'. 'Since so many have begun to write in their mother tongue', Otfrid says, 'why should the Franks be the only people not to sing the praises of God in their own tongue?' (I.1, 31–4). 'They are as brave as the Romans, and it is vain to assert that the Greeks could rival them' (I.1, 57–60). Who these 'many' others are who have begun to write in the vernacular is not clear – Foerste, detecting a certain polemical note against the poet of the Old Saxon *Heliand*, has argued that this refers to the English and the Saxons, with whose work Otfrid, as a pupil of Rabanus Maurus at Fulda, may have had some acquaintance.[8]

This gospel harmony, written in German and in rhyming verse, was a bold undertaking and Otfrid was well aware of it, as is evident from the Latin letter in which he commends the work to Liutbert, archbishop of Mainz, and from the section headed 'Why the author has written this book in German'. The letter to Liutbert – the most important statement on literary theory from the OHG period[9] – deals with three main themes: the purpose of the poem, the method of treatment of the material, and the question whether German is a suitable linguistic medium for such an undertaking. The aims are said to be to supplant heathen songs and the works of pagan authors of Antiquity and to enable those whose Latin was inadequate to become familiar with the gospels in German. As for method, Otfrid explains that he has divided the poem into five books; the number five represents the five senses whose sinfulness is shown up by the perfection of the number four of the gospels. The symbolism of the numbers was already long established, but this particular play on them appears to have been Otfrid's own idea.[10] As for Otfrid's views on language, he laments that, compared with Latin, German is 'uncouth' (*inculta*) and 'undisciplined' (*indisciplinabilis*). He remarks that he has not always been able to render a Latin masculine with a German masculine, a Latin feminine with a German feminine, a Latin plural with a German plural. He does not impose Latin on German but recognises – perhaps more clearly than anyone again until Luther 650 years later – that German has rules of its own.

---

[8] Foerste, 'Verhältnis', pp. 93–131, especially p. 130. On Otfrid's indebtedness to the phrases and syntagma of alliterative verse, see Stutz, 'Spiegelungen'.

[9] See Magoun, 'Ad Liutbertum'. On Otfrid's aesthetics see Ernst, *Liber Evangeliorum*.

[10] See Haubrichs, *Geschichte*, pp. 369–71. On number symbolism generally, see Meyer and Suntrup, *Lexikon*. On the structure of the *Evangelienbuch*, see Kleiber, *Otfrid*, pp. 163–340.

A comparison of the Latin letter to Liutbert and the opening section of the *Evangelienbuch* affords a glimpse of Otfrid's struggle to reproduce Latin rhetorical concepts in German. Speaking of his Latin models, he says:

> Tharána dátun sie ouh thaz duam: óugdun iro wísduam,
> óugdun iro cléini   in thes tíhtonnes reini.
> Iz ist ál thuruh nót   so kléino girédinot
> (iz dúnkal eigun fúntan,   zisámane gibúntan). (I.1, 5–8)

[Thus they did something worthwhile: they demonstrated their skill, they demonstrated their artistry in perfect verse. It is all presented so ornately: they have sought out complex figures and combined them.]

Cléini corresponds to *subtilitas* in the letter to Liutbert, *reini* means 'grammatically correct', and *fúntan* must be understood in the sense of Latin *inventio*. Otfrid remarks on the skill of ancient poets in metrical matters and in so doing is the first German to write of 'feet' (*fuazi*) and 'beats' (*ziti*).[11] In the lines that follow, Otfrid draws a parallel between subjecting the Frankish tongue to the constraints of verse and his compatriots subjecting themselves to the laws of God (I.1, 35–50). Thus the discipline of poetry becomes a metaphor for living in accordance with God's law. The Franks are God's own people, and Otfrid has composed his poem so that God may be praised in their language.

The *Evangelienbuch* is the most substantial monument in rhyming verse in OHG, and Otfrid has frequently been credited with its introduction into the vernacular – critics have spoken of the 'Otfridian revolution' – yet it is unlikely that he was in fact the originator of it. As Johann Christoph Gottsched (d. 1766) pointed out two centuries ago, had Otfrid introduced rhyming verse he would doubtless have apologised for this in his prefaces, just as he apologises for writing in German. Otfrid merely draws attention to rhyme – what he calls *schema omoeoteleuton* in the letter to Liutbert – as a constitutive feature of his work. The inference must be drawn that rhyme was already established in the vernacular. There are in fact a number of other short rhyming texts, such as the *Petruslied* and verses from Cologne and Trier, which have been held by some to be earlier than Otfrid. Furthermore it is improbable that Otfrid's poem was sufficiently widely distributed for it to exert any influence. The problem has recently been re-examined by Patzlaff who concludes that Otfrid stood in a pre-existing tradition. He points out that whereas Otfrid consistently employs strophes of two long lines (a form probably deriving from rhyming Ambrosian hymns or from Carolingian didactic Latin *ritmi*[12]), other OHG rhyming

---

[11] On Otfrid's terminology see Engel, 'Die dichtungstheoretischen Bezeichnungen'.

[12] On the origin of rhyming verse, see Haubrichs, *Geschichte*, pp. 363–518, and more generally the various contributions in Ernst and Neuser, *Genese*. It is worth noting that the manuscript of the *Ludwigslied* describes the poem as a *rithmus teutonicus*.

poems, such as the *Ludwigslied*, *138th Psalm*, *Christus und die Samariterin* and the *Georgslied*, all of which are probably later than Otfrid, mix some three-line strophes among the two-line ones. Unless one is willing to believe that the *Ludwigslied* introduced the three-line strophe (thus making the *Ludwigslied* poet an influential figure) one must conclude that Otfrid and the other poets stood in an existing tradition which permitted two- and three-line strophes, with Otfrid deciding to refrain from using the three-line form.

Notker Teutonicus

Besides Otfrid, the only other writer in the OHG period to emerge as a distinct personality is Notker of St Gall (= Notker Teutonicus, Notker Labeo; *c.* 950–1022). His obituarist said of him he was the first to write in German, a statement which seems to imply that the tentative beginnings of writing in the vernacular in the eighth and ninth centuries had already slipped into oblivion, even though the St Gall library probably already possessed manuscripts of the translation of Tatian's gospel harmony (made *c.* 835) and Otfrid's *Evangelienbuch*. There are sufficient eleventh-century records to show the monastery school set great store by command of Latin. So much the more remarkable is Notker's achievement, therefore.

Notker owed his reputation to his skill as a teacher through the medium of the vernacular. He was no theoretician, rather a practitioner. His stance is revealed most clearly in his letter to Hugo, bishop of Sion (Valais), written *c.* 1019–20, in which he outlines his programme. Hugo had recommended him to concentrate his efforts on the study of the liberal arts, but Notker responded by saying that he had to read the books of the church in his school; these were essential whereas the arts were merely desirable as aids to understanding the former. To this end it was necessary to help the students by providing them with German translations of the Latin texts 'because one may quickly understand in the mother tongue things which one can hardly or only imperfectly comprehend in a foreign tongue'.[13] This is the topos that underpinned Charlemagne's policies and Otfrid's endeavours, too, but of the three it was Notker who best succeeded in turning theory into practice. His works (not all of which are extant) included translations of the *De consolatione philosophiae* and the *De sancta trinitate* of Boethius, the *Disticha Catonis*, the *Bucolics* of Virgil, Terence's *Andria*, Books 1 and 2 of Martianus Capella's *De nuptiis Philologiae et Mercurii*, Boethius' Latin translations of the *Categories* and the *Hermeneutics* of Aristotle, as well as the *Principia arithmeticae*, the

[13] On the letter to Hugo, see Haubrichs, *Geschichte*, pp. 272–4, and especially Hellgardt, 'Notkers Brief'. On Notker's style as a translator, see Sonderegger, 'Notker'.

Psalter, and the Book of Job. As well as writing a number of pieces of his own in Latin he also wrote a treatise on music entirely in German. Whereas his approach to translation has often been thought to be deliberately rather free in the interests of simplification, Notker in fact worked strictly in accordance with the methodology of contemporary grammar teaching.[14] His translations are accompanied by exegetical commentaries in German. In all his writings, which are remarkable also for their use of a regular system of orthography, Notker employs a mixture of German and Latin, possibly reflecting the oral medium in which he conducted his teaching. The Latin elements are often technical terms, as in this example with numerous theatrical terms:

Tû bist keuuón, in *scenis* ze singenne diu sáng tero gescûohton *tragicorum* mit *coturnis*. – *Coturni* uuâren ze béiden fûozen geskáffene scúha. *Scena* uuas éin finster gádem in mittemo *theatro*. Dârinne gesâzen die *auditores* tero *fabularum tragicarum* álde *comicarum*.   (Martianus Capella, 3.13)

[You are accustomed to singing the songs of the tragedians wearing cothurns. – Cothurns were shoes made for both feet. The scene was a dark room in the middle of the theatre. This is where the audience sat to listen to tragedies and comedies.]

Unlike Otfrid, Notker was not creating a literature, he was using the vernacular for pedagogic ends. For him literary texts were vehicles for the teaching of rhetoric and dialectic. If one compares Notker's writings with earlier German translations from Latin, his skill becomes immediately apparent. Every linguistic difficulty has been overcome, he was able to grasp the sense of the original and present it in lucid German. Yet it is hard to see Notker's achievement as a direct development of what went before. For although we may recognise in his writing a similar commitment to a regularised orthography to that found in the anonymous OHG translation of Isidore of Seville's *De fide catholica contra Judaeos*, made in the closing years of the eighth century, a keen sense of form similar to Otfrid's in the mid ninth century, and an Otfridian passion to exploit the German language to praise God and to transmit Christian knowledge and values to his contemporaries in his cloistered community, he himself seems to have been unaware of standing in any tradition. Neither did he establish one: after his death in 1022 his efforts in regard to the German language were quickly forgotten, and henceforth writers at St Gallen reverted to Latin.

---

[14] As demonstrated by Backes, *Hochzeit*, pp. 27–64.

12

Literary criticism in Welsh before *c.* 1300

Marged Haycock

The majority of the Welsh poems extant from the medieval period were composed by praise-poets for oral performance at courts, religious foundations and noble houses. While the standing and livelihood of the poets depended mainly on their effectiveness in 'making fame' and on their technical ability, they also felt the need to explain and promote themselves, both as representatives of an august, ancient and autonomous bardic order, and as individuals vying for favour and position. These reflections, frequently conventional, are embedded in the verse, and in the absence of any treatise on Welsh poetics before the bardic grammar of the early fourteenth century, they are a guide to the practitioners' conception of their work. A corresponding emphasis on the poetic self, vis-à-vis the heavenly Patron, is evident in the religious poetry. Poems in the personae of the prophet Myrddin and especially the primordial poet and sage, Taliesin, are a subsidiary source, dramatic and perhaps archaising, which detail concerns such as inspiration, performance, competition, poetic worth and aesthetic criteria, and contain many technical terms. Prose criticism, by contrast, is minimal: native texts before *c.* 1300 are all anonymous and lack prologues, although they are usually assigned a name and a type in brief concluding colophons, which in rare cases elaborate on the nature of the text. Explicit translation theory is poorly attested, and must be inferred from working practice.

1. Early poetry

The earliest surviving written texts are two series of *englynion* (three-lined stanzas) in the heavily glossed Cambridge Juvencus manuscript (late ninth or early tenth century); a four-lined fragment about St Padarn's episcopal staff, in a late-eleventh-century copy of Augustine, *De trinitate*, was removed by a binder's knife in the 1950s. The main sources of early-medieval poems, however, are the manuscripts from the early thirteenth century onwards which W. F. Skene in 1868 styled as the Four Ancient Books. Modern scholarship follows the lead of the seventeenth-century antiquary, Robert Vaughan, who coined the term *Cynfeirdd* for the 'early poets' – Aneirin, Taliesin, Myrddin, and their anonymous brethren – setting them apart from the named individuals whose praise of the Welsh princes dominates the record from *c.* 1100 to 1282. (It is likely, however, that certain modes associated with the Cynfeirdd – prophecy and popular religious verse, in particular – continued across the apparent divide.) However, *hengerdd* ('old poetry') is a medieval designation, attested first in poetry *c.* 1220 (*Cyfres Beirdd y Tywysogion*, VI, p. 15, l. 33). Three-lined *englynion*, largely eclipsed by the four-lined versions used by the court poets, are styled in the grammars as being *o'r hengerdd* or *o'r hen ganiad*.

There is a striking range of Cynfeirdd material, including primary eulogy and elegy; retrospective 'saga' cycles spoken by figures imagined from the past; political prophecy; nature and gnomic and religious verse, and many poems about legendary and semi-legendary figures and events (including elegies for Cunedda and Dylan Son of Wave, poems about Hercules and Alexander the Great, and the prophet, Myrddin; and about the inundation of the land of Gwyddnau, and 'The Battle of the Trees'). Further items are of a mixed nature. Poetry was rarely used for narrative. The medieval editors' ordering of the manuscript compendia and their use of titles provide some clues about literary classification. The Black Book of Carmarthen (*c.* 1225–50), with its apparent disregard for arrangement by genre or metre or period, and its wide range of religious and secular material – including several Myrddin items, and five twelfth-century praise-poems – appears to have been put together over a long period. Daniel Huws has suggested that the impulse of this 'enthusiastic anthologist' (perhaps working at the Augustinian priory at Carmarthen) was literary rather than antiquarian, and that he may have taken some material directly from oral tradition.[1] By contrast, the Book of Aneirin (*c.* 1250–1300), copied by two scribes in the second half of the thirteenth century (perhaps at the Cistercian house of Strata Marcella), is a dedicated collecting up of Gododdin elegies (almost exclusively *awdlau*, series of rhymed lines) and other items from North Britain and Wales transmitted with them: 'This is The Gododdin: Aneirin sang it', is the confident assertion of scribe A's initial rubric. Four longer poems, the *gwarchanau* concerning Tudfwlch, Adebon, Cynfelyn and Maeldderw,[2] were copied into a fresh quire, with rubric differentiating them by name and by status 'in poetic contention' from the shorter *awdlau* of The Gododdin, each being worth 300 times more (*Canu Aneirin*, p. 55). The fourth poem, *Gwarchan Maeldderw*, which is attributed to Taliesin 'who sang it and

---

[1] Huws, *Medieval Welsh Manuscripts*, pp. 70–2.
[2] *Gwarchan* may mean 'counsel, teaching' (*Canu Aneirin*, ed. Williams, pp. 232, 361–2), or perhaps 'additional song'.

gave honour to it equivalent to *all* the Gododdin *awdlau* plus the three other *gwarchanau*',[3] is also mentioned in the Book of Taliesin (p. 25, ll. 18–19), perhaps confirming its one-time 'classic' or 'test-piece' status. Eight further poems in that manuscript are assigned a worth of twenty-four, ninety or 300.

The Book of Taliesin (*c.* 1325–50) contains no *englynion*. It appears to have been primarily a Taliesin collection, with a core group of early panegyrics to the sixth-century king, Urien Rheged, and other praise-poems to the rulers Cynan Garwyn and Gwallog. A body of later material is either explicitly or tacitly attributed to the Taliesin persona, or else appears to reflect 'his' especial interests, including prophecy (he claims the *armes* of Virgil), religious and scriptural material, and other international book-learning, as well as native lore. Elegies are diligently signalled by the title *marwnad* ('death-song') and placed together for the most part. *Canu* 'song' is generally praise; *dadolwch* is a poem of reconciliation. Prophecies are entitled *armes* (literally 'fore-measuring', used for both religious and secular pieces), *gwawd* (etymologically related to seeing, compare *vates*), *cathl* and *darogan*. The loan-word *cadair*, whose primary meaning is 'chair' (< Latin *cathedra*), appears to refer to a kind of metre in three titles (*Book of Taliesin*, pp. 31, 34, 35). The etymology of the rare term *trawsganu* suggests that it may denote a poem in which the final word or phrase echoes the beginning (a common feature in Irish).[4] *Edmyg*, literally 'repeated gazing', i.e. praise (compare the verbs *edmygu* and *ceinmygu*), in the title of a ninth-century *encomium urbis* to the fort at Tenby, is another unusual label. Other titles are extracted from key phrases within the poems.

The Cynfeirdd material in the Red Book of Hergest (*c.* 1400) – nothing of which is demonstrably earlier than the ninth century – is ordered by genre and metre. Myrddin prophecies (perhaps reflecting the special interest of Hopcyn ap Tomas, who commissioned this massive collection of prose and verse) are placed separately, with Sibylline prophecies and other prose texts. The first poetry block proper commences with mainly untitled *englynion* sequences including didactic, nature, and gnomic and proverbial verse, proceeding to poems about the Sick Man of Abercuawg, Llywarch, Urien Rheged and Heledd, which make extensive use of nature and gnomic lines, and a group of prophetic *awdlau* attributed to Taliesin. Religious verse, some anonymous, but mostly by named poets from the

---

[3] Huws, *Medieval Welsh Manuscripts*, p. 75, comments that 'the long rubric assigning fairytale-values . . . suggests that the real value of the contents of the Book of Aneirin was by now largely talismanic'. This obscure 'scoring' system is not paralleled in other medieval Welsh sources.

[4] *Poems of Taliesin*, ed. Williams, p. 1. But if *traws* is the noun 'oppression' rather than the preposition 'across', it may be construed rather as a term for a victory-song.

twelfth century onwards, stands at the head of a second, much larger block of *englynion* and *awdlau*.

The Cynfeirdd valued the poetic gift (*dawn*) and inspiration (*awen*) for they heightened the ability to see, hear and know, and to assign significance (*synnwyr* < Latin *sentire*), as well as facilitating poetic utterance. The *awen* is noted as being divided into seven score *ogrfen*, and its source as a cauldron (*pair*, which rhymes fortuitously with *gair* 'word, utterance'), associated twice with the female Ceridwen (*Book of Taliesin* 33.10, 36.9). But Christian syncretism is already apparent: 'The song of *ogrfen*, my Lord created it at one and the same time as milk and dew and acorns' (33.11–13, emended), as it is in a deft twelfth-century invocation by Prydydd y Moch: 'Lord God, grant me a gift of sweet inspiration like that which came from Ceridwen's cauldron' (*Cyfres Beirdd y Tywysogion*, V, p. 10, l. 2, and compare also I, p. 2, ll. 1–3). Although its etymology may pertain to breath and wind – or, according to Calvert Watkins (p. 117), to seeing – the *awen* is imagined as a liquid force, flowing from the depths, ebbing and boiling; poetic utterance is a 'river' or a 'torrent'. Inspiration could emanate from trauma and isolation, too. Myrddin's prophetic powers came to him after the horrors of battle and withdrawal to the forest; and according to a fragment of legend embedded in The Gododdin, Aneirin's muse was activated by an overnight sojourn in chains in an infested subterranean cell (*Canu Aneirin*, p. 22, ll. 548–52):

> mi na fi Aneirin –
> ys gŵyr Taliesin
> ofeg gywrennin –
> neu cheint (i) Ododdin
> cyn gwawr dydd dilin.

[I yet not I, Aneirin – Taliesin of skilful utterance is familiar with this – sang The Gododdin before dawn on the following day.]

The most common generic word for a poet singing secular or religious verse is *bardd*; it carries no connotations of a lower or an auxiliary function: 'I am a bard, I do not praise churls'. Compounds, such as *bargadfardd* 'sharp, perceptive poet', *posfeirddiain* 'riddling poets' and *oferfeirdd* 'vain poets', occur. Other terms for poets include: *eilewydd*, literally 'a weaver, plaiter'; *prydydd*, 'shaper, maker', infrequent, in marked contrast to the later period; *cerddor* and *cerddoliad*, who have mastery of the craft (*cerdd*) of music or poetry; *celfydd* and *cyfrwys*, the 'skilful' and 'wise'; *anant* 'supplicating poets'; *ceiniad* 'singer', and *puror* 'singer or declaimer', perhaps of light or entertaining verse.

A further group of terms is associated particularly with prophecy and arcane learning: two Latin borrowings, *dewin* (< Latin *divinus*) and *doethur* (< Latin *doctor*) supplement the native *derwydd*, *dryw*, *syw*, *sywyd, sywedydd* and *darogenydd*, whose meanings range across 'sage, learned poet; magus, prophet'. The terms *sywedydd llyfrau* and, less certainly, *llyfrawr* 'bookman; scholar; sage' (*Armes Prydein*, l. 193), refer to poets versed in book-learning, such as the Taliesin figure, and Myrddin who had 'read the book of Cato' and who recommends the study of 'the books of the *awen*' (in the twelfth-century 'Dialogue between Myrddin and Gwenddydd his Sister'; *Poetry in the Red Book*, cols. 580.25, 583.11).[5] In 1188, Gerald of Wales reported his discovery of a book of Myrddin prophecies at Nefyn on the Llŷn coast (*Journey* 2.6), and this aspect of poetic activity, whether written or oral, particularly attracted twelfth-century Latin authors. Gerald, for example, reported the case history of the unstable prophet, Meilyr Awenydd[6] of Gwent and the other *awenyddion* who behave 'as if they are possessed by devils' (*Journey* 1.5):

Words stream from their mouths, incoherently and apparently meaningless . . . but all the same well expressed: and if you listen carefully . . . you will receive the solution to your problem . . . They seem to receive this gift of divination through visions which they see in their dreams. Some of them have the impression that honey or sugary milk is being smeared on their mouths; others say that a sheet of paper with words written on it is pressed against their lips . . . they invoke the true and living God, and the Holy Trinity.

In a highly coloured but not unsympathetic passage, he elaborates on their rapture, comparing the Trojans, Calchas and Cassandra, and the Old Testament prophets, finally refuting the idea of evil possession in favour of divine grace. Geoffrey of Monmouth's *Vita Merlini*, written *c.* 1150, complements the 'Prophecies of Merlin' section of his *Historia regum Britanniae* by describing Merlin's madness, and his discourses with the sage, Taliesin, who, 'with the aid and direction of Minerva' – and, we may add, Isidore of Seville – instructs him about the mysteries of the natural world.

Terms for composing and externalising song are not always distinct. They range from the simple *dywedut* 'say', *llefaru* 'utter', through *canu* 'sing', with its compounds *dysgogan, darogan* for prophecy, to the more formal-sounding Latinate *traethu*, used frequently, together with its etymological partner *traethawd* (< *tractatus*) 'poetic utterance'. Ideas of fashioning, weaving and ordering or harmonising are reflected in verbs such as *prydu, dylifo* and *cywyddaid*. Many of the words for song relate to concepts which have already been noted: *canu, gorchan, cerdd, nad, awdl,*

---

[5] For a ninth- or tenth-century poetic reference to 'the writings of Britain' (which may have included poetry) kept at Tenby or nearby Penalun, see 'Two Poems', ed. Williams, p. 164, l. 45.
[6] There is only one (late) instance of the word *awenydd* in the Cynfeirdd corpus: *Poetry in the Red Book*, ed. Evans, col. 1054, l. 4, used of Aneirin, but Lloyd-Jones, *Geirfa* s.v., is probably correct in regarding this as a gloss.

prydest, cadair, barddgyfrau and *barddweddi*; with *marwnad, cwyn, er-ddifwl*, for lament, and *darogan, gwawd, cathl* and *armes* for prophecy. Aesthetic considerations turn on skill and efficacy: song must, above all, be *celfydd* 'artful', fluent and confident (*rhydd, ffraeth, llafar, huawdl, haer*), harmonious and well measured (*cywair, caw, cyson*), boundless yet not superficial. Clarity and radiance are the hallmarks of a successful poet and his composition alike. Bad poetry is 'shallow' (*bas*), futile (*ofer*), or simply *cam* 'wrong', literally 'twisted'. Many of the Taliesinic poems are hectoring in tone, and dismissive of the offstage opposition – whether ignorant poets, or churchmen and monks, or the books they read.

Formal panegyric, as already noted, tends to combine praise with self-conscious reflection and explication. Crucially, a poem which augments the patron's fame (*clod*, originally 'that which is heard') is a commodity to be exchanged for reward, protection and privilege, and the poets are not diffident in stressing its value, nor in affirming the autonomy of their own judgement, for 'it is the world's poets who adjudge men of valour' ('Beirdd byd barnant wŷr o galon'; *Canu Aneirin*, p. 12, l. 285). A late Cynfeirdd poem prophesies a world riven by social unrest when 'there will be no skilled poet' and, by implication, 'no one made famous in song' ('Ef a ddaw byd ni bydd cerddglyd, ni bydd celfydd'; *Poetry in the Red Book*, col. 1049, l. 34). Complaints, even satire, could thus be voiced, as in the 'Elegy for Cynaethwy' which castigates four shameless women who had exercised undue influence at an (eleventh-century?) Anglesey court, robbing the poet of his patronage. Taliesin's 'Appeasement of Urien' (sixth century) refers disingenuously to the poet's error in courting other patrons and 'making fun of the old boy' (literally 'throwing darts or splinters'), while confidently reaffirming the terms of the compact between them: 'Urien will not refuse me'; 'now I see how much I stand to gain': 'Mead from horns and boundless goods from the best king, the most generous one I have heard of' (*Poems of Taliesin*, p. 11).

Praise of God is the main concern of religious verse (attested from the late ninth or early tenth century onwards), but it is also accorded primacy in other items: 'Why would I utter an utterance save of Thee?' and 'God has created my *awen* so that I may praise my Lord'. Indeed, 'he who does not praise the Lord is not a skilful poet; he who does not praise his Father is no fit singer' (*Book of Taliesin*, p. 28, ll. 11–12; p. 80, ll. 4–5; p. 37, ll. 22–3). The author of the Nine Juvencus *englynion* is unusually mindful of the challenge this poses. By means of a 'well-wrought prayer' (*arawd* < Latin *oratio*) does he wishes 'to give praise to the Trinity which is commensurate with its power'. His choice of form (nine units of three) accords with the subject-matter. But while 'no praise can be too great in praising the Trinity' (and 'the son of Mary'), it must be rendered 'audibly and [yet] with humility' (*ufyll* < Latin *humilis*). And the ultimate inadequacy of song is indicated by variations on the biblical topos: 'the inhabitants of the world cannot express Thy wonders in clear, harmonious song – although the grass and trees proclaim it'. 'The extent of God's marvel [i.e. the Creation] cannot be contained or expressed in letters' ('Juvencus poems'; *Blodeugerdd*, pp. 7–9). One may compare the prologue to 'The Debate of the Body and the Soul':

> Cyfaenad celfydd
> cynnelw o Ddofydd,
> cyfaenad cynnan
> o Grist cain, diddan;
> *cy*fai gyfergynnan
> am <> gylchyn huan,
> a'r g'nifer pegor
> ysydd o dan fôr,
> a'r g'nifer edeiniawg
> a orug Cyfoethawg;
> ac *adfai [i]* bawb
> dri thrychan tafawd,
> ni ellynt-wy draethawd
> cyfoethau y Drindawd.
>
> (*Blodeugerdd*, pp. 211–2,
> ll. 1–14).[7]

[Here is a skilful harmonious poem in the service of God – a harmonious resonant poem to fair and gracious God. However eloquent it would be about the Sun's course, and all the creatures beneath the sea, and all the birds which the all-powerful created, and even if everyone had nine hundred tongues, they would not be able to express the riches of the Trinity.]

In similar vein, 'although this were a task encumbent on us until Doom, no one is able to express the miracles, the riches which are under God's decree' (*Blodeugerdd*, p. 220, ll. 160–3, and see also p. 106, ll. 17–18). Other poets, undaunted, were happy to continue in the worldly mode: 'Your praise is true; and I am your praiser. Profit results from singing under the patronage of Elöi.' 'I will sing a blessed song to pure God with the materials I possess so that I may be his blameless vassal.' 'Acknowledged profit comes through assiduous praise of Christ the Lord.' Effort will be rewarded: 'He will not reject nor spurn those who strive to praise God in the beginning and at the end' (*Blodeugerdd*, p. 19, ll. 11–12; p. 125, ll. 8–10; p. 94, l. 2; p. 157, ll. 1–2).

Within the Latin tradition, secular praise-poets were condemned as lying sycophants by the early-sixth-century churchman Gildas in his

---

[7] The diamond sign indicates that I have emended out a word from the MS reading; the italic letters that I have made minor emendations. Orthography has been modernised everywhere in quoting from the texts.

tirade against the usurping king, Maelgwn Gwynedd, castigated for murder and the appropriation of his dead nephew's wife. Maelgwn's 'parasites' – probably the bards – confirmed the legitimacy of the union at the wedding feast ('but from their lips only, not from the depths of their hearts'; *De excidio*, Ch. 35). Furthermore the king's ears were attuned, not to praise of God, but rather,

> empty praises of [him]self from the mouths of criminals who grate on the hearing like raving hucksters – mouths stuffed with lies and liable to bedew bystanders with their foaming phlegm.   (*De excidio*, Ch. 34)

By contrast, the ecclesiastic who wrote the *Historia Brittonum* around 829 looked back on the second half of the sixth century as something of a golden age when Aneirin, Taliesin, Blwchfardd, Talhaearn Tad Awen – 'the Father of the *awen*' – and Cian *simul uno tempore in poemate claruerunt*.[8]

2. The poets of the princes *c.* 1100–1282

Shortly after the Edwardian Conquest, the first extant anthology of the work of the poets who had sung the praise of the native Welsh princes (from Gruffudd ap Cynan to Llywelyn ap Gruffudd) was made by the main compiler of the Hendregaredd manuscript (*c.* 1300). The scheme of this 'able and incisive editor who precociously identified a chapter of Welsh literary history', a scheme which ordered poets and forms by quire, and had no place for prophecy and anonymous verse, was continued in the first quarter of the following century.[9] The Red Book of Hergest (*c.* 1400), less comprehensive than Hendregadredd for the court poets, took in the work of their successors who continued to used the *awdl* and *englyn* forms for praise of the post-Conquest nobility, the most prolific being Gruffudd ap Maredudd ap Dafydd, who sang to the family of Tudur ap Goronwy of Penmynydd, Anglesey.[10] Satires and prophecies were also admitted. Genre-specific titles in these two manuscripts include *marwnad* ('elegy'); *canu* and *awdl* (for eulogy); *dadolwch* ('reconciliation'); *arwyrain* ('exaltation'), *gorhoffedd* ('boast'); *breuddwyd* ('dream'); *rhieingerdd* ('poem to

---

[8] *Historia Brittonum*, p. 62. Dumville, 'The Historical Value of the *Historia Brittonum*', pp. 16–17, notes that the verb here reflects the usage of the late Latin annalists in referring to poets such as Virgil. Talhaearn's striking cognomen may be compared with that of the otherwise unknown Tydai Tad Awen: '"Stanzas of the Graves"', ed. T. Jones, p. 118, englyn 4a, and p. 136, englyn 13a.

[9] Huws, *Medieval Welsh Manuscripts*, pp. 75–7 and 193–226. The third stratum, copied *c.* 1325–50 in a secular milieu, is a contemporary witness to the work of the first generation of *Cywyddwyr*, and to the varied literary interests at the home of Ieuan Llwyd in the Aeron Valley.

[10] Iolo Goch's *tour de force* description of a beautiful maiden (*Gwaith Iolo Goch*, ed. Johnston, pp. 101–2) is the only poem in the new *cywydd* form in the Red Book.

a maiden'); *marwysgafn* ('death-bed poem'), and *bygwth* ('threat; satire'). The use of the *englyn*, clearly an established vehicle for elegy and eulogy, and sharing many of the stylistic features of the *awdl* form, is generally signalled in poem titles.

Although the Poets of the Princes inherited the traditional diction, craft vocabulary and topoi found in both the early *englynion* and *awdlau*,[11] there are only sporadic references to the Cynfeirdd in a corpus of some 12,500 lines. The twelfth-century Cynddelw Brydydd Mawr is unusual in referring to the 'historical' praise-poet, Taliesin, and indeed he mentions other poets, such as Afan Ferddig, whose work has not survived. Dafydd Benfras states that even if were 'a *dewin* possessing primacy of great bardic gift' he would be unable to express fully the battle prowess of Llywelyn ap Iorwerth – 'nor would Taliesin'. Other poets, such as Phylip Brydydd, mention his legendary fame in contention, especially when they are trying to establish their own primacy. Dafydd Benfras, again, wished to be replete with Myrddin's vigorous *awen* in order to sing praise 'like Aneirin did when he sang The Gododdin'.[12] On the whole, however, the court poets distanced themselves from the *awenydd* tradition, which may have contaminated the Cynfeirdd en bloc. Elidir Sais, for example, while claiming that his bardic utterance was 'radiant . . . in the style of Myrddin, a radiance from the cauldron of the *awen*', adds the caveat that 'to avoid the wrath of Judgment' he shall be a poet to God as long as he may live (*Cyfres Beirdd y Tywysogion*, I, p. 16, ll. 7–10).

The Lawbooks of the period show that both the *bardd teulu* ('poet of the warband', one of the court officials) and the visiting *pencerdd* (the head of the practitioners in the region where the itinerant court was in residence) were required to sing at court 'first of God' before proceeding to secular praise. Nevertheless, some religious poems indicate that this did not allay intermittent unease with worldly praise, whether expressed in the form of *contemptus mundi* and *Ubi sunt?* conventions, or in an apparently more heartfelt retraction. Meilyr Brydydd, for example, expressed his regret at having neglected the King of Kings: 'Many times have I received gold and brocade for praising mortal kings, and after the gift of the *awen*, a different impulse: poor is my tongue as I fall silent' (*Cyfres Beirdd y Tywysogion*, I, p. 4, ll. 21–4). But his son, Gwalchmai, and his grandson, Einion, echo the same idea, the one acknowledging the falsehood he

---

[11] Gerald of Wales' praise of their inventiveness, ingenuity and originality (*Description* 1.12) is presumably by comparison with Latin panegyric. He notes also the attractiveness of the language and sentiments, and the alliteration, a feature shared with English and Latin. He admires the rich rhetoric of the native lawyers, and the general predilection for 'plays on words, sly references, ambiguities and equivocal statements' (*Description* 1.14).

[12] References discussed by Owen, 'Chwedl a Hanes'. The prince-poet, Owain Cyfeiliog, who drew on Gododdin material in celebrating the success of his own warband in 1156 (*Cyfres Beirdd y Tywysogion*, II, p. 14), does not mention him by name.

mouths for venial intent, the other that worldly poems are not a worthy use of God's gift (*Cyfres Beirdd y Tywysogion*, I, p. 14, ll. 59–62; I, p. 27, ll. 35–6, 75).

Of the handful of poems addressed to poets before *c.* 1282, the only one which has any significant appreciation of the subject's literary activities is an anonymous request poem performed at a Calend-tide feast in praise of Cuhelyn Fardd, a chess-playing nobleman who lived in Cemais in north Pembrokeshire in the early twelfth century. He was the son of a poet, Gwynfardd Dyfed, and one of the forebears of Dafydd ap Gwilym. The poem is exceptionally artful and atmospheric. Cuhelyn is deemed the very 'marrow of fair song' (*mêr cerddau cain*), a master of 'honeyed versifying' (*mêl farddoni*), fully deserving of a bardic chair. Moreover, he appreciates 'measured, regular' poetry, and maintains standards of song 'in lively competition' (*cyfrysedd*) in the face of 'debased inspiration' (*Cyfres Beirdd y Tywysogion*, I, p. 2, ll. 28, 25, 41, 8, 43, 37).

The competition best attested during this period is the *amryson* held at Christmas 1176. Henry II had settled Ceredigion and Ystrad Tywi on Rhys ap Gruffudd, the prince of Deheubarth, in 1171, and work began apace on rebuilding the castle at Cardigan. Rhys' invitation to the feast there went out through Wales, England, Scotland and Ireland a year in advance, implying that that he was seeking a propaganda coup to consolidate his position and to establish himself as a culture king on the wider stage. Caerwyn Williams has suggested a possible imitation of the French *puys*. Two competitions were staged: one between the bards (*beirdd*) and the poets (*prydyddion*), and another between harpers, crowders, pipers and 'various types of musical craft'. This tallies with the etymology of *amryson*, lit. 'varieties of sound', and with other pieces of evidence[13] which suggest that like was not necessarily pitted against like in contentions for precedence of performance at the princely courts. How Cuhelyn Fardd and other poets had gained their 'chair' status is uncertain, however, but it is likely that this was regulated by the bardic order itself, who must have overseen training and the maintenance of rules or standards (*canon* is used in this connection); we know that some poets were teachers, and that there were a few bardic families.

The bardic grammars from the fourteenth century (Aberystwyth, National Library of Wales, MS Peniarth 20, from *c.* 1330, is the earliest manuscript) prescribe the correct use of the parts of speech, metrical rules, the appropriate attributes for praising individuals according to their station and gender, and the proper spheres of activity of the different kinds of poets (from the *clerwr* up to the *prydydd*). A poem is deemed faulty if

---

[13] *Cyfres Beirdd y Tywysogion*, VI, pp. 14, 15, discussed by Owen, 'Chwedl a Hanes', pp. 22–3.

it breaks metrical rules, conveys the wrong meaning or is disjointed, if it mixes praise and satire, or lacks 'soul' (i.e. a verb!) and sense and imagination (*dychymyg*). Profound meaning and copious Welsh were prized. Three things give rise to the *awen* – genius, practice and art. Another three can augment it: competition, and happiness, and praise! (*Gramadegau'r Penceirddiaid*, pp. 54 and 17).

3. Prose tales and translations

The commonality of traditional material underlying medieval Welsh prose and poetry is best witnessed by the Triads. Characters and events were classified in threes, with capsule information, which facilitated poetic allusions; the prose writers, too, were clearly familiar with the scheme. The Grammars indicate that the knowledge of stories (*cyfarwyddyd ystoriau*) – written stories, according to some versions – together with old verse (*hengerdd*) lent amplitude to song, and it is very likely that some of the native *literati* were skilled in both mediums. There is no clear indication, however, that prose and verse were regularly combined in prosimetrum form despite Ifor Williams' speculation that the early *englyn* cycles were originally embedded in a narrative prose matrix.[14] The written prose-tales – tailored in some cases, it would seem, for reading aloud – use *cyfarwyddyd* ('traditional knowledge; story, account') in referring to their source traditions, and a variety of self-referential terms: *chwedl* ('tale'), *cyfranc* ('[a tale about an] encounter'); *breuddwyd* ('dream'); and the problematic *mabinogi* (derived from *maban* 'son' – compare its use to render Latin *infantia*; or else from *Maponos*).[15] *Cainc*, literally 'branch; strand', commonly used for song and subdivisions generally, has been defined most recently, for the unique prose usage in the Four Branches of the Mabinogi, as a 'formally designated quasi-autonomous section of a complete narrative'.[16] The term *ystoria*, already noted, is used for translated works, and for tales indebted to written material. *Breudwyt Ronabwy*, which satirises the content and the conventions of stories about the past, and makes a jibe at the unintelligibility of bardic praise, styles itself as an *ystoria*, drawing attention to its literary nature in the closing colophon:

---

[14] Followed by Tristram, 'Early Modes', pp. 440–1, and, with important modifications, by Mac Cana, 'Prosimetrum', pp. 116–22. Rowland, 'Prose Setting', is more sceptical. The occasional *englynion* in the Four Branches of the Mabinogi can be viewed as 'quotations' from other realisations of the underlying *cyfarwyddyd*.

[15] Russell, *Celtic Word Formation*, p. 60, n. 89; Davies, *Crefft y Cyfarwydd*, pp. 45–9.

[16] Roberts, 'Where were the Four Branches Written?', pp. 61–2, who also reviews the question of whether its use may be influenced by the French *branche*.

And the reason why no one, neither a bard nor a storyteller, knows the Dream without a book is because of the multitude of colours of the horses . . . of the arms and their trappings, and of the costly mantles and the efficacious stones.[17]

Translated works, in general, show a high level of competence and – especially in the case of works from French – skill in adapting material to the literary expectations of the home market: native narrative formulas are used, structure is often simplified, and abstract and psychological reflection and the finer points of *courtoisie* are pruned in favour of action. Gruffudd Bola, who translated the Athanasian Creed for a fourteenth-century Cardiganshire noblewoman, Efa ferch Maredudd, is unusual in providing a comment on his translation from Latin, noting the commonplace that,

it is not always possible to translate word-for-word while at the same time sustaining the idiom of the language and the meaning of the phrase. For that reason I sometimes translated word-for-word, and at other times sense-for-sense following the mode and idiom of our own language.[18]

The 'mode and idiom' of medieval literary Welsh, as exploited and refined by translators, poets, prose writers and the skilled individuals responsible for a wealth of functional prose, was exceptionally rich and varied throughout our period. Literary criticism and self-criticism must have been highly developed amongst the practitioners, even if this is not always satisfactorily articulated by the evidence. In the final reckoning, their consummate mastery of their crafts must be their testimony.

[17] 'A llyma yr achaws na ŵyr neb y breuddwyd, na bardd na chyfarwydd, heb lyfyr, o achaws y gynifer lliw a oedd ar y meirch . . . ac ar yr arfau ac eu cyweirdebau, ac ar y llennau gwerthfawr a'r mein rhinweddawl' (*Breudwyt Ronabwy*, ed. Richards, p. 21).

[18] ' . . . na ellir yn wastad symud y gair yn ei gilydd, a chyd â hynny cynnal priodolder yr iaith a synnwyr yr ymadrodd yn deg. Wrth hynny y trois i weithiau y gair yn ei gilydd, a gweith[iau] eraill y dodais synnwyr yn lle synnwyr herwydd modd a phriodolder ein hiaith ni' (Lewis, 'Credo Athanasius Sant', p. 196; discussed by Lloyd-Morgan, 'Rhai Agweddau', pp. 137–8, and 'More Written about than Writing?', pp. 156–8).

13

Criticism and literary theory in Old Norse-Icelandic

Margaret Clunies Ross

In his *Edda* ('Poetics') of *c.* 1225 the Icelander Snorri Sturluson recorded an exchange of verses between a troll-woman and a poet, Bragi Boddason the Old, an archetypal figure of semi-divine status and the earliest named poet whose verses have survived in written form. The troll-wife challenged Bragi to identify himself as they met in a wood one dark evening and he did so in the following verse:

'Skáld kalla mik	'Poets call me
skapsmið Viðurs,	Viðurr's thought-smith,
Gauts gjafrǫtuð,	Gautr's gift-getter,
grepp óhneppan,	un-scant poet,
Yggs ǫlbera,	Yggr's ale-server,
óðs skap-Móða,	creating-Móði of poetry,
hagsmið bragar.	skilful smith of rhyme.
Hvat er skáld nema þat?'	What is a poet other than that?'[1]

Bragi's self-definition employs a list of kennings or poetic periphrases (*kenningar*) which reflect the two dominant indigenous Nordic conceptions of the art of poetry: poetry as the gift of the gods, particularly of the god Óðinn, and poetry as craft or skill (*íþrótt*), with the poet as a clever song-smith or craftsman of verse. The idea of the poet as a clever song-smith clearly contributes to the role of the court poet (*skáld*) of Viking Age Scandinavia and later as the pleaser of princes and the entertainer of their courts. The social and intellectual milieu of the courts gave an impetus to the development of a courtly or skaldic poetry that privileged abstruse diction, fractured syntax, riddling allusions to Old Norse myth and heroic legend and complex verse-forms. It is not therefore surprising that such a self-reflexive poetic art produced a corpus of indigenous poetic theory.

The history of literary theory and criticism in Old Norse is mainly one of an indigenous theory of poetry and poetics, partly encouraged

---

[1] Snorri Sturluson, *Edda, Skáldskaparmál*, ed. Faulkes, I, pp. 83–4; tr. Faulkes, p. 132. Viðurr, Gautr and Yggr are names for the god Óðinn, while Móði is the name of a son of the god Þórr, but here is the base word of a kenning for a poet. On the literary and folkloric genre of the exchange, see Almqvist, *Norrön niddiktning*, I, pp. 28–34.

by a knowledge of Latin grammatical rhetoric and metrics, rather than a theorising of prose literature. That this is the case is an indication of the great importance Icelanders placed on poetry and poets on the one hand, and the self-confidence of Norse vernacular prose literature on the other. The fact that much poetry is recorded within prose texts, as a kind of prosimetrum, is another complicating element. There are a number of prose texts in which we find a discussion or brief mention of specific prose genres, but these are mostly indigenous, and there is rarely any attempt to apply Latin genres or theory to vernacular literary kinds in a direct way. This is not to say that people in medieval Scandinavia were unaware of Latin literature and its genres; plainly, their many translations from Latin and other languages, including English, French and German, put them in touch with learned literature, with Christian religious literature, such as saints' lives and sermons, and with the literature of entertainment, such as romances, which they termed *riddarasögur*, 'sagas of knights'. However, such was the strength of their own vernacular prose, particularly the saga form, which, by its very name reveals its oral roots (*saga* means 'something said, narrated'), that they were rarely drawn to justify their own literary forms in terms of Latin precedents. In the prefaces to a variety of vernacular texts, there is often a discussion of sources, both indigenous and foreign, but rarely an overt interest in equating foreign and indigenous genres.[2] This literature is overwhelmingly Icelandic in conception and execution, even though traditions fundamental to its development must have derived from the Norwegian homeland.

One thing we can say about the scattered references to textual genres in Old Icelandic prose literature is that it was a literature concerned to distinguish genres according to how truthful they were about what had happened in the past and to a perhaps lesser extent in the present. A great deal of Icelandic prose literature is concerned to represent events of the Scandinavian past: the events of prehistory, the events of the Icelandic settlement age, and then what happened after *c.* 1000 when Icelanders accepted Christianity and, in time, literacy, using the Roman alphabet. Even though most names for the various genres of Icelandic literature are modern rather than medieval, we can perceive this distinction in the genres themselves; among the earliest prose writings, great stress is laid upon how wise a witness was in terms of historical knowledge (a reliable witness being described as *inn fróði*, 'the wise, learned').[3] And yet we also know, according to a remark attributed to King Sverrir of Norway

---

[2] Sverrir Tómasson, *Formálar*, is the standard work on this subject; see in particular Ch. 4 on Icelandic prose authors' approaches to their material and use of sources.

[3] For a discussion, see Tómasson, *Formálar*, pp. 222–7; Meulengracht Sørensen, *Fortælling og ære*, Ch. 2, and Whaley, 'A Useful Past'.

(reigned 1177–1202) in *Þórgils saga ok Hafliða*, in the context of a wedding at Reykjahólar in 1119, that some of the most entertaining stories were also recognised as the furthest from the truth (and the saga gives the term *lygisǫgur*, 'lying stories', for these). Moreover, the narrator goes on, some people believe fantastic narratives of heroes and monsters of prehistoric times to be actually true (implying that other people do not), and trace their own ancestry to the heroes of old. A similar attitude of disdain towards popular entertainment, particularly when provided by such sources as 'stepmother tales, which cowherds tell, and no one knows the truth of' (*stjúpmæðra sǫgur, er hjarðarsveinar segja, er engi veit, hvárt satt er*), is found in the preface to Oddr Snorrason's saga of King Óláfr Tryggvason (written c. 1190), but this does not stop Oddr from making ample and skilful use of a variety of popular stories in his own history.

To some people, the notion that a body of indigenous poetic theory exists for medieval Scandinavia, might be questioned. Stephen Tranter has argued that, in contrast to the situation of medieval Ireland, which also valued poets and poetry highly, 'technical literature on poetics in Icelandic is almost entirely lacking' ('Medieval Icelandic *Artes Poeticae*', p. 141). He did not mean that there are no works in Old Icelandic dealing with poetry and poetics, because there plainly are, but rather that there are no extant texts like the Irish bardic tracts that an apprentice poet could study as a kind of handbook to learn how to compose poetry 'according to a prevailing metrical system and how to distinguish different forms within that system' (p. 142). The sole exceptions to this generalisation are the third and fourth parts of Snorri Sturluson's *Edda*, *Skáldskaparmál* and *Háttatal*.

Another curious and paradoxical thing is that we get very little direct evidence from medieval Icelandic or other Scandinavian texts about how poets learned their craft, where and in what circumstances they performed it, and how they passed on what they knew to the next generation of poets, even though there is plenty of circumstantial evidence to tell us that medieval Icelanders regarded poetry and its practice as very important. We do not know directly how the transition from an oral poetic tradition to a written one came about. The closest we come to a representation of one poet talking to another about poetry and poetic composition is a well-known scene in *Egils saga Skallagrímssonar*, Ch. 78 (a saga that displays an intense interest in poetry, poets and poetics) in which the younger Icelandic poet Einarr Helgason skálaglam ('scales-tinkle')[4] visits

---

[4] He was called 'scales-tinkle' because the Norwegian Earl Hákon had given him a pair of scales that made a tinkling sound when a desired weight was placed in them.

the older Egill Skallagrímsson at the general assembly, and they have a conversation about poetry, *þeir ræddu um skáldskap*. Unfortunately, we are not told what issues they discussed.

The conceptual bases of Old Norse poetic theory may, however, be deduced from several kinds of evidence: from the corpus of extant poetry and the ways in which medieval Scandinavians classified it; from representations of poetry and poets in Old Norse literature generally; from the status of poetry in Old Norse myth, and from a group of thirteenth- and fourteenth-century Icelandic treatises on poetry and literary theory, which show the influence of medieval Latin handbooks of grammar and rhetoric but adopt an independent attitude to their subject-matter, revealing a wealth of technical terms that are unlikely to have been generated solely to translate Latin names. This and other evidence indicates that medieval Norwegians and Icelanders placed a very high value on poetry as an intellectual art and had evolved a corpus of poetic theory and sets of technical terms for poetry and poetics that are never likely to have been systematised in pre-Christian and pre-literate times, but which existed nevertheless and were brought together under the impetus of literacy and Christian learning. National pride was another motivating factor in developing a written vernacular poetics in which Icelandic could be used 'as a *Schriftsprache* with a suitable scholarly apparatus to that enjoyed elsewhere by Latin' (Tranter, 'Medieval Icelandic *Artes Poeticae*', p. 143).

Modern scholarship divides Old Norse poetry into two kinds, eddic and skaldic, and there is medieval authority for this division, though it is not an absolute one. In part it is based upon a metrical distinction, most eddic poetry being composed in the common Germanic alliterative verse-form whose basic metrical unit, the long line, breaks into two half-lines divided by a caesura and linked by alliterating staves, in which one or two syllables in the *a*-line alliterate with the first stressed syllable of the *b*-line. This verse-form can be found in the poetry of all European peoples who spoke Germanic languages, where early texts have been preserved, including Old and Middle High German, Old Saxon, Old and Middle English and Old Norse. There were several variants of the common Germanic verse-form in Old Norse, whose medieval names reveal their associations with particular operational frames of reference, like telling stories about gods or heroes, or recording various kinds of speech acts, ranging from a formal comparison of the merits of two men to the exchange of insults, or performing invocations, incantations and magical spells. The chief eddic verse-form was *fornyrðislag*, 'old story metre', with a major variant in *málaháttr*, 'speech-form'. Another important measure was *ljóðaháttr*, 'song form', with its augmented variant *galdralag*, 'incantation metre'.[5] Skaldic poetry, on the other hand, mainly used the syllable-counting measure *dróttkvætt*, 'court metre', and its many variants (there were normally six syllables to a *dróttkvætt* line). Like eddic poetry in Old Norse, skaldic verse was also stanzaic, an eight-line stanza divisible into two halves (*helmingar*) being the norm. Skaldic poetry also differs from eddic verse in its use of rhyme and assonance: odd lines bore assonance or *skothending*, while evens had full internal rhyme or *aðalhending*, each pair of lines being linked by alliteration.

Eddic poetry may also be distinguished from much skaldic verse on other grounds, including those of style, genre and subject-matter. An additional distinction is that eddic poetry is anonymous while most skaldic verse is attributed to named poets. A major medieval collection of eddic verse has tended to guide our modern views about the nature of this kind of poetry. This is the so-called Codex Regius of the Elder Edda,[6] a late-thirteenth-century Icelandic compilation of poems about the early Norse gods and Norse and Germanic heroes. It begins with *Vǫluspá*, 'The Prophecy of the Seeress', a sweeping overview of the creation of the world, of the giants, gods, dwarves and humans, which then continues to document the steady decline of that world, highlighting the death of the god Baldr before the catastrophe of Ragnarǫk, the fated destruction of the gods. Some poems in eddic measures are quoted in *fornaldarsögur*, 'sagas of ancient time', and in legendary histories of royal dynasties, while there are others (including some also found in the Codex Regius) in manuscripts containing Snorri's *Edda*. Their contextualisation and the frequent use of the adjective *forn*, 'ancient', to refer to this kind of poetry lends credence to the inference that eddic verse was regarded by medieval Icelanders as the more ancient type of Norse poetry, in contrast to skaldic verse which belonged to the historical period even though its composition antedated the era of written, Christian history in many cases. This view is endorsed by Snorri Sturluson's *Edda*, where eddic poetry is put in the mouths of gods and heroes in narrated myths while skaldic verse illustrates that section of the work (*Skáldskaparmál*, 'Poetic Diction', and *Háttatal*, 'List of Verse-Forms') which constitutes the treatise on poetics proper.

---

[5] For further details see Lehmann, *Germanic Verse Form*; Frank, 'Skaldic Poetry', and Harris, 'Eddic Poetry'. Frank and Harris offer a useful view of changing modern critical approaches to the two kinds of Old Norse verse.

[6] From the mid-seventeenth century to 1971 this codex was in the Royal Library, Copenhagen (Old Royal Collection MS 2365, 4to), but is now in the Stofnun Árna Magnússonar, Reykjavik, Iceland. It is sometimes (inaccurately) called *Sæmundar Edda*, a name that refers to the mistaken belief, held by Bishop Brynjólfur Sveinsson and others in the seventeenth century, that the compilation was the work of the early-twelfth-century Icelandic scholar Sæmundr Sigfússon.

Old Norse poetry and medieval Scandinavian attitudes to poetry developed in an oral society and display many signs of the close relationship between poetic genres and social interactions. Much of the verse is agonistically toned and represents direct interpersonal interaction and confrontation between protagonists, often of an aggressive kind. The nomenclature of eddic poems whose medieval titles are known indicates that they were classified as speech-related genres of various kinds, as narrative genres or as catalogue poems. The speech genres dominate and purport to represent the direct discourse of gods and heroes. Titles distinguish the *mál* ('speech, words') at the most general discourse level (e.g. *Hávamál*, 'Speech of the High One [Óðinn]') from the *spá*, 'prophecy' (e.g. *Vǫluspá*, 'Prophecy of the Seeress'), the *ljóð*, 'chant' (e.g. *Hárbarðsljóð*, 'Chant of Hárbarðr [Óðinn]'), the *senna*, 'flyting' (e.g. *Lokasenna*, 'Loki's Flyting'), the *hvǫt*, 'incitement' (e.g. *Guðrúnarhvǫt*, 'Incitement of Guðrún') and the *grátr*, 'lament' (e.g. *Oddrúnargrátr*, 'Lament of Oddrún'). Poems like *Hymiskviða* and *Þrymskviða*, whose titles' second element, *kviða*, probably denotes a narrative poem,[7] embody continuous narratives of one or more known myths but are less common than the speech genres. The *tal*, 'list', form, includes poems celebrating members of important Norwegian dynasties and, in one case, an Icelandic family, the Oddaverjar. Examples are *Ynglingatal*, 'List of Ynglingar', a Swedish and Norwegian dynasty, and *Háleygjatal* or 'List of the earls of Hálogaland'. Snorri Sturluson's *Háttatal* or 'List of Verse-Forms' is a catalogue illustrating a wide variety of skaldic and eddic verse-forms available to poets in the thirteenth century. It forms the final section of his *Edda*. Another catalogue form, of special interest to poets, was the *þula* or versified list of poetic synonyms (*heiti*) for the major subjects of skaldic verse, such as gods, men and women, ships, weapons and gold. Though *þulur* were of most use to skaldic poets, the extant examples use eddic verse-forms. The evolution of the *þula* is speculative, but in all probability is attributable to the need oral poets felt to have access to versified *aides-mémoire* which functioned like rhyming dictionaries (see Clunies Ross, *Skáldskaparmál*, pp. 80–91). At the same time some *þulur* recorded in manuscripts containing *Snorra Edda* (which is where most of them are found) are clearly of learned origin, as they include synonyms of Latin and even Greek origin.

Old Norse terms used to differentiate kinds of skaldic verse are largely based on formal criteria, including metrical and syntactic considerations, or refer to the context in which the poem was composed or the patron for whom it was intended. On purely formal grounds, a fundamental

---

[7] Heusler, *Die altgermanische Dichtung*, p. 154. For a review of the nomenclature, see Klingenberg, 'Types of Eddic Mythological Poetry', and Quinn, 'Naming of Eddic Mythological Poems'.

distinction was made between the *drápa* with its refrain (*stef*) and less elaborate sequences like the *flokkr* (literally 'a group [of stanzas]') without a refrain. The *drápa* was the most highly valued of the skaldic kinds, because of its formality and elaborate construction. *Stál* or inlay of intercalary clauses within the half-stanza was an admired syntactic feature of skaldic verse. Verses that regularised this feature could be termed *stælt* or 'inlaid', according to *Háttatal*, which provides a wealth of other technical terms for skaldic verse-forms. The diction and syntax of skaldic poetry were also important differentiating characteristics. The most notable feature of the diction was the *kenning*, a periphrastic noun phrase which poets used in place of a noun referent, as, for example, in the phrase 'fire of the sea' for gold. In order to understand many kennings it was necessary to know about the world of pre-Christian Norse myth, and this is why Snorri Sturluson prefaces an account of Norse mythology, *Gylfaginning*, to his treatise on poetics. The syntax and word order of skaldic poetry also differentiated it from other forms of discourse, for the various phrases and clauses of a skaldic verse often do not follow a prose word order but need to be fitted together mentally as one would reassemble the scattered pieces of a jigsaw puzzle.

As with eddic poetry, agonistic speech acts are never far from the surface of the classificatory vocabulary of skaldic verse. Thus it will come as no surprise that there are many Old Norse literary terms for poetry of praise and blame, which point to one of poetry's main social purposes, to serve as a public endorsement of the dominant values of early Norse, especially Norwegian, court society and of the figure of its ruler, in particular, as a leader in war, a tough fighter himself, and a generous rewarder of his personal entourage. Encomium or praise-poetry (*hróðr* or *mærð*), eulogy (*lof, lofkvæði*) and the memorial lay or *erfikvæði* are the modes of much courtly skaldic verse composed by Norwegian and Icelandic poets whose patrons included kings and princes in Scandinavia and abroad, King Athelstan of England among them. There also exist a small number of examples of poems in which poets express criticisms of their royal patrons, the best known of these being the *Bersǫglisvísur* or 'Plain-speaking verses' of the Icelandic skald Sighvatr Þórðarson addressed to King Magnús the Good. It is probable that the dangers inherent in composing and then recording poetry that was critical of its subject was the main reason why such a small number of examples of this kind have survived in written form.

The other side of praise, blame (*háð*, 'ridicule'), is, however, well represented in the corpus of skaldic verse, though less often in extant court poetry than in a variety of personal and public contexts recorded for Icelandic society between *c.* 900 and 1350. *Níðvísur* or verses of insult and calumny are reported in various contexts, from the verbal ammunition of the pro-pagan opponents of foreign missionaries in Iceland *c.* 1000 to the numerous personal quarrels represented in family sagas (see Almqvist, *Norrön niddiktning*). In all cases *níð* verses serve to undermine a person's (normally a man's) honour, usually by casting doubt on his sexuality as a measure of his manliness.[8] Underlying the psychodynamics of these poetic genres is the idea that poetry has the power to affect its victims with physical harm and mental hurt. It was often the vehicle for sorcery, that is, the practice of magical arts that were supposed to have particular effects upon their victims, whether physical or mental. *Mansǫngskvæði* or love poetry is mentioned in the Icelandic lawcode *Grágás* as something strictly forbidden, along with *níð* poetry, and there is no doubt that it was thought capable of turning a woman's affection to a particular man, without her knowledge and often against her will. Some of the runic scraps of poetry that have survived from the Bryggen quarter (the Hanseatic merchants' quarter) of Bergen in Norway reveal an active culture of such poetry even after the Viking Age.

An important attribute of poetry in Old Norse culture was that it was conceptualised as a vehicle for conveying major truths which, in pagan times, were believed to derive from the Norse gods. The myth of the origin of poetry as an intoxicating drink formed from the gods' spittle endorses this traditional view. Snorri Sturluson narrates a version of the myth in the early chapters of the section of his *Edda* dealing with poetic diction (*Skáldskaparmál*).[9] This mythic narrative is the basis for most of the many self-reflexive images for poetic composition in the works of Old Norse skalds. As Snorri's *Edda* puts it, 'því kǫllum vér skáldskapinn feng Óðins ok fund ok drykk hans ok gjǫf hans ok drykk Ásanna' ('Thus we call poetry Odin's booty and find, and his drink and his gift and the Æsir's [gods'] drink'; I, p. 5). Clever poets rang the changes on these basic kenning-types and applied them self-consciously to their own poetic efforts, as a certain Icelandic poet named Steinþórr did:

---

[8] See Meulengracht Sørensen, *Unmanly Man*, and Almqvist, *Norrön niddiktning*. Many associate the term *skáld* for a court poet with the satirical function (compare the English *scold*). See Steblin-Kamenskij, 'On the Etymology of the Word *skáld*'.

[9] Snorri Sturluson, *Edda, Skáldskaparmál*, I, pp. 3–5; tr. Faulkes, pp. 61–4. The story goes that two previously hostile groups of gods generate a wise being, Kvasir, from their own spittle which they mingle in a cauldron as a pledge of peace. Kvasir is killed and his blood fermented by a pair of dwarves who add honey to it: 'it turned into the mead whoever drinks from which becomes a poet or a scholar'. Then members of the giant race came to own the mead. A certain Suttungr immured it in a rocky fortress and placed his daughter Gunnlǫð in charge of it. Óðinn set out to gain the mead for the gods and, after various adventures, went to where Gunnlǫð was and lay with her for three nights and then she let him drink three draughts of the mead. He turned himself into an eagle and, with Suttungr in hot pursuit, also in eagle form, flew back to the home of the gods, where the deities had thoughtfully placed a series of containers in the courtyard to catch the regurgitated mead that Óðinn spat out. On the name Kvasir see Frank, 'Snorri and the Mead of Poetry', pp. 159–61.

Forngervan á ek firnum
farms Gunnlaðar arma
horna fors at hrósa
hlítstyggs ok þó lítinn

(*Skáldskaparmál*, I, p. 9).

[I am mightily proud of my ancient horn-cascade [mead of poetry] of the meanness-avoiding cargo of Gunnlǫð's embrace [Óðinn], though it be meagre.]

Here the antithesis between divine plenitude and human inadequacy provides an indigenous modesty topos that builds on the idea that poetry is a gift from the gods to human poets. Yet the gift does not come unsolicited or to the unprepared; only those who are skilled at composing poetry (*er yrkja kunnu*) can receive Óðinn's gift. Thus skill and inspiration both play their parts in the process of human poetic composition according to the Norse mythic model, with neither working well without the other.

The myth of the poetic mead may be interpreted in the following way. Poetry, being both a skill (*íþrótt*) and an inspiration from the gods (*óðr*, 'rhapsody'; compare Óðinn, 'Odin, the inspired one, the frenzied one'), belongs to two worlds envisaged in Old Norse mythological texts: the world of ordered intellectual control presided over by the gods and the world of natural processes, where the giants were dominant. Natural processes included birth, the unpredictable tenor of life (where fate was operative) and death. There was a tendency, in this as in other mythologies, to align the natural world with the feminine and see the world of culturally determined order as a masculine sphere. Poetry belongs to the male world but, in generating it, the gods mimic female processes of giving birth: their spitting into a cauldron generates the wise being Kvasir while Óðinn's swallowing and regurgitating of the mead makes it fruitful for the life of the mind. Poets, then, are creative beings, but their very creativity makes them unruly as well as powerful (hence the representation of poetry as an intoxicating alcoholic liquid).[10] Their ambivalent social role is expressed in many Icelandic sagas, where they are frequently portrayed as dark, difficult to deal with and inclined to be antisocial.[11]

There is another kind of evidence for Old Norse literary theory and poetics which is different from the often implicit, traditionally based sources we have considered so far. It is provided by a substantial group of overtly theorising texts, which include Snorri Sturluson's *Edda*, and are preserved within manuscripts that also contain the *Edda* in full or in part. Four so-called *Grammatical Treatises* and a fragment of a fifth

[10] I examine these aspects of the myth of the mead of poetry in *Prolonged Echoes*, pp. 150–2, 216–18.
[11] See Clunies Ross, 'The Skald Sagas as a Genre'.

have been preserved in these manuscripts.[12] The treatises date from the middle of the twelfth century to the mid-fourteenth century. They are all in Icelandic and display an independent attitude to their subject-matter, which derives from the Christian Latin educational tradition to a greater or lesser extent. It is possible, indeed, as Guðrún Nordal has suggested in *Tools of Literacy*, that Icelandic schools may have practised verse composition in Icelandic as well as in Latin in the medieval period. Recent approaches to the manuscripts containing these treatises emphasise that their parts should not only be seen as separate, free-standing works but as parts of a tradition of creative compilation and poetic commentary that extended into the modern period in Iceland.[13] The compilations reveal an interest in a variety of issues in medieval grammar and poetics, from phonology and orthography to poetic diction and metrics, and, in Snorri's *Edda*, the relation between poetic language and Old Norse myth.

At least a grounding in the Latin schoolroom tradition must be assumed for the writers of all the theoretical texts mentioned here, though the depth of their knowledge probably varied considerably. Snorri Sturluson's Latin education is the least certain, though he was undoubtedly a man whose knowledge of traditional Norse culture was encyclopaedic. It is likely that he had the rudiments of a Latin education, and some awareness of contemporary poetic theory, at least as hearsay. If he had had more, it has been suggested, he could not have composed such a free and original treatise as his *Edda*.[14] The authors of the four *Grammatical Treatises* were certainly acquainted with Latin sources, though in all cases they adopt an independent, if not an original, approach to their material.

Snorri Sturluson's *Edda* is without doubt the most important Old Norse contribution to medieval literary theory and arguably one of the most interesting and original theoretical works of the European Middle Ages.

---

[12] The major medieval manuscripts of Snorri's *Edda* are the Codex Regius (R, Reykjavik, Stofnun Árna Magnússonar, formerly Copenhagen, Old Royal Collection, MS 2367, 4to, written about the middle of the first half of the fourteenth century); the Codex Wormianus (W, Copenhagen, Arnamagnæan Institute, Arnamagnæan MS 242 fol., written *c*. 1350–70); the Codex Trajectinus (T, Utrecht, University Library, MS 1374, *c*.1600 but based on a lost medieval exemplar), and Codex Upsaliensis (U, Uppsala, University Library, MS De La Gardie 11, 8vo, of the early fourteenth century). W also contains the four *Grammatical Treatises* and a preface; U contains the *Second Grammatical Treatise*. Two other medieval manuscripts, both now in the Stofnun Arna Magnússonar, Reykjavik, Arnamagnæan MSS 748 1b 4to (A) and 757 a 4to (B), which contain parts of *Skáldskaparmál* (the third part of Snorri's *Edda*), also include parts of the *Third Grammatical Treatise*. For fuller details, see Snorri Sturluson, *Edda: Prologue and Gylfaginning*, ed. Faulkes, pp. xxix–xxx, and Snorri Sturluson, *Edda Snorra Sturlusonar*, ed. Jónsson, pp. iii–xvii.

[13] See Krömmelbein, 'Creative Compilers', and Johansson, *Studier i Codex Wormianus*. For the post-medieval tradition, see Sturluson, *Two Versions*, ed. Faulkes, and Jón Guðmundson, laerði, *Eddurit . . .* , ed. Pétursson.

[14] See Faulkes, 'The Sources of *Skáldskaparmál*'. Amory, 'Second Thoughts on *Skáldskaparmál*', also doubts whether Snorri had much knowledge of the Latin tradition.

Its date of composition is not precisely known but is probably *c.* 1225; the oldest manuscript that contains it (U) ascribes its compilation to Snorri Sturluson (1179–1241), a member of a powerful Icelandic family which was deeply involved in Icelandic and Norwegian politics. The work is in four parts. It begins with a prologue, which places Old Norse pre-Christian myth and religion in the context of medieval Christian explanations for pagan beliefs. *Gylfaginning* ('The Deception of Gylfi') follows, an account of Old Norse cosmology, cosmogony and eschatology set in a narrative frame, which allows a legendary Swedish king named Gylfi to question a fictional trinity of deities, High, Equally High and Third, about the major pre-Christian myths. The purpose of this section, which is illustrated with quotations from eddic mythological poetry, is to give an overview of Norse mythology as required background knowledge to the third section of the *Edda*, *Skáldskaparmál* ('Poetic Diction').

Skáldskaparmál begins with some discursive material, including the myth of the origin of poetry, but leads into a fairly systematic enumeration and exemplification of the major kenning-types of Old Norse skaldic poetry from the works of the chief skalds. Topics covered include kennings for the gods and goddesses, men and women, gold, weapons, battle, ships, animals and birds of various kinds. Some mythic narratives appear here to explain the origin of certain kennings. After the lists of kenning-types comes a list of *heiti* or poetic synonyms for major topics in Old Norse poetry. The fourth part of the *Edda*, *Háttatal* ('List of Verse-Forms'), is most like a formal school treatise and has clear associations with the type of Latin metrical treatise known as *clavis metrica* ('metrical key'). This may have been the first section of the *Edda* that Snorri composed. It takes the form of 102 stanzas in praise of the Norwegian king Hákon Hákonarson and his father-in-law Duke Skúli, each exemplifying a different Norse verse-form. The poem, with commentary, is preceded by an explanation of the formal characteristics of skaldic poetry (alliteration and rhyme), the various verse-forms and a brief account of rhetorical devices (including different kinds of kenning) which overlaps material in *Skáldskaparmál* to some degree. Snorri had at least one native model for *Háttatal*. A poem named *Háttalykill* ('Key of Metres') had been composed by the Icelander Hallr Þórarinsson and Jarl Rǫgnvaldr of Orkney some time in the 1140s and was almost certainly known to Snorri.

That Snorri intended his *Edda* as an *ars poetica* is indicated by the work's title, which has medieval authority and is probably an Icelandic formation upon the Latin verb *edere*, 'to write, publish or compose poetry'. At one point early in *Skáldskaparmál*, direct reference is made to 'young poets, who desire to learn the language of poetry [*mál skáldskapar*] and to furnish themselves with a wide vocabulary using traditional terms'. This declaration is followed by a passage which indicates how Christians are to use and understand pagan beliefs and the traditional poetry which was imbued with them. They should not consign these things to oblivion nor demonstrate them to be false; rather they should understand them as truths qualified by their forefathers' lack of Christian enlightenment. Such a detached and non-polemical approach to Old Norse myth (it also utilises euhemerism) informs the whole *Edda*. Snorri clearly wished to preserve the traditional myth and poetry of Iceland as a serious subject of study, though this does not prevent him from treating many of his mythic subjects with humour and possibly with irony.[15] There is no other work of medieval European vernacular scholarship which can compare with Snorri's in its breadth of treatment and independence of attitude to its material. Only the Irish, whose treatises on vernacular poetry were almost certainly unknown to him, produced metrical treatises about indigenous verse. Another, major, contribution to the *Edda*'s unique scope and form comes from its incorporation of a treatise on myth within the text in such a way that poetics and mythography form an integrated whole. Many people value Snorri's mythic narratives for their own sake, but they cannot be understood fully out of context. Moreover, he illustrates them with extensive quotation from his primary sources, the eddic and skaldic poetry which he knew from oral tradition and, possibly, in a few written compilations.

Of the four *Grammatical Treatises*, only the *Third* and *Fourth* concern poetic theory, the *First* and *Second* dealing with the sounds and spelling system of Old Icelandic.[16] The *Third* and *Fourth Grammatical Treatises* are fully within the Latin educational tradition. Though the *Third* includes material on the theory of sound and of writing, with a very interesting section on the runic alphabet, and offers some independent remarks on skaldic rhetoric, including a good deal of information on the native names of rhetorical figures, it largely follows the structure and content of the grammars of Priscian and Donatus. The *Third Grammatical Treatise* was written by Snorri Sturluson's nephew Óláfr Þórðarson some time between 1245 and the date of his death in 1259, doubtless for use in the school

---

[15] Holtsmark, *Studier i Snorres mytologi*, has argued for the latter and sees a deliberate parody of Christian doctrine in *Gylfaginning*.

[16] Two articles by Raschellà, 'Die altisländische grammatische Literatur' and 'Grammatical Treatises', give a good overview; individual editions of the four *Grammatical Treatises* are by H. Benediktsson (*First*, c. 1125–75), Fabrizio D. Raschellà (*Second*, c. 1270–1300) and Björn M. Ólsen (*Third*, c. 1245–52 and *Fourth*, c. 1340s). The *Third Grammatical Treatise* has recently become available in a new edition by T. Krömmelbein, though based on Ólsen's text, with a German translation, introduction and notes. Wills has a new edition and English translation of the first part of this work, while Collings provides an English translation of its second part. For Icelandic knowledge of European literary theory in Latin in the thirteenth and fourteenth centuries see Foote, 'Latin Rhetoric and Icelandic Poetry'.

he established at Stafaholt. Óláfr's chief debts are to Books 1 and 2 of Priscian's *Institutiones grammaticae* and to the third part of Donatus' *Ars maior*, but he clearly had access to other writings. In the first nine chapters his treatise gives a vernacular summary of Priscian's analysis of the various parts of speech, together with additional material, some of which seems to show a debt to near-contemporary logical treatises in its discussion of sound and voice. Óláfr then gives an Icelandic version of the third part of Donatus' *Ars maior*, in Chapters 10–16, a section that has been known in Iceland since at least the seventeenth century as *Málskrúðsfræði*, 'knowledge of the ornaments of diction'. The text of Donatus Óláfr used was probably mediated by a more recent commentary, which Micillo ('Die grammatische Tradition') has demonstrated is likely to have been in the ninth-century insular tradition.

Chapter 16 is an expansion of Donatus' treatment of figures and tropes, and attempts to show how the stylistic resources of skaldic poetry and native poetic terminology to some extent correspond to those of the classical inheritance. Óláfr's underlying argument, that both Latin and Old Norse poetics were derived from the language and literature of the ancient classical world, almost certainly builds on the thesis of the prologue to Snorri's *Edda*, but differs from it in an important respect. Unlike Snorri, who espouses the euhemerist theory of the translation of the Æsir (the Norse gods) from Asia direct to Scandinavia, bringing with them their language and poetry, which can therefore be seen to be one, Óláfr sees knowledge and learning coming to the north in the conventional *translatio studii* from Greece and Rome. In addition, and importantly, he argues that the equivalence between the Norse and classical traditions can be discovered from Donatus' book, a written source, which has set out the faults and ornaments of Latin poetry. It then follows that, in order to bring out the Norse parallels to these Latin figures, he must subject vernacular poetry to the model of Donatus' Latin, and this is what he does. The task Óláfr set himself was to follow Donatus in expounding the faults and beauties of poetic diction, and to illustrate them with examples from Old Norse poetry that supposedly revealed the same principles of composition as Donatus' Latin examples. The extent to which he was able – or not able – to do this constitutes the real interest and originality of Óláfr's *Málskrúðsfræði* as a work of literary theory.

Many of Óláfr's comparisons between classical and Norse rhetorical figures are more remarkable for the ingenuity of his arguments and what they reveal about Norse practice than for the scientific equivalences of the two poetic traditions. A number are inexact comparisons or stretch the classical definition somewhat (Collings, *Málskrúðsfræði*, pp. 67–8), while others are really comparing quite different things or, if there is a valid analogy, the phenomena are of very different importance in the two systems. This inequality is most obvious in Chapters 15, 'De scemalexeo', and 16, 'De tropo et metaphoræ', where Óláfr argues for the equivalence of some of the most important principles of Old Norse poetry with the rhetorical devices of the classical system. The analogy between *paronomasia* and *aðalhending* is quite misleading and fails to establish the central impor- tance of full internal rhyme to Norse poetics. Thus, both here and in his discussion of other central features of Norse poetics like the kenning and alliteration, Óláfr is obliged to add a prose comment on how structurally or conceptually important in Norse (but not in classical poetry) the feature is. We hear that alliteration 'holds together Norse poetry just as the nails hold together a ship', though the same could not be said for *paranomeon*, with which it is aligned in the classical system. Although, unlike Snorri, Óláfr equates the various forms of the kenning with the figure *metaphora*, the classical frame of reference within which he is obliged to discuss it fails to do justice to the complexity and vigour of the Old Norse kenning. He is hampered both by the classical definition of *metaphora* as a transfer of meaning from one word to another for various reasons and by the actual significance of *metaphora* in classical poetry, where it is far less important and far simpler than the Norse kenning, nor do all the features of the kenning appear in classical poetry. As Tranter has observed ('Medieval Icelandic *Artes Poeticae*', p. 146), Óláfr was probably aware that he was skating on thin ice in proposing this equivalence, and so attempts to bol- ster his argument (though in fact he weakens it still further) by quoting an example from Ovid which, as Tranter says, 'is almost laughable in its simplicity' when compared with the Old Norse kenning.[17]

The *Fourth Grammatical Treatise* was probably composed nearly a cen- tury after Óláfr's work, and is generally dated to somewhere between 1340 and 1350. It can be seen as a continuation and completion of the second part of the *Third Grammatical Treatise*, *Málskrúðsfræði*, using some of the newer treatises on poetics that had presumably by then become more widely available in Iceland than they were in Óláfr's day. Its unknown author drew on two of the most influential textbooks of the later twelfth and early thirteenth centuries, the *Doctrinale* of Alexander of Villa Dei (*c*. 1199) and the *Graecismus* of Évrard of Béthune (a little before 1212). Although these works were not part of the new speculative grammar, based on logical principles, that dominated some of the twelfth-century French schools, notably at the University of Paris, they did make available a new digest of the works of Priscian and Donatus, taking account of more recent commentaries. They were intended for students who had already

---

[17] This is the only place in *Málskrúðsfræði* where Óláfr actually quotes Latin verse examples, all the others being Norse. This strongly suggests special pleading.

mastered the rudiments of *grammatica*, and were both written in hexameter verse, which, however, was not imitated by the Fourth Grammarian. The inventories of medieval Icelandic religious houses indicate that these two influential works reached Iceland and were used by communities of scholars there. The Fourth Grammarian may also have been the author of a short preface to all four grammatical treatises in the Codex Wormianius (*Den tredje og fjærde grammatiske afhandling*, ed. Ólsen, pp. 152–5).

The *Fourth Grammatical Treatise* is based mainly on a section called 'de figuris grammaticis' which was appended to Chapter 12 of Alexander's *Doctrinale* and includes four figures, *brachylogia*, *climax*, *sinacriamos* and *teretema*, which were defined in Chapters 1–4 of Évrard's *Graecismus*. Aside from its sources, the treatise is noteworthy for its many verse quotations (sixty-two separate quotations), some of them quite long, which the author, like Óláfr Þórðarson, uses to exemplify his cited figures. A high proportion of these verse quotations are from Christian skaldic poetry, and, it is surmised, a number which are not attributed to a named author were probably composed by the Fourth Grammarian himself, who was almost certainly a cleric of some kind. Little recent research has been carried out on this work, but it would now repay study in the light of the current interest in the thirteenth- and fourteenth-century poetic tradition in Iceland.[18] Like Óláfr's treatise, the *Fourth Grammatical Treatise* is far from slavish in its use of Alexander and Évrard and – probably – other sources. We see here a witness to the continuing life of skaldic poetry and poetic theory in Iceland during the fourteenth century, particularly in the schools and religious houses of the island.

In summary, the Icelandic contribution to the subject of medieval criticism and literary theory was considerable. Icelandic historians and other prose writers showed an awareness of medieval Latin genres and were concerned to differentiate between kinds of text on the basis of their presumed truthfulness, but they were confident enough of their own traditions not to develop much in the way of overt comparison between their own and foreign genres. Theoretical discussion is recorded mainly in the field of poetry and poetics, subjects valued particularly highly in the native tradition and given a boost by the Icelanders' acquaintance with the Latin tradition of grammatical rhetoric taught in medieval Icelandic schools. Although little of this corpus has been influential outside Iceland and, from the seventeenth century onward, among scholars of Old Norse, medieval Icelandic ideas about poetry and poetics have a unique importance and contribute to our understanding of early Germanic

---

[18] Guðrún Nordal, *Tools of Literacy*, has included some discussion of this poetry, fifty-one out of sixty-two examples of which are of unknown origin, i.e. they are not attributed to named poets.

poetics, Old Norse poetry, both eddic and skaldic, and the myths that formed its conceptual base. Only in the Icelandic poetic treatises do we find a medieval vernacular account of indigenous poetics and an explanation of features such as alliteration, stress and rhyme, and other stylistic figures that appear in all medieval Germanic verse-forms and have been the subject of much modern scholarship in the fields of both metrics and poetic diction.

Part V

Vernacular critical traditions: the late Middle Ages

Latin commentary tradition
and vernacular literature

Ralph Hanna, Tony Hunt, R. G. Keightley, Alastair Minnis
and Nigel F. Palmer

'Translation [*translatio*] is the exposition of meaning through another language [*expositio sententiae per aliam linguam*]', claims Hugutio of Pisa
in the *Magnae derivationes* which he compiled between 1197 and 1201.[1]
That sentiment, which is rooted in grammatical theory, makes it abundantly clear that medieval 'translation' does not mean merely the production of a replacement text: exposition, exegesis, interpretation (however
one wishes to denote hermeneutic process) is involved as well. Hence in
a twelfth-century gloss on Priscian *interpretatio* is defined as the exposition (*expositio*) of one language through another, and in his *Summa
super Priscianum* Peter Helias describes *interpretatio* as 'translatio de
una loquela in aliam'.[2] Such theoretical discourse is echoed in one of
the most widely disseminated vernacular prefaces of the later Middle
Ages, Jean de Meun's introduction to his French Boethius (*c.* 1300). If
he had 'expounded [*expons*] the Latin by the French word by word', Jean
explains, the book would have been too obscure for laymen' and clerks of
moderate learning would have found it difficult to understand the Latin
from the French. Therefore he has opted for a freer form of translation –
an activity which, quite clearly, remains inseparable from *expositio*.

The activities of *expositio* or *interpretatio* and *translatio* were complexly interrelated. This chapter seeks to explore some of those relationships, with reference to late-medieval English, French, German and
Spanish literary traditions. It will range from quite pedestrian vernacular
renderings of standard glosses along with the texts which they expounded,
to exceptionally sophisticated exploitations of the techniques – and the
scholarly prestige – of commentary in the valorisation of texts composed
anew in the emergent European languages. What follows is, of course,
only part of the story, since the present volume cannot accommodate
either biblical exegesis or the vernacular translations and paraphrases of
scriptural texts in which biblical exegesis inevitably played a part. We

---

[1] Oxford, Bodleian Library, MS Bodley 376, fol. 84r. This statement is repeated in John
Balbus of Genoa's *Catholicon* (1286), s.v. *glossa*, a dictionary which is heavily dependent
on Hugutio's. When defining *interpres*, John explains that 'an interpreter is in between
two languages when he translates or expounds one language through another'.
[2] R. W. Hunt, 'Lost Preface', pp. 155, 156.

have, however, included a particularly striking and controversial case, the debate over the English Bible: here John Wyclif's followers were ranged against an ecclesiastical establishment (supported by kings both Plantagenet and Lancastrian) which sought to control access to the sacred text and vigorously rejected the notion that English could cope with its intricacies and do justice to its sublimities. Thus theoretical issues concerning the *translatio* of textual authority from Latin to vernacular were raised in a particularly acute, and dangerous, way.

The mainly secular texts which are discussed below amply illustrate the various ways in which translation could be seen as *expositio sententiae*, a kind of commentary, and how translation could draw on the resources of formal academic commentary to help it render an *auctor*'s words *in vulgari*. Such translation could itself be accompanied by glosses or a fullscale commentary, whether in Latin or some vernacular. Most remarkably of all, commentary proved that it was capable of change within new cultural contexts and in line with the needs of new audiences, some of which were lay and indeed mixed, including women readers. Socially, commentary found new sources of energy (as when Dante enlisted its services in the promotion of his 'illustrious vernacular') and of sponsorship (for example, in the ostentatious state-sponsorship of 'commentated translation' by King Alfonso X of Castile and King Charles V of France). Intellectually, commentary moved far beyond the pedagogic parameters of the schools to accompany vernacular works of a kind which were never (and never could be) part of a school curriculum. But, first things first: let us begin with some configurations of text and gloss which clearly bear the stamp of the schools.

1. Translating text and gloss

The major 'school' texts of the Middle Ages – those works prescribed for study in medieval schools of the arts and higher sciences (theology being the queen of the sciences) – were prime candidates for translation into the vernacular, and when this happened sometimes certain glosses were transmitted along with the texts they had accompanied. Major early examples of this phenomenon are afforded by the translations of Boethius' *De consolatione philosophiae* by King Alfred of England and Notker of St Gall (= Notker Teutonicus, Notker Labeo; *c.* 950–1022), both of which make heavy use of commentary materials. The Alfredian version, dating from the 890s and the first ever vernacular version of the work, is full of extensive interpolations from glosses and (it has been argued) certain authoritative texts of which the king's impressive circle of scholars had firsthand knowledge. Notker's version, the earliest continental translation, is a bilingual text where the Latin is quoted in full, usually with simplified word order, and each sentence or short section is followed by a free German paraphrase and commentary. During the Twelfth-Century Renaissance this kind of translation was frequent. Three Anglo-Norman translations of the *Disticha Catonis*, for example, were made during that century, by an anonymous scholar, by Everard, and by Elias of Winchester respectively, all of whom made use of the commentary attributed to the ninth-century polymath Remigius of Auxerre. This commentary, however, was not accorded any formal recognition within the verse translation. The Anonymous and Everard include the Latin text of the *Disticha* (but no part of the commentary), while Elias of Winchester, who provides a quite virtuoso versification, does not (though the Latin has been inserted in one of the manuscripts). In the following century a further three French translations are made on the Continent – by Adam de Suel, Jean de Chastelet and an anonymous Lotharingian. The first two certainly knew Remigius' commentary, but none of the three provides the Latin text of the *Disticha*; however, it has been inserted in a small number of the manuscripts of Adam's work. Thus, whilst exegesis is used to take these writers beyond literal translation, there is no formal recognition of text and gloss.

This level of use of commentary by translators continued throughout the Middle Ages – a point which may be illustrated in the first instance by reference to the French and English traditions of *De consolatione philosophiae*. Jean de Meun's dominantly literal prose translation makes occasional use of a version of the William of Conches commentary – but, interestingly, the French work draws on the Latin prologue to another commentary, that of William of Aragon, dating from the late-thirteenth century.[3] (The preface to a late-thirteenth or early-fourteenth-century prose translation, uniquely preserved in Troyes, Bibliothèque municipale, MS 898, also seems to have made use of this Latin prologue.[4]) William of Aragon had made ostentatious reference to the new Aristotelian learning, and presumably it was that up-to-date quality which attracted Jean to it, in preference to the prologue of the Neoplatonist William of Conches. Subsequently Jean's version of the Aragon prologue, with its dedication to Philip the Fair, was used as the introduction to the most popular of all the Old French translations of the *Consolatio*, the so-called 'Anonymous Verse-Prose Version' (*c.* 1360) which in its two states survives in some fifty-nine manuscripts.[5] Geoffrey Chaucer made use of Jean's version and Nicholas Trevet's highly popular Latin commentary (before 1307) in producing his Middle English *Boece*; it is possible that a few details not

3 See Crespo, 'Il Prologo'.
4 See [Boethius], *Eine altfranzösische Übersetzung der 'Consolatio philosophiae'*, ed. Schroth.
5 See Cropp, 'Le Prologue'. No modern edition is yet available of this translation.

paralleled in either of these sources came from interlinear glosses deriving from the Boethius-commentary associated with Remigius of Auxerre.[6] These sources Chaucer wove together with some dexterity. Typically, he seems to have begun by translating the French, perhaps because its syntax more closely resembled English than did the Latin. But he then read the results of this preliminary Englishing against the Latin and corrected the translation to reflect the source text. The major alterations occur in the lexis, which Chaucer brought into close accord with the original, either by rejecting Jean's equivalents or by supplementing them with doublets from the Latin. And finally, Chaucer interpolated a vast amount of material, designed to explain a variety of obscurities, from the commentary tradition.

Some of Chaucer's readers sought to extend these glossarial activities: a sporadic series of interlinear glosses is found in most of the surviving *Boece* manuscripts (but is not authorial). The work seems to have been particularly subject to such treatment, since many copies belonged to persons who were learned, if not academics; they apparently intended to use the text as an English aid to Latin obscurities. This purpose may explain the most elaborate layout in which the *Boece* figures, as found in Cambridge, University Library, MS Ii.3.21, originally owned by John Crowcher, Dean of Chichester. It provides the Latin text alongside the English, the Latin being indexed and glossed with very substantial portions of Trevet's commentary; all this is followed by a second (and this time a complete) commentary, that of William of Aragon.

Chaucer provided no prologue to his translation, an omission which two redactors of his work sought to remedy. First, the version of Book 1 of the *Boece* found uniquely in Oxford, Bodleian Library, MS Auct. F. 3. 5 begins with an extensive prologue which partly corresponds to one of the typical forms of the *accessus ad auctorem*. The anonymous writer declares his respect for 'the entent of the auctour' and discusses Boethius' 'name' and 'the titil of this boke' (compare the *accessus* headings *intentio auctoris*, *nomen auctoris* and *titulus libri*), and provides details of the author's life, death and works of the kind traditionally found in medieval *vitae Boethii*. Secondly, the epilogue in William Caxton's 1478 printed edition of the *Boece* contains information which one would normally expect in a prologue: the name of the book, its material, the life of the author, and the authorial intention (compare the headings *nomen libri*, *materia*, *vita auctoris* and *intentio auctoris*). Caxton's life of Boethius bears strong resemblances to one of the standard *vitae Boethii*. Furthermore, when John Walton made his all-verse English translation of *De consolatione philosophiae* (1410) he used both the Chaucer translation and Trevet's

---

[6] See Minnis, '"Glosynge"'. The commentaries by Remigius, Trevet and William of Aragon remain unedited.

commentary; moreover, one of his prologues draws on the Latin prologue with which Trevet had introduced his commentary.

Another variant can be found in the 'anonymous interpolated' Spanish version of the *Consolatio* which survives in two fifteenth-century manuscripts. The text keeps quite close to the Latin, but regularly adds glosses (which usually can be traced back to Trevet) to explain proper names or unfamiliar terms. The truly distinctive feature of this version is its prologue, which, unlike those of other Spanish translations of the *Consolatio* (which also rely principally on Trevet for their material), resembles most closely the prologue which introduces the 'Pseudo-Aquinas' Boethius commentary as it appears in various early printings. But there are some important modifications. Pseudo-Aquinas had replaced Trevet's neat Aristotelian set of four causes with five *premittenda*; the Spanish text presents 'seven matters or roots which need to be known before beginning a book, the better to understand what it has to say'. First comes a statement of the subject-matter of the work, followed by its purpose and the circumstances in which it was created. Next comes the identity of the author and the title of the work; on the latter an unnamed philosopher's remark is quoted: 'if the book's title is lost, the page remains silent and darkened, and no man knows what it is about'. The sixth 'root' is the work's philosophical category: natural, logical or moral. Finally there is the notion of mode and form, which in this instance is didactic dialogue in five books, which are briefly summarised. The attempt to restrict the categories to seven is somewhat spoiled by a second and fuller statement of the central moral lesson of the *Consolatio* with which the prologue ends.

A similar level of glossing is evident in a mid-thirteenth-century Spanish translation of Lucan's *Pharsalia* (*De bello civili*), which forms a major part of Book 5 of King Alfonso X's *General estoria* (on which, more later). In all five of the extant manuscripts the text is presented in essentially the same manner, beginning with an exiguous *accessus*. Lucan's Andalusian origin and the subject-matter of his poem lead into brief definitions of the kinds of war, by way of explaining the first line of the poem, 'Bella plus quam civilia'. Thereafter the text follows the poem, in loose paraphrase rather than direct translation, and drawing on glosses from time to time. Identifications of the various speakers are regularly included. Other standard glosses supply the basic facts on people, places and movements of the heavenly bodies; given Lucan's traditional status as historian rather than poet, allegory is apparently off the agenda. This attitude is particularly remarkable in Book 4's account of Hercules and Antaeus, where the readily accessible euhemeristic and allegorical treatments of the myth are simply ignored.

Not all translators, of course, were content to stay with the basic commentary. Some went farther afield in their search for material with which the original text could be amplified. Jacob van Maerlant's *Alexanders geesten* (*c.* 1260), a Dutch verse adaptation of Walter of Châtillon's Latin poem the *Alexandreis*, makes extensive use of the interlinear and marginal glosses which accompany the *Alexandreis* in most manuscripts. Some of the marginal glosses draw on Peter Comestor's *Historia scholastica*, and much of this material has been taken over by Jacob. But those particular glosses seem to have also served as a signpost to the Dutch author, who apparently went back to the *Historia* itself to find further information to incorporate into his Alexander poem. Another enterprising translator was the Picard scholar responsible for a fourteenth-century translation-commentary of the *Consolatio* (probably from Hainaut).[7] In addition to a commentary in the William of Conches tradition he also consulted, for the historical part of his prologue, the *Chronicon* of Sigebert of Gembloux, and for his interpolated comments, Helinand of Froidmont's *Chronicon*, Fulgentius, the Vatican Mythographers, the 'Bernard Silvester' commentary on the *Aeneid*, and perhaps William of Aragon's Latin commentary on *De consolatione philosophiae*. This scholar is very much an interpreter as well as a translator. His commentary is original in the same sense as a typical Latin commentary, in that it comprises a selection and adaptation from within an already established tradition of commentary, new materials being assimilated within the standard pattern.

Even greater intellectual enthusiasm and editorial energy mark Gavin Douglas' plan to write a commentary to accompany his Middle Scots translation of the *Aeneid* (1553):

> I haue alsso a schort comment compylyt
> To expoun strange histouris and termys wild . . .
>
> (conclusion, 'Heir the translatar . . .', ll. 141–2)

In his text and gloss Douglas refers to, and draws on, the commentaries of Servius, Cristoforo Landino ('that writis moraly apon Virgill'),[8] Lorenzo Valla, and Josse Badius Ascensius in the 1507 version. Either all of these accompanied the original text in the printed edition of Virgil that he used – printed editions containing as many as five commentaries had been published – or Douglas brought together materials which he found in separate copies of the *Aeneid*. Yet he was not content to rely on the commentaries of others; it is evident that scholarly sources were consulted at first hand, such as Augustine's *De civitate Dei*, Boccaccio's *Genealogia deorum gentilium* and Livy's *Ab urbe condita* (which, Douglas assures us, has greater authority than the 'pevach [peevish] and corrupt' Guido delle Colonne). Unfortunately, as we have it the commentary ends halfway

---

[7] See Atkinson, 'A Fourteenth-Century Picard Translation-Commentary'.
[8] Gloss on I.iii.100; ed. Coldwell, II, p. 29.

through the translation of Book I. Presumably this is all that Douglas wrote, but his intention of continuing the commentary is indicated by the promise, 'of Venus and hir son Cupyd I sall say sum thyng in the x c. of this sam buke' (2.41). Moreover, it may be noted that Douglas regarded his entire translation-project as, in some measure, a work of academic commentary. This comes out, for example, in his remark that one 'proffit' of his book will be its usefulness to those who 'Virgill to childryn expone'. Such teachers should acknowledge their debt to him: 'Thank me tharfor, masteris of grammar sculys' (conclusion, 'Heir the translatar . . .', ll. 41–8).

2. Elaborating the gloss

Moving to consider more elaborate uses of school glosses and glossing techniques, we may begin with a fourteenth-century French translation of a grammar-school text, the *Ecloga* of 'Theodulus', which (along with the *Disticha Catonis*) formed part of the standard group of authors known as the *Liber Catonianus* (compare the relevant discussion in Chapters 1, 5 and 6 above). The French adaptor, possibly the minorite Jaquemon Bochet (writing in the first third of the fourteenth century), sets out to render the *Ecloga* in octosyllabic couplets, but he was careful to distinguish text and gloss, and the formal distinction has been attentively observed by the scribe of the unique surviving manuscript, in which each translated stanza is boxed in red and followed by the word *gloze*, rubrics and explicits being also marked in red. The adaptor calls his work *Tiaudelet* and prefaces it with his own prologue of 136 lines, in which he follows one of the standard *accessus* models by discussing the author, the title of the work, and, in this case, a major source, which is said to have been 'Ovide le grand' (i.e. the *Metamorphoses*; l. 33). Ovid, we are told, expressed himself subtly, describing actions 'en exemplez couvertement / par tres soubtil entendement' (ll. 39–40). Through such *samblanches* and *exemplez* it is possible to penetrate to the inner sense ('au sens / qui estoit couvers par dedens'; ll. 43–4). The adaptor goes on to explain that when 'Theodulus' had digested the *Metamorphoses* and fully imbibed its meaning ('le sens cognut'), he studied Holy Scripture which is inexhaustible in its richness and its transparency ('sans falasse et sans fiction / et sans nulle deception'; ll. 53–4). 'Theodulus' saw that the two works resembled each other, partly following the same path, and he therefore drew on both and placed comparable passages side-by-side in units of four verses. In admiration of the resulting work the French translator has sought to reveal and expound the 'sens grans et parfond couvers' (l. 104). Latin, he claims, is more concise than French ('Latin parolle plus briefment /

que romman') and he has therefore expanded the four-line strophes of the original to twelve-line units (ll. 113–14). After this explanation of his task he renders the prologue of the *Ecloga* (thirty-six lines) in 118 lines, the final fourteen of which are his own defence of the *gloze*. The dispute of Pseustis and Alithia is that between falsehood and truth and so the translator has sought in his *gloze* to expound (*exposer*) what has been said allegorically (*en figure*) so that nothing remains obscure. This *gloze* certainly draws on medieval Latin commentaries, most of which are still in need of investigation.

Three different Old French translations of the *Parabolae* attributed to Alan of Lille, which formed a component of the *Liber Catonianus* in the enlarged form known as the *Auctores octo*, differ from each other in their adoption of exegetical techniques.[9] A partial Anglo-Norman translation of the thirteenth century presents alternating Latin and French sections of text, the latter being written in the unique manuscript in red (more normally reserved for Latin). The translation is in prose and does not always render the original accurately. This is partly because the vernacular is less a literal translation than a guide to the sense of the original. The moral sense is conveyed by prose résumés written in the margin in Latin, and it is interesting to note that they are sometimes incorporated in the vernacular translation. There is no question of the latter being an aid to construing the Latin distichs in a grammatical manner, but rather the Anglo-Norman functions as a guide to the moral sense of each distich. The formal distinctions of text and moral résumé are thus blurred in the translation. In the fourteenth century, a writer called Thomas (Maillet?) translated the whole text of the *Parabolae* into 1,286 octosyllabic verses, without the Latin and without any evident knowledge of a gloss or commentary. Much more interesting is the extensive adaptation into French verse and prose published by Antoine Vérard in 1492 (1493 new style) and, with modifications, by Denis Janot in 1534. This adaptation is dedicated to King Charles VIII of France. The author drew on a Latin commentary which appeared in early prints from about 1490 onwards, and he places a French adaptation of this commentary before his verse translation of each Latin distich of the original. His procedure is to follow the sequence: illustrative woodcuts (usually in pairs), French prose commentary, French verse translation with the original Latin distichs placed alongside. The correct understanding of the original is thus ensured by the provision of the explanatory prose commentary first, whilst the translator's formal achievements are given prominence by placing alongside his translation the Latin original. When, however, this translation was issued by Denis Janot in 1534–5 the layout was changed. First comes the original Latin

9 On these *Parabolae* versions, see Hunt, 'Les Paraboles' and 'Une traduction partielle'.

text of the *Parabolae* distich by distich, which is thus restored to primacy. Then there is (usually) a woodcut, next the French translation (*le texte*) and finally the commentary (*sens moral*). This is perhaps the more logical layout in theory, but neither this nor the Vérard version is entirely organic, for the printed Latin distichs differ in some cases from the readings predicated by the French translation.

The fact that grammar texts and their academic apparatus could provide the occasion for experimentation in, and theorising about, vernacular prosody, may be illustrated by the Spanish translations of the *Disticha Catonis*. An anonymous late-thirteenth-century version, written in *cuaderna vía* (monorhymed quatrains of fourteen-syllable alexandrines), favoured for narrative verse, was one of the very few works in this form to be printed, running through at least ten editions. It proved far more popular than the versions of Martín García (1467, printed around twenty years later) and Gonzalo García de Santa María (late 1493, printed shortly afterwards). Martín García turned the Latin distichs into stanzas of *arte menor* (a lyric metre) in a variety of Aragonese dialect, but García de Santa María, by his own confession no poet, attempts *arte mayor* (a late-medieval narrative metre, octaves of dodecasyllabics) and rarely manages to scan a line correctly. In a prose preface he excuses his lack of aptitude for verse, recalling Cicero's similar weakness and Virgil's poor oratory in the Senate, and remarking that no ancient achieved perfection in both prose and verse. Claiming to be by nature inclined to prose, he discusses the subject of natural gifts, since it was the practice of the ancients (he claims) to encourage every man to follow his own natural bent, provided it were honest. That practice he finds sadly not honoured in the Spain of his day, so that there is a consequent dearth of outstanding figures in the arts. The reason is simple: children are brought up to suit the estate and desires of their parents rather than according to the abilities they are born with. Thus, he claims, many promising talents are lost to the arts, while their possessors fail to achieve success in the careers forced upon them in the military, the church or the law. Potential poets end up mismanaging their estates and many abbots are good crossbowmen though poor members of religious orders.

García de Santa María offers two reasons for his excursion into verse. The second is an adaptation of a commonplace: he wished to make profitable use of the leisure forced upon him by the exceptional heat during the summer of 1493 which, together with the threat of plague, brought business in Saragossa to a standstill and virtually confined him to his house. The principal cause of his unwonted versifying, however, is highly original: he feared that, finding little or no work, the excellent printer Paulus Hurus would abandon Saragossa, which would be a serious blow to that city. Praising Hurus' work, potentially as good as anything coming out of Venice if only his paper were of better quality, he singles out the correctness of his orthography and punctuation in Spanish – a virtue which many underestimate, in García's opinion.

García goes on to explain his choice of the *arte mayor* stanza, declaring it the most suitable vernacular equivalent of hexameters, just as elegiac couplets are best turned into *arte menor*. This leads into a brief survey of Latin prosody, with particular regard for fitting form to content, as Horace recommends. (Following his usual practice in this preface, García gives no reference here; the passage in question is *Ars poetica* 73-92, roughly paraphrased – and with some reminiscences of Isidore of Seville, *Etymologiae* 1.39.) By contrast, the vernacular poets of the day versify according to no art whatsoever, but simply imitate; some works employ forms quite unsuited to the context, He makes special mention of the misuse of *pie quebrado* (stanzas combining tetrasyllabics and octosyllabics), a metre often used for serious subjects, where the lyrical *arte menor* would be more appropriate. As it turned out, the first tentative steps towards an *arte* or poetics which sought to regulate such matters were to be taken only three years later, in the brief treatise which serves as preface to Juan del Encina's collected works.

The prologue next shifts attention to the author of the Latin original, correctly rejecting both the Censor and Cato of Utica as candidates, on the grounds that the work mentions Virgil and Lucan, who lived after the two Catos. Rather than speculate further, he muses on the lack of contemporary writers who might match the giants of Antiquity. The fault does not lie in any scarcity of information, when there is so great an abundance of Latin, Greek and Arabic books on all matters; perhaps the fewer books of earlier times served to stimulate the great minds of the day. What the modern age lacks are the prizes and rewards available to the ancients. Citing Maecenas as an example of a good patron, he recalls Martial's response to Horace on the absence of a second Virgil (*Epigrammaton* 8.55[56], 5–6) and appears to echo the Ciceronian tag 'honour nourishes the arts' (*Tusc. disp.* 1.2.4) as he concludes, 'thus honours and benefit maintain the arts and sciences'. Without enlightened rulers in the mould of Alexander and his like, writers must struggle to rise above the lowly status assigned to them.

Commenting on his translation as he brings this rambling preface to a close, García explains that he has written out words in full even where elision is required by the rules of prosody. In this he has followed the model of Latin, he claims; by implication, the common habit in the *cancioneros* (i.e. poetic anthologies) of the day of matching the spelling to the sound (e.g. *ca* for *que a*) is condemned. Would-be critics are disarmingly informed that his verses will not always scan in any case; there was much to translate, and the translator lacks the freedom of the original poet.

García's lines indeed limp along, both metrically and syntactically. Each Latin distich is set out in large type and followed by the eight dodeca-syllabics of the *arte mayor* stanza; the threefold increase in expressive material available allows for each detail or allusion to be expanded, or for an illustrative example to be added, in what amounts to a virtual gloss incorporated into the text of the rendering.

The Old French Boethius passed through similar permutations of lay-out. Some manuscripts of Jean de Meun's translation contain a version of the William of Conches commentary, in Latin, written in the margins of a French and Latin 'parallel text' presentation of the *Consolatio*. Turning to the 'Anonymous Verse-Prose Version',[10] it may be noted that French glosses, derived in the main from a recension of the William of Conches commentary, were added to it sometime before 1383; it was this version of Boethius which was the most popular in the fifteenth century. In some of its manuscripts the Latin *Consolatio* and Latin glosses alternate with the French glossed text.

The unique manuscript of Jacob Vilt's Middle Dutch Boethius (made between 1462 and 1466 from the same French 'Anonymous Verse-Prose Version') presents the vernacular text surrounded by a marginal vernac-ular commentary keyed into the text by vernacular lemmata. The second Dutch version, the so-called 'Ghent Boethius', has the same layout in the massive printed edition of 1485 (from which two manuscripts were copied). Here the vernacular text – made directly from the Latin this time – is accompanied by the Latin *Consolatio* and an exceptionally extensive Middle Dutch commentary which draws on the Latin Boethius commentary of Renier of Saint-Trond, but 'departs from Renier so signif-icantly' that it should probably be regarded 'as an altogether new com-mentary' (Goris and Wissink, 'Medieval Dutch Tradition', p. 127).

However, the first printing of the *Consolatio* in northern Europe was that of Anton Koberger, at Nuremberg in 1473.[11] This is a bilingual edi-tion in which each prosa and metrum is followed by a German prose translation; the second part of the book offers the Pseudo-Aquinas Latin commentary. Much less elegant is the layout of Latin text and partial German translation in Oxford, Bodleian Library, MS Hamilton 46, a late-fifteenth-century compilation. Here the vernacular rendering (apparently in the translator's own hand) serves as a sort of commentary on the Latin text, which indubitably has pride of place; it is also served by Latin inter-linear glosses and an interleaved Latin commentary. By contrast, Thomas Richard's 1525 *editio princeps* of Walton's Boethius is an all-English pro-duction, the English verses being accompanied by an English commentary

[10] On which see the articles by Cropp.
[11] On these German versions see Palmer, 'Latin and Vernacular'.

which derives in the main from Nicholas Trevet's exposition, this source being acknowledged at one point. (The fifteenth-century manuscript actually used by the printer has recently been identified – it does include the Middle English commentary.[12]) None of the Spanish Boethius versions includes the Latin original and only one of them separates text from gloss.

These translators and redactors spared no pains in ensuring the fullest understanding of their original texts by their readers, and to that end they willingly adopted the formal procedures of their Latin models. The opposite extreme occurs when vernacular translators made such extensive use of the commentaries that accompany the standard texts that in some passages the *originalia* (i.e. the original texts, in their entirety) seem hardly to have been followed at all. An excellent example of this is afforded by a German prose rendering of the *Memorabilia* of Valerius Maximus, the work of Heinrich von Mügeln (*c.* 1320–72).[13] Heinrich makes extensive use of the commentary on Valerius by Dionysius de Burgo O.E.S.A. (*c.* 1280–1342); he draws on it selectively, but to such an extent that in some passages he provides a version of the commentary rather than of the original text. The problems that could arise from the blurring of text and gloss are well illustrated by the complaint of Ruy López Dávalos, Constable of Castile in the late-fourteenth century, who grumbled that he was confused by the mingling of Boethius' own words and the explanations of the commentator in the version of *De consolatione philosophiae* known to him. The Constable's criticism in fact arose from a misunderstanding: what he took for a translation of Boethius' work, 'put into Romance by the famous Master Nicolas', was an anonymous translation of Trevet's commentary, presented in its initial rubric as '*The Book of Consolation* glossed by a doctor in Theology named Fray Nicolas Trebet, of the Order of Dominican Friars'. Nowhere in the three known manuscripts of the Spanish Trevet is the work identified as a translation of what Trevet had produced in Latin – a treatise wherein the original text of Boethius features only in the form of lemmata.

Other vernacular translations offer interesting blends of tradition and originality in which standard glosses and commentary procedures play a major part. A good example is afforded by a continental French adaptation of Ovid's *Ars amatoria*. The twelfth century has, with some justice, been called an *ætas ovidiana*, and such a major vernacular poet as Chrétien de Troyes appears to have initiated his writing career with translations or adaptations of Ovid. In the thirteenth century four French authors made verse adaptations of the *Ars amatoria*, displaying a considerable degree

---

[12] See Donaghey and Taavitsainen, 'Walton's Boethius'.
[13] On this text, see Stackmann, 'Heinrich von Mügeln', cols. 819ff.

of freedom in their handling of the source. None of them seems to have known the work of the others, but all four operated under the influence of courtly conventions which coloured their approach to the original. A fifth adaptation is quite different from these *ars d'aimer*. It is in prose and bears the imprint of a wide variety of learned sources.[14] Books 1 and 2 were composed in the first third of the thirteenth century and the third book (which occurs in only one of the four manuscripts) was added by a different writer in the last third of the same century. The translator of the first two books employs an argument which was quite familiar from Augustine's *De doctrina christiana* (and which had appeared in the prologue to Marie de France's *Lais*), namely that what is easily accessible to all loses its value, whilst a degree of obscurity encourages careful attention and reflection. He then lists Ovid's *causae scribendi* and announces that he is translating both Ovid's text (*moralite*) and a gloss (*sentence*). This prologue is modelled on the Latin *accessus Ovidiani*; it is followed by the translation (*texte*) and a commentary (*glose*). The translation often comes after the gloss. In one of the manuscripts the Latin text is frequently interpolated (369 lines for Books 2 and 3) and there is some interlinear glossing, and even, on occasion, a more developed moralising gloss. The *glose* is based on a different text of the *Ars amatoria* from that used for the *texte* and seems to be indebted to Latin commentary materials which have not yet been identified. It is essentially of three types: glosses which paraphrase the text, those which explain mythological details, and those which introduce material from outside the text. The last category includes over a hundred vernacular proverbs and lyric insertions (mostly refrains, and generally described as *chançons*, *chançonnetes*, *karoles*) which form part of an expository technique for commenting on courtly aspects of the text; there are also references to the romances of *Blancandin* and *Athis et Prophilias*. Here, then, the formal distinctions of exegesis are preserved even in the case of a text which has on more than one occasion already been adapted to courtly, vernacular conventions and thus has penetrated far beyond the schools.

On the other hand, some vernacular translations of authoritative texts contain literary theory and criticism which go far beyond the matter or the methods of the standard glosses, although some of the principles inherent in scholastic literary discourse may still be influential. As examples we may take two very different treatments of that highly popular grammar-school text, the fables associated with Aesop. Aesop, according to the quite typical account given in Conrad of Hirsau's *Dialogus super auctores* (on which see pp. 125–6, 152–3 above), was famous in Phrygia for

[14] *L'Art d'amours*, ed. Roy.

his expertise in secular learning; his fables teach sound moral doctrine. In other words, he was regarded as a kind of philosopher-poet. He is ostentatiously presented as such in the Middle Scots version of 'Aesop's Fables' by Robert Henryson, who flourished in the later fifteenth century and is generally assumed to have been the master of the grammar school in Dunfermline's Benedictine abbey. (His knowledge of standard school-texts – Évrard of Béthune's *Graecismus* and the *Disticha Catonis* – is not in doubt, and Trevet's commentary on *De consolatione philosophiae* is, as Henryson himself acknowledges, substantially used in his poem *Orpheus and Eurydice*.) The main source of Henryson's Aesop is the fable-collection known as the *Romulus* and attributed to 'Walter of England' (Galterius Anglicus), a work with which he would have been intimately familiar as a teacher. In a dream-vision which constitutes a prologue to the text's central fable, that of the lion and the mouse, 'maister Esope, poet lawriate' appears to the Scotsman's first-person narrator as 'the fairest man' he ever saw (ll. 1377, 1348). Dressed as a university graduate, with his large stature, awe-inspiring countenance, white beard, grey eyes and long hair, he cuts an impressive figure. (Similarly, in *Inferno* 4.83, Dante describes the shades of the major classical poets as being great of stature.) Henryson has here painted a picture of a typical *auctor*, all the status and reverence which that position implies being rendered in iconographic terms. A sort of priest, 'Esope' is addressed by the narrator as 'father' (1366) and addresses the narrator as 'my son' (l. 1370). This priestly role may be related to the character's statement that 'now my winning is in heuin for ay' (l. 1374), i.e. he is one of those righteous heathen who, even though Christ was unknown to him and therefore he was in ignorance of His truth, has somehow been granted a share of eternal bliss. His residence in heaven has obviously taught him a much more comprehensive morality than that which he held while alive on earth: 'Esope' can complain that nowadays there are few or none who heed the word of God. Initially he evokes the traditional distrust of fables as fictions or indeed lies (why should he tell a feigned tale when not even holy preaching is efficacious?), but proceeds to narrate and then moralise the story of the lion and the mouse. Whatever the differences and tensions between the bumptiously enthusiastic first-person narrator and the *auctor*-construct, there is no fundamental difference in technique between their moralising enterprises – though their common reliance upon an ethically orientated study of school-texts does not exhaust the narratives which they seek to explain. Henryson presents his *auctor*-figure and I-persona as engaged in a common enterprise as they expound a shared source, seeking to bring out the profound *intentio auctoris* which is, as it were, bigger than all of them. In theory, the shared goal is simple and single Truth, pagan ethics leading naturally into the much more comprehensive Christian system of morality. But the 'inward sentence and intent' (l. 117) of Henryson's text sometimes proves more disquieting than the overt and sombre moral would suggest.

This attitude to 'Aesop's Fables' was commonplace and persistent, but Henryson's reverential *auctor*-portrait finds its diametric opposite in the depiction of Aesop as a deformed hunchback, which appeared first in English in the *vita Aesopi* that forms the first part of Caxton's 1484 printed edition of the fables of Aesop and others. Caxton took the biography from his primary source, Julien Macho's French translation (printed 1480) of the fable-collection of the German physician Heinrich Steinhöwel. The *vita* itself had been translated into Latin from the Greek by the Italian humanist, Rinuccio da Castiglione of Arezzo; its transmission in the West seems to stem from an eleventh-century Byzantine reworking of an ancient version of the biography. Its reappearance and circulation may be regarded as part of the process whereby medieval scholars and readers became more prepared to accept the shortcomings and sins of their *auctores*.[15] The *vita* consists of a string of anecdotes: the dumb slave is given the powers of speech and wisdom by the goddess of hospitality; is sold to the philosopher Exantus, whom he constantly surpasses in wisdom; gains his freedom by explaining an augury; wins the respect of King Croesus; goes to live in Babylon, where he composes many fables which the king of that country uses to gain tribute from other kings; is wrongly condemned to death – because of the false accusation of his adopted son – but is spared and subsequently honoured even more greatly when he answers a riddle posed by Nectanabus, king of Egypt, and, finally, visits Greece and upsets the citizens of 'the Cyte of delphye' who fear he will destroy their reputation, whereupon they accuse him of robbing the Temple of Apollo and throw him over a cliff to his death. Aesop has a fable for every occasion, but there is no literary analysis of his style and technique and his morality is consistently basic.

The issue of the authority of *auctores* is the subject of an extraordinary passage in Gavin Douglas' *Aeneid* translation, which also constitutes one of the most significant comments on Chaucer's poetry to date from the period. Douglas complained that Chaucer had gone too far (in his *House of Fame* and *Legend of Good Women*) in condemning Aeneas in order to cast Dido in the role of wronged woman, though he was prepared to excuse his 'mastir' on the grounds that this was predictable behaviour from one who was a friend to all women ('all womanis frend'; Bk. 1, Prol. 445–9). If, Douglas declared, Chaucer's charge that Aeneas was 'forsworn' was true, then Virgil's construct is utterly ruined and his twelve years' labour on the poem are not 'worth a myte' (ll. 423–4). Here we may

---

[15] See Minnis, *Authorship*, pp. 103–12, 214–16; *Magister amoris*, pp. 247–54.

detect the scholastic view that a true *auctor* must have impeccable moral credentials, anyone who wrote with evil or suspect intent being utterly unworthy of that accolade. Douglas offers four arguments in Virgil's defence: Aeneas was simply obeying the gods' command; he never concealed the fact that his destiny lay in Italy; he never promised to stay with Dido, and hence was not forsworn; far from being callous, he was regretful and sorrowful on departing but had no choice in the matter. By these means the translator seeks to save the *auctoritas* of 'Maist reverend Virgill, of Latyn poetis prynce, / Gem of engyne [i.e. ingenuity, compare the Latin *ingenium*] and flude of eloquens . . . ' (Bk. 1, Prol. 3–4).

In other cases the amplification of a school-text takes it far beyond the realms of traditional commentary, resulting in a transformation rather than a translation of the original and its glosses. An excellent example of this process is the French *Ovide moralisé*, a text already discussed in Chapter 6 above. This massive poem of around 70,000 verses, in the form of octosyllabic couplets, was composed between 1291 and 1328 by an anonymous Franciscan who took the existing structure of Ovid's *Metamorphoses* and recompiled its constituent parts, inserting explanations of the moral and allegorical significance of each part. The prologue begins by echoing Romans 15:4, 'all that is written is written for our doctrine'. Evil is there so that one might beware of it, and good that one might do it. And he to whom God gives the good fortune and grace to acquire wisdom should not be reluctant to speak and expound (*espondre*) in a good manner, for wisdom which is locked up is worth no more than treasure buried in the earth. Therefore, the anonymous writer continues, he will translate 'en romans' the 'fables de l'ancien temps', as transmitted by Ovid, and say what he understands by them. These fables all seem to be false, but there is nothing in them which is not true. To the person who could get to know the sense, the truth which is 'covered' (*couverte*) with these tales would be patent; he himself will concentrate on unravelling those which are good and profitable. Hence the Franciscan justifies a work which will please and profit 'those who are to hear it', protesting that he himself is of little wit ('je me sens / De foible engin') and open to correction. The *Ovide moralisé* thus represents its purpose very much as commentary, but it is obvious that, despite the modesty formula, the translator's own privileged knowledge is being affirmed; here we are reading an '*accessus ad commentatorem*' rather than an *accessus ad auctorem*. In Book 15 he reiterates his claim that the expert interpreter can 'derive from the fable a meaning that is good and consistent with truth', and cites the precedent of holy Scripture: 'even sacred Scripture is difficult and obscure in many places and seems to be mere fable' (ll. 2525–57). Indeed, he goes so far as to say that 'whoever would take Ovid's texts at the literal level [*a la letre*] and not understand another sense, another meaning than what the author crudely presents in recounting the story, to this person everything would be a lie, of little profit and great obscurity'. These attitudes are manifest in his very exegetical method, whereby the original character of the Latin text is largely ignored as Ovid is ahistorically 'Christianised' far beyond anything which the pagan author himself could have meant. It would seem that Ovid does not have exclusive rights over the meaning of the tales he transmitted; we are in the world of inventive mythography rather than that of textual explication. Throughout the poem the *fabulae* are interpreted both morally and in accordance with Christian allegory, the latter sense sometimes being described as 'more noble and of greater profundity [*de meillor sentence*]'.

One later writer who made substantial use of the *Ovide moralisé*, namely Christine de Pizan in her *Epitre d'Othéa la déesse à Hector* (c. 1400), attempted to segregate the moral and allegorical senses of mythography. In each of its hundred chapters we first have the *texte* or the basic myth itself. Then comes the *glose*, which generally expands the literal/historical narrative and spells out its moral implications in the manner characteristic of exemplification, often relying on philosophical authority. Finally Christine provides an *allegorie* or spiritual interpretation which cites theological authority and ends with a reference to holy Scripture.

Within this same category of transmuted commentary we may include *Los doze trabajos de Hércules*, one of the earliest works of Enrique de Villena (c. 1384–1434). It is not usual to consider this as a commentary or gloss, but it does display most of the external features of the mode. The basic text is Boethius' *De consolatione philosophiae*, 4 met. 7, which Villena uses to identify the twelve labours, helped by Nicholas Trevet's gloss on this passage (to which he makes specific reference in his *Aeneid* commentary for this same purpose). The few words devoted to each labour by Boethius are here replaced by a longer narrative, drawn from a classical source where one is available (e.g. Achelous from *Metamorphoses* 9, Cacus from *Aeneid* 8 and Antaeus from *Pharsalia* 4). These form the 'bare histories' (*historias nudas*), for each of which Villena supplies a *declaraçion* or moralisation, a *verdad* or euhemeristic explanation, and an *aplicaçion*. This last is, in most instances, his own original contribution, suggesting the social and/or moral lesson to be drawn from a particular labour for one of the twelve sectors into which Villena divides human society. In one manuscript (Madrid, Biblioteca Nacional, MS 6599) these four divisions are indicated by marginal headings, but here *historia nuda* is replaced by *fabula*, which reflects rather better the categories Villena employs to classify the narratives: *ficçion (poetica)*, *semejança metaforica* and *fabulosa*. That these terms are not used indiscriminately can be argued on the grounds that *ficçion (poetica)* and *fabulosa* usually correspond to *figura(tiva)* in the *declaraçion*, while *metafor(ic)a* tends to be paired with *parabol(ic)a*. These associations indicate a measure of distinction between the impossible (poetic fiction, fable, figure) and the improbable (metaphor and parable).

Though there are some discrepancies, as when Cacus is accepted as historically factual (as he was by most peninsular historians before the seventeenth century), the scheme holds up fairly well on analysis and the oddities can be explained in context. One fascinating aspect of the *aplicaçion* is its open-endedness. Villena offers in each chapter only the moral/social lessons to be drawn from the Labour for the particular social sector with which he is concerned therein, explicitly leaving it to the reader to apply it to any or all of the remaining eleven sectors, though his original intention had been to carry out the task himself in its entirety.

An extreme case of the use of commentary material in a work serving a very different purpose is the *General estoria*, or universal history, compiled under the direction of Alfonso X 'the Learned' of Castile (1221–84). The king did not direct his team of scholars and translators to produce a vernacular gloss or commentary on Eusebius' universal chronology, but the *Chronici canones*, either directly or through one of its imitations and continuations, provides a chart to which he constantly turns for guidance through his *mer des histoires*. Whenever possible, Alfonso seeks to fill in, as fully as available sources permit, the details of events summarily recorded by Eusebius and repeated down the centuries in his terse statements. For this purpose he draws heavily on biblical and classical materials, but also on Jewish and Islamic traditions. Thus we find the story of Moses and the exodus from Israel told according to both the Old Testament narrative and the *Kitāb al-masālik wa-l-mamālik* of Abū 'Ubayd al-Bakrī. Where the sources record nothing further for a period represented by blanks or bare lists in Eusebius' tables, Alfonso is content to note their silence and pass on to the next event of which he can find some fuller account. The pattern thus established, especially for parts 1 and 2, is essentially one of extended narratives interspersed with rapid catalogues of names drawn from the *Chronici canones*. The major narratives included in these first two parts comprise Old Testament history up to the death of King David, with the biblical sources frequently supplemented from Islamic works and Josephus, and the matters of Thebes, Hercules, the Argonauts and Troy, drawn from both classical and medieval sources, some of the latter already in vernacular versions.

One of the more remarkable features of the *General estoria* is the even-handed treatment of sources. Even the Bible is rarely allowed to speak entirely for itself, each matter being introduced by a listing of relevant *auctores*. A similar technique is employed for secular material, which in the first two parts is very largely mythological. The authority for the inclusion of such material comes from the *Chronici canones*, by virtue of the status of its author, a bishop of Caesarea and a holy man, and Jerome, likewise a saintly bishop and the translator of the Bible. Reassurance against fears of doctrinal error follow immediately: pagan authors knew very well how to say one thing intending to convey another, just as the writers of both Old and New Testaments, the former especially, 'which dealt always in *figura*'. When Ovid is introduced as source, treating of Io, the narration pauses shortly after the opening of his version of the myth in order to inform us that 'Ovid . . . was very learned and a most accomplished poet among the *auctores*; by "poet" is meant the new finder of a concept, the one who draws it out and wraps it in a fiction, to provide pleasing ideas by his words on the matter and also the words and ideas full of truth they wish to convey, as you will see' (1.156a). There follows a full account of Io and related matters based on *Metamorphoses* 1, heavily supplemented from glosses, before the compiler intervenes to establish Ovid's credentials, building on the earlier remark defending pagan authors in general. In a famous passage, Ovid's great poem is accorded all the respect due to the 'pagan Bible': 'The pagans' *auctores* were very learned men and spoke of great matters and in many places used *figura* and metaphor, one thing standing for another, as do today the Scriptures of our Holy Church. And above all other *auctores* is Ovid, in his larger book, which depends upon the theology of the pagans more than upon any other ideas of theirs; and Ovid's larger book is among them nothing less than the theology and bible of the pagans' (1.162b-3a).

After a rapid summary of the principal elements of the myth of Io, the text continues: 'Let nobody take this for a mere tale [*fabliella*] simply because these are Ovid's words, for whoever looks closely at his words and understands them will find that this is no tale; nor, if such were the case, would our Dominicans and Franciscans who have laboured to express it in terms of our theology have done so. All is written in *figura* and metaphorically of something else' (1.163a). The following chapter begins a lengthy exposition drawn from the 'integumentos' (compare the Latin term *integumenta*) attributed to 'Master John and the Friar' (a glossed version of John of Garland?) but also referring to 'Ramiro's' commentary on the Bible, Augustine's *De civitate Dei*, Horace and glosses on him, and Eusebius-Jerome. The *integumento* is defined as an uncovering, because it analyses, uncovers and defends the words and concepts of the pagans' learned men, seeking what they intended when they spoke indirectly of one thing in terms of another. The exposition of the myth of Io which follows is mainly moralising, though with touches of simple euhemerisation and occasional references to the interplay of elemental forces. Once firmly established, the system here described is regularly resorted to in later chapters without further justification. Ovid, through his *Metamorphoses* and *Heroides* (the 'lesser book of Ovid' or 'Book of the Ladies'), dominates the first two parts; thereafter the sources of non-biblical material are more varied, as the subject-matter lies increasingly outside the scope of the Ovidian corpus. Non-classical texts, some of them in vernacular languages, often provide the main narrative; already in the *Segunda parte* a text of the *Roman de Thebes* is preferred to Statius, and the *Roman de Troie* underlies most of the Trojan cycle. For the matter of Britain, Geoffrey of Monmouth is the natural source, and for Alexander in the *Quarta parte* Walter of Châtillon's *Alexandreis* competes with the *Roman d'Alexandre* and their Spanish epigone, the *Libro de Alexandre*.

The *General estoria* stands as the first universal history in a vernacular European language, a major monument of Castilian cultural hegemony and regal self-promotion on the part of Alfonso *el Sabio*, a despot who liked to style himself 'King of the Three Religions'. The politics of his literary patronage bear comparison with those of Charles V *le Sage*, king of France from 1364 until 1380. Charles commissioned 'over thirty translations of authoritative classical and medieval works as part of a conscious policy to legitimate the new Valois dynasty',[16] including Bartholomew the Englishman's *De proprietatibus rerum* (by Jean Corbechon, 1372), Valerius Maximus (a translation of the first four books, by Simon de Hesdin, is extant; 1375), Augustine's *De civitate Dei*, portions of the Bible (by Raoul de Presles, between 1371 and 1375), Giles of Rome's *De regimine principum* (by Jean Golein, 1379), and of course the Aristotle translations of Nicole Oresme (d. 1382). Charles' physician, Evrart de Conty (d. 1405), translated another work believed to be by Aristotle, the clumsy collection of medical questions known as the *Problemata*, though this did not appear until after the king's death. These translations evince striking confidence in the future of French as 'the new Latin', as for instance in Nicole Oresme's assertion, 'thus in those times for the Romans, Greek was in relation to Latin what Latin is for us in relation to French. And at that time the students in Rome and elsewhere were introduced to Greek, and the sciences were usually presented in Greek; while the common mother language ("langage commun et maternel") in that country was Latin' (*Le Livre de éthiques*, ed. Menut, p. 100; compare *Le Livre de politiques*, ed. Menut, p. 27). The mother language of his own country being French, Oresme can conclude that the project of 'our good King Charles, who has good and outstanding books translated into French, is to be commended'. Oresme is, in effect, proclaiming a *translatio studii*, the transition of scholarship from Rome to France, from Latin to French. And an engagement with Latin academic commentary was essential for that transition. In preparing his translation of *De civitate Dei*, Raoul de Presles consulted the commentaries on Augustine's text by Nicholas Trevet and Thomas

Waleys. Evrart de Conty equipped his rendering of the *Problemata* with extensive vernacular glosses which are indebted to (and often seek to improve upon) Peter of Abano's erudite commentary on the Latin text. Oresme's debt to Latin commentary tradition was substantial; indeed, his *Livre de éthiques*, *Livre de politiques*, *Livre de yconomiques* and *Livre du ciel et du monde* have been termed 'commentated translations' of Aristotle's works.[17] It can be difficult to determine what Oresme has taken from Latin commentaries and what he has provided himself, though some influences are obvious: for his *Livre de politiques* he consulted the *Politics* commentaries of Albert the Great and Walter Burley, along with the *De potestate regia et papali* of John of Paris and the highly controversial *Defensor pacis* of Marsilius of Padua. There is little if any evidence of simplification to suit the supposedly lesser capacities of his wider audience; Oresme's vernacular scholarship carries on the business of Latin commentary – as when, for example, in his *Livre de politiques* he criticises the views of Albert the Great. Furthermore, Oresme was acutely aware of the procedures and status of commentary itself. Manuscripts of his Aristotle translations attempt, in various ways, to distinguish between text and gloss, and we need not doubt that this reflects the translator's own wishes. The care with which he annotated his translations is evident by the extent to which he sought to make them even better. Copies of the *Livre de politiques* and the *Livre de yconomiques* indicate an ongoing process of revision of the commentary; we have no fewer than three redactions of the *Politiques* in eighteen manuscripts, wherein the text remains largely the same but the gloss is changed substantially. Evrart de Conty shared Oresme's concerns: in the autograph manuscript of *Le Livre des problèmes d'Aristote* the French text of each and every problem is organised into *texte* and *glose*. Thus Evrart, like Oresme before him, plays his part in the grand enterprise of state-sponsored hermeneutics.

3. Translations of commentaries, and new vernacular commentaries

There were cases in which a Latin commentary was translated into the vernacular as a treatise in its own right, not necessarily to accompany the original text which it was explaining. For instance, there are fourteenth-century Italian and Spanish translations of Trevet's commentary on *De consolatione philosophiae*. The Spanish translation often severely prunes the original. Although the metrum/prosa distinction is kept in the presentation, Trevet's discussion of metrical matters is wholly omitted; a similar

---

[17] By Menut; Oresme, *Le Livre de politiques*, p. 20.

silence is maintained over the purely linguistic material in the original Latin text. These elements would, of course, be pointless when dealing with a vernacular version of Boethius.

Trevet's commentary is by no means an isolated example of scholastic Latin commentary rendered in Spanish. The later redaction of the exposition of Ovid's *Metamorphoses* which forms Book 15 of Pierre Bersuire's *Reductorium morale* was among the many translated works in the library of Iñigo López de Mendoza, first Marquis of Santillana (1398–1458). He almost certainly had also the *Biblia de Osuna* and the Spanish translation of Old Testament prophetic and wisdom literature (Madrid, Biblioteca Nacional, MS 10288) on his shelves, along with two Latin Bibles and a concordance of the Latin text; accompanying them was a translation of parts of Nicholas of Lyre's *Postilla* on the Old Testament, made at the behest of Alfonso de Guzmàn, son of the first Count of Niebla. The translation of Lyre, which occupies six large folio volumes in Santillana's copy, took nearly eight years to complete, though the bulk of the work was done between 1420 and 1422.

The Marquis also possessed translations of two Latin commentaries of a more recent work, Dante's *Commedia*: an anonymous translation of Pietro Alighieri's commentary on the entire work and, commissioned from his physician, Martín González de Lucena, a translation of Benvenuto de Imola's commentary on the *Purgatorio* and probably Benvenuto's commentary on the *Inferno* as well, the latter surviving in an incomplete copy with no indication of translator or dedicatee. In both instances the original author's prologue is translated, with no additions. These commentaries complemented two copies of Dante's poem in the library, one of them a curious manuscript with Latin glosses in at least two hands and still later annotations in Castilian, many of them by Santillana himself. Around all this is fitted a translation of the poem, the work of Enrique de Villena (completed 1427–8, during the period which also saw his translation of the *Aeneid*). It is quite possible that Villena was responsible for the later Latin glosses as well, and that he was asked by Santillana to undertake the translation while he was in the process of reading and annotating the *Commedia* for himself. This working draft is the only text of Villena's translation to have survived, and Santillana's own annotations suggest that he was content to have the work in this form, with its marginal translation and glosses, and indeed that he preferred it to the more elegantly presented copy also found among his books.

New commentaries on major authors written originally in a vernacular language were rare, but a remarkable number of them survive from Spain. Villena's vernacular exposition of the first three books of the *Aeneid*, which survives in only two manuscripts (Madrid, Biblioteca Nacional, MSS 17957 and 10111), is a distinguished example. Whether he commented on the subsequent books is not known. It is clear, however, that Villena had planned the work as a whole and knew precisely where material would be placed later, as when, glossing *Aeneid* 3.210-5, he declares that the Stygian marsh will be dealt with more fully at the proper time, 'in the glosses to the thirteenth chapter of the sixth book'; moreover, the final extant gloss notes that even greater difficulties than those so far traversed lie ahead in Book 6. At any rate Villena's translation of the entire *Aeneid* has come down to us. This project was completed in October 1428, after a year and twelve days of astonishing activity which produced, among other works, the translation of the *Commedia* in the margins of Santillana's copy and a translation (now lost) of the *Rhetorica ad Herennium*. A work of extraordinary density and erudition, the partial *Aeneid* commentary seems to have attracted little attention in its own day and was never printed; this may in part be attributable to the temporary fall from grace of its original dedicatee and Villena's own attempt to use the work to improve his somewhat shaky case for having his former estates restored.

Villena prefaces his work with an epistle to Juan de Aragon, who had commissioned it soon after ascending the throne of Navarre, and a *prohemio ho preambulo*; both epistle and prologue are extensively glossed. The epistle, whose formal structure is carefully analysed in an early gloss, is concerned with the circumstances of the work's creation, while the *prohemio* comprises a rather confused and unbalanced *accessus*, which, though it begins by setting out the standard divisions of author, title, subject-matter, purpose and philosophical category, lingers over a protracted biography of Virgil and reorders later categories (merely mentioning the title), and adds such material as: the opinions on Virgil to be found in the work of Ovid, Statius and Dante; Villena's own ideas about translation, and his strongly individual views on Spanish orthography and punctuation.

From all this certain issues emerge as central to Villena's approach. Foremost is his defence of scholarly activity, a topic already explored at some length in his *Los doze trabajos de Hércules*. Early in his epistle to the king of Navarre he expresses the desire to serve him not only in intellectual labours but also with his person, even to shed his blood for the king, scorning the opinion of those who hold that 'those who are dedicated to the cultivation of knowledge cannot understand worldly matters and action' (Madrid, Biblioteca Nacional, MS 17957, fol. 2r). On the contrary, learning better fits a man for the life of action by supplying the theory underlying the practice; only the predominance of the ignorant in high places prevents recognition of this self-evident truth. The learned can also perform the useful function of recording and interpreting the actions of the powerful as historians: Villena laments the poverty of contemporary chroniclers, who seem to him barely to have passed the portals of Orthography, let alone to have been suckled by Rhetoric. The real meat of Poetry ('vianda poethyca nutritiva') is reserved for magnanimous minds ('generosos entendimientos'), a concept which Villena stoutly defends in the gloss on *generosos*: 'for just as those who are descended from noble and great ancient families are called magnanimous, so too minds accustomed to seeking out and caring for ancient, remote knowledge are called magnanimous and noble' (fol. 12v). Only these minds are capable of poetry, so that 'poetry ought not to be the first [level of] instruction, but rather the last, after [the mind] has been instructed in the other branches of knowledge'. For this reason Virgil's masterpiece can provide the basis for expositions ranging over all of human experience, of all times and in all places.

One major consequence of this high concept of poetry is the firm belief that the 'romançista' reader, lacking Latinity, is denied a full understanding of Virgil's poem by virtue of the vernacular's relative poverty of expression. This requires the translator to build into the text brief explanatory glosses, as when, for example, the translation 'says "Tydydes" which it explains as "son of Thideo, that is, Diomedes"' (fol. 16r). The result is seen as an advantage for the vernacular text, in terms of practical value for the diligent reader, who is thereby enabled the better 'to taste the fruit of its latent doctrine' (fol. 16r–v). Villena's choice of the word 'latent' is deliberate; as the attached gloss on the word informs us, 'the word "latent" [*latente*] signifies a deeper level of covering than "hidden" [*encubierto*], for "latent" indicates very considerable covering and difficulty of discovery and "hidden" simply hiding away [in a place] not hard to find' (fol. 16v). The latent meaning is the primary justification for the commentary, to such an extent that a special gloss on the first page strictly enjoins scribes never to copy the text without it, 'so that the secrets of the narrative [*secretos ystoriales*] and the poetic coverings [*yntegumentos poethicos*] may become known to the readers'. Scribes are sternly warned that, should they feel 'a wish or desire to copy [the work] without the gloss, it is through diabolical temptation or control designed to prevent the fruitful teaching contained in the gloss coming to the attention of readers' (fol. 1r).

When dealing with Virgil's intention in writing the *Aeneid*, Villena points out clearly the difference between the surface text, ostensibly the story of *Aeneas*, and the subtext, concerned to enhance the worth of the Emperor Octavian by linking him to the foundation of the Roman state, its laws and its religion. This message is subtly conveyed 'beneath the veil of poetry and rhetorical colouring ("so el velo po[e]ticho et colores rectoricales"), discreetly and covertly' (fol. 10v). The nature of this veil is explored in a gloss: '"veil" is the name given to the covering or cloak commonly used in poetic language, for just as a veil covers the thing upon which it rests, yet not so much that through its thinness it cannot be discerned that something is beneath it and is evident, though less so than without the veil, so poetic language speaks through such coverings, so that to the uncomprehending all seems dark and veiled and to those who know [all is] clear and manifest' (fol. 10r). The poet's purpose in writing thus is fourfold, as a gloss prefixed to the text proper explains: 'The reasons why poets wrote their works figuratively were four. First, so that [a work] should be common to all, so that young people could treat it as a mere tale; older, unlettered people as a history; and the learned as an allegory behind which they could speculate on the secrets of nature and the moralisations contained therein. Second, for brevity of speech, so that they might convey much substance in few words. Third, so that commentators [*exponedores*] might have some general material on which they could base diverse commentaries. Fourth, to hide from the wicked the details of any vices they had to mention disapprovingly, so that they would be unable to learn new manners of wrongdoing' (fol. 20r). The presumption which appears to underlie the third of these reasons suggests that it should be read in the light of the first reason: a poetic text should not only please different readers at different levels in its superficial aspect; it should also offer a variety of subtexts to serve the purposes of different scholars – for example, the secrets of nature or social morals. The poet therefore seeks to be all things to all men at both levels.

Certainly Villena's own practice concentrates on the two modes specifically mentioned when he offers an interpretation of the text, though much of his commentary deals with the simpler matters of explaining allusions and supplying information on the people and practices mentioned in the text. Thus the long gloss (fol. 28r) on *Aeneid* 1.154–6, describing Neptune's calming of a storm, divides its attention equally between the *secreto natural* and the *doctrina moral*. In terms of natural phenomena, the operation concerns four aspects of rain and their relationship with the four elements, while morally it is a question of the interplay in the human conscience of the four cardinal virtues and the four modes of silence. In other instances the moral aspect is developed through extended sequences of glosses covering long passages of the text; these moralisations grow longer as the commentary progresses. The erudition displayed is vast, nowhere more so than on scientific matters, where Villena comes into his own, most remarkably when he attempts to identify the incense used at Dido's banquet for Aeneas (*Aeneid* 1.726–7), concludes that the most likely substance is one described by 'Ballianos the Indian . . . in the book which the Arabs call *Mucaf alcamar*', and puts it to the test: 'I tried it and found it a very soft and pleasant odour' (fol. 50v). One can only wonder at Villena's dedication and speculate on what he might have made of Book 6.

Some twenty-five years later, Alfonso de Madrigal el Tostado broke off, after five closely written folio volumes, his *Comento de Eusebio*, when scarcely one-third of the text had been dealt with. As far as can be ascertained, El Tostado completed a Castilian translation of Jerome's Latin version of Eusebius' *Chronici canones* for the Marquis of Santillana in 1449–50, and began a Latin gloss soon afterwards, only to abandon it in favour of the Castilian *Comento* less than a year later. Although the *Comento* enlarges to a considerable degree upon the *In Eusebium*, work on it stopped just before it became necessary to tackle the myth of Hercules, a matter which alone occupied one-sixth of the existing Latin gloss, though that work had got no further than a point half-way through Eusebius' prologue, so vast had the exposition become. Alfonso de Madrigal was no stranger to glossing. His intention to write a commentary on the *Chronici canones* had been announced in 1436 in his voluminous exposition of Genesis, and over the next dozen years or so he had worked his way through the historical books of the Old Testament, beginning with the Pentateuch, and seven volumes on Matthew – left unfinished (!) in 1449 – producing some twenty-four large folio volumes in all, a substantial portion of his Latin output. From time to time in these works he had reason to mention events in contemporary pagan history, and from Genesis onwards the exposition of Eusebius was a target for the future, to complement the Bible commentaries.

The prologue to the Eusebius/Jerome translation (called *Libro de los tiempos* by El Tostado) dwells briefly on the linguistic problems involved, lamenting the poverty of the vernacular as regards grammatical rules, including those for word-formation, and the *figuras et modos* necessary for multiplying meanings, whether in rhetoric or plain style. Such problems increase when one attempts word-for-word translation, which he considers more authoritative because it adds nothing to what the original author wrote. For El Tostado, sense-for-sense translation is not so much *interpretaçion* as *exposiçion o comento o glosa*, designed to make the text easier to understand for those of lesser abilities. Such versions cannot truly be called the work of the original author; they are better viewed as the work of the translator/*glosador*. As he purposes to offer a word-for-word translation, he will need to add brief glosses on particular points; these were to follow in the text, but neither they nor the red virgules in the text which would indicate the availability of such annotation are to be found in the autograph manuscript. Indeed, the prologue to the subsequent *Comento* suggests that this new work is designed to take the place of the glosses originally promised; the *Comento* will still be limited to what is strictly necessary, eschewing a full account of every person, creature or event appearing in the *Chronici canones*. In particular, some matters treated in Latin are unnecessary or inappropriate in the vernacular; this proves especially true of Latin prosody, to which several pages are devoted in the Latin commentary *In Eusebium*, while the vernacular *Comento* dismisses the subject as incomprehensible to those unskilled in Latin and in any case inapplicable to Spanish verse.

The purpose of the *Comento*, then, is to facilitate understanding of the *Libro de los tiempos* by fleshing out the events listed in Eusebius' time-charts, supplying further details of places, people, causes and events. Above all, El Tostado is concerned to resolve chronological contradictions created by the differing accounts transmitted by the writers of Antiquity and compounded by those dependent upon them in later centuries. Conflicting versions are set out and subjected to rigorous logical analysis, aided by reference to a powerful arsenal of *auctores*, until a convincing conclusion can be reached. The euhemeristic version of myths is preferred, because it reduces supernatural elements in a given narrative to action readily conceivable in a 'real' world. An early opportunity is taken to explain how, according to Euhemerus, men and women of outstanding achievement came to be venerated as gods (2.52), after which the principle is taken for granted and other interpretations summarily dismissed. A good example comes in discussion of Hercules and Antaeus, where the problem revolves around the identity of the Hercules in question and the date of their encounter. A summary of Fulgentius' version is included (3.90), followed by the comment: 'This is the moral sense, with which we are not concerned, because we know that the creators of this fable had no such intention in their fiction; we shall follow the literal sense, as intended by them'.

The impressive array of sources is difficult to evaluate, no less so because of El Tostado's own flow of comment on the worth of their testimony. When Eusebius cites Homer on Dardanus, the gloss comments at length on Homer's supposed lack of neutrality, as a Greek, on matters concerning the Trojan war, refers briefly to the structure of the *Iliad* and for good measure throws in a brief mention of the *Odyssey*, described as written to favour Ulysses. A later eulogy of Homer gives him the credit for preserving the fame of the heroes on both sides in the Trojan War. Yet it is unlikely that Alfonso de Madrigal knew Greek: when he cites Euhemerus, it is from Ennius' Latin version as relayed by Lactantius. A fascinating paragraph comparing the merits of Plato and Aristotle refers three times to Cicero's translations of Plato, while showing how Aristotle's ability to demonstrate and defend his propositions has given him the upper hand for some 800 years over the philosopher who was 'more of a theologian than a natural philosopher, and said many reasonable things worthy of the highest consideration but could not prove them'.

What is quite clear is El Tostado's use of Boccaccio's *Genealogia deorum gentilium*, cited on several occasions by name as well as being the most likely source for material attributed to writers such as Theodontius. Although Latin quotations, followed by vernacular translations, are not infrequent in the *Comento*, Boccaccio is consistently quoted in Spanish, but any suspicion that El Tostado knew only the vernacular translation of Boccaccio's treatise in his patron's library (the work of Martín de Avila) is quickly dispelled by an examination of the *In Eusebium*. A telling example comes near the end of that work, where the treatment of the myth of Hercules consists essentially of *Genealogia* 13.1, more or less complete, but subjected to a painstakingly thorough critical assessment from which El Tostado emerges as clear victor in terms of knowledge and scholarship. The abandonment of the *Comento* before this had been reworked in the vernacular was a minor tragedy for the diffusion of classical mythography in Spain.

One of the oddest new commentaries on a vernacular translation of a classical text must surely be Francesc Alegre's on his *Transformacions*, printed in 1494 by Pere Miquel of Barcelona and fulsomely dedicated to Joana of Aragon, the future 'Juana la Loca', queen of Castile, but at that time a girl of fifteen. This Catalan version of the *Metamorphoses* is unremarkable as such, but for the commentary Alegre hit upon the highly original idea of adapting to the structure of Ovid's poem a large part of Boccaccio's *Genealogia*. Boccaccio's material is reassigned to its appropriate points in the poem; moreover, what Boccaccio had taken from earlier authorities is put into their own mouths in a simulated dialogue. Alegre recounts how, when planning his commentary, he walked out early one Wednesday morning on the slopes of Montjuic, looking down on Barcelona, only to be assailed by Age, Ignorance, Timidity and Time, followed by a vision of ancient Rome in flames. As morning sunlight strikes his eyes, he prays to the Virgin for mercy and help. Immediately a gentle breeze announces the arrival of twenty ancients, led by Boccaccio, who proceeds to introduce his companions to the dazed Alegre. By agreement, Alegre puts questions and Boccaccio marshals his *auctores*' responses, directing who may speak to the point at issue at any given moment. The commentary therefore has little need to go far beyond the bounds set by the *Genealogia*, so that interpretations are predominantly euhemeristic, though Alegre appears to have pursued further some topics of a philosophical nature.

The presentation of the entire work is complex. The dedication to the young princess is followed by a prologue to the translation, beginning with a eulogy of the ancients' breadth of knowledge, as revealed in the store of books inherited by the modern age. All that is left to writers of the present day is the collection and translation of ancient works, and 'the refurbishing and painting of the mansions founded by our learned forefathers, to the end that through the diversity of writings and the variety of style those now living may be stimulated by the desire to read, embracing knowledge, to which alone, as the mother of virtue, honour is due'. By their writings the moderns can hope to win the rewards granted to the writers of Antiquity. After a brief explanation of the title, *Transformacions*, Alegre states his intention to provide a matching set of fifteen books in which he will declare the truth of the matters contained in Ovid's text. His purpose in doing so is threefold. In the first place, to reveal the truth hidden beneath *les fictes colors de poesia*, he rapidly sketches the standard euhemeristic version of the creation of the pagan pantheon, designed by poets in ancient times to flatter rulers and magnates. Second, intellect and memory will be trained in their tasks of understanding and retaining, through being led to appreciate the careful ordering of Ovid's work as it moves from primeval chaos to the dedication of Caesar. Finally, the moral value will be shown in the rewarding of virtue and punishment of wickedness as told in the poem's numerous examples.

Alegre prefaces his *allegories e morals exposicions* with a recollection of the promise to provide interpretations which he made in the prologue to the entire work, and goes on to define the three key terms: poetry, *fabula* and allegory. As to the first, he prefers to translate the cognate Greek verb as signifying 'create', rather than merely 'make' – and still less 'feign', as many would have it. Thus he offers as his definition: 'Poetry is a fervour of exquisite song-making, guiding the imagination in writing down prettily what one has conceived from out of the bosom of God, [a thing] granted to few minds in all creation. For this reason few are true poets, because only rarely are revealed the great effects of this divine *furor*.' Citing a remark by Cicero, he continues by noting the use of *vates* to signify 'poet' before turning his attention to those who scoff at poetic fable, sweeping aside 'the cloud, arising from the thick vapours of ignorance and presumption, which blocks their understanding'. Following Boccaccio, he recalls the etymological root *fari* and the senses of the cognate *(con)fabulare*, for which he suggests the meaning 'reasoning together'. Thus a fable is to be understood as 'an illustrative example in the form of a fiction from which, once the outer covering has been removed, can be seen clearly the intention of the one who constructed it'. This leads into a brief dissertation on the four classes of *fabula*: animal fable, myth and exemplary tale (all of which serve to conceal a truth or moral), and old wives' tale, which has no value and scarcely merits consideration. The low esteem in which the fourth category is held is indicated by its absence from the Bible, where many instances of the other three forms may be found. Allegory gets short shrift here. Noting that the Greek *allon* signifies the same as the Latin *alienum*, i.e. 'different', he rapidly concludes that all meanings except the *hystorial e literal* can be broadly categorised as allegorical.

At the conclusion of the vision, which lasts a full day and night, ending with the Morning Star shining at daybreak on Thursday, Alegre offers a prayer of thanks on completion of his task. But the work does not end there, for *Lo libre* – the book itself, personified – is allowed the last word, in a spirited address to the princess in defence of its author against detractors. Some have complained because Alegre has written on serious matters which older and more learned men have feared to treat. The most frequent objections were those raised against the translation, on a variety of grounds which Book proceeds to enumerate, before giving brief answers to all of them in turn. Book's most forceful comments come in response to questions about the propriety of the translation; he vigorously defends its priority in any vernacular, since what had hitherto appeared in both Italian and Catalan was not a translation of the *Metamorphoses* itself but rather a version of Giovanni del Virgilio's Latin commentary on the work. In any case, both Jerome and Leonardo Bruni in their day had thought retranslation a worthwhile practice. As regards quality, Book observes that word-for-word translation of Latin verse results in awkward, disjointed vernacular prose. Passages were indeed omitted – not because Alegre was unable to translate them, but in order to avoid offending the young princess' sensibilities. Finally, the use of Boccaccio's *Genealogia* is fully acknowledged, and defended as being from any point of view far from slavish, as should be obvious from the difference between the structures of Ovid's poem and the mythological compendium.

4. Commentary and controversy over translation

Many of the issues which have been considered above were discussed in medieval debates on the pros and cons of making available in the vulgar tongue the most authoritative text of all – holy Scripture – and its expository apparatus. Space allows only one example, the well-documented controversy concerning Wycliffite Bible translation, which must be accorded pride of place in any account of English vernacular appropriations of the academic commentary tradition. This work, whoever its exact producers, is certainly an Oxford product, and its academically trained authors knew intimately the contents of the commentary tradition, how to acquire the necessary materials, and precisely how to use them – in particular, how to use the tradition to forestall objections to the transformation of holy writ into the vernacular. The meticulousness of these procedures is described in the 'General Prologue to the Wycliffite Bible':

First this simple creature worked very hard, along with various companions and helpers, to gather old Bibles, and other doctors and common glosses, and to make a single Latin Bible with a somewhat faithful text. And then he studied it anew, the text with the gloss, and with whatever other doctors he might obtain, and especially Nicholas of Lyre's gloss on the Old Testament, which helped a great deal in this work. Third, he consulted the books of old grammarians and theologians about difficult words and expressions, to find how those might be understood and translated. Fourth, he translated 'sense-for-sense' as clearly as he might, and he had many good and wise companions correct the translation.[18]

For the translators, all these steps served the goal of a faithful literal text, designed to be available to universal consultation.

At the initial stages, the translation team was concerned simply with the quality of the text itself. The Vulgate had been recognised as subject to gradual corruption; Parisian correction tables had been developed in the later thirteenth century to arrest this process. However, the Wycliffite translators chose not to use these and preferred to return to the primary documents. In this procedure, as virtually everywhere in their work (and in contemporary discussions of translation generally), they were guided by the model of Jerome and by his various discussions of the need to consult the *originalia* (the original texts in their entirety). As the prologue indicates, such consultation was not limited to available manuscripts of the scriptural text. The translators recognised that much of the text in its antique form could be recovered from the lemmata glossed in the exegesis of the Fathers. Although, as the prologue discussion of the second stage of translation indicates, much of the material included in their Bible represents a single source, Lyre's *Postilla litteralis*, they certainly read more widely. The translation appears to include a large number of readings supplied by the exegetical tradition, not the ostensible biblical source. On this basis, the author of the prologue can claim with some justice (ll. 66–75) that his English Bible offered a more accurate text than most copies of the Vulgate.

The influence of the commentary tradition was not limited to arresting textual corruption. The translation appears to have proceeded through a number of stages not fully captured by the four steps outlined in the quotation above. Initially, in what is usually considered the first stage of the Earlier Version of the Bible, the concern to reproduce the exact verbal texture of the source was extreme. What the author of the prologue indicates as the fourth stage of the work, the movement from such 'word-for-word' constraints to a translation for the sense, gradually produced a text freer of Latinate syntax (one may compare the techniques for 'resolution' discussed in the prologue, ll. 40–66), which included progressively greater amounts of detail derived from the commentary tradition.

A fairly large number of phrases from glosses (particularly Lyre's, as the author notes) were incorporated into the text, most frequently to explain obscurities in transitions or references deemed implicit but unstated in the Latin. Moreover, Lyre also fed the translators' interest in the literal

[18] Tr. by Ralph Hanna from Hudson, *Selections*, sel. 14, ll. 26–35.

words of Scripture by providing considerable information on the *veritas Hebraica*, where that differed from the Latin received text. As the author of the prologue promises (ll. 75–9), notes on such matters appear in the margins of some copies. There they are intermixed with a variety of other materials. Substantial portions of the text, particularly Old Testament wisdom literature and the New Testament epistles, were given – although at different stages in the work – fairly extensive marginal glosses, in most cases from Lyre.

The emphases of this marginal gloss are particularly interesting. Lyre appealed to the Lollard translators as the great expositor of the literal sense, and for the most part they emphatically rejected glosses referring to spiritual senses. Typically, the glosses attend to such details as the explanation of figurative language, a response in which the biblical propensity for metaphor is explained rhetorically (as a literal relationship of tenor to vehicle); logical explanations of the progress of the narrative (for example, the relation of Job's claims to those of his tempters, and the way his false friends misrepresent his views); indications of Latin tonality obscured by English syntax (whether questions expect negative answers, for example), and of impersonated speech (moments when characters speak as if in another person).

But the translation, however augmented by such material from the commentary tradition, was never quite intended to stand by itself. Typically, the author of one Lollard tract prays that 'every parish church in this country have a good Bible and good expositors on the Gospels' (*English Works of Wyclif*, ed. Matthew, p. 145). This motivation lies behind another monumental effort of Wycliffite scholarship, a group of works known collectively as 'The Glossed Gospels'. This was derived from standard patristic exegesis, in many cases by choosing prestigious commentaries (for example, the Pseudo-Chrysostom *Opus imperfectum* on Matthew) and selecting excerpts from them. Other portions reproduce Thomas Aquinas' *Catena aurea*, but, with their usual zeal, the Wycliffite writers appear to have tracked down many of Aquinas' excerpts to their sources in manuscripts of the *originalia* and to have expanded or condensed the exegesis as they felt necessary. The form of the text commented upon (the second stage of the Earlier Version), as well as the general absence of marginal glosses to the gospels in manuscripts of the Bible, suggests that this production was indeed conceived as central and undertaken at a relatively early stage.

The presence of Lollard Scripture of course attracted interest and inspired concern, the most formal aspects of which involved open disputations at Oxford in 1401 over the legality of biblical translation into the English vernacular. The official possibility for open discussion implicit in these disputations was closed peremptorily in 1408 when Archbishop

Thomas Arundel promulgated his constitution banning all biblical translation.

From these public debates a range of documents survives. William Butler, a Franciscan, prepared in 1401 a *determinatio* in six articles. In his 1401 *Tractatus*, the most extensive surviving document of the debate, the secular master of theology Richard Ullerston described a disputation between two doctors. He recorded thirty arguments defended by the disputant opposed to translation, and his lengthy refutation presumably represents the positive contribution made by himself, the unnamed second doctor. (Substantial excerpts from Ullerston's work were translated into English before 1407 as the anonymous Lollard tract 'Aȝens hem þat seyn'.) In addition, a series of rough notes, sketching opinions both favouring and opposing translation, is ascribed to the London Dominican Thomas Palmer; it probably dates from shortly before 1407.

The Oxford debate was of course not confined to matters of literary theory in any narrow sense; much of the discussion inevitably involved topics associated with social discipline. By policing access to the sacred text ecclesiastical authority hoped to avert potential (in the English situation, more than merely potential) lay heresy. Pope Innocent III had largely determined the shape of subsequent discussion in a pastoral letter of 1199 to the faithful of Metz, 'Quum ex injuncto'.[19] Innocent found that vernacular bibles were apt to be so socially disruptive as to necessitate active discouragement, if not suppression, and echoes of his arguments recur throughout the English documents. But here they typically confront other imperatives, equally social in nature. As a later Lollard puts the case, 'If we are to be judged by Christ's word, we must learn His word and know it. Why then should not unlearned men read and write and speak His word?' (Cambridge, University Library, MS Ii.vi.26, tract 7, fol. 46r). Whereas Innocent had insisted upon the dangers of lay heresy, the Wycliffites saw an even graver danger in lay ignorance. Thus, substantial portions of the debate treated problems which, however they might be couched, essentially reflected clerical suspicion of possible lay readership, and – it was felt – consequent abuse of Scripture. Palmer, for example, makes the perfectly reasonable point that translation may seriously misrepresent the sense of Scripture, but he does so in language that indicates not a literary perspective but a clerical contempt for the learning of putative translators. Since both Jerome and the Seventy erred, he asks, 'Why should those who are simple, those who in general understand grammatical rules alone, and scarcely even those, not err also?' (Deanesly, *Lollard Bible*, p. 429).

Then there was the nationalistic argument. The most extensive treatment occurs in Ullerston, who adduces a lengthy list of English biblical

---

[19] Included in Gregory IX's *Decretals*, 5.7.12 (*Corpus juris canonici*, II, cols. 784–7).

translators and takes great pride in citing English authors who have spoken on the issue, particularly Bede. 'It is no less permissible', he states, 'for the people of England to have holy Scripture translated into their vernacular than it is for the French, the Germans, the Wends, or the Armenians. This is evident because of the freedom of the English people, a freedom equal to that of other nations' (Vienna, Nationalbibl., MS 4133, fol. 207v). Similar attitudes had, of course, been found in earlier and non-Lollard works – and they also feature, for example, in the prefaces to the French versions of major philosophical and religious works produced by Charles V's team of translator-commentators, the most prominent being Nicole Oresme (see pp. 382–3 above). But in the mouths of heretics such words amounted to a challenge to the authority of both church and state.

Necessarily, considerations of the nature of language played some role in the 1401 Oxford discussions. Many of these ideas were introduced by those who were opposed to Bible translation; Butler and Palmer were at pains to question the very possibility of translation and therefore invoked various features of the English language which, because non-comparable with those of Latin, made exact rendition of the original difficult if not impossible. Points like that had already been answered implicitly within the Lollard Bible itself: in their reliance upon commentary materials, the translators appear to have consciously attempted to forestall certain negative views. Examples would include the insistence upon the ambiguity and obscurity of the Vulgate, answered by the translators' use of commentary to identify the true sense of problematic passages or of individual 'wordes equiuok'. Similarly, marginal glosses may be taken as an answer to Butler's claim that Scripture cannot always be accurately translated through attention to the words themselves.

Stronger objections included the lexical poverty of English, the absence of an English tradition of figural speech, and the quality of the English stress accent. The supporters of English were unable to answer such attacks constructively; the best they could offer were the practical suggestions, made in the Old Testament prologue, about finding English syntactic equivalences for Latin constructions. Indeed, the defenders of translation most frequently approached the disparity between languages as a matter of common sense. Translation, including Jerome's of the Vulgate, had proceeded with success for centuries and might well continue. Thus Ullerston argues that the activities of the translator simply extend those procedures which are normal in the basic teaching of Latin grammar; masters command their charges, 'Construe this for me in Latin' and receive acceptable responses (fol. 201v). He also argues that early biblical translations had been made into vernacular tongues, including languages which had not corresponded in grammatical features to the original forms of the text. Moreover, just like 'learned and grammatically regulated languages', supposedly 'barbarous tongues' like English in fact are essentially grammatical, having their own rules of construction which are known to their speakers, even if not dignified by descriptions in formal grammatical tracts.

In another context (fol. 196v) Ullerston indicates a psychological grounding for his commonsense views. He cites with approval Augustine's argument that spiritual comprehension of God's meaning is pre- or super-linguistic (*De trinitate* 15.10.18–11.20). Concepts, according to this view, exist before language. Thus, a biblical translator is in touch with a universal Idea, the Incarnate Word, to which he discovers that the linguistic forms of two languages correspond. He therefore translates a prelinguistic perception which joins him to divinity, rather than to mere words.

More normally, however, linguistic objections were, on theoretical grounds, simply not a serious anxiety in the translation process. Medieval translators, whatever the rhetorical claims for accuracy and exactness of reproduction they might make, always assumed that they offered interpretations of the sense. Hugutio of Pisa, in his *Magnae derivationes*, relies upon this common view when he defines translation as 'the exposition [*expositio*] of meaning through another language' (cf. p. 363 above). By calling translation an *expositio* he underlines what we have seen often throughout this chapter, that the act of translating is an act of interpretative commentary. Ullerston indicates the strength of this tradition in his analysis of *translatio*. He places equal emphasis upon two pairs of words – not just *translator* and the parallel verb *transferre* but also *interpres* ('translator') and its parallel verb *interpretari*. And the connection of translation and commentary becomes explicit when he comments that *interpretari* is sometimes used as a synonym for 'to expound or interpret, to reveal, to explain, or to disclose the sense hidden within words' (fol. 196v). In Ullerston's view the translator does not blandly give his readers word-for-word equivalents: his choices constitute a more total textual appropriation, which everywhere is conscious of the source's meaning in its deepest sense. He seeks, as commentators regularly claimed they did, the author's hidden meaning, which his translation explains, interprets. In such a context, the behaviour of the Lollard translators, their care in intercalating glosses to provide an authoritative guide to the original sense, appears a highly principled decision. For them, fidelity to the source depended upon exposition, interpretation – and the more authoritative it was, the better.

Moreover, Ullerston adopts a position which minimises the difficulties of translation. 'One cannot properly conclude', he says, 'that the plainly stated histories in Scripture, the life of Christ, His miracles, and His doctrine may not be explained to the populace in the vernacular' (fol. 204v).

Like Butler and Palmer, he believes that certain 'arcane' scriptural discussions may be untranslatable – but the greater and more useful part of Scripture, which he elsewhere describes as 'histories, laws, and admonitions pertaining to salvation' (fol. 201v), relies on direct statements and hence does not involve such translational difficulties.

Here we approach one of the major cruxes of the matter. The opposition's belief that the Bible was untranslatable rested upon a belief that the text was most meaningful at a latent level; it involved multiple senses simultaneously and was not exhausted by attention to its patent *sensus litteralis*. Palmer, among several arguments which insist upon the greater value of the traditional three 'spiritual' senses of Holy Writ, cites with approval the traditional Gregorian formulation that Scripture is 'a river both shallow and deep, in which the lamb may walk and the elephant swim' (Deanesly, *Lollard Bible*, pp. 424–5). For him and others like him, this multiplicity formed the verifiable miracle of divine textuality, a marvel which translators had inevitably to jettison in their effort to convey the literal sense. But Palmer's formulation presupposes two separate audiences: it identifies Scripture as providing mysteries for the adept (who, gigantic in their learning, are like elephants), with the surface sense of the text catering for the childlike lambs. This is quite antipathetic to the Lollard belief in a single form of life and a single way to salvation: multiple understanding of the Bible violates this unity by creating diverse readerly communities. And, of course, Palmer's communities are graded, since the surface of the text explicitly appeals to the ignorant and the deeper spiritual readings appeal to clerical *cognoscenti*.

The Lollard response strives to re-create this single community of the faithful through an insistence upon the literal biblical text, universally available through a translation for sense. Indeed, from certain extremely strict Lollard points of view, any interference with the literal word of Scripture could be viewed as a serious dereliction of responsibility. Wycliffite writers often insist that adversaries who uphold the value of the traditional 'four senses' of Scripture misrepresent the nature of the sacred book; they claim that their adversaries suppose 'that holy writ is false' or that it 'is false so far as the literal sense', thereby adopting the heretical view that God deliberately lies. Such sinister misreading represents, in their view, a conspiracy usually of papal or fraternal origin. Lollards associated glosses relying on the spiritual senses with the defence of perverse modern institutions dependent for their sanction on extended readings of the Bible. Thus, Ullerston identifies a 'carnal motive' (fol. 199r), a solidarity with those belonging to the same social group, including the same order, as one of the efficient causes which might have induced his adversaries' opposition to translation.

The importance of the traditional four senses of Scripture is questioned in the Wycliffite prologues. The literal sense is said to provide 'the ground and foundation' of all other forms of understanding, a point with which most late-medieval commentators would concur. But by this statement, the Lollard writers mean to limit severely the range of licit commentary through the 'higher' senses: 'These three spiritual senses are neither authentic nor do they compel belief, unless they are manifestly based upon the literal text of holy Scripture in one or another place, or are based upon a manifest logic beyond confutation, or are based on passages where the Evangelists or other apostles draw upon an allegory in the Old Testament, and thus confirm it, as Paul does in Galatians 4' (*Holy Bible*, I, p. 43). The value of such spiritual readings is sharply curtailed. Following a view popularised by Aquinas (although here derived from Lyre), the Lollard General Prologue states that 'only by the literal sense, and by no spiritual senses, may someone make an argument or proof in order to prove or resolve a doubtful issue' (*Holy Bible*, I, p. 53). The textual basis for papal and fraternal claims, predicated upon spiritual glossing, becomes significantly eroded. And the prologue to the prophetic books includes a strenuous warning against any such efforts: following Lyre's claim that spiritual senses which diverge from the literal text should be considered *indecens et inepta*, it goes so far as to gloss 'spiritual understanding' as 'moral fantasy', potentially an act of self-deception and intellectual pride. Of course, some kinds of spiritual reading were hallowed by tradition and of too great a power merely to be rejected. Consequently, the demolition of 'higher senses' could only function with a concomitant expansion of the notion of the literal sense, and the prologues give ample guidance towards such reading strategies. They resuscitate a variety of reading techniques originally conceived as guides to common spiritual senses which are then taken as expansive metaphorical devices. Traditional allegories are often to be taken as analogical metaphors inherent in the literal sense.

The debate associated with Wycliffite Bible translation thus raised a wide variety of literary issues both traditional and novel. And among the most important novelties was the language of much of the discussion, the vernacular: indeed, the quarrel (leading to the eventual suppression of the Lollard Bible) became so heated in large measure because of the social tensions underlying the provision of commentary theory and methodology to those untrained in Latin. These social imperatives also functioned to render the controversy uninfluential during the remainder of the Middle Ages. Suppression of Lollard writings inevitably qualified the value (and reduced the vernacular dissemination) of the sophisticated ideas raised here. Only with the controversy over Tyndale's translations (and the nearly contemporary printing of the Lollards' Old Testament prologue) did such issues regain social currency.

5. Commentary and vernacular creativity

Now we may move far beyond the schools to consider the influence of commentary on works of vernacular literature which may be described as more original, though often they were dependent on common narrative forms and contents. The artistic resources and implications of commentary were many. In glosses on classical authors – either communicated in their education and/or consulted in manuscripts of their source-texts – medieval writers gained much of the information which informed their sense of the past, a sense which is well attested by the twelfth-century French *romans d'antiquité*, which medievalised the stories of Thebes, Troy and Rome. The assimilation of text and gloss in such works can often be taken as evidence of considerable scholarship, as may be illustrated by *Li Fet des Romains* (dated 1213–14), one of the most popular translations of the Middle Ages (surviving in at least fifty-nine manuscripts). This comprehensive prose history of Rome from Julius Caesar to Domitian draws directly on Sallust, Caesar, Suetonius and Lucan – and many of the explanatory additions have been proved to derive from glosses on the *Pharsalia* (*De bello civili*). Given the anonymous nature of so much medieval glossing, and the varying forms in which so many glosses appear, precise identification of which gloss influenced a given vernacular passage is sometimes difficult if not impossible, but where major commentaries exist in standard redactions exact parallels may certainly be offered. Clear evidence of the influence of glosses on Ovid's *Heroides* may be found in some of the verse narratives in two Middle English anthologies, Chaucer's *Legend of Good Women* (dating from the 1380s) and John Gower's *Confessio amantis* (from the 1390s). The class of commentary known to Chaucer has even been identified.[20] Theological commentaries were also consulted – and not just for theology. To take one well-documented case, Robert Holcot's popular 'classicising' commentary on the Book of Wisdom (mid-1330s) was known to Chaucer, Thomas Hoccleve, and perhaps to Gower.

Major theoretical ideas which the commentary tradition transmitted could come to have an influence which extended far beyond the boundaries of that tradition. A good example is afforded by the idea that characters (*personae*) who say different and apparently discordant things within a text can function to serve an ultimate and unifying moral objective. This

[20] By Edwards, 'Six Characters'.

had its origin in the medieval distinction between three styles of writing (the *characteres scripturae*), which goes back to the fourth-century commentary by Servius on Virgil's *Bucolics*. The style of a work is called 'exegematic' when the author speaks in his own person; 'dramatic' when he speaks in the persons of others; and 'mixed' when both these styles are used (*In Verg. comment.*, ed. Thilo and Hagen, III, p. 1). Some scholars built on these commonplaces an interpretative method capable of distinguishing between types of literary responsibility and of placing the responsibility for the diverse statements made in a given work where it belonged, whether to a specific character or to the author speaking *in propria persona*. Boethius commentary is a major focus for such theory – as one would expect, given the way in which Boethius conveyed his philosophy on fate and free will through two major characters, the lamenting and limited Boethius-persona (who is not to be confused with the author himself) and Lady Philosophy, in whose mouth Boethius put his own most profound insights. William of Aragon explained that in this work two *personae* are feigned ('duplex persona confingitur . . . '), namely, the learned and the learner, or the sufferer along with the physician.[21] This account enjoyed a wide dissemination in the Romance world, since, as already noted, part of William's prologue to his commentary – wherein it is to be found – was translated and incorporated in the prologue to Jean de Meun's French translation of Boethius, and in its turn Jean's prologue was appropriated by those responsible for the 'Anonymous Verse-Prose Version' of *De consolatione philosophiae* (already discussed earlier in this chapter) to serve as its preface. Similarly, in his commentary on the *Consolatio*, Nicholas Trevet distinguished between the *persona indigens*, the person in need of consolation, and the *persona afferens*, the person effecting that consolation. What is especially interesting about these accounts is the recognition of the fictionality of the characters and their distance from the author himself.

Vernacular writers drew on such methods of assigning, devolving – or indeed avoiding – responsibility. In the Latin commentary which (it would seem) John Gower wrote to accompany his Middle English *Confessio amantis* the distance between the passions of the narrator and the wisdom of the author is emphasised. Gower is not speaking *in propria persona*, but rather is conveying the emotions of others. The key gloss explains that 'Here as it were in the person of those other people ['quasi in persona aliorum'] whom love constrains, the author, feigning himself to be a lover ['fingens se auctor esse Amantem'], proposes to write of their various passions one by one in the various distinctions of this book'. Similarly, in *Il Convivio*, Dante had asserted that the 'literal story' of his

---

[21] See the prologue to this commentary, ed. Crespo, 'Il Prologo'.

lyric 'Voi che'ntendendo' was in fact fictitious, its true meaning relating to the love not of an earthly woman but of philosophy. In both cases, the emphasis on the fictionality of the text serves to preserve the authority of the writer. But perhaps the most elaborate vernacular appropriation of persona-theory occurs in the *querelle de la Rose* (*c.* 1401–*c.* 1403), when the supporters of Jean de Meun sought to defend him by arguing that certain controversial statements in the *Roman de la Rose* were made not by the writer himself but by personae of limited standing or indeed of reprehensible character.

Moreover, the commentary tradition had to offer the late-medieval writer various *modi agendi*, i.e. stylistic and generic forms. Some modern historians of literary criticism have suspected that medieval literature is 'a generic wasteland or labyrinth'. 'There are signposts', it has been suggested, 'but these only confuse matters further by their baffling ambiguities. They may be classical, or classical misunderstood, or classical reinterpreted, or vernacular equivalent, or vernacular oblivious, or vernacular artful and innovative' (Fowler, *Kinds*, p. 146).

The medieval mode of tragedy – which has already been discussed at some length in Chapter 6 above – is a good test-case for this view. In his *Magnae derivationes* Hugutio of Pisa, following in the footsteps of Papias and Isidore of Seville, sums up many of the grammarians' commonplaces by describing tragedy as being about great crimes, proceeding from joy to sorrow (whereas comedy moves from sorrow to joy), dealing with great individuals (whereas comedy treats of private persons), and being written in the high style, in contrast with the low style which is appropriate for comedy. Most medieval notions of tragedy moved within these narrow parameters, and some writers did not even know that much. More knowledgeable individuals were confused about whether tragedy's victims deserved their downfalls or not.[22] In *De consolatione philosophiae* (2 pr. 2) Lady Philosophy envisages tragedy as dealing with disasters which unexpectedly befall the innocent as well as the guilty. But in Boethius commentaries (such as Trevet's), Isidore's definition of tragedy as a record of the ancient deeds and crimes of wicked kings is reported, to which is added a statement that a tragedy is a poem dealing with great iniquities, which begins in prosperity and ends in adversity. Medieval 'narrative tragedies' (if so they may be called), like Boccaccio's *De casibus virorum illustrium* and Chaucer's *Monk's Tale*, feature people who deserved their downfalls alongside those who did not. But Boccaccio, it should be emphasised, did not call his *De casibus* a tragedy or a collection of tragedies; when he uses the term it designates in general an ancient (and, to Boccaccio *cum suis*)

---

[22] See Kelly, 'Non-Tragedy of Arthur', and *Tragedy and Comedy*.

very obscure dramatic form, and in particular the plays of Euripides and Nero's stage productions.

The extent to which the two most sophisticated medieval documents on the subject, Averroes' 'Middle Commentary' on Aristotle's *Poetics* as translated by Hermann the German and Nicholas Trevet's commentary on Seneca's tragedies, were actually known and used in the later Middle Ages is a matter of some controversy among modern critics; suffice it to say that no incontrovertible evidence has been produced for either of these documents having influenced any of the major vernacular writers, including Boccaccio and Chaucer. Instead, what we seem to be dealing with is a small body of received ideas which, in the hands of different interpreters, could take on different meanings.

This may be illustrated by two substantial but quite contradictory medieval realisations of tragedy, the first being found in John of Garland's *Parisiana poetria* (on which see Chapter 2 above). John actually writes a tragedy, a non-dramatic one in hexameters, which, he declares, is only the second work of this kind ever written, Ovid's lost *Medea* being the first. John's poem tells the sordid tale of two washerwomen who serve the sexual needs of a besieged garrison: its qualifications as a tragedy seem to consist simply of its unhappy ending and martial terminology. Here practice is striving to imitate theory.

Our second text indicates a writer seeking in what he knows of classical literary theory principles with which he can elevate, and indeed encourage, literary practice in the 'illustrious vernacular'. Tragedy is a major focus of the finished portion of *De vulgari eloquentia*, and Dante had planned to write about comedy in its fourth book – and of course he bestowed upon his greatest work the title of *Commedia*, or at least considered it as such. Dante seems to understand these terms to refer to non-dramatic works written in styles which are appropriate for specific subjects: 'by "tragic" I mean the higher style, by "comic" the lower, and by "elegiac" that of the unhappy' (2.4; ed. and tr. Botterill, pp. 56–7). In the vernacular, tragic style is attained when exquisite verse-forms, elevated construction and excellent vocabulary are joined with gravity of substance (*gravitas sententie*). Thus, only the gravest subjects – love, virtue and arms – are appropriate for the tragic style: here the influence of the work which Dante was later to term *alta tragedia* (*Inf.* 20.112–3), the *Aeneid*, is obvious, for in the medieval reception of Virgil's poem all three of these aspects were emphasised, particularly its celebration of virtue. Here the classical genre of epic is being reconstructed in terms of a quite individual definition of tragedy – a definition which, indeed, would allow a love-lyric with the right style and the right *sententia* to be termed a tragedy.

Here, then, is a clear case of 'vernacular artful and innovative' arising out of 'classical misunderstood', though the notion of 'misunderstanding' is quite inappropriate in an investigation of how medieval textual culture made sense of earlier texts in the light of its own priorities and values. Then-current notions of genre could accommodate a considerable number of permutations and cross-influences. This fact is further borne out by the literary theory and practice of Boccaccio's attempt at a 'vernacular epic', the *Teseida* (probably written between 1339 and the mid-1340s). Dante's triumvirate of gravest subjects – love, virtue and arms – is echoed in the envoy to this work. Since the Muses began to walk naked in the sight of men (i.e. since poetry began to be written in the vernacular, as Boccaccio's own gloss explains), some have employed them in fine style for moral composition while others have enlisted them in the service of love-poetry. But Boccaccio's own work is the first 'to make them sing the long labours of Mars' in the Italian vernacular.[23] This claim should not, however, be taken as exclusive of love and virtue. For in the poem's invocation Boccaccio invokes Venus and Cupid along with Mars and the Muses, and in general the poem depicts and celebrates the achievements of virtuous heathen (the soul of Arcite, for instance, seems to journey to Elysium, described by Boccaccio as the home of valiant and good men). This range of subjects is further indicated by the *accessus*-style introductions to two mid-fifteenth-century Italian commentaries on the *Teseida* (Boccaccio's self-commentary lacks a formal prologue).[24] According to one of these, the work of an anonymous Neopolitan, in its various parts the poem comprises elements of tragedy, comedy, satire and elegy. He explains that it can be called a comedy because its main action ends with a marriage. (The unsuitability of this designation, inasmuch as the poem's characters are of high rather than low birth and status, is ignored.) The other commentary, written by Pietro Andrea de'Bassi (a scholar in the service of the d'Este of Ferrara), describes the *materia* of *Il Teseida* as follows: 'we know the author wants to treat of and to be the subject: his presentation of battles, of the power of love, of the effects of Venus, which things mixed with infinite poetic fictions and histories he puts forward most elegantly'. The part of philosophy to which the work pertains is then identified as ethics – thus de'Bassi emphasises the poem's conformity to the 'ethical poetic' as defined in generations of *accessus* to Latin writers (see Chapters 5 and 6 above). The mixed style of the *Teseida*, it would seem, accommodates all three of Dante's superior subjects, and this range is a strength rather than a weakness.

---

[23] Tr. Anderson, *Before The 'Knight's Tale'*, p. 17.
[24] On these commentaries, see Anderson, *Before The 'Knight's Tale'*, pp. 18–21, 33–4.

Satire was perhaps the secular literary mode which attained the highest level of definition in the later Middle Ages.[25] Generations of *accessus* described the subject-matter of the Roman satirists as being vice, their intention being the censure of vice and the fostering of virtue. Their moral credentials were impeccable: quite clearly, satires pertain to ethics and possess considerable *utilitas* inasmuch as they teach good behaviour. Other poets, the commentators declare, may begin their works with some delightful device, but satirists get straight to the point and begin suddenly (*ex abrupto*), such directness being a distinguishing feature of the mode. Given that satirical theory remained remarkably stable and monolithic throughout the period, the critical consensus may be summarised as follows: 'Satire is that type of ethical verse, ranging in tone between bitter indignation, mocking irony, and witty humour, which in forthright, unadorned terms censures and corrects vices in society and advocates virtues, eschewing slander of individuals but sparing no guilty party, not even the poet himself' (Miller, 'Gower, Satiric Poet', p. 82). In the school exercises in which they imitated the ancient works they studied, medieval students were influenced directly by this medieval theory of satire and only indirectly by the actual satires of Horace, Persius and Juvenal. Thus were established the parameters within which many medieval satires were written. In the period between 1050 and 1250 a corpus of Latin poetry was produced which complied with important aspects of medieval satirical theory. This includes the *De contemptu mundi* of Bernard of Cluny, the satiric poetry of Walter of Châtillon and his so-called 'school', the *Speculum stultorum* of Nigel Wireker ('de Longchamps'), and the *Morale scolarium* of John of Garland. Some of the vernacular satirists were as critically well-informed as those scholar-poets. Satiric theory is echoed in Jean de Meun's *apologia* for his part of the *Roman de la Rose*.[26] And the anonymous author of the Middle English poem *Mum and the Sothsegger* (*c.* 1400) emphasises, after the manner of the *accessus ad satiricos*, that his *tente* (compare the Latin term *intentio*) is not to slander maliciously but to correct those whom he censures (ll. 72–5). Moreover, important sections of John Gower's three major works – the Anglo-Norman *Mirour de l'omme* (*c.* 1376–8), the Latin *Vox clamantis* (*c.* 1379–81) and the Middle English *Confessio amantis* – conform to medieval satirical theory and practice in significant aspects of content, structure and style.

The way in which descriptive critical discourse tended to provide prescriptive literary models is also illustrated by the theory of a very different medieval mode, namely prophecy. This had as its determining source

---

[25] See further the discussion of satire included in Chapter 6 above.
[26] See Minnis, *Magister amoris*, pp. 82–118.

medieval scriptural exegesis, though the influence of secular commentary, particularly Macrobius' commentary on Cicero's *Somnium Scipionis*, must also be given its due. Theologians 'discovered' and provided much of the literary theory for new literary forms, forms for which there was little if any basis in traditional rhetoric and poetics. One of these was the *forma* (or *modus*) *prophetialis*: the prophetic books of the Bible possessed certain literary properties which, according to the expositors, constituted a literary form. Once defined as a viable form, it could be exploited in 'modern' writings of many different kinds, including the Latin prophecies of 'John of Bridlington' (described in the anonymous commentary which accompanies them as having an obscure and prophetic formal cause)[27] and Gower's *Vox clamantis*. Dante, and the commentators on the *Commedia*, were indebted to theological discussions of the *forma prophetialis*, and the issue of whether Dante's vision was 'real' or 'imaginary' (i.e. fictional) was a matter of hot debate. Moreover, in theologians' disquisitions on prophecy may be found literary ideas of considerable relevance to the vernacular dream-vision poetry which abounded in the later Middle Ages, particularly in French and English. This type of information mingled with that characteristic of the Macrobian tradition to create a considerable body of theory upon which medieval vernacular writers drew at will, and sometimes wilfully.

One of the most interesting manifestations of such theory is the late-fourteenth-century French commentary on an anonymous French poem, the *Eschez amoureux*, which recently has been attributed to Evrart de Conty,[28] physician of King Charles V and the author of the *Livre des problèmes d'Aristote* which has been discussed above. Although not, technically speaking, a dream-vision itself, the *Eschez* is very much a derivative of what was indubitably the most widely influential work composed in that mode, the *Roman de la Rose* (a work which, incidentally, is itself remarkably reticent about affirming theoretically its own visionary genre; see Chapter 7). Evrart describes literary dreaming as one of the types of reasonable 'feigning' or fiction-making which can be practised in order to speak in a way which is safe and secure (in situations where plain speaking is unacceptable; *Eschez amour moral*, ed. Guichard-Tesson and Roy, pp. 23–4). This method was preferred by Cicero to Plato's use of myth, which was ridiculed by the ignorant; by using 'the manner of a dream' (*maniere de songe*) he sought to avoid all unreasonable objections (compare Macrobius, *In Somnium Scipionis* I, 1–2). Cicero therefore feigned that King Scipio saw his ancestor Scipio the African and with him his father in a dream, and that 'those two told him of great wonders and

[27] On 'John of Bridlington' see Meuvaert, 'John Erghome'.
[28] By Guichard-Tesson, 'Evrart de Conty'.

secret things of the heaven and of the earth', and of other matters concerning his situation and person. In particular, they confirmed that those who sustain, defend and govern the country well by reason and justice, are finally translated to the heavens, and this is their right and proper dwelling place, where they live forever in great beatitude. Those who, on the contrary, fail in these duties, are left below on the earth. 'And this', declares Evrart, spelling out the message for his Christian audience, is 'what we mean when we say that the good and just go to paradise after death and the bad, on the contrary, go to hell'. He also notes that the dream-form sometimes excuses 'the person who speaks of many things that would be considered badly said' if they were taken as actually having happened or in a literal way. For the dreamer can always excuse himself on the grounds that he himself cannot be held responsible for what he dreamed about, answering that 'it seemed that way to him while he slept and that it was imposed on him in a dream'.

The *Rose* is then compared to the *Somnium Scipionis* in that here too the dream-form is employed. Unfortunately there is no ensuing discussion. One may recall, however, how Guillaume de Lorris, at the very beginning of the *Rose* (ll. 1–20), had sought to validate his own dream by appealing to Macrobius, 'who did not take dreams as trifles'; his argument that 'a dream signifies the good and evil that come to men' certainly matches Cicero's poem. At no point does the *Rose* actually use the defence that one cannot help what one dreams – indeed, Jean de Meun takes rather a rationalist view of the problem, mentioning Scipio in the course of an account of how certain men through an excess of contemplation 'cause the appearance in their thought of the things on which they have pondered' (ll. 18,357–70). But the defence was an obvious one and some practitioners of the dream-form were certainly aware of its advantages, including William Langland, who, at the end of the 'Visio'-section of *Piers Plowman*, presents his dreamer-figure as being utterly bemused by his experience. He cannot interpret it, for he has no expertise in dream-interpretation; all he can do is cite the warning of 'Cato and canon-lawyers' that one should take no account of dreams (compare *Disticha* 2.31), yet note that the Bible bears witness that dreams can signify future truth, as in the cases of the dreams of Nebuchadnezzar and Joseph. But he himself is no Daniel or Jacob; all he can do is 'study' what he 'saw sleeping' (B-text, 7.144–67). The literary dream-vision was, in sum, a consummately ambiguous genre, which could either be elevated by reference to biblical visions or denigrated by reference to scientific and medical scepticism about the validity of dream experiences. (See further the discussion of medieval theory of imagination, in Chapter 7 above).

Turning now from the commentaries proper to the prologues which introduced them, it may be said that academic Latin prologues exercised a profound influence on the prologues – and, more generally, on the literary attitudes – of late-medieval authors, whether they were writing in Latin or *in vulgari*. The direct transfer of Latin academic prolegomena as part of the translation of Latin works into European vernacular languages has been considered above. Here our subject is the adaptations and developments of standard idioms and vocabulary to suit new needs. Prologue paradigms which had developed most fully as introductions to Latin commentaries on *auctores* were altered to serve as prefaces to many different kinds of text, written both in Latin and in the vernaculars, ranging from treatises and reference-books on a wide range of subjects to *exempla* collections and legendaries, and indeed to 'modern' poems and prose works written in the several European languages.

Hence, the technical vocabulary and formal patterns of the several types of prologues were put to a variety of uses – as may be illustrated by the permutations of one of the ideas associated with the 'Aristotelian Prologue' (on which see p. 52 above), the theory of efficient causality, which encouraged the description of different levels of authorship and authority. What could be done is well illustrated by the elegant prologue to Robert of Basevorn's *Forma praedicandi* (dated 1322), a work in the *ars praedicandi* tradition (on which see Chapter 4 above). Here God is identified as the final cause of this work; He is, after all, the ultimate goal of every right-thinking man. May God also be the primary efficient cause who influences this work throughout, Robert adds. With appropriate humility, he protests that nothing proceeds from himself alone: he would say with the Apostle, 'I dare not speak of any of those things which Christ works in me' (Rom. 15:18), and 'And I live, now not I, but Christ lives in me.' (Gal. 2:20).[29] In other words, Robert is a self-declared secondary efficient cause working under the primary *causa efficiens*, God. He has manoeuvred himself into the position occupied by the human authors of holy Scripture, as described in the 'Aristotelian Prologue' to commentaries on many Aristotelian and biblical texts. Similar strategies were adopted by the compilers of various kinds of reference-book. For example, in the prologue to Pierre Bersuire's *Reductorium morale* (begun *c.* 1320), the *causae* function as part of an elaborate protestation of humility in which all that is useful and worthwhile in the compilation is decorously attributed to its primary efficient cause, God.

These procedures carried over into the vernaculars. In the prologue to an Anglo-Norman compilation, the *Lumière as lais*, which was completed in 1276, the anonymous writer (perhaps Pierre d'Abernon of Fetcham?) describes himself as an instrument employed by the principal *autur*, our Lord. The most systematic 'Aristotelian Prologue' to have originally been written in Middle English appears at the beginning of the *Legendys of Hooly Wummen*, an individual compilation of lives of female saints by an Augustinian friar, Osbern Bokenham (*c.* 1390–*c.* 1447). This is particularly interesting because it assimilates to the scheme of the four causes two of the literary *circumstantiae*, the 'what' and why' of a text. These are the things, Bokenham declares, which every clerk ought to explain at the beginning of a work, if he wishes to proceed in an orderly fashion. In these two words 'The foure causys comprehendyd be' – which, as philosophers teach us,

> In the begynnyng men owe to seche
> Of euery book; and aftyr there entent
> The fyrst is clepyd cause efficyent,
> The secunde they clepe cause materyal,
> Formal the thrydde, the fourte fynal.
>
> (8–12)

A rather different kind of example is provided in an early-fourteenth-century manuscript of Thomasin von Zerklaere's Middle High German *Der welsche Gast* (written 1215–16). This long didactic poem has a prose summary which begins with a *materia operis* or *divisio operis* of a type characteristic of twelfth-century scholasticism. But Gotha, Forschungs-bibliothek, MS memb. I.120 includes an author-portrait at the beginning of its cycle of illustrations in which the author, labelled as *causa efficiens* (all the other inscriptions on the pictures are in German), hands over a copy of his book to 'the German Language' (*div tvtsche zunge*). This picks up a passage in the verse prologue in which the German Lands (*Tvtsche land*) are addressed in the first person as the mistress of a household. Although the verse prologue itself is free of scholastic terminology, clearly the person responsible for that Latin inscription felt it appropriate to use the current technical term.

Far more complicated is the case of the presentation of Mechthild von Magdeburg's *Das fliessende Licht der Gottheit* (completed *c.* 1282 but written over the period 1250–82). These revelations were written down in Low German, no doubt under the supervision of her confessor. The seven-book version, which has been preserved only in a High German translation from Basel (and is the only full text extant in German), was edited by a Dominican friar who provided a Latin and German preface and must have been responsible for the Latin book- and chapter-headings and the table of contents. The prologue to the Latin translation of this work (made sometime between 1282 and 1298) discusses, in the manner of the earlier *accessus* model, its *auctor*, *materia*, *modus agendi* and *finis*. The author is identified as the Trinity; the material is Christ and the church (traditionally described as Christ's mystical body) on the one hand, and Satan along with his body on the other; the mode is both historical and mystical, while the objective is the regulation of life here and now, the useful memory of things that are past and prophecies of future things. The strong emphasis here on divine authorship is remarkable. Similarly, in the German prologue to Book 1 we are assured that the book has been composed ('made', *gemachet*) by God Himself. The first heading states, 'This book should be received gladly, for the words are spoken by God Himself'. However, it is disputed whether the words 'It signifies me alone and it reveals most wonderfully my secrets' are to be taken as spoken by God or by Mechthild. If the words are God's, as seems likely in view of the immediate context, then they express the idea that Mechthild is to be seen as a mere instrument rather than as the 'human author' of the work who is functioning alongside God as the 'divine author'. What is indisputable is that, in his prologue, the Latin translator records the devotion and simple piety of the woman through whom the revelation came to be known, which chimes with a statement in the German text that, 'This book has come from God in love, and it is not derived from human thoughts' (rendered in the Latin as 'it has not been put forth by human sense or understanding'). Here the idea of instrumental efficient causality functions to diminish the status of the human author. In personal records of mystical experience such as this, the issues of authorship and authority were particularly delicate (and no doubt further exacerbated in this case by the sex of the recipient of His grace).

The way in which technical prologue vocabulary could take on different forms in both Latin and vernacular works may be further exemplified by tracing some of the developments of a distinction which in large measure owed its popularity to its memorable formulation in the *apologia actoris* of Vincent of Beauvais, the 'king of compilers' (on whom see further Chapter 6 above). According to Vincent, the *auctor* affirms whereas the *compilator* repeats and reports; to the author belongs the authority, whereas the lot of the compiler is to excerpt, collect and organise. This became the required stance of the *compilator*, reiterated at the beginning of many a later compilation, whether in Latin or in a vernacular language. The same method of professing personal humility, the same ostentatious deference to sources, occur in the prologue to Brunetto Latini's French *Trésor* (c. 1260): 'I do not say that the book is drawn from my poor wit or my scanty learning: but it is like a honeycomb gathered from different flowers, for this book is compiled exclusively from the marvellous sayings of authors . . .' (pp. 17–18). Bartholomew the Englishman explained his intention in composing the popular *De proprietatibus rerum* (begun 1225–31) in words very similar to Vincent's, protesting that he had added 'little or nothing of my own', or, as John Trevisa's English translation (of 1398) puts it, 'of myne owne wille litil oþir nouȝt' (I, p. 43). In the prologue to a work clearly indebted to the *Speculum maius*, Ralph Higden's *Polychronicon* (finished *c.* 1352), Vincent's ideas are amplified and presented even more aggressively. The mighty compiler, Higden declares, has taken the mace from the hand of Hercules (no excessive humility here!); he continues the martial metaphor by claiming the names of his *auctores* as a 'shield and defence' against detractors (I, p. 20). A 'sword to slay envy' – that is how Chaucer, addressing his *Treatise on the Astrolabe* (1391?) to his son Lewis, saw the traditional stance of the compiler. He is not claiming to have 'founden this werk of my labour or of myn engyn. I n'am but a lewd compilator of the labour of olde astrologiens, and have it translatid in myn Englissh oonly for thy doctrine. And with this swerd shal I sleen envie' (p. 662, ll. 60–4). One may also recall Boccaccio's declaration that he could only transcribe the tales in the *Decameron* as they were actually told, the implication being that he should be regarded as their scribe (*lo scrittore*) rather than their originator (*lo 'nventore*).

Many of the applications of scholastic literary idioms which we have considered so far are clearly appropriate, perhaps even to some extent predictable, extensions of the theory disseminated by commentary tradition. For we have often been dealing with indubitably didactic works of one kind or another. Now we may proceed to consider far more daring and controversial applications of scholastic literary theory, namely the uses to which certain vernacular love-poets put ideas and idioms which were characteristic of commentary on that most ambiguous – not to say dubious – of all *auctores*, the poet Ovid. (The hermeneutic difficulties presented by Ovid have been discussed in Chapters 5 and 6 above.)

Many late-medieval commentaries and treatises were introduced by linked pairs of prologues (or bipartite prologues), wherein the first, 'extrinsic' component would offer general discussion of wisdom (in the Aristotelian sense of *sapientia*) while the second, 'intrinsic' component would provide discussion of the text itself. John Gower's *Confessio amantis*, an anthology of stories which have love as their main subject and Ovid as their main source, opens with elaborate prolegomena which seem to have been influenced by these types of academic prologue. Its long, admonitory Prologus may to some extent be regarded as an extrinsic prologue which is about wisdom ('this prologue is so assised / That it to wisdom al belongeth', ll. 66–7), while the first ninety-two lines of Book 1 function as an intrinsic prologue which focuses on the writer's plan and purpose in the following work. *Sapientia* and *amor* are linked through the donnish joke that love has 'put under' many a wise man (ll. 75–6). Hence, it seems fitting that a Prologus on wisdom should be followed by a treatise about love. Gower's declared intention is 'in som part' to advise 'the wyse man' (ll. 64–5), and so the Prologus warns of the ways in which the temporal rulers, the church and the commons have ceased to

follow wisdom. It is emphasised that God alone has the wisdom necessary
for full understanding of worldly fortune. Then, in his intrinsic prologue
Gower proceeds to explain precisely what is within his compass. He cannot stretch his hand up to heaven and set the world to rights; instead he
will change the style of his writings and speak of a matter with which all
the world has to do, namely Love.

Our second case is the Spanish prose preface found at the beginning of
the final version of another work which in its content is often indebted
to Ovid, Juan Ruiz's *Libro de buen amor* (preserved in the Salamanca
manuscript, dated 1343). This takes the form of a 'sermon-type' prologue,
the initial *auctoritas* being Psalm 31:10, which is interpreted as meaning
that by true understanding man knows the good and consequently knows
the bad. The biblical quotation is divided and discussed in the traditional
manner; finally, the extrinsic treatment gives way to an intrinsic discussion of the *Libro de buen amor*. Here Ruiz manages both to condemn and
commend human love, combining ideas which traditionally figure in the
accessus to Ovid's *Heroides, Ars amatoria* and *Remedia amoris*. These
transitions would have seemed far less surprising to those readers who
knew the 'Medieval Ovid' who was his source – i.e. Ovid as interpreted
in the Middle Ages, entailing systematic moralisation together with an
ultimate harmonising of discords by appeal to the poet's eventual repentance, as recorded in the *Remedia amoris*, and indeed (for those who
knew and accepted the Pseudo-Ovidian *De vetula*) to his conversion to
Christianity. (For a fuller account of the Ruiz prologue see Chapter 17
below.)

The Ovid commentators' ideas keep surfacing in the 'quarrel over the
Rose', with regard to both Ovid himself and to his great imitator Jean
de Meun, identified by both his defenders and attackers, for better or
worse, as a medieval Ovidian. Christine de Pizan and Chancellor Jean
Gerson made the connection not least because in their view Jean de Meun
was replicating Ovid's great fault. Reading books which stimulate lust
is particularly dangerous, declares Gerson in a sermon preached on 17
December 1402; men who own them should be required by their confessors to tear them up – books like Ovid's, or Matheolus, or parts of the
Roman de la Rose (*Le Débat*, ed. Hicks, p. 179). Similarly, in a letter to
Jean de Montreuil (author of a lost treatise in defence of Jean de Meun),
Christine asserts that the *Rose* has no *utilité* (*Le Débat*, ed. Hicks, p. 20).
Apparently she is using the term in the technical sense which the Latin
form *utilitas* bears in the *accessus*, as designating the didactic effect and
moral worth which one requires in an authoritative work of literature.
The connection between the *praeceptor amoris* and Master Jean de Meun
is made quite explicit in Gerson's version of this form of accusation. In his
1402 treatise against the *Rose*, he imagines one of its supporters saying

that, while there is some evil in the book, it contains much more that is good, and so 'Let every man receive the good and reject the evil' (*Le Débat*, ed. Hicks, p. 65). Gerson retorts, are the evil things in the book thereby deleted? Indeed not – a hook does not injure the fish less if it is covered in bait; a sword dipped in honey does not cut less deeply. Indeed, the good things contained in the book actually make it more dangerous. St Paul (1 Cor. 15:33), Seneca and experience all teach that evil speaking and writings corrupt good morals. Gerson proceeds to consider the edifying example of Ovid's exile (*Le Débat*, ed. Hicks, p. 76). The *Tristia* proves that he was exiled on account of his wretched *Ars amatoria*; even his refutation of its false teaching, the *Remedia amoris*, could not save the poet from this fate. How amazing it is that a pagan and infidel judge (i.e. the Emperor Augustus) should condemn a book which incites to foolish love, while among Christians such a work is supported, praised and defended!

For the poem's opponents, the fact that it was more comprehensive and thoroughgoing than the *Ars amatoria* made it all the more dangerous. 'It is clear', declares Gerson, 'that this work is worse than that of Ovid', because the *Rose* contains not only Ovid's *Ars amatoria* but also other books 'which are not any the less dishonest or dangerous' (*Le Débat*, ed. Hicks, pp. 76–7). Gerson proceeds to argue that Jean de Meun had fewer scruples than his Roman predecessor. Ovid clearly declared in the *Ars* that he is not writing about good matrons or of ladies joined in marriage, or of those who could not be loved lawfully (see *Ars amatoria* 1.31–4, 2.599–600). But the *Rose* is no respecter of persons: 'it mocks all, blames all, despises all without any exception'.

For the poem's supporters, however, Jean's amplification of Ovid made his poem all the more praiseworthy, as may be seen from Pierre Col's ingenious appropriation of a common defence of Ovid (*Le Débat*, ed. Hicks, p. 104). By describing the way in which the Rose's castle was captured, he claimed, Jean de Meun actually was aiding its defenders. Because they then knew how their fortress could fall, in the future they would block the gap or place better guards there and thus lessen the chances of the assailants. Moreover, Jean made this information widely available by writing in 'the common language of men and women, young and old, that is, in French'. By contrast, the *fin* of the *Ars amatoria* was exclusively to teach men how to assault the castle – being in Latin, he declares (reflecting medieval values rather than those of Ovid's day), this work was not available to women. Here *fin* is used in the technical sense carried by *finis* or *finalis causa* in the *accessus*; one may compare a representative glossator's statement that Ovid's objective in the *Ars* was to make 'clear to young men' the 'course they should follow in a love affair', the authorial intention being 'to instruct young men in the art of love' (tr. Minnis and Scott, p. 24).

Ovid, then, served only the assailants, whereas Jean de Meun has taken the side of the defenders in preparing them for the stratagems which they will face. But Christine de Pizan was not impressed. Pierre Col's claim that Jean was on the side of the defenders of the castle was, in her view, *mervilleuse* ('incredible'). Master Jean, she retorted, does nothing at all to help the defenders in closing up the gaps, for he does not speak to them at all and is not of their counsel; rather, he aids and abets the attackers in every form of assault (*Le Débat*, ed. Hicks, pp. 136–7). If you were to suggest that the poet is simply recounting how the castle fell rather than recommending it, she warns Pierre Col, she would reply that a man who described an evil way of making counterfeit money would be teaching that method quite sufficiently. By identifying Ovid's *Ars amatoria* as a source of the *Rose*, she continues, Pierre has been caught in his own trap, for a bad work cannot be the foundation of a good one. Furthermore, Pierre's argument that Meun drew upon works other than the *Ars* does not help his case, for a proliferation of evil material does not make for a good *fin*. Pierre had said that the more diverse the methods of attack which are revealed to the guards the better they are taught the art of defence. This, Christine asserts, is tantamount to saying that a man who attacks you and tries to kill you is merely showing you how to defend yourself!

Here, then, is clear evidence that one and the same body of critical ideas could be manipulated to serve two utterly opposed and irreconcilable points of view. When the *Rose*'s opponents castigated it as lacking utility, or when its defenders affirmed its great value, they had in common certain paradigms, and revealed themselves to be influenced by certain principles, which figure largely in medieval commentary tradition, most relevantly in the *accessus Ovidiani*.

6. Commentary and vernacular authority

Latin commentary tradition was often drawn upon by those who wished to provide vernacular texts with an apparatus which at once described certain aspects of those texts and tacitly claimed a degree of prestige for them, because that apparatus was of the type which conventionally had accompanied the works of the revered Latin *auctores*. Academic commentary became a precedent and source for 'modern' commentary (i.e. commentary on writers who were *moderni*) and even 'self-commentary': certain writers set about the business of producing exegesis of texts which had been written by their contemporaries and even by themselves.

Some of these appropriations of method and matter were more daring than others. Various moral and didactic vernacular works received, quite naturally, moral and didactic glossing. A good example of this is provided by one of the most heavily glossed original works in Middle English: two copies of the mid-fifteenth-century *Court of Sapience* contain an erudite apparatus of Latin glosses, probably the work of the poet himself. Similarly, the Low German printed edition of the poem *Reynke de vos* (Lübeck, 1498), which is based on a lost Dutch recension, has extensive glosses in prose which itemise the moral points to be derived from the poem on a chapter-by-chapter basis. They are usually structured according to the following scheme: 'In the preceding chapter there are four points to be learned; the first is . . .'. In content, the glosses are overwhelmingly of a general moral nature, only occasionally are allegories offered (e.g. the gloss on ll. 717–608 interpreting Reynard as signifying the devil). The prose prologue claims that the *poete* who composed the Reynard story was one of the *phylozophy* of Antiquity, who lived before the birth of Christ, thus associating the poem with the traditional Latin school-texts, on whose commentaries the prose gloss on *Reynke de vos* is based. The use of Reynard as a school-text is further documented by a later sixteenth-century synoptic French–Dutch edition (Antwerp, 1566). This example shows how a vernacular poetic text of the high Middle Ages could be taken over into the tradition of school literature.

Far more significant are the commentaries on texts of a more innovative kind, including poems which contain an erotic element. And here we must turn to late-medieval Italy, where the most sophisticated traditions of 'new' commentary and 'self-commentary' are to be found. Much of the credit must go to Dante – arguably the greatest medieval poet, he was also one of the most innovative of medieval literary critics. Dante's confidence as self-commentator provided a powerful precedent for lesser mortals; the commentaries on the *Commedia* constitute the single most important corpus of contemporary criticism on any medieval writer (see Chapter 22 below). In his first attempt at 'autoexegesis', the *Vita Nova*, Dante employed the scholastic technique of 'exposition by division' (*divisio textus*). But the affinities of that work are rather with the *vidas* of the troubadour poets (on which see Chapter 16 below). The later *Convivio* represents a thoroughgoing appropriation of the principles and terminology of academic literary criticism; Dante rightly calls it 'quasi comento', a kind of commentary in the technical sense of the term. The work begins with an Aristotelian extrinsic prologue which features the theory of causality, and proceeds with a sophisticated commentary on commentary itself, wherein it is concluded that it is most appropriate for vernacular poems to be accompanied by a vernacular commentary. After a well-known and highly controversial excursus on the two kinds of allegorical interpretation ('the allegory of the poets' and 'the allegory of the theologians': see Chapter 20 below), Dante proceeds to apply an extraordinary amount of erudition to the matters allegedly raised by the *canzoni*. No one, after reading all this, could fail to take the *canzoni* seriously, or take them with the wrong kind of seriousness. One aspect of Dante's ambition was, quite clearly, to be regarded as a vernacular *auctor*. Hence he sought that validation which academic exegesis could bring to his art.

Following in his master's footsteps, Boccaccio (who in the last years of his life was to comment on the *Commedia*) equipped his own *Teseida* with a commentary. The beginning of his work on this poem is marked by a letter to an anonymous friend in which he complains that he has been having difficulty in reading Statius' *Thebaid* 'without guidance or glosses', and expressed his wish (later realised) to have a copy of the commentary on that work by Lactantius Placidus. Subsequently he made sure that his own vernacular epic came equipped with an extensive commentary. These vernacular *chiose*, and indeed the poem itself, display no marked dependency on Lactantius; the point is rather that Boccaccio felt his poem merited an apparatus of the kind which accompanied its Latin counterparts in manuscript (the scholia on the *Thebaid*, *Aeneid*, and that highly popular medieval facsimile of a classical epic, Walter of Châtillon's *Alexandreis*), an apparatus designed to dispose the discerning reader in favour of the poem and underline for his benefit the superlative literary criteria in accordance with which it should be judged and esteemed.

In his later *Genealogia deorum gentilium* Boccaccio laments that while other kinds of texts (legal, philosophical, scriptural, etc.) have their commentaries, 'Poetry alone is without such honour. Few – very few – are they with whom it has dwelt continuously' (15.6; tr. Osgood, p. 117). This is rhetorical exaggeration (although the scale of commentary on poetry was indeed relatively minor), and Boccaccio was well aware of previous attempts to remedy the deficiency – the influence of *De vulgari eloquentia* on the poetics of the *Teseida* has already been noted, and in the *chiose* on its seventh book Boccaccio cites Dino del Garbo's (Latin) commentary on 'Donna mi prega', the *canzone d'amore* of Guido Cavalcanti (*c*. 1259–1300). Hence it seems reasonable to assume that here Boccaccio saw himself as writing within a tradition of vernacular criticism.

The efforts of Dante and Boccaccio at self-commentary are overshadowed, however, in quantity if not in quality, by the Latin commentary which Francesco da Barberino, lawyer and episcopal notary, wrote to accompany his *Documenti d'amore* (apparently produced during the period 1309–13). Here Barberino set out to do for 'the laws of love' what Justinian and Gratian had done for Roman law and canon law respectively, i.e. the collection and harmonising of diverse and discordant documents. His overall purpose as commentator, he says, is to expound the text diligently with regard to divine love and spiritual intention (*intentio*).

There follows an intrinsic prologue in which a discussion of the *Documenti d'amore* is conducted under four of the standard *accessus* headings (*intentio, materia, utilitas* and *cui parti philosophie subponatur*), to which a fifth, *modus agendi*, is added later. Barberino's professed ambition is to teach the form of love, providing documents whereby the vices may be known for what they are and thence eschewed, and the virtues may be loved. This is the principle which underlies his attempts at reconciling authorities which are very different in status and in kind, love being regarded in its most universal aspect. Throughout the commentary philosophers and theologians (for example, Aristotle, Augustine, Jerome, John Chrysostom, St Bernard, Hugh and Richard of St Victor) rub shoulders not only with the poets of Antiquity but also those of the writer's own time, including a formidable array of Provençal poets, several of whom are unknown apart from Barberino's citations. 'The greatest virtue of our superior, Love, has recently fired my intellect to call his servants to his greater citadel from each and every country', declares Barberino in the very first lines of the Italian poem and the corresponding Latin translation (ed. Egidi, I, pp. 3–4). Never before had a 'legislator' sought to collate and codify so many different laws from so many different countries and – more to the point – so many different literary contexts. In the entire *Documenti d'amore* (taking its Latin and Italian components together), the troubadour love-poetic has been assimilated to the 'ethical poetic'. The physical aspects of human love have been transcended or at least obscured; the subversive element of medieval Ovidianism has been moderated.

By contrast, in the commentaries on texts which do retain something of that subversive element of medieval Ovidianism, the distance between the text and the gloss is sometimes marked. Thus, Boccaccio's *chiose* to his *Teseida* amplify the negative aspects of the text's depiction of the passions which Arcita and Palamon feel for the same woman, Emilia. An even greater disjunction often exists between the French *Eschez amoureux* and Gower's English *Confessio amantis* and the commentaries which seek to bring out their moral significance.

Evrart de Conty's *Eschez amoureux* commentary appears to be the first full-scale exegesis of any original work in French, both the poem and its commentary dating from the late fourteenth century. At the outset he declares that his author, following the precedent of the ancient poets, wishes to offer profit and delight (a variation on the Horatian dictum); the commentator's own emphasis is on the profit, as is indicated by his version of a conventional apology for poetry: 'the principal intention [*entente*] of the author in question and the end [*fin*] of his book, is to concentrate on virtue and good works and to flee from all evil and all foolish idleness' (*Eschez amour. moral.*, ed. Guichard-Tesson and Roy, p. 3). With this end in view, Evrart is anxious to put some distance between the author and the *personae* he deploys, including the persona of the amorous young man who plays the chess of love with his lady. 'We should know first of all', he explains, 'that the author of this poem . . . feigns [*faint*] and says things that are not to be taken literally, although they may be invented in a reasonable manner, and that there may be some truth secretly hidden beneath the letter and the fiction' (p. 22). Because of this, Evrart continues, the poet feigns and introduces several characters (*personnes*), each of whom speaks in his turn as is appropriate to his nature, in the 'manner of feigning' used in the *Roman de la Rose*. And no doubt one can sometimes 'feign' and speak figuratively and in fable in a way which is beneficial and to a good end.

The end of the commentary echoes its beginning. What the author 'says about having mated' (as in chess) should not, Evrart declares, be understood to mean that he really was maddened and overcome by love (pp. 764–6). 'Rather', we are assured, 'he feigns this, to take the occasion for speaking of love better, more pleasantly, and more beautifully'. For thus the subject is made more pleasant and agreeable to many people. Evrart is quite consistent, therefore, in his desire to sunder the author from his persona. The moral note is struck as Evrart adds another justification: this was also done to show better the error and deception that exist in mad, passionate love and the great, innumerable dangers in which those who are too bemused by it place themselves. 'It is the principal intention of the above-mentioned author and the end of his book to reprehend and blame their folly as a thing contrary to reason, as can clearly appear by the procedure of his rhymed book'. We are back in the world of the *accessus Ovidiani*.

The commentary ends long before the poem does. The Lady Pallas comes, as Evrart puts it, to 'reprove and blame' the lover's 'folly and to show him primarily how the life of pleasure that Venus and Love and Delight and Idleness teach [people] to follow is a deceptive and perilous life'. Then he offers a rapid summary of what is in fact a major part of the poem. 'And here the lady Pallas told and showed him many beautiful lessons and fine things profitable to ethics and to honest life, and which it would be good to explain. But since the cause [of his poem] has been rendered understandable I shall say no more at this [point] at present. Amen.' Perhaps this silence is appropriate because the text has rendered the gloss redundant, by becoming explicitly moral itself. And thus the commentator can in the final stretch take his leave of his author, having helped him over the earlier hurdles.

The relationship between Gower's *Confessio amantis* and what seems to be his own Latin commentary on it may be described in remarkably similar terms. The gloss which appears at the head of the first book employs traditional *accessus* headings, namely *intentio auctoris*, *nomen libelli* (a variant on *titulus/nomen libri*) and *materia*:

... the author intends [*intendit auctor*] presently to compose his book, the name [*nomen*] of which is called 'The Lover's Confession', about that love by which not only human kind but also all living things naturally are made subject. And because not a few lovers frequently are enticed by the passions of desire beyond what is fitting, the subject-matter [*materia*] of the book is spread out more specially on these topics throughout its length.

This stance is maintained throughout the commentary, these very sentiments being echoed in the very last gloss on the poem, which declares that 'the pleasure of all love apart from charity is nothing. For whoever abides in charity, abides in God.'

The English poem gradually reveals all the problems and preoccupations of a typical 'courtly lover', Amans, thereby instructing its audience in love-doctrine, in the then-fashionable way of conducting an affair. Such is the perspective offered by the text. But a far wider perspective is offered by the Latin commentary: here we are taken beyond 'the case of love' to a larger world of ethical verities. On occasion it anticipates ethical views which will subsequently be made abundantly clear in the text; it may be said in general to link up with, and consolidate, the moral highlights of the English text, and on occasion (as in that final gloss) to go beyond what the text is recommending. Writing in English, Gower offers himself as an example of the committed lover. Writing in Latin, he assures us that this is all a fiction; he is only pretending to be an Amans – *fingens se auctor esse Amantem*. ... As (would-be) *auctor*, Gower of course has not been fooled. He knows the limits and limitations of human love, that in the very nature of things love is subject to wisdom.

The crux of the matter should by now be clear. Certain vernacular writers wished to locate and define their writings in relation to the systems and strategies of textual evaluation which scholasticism had produced. But vernacular secular literature had human love as one of its main subjects; indeed Dante, in the *Vita Nova*, speculated that it had its origin therein: the first vernacular poet was motivated by his wish to make his verses intelligible to a lady who found it difficult to understand Latin. How, then, could such literature possibly win the approval of the commentary tradition's literary theory, with its strong moral bias and conviction that heterosexual desire was at best an inferior good and at worst a major evil? According to the troubadour *vidas* and the poetics of the 'school of Machaut', expertise in love was essential for expertise in poetry; *fin'amor* ennobled the lover and created in his psyche the correct sentiments for the production of fine love-poetry (this is, of course, very much the tradition which Dante drew upon in the *Vita Nova*). But this method of 'authentication by experience' failed to satisfy some writers, particularly Dante. The technical term *auctor* was, according to the common etymology (as recalled in the *Convivio*), related to the Greek noun *autentim*, 'authority'. It was this sort of authentication which some vernacular poets were seeking for 'modern' literature, a '*translatio auctoritatis*' – a transference of textual authority – from Latin into the vernacular. Their sense of the worth of the vernacular in general and their own writing in particular impelled them irresistibly in that direction. But there was a price to pay: love had to recede before wisdom.

This is what seems to have happened in Dante's exegesis of the first poem he discusses in the *Convivio*, 'Voi che'ntendendo'. The compassionate *donna gentile* who, according to the *Vita Nova*, had comforted the poet for a short time after Beatrice's death is now allegorised as Lady Philosophy (here Dante is, as he himself admits, influenced by the female personification created by Boethius); no rival to Beatrice, but rather a means to her now-glorified self. Similarly, in Thomas Usk's *Testament of Love* (1388?), the authority-figure 'lady precious Margarit' talks like Lady Philosophy, the *Consolatio philosophiae* being a major source of this English 'allegorised autobiography'. Its conclusion assures us that 'Margarite, a woman, betokeneth grace, lerning, or wisdom of god, or els holy church' (3.9). Here Usk has somewhat over-reached himself; in his eagerness to make a grand claim for his treatise he has proffered a tenor which is far too heavy to be carried by the vehicle. But no one could possibly mistake Margarite for a flesh-and-blood woman: her eventual identification as a sexless symbol is utterly predictable, in marked contrast with the literally realised gentle lady of 'Voi che'ntentendo'. This accounts for the modern critical controversy over the meaning of that *canzone*, some claiming that Dante originally intended it to mean what he says it meant in the *Convivio*, while others suspect that he retrospectively allegorised a poem which was written in (or near) the heat of the moment of human love. Whatever the truth of the matter is, it may be accepted that, in Dante's aggrandising explication of 'Voi che'ntendendo', the human love-object has been *replaced* by an edifying personification. Dante's other way out of the dilemma is recorded in the *Commedia*, wherein the human love-object is *equated* with the edifying personification, as Beatrice leads the narrator through paradise, even unto the Empyrean heaven. Here, it may be said, is Dante's ultimate reconciliation of the matter of vernacular poetry with the method of late-medieval commentary tradition.

When the writers of 'new' commentary and 'self-commentary' drew on the academic techniques of literary exposition they inherited an approach which was as prescriptive as it was descriptive. Those techniques were themselves suffused with distinctive values, values which defined the commentators' terms of reference and made his moral conclusions inevitable, whether he was expounding an 'ancient' or a 'modern' text, someone else's work or his own. The most self-aware of the 'new' and 'self-' exegetes of the later Middle Ages were perfectly aware of this fact; they wished to appropriate the values of academic literary criticism and bestow them on their own writings and those of distinguished medieval contemporaries. Full understanding of their attempts at valorising 'modern' literature involves the sense of being present at the birth of the vernacular author.

15

Vernacular literary consciousness
c. 1100–c. 1500: French, German and
English evidence

Kevin Brownlee, Tony Hunt, Ian Johnson, Alastair Minnis
and Nigel F. Palmer

Whilst it is reasonably assumed that there extended from the Merovingian
period a long tradition of oral poetry in France which embraced the lyric,
hagiography, epic and drama, a tradition which drew on Indo-European
traditions, more localised folklore, and historical events, it is certain that
vernacular French literature (i.e. what has been set down in letters) owes
its emergence entirely to the church. It is doubtful whether the *romana lingua* of the Strassburg Oaths (as sworn by Louis the German and Charles
the Bald in June 842) can really be called French, but the short *Sequence of
Saint Eulalia* (*c.* 881–2) from the area of Valenciennes is certainly French,
as are parts of the Sermon on Jonah, also produced near Valenciennes,
towards the middle of the tenth century. A Passion narrative and a Life of
St Ledger copied *c.* 1000 have been preserved in the south-west of France,[1]
whilst in the following century we have fragments of Occitan and, from
Normandy, two literary masterpieces, the *Vie de Saint Alexis* and the
Chanson de Roland. With the exception of the last two we are dealing
with works written in a supra-dialectal koiné or *scripta*, designed to find
favour with supra-regional audiences who could not tackle whatever Latin
originals were available. Secular French literature written in a relatively
standardised language (ultimately identified with that of the Ile de France)
is the product of the twelfth century. It was preceded in England by the
curiously precocious literary productions that owed much to the patronage of Henry I and II. Thus in the first quarter of the twelfth century the
rhyming couplets of the *Voyage de Saint Brandan* by Benedeit anticipate
the appearance of the romance genre and a little later Geoffrey Gaimar's
Estoire des Engleis, written for Constance FitzGilbert, paves the way for
courtly values. In France political, economic and educational changes led
to the flowering of a remarkable courtly literature that became a model
for other European vernaculars. Within a community of shared values

---

[1] On the early texts mentioned thus far, see Paris, *Les plus anciens monument*, Stengel, *Die
  ältesten französischen Sprachdenkmäler*, and Sampson (ed.), *Early Romance Texts*.

poets vied with each other to refine and vary their literary techniques
of allusiveness, critical irony, playful humour and rhetorical strategies.
There arose a literary self-consciousness that sought gradually to evolve
a technical and conceptual vocabulary adequate to the expression of its
ambition.

In Germany we observe the rise of a new vogue for biblical and hagiographical poetry from the late eleventh century onwards, whereas, apart
from an extensive vernacular verse chronicle (the *Kaiserchronik*) composed in the 1140s, the secular subject-matter of adventure, war and love
does not emerge as a literary theme until the mid-twelfth century. Whilst
two Old High German works continued to be widely copied (Notker's
commentary on the Psalter and Williram von Ebersberg's Latin–German
bilingual commentary and paraphrase of the Song of Songs), there is no
sense in the period before this new beginning of any literary self-awareness
in the vernacular. Vernacular self-consciousness in the period before 1100
manifests itself in Latin texts that derive their subject-matter from oral
tradition, and anticipate literary genres that were later to play a major
part in the literature of vernacular languages: the *Ecbasis captivi* as a
precursor of the *Roman de Renard*, the *Waltharius* which heralds heroic
epic in the manner of the *Nibelungenlied*, and the *Ruodlieb*, which points
forward to the courtly romance and the folk tale.

In the British Isles, a developed literary consciousness does not, with
some notable exceptions, make itself felt in Middle English writing until
the latter half of the fourteenth century, this being concurrent with the
rise of national consciousness and the firm establishment of English as a
literary vernacular.

The following discussion will not attempt to describe the literary consciousness implicit in the practice of individual writers, this being too
large a topic to be treated in a single chapter. Instead, we shall synthe-
sise the explicit comments about literature found in vernacular works,
often, though not exclusively, in prologues. These comments are designed
to situate the given work in relation to its sources, its audience, and its
technical, rhetorical traditions, and also to define the writer's status and
his relationship with his matter. These are not exclusive categories and so
some overlap is unavoidable; moreover, discussion of smaller topics may
conveniently be grouped under these four heads. It should be stressed
at the outset that such literary comments or deliberations – which we
are in effect viewing as a corpus of 'internal literary criticism' – do not
necessarily reflect the actual practice of the writers here cited. Of course
they often do, but it is also true that the standards defined therein may
serve as norms which the writer then goes on to manipulate or even
subvert.

1. Sources

The fundamental sources of knowledge for the late-medieval poet are twofold: 'experience' and 'authority', knowledge that is gained by observation of the world on the one hand, and from authoritative books on the other. The majority of French, German and English writers of the period *c.* 1100-*c.* 1500 claim the second of these as their point of departure. 'Olde appreved stories', declares the narrator of Chaucer's *Legend of Good Women* (dating from the 1380s), reveal information on matters of which we can have no direct experience; when we can have no other 'preve' (by experience), these books merit our belief and our reverence, since without them, 'of remembrance the keye' would be lost (Version F, ll. 1–28).

This ostensible (and in many cases genuine) reverence for sources which are variously described as 'authentic', 'approved' or 'authorised', is clearly of importance in historical writing, as one would expect in a genre where personal invention is not deemed an admirable quality. Guido delle Colonne, for example, claimed to be following 'the writings of the ancients, faithful preservers of tradition', who 'depict the past as if it were the present, and, by the attentive readings of books, endow valiant heroes with the courageous spirit they are imagined to have had, just as if they were alive – heroes whom the extensive age of the world long ago swallowed up by death' (*Historia destructionis Troiae*, Prol. [dated 1287]; tr. Meek, p. 1, and compare pp. 265–6 above). Those sentiments were echoed by generations of vernacular poets.

In particular, the poets' sense of standing within a chain of authorities, in which each writer handed on what he could derive from his source, whose author was similarly placed, emerges clearly in the work of those twelfth-century authors whose narrative material derived from the ancient world. German authors in particular, who in the twelfth and thirteenth centuries often followed French sources, felt that they were many removes from the ultimate source of their material, at the very end of the process of cultural transmission. Hence Herbort von Fritzlar in his *Liet von Troye* (1190–1215?) says: 'This is a French and Romance book; its composition is whole and perfect; it first took root in Greece, and passed thence into Latin and from there it passed into Romance. . . . If I am to observe the form of my material [*die formen merken*] I must have a triple sense, Greek, Latin and that of the Romance book; of the two latter senses I shall now take the third and follow it so that it is my true guide in the composition of the German book' (ll. 47–70). When Konrad von Würzburg (writing before 1287) deals with the same theme he describes the literary tradition as a chain of authorities deriving ultimately from a reporter who experienced the events himself: 'Dares, a splendid knight, who himself fought a good deal at the siege of Troy – whatever he spoke in Greek about that royal city was set out in a final written version [*mit endelicher schrift*] in Romance and in Latin; I in turn am intent on elaborating [*breiten*] it and taking it with my poetic skill [*mit getihte leiten*] from Romance and from Latin and turning it [*wirt . . . verwandelt*] into the splendour of German words' (*Trojanerkrieg*, ll. 296–306). Whereas a century earlier Pfaffe Lamprecht, the author of the first German Alexander romance, had used his intermediary status as the basis for a disclaimer ('Let nobody blame me: if he [Alberic, the author of the Occitan source] was lying, then I am lying'; *Alexander*, ll. 17–18), Konrad von Würzburg sees his own role in the process of 'breiten', 'leiten' and 'verwandeln' in a self-consciously positive light. Similar attitudes to the tradition of authorities can be found in French and English writers. Ultimately they are inspired by such texts as the prologues to the late-antique *Ephemeris belli Troiani* attributed to Dictys Cretensis, which tells a remarkable tale of how his source barely survived, having been translated and even transliterated several times before it came into his hands.

But the truth derived from literary authority, in the sense here defined, did not necessarily stand in opposition to the truth that could be gained from experience. According to a common medieval etymology, the technical term *historia* derived 'from the Greek *historein* which in Latin is *videre* (to see) or *cognoscere* (to know). For among the ancients no one wrote history who had not been present and had seen the events which had to be written about' (Isidore of Seville, *Etymologiae* 1.6.1). Non-historical types of knowledge originally gained from experience, and verifiable by present-day experience, were also, of course, preserved in books. John Lydgate, monk of Bury, makes this explicit in the *Troy Book* which he produced between 1412 and 1420: without writers, all true knowledge would have died, 'nat story [i.e. history] only, but of nature and kynde' (l. 160). Indeed, citation of ancient experience could be useful by way of justifying one's own writing. Thus Jean de Meun defends the views on women expressed in his portion of the *Roman de la Rose* (*c.* 1269–78) on the grounds that his authors 'knew about the ways of women, for they had tested them all and had found such ways in women by testing at various times'. 'For this reason', Jean advises his audience, 'you should the sooner absolve me': he himself is not telling 'fables' (compare the Latin term *fabulae*) or lies as long as 'the worthy men who wrote the old books did not lie'. The veracity of these sources is confirmed by the fact that they are in total agreement on the subject of female frailty (ll. 15,195–242). Reverence for authentic sources was, therefore, certainly not restricted to specifically historical writing; we find declarations of fidelity to written sources in very many texts in a wide range of genres, from the fourteenth-century *Middle English Stanzaic Life of Christ*, whose writer declares that he is faithfully repeating his authorities ('myne Aucteres fully rehersynge' [l. 19]), to the historical 'tragedye' *Troilus and Criseyde* (1382–6), whose narrator repeatedly states that he will not write anything 'forther than the storye wol devyse [relate]' (V.1094), to the *Fables* of the Middle Scots poet Robert Henryson (*fl.* 1460–80), the prologue of which points both to the fictional quality of the work and to the fact that Aesop is the 'author' (ll. 43–56; compare pp. 376–7 above).

It is clear, however, that writers did not consider all apparently authoritative sources with equal reverence. Problems arose when their sources did not agree, and they were faced with differing versions of the same story. In this situation poets were bound to accept a degree of selectivity as a prime artistic criterion. The actual principles of selection were, unfortunately, rarely made explicit, though historical authenticity and moral exemplariness were often invoked. The situation is best illustrated by one of the most famous stories of the Middle Ages, that of Tristan and Isolde. The insular poet Thomas, possibly writing in the 1180s, includes in his highly influential version of the tale an excursus (Douce fragment, ll. 835ff.) on the theme of selection from diverse source material (the old *ex pluribus pauca* topos). In a direct address to the audience ('seignurs') of his *Tristan* he explains that there are many versions of the tale he relates ('cest cunte est mult divers') and from the disparate, heterogeneous materials he has tried to harmonise or unify his selection, whilst leaving out much material, for he does not wish to be too inclusive ('Ne vol pas trop en uni dire'). In the language of scholastic literary theory we might say that he has brought together (*in unum redigere*) from the mass of the sources (*materia remota*) only what is germane to his purpose (*materia propinqua*), rejecting certain parts of the sources concerning Tristan's death because they contain incongruities or improbabilities.[2] For example, he can show logically ('par raisun') that the version containing the visit to King Mark's court of Governal disguised as a merchant cannot be right – Governal would have been recognised by Mark who hated him (Douce fragment, ll. 852ff.). Thomas regards the *invraisemblance* (our term) of Governal's undetected visit as the product of writers who have departed from the true tale ('sunt del cunte forsveié / e de la verur esluingné'), but he will not engage in a polemic ('Ne voil vers eus estriver'): let them stick with their version and he will stick with his, and reason will tell (Douce fragment, ll. 879–80, 882). Specifically, he will follow the version of 'Breri' (Bledhericus or Bledri ap Cadivor, *c.* 1075–1133, a celebrated Breton *conteur*). What he himself is concerned to do is to maintain the coherence and verisimilitude of his narrative and to avoid contradictions produced by disparate sources. Here, then, is an author's assertion of his discriminating intelligence at a moment in his tale when he realises that his audience

[2] See Kelly, '*En uni dire*'.

may be familiar with other versions which are in his view unsatisfactory. Narrative and psychological coherence is upheld as an important artistic desideratum. Other authors of Tristan poems, notably Béroul (1160s?), Eilhart von Oberge (1190s?) and above all Gottfried von Strassburg (c. 1210) echo this problem of selecting the right features from conflicting accounts of the material and defend the superiority of their own version. Béroul, for example, argues that storytellers (*conteors*) who claim that Tristan drowned the leper Yvain are quite disreputable (*vilain*). Tristan was too courtly (*cortois*) to do such a thing; he, Béroul, remembers the correct details better (ll. 1265–70).

Gottfried von Strassburg, who sets out his response to the problem of the multiple versions of the Tristan romance in his prologue, styles himself as a historian who has researched into the authentic version of the story. His choice falls on the version by 'Thomas von Britanje' whose narration of the Tristan story was based on his study of 'britûnschen buochen' that set out the history of the lords of Britain. Gottfried claims to have made an extensive study of Romance and Latin books himself in search of this authentic rendering of the story (*Tristan*, ll. 149–66). This stated preference for an authentic version of the (fictitious) story, which is in line with the historiographical sources, is in continuation of the position stated by Thomas himself, who, as already noted, claimed to be indebted for his story to Breri, 'who knew the deeds and stories of all the kings, of all the counts that had lived in Britain' (ll. 849–51).

A further context in which source criticism was crucial was the story of the siege of Troy, for here medieval authors had to choose between two versions, that deriving from Homer, who took the side of the Greeks, and that embodied in the work of Dares Phrygius, who took the side of the Trojans. In his *Roman de Troie* Benoît de Sainte-Maure (writing c. 1160) praises Homer for having been 'clers merveillos e sages e escientos' and thus a potentially reliable authority, but he points out (here following Dares) that as he was not even born until a hundred years after the siege, it is not surprising that he made some mistakes. He adds that some listeners to the tale take exception to the way that Homer allows his gods and goddesses to take part in the combat as if they were humans (ll. 45–74). This critical appraisal of Homer as a source for the story of Troy passes from Benoît's poem into the Latin *Historia destructionis Troiae* of Guido delle Colonne and thence into vernacular versions of this work in English, French, Italian, Dutch and German.

Awareness of the distorting predispositions of *auctores* is also found in writings about the nature of women. Christine de Pizan's extended polemical defence of women involved a sustained attack on Ovid as inaccurate and duplicitous. In her *Epistre au Dieu d'Amours* (1399) she has her character Cupid state that 'If women had written the books, I know for a fact that it would have been done differently, for they know well that they

were wrongly defamed' ('se femmes eussent les livres fait / je sçay de vray
qu'autrement fust du fait, / car bien scevent qu'a tort sont encouplées';
ll. 417–19). This critical stance is of course particularly effective in
strengthening the authority and legitimacy of Christine herself, a female
clerkly author engaged in defending the status of the female sex. Chaucer's
Wife of Bath complains that antifeminist writing exists only because
'clerkes' have been writers; 'if wommen hadde writen stories', she says,
there would be a literature against men (*Canterbury Tales*, III(D), 688–
710). In his *Legend of Good Women* Chaucer, writing in ostentatious
defence of women (having been prompted by Machaut's *Jugement dou
roy de Navarre* of 1349), attempts to provide such a literature.

But it is in the *House of Fame* (1378–80) that his most sophisticated and
sustained critique of apparently unimpeachable *auctores* is to be found.
After having highlighted the discrepancies between the Virgilian and
Ovidian accounts of Aeneas, the narrator goes to the house of Fame,
where many great classical poets, along with historians from other traditions, are associated with the whimsical goddess Fame, whose authority is
certainly questionable. The narrator ends up visiting the house of Rumour,
where he will find matter for his poetry not from the great sources of textual authority but rather from the transient world of street gossip, where
truth and falsehood are inevitably mixed. This might seem like a negligent or indeed perverse choice of source beside the great classical poets
and the historians the poem has mentioned; but what Chaucer has done
is to reveal that all sources of authority (all secular sources, at any rate)
are ultimately derived from the struggle of competing interests. This is
a condition from which even great poets do not escape, and to choose
the 'tydynges' of rumour is simply to recognise the inescapable condition
of secular knowledge, and to take responsibility for one's reporting of
that knowledge, instead of hiding behind the false absolute of *auctoritas*. So, while many texts, and particularly popular romances of the most
patently fictional kind, do claim that their matter is certainly true, it is
also the case that some texts of a more sophisticated and self-analytical
kind manifest a caution towards claims of absolute authority and
truthfulness.

Just as we have been able to offer evidence of a critical attitude towards
authoritative sources in French, German and English vernacular writing,
so too we may detect a firm belief in the importance of individual skill
in the rewriting of received matter. A number of writers regarded their
common mission of perpetuating past culture as, far from being a passive
or subservient activity, actually a means of elevating their own contribution to the process of transmission. In the twelfth-century Anglo-Norman
chronicles of Wace, for example, the identity of the *clerc* as the guardian
of the values of civilisation is already well established and clearly articulated, particularly in the *Roman de Rou* (III. Prol. 1–66; composed

during the period 1160 – after 1170). In the prologue to his *Roman de Troie* Benoît de Sainte-Maure went so far as to say that, without collective cultural memory, men would all live like beasts (Prol. 11ff.) – and the role of clerkly activity in conserving this is, of course, crucial. The topos of *translatio studii* linked to that of *translatio imperii* could, therefore, be employed to bestow immense value on one's own literary labours. An excellent example of this is afforded by the introduction to Chrétien de Troyes' *Cligés* (*c.* 1176 or 1185–7), where the poet (apparently influenced by Wace) praises old books for having recorded ancient deeds and times and proceeds to describe his translation of the source as part and parcel of the most recent stage of the process whereby chivalry and learning have passed from Greece to Rome – and that 'highest learning' has now come to France. This idea was also taken up by the German author of *Moriz von Craûn* (*c.* 1210–15?), which begins with a declaration that the art of chivalry was invented in Greece, when, for the sake of a woman, Troy was besieged. Subsequently the art took up residence in Rome, thanks to Julius Caesar's exploits, but 'she' fled during the reign of Nero – moving to Carolingia, where she suffered deprivation until the time of Charlemagne. Oliver and Roland made her their concubine on account of her courage, cherishing her in a knightly fashion.

Supposedly inferior writers were roundly accused of corrupting the process of transmission. Chrétien is supremely conscious of the superiority of his careful artistry to the slapdash methods of mere storytellers (*contors*) who frequently spoil their material; his authorial pride is illustrated by the list of his compositions to date that he furnishes in the prologue to *Cligés*. At the beginning of the thirteenth century, the author of the continental *Bueve de Hantone* (Bevis of Southampton) complains that the *jogleors* do not know the story properly and hence distort and spoil the tale ('Del mieus en ont grant partie oubliee, / le canchon ont corrompue et faussee'; ll. 10–11). They have neglected the best features – what he calls 'the flower of the tale' ('de l'estoire la flour'; l. 50). The remedial process – which in this case involves (as the poet sees it) reassembling the two parts of the tale in a logically coherent and morally exemplary way – is often understood by medieval writers as 'renewing' or 'making new' (*renoveler, niuwen*) the material. In the German *Minnesang* the adjective 'new' is used in a positive sense with associations of happiness and springtime, as when Heinrich von Morungen cries out for someone to teach him a 'niuwen sanc' to put the season of loveless gloom behind him (II, 3,11–12; MF 124,6–7).

Much medieval writing is, indeed, a renewing of what already exists. The Middle High German poet Wolfram von Eschenbach, writing in the first decade of the thirteenth century, introduces the main themes of his *Parzival* with the words 'ein maere wil i'u niuwen / daz seit von grôzen triuwen' ('I shall renew for you a story which tells of great loyalty . . .';

4, 9–10). The narrator of Chaucer's *Parlement of Foules* (1380–2) recounts at the beginning of the poem that he picked up a book, 'write with lettres olde'; this might seem like the occasion for a profession of fidelity to this authoritative source, but instead the narrator defines a more nuanced position: he says that just as new corn comes from old fields, so too does 'newe science' come from 'olde bokes' (ll. 22–8). Similarly, in the prologue to his English *Confessio amantis* (1386–93) John Gower begins by stating that he will write 'of newe som matiere'; this will not be wholly original, however, since (as he goes on immediately to say) his 'newe' work will be 'essampled of these olde wyse' (ll. 1–7). Later, Gower specifies the rationale for new matter: he will write a book according to the world which once existed, but, since men say that the world has now changed and degenerated, he will also treat 'the world wich neweth every dai' (ll. 52–60).

Another justification for writing new matter is to be found in works that claim to be written through inspiration. Margery Kempe says that it was decided to 'makyn a booke of hyr felyngys & hir reuelacyons' only after it had been agreed that these visions were 'inspyred with [by] the Holy Gost' (*The Book of Margery Kempe* (1436–8), p. 3). The recording of visions from God draws on a well-established tradition. What is new in England during the period under review, although already anticipated in German in the early thirteenth century by Gottfried (see Chapter 18), is an appeal to the Muses for inspiration. Imitating the model of Dante's *Commedia*, Chaucer makes the first English invocation to the Muses for inspiration in *The House of Fame*, in a context where he is possibly claiming an authority of personal, visionary experience for his poem (ll. 520–2). However, this claim is undercut with characteristic self-irony. The most striking use of the Muses in late-medieval French also involves a response to Dante. In Christine de Pizan's *Livre du chemin de long estude* (1402–3) the key scene in the first-person protagonist's literary initiation takes place on Mount Parnassus where the 'nine Muses hold their holy school, which is enclosed by great learning' (ll. 992–6). In Christine's regendered transformation of the Dantean Limbo, the *bella scola* of the classical epic poets in *Inferno* 4.94 becomes the *escole sainte* of the Muses who rule the 'Fontaine de Sapience' ('fountain of wisdom') from which the French writer is instructed to draw the water of inspiration (ll. 1081–8). On the other side of the coin, Chaucer, at the opening of his *Troilus*, has his narrator appeal for inspiration not to the Muses but to the Furies: a sure sign that his 'enditing' is to be suspected of love-fraught unwisdom and unBoethian affective excess. A few years later John Walton, in the *Prefacio* to his Middle English Boethius translation, overgoes Chaucer's narrator by pointedly scorning the selfsame Furies (ll. 60–2); and for all the modesty of his statement that he has 'tasted wonder lyte / As of the welles of calliope' (ll. 57–8), he outdoes the Muses too by praying that 'god of hys benignite / My spirit enspire wiþ hys influence' (ll. 63–4), thereby putting himself in the way of grace in his devout labours in the field of *sapientia et eloquentia*. The possibility of an all-seeing God's aid and interest in the making of texts coloured not only conceptions of literary production but of textual authority and of the seriousness of any audience's duty to heed such works.

2. Audience

Medieval writing is in many instances presented as a social act, conceived with regard to, and often requested or sponsored by, a particular audience. The most isolated English poet-figure of the period, Thomas Hoccleve, who suffers from an acute sense of social alienation, portrays himself (in *Dialogue with a Friend*, 1422) as being prompted not to write: this is quite uncharacteristic. On the whole, poets and writers represent themselves as figures functioning within a social context. Perhaps this is clearest of all in the lyric, where singing is presented as a social activity dependent upon recognition and demand. The *locus classicus* in German is Walther von der Vogelweide's poem 'Lange swîgen', where the poem begins with the statement that the singer, having been rejected, resolved to abandon his profession; now he is singing again only in response to a specific request from the 'good people' in the audience. What is explicit in the lyric may apply more widely to other forms of writing. Certainly there are many instances of 'internal literary criticism' which reflect several aspects of the social context of texts.

Patronage

Whatever the truth of the matter may have been, writers often describe themselves as writing not at their own initiative, but rather at the command of a patron or at the suggestion of others. In texts produced by religious, the topos often takes the form of a request by brethren or sisters who require instruction.

Jean Froissart, poet and chronicler, was particularly fond of emphasising his connections with royalty: in his *Temple d'honneur* (1363) he claims that he has met no less than ten kings, and an emperor at Rome. His *Roman de Méliador* (c. 1385) was written in collaboration with his noble patron Wenceslas de Brabant who composed the romance's lyric intercalations, as Froissart proudly states both in the *Dit dou Florin* (1389) and in the so-called *Voyage en Béarn* (*Chroniques* 3.19; first version, 1390–2). The naming of often-powerful patrons reveals that many writers were aware of presenting their works in a political context, and writing within the constraints of political power. In some cases this awareness becomes part of the fiction of the poem itself. Guillaume de Machaut (*c.* 1300–77), for example, was adept at projecting himself as the servant of his patrons, who themselves – in flatteringly idealised forms – sometimes play a dominant, judgmental role within his works, as with the kings of Bohemia and Navarre, and the Duke de Berry. The contemporary Holy Roman Emperor Charles IV (1346–78) plays a similar role as judge of the virtues in Heinrich von Mügeln's poem *Der meide kranz*. Eustache Deschamps, in his *Lay de franchise* (1385), has a youthful king of France parade his many virtues, while the self-effacing poet looks on – as in Machaut's *Behaingne* – from a bush. Chaucer represents his legends of good women as a literary penance imposed on him by Alceste, exemplary wife and queen of Love, for his apostasy against Cupid's 'lawe', and this fictional power which commands the poem is allied with historical centres of power: after Chaucer has finished the book, he is, commands Alceste, to 'yive it the quene [presumably Anne of Bohemia, Richard II's queen], / On my byhalf, at Eltham or at Sheene' (Prol., Version F, ll. 496–7).

Often a writer will present his work not as the result of a request by the powerful, but rather as an entrée to political influence, or simply as a way of claiming financial support from a patron. Satirical works in particular may presume to address a king, calling his attention to the voice of one who tells him the truth. But more often the address to the powerful takes the form of a call for payment. This is true of many genres: frequently in popular romances we find minstrels praising those who pay well. Such a conception of literary entertainment as a commodity is transformed in more sophisticated traditions, but the idea of payment for poetry is still retained. More professional poets like Lydgate elaborate notions of princely support for poor poets from a historical perspective: in his *Fall of Princes* (1431–9), he asserts that Virgil, Dante, Petrarch and Chaucer all received the patronage of princes, before he begs his own patron to relieve his anxiety with payment (III.3858–71).

In texts with a ludic or ironic strain, however, there is no reason to suppose that references to patrons have a privileged immunity from burlesque treatment. In the prologue to Chrétien's *Chevalier de la charrette*, for example, the author displays a highly ambiguous attitude to courtly flattery of his patroness, Marie de Champagne, by both disdaining it and corroborating it, and it has been argued that he is trying to write two romances in one – one of his own stamp dealing with an 'héros libérateur' and another, made according to the requirements of Marie, based on the concept of the 'fin amant'.

Addressing the audience

Many writers of the period are conscious of their work not only in terms of its patronage but also in terms of its more general audience, which will often be represented in the work itself. Where a man has no audience, says Chaucer's Host in the *Canterbury Tales*, 'noght helpeth it to tellen his sentence' (VII, 2800–2). Some of the discourses that inscribe this social relationship may now be considered.

Texts are often presented as having been produced within a specific social context, and as catering for particular tastes, needs or interests. The author of Branch IV of the *Roman d'Alexandre* (1180–90) envisages clerks, knights, ladies and young women as the members of his ideal audience. On the other hand, the anonymous author of the mid-twelfth-century *Roman de Thèbes*, drawing inspiration from Homer, Plato, Virgil and Cicero (he claims), desires only clerks and knights (ll. 13ff.). Raoul de Houdenc considers no one worthy of hearing his work who is not courtly and upright ('courtois et vaillanz'; *Meraugis de Portlesguez*, ll. 30ff.). In the crusading epic *La Fin d'Elias* the author addresses himself to 'ladies and valourous knights' ('dames et cevalier de pris'; ed. Nelson, l. 20). The monk Gautier de Coinci (*c.* 1171–1236), Grand Prior of the church of Saint-Médard at Soissons, addresses his Marian miracle tale *Des nonains de Nostre Dame de Soissons* 'a mes dames que mout ai chieres, / As damoyseles, as cloistrieres / De Nostre Dame de Soissons' (ii.460; ll. 3–5), but in other tales addresses a mixed audience and sometimes just 'seignor'. Whilst many French writers inveigh against the boorish ('vilains') and envious detractors, the author of *Durmart le Gallois* (produced in the first half of the thirteenth century) says that he does not mind criticism if it is well-founded and constructive, but rejects critics who are purely negative or spiteful (ll. 5ff.).

Of course very many works are preserved in a form designed for performance before a live audience, to create the context of an impromptu performance, where poet and reciter are one: 'Oiez, seignors, quel aventure', 'Nû vernemet, ir lieben liute' and 'List[n]eth lordynges!' are typical forms of audience address in the popular romances. Even where the text seems clearly the product of a scholarly hand, and designed for private reading, the writer will still preserve the fiction that he is not a writer so much as a reciter before a live audience. Thus the author of the alliterative *Wars of Alexander* (*c.* 1450), an extremely long text unlikely to have been recited before a listening audience, presents himself as addressing a gathering after dinner (l. 1). And within this probably imagined social setting, the poet presents himself as participating in a social decorum; after he says that some people 'couettis & has comforth' to hear of courtesy and knighthood, and conquering kings, he will rehearse such a tale, if his audience will fall silent for him (ll. 1–22). So he pictures himself not as forcing matter on his audience so much as satisfying audience-demand. And just as many works imply a social decorum existing between poet and audience, so too is a connection made between literary and social decorum. Works written in a high style, containing noble matter, are fit for noble audiences, and vice versa: it is especially the 'gentils [nobles] everichon' (I(A), 3113) who admire the *Knight's Tale* as 'a noble storie' (3111), and it is to 'every gentil wight [person]' (3171) that the narrator apologises for having to repeat the *Miller's Tale*. Gottfried von Strassburg addresses his *Tristan* to an exclusive audience of 'noble hearts' ('edele herzen'; 47), adapting the social concept of nobility to convey the aesthetic and moral refinement of those who are able to bring an adequate response to the dialectic of joy and sorrow which underlies the poem, uniting poet, audience and the characters Tristan and Isolde.

And just as works are represented as being offered to a particular audience, so also do writers (drawing on a topos found in Latin dedicatory epistles) defer to the questions and to the supposed expertise of that audience. Throughout the entire range of medieval literature we find writers deferring to their audience by presenting themselves as speaking under 'correccioun' (a corollary of their denying authorial status for themselves); sometimes the expert audience might change within the single work, as in Chaucer's *Troilus and Criseyde*, where lovers are asked to exercise their 'discrecioun' to 'encresse or maken dymynucioun' of the narrator's description of the lovers in the third book (ll. 1331–7), whereas at the end of the final book his friends 'moral Gower' and 'philosophical Strode' are enjoined to 'correcte' the entire work (V.1856–62).

Although many works are written for a listening audience (or at least presented thus), others are presented specifically as books to be read from, whether publicly or privately. But books designed for a private reader do not abandon a sense of social relationship between author and audience; rather, they offer new possibilities for such a relationship. In particular, the private reader has greater freedom with regard to the text, and writers of the period respond to this fact in different ways. Robert Mannyng, in the prologue to his translation *Handlynge Synne* (1303), tells his reader that wherever he wants to open the book he shall 'fynde a begynnyng', since the beginning of sin is everywhere (ll. 119–24). Again, in the prologue to Chaucer's *Miller's Tale*, the narrator tells his reading audience that they are free to choose another tale: whoever does not want to 'hear' the tale, he says (sustaining the fiction of a listening audience), should 'turne over the leef [page] and chese another tale', where the address is to a private reader (I(A), 3176–7). Some books are clearly designed both for private reading and to be read to an audience. The author of the Middle English mystical work *The Cloud of Unknowing* (late fourteenth century) shows his awareness of all the possibilities of dissemination, including private reading, by insisting that his work be absorbed in its entirety, and in the order in which it was written. Whoever shall 'rede it, write it, or speke it, or elles here it be red or spokin', he says, should cover the book 'al ouer', since perhaps there is matter 'hanging' in either the beginning or middle which is not 'fully declared' where it stands, but explained elsewhere (p. 2). On rare occasions the failure of readers to 'cover the book all over' is dramatised in medieval literature, the most sophisticated example occurring in *Inferno* 5. Here Dante has Francesca recount how she and her lover Paolo read the tale of Lancelot and Guinevere (apparently in the highly moral Vulgate Cycle *Lancelot del Lac*), but stop at the point at which the literary lovers kiss; they themselves imitate that action, rather than finding out that the story progresses to reprove adulterous love. Improper reading, it would seem, can encourage improper behaviour.

The written book changes literary consciousness in one further way. The reality, or the fiction, of a listening audience implies that the work is for immediate use, whereas the book for a private reader is not tied to the present in this way, and can be imagined as being read in the future. Some works of the period absorb this fact, and present themselves as being written for future readers. In the prologue to Gower's *Confessio amantis* (ll. 1–11) the narrator says that just as he is taught by books of the past, so too is it good that he should write a book which will be believed 'in tyme comende after this'. This development is further associated with the commonplace whereby an author asks the audience to pray for his soul. A famous example in German literature is found in Hartmann von Aue's *Der arme Heinrich* (*c.* 1195), where the author requests that whoever hears or reads this tale after he is dead should pray to God for the salvation of his soul (ll. 22–5).

The effect of literature

Beyond these remarks designed to indicate the kinds of audience for whom a vernacular work is written, there are many commonplaces that specify the intended effect of the work on the audience. Medieval literature is very frequently instrumental, designed to have a particular effect on its audience, of moral or intellectual 'information' or of affective persuasion. The most general formula for the range of effects which literature might have is that used by Jean de Meun in his apology for the *Roman de la Rose*. He is following the example of the ancient poets, he declares, who sought to delight and profit their readers (ll. 15,210–12). The *locus classicus* of this binary pair is of course the Horatian dictum that literature is designed both to instruct and delight (*prodesse et delectare*; *Ars poetica*, l. 333), although it does have roots in patristic authors also. A wide variety of late-medieval French, German and English literature consciously works within these terms.

Many works lay claim to both these qualities, of instruction and delight, without privileging one over the other. The prologue to one of the most popular romances of the Middle Ages, *Partonopeu de Blois* (before 1188), cites St Paul's statement that all that is written is written for our profit (Romans 15:4), for it either attracts us to virtue or deters us from vice.[3] Foolish men detect only the crude (literal) sense ('le gros sens'; l. 118) whilst the wise man draws out the deeper sense just as a bee draws honey from a plant, even from the bitterness of a nettle. The metaphor of the bee is itself drawn from the exegetical tradition. Whilst the author of *Partonopeu* emphasises the importance of the moral sense on the authority of St Paul, and Gautier de Coinci in his *Miracles de Nostre Dame* stresses plain speaking ('dire rudement' (II pr.1, 55–62)) on the authority of St Jerome, the thirteenth-century French adaptor of Aesop's fables in the version known as the *Isopet de Lyon* cites Cicero the rhetorician in support of his claim that what we should now call 'presentation' is of great importance, 'for argument [*raisons*] which is beautifully adorned is the more willingly listened to' (ll. 3–4). Thus, the assimilation of moral truth is compared with the flower and the fruit. The former is 'delitable, plaisanz et bele', whilst the latter represents 'doctrine profitauble' (ll. 11–14); the one can be taken without the other. Many medieval writers employ a series of venerable exegetical metaphors – wheat/chaff, kernel/husk, pith/bark – but in non-religious works they are applied only in a general way to distinguish between surface attractiveness and deeper moral truth.

A particularly bold statement about the effect of literature is made by the German poet Konrad von Würzburg in the prologue to *Partonopier und Meliur* (late thirteenth century). He lists three benefits to be derived from poetry and song: 'one is that sweet sound delights the ear with its pleasing quality' (*delectatio*); 'the second is that courtly refinement conveys its teaching to the heart' (*utilitas*); 'the third is that the tongue becomes most eloquent [*gespraeche sêre*] as the result of the first two benefits' (ll. 8–15). Konrad offers a model for the interaction of the traditional effects of poetry, instruction and delight, in which they combine to instil the almost proto-humanist quality of *eloquentia* into the audience. This is conceived of as an important aspect of courtly and virtuous behaviour.

In English literature, many writers lay claim to both terms of the pair for the single work. Gower says that his *Confessio amantis* offers both 'lust' (i.e. pleasure) and 'lore' (Prol. 19), and that it 'stant betwene ernest and game' (VIII.3109). Similarly, William Caxton declares that his edition

---

[3] See Chapter 6 above on the use of this biblical quotation in the *Ovide moralisé*.

of Malory's *Le Morte Darthur* (1485) offers both moral examples and a pleasurable read: 'Doo after [imitate] the good and leve the evyl, and it shal brynge you to good fame and renommee. And for to passe the tyme thys book shal be plesaunte to rede in' (ed. Vinaver, p. xv). He defends his translation of *Reynard the Fox* (1481) in the same terms: for those who understand it, the work shall be 'ryght Ioyous playsant and prouffitable' (p. 6). The very same combination is invoked by the prose preface to the Low German *Reynke de vos* (1498), when it is said that the 'history and fable of Reynke the fox was written for the benefit and instruction ['nutte unde lere'] of men' and that it is 'very enjoyable to read and listen to' ('de seer ghenoechlik is to lesen vnde to horen'; pp. 3, 5).

Both the terms of the instruction/delight pair have their own particular defences. The 'cheeff labour' of poets is 'vicis to repreve', says Lydgate in his *Fall of Princes* (III.3830), and this defence of poetry as a moral instructor is found in many genres. In historical writing the point is often made that in chronicles 'blaseth and schyneth clerliche the right rule of thewes [virtues])' (*Polychronicon*, trans. John Trevisa, p. 5), and this sense of the exemplary, moral value of history extends to other genres which use historical materials, without being strictly historical. Romances, for example, often claim that the actions of their heroes are exemplary. The moral benefit to be obtained from following the examples of literary figures is discussed extensively in *Der welsche Gast* (1215) by the Friulan poet Thomasin von Zerklaere. There it is recommended, for example, that maidens should model themselves on Andromache, Enit, Penelope, Oenone, Galjena, Blanscheflor and Sordamor, young men on Gawein, Clies, Erec, Iwein, Artus and others (ll. 1029–52). Works concerned with contemporary corruption and vice obviously claim legitimacy from their moral effect: this is true of both satire and of the large body of penitential writing produced by representatives of the church. A moral defence of writing is also found in works that are declaredly fictive on the surface, such as animal fables. Thomasin goes as far as to say that lies are the crown of beauty ('gezierde krône') of adventure stories. These lies are not to be disparaged, because they signify good teachings and truth: 'wan si bezeichenunge hât / der zuht unde der wârheit' (ll. 1124–5). Poets who have translated such adventure stories into German are to be praised, but they would have deserved even greater honour if they had written works that contained no untruth at all ('vil gar ân lüge'; l. 1141).

But the pleasurable effect of literature is not without its own defence. Sometimes this is made within the larger moral defence. Chaucer's Host criticises the Monk's tale because, although full of commendable 'sentence', it lacks 'desport or game', and it is no use telling one's 'sentence' if an audience is not attracted with pleasure (VII, 2789–804). Alternatively, taking pleasure in literature could be presented as a means of relaxing from, but not subverting, serious matters (see above, Chapter 8). Thus, in *Piers Plowman* the narrator defends his poetry by citing the *Disticha Catonis* to the effect that even the serious scholar should 'solacen hym som tyme' (B-text, 12.20–4), and in Henryson's *Fables* the same point (a metaphor going back at least to St John Cassian's *Collationes*) is elaborated with the image of the bow that is always taut – the mind which is constantly in 'ernistfull thochtis [thoughts]' becomes slack with too much strain (ll. 19–28). More ingenious are the defences of pleasurable literature which say that such literature is worthless, but valuable insofar as it provokes its audience to recognise that worthlessness! This is the argument of the prologue to the Old French romance *Partonopeu de Blois* (ll. 107–14). Another version of this strategy is that of the Nightingale in the Middle English *Owl and the Nightingale* (written between 1189 and 1216?), who resourcefully argues that her pleasurable love-lyrics teach of the shortness of love through their own brevity, and thus instruct the young to be wary of love (ll. 1449–66).

Sometimes the pleasurable in literature is seen not merely as the sugar which coats the moral pill, however, but as having a positive value in itself – vernacular writers were not reluctant to embrace *delectatio*. Gerbert de Montreuil, in his *Roman de la Violette* (1227–9), presents 'un conte biel et delitable' (l. 33), and Philippe de Beaumanoir (*c.* 1250–96) says that his romance *La Manekine* is a work 'in which those who hear it will take great pleasure' ('se deliter'; ll. 2–3). Adenet le Roi describes the story of *Cleomadés* (late thirteenth century) as 'charming to listen to' ('a oyr mout gracieuse'; l. 13). The Old French author, Gervaise, in his *Bestiaire* (*c.* 1215), admits that the purveyor of tall stories is often listened to, for 'fables are attractive and pleasurable' ('fables sunt delitouses et plaisables'; l. 20): the writer concerned with truth, however, must follow the letter ('sevre la letreure'; l. 26). The preface to the Anglo-Norman *Life of St Edmund* (*c.* 1200) is far more comprehensive. Its author, Denis Piramus, begins in conventional monkish fashion by regretting his misspent youth in which he composed verses for lovers (*serventeis, chanceunettes, rimes, saluz*; ll. 6–7). But then he draws attention (ll. 25–34) to the enthusiastic reception accorded to the romance of *Partonopeu*, the author of which is praised as a master whose verses were much appreciated and praised at court, and yet whose subject-matter is fanciful ('la matire resemble sounge'; l. 30), not truth, but 'fable e menceonge' (l. 29). The same is true, continues Piramus, of Marie de France, whose work is similarly approved by men and women, for almost all people enjoy 'cuntes, chanceuns e fables / e bons diz qui sunt delitables' (ll. 51–2): such works are known to banish cares and sorrow. In this digressionary preface Denis Piramus expresses as clearly as could be desired the medieval idea of literature as recreation and consolation (on which see Chapter 8 above). This idea seems also to form the substance of the epilogue to the *Tristan* romance of Thomas, which represents a *commendatio operis* in which consolation is offered to different categories of lovers, there being no attempt to defend the work on the grounds of its moral usefulness. Literary consolation is identified by Chaucer's Host as one of the criteria by which the tale-telling competition will be judged and won: whoever tells the tale 'of best sentence and moost solaas' ('the most edifying and consoling tale') will win the free supper (I(A), 796–8). The type of *consolatio* conceived of in these examples is rather far removed from that offered by the ancient genre, as influenced by epideictic oratory and finding its supreme medieval example in Boethius' *De consolatione philosophiae*, which taught that true consolation comes with the recognition that death comes to us all and that the pleasures of this world are transitory.

The pleasurableness of literature may be defended in various ways. It is, for example, presented simply as an agreeable way to pass the time – the entire *Canterbury Tales* is proposed, after all, as a vacation, a diversion 'to shorte with oure weye' ('to shorten our journey with'), as the Host says (I(A), 791). And there are defences of the pleasure of poetry in terms of its therapeutic qualities: this can either be on a political level, as in the prologue to Gower's *Confessio amantis*, where the classical harper Arion is held up as one who created social harmony through his capacity to 'putte awey malencolie' (Prol. 1053–88); or it can be on a personal level, where the melancholic Black Knight of Chaucer's *Book of the Duchess* (1368–72) complains that neither the doctors can help him, nor the poets – not 'the remedyes of Ovyde', nor Orpheus, 'god of melodye' (ll. 567–72). This implies that normally such pleasures could indeed help him; their failure is therefore a measure of his extreme grief. A particularly sophisticated example of 'literature as therapy' in Middle High German is afforded by the prologue to Gottfried's *Tristan*, where the *utilitas* from the love story is presented as emerging from a pleasurable pastime. The poet offers his love story 'to all noble hearts, so that they may find distraction in it [*unmüezic wesen*]: it will be very good reading for them. Good? Yes, profoundly good: it makes love lovable and ennobles the heart; it fortifies constancy and makes living virtuous; it has the power to bestow virtue on life' (ll. 169–76).

Defences of pure pleasure to the deliberate exclusion of any instruction are much less likely to find a voice in a culture where the defence of literature on moral grounds is so strong, but such defences do exist. Some worldly writers were happy to give audiences what they wanted. The author of Branch IV (*c.* 1175–80) of the satirical *Roman de Renart* promises that he will make his audiences laugh, for he realises that they have no desire for a 'sermon' or for the life of some holy personage ('de cors seint la vie'; ll. 4–5). Similarly, Boccaccio declares that the stories of his *Decameron* were told neither in a church nor in a place where either churchmen or philosophers were present, but rather 'in gardens, in a place designed for pleasure, among people who, though young in years, were nonetheless fully mature and not to be led astray by stories' (tr. McWilliam, p. 830). And in English, Chaucer's Shipman disallows the possibility of any preaching by the Parson, and at the same time expressly states that his 'mery' tale will not contain anything of philosophy, medicine, or law (II(B1), 1178–90).

However, even if these two criteria could be defended, and could meet, within the same works, it remains true that writers with a moral or religious intention often express hostility to the literature of pleasure. In his *L'Escoufle* (c. 1200) Jean Renart complains that many of the storytellers' ('conteors') tales are unacceptable to his intelligence ('raison' (ll.10–13)), and a thirteenth-century writer on the goodness of women says that he is tired of those who rhyme, sing, read and recite nothing but fables: instead he will offer 'un dit creable'.[4] There was, of course, straight competition between secular and religious writers: early on, the *chansons de geste* and vernacular saints' lives display mutual interference – the author of the Old French *Poème moral* (c. 1200) draws a picture of 'jugleires' waiting at the doors of the church to lure the faithful to a performance of the *Chevalerie Ogier de Danemarche* or some such entertainment (ll. 3131–6). The author of the *Quinzes signes du jugement dernier*, written towards the end of the twelfth century, complains that the proud man would rather hear the story of how Roland fought with his companion Oliver than attend to the account of Christ's Passion (ll. 21–9). In fact, the author of the *Poeme morale* mentions not just Roland (and his defeat of Fernagu), but also the stories of Apollonius of Tyre, Aye d'Avignon, Aiol, Folque de Candie and others that he regards as useless to the soul (ll. 2309ff., 3141ff.). In similar vein the thirteenth-century English Passion poem in Oxford, Jesus College, MS 29 tells us in the manner of the *chanson de geste* a 'lutele tale' (l. 1) of Christ's suffering rather than one of Charlemagne and his twelve followers. Here, standard-issue *chanson de geste* declarations of non-fictionality, normally the very hallmark of the fabulous, are the literal Gospel truth: 'nys hit no lesynge' (l. 20).

It is, furthermore, not just the taste of male audiences that is deplored or piously rerouted in the critical statements of works aiming at spiritual edification. The author of a prose translation of the *Vitae patrum* [the *Vie des pères*] who worked in the first quarter of the thirteenth century at the instance of Blanche de Navarre, Countess of Champagne, praises her for not being like 'the women of this world' whose thoughts turn to the low rather than the lofty and have lies set to rhyme and words so polished that

4 Ed. in Meyer, 'Les manuscrits', p. 316.

their own heart is tarnished: such lies darken the heart, compromising the light of the soul (ll. 23–31). 'Abandon', he adjures her, 'Cligés and Perceval, who deaden and cause suffering to the heart, and all vain romances' ('les romanz de vanité'; ll. 33–5). The author of the thirteenth-century *Évangile de l'Enfance* similarly seeks to turn his audience away from the romances, the falsehoods of this world, the Round Table maintained by Arthur, where there is no truth (ll. 13–19). Whereas these examples document the longevity of a monkish attitude that had been stated as early as the fourth century by Sulpicius Severus in his life of St Martin, and propagated in the vernaculars from the later eleventh century onwards, from the later twelfth century onwards a new variant is attested: writers such as Aelred of Rievaulx, Peter of Blois and Hugo von Trimberg (the last of these writing in 1300) castigate those who bring the same emotional response to secular poetry as to the Passion of Christ.

The opposition of the value of religious literature and the failings of secular literature is sometimes internalised by the poet, so that he presents a change from secular to religious subject-matter autobiographically as a 'conversion'. The *locus classicus* in German literature is the prologue to Hartmann's *Gregorius* (from the last decade of the twelfth century), which opens with the statement that often, out of youthful folly, he has felt the desire to compose poetry that will earn worldly rewards: now he sees the folly of this and wishes to proclaim the truth, to do God's will and make good the sin incurred by those vain compositions ('diu grôze swære / der süntlîchen bürde / . . . die ich durch mîne müezikeit / ûf mich mit worten hân geleit'; ll. 38–42). Rudolf von Ems makes a similar gesture in his *Barlaam und Josaphat* (c. 1230), when he regrets that in the past he has often 'lied and misled people with deceitful stories [*trügelichen mæren*]': the rendering of the Barlaam story is an act of atonement and he seeks the audience's prayers (ll. 5, 10–24). The function of such 'autobiographical' passages is clearly not to document the poet's own inner life, but rather to draw attention to the special qualities of the religious story offered in the poem.

The tension between pleasure and profit in Middle English writing is apparent from its first examples. In *The Owl and the Nightingale* the competing claims of a morally committed but unpleasurable poetry against a pleasurable but morally uncommitted poetry are represented in the respective claims of the Owl and the Nightingale, even if these claims are left unresolved. The tension between these claims runs throughout the period, often with one side of the pair claiming to suppress the other. Chaucer's *Nun's Priest*, after telling his animal fable, exhorts his audience to take the 'moralite' of the tale, in accordance with the Pauline idea (Romans 15:4) that everything that is written (even, in this instance, the 'folye' of a cock, fox and a hen) is written for our doctrine – the audience is asked to take the 'fruyt' (i.e. the moral meaning) and 'lat the chaf [meaning the pleasurable story] be stille' (VII, 3438–46). Many works of the period, especially those with a moral, didactic intent, attack the purely pleasurable verse of minstrels. Robert Mannyng attacks the 'talys and rymys' that men love to hear, that lead them to deadly sin, and proposes as an alternative his own, morally valuable work (*Handlynge Synne*, ll. 43–56). Langland pictures Sloth as knowing the 'rymes of Robyn Hood' while being ignorant of the Lord's Prayer (*Piers Plowman*, B-text, 5.395–97), and consistently attacks 'japeres and jangleres' who lead men to Hell. But the attack on pleasurable literature can extend well beyond low-brow minstrelsy: Chaucer's Parson implicitly attacks many of the Canterbury tales that have preceded his by rejecting 'fables and swich wrecchednesse' in favour of 'moralitee and vertuous mateere' (X(I), 30–41). It is true that he promises licit 'plesaunce', but this is pretty hollow given the tract that follows. An even harsher judgement of at least some of Chaucer's secular, fictional work occurs in his *Retractions*.

Friction between pleasure and profit is clearly in evidence, although it may not always be intended, where an essentially immoral or a totally hilarious story is avowedly offered to the readers for the moral lessons it contains. The remarks made by the German poet Eilhart von Oberge in the prologue to his *Tristrant* (*c.* 1170) about the 'moral blindness' of those listeners who disparage his tale and the benefit ('nutz') to be gained from listening to it fall rather flat when one considers the actual nature of the story to follow (a story of adultery). Thomasin von Zerklaere may have been aware of such problems of the Tristan story when he restricts the exemplary nature of Tristan to his *gevuoc* ('adroitness') (*Der welsche Gast*, l. 1051). Of course, matter that was in itself dubious could be defended as illustrating what one should avoid rather than what one should actually do. In Chrétien's *Cligés* for instance, a poem which modern critics have seen as a sort of *Anti-Tristan*, the heroine Fénice, Cligés' beloved and the wife of his uncle, refuses to model her behaviour on that of Iseult, whom she sees as a negative example. All that is written is indeed written for our doctrine – providing the reader has the right response.

Audience and meaning

An audience requires no special skills to enjoy either the pleasure or the 'solace' of literature, but if the 'sentence' of any given work is to be interpreted correctly, then the audience should be skilled. The qualities of the critically skilled judge are neatly summed up in *The Owl and the Nightingale*, when both contestants agree to let one Nicholas of Guildford (probably, in fact, the poem's author) judge their dispute. The qualities that recommend him are that he is both prudent and intelligent in judgement, he cares for morality, and that he has 'insight in eche songe, / Wo singet [who sings] wel, wo singet wronge' (ll. 187–214). In French writing, a universal criticism of the allegedly second-rate storyteller is that he fails to perceive or to elucidate the deeper meaning (*sens*) of his material (*matiere*), thereby trivialising it and reducing it to the level of an idle yarn, a mere fiction, sometimes simply 'made up'. The terms 'sens' and 'matiere' are definitively established in critical usage by Chrétien de Troyes in his *Chevalier de la charrette* (l. 26). The word 'fable' is used by almost all writers to denote what might be called *Trivialliteratur*. The word is most commonly used as part of the binomial 'mençonge et fable' in opposition to truth ('le voir') and usually indicates 'made up' tales which might also be referred to as lies (*menconges, gaberie*), 'cock and bull stories' (*fabliaux*), indecent acting (*lecherie*), frivolity (*legerie*), fantasies (*songes*), jests (*bourdes*), fibs (*losenges*). In direct opposition stands another binomial expression 'sens et essample' – 'exemplary moral truth'. A fundamental assumption is that both the artistic skill of the poet and the critical appreciation of the recipient reside in the elucidation of the deeper meaning of a fable and what can be learned from it. The phrase 'atorner a fable' is used constantly to denote the degeneration or 'watering down' of stories at the hands of the *jogleors*, and the serious-minded poet will proclaim, as does the author of the early-thirteenth-century *Chanson d'Antioche*, 'there is no untruth in my tale' ('n'a point de fable ens en nostre cançon'; l. 66) and, like Robert de Blois, in his *Beaudous* (mid-thirteenth century), that what he has to say is emphatically not 'pure invention' (*controvure*; l. 283).

More nuanced attitudes sometimes are expressed. Wace argues that the adventures of Arthur are neither wholly true nor wholly false, neither simple foolishness nor strict sense; but they have been retailed so many times by storytellers that they have degenerated into lies ('fables') through the storytellers' constant attempts to embellish or embroider the tales (ll. 1247–58). Similarly, the author of the early-thirteenth-century romance of *Yder* complains that many *troveors* distorted their tales by giving excessively self-indulgent descriptions of such things as orchards and tents, with the result that everybody could see through them, for such embroidery makes a story seem fanciful, like a dream, whether the story itself is actually true or false. Such an accumulation of words is hyperbole (*iparbole*; l. 4455), the definition (*difinicion*; l. 4458) of which is something untrue that never was and is not to be believed (ll. 4466–8). This realisation that it is not so much the matter as the manner which determines the value of the stories is shared by an early-fourteenth-century translator of John the Deacon's life of St Gregory the Great, who emphasises that the lives of the saints must be reported as they really were, without lies or exaggeration ('sanz mentir, sanz dire en seurfez'; p. 512, l. 28), for no service is rendered to these holy men by embellishing their lives in an attempt to increase their glory in the way that has been done for Hector or Achilles, Perceval or Lancelot: that is the path of vainglory, lies ('grans menteries'), the product of rascals ('coquarts') who invent as if in a dream (ll. 35–66). But what is worthy of belief? In his *Paris et Viene* (1432) Pierre de la Cépède, a Marseillais, quotes the dictum 'hoc crede quod tibi verum esse videtur' (p. 391, l. 2) and confesses that he has read with pleasure romances and chronicles on subjects from the past like Lancelot, Tristan and Florimont (ll. 1–4), whilst at the same time resisting some elements as incredible ('pluseurs chouses y ay trouvees qui moult sont impossibles a croyre'; p. 392, ll. 4–5). On the other hand, the tale of Paris and Viene he finds enjoyable ('assés plaisant'; l. 15) and notes that the subject-matter is within the bounds of reason and credibility ('la matiere me semble estre bien raisonnable et assés creable'; l. 14). His readers are invited to correct, according to their judgement, whatever does not seem fitting (ll. 18–21).

That interpretative 'insight' is required for many Middle English works is certain from the frequency with which writers claim that they have an 'entention', or 'purpose', which may or may not be made explicit. Thomas Usk, placing himself within a Pauline aesthetic (compare 2 Cor. 3:6) of 'the letter sleeth ['kills']' but 'the spirit yeveth lyfelich understanding ['gives a living meaning']', prays that the reader may perfectly know through what 'intencion of herte' he has composed his *Testament of Love* (III.ix; p. 145). And writers often invite the audience to seek out the 'sentence'; this is particularly true of such works as animal fables and personification allegories. In the prologue to his English version of the *Pilgrimage of the Life of Man* (1426–8), for example, Lydgate asserts that each reader who sets diligently to 'vnderstonde clerly the sentence, – / What hyt menyth, and the moralyte', shall know the truth (ll. 81–5).

The reciprocal obligation of author and audience concerning the *sens* is frequently derived from biblical sources and the principles of patristic exegesis. Following Ecclesiasticus 20:32 numerous French writers begin their works by affirming the obligation of those possessed of wisdom and knowledge to impart it. The author of the *chanson de geste, Aymeri de Narbonne* (*c.* 1170), Bertran de Bar-sur-Aube, reflects that wisdom concealed is like a fire heaped with ashes, burning within, but without a tangible flame (ll. 4–8). Similarly, the obligation of the audience to attend to the deeper meaning within is derived from theological sources, as the ubiquitous phrase 'de cuer entendre' shows, and from the famous dictum of Pseudo-Cato, 'legere et non intelligere negligere est' (*Disticha Catonis*, opening epistula). The author of the late-thirteenth-century *Richars li Biaus* puts it this way: the listener who hears but does not understand is like the huntsman who catches nothing (ll. 3–4). As clerks were bidden to chew over and digest the divine precepts (*divina ruminare praecepta*) secular audiences are to 'digest' what they hear, 'de cuer entendre', the heart being the seat of true knowing, just as it appears in certain theological writings. Where this reciprocal obligation breaks down, authors promptly revive the biblical metaphor of casting pearls before swine (Matthew 7:6) and abjure their duty to unworthy audiences. An author will recommend his work over that of others as 'de sens bien enluminé' – illuminated with wisdom – whereby the audience will profit, be better for it ('amender'). But performing to an unworthy audience invites reminiscences of the famous Boethian image of the ass listening incomprehendingly to the harp (e.g. in the *Roman de Thèbes*, ll. 15–16 and *Roman d'Alexandre*, Br. IV, ll. 1686–7). The German lyric poet Neidhart varies this image by claiming that his singing to an unreceptive lady is like playing the harp amidst the din of the mill (WL 23 II, 1–2.).

There are many examples in the period of meanings being imposed on stories in an authoritarian way; stories will often 'enden in som vertuous sentence' (*Canterbury Tales*, X(I), 63), where the meaning is simply presented to a presumably compliant audience. This topos can be exploited when the meaning is imposed ironically, for the audience to question, as in Chaucer's *Clerk's Tale*, where the story is given an allegorical significance with which we may want to take issue. But there are, nevertheless, many cases in which the burden of judgement is explicitly presented as being left to the audience. A particularly striking instance is found in the conclusion of Boccaccio's *Decameron*: 'stories, whatever their nature, may be harmful or useful, depending on the listener' (trans. McWilliam, p. 830). Gower writes his *Confessio amantis* as a book which may be 'wisdom to the wise / And pley to hem that lust to pleye' (first version Prol. 81–5); the audience, it would seem, is free to use the book as they like. French and English writers also exploit the dream-vision for its multiple interpretative possibilities. This is particularly true of Chaucer's, and Chaucerian, dream-visions, where readers are often allowed to read the dream within different interpretative frames. Drawing on categories of dreams defined by Macrobius, writers in this tradition offered readers the freedom to interpret dream poems either within Macrobius' categories of truth-bearing dreams, or within his categories of trivial dreams without cognitive value (see Chapter 7 above). Thus, readers were alerted to the possibility that the meaning of such a poem is not immutably fixed.

When the meaning of a work is left to its audience to determine, according to what principles should this determination be made? Aspects of the influence of exegesis have been discussed in the previous chapter, but it is important to emphasise here the general late-medieval approach to the relation between *sentence* (compare the Latin *sententia*), or profound meaning, and the surface of a text, between its spirit and its letter. The most powerful current of thought in the period concerning the relation between textual surface and *sentence* is that they are separable. The meaning of a text can remain the same, that is, despite changes in its organisation and style; or as Reginald Pecock put it in his mid-fifteenth-century *Reule of Crysten Religioun*, 'þe dyuers ententis of the treter in oon book and in an oþer, þe ordris of þe same maters tretid bi him in þe oon book and in þe oþir may conueniently and allowabily be chaungid and dyuersid' (p. 22). This position is also well exemplified by the Chaucer-figure in the *Canterbury Tales*, in the prologue to his *Tale of Melibee*. The narrator says that although the story is told 'in sondry wyse' ('in various ways'), it is nevertheless 'a moral tale vertuous', whose morality remains the same in different tellings. Such a discrepancy between surface and underlying meaning is also evident, he says, in the Gospels, which give different accounts of Christ; although there is 'in hir [their] tellyng difference', they all 'acorden as in hire sentence' (VII, 936–64). The same sense of a variable style and a stable meaning is manifest in Lydgate's praise of Chaucer's 'rethorike': he says that Chaucer refreshed his matter through his eloquence, while keeping 'the sentence hool withoute variance' (*Siege of Thebes*, ll. 41–57).

This aesthetic can take more and less sophisticated forms. The less sophisticated form might propose simply to give the meaning of a story at its end, and ask the reader then to dismiss the story itself as 'chaff'. The character Pandarus in Chaucer's *Troilus and Criseyde* gives a neat formulation of this position. Although some men take delight in composing their tales 'with subtyl art', tales are, he declares, in their composers' 'entencioun', 'al for som conclusioun'. The end, he says, 'is every tales strengthe' (II.255–63). This could serve as the theoretical underpinning of works such as animal fables, which reflect the separability of story and meaning in their binary structure of fable followed by *moralitas*. 'Subtyl art' within such an aesthetic is regarded as an optional element in composition, incapable of changing the meaning of the story in one way or another; the frequent assertions that a writer has not taken any trouble with the style or 'craft' of his work, but only with its 'sentence', imply the same idea of meaning being unaffected by style.

The more sophisticated form of this position does not necessarily reject the body of a work, but posits the perception of meaning as being dependent on the intuition of the author's intention, which is not adequately embodied in the actual text. Meaning here is always beyond the words themselves. Thus, when Usk prays that men might understand his good intention in composing his *Testament* (compare pp. 420, 444 above), he also prays that they should look to the spirit of the work, and that here the Holy Ghost should aid them (III.ix; pp. 144–5). Julian of Norwich, too, says that one of her visions was composed of three elements, a bodily sight, a word formed in her understanding, and a 'gastely syght' ('spiritual vision'). The last of these is impossible to communicate adequately, and she prays to God that He may make the reader 'take it mare gastelye [more spiritually] and mare swetly [sweetly] than I can or maye telle it' (p. 224).

The gap between surface and meaning, then, requires an interpretative act. And writers of the period were certainly aware of ways in which this fact could be exploited. It is one of the commonplaces of anti-fraternal satire that friars 'glosed [interpreted] the gospel as hem good liked' (*Piers Plowman*, B-text, Prol. 60). The distrust, within the Lollard movement, of certain kinds of glossing that this obfuscating exegesis produced, finds expression in works of Lollard sympathy, like *Pierce the Ploughman's Crede* (1394–9), where the ploughman argues that the friar glosses 'godes wordes', and 'toucheth nought the text but taketh it for a tale' (ll. 585–94). When comments like this appear in vernacular literature, they generally are referring to the practice of biblical exegesis rather than giving instructions concerning how the vernacular texts should be read. But vernacular writers could themselves exploit the possibility of imposing meanings on texts which cannot be said to be 'really there'; thus, despite claims that a doctrine 'full of frute' lies under a fictive tale (Henryson's *Fables*, ll. 8–14), the actual application of moralities in collections such as the *Gesta Romanorum* (which was translated into several vernaculars) often implies the imposition of meanings according to the demands of the moralist rather than a pursuit of any interpretative clues which may be inherent in the tales themselves.

Needless to say, sophisticated writers of the period took issue with the position outlined by Pandarus, that meaning is easily separable from style. In that very example, Chaucer has Pandarus use an extremely subtle and meaningful 'art'. But a more subtle aesthetic that sees meaning as inseparable from style does not find explicit formulation.

3. Rhetoric: composition, style and versification

In his *Regement of Princes* Thomas Hoccleve eulogised Chaucer by calling him both the 'flour of eloquence', and the 'mirour of fructuous entendement [profitable significance]' (ll. 1962–3).[5] These two forms of praise are often correlative with the pleasure/profit pairing considered above: as the eloquence gives pleasure, so the 'fructuous entendement' has moral *utilitas*. When, after Chaucer, a heightened sense of a distinctive vernacular literary tradition develops in England, these terms form the standards by

---

[5] Here, as elsewhere in this section, we draw on materials in Burrow, *Chaucer: A Critical Anthology*.

which poets of the past are praised. Whereas the discussion of meaning above might lead us to expect that praise of Chaucer's 'fructuousness' would take precedence over praise of the mere surface, or style, of his poetry, in fact the reverse is true in the fifteenth century: it is particularly Chaucer's rhetorical achievement which is singled out for commendation. Lydgate, for example (drawing on Neoplatonic metaphors essential to late-medieval rhetorical theory), repeatedly praises Chaucer for having rid the language of all 'reudnesse', and having 'reformed' it 'with colours of suetnesse' (*Fall of Princes*, 1, Prol. 274–80). The role of rhetoric in these formulas is seen as one of 'refreshing' and 'enlumynyng' the stable *sentence* of poetic matter with 'crafty [skilful] writinge' of 'sawes swete' ('sweet maxims') (*Siege of Thebes*, Prol. 39–57).

Different genres of writing in the period work within different rhetorical traditions, both ecclesiastical and secular. But the most influential and specifically literary body of rhetorical theory in the Middle Ages, that embodied in twelfth- and early-thirteenth-century manuals like those of Matthew of Vendôme and Geoffrey of Vinsauf, seems to have been assimilated by many writers, including Chaucer (despite the doubts expressed by some modern critics). Our interest here is not so much in the technical detail of this assimilation, but rather in how it affected literary consciousness in matters of composition, style and versification. Chaucer's Nun's Priest apostrophises Geoffrey of Vinsauf as his 'deere maister soverayn' (*Canterbury Tales*, VII, 3347), an attitude that was widely held. The rhetorically hyperactive Osbern Bokenham, in the opening prologue to his *Legendys of Hooly Wummen* (1443–7), declares he will not be poetical in the manner of the school of 'Galfridus Anglicus, in his *Newe Poetrye* / Enbelyshyd wyth colours of rhetoryk / So plenteuously' (ll. 88–90). The (quite conventional) disclaimers of rhetorical knowledge or ability by writers of the period should not obscure their very considerable debt to that branch of medieval literary theory.

Some medieval French vernacular writers manifest a concern for composition, or what rhetorical manuals called *dispositio* (see Chapter 2 above). A common accusation against rivals is that they 'make a mess of' (*corrompre*) whatever they handle, and travesty (*fausser*) or trivialise (*aviler*) their subject-matter. A major *locus classicus* for this kind of criticism is the prologue to Chrétien de Troyes' Arthurian romance *Erec* (*c.* 1170), where he points out that the basic story is frequently retailed by 'those who simply wish to make a living out of storytelling' ('cil qui de conter vivre vuelent'; l. 22). In reality they make a mess of it ('depecier et corrompre'; l. 14). What Chrétien will do is to take the basic story ('conte d'avanture'; l. 13) and fashion it so as to produce a perfectly proportioned and meaningful whole ('une mout bele conjointure'; l. 14). This *conjointure* may owe something to Horace's *callida iunctura* (*Ars poetica*, ll. 47–8), but it is by no means synonymous with it. There is no doubt that medieval poets, though leaving behind few theoretical pronouncements on overall structure or composition, saw their task as 'polishing' their materials and then 'fitting' them together (OF *ordener*) in a meaningful whole. A symbolic indication of the care that might be afforded to literary composition is given by Benoît de Sainte-Maure in his *Roman de Troie*, where his adaptation of the basic story is expressed in terms of *controver* ('conceive'), *faire* ('produce'), *dire* ('express') and the subsequent arrangement of words described in a varied terminology: *escrire* ('write'), *taillier* ('fashion'), *curer* ('polish'), *aseeir* ('situate'), *poser* ('place'). Conversely, in *Les Enfances Ogier* Adenet le Roi (*c.* 1240-*c.* 1297) criticises the *jogleors* for regarding their task as mere entertainment and failing to order and apportion appropriately the themes of love, chivalry and honour. Equally they were unable to find the right combinations of words ('les paroles a leur droit enarmer'; l. 18). Thus they falsified the tales they related (ll. 15ff.). In *Berte aus grans piés* Adenet refers to them as 'apprentices and disappointed writers' ('aprentiç jougleour et escrivain mari'; l. 13). The author of the *Chanson d'Antioche* (*c.* 1180) acknowledges that his audience will have heard another song on the same theme, 'but its verse was not like mine, which is newly executed and written down in quires of parchment' ('n'estoit pas rimee ensi com nous l'avons: / rimee est de novel et mise en quaregnon'). In the development and composition of his material the poet was, of course, guided by the principles of *abbreviatio* and *dilatatio materiae*. The German poet Herbort von Fritzlar begins the prologue to his *Liet von Troye* with a statement about the poet's art: 'Whoever is master of his art is in control of his skill. He knows how to modify, abridge, expand, broaden, shorten and lengthen. He shows wisdom and skill in doing this' (ll. 1–8). The author of *Durmart le Gallois* (*c.* 1240) promises to tell his tale succinctly (*briement*) 'without tedious expansion' ('sens annioz alongement'; l. 16). Again and again medieval writers claim to have neither added to nor subtracted from their source. Such pronouncements are valuable for tracing literary attitudes rather than for establishing the facts. Hue de Rotelande playfully manipulates these attitudes when he says, speaking of his (invented) Latin source, that he will add nothing to it save truth, but ought not to be criticised for failing to retain the grammatical cases of his original and to form all the proper tenses (*Ipomedon*, written in the 1180s; ll. 33–42). Amplification and abbreviation remain the essential compositional operations that medieval writers perform on their sources.

In keeping with classical and medieval rhetorical theory, the rhetorical register of a work should conform to both a social and a literary decorum, and Middle English writers are aware of these constraints. Chaucer's Host asks the Clerk to tell a tale, but in a 'pleyn' style; he asks him to keep his 'termes', 'colours' and 'figures' for the time when he composes in 'heigh style, as whan that men to kynges write' (*Canterbury Tales*, IV(E), 16–20). And just as style should be shaped to the social level of its audience, so too should it befit the literary level of its matter. Quoting Plato (in fact Plato's opinion as recorded in Boethius' *De consolatione philosophiae*, 3 pr. 12 – but see also the *Roman de la Rose*, ll. 15160–2), Chaucer's Manciple says that 'the word moot nede accorde with the dede' (*Canterbury Tales*, IX(H), 208), a dictum given different versions by the Squire, in his earnest attempts to implement it: it would need, he says, a 'rethor excellent' to describe so 'heigh a thyng' as the beauty of his heroine, for example (*Canterbury Tales*, V(F), 35–41).

In medieval German literature it is useful to distinguish two traditions, one which esteems and consciously practises ornate rhetorical language (headed by Gottfried von Strassburg), and another which styles itself as essentially non-clerical, 'illiterate', and orientated towards oral tradition (headed by Wolfram von Eschenbach). Gottfried's literary excursus, where he extols contemporary poets for their rhetorical eloquence, is discussed in Chapter 18 below. Konrad von Würzburg sets out an ideal of true eloquence in the prologue to his *Trojanerkrieg*: 'gebluomter rede . . . , diu schœne ist unde wæhe' ('florid language, fine and ornate'); works of such finesse as he promises are scarce, and rarity ('sine tiuren fremdekeit') is a literary value in itself (ll. 8–31). Heinrich von Freiberg, the continuator of Gottfried's *Tristan*, praises his predecessor's eloquence in terms which make particular use of floral metaphors: 'Where have that fine language, those blossoming words, gone? Where that poetic invention the colour of violets? Where the phrases bright as roses?' (ll. 2–4). Reinbot von Durne writes in the prologue to *Der heilige Georg* that he could have fashioned and ornamented the poem 'much better' and filled it out with florid lies (in the rhetorical tradition), but the Duchess of Bavaria, wife of his patron Otto II (who died in 1253), forbade this (ll. 46–56), presumably because such style was thought inappropriate for a saint's life.

The opposite position is that of Wolfram von Eschenbach (*c.* 1170–*c.* 1220), who emphasises his knightly status and denies his literacy. 'My work isn't to be considered a book', he declares; 'I don't know a single letter of the alphabet. Many poets take a book as their starting-point: these adventure stories of mine get along without the guidance of books' (*Parzival*, 115, 26–30). The layman's attitude that Wolfram adopts here is in line with the complete absence in his work of any statements expressing admiration of rhetorical language and eloquence. A similar appraisal of Wolfram's work underlies Ulrich von Etzenbach's remark in the prologue to his *Alexander* (begun *c.* 1271): 'Whatever poetry Sir Wolfram composed was based on good sense; everyone has to admit that no layman ever wrote better poetry' (*Alexander*, ll. 124–6).

Just as many late-medieval writers are acutely aware of rhetorical theory in matters of style, so too are they aware of traditions concerning versification. The author of the twelfth-century French *Destruction de Rome* claims that in the work of his rivals – inevitably described as 'altres jougelors' (l. 5) – 'the song is gone and the rhyme false' ('le chanchon est perdue et le rime fausee'; l. 7). At about the same time Jean Bodel in his epic, *Chanson des Saisnes* (*c.* 1200), argues that common entertainers ('vilains jougleres, bastart jougleour') could never emulate his verse or melody and, indeed, are ignorant of his 'new rich verses' ('les riches vers nouviaus') and his 'rhymed song' (*chançon rimee*; ll. 24ff.). The awareness of a desired harmony or fit between music (*chant*) and verse (*dis*) is common. The author of the early-thirteenth-century romance *Hunbaut* boasts that his audience will never hear 'verses rhymed like these' ('vers / de nule rime qui cels sanblent'; ll. 34–5) and begs it to listen to 'how they chime with each other and are grateful to pronounce' ('con il asanblent / et con il sont a dire fort'; ll. 36–7). He knows what he is doing. A person who cannot achieve great things 'need not strain to write a book' ('ne doit baer a livre faire'; l. 41). The author acknowledges the mastery of Chrétien de Troyes (ll. 186–90), as do a number of other thirteenth-century writers.

Words and music[6]

The interest in music and metre as crucial ingredients of the successful literary work gave rise to an interesting vogue, particularly prominent in the north-east of France in the thirteenth century, for inserting sung *chansons* – original or borrowed – into recited narratives, in verse and in prose. Jean Renart in his *Roman de la Rose ou de Guillaume de Dôle* (*c.* 1200–10) boasts that he is the first to do this ('qui est une novele chose'; l. 12), including 'songs and sounds' ('chans et sons'; l. 10) which will afford infinite refreshment to the listener who will enjoy both 'song and recitation' ('chanter et lire'; l. 22). So, too, in the *Roman de la Violette* Gerbert de Montreuil argues that his audience will appreciate what he offers, 'for it may read and sing' ('car on i puet lire et chanter'; l. 38), and the melody fits the words beautifully ('si est si bien acordans / li cans au dit'; ll. 39–40). On occasion an unusual or even unique text gives us a rare glimpse of theory that may irrecoverably be lost. The anonymous author of the prose-and-verse *Aucassin et Nicolette* (dating from the first half of the thirteenth century) calls his composition a 'cantefable', but we cannot tell if he invented the term or whether this work is the sole survivor of a particular genre which combined prose narrative and song. In southern

---

[6] The specific issue of the singing of troubadour poetry is discussed in Chapter 16 below.

Austria the poet Ulrich von Lichtenstein includes a sizeable corpus of songs in his elaborate pseudo-autobiography, *Frauendienst* (completed in 1255). This work is based on the literary conceit, essential to the love-lyric, according to which the singer insists on the autobiographical truth of his love, taking this to an extreme by situating the fifty-two songs that make up the principal body of his *œuvre* in the context of a semi-fictional life-story. The result is a composite work in which the juxtaposition of a range of literary forms, such as the prose charter, the 'discourse on love' in couplet verse, the love letter, the 'Leich', and a wide range of different types of love-song (such as 'tanzwîse', 'lanch wîse', 'ûzreise' and 'reye') takes its place in a book-length narrative of couplet verse in twelve-line stanzas. It is a testimony to the self-consciousness which marks out the work of a generation of poets who were able to look back on a tradition of court love poetry which had flourished for seventy or eighty years.

A particularly interesting development may be discerned in late-fourteenth-century France, whereby words become progressively detached from music. Guillaume de Machaut stands as the dominant French lyric poet of that century, the systematiser of the new lyric practice that replaced the twelfth- and thirteenth-century *grand chant courtois* of the *trouvères*. At the same time, he was fourteenth-century France's major composer. The link between music and words thus constitutes an impor-tant – indeed, defining – part of his authoritative self-presentation as a new kind of vernacular poet figure, which occurs most explicitly in his *Prologue* (*c.* 1372). Here, 'Musique' is one of the three constitutive parts (along with 'Retorique' and 'Scens') of Machaut's poetic vocation, given to him (within the fiction of the text) by Dame Nature. These three 'tools' are presented as operating together. *Scens* represents the overall ordering principle of Guillaume's art, derived from his individual talent (his *engin*).[7] It is his capacity to provide a harmonious organising pattern (*ordenance*) for his basic subject-matter (*matere*), itself provided by the God of Love. *Scens* is articulated both through Rhetoric (which here signifies the full range of versification and metrical possibilities available to Machaut) and through Music (characterised as a 'science', i.e. a category of knowledge with practical, material results). As a principle, Music is celebration; it results in joy. As a practice, Music is presented as an integral part of poetry as Machaut chooses examples of instrument-accompanied song to illustrate and valorise his own activity. Sacred music is epitomised by the figure of David performing on his harp before God. David 'harped so well and sang hymns, psalms and prayers so devoutly' (ll. 129–31) that the resultant delight appeased God's anger. Secular music is epitomised by Orpheus' rescue of Euridice (presented as a courtly lady: 'la cointe, la

7 See Cerquiglini, 'Un Engin', pp. 17–21.

faitice'; l. 136) from the underworld 'by his harp and by his sweet singing' (l. 137). Both David and Orpheus are, of course, the key medieval figures of 'originary' poets in the biblical and the classical registers respectively. They authorise Machaut's self-presentation as a new vernacular poet for whom words and music are coterminous.

If the *Prologue* constitutes a general (even 'theoretical') treatment of Machaut's poetics, his *Remède de Fortune* (*c*. 1350) functions as an implicit *ars poetica*, a poetic *liber exemplorum*. The series of lyric poems embedded in – and integrated into – the narrative of the *Remède* functions as an exemplary collection of the new lyric *formes fixes*. There is one superlative example of each of the major lyric forms of the fourteenth century, which are here presented as models to be imitated: *lay, complainte, chant roial, balladelle* (*duplex ballade*), *balade, virelay* (*chanson balladée*) and *rondeau*. And each of these key examples is musical as well as verbal. It is evident, then, that poetic activity involves both *dis* and *chans*, words and music.

However, it is important to add that both of these works – so central to Machaut's identity as *caposcuola* – inflect this 'official' self-presentation by incorporating the other side of Machaut's lyric corpus: words without music. The *Remède* contains an eighth intercalated lyric form that is not set to music: the *priere* (ll. 3205–348). And the *Prologue* opens with four non-musical ballades in which Guillaume receives his charge from Nature and Amours to produce 'nouviaus dis amoureus plaisans', new, delightful love poems (*Prologue*, Ballade 1.5).

It is in Machaut's literary masterpiece, the *Voir-Dit* (1363–5), that we have the most extensive treatment of the work habits of the poet-composer. Indeed, this elaborate portrait of the artist at work is one of the central themes of this 'autobiographical' text. A narrative poem with intercalated lyrics and prose letters, the *Voir-Dit* consistently uses different terms for the words and the music of Machaut's lyric poems. Poems set to music are referred to in general as 'diz notez' (Letter 1; ed. Imbs and Cerquiglini-Toulet), or as *dis* plus *chanson* (e.g. in Letter 3). In particular cases, the specific generic term (*ballade, virelay, rondel*, etc.) identifies the verbal artefact and the term *chanson* or *musique*, the music. In addition, the plot consistently presents the composition of the verbal artefact as preceding that of the music in Guillaume's artistic work-routine. The first-person protagonist repeatedly describes this sequence, starting from the very beginning the lovers' correspondence: in Letter 2 he sends his Lady a *ballade* for which he promises to send the music later, as soon as he has composed it; in Letter 4, he sends her the music for a poem that she has already received. The Lady, for her part, repeatedly and urgently requests musical settings for lyric poems that Guillaume has sent to her. The musical setting appears as a 'supplement' that 'completes' the work of art. In qualitative terms, the poem set to music is richer, more 'autonomous', and more prestigious, than the verbal arte-fact alone. In quantitative terms, however, it is the poem without music that overwhelmingly predominates: of the sixty-three intercalated lyrics in the *Voir-Dit* only ten are set to music. While an equally high ratio does not obtain for the Machauldian lyric corpus as a whole, non-musical poems consistently outnumber those set to music (see Earp, *Guillaume de Machaut*, especially pp. 241–3, 273–7). What emerges then is a two-tiered system: Machaut privileges poems set to music, giving them a special 'offi-cial' status vis-à-vis his identity as master-artist figure (for they involve the realisation of both of his defining talents). On the other hand, Machaut's exclusively verbal lyric poetry is valorised by virtue of its being more numerous and more versatile. In addition, it clearly constitutes a 'legiti-mate' category of artistic activity for Machaut *qua* master-poet figure.

This functional but implicit Machauldian opposition between sung and spoken poetry is made fully formal and explicit in the *Art de dictier* (1392) of Eustache Deschamps, Machaut's self-proclaimed disciple and succes-sor. In his chapter on music, the seventh liberal art, Deschamps makes a fundamental distinction: 'artificial music' involves vocal or instrumental melody (*melodie, chans*); 'natural music' involves the sonorous recitation of poetry, 'une musique de bouche en proferant paroules metrifees' ('music made by the mouth as it articulates words in metre'; ed. Sinnreich-Levi, p. 126; ll. 125–6). Artificial music is so-called because it constitutes a set of specific categories and techniques (an 'art') by means of which any human being (even the most ignorant, 'le plus rude homme du monde'; p. 60, ll. 106–7) can be taught to sing or to play. Natural music, by contrast, can only be taught to those who have a pre-existent natural inclination for it. Deschamps repeatedly stresses that the term 'music' is equally appli-cable to both categories, covering on the one hand the 'sweetness of the melody [chant]' and on the other the 'words that are all pronounced and made distinct by the sweetness of the voice and the opening of the mouth' (p. 64, ll. 159–61).

Having set up his two categories of 'music' Deschamps explicitly con-siders the three resulting possibilities. On the one hand, there is the perfect union of text and (polyphonic) song. On the other, 'each of these two is pleasing to hear by itself' (p. 64, ll. 167–8): artificial music 'may be sung with the voice in an artistic way without words',[8] and natural music, that is poetic texts (*diz*), 'may be recited in many places where they are very willingly heard, and where artificial music would not be appropriate' (p. 64, ll. 168–72).

---

[8] Tr. Page, 'Machaut's Pupil', p. 489, who makes the important point that Deschamps' phrase *par art* implies polyphony.

In this context it is important to note that Deschamps stresses that poets are no longer composers: 'Those who make natural music generally do not know artificial music or how to give their texts an artful melody ('ne donner chant par art de notes a ce qu'ilz font'; p. 62, ll. 137–9). Their works are not meant to be sung, but to be 'read out loud and articulated by a non-singing voice in such a way that the sweet words thus composed and recited aloud are pleasing to those who hear them' (pp. 62–4, ll. 141–4).

We end up, then, with Deschamps having in effect split Machaut's unified public self *qua* poet in two, definitively separating out what had been merely different components of the master's comprehensive poetic identity. Deschamps explicitly establishes a fundamental difference between the composer of music and the poet who produces 'musical' words. And he situates his own practice squarely in the latter category. Thus, in the *Art de dictier* Deschamps presents as self-sufficient and authoritative the non-musical poetics that had already become dominant among the younger followers of Machaut, and in particular Jean Froissart. The treatise therefore signals an important shift in vernacular literary consciousness during the late fourteenth century and beyond. For the French poets who followed Machaut, poetic practice no longer had to involve music.

Arts of the 'Second Rhetoric'

Deschamps' *Art de dictier* of 1392 may also be seen as the key point of departure for the fifteenth-century 'Arts of the Second Rhetoric', so named in contradistinction to the dominant medieval tradition of Latin Arts of Poetry (considered as the 'First Rhetoric', and discussed in Chapter 2 above). The Arts of the Second Rhetoric, by contrast, were written in the French vernacular as practical manuals for composing verse in the recognised French metres, rhymes and genres of the fourteenth and fifteenth centuries. Within this context, Deschamps' *Art* is, on the one hand, the first *ars poetica* written in French. (Book 3 of Brunetto Latini's *Livre dou tresor* of 1267, the first French-language rhetorical treatise, does not deal with 'practical' poetics, i.e. verse-forms and genres.) On the other, the *Art de dictier* anticipates the exclusively 'contemporary' vernacular corpus of the Second Rhetoric treatises by considering only the new fourteenth-century lyric *formes fixes* initially systematised fifty years earlier by Machaut in his *Remède de fortune*. Deschamps' treatise is thus the first French handbook of vernacular verse-forms, a presentation of exemplary *ballades*, *virelais*, *rondeaux* and *lais* written by Deschamps and by his *magister* Machaut. Finally, as discussed above, Deschamps places *rhétorique* (here to be understood as the rules for the written forms of lyric poetry and the relation between these forms and oral performance) under the rubric of music.

Jacques Legrand's *Archiloge Sophie* (*c.* 1405; a French adaptation of his earlier, Latin, *Sophilogium*) is a key link between Deschamps and the somewhat later *seconde rhétorique* corpus. An ambitious but incomplete treatise on human knowledge, its second and final part, devoted in principle to all of the Seven Liberal Arts, treats only the trivium (and the first branch of the quadrivium, arithmetic). In Part 2, Chapter 25 ('Des rimes et comment se doivent faire'), in contrast to Deschamps' taxonomy, Legrand makes rhyme a subset of rhetoric, rather than of music: 'rime peut estre nombree entre les couleurs de rethorique' (p. 141). And although Legrand asserts that rhyme functions in prose as well as verse, it is the latter (i.e. versification in the French vernacular) that is the chapter's primary focus, involving exclusively formal and practical matters. First, there is the ambiguity in pronunciation and orthography caused by the possible elision of French mute 'e', which allows two different ways of counting the syllables in a line of verse. Second, a brief descriptive presentation is provided of the 'three rules' for functional vernacular rhyming. Third, Legrand offers a set of short descriptive definitions (without examples) of the *rondeau, ballade, serventois* and *lais* (four key *dis*, or lyric *formes fixes*) in terms of syllable-count and rhyme-pattern. Finally, in the chapters that follow, Legrand distinguishes between, on the one hand, rhyme and metre and, on the other, what he calls 'poetrie', understood not as the 'science de versifier' but as 'science qui aprent a faindre et a faire fictions fondees en raison et en la semblance des choses desquelles on veult parler' ('science that teaches how to feign and to make fictions based on reason and on analogies with the things about which one wishes to speak'). Within the didactic context of the treatise, the *poetries* (listed in 2.28–2.30) constitute a compendium of morally and/or spiritually exemplary personages and narratives (mythographic, biblical, historical) that the French vernacular writer can use as subject-matter (or 'raw material') for versification (see Kelly, *Medieval Imagination*, pp. 50, 56).

It is with the anonymous *Règles de la seconde rhétorique* (1410–20)[9] that the distinctive features of the Second Rhetoric – including its valorisation of vernacular verse-making, detached from Latin poetics – appear explicitly as such. A clear distinction is made here between a rhetoric for (Latin) prose and one for vernacular versifying. This treatise deals with the rules for making 'choses rimées', and therefore 'est dicte seconde rhethorique pour cause que la premiere est prosayique' ('is called second rhetoric because the first involves prose') (ed. Langlois, p. 11). It presents itself as a teaching manual for aspiring French poets, who are to learn

9 See Mühlethaler, 'Un poète', p. 408.

by following the examples of their predecessors, authoritatively listed by name. This list constitutes an extended canon of French vernacular poets with no reference to the Latin *auctores*, as opposed to the standard practice in earlier medieval texts where *translatio studii* constructs were used to authorise a vernacular writer's new project by references to Greek and Latin predecessors (as in, for example, the prologues to Benoît de Sainte-Maure's *Roman de Troie* and to Chrétien de Troyes' *Cligés*; or the God of Love's speech to his troops in Jean de Meun's *Rose*, ll. 10,465–648). The *Règles*' list includes narrative and satiric as well as lyric poets, but French verse as form is the defining factor. While the list's order is meant to be chronological, it begins by presenting William of Saint-Amour (*fl.* 1252–6) as a vernacular poet and the first of the 'new rhetoricians' ('fut le premier qui traitta de la nouvelle science [i.e. "la Seconde Rettorique"]'; ed. Langlois, p. 11). This portrait of the mid-thirteenth-century religious polemicist results entirely from his association with the *Roman de la Rose* (where he is repeatedly mentioned in Faux Semblant's speech – see especially ll. 11476–7), and culminates in the attribution to him of a vernacular 'dit' (poem) of which the first three verses are cited (ed. Langlois, p. 11). What follows directly are the names of the two authors of the *Roman de la Rose* itself: Guillaume de Lorris who started the poem (*c.* 1225–30), and Jean de Meun who completed it. Then come Philippe de Vitry, Guillaume de Machaut, and, among others, Jean Le Fèvre, Eustache Deschamps and Jean Froissart. Thus we move from the early 1200s to the late 1300s, before concluding with living early-fifteenth-century poets contemporary with the composition of this treatise. The introduction provides a context for the treatise's primary content: extensive lists of rhyme-words of different categories, formal descriptions of lyric and narrative genres complete with models to be imitated, and finally, catalogues of biblical and classical *exempla* ('poetries') to be used in vernacular verse-making.

Baudet Hérenc's *Doctrinal de la seconde retorique* is dated 1432 in its opening rubric. The treatise is carefully and coherently divided into two sections. The first presents an alphabetised list of vocalic examples, followed by an extensive rhyme-word dictionary. The second is devoted to definitions and examples of lyric and narrative verse genres, with lucid exposition of formal patterns of rhyme and metre complemented by rules for genre-appropriate subject-matters. The explicit definition of Second Rhetoric articulated in the *Règles* functions to introduce the *Doctrinal's* final section: 'est nommée Seconde Rethorique pour ce que la premiere est prosayque' (p. 165).

The modest *Traité de l'art de rhétorique* (anon., *c.* 1450) includes a brief discussion of the vowels, the mute 'e' (called a 'demi-vowel') and the aspirate 'h', linked to syllable-count in speaking and writing, and a short consideration of rhyme possibilities restricted to the *rondeau* and the *ballade*. A rhyme word-list concludes the work.

The *Art de rhétorique* (*c.* 1493) of Jean Molinet (1435–1507) can be seen as the culmination of the fifteenth-century Second Rhetoric tradition. For the first time since Deschamps' *Art de dictier*, a major, active, professional French poet writes a treatise on making poetry in the vernacular. Molinet is also, of course, one of the *chefs de file* of the group of late-fifteenth-century French poets known as the *Grands rhétoriqueurs*. Because of his status as a professional poet, Molinet's didactic intent in the *Art* is incorporated into his dedication to the noble patron who has commissioned the treatise in order to learn how to compose vernacular poetry. Molinet opens the dedication with a flattering comparison in terms of social class: the aristocratic patron's superiority with regard to his noble vocal talents (his 'bouche') is contrasted with the non-noble Molinet's 'mere' writerly skill (his 'mettre par escript'); the patron's 'vive eloquence' (vital eloquence), with the poet's lowly 'rymes'.

Also at issue in this dedication, however, is the Second Rhetoric's constant and fundamental concern with the gap between vocal and written poetic practice in French.[10] And this concern becomes explicit as Molinet shifts registers at the opening of the treatise proper. Speaking here in an authoritative clerkly-didactic tone, he clarifies this vocal/written discrepancy in the vernacular by explaining what for the Second Rhetoric is the key dichotomy between Latin and French: ' . . . and while all Latin phonemes are pronounced, in the vernacular there are some phonemes or syllables which are imperfect, that is, which are not sounded . . .'.[11] These 'feminines ou imparfaites . . . dictions' all involve the mute 'e', which leads Molinet to the first section of the treatise: an analytical and evaluative list of rhyme-forms, in which special emphasis is given to the *Roman de la Rose*, Alain Chartier (*c.* 1390–1430), Georges Chastellain (1405–75), and Molinet himself. This list leads seamlessly to a particularly comprehensive presentation of the major lyric genres (fourteen basic forms plus subcategories), each illustrated by an example. Arnoul Gréban (*c.* 1425–*c.* 1495) is named as an exemplary practitioner of the first (the *complainte amoureuse*) and Georges Chastellain of the penultimate (the *riqueracque*). The treatise concludes with a short, analytical, and clearly evaluative list of rhyme-words, in which various overly repetitive rhymes are condemned 'pour vice de rethorique . . . si les fault eviter de toute puisance, et querir termes plus riches et mieulx recommendez' ('as rhethorical

---

[10] See Méchoulan, 'Les Arts', especially p. 216.

[11] Ed. Langlois, p. 216: ' . . . et ja soit ce que toute diction latine ait parfait son, touteffois en langaige rommant . . . sont trouvéez aucunes dictions ou sillabes imparfaittes, c'est a dire qui n'ont point parfaitte resonance . . .'.

vices . . . thus they must be avoided at all costs in favour of richer and more highly recommended rhymes'; p. 251).

The anonymous *Traité de rhétorique* (*c.* 1495–1500) is basically a versified re-presentation of Molinet's work. The major rhyme-forms (and their variants) are defined and illustrated in the appropriate verse-forms, with exemplary stanzas at times employing first-person discourse, for example, for the 'rime de equivocque': 'Quant du verbe et du nom je rime / L'ung contre l'autre, j'equivocque' ('when I rhyme the same word as noun and as verb, I "equivocate"'; p. 254). Building from the points made in its first section, this short treatise concludes with explicitly didactic rhymed and metrical examples of the major lyric genres (*lai, regrets, rondeau* and *ballade*).

The *Instructif de la seconde rhétorique* (published by Vérard in 1501 but possibly written some twenty years earlier) is an important summing up of both the theory and the practice of poetry as rhetoric over the course of the preceding century. It also confers a new and more solid authority on what had become a vernacular poetic canon. First, this vernacular canon of French poets as rhetoricians is here (for the first time in the Second Rhetoric tradition) grounded in Antiquity through a classic deployment of the *translatio studii* topos. Rhetoric began with the Greeks: Hermagoras of Temnos first discovered 'les nobles degrez / de la science' ('the noble stages of this science') and set forth its 'decretz' ('decrees'); Aristotle revealed its 'secretz' ('secrets'). Then Cicero, 'le poet notable / et treselegant ortateur / fist translation honnorable' ('the notable poet and elegant orator honorably "translated"') his Greek predecessors (ed. Droz and Piaget, I, fol. 3r, and II, p. 251). The other named Latin *auctores* are Quintilian, Virgil, Seneca, Horace, Ovid and Boethius. The final step in the *translatio* chronology, of course, places the contemporary abode of the 'noble science of Rhetoric' in France:

> Pource est elle [i.e. Rethorique] de present advenue
> En la langue galicane fertile
> Par pluseurs bons clers engins retenue.
>
> (ed. Droz and Piaget, I, fol. 11v)

[thus does Rhetoric at present reside in the fertile Gallic language, held there through the work of many good, intelligent clerks]

The canonical list of fifteenth-century French vernacular poets that follows begins with Alain Chartier, as a kind of founding father. Then come Arnoul Gréban, Christine de Pizan, Jean Castel (a conflation of Christine's son [d. 1425] and grandson [d. 1476] of the same name), Pierre de Hurion (known as 'Ardant Désir', a familiar of René d'Anjou (1409–80)), Georges Chastellain (here called 'l'Aventurier'), and (Jehan?)Vaillant (*fl.* 1445–70; linked to the courts of Gaston IV de Foix, Charles d'Orléans and King René).[12]

The author of the *Instructif* names himself from the beginning only as 'L'Infortuné' (ed. Droz and Piaget, I, fol. 12r); his modern editors identify him as Regnaud Le Queux (see Droz and Piaget, II, p. 39). His treatise, entirely in verse (like the *Traité de rhétorique*; ed. Langlois, VI), is divided into ten chapters. The first three are introductory: a short definition of Rhetoric as the 'science' of persuasion by beautiful and effective verbal means (Chapter 1); a brief, opening consideration of Rhetoric's origins (Chapter 2); a statement of Rhetoric's prose/poetry division plus a résumé of the more substantive chapters to follow (Chapter 3). Chapter 4 enumerates seven poetic 'flaws' (*vices*); Chapter 5, six key rhetorical figures. Chapters 6 to 9 involve the key topics of Second Rhetoric as vernacular versification manual: masculine versus feminine rhymes (Chapter 6); syllable-count in different lines (Chapter 7); proper use of different rhyme-patterns (Chapter 8). Chapter 9 (by far the longest in the treatise) presents definitions and examples of different types of rhymes and of the lyric fixed forms in which they can be employed (*rondeaux, ballades, serventois*). Chapter 10 represents something of a new departure for a Second Rhetoric treatise: an extended didactic presentation of the discursive rules for composition in the period's major dramatic (and narrative) genres: morality plays, comedies, and mystery plays (which are grouped with chronicles, romances and histories). A second new departure occurs at the very end of Chapter 10, as aspiring poets are instructed to open themselves to the divine inspiration of Clio, Fronsis and Minerva; to the 'bright flashing rays of eloquence' coming from Apollo. This is the first time that what will become the doctrine of 'fureur poétique' appears in a French rhetorical treatise.

It is particularly important to note that the *Instructif* as a whole constitutes the introduction to an extensive anthology (672 separate items over 258 folios) of fourteenth- and fifteenth-century courtly French poetry from Guillaume de Machaut to the court of Charles d'Orléans, and beyond: the *Jardin de plaisance*, compiled by l'Infortuné (as the author of the *Instructif de la seconde rhétorique* styles himself), in collaboration with André de la Vigne (1470–1515) for the final sections. The *Jardin* is the largest and most important of the many poetic anthologies produced in late-medieval France, and was republished seven more times during the first half of the sixteenth century.

The fifteenth-century Second Rhetoric tradition thus culminates in a highly significant 'hybrid' form. The discourse of practical didacticism

---

[12] This biographical information comes from *Œuvres de Pierre Chastellain et de Vaillant*, ed. Deschaux, pp. 11–13. Deschaux also provides a summary of the scholarly debate on Vaillant's historical identity.

in the French vernacular (the *Instructif* as treatise on verse-making) here serves as a kind of gateway to an extensive and prestigious French vernacular poetic corpus (the *Jardin de plaisance*) which is implicitly presented as both authorising and illustrating it.

The distortions of rhyme

It remains to comment on a difficulty that is mentioned frequently in French and German (though not in English) texts: the distortions produced by the need to find rhymes (Verlaine's 'les torts de la rime'); the tensions between strict adherence to the source and the degree of elaboration necessitated by the rhyme. The prologue to the German *Lucidarius* (*c.* 1195?) reports that Duke Henry (the Lion), who commissioned his chaplains to compose the work, ordered them to 'compose it without using rhymed verse [*ane rimen*], for they were to write nothing but the truth, as it is set out in the Latin' (ll. 14–18). Here the truth-value of prose is deemed to be superior. But in his romance of *Beaudous* (mid-thirteenth century) Robert de Blois speaks for many poets in assuring his audience that he will add nothing of his own to his source save in putting it into rhyme (ll. 289–90). Similarly in *La Manekine* Philippe de Beaumanoir (*fl.* 1270–85) claims that he will not add a word of a lie, except when he has to find a rhyme (ll. 46–8). In the German prose *Ackermann aus Böhmen* by Johannes von Tepl (written shortly after 1400) Death tells the Ploughman: 'Your inditement is composed without melody or rhyme: from that we observe that you do not wish to compromise the content of your statement for the sake of the rhyme or the melody' (*Ackerman*, Ch. 2, 12–14). The same problem is faced by the author of *La Chevalerie de Judas Machabée* (1285) who remarks that it is not surprising that he does not always achieve rich rhyme (*lionime*), since he is dealing with truth and hence the meaning (*sens*) requires that he does not insert inventions (*mençoigne*) merely to procure a rhyme (ll. 6–11). However, three of the manuscripts of this work say 'I do not claim that I never insert an embellishment [*beau dit*] to make the rhyme more pleasing and rich'. This is an echo of Benoît de Sainte-Maure, who had said in the prologue to his *Roman de Troie*, 'I shall follow my source, but I'm not saying that I won't add any embellishment [*bon dit*], if I feel up to it'. One author of a prose translation of the Pseudo-Turpin chronicle goes so far as to reject many of the tales of Charlemagne with the dictum 'no story in rhyme is truthful' ('nus contes rimés n'est verais'). Yet the author of the epic *La Mort Aymeri de Narbonne* (between 1180 and 1220) declares that no composer of a *chanson de geste* can avoid untruth when he comes to the end of a line and must accommodate the words and fashion a rhyme (ll. 3055–7). The Old French translator of Psalm 44 claims that all he has provided of his own is an appropriate word for the rhyme (*Eructavit*, ed. Jenkins, ll. 139ff.).

The problems associated with rhyme may generate a tension between the audience's requirements and the author's own artistic conscience. In concession to the taste for versification the author of a lost prose *Histoire de Philippe-Auguste* (first half of the thirteenth century) composes a verse prologue in which he declares that his story will be 'not rhymed' (l. 100) and 'like the book of Lancelot where there is not a single rhyme-word, the better to adhere to the truth and avoid distortion, for it is very difficult for a story to be rhymed without lies being added to supply the rhyme' (ll. 101–7). In a translation of the Pseudo-Turpin chronicle commissioned in 1206 by Renaud, Count of Boulogne, the translator declares that the count wished it to be unrhymed, since rhyme always attracts 'words gathered from outside the story' (ll. 10–12), a claim which echoes the concern expressed in the German *Lucidarius* (as quoted above) and which was to be repeated by Pierre de Beauvais in his *Bestiaire* (before 1217; ll. 6–8). These statements are sufficient to convince us that the aural pleasure afforded by recited narratives was taken seriously as an element of the poet's art, even though there was some anxiety about its interference with the principle of fidelity to truth and to the source.

In Middle English writing, the situation with regard to metrics is neatly encapsulated by Chaucer's Parson in the prologue to his tale. He says that he is a Southern man, and therefore unable to 'geeste "rum, ram, ruf" by lettre'; neither does he esteem 'rym' more highly; therefore, he says, he will tell 'a myrie tale in prose' (*Canterbury Tales*, X(I), 42–6). Alliterative verse, rhyme and prose: these were the three main possibilities for a Middle English writer, although one should also mention rhythmic prose as a separate category.

The actual practice of Middle English writers within each of these categories is much more complex than their statements about it; here we are concerned not to define the technical possibilities or their provenance, so much as to state what writers said about versification. Two currents of thought are contained in the Parson's statement. On the one hand, he sees metrical traditions in geographical terms: as a Southern man, he is unable to produce the alliterative metre characteristic of north- and south-western England from the mid-fourteenth century. On the other, he does not 'holde' rhyme in esteem; he seems to regard prose as the ideal teaching medium, and rhyme as an unnecessary adjunct to his 'sentence'. The same sentiments are expressed by John Trevisa, in his *Dialogus inter dominum et clericum* (c. 1387), where he says that he translates in prose, 'vor comynlych [because commonly] prose ys more cleer than ryme, and more esy and more pleyn to knowe and vnderstonde' (p. 293). Other writers concerned with 'sentence' do not necessarily reject rhyme, but, like the Parson, consciously choose simplicity of metre in the interests of clarity. Thus Robert Mannyng says he writes his history specifically for the unlearned, in an English which is 'lightest in mannes mouthe', and not for 'disours', 'seggers' or 'harpours', who employ more complex metrical resources. He goes on to say that English is made 'strange' by difficult rhyming patterns, and to blame minstrels for distorting the metre of famous poems through 'quaynte', 'or 'strange' rhyme, simply out of pride (*Chronicle* (1338), ll. 71–120).

However much some didactic writers might dispraise metrical skill, it is nevertheless true that such skill was highly regarded. Chaucer's Host attacks the narrator's own *Tale of Sir Thopas* because he cannot tolerate the 'drasty rymyng' (*Canterbury Tales*, VII, 919–35). This attack implies metrical skill as a basic minimum for anyone attempting to entertain an audience with poetry. A more profound sense of technical poetic skill can be found in *Piers Plowman*, where the narrator laments the general decline in educational standards. Grammar, from which derives both the analysis (or 'construing') and the composition of texts, now perplexes children, he says, such that these 'newe clerkes' cannot 'versifye faire ne formaliche enditen' (B-text, 15.370–4); here beautiful and skilful poetic composition is clearly regarded as a praiseworthy accomplishment of the learned.

4. Minstrels, makers and poets

Much medieval writing is anonymous, both literally and in spirit. The writers of very many religious works designed either for moral instruction or to arouse salutary emotion do not usually draw attention to themselves and their interests. The same is true of the speakers of very many popular romances and the heroic epic, where the narrator is presented simply as a minstrel, whose only interest lies in entertaining his audience, and, perhaps, in being paid to do so. But some exceptional poets had a quite elevated view of their role, and in the later Middle Ages this may be identified as a definite trend, though its manifestations were various and often very different in character.

Some writers affirmed their sense of their own importance by attacking mere minstrel entertainers. Raoul de Houdenc, in his romance *Meraugis de Portlesquez* (first quarter of the thirteenth century), disparages the *jogleors* as 'rhymsters of empty words' ('rimeor de servantois') who have nothing to say (ll. 10–11). The first Castilian poet known to us by name, Gonzalo de Berceo (*c.* 1190-after 1264), declares that his art falls within the category of *clerecia*, not *joglaria*, i.e. that he is a poet of the schools rather than a travelling minstrel, and that his subject-matter is more likely to be sacred or ancient rather than the deeds of some relatively recent local hero. The same bias is evident in Chaucer's *House of Fame*, where minstrels and 'gestiours' are positioned on the outside of Fame's castle, whereas the places of pride, and the great 'matters' of poetry, are reserved for great poets within Fame's palace. In *Piers Plowman* the idea of minstrelsy is preserved, but transformed to apply to poetic composition of the highest importance: in contrast with minstrels who entertain simply to pass the time, Langland presents an image of the minstrel as 'Goddes gleman', who with his 'game of hevene' does not 'spille speche' or waste time (B-text, 9.99–104).

Returning to the notion that there are several great 'matters' of poetry, it should be noted that certain writers made much of this in order to claim prestige for their own work within one or another of the major subject-areas. Jean Bodel in a celebrated pronouncement in his *Chanson des Saisnes* (ll. 4–6) proposed there were three worthy subjects ('trois matieres') for poets to take up: the *matiere de France*, i.e. *chansons de geste* dealing with Charlemagne and his descendants; the *matiere de Bretagne* based on the Arthurian legends; and the *matiere de Rome le grant*, the history of the founding of Rome. The first Bodel characterises as true, the second as fictitious, entertaining but vain, and the third as instructive and profitable (ll. 9–11). With more than a reminiscence of 'Arma virumque cano' (Virgil, *Aeneid*, 1.1), the epic poets celebrate arms and chivalry ('armes et chevalerie'), great deeds ('bons gestes'), valour and nobility ('seignorie, barnage') and reject stories of pride, folly, treachery and deceit, as is made clear in Bertran de Bar-sur-Aube's *Girart de Vienne*, written at the beginning of the thirteenth century. Bertran distinguishes three epic cycles or *gestes*, dealing respectively with kings of France (ll. 13ff.), with Doon de Maience (ancestor of the traitor Ganelon and other traitors), and Garin de Monglane, whose family nobly served Christianity and the kings of France. The Doon branch is considered unworthy because it deals with treachery (ll. 21ff.). In contrast, writers like the author of the AB redaction of the *Prise d'Orange* wished to offer a 'chancon de bone geste' (l. 32).

Elsewhere the emphasis is placed on the merits of the writer himself rather than those of his traditional matter, an excellent example of which is provided by Chrétien de Troyes' self-presentation. In his *Cligés* he proudly lists his compositions to date (or at least those which are relevant to the themes of that romance). In *Erec* he distinguishes himself from storytellers who merely serve up episodes by affirming his central concern for 'un bele conjointure', for the architecture of his work, i.e. the textual organisation in its entirety. Such is his authorial confidence, in this his earliest surviving work, that he can issue the punning claim that his story 'will be remembered for as long as "Christiandom" endures – this is "Christian's" boast' (ll. 24ff.). In the extremely ambiguous *Le Chevalier de la charrette* new critical terminology – *matiere* (subject-matter), *sen* (meaning), *antancion* (purposeful effort), *painne* (labour) – is applied to composition. There is no formal introduction to *Le Chevalier au lion*, but at the end Chrétien takes pains to stake out the limits of the authentic text, warning his readers/listeners that if they hear any more, it must be lies.

Other writers boldly identify with their art, as, for example, in a song by the German Heinrich von Morungen (early thirteenth century), where the lyric persona states that he was 'born into the world to sing' (XIII, 1,7; MF 133,20). Perhaps the finest elaboration of this commonplace is found in Konrad von Würzburg's *Trojanerkrieg*. No matter how little reward he receives for his work, Konrad says, he just cannot deny his tongue its proper office (*ambet*). Poetry has a total grip on his life; he has a total compulsion to practise his art (*kunst*) as a reward and rich gift to himself, whatever his audience may think. Indeed, if he was the only person alive he would 'still go on composing and singing, so that my words and the resonance of my voice would sound just for me' (ll. 176–91). This remarkable statement of the poet's position claims an autonomy rarely expressed in medieval poetry.

Further evidence of a growing artistic self-consciousness among certain vernacular writers is provided by their descriptions of themselves as 'makers' (i.e. skilled craftsmen) or indeed as 'poets'. The anonymous author of the Middle English *Winner and Wastour*, for example, pictures himself as an experienced 'maker' who can invent poetic matter (who 'matirs couthe fynde') against the young entertainer who can merely 'jangle als a jaye and japes telle' (ll. 19–30). Far more sophisticated are the self-descriptions of the Middle French poets who followed in the wake of the *Roman de la Rose*, particularly Guillaume de Machaut, who, by the end of his life (1377), had become the reigning lyrical presence on both sides of the English Channel. Machaut sought to establish a consistent image of himself as artist: as 'poète' and hence as 'auctour' in the sense of a writer whose work commanded total respect in moral as well as literary terms. In fourteenth-century French the term 'poète' seems to have extended its sphere of reference to classical *auctores* to include vernacular, contemporary poets. Dante had shown the way here: he initially treated the matter in *Vita Nova* 25, and returned to it in the *Commedia*, whose thirty uses of the term *poeta* begins with 'Virgil' saying 'I was a poet . . .' (*Inf.* 1.73) and concludes with the Dante-persona saying 'a poet will I return' (*Par.* 25.8). This new attitude is well illustrated by two elegiac ballades in memory of Machaut which Deschamps composed in 1377. In one both the ancient *auctor* Ovid and the late French writer are described as poets and 'makers'; in the other, Machaut is represented as having drawn inspiration from the very same sources ('Circe's fountain and the spring of Helicon') that the classical *auctores* used.

But there was a definite hierarchy for the terms 'maker' (OF *faiseur*) and 'poet', the latter being the more prestigious, indeed a veritable accolade. Basically, the courtly maker was supposed to be concerned with a limited goal, the perfection of his craft, which met immediate social demands; only when he exceeded this function and wrote wisely could he be considered a 'poet'. The anonymous *Règles de la seconde rhétorique* generally relies on the terms 'rethorique', 'faiseur' and 'ouvrier' in its accounts of lyric forms, but singles out the work of Jean Le Fèvre for its ethical purposefulness, this being identified as characteristic of poets ('les bonnes menieres qui furent en li est apelez poetes'). Similarly, in his *Art de dictier* Deschamps used only the term 'faiseur' – which reveals the true significance of his application of 'poéte' to Machaut. Here is a conscious attempt by a younger writer to elevate the achievement of his master (and perhaps his uncle) to the highest level of verbal art – a level to which Machaut himself had aspired – by applying a term in which moral as well as literary excellence is implicit. And this also indicates Deschamps' personal ambition to be a hailed as a 'poète'.

The key model here is Machaut's own self-presentation as a writer, which involved a number of important new developments for the late French Middle Ages in terms of the very conception of the vernacular author. First, there is Machaut's consistent self-depiction, within the context of his longer narrative works, as a professional writer directly involved in the physical production of his own artistic works, i.e. the transcription and circulation of manuscripts. This is particularly evident in the *Voir-Dit* (discussed previously in this chapter from a different viewpoint), where the progressive physical production of the text itself becomes an essential part of the plot. Second, there is Machaut's explicit self-presentation as a professional writer (in the *Voir-Dit*, as well as in the *Jugement dou roy de Navarre* and the *Fonteinne amoureuse* of 1360–1) visibly concerned with the business of patronage, which simultaneously confers prestige on his writerly activity and differentiates him from the class for which he writes. Third, Machaut's self-representation as author figure in the global *Prologue* to his *œuvres complètes* serves as the unifying principle for a strikingly heterogeneous body of work: love-poetry (both lyric and narrative), didactic texts, contemporary historiography. Fourth, this *Prologue* invests his status as a writer with a new kind of dignity and prestige. In effect, we have a ceremonial staging of the writerly vocation, as the allegorised figures of Nature and Love single out Guillaume de Machaut as their privileged servant (1.1–5; 2.1–8), while he solemnly vows full devotion to this calling (5.21–4). His creation of poems is clearly made to be analogous to Nature's creation of him: the same verbs are used in both cases: *fourmer, ordener, faire*.

Jean Froissart's literary self-consciousness builds on Machaut. In the prologue to the *Joli buisson de Jonece* (1373), Froissart depicts himself as having been created by Nature with the 'mission' to write: 'for she has made me for this . . . that I compose beautiful poems *(faire biaus dittiers*; ll. 33, 37). This imperative involves the revelation of the experience of the writer's intellectual self, presented as a source: 'Nature motivates me to represent and to articulate what I think about and study' (ll. 54–6). In the *Joli buisson* Froissart refers to himself indirectly as *poëtes* by using the term (ll. 2013, 2103) to designate the creator of the work's two pseudo-Ovidian fictions, who is none other than Jean Froissart himself, wittily presented as a new vernacular Ovid.

The opening sequence of the third book of the *Chroniques* (the so-called *Voyage en Béarn*; *Chroniques* 3.1–27) involves an elaborate self-portrait of Froissart the writer. A three-stage process is involved. First, he obtains his basic historical material orally. Next, he writes it down in a first draft: 'I wrote these words down either at night or the next morning in order to preserve them for the future in my memory, for the best way to retain things is by writing' (*Chroniques* 3.16; p. 65). Finally, he transforms these notes into art, into the Book. In this last stage Froissart the writer seeks to 'clarify through beautiful language [*bel langaige*] all the information I had obtained' (*Chroniques* 3.1), at the same time adding an exemplary dimension. Linguistic craftsmanship is linked both to intellectual understanding and to a moral valence. The privileged setting for this final stage is the workshop of the professional writer, whose labour is presented in terms analogous to those used by Jean de Meun for the creative work of Nature who 'within her forge always hammers and forges' (*Rose*, ll. 15,979–80). The figure of the vernacular writer is thus (self-)invested with great prestige: 'I, Jean Froissart . . . have once again entered my forge in order to work upon and forge this high and noble subject-matter' ('haulte et noble matière'; *Chroniques* 4.1).

In *Chroniques* 3.19 Froissart depicts in strategically prestigious terms the performative aspect of his status as professional writer: a public reading from an earlier work (the *Roman de Méliador*) at the court of Gaston Phébus. Here, Froissart explicitly appears as the author of the work he reads from, referring to 'the master-plan I had from which to write and compose the book' ('la ymagination que j'avoie eu de dicter et ordonner le livre'; p. 76). The Count of Foix bestows special honorific status on Froissart's performance (for example, enforced silence on all other courtiers during the readings), for which he provides the privileged audience. In the *Dit dou Florin*'s description of the same scene, the Count responds to Froissart's reading by complimenting him on his writing: 'and he said to me: "it is a fine vocation, fair master [*uns beaus mestiers, beaus maistres*], to compose such works"' (ll. 298–9). In addition, Froissart's performance *qua* author (in the *Voyage*) is clearly differentiated from (and elevated above) that of the minstrels who are also present at Phébus' court ('menestrandies', 'menestrelx qui tous firent mestier'; pp. 78, 117).

Christine de Pizan's self-depictions *qua* writer continue the move away from the categories of 'ministrel' and 'maker'. The *faiseur* identity of her early courtly production (especially her *Cent ballades*, *c.* 1400) quickly gives way to a learned authorial persona with a strong moral dimension, linked to a self-authorising autobiographical fable which emphasises her newly authoritative status as female writer. Her narrative works repeatedly present her literary career as a high vocation for which she has been specially chosen. In the *Chemin de long estude* (1402–3) the Cumean Sibyl singles out Christine for a journey of literary initiation on the basis of her exceptional love of knowledge (*science*, l. 492) which will guarantee her future fame: 'your name will be resplendently remembered long after your death' (ll. 496–7). In the *Livre de la cité des dames* (1405), the allegorical character Droitture (Rectitude) affirms the uniqueness of Christine's literary mission vis-à-vis earlier female writers: 'the construction of this work was reserved for you and not for them' (2.53; p. 253).

A further development of the vernacular writer's status occurs in Christine's establishment of a 'personalised' canon of model authors in which French and Italian writers (treated, in effect, as *auctores*) mingled with Latin ones: Ovid, Boethius, Jean de Meun, Dante and Boccaccio. Of particular importance is Christine's explicit (and contrastive) self-definition as learned, female writer in contradistinction to Jean de Meun (especially in the *Querelle de le Roman de la Rose* of 1401–2, on which see Chapter 14 above). Furthermore, Christine ends by treating herself as a vernacular *auctor*, repeatedly citing her own earlier works in the course of her evolving *œuvre*. Particularly striking examples of this are found in the *Cité des dames* (1.17 and 2.54), the *Advision Cristine* of 1405 (2.14, 15, 17) and the *Livre des trois vertus*, also written in 1405 (1.26–7). By the mid-fifteenth century, this commingled Latin, French and Italian canon is explicitly figured in the famous 'cemetery' of the Ospital d'Amours in René d'Anjou's *Livre du cuer d'amours espris* (1457). We have here a set of six tombstones, each with a first-person verse epitaph. Right next to the tomb of Ovid is that of 'Machault, poethe renommé' (p. 142), followed by those of Boccaccio, Jean de Meun, Petrarch and Alain Chartier, each designated as a 'poethe'.

Turning to the English poets who were influenced by 'the School of Machaut', Gower uses 'makynge' to describe his own writing but calls Ovid a 'poete'. Chaucer shares this ostensible modesty, always referring to himself as a 'maker' and using the term 'poet' of only two among the vernacular writers he does mention: Dante is described as a 'grete poete'

and a 'wise poete' (*Canterbury Tales*, VII,2460, III(D), 1125) and Petrarch
as 'the lauriat poete' (IV(E), 31). But this humility is largely conventional,
as is evidenced in Gower's case by his efforts at self-commentary (see
Chapter 14 above) and in Chaucer's by subtle implications of self-worth.
In *The House of Fame*, for example, Chaucer 'himself' (the narrator is
called 'Geffrey') momentarily joins a company including many great classical poets. It is true that he chooses to leave it, and disclaims any desire
for personal fame (ll. 1875–82), but the very act of entering in the first
place indicates the awareness of the possibility of joining such a tradition,
with its attendant fame. And if a poet might join a tradition, this entails
a decorum between himself and other great poets. In the envoy to *Troilus
and Criseyde*, Chaucer enjoins his 'litel book' not to 'envie' ('compete
with') other poets, 'but subgit be to alle poesye'. Instead, Chaucer's poem
is to 'kis the steppes' where Virgil, Ovid, Homer, Lucan and Statius walk
(V.1789–92). At the same moment as he registers his humility before such
poets, he implicitly calls attention to the possibility that he might join
them. This is the mark of high self-esteem by a poet who rarely mentions
vernacular authors, even when they are his real sources – the most striking
example being his refusal to give Boccaccio the credit for having provided
the main source of Troilus. Indeed, he goes so far as to disguise this debt
by ostentatious references to 'myn auctour called Lollius' (I.394), who
sounds like an ancient and venerable *auctor*, an impression reinforced by
Chaucer's claim that he is translating from a Latin source (II.14). This
strategy, along with the self-ironies of *The House of Fame*, may be taken
as revealing Chaucer as a writer standing at a cultural crossroads – from
which he can view both the old and the new senses of poetship and *auctor*-
ship. The 'grete' and 'wise poete' himself, Dante, had fewer qualms about
signalling his own literary and moral worth – witness the extraordinary
passage in *Inferno* 4 (which may well have influenced Chaucer in the two
poems cited above) wherein Dante's *maestro e autore* Virgil (*Inf*. I.85)
presents the new poet to his 'fair school' of famous poets, which consists of Homer, Horace, Ovid and Lucan, Virgil himself being hailed as
l'altissimo poeta (4.80). 'They turned to me', Dante declares, 'with sign
of salutation, at which my master smiled; and far more honour still they
showed me, for they made me one of their company, so that I was sixth
amid so much wisdom' (4.98–102). But at the end of the entire *Commedia* there can be no doubt of the force of the implication that Dante is
primus inter pares, having – literally and allegorically – left Virgil behind,
to attain a vision of true deity which the best of pagan poets could only
gesture towards.

What is common to these creations of self-image is the principle
that the right kind of self-effacement could in fact be self-promotion.
The ability to deny one's worthiness for the accolade of 'poet' and yet

elsewhere – or indeed in the very act of denial – to embrace it is characteristic of that class of medieval poets who are demonstrably self-conscious
about their poetship. As 'lauriat' Petrarch knew, one does not give oneself
the title 'poet', any more than one could describe oneself directly as an
auctor. But one could at least conspire to be crowned. Dante (to cite the
most spectacular case again) certainly did, and he got what he believed
he deserved (see Chapters 20–22 below). The 'crowning' of Chaucer took
a rather different form, for he came to be credited with the paternity of
English poetry. For Gower he was the 'disciple and . . . poete' of Venus
(*Confessio amantis*, VIII.2942), whereas Thomas Usk saw him as the servant of a higher form of Love, 'the noble philosophical poete in Englissh'
who in 'wit' and 'sentence' surpassed 'al other makers' (*Testament of
Love*, III.iv; p. 123). But in the next century Thomas Hoccleve began
his paean (1412) by addressing Chaucer as 'O maister deere and fadir
reverent!' (*Regement of Princes*, l. 1,961), while the anonymous writer of
the *Book of Courtesy* (1477) termed him the 'fadir and founder of ornate
eloquence' in Britain (l. 330). (Much later, in 1700, John Dryden was to
hail him as 'the father of English poetry', to be held in such veneration
as the Greeks held Homer or the Romans, Virgil.) These and other writers of the same period set about claiming kin, declaring that they while
they cannot hope to compete with 'The firste fyndere of our faire langage'
(*Regement of Princes*, l. 978), nevertheless they can at least presume to
follow in his footsteps. Hence Walton (in his Boethius translation of 1410)
and John Lydgate can praise Chaucer as a 'poete' and use 'makynge' to
describe their own work. The inevitable happens when Caxton (in his
1484 edition of the *Canterbury Tales*) declares that Chaucer was a sort
of laureate poet in his time, and King James I of Scotland, throwing qualification to the winds, describes Chaucer and Gower as 'superlatiue as
poetis laureate' (*Kingis Quair*, ll. 197–101, written *c.* 1435), though of
course the title has no historical basis in Chaucer's own age. John Skelton
(1460?–1529) was the first English poet to have the legal right to use the
title, since it was conferred on him, as an academical distinction, by the
universities of Oxford, Louvain and Cambridge; his *Garlande of Laurell*
is a self-laudatory allegory which describes how he was crowned among
the world's great poets. Here is self-promotion with little self-effacement.

When English writers aligned themselves with Chaucer, or French poets
with Chrétien (rarely named but clearly dominant), de Meun or Machaut,
or Italian poets with Dante (though certain humanists – even Petrarch –
could scarcely forgive him for having written in the vernacular rather than
Latin), they seem to have been guided by the same fundamental motivation. By distinguishing a true poet from the crowd they were laying
implicit claim to knowing the true nature of poetry; that superior knowledge, operating in their own writing, should produce superior poetry, to

be recognised as such by those of superior discernment. By conferring the title 'poet' on another writer in his own poems, the ambitious writer was suggesting that in due course the title could be applied to himself. Personal fame, then, was sought through the recognition of one's peers; hopefully posterity would do the rest, the application for membership of the select society having, as it were, been made. And this level of artistic self-consciousness clearly anticipates certain aspects of the Renaissance conception of the poet. But then the terms 'maker' and 'poet' merged, as critics explored the derivation of the latter from the Greek verb '*poiein*, which is to make'. 'Wherein I know not', adds Sir Philip Sidney, whose *Apology for Poetry* (*c.* 1583) we are quoting here, 'whether by lucke or wisedome, wee Englishmen haue mette with the Greekes in calling him a maker', this being a 'high' and 'incomparable . . . title'. For, as George Puttenham explains, inasmuch as poets 'make' and devise so many wonderful things by themselves, 'they be (by maner of speech) as creating gods'. We have come a long way from the minstrels and makers of the later Middle Ages.

16

Occitan grammars and the art of troubadour poetry

Simon Gaunt and John Marshall[1]

One of the most dazzling and influential vernacular literary traditions of the twelfth and thirteenth centuries is that of the troubadours. The troubadour lyric quickly developed its own sophisticated poetics that was in turn to have a great impact on the development of lyric poetry and love casuistry in the literary traditions and cultures of Italy, Spain, northern France, Germany and England: Dante, for example, devoted a good portion of his literary criticism to the troubadours and similarly expounded his literary theory in part at least on the basis of his reading of troubadour *chansonniers*. The troubadours composed in a language that today we call Occitan, though earlier in the twentieth century it was (somewhat erroneously) known as Provençal and in the Middle Ages it could be designated by a variety of terms, some reflecting dialect (e.g. *Lemosi*), others merely vernacularity (*Romans*). Occitan was spoken until the early twentieth century in roughly the southern half of present-day France, but in the Middle Ages it was also used as a literary language at least in the twelfth century at the culturally crucial court of Poitiers and at a variety of courts in Catalonia, other parts of northern Spain, and then, in the thirteenth century, in Italy. Occitan was therefore a literary language with an international following, a language that some foreigners learnt, again particularly in the thirteenth century, with the specific intention of composing poetry.

No critical or theoretical text on literature in Occitan survives from the richest period of troubadour poetic activity. The earliest such text, Raimon Vidal's *Razos de trobar*, was composed between 1190 and 1213, in other words either after or towards the end of the literary careers of the troubadours of the so-called classical period (*c.* 1160–*c.* 1200). The texts themselves are the only sources for critical or theoretical comments on troubadour poetry from the twelfth century.

Prescriptive theoretical texts for would-be troubadours, often concentrating on linguistic or formal aspects of composition such as grammar or versification, proliferate in the thirteenth and fourteenth centuries, but the poetic tradition is by this time in decline. The reasons for the slow

---

[1] Simon Gaunt wrote the first part of this chapter, John Marshall the second, but the final version of the conjoined chapter was the responsibility of Simon Gaunt.

demise of the vibrant poetic tradition of the twelfth century are unclear, an obvious socio-political explanation being the Albigensian Crusade which began in 1209, but it is apparent that the turn of the twelfth and thirteenth centuries is a watershed in the history of troubadour poetry. In the twelfth century, the troubadour lyric is constantly evolving and there are a great many innovative and individualistic figures; in the thirteenth century (despite some notable exceptions like Peire Cardenal) troubadours are content to rework old themes in a manner that becomes increasingly repetitive and this despite the large quantities of texts still being produced.[2] The literary theory and criticism of the two periods reflect this historical shift and will consequently be given separate treatment. Twelfth-century theory and criticism are contained within the texts of poets working in a rich and living tradition comprising not just the love-poetry which most modern scholars (and indeed later medieval readers) prefer to read, but also political and moralising lyrics; twelfth-century poets rarely touch upon formal problems, for they are not concerned to provide prescriptive rules, but to give an account of their own creative enterprise and to situate it in relation to the work of their colleagues. In contrast, thirteenth-century criticism and theory are the work of writers attempting to preserve a tradition which was already in decline. (In Raimon Vidal's 'Abrils issia', for example, a *joglar* looks back nostalgically on the golden age of troubadour courts.) They were seeking to instruct people in how to write poetry in the literary language of a world which was slipping away from them, indeed which in some cases they had never known. This language had already evolved from the mid-twelfth-century form they were encouraging people to emulate, and this perhaps explains the conjunction of love-poetry and grammar in their texts. It is also significant that at least some of the surviving Occitan grammars were probably intended to teach foreigners (Catalans, Italians and so on) how to write passable troubadour poetry in an archaic style, for Occitan was a fashionable literary language in certain parts of Spain and Italy for some time after the decline of troubadour poetry was irreversible in southern France.

1. The *trobar* of the troubadours

One salient feature of the troubadour lyric is the frequency of intertextual play, often parodic. Where a troubadour is referring to a specific text or poet intertextual play can amount to literary criticism, and there are numerous examples of songs composed as replies to other songs. For example, in one trio of poems Bernart de Ventadorn (*fl. c.* 1147–*c.* 1170),

---

[2] For an overview of the later period, see Routledge, 'The Later Troubadours'.

Raimbaut d'Aurenga (*fl. c.* 1147–73) and the French *trouvère* and *romancier*, Chrétien de Troyes, debate the love of Tristan and Iseult. The chronology of the exchange is uncertain and obviously the poems may be appreciated separately, but each is the richer for being placed alongside the other two, which can be read as contemporary commentaries on the poet's views. Similarly, several poems by Marcabru (*fl. c.* 1130–*c.* 1149), the dominant figure of the first half of the twelfth century, can be read as glosses on texts by other troubadours: 'D'aiso laus Dieu' (XVI), a parodic boasting poem, can be interpreted as a polemic reaction to 'Ben vueill' (VI), in which Guilhem IX (1071–1126) vaunts his poetic and sexual prowess; 'Estornel, cueill ta volada' (XXV), in which an immoral lover sends a message to his lady with a starling, is a parody of 'Rossinhol en son repaire' (XIX), where a nightingale acts as a more courtly messenger for Peire d'Alvernhe (*fl. c.* 1149–*c.* 1168).[3] Elsewhere Marcabru criticises his contemporaries for abusing the power of language, mistrusting the courtly veneer which in his view masks the immorality of their songs. In this light, his parodic imitations of Guilhem and Peire are comments on their work.

Marcabru probably has the smooth, courtly style in mind when he attacks 'childish troubadours' for composing words which are *entrebescaz de fraitura*, 'interwoven with fragmentation' (XXXVII, 7–12). Peire d'Alvernhe uses the same terminology when he claims that there are no *motz romputz* ('broken words') in his work and that he is the first troubadour to compose *vers entiers*, 'whole poetry' (XVI, 31–40; XX, 1–4). The idea that a poem is 'fragmented' or 'broken' unless it combines formal perfection and moral integrity may bear the mark of rhetorical and scholastic thinking: Thomas Aquinas, for example, maintains that the unity of beauty and rectitude in a work of art gives it *integritas*. Bernart Marti (mid-twelfth century) seems familiar with this concept, for he criticises Peire's use of the term *vers entiers*. How can a poem be 'whole' when it is the product of vanity (V, 13–18)?[4] However, Bernart does not dwell on this analysis of the relationship between aesthetics and ethics; his poem quickly degenerates into personal insults of a more mundane

---

[3] Each troubadour's known period of literary activity is given in brackets after the first occurrence of his name. On the specific instances discussed here, see Roncaglia, 'Carestia'; di Girolamo, *I trovatori*, pp. 120–41; Rossi, 'Chrétien' (on the Bernart–Raimbaut–Chrétien exchange); Topsfield, *Troubadours*, pp. 93–4; Paterson, *Troubadours*, pp. 20–8; Léglu, *Between Sequence and Sirventes*, pp. 34–62 (and pp. 89–103 on Marcabru XVI, also imitations of Marcabru); Lejeune, 'Thèmes communs', pp. 287–98; Harvey, *Marcabru*, pp. 158–93 ; Meneghetti, 'Uno stornello' (on Marcabru XXV). Marcabru also attacks and comments upon Jaufre Rudel: see poems XV and XXVIII. Continuations and interpolations, a related form of criticism, are the subject of Kay, 'Continuation'.

[4] On this terminology and the *vers entiers* controversy, see Paterson, *Troubadours*, pp. 58–74.

nature (V, 31–6) and this reluctance to engage in intellectual debate is typical of the early troubadour tradition. Troubadours were competing, if not for patrons, at the very least for popularity. Is it surprising that they often preferred blackening the character of competitors to abstract literary criticism?

Indeed, when troubadours name other poets, literary judgements are vague in the extreme, and the purpose of singling out a colleague is often to create humour at his expense, frequently with his complicity. We possess, for example, two twelfth-century literary 'reviews', one by Peire d'Alvernhe, composed in 1161 or 1162, and another by the Monk of Montaudan (*fl. c.* 1193–*c.* 1210), composed in 1195. In each song the poet publicly defames a series of contemporary troubadours, before humorously disparaging his own work in the last stanza. Although some stanzas involve play on texts by the poet in question, such literary criticism or theory as there is in these poems cannot be taken seriously, for it is likely that the troubadours mentioned were present for the first performance, and that they were conceived as satirical entertainment. Indeed, Peire announces that his poem was composed *tot iogan rizen*, 'all playing and laughing' (XII, 85–6). He does offer some value judgements on his colleagues' poetry. Giraut de Borneil (*fl. c.* 1162–*c.* 1199), for example, is said to compose 'thin and whining' songs (XII, 15). However, Peire's taunts are generally of a non-literary, but more scabrous nature, as when he casts aspersions about Bernart de Ventadorn's legitimacy (XII, 19–24). Similarly, the Monk mocks Arnaut Daniel (*fl. c.* 1180–*c.* 1195) for composing incomprehensible songs (XVIII, 43–8), but otherwise he prefers personal attacks: Peirol (*fl. c.* 1188–*c.* 1222), he claims, has not changed his clothes for thirty years (ll. 25–6).

Despite this tendency to dismiss each other's work rather frivolously, troubadours possess a rich vocabulary for theorising about their poetry, and it is in this context that the most interesting terminology and ideas are found. Several broad categories of vocabulary can be discerned: metaphors that acquire a pseudo-technical sense, generic terms, words describing rhymes, terms relating to the moral content of a song, terms concerned with sound-texture, and finally terms indicating the presence or absence of different levels of meaning. It is noteworthy that although troubadours like Marcabru, Peire d'Alvernhe and Giraut de Borneil probably had a training in rhetoric, their technical vocabulary represents, on the whole, an independent vernacular tradition. If the influence of rhetoric is evident in the *dispositio* of some poems, in a troubadour's debating technique or in his use of tropes, few of the troubadours' technical terms bear a direct resemblance to Latin terms. *Razo* (from *ratio*, 'argumentation', 'reasoning') and *colors* ('rhetorical colours') are perhaps the only two obvious borrowings from the Latin tradition that are used regularly.

Metaphors describing the art of composition are common. For instance, poets frequently liken their work to that of a craftsman. Guilhem IX tells us that one poem has been 'brought forth from a good workshop' (VI, 3); he says the same song is 'bound up' (*lasatz*), possibly a technical term in weaving. Weaving is certainly the frame of reference when Marcabru attacks troubadours whose songs are 'interwoven with fragmentation' and when Raimbaut d'Aurenga claims to 'weave rare, dark and tinted words' (I, 19), in an allusive poem which uses 'derived rhymes': pairs of rhyme-words based upon the same radical, but with different rhyme-sounds, for example *pesc/pesca, laire/laira*. Indeed the image of 'word-weaving' (*entrebescar los motz*) may have been associated in a technical sense with 'derived rhymes'.[5] The best-known metaphors relating the troubadour to the craftsman occur in Arnaut Daniel's poetry, and it is perhaps the image of Arnaut planing and filing away at the words of his songs that prompted Dante to call him 'il miglior fabbro del parlar materno' ('the finest craftsman of the vernacular tongue'; *Purgatorio* 26.117).[6]

Twelfth-century troubadours use a variety of generic terms to designate their poems. Several genres, apart from the love poem, emerge from the early twelfth century, notably the *planh* (lament), the *pastorela* (pastourelle) and the *tenso* (debate poem), but specific terminology distinguishing them from other poems develops only later in the century. Until the 1150s *vers* (from *versus*) seems to be a blanket term for poetry; from about 1160 *canso* is the usual term for a love poem, though there is no obvious difference between many *vers* of the first half of the century and the *cansos* of the second. If, in the early thirteenth century, some troubadours were to argue about the relative merits of the *vers* and the *canso*, their confusion as to what the words meant suggests that they were no clearer on the matter than modern scholars. These later poets associate the *vers* with moralising poetry, but several troubadours from the key decade of 1160–70 use the terms indiscriminately. Perhaps *vers* as a generic term simply went out of fashion as it gradually became associated with the early troubadours, whose melodies may have been inspired by the *versus* of the Aquitanian school of Saint-Martial de Limoges and whose poems may have seemed quaint and archaic by the 1170s. Raimbaut d'Aurenga certainly implies as much in the 1160s when he opens a poem, 'I will call my *vers* a *chansso*' (XXX), which suggests that his preference for *chansso* is simply a question of terminology. In any event, in the latter half of the century generic distinctions seem to have sharpened

---

[5] On 'word-weaving', see Shapiro, '*Entrebescar*'; Kay, 'Derivation'.
[6] On these metaphors, see Spence, 'Rhetoric and Hermeneutics', pp. 170–1; Gaunt, 'Orality and Writing', p. 234.

as the troubadours began to distinguish between the *canso* and the *sirventes*, a moralising or satiric poem. As the century advanced, new genres appeared: the *alba* (dawn song), the *descort* (a poem in which the stanzas are irregular) and the *partimen* (similar to a *tenso*).[7]

Regular and precise versification was an important feature of the troubadour lyric by about 1150, and there is a dazzling array of complex verse-forms, unusual rhyme-sounds and rhyme-schemes. A freer attitude towards versification is no doubt the cause of the 'irregularities' that have unnecessarily troubled editors of some early poems, but after 1150 troubadours composing in the 'high' style of the *canso* (as opposed to the so-called 'popularising' genres like the *pastorela*, or the satiric *sirventes*) seem to become more meticulous about regular versification and rhymes. It would be surprising, however, if the poets themselves were to draw attention to this aspect of their craft. Only the most self-conscious of painters allows brush-strokes to be visible as brush-strokes; similarly the vocabulary used by later theoretical writers to classify versification, is not found in the troubadours' own poems. When they allude to their rhymes they are eager to extol quality, but vague on technique. Raimbaut d'Aurenga says his rhyme is 'delicate' in one poem (II), and he alludes, in a poem which parodies the allusive style, to his *rima braca*, 'slimy rhyme' (X, 52). With equal imprecision Arnaut Daniel stresses the perfection of his rhymes (XII, 6–8) and Raimon de Miraval (*fl. c.* 1191–*c.* 1229) may have botched rhymes in mind when he accuses one Villemin of composing 'songs and *sirventes* with wretched words that are badly placed and put together' (XLIII, 5–6).[8]

Several terms which apparently designate style or poetic technique in fact refer to content and moralising tone. *Vers entiers*, the subject of the dispute between Peire d'Alvernhe and Bernart Marti, is one such term, but the most interesting is *trobar naturau*, a 'style' only alluded to and practised by Marcabru (XXXIII, 6–12). *Trobar naturau* is poetry which avoids the confusion of 'fragmentation' and what Marcabru calls *la falsa razos daurada*, 'false gilded speech' (XXV, 24); it seeks instead to explore the lessons offered by the natural world. Often drawing on imagery derived from patristic and contemporary theological texts, Marcabru

---

7 On the *vers*, see Chailly, 'Les premiers troubadours'; Marshall, 'Le *vers*'. On the *sirventes*, see Rieger, *Gattungen*; Léglu, 'Moral and Satirical Poetry'. On genre, see Bec, 'Le problème'; Spence, 'Rhetoric and Hermeneutics'.

8 Frank, *Répertoire*, classifies the versification of the entire troubadour corpus, though this has now been supplemented by Beltrami and Vatteroni, *Rimario*. Paterson, *Troubadours*, pp. 213–18, provides invaluable statistical data on frequency of rhyme-sounds and on versification. There is no satisfactory study of rhyme in troubadour poetry, but Chambers, *Introduction*, is the best to date; see also Billy, *L'Architecture*. On irregular rhyming and versification, see Marshall, 'Versification'; Marcabru, *Critical Edition*, ed. Gaunt, Harvey and Paterson, pp. 20–6.

accords immense importance to the moral truths nature reveals, condemning what he deems 'unnatural'. Each creature has its place in a carefully regulated universe: thus the donkey who seeks to play with his master like a dog is ridiculous (XXXIX, 53–6), and, as in medieval bestiaries, some creatures are naturally noble, others naturally proud, treacherous or stupid. The animal world, as Marcabru portrays it, is an allegory of the human world: thus the lady who takes a servant as her lover is likened to the greyhound bitch who mates with a mongrel (XXXI, 46–9).[9]

Troubadour poetry was originally intended to be sung. However, the poor survival rate of melodies suggests that texts were considered more important than tunes, even though troubadours continually refer to the act of singing. It is nevertheless no accident that, in a tradition that was musical as well literary, poets should be intensely aware of the musicality of language. In contrast to Marcabru's harsh alliterations and rhymes, which bristle with dentals, sibilants and glottal stops, Cercamon (*fl. c.* 1137–*c.* 1149) boasts of the smoothness of his poetry which, he claims, uses *motz politz*, 'polished words' (III, 31–4). Later poets were to find that the 'harsh style', for which the term *trobar brau*, 'rough poetry', was to be coined, lent itself readily to parody. Unfortunately, the absurdity of the accumulation of harsh alliterations in a poem by Guilhem Ademar (*fl. c.* 1195–*c.* 1217), which advertises its formal dexterity by using derived rhymes, is difficult to convey in translation:

> Al prim pres dels breus jorns braus,
> Quan branda·ls brueils l'aura brava,
> E·ill branc e·ill brondel son nut
> Pel brun tems sec que·ls desnuda,
> Per us, brus braus brecs de cor
> Trobadors a bric coratge,
> Fauc breus menutz motz cortes,
> Lasatz ab rima corteza.   (XIII, 1–8)

[When the brief, harsh days first set in and when the sharp wind shakes the boughs, and the branches and twigs are naked, because the dark, dry season strips them bare, I, a dark, fierce, broken-hearted troubadour of foolish demeanour, compose, as is my custom, brief, delicate, courtly words, bound up with a courtly rhyme.]

Trobar brau had its dedicatees amongst moralising poets well into the thirteenth century, but the smooth alliterations and assonances of what modern critics have called *trobar prim* were more popular in courtly circles. Arnaut Daniel was a master of this style, combining smooth,

---

[9] On *trobar naturau*, see Roncaglia, 'Riflessi'.

delicate sounds with unusual rhymes to produce exquisitely languid sound-textures. His versatility in creating and exploiting sound-patterns was undoubtedly at least partly responsible for the high regard in which Dante held him.[10]

A considerable amount of modern scholarly debate has focused on the meaning of the terms *trobar clus* and *trobar leu*, and on related terminology, for instance, *trobar ric*, *trobar car*, *color*, *cobert* ('covered'), *clar* ('clear'), *plan* ('plain'), *leugier* ('light') and *escur* ('dark'). The origins of the *trobar clus*, variously defined as a 'closed', 'dark', 'obscure' or 'hermetic' style have been located in Arabic hermetic poetry, in the *ornatus difficilis* of classical rhetoric, and in techniques drawn from biblical exegesis; its practice has been attributed to moralising poets and to aristocrats seeking a discerning public. The *trobar leu*, an 'easy', 'limpid' or 'open' style, is compared to the *stilus levis* of the Latin tradition and is thought to be best typified by limpid and smooth *cansos*. Discussion has centred on a *tenso* composed between 1162 and 1173, 'Era·m platz' (LIX), in which Giraut de Borneil defends the *leu* style and Raimbaut d'Aurenga the *trobar clus*: it has been suggested that the *trobar clus* was fashionable in the mid-twelfth century, before being displaced, following a public controversy, by the more accessible *trobar leu*. Terms associated with the *clus/leu* debate occur frequently in the work of Raimbaut and Giraut, the protagonists of the *tenso*, and they are therefore thought to be the key figures in the controversy, which, it is supposed, subsided shortly after 1170. *Trobar ric*, 'rich poetry', and *trobar car*, 'precious poetry', are considered to represent attempts by a few troubadours to combine the best features of the two opposing styles.[11]

Some troubadours did draw a distinction between 'allusive' and 'clear' poetry, yet terms like *trobar clus* and *trobar leu* are rare in troubadour poetry, occurring far more frequently in modern criticism, whilst other categories used by scholars, such as *trobar car* or *trobar ric*, are found only in isolated instances in contexts that suggest they were coined for the occasion. In the best account of troubadour literary terminology and stylistic theory, Linda Paterson analyses the technique of five poets to conclude that although each one has his own individual view of style, the *trobar clus* is distinguished by the presence of different levels of meaning

---

[10] On sound-texture, see Paterson, *Troubadours*, pp. 52–4, 74–6, 178–85, 201–2; Makin, 'Pound'. On the troubadours' music, see Page, *Voices*, pp. 12–28; Switten, 'Music and Versification'.

[11] The most notable contributions to the huge bibliography on this subject are: Bossy, 'The *trobar clus*'; di Girolamo, *I trovatori*, pp. 100–19; Köhler, *Trobadorlyrik* and 'Marcabru'; Milone, 'Retorica'; Mölk, *Trobar clus*; Paterson, *Troubadours*, pp. 41–52, 77–85, 90–117, 145–79, 193–201; Pollmann, *Trobar clus*; Roncaglia, 'Trobar clus'; Spence, 'Rhetoric and Hermeneutics'; Van Vleck, *Memory*, pp. 133–63. I refer to Sharman's edition of the Giraut/Raimbaut *tenso*.

(*colors*) and the gradual unfolding of a theme. The *trobar leu*, she suggests, is characterised by lightness of touch, limpidity and smoothness (*Troubadours*, pp. 207–12). These conclusions are undoubtedly correct with regard to poetic practice, providing an invaluable framework with which to approach the aesthetics of the troubadour lyric. But did the troubadours themselves think in terms of rigid and prescriptive distinctions between styles? Furthermore, did the *trobar leu* displace the *trobar clus* because of popular demand for 'easy' poetry? Giraut de Borneil is thought by some scholars to have given up composing in the *trobar clus* early in his career in order to take up the more popular *trobar leu*. Yet the little we know of the chronology of his poems belies this supposition and it is often difficult to tell the two styles apart in his work, particularly on the basis of his use of *clus* and *leu* terminology (Paterson, *Troubadours*, p. 89).

Some commentaries on the *tenso* at the centre of the *clus/leu* controversy suggest that far from being a highbrow debate on aesthetics, as many scholars have thought, it is a literary joke.[12] Neither protagonist defines the style he purports to defend. Indeed the poem is not about style at all: of greater concern is the question of public acclaim. Should a troubadour aim to please only a discerning public with the *trobar clus* or should he seek the applause of the widest possible audience and compose in the *leu* style? Raimbaut, a relatively powerful aristocrat, claims to be indifferent to public approval, while Giraut, a professional troubadour, is apparently concerned that his work should be liked by everyone. But the tone of the exchange is parodic and burlesque. Raimbaut, defending the *clus* style, is limpid and to the point, whereas Giraut, defending the *trobar leu*, is allusive and circumlocutory. Each poet parodies his own work and at the end of the poem the debate degenerates into an obvious pastiche of Guilhem IX and a discussion of Giraut's plans for Christmas. How seriously can this poem be taken? Giraut is ambivalent about the taste of the public whose approval he claims to be seeking, calling the style it prefers *levet e venansal*, 'facile and common' (LIX, 13). Is he really defending the *leu* style, or is he mocking an audience that is unwilling to make an effort to understand the complexities of his work? Is Raimbaut offering a serious defence of the *trobar clus*, or is he making a joke of stylistic labels?

Many of Giraut's most limpid poems are viewed by his latest editor as parodies, indicating that he in fact had scant respect for the style he purports to defend in 'Era·m platz'. Similarly, although Raimbaut did compose one serious *clus* poem, his other songs in which terminology associated with the *trobar clus* occurs are burlesque, the best example being the

[12] Kay, 'Rhetoric', pp. 125–59; Gaunt, *Troubadours*, pp. 167–8.

outrageously comic 'Lonc temps' (XVIII), in which the 'covered' theme he hesitates to reveal is his own castration. Both Giraut and Raimbaut chide their public for not making an effort to understand and appreciate a song, mocking its taste for simple poetry, and both claim to yield reluctantly to public pressure for *leu* or *plan* ('plain') poetry. In a poem that is allusive, if not obscure, Giraut ironically claims to use words that are 'entendables e plas', 'understandable and smooth' (XLVI, 12) and, as if deliberately to disorientate his audience, Raimbaut often mixes *clus* and *leu* terminology in a haphazard manner, as for instance in 'Una chansoneta fera' (III), which he opens by stating his intention to write limpidly only to change his mind before he is half way through the first stanza in order to 'conceal meaning'. It is as if Raimbaut and Giraut, the two poets at the centre of the *clus/leu* controversy, were in league against those of their listeners who sought to classify their work using these categories.

Significantly, terms evoking the *clus/leu* dichotomy frequently occur when troubadours allude to audience reception and response; witness Giraut XXXIII, 1–7, and Raimbaut XVI, 1–8. Many of the terms used by critics to classify troubadour style do not in fact serve this function in the troubadours' own lyrics; their use is rather a product of the troubadours' uneasy response to the reception of their work amongst audiences whose judgement they were disinclined to respect, and who were attempting to impose their taste for 'easy' poetry on the literary world as a whole. Giraut de Borneil, often held to be the 'inventor' of the *trobar leu*, is frequently as disparaging about the 'easy' style and its audience as Raimbaut d'Aurenga, his adversary in the *tenso* (for example XXIX, 8–19). Despite their ostensible opposition to each other in 'Era·m platz', the two poets in fact share similar views on poetry: they are united in the view that all poetry should be demanding, requiring an attentive and discerning audience.

The division of audiences into the discerning and the undiscerning is common from the early years of the tradition:

> E tenhatz lo per vilan, qui no l'enten,
> qu'ins en son cor voluntiers [res] non l'apren.
>
> (Guilhem IX, I, 4–5)

[And consider the man who does not understand the poem, and willingly learn it in his heart, to be a rustic.]

Guilhem's poem turns out to be bawdy, but the import of these lines is nonetheless clear: poetic language lends itself naturally to the production of different levels of meaning. Thus Marcabru declares that language resists his attempts to produce clear thoughts and meanings (XXXVI, 1–6). In a similar vein, Giraut de Borneil suggests that making poetry simple (*esclarzir*, 'to make clear'), is much harder than making it difficult (*escurzir*, 'to make dark'), the implication being that language is not a medium that lends itself to simplicity or clarity (XLVIII, 1–10). On the contrary, language is by its very nature allusive and ambiguous. Other troubadours echo this sentiment and it is thus hardly surprising that they wanted audiences to be attentive and discerning.

A sophisticated critical tradition emerges from twelfth-century troubadour poetry, indicating a lively interest in literary theory. Yet most poets do not participate in critical debates in their texts. Bernart de Ventadorn, for instance, perhaps one of the finest poets of the Middle Ages, does not touch upon stylistic issues. Instead, he claims that the quality of his poetry is intrinsically bound to the quality of his love, presenting himself to his audience as the perfect lover, and consequently, as the perfect poet (XXXI, 1–4).[13] The first requirement of the rhetoric of sincerity is to appear to have no rhetoric. Feigning to compose ingenuously, without technical or rhetorical skill, thus becomes a rhetorical device in its own right, and in the *canso* poetry and love become reciprocal metaphors. But if a poet like Bernart de Ventadorn offers no explicit discussion of his *eloquentia*, we have a more precious testimony to his literary skill: his songs.

2. Grammarians and biographers

The theorists to be considered in this section differ greatly in the scale and scope of their work, in the extent of their knowledge of troubadour poetry and in the public for which they wrote. The single feature common to all is their awareness of the terminology of Latin grammar and rhetoric: even the least systematic of these writers were deeply indebted to the models offered by the learned tongue, which provided them with a ready-made framework and vocabulary in which to express their reflections on vernacular poetry.

The earliest theoretical work, the *Razos de trobar* of the Catalan Raimon Vidal, dates probably from the last decade of the twelfth century. Nothing is known of the public for which the work was intended: certain emphases in the grammatical material strongly suggest that Vidal was aware of particular linguistic difficulties encountered by those whose native speech was Catalan, not the Occitan of the troubadours. The success of his work in Catalan and Italian circles is attested by the provenance

---

[13] On the theatrical presentation of the subject in the troubadour lyric, so important to an appreciation of its aesthetic, see Sutherland, 'L'élément théâtral'; Kay, *Subjectivity*, pp. 132–70.

of the surviving manuscripts, as well as by a number of later adaptations. Between 1282 and 1296 Terramagnino da Pisa, writing perhaps for some literary circle in Sardinia, modernised Vidal's work by turning it into verse (under the title *Doctrina d'Acort*) and furnishing it with new illustrative examples. And in the last decade of the century the Catalan cleric and diplomat Jofre de Foixà extended and corrected it in his *Regles de trobar*, explicitly attempting in the process to make grammar accessible to those ignorant of Latin terminology. Jofre may well also have been responsible for the survey of the poetic genres (*Doctrina de compondre dictats*) which treats an area untouched in the other works mentioned. The same field is much less adequately covered in the first of two short anonymous Catalan treatises (the second surveys types of rhyme in an equally sketchy manner).

Though Vidal and his successors all dealt with aspects of linguistic correctness none of them provided a full grammar of Occitan. The earliest work to do so was the *Donatz Proensals* of Uc Faidit, written *c.* 1240 at the request of two Italian noblemen who, presumably, were desirous of understanding and perhaps (like many of their compatriots) imitating troubadour verse. Adopting the framework and terminology of the *Ars minor* of Donatus, Faidit expounded the morphology of Occitan, paying particular attention to the inflection of nouns and verbs. To this he added a list of verbs, classified by infinitive-type, and an extensive dictionary of rhymes. The whole work was accompanied by an interlinear Latin translation, perhaps added by Faidit himself. Thus the *Donatz* can be said to cover phonology (in the classification of rhymes) and lexis (in the verb-lists and the rhyming dictionary) as well as morphology. For all its shortcomings, both practical and theoretical, it was a remarkable achievement, all the more so since Faidit can hardly have had any vernacular model.

By the last decades of the thirteenth century the tradition of troubadour poetry was all but extinct. The setting-up of the *Consistori del Gai Saber* at Toulouse in 1323 by seven citizens who were its first *mantenedors* ('upholders') was an attempt to revive that tradition by regular poetic competitions. Such enterprises require rules, and the various versions of the *Leys d'Amors* (the earliest completed between 1337 and 1341) attempt to codify language and poetics and to place the composition of poetry within the framework of traditional rhetoric and grammar.[14] Of necessity, the *Leys* is in some measure backward-looking, since it was endeavouring to revive a tradition already dead. Thus, like the thirteenth-century

---

[14] For the chronology of the versions, see Jeanroy, 'Les *Leys*', pp. 144–61. Version A (between 1337 and 1341) was edited by Gatien-Arnoult, *Monumens*; version B (between 1337 and 1343) by Anglade, *Las Flors*; version C (1355–6) by Anglade, *Las Leys*. References are given here solely to version A, which is the clearest and fullest.

theorists, the authors of the *Leys* insist on the two-case system in treating the morphology of nouns and adjectives, although this could hardly have been a living feature of the contemporary spoken tongue (if indeed it was ever a consistent feature of the language of troubadour poetry). And their extensive description of the poetic genres is a retrospective survey of troubadour practice insofar as they were acquainted with it. Yet they hardly ever quote from troubadours of the 'classical' period, and their detailed treatment of versification is largely prescriptive, their notions of what is correct or permissible being often less liberal than the usage of good twelfth-century troubadours.

The considerable influence of the *Leys* is shown by a number of texts directly reflecting the doctrines of the *Consistori*. The *Doctrinal de trobar* of Raimon de Cornet (1324) is a verse epitome of some of those doctrines, to which Joan de Castellnou, one of the *mantenedors* of the *Consistori*, added in 1341 a prose *Glosari* to correct and amplify the earlier work. The same Joan was responsible for the mid-fourteenth-century *Compendi*, a handbook on rhetoric and versification taking the *Leys* as the sole source of orthodox doctrine. Only the undated *Mirall de trobar* of the Catalan Berenguer de Noya, which uses troubadour quotations as examples in an epitome of traditional rhetoric, seems independent of the *Leys*, which it may antedate.

The Provençal tradition revivified by the Toulouse *Consistori* was vigorously prolonged in Catalonia: this is attested by the foundation of a similar *Consistori* in Barcelona (1393) and by the works of its two founders: an extensive *Diccionari de Rims* by Jaume March (1371) and the encyclopaedic *Torcimany* of Luis de Averçó (*c.* 1370–1400). It may well be to this cultural phenomenon that we owe the preservation of a number of the earlier theoretical works on language and rhetoric, nine of which, stretching chronologically over almost two centuries, are brought together in a late-fourteenth-century manuscript possibly compiled for the Barcelona *Consistori* (Barcelona, Bibl. de Catalunya, MS 239).

Of all the theorists listed above, Raimon Vidal was closest in time and perhaps also in spirit to the great flourishing of troubadour lyric poetry in the late twelfth century. He was more willing than his successors to set the details of grammar within a wider cultural context. A central issue in his presentation of language is the notion of correctness in a tongue used for literary purposes.

Every man wishing to write verse or appreciate it must first understand that no tongue in our vernacular is perfect or correct except that of France and that of Limousin and Provence and Auvergne and Quercy. That is why I say that when I shall refer to *lemosi* you are to understand all those provinces and all the neighbouring ones and all those lying between them. And all men born and bred in those lands have the perfect and correct tongue.[15]

Within the Gallo-Romance area, then, French and Occitan were 'correct'. Gascon and Catalan (by implication) were not. The reason becomes clear in Vidal's famous distinction between the literary aptitudes of French and Occitan:

> The French tongue is more esteemed and agreeable in the composition of romances and *pastourelles*, whereas that of *lemosi* is more esteemed for making *vers* and *cansos* and *sirventes* [i.e. the pre-eminent forms of troubadour lyric poetry]; and throughout the lands of our vernacular the songs of the *lemosi* tongue are of greater authority than those of any other idiom.[16]

A distant foreshadowing of Dante's *vulgare illustre* is perceptible here, in that it is the existence of an esteemed literary tradition which confers on certain forms of the vernacular an 'authority' analogous to that conferred on Latin by the classical *auctores*. But, if French and Occitan are both regarded by Vidal as established literary languages, their forms, as some of his examples underline, are not to be mingled: thus the language of the troubadours is not only 'correct' but autonomous. Its correctness resides in an adherence to a two-case system in the inflection of nouns and adjectives (which Vidal illustrates at length) and in clear-cut distinctions between various pairs of alternative forms, notably within the conjugation of the verb. In illustration of the last point Vidal quotes and condemns a number of 'erroneous' forms used at the rhyme by good twelfth-century poets. The grammarian, therefore, was more doctrinaire than the literary tradition itself: he suffered from the delusion (common amongst grammarians) that where two alternatives exist one must of necessity be incorrect or, at best, less correct. Such judgements can hardly have stemmed from anything more reliable than Vidal's personal preferences. But at least he was aware of a characteristic feature of troubadour usage, namely the coexistence of alternative forms, the existence of which is authenticated by their use as rhyme-words, even though his condemnation of good poets

---

[15] 'Totz hom qe vol trobar ni entendre deu primierament saber qe neguna parladura non es naturals ni drecha del nostre lingage, mais acella de Franza et de Lemosi et de Proenza et d'Alvergna et de Caersin. Per qe ieu vos dic qe, qant ieu parlarai de "Lemosy", qe totas estas terras entendas et totas lor vezinas et totas cellas qe son entre ellas. Et tot l'ome qe en aqellas terras son nat ni norit an la parladura natural et drecha' (Raimon Vidal, *Razos*, p. 4).

[16] 'La parladura francesca val mais et [es] plus avinenz a far romanz et pasturellas, mas cella de Lemosin val mais per far vers et cansons et serventes. Et per totas las terras de nostre engage son de maior autoritat li cantar de la lenga lemosina qe de neguna autra parladura' (Raimon Vidal, *Razos*, p. 6).

for availing themselves of them rests on a theoretical basis which is at best shaky and in all events not borne out by troubadour practice.

Jofre de Foixà, almost a century later, intelligently took Vidal to task for these criticisms of certain troubadours. In an interesting passage of the *Regles de trobar* discussing the relative importance of usage (*us*) and strict grammar (*art*), he reports his predecessor's view and then, with an appeal to usage which foreshadows Vaugelas three and a half centuries later, demolishes it:

> I grant him that according to strict grammar he spoke the truth . . . but I do not grant that the troubadours were in error, because usage prevails over strict grammar and custom is held to be law for so long that it prevails through usage. And as it is the usage, in certain lands where the language is appropriate to composing poetry, that people as commonly (or more commonly) say *eu cre* as *eu crey* in the first person and as commonly *ausi* as *ausic* in the third person, I therefore maintain that the troubadours did not err in this matter, for they followed the usage and custom of the language. And since all the troubadours have spoken so in their compositions, this is usage and confirmation of the language; but if only one or two had so spoken, one might well say it was an error.[17]

By Jofre's time, of course, the tradition of troubadour poetry must have seemed complete and its linguistic usage unassailable, whereas in Vidal's time both were still evolving. Nevertheless, it was intelligent of Jofre, who in many other passages draws extensively on Vidal, to see that on this point his predecessor had left himself open to criticism. He perceived, then, that literary usage was not absolute and immutable but relative and fluctuating and that its relationship to the spoken vernacular was more protean than Vidal had allowed.

The compilers of the *Leys d'Amors* often refer to 'established usage' (*lonc uzatge*) and to the practice of the 'ancient troubadours (*li antic trobador*) when offering decisions on matters of morphological correctness: they, like their predecessors, found difficulty when faced with the multiplicity of alternative forms offered by the language. They were not entirely consistent in the ways in which they invoke practice as authority and also on occasion invoke conformity with Latin as a further criterion.

---

[17] 'E eu altrey li que segons art el dix ver . . . mas no li altrey que li trobador errason, per ço car us venç art, e longa costuma per dret es haüda tant que venç per us. E con sia us en algunes terres on le lengatges es covinentz e autreyatz a trobar que tuyt cominalment diguen aytant o plus en la primera persona *eu cre* com *eu crey*, e en la terça persona diguen aytant *ausi* com *ausic*, per aquesta raho dic eu que li trobador no y falliron, car ill seguiren lo us del lengatge e la costuma. E pus tuyt li trobador ho han ditz en llurs trobars, es us e confermamentz de lengatge; mas si us o dos ho haguessen ditz, assatz pogra dir que fos enrada' (Jofre de Foixà, *Regles*, in Raimon Vidal, *Razos*, p. 84). Vidal had specifically condemned the first-person singular present indicative form *cre* and the third-person singular preterite form *ausi*.

No doubt the members of the *Consistori* had debated individual points of grammar: the echo of such *ad hoc* discussions (not unlike those of the French Academy in later centuries) is often perceptible in the *Leys*. One passage is particularly revealing. After indicating their preferences among the forms of *dimenge* ('Sunday') and between the forms *menhs* and *mens* ('less'), they continue:

... and so with many others, which a man may have by usage. And when it is doubtful whether they can be said in one fashion or in two, a man should then have recourse to the songs of the ancients. . . . And if by this means a man cannot arrive at certainty, he should have recourse to the manner of speech found commonly throughout one diocese, that is one bishopric. And this is the most difficult matter in writing verse in the vernacular, more difficult than any other matter we can find, for a word that I understand you will not understand; and this is through the diversity of one and the same language.[18]

The grammarians' difficulty is honestly faced, though not resolved: the reader is not informed whether these linguistic criteria form a hierarchy or what he should do when they conflict. But the mention of the 'common usage of one diocese' shows intelligent awareness of a criterion of a type which probably did operate in troubadour practice. The latter had not been based on the dialect of any one province, but on a dialect mixture avoiding narrowly parochial features. This must have made practical sense in songs widely diffused by travelling performers. Its theoretical basis seems to have been intermittently envisaged in the *Leys*.

All theorists who discuss the matter agree on the central notion of phonetically exact rhyme: rhymes involved the exact correspondence of the tonic vowel and all that followed it. In this they were true to the practice of the troubadours, who were seldom content with imperfect rhyme or mere assonance. Here again, however, the relation between rhyming and correct language is less straightforward than it seems. In the *Donatz* and the *Leys* the Occitan reflexes of Latin -L- and -LL- are different, so that *tal* (< *talem*) and *caval* (< *caballum*) do not constitute an exact rhyme. In the lyrics of most troubadours such words rhyme freely together (Uc Faidit, *Donatz*, pp. 299–300; *Leys*, I, p. 36; and see [under *Leys*] *Las Flors*, ed. Anglade II, p. 44). But a few poets, notably Peire Vidal (who, like the authors of the *Leys*, came from Toulouse), do observe the distinction made by the grammarians. Thus the phonetic usage of a part of

---

[18] '. . . et en ayssi de trops autres, los quals hom pot haver per uzatge de parlar. E cant es doptes si·s podon dir en una maniera o en doas, adonx deu hom recorre als dictatz dels anticz . . . E si per aquela maniera no s'en pot hom enformar, hom deu recorre a la maniera de parlar acostumat cominalmen per tota una diocezi, so es per un avesquat. Et aysso es la cauza mays greus cant a dictar en romans que deguna autra que puscam trobar, quar un mot qu'ieu entendre tu no entendras, et aysso es per la diversitat d'u meteysh lengatge' (*Leys*, II, p. 210).

Languedoc might be reflected in the rhymes of poets born in that area but was not a constraint on the rhyming of poets born elsewhere.

Rhyming constituted the armature on which the lyric stanza was constructed and, through the echoing of the same pattern in succeeding stanzas, provided the formal unity of the whole song. In their exposition of these matters, the authors of the *Leys* were evidently the true inheritors of over two centuries of poetic tradition. They were, however, inclined towards hyper-correctness, as is suggested by their treatment of *mot tornat* or repeated rhyme (*Leys*, III, pp. 94–102). The use of the same word twice in a rhyme-series within the body of a song (the *Leys* expressly excludes the *tornadas* or *envois*) is more common in troubadour poetry than many editors, following the Toulouse theorists, have supposed: in this matter it is unwise to trust the word of the grammarians (or the practice of certain copyists, their approximate contemporaries), for many good twelfth-century poets clearly did allow themselves some licence in this matter.

The *Leys* offers an extremely long classification of the types of *cobla* or stanza, most of which depend on the way in which the rhymes are arranged (*Leys*, I, pp. 208–338). This reliance on rhyme-schemes to the exclusion of other metrical factors, in particular the syllabic count of the lines and the disposition of masculine and feminine endings, must be accounted a weakness, though it is one widely echoed amongst nineteenth- and twentieth-century scholars. The authors of the *Leys* attempted a classification on the basis of recognisable external factors, of which the rhyme-scheme is the most obvious. But it can be argued that the aurally perceived metrical shape in troubadour poetry was in the first instance numerical (syllable-count, gender of rhymes) rather than literal (rhyme-scheme).[19] One fundamental element is missing from all the lucubrations of the Toulouse theorists, namely the fact that the cunning symmetries and asymmetries of troubadour stanzas existed because each verse-form fitted a tune offering specific freedoms and imposing specific constraints.[20] If this was no longer evident in fourteenth-century Toulouse (the *Leys* never mentions the matter), modern scholars ought not to be imprisoned within the same limited perspective.

The authors of the *Leys* offer more reliable guidance when they expound the ways in which rhyming was used to create the unity of the whole song. In defining *coblas singulars*, where the rhyme-endings changed from stanza to stanza within a constant rhyme-scheme, *coblas doblas*, in which the endings were renewed after each pair of stanzas, and *coblas unissonans*, where the same endings were maintained throughout

---

[19] Marshall, '*Contrafacta*', pp. 290–1.
[20] On the relation between verse-form and music, see Switten, 'Music and Versification'.

the whole song, the *Leys* launched a clear metrical terminology for which scholars are still grateful.[21] These terms are still commonly used as convenient and unambiguous labels, as are those which identify various means employed by the troubadours for linking the stanzas of a song to form a unified metrical construct, for example *coblas capcaudadas*, in which the last rhyme-ending of each stanza is echoed in the first rhyme-ending of the following one, and *coblas capfinidas*, where the final word of each stanza reappears, sometimes in a different grammatical form, within the opening line of the next stanza.[22] It is not difficult to see why the mania for classification so evident in the *Leys* should in this instance have yielded a permanently valuable terminology: a taxonomy based on the surface structure of poetic texts was here perfectly adequate. That such theorising was indeed so based is clear from the way in which the *Leys* treats the widespread phenomenon of contrafacture, i.e. the borrowing, in poetic genres lying outside the courtly love-song, of the tune, the metrical form and (commonly) the rhyme-endings of a pre-existent courtly song on which the new text was constructed.[23] For each poetic genre, the authors of the *Leys*, like other theorists, are content either to prescribe a new tune or to permit the use of a pre-existent one, noting that in this latter case the imitation of the metrical form of the model may optionally include reproduction of its rhyme-endings.

In attempting an extensive series of definitions of the form and content of the poetic genres practised in troubadour poetry, the *Leys* was on relatively firm ground (*Leys*, I, pp. 338–50). While its definitions (reproduced in the treatises dependent on it) seem independent of those offered by the *Doctrina de compondre dictats* and the anonymous Catalan treatise on the subject (preserved in Ripoll MS 129), they all present a broadly similar type of material: all were perhaps aiming at a vernacular equivalent of a feature found in some medieval Latin treatises (e.g. the section *De differencia* in the *Poetria parisiana* of John of Garland). It is only for the principal poetic types that we find definitions in all three sources. Thus the *canso* – the 'song' *par excellence* being the love-song – celebrated love for and praise of a lady expressed in verse set to an original tune. Though they differ somewhat over the number of stanzas required in such a song, the theorists agree with one another and with classical troubadour practice in defining the characteristics of what had become, from the 1180s at the latest, the pre-eminent Occitan lyric type. The proper use of the terms *vers* and *canso*, which had been a subject of controversy for certain troubadours around 1200, offers no difficulty for the theorists, for

---

[21] *Leys*, I, pp. 212–36 (*coblas singulars*), 264–6 (*coblas doblas*), 270–2 (*coblas unissonans*).
[22] *Leys*, I, pp. 236–8 (*coblas capcaudadas*), 280–2 (*coblas capfinidas*).
[23] Chambers, 'Imitation'; Marshall, 'Imitation', and '*Contrafacta*'; Gennrich, *Kontrafaktur*.

whom the term *vers* referred, as it did in thirteenth-century practice, to a song of moralising or didactic content. Evidently, it was the practice and terminology of the later period, not the much more fluid usage of the earlier generations of troubadours, which is reflected in the views of the theorists. Indeed, it can plausibly be argued that the desire to constitute a terminology of poetic genres is hardly evinced by practising poets much before 1200 and stems directly from the aesthetic dominance acquired by the courtly *canso*.

The evolution of the *sirventes* by a sort of polarity with the *canso* is evident in the theorists' definitions. According to the *Leys*,

it must deal with reproof [of individuals] or with general satires to chastise the foolish and the wicked, or it may deal, if you will, with the circumstances of some war.[24]

The longer definition given by the *Doctrina de compondre dictats* says much the same thing and may reflect some knowledge of the work of Bertran de Born (*c.* 1159–1215), whose example had a decisive influence on the development of the genre. Where the *canso* praises, the *sirventes* reproves and satirises. One sings of love, the other of war. One belongs to the realm of ideals, the other to the real world. And yet, as no theorist deemed it necessary to point out, the courtly and moral and social values expressed in both are fundamentally of the same kind. Though superficially contrasted, the two genres are at a deeper level united. And this paradox is reflected in the second element of the theorists' definitions: the *sirventes* commonly takes over the tune of an existing love-song, from which it borrows its metrical form, including often some or all of its rhyme-endings. This procedure, amply attested in the troubadours' practice from the time of Bertran de Born (who may have originated it), had evident practical advantages but also corresponded with the true nature and function of the *sirventes* in the courtly world: it defended polemically what the *canso* celebrated. But for the theorists the borrowing of tune and versification was no more than an optional technical procedure.

The *dansa*, a verse-form akin to the Old French *balete*, was practised mainly in the thirteenth and fourteenth centuries and seems to have been well known in Catalonia. It is not surprising, therefore, that all theorists who attempt to define the poetic genres give extended and circumstantial descriptions of its characteristic form. The second part of each of its three stanzas corresponded metrically with the *respos* (literally 'response'), which was placed before the first stanza and often repeated

---

[24] 'Deu tractar de reprehensio o de maldig general, per castiar los fols e los malvatz, o pot tractar, qui·s vol, del fag d'alquna guerra' (*Leys*, I, p. 340).

textually as a refrain after each stanza. The first part of each stanza used rhymes different from those of the second part and the *respos*. Schematically, if the *respos* is called A each stanza is *bba* or, with the refrain-like repetition, *bbaA*. This basic *virelai*-form depended on a musical structure which mirrored the metrical structure and was its *raison d'être*. This is revealed only by study of the surviving examples, for, astonishingly enough, the theorists do not refer to the matter. Their painstaking expositions of the metrical intricacies of the *dansa* are accompanied by no indication of how music and metre fitted together. Their technical limitations are evident here.

The failure to expound, even in broad outline, the nature of metrical structures in poetic genres whose construction was primarily musical is not limited to the *dansa*, for the theorists' definitions of the *estampida* and the *descort* are defective in the same way. Indeed, the protracted definition of the latter in the *Leys* is vitiated by the fact that it is largely based on a single example, the famous plurilingual *descort* of Raimbaut de Vaqueiras (*fl. c.* 1180–*c.* 1205), which is atypical of the genre. Exceptional cases make bad law. For some at least of the poetic types, the theorists' sources of information would seem to have been more restricted than our own.

For poetic genres of which few examples are extant, the theorists are a valuable source of information. Though the compilers of the *Leys* offer only a dismissive observation on what are there called *viandelas* (*Leys*, I, p. 350), finding them of uncertain authorship and unregulated verse-form ('cert actor ni cert compas no y trobam'), the anonymous Catalan treatise on poetic genres attempts a detailed description of the *viadera*, which it calls 'the lowest type of song' ('la pus jusana species qui es en los cantas'), and even cites the first two lines of an otherwise unknown specimen. This definition, together with the single complete *viadera* now extant – by Cerveri de Girona (*fl. c.* 1259–*c.* 1285) and therefore also of Catalan provenance – enables us to gain some insight into the nature of a poetic type which, being no doubt a popular and not a learned verse-form, had little chance of attracting the attention of either the theorists or the compilers of *chansonniers* (see Poem 99, ed. Coromines, I, pp. 219–22). Again, it is to Catalan theorists that we owe such knowledge as we have of the *gaita* (literally 'watchman'), a genre which, to judge from the brief definition offered by the *Doctrina de compondre dictats*, would seem to have been a sub-species of the *alba*. The only surviving text of this type is found in the *Mirall de trobar* of Berenguer de Noya, where the author quotes the first stanza of 'a *gaita* composed by whoever you please' ('una guayta que feu qual que us placia'). Such material constitutes a valuable testimony to the continued existence, on the margins of the major genres of courtly poetry, of more popular types of anonymous song which, when they survive at all, do so by pure chance.

The discussion of poetic genres in the *Leys* and its successors is intended to be prescriptive, whereas the surveys offered by the other two sources is probably descriptive in intention. The desire shown in all these texts to elaborate a static genre-system is a characteristic feature of the long decline of the troubadour tradition. A similar tendency is perceptible in the rubrics attached to the songs of some troubadours of the second half of the thirteenth century, notably Guiraut Riquier (*fl. c.* 1254–92) and Cerveri de Girona. The provision of such labels indicates that a once fluid and evolving system of poetic types had become ossified. It is striking that much of the terminology used in the rubrics refers to characteristics of content rather than form. The theorists too place much emphasis on content, which they are able to define with reasonable accuracy; when faced with the need to define metrical and musical structures they are often at a loss.

The compilers of theoretical handbooks were not the only later prose-writers to examine aspects of troubadour poetry and its practitioners. In the course of the thirteenth century, the works of individual troubadours were brought together in wide-ranging anthologies, which constitute the sources whereby the songs were preserved and transmitted in written form. In some of these *chansonniers*, the works of a troubadour are preceded by a *vida* or 'life' of the author. In addition, several of them include *razos* or 'explanations' for a certain number of individual songs. For the most part, the *vidas* and *razos* are anonymous. From geographical references in the texts it is clear that many were composed in Italy, where a good proportion of the *chansonniers* were compiled. All are written in Occitan, some probably by writers who were not native speakers of the language, many others no doubt by Occitan-speaking exiles residing – like a number of thirteenth-century troubadours – in Italy. Whether *vidas* and *razos* had an independent existence outside the written sources which have preserved them can hardly be decided on the basis of the evidence that survives. It seems likely that performances of the songs of twelfth-century troubadours given fifty or a hundred years after the poet's death required some prefatory explanation of the circumstances of composition or at the least some brief presentation of the poet whose song was about to be performed. Some of the extant *vidas* and *razos* may derive from an oral tradition of this kind.[25]

Though many *vidas* and *razos* have the humble practical aim of satisfying curiosity about poets of the recent past, their authors were no doubt conscious of having a learned model in the *vitae auctorum* which formed part of the *accessus ad auctores*.[26] The structure of a number of

[25] On the *vidas* and *razos*, see particularly Burgwinkle, *Love for Sale*.
[26] See Egan, 'Commentary'; Meneghetti, *Il pubblico*, pp. 277–321. On the *accessus* tradition see Chapters 5, 6 and 14 above.

the more elaborate *vidas* and *razos* shows striking similarities with certain *accessus* texts, especially those relating to the works of Ovid. Specifically, the techniques of extrapolating significant elements of a poet's life from his works and of quoting short passages from these as evidence are so closely paralleled in the Latin texts as to suggest conscious imitation on the part of the vernacular writers.

Although *vidas* differ considerably in scale and scope, they show a number of common features: all indicate the poet's social and geographical origins, all but the briefest detail some of the circumstances of his life, especially his real or imagined love-life, and many offer some succinct characterisation of his work. This may involve no more than 'he composed well', 'he sang well', 'he was known for his courtliness', and the like; but a few *vidas* are more specific. When the *vida* of Marcabru states that 'at that time people did not use the term *canso*, but everything that was sung was called *vers*', or when that of Peire d'Alvernhe asserts, 'He made no *canso*, for no song was called *canso* at that time, but only *vers*; it was Sir Giraut de Borneil who made the first *canso* that was ever made',[27] the writers show some awareness of the evolution of the poetic tradition. When they note that Cercamon 'wrote *vers* and little *pastorelas* in the ancient manner' or that Peire de Valeira 'was a jongleur in Marcabru's time, and he made *vers* of the sort people made in those days, of poor quality, all about leaves and blossom and bird-songs: his songs had little value, nor did he',[28] they reveal a sovereign contempt for songs which, by the thirteenth century, must have appeared painfully old-fashioned. When the author of the *vida* of Rigaut de Berbezilh (probably of the late twelfth century) notes that he 'took great delight in using in his songs similes involving beasts and birds and men and the sun and the stars, to find fresher themes which others had not used',[29] he singled out for comment one strikingly individual feature of that poet's songs. At such moments the *vida*-writers offer us a suggestive thirteenth-century critical perspective on the work of poets of the preceding generations.

The aim of those responsible for the *razos* was of a somewhat different kind. A *razo* sought to explain the circumstances in which an individual

[27] 'Et en aqel temps non appellava hom cansson, mas tot qant hom cantava eron vers' (*Biographies*, p. 12). 'Canson no fetz qe non era adoncs negus cantars appellatz cansos, mas vers: qu'En Girautz de Borneill fetz la premeira cansos que anc fos faita' (*Biographies*, p. 124).

[28] 'Trobet vers e pastoretas a la usanza antiga' (*Biographies*, p. 9); 'Joglars fo el temps et en la sason que fo Marcabrus; e fez vers tals com hom fazia adoncs, de paubra valor, de foillas e de flors, e de cans d'ausels. Sei cantar non aguen gran valor, ni el' (*Biographies*, p. 14). The strictures on Peire de Valeira are based on the first stanza of a song by Arnaut de Tintignac, misattributed to Peire by the two manuscripts which contain the *vida*.

[29] 'El si se deletava molt en dire en sas chanssos similitudines de bestias e d'ausels e d'omes, e del sol e de las estellas per dire plus novellas razos qu'autre non agues ditas' (*Biographies*, p. 150).

song (or occasionally two or more pieces thought to be related) had been composed: the poetic text is thus provided with a setting within the (real or imagined) events of the poet's life. The technique of embedding a song within an expository prose context may have suggested the structure adopted by Dante in the *Vita Nova* (or indeed by Old French writers such as Jean Renart who interpolate lyrics into romance narratives), though the *razo*-writers never offer the kind of textual commentary provided by Dante. Indeed, their interest lies almost exclusively in the forging of links between life and works: they explain in circumstantial detail how the *sirventes* of Bertran de Born fitted into the vicissitudes of his existence as an embattled nobleman or how the *cansos* of a Folquet de Marselha (*c.* 1178–1231) or a Gaucelm Faidit (*fl. c.* 1172–*c.* 1203) reflected the ups and downs of the poet's love-life. The troubadour who composed love-songs is thus constantly seen as an aspect of the man involved with his contemporaries (patrons, lady-loves, courtiers). The *razo* explaining the celebrated *estampida* of Raimbaut de Vaqueiras recounts how two visiting French jongleurs played on their viols an *estampida*-tune which pleased the whole court of the Marquis of Montferrat and how the troubadour composed his text to this instrumental tune ('Aqesta stampida fu facta a las notas de la stampida qe·l joglars fasion en las violas').[30] But this technical account of the genesis of the piece (which may or may not be true) forms part of an extended narrative concerning a breach between the troubadour and Beatrice of Montferrat, his beloved, engineered by the machinations of slanderers and brought to an end only when the depressed poet was prevailed upon to compose a new song, namely the *estampida* itself. For the *razo*-writers, every love-song tells a story.

The constant preoccupation of the authors of *vidas* and *razos* with the construction of links between a poet's life and his work answered a need which must have been widely felt by the thirteenth century. Many twelfth-century troubadour songs must, at the moment when they were first launched before a courtly audience, have derived much of their effect from the presence of the living poet, either literally as singer or by proxy in the person of a paid performer: listeners knew who and what the poet was. Such links between poet and public necessarily vanished with the passage of time. The function of *vidas* and *razos* was to reconstruct them for the benefit of a later age by assembling biographical information, some of it extrapolated from the texts of the songs themselves. It is for this reason that the biographers place the flesh-and-blood individual, rather than merely the maker of verses and tunes, in the forefront of their attention. To invent that mythical Countess of Tripoli with whom Jaufre Rudel fell

---

[30] For the *razo*, see *Biographies*, pp. 465–8; for the song, see Raimbaut de Vaqueiras, XV.

in love without ever seeing her, the author of the most famous of all *vidas* had only to read Rudel's celebrated song of 'distant love' (*amor de lonh*) and to take *vezer* ('to see') in the sense of 'see for the first time' instead of 'see again':[31] how can we castigate so creative a misreading, when most modern scholars, seeing Rudel's love as anything but fleshly, apparently concur in it?

Vernacular discourse on grammar and rhetoric in the Middle Ages could exist only by adapting the established Latin terminology. Even Jofre de Foixà, whose avowed aim was to expound vernacular grammar in a fashion comprehensible to those ignorant of *grammatica*, is no exception. And the treatment of Occitan grammar in the *Donatz* or the *Leys* relies heavily on the terms and concepts available in the learned tongue. The originality of the texts resides in the skill with which pre-existent categories were used as a receptacle for the linguistic substance of the vernacular, not in the invention of a fresh series of categories.[32] Similarly, the extensive survey of rhetorical tropes offered by the *Leys* brings together elements from the *Ars maior* of Donatus, the *Etymologiae* of St Isidore, the *Rhetorica ad Herennium* and other Latin sources.[33] Such a compilation of inherited erudition was original only in the sense that the Occitan exemplification of the various tropes demonstrated the ways in which the latter were as valid for the vernacular as for the learned tongue. The idea of rhetoric as a craft whose object was to produce a particular effect on a particular audience was evidently familiar to the troubadours and underlies much of their theorising and their practice. Nevertheless, a good proportion of the vocabulary in which matters of style and versification were discussed is of vernacular origin: at the most, one can point to parallels, rather than sources, in Latin terminology. This was no doubt because the practice of troubadour song had evolved in parallel with medieval uses of the learned tongue, rather than as a derivative of any one of them. The extent and the accuracy of the theorists' erudition were evidently variable, as were their knowledge of the vernacular poetic tradition and the intelligence behind their response to it. The utterances of any theorist on the matters which concern us here were subject to the limitations of human fallibility, as well as to those of time and place. But if the insights they offer us into the language and literature of the troubadours are partial in both senses of the word, they are nevertheless the insights of near-contemporaries of the world in which the poets themselves had functioned.

---

[31] For the *vida*, see *Biographies*, pp. 16–19; for the song, see Jaufré Rudel, *Canzoniere*, 4. On the relationship between Rudel's *vida* and his songs, see Monson, 'Jaufré Rudel'.

[32] See Law, 'Originality'.

[33] See Marshall, 'Observations'; Jeanroy, 'Les *Leys*', pp. 203–11.

17

Literary theory and polemic in Castile,
c. 1200–*c.* 1500

Julian Weiss

The first signs of a critical stance towards poetic composition in the Castilian vernacular are to be found in the clerkly metre of *cuaderna vía*, which accompanied the emergence in the early thirteenth century of a new class of university-trained clerics. Writers such as Gonzalo de Berceo and the anonymous poets of the *Libro de Alexandre* and *Libro de Apolonio* introduced their narratives with self-conscious statements about their 'clerical ministry' (*mester de clerecía*) and their role as intermediaries between the laity and the received wisdom of bookish authority. Theirs, they claimed, was a new poetic movement, superior to the work of *juglares* (minstrels), and characterised by its metrical polish and civilising goals. These prefatory remarks are undeveloped (and have been variously interpreted), but they are nonetheless significant. They are evidence for the fact that, for the period in question, what may loosely be called 'literary theorising' was undertaken fundamentally in order to establish a social relationship: it is, so to speak, literary theory 'in action'. This is to say that those who wrote for a lay public were less concerned with philosophising about an abstract category later to be called 'literature', than with defending their status as writers, and confronting the problems that attended the composition and interpretation of their own work. Thus, although theoretical treatises were written during this period, theory and criticism find expression principally through the medium of the literary text itself, prologues and, later, commentaries on specific works in the Castilian vernacular tradition.[1]

From its inception at the start of the thirteenth century, the Castilian court lyric (written until *c.* 1370 in Galician-Portuguese) was conceived as a social act. As in the older Occitan tradition, the association

---

[1] For reasons of space what follows does not encompass the totality of literary thought in the Iberian peninsula of the Middle Ages. Hispano-Arabic and Hebrew poetics have been excluded, but for examples of metrical treatises (in Spanish translation) see Moses Ibn 'Ezra, *Kitab al-muhadara wal-mudakara*, and Valle Rodríguez, *El diván poético de Dunash del Labrat*; for an overview of grammatical theory, see Sáenz-Badillos, *Gramáticos hebreos de Al-Andalús*, and for a major study and ample bibliography of the literary thought of practising Hebrew poets, see Brann, *The Compunctious Poet*. The present focus on Christian Castile also means that the literary thought in the Occitan-Catalan tradition is dealt with elsewhere in this volume; see Chapter 16 above.

of aristocratic poets and minstrels in the competitive and self-assertive atmosphere of the courts generated debates over certain aspects of the composition and nature of poetry. The two main centres of debate were the courts of Alfonso X of Castile (reigned 1252–84), and his grandson Dinis I of Portugal (reigned 1279–1325), and the favoured medium were the *tenções* (debate poems) and *cantigas d'escarnho e maldizer* (poems of often highly scurrilous personal invective). To a great extent, literary polemic was part of a larger struggle over social status.

Although the poets do not articulate in systematic form their underlying theoretical assumptions, the corpus as a whole reveals certain recurring patterns of concern. The most prominent are polemics over what it meant to be an authentic troubadour, and their paradigm is in the attacks on the *jogral* ('minstrel') Lourenço. In poems that parallel the Occitan *sirventes joglaresc* ('satire on minstrels'), Lourenço was chastised by members of the upper and lower nobility, primarily for his social climbing, inadequate musicianship and plagiarism.[2] These were familiar accusations, and examples could be multiplied by reference to the invectives by such poets as Pero da Ponte and Afonso Eanes do Coton (no. 53, on the relative status of the *trobador* and *segrel*; on these classes of poet, see below); Martin Soares (no. 285, a satire on vulgar versifying and breaking the code of poetic and social exclusivity); and Afonso Eanes do Coton's sneer at Suero Eanes's inability to 'count his metre' ('cantar igual'; no. 43). Equally widespread and complementary criticisms concern the poet's *saber* ('knowledge') and morality. References to poetic *saber* often seem deliberately allusive, functioning simply as a strategy for undermining an opponent's claim to poetic prestige. But according to Alfonso X, in the preface to his *Cantigas de Santa Maria* (poems in praise of the Virgin Mary), poetry is based on the faculty of understanding (*entendimento*), which empowers the judicious and rational expression of one's will. In other cases, this knowledge is explicitly said to entail both technical control and the tenets of courtliness (e.g. nos. 364 by Pero da Ponte and 398 by Pero Mafaldo). Courtliness, which comprised both wisdom and morality, helps to account for the invectives that appear to link poetic and sexual 'corruption' (nos. 132–3 and 377, on the incompetence of allegedly homosexual minstrels).

These debates inspired the intervention of the Occitan poet Guiraut Riquier, who was at the court of Alfonso X during the years 1271 and 1280. Motivated in part by the economic self-interest of a poet who lived from his verse, his *Supplicatio* to King Alfonso, and the latter's reply, the *Declaratio* (written, however, by Riquier between 1274 and

---

[2] See *Cantigas d'escarnho e de mal dizer*, ed. Rodrigues Lapa, poems 208–9, 216–17, 220, 238, 270–3, 318. All further references are also to poem-numbers in this edition.

1275), attempt to establish a rigid hierarchy of poets and court entertainers. Employing scholastic argumentation, etymological definitions and a structure based on the *ars dictaminis*, Guiraut sets forth a range of poetic categories that, he claims, is far superior to the narrow dichotomy between *joglars* and *trobadors* existing in Languedoc, where social distinctions are consequently blurred (*Declaratio*, ll. 188–99). On the lowest rung are the vulgar entertainers called *cazuros* (l. 183), followed by the *remendadors* (l. 171), who imitate instrumentalists and performers of other poets' compositions, the *joglars*. Unlike these itinerant groups, the *trobadors* are closely tied to a particular court, where they dedicate themselves exclusively to composing original lyrics and music (Guiraut relates the term to *inventores*, l. 136). Their craft is divine; they are endowed with a natural talent and polished technique, and they purvey moral and spiritual instruction to the court (ll. 246–83). Because of their power to supply doctrine (*doctrinar*), the finest *trobadors* qualify for the rank of *doctors de trobar* and become especially valued court advisers. Guiraut also makes an enigmatic reference to the *segriers* (l. 173; *segrel* in Galician-Portuguese). This category may be a combination of *trobador* and *jogral*, that is to say a peripatetic poet from the minor nobility. But, influenced by the Latin *saecularis*, Guiraut may have been attempting to revive an earlier meaning, that of a poet who wrote in an exclusively secular mode.

The poets writing in Occitan at Alfonso X's court added an extra dimension to poetic debate. In an otherwise conventional satire of the troubadour Pero da Ponte (*c.* 1255), Alfonso embellished his accusation of moral turpitude with the claim that Pero did not compose like 'a Provençal', but rather like the *jogral* Bernal de Bonaval (no. 17). Consequently, his verse was not 'natural' ('por en non é trobar natural'). *Trobar natural* is not defined (nor is it in Occitan where it also occurs), but in the context, it probably alludes to formal and moral perfection, a sign of the poet's 'natural', God-given nobility. Some argue that this poem is an attempt to contrast two competing schools, the native and the Occitan, and that Alfonso had a preference for the latter. Others believe the issue to be essentially moral, rather than nationalistic, or that the king's criticism cannot be taken seriously on an aesthetic level (given that Pero da Ponte was a noted practitioner of Occitan genres). Although it is not possible to define the precise terms and scope of the king's criticism (whether intended in earnest or in jest), it seems clear that Occitan verse was held up as an aesthetic and moral ideal.[3]

Alfonso's grandson Dinis I also compares the native and Occitan lyric in two *cantigas d'amor*. He declares in one that the Occitan poets write

---

[3] See d'Heur, *Troubadours d'Oc*, pp. 291–9; Beltrán, 'Los trovadores', pp. 498–503.

good verse, and this they attribute to love; but those who compose only in spring experience a love inferior to his. Thus, although Dinis emulates the older school, he opposes the truth of his own love to the latter's alleged conventionality. As a critical statement, this poem operates on two levels: first, it implies the desire to assert the autonomy of the Galician-Portuguese lyric, in which the spring topos was quite rare; and second, it expresses the belief that good love-poetry is the product of authentic experience, and not the mere manipulation of rhetorical topoi. In this respect, Dinis echoes a concern for poetic sincerity expressed by such poets as Afonso Sanchez (no. 66) and Pero d'Ambroa (nos. 337 and 339). In other quarters, poetic sincerity was subjected to playful scepticism, the best-known examples being the satires written at the expense of Ruy Queimado, who was mocked for overusing the motif of 'dying of love' in order to appear an authentic troubadour (e.g. no. 380 by Pero Garcia Burgalês).

Some of the above issues are taken up in the fragmentary *Arte de trovar*, copied *c.* 1500 from an acephalous and mutilated fourteenth-century original by Angelo Colocci, the Italian humanist responsible for the preservation of most Galician-Portuguese verse. Positioned at the start of the *Cancioneiro da Biblioteca Nacional* (Colocci-Brancuti), the treatise originally comprised six sections, each of which is subdivided into an irregular number of short chapters. The extant fragment (only 200 lines have survived) begins a third of the way through section three, which is devoted to genre. To judge from authorial cross-references, this section began with an account of the two main kinds of love lyric, the *cantigas d'amor* and *d'amigo*. It then summarily describes the love lyric in dialogue form, and distinguishes between the two kinds of satiric verse, *cantigas d'escarnho e de maldizer*: the former is indirect and ambivalent, making use of 'what the clerics call *equivocatio*', while the latter is open invective (a theoretical distinction also debated by Pero da Ponte and Estevan da Guarda, in nos. 364 and 112). There follows an account of debate verse (*tenções*), *cantigas de vilãos* (possibly a form of *pastourelle*: the passage is mutilated), and, finally, *cantigas de seguir*, a form of *contrafactum*, of which there are three kinds (see below). The fourth and fifth sections cover the basics of versification, rhyme and the proper use of tenses (temporal inconsistency is also satirised by Eanes do Vinhal; no. 173). The treatise closes with remarks on the two commonest errors, hiatus and *caçafaton* (lexical vulgarity).

This poetic was clearly conceived as a schematic guide to Galician-Portuguese verse, written to help the public discriminate good from bad poets. Although no examples are cited, as a practical guide it is similar to Raimon Vidal's *Razos de trobar* (*c.* 1200). Unlike this text, however, the Galician-Portuguese treatise generally avoids technical grammatical explanations. Although occasionally prescriptive in tone, the author mainly describes accepted aesthetic practices. His principal concern seems to be the proper harmony of parts within the poem, achieved either by means of temporal coherence, or by clever manipulation of the refrain, or by the structural technique called *atafiinda*, which confers syntactic unity throughout the poem. Finally, it is worth noting the relatively large space given to enumerating three kinds of *contrafactum* (*cantiga de seguir*). They are: (i) the poet appropriates a colleague's music and sets new words to it; (ii) the music and versification are both appropriated; (iii) a variety of elements is taken, and the original idea is given a new slant – particularly when the refrain is taken verbatim but its meaning altered in its new context. Taken in conjunction with the author's interest in debate and satiric verse, the emphasis placed on the *seguir* reveals an eminently social concept of poetic creativity. As a form of interplay between the various levels of court society, poetry is both a means of social bonding and of acquiring individual distinction by expressing variety and originality within an all-enclosing convention.[4]

Before continuing with the fourteenth century, it is necessary to return to Alfonso X and describe his role in the vernacular transmission of literary thought. Not only did he consolidate Castilian as the official language of the chancery, but he also commissioned in the vernacular a wide range of historical, scientific, legal and literary works, all of which earned him the sobriquet 'el Sabio', 'The Wise'. This enterprise was undertaken in large measure to make Castile central to the *translatio studii* from Antiquity to the modern age (e.g. he promoted the myth that Aristotle was a Cordoban). And since his patronage also bolstered his claim to become Holy Roman Emperor, his cultural nationalism implicitly anticipated Antonio de Nebrija's view that language should be the 'companion to Empire' (see below).

Alfonso's involvement with literary theory and criticism was not limited to his patronage of poets and rhetoricians (Geoffrey of Eversley's *Ars epistolaris ornatus* of *c.* 1270 was dedicated to him, and Juan Gil de Zamora, author of another *ars dictaminis*, was a close acquaintance). Also relevant is the *General estoria*, one of the greatest products of Alfonsine scholarship. This universal history displays an impressive range of *auctores*, many of whom are subjected to scholastic techniques of literary study. Since it was one of the king's most widely read works, it passed on to a lay audience the methods of biblical exegesis, grammatical *accessus* and *enarratio poetarum*. The *General estoria* draws heavily on the Bible and the

---

4 On the ideological and theoretical implications of convention in this school, see Weiss, 'On the Conventionality'.

classics, and both sets of sources are accompanied by commentaries, some named, others anonymous. For the Bible, Alfonso's team referred to the exegetical work of Augustine and Jerome, as well as the latter's reworking of Eusebius's *Chronici canones*. For classical mythology, Ovid ('the gentile theologian') is a major authority. Although other Ovidian texts are used, the *Metamorphoses* figures conspicuously, often explained at the three levels of *sententia*, *sensus* and *littera*. One of the principal sources for this allegorising is John of Garland's *Integumenta Ovidii* (possibly via an intermediary compilation).

Also characteristic of the *General estoria* is an interest in language. Though there is little truly systematic treatment, the work is pervaded by observations on such matters as the origins, nature and function of human speech and writing (important sources here are Donatus, Priscian, Évrard of Béthune and Vincent of Beauvais' *Speculum maius*). Although the emphasis falls on the features common to all languages rather than on specific ones, the work is rich with comments on Castilian etymology and lexicography.[5]

Alfonso's concern for the liberal arts as an essential programme of studies links him with the ideals of twelfth-century humanism. However, much remains to be done to clarify the details of his cultural position. Little is known of the Castilian schools at this time, which makes it harder to situate the kingdom in relation to intellectual developments elsewhere in Europe, notably to the battle over the relative importance of the quadrivium and trivium. Grammarians such as John of Garland, Thierry of Chartres and Arnulf of Orléans are deployed primarily as historical sources, so their presence may not necessarily imply a conscious defence of the grammar curriculum in face of the challenge posed by the newer scholastic developments in Paris, with their emphasis on logic.

One of the works Alfonso had translated into Castilian (in 1251) was the famous collection of Oriental fables, *Calila e Dimna*. Its prologues are important for the way they thematise the dissemination of knowledge and the acquisition of wisdom, orally and through the written word. It shares these concerns with other didactic texts (like the romance *El caballero Zifar*, c. 1300), and as such it anticipates the main current of vernacular literary criticism of the fourteenth century. At the heart of this lies the work of two men: don Juan Manuel (1282–1348) and Juan Ruiz, Archpriest of Hita (*fl.* 1330–50). Both were deeply preoccupied by the nature of didacticism and the relationship between author, text and public. Differences in temperament, literary medium and social and intellectual background, however, meant that they approached their common problems in radically different ways.

---

[5] On the *General estoria*, see further, pp. 380–2 above.

Juan Manuel wrote numerous treatises on the education, pastimes and social duties of the nobility, among them an *ars poetica*, the *Libro de las reglas de cómo se debe trobar*. This is now lost, and we can only speculate whether it was modelled along the lines of the extant Galician-Portuguese treatise or whether it owed a more direct debt to the poetics of the Occitan-Catalan school. Given his contacts with the east of the Iberian peninsula, the latter is not an unlikely hypothesis. Not only does his title evoke Jofre de Foixà's *Regles de trobar* (*c.* 1286–91),[6] but Jofre's work was commissioned by Jaime II of Aragon, to whom Juan Manuel was related by marriage.

Indeed, as nephew of Alfonso X and cousin of Sancho IV, don Juan was acutely sensitive to his status as an aristocratic man of letters. Anticipating the 'arms *versus* letters' debate of the following century, he gave an unambiguous riposte to those who complained that his literary interests compromised his noble position. In his books, he claimed, there was both *pro e verdat* ('profit and truth'). The pride he took in his literary pursuits is reinforced by the importance he attached to textual authenticity. The general prologue to his complete works reflects, for the first time in Castilian literature, the belief that the authority of the writer depended upon the textual authority of his manuscripts. His remarks on the consequences of scribal corruption stem from the prologue to Nicholas of Lyre's *Postilla litteralis* (1322–9).[7] But in spite of this learned source, Juan Manuel did not set himself up as a contemporary *auctor*, as some fifteenth-century noble writers did. Rather, he presented himself as a compiler, comparing his methods on one occasion to those of the biblical commentator who revised accumulated wisdom and passed it on to future generations.[8] These comparisons apart, there is little that is bookish about his literary self-image. He established himself as the epitome of what may be called the 'authoritative layman': that is to say, as a non-professional who claimed the power to act as a mediator of received wisdom, writing to instruct those of equal or lesser intellect and experience. In Juan Manuel, the vernacular lay writer found a conceptual paradigm with substantial autonomy from clerical models.

As to the function of literature, Juan Manuel's remarks on the therapeutic value of reading are by and large conventional (conforming to the theories described in Chapter 8 above on 'The Profits of Pleasure'). Of greater interest are his views about the way his own writing supplies a secular education (the 'profit and truth') for his fellow nobles. In this regard, two books stand out: the *Libro de los estados* (on the social estates, 1328–30) and his most famous work, *El conde Lucanor* (a collection of *exempla*,

---

[6] See the discussion of this text in Chapter 16 above.
[7] *El conde Lucanor*, ed. Blecua, pp. 45–7; Rico, 'Crítica de texto'.
[8] Macpherson, 'Don Juan Manuel', p. 5.

maxims and proverbs, 1335). The prologues to the latter provide a commentary on the work's five parts and, buttressed by remarks drawn from *El libro de los estados,* form a coherent aesthetic of exemplary literature.[9]

El conde Lucanor is divided into five parts, and, as don Juan carefully explains, is structured upon an ascending scale of obscurity. The first and largest section contains fifty *exempla,* the moral of each being hammered home in two lines of doggerel. The proverbs and maxims of parts 2 and 3 become increasingly obscure, while remaining at an intermediate level of difficulty (they are only 'yaquanto sotiles', 'somewhat obscure'). The final stage is reached in part 4, in which Juan Manuel disrupts conventional word-order to produce the hardest stylistic level, before he returns, in part 5, to the 'easy' expository style of the *exempla.* Thus, *El conde Lucanor* puts into partial practice theories elaborated in the *Libro de los estados.* Here he explains that there are three levels of style: (i) prolix and clear (which corresponds to parts 1 and 5 of *El conde*); (ii) brief and obscure (parts 2–4), and (iii) brief and clear (a rare stylistic ideal practised, he observes, by his uncle Alfonso X, and which he himself attempted only in his *Libro del cavallero et escudero*).

Broadly speaking, Juan Manuel differentiates these three styles according to the effort required to interpret them. And of the three, the bulk of his remarks concern the prolix and clear (i) and the brief and obscure (ii) styles. Whereas for classical and medieval rhetoricians excessive brevity was considered a vice, for Juan Manuel it served a particular didactic function. In line with the concept of 'useful obscurity' elaborated by the biblical exegetes and the church Fathers (e.g. St Augustine, *De doctrina christiana* 2.6.7–8 and 4.8.22), the extreme brief style of *El conde Lucanor,* part 4, was designed to tax the readers' intelligence in such a way that the more they strove to understand the text, the more they would prize its wisdom. A further value of stylistic obscurity was that knowledge, especially in theological matters, would be protected from the gaze of the stupid. (Juan Manuel's use of cipher in the *Libro de los estados* suggests that this concept was no mere topos.) This stylistic level implies that the readers themselves bore the responsibility for extracting the moral – an implication confirmed by the author's remarks to the readers of the second part of *El conde,* where he lays the fault for any potential misunderstanding at the door of those who 'cannot or *do not wish* to comprehend' (p. 278; my emphasis). Likewise, in a number of *exempla,* Juan Manuel encourages the readers to judge for themselves whether his messages were appropriate for their own circumstances. His views may have been shaped in part by the dialectical

---

[9] The following discussion owes much to Taylor, 'Don Jaime de Jérica', and 'Juan Manuel's Cipher'. See also Palafox, *Las éticas del 'Exemplum'*, pp. 61–97.

relationship between pupil and mentor, which influences his *Libro de los estados* (ed. Tate and Macpherson, pp. xvi–xviii). However, although he is certainly aware of the readers' role in the communication process, and of the relationship between understanding and will in the production of meaning, he does not raise these ideas to the same prominence as Juan Ruiz, and is more interested in foregrounding authorial control over a potentially wayward text.

More characteristic by far is his emphasis on the need to employ a clear and prolix style when communicating with his lay readers. The theoretical premise for the use of *exempla* and 'palabras apuestas' ('elegant words') is straightforward enough: 'plus docent exempla quam verba subtilia' ('examples teach more than subtle language'). As explained in his *Libro de los estados* (p. 226), Man in his carnal state grasps abstract notions more easily when expressed in concrete and attractive form. And don Juan's recourse to pictorial illustration in *El conde* suggests an attempt to circumvent linguistic mediation altogether.[10] Accordingly, the burden of responsibility for communicating the message shifts onto the author, who takes on the duties of a doctor. Though he adapts the 'sugared pill' commonplace, the extreme form in which it is expressed gives it special significance: for such is the power of his 'beguiling and beautiful words' even those of minimal understanding will be unable to avoid swallowing the moral message and deriving benefit from it (*El conde*, p. 51). This notion of authorial coercion marks an important stage in the development of the concept of the author. It provides the platform for Juan Manuel's belief in his power as a writer who, working within lay circles, derived authority not from bookish learning but from the efficacy of his style and the validity of his personal experience.

Strikingly distinct attitudes emerge from *El libro de buen amor*, written prior to 1343 in *cuaderna vía* by Juan Ruiz, archpriest of Hita. The poem is structured on the framework of a pseudo-Ovidian erotic autobiography, and is interspersed with edifying digressions, *exempla* and salacious *fabliaux*. An elusive blend of seriousness and parodic jest, it is intensely self-conscious of its own originality and poetic artifice. On a formal level, in one of the few transparent statements of intent, Juan Ruiz presents his 'new book' – 'este nuevo libro' (Prologue, p. 109) – as an *ars versificatoria*, designed to teach a wide range of genres and metres (see also st. 1634). Indeed, it has been suggested that one of the main targets of Juan Ruiz's parody are the poetic conventions of the 'mester de clerecía' itself.[11] Though not in the strict sense didactic, the poem takes didacticism as one of its themes: to a great extent it is about language and the

---

[10] See Seidenspinner-Núñez, 'On "Dios y el mundo"', p. 258.
[11] Walsh, 'Juan Ruiz and the *mester de clerezía*'; but see Joset, *Nuevas investigaciones*, pp. 74–8.

way we interpret it. Although this issue is implicit in much of the narrative, Juan Ruiz occasionally acts as his own glossator: his critical asides, though often enigmatic, constitute one of the most important series of remarks on textual ambiguity and audience response that we possess in any medieval vernacular.

The prologue is based on the patterns of a sermon, taking as its theme 'Intellectum tibi dabo' (Psalm 31). After an account of the relationship between the will, understanding and memory, the author explains that his descriptions of sinful love will encourage those of 'good understanding' to choose the path of salvation and deter those of 'little understanding' from persevering in their evil ways. However, 'because to err is human' ('porque es umanal cosa el pecar'; p. 110), Juan Ruiz adds that, for those who choose it, the book will also serve as a manual for the art of seduction. He has thus 'given understanding' to all men, the wise and the foolish. Calling on his public to heed the 'sentence', not the 'ugly sound of the words', he concludes by declaring the honesty of his intentions. The distinction between inner and outer meaning, the polysemous nature of the work and the general applicability of its content are all reaffirmed in the poem's opening and closing verses.

The apparently incongruous statements of intent, often cast as challenges to the audience's will and capacity to understand, can be explained in part by reference to scholastic commentaries on Ovid. Ovidian and Pseudo-Ovidian material (*De vetula* and *Pamphilus*) make up an important part of the *Libro*, and Juan Ruiz was clearly familiar with the *accessus* that customarily prefaced Ovidian texts. Of the guidance offered by these prologues, the most relevant here is what the authors said about *intentio* and *utilitas*. In accordance with the thirteenth- and fourteenth-century trend to moralise Ovid, the general thrust of most *accessus* was to search for ethical intent, and the grammarians' recurring conclusion was that Ovid's poetry pertained to ethics: *ethice supponitur* (see Chapters 5 and 6 above). But explanations of moral significance often sit ill-at-ease with explanations of the poems' *materia*, or content. For example, the *accessus* to the *Heroides* commonly held that Ovid's intent was to praise virtuous love and reprehend illicit love by setting forth examples of female vice and virtue. In one of the longer prologues, however, there is an important extra detail: besides the epideictic intent, Ovid offered lessons in epistolary seduction. There is an obvious parallel here with Juan Ruiz's disingenuous claim that although his book is designed to inculcate *buen amor* it also contains the precepts for *loco amor*. The parallel is reinforced by the *accessus* to the *Ars amatoria* and *Pamphilus*. Both were said to offer instruction in earthly love; but both were also classified under ethics, for the simple reason that 'de moribus puellarum loquitur' ('it speaks about the morals of young girls'). The perfunctoriness of this explanation raises doubts about whether an ethical reading of poetry – particularly erotic poetry – was really that straightforward. The grammarians seem to take a lot on trust, expecting readers to interpret Ovid piously, agree over which was licit and which illicit love, and, having done so, self-righteously ignore the lessons in seducing young girls. Juan Ruiz's poem, and his interventions in it, suggest that the process was not that simple.

The Castilian's scepticism towards facile didacticism may also be related to Augustinian hermeneutics (both *De magistro* and the *Confessions* have been cited as Juan Ruiz's points of reference).[12] Especially important is the notion of voluntarism; according to this, human understanding is controlled by one's moral state, which is the domain of the will, which in turn is influenced by divine grace. This is the central theme of the sermon prologue, and as such it has a bearing on what Juan Ruiz says about the moral intentions of his book. Morality is outside authorial control, he implies, and is wholly dependent upon the reader's will and understanding – a point reinforced in the first *exemplum* of the poem, the dispute between the Greeks and the Romans (sts. 44–70). This parable relates the latters' attempts to acquire laws from the Greeks, and in order to achieve this they agree to debate in sign language. Their representative, an aggressive dimwit, is pitted against the most learned Greek. Each makes three signs of the hand: the Greek to prove the unity of the Holy Trinity, the Roman to threaten violence. Both misunderstand, and both appear foolish, because of their willingness to read into the other's sign the message they are predisposed to find. Commenting that 'there is no evil word, unless it is badly taken' ('non ha mala palabra si non es a mal tenida'; st. 64), Juan Ruiz concludes with the image of the book as musical instrument, whose effect depends upon one's ability to play it (st. 70).

But this *exemplum* contains an equally fundamental idea about the difficulty of communicating. Other considerations apart, the Greek and the Roman misunderstand each other because of the ambiguity of the signs themselves. Thus, not only does meaning vary according to the *voluntad* and *entendimiento*, it is also subject to the inherent slipperiness of language. It would be hard to specify the sources of Juan Ruiz's linguistic beliefs (they are probably shaped by a multiplicity of factors), but they are similar to views that underpinned much of scholastic logic. Of the texts which formed the *Organon*, the canon of Aristotelian dialectics, the most relevant here is *De sophisticis elenchis* (*On Sophistical Refutations*). In this, Aristotle says that true reasoning or refutation is obscured by the 'certain likeness [which exists] between the genuine and the sham'. And the most prolific source of fallacy 'is the argument that turns upon names

---

[12] Though the Augustinian influence is challenged by Walsh, for whom St Bonaventure is equally relevant (review of Brownlee, *Reading Subject*).

only . . . . Inevitably, then, the same formulae, and a single name, have a number of meanings.'[13] It is not difficult to see similar notions at work in the *Libro de buen amor*, where much of the ambiguity arises from the polysemy of individual words and phrases (e.g. 'buen amor' itself). The prevalence of fallacious arguments and misapplied *exempla* sets Juan Ruiz apart from the glib didacticism of much wisdom literature, which acknowledges the role of man's *voluntad* and *entendimiento* in the learning process, but which seems to pass over their potential recalcitrance. For the sceptical Archpriest, however, between man and the moral lies not just the variable inclination of the human will, but language itself – the 'meretricious word'.[14]

With the advent of the Trastamaran dynasty in 1369 Castilian culture took a new turn. The monarchy's policy of rewarding its supporters by raising them to the ranks of the upper nobility created a class of landed aristocracy who were eager to consolidate their newly won political power by projecting an image of courtly and chivalric values. In some noble quarters the ideal had a more emphatically literary dimension, reflected, for example, in the creation of libraries and the patronage of classical translations. These pursuits, which are related to the more general spread of lay literacy throughout late-medieval Europe, form part of the broad movement of Castilian vernacular humanism that was fostered by the nobility and their entourage. The precise scope of this brand of humanism, its debt to Italian cultural models, its relationship to the other forms of professional Latin humanism, and whether or not it merits the epithet 'Renaissance', have all been the subject of debate. Nonetheless, the union of the active and contemplative lives embodied by the literate *militares viri* (the theme of *armas y letras*) clearly provides the framework for a substantial portion of the literary thought before the final decades of the fifteenth century. On a theoretical level, there was now no question that the aristocracy should draw on the power of the written word; in practice, the problem was the kinds of literary pursuit appropriate for the cultured layman. A second, and related, current of thought concerns the emancipation and status of vernacular literature and lay authorship.

With regard to formal literary treatises, fifteenth-century Castile offers the following: the critical prologues of Juan Alfonso de Baena and the Marquis of Santillana; two preceptive poetics by Enrique de Villena and Juan del Encina respectively; Alonso de Cartagena's epistle on aristocratic education and book-collecting, and a chapter on metre in Antonio de Nebrija's Castilian grammar. Yet the theoretical and critical vitality

---

[13] I follow the translation in Murphy (ed.), *Three Medieval Rhetorical Arts*, pp. 227–8.
[14] I adapt the happy phrase of Catherine Brown; see her *Contrary Things*, Ch. 6.

of this period must also be gauged by reference to the frequent discussions contained in prefaces and the literary texts themselves. The composition of vernacular commentaries and glosses was also widespread, and some of these offer extended passages of literary criticism (particularly the commentaries of Enrique Villena, Juan de Mena and Hernán Núñez, which I discuss below). Also significant are the Castilian translations of classical and modern treatises: *De inventione* (by Cartagena), *Ad Herennium* (by Villena, now lost), St Basil's homily on reading pagan literature, Isidore's *Etymologiae*, Petrarch's third invective, Boccaccio's *De genealogia gentilium deorum*, Bruni's *Vite di Dante e di Petrarca*, and extracts from the Dante commentaries by Benvenuto da Imola and Pietro Alighieri (on which see Chapter 22 below). There is also a rhyming dictionary in the Occitan-Catalan tradition, *La gaya sciencia*, by Pero Guillén de Segovia (1475), and a lost poetic treatise attributed to Juan de Mena.

Chronologically, the first significant work is the *Cancionero* compiled by Juan Alfonso de Baena shortly before his death around 1430 (though the sole extant manuscript was copied *c*. 1470). This anthology draws on verse that dates back to the final decades of the previous century, when the aristocracy began to display the trappings of literacy as a vehicle and sign of their recent re-empowerment. A mark of their courtly learning was the poetic debates (*preguntas y respuestas*) over scholastic or theological issues, in which members of the church and university often participated. In spite of their often mock-serious tone, the theological debates in particular provoked a negative response from theologians. They claimed that the nobility had no right to comment on such matters, and that poetry and theology were incompatible. As the Franciscan Fray Lope del Monte put it, 'I never saw God's secrets in verse' ('Nunca vy ssecretos de Dios en ditar').[15]

To counter this view, several lay poets claimed divine inspiration for their work, stating that, in Baena's words, they possessed 'a grace infused by God' ('gracia infusa del señor Dios'; I, p. 14). Unlike Italian humanist defenders of poetry, they did not derive their arguments directly from the concept of the *poeta theologus* first elaborated by Aristotle (*Metaphysics*) and Augustine (*De civitate Dei*). Possibly influenced by contemporary currents of popular spirituality, their stated authority was St Paul, Ephesians 4:7: 'But unto everyone of us is given grace according to the measure of the gift of Christ' ('Unicuique autem nostrum data est gratia secundum mensuram donationis Christi'). Baena adapted this quotation as a rubric to his *Cancionero* (I, p. 3; see also his poem 359), and thus implicitly endorsed

---

[15] Baena, *Cancionero*, II, p. 553 (no. 273). Another example is the debate over predestination instigated by Ferrán Sánchez Calavera (poems 517–25).

the two basic assumptions of those who claimed divine inspiration: first, that their special verbal powers as laymen were a sign of God's favour, which gave them the authority to speak on learned matters, and second, that the divine aura with which they surrounded their verse conferred upon them greater social prestige over their non-poetic peers.[16]

However, within the *Cancionero* itself one can detect a more nuanced variety of strategies underlying the concept of 'gracia infusa'. Alfonso Alvarez de Villasandino, for example, uses it to defend his special status as a professional troubadour. Echoing complaints made in Guiraut Riquier's *Supplicatio*, he attacks noble poets who plagiarise his original verse and vulgarise the art of poetry (no. 80; see also 96 and 200). In his exchanges with the minor nobleman Ferrán Manuel de Lando (nos. 253–9), the notion of poetry as *ars divina* is central to their arguments over the relative importance of originality, natural talent and craftsmanship. Ferrán Manuel also exploits it in his debates with theologians in order to justify his pronouncements on such topics as astrology (e.g. no. 272). Arguing that God revealed His secrets to the simple, he asserts that as a poet he has verbal powers denied to the incoherent friars (no. 274).

As the above debates indicate, the poets of this *Cancionero* frequently commented on their own or each other's literary abilities. Their aesthetic ideals fall within the broad traditions of medieval rhetoric: comments range over such issues as decorum, metre, structural coherence, intellectual or doctrinal authority, invention and wit (often the ability to compose obscure metaphors). These basic ideals are encapsulated in Baena's rubrics, of which there are of two kinds: the occasional biographical introductions to the work of individual poets, and the much briefer rubrics attached to almost all the 588 poems.[17] Although these and the biographical rubrics are similar in function to *vidas* and *razos*, they are almost certainly not directly inspired by them. However, one partial influence on Baena's critical terminology is the *accessus*, from which he derives his sporadic observations on a poet's *materia* or *intención*. For the most part, the briefer rubrics have a two-part structure, in which Baena names the type of poem and its author, and then evaluates its quality and/or mentions the circumstances of its composition. As a justification of the selected poets' *savoir-faire*, they also validate the compilation's social and aesthetic authority as a mirror of court wit and manners.

---

[16] Fraker, *Studies on the 'Cancionero de Baena'*, pp. 63–90; Weiss, *The Poet's Art*, pp. 25–40. The notion of poetic grace was also common in the earlier Catalan consistories, and recurs, in various modulations, throughout the fifteenth century; see Potvin, *Illusion et pouvoir*, pp. 43–7.

[17] On Baena's debt to the *artes poeticae* and the Occitan-Catalan poetic consistories, see Nepaulsingh's introduction to Imperial, 'El dezir a las syete virtudes', pp. xxxvi–lxvii; also Potvin, *Illusion et pouvoir*, pp. 47–61.

Baena was much more than a simple scribe. As the first critical compiler of Castilian vernacular verse, he attempted to organise the literary production of the new Castilian lyric, and also to control its reception by acting as an arbiter of taste for his literary community. The extent to which he went further than earlier European compilers is emphasised by his very unusual step of prefacing his anthology with a prologue, divided into a dedication to Juan II and a *Prologus Baenensis*. In the former, after declaring his own thoroughness as compiler, he claims that his book will give pleasure and relief from care (I, pp. 2–3) to those of the royal household who wish to understand the art. This qualification is significant; by making critical understanding essential to the therapeutic effect of poetry, he validates the role of the theorist and critic in literary circles. Thus, the prologue that follows is designed to serve as the 'foundation and root' ('fundamento e rayz') of the whole anthology.

The bulk of the *Prologus Baenensis* is an unacknowledged paraphrase of the prologues to Alfonso X's *General estoria* and *Estoria de España*, being a eulogy of history, writing and books.[18] Having expounded the role of history in preserving and disseminating wisdom, Baena emphasises its moral and political value to rulers and the nobility. He then describes how the nobility own and read other books of doctrine and delight, the more varied the better. Although they have many courtly pastimes, they derive greater pleasure and benefit from reading and listening to books of great deeds, whose recreational value is moral, physical and spiritual. Finally, he declares, poetry is a particularly subtle and pleasurable ('sotil e graciosa') form of writing. As this paraphrase indicates, in spite of his theoretical intentions, Baena's method up to this point has been far from analytic. Nonetheless, he allows the reader to infer that poetry shares the value of all writing, even though he avoids specifying its relation to other branches of knowledge and written discourse. His central purpose is to elevate the status of poetry, and to make it appear more than a trivial courtly pursuit. This point is further illustrated in the closing lines of the prologue, where Baena prescribes the qualities that define a true poet. The 'gay science', he writes, depends upon the 'grace infused by God' ('gracia infusa del señor Dios'), who imparts it to those who already possess expert metrical and versificatory skill. It is such a subtle art that it can be mastered only by those who possess the following qualities: powers of invention and critical judgement; extensive knowledge of books and languages; practical experience of the courts and the world at large; nobility and courtliness;

---

[18] See *Las poéticas*, ed. López Estrada, pp. 29–33. For general studies on the prologue, see Kohut, 'La teoría de la poesía cortesana'; Potvin, *Illusion et pouvoir*, pp. 33–9; Weiss, *The Poet's Art*, pp. 40–54, and the important critique of these studies by Johnston, 'Poetry and Courtliness'.

eloquence and wit; and finally, poets must simulate being in love, because love is considered to be the source of all worthy doctrine.

Baena's account of the ideal poet owes much to earlier medieval concepts of courtliness; for him, poetry is essentially a mark of social exclusivity, and possesses a less emphatically philosophical dimension than it was to acquire at the hands of Enrique de Villena, Juan de Mena and Santillana. Though he gestures in their direction, Baena does not go as far as these writers, who moved beyond the concept of the poet-courtier to promulgate that of the philosopher-poet. This distinction may be illustrated by contrasting Baena's treatment of Villasandino and Imperial with that of Santillana. In his dedication and rubrics, Baena eulogises the troubadour Villasandino as the divinely inspired monarch of all Spanish poets (I, p. 16), yet makes only perfunctory comments on the verse of Imperial, the poet of Genoese origin who introduced to Castile the fashion for Dantesque allegory. For Santillana, on the other hand, Imperial epitomised the higher ideals of the *poeta*, against those of the *dezidor* or *trobador* Villasandino (see below).

More ambitious than that of Baena, and certainly grounded on more solid intellectual resources, was the work of the nobleman Enrique de Villena (1384–1434). The political and intellectual career of this remarkable polymath embodied the fifteenth-century polemic between arms and letters, and his ideas about the social function of literary study helped shape the outlook of such major figures as the Marquis of Santillana and Juan de Mena.

A belief in the ethical and political value of letters pervades Villena's writings, but is most forcefully expressed in his translation of, and commentary on, the *Aeneid* (1428). This work has already been discussed in relation to the vernacular commentary tradition (see above, Chapter 14). In the present context, it is important to note how he sets poetry apart as one of four main branches of knowledge, alongside theology, the mechanical arts and philosophy (all with numerous subcategories). As an architectonic science, poetry can be appreciated only by a mind which is mature and already shaped by preparatory training, and literary study is a form of spiritual ennoblement (*Traducción y glosas de la 'Eneida'*, I, pp. 39–40, 56).[19] Although in itself the idea that poetry was a form of overarching philosophy has a long history, Villena's formulation is conditioned very much by contemporary concerns. Self-interest apart (he often presents himself as the ideal aristocratic intellectual), he was responding to the changed configuration of the Castilian aristocracy. By reworking the argument that one's nobility need not depend

---

[19] See Weiss, *The Poet's Art*, pp. 73–83; Miguel Prendes, *El espejo y el piélago*.

exclusively upon inherited status, but upon a nobility of the mind, he no doubt thought he could appeal to the interests of a caste in the process of rapid expansion.

Traces of these ideas may also be detected in what remains of his poetic treatise, *El arte de trovar* (1433), dedicated to the Marquis of Santillana, and surviving only in the excerpts of the sixteenth-century humanist Alvar Gómez de Castro. Though a mature work, *El arte* harks back to a youth and early manhood spent partly at the Aragonese court of his cousin, Martin the Humane. Modelled on the preceptive treatises of the Occitan-Catalan school (on which see Chapter 16 above), it reflects Villena's ambition to set standards for the emerging Castilian lyric. Most of the extant text was probably extracted from the original work's prologue. In it, Villena gives an account of his prominent role in the Barcelona Poetic Consistory at the turn of the century, and describes its elaborate ceremonies in fascinating detail. He also surveys earlier poetic treatises such as those by Raimon Vidal, Jofre de Foixà, Berenguer de Noya and Guilhem Molinier (though he was probably aware of numerous other treatises whose manuscripts were available to him at the Barcelona Consistory).

Apart from the prologue, Gómez de Castro took notes from the first part only, which is grammatical. (His source may have contained no more, for it possible that *El arte*, like the *Aeneid* commentary, was an over-ambitious project, left unfinished at the author's death.) These fragments from part 1 do not support the oft-repeated view that the work was modelled on the *Mirayll de trobar* by Berenguer de Noya. Indeed, the state of the text and the nature of its contents render otiose any attempt to pin down specific sources. The ten sections of the extant *Arte* deal with orthography and punctuation, subjects which Villena had already discussed in a briefer, though more polemical, fashion in an excursus of his *Aeneid* commentary (ed. Cátedra, I, p. 7). His method is partly prescriptive and partly descriptive, the latter being of special interest for the occasional comparative side-glances at Catalan phonetic and orthographic practice (e.g. ed. Sánchez Cantón, p. 177).

Villena's dual concern for correct spelling and lucid declamation owes a general debt to the Barcelona consistories which, as he himself describes, placed considerable emphasis on the proper written and oral presentation of the poetic text. It would be wrong, however, to characterise *El arte* as a consciously archaising treatise, because Villena had contemporary cultural concerns very much in mind. This is evident in three issues that dominate the prologue and the treatment of grammar: poetry was a vital form of communication; it was a legitimate branch of knowledge, and modern Castilian verse required the dignity of an authoritative past.

El arte opens with a critique of those who believe that poetry is simply a matter of correct rhyme and metre. Commenting on Santillana's early verse, he states that because of this poet's inexperience with the fundamentals of the *gaya dotrina*, he has been unable to communicate to his listeners 'the excellent inventions which Nature administers to your noble mind with the aptness with which they were conceived' ('las escelentes invenciones que natura ministra a la serenidat de vuestro ingenio, con aquella propiedat [con] que fueron concebidas'; p. 164). This formulation, which has antecedents in the *Leys d'Amors* and other works of the Catalan school, places emphasis on poetry as the effective communication of thought. It reflects the importance of *inventio* in the troubadour tradition and recalls the theory of composition whereby, according to Geoffrey of Vinsauf, the poem is a faithful reproduction of a mental archetype (*Poetria nova*, Prol.). But this rhetorical emphasis also needs to be understood in the particular context of Villena's literary theorising. Although he mentions the ludic value of poetry (e.g. pp. 164, 166), it is clear that there was a stronger bond between poetry and rhetoric, and that this was part of his well-attested concern for the communication of wisdom and the social value of an intellectual elite of noble minds ('generosos entendimientos'). The sort of rhetorical skills harnessed by poetry enabled the truly gifted to emerge in society, to ascend the God-given intellectual hierarchy, and to stand out from the ranks of the 'ediothas' for whom Villena displays such contempt in the opening pages of *El arte* (pp. 163, 164, 169). In short, his declaration that poetry bestows great benefit upon 'la vida civil' (p. 166) reveals how *El arte* is motivated by the same social concerns that inspired his *Aeneid* commentary and his earlier exegesis of classical myth, *Los doze trabajos de Hércules* (1417). In this regard Villena may be influenced by Italian civic humanism.[20]

Secondly, the treatise attempts to set Castilian, a new lyric language, within a national and historical context – a goal shared by other writers of the time, most notably Santillana, whose defence of Castilian verse is based in large measure on the claims of its history. Though don Enrique was not the only theoretician to preface his work with a list of previous poetics (the anonymous author of a contemporary French *Art* did the same), he does so not merely out of deference to convention; the list is there to project the sense of an authoritative – and continuing – tradition. This he does by setting his own treatise firmly within the Occitan-Catalan school, and also by affirming that the torch of true poetic learning will then pass to its dedicatee, Santillana, who will light the way for a new generation of poets (p. 164). The obvious influence of *translatio studii* also

---

[20] See Di Camillo, *El humanismo castellano*, pp. 101–2; Cátedra, 'Enrique de Villena y algunos humanistas', p. 202.

shapes his account of the development of the various alphabets, derived in part from Isidore (*Etymologiae* 1.3–4). But Villena gives the topos a sense of historical authenticity by relating Spain's alphabet to its political history: the bastard Gothic script was lost upon the Moorish conquest, so the Christians sent to England for the Anglican script, and what resulted was a wholly individual blend of Western and Moorish writing (pp. 172–3). Though fanciful, this account bears the stamp of an incipient cultural nationalism.

Finally, the use of *translatio studii* is predicated on Villena's conviction that poetry should be afforded the dignity of a *scientia*, defined, following Walter Burley, as the 'full order of immutable and true things' ('complida orden de cosas immutables e verdaderas'; p. 169). This conviction recalls the attempt made in the *Aeneid* commentary to classify poetry as a specific branch of wisdom, and it influences *El arte* on all levels. From an epistemological viewpoint, his survey of earlier treatises is phrased in such a way as to show that knowledge of poetry has progressed according to well-known scholastic theories. Like every true *scientia*, poetry constitutes a fixed body of learning; what develops is not the unchanging framework, or laws, of the subject, but man's understanding of it, which generations of practitioners build up by a gradual process of accretion and refinement.[21] On a more specific level, to illustrate his precepts on euphony, the main aesthetic principle of the extant text, Villena invokes the authority of the 'ancient troubadours' (pp. 177–9). Although the few lines cited cannot be identified, his point is clear enough: to teach Castilian poets that although their own lyric tradition was new, the laws that govern poetic composition and style were pre-ordained and could be transferred – like the laws of any science – from one nation to another.

If anyone aspired to Villena's ideals of intellectual nobility and the conjunction of the active and the contemplative life, it was Íñigo López de Mendoza, marquis of Santillana (1398–1458). Head of one of the most powerful political clans, he was a notable and adventurous poet and bibliophile, whose substantial library epitomised the lay reading habits of his day. Although his outstanding contribution to literary criticism is his *Proemio e carta al condestable don Pedro de Portugal*, his other prose prologues bear witness to his interest in literary theory and, above all, history.[22]

The prologue to his *Proverbios* (1437) is famous for its polemical defence of the unity of arms and letters. His case is based on examples drawn from biblical, classical and Spanish history, reinforced by the

---

[21] Compare Boccaccio, *Genealogia deorum gentilium* 14.4. For discussion, see Weiss, *The Poet's Art*, Ch. 2, and, for the notion of poetic 'tradition' more generally, see Johnston, 'Literary Tradition' and 'Troubadour Tradition'.

[22] All quotations are from López de Mendoza, *Obras completas*, pp. 435–60.

popular argument of virtuous *otium* (Cicero, *De officiis* 3, introd.), and summed up in his dictum: 'wisdom does not blunt the tip of the lance, nor weaken the sword in the hand of the knight' ('La sciencia non enbota el fierro de la lança, ni faze floxa la espada en la mano del cavallero'; *Obras*, pp. 218–19). Typically, Santillana offers his own poem, with his own glosses, as an example of the literary learning to which his fellow nobles should aspire. He rejects the allegation that his proverbs merely plagiarise the *auctores* by taking on the persona of the compiler: this reliance on the past, he claims, is not unoriginality but a source of authority. Similarly, he forestalls any criticism of his versification by referring to the precepts of Raimon Vidal and others, in a passage cribbed almost verbatim from Villena's earlier treatise.

Santillana wrote the *Carta a doña Violante de Prades* (1443) to accompany copies of his *Proverbios*, sonnets 'al ytálico modo', and the allegorical *Comedieta de Ponza*, whose title reflects the author's deference to Dante, and whose content his fondness for Boccaccio. This letter explains the meaning of the term *comedieta* in the light of the three classical genres of tragedy, satire and comedy, whose content and narrative structure were related to the three levels of style: thus, like the *comedia*, his poem begins sadly but ends in joy. These definitions could have reached him via several channels, such as Isidore, Boccaccio (both of whom he exploited for his *Prohemio e carta*), or Benvenuto da Imola's commentary on Dante (which he owned in translation and whose genre definitions were cited by Juan de Mena, in the prologue to his *Coronación*; see below). However, although the *Carta* betrays familiarity with these basic notions of genre, it is more significant that his account is even briefer than the generally schematic versions of his contemporaries. Characteristically, Santillana is less interested in expounding theory than in giving particular examples of the genres – a method which allowed him to enhance his own status by parading his wide reading and creating a historical framework for his own verse. The same is true of the few lines he dedicates to the sonnet, which he himself introduced to Castile. Rather than define it, he traces its origins back to Guido Cavalcanti, and names its most notable exponents, Cecco d'Ascoli (i.e. Francesco Stàbili, 1269–1327), Dante and Petrarch.

Two other letters deserve a note in this regard: one to his son, Pero González de Mendoza, requesting a Castilian translation of Decembrio's Latin version of the *Iliad*; and the other to his nephew, Pedro de Mendoza, accompanying a manuscript of his *Proverbios*, sonnets and a vernacular version of Seneca's *Epistulae ad Lucilium*. Various critical commonplaces surface here (concerning, for example, vernacular translation, 'arms *versus* letters', and the notion of reading for consolation and profit); but these letters are valuable mainly as evidence for the rhetorical use of literary theory as a means of striking a particular authorial pose. In Santillana's case, they validated his self-image as an energetic literary patron, as a noble who had conjoined the active and contemplative lives, and as a poet whose verse was at once avant-garde and yet cast within authoritative literary traditions.

This point applies with special force to Santillana's most famous literary prologue-epistle, sent with a collection of the poet's verse to the young Pedro de Portugal between 1445 and 1449. Though the *Prohemio e carta* contains a much broader range of theories than other Castilian treatises, it is not theoretical in an analytic sense. It is a eulogy of poetry, designed to celebrate the dignity of modern verse and justify literary pursuits as an essential ingredient of true nobility. A striking example of *ars dictaminis*, its stylistic polish and broad scope make it a landmark of aristocratic culture of late-medieval Europe.[23]

The prologue is framed by remarks on the appropriateness of poetry during the course of life. Citing the biblical tag 'cum essem parvulus' (I Cor. 13:11), Santillana opens by apparently dismissing his own work and relegating poetry to the role of another court pastime. Yet for various reasons it is clear that his self-criticism was shaped by the exordial demands of affected modesty rather than by a coherent theoretical stance. For Santillana, poetry itself is not morally suspect. Divinely infused into the best and most noble minds, poetry does not consist simply of 'vain and lascivious things': poets write in a way that reflects and is determined by their own age and times (pp. 439–40). This line of argument – exploited to the full by such writers as Petrarch (*Invectiva* 3) and Boccaccio (*Genealogia* 14.6) – frees poetry from the guilt of its practitioners. It also prepares the ground for Santillana's conclusion, where he claims that there is a kind of poetry suitable for each age. Arguing from personal experience, he asserts that verse had been as pleasurable in his youth as it was necessary in the turbulence of his later years (p. 454). His supporting aphorism, 'Quem noua concepit olla seruabit odorem' (derived ultimately though not directly from Horace, *Epistles* 1.2.69–70), reinforces one of the prologue's central themes: the composition and study of verse provide enduring wisdom and delight for a dedicated and select few.

These ideas are implicit in Santillana's definition of poetry. In a phrase that combines theories of inspiration with the rhetorical concept of *studium* (the enthusiasm which sustains arduous pursuits), he defines it as 'a celestial zeal, a divine passion, a food that never sates the soul' ('Un zelo celeste, una affección divina, una insaciable cibo del ánimo'; p. 439). As such, it is the mark of both social and spiritual nobility (pp. 439–40). With regard to form, Santillana draws on equally well-known concepts

---

[23] On its rhetorical structure, see Gómez Moreno, *El 'Prohemio e carta'*, pp. 24–43, 149–50.

of allegory and metrical balance to define poetry as 'an imagining of useful things, veiled with a most beautiful covering, composed, ordered and scanned according to true weight and measure' ('un fingimiento de cosas útyles, cubiertas o veladas con muy fermosa cobertura, conpuestas, distinguidas e scandidas por cierto cuento, peso e medida'; p. 439). It is generally held that the source for this passage lies in Boccaccio's *Genealogia* 14.7, a work which Santillana owned in Castilian translation (though his copy lacks Books 14 and 15). Less convincingly, Cicero's *De oratore* and Horace's *Ars poetica* have also been suggested as influences. However, the ideas were commonplace and were expressed in very similar form by other authors whose works were also in the Spaniard's library, such as Leonardo Bruni's *Lives of Dante and Petrarch*, and the Dante commentaries by Pietro Alighieri and Benvenuto da Imola. More important than the quest for specific sources is how the Italians supplied Santillana not simply with the inspiration but – principally through their association with Dante – with a powerful confirmation of the pre-existing movement to ennoble and expand the range of vernacular verse.

A eulogy of eloquence as a mark of human dignity, and of verse as its most ancient and authoritative form, signals the transition to the historical survey. After an account of Bible poetics based largely on Isidore, followed by brief remarks on the earliest Greek and Latin poets, Santillana develops a previous point about poetry's essential role at all levels of human life, both spiritual and secular. To prove his case, he cites the examples of epithalamia, bucolics, elegies, and the literary patronage of Roman emperors and modern monarchs (Robert of Naples and Hugh of Cyprus). These passages illustrate the principal character of Santillana's historical method: he attempts to perceive historical change, and at the same time to subordinate difference to an underlying unity. After pausing to recognise the difficulty of describing poetry's *translatio* from Antiquity to the modern age, he then establishes a universal scheme of poetic practice. This scheme, an adaptation of the *rota Virgilii*,[24] divides all poetry into three levels: 'sublime' (Greek and Latin, though with no explicit distinction between classical and medieval); 'mediocre' (vernacular verse, such as that by Guido Guinizelli and Arnaut Daniel) and 'infimo' (represented by the metrically irregular *romances* and *cantares* which delight 'those of a low and servile condition'; p. 444). The last category embraces a wide range of popular lyric (such as the ballads), and it has been subjected to many interpretations.[25] But the disputes over the precise generic application of the terms *romances* and *cantares* – and over Santillana's attitude

---

[24] 'Virgil's wheel', the diagram commonly used in rhetorical manuals to illustrate the theory of decorum.

[25] On the three levels of style and the meaning of *romances e cantares*, see the critical survey in Gómez Moreno, *El 'Prohemio e carta'*, pp. 115–25.

towards them – have obscured something more fundamental: by being assigned a place, albeit a low one, in a scheme of poetic values, oral verse is at least recognised *qua* poetry. Moreover, its position breaks down the binarism between literature composed in classical and vernacular tongues: modern vernacular poetry no longer suffers in exclusive comparison with its Latin counterpart but achieves a dignity of its own, and expresses the superiority of the noble class over the third estate with its outpourings of allegedly artless verse.

Santillana once more takes up the thread of his historical survey and, after references to the Italian triumvirate of Dante, Petrarch and Boccaccio, he traces the passage of poetry west to France. His evaluative criticism, like that of his contemporaries, is usually perfunctory; but mention of the *Roman de la Rose*, Machaut's *chansonnier* and some narrative *dits* by and attributed to Alain Chartier prompts a value judgement of special interest. The Italians are preferred over the French because their works display greater intellect and narrative inventiveness; the French over the Italians because of their respect for poetic form and the brilliant richness of their music: they are the inheritors of Orpheus, Pythagoras and Empedocles (p. 446). Under this balanced appraisal perhaps lies the suggestion that Castilian taste, capable of appreciating the merits of both form and content, was less one-sided than that of its two main poetic rivals.

Notes on Catalan, Valencian and Aragonese poets follow, and after listing a group of Castilian narrative poems composed in *cuaderna vía* during the previous two centuries, Santillana moves back in time to describe the lyric school of Galician-Portuguese. Acknowledging its early dominance within Iberia, he stresses Castile's special debt to its metres and genres. His own youthful memories of a Galician-Portuguese *cancioneiro* assume special importance in view of this school's slender manuscript tradition. Although he seems ignorant of Alfonso X's religious *cantigas*, written in Galician-Portuguese, he places this monarch at the head of a long list of Castilian poets – some of whom are well known to us, others less so – which stretches down to the generation immediately preceding Santillana. From a critical point of view, the most significant aspect of this survey is the comparison between two kinds of writer: the *dezidor o trobador*, exemplified by the prolific Villasandino, and the *poeta*, embodied by Francisco Imperial. Though the distinction had become a common one in European terms, it projects Santillana's pride in the maturity of his native tradition, now capable of producing writers to rival the philosopher-poets of old.

The value of this historical survey lies in a number of factors. Obviously significant are the insights into texts available at the time, or thought worthy of mention (e.g. the reference to the *Libro del Arcipreste de Hita*, evidence both for the early dissemination of this work and for the

questionable validity of the modern title). Although there is some evaluative criticism, mainly eulogistic, Santillana does not try to establish canons
of 'great poets' within the various branches of the European poetic tradition. His primary concern was to demonstrate its long history, breadth
and current vitality, as well as to situate his own school of writing within
the larger whole. The desire to forge a tradition is clearly a function of
the eulogistic aims of the prologue: that poetry has its own history sets it
apart as an autonomous branch of knowledge. But the depiction of that
history also confers an identity upon the culture of the nation and (perhaps more importantly for Santillana) of the class to which he belonged.
Implicitly then, the writing of this history is a statement of belief that the
nobility could, without fear of compromising their estate, exploit poetry
as a symbol of prestige for their class and country.

A radically different perspective is supplied by the Latin epistle dedicated to Pedro Fernández de Velasco, Count of Haro, and written c. 1440
by the bishop of Burgos, Alonso de Cartagena.[26] Cartagena's diplomatic
missions brought him in contact with Italian humanists, notably Leonardo
Bruni. Nonetheless, his treatment of aristocratic literary education does
not match the depth of Italian treatises (some of which were known in
Castile: for example, Maffeo Vegio's *De educatione liberorum*, Matteo
Palmieri's *Libro della vita civile*, and Leonardo Bruni's *De studiis et litteris*, dedicated to Juan II). Moreover, his guidelines set him apart from the
cultural beliefs of the Italians, and ally him with a figure such as the French
theologian Jean Gerson, whose two treatises on noble education are similar in tone and content. Significantly prefacing a copy of the *Cathoniana
confectio* (i.e. the *Disticha Catonis* and *Contemptus mundi*), Cartagena's
epistle is divided into twelve short chapters, and its main authorities are
the Bible and Gratian's *Decretum*. After a preamble (Chs. 1–2), structured around such well-worn topics as *scripturae tenacitas* (the durability
of writing), and the notions that man has a natural desire for knowledge,
and that all that is written is for our profit, Cartagena arranges society into three groups: those whose responsibilities to the state preclude
the study of books (the majority); the professional *scholastici viri*, and
a *medium genus*, who are able to combine the active and contemplative
lives, and cultivate man's higher instincts, by moderate and apt literary
study in times of leisure (Chs. 3–5). After warning against the deceptions
of empty eloquence and the confusion between idle curiosity and true
wisdom, the author sets boundaries to noble reading (Chs. 6–7). Three
criteria are established: that which is spiritually healthy, morally correct, and suitable for lay intellects. The rest of the treatise is a practical

---

[26] *Un tratado sobre la educación*, ed. Lawrance. On Cartagena's literary attitudes, see also
Kohut, 'Der Beitrag', pp. 183–202.

application of these principles. Adopting the role of a spiritual doctor, Cartagena emphasises what books to avoid rather than what to read. Strictly forbidden are the 'amatoria bucolica aliaque poetarum figmenta' (p. 50), whose eloquence and sophistication mask lewdness and pagan error. Forbidden too are Arthurian romances and any work that masquerades as historical fact. Chronicles, though, are 'perutiles', as are unspecified works of lay piety, most of the Bible (with the principal exception of the Song of Songs, whose allegorical intent is closed to laymen), and certain ethical books by pagans (Aristotle, Cicero and Seneca). After stressing that nobles should stay within their intellectual limits and not dabble in theological speculation (a possible allusion to *preguntas y respuestas* like those recorded by Baena; see above), Cartagena sets out a curriculum of lay studies based on the authority of Giles of Rome's *De regimine principum*. The noble should first acquire the principles of grammar, logic and rhetoric, then move on to the study of ethics. Some Latin is expected, but the texts can be read in rough translations. The treatise closes with a eulogy of the *Cathoniana confectio*, a work whose style and content fulfil all the criteria previously set out.

Cartagena's distrust of eloquence is just one aspect of his conservatism in literary matters, and his attitudes brought him into direct conflict with his Italian humanist acquaintances. Leonardo Bruni's new translation of Aristotle's *Nicomachean Ethics* inspired from him a vigorous defence of the old version and the scholastic methodology that produced it (Birkenmajer, 'Der Streit', pp. 162–86). Although the Spaniard had many perceptive criticisms (which were mostly sidestepped in Bruni's reply), his main bone of contention was the apparent subordination of ethics to the claims of rhetoric. In this regard, he had no serious cause for debate with contemporary Castilian nobles, whose position may be summed up in the remark made by Santillana when faced by the prospect of reading Homer in a Castilian adaptation: 'If we lack form, let us be content with matter'.[27] Although they did not voice much theoretical interest in the relation between eloquence and wisdom, manuscripts of classical treatises have survived in increasing numbers from 1400 onwards: Santillana, for example, owned a copy of Cicero's *De oratore*. However, it has yet to be determined exactly how far this indicates a renewed and more sophisticated practical interest in the nature and function of rhetoric.[28]

[27] 'Si careçemos de las formas, seamos contentos con las materias'; *Obras completas*, p. 456. Though fifteenth-century theories of translation cannot be dealt with here, it is a fertile field: for an overview see Russell, *Traducciones y traductores*, and Recio, *La traducción*. For the ideas of Madrigal in his commentary on the *Chronici canones*, see Recio, 'Alfonso de Madrigal', and Ch. 14 above.

[28] See Faulhaber, *Latin Rhetorical Theory*, p. 9, and *Retóricas clásicas y medievales*, p. 159; also Di Camillo, *El humanismo castellano*, Ch. 2.

As mentioned above, increased literacy and political power combined to enhance the status of vernacular literature and the contemporary lay author. Further evidence for this is the large number of commentaries and glosses written in Castilian to accompany all kinds of work, both prose and verse, original compositions and translations of classical and patristic texts. This critical apparatus was used mainly to explain the text's literal level to the lay reader and to buttress it with a framework of *auctoritates*. An interesting feature of this trend are the commentaries and glosses added by the authors themselves. Their implicit function was to bolster the stature of the poet (as in the case of Santillana's glosses to his *Proverbios morales*, later extended into a full-scale commentary by Pero Díaz de Toledo, a cleric who frequently worked under this nobleman's patronage); or to use the commentary as a literary form, to develop the narrative potential of the mythical or historical allusions of the main text (e.g. don Pedro de Portugal's *Sátira de infelice e felice vida*). Some of these commentaries contain important critical or theoretical statements: obvious examples are Enrique de Villena's *Aeneid* commentary, Alfonso de Madrigal's Castilian version of his commentary on the *Chronici canones*, and Juan de Mena's commentary on his moral poem *La coronación del marqués de Santillana*.

The exegetical methods and literary attitudes of Villena and Madrigal have been discussed in a previous chapter (Chapter 14), in connection with European traditions of textual commentary. Here, it is important to note the national context of their work. First, with regard to their biblical commentaries, their methods and theoretical asides suggest traces of a polemic over the application of exegesis in the first half of the fifteenth century. Villena's emphasis on the literal interpretation of the sacred text, and his concomitant defence of Nicholas of Lyre (whose *Postillae* were in several contemporary noble libraries), set him apart from a figure such as Pablo de Santa María, a strict proponent of the allegorical method. Another hint of an underlying polemic is the fact that both Villena and Madrigal seemed in conflict with the Thomistic views of the popular Valencian preacher Vicente Ferrer, who wrote a sermon denouncing the application of the allegorical method to secular texts (Cátedra, *Exégesis*, pp. 29–43).

Although they wrote from different social perspectives and expressed contrasting views on many literary matters, Madrigal and Villena responded in a similarly positive fashion to the growth of lay literacy. Their commentaries on the *Aeneid* and the *Chronici canones* present more than information about specific texts: they also supply a literary education for the new lay reader and a justification for literacy. As explained above, Villena extols poetry as the sustenance for the noble mind, and the final goal for the cultured layman (in sharp contrast with Cartagena's sequence of studies incorporated in his Latin epistle; *Tratado*, p. 57). But in one striking passage of his *Aeneid* commentary, he also exalts the role of the exegete: explaining the function of the 'poetic veil', he writes that poets employ allegory to provide exegetes with *materia general* for multiple interpretations (ed. Cátedra, I, p. 76). The advanced reader acquires an autonomy and a status almost on a par with the original author. To this end Villena intersperses his commentary with guidance on how to read the text, explaining to 'el nuevo leedor' the intellectual processes by which the meanings of the poem can be extracted. Madrigal also responds to the specific needs of the lay reader, adapting his Latin commentary specifically to suit the abilities of the *romancistas*. He dedicates the work to Santillana as a 'llave' ('key') to all commentaries: a sort of encyclopaedic reference manual, including, rather like Boccaccio's *Genealogia* on which he frequently draws, a vast repository of antique myth to help the new class of readers decipher contemporary and classical texts (see Schiff, *La Bibliothèque*, p. 42).

The most important example of self-exegesis is Juan de Mena's *La coronación del marqués de Santillana* (1438). Originally entitled *Calamicleos*, it is an allegorical eulogy of the moral and political virtues of Santillana, the embodiment of the union of arms and letters (*Obras completas*, ed. Pérez Priego, pp. 105–208). In addition to adding a long commentary, Mena prefaced his poem with a prologue ('un exordio començual') which comprised an encomium of the dedicatee, and four brief *preámbulos* (pp. 105–9). Although it is not patterned explicitly or rigidly upon the *accessus*, an academic model underlies Mena's explanation of the poem's allegorical conceit, style and significance ('la invención, estilo e consecuencia'; p. 106). The first of the four *preámbulos* explains, by etymology, that the work's title *Calamicleos* means 'misery and glory', and that this juxtaposition is intended to highlight the contrast between virtue and vice. In the second, and following Benvenuto da Imola's commentary on Dante, Mena defines the three poetic 'maneras de escrevir' ('modes of writing'), tragedy, satire and comedy. For Mena, three factors make his poem a blend of comedy and satire: its humble style, its narrative progression from sadness to joy, and its criticism of vice and eulogy of virtue (pp. 107–8). Thirdly, Mena explains that his poem will describe how and why Santillana is crowned by the Nine Muses, and finally he clarifies the explanatory procedure adopted in his commentary (i.e. his use of Latin authorities, etymology, and allegorical exegesis of classical myth; pp. 108–9).

In part, Mena exploits his commentary to control the interpretation of his poem. Although he often expounds classical myths at the three levels of fiction, euhemeristic truth and moral application (*moralidad e aplicación*), he also carefully points out those tales which are included only to decorate and develop the narrative, without moral significance. Occasionally, his versions of the fables are themselves self-contained narratives. Mena does not comment on isolated figures of thought and speech: an interest in rhetoric is rare in vernacular commentaries before Hernán Núñez (see below). His primary artistic concern is to defend the appropriateness of his avant-garde poetic diction and to demonstrate the structural and thematic coherence of the narrative. On occasions, he also clarifies the structure of individual stanzas according to their syntactic or thematic units (just as Dante had done in his *Vita Nova* and *Convivio*, borrowing the scholastic technique of *divisio*).

One underlying goal of his commentary is to teach the lay reader by example how to understand the workings of allegory – a mode which, though new to vernacular verse, he considers central to the definition of true poetry (p. 155, where his authority is Isidore's *Etymologiae*). This pedagogic dimension is exemplified by his exhortation to the reader to cultivate an alert and reflective reading of allegory, in order fully to appreciate the poem's style and intentions (p. 145).

In short, the commentary allowed Mena to assume the role of teacher, as well as poet, and hence to stake a claim for the title of *poeta* or philosopher-poet. This self-image was further promoted by his most famous poem, *El laberinto de Fortuna* (1444), a complex moral and political allegory accompanied by explanatory glosses which elucidate the poem's Latinate vocabulary and historical and mythological allusions. Mena himself may have had a hand in their composition. But this apparatus also implicitly reinforces the notion that vernacular literature could be worthy of the kind of meditative study advocated by Villena and Mena himself. This implication is brought to the fore in two of these glossed manuscripts (the *Cancionero de Barrantes* and Paris, Bibliothèque nationale de France, fonds espagnol 229), in which the poem is also surrounded by commentaries.

The *Cancionero de Barrantes* (*c.* 1479) contains works by, amongst others, Santillana, Mena and Fernán Pérez de Guzmán, and to all their works the compiler added extensive notes, both in Latin and Castilian. The most extensive are those on *El laberinto* (Madrid, Biblioteca de Bartolomé March, MS 20–5–6, fols. 39r–68v). In his preface, the commentator elucidates the etymology of the poem's title in order to clarify Mena's intentions. It means 'trabajo de dentro' (or 'inner toil', derived from *laborintus*), which indicates that the poem is an almost encyclopaedic compilation of wisdom (fol. 39r). He then compares his annotation to a thread which guides the reader around the poem's labyrinthine intellectual intricacies. In the commentary itself, he buttresses the text with a framework of medieval authorities, such as Alfonso X's *General estoria*, scholastic jurists, and Isidore's *Etymologiae*, whose account of the alphabet (fol. 51r–v) and metre (fols. 57v–8r) are adapted almost verbatim.

An insight into the way he conceived his role is afforded by his treat-ment of the poem's cosmographical section (sts. 34–62). Calling himself 'copilador' and his notes 'adiciones', he incorporates passages from the *Imago mundi* (attributed to Anselm) in order to describe lands not men-tioned by Mena. In other words, he works not as the author's subordinate, but rather in tandem with him, so as to create a fuller cosmographical compilation.

The commentator of the Paris manuscript inhabited quite a different intellectual world. Probably writing in the last third of the century for the Aragonese court in Naples, his authorities are classical rather than medieval. But not only does he simply explain passages by pertinent ana-logues from Virgil's *Aeneid*, Ovid's *Metamorphoses* and Lucan's *Pharsalia* (*De bello civili*); more significantly, he also suggests that *El laberinto* was in large measure a conscious *imitatio* of this classical triumvirate. In cer-tain respects he was correct, and he identified Mena's imitation of Lucan to a hitherto unnoticed extent, thus anticipating the more widely acknowl-edged work of the humanist Hernán Núñez (see below). He also antic-ipates Núñez in his occasional references to textual variants, although there is no comprehensive attempt at textual criticism as there is in the commentary of the humanist editor.

The history of vernacular literary criticism in medieval Castile closes with the work of three crucial figures. Antonio de Nebrija (1441–1522) was widely famed as the man who 'banished barbarity' from the shores of Spain ('el debelador de la barbarie'). Not only did he revolutionise the study of Latin in university circles, his grammars, dictionaries and com-mentaries on the Christian poets Sedulius, Prudentius and Persius were the pillars of early Spanish Renaissance humanism, in both its classical and Christian dimensions. Though less of a self-publicist, Hernán Núñez (1477–1550) was no less important in advancing the cause of the classical *studia humanitatis*. His strength was textual criticism, and his editions of Greek and Latin authors are still considered major contributions to European scholarship. The classical and biblical commentaries and edi-tions of these two men must be seen in the full context of Renaissance literary criticism and cannot be adequately treated here. Nonetheless, as humanists with a strong pride in their nation's new political identity, part of their endeavour was to show how their native vernacular literature could be worthy of the triumphant new regime of Ferdinand and Isabella. In this they were joined by the versatile poet, dramatist and musician Juan del Encina (1468–1529). Though not a humanist scholar, he was influenced by his Salamanca University background and his acquaintance with Nebrija. His treatise on Castilian poetry is a major attempt to capture contemporary poetic ideals and hand them on to a new age.

The prologue to Nebrija's *Gramática de la lengua castellana*, the first humanist vernacular grammar, and written in the *annus mirabilis* of 1492, sets forth the seminal concept of language as 'compañera del imperio', according to which the fate of a language hangs upon the rise and fall of a nation's political power. Arguing that Castilian had reached a peak of perfection under the new regime of the Catholic Monarchs, and that the future could bring only linguistic decay, Nebrija proposed to standardise Castilian and give it the same advantages as Greek and Latin, which survived over the centuries 'through having been subject to the rules of art' ('por aver estado debaxo de arte'; p. 101). By fixing his own language in the same way, Nebrija hoped to fulfil a number of patriotic goals. Not the least of these was to ensure the preservation of the literature of his time. Although he avoids any detailed discussion of the matter, there are no surprises as to the kinds of writing he thought most worthy of protection. Like Cartagena before him, he attaches considerable importance to vernacular chronicles and denigrates his compatriots' fondness for the *mendacia poetarum* (pp. 100–1).

Divided into five books, the treatise covers the rudiments of orthography, prosody, morphology, syntax and concludes with an introduction to Castilian for the benefit of non-native speakers. The second book, on prosody, constitutes a brief metrical treatise, containing Nebrija's most important statements on vernacular poetry and aesthetics. Beginning with a definition of the syllable, he explains that Castilian lacks the quantitative metrical system found in Greek, Latin and (following the customary authority of Origen, Eusebius, Jerome and Josephus) biblical Hebrew. This point leads into a discussion of the rules of Castilian accentuation (Chs. 2–5), which is the basis of the vernacular metrical system (Ch. 5). He next describes the principles of Castilian rhyme (Ch. 6), and, after commenting on the nature of elision (Ch. 7), he devotes the following two chapters to the six kinds of verse sanctioned by correct Castilian usage. Finally, he defines the *copla* and offers a few observations on the main strophic forms of Castilian poetry (Ch. 10).

The significance and originality of Nebrija's exposition lie in a number of factors. Of obvious note is the consistent use of the poetry of Juan de Mena (*El laberinto*, and to a lesser extent *La coronación*) to exemplify the metrical principles under discussion. In spite of Nebrija's apparent reservations over some aspects of Mena's classicising verse, the attention he gave to this poet was clearly influential in cementing his status as a national classic. Also significant is the comparative method adopted throughout the four main books of the treatise. Both the characteristics and the terminology of Castilian grammar are compared with those of Greek and Latin. This is the source of what has often been considered as the main theoretical weakness of Nebrija's analysis of Castilian prosody. Though he states on several occasions that the vernacular cannot accommodate the classical quantitative system, he nevertheless persists in applying classical metrical patterns to Castilian verse with forced and occasionally confused results. Clearly, one of the motives that underlie this procedure is the desire to elevate the status of the vernacular. For although he recognises the autonomy of Castilian which, like the classical languages, has its own strengths and weaknesses, he evidently believes that it acquires greater dignity by being set within a classical context. Another factor, to which scholars have not given due credit, is his prefatory claim that the treatise will be an indispensable guide to the study of Latin (p. 101). Thus, his metrical instruction paves the way for the study of both Latin and Castilian verse. Nebrija himself draws attention to the surge of interest in classical metres elsewhere in Europe: his efforts, he hopes, will enable his compatriots to participate in this current revival (p. 135).

Nebrija's perspective on metre was no doubt influenced by aesthetic preferences and not just by pedagogical goals. Much of this book (and indeed the whole treatise) is pervaded by a sense of dissatisfaction with the practices of *nuestros poetas*. However, this surfaces most clearly in the chapter on rhyme, where he associates the loss of the quantitative metrical system with the decay of *las buenas artes*. The early composers of Latin hymns, whose art consisted of mere syllable-count and the devising of rhymes, perpetrated an 'error' which, he alleges, modern vernacular poets eagerly transformed into an aesthetic virtue (p. 146). He backs up this observation with criticism firmly grounded in contemporary literary reality. While he admits that *similiter cadens* is a legitimate rhetorical colour, he finds the current emphasis on rhyme tedious and obtrusive, and he castigates modern poets for using it to conceal a poverty of intellectual content (pp. 146–7). Nebrija's barbs are clearly aimed at late-fifteenth-century lyric, which relied for much of its effect on the virtuosity of rhyme and the narrowness of its abstract vocabulary. His ill-concealed distaste anticipates by a couple of decades the equally negative, but much better known opinions of Boscán and Garcilaso, the two Renaissance poets responsible for introducing Italianate metres to Castilian verse and liberating it, in their view at least, from the dominance of rhyme.

By contrast, one aspect of contemporary aesthetics did not draw Nebrija's criticism, and it is enshrined in his definition of the *copla* ('stanza') as 'a binding together of lines which enclose a notable concept' ('un rodeo e aiuntamiento de versos en que se coge alguna notable sentencia'; p. 158). The fact that this notion stretches back though Occitan poetics to Antiquity enabled the humanist to stamp his approval upon the sententious and 'witty' verse cultivated in the courts of late-medieval

Castile. Nebrija himself may not have found much to enjoy in the reality of *cancionero* verse, but this definition recognises and endorses one of its essential ideals.

Prefixed as a prologue to the first printed edition of his work (1496), Juan del Encina's *Arte de poesía castellana* is made up of nine chapters (*Las poéticas castellanas*, pp. 67–93). The first is an introductory statement of goals and a eulogy of poetry (especially Castilian verse). The eulogy carries implicitly through Chapters 2–4, which contain general observations about the ideal poet and the nature of the art. Technical aspects of composition are treated in the next four chapters, and the ninth closes with a few significant remarks on the punctuation and the reading of printed verse-texts.

Like Nebrija's prologue to his Castilian grammar, by which Encina was deeply inspired, the initial chapter of *El arte* projects a sense of a culture in movement. With the new political stability imposed by the Catholic Monarchs, Encina considered the time ripe for a treatise devoted to poetry, one of the supreme 'arts of peace'. Adapting Nebrija's dictum about the rise of the Castilian language, he asserts that the native poetic tradition had also touched perfection, at least with regard to technique. This boast is inspired in part by the sheer abundance and technical polish of *cancionero* verse; but like the later claim that poetry flourishes in Spain more than elsewhere in Europe, it is also coloured by the eulogistic aims of the introduction and the author's teleological concept of national history.

Aware that his treatise shared common ground with Nebrija's *Gramática*, Encina carefully stressed his own peculiar goals: to treat only what was relevant to Castilian, and to publicise the dignity of poetry. This eulogistic aim may account for the brevity of the purely technical sections (Chs. 5–8). Rather than give detailed account of the precepts, he describes only the main points to support the notion (treated in Ch. 2) that poetry was indeed an art, requiring natural talent, training and thoughtful deliberation. Thus, Encina hoped to teach aspiring poets not just how to write verse, but, equally importantly, poetic discrimination. Chastising those who learned their craft by careless imitation of what they had merely heard (p. 84), he goes on to make the critical appreciation of poetry – in all the finer points of its written form – an essential element in the formation of the ideal poet (p. 85); and it is this concern that underlies his concluding advice on how to interpret the printed page.

The opening praise of poetry draws on well-known arguments: for example, the dignity of human speech (here taken from Cicero, *De oratore* 1.8); Jerome's concept of biblical poetics; the hackneyed claim that art is innocent of the abuses of its practitioners. Most of these had already been used – and with greater rhetorical effect – by Santillana. Contemporary cultural and political developments, however, invest several of these old topoi with new life. This is true of the claim (supported by classical and biblical examples) that the three principal effects of poetry were to inspire men to religious devotion and, when appropriate, to both peace and war. The relevance of this idea to a regime flushed with military success and crusading zeal hardly needs to be stressed. A similar attempt to adapt the commonplace to the contemporary is his handling of the concept of *translatio studii*, which he incorporates into his eulogy to strengthen his defence of the historical authority of verse. In writing that Spain inherited the art directly from Italy (and ultimately from the Bible) he must have been aware that he was overlooking the contribution of other nations to his native tradition. In comparison with Santillana, his simplification of history was governed by a more obvious patriotic – and almost oedipal – motive: to prove that, as the leading exponent of the art, Spain had overtaken Italy, the country that had produced those two great 'modern classics', Dante and Petrarch, and was currently inspiring a good deal of his own country's humanistic endeavours.

That poetry possessed the status of an art was essential to its defence: this point and its implications are dealt with in Chapters 2–4 of *El arte*, in which Encina emphasises that although poetry, like rhetoric, aims to persuade and soothe the ear ('persuadir y demulcir el oýdo') it is ultimately a rational art (p. 83). Adapting Boethian notions of the superiority of theoretical over practical knowledge and of reason over the senses (*De musica* 1.1), he distinguishes between the poet and the troubadour: the former commands the theoretical essence of the art, the latter is a mere artisan. From this premise, he invokes Quintilian to support the value of cultivating natural talent by close and critical study of the works of recognised authors. It is therefore interesting that, apart from drawing examples from the work of Juan de Mena, Encina should include extracts from his own verse to illustrate certain rhetorical tropes (Ch. 8), reminding us that the treatise served as a prologue to his own *cancionero* and, as such, was designed to publicise the talents of its author.

In spite of its brevity, Encina's treatment of Castilian versification is enlivened by a number of critical asides which present a coherent aesthetic outlook and establish him as an eloquent spokesman for contemporary poetic taste. They are also further evidence of the fact that, although he covers some of the same ground as Nebrija, he writes from an independent perspective. Perhaps the best example is his approach to the process of poetic composition. Pointing to the etymology of *trobar* (which he derives, characteristically, from the Italian), he makes *inventio* central to the act of poetic creation. To compose in verse means finding the right words and metrical form in which to 'enclose' ('encerrar') an idea, and spicing it judiciously with rhetorical *galas* (pp. 82, 91–2). Although Nebrija and others had made similar points, Encina, as a practising poet and musician, gives the idea far greater prominence. For example, he adopts radically different views about one basic aspect of this process – rhyme – and goes beyond the humanist in his assessment of its aesthetic effect. He acknowledges that rhyme was not sanctioned by antiquity, but finds it justified on two counts: its use by the Christian poets, and its power to communicate thought. For Encina, a poem's very force and meaning resides in the combination itself of words and sounds, since this combination imparts to the memory an 'image' (*semejança*) of the past (p. 82). Although he may be reworking certain grammatical theories about the ideal correspondence between sounds, letters, things and mental concepts (e.g. Nebrija's *De vi ac potestate litterarum*, Ch. 1 [1503]), his formulation is more novel than has previously been supposed. The new twist he gives to old views about the mnemonic function of verse suggests that he is conscious of the unity of poetic form and content in a way that was rare in Castilian utterances on the subject.

Overall, Encina's emphasis on *ocio* (especially in Ch. 1) indicates how, in spite of his emphasis on its speculative aspects, he viewed the writing of poetry as an activity for relaxation, the mark of the well-bred courtier. Thus from a different cultural perspective and with new authorities, he revised and kept alive an attitude that was popularised earlier in the century by Baena and which received its most eloquent formulation in Castiglione's *Il Cortegiano*, soon to be translated by Boscán for the benefit of the next generation of Castilian nobles. It was up to Hernán Núñez to publicise the weightier, more philosophical achievements of the native poetic tradition.

The fondness for adding commentaries and glosses to vernacular texts culminated in the publication, in 1499, of the first critical edition of Juan de Mena's *Laberinto de Fortuna*, in which Hernán Núñez endowed the poem with an *accessus* and a long and erudite commentary. The second, revised, edition (1505) became a sixteenth-century bestseller, under the title *Las trezientas del famosíssimo poeta Juan de Mena con glosa*, and made the poem central to the canon of Spanish classics. A 'moral epic' espousing the cause of national unity, it possessed, as Núñez observed in a decidedly double-edged compliment, formal and philosophical qualities that were remarkable given the unenlightened age in which it was composed. No other Castilian work, he enthused, matches its eloquence, all-embracing wisdom, abundant aphorisms, and wealth of myths and legends (1499, fol. 2v). It was proof enough of poetry's educational value which, citing the Greek geographer Strabo, he described later in his commentary (gloss on st. 123).

In part, Núñez considered his task to be a salvage operation. He hoped to rescue the poem from the obscurity caused by the 'crass ignorance' of recent publishers and their compositors, and (paralleling Nebrija's interest in local antiquities) he tried to restore a literary monument for the edification of a broad reading public. His twin goals of restoration and dissemination are neatly summarised by his play upon the architectural metaphor prompted by the title of the poem itself. Like the Barrantes commentator (see above), Núñez believed that the work's title alluded to its complexities of form and content; yet unlike him, the humanist did not remain simply an admiring guide, leading his readers through this awesome labyrinth. In restoring the edifice, he rebuilt it, turning it into 'a clear and open amphitheatre, into which both learned and unlearned may pass without fear' (1499, fol. 2v).

For the second edition, Núñez made various changes to the text and commentary. Aiming more directly at the unlearned, he did away with practically all the Latin quotations, and discarded as irrelevant the formal *accessus* tacked on the end of the earlier prologue. These changes indicate that he had formed a clearer picture of his intended reading public; but, together with other evidence, they show how although his esteem for the poem had not diminished, his attitude towards expounding a vernacular classic had become, as it were, less reverent (see below). The lay readers whom Núñez addressed would already have been familiar with his basic approach: he glosses obscure vocabulary, paraphrases difficult syntax, dwells on the moral significance of key passages, and offers discursive explanations of the many historical, geographical and mythological references. They would have been less familiar, however, with his concern for textual emendation and the occasional, but fascinating, passages of an evaluative nature. The latter aspect was encountered very rarely in previous Castilian commentaries, and the former not at all.

Núñez's admiration for the poem's merits may be classified under two heads: literary decorum, or *propriedad*, and imitation. Like Mena himself in his *Coronación* commentary, Núñez drew attention to the apt choice of vocabulary and to the logical structuring of episodes. But – and this is a new feature in the native tradition – he was particularly struck by the appropriateness of Mena's metaphors and similes. Indeed, he claimed that Mena's skill in poetic comparison put him on a par with 'los más excelentes latinos' (1505, fol. 90v). These three levels of *propriedad* (diction, structure and metaphor) laid the basis for the power of Mena's literary depiction, and were also a source of elegant wit ('gracia y sal'; 1505, fol. 127r). Núñez believed that the epitome of Mena's skill in writing 'propriamente' was the description of the death of Lorenzo d'Avalos and his mother's lament (sts. 201–7), a scene that comes to life before the readers' eyes and hence silences all commentary (1505, fol. 99v).

Throughout, Núñez identifies examples of Mena's 'youthful fervour' (1499, fol. 4v) in imitating poets from Antiquity, mainly the Latin epic poets Virgil, Statius, Ovid and, most consistently of all, 'our Lucan' (following the common practice of claiming Spanish nationality for the Iberian writers of the Roman Empire). Mena's imitation was largely, he thinks, a question of subject-matter and wording. But he also took pains to show how style and form, especially the exploitation of poetic licence and certain rhetorical devices, owed a general debt to the ancients. Although he brings out the poem's classical dimension (often in ways that Mena would not have recognised), he does not ignore medieval Latin sources, principally Pseudo-Anselm's *De imago mundi* and, to a lesser extent, Isidore's *Etymologiae*. Although some of his points had been anticipated by the anonymous commentators of the Paris and Barrantes manuscripts, he was the first to set *El laberinto* within a balanced framework of classical and medieval Latin authorities, and thus to present the poem both as a philosophical compendium as well as a celebration of national heroes modelled along classical lines.

This fact alone, however, would not do justice to the novelty and significance of Núñez's treatment of sources. He did not investigate them just to lend authority to the text and place it within its supposed intellectual tradition: he also used Lucan and Pseudo-Anselm to restore readings garbled by previous scribes and compositors. Equally important, though for different reasons, is his critical approach. The Paris commentator had already pounced on a few of Mena's historical and geographical errors. Núñez, on the other hand, when he does not put them down to poetic licence, attributes them not to Mena's personal ignorance but to his reliance on inadequate sources. For the most part, this entails a critique of Anselm, whom he regards as a dubious authority on cosmographical matters. In one minor but telling detail, however, he suggests that Mena was misled by a corrupt manuscript of Lucan, which illustrates the new philological concerns that Núñez was keen to advertise. This judicious combination of criticism and praise is crucial to our understanding of the commentary, since it points to the changing style of 'reverent exposition' that began to develop throughout late-medieval Europe. On the one hand, Núñez exonerates Mena from direct responsibility for errors of erudition, and thus goes some way towards protecting the classical status of the vernacular poet. But he also shows how, in matters of learning at least, the times were changing: Anselm ('un escritor proletario') is less authoritative than the classical geographers Strabo, Pliny and Pomponius Mela, whom Núñez himself would later teach and edit. In short, he leaves the reader in no doubt that although Mena should be afforded respect, this should be tempered by an awareness that this particular classic, indeed classics in general, were not infallible. Ultimately, Núñez's project was to prove that although Mena often rose above the intellectual limitations of his age, he was, in the final instance, hemmed in by corrupt manuscripts and a reliance on authorities who did not belong to the canon of the new age of humanism.

18

Literary criticism in Middle High German literature

Nigel F. Palmer

Among German poets of the early thirteenth century there emerges a new literary self-consciousness which manifests itself in references to the author's own person in the body of his poem and in allusions to other writers and their work.[1]

Such references to other poets may be implicit. That is the case, for example, when the narrator in Wolfram von Eschenbach's *Parzival* (*c.* 1210) claims in 436, 4ff.[2] that Sigune's love for the dead knight Schionatulander was such that, if the couple had been married, lady Lunete (a character in Hartmann von Aue's *Iwein, c.* 1200) would have been more reticent in advising Sigune to remarry than she was towards her bereaved mistress Laudine. The critical comment on the behaviour of Lunete, who presses her mistress to remarry on the very day of her husband's death, remains at the level of a playful critique of a character in another poem (as distinct, say, from being a comment on Hartmann's character motivation). By the contrast between his own characters' behaviour and that attributed to the characters of another fictional work Wolfram's narrator claims a special seriousness for the qualities of *triwe* ('fidelity') and *minne* ('love') displayed by Sigune (and later also by the hero Parzival); he marks out the divide between the values of his own literary world and those of 'traditional' Arthurian romance. At the same time the author establishes a relationship between the ethical constructs of his literary fiction and the real world, the world in which the composition and reception of *Iwein* and *Parzival* is to be situated.

Wolfram's narrator makes numerous explicit references to other poets, as for example when in *Parzival* (404,28–30), instead of describing the qualities of the lovely queen Antikonie, he regrets the passing of Heinrich von Veldeke (*Eneide, c.* 1170–85), who could have written a better description of her. There is a comparable, but slightly more elaborate, passage

---

[1] These are conveniently collected together in the anthology by Schweikle, *Dichter über Dichter*. On the concepts of authorship and intertextuality in Middle High German literature, see Coxon, *Presentation of Authorship*, and Draesner, *Wege durch erzählte Welten*, both of which were written after the present study was conceived.

[2] For Wolfram's *Parzival* and *Willehalm*, numeration refers initially to the *Dreissiger* or thirty-line unit and then to the line within the unit.

in Wolfram's *Willehalm* (*c.* 1220) where, having alluded to the exceptionally splendid appearance of the heathen knights Tenebruns and Arofel,
the narrator declares that if it had been expected of him that he should
describe them he would have been obliged to lament his *meister von*
Veldekîn (i.e. Heinrich von Veldeke), who could have done the job so
much better (*Willehalm*, 76,22–9). The function of such allusions is not
to provide objective assessments of the work of other authors or to comment on their handling of plot and character-motivation, but rather self-
referential, to establish the poet's own text as a literary artefact which
itself forms part of the literature to which the works cited belong, to create a bond between himself and an audience to whom these other works
are familiar. In the case of Wolfram's Veldeke citations the reference to the
work of another author occurs at a point in the text where, by the conventions of late-twelfth-century poetics, a rhetorically elaborated description
might have been expected, and so in a sense one kind of self-consciously
artificial literary discourse (the literary allusion) stands in lieu of another
(the *descriptio*).

The sense of writing within a German vernacular literary tradition,
by no means a self-evident authorial position, gives rise to the literary
excursus, the review of canonical authors in relation to whom the author
implicitly or explicitly places himself. The first is that of Gottfried von
Strassburg (*Tristan*, ll. 4621–820), written in south-west Germany *c.* 1210;
the second that of Heinrich von dem Türlin in his romance *Diu Crône*
(Austrian, *c.* 1220). The Swabian author Rudolf von Ems includes literary
reviews in his *Alexander* (written *c.* 1230 onwards) and in his *Willehalm*
von Orlens (*c.* 1240). The later writers are heavily indebted to Gottfried,
although the use they make of the literary review is different. Gottfried's
literary review is of particular importance here, as it is the first piece
of extended 'literary criticism' in a European vernacular. The genre of
the 'literary review' is taken much further here than, for example, in Peire
d'Alvernhe's playful presentation of the troubadours in his poem *Cantarai*
d'agestz trobadors (cf. p. 475 above).[3] The similarity between Gottfried's
literary review and the medieval tradition of catalogues of authors and
literary texts, which are sometimes contained in literary works or cast in
poetic form, is at most superficial.[4]

The literary review in *Tristan* forms the first part of an excursus which
Gottfried integrates into his poem in lieu of a description of the knightly

---

[3] Ed. Del Monte, no. XII. See Pattison, 'Background'; Gaunt, *Troubadours*, pp. 119ff.

[4] See, for example, the versified list of Latin school authors in: Hugo von Trimberg, *Reg-*
istrum multorum auctorum and *Der Renner*, ll. 1179–308; Eneas Silvius' *Epistola ad*
Ladislaum Posthumum (1450) with a critique of Latin texts suitable for reading by
young people; the catalogues of books contained in the *Ehrenbrief* of Jakob Pütrich von
Reichertshausen (1462); the Old Norse *Allra kappa kvæði* in thirteen strophes with a
catalogue of literary themes (*c.* 1500).

costume and equipment prepared for Tristan's investiture.[5] Although it contains the most sophisticated discussion of vernacular writers to have survived from the period, this passage does not yet provide evidence of vernacular 'literary criticism' as an institutionalised form of writing, with its own specific traditions and conventions: it forms part of a programme specific to the *Tristan* poem, whereby the literary claims for a new and exceptional poetic composition are shown to be analogous to the singularity of the hero Tristan – and by implication analogous to the exceptional love experienced by Tristan and Isolde.

Tristan's excellence and singularity, which only at a later stage in the poem will be made manifest in the excellence of his love, is a central theme. The young prince has a remarkable childhood, being brought up ignorant of his true identity by foster parents, then kidnapped by pirates and adopted as favourite minstrel and huntsman at the Cornish court. The moment when he is at once identified as the child of Riwalin and heir to Parmenie, reunited with his guardian Rual, and then integrated into this court society through knightly investiture, is of great potential and significance for him. Tristan is to be knighted along with thirty companions, whom he surpasses in excellence. Faced with the task of describing the clothing and equipment of Tristan's companions the author playfully claims that he must restrict himself to the material in his source, and he offers not a *descriptio* but an allegorical account of how the clothes were tailored through the interplay of four specifically courtly values: *hoher muot* ('lofty aspirations'), *vollez guot* ('wealth and riches'), *bescheidenheit* ('discernment') and *höfischer sin* ('courtly disposition'). This vocabulary harks back to that used to describe the agreement of will and wealth established between Tristan and his uncle King Marke (ll. 4402–88), and then between Tristan and Rual (ll. 4500–49), but it is also the vocabulary of literary metaphor – tailoring, *sin*, *bescheidenheit* – and leads into the literary review.

Having described the companions fittingly ('mit bescheidenlicher richeit'; l. 4590) Gottfried turns his attention to how Tristan can be prepared for the ceremony so that it will please the listener and be found fitting in his story. He regrets that he cannot do this, for his contemporaries and predecessors have been so adept in their *descriptiones* that, if his is to be the most excellent description of all, then he does not know how to begin; the theme of knightly splendour has become so hackneyed and commonplace ('mit rede also zetriben', l. 4618; 'so worn down with

5 See Chinca, *Gottfried von Strassburg*, pp. 58ff.; Chinca and Young, 'Literary Theory', pp. 639–44; Fromm, 'Tristans Schwertleite'; Hahn, 'Literaturschau'; Huber, *Gottfried von Straßburg*, pp. 61–5; Kellner, 'Autorität und Gedächtnis'; Schulze, 'Literarkritische Äusserungen'; Stein, 'Tristans Schwertleite'. Quotations and line-numbering follow Ranke's edition.

words') that no pleasure can now be derived from such a description. Whereupon Gottfried makes an abrupt break and begins the excursus, which opens with the literary review: 'Oh, how Hartmann von Aue dyes and ornaments his tales through and through, externally and internally, with words and meanings . . .'. The excursus, of which the literary review forms the first half, stands in lieu of the *descriptio*. It is a comparable, but much more elaborate, gesture to that whereby the author avoided a description of Tristan's companions' equipment. He moves from the making of clothes for literary characters to the making of literature, from a claim for Tristan's excellence (for Tristan surpasses his companions and all literary figures hitherto described in German literature) to a claim for his own literary excellence, which in turn reflects back on the subject-matter of his story. Discussion of the literary review has often neglected to consider its function in Gottfried's narrative, and the association between the literary aesthetic and the special qualities of the love of Tristan and Isolde has rarely been noted.

Gottfried's claim that a certain mode of literary discourse had become hackneyed has been described as a landmark in the development of the perception of literary language in the Middle Ages.[6] Having characterised the literary art of those authors whose works he admires and would wish to emulate Gottfried objectivises the literary achievement for which he himself is aiming. He sees this not as a literary creation to be judged simply on its own merits by the reader but rather to be read in the context of a German literary tradition:

> man sprichet nu so rehte wol,
> daz ich von grozem rehte sol
> miner worte nemen war
> und sehen, dazs also sin gevar,
> als ich wolte, daz si wæren
> an vremeder liute mæren
> und alse ich rede geprüeven kan
> an einem anderen man.

(ll. 4845–52)

[Such fine poetry is being written at the moment that I am truly justified in taking a look at my own literary composition to see if it has the quality that I would wish such writing to have in the work of other writers and to subject it to the same judgement that I would bring to bear on another man's work.]

---

[6] By Fromm, 'Tristans Schwertleite', p. 341, who suggests that Gottfried's theoretical position presupposes Aristotelian views of language and Abelard's redefinition of the relationship between *vox* and *res*. See also Fromm, 'Gottfried und Abaelard'; Stein, 'Tristans Schwertleite', p. 322. Okken, *Kommentar*, I, pp. 227–8, compares Virgil's *Georgics* 3.3, 'cetera quae vacuas tenuissent carmine mentes, / omnia iam volgata' ('the remaining themes, which might otherwise have captivated carefree minds, have now become all too commonplace').

At the beginning of the second part of the excursus Gottfried restates his position. Faced with so many and such eloquent exponents of the art of poetry as those whom he has mentioned in the literary review he finds himself tongue-tied. He pins his hopes of holding his own among the writers of German literature on a prayer for divine inspiration to Mount Helicon, where Apollo holds his court, and to the Nine Muses. In the literary review each of the authors considered had been presented as a quasi-classical poet or endowed with gifts of classical/mythological origin: Hartmann the winner of the competition for the laurel wreath, Bligger von Steinach's work purified in a fairy spring, Veldeke's wisdom drawn from the fountain of the Muses ('uz Pegases uzspringe'; l. 4731), the nightingale of Hagenau inspired by Orpheus, Walther von der Vogelweide by Venus herself. Now Gottfried appeals to *der ware Elicon* ('the true Helicon') the very fountainhead of all Christian and classical eloquence,[7] and is endowed with the gifts of 'words and meaning' ('der worte unde der sinne'; l. 4869) by the Muses so that his 'tongue and creative talent' ('beidiu zungen unde sin'; l. 4887) may have free rein. What follows is an elaborate exercise in hyperbole. It is argued that if Gottfried were to exercise all his skill to describe how Tristan's armour and clothing were fabricated by Vulcan and Cassandra (with an elaborate account of what they might achieve), then the result would be no more splendid than the handicraft of the four allegorical tailors of Tristan's companions' clothes. And yet Tristan, when decked out in these clothes, which make him outwardly identical to his companions, remains vastly superior through his inborn qualities, which manifest themselves in manners and deportment. If Gottfried claims to surpass the literary models he admires, then he does so implicitly on the basis of the analogy between Tristan's ultimate superiority over his companions and the superiority of his own literary demonstration of Tristan's excellence over the descriptions of writers such as Hartmann and Veldeke. That superiority, according to Gottfried's literary theory, is not simply a matter of greater skill, but also of 'standing higher' and coming later in the literary tradition.

An additional, but essential, dimension to the interrelationship between Gottfried's discussion of literature and his presentation of narrative can be seen if the literary excursus is understood in its relationship to the cave-of-love episode, which occurs much later in the romance, and to the allegory of love presented there.[8] It is not simply that terms we will see Gottfried employ to define his literary ideal (such as crystalline purity, translucence and lack of deviousness) are there attributed to love, but there exists a whole set of parallels between the way Tristan and Isolde's love is described – with its connection to music, the celebration of the

---

[7] Kolb, 'Der ware Elicon'; Stein, 'Tristans Schwertleite', pp. 325ff.
[8] See Grundlehner, 'Gottfried von Strassburg'.

tales of classical lovers, its verdant natural setting, its exclusivity – and his programmatic statements about literature. This suggests that it was Gottfried's intention to establish a meaningful analogy between the nature of true love and the aesthetics of his literary discourse.

Gottfried's literary review begins with a discussion of Hartmann von Aue (ll. 4621–90), Bligger von Steinach (ll. 4691–722) and Heinrich von Veldeke (ll. 4723–50), and continues with an appraisal of the principal *Minnesänger* (ll. 4751–820).[9]

The section devoted to Hartmann consists of a passage in praise of his literary techniques and their effect upon an audience. Hartmann is then contrasted with an unnamed rival for the laurel wreath, *des hasen geselle* ('the companion of the hare'; l. 4638). The passage is usually taken as a reference to Wolfram von Eschenbach.[10] Hartmann's special quality is the intricacy with which the words and meanings are united so as to achieve the translucence of *cristalliniu wortelin*, whilst at the same time expressing the underlying meaning of the story:

> ahi, wie der diu mære
> beid uzen unde innen
> mit worten und mit sinnen
> durchverwet und durchzieret!
> wie er mit rede figieret
> der aventiure meine!
> wie luter und wie reine
> siniu cristallinen wortelin
> beidiu sint und iemer müezen sin!

> (ll. 4622–30)

[Oh, how he dyes and ornaments his tales through and through, externally and internally, with words and meanings! How he captures the meaning of the story through his use of language! How transparent and pure his crystal-clear words are and shall ever be.]

The literary ideal formulated in Gottfried's praise of Hartmann is indebted to the contemporary Latin rhetorical doctrine of *colorare intus et exterius* ('to colour inwardly and outwardly') which is first formulated by Geoffrey of Vinsauf in ll. 742ff. of the *Poetria nova* (generally dated *c.* 1200–15), that is to say painting or dying the literary subject-matter with verbal

---

9 Müller, *Literarische Kritik*, pp. 4–10; Jackson, 'Literary Views'; Haug, '*Der aventiure meine*'; Müller-Kleimann, *Gottfrieds Urteil*; Okken, *Kommentar*, I, pp. 235–67; Nellmann, 'Wolfram und Kyot'. See also the studies listed in note 4 above; for further literature see Steinhoff, *Bibliographie*, I, pp. 75ff.; II, pp. 162–4; Huber, 'Bibliographie zum *Tristan*' (index, under 'Literaturexkurs').

10 Nellmann, 'Wolfram und Kyot'; Hoffmann, '*Vindaere wildere maere*'.

ornaments (*wort*) and enriching it with inner meaning (*sin*, Latin *sensus*).[11] This is combined with a stylistic ideal of *perspicuitas* ('transparency'), which is a specific feature of Quintilian's doctrine of *elocutio*, but not of the medieval rhetorical tradition.[12] Those who write in the manner of Hartmann's rival, the *vindære wilder mære* ('inventors of wild tales'), are chided for writing in a manner so opaque that they have to send out interpreters to explain the meaning of what they have written:

> die selben wildenære
> si müezen tiutære
> mit ir mæren lazen gan:
> wirn mugen ir da nach niht verstan,
> als man si hoeret unde siht;
> son han wir ouch der muoze niht,
> daz wir die glose suochen
> in den swarzen buochen.

(ll. 4683–90)

[These trap-setters have to send out interpreters with their work. We cannot understand it just by hearing it and reading it, and yet we are not men of such leisure as to be able to seek out the gloss in the handbooks of necromancy.]

These statements amount to a clear commitment to Gottfried's fundamental literary principle of the congruence of the literary form and the underlying meaning.[13]

Gottfried places particular emphasis on audience response to Hartmann's work when he writes of the *cristalliniu wortelin*:

> si koment den man mit siten an,
> si tuont sich nahen zuo dem man
> und liebent rehtem muote.
> swer guote rede ze guote
> und ouch ze rehte kan verstan,
> der muoz dem Ouwære lan
> sin schapel und sin lorzwi.

(ll. 4631–7)

---

[11] Nellmann, 'Wolfram und Kyot', pp. 34–43. See further Sawicki, *Poetik*, p. 57. Some writers have held that the duality of words and meaning is indebted to the distinction between the *sensus litteralis* and *sensus spiritualis* in biblical hermeneutics; see Ohly, 'Vom geistigen Sinn des Wortes', p. 19. Nellmann, 'Wolfram und Kyot', p. 41, argues that the *sensus litteralis* cannot be compared with verbal ornament imposed on literary material. See also Huber, 'Wort-Ding-Entsprechungen', pp. 284–90; Chinca, *History*, p. 77.

[12] Sawicki, *Poetik*, p. 58; Nellmann, 'Wolfram und Kyot', pp. 43ff. For the medieval aesthetic ideals of clarity and translucence see De Bruyne, *Études*, III, pp. 3–29 ('L'esthétique de la lumière').

[13] On *wort* and *sin* see Huber, 'Wort-Ding-Entsprechungen'; Haug, *Vernacular Literary Theory*, pp. 213–17 (German edn, pp. 214–18).

[They approach you with decorum, they sidle up to you and delight the just heart. The man who has a good and just understanding of good poetry will not begrudge Hartmann von Aue his crown and his laurels.]

His criticism of Hartmann's rivals is couched in similarly audience-orientated terms:

> die bernt uns mit dem stocke schate,
> niht mit dem grüenen meienblate,
> mit zwigen noch mit esten.
> ir schate der tuot den gesten
> vil selten in den ougen wol.
> ob man der warheit jehen sol,
> dan gat niht guotes muotes van,
> dan lit niht herzelustes an:
> ir rede ist niht also gevar,
> daz edele herze iht lache dar.

(ll. 4671–80)

[They offer us shade just with the trunk of the tree, not with the green foliage of May and with the twigs and branches. It is not often that their shade affords pleasure to the visitor. To tell the truth, there's no fine emotion to be had there, no delight of the heart. Their poetry is not of such a hue that a noble heart can take delight in it.]

Such interaction between poet/poetry and audience can be placed broadly in the Middle Ages' essentially social conception of literature as communication. But in the context of *Tristan* it relates to the specific claims Gottfried makes for his own poem. In ll. 208–40 of the prologue Gottfried presents a more elaborate account of the interaction between his poem and an exclusive audience of 'noble hearts', who are sustained by the bitter-sweet story of the death of the lovers Tristan and Isolde, who thus in turn live on in poetry through the story of their death:

> Ir leben, ir tot sint unser brot.
> sus lebet ir leben, sus lebet ir tot.
> sus lebent si noch und sint doch tot
> und ist ir tot der lebenden brot.

(ll. 237–40)

[Their life and their death are our bread. So their life lives on and their death lives on. In this way they still go on living and yet they are dead, and their death is the bread of the living.]

Without the audience response there is for Gottfried no value in poetry:

> Gedæhte man ir ze guote niht,
> von den der werlde guot geschiht,
> so wærez allez alse niht,
> swaz guotes in der werlde geschiht.

Der guote man swaz der in guot
und niwan der werlt ze guote tuot,
swer daz iht anders wan in guot
vernemen wil, der missetuot.

(ll. 1–8)

[If one failed to hold these people in good memory[14] through whom good was given to society, then whatever good is done in society would be entirely worthless. . . . Whatever the good man does with good purpose and selflessly, only for the benefit of society – whoever is determined to take that other then in good part does wrong.]

Whether or not Gottfried intended his account of Hartmann as an accurate appraisal of this poet's distinctive literary style remains an open question. Hartmann certainly writes clearly and comprehensibly, but could Gottfried, as a reader of Hartmann's *Erec*, truly have considered that author to be an exponent of the unity of rhetorical form and inner meaning? Hartmann's narrator himself often poses as an interpreter commenting on the story, thus separating narration and interpretation. And for the modern reader the 'inner meaning' of the story is certainly not always clearly evident. What is clear is that in praising Hartmann Gottfried is setting out his own stylistic ideals and aims.

With Bligger von Steinach no such comparison is possible, for this author's work is lost. Gottfried's praise of Bligger begins with an account of the purity of his poetry and the delightful interplay of *wort* and *sin* that he achieved. He then continues with a discussion of his metrical skill:

wie er diu mezzer wirfet
mit behendeclichen rimen!
wie kan er rime limen,
als ob si da gewahsen sin!

(ll. 4714–17)

[Oh, how he throws the knife with his deft verses! How he binds the rhyme-words together as if they had grown there!]

The discussion of Heinrich von Veldeke is of central importance for an understanding of the literary review, for Veldeke stands at the head of the tradition which has, according to Gottfried's claim, made it impossible for him to write a description of Tristan:

er inpfete daz erste ris
in tiutscher zungen:
da von sit este ersprungen,

[14] Later printings of Ranke's edition have the conjecture *Gedaehte mans . . . / von dem . . .* ('If the source of all good were not held . . .', or 'If everything through which good comes about . . .'). See the note in the edition of Bechstein and Ganz, I, p. 342.

von den die bluomen kamen,
da si die spæhe uz namen
der meisterlichen vünde;
und ist diu selbe künde
so witen gebreitet,
so manege wis zeleitet,
daz alle, die nu sprechent,
daz die den wunsch da brechent
von bluomen und von risen
an worten unde an wisen.

(ll. 4738–50)

[Veldeke grafted the first branch in the German language. From this branch the boughs have sprung which have produced the flowers from which in turn the poets have extracted the artistry of their masterly inventions; and this skill has spread its branches so broadly and has been trained in so many varieties that today everyone who composes poetry can pluck the finest flowers and sprigs, words and melodies.]

Veldeke is introduced as no longer among the living, and Gottfried's report of him is attributed not to his own reading of the poems but to masters who heard the poet himself perform. Here, as often in the Middle Ages, literary comment refers principally to the poet rather than to the poetry. Veldeke is presented as a performer who used to sing fine love-songs ('wie wol sanger von minnen'; l. 4728). It is not certain whether this is intended as an appraisal of Veldeke's *Minnesang* or whether *singen*, like *wise* in l. 4750, is a metaphor for poetic composition (with reference to his handling of the love theme in the *Eneide*), in which the performance aspect of Veldeke's epic composition is stressed. The death of the poets is a theme repeatedly treated in German literature, for example in Walther von der Vogelweide's famous elegy on the death of Reinmar (L.82,24), or in Hermann Damen's poem (early fourteenth century) in praise of Frauenlob and Konrad von Würzburg:

Reimar, Walther, Rubîn, Nîthart,
Vridrich der Sunnenburgære,
dise alle sint in tôdes vart.
âne swære gebe got,
daz sie dort leben!
Der Marner der ist ouch von hin,
und der von Ofterdingen:
dise alle hêten wîsen sin
Ûf daz singen;
des ist in prîs gegeben.

[Reinmar, Walther von der Vogelweide, Rubin, Neidhart, Friedrich von Sonnenburg, these poets are all dead. God grant that they may live peacefully in the world beyond! Der Marner has also passed away, as has Heinrich von Ofterdingen. These poets all had the gifts of wisdom and song; they earned renown thereby.]

We have already seen that Wolfram von Eschenbach makes references to the death of Heinrich von Veldeke in *Parzival* (404,28–30). In such passages the poets are treated not just as authors but as men who live and die. This aspect of medieval literary comment is a clear indicator of the mixed oral-literary culture of the period.[15]

The account of how Veldeke grafted the first (German) branch on to the tree of poetry, an image which has been variously translated and interpreted,[16] is important for revealing Gottfried's conception of German literary tradition as a discrete cultural entity. Gottfried and his successors restrict their 'literary criticism' to German authors. Even the fourteenth-century poet Hugo von Trimberg, who praises Der Marner's bilingual literary production –

> der lustic tiutsch und schone latîn,
> alsam frischen brunnen und starken wîn
> gemischet hât in süezem gedæne
>
> (*Der Renner*, ll. 1199–1201)

[Der Marner, who in his sweet song mixes pleasant German with fine Latin, like fresh springwater and strong wine]

– and himself wrote in German and Latin, restricts himself to poets who use the vernacular. Gottfried's literary excursus is the clearest evidence we have that German poets of the High Middle Ages came to have a clear sense of standing in a distinct national tradition. The image of the branch grafted on to the tree of poetry, like the Lucan quotation (*Pharsalia* [*De bello civili*] 1.135–43) used to criticise the poets who only offer such shade as is afforded by the bare trunk of the tree (ll. 4673ff.),[17] is a metaphor which Gottfried must have derived from the Latin poetological discussion of his own day.[18] A somewhat similar example of arboreal literary metaphor occurs in the *Poetria nova* of Geoffrey of Vinsauf, where

---

[15] Green, 'On the Primary Reception'; Green, 'Zur primären Rezeption', with further literature. See also Green, *Medieval Listening and Reading*.

[16] Minis, *Er inpfete das erste ris*; Winkelman, 'Baummetapher'; Haug, *Vernacular Literary Theory*, p. 219 (German edn, p. 219).

[17] See further Abelard, *Historia calamitatum* (ed. Monfrin, p. 68); Matthew of Vendôme, *Ars versificatoria*, Prol. 7 (ed. Faral, p. 110); Eberhard the German, *Laborinthus*, 111ff. (ed. Faral, p. 341); Worstbrock, 'Lucanzitat'; Okken, *Kommentar*, I, pp. 252–4.

[18] Winkelman, 'Baummetapher'; Okken, *Kommentar*, I, pp. 252–4.

the *ordo naturalis* and the eightfold *ordo artificialis* are compared to the branches of a tree:

> Ordinis est primus sterilis, ramusque secundus
> Fertilis et mira succrescit origine ramus
> In ramos, solus in plures, unus in octo.

> (ll. 101–3)

[The one branch of organisation, i.e. the natural sequence of a narrative, is sterile, whereas the other, i.e. the artificially varied sequence, is fertile and the branch grows into branches of wonderful origin, a single branch into several, one into eight.]

It is not clear that Gottfried could have had access to a copy of the *Poetria nova*, which is thought by some authorities to date from after *c.* 1208, but a comparison of the two passages is useful as an aid to the clarification of Gottfried's intentions. Gottfried's text, unlike the *Poetria nova*, stresses the process of grafting, where two species are combined. It is not of particular significance for the interpretation whether a branch of the Latin or French rhetorical tradition is grafted on to the rough briar of German poetry, or a branch of German-language composition on to the vigorous root-stock of European poetry. The flowering of poetry in his own day is all seen as going back to Veldeke's translation of poetry from the Romance (or Latin) world to Germany. Today the poets suck the *spæhe* (literally 'cunning') from the flowers like bees (compare p. 436). The branches have been trained[19] so that all modern practitioners of the art of poetry can pluck flowers and sprigs from Veldeke's compositions to use in their own work.

The final passage of the excursus is devoted to *Minnesang*. Gottfried marks out a clear generic distinction between epic composition and the love lyric. *Diu von Hagenouwe*, who is to be identified as the poet Reinmar, is identified as the former leader of the nightingales, the *Minnesänger*, because of 'her' melodic gifts. But Reinmar is now dead, and *Diu von der Vogelweide* (Walther von der Vogelweide) is the new leader and marks the culmination of the *Minnesang* tradition. Whereas the voice of Orpheus lived on in Reinmar, Walther is said to derive his melodies from the court of Venus herself, *diu gotinne Minne*, on Mount Cithaeron. The social function of the *Minnesänger* is particularly stressed:

---

[19] Translating *geleitet* or *zeleitet* as a horticultural term 'trained', which is born out by Rudolf von Ems' development of the thought of this passage in *Alexander*, ll. 3116–22: 'des stam hât wol gebreitet sich . . . driu künsterîchiu bluomenrîs / hat sich dar ûf in mange wîs / vil spaehlîche zerleitet / und bluomen ûz gespreitet'. For the alternative translation 'thinned out', see Fromm, 'Tristans Schwertleite', p. 341, who relates it to the idea that rhetorical descriptions had become hackneyed; and also Krohn, *Kommentar*, p. 67.

> ir stimme ist luter unde guot,
> si gebent der werlde hohen muot
> und tuont reht in dem herzen wol.

(ll. 4759–61)

[Their song is pure and good, they give noble aspirations to the world and are comforting to the heart.]

It is their particular role to turn sorrow to joy:

> si unde ir cumpanie
> die müezen so gesingen,
> daz si ze vröuden bringen
> ir truren unde ir senedez clagen:
> und daz geschehe bi minen tagen!

(ll. 4816–20)

[May Walther von der Vogelweide and his company sing with such effect that their sorrow and heartfelt lamentation are turned into joy – and may I live to experience it!]

This aim of poetry and song to convert sorrow into joy, with which Gottfried brings the literary review to a close, is only one part of the poetological theory which he regards as underlying his own poem. As an aim it is legitimate and essential, but Gottfried dwells not on the achievement of happiness but on the dialectic of sorrow and happiness. His poem is not written for those who merely wish their sorrow to be turned to joy, but who rather as truly 'noble hearts' voluntarily assent to that union of joy and sorrow which lies at the centre of Gottfried's own ethical-aesthetic conception of literature:

> der edele senedære
> der minnet senediu mære.
> von diu swer seneder mære ger,
> dern var niht verrer danne her;
> ich wil in wol bemæren
> von edelen senedæren,
> die reiner sene wol taten schin:
> ein senedær unde ein senedærin,
> ein man ein wip, ein wip ein man,
> Tristan Isolt, Isolt Tristan.

(ll. 121–30)

[The noble sorrower in love loves sorrowful love stories. So that man who desires sorrowful love stories need go no further than this. I will tell him a tale of noble sorrowers in love who showed pure love in sorrow: a lover and his lady-love; man and woman, woman and man; Tristan and Isolde, Isolde and Tristan.]

Heinrich von dem Türlin introduces a passage in praise of Hartmann von Aue and other poets (Reinmar, Dietmar von Eist, Heinrich von Rugge, Friedrich von Hausen, Ulrich von Gutenberg and Hug von Salza) in an excursus towards the beginning of *Diu Crône* (ll. 2348–492).[20] Here too the opportunity for praise of modern German poets is afforded by a passage of rhetorical display, the list of sixty knights who drink from a magic cup at Arthur's court. This list is an imitation of the catalogue of knights in Hartmann's *Erec*, and Heinrich cuts his list short, saying that he is omitting the names cited by Hartmann von Aue in *Erec* on the grounds that it would be repetitious ('Vberich vnd vnlobelich'; l. 2356) to give them again here. The passage devoted to Hartmann laments his death and includes an elaborate prayer for his soul inspired by Heinrich's reading of Hartmann's work: 'For when that untainted poet Hartmann takes possession of my heart, it goes hot and cold and swells to bursting; it is his virtue, which possessed him all his life, which has this effect' (ll. 2406–11). We have here an ethical rather than a stylistic concept of fine literature: poetry is imbued with the virtue possessed by its creator. Hartmann and the *Minnesänger* Reinmar are praised for having provided 'Tugend bilde vnd werdes lere' ('models of virtue and noble teaching'; l. 2421). In particular they and their supporters, the other *Minnesänger* named above, have done this through their praise of noble women. Hartmann was both an author of courtly romances and a *Minnesänger*, and Heinrich von dem Türlin uses this double aspect of Hartmann's *œuvre* to make a transition from the narrative poet's considerate treatment of his characters in fiction, which stems from his virtue, to the ethical ideal embodied in love-poetry, which is presented as the essence of poetic creation. This same ideal of poetic creativity underlies the passage at the beginning of the poem (*Diu Crône*, ll. 246–8), where Heinrich gives his name as author of the poem and claims that same distinction for himself: 'Ez ist von dem Türlin / Heinreich, des zvng nie / Weibes gantzen lop verlie' ('It is Heinrich von dem Türlin, who has unceasingly spoken in praise of women').

The first literary review in the work of Rudolf von Ems is contained in the prologue to Book 2 of his *Alexander* (ll. 3063–309).[21] Rudolf presents himself as belonging to the post-classical generation of German poets. He presents his own work as an offering to the 'masters' of poetry and subjects it to their judgement. The review consists of two sections. In the first he describes the three branches of poetry which have sprung from the stem established by Heinrich von Veldeke: the work of Hartmann von Aue, Wolfram von Eschenbach and Gottfried von Strassburg. In a second

[20] Cormeau, *'Wigalois und 'Diu Crône'*, pp. 212–14.
[21] See Haug, *Vernacular Literary Theory*, pp. 311–14 (German edn, pp. 310–12).

section he offers a catalogue of notable German poets and their work, in which he includes his own previous poems as the last item.

The first section is notable for the characterisation of the style of the three authors, in which he draws on the literary terminology and metaphor of Gottfried's own literary review.

Hartmann von Aue:

> daz eine ist sleht, süeze und guot,
> des vruht den herzen sanfte tuot.
>
> (*Alexander*, ll. 3123–4)

[The first branch is smooth, delightful and excellent, its fruit soothing to the heart.]

Wolfram von Eschenbach:

> daz ander rîs ist drûf gezogn,
> starc, in mange wîs gebogn,
> wilde, guot und spæhe,
> mit vremden sprüchen wæhe.
>
> (*Alexander*, ll. 3129–32)

[The second branch is grafted on to it, strong, somewhat twisted, extraordinary, excellent and of wonderful artistry.]

Gottfried von Strassburg:

> dêst spæhe guot wilde reht,
> sîn süeziu bluot ebensleht
> wæhe reine vollekomn,
> daz rîs ist eine und ûz genomn
> von künsterîchen sinnen.
>
> (*Alexander*, ll. 3143–7)

[It is wonderful, excellent, extraordinary, exactly right; its delightful blossom is quite smooth, brilliant, pure, perfect; this branch alone is of exceptionally subtle artistry.]

The notion of Wolfram's devious style, which in Gottfried's literary excursus is said to be a vice, is made positive here, and Gottfried's own style is described as combining the smoothness of Hartmann with the twistedness that characterises Wolfram.

The elaborate account of the three principal exponents of the classical period, in which Rudolf's own Gottfridian stylistic ideal is implicitly set out, is followed by a list of notable authors. He mentions thirteen authors whose works range from biblical epic and the lives of the saints through courtly romance to the didactic poetry of Freidank. Unlike Gottfried and Heinrich von dem Türlin he does not include *Minnesang*. Some of the authors mentioned are Rudolf's own contemporaries and he claims a personal association with a certain Absolon, the author of a lost poem about Frederick Barbarossa, and Wetzel, the author of a verse life of St Margaret. The names are set out as a catalogue, each accompanied by details of the poet's work and occasional words of praise.

Rudolf's second literary review is contained in his poem *Willehalm von Orlens*, where it is contained in the prologue to the second book (ll. 2143–334). The book opens with a dialogue between the poet and Frouwe Aventiure, in imitation of a passage in Wolfram's *Parzival*, in which Aventiure demands that he should press on with the story. Rudolf feigns modesty and claims that she would do better to approach other poets, whereupon he introduces a catalogue of eighteen authors including Veldeke, the poets of the classical period, and a number of his own contemporaries. At the end of the catalogue, pressed again by Frouwe Aventiure, he agrees to continue if his work finds favour with the scribe Meister Hesse von Strassburg, who is renowned for his literary judgement, and with his friend Vasolt and other unnamed literary critics (*merkære*). The function of the passage is to provide the context of a literary tradition within the poem, within which Rudolf implicitly places his own work: Frouwe Aventiure has after all turned to him to render her story from French into German rather than to one of the others. The context requires that only exponents of courtly narrative literature (including religious poetry) should be included in the catalogue. There is no discussion of style here, only content.

Within the short span of the tradition of the Middle High German literary review from Gottfried through Heinrich von dem Türlin and Rudolf's *Alexander* to *Willehalm von Orlens* it is possible to perceive a development from genuine 'literary criticism', based on an assessment of the stylistic and thematic opportunities open to a writer who occupies a particular place in the literary tradition, to mere catalogues which set out the authors who have come to be regarded as canonical within the German tradition.[22]

[22] Heinzle, *Wandlungen und Neuansätze*, pp. 42–3.

19

Later literary criticism in Wales

Gruffydd Aled Williams

Though late-medieval Wales produced no *Ars poetica* it did produce texts which enunciated principles and standards relevant to literary composition and which highlighted matters at issue in contemporary literary life. Foremost among these were the various recensions of the bardic grammar (*gramadegau'r penceirddiaid*) and the contentions (*ymrysonau*) involving some of the leading poets of the age.

1. The bardic grammar

Copies of the bardic grammar survive in four medieval manuscripts: Aberystwyth, National Library of Wales, MS Peniarth 20 (*c.* 1330); Oxford, Bodleian Library, MS Jesus College 111 [the Red Book of Hergest] (*c.* 1400); Aberystwyth, National Library of Wales, MS Llanstephan 3 (*c.* 1425), and Bangor, University of Wales, MS Bangor 1 (*c.* 1450).[1] The relationship between the texts is complicated: the manuscript copies represent different recensions with considerable variation in wording, order and substance, the Red Book, Llanstephan 3 and Bangor 1 texts displaying an affinity which is not shared with the Peniarth 20 version. Paradoxically, in view of its date, it is the Red Book text which preserves the earliest recension of the grammar; notwithstanding its status as the earliest manuscript text the Peniarth 20 grammar represents a later, more developed recension. Peniarth 20, however, provides a *terminus ante quem* for the composition of the grammar, and this, together with internal evidence – a metrical example dated to 1316–17 – makes it likely that it was composed during the second decade of the fourteenth century.

Though primarily concerned with bardic matters, the tone of the grammar identifies it as a work of clerical origin. Two clerics – who both wrote poetry – are cited as the inventors of metres exemplified in the grammar, Einion Offeiriad (Einion the Priest) being named in the Red Book and

---

[1] Texts from the first three manuscripts are edited, with an extensive introduction, in *Gramadegau'r Penceirddiaid* (hereafter = *GP*). The Bangor 1 text is edited in Jones, 'Gramadeg Einion Offeiriad'. Manuscript dates cited follow Gruffydd, 'Wales's Second Grammarian', p. 4, which supersedes earlier accounts.

Llanstephan 3 and Dafydd Ddu Athro (*athro* = *magister*) in Peniarth 20. Einion held land in Cardiganshire and Carmarthenshire and was parson of Llanrug in Caernarvonshire when he died in 1349. Dafydd Ddu, a native of north-east Wales, was appointed a canon at Bangor in 1318, later transferring to St Asaph where he became Vicar-General of the diocese in 1357.[2] Later poets explicitly associate the grammar with Dafydd, but early in the seventeenth century the antiquary Robert Vaughan cited both Einion and Dafydd severally as its authors.[3] Having regard to the textual history of the grammar it is likely that the work was composed by Einion and later revised by Dafydd, although there is tenuous evidence which suggests that Dafydd may also have collaborated to some extent in the original composition. Vaughan claimed that Einion composed the grammar in honour of the powerful nobleman and literary patron Sir Rhys ap Gruffydd, Deputy Justice of South Wales (d. 1356); the fact that Einion composed an ode praising Sir Rhys, coupled with suggestive internal evidence found in the grammar, renders this highly plausible.[4]

In common medieval fashion the grammar combined instruction in grammar as now understood with instruction in poetry; its orientation, however, was predominantly bardic, its intended audience being professional bards or aspirants to the bardic profession. Whilst clearly meant to be of direct practical use, it also represented a conscious attempt to enrich and elevate bardic instruction by fusing to it elements derived from Latin learning, which comprised the dominant intellectual culture of the age. The section on grammar proper was an adaptation of material derived from the late Latin grammars of Donatus and Priscian, though no source is cited and the precise affiliations of the Welsh work have not been determined. Interestingly, *dwned* (< Donatus, through English *donet*) came to be used generically of a bardic grammar in the fifteenth century. This usage, however, may have evolved soon after the compilation of the Welsh grammar and may reflect what informed contemporaries knew to be one of its prime sources: the fourteenth-century poet Dafydd ap Gwilym, who was familiar with the grammar and moved in the same literary circles as Einion Offeiriad, addressed his uncle and bardic teacher Llywelyn ap Gwilym as *Llyfr dwned Dyfed* ('the donet book of Dyfed').[5]

The *ars grammatica* section of Einion's work includes sections devoted to the letters, syllables and diphthongs, parts of speech, syntax and figures.

---

[2] Gruffydd, 'Wales's Second Grammarian', replaces earlier biographical accounts.

[3] In Aberystwyth, National Library of Wales, MS Mostyn 110. See *GP*, p. xvii, where the manuscript is wrongly attributed to Thomas Wiliems. This is corrected in *Gwaith Einion Offeiriad a Dafydd Ddu*, p. 3.

[4] MS Mostyn 110, quoted in *GP*, p. xvii. Einion's ode is edited in *Gwaith Einion Offeiriad a Dafydd Ddu*, pp. 7–32.

[5] *Gwaith Dafydd ap Gwilym*, ed. Parry, p. 31. On Dafydd and the grammar, see Bromwich, *Aspects*, pp. 105–31.

Unsurprisingly, much of the terminology leans on Latin, examples being the borrowings *bogal* (< *vocalis*), *berf* (< *verbum*), *ffutur* (< [*tempus*] *futurum*) and the calques *cytsain* ('consonant', < *cyd-* + *sain*) and *anterfynedic* ('infinitive', < *an-* + *terfyn* + *-edic*). The influence of a Latin template is also evident in much of the discussion, *q* and *x*, for example, being superfluously (as regards Welsh) included among the letters, substantives being divided into physical and spiritual subcategories (Latin *corporale* and *incorporale*), and five verbal moods specified (including the optative and the infinitive, inapplicable to Welsh). Sensitivity to the characteristics of the language is displayed, however, in features such as the specification that there were seven vowels in Welsh, and in the omission (unlike some Welsh Renaissance grammars) of the irrelevant Latin categories of declensions and cases. A long section on syllables and diphthongs deviates from classical grammatical practice; the terminology used is native, and an origin in traditional bardic instruction likely. The brief section on figures of speech which follows has been shown to reflect the influence of Priscian.[6]

Moving explicitly to poetry, the grammar defines it as 'a composition of regular constructions of splendid ornate words, made fair by fine and well-appointed adjectives, which denote praise or satire, and that in commendable poetic art',[7] thus recognising it as a refined verbal artifice subject to both grammatical and prosodic rules and indicating its primary subject-matter in medieval Wales. There follows a threefold division of the 'branches' of poetry (amplified in a later section in Llanstephan 3 and Peniarth 20): *klerwryaeth*, whose attributes included satire and parody; *teuluwryaeth*, whose output included love-poetry featuring ambiguity, and *prydydyaeth*, which entailed proficiency in all branches of Welsh metrics (*englynion*, *awdlau* and *cywyddau*) and whose output was characterised by a complexity both of form and imaginative conception. This is followed by a classification of metres encompassing *englynion*, *awdlau* and *cywyddau*, illustrated with metrical examples, and amounting to a total of twenty-four. It has long been recognised that this classification was arbitrary and idiosyncratic and divorced from contemporary bardic practice. The number twenty-four occurs in other formulations in Welsh lore and a total of twenty-four metres was achieved through conflation and duplication, the devising of new metres and the inclusion of a borrowed Latin hymn metre (designated *cywydd llosgyrnog*). Interestingly, some of the metres featured were not used by contemporary high-grade bards, being derived from popular or semi-popular verse, an indicator that

---

[6] By Russell, 'Figures of Speech'.

[7] 'kyuansodyat ymadrodyon kyfyawn o eireu adurn arderchawc, a deckaer o eireu gwann adwyn, kymeredic, a arwydockaont molyant neu ogan, a hynny ar gerd dafawt ganmoledic' (*GP*, p. 6).

the grammar's author was an informed dilettante – as clerics like Einion or Dafydd Ddu would have been – who did not share the preconceptions of members of the bardic order. The listing of metres is followed by a section on the faults – of language, prosody and sense – to be avoided in verse. Manifestly traditional, some of this material was anachronistic by fourteenth-century standards. A statement that *cynghanedd* – the system of consonance and internal rhyme which was a regular feature of contemporary high-grade verse – occurs in mid-line pertains only to proto-*cynghanedd* far removed from the use of the age. It must be presumed that the lack of a full discussion of *cynghanedd* in the *ars metrica* section would have been remedied by oral instruction in the case of pupils under the tutelage of a master-poet.

The primacy of panegyric in the Welsh literary tradition is illustrated in the section of the grammar known as the *prydlyfr* ('book of poetry') in which poets are instructed 'how everything is to be praised'. Set attributes deserving of praise are attached to a hierarchy of subjects – God, Mary, and the saints, men and women – both ecclesiastical and secular (the emphasis on the religious probably reflecting the author's clerical status). It has been claimed that the *prydlyfr* was expressly meant to provide a philosophical justification for panegyric,[8] but this view seems exaggerated. A clerical concern with propriety is doubtless reflected in the stipulation that love-poetry addressed to a married lady (*gwreicda*) is improper; similar verse addressed to an unmarried girl (*riein*) is explicitly licensed.

A section found only in Peniarth 20 and Llanstephan 3, apparently interpolated into Einion's original text, is of interest in illustrating a concern to maintain the dominance of eulogy possibly threatened by an exaggerated contemporary vogue for satire (probably an ancient feature of Welsh bardic tradition, though little evident until the fourteenth century). It amplifies the distinction made earlier between the three branches of verse, *klerwryaeth*, *teulwryaeth* and *prydydyaeth*. The main concern is to establish a strict demarcation between the highest grade of poet, the *prydyd* (= Modern Welsh *prydydd*) expressly associated with eulogy, and the low grade *klerwr* (compare Irish *cléir*, 'wandering poets', Old French *cler*, *clers*) whose activity centred on satire, ridicule and lampoon. (There is less concern with the *teuluwr* [compare the *bardd teulu*, 'war-band poet' of the Welsh Laws, a court functionary obsolete by the fourteenth century] who is described in Peniarth 20 as 'the pupil of a *prydyd*'.) The *prydyd* is enjoined to refrain from satire, the *klerwr*'s speciality, which is characterised as being 'unclassifiable' (*anosparthus*) and stigmatised in Peniarth 20 as 'foul spittle-verse' ('ymboergerd vvdyr'; *GP*, p. 56). The *prydyd*'s eulogy is declared to be superior to the *klerwr*'s satire as good is

---

[8] In particular Lewis, in *Braslun*, pp. 55–64, and *Gramadegau'r Penceirddiaid*.

superior to evil. An interesting stipulation that the *prydyd* should abstain from charms, sorcery and magic may implicitly associate these with the *klerwr*, or, alternatively, may represent a renunciation of older bardic mantic functions. The *prydyd* is further distinguished from the *klerwr* in being a learned (and specifically literate) poet; his learning according to Llanstephan 3 ought to include knowledge of ancient poetry (*hengerd*) and written tales (*ystoryaeu yscriuenedic*), and, according to Peniarth twenty arts and laws. The social orientation of classical Welsh poetry is reflected in the stipulation that such learning should be deployed in conversing with and entertaining high-born patrons, both male and female. The issue of the origin of poetic inspiration is touched upon in Llanstephan 3 where *prydydyaeth* is designated 'a portion of natural wisdom . . . originating in the Holy Spirit'[9] characterised by genius, art and practice. A moral code is prescribed for the *prydyd* in this manuscript, where it is stipulated that he should be obedient, generous and chaste, display spiritual love, exercise moderation with regard to food and drink, be kind, and attend to his divine duties, virtues declared to be the antithesis of the seven deadly sins. Both Llanstephan 3 and Peniarth 20 briefly identify the *prydyd*'s art with truth; according to the latter manuscript it was his duty to suppress the lies of buffoons and unskilled poetasters.

The grammar's final part consists of triads of verse (*trioedd cerdd*), many of them recapitulating the preceding material. Whilst some refer to technical linguistic and prosodic features, others are broader in application. Of the latter the following may serve as examples:

Three things which strengthen a poem: depth of meaning, and copiousness of Welsh, and splendid imagination.[10]

Three things which dignify a poem: clear declamation, and refined workmanship, and the authority of the poet.[11]

A prominent concern in the triads is the desire to affirm the dignity and exalted nature of poetry and the poet's calling. One triad affirms poetry's incompatibility with foolishness and frivolity, whilst another aligns it with truth by prohibiting a poet from disseminating lies. Another triad, echoing the earlier stipulation in Llanstephan 3 that a poet should be learned, lists as features which promote poetic amplitude lore relating to stories, poetry and ancient verse. A series of triads reinforce the previously established distinctions between the *klerwr*, *teuluwr* and *prydyd*, and another explicitly reiterates the precedence of eulogy over satire. Satire is further

---

[9] 'kyffran o doethineb anianawl . . . ac o'r Yspryt Glan y pan henyw' (*GP*, p. 35).

[10] 'Tri pheth a gadarnhaa kerd: dyfynder ystyr, ac amylder Kymraec, ac odidawc dechymic' (p. 17).

[11] 'Tri pheth a hoffa kerd: datkanyat eglur, a chywreint wneuthuryat, ac awdurdawt y prydyd' (p. 17).

demoted by being associated with drunkenness and adultery in a triad which lists 'the three things which corrupt a poet's muse' ('Tri pheth a lwgyr awen kerdawr'; *GP*, p. 17). A triad which occurs only in Peniarth 20 interestingly proclaims a hierarchy of poetic genres according to subject-matter by stipulating that religious poetry, love-poetry and poetry in praise of lords were the three pre-eminent forms of verse (*teir prifgerdd*). Practical considerations previously unmentioned in the grammar intrude in a triad which concerns the etiquette to be observed in a poet's dealings with patrons. The untimely and unsolicited presentation of a poem and the presentation of a poem to an undeserving patron are declared shameful; these strictures anticipate the more detailed regulations contained in the Statute of Gruffudd ap Cynan (1523) which sought to govern bardic practice in sixteenth-century Wales.

Later copies of the grammar, together with references to it in poetry, testify to its use and acquired authority among poets. It may have influenced poetic subject-matter by emphasising the pre-eminence of eulogy; satire of the more uninhibited kind often found in fourteenth-century poetry, whilst still occurring, appears to recede in the following two centuries, although the poetic record could be misleading in this respect. The grammar's vogue, however, is unambiguously illustrated by its continuing evolution. In the mid-fifteenth century it was revised to accommodate metrical regulations promulgated by the poet Dafydd ab Edmwnd at the Carmarthen eisteddfod: these are evident in a copy written by his pupil, Gutun Owain, which also contains a fuller *ars grammatica* with Latin examples.[12] The grammar achieved its fullest form in the *Pum Llyfr Kerddwriaeth* ('Five Books of Poetry') compiled by the poet Simwnt Fychan *c.* 1570.[13]

2. Bardic contentions

Contentions were an old feature of Welsh bardic life, but early examples largely concerned contests for patronage or office. The late-medieval period, however, produced contentions which aired broader issues relating to literary composition.[14]

The earliest of these was the fourteenth-century debate between the Anglesey poet Gruffudd Gryg and Dafydd ap Gwilym,[15] a poet renowned for popularising the new *cywydd* metre and for love-poetry influenced by

[12] For the text of the *ars metrica* section of Gutun's grammar see Williams, 'Gramadeg Gutun Owain'.
[13] For the text of the *Pum Llyfr*, see *GP*, pp. 89–142.
[14] The best general discussion is Matonis, 'Later Medieval Poetics'.
[15] Text in *Gwaith Dafydd ap Gwilym*, ed. Parry, pp. 388–413.

the continental tradition of *amour courtois*. The contention – extending to eight poems in all – was initiated by Gruffudd who chided Dafydd for the repeated references in his poetry to love's spears and their torment. If Dafydd were to be believed, his body was pierced by spears as numerous as the stars, sufficient to slay even the mighty Arthur. Gruffudd asserted that Dafydd's exaggerated use of such imagery amounted to falsehood, accusing him of 'a great lie' (*mawr o gelwydd*; p. 389) and of betraying his bardic calling. In response, having charged Gruffudd with inexperience in the ways of love-poetry, Dafydd claimed that his love *cywydd* – which he explicitly associated with Ovid (*cywydd gwiw Ofydd*; p. 392) – was the equal of praise-poetry in dignity, a radical assertion in view of the pre-eminence of panegyric in Welsh bardic tradition. To justify the new love-poetry he cited its popularity: such verse was the favourite of maidens and tavern audiences; an old discarded manuscript would be retrieved from a waste-heap if known to contain love-poetry. Turning to Gruffudd's alleged poetic defects, having accused him of 'perverting poetry' ('Gwyraist â'th ben gerdd y byd'; p. 393), a charge which he did not amplify, Dafydd – himself a highly original poet – chided him for imitating other poets. Employing the metaphor of the poet as carpenter of song, he urged Gruffudd to fashion a song from his own timber, further castigating him as 'an echo-stone of poets' (*craig lefair beirdd*; p. 393).

Having refuted Dafydd's implied charge of plagiarism, Gruffudd's second *cywydd* centred on the depiction of three erstwhile novelties, now no longer esteemed: a wooden hobby-horse, impressive from afar, but perceived at close hand to be flimsy; the recently acquired organ in Bangor cathedral, a nine days' wonder which now attracted no offerings; and, lastly, Dafydd's *cywydd*, popular in north Wales when new but now sadly *passé*. Dafydd later cited these examples to renew the charge of plagiarism, claiming that they were inspired by another poet. Subsequent poems added little of substance to the debate, being largely devoted to personal invective. Whilst there may have been an element of role-playing in this exchange – Gruffudd, in fact, himself composed accomplished love-poetry – the contention may reflect contemporary tensions between the new poetry influenced by foreign modes, of which Dafydd was the main exponent, and more conservative bardic elements. The question of poetic veracity, touched upon by Gruffudd but barely developed, echoed values proclaimed in the grammar's *trioedd cerdd* and would engage later Welsh critics.[16] Dafydd's charge that Gruffudd's muse was derivative indicated an emphasis on originality which may reflect Dafydd's awareness of his own poetic strength.

[16] See Jones, 'Pwnc Mawr'.

A later debate (*c.* 1425) between Rhys Goch Eryri and Llywelyn ab y Moel eventually focused on the issue of the origin of *awen* or poetic inspiration,[17] a phenomenon attributed by Llywelyn to the workings of the Holy Spirit at Pentecost. Having accounted for its origin, he affirmed it as a prerequisite for true poetic composition: citing the example of the Taliesin of legend as the archetypal inspired poet, Llywelyn asserted that there were a thousand versifiers (*cerddwyr*) for every poet (*awenydd* < *awen*).[18] In a retort designed to impress his adversary with learning, Rhys agreed that the muse was of divine origin, but claimed that it had been given by God to Adam 5,200 years before the Pentecost, a date derived from estimates of the year of Creation based on the Septuagint.[19] He also indulged in linguistic speculation, associating the word *awen* with *Ave*, the archangel Gabriel's greeting to Mary. The debate is interesting as evidence for the influence of book-learning on bardic perceptions, such material in this case being probably acquired through an intermediary. It should be added that whilst both poets subscribed to an apparently thoroughly Christian poetic, Llywelyn's reference to the legendary Taliesin – a figure ultimately deriving from pre-Christian mythology – indicates the syncretic nature of the bardic concept of poetic inspiration.

The dispute concerning the *awen* stimulated a further contention.[20] This time Rhys was confronted by Siôn Cent, a poet of an intensely moralistic disposition.[21] In a trenchant poem, he mounted what has been described as 'one of the most bitter criticisms of secular bardic practice found anywhere in medieval literature' (Matonis, 'Later Medieval Poetics', p. 654). He posited the existence of two contrasting muses, the Christian Muse which had inspired the prophets and the lying Muse which inspired Welsh professional poets. The mendacity of the latter Muse is scathingly illustrated with examples drawn from the main secular bardic genres. The bards, he claimed, praised providers of whey as dispensers of wine and mead and falsely compared them to Arthur and Roland for alleged feats in the French wars; they likewise transgressed in comparing women to the Virgin Mary and to the sun; their satire too was similarly exaggerated. The inspiration of Welsh poets derived, he alleged, not from the Holy Spirit but rather from 'the infernal furnace of nature' ('O ffwrn natur uffernawl'; *Cywyddau*, p. 182). Siôn ended his broadside by citing

---

[17] Text in *Cywyddau*, pp. 157–78.

[18] *Cywyddau*, p. 167. The references to Taliesin at the court of Maelgwn (*yn llys Faelgwn*) and his association with Elffin identify him as the Taliesin of legend rather than the historical poet, although medieval Wales did not make this distinction.

[19] Found in early Christian chronological works, e.g. Eusebius' *Chronicon*.

[20] Text in *Cywyddau*, pp. 181–6.

[21] Lewis, *Braslun*, pp. 95–114, advances the theory that Siôn was educated at Oxford where he absorbed Ockhamist doctrine; for reservations see Williams, *The Welsh Church*, p. 237, n. 8.

Peter Lombard, Alexander of Hales and 'the Book of Decrees' as authorities who had denounced mendacity as sinful.[22] Rhys's response appears
to lack focus, for he concentrated on rebutting an insult which probably
featured in a lost poem by Siôn, namely his depiction as a rustic herdsman
tending his mother's goats in Snowdonia! But towards the end of his poem
he energetically refuted the existence of two contrasting Muses, asserting
that 'there is . . . but one Muse'[23] and that deriving from the Holy Spirit in
heaven. It is noteworthy, however, that he did not address his adversary's
specific charges of mendacity, charges which would be renewed by Welsh
Renaissance critics.

Siôn Cent's morally based condemnation of poets exemplified a well-
established critical tradition. In the specifically Welsh context, Bishop
Anian II of St Asaph (d. 1293) is credited with the authorship of a
tract called *Commentum in fabulas poetarum* ('A Commentary on the
Fables/Lies of Poets'). That the application of moral criteria in judging
poetry was a recurrent phenomenon in late-medieval Wales is suggested
by the grammar's repudiation of satire; further evidence is provided by
Dafydd ap Gwilym's mock dialogue between himself and a grey friar in
which he defended his love-poetry against the friar's moral strictures.[24]
The poets' insistence on the Holy Spirit as the fount of their Muse – a
claim incorporated in the grammar – may have been in part a defensive
reflex meant to counter such criticism. Significantly, in the late fourteenth
century the *awen*'s divine origin was cited by the poet Gruffudd Llwyd
in defending his calling against the condemnation voiced in the *Elucidarium*, a popular religious tract which had stigmatised poets (*clêr*) as beyond
redemption.[25]

---

[22] The names are somewhat mutilated in the poem. The first two are identified by Lewis,
Braslun, pp. 103–4 (who provides the relevant passage from Peter Lombard's *Sententiarum libri quatuor* [*c.* 1155–8]). Lewis's identification of the poem's *Durgrys* as Dietrich
of Freiberg is refuted by Breeze, 'Llyfr durgrys', who shows it to refer to the 'Book of
Decrees' (*Liber decretalium*), probably Gratian's *Decretum* (*c.* 1140).

[23] 'Nid oes chwaith awen ond un./ O'r Ysbryd Glân . . . Y tyf honno i'r tafawd' (*Cywyddau*,
p. 186), but these are challenged by Bryant-Quinn, 'Trugaredd Mawr'.

[24] *Gwaith Dafydd ap Gwilym*, ed. Parry, pp. 362–4.

[25] *Cywyddau*, pp. 119–21. The *Elucidarium* was a work by Honorius 'of Autun' (*fl.* 1106–
35). In the Welsh translation (pre-1346) *clêr* renders Latin *joculatores*.

Part VI

Latin and vernacular in Italian literary theory

20

Dante Alighieri: experimentation and (self-)exegesis

Zygmunt G. Barański

Dante Alighieri (1265–1321) reflected on matters of literature throughout his *œuvre*. His earliest compositions (the *tenzone* with Dante da Maiano, and the sonnets 'A ciascun'alma presa e gentil core' and 'Com più vi fere Amor co' suoi vincastri' (*Rime* 39–47, 1, 62)), written before he was twenty, are lyric 'correspondence' poems, examples of a genre whose self-reflective concern with questions of literature has been amply documented.[1] Dante's youthful *rime* are largely mechanical and conventional; yet, looked at in terms of his overall development and his general approach to literature, they acquire greater significance. It is suggestive that the poet should have begun writing in a 'style' which allowed him to establish direct textual contact with other poets and their works. From the very start, Dante was intrigued by the 'mechanics' of his art and by the 'discourses' which could accompany a literary text.

In the months before his death, Dante once again returned to the formulas of the poetic 'debate' (as he had on other occasions, most notably when he exchanged sonnets with Forese Donati and with Cino da Pistoia; see Dante, *Rime* 73–8; 110–15). Attacked in verse by the Bolognese *magister* Giovanni del Virgilio for having gone against traditional usage when he employed the vernacular instead of Latin, namely, a 'low' language instead of a 'high' one, to present the intellectually demanding subject-matter of the *Commedia* (see Dante, *Egloghe* I, 1–34), Dante defended his choice of language through a complex and multi-layered literary strategy. Although, especially in the first of his two replies, the poet explicitly and ironically rejected the idea that he had behaved improperly (*Egloghe* II, 51–4; pp. 44–5), he developed his full critique of Giovanni in a rather more subtle and implicit way: one, in fact, which underlined his poetic sensibility. Instead of conventionally replying to his interlocutor in the same metrical form as that in which he had been addressed, Dante, in a move of considerable novelty, substituted the eclogue for Giovanni's Horatian epistle. The poet thereby gave substance to a genre which the Middle Ages often discussed, but in which it refused to compose. The eclogue was accorded a key position in discussions of the *genera dicendi*,

---

[1] See Gorni, 'Le forme', pp. 475–7.

in which its status as an emblematic example of the 'low' style was firmly enshrined.[2] It is thus likely that when, unexpectedly, Dante selected this metre, his idea was that it should serve as an integral part of his self-defence, thereby bringing together and harmonising the literary-critical associations both of the poems' content and of their form. By resuscitating the eclogue, the poet clearly demonstrated that he was well aware of the traditional conventions of the 'low' style. His point seems to have been that he – unlike other authors – could in fact write in one of its classic yet unused forms. Therefore, if he had chosen – as Giovanni del Virgilio complained – to deal with 'lofty' topics in a *carmen laicum*, this was not out of ignorance. He not only knew what he was doing, but it was also evident that the *Commedia* could not be judged simply in traditional terms. The approach taken by Dante in his two Latin eclogues, whereby he merged his critical thinking with the formal texture of his writing, is a major hallmark of his illustrious artistic career; and it is suggestive that Dante should have brought his *œuvre* to a close as he had begun it, writing a kind of literature which highlighted what had arguably always been closest to his heart: the *ars poetica*.

This same deep-felt concern is present in just about all his other works, which, whatever their formal and ideological differences, are nevertheless united by a shared fascination with literature. They are among the best-known and most original works in Western culture: the *Vita Nova*, the *Convivio*, the *De vulgari eloquentia*, the *Commedia* and the *Monarchia* (even this overtly historical-political treatise makes important observations, for instance, on allegorical exegesis, on the textuality of the Bible and on the processes of signification).[3] And it is no exaggeration to claim that, taken together, Dante's writings embrace all the major questions which might be included under the rubric of medieval literary criticism. The poet had much to say on the social and personal functions of literature, and on its relationship to the arts of the *trivium*, to semiosis in general, and to aesthetics. He explored, too, the interconnections and differences between prose and poetry, between Latin and the vernacular, between literary and non-literary language, and between divine and human writing. He reflected on the theory of *convenientiae* (the question of the proper relationship between form and content), on the functions of allegory, on the implications for literary composition of the doctrine of the *genera dicendi*, and on the different ways in which literature might be categorised. He explored the nature both of authorship and of readership; and, drawing on heterogeneous methods of exegesis from the gloss to the

[2] See Quadlbauer, *Die antike Theorie*, pp. 58–9; Mengaldo, *Linguistica*, pp. 215–17.
[3] See Dante, *Monarchia* 3.4.6–11 (on allegoresis); 2.7.4, 12 and 3.3.11–4.1–11 (on the Bible); 2.2.7–8 (on signification).

vita auctoris, and from the *accessus* to the commentary, he examined the ways in which what we would now call literary traditions are established and function.

More significantly, Dante's critical interests helped structure both individual texts and his work as a whole. His observations on literature are insistently present at every level of his *œuvre*, surpassing in number, and probably in importance, any of his other preoccupations, whether religious, political or philosophical (and it is thus surprising that scholars should have largely ignored this area of his writing). As has been justly noted, 'a constant feature of Dante's personality is . . . the way in which technical reflection perpetually appears alongside poetry' (Contini, *Un'idea*, p. 4). This represents more than a mere interest in literary matters on Dante's part; what is crucial is the fact that poetics and poetry, 'literary criticism' and literature were indissolubly linked in his work. During the course of his life, Dante displayed a coherent yet continually evolving and increasingly original understanding of the nature of writing, which culminated in the composition (and exegesis) of the *Commedia*. The poet's constant reflection on literature was not only the major stimulus behind his artistic experimentation, but it was also the means whereby he explained and legitimated the *novitas* of his writings. It is now widely accepted that just about all Dante's works, from the *Vita Nova* onwards (*c.* 1293–5), mark major new departures in literary history. Only a writer who had an acutely sophisticated understanding of the literary tradition could have undertaken such a creative enterprise; and Dante was always careful to account for his experimentation by measuring his artistic solutions against those of other writers.

This is the key point regarding Dante's interest in literary theory and criticism. Regardless of his many allusions to a rich variety of authors and their works and to matters of general literary interest, the poet's main focus was always the nature of his own writing and his own position within the tradition. However much Dante's literary criticism draws on (and can illuminate) contemporary values and ideas, it remains on the fringes of the tradition, since it constitutes a kind of self-referential, 'closed' system. This is probably why, despite the poet's fundamental concern with and contribution to the development of literary criticism, it is questionable whether any of his works – especially if one does not accept the authenticity of the *Epistle to Can Grande* – can strictly be defined, either formally or in their intent, as exegetical texts.

There seem to be two principal reasons why Dante idiosyncratically exploited the general critical discourses of his culture for explicitly personal ends (at times challenging and overturning the most-cherished of beliefs). First, in order to clarify the novelty of his writings, he needed an exegetical language and terminology which was intelligible to his audience. Aware of the difficulties which his experimentation would create for his readers, especially in a traditionalist literary culture such as the one in which he was writing, Dante wanted to underline the continuing interpretability of his works. As he declared himself, there were few things more shameful than an 'uninterpretable' text: 'since great shame would attach to whoever might write verse about things concealed under a figure or a rhetorical colour [*rimasse cose sotto vesta di figura o di colore rettorico*], and, subsequently, having been asked, might not be able to strip away his words of such covering, in order to reveal their true meaning' (*Vita Nova* 25.10). He thus maintained visible links between his writings and exegesis. The broader implications of this manoeuvre are clear. His fourteenth-century readers were meant to imitate his example and, following standard exegetical procedures, they were supposed to understand for themselves the reasons for and the mechanisms behind the *novitas* of his texts. Dante would provide help in this task by introducing a constant flow of metaliterary prompting into his writings, which would thus additionally benefit from a regular 'auto-commentary'. Second, and more originally, beginning cautiously in the *Vita Nova*, Dante was consistently engaged in an operation of revolutionary dimensions. In an environment where the authority of Latin and its culture was just about total, his aim was to establish his credentials not just as an *auctor*, but as a vernacular *auctor*, the equal of his classical forebears. 'No one worked harder at becoming an *auctor* – not just a maker of verses but an authority – than Dante, and his self-promotion was inextricably intertwined with the promotion of the Italian language' (Minnis and Scott, p. 374). One simple way of doing this was to show that the exegetical vocabulary and methods which for centuries had been almost exclusively restricted to classical and biblical literature in Latin were also appropriate for his 'contemporary' writings. By extension, the very fact that Dante had no difficulty in associating his Italian texts with the critical techniques and register normally reserved for the work of the *auctores* provided immediate evidence of their 'prestige' and of the 'correctness' of the poet's self-exegetical ambitions.

With Dante, Western literary criticism reaches a watershed. Not only did a vernacular writer claim the same artistic rights and status as the great authors of Antiquity, but he also founded a tradition of interpretation whose specific aim was to talk about vernacular literature. It is precisely because Dante had so carefully prepared the ground that a rich tradition of commentary to the *Commedia* grew so rapidly during the course of the fourteenth century, thereby establishing the basis for a 'modern' analysis of literature in general, whose benefits continue to be enjoyed to this day. Given Dante's ambitions, it is obvious why he felt he needed to challenge, both critically and artistically, the conventional literary wisdoms of his culture, despite the latter's obsessive concern with the proper respect for

precedents and *auctoritates*. The way in which he concretely achieved his
aims constitutes the history of Dante as poet and critic.

The progress of Dante's reflection on literature is marked by a clear
movement from the orthodox to the unorthodox, although within individual works elements of both perspectives are normally discernible. The
Vita Nova, through a combination of prose and poetry, tells of the unfolding of the narrator's love for Beatrice, and of the effects of this love on
his spiritual, intellectual and artistic development. While many elements
associated with the standard conventions and ideas of medieval literary
criticism are discernible in its pages, it is their synthesis which is a first clue
both to their novel reutilisation and to the *prosimetrum*'s overall *novitas*.
The *Vita Nova* is introduced simply as an extended gloss upon a 'book':

> In that part of the book of my memory before which there would be little to
> read, is found a heading [*rubrica*] which says: *Here begins the chapter entitled
> 'Vita Nova' / Here begins the new life* [*Incipit vita nova*]. Beneath this heading I
> find written the words which I intend to copy into this book [*libello*]; and if not
> all of them, at least their meaning (*sentenzia*).   (I.1)

The narrator metaphorically presents himself as the copyist from ('è mio
intendimento d'assemplare') and commentator on ('la . . . sentenzia [delle
parole]') the 'book of his memory' (a traditional topos);[4] and it is significant that, in the *Vita Nova*, Dante was careful to give concrete expression
to both these activities. He transcribes the verse which he had apparently
written previously as the immediate record of his love, and accompanies this with a prose commentary which analyses the formal patterning
of his poems and explains the providential and exemplary nature of his
relationship with Beatrice – a relationship, whose aim is to lead him to
salvation by teaching him a properly Christian way of loving. Dante's
prosimetrum thus finds its most obvious structural source in the make-up
of the glossed poetic manuscript, and when it clarifies the organisation of
individual compositions, it especially draws on the techniques of *divisio
textus* (the subdivision of a work in order to enhance understanding of
its meaning). Yet, given that, rather than being strictly analytical, much
of the *Vita Nova*'s prose is of a narrative, biographical and critical character, it establishes connections too with the Provençal *vidas* and *razos*.
At the same time, the sustained ideological sophistication of Dante's presentation and the rigorously organic quality of his work (in many ways,
the *Vita Nova* can be regarded as the first 'novel' in Italian) clearly separate it from any previous commentary to a secular text. The *libello*'s
prose, not least because of its strong religious and narrative sense, has
ultimately little in common with the introductory ambitions of the *vitae*

---

[4] See Curtius, *European Literature*, p. 326, and Chapter 7 above.

auctoris and of the academic prologues to the *auctores*. In some ways, it has something of the greater wealth of biblical exegesis, which would fit in well with the *Vita Nova*'s claim to participate in the processes of salvation. It is thus highly significant that, recently, it has been persuasively demonstrated that, both formally and ideologically, the *Vita Nova* is closely modelled on the Song of Songs and its commentaries, a tradition which, like Dante's *prosimetrum*, integrated verse and prose.[5] The *Vita Nova* thus brings together religious and secular elements not just at the levels of content and ideology, but also in its understanding of literature, thereby giving concrete artistic expression to the *rapprochement* between poetic and scriptural ideas on writing which, since the twelfth century, had increasingly marked medieval critical thought.

Dante's views on the relationship between Latin and the vernacular in the *Vita Nova* at first seem to be rather conservative, although, like his reworking of exegetical models, these soon progress in unexpected directions. The *libello* supports the traditional view that vernacular writing is subordinate to classical literature. Chapter 25 announces the superiority of the 'litterati poete' over their imitators, the 'dicitori . . . in lingua volgare' who, furthermore, according to Dante, are restricted to amorous themes. Similarly, the choice of the vernacular as a literary language is explained in purely utilitarian terms: to ensure that women, who lack a knowledge of Latin, can understand the poetry which is addressed to them (§6). Yet Dante himself, already within Chapter 25, begins to deconstruct these positions. Thus, he is almost certainly the first in Italy to bestow the tag *poeta*, which for centuries had belonged exclusively to classical *auctores*, to writers in the vernacular ('questi poete volgari').[6] Similarly, the fact that he himself used the vernacular to talk about literary history and practice, and furthermore utilised it, probably for the first time in the history of the Romance *vulgari*, to write an extended critical commentary, amply demonstrated that Italian could not be restricted to talking about *Amore*. In fact, despite first appearances, Chapter 25 is ultimately 'bent on ennobling and . . . granting the status of classic . . . to vernacular poetry'[7] in general, and to Dante's own verse in particular; indeed, the same can be said of the *Vita Nova* as a whole. Within what is basically a conservative and reductionist general theory of literature and language, Dante fashioned an original system of critical analysis and evaluation which was to stand him in good stead for the rest of his creative life. The structure of the *Vita Nova* is organised in such a way as to give both an idealised picture and a personal assessment of the history of the fledgling

---

[5] See Nasti, 'La memoria'.
[6] See Bargagli Stoffi-Mühlethaler, '"Poeta"', pp. 68–165; Berisso, 'Per una definizione', p. 123.
[7] Berisso, 'Per una definizione', p. 122.

Italian vernacular love lyric. Dante anthologised his poems according to their most obvious literary influences. The poetry of the *Vita Nova* moves from neo-Provençal compositions with formal and thematic connections to the schools of Guittone d'Arezzo and Bonagiunta da Lucca, through to the pessimistic and refined verse of Guido Cavalcanti, before culminating, under the stimulus of the optimistic and urbane elegance of Guido Guinizzelli, in Dante's own Christianising *stilo de la loda* ('praise style'). In addition, it has been convincingly demonstrated that the *Vita Nova* also implicitly includes a critical appraisal of most of the major moments and topoi of the Romance erotic tradition.[8] In this light, the *libello* is a *summa* of both a national and an international literary culture.

More importantly, by presenting his own writing on love – embodied not only in the 'praise style' (the altruistic celebration of Beatrice modelled on the Christian love of God) but also in the *Vita Nova* as a whole – as the pinnacle of the tradition, Dante pointed to his own pre-eminence in the field. Drawing on the standard idea about the intimate relationship between the quality of an author's love and the quality of his writing, the poet guaranteed his ideological and artistic primacy by showing that his love, the source of his writing, was uniquely free from any earthly desire and in close harmony with Christian *caritas*. Only the *Vita Nova*, according to Dante, successfully blends religious and secular elements, and thus gives a proper perspective on the nature of love and on how this should be poetically presented.

The approach Dante developed in the *Vita Nova*, whereby he tested the ideological and formal boundaries of a genre in order to demonstrate his own superior application of its conventions, was to become a hallmark of his subsequent writing. Typical, too, was the way in which he incorporated and judged, within his own text, the work of other writers in order to pinpoint their limitations, while, simultaneously, proposing personal solutions as to how these deficiencies could be overcome. Thus, until he discovers his own *stilo de la loda* in Chapters 17 and 18 of the *Vita Nova*, Dante experiments with poems in the style of a number of his peers, rejecting each in turn, since they all lack a properly spiritualised view of love. In this way, his experimentation could be considered both necessary and to have been legitimated in terms of the tradition. Similarly, although in the *libello* Dante was indubitably interested in establishing his own poetic standing and identity, this did not diminish his respect for other authors. And this attitude, too, evolved into a personal commonplace. In the *Vita Nova* and elsewhere, Dante always acknowledged that his own successes were dependent on the work of others. The respectful manner, for example, in which, in the *prosimetrum*, he addresses Guido

---

[8] Picone, '*Vita Nuova*'.

Cavalcanti[9] is evidence of this. Ultimately, one of Dante's achievements was to have restored life to two such fossilised concepts as *imitatio* and *aemulatio* (the rigidly hierarchical rhetorical doctrines of strict creative dependence on, and limited independence from, the literary practices of one's artistic models).

The formal structure of the *Convivio* (1304–7), too, is based on that of the glossed poetic manuscript. Dante's overt aim was to provide a literal and a 'philosophising' allegorical commentary to fourteen of his *canzoni* (he actually abandoned the treatise after analysing just three of his poems). However, as occurs in the *Vita Nova*, the *Convivio* in fact deals with a much richer array of critical problems than would appear from its statement of intent. In the introductory first book of the treatise, Dante went much further than he had done in the *libello* to emphasise his credentials as the best possible *lector* of his own verse. Thus, unlike others, he was not likely to misunderstand his own work (1.1.14–15, 18), and only he could set the record straight as regards his ideological intentions (1.2.15–17). In order to deflect accusations of self-centredness in talking about his own poetry, Dante appealed to the authority of the autobiographical writings of Augustine and Boethius, and, in keeping with a long-established tradition, repeatedly emphasised the social usefulness of his doctrinal 'exposition'. At the same time, however, in apparent contradiction with his earlier modesty, he also proposed his *canzoni* as models of allegorical verse and his commentary as a model of hermeneutical analysis (1.2.17). Despite the apparent altruism of his intentions, there is little doubt that, once again, the poet was concerned to establish his own 'authoritativeness' and his own uniqueness as a writer (1.9.2–3; 10.10). As in the *Vita Nova*, he bent the conventions of his day to his own ends, at times making them support positions which were the opposite of their accepted usage.

Dante's very choice of the literary commentary as the structure for his treatise is an obvious case in point. Even though he repeatedly labelled the *Convivio* a *comento* and an *esposizione*, gave the first book links with the *accessus ad auctores* and in particular, though far from exclusively, with the Aristotelian 'extrinsic' prologues on causality,[10] and, during the course of his introduction, reflected on the nature of commentary, the treatise has little in common with other poetic commentaries. The breadth of Dante's analyses places the *Convivio* in a quite new category of literary exegesis – and it is indicative that the poet laid emphasis on the profundity of his *esposizione* even as he ostensibly apologised for this supposed 'flaw' (1.2.1–2).[11] The treatise's interests range across astronomy, angelology,

---

9   See for example 3.14; 25.10; but see also Picone, '*Vita Nuova*', pp. 64–72; Barolini, *Poets*, pp. 123–53; Iannucci, *Dante*.

10   Trovato, 'Il primo'; Minnis and Scott, *Medieval Literary Theory*, p. 377.

11   Barański, 'Il *Convivio*'.

the *trivium* and *quadrivium*, love, light metaphysics, philosophy, nobility, history, politics, creation and classical literature. As a result, the poems, the apparent source of Dante's discussion, are almost forgotten, overwhelmed by the variety and complexity of the prose, thereby subverting the traditional hierarchical relationship between text and gloss ('this commentary, which is composed to act as a servant to the *canzoni* written below, must be subject to those in every respect'; 1.5.6). It is, in fact, at least open to question whether *comento* is the most appropriate designation for the *Convivio*, given that, formally, it has several of the traits of the encyclopaedic doctrinal *summa*. If it is regarded in terms of the exegetical tradition, which, in the light of Dante's definition, is how it ought to be regarded, the *Convivio*, like the *Vita Nova*, is closest to the commentaries on the Song of Songs, though it also has links with commentaries on theological and philosophical texts. Once again, Dante was applying to his vernacular *canzoni* structures which traditionally had had little to do with the explication of poetic *fictiones*. And it is not unlikely that one reason why, in Book 4, he interpreted the works of the great classical *auctores* according to the standard conventions of 'moral' allegory, was to hint at the ideological differences between his poetry and theirs. Dante was not just applying to his poems the critical techniques associated with Latin poetry, he was actually hinting, and fairly strongly at that, at the greater *auctoritas* of his compositions.

As well as the poet himself, the other main beneficiary of Dante's critical operations in the *Convivio* is the vernacular. There is no longer any suggestion that, as a literary language, it should simply be restricted to matters of love. The whole thrust of the treatise is to prove that it is a suitable medium for the dissemination of knowledge and for the composition of intellectually demanding texts. On the surface, Dante continued to acknowledge the superiority of Latin over the *vulgare* 'on account of its nobility, virtue and beauty' (1.5.7). He particularly stressed the former language's special associations with exegesis ('Latin, which has already been asked to act as commentary and glosses on many works'; 1.9.10). As a result, he put forward three reasons for his unexpected yet logically necessary choice of the vernacular for his exposition: (i) if the commentary had been written in Latin, it would have found itself in an inappropriate position of pre-eminence in relation to the vernacular poems it was meant to 'serve'; (ii) amplifying an idea he had already begun to develop in the *Vita Nova*, using the vernacular meant that many more people could benefit from the teachings of his commentary, and (iii) his decision was dictated by 'his natural love for his own speech' (1.5.2). Paradoxically, the more Dante excuses himself for having made recourse to the vernacular, the more he highlights the *novitas* and radicalism of his decision ('the vernacular will give a gift without being asked, which Latin would not have given: since it will give itself for the writing of commentary, which it was never asked by anyone'; 1.9.10 and see also 1.10.1–5). And this same tension is apparent elsewhere in the treatise. Dante scrupulously catalogues Latin's traditional advantages over the vernacular: 'Latin is perpetual and incorruptible, while the vernacular is unstable and corruptible' (1.5.7); 'Latin reveals many things conceived in the mind which the vernacular cannot, . . . [thus] its virtue is greater than that of the vernacular' (1.5.12); 'that speech is more beautiful, in which [words] more properly accord with each other [; and they more properly accord] in Latin than in the vernacular, since the vernacular follows usage, while Latin follows art' (1.5.14). Yet, at the same time, the *Convivio* – as the poet underscores – provides concrete evidence of the vernacular's 'solidity' and expressive power (1.10.12–13). In order to appreciate the logic and the force of Dante's arguments, his statements need constantly to be seen not in isolation but in relation to their total context. His celebration of the vernacular reaches its climax in his great and moving declaration of love for his maternal language in the last four chapters of Book 1, which he couples with a fierce attack on those *malvagi* who disdain the *vulgare*. Dante closes his introduction with a clear and remarkably accurate prophecy, whose biblical terminology only serves to enhance its force and solemnity: 'This [the vernacular and/or his commentary] will be the new light, the new sun, which will rise there where the old one [i.e. Latin and/or its elitist culture] will set, and it will give light to those who are in darkness and obscurity, since the old sun gives them no light' (1.13.12) – the fundamental reason, in brief, why Dante could aspire to transcend the achievements of the classical *auctores*.

In the *De vulgari eloquentia* (1305–7), Dante further opened out what was creatively permissible to a *poeta vulgaris*. On the surface, like the *Vita Nova*, the treatise upholds an essentially conservative critical frame. It vigorously subscribes to the doctrine of the three 'styles'. However, by discussing these not only in terms of Latin but also of vernacular literature, Dante suggested that the vernacular poets could deal with the same topics as the writers of Antiquity. In line with this suggestion, Dante once more boldly modified his thinking on the relationship between Latin and the *vulgare*, by openly stating what had already begun to be implicit in his earlier two works, namely, that, from a linguistic point of view, 'nobilior est vulgaris'. It was 'nobler' because 'it was first used by the human race; then because the whole world makes use of it, even if it is divided into different pronunciations and words; finally, because it is natural to us, while the other has a rather artificial origin' (1.1.4). To champion the vernacular, Dante thus had to reverse one of the reasons which he had given in the *Convivio* for Latin's primacy (compare 1.5.14). At the same time, and despite the change in his relative opinion of the two languages, on the surface at least, he left the supremacy of Latin literature unchallenged (it was only in the *Commedia* that he explicitly called this fundamental belief into question). The duty of the vernacular writer was – as it had always been – to imitate his classical forebears (2.6.7).

In the *De vulgari eloquentia* Dante is not, in fact, primarily concerned with the traditional relationship between classical and vernacular literature. His aim was to establish a new 'modern' literary hierarchy by exploring the respective artistic merits and achievements of French, Provençal and Italian. Dante was thus continuing and broadening out his analysis of the Romance tradition which he had initiated in the *Vita Nova*. No other work before the treatise's original mix of literary history, evaluation and prescription had considered vernacular writing with the same care and sophistication. Indeed, the map which Dante drew in the treatise of the development of the Italian love lyric holds good to this day.

For the poet, the critical assessment which he was undertaking in the *De vulgari eloquentia* must have seemed crucial, since it directly affected his own status as a writer. Given the late appearance of Italian vernacular literature, the range and number of its accomplishments were bound to appear lacking in comparison to the works produced by the older French and Provençal traditions. A contemporary topos – repeated by Dante – ascribed pre-eminence to French in the field of prose, and to Provençal in that of the lyric (1.10.2). In addition, the variety of different regional languages which could be heard in the peninsula inevitably put into doubt the very existence of an Italian literary language. Yet, despite this state of affairs, Dante succeeded in turning these potential weaknesses, which also represented a major threat to his own poetic standing, to his own advantage and to that of Italian.

Dante's vivid sense of the plurilingualism of his world made him aware of the fluidity of the cultural situation at the beginning of the fourteenth century. He perceived the jockeying for position of the different Romance languages as the opportunity to establish a new linguistic and literary canon, where Latin and its traditions were still the measure, though in more direct competition than hitherto with a pre-eminent vernacular culture. For Italy to enjoy this rank ahead of France and Provence, Dante had to establish that its tongue was more than just a collection of regional *sermones*. He had to show, as he did in Book 1 of the treatise, that not only did a *vulgare latium* exist as an independent language, but also that it was this that the best writers used in their works. Additionally, he had to prove that Italian was artistically the most efficacious of the Romance languages. Dante argued, therefore, after assessing the writings of others, that only poets writing in Italian (namely himself and Cino da Pistoia) had successfully imitated the *ars* of Latin, thereby obscuring one of the crucial differences between the two languages which he had noted in the *Convivio*. Thus, given that 'those who have most sweetly and subtly written poetry in the vernacular' ('qui dulcius subtiliusque poetati vulgariter sunt') belong to the language of *sì* (1.10.2), the present superiority of Italian was assured. Furthermore, Dante also implied that, on account of the special potential of literary Italian to match Latin, particularly in the works of its two leading practitioners, it was only a matter of time before Italian literature surpassed its competitors in every genre, and not just in love-poetry.

The *De vulgari eloquentia* undoubtedly marks a major step forward in Dante's critical thinking in comparison to the *Vita Nova* and the *Convivio*. Neither of these works can match the breadth of its literary allusions or the manner in which it explores literature's relationship to other spheres of human activity: most notably, language (as we have just seen) and politics. Dante's growing sense of the social functions of literature is another mark of the sophistication and originality of his critical vision. The poet's desire to transcend Italy's dialectal fragmentation was, in part, born from the experience of his exile. It was expressed as a desire for linguistic unity to counter both the country's political factionalism and the widespread external interference in its affairs (a factionalism and interference, which, as the poet noted, were reflected at the cultural level, since many Italian writers preferred to use either their *vulgare maternum* or another Romance language rather than the *vulgare latium*). According to Dante, the best Italian poets had shown the way not only to how a form of national unity might be achieved, but also to how hegemony could be established over Italy's neighbours. It was now the responsibility of politicians to build on this success and to follow suit. Dante was adapting the traditional idea of the 'poet-guide' to the contemporary situation, and, in one magisterial sweep, he proposed solutions to the literary and political problems which so preoccupied him.

After the 'lyrical privacy' of the *Vita Nova*, Dante gave an increasingly practical and public slant to his views on literature. Although their concreteness can be linked to his growing political awareness and to the ever-greater 'realism' of his work, their main stimulus remains Dante's refined sense of his own artistic persona, which he began to define not just in literary but also in socio-historical terms. It is this persona which is at the centre of things in the *De vulgari eloquentia*, and it has close links with the treatise's investigation of the relationship between language and ethics, which is probably its main concern. Other poets revolve (as do various contemporary political and cultural questions) around Dante Alighieri and his position of supreme authority as the 'sweetest and most subtle' of vernacular writers. Cino da Pistoia, with whom he pairs himself, actually serves to underline Dante's importance. As the younger of the two poets, he is necessarily following in Dante's footsteps. Cino is given a place in the treatise to prove that Dante's brand of 'illustrious' Italian poetry was capable of generating a living tradition, something which was fundamental if his arguments on the supremacy of Italian and its literature were to be persuasive. Once again, Dante is exploiting other writers to enhance his own standing; and, time and again during his artistic career, he shifted his literary alliances to suit his personal ends. Thus, Guido Cavalcanti, with whom he had associated himself in the *Vita Nova*, is marginalised in the *De vulgari eloquentia*. The complex toughness of Cavalcanti's syntax and his negative personalised philosophy of love, which Dante had already criticised and left behind in the *libello*, were clearly antithetical to the treatise's ideal of poetic musical elegance and to its abstracting vision of the uplifting power of love. Cavalcanti's place, as I have mentioned, was given to Cino, who, on account of his subordinate standing as a writer, in his turn, would be dropped in the *Commedia* in favour of more substantial figures such as the biblical authors, Virgil, Arnaut Daniel and Guido Guinizzelli.

What basically unites Dante's discussion of literature in the *Vita Nova*, the *Convivio* and the *De vulgari eloquentia* is the fact that, regardless of the novelty of so much of his art and of the details of his critical reflection, he always managed to remain within the broad limits of established theory and practice. At the most general level, both their poetics and the critical ideologies they propound can be explained in terms of such traditional systems as the dichotomy between Latin and vernacular culture or the *genera dicendi*. In fact, all three works clearly acknowledge and support the necessary superiority of the 'tragic' 'high style'. In the *De vulgari eloquentia*, Dante gave his fullest definition of this register: 'We . . . make use of the tragic style when the weight of the subject [*gravitate sententie*] accords with the magnificence of the verses as well as with the loftiness of the construction and the excellence of the vocabulary' (2.4.7). Earlier the poet had presented its subject-matter as limited to three topics: 'safety [*salus*], love, and virtue . . . [and] the things which are most closely connected with them, such as prowess in arms, the fire of love, and the right direction of the will' (2.2.7).

In the *De vulgari eloquentia*, Dante became ever more intent on the 'tragic' style. By doing this, he inescapably restricted the potential range of his art more and more. As Book 2 of the *De vulgari eloquentia* advances, this constraint becomes increasingly apparent. First, Dante transformed the *vulgare latium* from a living national language into an exclusively literary medium, the 'illustrious vernacular', which he equated with the rhetorical 'high style'. Second, only this refined language appears as the proper medium for poetry, on account of Dante's withering critique of Italy's regional languages in Book 1. As a result, it is not at all clear what the poet thought might in practice constitute the linguistic character of the other two literary styles to which he alluded in Chapter 4 of Book 2, and which he promised to discuss in the treatise's subsequent books. Thus, paradoxically, both the 'comic' – the 'inferior' style employing either the 'middle' or 'low' vernacular (2.4.6; but see below for Dante's highly original reworking of this *stilus* in the *Commedia*) – and the 'low' *vulgare* – the 'style of the unfortunate' written in the 'low' vernacular – appear as styles bereft of a language. Yet, once Dante had closed the *vulgare latium* in the trap of the 'high style', it is difficult to see how this alone could have ever been flexible enough to challenge Provençal and French literature in every genre, as he had declared in Chapter 10 of Book 1; nor how it could deal with that multilayered reality which had become the focus of his attention. If Dante was not to be doomed to remain forever a 'tragic' poet, he needed to reconsider both his own literary values and those of his culture. When he became aware of this, he symbolically abandoned the *De vulgari eloquentia* in mid-sentence, and, less dramatically, left off the *Convivio* at the end of its fourth book.

Dante resolved his problems by inventing the 'plurilingual' and eclectic style of the *Commedia* (*c.* 1307–21), which rejected the traditional grading and separation of literary *genera*, and instead supported integration. The ways in which Dante applied this notion when he composed and tried to clarify his poem are so novel that only now are we beginning to have a sense of their complexity. To put it simply, basing himself not on a rhetorical construct such as the 'illustrious vernacular' but on his 'maternal' Florentine, which he enriched with terms taken from all the languages and jargons with which he was familiar, Dante tried to find a register with which he could come to grips with the complexities of the world. As a result, he called into question the criteria which, for centuries, had served as the basis for all writing. He cast doubt on the efficacy and desirability of that artificial hierarchy of *auctoritates*, subject-matter, style and language on which rhetoric and poetics, and thus literature, stood.

The *Commedia*, unlike Dante's other works so far discussed, has no overt structural connections with the normal conventions of exegesis. The poem is the first-person account of the divinely willed journey through the three realms of the afterlife which the Florentine poet, Dante Alighieri, undertook bodily in the thirty-fifth year of his life. Formally, the *Commedia* is a narrative poem whose division into 100 *canti* of approximately 140 lines each and into three *cantiche*, one for each part of the otherworld, is an original invention of the poet's. At the same time, like many other medieval literary works, it contains internal allusions which provide critical aids to its interpretation. Such explanations tend to be closely integrated with the development of the action and with Dante's stylistic presentation of this. Literature and reflection on literature are tightly fused, so that it is rare to find examples of explicit and independent commentary in the poem. On the other hand, however, the reader is often encouraged to interpret by Dante's judicious and telling use of one or more technical critical terms as part of his overall formal presentation of an episode.

Paradoxically, the *Commedia*'s critical vision is both broader and more specific than that of any of the poet's other works. In the light of his challenge to the tradition, Dante's critical eye takes in what might loosely be termed literature in general. On the other hand, given the *novitas* of the alternative solutions he put forward in the *Commedia*, his critical reflection is on the whole directed at explaining his own poem. In his earlier works, because of their conventional nature, the tension between Dante's discussion of his own writing and that of other authors was much less apparent. His judgements, therefore, even at their most self-referential, appear to have an air of 'objectivity'. This was almost impossible when Dante attempted to account for his uniquely personal 'comedy' ('questa . . . mia comedía'; *Inf.* 16.28, and compare 21.2). In effect, the *Commedia*'s 'literary criticism' is basically equivalent to an act of self-justification. As Dante reached the peak of his thinking on literature, so this became indistinguishable from the poetics underlying his own poem. The whole of his artistic career had been steadily moving to this point, and thus it is significant that he was able to carry on employing in the *Commedia* critical structures which he had developed in his earlier works.

At the heart of the poem lies the explanation for its unorthodoxy; and it is misleading to try to minimise either the range or the nature of its experimentation. The *Commedia*'s hybrid style and content should not simply be reduced to a rhetorical exercise, as has been suggested by several critics. While it is undoubtedly true that the poem does include elements drawn from each of the three 'styles', and that certain passages can best be understood in terms of the conventions of the *artes poeticae*, there is much, even at the formal level, that cannot be accounted for in standard rhetorical terms. Thus, it would be interesting to know where precisely in the catalogue of 'styles' one would locate, for instance, Dante's description of Mohammed in *Inferno* 28 which, *inter alia*, draws on elements taken from the spoken language: scatological terms such as *trullare* ('to fart') and *merda* ('shit'), and examples of the barrel-maker's jargon (*mezzul* ['stave'] and *lulla* ['cant']) – the type of discourses which lay outside the lexicon sanctioned by the *genera dicendi*. Furthermore, the opening of Canto 28 is full of technical literary references (ll. 1–27) by means of which Dante points out that his language, which draws on forms traditionally lying outside the written language, is more effective at presenting the bloody horrors of the eighth *bolgia* ('ditch') than either historical prose or the 'tragic style' which conventionally had been linked to martial themes. As he had done in his earlier works, so in this canto too, the poet is both highlighting deficiencies in two specific traditions, and proposing new alternatives. What distinguishes this critique from, say, the *Vita Nova*'s discussion of love-poetry is that the solutions it offers stand squarely outside the boundaries of custom.

In addition, the *Commedia*, on account of its stylistic eclecticism and the carefully selected range of its intertextual allusions, does not limit its analysis to a particular genre or tradition, but encapsulates writing in general. The poem challenges both the system of *genera dicendi* and the literature this produced. In order to underline the *Commedia*'s superiority Dante consistently highlighted the differences between it and other texts: from the works of the Greek and Latin classics to those of the Provençals, and from those of the jongleurs to his own 'pre-comic' writings. The *Commedia* is concrete proof that alternative literary forms are eminently possible; and Dante's whole point seems to be that he could not find adequate formal and ideological support for his new poetry in the theory and practice of classical and medieval literature. It is thus indicative that no medieval rhetorical work can justify the *Commedia*'s original syncretism. On the other hand, Dante could have found some limited encouragement for this in brief asides by Cicero, Horace, Quintilian and Augustine,[12] whose works it can be shown he was probably studying at about the time he was planning the *Commedia*. However much Dante was his own man artistically, and however much he was aware of the unnecessary constraints which a rigidly codified approach to literature could impose, he always tried to maintain links with the tradition: this is the key critical tension which organises his *œuvre*.

The poet never forgot that he had to communicate in a society which, for centuries, had intimately associated certain forms with specific subjects and connotations. This was all the more crucial for a work of universal reform such as the *Commedia*. Dante's aim was to innovate and challenge from within the tradition, rather than to reject this unconditionally; hence the constant questioning appreciation of other writers, with Virgil at their head. Ultimately, if the poet had not created a dialectic between traditional forms and his own text, it is difficult to see how he could have underlined the newness of the *Commedia*. As was suggested earlier, he expected his readers to follow his metaliterary suggestions and be actively involved in interpreting his 'new' poem – just as they would have done with a more 'conventional' text. Exegesis was central to the medieval literary experience, and in the *Commedia* Dante called his readers to this in ways which would have been immediately recognisable. Thus, he tended to discuss other writers and their works according to standard definitions (Livy was he 'who did not err', *Inf.* 28.12; the *Aeneid* was

---

[12] Cicero, *De oratore* 1.16.70 (also 3.8.30, 32); *Orator* 20.70 (and compare 22.74); 27.97–9, 31.110–11; Horace, *Ars poetica* 9–11, 93–6; Quintilian, *Instit.* 8.3.21, 11.3.181; Augustine, *De doct. christ.* 4.22–3.

'the high . . . tragedy', *Inf.* 20.113), not least because such tags could immediately highlight an author's or a text's dependence on traditional criteria. Dante's very recourse to critical references and to an internal 'auto-commentary' as prompts to interpretation are typical of contemporary vernacular literature from the lyric to the *chanson*, and from the *roman* to the *novella*. At the same time, no other writer introduced these in such a programmed and subtle manner or in such numbers (just about every canto includes critical allusions of one kind or another). The poet talked about the *Commedia* in a language and in structures which he felt would be familiar to his culture. It is crucial that Dante did not invent a single new technical term with which to describe his poem. Yet, a semantic discrepancy is nearly always present between the content and form of the *Commedia* and the conventional associations of a particular literary critical allusion. Dante assumed that an ideological 'gap' would appear, for instance, between a reader's normal literary expectations at finding the poem defined as a *comedìa* and what he actually discovered in its pages. To overcome his confusion, the *lettor* would be forced to interpret.

The mechanics of this operation become clear if one considers, for instance, the logic of Dante's choice of the title *Comedìa* for his poem (the epithet *divina* was only added in the Venetian edition of 1555 printed by Gabriele Giolito and supervised by Ludovico Dolce). It is more than self-evident that the basic, widely diffused definitions of 'comedy' in terms of its 'low' (*humilis*) or even 'middle style' (*mediocris*) and of its structure ('Comedy . . . begins with various difficulties, but its subject-matter ends well'; *Ep.* 13.10) offer, at best, only a most partial elucidation of the *Commedia*. Ever since the fourteenth century scholars have tried to find other, more persuasive reasons for Dante's intriguing title. For example, his choice is explained as an act of modesty, as underlining the difference between Dante's poem and Virgil's 'high . . . tragedy' (*Inf.* 20.113), and as establishing links with 'satire', and so pointing to the poem's political concerns. What is striking about these and similar proposals is that they can all find support in contemporary discussions. Thus, it can be demonstrated that 'comedy' was both the most wide-ranging and most flexible of all the literary genres. In addition to the interpretations mentioned, it also embraced, for example, characters and emotions of every kind (see Quintilian, *Instit.* 1.8.7), it was associated with prose (see John of Garland, *Parisiana poetria* 1.51–2), and included a rich array of registers.[13] The 'comic' seems to have touched on every subject and style, seemingly standing for literature *tout court*, especially as, in the Middle

---

[13] See, for instance, Horace, *Ars poetica* 95; Quintilian, *Instit.* 10.1.65; Matthew of Vendôme, *Ars* 2.7.

Ages, it had lost contact with its original dramatic characteristics. It was therefore the ideal term with which Dante could suggest the variety and wealth of his poem. In one sweeping move, Dante brought together, within a single work, all those features of the 'comic' which the tradition recognised, but which both in its practice and in its theorising it never actually brought together and reconciled.

In addition, the notion of *comedía* also pointed to the poem's religious dimension, since it had contacts with the Bible and Christian literature. St Jerome praised 'comedy' for its moral vigour, while biblical *sermo humilis* established clear bonds with 'comic' *stilus humilis*. By the Duecento, the Bible was, in fact, being given as an example of both the 'middle' and 'low styles', the same ones to which 'comedy' had been conventionally linked.[14] Dante could not have found a more effective traditional tag to describe his poem than *comedía*; and by selecting this for its title, he immediately gave a hint of his work's synthesising ambitions and a clue to its interpretation in a textual space which the *accessus ad auctores* highlighted as important in understanding a work as a whole. 'Comedy' was the only 'style' which could give life to the ancient rhetoricians' cautious hints on artistic freedom; and, most of all, it could accommodate the poet's divinely instituted responsibility to present and explain in a single work the multiformity of 'that which is scattered in pages through the universe' (*Par.* 33.87).

This was the basic ideological reason why the *Commedia* was inescapably different. Since God's hand lay behind the poem ('the sacred poem / to which heaven and earth have set their hand'; *Par.* 25.1–2), it could not be judged in the same way as other human works. Similarly, since both the journey and the poem were presented as part of God's providential plan for humanity, Dante had to report as accurately as possible on every aspect of his otherworldly adventure (*Purg.* 33.52–7; *Par.* 17.127–9), an experience which seems to have embraced the whole of creation. Dante clearly could only achieve this end if he was not tied to standard literary conventions. It was because other authors were limited ideologically and formally in their focus, on account of their dependence on the hierarchies of the *genera dicendi*, that they could not supply Dante with adequate models for his kaleidoscopic 'divine' comedy. Instead, the *Commedia* turns to God for its legitimation, the one authority, Who could ensure that the poet's experimentation would not be dismissed as a catalogue of *vitia*. Dante's most explicit textual *auctoritates* in the *Commedia* are God's two 'books': the universe which includes the whole of creation 'in un volume' (*Par.* 33.86), into whose pages the pilgrim had been allowed to peer, and the Bible, which is written according to the stylistically and

---

[14] See, for instance, Bene of Florence, *Candelabrum* I.6.

thematically all-embracing conventions of the *sermo humilis*. Dante, imitating his models, attempted to create a similar harmonious synthesis by drawing on and remodifying 'all' the books, 'styles' and languages of his culture, and by placing these in a numerically balanced structure which recalled the order of God's 'art'. The poet had found unimpeachable 'authoritative' precedents for the broad eclecticism of his 'comic' form.

Dante repeats the macroscopic synthesising model of divine origin at every level of the *Commedia* in a continual interplay of the poem's form and content. Thus, he forged its allegory out of a combination which includes 'allegory of the theologians' and that 'of the poets' (see *Convivio* 2.1 and the discussion below) together with conventional and personification allegory. As with other aspects of his literary criticism, Dante's attitude to allegory became increasingly complex and totalising as his *œuvre* developed. The issue of Dante's relationship to the allegorical tradition and, in particular, of the *Commedia*'s dependence on its forms has, for centuries, represented the major area of disagreement between his readers.[15] The main reason for this critical dissension can be traced back to the simple fact that Dante's three explicit comments on the subject are neither particularly original and illuminating, nor can be said to cast light on the seemingly scriptural bias of the *Commedia*'s allegorical framework – its claim to tell of things directly involved in the unfolding of divine providence.

First, in Chapter 25 of the *Vita Nova*, the poet defended his use of the personification of Love as a 'figure or colour of rhetoric' (§7) and stressed the need for authors to be able to explain the rationale behind their own rhetorical inventions, noting that these had to be constructed 'with reason which can then be revealed [*aprire*] by means of prose [i.e. exegesis]' (§8). There is nothing really new here.

Second, things are somewhat more complicated as regards Dante's presentation of the differences between the 'allegory of the theologians' and that 'of the poets' in Chapter 1 of Book 2 of the *Convivio*, not least because a major lacuna and other textual cruces mar his definition (1.3). The problem revolves around whether Dante intended exclusively to analyse his *canzoni* according to the twofold canons of the 'allegory of the poets' ('my intention here is to follow the way of the poets'; 1.4), or whether he wanted to interpret these according to the fourfold structures of 'theological allegory' ('as regards each *canzone*, I will first explain [*ragionerò*] its literal meaning and then I will explain its allegory, namely its hidden truth; and occasionally I will touch incidentally on the other senses [i.e. the 'moral' and the 'anagogical'], as place and time will dictate'; 1.15). These two

---

[15] See Pépin, *L'allégorie*; Picone, *Dante e le forme*.

statements are not as difficult to reconcile as might be imagined. By the beginning of the fourteenth century, it had long been acknowledged that a few privileged secular works – most notably, Virgil's Fourth Eclogue, which was read as prophesying the coming of Christ – could not entirely be contained within the confines of the 'allegory of the poets'. In the *Convivio*, Dante appears to claim a similar limited flexibility for his *canzoni*, while at no stage denying their intrinsic 'fictionality'. And it is important to note that he was not alone in doing this: Alan of Lille had previously made a similar declaration on behalf of his *Anticlaudianus* (ed. Bossuat, p. 56; see also 5.265–305).

Third, in the *Monarchia*, in line with St Augustine, Dante warned against excessive and over-subtle allegorical interpretations (3.4.6–11).

What is important to recognise about these three largely traditionalist discussions of allegory is that none of them tells us anything directly about the specific nature of the *Commedia*'s allegorical make-up. Since Dante did not explicitly address this problem in the poem, it has been customary to explain its allegory by making recourse to the *Epistle to Can Grande*. Whatever one might think about the status and exegetical efficacy of the letter, this is unsatisfactory for one crucial reason. The *Epistle* is far from being the indispensable sole prerequisite which legitimates the interpretation of the poem according to the 'allegory of the theologians'. Given that 1315 has been proposed as the letter's earliest possible date of composition, this means that the first two *cantiche* were already completed and circulating before they could count on the *Epistle*'s support. It is extremely likely, therefore, that *Inferno* and *Purgatorio* contain internal indications as to their allegorical status; otherwise, they would be open to misinterpretation. And both canticles do indeed include such indications. To help his readers understand the epistemological and ontological complexity of his text, Dante organised various episodes, beginning with *Inferno* 1 – the prologue to the poem as a whole – in such a way that they revealed the variety of its allegorical levels. Thus, in order to underline the veracity of his poem's account, its God-given attributes, and its contacts with the Bible, Dante suggested that the journey, since it was part of God's providential scheme, had to be interpreted in the light of fourfold biblical allegory, although all those sections of the poem which did not directly refer to this event had to continue to be viewed in terms of its twofold secular model. In his treatment of allegory, as elsewhere in the *Commedia*'s critical structure, and as he had first done in the *Vita Nova*, Dante brought together religious and secular culture. His was the most original and systematic expression of that convergence of biblical and literary exegesis which was a key feature of the literary thought of his day. It was in the space between these traditions that he tried to locate the *novitas* of his own poem. Since Dante never claimed that he could match the perfection of God's 'poetry', he had to draw on every literary tradition and on the whole gamut of language, so as to make his defective human voice as forceful as possible in proclaiming the divine message. With God, the supreme *auctor*, on his side, Dante could both permit his literary sensibilities to have total freedom and present the *Commedia* as the archetypical 'earthly' text for others to 'imitate'. His was a literary form which offered practical confirmation of how human *verba* benefited from participating as directly as possible in the divine *Verbum*. Once more, Dante was pushing a key medieval critical concept – that of God as the ultimate source of all writing – to its logical conclusion.

The *Commedia* was to be the 'new' book for a modern, Christian culture; and, as such, it was intrinsically superior to even the 'highest' Latin 'tragedy', Virgil's *Aeneid*. Dante's energies in the poem are directed towards establishing this fact. The question of its language is no longer an issue. The problem of the literary efficacy of the vernacular had been theoretically settled in the *De vulgari eloquentia* – a proposition which finds practical confirmation in the *Commedia*'s poetry. In *Paradiso* 26 Dante did, however, briefly return to the question. By having Adam, the first speaker, acknowledge that language, as a human invention, was inescapably subject to change (ll. 124–38), Dante re-emphasised that the vernacular's 'instability' was not a flaw but something quite 'natural', thereby 'auto-justifying the paradox of the sacred poem in a perishable language' (Contini, *Varianti*, p. 343).

The range and ambition of Dante's critical operations are impressive. It is doubtful whether any other Western writer or literary thinker comes close to the breadth and daring of his reflection on literature. Quite simply, Dante not only assessed and systematised a tradition which had been unfolding for about 2,000 years, but he also used his reflection as the springboard for a series of artistic experiments which were meant to indicate ways in which this same tradition could renew itself. Although every word any author writes can be said to have literary critical reverberations, as twentieth-century structuralist and post-structuralist thinkers have suggested, it is the degree of control and order which he can impose on his artistic reflection that distinguishes one writer from another. Dante's reflections on literature show perfect timing, not least because they bring together so effectively the literary and the critical, and merge these with his other concerns. However necessary, it is mechanical to compartmentalise the poet under discrete labels such as 'Dante the literary critic'. A major facet of his thinking on literature was to show how this had contacts with the whole of human experience. Yet, despite Dante's 'realism', his literary reflection is largely inward-looking. It illuminates brightly an author's original view of his own work and artistic self; and it represents the apex of such contemporary concern with the authorial *officium*. By taking note of his 'literary criticism', we are at last beginning to read Dante as he wanted us to read him. Like the most consummate *magister*, the poet guides our interpretations of his texts, so that the prose commentaries which, in the *Vita Nova* and the *Convivio*, delimit an independent exegesis of his poems are, in many ways, the most revealing signs of the nature of his critical reflection.

21

The *Epistle to Can Grande*

Zygmunt G. Barański

Modern editors divide the *Epistle* into thirty-three paragraphs or chapters. These fall into three main sub-sections: paragraphs 1–4 dedicate the *Paradiso* to Can Grande; paragraphs 5–16 begin by presenting a general introductory discussion of allegory with reference to the four interpretative 'senses' of biblical exegesis (§7), and then analyse the *Commedia* as a whole and the third *cantica* in particular under six headings drawn from one of the standard models of academic prologue to an *auctor* ('There are six parts . . . which need to be discussed at the beginning of every didactic work, namely, the subject, the author, the form, the aim, the book's title, and the branch of philosophy to which it belongs'; §6); finally, paragraphs 17–33 offer a close 'literal' reading of the opening twelve lines of *Paradiso*, concentrating in particular and with considerable expertise on many of their philosophical and theological allusions.

One of the most controversial issues in present-day Dante studies concerns the authorship and significance of the *Epistle to Can Grande*,[1] whose apparent addressee was the Lord of Verona between 1311 and 1329. Unlike most other critical disputes, the question of whether the letter is or is not by the poet has a direct and fundamental bearing upon our appreciation of the *Commedia* and of its author's intellectual development. If genuine, then, the *Epistle* is a key auto-commentary to the poem, second only in importance to the *Commedia*'s own self-reflexive critical system, although any comparison between them confirms the undoubted greater exegetical range and sophistication of the poem. Thus, a major issue in the debate concerning its authenticity is why Dante should have felt the need to compose a work which was not just less effective as a *commentarium* than the *Commedia* itself, but was also frequently at odds with the poem's interpretative, artistic and ideological aims.

A more general problem involves the letter's position in the history of Trecento Italian discussions of vernacular authors. Supporters of the

---

[1] For surveys of the main points in this debate, see Mazzoni, 'L'Epistola'; Brugnoli, 'Epistole: Introduzione', with the notes in his edn of Dante, *Epistola* XIII; Paolazzi, *Dante*, pp. 3–10; Barański, '*Comedìa*'; Hollander, *Dante's 'Epistle'*; Cecchini, 'Introduzione', pp. x–xxv. See also Ricklin, *Das Schreiben*.

Epistle's authenticity claim that it is the oldest commentary on the *Commedia*, and propose the years 1315 to 1317 for its composition.[2] However, the philological evidence in support of this view is not compelling. Only a very small number of possible lexical similarities between the *Epistle* and other commentaries has been adduced. Furthermore, it is not at all clear from these verbal repetitions whether the commentators depend on the letter or whether the process of influence flows in the opposite direction. The fact that the *Epistle* was quoted for the first time and assigned to Dante solely around 1400, in the *praefatio* to Filippo Villani's *lectura* on *Inferno* I,[3] undermines the positions of those who argue in favour of its genuineness and its early composition. Finally, its manuscript tradition does nothing to clarify matters, but is itself a source of further uncertainty. The three oldest fifteenth-century manuscripts merely transmit its opening four paragraphs, the complete work appearing only in six sixteenth-century exemplars. All these difficulties have led to suggestions that the letter is a late-fourteenth-century compilation made up of several different texts written during the course of the Trecento.[4] A variation of this hypothesis acknowledges the genuineness of the first four paragraphs, but considers the remainder a forgery, the work of an unknown author who merged Dante's original brief letter with his own much longer invention.[5]

Given the present state of our knowledge, it is impossible to give definite answers to the questions of the *Epistle*'s date, manner of composition and influence; thus, little if any help can come from these three areas in deciding whether or not it should belong in Dante's *œuvre*. More substantial evidence against its authenticity has been presented by those who have examined its style (in particular, its use of the *cursus*)[6] and its philosophical preferences which often run counter to what is known about Dante's ideological formation.[7] The arguments against the letter's authenticity have not been convincingly refuted; nevertheless, it is also important to note that a majority of Dante scholars, albeit a decreasing one, continues to believe in its genuineness. One aspect of the *Epistle*, however, can yield telling information about its possible provenance and cultural identity. Whatever else the letter might be, it is undoubtedly a *commentarium* on a particular text and author. All its most important students, regardless of their other views on the *Epistle*, concur that attention should focus on

---

[2] Mazzoni, 'L'Epistola', pp. 187–93.   [3] Villani, *Expositio*, Prefatio, 32 (p. 38).
[4] See Hardie, 'The Epistle'; Paratore, *Tradizione*, pp. 110–11; Kelly, *Tragedy*.
[5] See Mancini, 'Nuovi dubbi'; Nardi, *Il punto*.
[6] See Dronke, *Dante*, pp. 103–11; Kelly, *Tragedy*, pp. 79–111; Hall and Sowell, '*Cursus*'.
[7] See Brugnoli's notes to his edn of Dante, *Epistola* XIII; but see also Padoan, 'La "mirabile visione"'; Martinelli, 'La dottrina'; Botterill, ' "Quae non licet" '.

its status as a commentary.[8] Yet, until very recently, little progress could be made in assessing the letter's status as an exegetical text.

Thanks to the rapid development in the 1980s of work on medieval literary criticism, we are now in a much better position both to define its characteristics as a *commentarium*, and to measure its interpretative solutions against the *Commedia*'s critical self-explanations and its overall stylistic and ideological make-up. Many Dante scholars assume that the *Epistle* presents vital information on the poem's allegory (§§7–8) and on its genre (§10), thereby resolving problems to which the poem itself does not appear to provide obvious solutions. If this is true, then supporters of its authenticity are correct in assuming that it is an exegetically sophisticated text, and that its author could only have been Dante himself. Yet one can argue that the analyses of the *Commedia*'s allegory and its title are neither especially significant in themselves nor relevant to an understanding of the poem; in fact, the opposite would seem to be the case. As was suggested in the previous chapter, Dante selected the title *comedía* for his work, because he believed that the term's wide-ranging connotations could give an immediate impression of his work's unique formal and ideological range. At the same time, in the *Commedia*, he fashioned a highly complex self-reflexive critical system which was meant to vindicate and clarify his 'experimental' view of the 'comic'. In stark contrast to the poem, the *Epistle* presents a highly reductive and conservative treatment of 'comedy', which closely follows the most conventional of contemporary discussions, such as those found in medieval Latin glossaries and in the commentary tradition to Terence:[9] 'comedy comes from *comos*, village, and *oda*, which means song, thus comedy is as it were "country song"'; 'Comedy begins with various difficulties, but its subject-matter ends well, as appears from Terence's comedies'; and 'in its style of language ... comedy is ... unstudied and low [*remisse et humiliter*]' (§10). On the basis of these definitions, it is difficult to see how the *Commedia* actually differs from any other vernacular work of fiction with a 'comic' structure. Furthermore, the manner in which the *Epistle* dismisses the *vulgare* ('as regards its style of language, this is unstudied and low, since it is the vulgar tongue, in which even women [*muliercule*] communicate'; §10) runs counter both to Dante's elevation of Italian in the *De vulgari eloquentia* and to the wealth of uses to which he put his 'maternal' language in the *Commedia*. Nor is the fact that paragraph 10 quotes Horace's

---

[8] See Moore; 'The Genuineness', pp. 351–3, 363–9; Curtius, 'Dante', pp. 163–71, and *European Literature*, pp. 221–5; Mazzoni, 'L'Epistola'; Nardi, 'Osservazioni'; Hollander, *Allegory*, pp. 237–8; Brugnoli, 'Epistole: Introduzione'; Ascoli, 'Access'.

[9] On medieval discussions of comedy, see Cloetta, *Komödie*; Quadlbauer, *Die antike Theorie*; Bareiss, *Comoedia*; Villa, *La 'Lectura'*; Kelly, *Tragedy*; Barański, '*Comedía*' and '*Libri*', pp. 61–99; also the relevant discussion in Chapter 6 above.

Ars poetica 93–6 significant as far as Dante's poem is concerned: 'Similarly they differ in their style of language: tragedy is high and sublime, while comedy is unstudied and low, as Horace says in his *Poetria*, where he allows comedians occasionally to speak like tragedians, and vice versa: "Yet sometimes comedy raises its voice / and angry Chremes reproaches with swelling language / and in tragedy Telephus and Peleus often lament in pedestrian language, etc"' (§10).[10] The allusion to the Latin poet in no way legitimates the poem's unique mingling of 'styles'. First, looked at *per se*, Horace's lines advise caution when mingling genres, while allowing some limited licence to both tragedians and comedians. Second, the letter does not actually use the 'authority' of the *Ars poetica* to argue for a relaxation of the *genera dicendi*, but to illustrate the necessary formal separation between genres – precisely the same conventional end to which ll. 93–6 were put in a large number of *commentaria*.[11]

The *Epistle*'s discussion of allegory divides into two parts. Most Dante scholars believe that what makes the letter impressive is the way in which, in paragraph 7, it boldly asserts that the poem depends on the scriptural 'allegory of the theologians', thus separating it from the 'beautiful lies' of other poets. As a result, they pay less attention to paragraph 8, since its claims are rather less dramatic. Yet, it is only in this paragraph, and not in the preceding one, that we are explicitly given the 'subject' of the *Commedia*'s allegory: 'But if the work is considered allegorically, the subject is man according as by his merits and demerits, the result of his free will, he deserves rewards or punishments from [divine] justice' (§8). It has been shown that there is little to distinguish this particular ethical interpretation of Dante's poem from all the other moralising literary analyses of classical and medieval texts pursued under the aegis of the 'allegory of the poets'.[12] In fact, to have stated that the *Commedia* dealt with a moral subject was to lower it to the most common of contemporary exegetical denominators, since a common view held that literature in general could be classified under ethics.[13] The rest of the letter's *accessus* section takes its interpretative lead from the exposition of the poem's *subiectum*. 'Philosophically', the *Commedia* is classified under ethics, since its aim is largely 'practical' (§16); its *finis* is expressly seen in moral terms: 'to remove the living in this life from a state of misery and to lead them to a state of happiness' (§15); its *forma tractandi* underlines its secular

---

[10] 'Similiter differunt in modo loquendi: elate et sublime tragedia; comedia vero remisse et humiliter, sicut vult Oratius in sua Poetria, ubi licentiat aliquando comicos ut tragedos loqui, et sic e converso: "Interdum tamen et vocem comedia tollit, / iratusque Chremes tumido delitigat ore; / et tragicus plerunque dolet sermone pedestri / Telephus et Peleus, etc.".'

[11] See Quadlbauer, *Die antike Theorie*, pp. 138–9, 173, 214, 223–4; Mengaldo, *Linguistica*, pp. 211–12; Villa, *La 'Lectura'*, p. 40.

[12] Minnis and Scott with Wallace, *Medieval Literary Theory*, pp. 385–6.

[13] See Allen, *The Ethical Poetic*.

content and traditional style (§9);[14] its *titulus* (as we have seen) points to its rhetorically constrained fictional genre and to its dependence on Terence, traditionally one of the most 'moral' of poets; finally, Dante's 'total' authorship is emphatically highlighted (§14), thereby negating the possibility that the *Commedia* might in any way be divinely inspired. The *accessus* pursues a remarkably consistent exegetical line, which is further supported by the subsequent analysis of the opening of *Paradiso*. Its interpretative homogeneity has two main ideological corollaries, both of which are at odds with the *Commedia*'s poetry and its internal critical explanations. First, the *Epistle* presents the poem as if it were a standard fictional work conventionally composed according to the norms of 'poetic allegory' and those of the *genera dicendi*. Second, and stemming from the previous position, its aim is to deny that the *Commedia* can in any way be read, like the Bible, as a divinely inspired work. In relation to the standard assumptions of medieval exegesis, there is nothing remarkable about the *Epistle*'s presentation either of the poem's allegory in paragraph 8 or of its general literary characteristics.[15] Its author belongs to the conservative wing of fourteenth-century Dante exegesis. Like nearly all the Trecento commentaries, the letter conventionally standardises the poet's formal and ideological innovations (though to a greater degree than the others, as a comparison of their *accessus* reveals). Similarly, like several of the commentators (most notably, Pietro Alighieri), the author of the letter felt extremely disturbed by the *Commedia*'s religious connotations (though it is equally noteworthy that, in his commentary, the Carmelite friar, Guido da Pisa, interpreted the poem as the work of a *scriba Dei*).[16] In the key contemporary debate on the relationship between poetry and theology,[17] one of whose central questions concerned the status of Dante and the *Commedia*, the *Epistle*'s anonymous author rejected the possibility that an inter-relationship might exist between literature and 'divine science'. He simply and conventionally dealt with the poem's religious dimension by resorting to a rhetorical commonplace. He defined the *Paradiso*'s subject-matter as *sublimis* (§3; see also §19), namely, as belonging to the 'tragic' 'high style'. (And it is far from insignificant, when deciding on the letter's authenticity, to remember that, in the *Commedia*, Dante never described either his last *cantica* or the poem as a whole by means of this ideologically and stylistically selective term.)

The letter's conservative attitude returns in its treatment of the relationship between Latin and the vernacular – another crucial fourteenth-century issue. Its traditionalist championing of the classical

---

[14] See *Epistola* XIII, ed. Brugnoli, pp. 613–14.
[15] For recent dissenting views, see Pertile, '*Canto-cantica-Comedía*', and Ascoli, 'Access'.
[16] See Nasti, 'Autorità'.
[17] See Minnis and Scott with Wallace, *Medieval Literary Theory*, p. 390; Boli, 'Boccaccio's *Trattatello*'.

language, already obvious in paragraph 10, is best exemplified by the fact that its author translated into Latin any lines he quoted from the *Commedia*. In this way, he traditionally attempted to match its *sublimis materia* and its linguistic form. If the *Epistle* were by Dante, then, this would be an astonishing procedure. It would mean that the poet, against his own practice in the *Commedia* and his self-defence in the eclogues, accepted the proposals of those, like Giovanni del Virgilio, who appealed to him to use Latin, and not the language of the common people, when dealing with 'sublime' matters. Overall, a gulf separates Dante's views from those of the author of the *Epistle* as regards not only the *Commedia*, but also literature in general. The letter's limitations as a literary *commentarium* call into question the claim that only a Dante could have written it. Yet, as was noted earlier and as Dante scholars have long argued, paragraph 7 would appear to countermand my thesis. In its opening, the letter implies that the *Commedia* has a complex, biblically inspired allegorical organisation: 'the meaning of this work is not simple, rather it can be called polysemous, that is having various senses' (§7).[18] Several major complications accompany this claim: (i) it is contradicted by the specific definition of the poem's allegory in the following paragraph; (ii) it runs counter to the letter's general secularising interpretation of the *Commedia*, and (iii) the letter illustrates the workings of 'polysemous' allegory solely with reference to the Bible (and it is noteworthy here that both Guido da Pisa and Jacopo della Lana felt able to draw on the *Commedia* to demonstrate its contacts with 'fourfold allegory').[19] These problems, however, can be resolved and the letter's logical coherence can be restored, if we consider the argumentative structure of its central panel. It can be argued that paragraph 7 has rather less to do with the *Commedia* than has been widely assumed. It is, in fact, a general introduction ('To clarify, therefore, what has to be said . . .'), which attempts to give an overview of allegory's full range. In order to do this, it inevitably has to turn to the Bible for its examples, and, in the process, moves ever further away from Dante's poem. The *Commedia*'s actual exegesis, as would have been acknowledged by readers versed in the conventions of *poetarum enarratio*, only begins in paragraph 8, when it is considered under the first of the *accessus* headings, that of the *subiectum*. Rather than being complementary, the two paragraphs stand in opposition to each other, and thus the Bible and the *Commedia* exemplify the two main kinds of allegory. By implication, the poem's allegory is shown to be inferior to that of the Bible; in fact, as the letter evinces, a few scriptural verses are exegetically richer than an entire human text. Once again, the letter's author puts the *Commedia* in its place.

[18] '. . . istius operis non est simplex sensus, ymo dici potest polisemos, hoc est plurium sensuum.'

[19] Guido da Pisa, *Expositiones*, pp. 6–7; Jacopo della Lana, *Comedia*, I, pp. 104–5.

As was suggested in the preceding section, the *Commedia* does not, in fact, need the *Epistle*, or any other text, in order to highlight its reliance on the 'allegory of the theologians'. Its system of critical allusions reiterates this point throughout its length. Nor was the *Commedia* the first literary work to claim to have similarities with the Bible; for instance, Alan of Lille's *Anticlaudianus* declares a not-dissimilar ambition (ed. Bossuat, p. 56; see also 5.265–305). Nor is there anything particularly exceptional in the fact that the author of the *Epistle* should have discussed religious and secular exegesis in a *commentarium* to a literary work. Such overlapping of critical interests had been a characteristic feature of exegesis at least since the twelfth century, and had reached its apex in Trecento Italy. If anything, the *Epistle* shows itself rather resistant to the fusion of the human and the divine. All in all, there seems to be little that smacks of Dante in its pages.

Postscript

An important discovery regarding the *Epistle to Can Grande* has very recently been made.[20] A reference to the letter has been found in a Florentine manuscript (Florence, Biblioteca Nazionale Centrale, II I 39), which – it is claimed – was written in the 1340s and contains the commentator Antonio Lancia's autograph vernacular glosses to the *Commedia*. At fol. 133r, and more than fifty years before Filippo Villani, Lancia, who had a very good knowledge of Dante's 'minor works', presents the poet as the author of the *Epistle* ('as the author himself wrote to *messer Cane della Scala*') and precisely translates into Italian the letter's explanation of the twofold division of the *Paradiso* into a 'prologue' and an 'executive part' (§17). Until now, the manuscript had been assigned to the fifteenth century and had been judged a collection of miscellaneous glosses to the *Commedia*. If both the new dating and the ascription are correct, then it is somewhat more likely that the letter is by Dante. At the same time, there is nothing in Lancia's statement to prevent one from concluding that the *Epistle* is an early rather than a late Trecento forgery, since the commentator's recourse to the letter does nothing to resolve the many technical and ideological problems associated with it. In particular, even if it could definitively be demonstrated that the *Epistle* were Dante's, this in no way would change the fact that it is a conservative commentary largely at odds both with the *Commedia*'s exegetical structures and with its poetic and intellectual character. The fascinating question would arise, however, of why Dante had felt compelled to compose a misleading commentary on his masterpiece. Perhaps the beginnings of an answer might be sought in the poet's relationship to the *Epistle*'s addressee.

[20] See Azzetta, 'Le chiose', in particular pp. 37–47.

22

The Trecento commentaries on Dante's *Commedia*

Steven Botterill

Copies of *Inferno* and *Purgatorio* were already circulating in northern Italy when Dante died in September 1321, and these lost early exemplars were the forerunners of hundreds of fourteenth-century manuscripts of the *Commedia*, complete and partial. Few vernacular texts achieved so rapid or widespread a diffusion anywhere in medieval Europe. But Dante's poem was not long allowed to go about unaccompanied. By 1322 commentators were working on *Inferno*; by the decade's end a commentary on the whole *Commedia* had appeared, and the first century of Dante criticism eventually yielded a vast crop of exegesis. It includes full-scale commentaries, in which theoretical prologues, proems to each canto and textual glosses are combined to form an organic whole; sets of individual glosses (*chiose*), either discontinuous or in connected prose; and a variety of paraphrases, summaries, introductions, biographies, and other prolegomena, frequently in verse, which flourished on the margins of commentary proper, especially in the 1320s. New material continues to come to light: a long-lost Neapolitan commentary on *Inferno*, of 1369–73, was published in 1998.[1] Commentators wrote in Italian and Latin, all over Italy (Naples, Milan, Bologna, Venice, Verona, Pisa) and abroad (Germany). Even Dante's loved and hated native city paid tribute to the poem that so ruthlessly dissects it: Giovanni Boccaccio and Filippo Villani lectured and wrote on *Inferno* in Florence, while the *Ottimo commento* and the work ascribed to the 'Anonimo Fiorentino' almost certainly originated there.

This imposing mass of material did not, however, come out of nowhere. Although the response generated by the *Commedia* is unparalleled for sheer volume, the idea of commentary itself was familiar in Trecento Italy, where the late thirteenth century had seen a growing willingness to equip readers of vernacular texts with the guidance they were used to finding in commentaries on the Bible and the major Latin authors. Dante himself was active in this field: both the *Vita Nova* and the *Convivio* are, essentially, commentaries on vernacular lyrics, the one providing structural analyses (*divisiones*) and a narrative matrix, the other

---

[1] Maramauro, *Expositione*; for a still more recent discovery, see Seriacopi, 'Un commento'.

exploring the poems' allegorical significance and philosophical background (see Chapter 20 above). In the early Trecento, Francesco da Barberino and Niccolò de' Rossi glossed their own vernacular poetry (in Latin), and the physician Dino del Garbo wrote a commentary on Guido Cavalcanti's notoriously elusive *canzone* 'Donna mi prega', arguing that it speaks 'in a scientific and accurate way, based on the precepts of natural and moral science', and explaining it in terms that owe much to both Aristotelian thought and medical training (p. 359). A debt to Avicenna, for instance, has been identified in this representative gloss on ll. 39–41:

So we see from experience that love often kills, when someone is fervently dedicated to it; and also that, when human beings forget about love, the act alone enables them to revert to their natural disposition; wherefore doctors claim that the best cure for this passion of love is that the lover be distracted from thoughts of the beloved object and forget about it.   (p. 370)

Dante's Trecento commentators could, then, easily find precedents for their undertaking; but the *Commedia* was longer, structurally more complex, and intellectually more demanding than any vernacular text tackled by their predecessors. Its first critics were constantly required to extend the boundaries of their critical tradition, to develop accepted modes of reading in unexpected directions, and to invent new concepts and vocabulary, in order to cope with the startling originality of the text before them. The result was an extraordinarily diverse body of criticism, which offers multiply-refracted images of poem and author alike, ranges widely in method and conclusions, but is unified by the conviction that the *Commedia*'s manifold meanings can – and should – be made clear through acts of interpretation. This energetic confidence is the hallmark of Trecento commentary on the *Commedia*.

The tradition's basic and most influential text was undoubtedly the *Epistle to Can Grande*, discussed in detail above (Chapter 21). Throughout the Trecento, it remained a touchstone for commentators, many of whom drew on its methodologically conservative analysis – though whether directly or indirectly is rarely clear. Whatever the truth about its disputed authorship, the *Epistle* definitely dates from the final years of Dante's life. Within a year of his death, his son Jacopo, in exile at Verona, had begun a commentary of his own in defence of his father's memory; his vernacular *chiose* on *Inferno*, completed by 1324, are preserved in several manuscripts. They show some textual affinity with two obscure sets of Latin glosses, also apparently produced before 1324. A recent and still controversial 'reconstruction' of these proposes them as originally the work of a single author, the 'Anonimo Latino'; but whatever the truth of this, or of their relationship with Jacopo's *Chiose*, they have survived only in fragmentary form.

More lastingly significant was the work of Graziolo de' Bambaglioli, a distinguished politician and jurist from Bologna, whose Latin glosses on *Inferno*, also dating from *c.* 1324, are found in three manuscripts (one complete, two partial) and several contemporary *volgarizzamenti*. The 1320s were fruitful years indeed for Dante commentary, and their crowning achievement was the earliest surviving commentary on the whole *Commedia*, by Jacopo della Lana, probably composed in Venice between 1323 and 1328. Lana's work soon became popular (more than eighty manuscripts are extant, and at least two Latin versions of the vernacular original also circulated), and was widely used and cited by later commentators.

It should perhaps be stressed, at this point, that much is still uncertain about the dating, provenance and authorship of many of the Trecento commentaries, and about the complex network of influences and borrowings that links them. No one chronological ordering is universally accepted; and, in the present state of the texts – most are available only in inadequate nineteenth-century editions, and a few even remain unedited – conclusions based on anything other than close study of individual manuscripts must often remain provisional. Probably the most controversial case in point is that of Guido da Pisa, author of a poetic paraphrase (*Declaratio*) of the *Commedia*, and of a Latin prose commentary (*Expositiones*) on the *Inferno*, which occurs in at least five manuscripts. The *Declaratio* can plausibly be dated to 1325–8, but the commentary's date is still highly contentious. The most authoritative modern student of the material, Francesco Mazzoni, has consistently argued for a late dating, to about 1343–50; but recently the balance has shifted towards general acceptance of a date in the late 1320s (perhaps 1327–8), on the basis of compelling, mostly internal, evidence presented by other scholars.

The consequences of such uncertainty for our understanding of the commentaries will be obvious. To take a pertinent example: the numerous resemblances between Guido's *Expositiones* and the first of the three redactions of the so-called *Ottimo commento* can be explained as borrowings; but the question of who borrowed from whom can only be resolved after deciding which dating of Guido's work is correct, since the *Ottimo*'s first version is known to date from *c.* 1330. The second redaction (1334–7) and the third (1337–40) remain unpublished *in extenso*. All three are in the vernacular, cover the *Inferno*, *Purgatorio* and (in fragments) *Paradiso*, and seem to have been written in Florence, probably by 'Andrea Lancia, notaio fiorentino' – the conventional explanation of the enigmatic initials 'A. L. N. F.' found in several of the twenty-odd manuscripts. The redactions differ considerably, especially in their theoretical prologues, and are distinguished below as *Ottimo* I, II and III.

Pietro Alighieri's *Commentarium* on his father's poem also exists in three redactions (of 1340, 1350–5 and *c.* 1358; = Pietro I, II and III as discussed below). It was written, in Latin, at Verona, and quickly established a high reputation for authority and critical acumen. Its appearance also coincided with – perhaps provoked – a crisis in the history of the *Commedia*'s interpretation. For more than a decade after the completion of Pietro's third redaction, no serious effort to continue the tradition was made. Several sets of *chiose* appeared in the middle decades of the Trecento, but Pietro's was the only attempt at coherent, theoretically based commentary. As early as 1337, a glossator, probably Sienese, had produced the vernacular *Chiose Selmiane* on the *Inferno* (a fuller version in another manuscript is called the *Chiose Marciane*); the *Chiose Cagliaritane*, also in the vernacular, on the whole *Commedia*, originated in Arezzo or Cortona after 1345; in about 1355 another (possibly Milanese) author was responsible for the Latin *Chiose Ambrosiane*, also on the whole poem; and, after 1360, two scribes in the abbey of Montecassino concocted the modified transcription of Pietro II and III sometimes referred to as the *Chiose Cassinesi*. Of these *chiose*, only the *Selmiane/Marciane* exist in more than one manuscript, and their influence was correspondingly small.

This relatively barren period is significant, in that it marks the start of the long, slow process in which commentators on the *Commedia* gradually became estranged from their text. When the elderly Boccaccio began work on his vernacular *Esposizioni* (interrupted, at *Inferno* 17, by his death in 1375), half a century had passed since Dante's death; scholastic culture had entered a decline that was to prove terminal, and the new interests and approaches later to be labelled 'humanist' were already encouraging – if not actually imposing – new ways of reading.

An innovation in method, related to these developments, was the *lectura Dantis*, the public reading and exposition of a single canto. This practice inspired the three major commentaries of the late Trecento. Boccaccio lectured on the *Inferno* at Florence in 1373–4; Benvenuto da Imola (Bologna, 1375) and Francesco da Buti (Pisa, *c.* 1385) both discussed the whole *Commedia*. In each case the lectures were followed, after a short interval (though Buti took ten years), by the commentary's appearance in written form (Boccaccio's and Buti's in Italian, Benvenuto's in Latin). We also have a preliminary version of Benvenuto's work (the – unpublished – Florence, Laurenziano Ashburnhamiano, MS 839), and a *recollectio* of his lectures prepared by another hand; this was mistaken, by its first editors, for an original commentary by Stefano Talice da Ricaldone, the (fifteenth-century) copyist of the work's unique manuscript. These three commentaries were well received (more than thirty manuscripts exist of both Benvenuto and Buti), and Boccaccio in particular found posthumous disciples: as well as Benvenuto himself, his *Esposizioni* inspired the unknown author of the Latin *Chiose Filippino* (Naples, late Trecento), and an anonymous Florentine ('Falso Boccaccio'), whose mediocre and imitative vernacular *chiose* have been dated to about 1375.

Imitation, indeed, was a major feature of *Commedia* commentary at the century's end, and the result was critical stagnation. The vernacular commentary attributed to the 'Anonimo Fiorentino', dating from about 1400 and attested in a handful of manuscripts, is heavily reliant on Buti in the *Inferno* and *Purgatorio* sections and in the *Paradiso* section merely transcribes Lana. The solitary manuscript of Filippo Villani's Latin commentary of 1402–4 (based on his experience as *lector Dantis* in Florence between 1391 and 1402) provides an enormously lengthy preface and glosses limited to *Inferno* 1; this top-heavy reading offered no real way forward. Glossators were still active (Benedetto, in Pisa, 1408; Frate Stefano, in Bologna, 1408; both in Latin); but, as late as 1417, Giovanni da Serravalle's Latin *Comentum*, written at the instigation of two English bishops during the Council of Constance, responds to the *Commedia*'s challenge with close, even slavish, dependence on Benvenuto. The critical methods and values that had underpinned Dante commentary since the 1320s had finally ossified, and study of the *Commedia*, like many other cultural activities, was to be radically transformed in the late fifteenth century.

What, then, were these methods and values? The methods, of course, are best studied in practice; some examples of how the commentaries actually work are considered below. But many commentaries include an explicit statement of theoretical intent, usually in a separate prologue, and from these it is possible to gain some idea of the assumptions that precede and condition the commentators' engagement with Dante's poem. Sixteen such statements will be analysed here: those of Jacopo Alighieri, Graziolo, Lana, Guido, *Ottimo* I, II and III, Pietro I, II and III, Boccaccio, 'Talice', Benvenuto, Buti, Villani and Serravalle (none exists for the 'Anonimo Fiorentino' or the mid-century *chiose*). Most of these share with the *Epistle to Can Grande* a hermeneutic scheme based on the established procedures of the *accessus ad auctores*, but there is frequent, and frequently revealing, variation among them. The *Epistle* superimposes on this scheme that of the *quadruplex sensus* (interpretation according to the literal, allegorical, tropological and anagogical senses of a text); this too appears in some Trecento commentaries. The presence and treatment of these paradigms form a convenient starting-point for comparative study; but three early commentaries exempt themselves immediately. Jacopo Alighieri asks only two preliminary questions of his text: the meaning of its title and how it is divided; he answers with definitions of tragedy, comedy, satire and elegy, and a description of the *Commedia*'s narrative structure in the form of a *divisio*. Graziolo too is interested chiefly in *divisio*: 'the material of this book', he announces, 'can be divided into two parts', and the crucial point is the appearance of Virgil (*Inf.* 1.61–3), which separates Dante's bewilderment in the 'selva oscura' from his education in the circles of Hell (ed. Rossi, p. 5). The prologue to *Ottimo* I declares baldly that 'to uncover the author's intention one must understand the images [*figure*] that he uses', and accordingly supplies allegorical elucidations of Virgil, Beatrice, the 'donna gentile' and Lucia (I, p. 4).

The remaining commentators ask some or all of the six questions of the *accessus*, which the *Epistle* calls those 'asked when beginning to read any work of doctrine' (*Ep.* 13.6): what are its subject (*subiectum*), authorship (*agens*), form (*forma*), purpose (*finis*), title (*titulus*) and branch of philosophy (*genus phylosophie*)? Although the commentaries often show strong verbal similarity to the *Epistle*'s questions and answers, this does not prove that every commentator knew it. The *accessus* scheme was a commonplace in the late Middle Ages (as Chapters 5, 6 and 14 above have demonstrated), and the use, in a given commentary, of categories based upon it, is of strictly limited assistance in establishing derivation from any earlier text. Moreover, formulations traceable to the *Epistle* are not infrequently so transformed in the commentaries – even garbled – as to suggest either deliberate reworking of the original or, in many cases, the intervention of other texts. The commentaries' reliance on the *Epistle* is neither automatic nor consistent. As the decades slid by, it became an increasingly distant landmark, more likely to be assimilated through textual intermediaries than at first hand – if indeed it was known at all. It is worth noting that no commentator before Villani either mentions the *Epistle*, as such, or attributes it to Dante, unless the recent 'discovery' of a reference by Andrea Lancia in the 1340s can be confirmed (see 'Postscript' to Chapter 21).

It need not, then, seem surprising that by no means all the Trecento commentaries follow the *Epistle* in employing both the *accessus* scheme and the *quadruplex sensus* in their standard form. The most faithful is Guido's *Expositiones*, whose definitions (apart from a broader conception of the *Commedia*'s *finis*) are also markedly similar to the *Epistle*'s. Lana almost matches Guido's fidelity, but discusses the poem's title under *forma* and its allocation to a branch of philosophy under *finis*, thereby blurring two of the six conventional categories. He does, however, mention the *quadruplex sensus*, and adds a *divisio* of the *Inferno* (Guido has one of the whole poem). Pietro Alighieri uses the six *accessus* questions (though *genus phylosophie* is missing from Pietro III), but in Pietro I the four senses become seven, with the addition of *sensus historicus, apologeticus* and *metaphoricus*. These refinements disappear from Pietro II and III, where the *quadruplex sensus* is absorbed into the discussion of *forma*. In Boccaccio, Buti and Serravalle the *accessus* scheme takes its familiar form, but Boccaccio postpones consideration of the *quadruplex sensus* to the commentary on *Inferno* 1, while Buti appends it to his preliminary *divisio* of the same canto.

Other commentaries differ more substantially. *Ottimo* II enquires into three of the *accessus* questions under their usual names (*materia, titolo* and *parte di filosofia*), and two more under unusual ones (*agens* becomes *nome* and *finis* is divided into *intenzione* and *utilità*); the *quadruplex sensus* and the poem's *forma* are combined in a separate category, *forma del trattato*. *Ottimo* II also offers a *divisio* of the *Commedia* and an examination of 'the cause that moved the author to write' (see Jacopo della Lana, ed. Scarabelli, I, p. 97); these also appear in *Ottimo* III, which, however, omits the *forma del trattato* section (and hence the *quadruplex sensus*) and the *agens*.

'Talice' and Benvenuto, so closely linked in origin, form a case apart. 'Talice' covers all the usual points except *forma* (splitting *finis* into *intentio* and *utilitas*, like *Ottimo* II and III), and divides the poem into *cantiche*. Benvenuto dispenses with this *divisio*, and, although he asks all the *accessus* questions, his discussion of *forma* appears under the rubric *titulus*.

Finally we come to Filippo Villani. His achievement is to give conventional models a spurious novelty by inventing his own technical lexicon. Having surveyed his predecessors' methods – the *quadruplex sensus*, various forms of the *accessus* (including, specifically, that used in the *Epistle to Can Grande*) and the four Aristotelian causes (efficient, material, formal and final) – he stakes a claim to originality: 'I prefer to recall the diligence of the ancients to modern attention, and to mix the new with the old' (p. 38). But Villani's headings turn out, on examination, to be exactly equivalent to the six *accessus* questions: *res* to *subiectum*; *qualitas* to *forma*; *locus, tempus* and *persona* to *agens*; *causa* to *finis*; and *facultas* to *genus phylosophie*. *Titulus* alone is common to both schemes.

If the commentators' questions about the *Commedia* are diverse, their answers are still more so. The two points on which all agree are that the poem's *agens* was Dante (most supply long and sometimes fanciful biographies), and that its *titulus* is *Commedia* (variously spelled). Thereafter, a hundred flowers bloom. Definitions borrowed or derived from the *Epistle* retain a powerful influence at both conceptual and lexical levels, but often serve only as points of departure. For example, the *Epistle* defines the *Commedia*'s *subiectum* as (literally) the state of souls after death, and (allegorically) human beings sinning or doing good according to their use of free will (*Ep.* 13.8). This definition is reproduced without significant changes in vocabulary by Lana, Guido, Boccaccio and Buti, and with verbal alterations that do not affect the concept by Villani. *Ottimo* II adds 'human behaviour' (see Jacopo della Lana, ed. Scarabelli, I, p. 96);

Ottimo III mentions only the state of souls. 'Talice' (I, p. 4), Benvenuto (I, pp. 15–16) and Serravalle (p. 21) collapse the literal and allegorical meanings into one, depriving the latter of much of its force; for them the poem's subject is 'the state of the soul, when united with and when separated from the body', a tripartite condition expressed in the *Commedia*'s tripartite construction. Only Pietro Alighieri is clearly independent of the *Epistle*; Pietro II and III do no more than embroider on Pietro I's pithy remark that the *causa materialis* is 'that which our poet has said in this poem' (p. 3).

The commentaries' conceptions of *forma* likewise show traces of the *Epistle*'s distinction between *forma tractatus* (the structure of *cantiche*, *canti* and *versi*) and *forma tractandi* (*Ep.* 13.9). This latter, the poem's 'mode of procedure', is defined in a famous series of adjectives as 'poetic, fictive, descriptive, digressive, transumptive, and also definitive, divisive, probative, improbative, and rich in examples'. Not all the commentators, however, observe the distinction precisely. *Ottimo* III and 'Talice' ignore it altogether; Serravalle mentions only *forma tractandi* (while his phrasing reflects the *Epistle*'s definition of *forma tractatus* – perhaps an indication of just how muffled its message had become as it was transmitted across the Trecento). Even those who do make the distinction show many lexical divergences from the *Epistle*, and do not always discuss it under *forma*. Once again, the most independent – and commonsensical – voice is Pietro Alighieri's. In Pietro I *forma tractatus* is simply 'the division of this book', and *forma tractandi* is the *septemcuplex sensus* mentioned above (p. 4); in the more elaborate versions II and III, *forma tractatus* becomes 'the unity of the parts of this volume', *forma tractandi*, the *sensus* model in its fourfold form (pp. 5–6).

As with *forma*, so with *genus phylosophie*: the *Epistle*'s definition ('the moral sphere, or ethics'; *Ep.* 13.16) is quoted verbatim by Guido da Pisa and, with frequent but insignificant variations in wording, by all the other commentators. Some, however, expand it: *Ottimo* III also allocates the *Commedia* to natural philosophy, metaphysics and theology, and Benvenuto's declaration that it belongs to 'all kinds of philosophy: ethical, metaphysical, and physical, but chiefly and most properly ethical' (I, p. 17) is sketched in 'Talice' and repeated by the loyal Serravalle.

Treatments of the *Commedia*'s *finis* are more varied. All the commentators allude to the *Epistle*'s phrasing ('rescuing those living this life from their wretched state and leading them to a state of bliss'; *Ep.* 13.15), but most modify its sense. Pietro I and III delete the reference to eternal life, though Pietro II speaks vaguely of 'rewards' and 'penalties'; according to both later redactions, the poem intends 'to show by example how human beings should behave in this world and what they should avoid; in short, in what the good of mankind may consist' (pp. 3–4). 'Talice' and Benvenuto divide *finis* into *intentio* (making people good) and *utilitas* (leading them to know happiness); Villani calls the former purpose *causa propinqua* and the latter *causa remota*, borrowing the terms but not their meanings from the *Epistle*.

Other commentators add emphases of their own. Most important is the literary and stylistic interest shown by Lana, Guido and *Ottimo* II, who all include the promotion of oratory in their conceptions of *finis*; Guido also adds 'the renewal of poetry' and, more moralistically, 'the condemnation, through examples, of the wicked lives of evil men, and especially of prelates and princes' (p. 128). Meanwhile, *Ottimo* II and III join Lana in claiming that 'the telling of many tales' is another of the poem's functions, and both examine under this heading the *Commedia's utilità*, which for *Ottimo* II lies in its 'instruction in honest living' (see Jacopo della Lana, ed. Scarabelli, I, p. 97), and for *Ottimo* III in its wealth of doctrine.

Finally, even the seemingly straightforward question of the poem's *titulus* is not without controversial implications. Most of the commentators take it as a pretext to discuss comedy as a genre, following the *Epistle*, which defines comedy, contrasts it with tragedy, lists other genres, and cites Horace as its authority (*Ep.* 13.10). The commentators' response is, as ever, broadly differentiated. Lana and Boccaccio define comedy alone; Buti considers the choice of the comic genre without defining it; Villani defines comedy and tragedy; Pietro defines both these and lists other genres; 'Talice', Benvenuto and Serravalle define comedy, tragedy and satire; Guido adds lyric to this list, and *Ottimo* II and III define comedy, tragedy, satire and elegy.

It should be clear, even from this brief survey of their prologues, that the Trecento commentators display a remarkable openness to innovation, an eagerness to explore to the full the possibilities offered by the critical tools they inherit from their predecessors and each other. Their quest for completely satisfying exegesis, and their attempt to devise new methods with which to achieve it, explain many features of their commentaries, from the numerous adaptations of the *accessus* scheme through the repeated rewritings of the *Ottimo commento* and Pietro's *Commentarium* to the lexical inventiveness of Filippo Villani. But the commentaries' boldness and diversity only become fully apparent beyond the confines of prologue, at the point of contact with the *Commedia* itself. The conversion of theory into practice will be the subject of the rest of this chapter.

If there is one problem with which all the commentaries had to come to terms, consciously or otherwise, it was the relationship between literal and allegorical reading – between exposition of what the *Commedia* says and explanation of what it means. Following the *Epistle to Can Grande*, most Trecento readers accepted that the poem's meanings are not exhausted by explication of its literal sense ('the meaning of this work is not simple, indeed it may be called polysemous, that is, having many meanings'; *Ep.* 13.7). But the extent to which it was legitimate to look for meanings beyond the literal, as well as the nature of such meanings, never ceased to be controversial. Solutions ranged from one extreme (the identification of an allegorical correspondence for the poem's every detail) to the other (the consistent avoidance of allegorical interpretation), through a variety of compromises, in which literal and allegorical approaches were more or less felicitously harnessed together. The extreme positions were delineated as early as the 1320s, by Jacopo Alighieri and Graziolo de' Bambaglioli.

Jacopo proclaims that his father's intention was 'to show, in allegorical guise [*sotto allegorico colore*], the three qualities of human kind' (p. 87), and the primacy of allegory in his reading is apparent from his comment on *Inferno*'s opening lines:

The author . . . noticed that he was in a dark wood, where the straight path was lost. By which, figuratively, he means the many people who dwell in the darkness of ignorance, unable to advance towards human happiness; so he calls them a wood, to show that there is no difference between their sensible and rational nature and the merely vegetable.   (pp. 89–90)

Thereafter, Jacopo's procedure is to advance through the narrative, explaining historical and mythological references as they occur, and missing no chance to interpret them allegorically. Thus Icarus (*Inf.* 17.109) teaches us that 'any son who acts contrary to his father's instructions will eventually bring about his own downfall' (p. 156); Narcissus (*Inf.* 30.128) that 'he who pays too much attention and regard to the beauty of the body causes the death of the mind' (p. 208). Though sometimes arid, this method, at its best, can produce readings both coherent and illuminating. Particularly suggestive examples include Jacopo's lengthy explications of Minos, as a figure of human conscience, or of the size and appearance of Lucifer:

He is depicted as enormous, with three faces and three enormous wings, to show that all the sin in the world is embodied in him. . . . Of the three coloured faces, the middle one, which is red, is an image of [*si figura*] sinful and hateful rage; the white and yellow one is an image of impotence; and the black one, of the darkness of ignorance.   (pp. 220–1)

Graziolo's commentary, on the other hand, evinces scepticism about the importance of allegorical reading. Dante's initial predicament is explained in allegorical terms, which establish a framework for the commentary as a whole ('the author shows how, borne down by the weight of his grievous vices in this life and vale of wretchedness, wandering from the path of light and the truth, he had fallen away from virtue'; ed. Rossi, p. 5); but from *Inferno* 2 onwards the framework is increasingly taken for granted, and Graziolo devotes most of his energy to expounding the poem's literal meaning, drawing on his wide reading (his *auctores* include Augustine, Boethius, Gregory and Aristotle, as well as Dante himself) and philosophical interests (which inspire, for instance, an extended discussion of the figure of Fortuna in *Inferno* 7). Allegorical interpretations are reserved, henceforth, for particularly thorny problems like that posed by the 'Veglio di Creta' (*Inferno* 14): 'It should be noted that in this old man is signified and figured the whole history and decline of the world, and also the whole empire, and the lives of emperors and princes from the beginning of the reign of the above-mentioned Saturn to the present day' (ed. Rossi, p. 112).

Graziolo's aversion to systematic allegorical reading appears especially clearly when his treatment of Lucifer is compared with Jacopo's. For Jacopo, every aspect of the portrayal (Lucifer's size and posture, his three faces, their differing colours) has a hidden significance, which must be carefully elucidated. Graziolo, however, is concerned with narrative, poetics and plain fact:

Here the author describes how Lucifer, father and prince of the other unclean spirits, dwelt in those depths, and he says that he was frozen in the ice of Cocytus, the infernal river. . . . Lucifer's left-hand face is black, and this is expressed in a simile, for he says that this face was like those of men who live or are born on the banks of the Nile, the greatest of rivers. . . . He says that Lucifer was devouring and destroying a certain sinner in the manner of a *maciulla*. A *maciulla* is a device for breaking flax, also called *spadola* or *cramola*.

(ed. Rossi, pp. 214–15)

In the face of such divergent possibilities, some commentators seek to reconcile the demands of literal exposition and allegorical interpretation. Jacopo della Lana's solution is based on an innovation in method: beginning with *Inferno* 6, he provides every canto with a *proemio*, summarising its subject-matter, structure and deeper significance, and thus uncovers what he calls the canto's *intenzione*. These proems, which vary in length from a few lines to over twenty printed pages (*Paradiso* 6), are accompanied by glosses of problematic words, phrases and lines, in which free rein is given to Lana's well-developed didactic impulse. The *proemio* to *Inferno* 14 is typical of his approach:

In this canto the author intends to discuss those whose pride caused them to hold God in contempt and hatred, and he punishes them according to the division made above. . . . He divides them into three groups. The most contemptuous are supine on the sand, and the [fiery] moisture falls on them; those in the second group are seated, hunched up so as to occupy as little space as possible, and continually doing their best to shield themselves from pain with their hands; and the third group is running around the others, in ceaseless movement without respite. The author adopts this scheme in his allegory to show that pride against God must be punished by God, and that his justice is so righteous that even the lowest created things share in his judgement, like the sand. The author also introduces, as will be clear in the text, some poetic fables. . . . Having declared the intention of the present canto and the condition of those it mentions, it is time to expound the text, where necessary.

(Jacopo della Lana, I, pp. 262–3)

The reader is thus furnished, by way of introduction, with a survey of each canto's major issues, and informed reading is further assisted by the detailed glosses, which range from linguistic notes on obscure or regional words to the theological excursuses that abound in Lana's notes on *Paradiso*. This pragmatic combination of literal and allegorical reading (which Lana achieves, paradoxically, by treating the two approaches as separate stages in the act of reading itself) was to be highly influential in the Trecento – thanks, no doubt, to the scope the method offers for both theoretical synthesis (in proems) and textual analysis (in glosses).

Its influence is, for example, clearly discernible in the *Ottimo commento*, whose frequent echoes of other commentaries (especially in *Ottimo* I) strongly suggest that it was conceived, in both method and substance, as a synthesis of existing *Commedia* commentary. The *Ottimo commento* distinguishes less sharply between *intenzione* and *esposizione* than does Lana. Its proems are usually based on *divisio*: 'The first part [of *Purgatorio* 15] completes the treatment of envy; in the second begins the treatment of anger. . . . The first part can be divided into six parts . . . the second into three' (II, p. 257). Its glosses, meanwhile, are used as vehicles for literal *or* allegorical commentary, according to the perceived requirements of the text. Occasionally the two are linked, as in this note on *Purg.* 30.121, which also exemplifies the *Ottimo commento*'s characteristic readiness to read the *Commedia* through Dante's other works:

This text [*lettera*] has two explanations: in one you may say that he speaks of Beatrice, as she was in her bodily existence among mortals, when her beauty had so much influence on Dante that it took from him every evil thought, and inspired thoughts of good, as is clear from his *canzoni* and sonnets. . . . The other refers to his spirit and intellect, saying that the author began the study of theology as a youth, and was excellently trained in it, as he says in *Inferno* 15 . . . and this study sustained him for a long time, and saved him from falling into the luxury and vices of the world.   (*Ottimo I*, ed. Torri, II, pp. 539–40)

Lana's structural model was not, however, universally adopted. Guido da Pisa works, instead, with a modified scheme in which each canto is first summarised and paraphrased in detail (*deductio textus*), then glossed (*expositio lictere* [*sic*]), and finally examined for similes (*comparationes*), theological problems (*questiones*), prophecies (*vaticinia*) and other points of interest (*notabilia*). As the (admittedly sporadic) presence of *questiones* and *vaticinia* implies, for Guido the *Commedia*'s dominant meaning is that of an inspired vision granted to a prophetic Dante, which expresses truths in words not themselves necessarily true. The problem of veracity – the sense in which *Inferno* can be said to be 'true' – becomes all-important.

Commenting on *Inferno* 1.1, Guido borrows terms and definitions from Macrobius to argue that the *Inferno* has the characteristics of *oraculum*, *visio* and *somnium*, all of which 'signify and express something true' ('aliquid veri significant et important'), but not of *insomnium* or *fantasma* which, being false, are 'unworthy of the task of interpretation'. His conclusion is unequivocal: 'Therefore, at the mid-point of our life, that is, in a dream . . . the author claims [*fingit*] to have seen his visions' (pp. 18–21). This visionary framework enables Guido to establish two ways of reading the *Inferno*, which at once relate it to, and differentiate it from, the 'divine page' which is the ultimate standard of truth:

Note that the author, after mentioning the vices that prevent men from doing good, describes how Virgil, greatest of poets, appeared to him, and how he freed him from those three vices. Here it should be noted that, in this passage, Virgil is an image and likeness [*tenet figuram et similitudinem*] of human reason, with which the author makes his penalties fit his crimes. So if, in some place or passage, he seems to speak against the Catholic faith, let no one be surprised, for he goes along his way writing poetically, according to human reason. And I, expounding and glossing likewise, will follow no path but my author's. So where he speaks poetically, I shall speak poetically; where theologically, theologically, and so on in each instance. I do not, however, intend to say or utter anything contrary to the faith or to Holy Church. . . . Therefore I beg you, reader, not to judge or blame the author, if he seems in some place or passage to contradict the Catholic faith, for he speaks poetically and fictively.   (pp. 30–1)

'Poetic' writing (and reading) are thus exempt from the 'theological' requirement to be truthful, but they can – and do – sometimes fulfil it. For Guido, the essence of allegory is not just that one thing shall stand for another, but that the thing for which it stands shall be the truth. In this way his reading fuses the literal and the allegorical, for the letter of Dante's text conveys an allegorical meaning that is in turn expressive of the true letter of the 'divine page'. His commentary's close relationship with Scripture is also confirmed by his frequent quotations from the Bible and the Fathers, although he by no means disdains classical culture (the 'pagan' page is regularly cited alongside the 'divine'), or, indeed, empirical observation ('Carrara marble is the whitest and most precious found anywhere in the world'; p. 389).

If for Guido Dante is a visionary and his text prophetic, for Pietro Alighieri he is a poet and his text a fiction. Especially in its later redactions, Pietro's *Commentarium* is firmly founded on the concept of *fictio*, carefully distinguished from any notion of the true (with the help of Papias, Isidore, Horace and Augustine), and consistently used to explain the *Commedia* in terms of secular, not sacred, writing and experience (pp. 5–7). Forms of the key verb *fingere* recur continually, a constant reminder of the poem's fictional status, and an implicit rebuke to any pretensions, on the text's part or the reader's, to divine authority. In Pietro's vocabulary, allegory has none of the connotations of truthfulness so vital to Guido: 'Allegory means speaking otherwise, that is, when the text [*litera*] says one thing and something else is to be understood' (p. 7).

This does not mean, however, that allegory is unimportant. Indeed, the progressive revisions of the *Commentarium*, as well as adding to the somewhat scanty cultural material in Pietro I's annotations, incorporate an increasingly profound exploration of allegory and the ways in which it combines with the letter to produce *fictio*. In Pietro I, for example, Capaneus (*Inferno* 14) is dealt with succinctly and literally: 'Capaneus was so arrogant before the gods that he blasphemed them as if they had been men, especially Bacchus, god of the Thebans; and for this Jove struck him down . . . and slew him' (p. 238). Pietro II expands the narrative, building on Pietro I's idea that Jupiter, Vulcan and Vesta may be images (*poetice . . . accipitur*) of fire; but Pietro III introduces the technical lexicon of allegory ('if anyone wishes, the story may be allegorised [*posset . . . allegorizzare*] in this way'), and reads Capaneus himself figuratively, in a moral context, as representing 'the life and condition of many powerful rulers in this world, whose pride swells to such a degree that, despising and blaspheming God, they think Him unable to harm them in any way' (p. 240).

Here both the focus on this world and the reluctance to impose an interpretation on the reader (*si quis enim vellet . . .*) are characteristic of Pietro's undogmatic approach. The *Commentarium*'s lasting influence may partly be owed to this flexibility, which frees the poem from the stricter categories to which earlier readers (Jacopo Alighieri, Guido da Pisa) had sought to confine it, and links letter and allegory in a relationship that is dynamic and open to a variety of interpretations. Pietro's own method is also indicative of this unwillingness to construct rigid categories: he dispenses with the arrangement in *proemio* and glosses, which Lana and others generally use to embody the division between allegory and letter, and simply begins each canto's commentary with a brief *divisio* and supporting quotations from *auctores*.

Guido links literal and allegorical reading in his concept of *visio*, Pietro in his concept of *fictio*; Boccaccio breaks the connection. His *Esposizioni* are based, in fact, on a well-nigh absolute cleavage between letter and allegory: most cantos are glossed twice, once for *senso letterale* and once for *senso allegorico*, and Boccaccio's findings are presented under separate rubrics. Usually the literal exposition is considerably longer than the

allegorical: the major exception is *Inferno* 1, where the allegorical meaning of the 'selva oscura' is subjected to searching examination. This is
preceded, however, by a literal reading:

Here he describes the three qualities of this wood: he says first that it was 'wild',
meaning that it contained no human habitation, and was frightening on that
account; then he says that it was 'harsh', to show the nature of the trees and
plants therein, which must have been ancient, with long, twisted branches,
tangled and woven together, and likewise thick with thorns, brambles and twigs,
growing unchecked and extending in all directions; and for this reason the wood
was 'harsh' and difficult to traverse. And when he says 'stubborn', he means the
difficulties already mentioned, since the wood's harshness makes it stubborn,
that is, hard to walk through and get out of. And he says all this was so terrible
that 'in my thoughts', that is, in the memory of his experience, 'fear is reborn'.
For it is human nature to be afraid all over again whenever one remembers the
perils in which one has been.   (pp. 20–1)

Only after the whole canto has been expounded in this fashion does
Boccaccio change tack: 'Since, by the grace of God, that which may be
explained according to the literal sense has been dealt with, it is time to
return to the beginning of the canto and uncover and expound what is
hidden under the coarse rind of the words, that is, the allegorical meaning'
(p. 53). Here the reason for Boccaccio's ruthless separation of letter and
allegory becomes clear: the two kinds of reading are suitable for different
audiences. 'Those of lesser sensibility' can not only 'take pleasure in the literal meaning but also develop their abilities and become better equipped'.
Understanding of the hidden, allegorical sense, however, is reserved for
'the most powerful intellects' (p. 59).

Readers of the literal sense, then, will be content with the story
recounted in the text, while the 'ingegni più sublimi' identify Dante's sleep
as that of a soul steeped in vice, the 'diritta via' as the path leading to eternal life, the 'selva oscura' as Hell itself, the sunlit mountain as Christian
doctrine illuminated by the Holy Spirit, and so on. *Inferno* 1, however,
shows this method at its most fully developed. Elsewhere literal exposition
dominates, and allegorical reading can seem perfunctory in contrast. It is
far from indispensable, in fact, to Boccaccio's scheme (hence its absence
from the commentary on cantos 10 and 11, neither of which contains 'any
allegory whatsoever'; pp. 537, 558), and his proto-humanist devotion to
the letter is evident throughout, in the treatment of etymologies, classical
allusions and poetic tropes, and in the extended definition and defence
of poetry, against detractors both Platonist and patristic, occasioned by
Virgil's 'poeta fui' at *Inferno* 1.73 (pp. 33–43).

By the end of the Trecento, the critical issues that had excited the
Commedia's earliest commentators were losing some of their urgency.

Benvenuto da Imola, for instance, is not greatly exercised by the relationship of letter and allegory, though he insists on the figural interpretation of Beatrice and acknowledges his debt to Boccaccio (I, pp. 89–90). No trace of his mentor's separation of literal and allegorical reading survives, however, in Benvenuto's massive work, where commentary on each canto begins with a *divisio*, followed by glosses in continuous prose that include explication of both literal and allegorical senses.

The complex ingenuity of Benvenuto's technique is apparent in this gloss on *Par.* 1.46–8, which also gives a hint of the erudition and scientific interests that led Francesco Mazzoni neatly to define Benvenuto's as a commentary '*ad usum humanistae*'.[2] The analysis rests on Benvenuto's basic identification of Beatrice with theology; Dante's text here compares her to an eagle:

First, the eagle is a great bird, as sacred knowledge is great, and it has huge wings, a large beak, and strong claws, so that the noble eagle is queen over the other birds; and theology is above all things, for the divine rules and governs everything human. The eagle flies higher than other birds, and sees more clearly, as Beatrice alone ascends into heaven and sees God; for the enquiries of theology are the means of knowing God. Wherefore theology is called knowledge by its very nature, which is to be the end of all knowledge and its perfection; for theology itself is the goal to which all enquiry tends and in which it rests. The eagle is the only bird that is not struck by lightning (so Pliny asserts), as the laurel is the only tree; and theology, alone among the branches of knowledge, cannot be eclipsed. . . . The eagle alone can gaze upon the sun's rays, and those of its offspring that cannot do this it does not feed, but casts out; and so does Beatrice. . . . So we have the most noble eagle, which feeds only on the hearts of other birds, which it consumes for its nourishment; and thus this noblest of branches of knowledge alone embodies the principles of all the others. Therefore the poet says, literally, 'no eagle ever gazed upon it thus', that is, with such fixity; as if to say, that no physical eagle could gaze so constantly at the physical sun, as this spiritual knowledge gazes, contemplating the spiritual sun that is God. And here notice that the author speaks very justly: for the eagle could not gaze upon the sun's sphere with the mere purity of its eyes. The sun's scorching, burning light produces many reflections of its rays on the eye's polished sphere, reaching even the centre of the eye, where is the glacial humour in which the images of visible things are sealed. This reflection heats and dissolves that humour; and so the eyes weep when one sees anything outstandingly bright. . . . So the poet rightly says that no eagle ever gazed upon the sun as Beatrice now does; for the longer and more fixedly that lady's pure intellectual eye regards the eternal sun, the more it is invigorated and strengthened.   (IV, pp. 312–13)

[2] Mazzoni, 'Critica', p. 295.

Almost baroque in the elaboration of its detail, this gloss is typical of Benvenuto at his most professorial. Some notion of the difference between the written commentary and the oral version of Benvenuto's *lecturae* can perhaps be obtained by comparing it with the equivalent gloss in 'Talice': 'And he shows this in a comparison with the eagle, which sees more clearly and flies higher than any other creature. So sacred theology is more noble than other branches of knowledge' (III, p. 10).

The accumulation of detail and the display of erudition, especially in theology and grammar, are also the hallmarks of Francesco da Buti's roughly contemporary lecture-based commentary. Like Benvenuto, Buti approaches each canto by way of a *divisio* of its content, after which he glosses very nearly every word of the text, even those (such as pronouns whose referent is unambiguous) where explication seems redundant. This exhaustive and often exhausting method is, perhaps fortunately, not tied to any rigid interpretative scheme: 'And so I shall expound first the letter and then the allegory or the moral, according to what I believe to have been the author's intention' (I, p. 45).

In the *Inferno* Buti's literal exposition precedes his allegorical analysis, but in *Purgatorio* and *Paradiso* the two proceed simultaneously, in order 'to reduce the writer's labour and the reader's boredom' (II, p. 3). These comments on *Purg.* 8.43–60 are a good example both of the scope and penetration of Buti's allegorical readings and of the minute, even otiose, detail that characterises his treatment of the letter:

In these six tercets our author depicts [*finge*] how Sordello led him and Virgil down into the valley of the princes, and how he recognised some of them; and he says . . . *Sordello*, the Mantuan who had brought them to the valley of the princes, *allora*, after the angels had come down from heaven to protect the valley against the serpent, said to Virgil and Dante, *Or*, (we use this vernacular word to encourage someone, as we use *deh* to make a request) *valichiamo omai*, down into the valley, *tra le grandi ombre*, among the princes; for they had all been princes in the world, as I said above, *e parleremo ad esse*, when we reach them; *Grazioso fi' lor vederte assai*, they will be very pleased to see you. *Solo tre passi credo ch'io*, that is Dante, *scendesse*, from the mountain-side down into the valley. This is what he says according to the letter, to show how much lower the valley was than the mountain-side; but according to the allegory our author had different intentions; since, as is mentioned above, the ascent of Mount Purgatory signifies in our author the ascent that he made to the heights of purity by means of the effort of penitence, and he ascended to those heights by three steps: the contrition of the heart, the confession of the mouth, and the satisfaction of works.

(II, p. 177)

Buti's insistence on annotating the *Commedia*'s every word sometimes overwhelms the text (especially in passages of linear narrative) with its sheer volume of plodding explanation of the obvious. But it appears to better advantage in the philosophical and theological discussions of the *Purgatorio* and *Paradiso*, where the painstaking dissection of some of the poem's more convoluted passages achieves results remarkable for their clarity:

In these three tercets [*Par.* 2.64–72] our author depicts how Beatrice, combating his opinion with an argument that applies to all heavenly bodies, shows that, if Dante's thinking were right, an inconsistency would arise; and that if this were removed its antecedent would have to be removed also. But she puts forward a proposition that is true: saying that the eighth heaven has many stars that can be seen to differ in quality (for some are brighter than others), and in quantity (for some are bigger than others).   (III, p. 53)

Although it is still, perhaps, most helpful to see the 'Anonimo Fiorentino' commentary, like the *Ottimo commento* of nearly seven decades earlier, as a *summa* of contemporary thinking about the *Commedia* (since so much of it is taken directly from other commentaries), its original sections consistently manifest a sophisticated sense of the problematic relationship between letter and allegory. Its usual practice is to begin commentary on each canto with a *divisio materiae* and some remarks on its allegorical meaning:

This canto [*Inferno* 8] is divided into four parts. The second begins at *Com'io vidi una*; the third at *Mentre noi correvamo*; and the fourth at *Uscite, ci gridò*. In the first part he wishes to say that the three flames mentioned above, and the tower, have no meaning other than the literal; and that these things are included to embellish what follows, and for the adornment of the poem. And let no one be surprised at this, for Saint Augustine says in the *City of God* that not every word of Holy Scripture is allegorical; and many have no other meaning than the literal and parabolical; and there are many that have no purpose beyond the embellishment and adornment of those that follow; and he gives two examples, of which one will suffice for the present. He who makes a plough-share, and he who uses it, do so with the intention of tilling the soil; and the plough-share is what tills it; and yet men make the plough, and the shaft in which one fixes the plough-share, and the plough-tail, and the handle where the ploughman rests his hand; and all these things are made for their own sake, and they do not till the soil, but serve to embellish the plough-share. Likewise poets, when they are able, follow the practice of prophets, who speak in certain images [*figure*]; and some images have an allegorical sense, and some a literal, and some words have meanings [*significazioni*], and some have no other purpose than to add to the poem's beauty and adornment, like those that the author places here.

(I, pp. 202–3)

This reluctance to enforce any one kind of interpretation of every detail of Dante's text sets the 'Anonimo' commentary squarely in the eclectic tradition with which several of the major Trecento commentaries – Lana, the *Ottimo commento*, Benvenuto, Buti – might be identified, a tradition whose techniques and conclusions are adaptable to the nature of the examined material, rather than being conditioned in advance by the adoption of an interpretative programme. Other commentators, however – Guido da Pisa, Pietro Alighieri, Boccaccio – do work with a single governing idea; and there are also indications in Filippo Villani's truncated *Comentum* of more radical departures, through which the terms of the critical debate around the *Commedia* will soon be transformed.

Villani's long introduction ranges far beyond the scope of the *accessus* scheme, dealing with problems of interpretation both literal (the nature and structure of Hell) and allegorical (the 'mystical sense' of the poem's characters). It also includes a spirited defence of allegorical reading against those who confine their study to the literal: 'A false opinion about such great spirits [poets] is held by those who do not dare slice through the beautiful surface of a work in order to discover whatever may lie within. Whence it comes about that, puffed up with empty wind, they fall into catastrophic error' (p. 70).

The centrality of allegory in Villani's scheme is again apparent when he turns from the initial *divisio* of *Inferno* I to its explication: 'Having seen how this first canto is divided, I shall undertake the exposition of the text according to its allegorical meaning, as far as my intellectual capacities will allow' (p. 81). He goes on to compare Dante to the author of Ecclesiastes and the prophet Jeremiah, and thereby strikes the keynote of his commentary, in which allegorical meanings are regularly presented in terms of biblical typology. Although his text is liberally sprinkled with allusions to classical culture and authors, as well as observations on contemporary history, customs and language, it is the Bible that provides most of Villani's authorities and illustrations, and the tradition of biblical exegesis that supplies his interpretative model:

Veltro means 'swift and savage' [*velox trux*], and this is the vernacular word for the dog used to hunt hares, which some call *veltro* and some *levriere*. And this dog also hates foxes and chases them whenever it can. And this name is no less apt for Christ coming to judgement than is the name of 'lion' for Christ in His passion. For when the Son of God came in the flesh, he did not come to judge the world, but to be judged, and judged by the world; and so he came not to pursue, but to be subject to persecution. But when he comes to do justice, he will pursue the cowardly hare and the sagacious fox, as he will separate the sheep from the goats.

(pp. 174–5)

Where Guido da Pisa, calling on the 'divine page' to illuminate the *Inferno*, had carefully distinguished between it and the *visio* embodied in Dante's poem, Villani reads the *Inferno* itself as a *figura* of Scripture, and its details as *figurae* of Christian doctrine. He is even prepared to extend this treatment to the pagan *Aeneid*, which becomes an allegory of Christ and the foundation of the church (pp. 148–59). Moreover, Villani is scathing about those (such as Guido) who read the *Inferno* as a vision (however 'true'), and interpret the 'mezzo del cammin' as a dream:

Many say that this 'middle' means a dream; because dreams are midway between life and death. . . . Yet it was not in dreams, but through the workings of divine inspiration, the revelation of the Spirit that opened the poet's mouth, that this divine work was brought into being. Wherefore it seems to me that those who assert so much to have been done in a dream, are dreaming themselves.   (pp. 83–4)

Villani's strict adherence to allegory connects him with medieval critical tradition, but his obvious debt to humanist learning is equally revealing. Plato and Socrates make more than incidental appearances in his commentary, and the Greeks are credited with the invention of the *accessus ad auctores*: 'According to ancient custom, writers of commentaries . . . would enquire into seven aspects that the Greeks called *periochyas*' (pp. 37–8).

Other commentators in the early fifteenth century found themselves similarly placed, on the critical fault-line where Trecento tradition ground painfully against Quattrocento innovation. Giovanni da Serravalle takes both his interpretative scheme and many of his individual readings from Benvenuto, borrowing even some of his predecessor's most idiosyncratic ideas (such as the identification of the rapt old man of *Purg.* 29.143 with Bernard of Clairvaux).[3] Guiniforte Barzizza (or delli Bargigi), author of a vernacular commentary on *Inferno* written at Milan in about 1440, uses the eminently medieval methods of *divisio* and literal exposition (*sposizione del testo*) as the basis for his substantially allegorical readings. However, his interest in the workings of *fictio* occasionally inspires him to read the text against itself – a subtlety not common in the Trecento. His gloss on *Inf.* 15.79–99, where the Trecento commentators take Dante's tribute to Brunetto Latini at face value, is especially original:

I believe the truth is, that when Dante makes this great show of praising Ser Brunetto, he wishes to stain him forever with such infamy as to silence and drown any praise, and he does this by introducing him among the sinners against nature. And it may be that Dante speaks ironically, wishing to be understood as meaning the opposite of what he says, perhaps because Ser Brunetto, under pretence of teaching him wisdom, had sought to lead him into some evil. This is what I am led to believe by what Dante says when he promises to reward him according to his deserts.   (p. 367)

---

[3] Serravalle, *Translatio*, p. 768.

The echoes of Trecento practice linger to the very end of the following century. Cristoforo Landino's vernacular commentary of 1481, though perfused with its author's celebrated Neoplatonism and with evidence of interests and beliefs considered aberrant or worse in the Trecento, still takes the *Commedia*'s doctrine seriously and refers favourably to Trecento commentators, though stressing the need to 'liberate' Dante's poem from 'the barbarism of many foreign dialects [*externi idiomi*]' with which they had corrupted it (fol. 1r). Much of the commentary's long *proemio* consists of a 'defence of Dante and Florence against false slanderers', in which Landino reviews Florentine history and its great men. To this he adds a life of Dante, a definition and history of poetry (which he, like Villani, sees as a divine inspiration akin to prophecy), and a description of the arrangement of Dante's Hell. The *proemio* begins, however, with Landino's declaration of intent:

Now, because I had recently interpreted and rendered in Latin the allegorical sense of Virgil's *Aeneid*, I judged it would be neither useless nor uninteresting to my fellow-citizens if I tried, with all the learning and diligence at my command, to investigate likewise the arcane and secret, but wholly divine, meanings of the *Comedy* of the Florentine poet Dante Alighieri; and, since I had expounded the Latin poet in Latin, I would expound the Tuscan in Tuscan.   (fol. 1r)

Allegorical arcana, reverence for poets and poetic eloquence, civic and linguistic patriotism verging on propaganda: the recurrent themes of Landino's commentary are all announced on its opening page. Its immense popularity (witnessed by more than a dozen editions between 1481 and 1536) marks it as the characteristic *Commedia* commentary of the early Renaissance; and that fact alone illustrates the transformation that was overtaking *Commedia* criticism at the turn of the fifteenth and sixteenth centuries.

For all its nods to Trecento precedent, Landino's work shows clear signs of increasing detachment from that context. It assumes the superiority of allegorical interpretation, without defending it; it does no more than glance at the *quadruplex sensus*, and ignores the *accessus* altogether; its presiding genius is 'Platone singulare'. Landino feels, in fact, a need to rescue Dante from the Trecento commentators: though they had said 'many things worthy of their learning and by no means useless to the listener', he wants to 'examine Dante's mind and intentions from a loftier starting-point, and . . . to investigate his more abstruse doctrine' (fol. 1r).

The signs are unmistakable. Under the pressure of a historical and intellectual movement from the climate loosely called 'scholasticism' to that equally loosely called 'humanism', the cultural affinity between commentators and *Commedia* had weakened, by Landino's time, almost to vanishing point. The hermeneutic and methodological questions so crucial in the 1320s seemed, to many of Dante's Italian readers, outmoded and irrelevant by 1500. By then, at least among those intellectually nourished by Quattrocento humanism, the universe of Guido da Pisa or Benvenuto da Imola, let alone of Dante himself, had come to seem unimaginably distant. Dante's poem had taken on the alterity that remains its abiding challenge and its most powerful attraction to readers today. The Trecento commentaries were to suffer centuries of neglect and disdain before they could emerge, in all their rich diversity, to show themselves still capable of expressing the central truth about the *Commedia*: for, even at the beginning of the critical history of Dante's poem of many meanings, it is already clear that the last word can never be said.

23

Latin and vernacular from Dante
to the age of Lorenzo (1321–*c.* 1500)

Martin McLaughlin

The previous chapter stressed the ways in which Dante's achievement represented a challenge to prevailing orthodoxies: he had chosen the vernacular for a major poetic work, and the *Commedia* itself had engendered a tradition of commentary on a par with that usually reserved for classical texts. Petrarch's literary hegemony, which from 1350 onwards restored Latin to its privileged position, in a sense constituted a linguistic counterrevolution. The rivalry between the two languages was to continue for two centuries from the death of Dante, and since it represents an obligatory topic in critical thinking in this period it seems best to treat the question in this separate chapter. There are four major stages in the debate: first the Petrarchan revolution; second the arguments for and against the vernacular around 1400; third the crucial decade 1430–40; and finally the age of Landino, Poliziano and Lorenzo de' Medici.

The conflicting currents, set in motion on the one hand by Dante's enhancement of the status of the *volgare* and on the other by the new humanist conviction of the superiority of Latin, were already visible in Dante's last years in his exchange of Latin hexameters with Giovanni del Virgilio (*c.* 1320). Giovanni criticised Dante for writing serious poetry for the masses, bemoaning their ignorance, their tendency to distort the poet's words in the street, and the fact that the vernaculars are too many and transitory to be the vehicle of serious work (*Eclogues* 1.6–16). Dante replied to Giovanni in the same metre but reviving the ancient genre of the eclogue (*Eclogue* 2), possibly to couch the content of his reply (defence of the layman's language and the comic genre of the *Commedia*) in an appropriate form (pastoral was the lowest genre, according to the *rota Virgilii*; see p. 517 above). Giovanni's reply (*Eclogue* 3) acknowledged Dante's Latin skill in reviving the eclogue but made no further mention of his use of the vernacular.

Although this exchange ended on a note of reconciliation, the chorus of disapproval at the language of the *Commedia* was to grow throughout the century, largely due to the increasing prestige assigned to Latin by one of Giovanni's pupils in Bologna in the 1320s, Francesco Petrarca (1304–74). Despite writing two major poetic works in the *volgare* (his *Canzoniere* or *Rerum vulgarium fragmenta*, and the *Trionfi*), Petrarch in his public pronouncements attached more weight to his Latin writings and acted as the influential spokesman of a cultural movement which reversed the synthesis between Latin and the vernacular epitomised by Dante's masterpiece, and drove a wedge between the two cultures which would not be removed until the end of the Quattrocento.

The first crucial document in linguistic as well as literary criticism after Dante is Petrarch's 1359 letter to Boccaccio about his predecessor (*Familiares* 21.15). The epistle is Petrarch's reply to Boccaccio's previous letter (now lost) which had been an *apologia* for Dante and which had accompanied Boccaccio's gift of a copy of the *Commedia* and his Latin poem in praise of Dante's masterpiece. The content of Petrarch's letter remains, perhaps intentionally, ambiguous, most elements of criticism being hedged about with praise. However, the letter ends with three largely negative points which were to become critical commonplaces in the next generation of humanists. First Petrarch claims that his admiration for his predecessor is such that he believes Dante could have (later humanists will say he should have) written the poem in Latin. Secondly he distances himself from the *Commedia*'s audience of 'fullers, innkeepers and woolworkers', and aligns himself instead with Homer and Virgil who are also ignored by this 'vulgar' public: this move effectively decoupled Dante from the classical epic tradition epitomised by the two poets. His third and major criticism is of the uneven quality of Dante's work, for 'his style had greater clarity and sublimity in the vernacular than in Latin prose and verse', though this too is attenuated by adding the formula derived from Seneca the Elder (*Controversiae* 3, Pref. 8) that even Cicero and Virgil did not excel in more than one genre. These critiques of Dante's linguistic medium, his literary public, and his defective Latin will be developed in future years, particularly the notion that it is impossible to be outstanding in both prose and verse, or in both Latin and the *volgare*. But despite starting out by agreeing with Boccaccio's claim that Dante's poem is appreciated by both the learned and the populace, the thrust of the whole epistle is to separate the two cultures.

Another of Petrarch's many pronouncements on the two languages reinforced the divide. In a later letter to Boccaccio (*Seniles* 5.2, written in 1364) Petrarch portrays himself as having initially turned to the vernacular because all the great works had already been written in Latin and thus left no space for the modern writer to add anything; but although he had started writing a work in the *volgare* that he hoped would rival classical literature (either the *Canzoniere* or the *Trionfi*), the populace's oral distortion of his verses forced him to abandon the project and concentrate instead on writing in Latin. This relegation of his vernacular poetry to the period of his youth is clearly disingenuous, since we know that Petrarch continued to revise his *rime* until his death, and many of them represent, like the *Commedia*, an attempt at synthesis between the two literary traditions. But although inaccurate as far as Petrarch's own poetic development was concerned, this literary myth was publicly so powerful as to effect a cultural crisis amongst the intellectual elite of the late Trecento.

The most spectacular example of Petrarch's influence in reshaping linguistic priorities was his closest disciple, Giovanni Boccaccio (1313–75), who in assimilating the master's ideals was forced into a series of recantations regarding his sympathy for the vernacular in general and his admiration for Dante in particular. Before 1346 Boccaccio had been responsible for the translation into the *volgare* of Valerius Maximus and of the third and fourth Decades of Livy. But after his first meeting with Petrarch in 1350, Boccaccio accepted the impropriety of translating the great authors into the common language and removed his name from those early *volgarizzamenti* as well as repudiating his other vernacular works. The early Trecento vogue for translations from Latin into the *volgare*, which could be seen as parallel to Dante's synthesis of classical and vernacular culture in the *Commedia*, peters out after Petrarch erects an insuperable barrier between the two traditions.

As for Boccaccio's relationship to his first master, Dante, the two redactions of his biography of the poet, the *Trattatello in laude di Dante*, are a significant barometer of his change in literary ideals: the first version (1351–4) had been composed before he had fully absorbed the import of Petrarch's linguistic division, but the second redaction (1361–4) registers changes which are clearly determined by the key ideas in Petrarch's 1359 letter about Dante (*Fam.* 21.15).[1] This 'Petrarchan' rewriting of the *Trattatello* significantly omits all mention of Dante's bridging of the two cultures, his writing for both the 'letterati' and the 'idioti' (*Trattatello* 1.191). Instead the separation of the two languages and their audience, emphasised in Petrarch's letter, is evident in the omission of the earlier portrayal of Dante as the poet who recalled the Muses to Italy (1.19) and who had been linked with the two greatest classical poets, Homer and Virgil, in making his own language capable of dealing with any subject (1.84–5). Perhaps most significant of all in the light of Petrarch's division of the two literatures, Dante is no longer even considered as having imitated the classical poets (1.22): such *imitatio* now belonged only to those who, like Petrarch, wrote serious works in Latin. Although Boccaccio subsequently tried to maintain a compromise position by suggesting that both Dante

---

[1] Both redactions are edited by Ricci in Boccaccio, *Opere*, III, pp. 437–538. References in parenthesis in the text will be to the paragraphs of Ricci's edition. For the main differences between the various redactions, see Ricci's introduction (pp. 425–35); for their relationship to the Petrarch letter, see Paolazzi, 'Petrarca, Boccaccio', and McLaughlin, *Literary Imitation*, pp. 53–8.

and Petrarch had sought to revive Antiquity by different routes (*Ep.* 19; ed. Auzzas, p. 666), his late repudiation of his own vernacular works (*Ep.* 21; p. 706) and his conviction that his illness in 1374 was a punishment for his 'prostitution of the Muses' in expounding Dante's *Commedia* to the masses (*Rime* 122–5; ed. Branca, pp. 95–6) were symptoms both of a personal crisis and of a wider intellectual aporia. Boccaccio, like other disciples of Petrarch, had learnt from his mentor that ideally there should be no *contaminatio* between Latin and vernacular culture.

Petrarch's final letter to Boccaccio (*Sen.* 17.2) shows how the latter had developed one of the critical notions outlined in the 1359 letter. Although Petrarch had pointed out in *Familiares* 21.15 that not even Cicero or Virgil, far less Dante, could hope to be proficient in more than one genre or language ('stilus' meant both genre and language), it is clear from Petrarch's last letter that Boccaccio had made this very claim for Petrarch, asserting that he equals Cicero in prose and Virgil in verse. The notion of Petrarch's brilliance in both prose and poetry is propagated by the leading humanist of the next generation, Coluccio Salutati (1331–1406), chancellor of Florence.[2] Salutati first makes this claim in the encomiastic context of a letter of 1374 (Salutati, *Ep.* I; pp. 176–87) about the recently dead poet. The claim is accepted in the 1370s, when nobody had seen much of Petrarch's major Latin poem, the *Africa*, but by the end of the century, once copies of the epic begin to circulate, critical disillusionment with the poem, and with other aspects of Petrarchan humanism, is strongly articulated by the new generation of humanists.

Salutati began as Petrarch's most outspoken admirer, but it was Dante's vernacular work rather than Petrarch's which exemplified for him the power of that idiom. In 1383 he criticised Benvenuto da Imola's commentary on Dante on the grounds that his 'low' Latin belittled Dante's sublime poem (*Ep.* II, p. 77). The *Commedia* thus became associated in Salutati's mind with high humanist culture, since it deserved a commentary in humanist not scholastic Latin, and it required a text as incorrupt as that of any classical author (*Ep.* III; pp. 371–5). In the late 1390s Salutati even translates part of the *Commedia* into Latin and apologises that his Latin has failed to match the 'ornatus' of the vernacular (*De fato et fortuna*, p. 193); and by 1401 he is advancing claims similar to those made for Petrarch in 1374: that if Dante had written his poem in Latin, he would have surpassed both Homer and Virgil (*Ep.* III; p. 491).

Around the same time, Filippo Villani (1325–1405) began his commentary on the *Inferno*, in which he included a (poor) Latin translation of the whole of the first canto. Villani also subscribed to the fiction that Dante

[2] See Witt, *Hercules at the Crossroads*, pp. 266–71, 403–5; Seigel, *Rhetoric and Philosophy*, pp. 86–98. References in what follows are to Salutati, *Epistolario*.

began the poem in Latin, and even claimed that when the poet compared his vernacular verse with that of the great Latin poets it seemed like 'sackcloth beside purple silk' (*Expositio*, p. 77). But Villani does not openly criticise Dante's Latin. Indeed he seems unaware of the barrier that Petrarch had tried to erect between Latin and vernacular culture: in his *De origine civitatis Florentie et de eiusdem famosis civibus* (*c.* 1395) he draws a distinction not between vernacular and Latin writers but merely between 'poete' and 'semipoete' (pp. 398–9).

These attempts to equate Dante and Petrarch with ancient authors aroused the obloquy of the 'humanist avant-garde', the younger generation of humanists such as Leonardo Bruni (1374–1444), Poggio Bracciolini (1380–1459) and Niccolò Niccoli (1364–1437). Bruni's *Dialogi ad Petrum Paulum Histrum* (1401–6) constitute the key text of this polemical period. In the first book Bruni portrays Niccoli adopting an extremist attitude, attacking Salutati's defence of the Tre Corone and castigating vernacular culture for its inadequacies compared with classical literature. In Book 2, however, Niccoli recants, claiming that he had merely attacked the *volgare* in order to provoke Salutati into an encomium of the three writers. Niccoli's recantation, however, is not very convincing since his defence of the vernacular writers is much more generic than the detailed criticisms he had made in Book 1. Critics have argued whether Bruni's own view is represented by the extremist approach of Book 1 or the more conciliatory tone of the second book, or indeed by both, with a change of heart occurring between the composition of the two parts of the dialogue.[3] But however one interprets this volte-face, it is clear that the *Dialogi* represent a crisis within early Quattrocento humanism, a divergence of opinion between the radical anti-vernacular wing and the more conciliatory grouping around Salutati.

The *Invettiva* (1405–6) of Cino Rinuccini (1350–1417) is a contemporary document which attempts to rebut the charges of that radical wing and to defend not only the *volgare* but also that synthesis of the vernacular, scholastic and humanist traditions epitomised by Salutati. Rinuccini's opponents were extreme humanists who attacked the traditional, scholastic curriculum of the seven liberal arts as well as the Tre Corone. They criticised Boccaccio for his insecure Latin; they condemned Petrarch's *De viris illustribus* as a scholastic exercise; while Dante was dismissed as a 'shoemakers' poet' (Lanza (ed.), *Polemiche* [1971], pp. 261–7). Rinuccini's defence begins with an attack as he makes the extravagant claim that Dante's poem outdoes all classical poetry, achieving more in three lines

---

[3] Baron, *The Crisis*, pp. 225–69, assumes a chronological gap between the two books, but most recent critics have contested this: see Seigel, ' "Civic Humanism" '; Quint, 'Humanism and Modernity'; Lanza (ed.), *Polemiche* (1989), pp. 28–41.

of *terza rima* than Virgil manages in twenty hexameters. He is on surer ground when observing that there is greater variety of ancient and modern 'istorie' in Dante than in Virgil, and when he associates the *Commedia* with the scholastic tradition by pointing to the wealth of ethics, natural philosophy and theology it contains. But the defence closes with the aggressive hyperbole with which it had begun, arguing that Dante's poem outdoes even Peter Lombard's *Libri sententiarum* in its treatment of theological matters, and remains superior to any work in Greek or Latin. The rest of the document demonstrates that Rinuccini, who may well have been the intended target of the first book of Bruni's *Dialogi*, is defending not just vernacular literature but its links with scholastic learning and the allegorical reading of poetry that was associated with Salutati.

Rinuccini's invectives survive only in vernacular versions, but they were originally written in Latin. However, there were also defences written directly in the *volgare*. Domenico da Prato (*c.* 1370–1435), in a later anti-humanist invective of the 1420s, cites similar accusations against Dante: 'they say that Dante's books should be given to the spice-merchants to use as wrapping paper, or rather to the fish-vendors to put salted fish in, since he wrote in the vulgar tongue' (Lanza (ed.), *Polemiche* [1971], p. 241). This jibe, which had come from Petrarch's 1359 letter via Boccaccio's second redaction of the *Trattatello*, was to continue to circulate in the first half of the Quattrocento, but it would disappear in the second half of the century with the enhanced prestige of the vernacular. The other charges specified by Domenico are that Dante had not read certain Latin and Greek texts which would have helped him in the writing of his poem, and that he had even misunderstood Virgil in his discussion of the origins of Mantua – an accusation which we know was levelled at Dante by Bruni in 1418 (Lanza (ed.), *Polemiche* [1971], p. 242). The general humanist prejudice that nothing could be written that was not inferior to ancient literature is countered by Domenico simply claiming that the *volgare* in which Dante wrote is more authentic and praiseworthy than the Latin and Greek used by his critics. The same document also reveals that Petrarch's *rime* were under fire for being 'mere fragments, worthless trifles', and that even Salutati was attacked along with the Tre Corone by those humanists who wrote nothing original themselves, but merely translated from Greek into Latin and admired humanistic calligraphy. Domenico's contemporary and fellow-citizen, Giovanni Gherardi da Prato (1367–1444), also saw himself, in *Il Paradiso degli Alberti* (*c.* 1426), as following in the wake of the 'tre corone fiorentine', and adopts the more aggressive line, which will be later resumed by Poliziano and Lorenzo, that Florentine is 'so polished and copious' that it can deal with even the most profound subjects (*Il Paradiso*, p. 217). But unlike Poliziano and Lorenzo, Gherardi merely states his claim without substantiating it.

These polemics for and against the vernacular came to a head in the crucial decade of the 1430s. In 1434 Matteo Palmieri (1406–75) took the unprecedented step of composing in Tuscan a serious dialogue, the genre which had hitherto been the flagship of humanist Latin. He justifies his linguistic choice for his *Della vita civile* by adopting both Dante's motive in the *Convivio* of sharing ancient wisdom with those who know no Latin, and the humanist complaint about the poor quality of the *volgarizzamenti* of classical texts dealing with the good civic existence. Although appreciating their achievements, Palmieri also noted that none of the Tre Corone had treated the subject in a satisfactory manner (*Vita civile*, pp. 5–6).

The following year, 1435, witnessed the famous debate between Bruni and Flavio Biondo (1392–1463) about whether the language spoken in ancient Rome was Latin or a form of the vernacular. Bruni subscribed to the latter view, which suggests that, like Dante, he saw Latin as an immutable, artificial language. Although the dispute was not definitively settled in 1435, two important points emerged. First both theses enhanced the status of the vernacular, Bruni's by suggesting that it dated from Antiquity and was not the bastard creation of the barbarian invasions, Biondo's in that both Latin and the *volgare* were seen to be natural languages which had a beginning, an evolution, and, in the case of Latin, a decline. Second, the resonance of the debate caused many contemporary intellectuals to reconsider the whole question of the relationship between Latin and the vernacular. One of the key motives in prompting this linguistic revaluation was the discovery at Lodi in 1421 of the complete texts of Cicero's *Orator*, *De oratore* and particularly the unknown *Brutus*, with its important history of the evolution of Latin up to the time of Cicero.[4] Biondo had transcribed these texts in the 1420s and was able to make telling use of them in the dispute.

That Bruni's thesis was also compatible with defending the vernacular is confirmed by the fact that in the following year, in his *Vite di Dante e del Petrarca* (1436), despite conceding that the vernacular could not cope as well as Latin with questions such as the definition of key words like *poeta*, Bruni actually formulated a theory of the parity of the two languages, observing that whether a work is written in Latin or the *volgare* is immaterial, and makes no more difference than whether it is written in Greek or Latin: every language, claims Bruni, has its own perfection, its own sound, and its own polished and learned style (*Le vite*, p. 550). The important point here is that, unlike Rinuccini and Domenico da Prato, Bruni does not simply argue that the *Commedia*

---

[4] In Silvio Rizzo's elegant paradox, 'Latin became a dead language only when humanists realised that it had been a living language' (Rizzo, 'Petrarca, il latino e il volgare', p. 32).

outdoes all classical poetry, or that vernacular verse is more difficult to compose or nobler than Latin poetry; instead his study of Greek and his translations from Greek into Latin allow Bruni to evaluate Latin more objectively, as a language less rich than Greek, and to conclude that the actual language of literature does not matter, it is stylistic *perfezione* which is crucial.

In the same decade, the 1430s, Leon Battista Alberti (1404–72) put forward the most forceful theoretical defence of the vernacular articulated so far, and rejected Bruni's thesis about the origin of the *volgare*, in the proem to his third book of *Della famiglia* (1437). Alberti also provided practical demonstrations of the capabilities of the language in a series of initiatives: in the moral prose of his vernacular dialogues, in the technical prose of *Della pittura* (1436), in his brief Tuscan grammar (*c.* 1440) and in his organisation of the 'Certame Coronario' (1441). The major significance of Alberti's contribution to the debate was that he defended the vernacular, not like his predecessors by pointing solely to the achievements of the Tre Corone, but by adopting rigorously humanist criteria. Like Petrarch, he was conscious of the difficulty of composing anything new in Latin, and consequently his passionate quest for originality led him to use Latin for technical subjects rarely touched on by the ancients, and the *volgare* for matters usually dealt with in Latin. Thus the vernacular, which since the 1370s had been used only for popular poetry, chronicles and *novelle*, was now in practical terms being equated with Latin since in the hands of Palmieri and Alberti it was also the vehicle for serious moral dialogues. On the theoretical side, Alberti's grammar of Tuscan, or *Grammatichetta* (*c.* 1440), which also stems from the 1435 dispute, attempts to prove that the *volgare* is as regular a language as Latin.

The Certame Coronario was a literary contest organised in Florence by Alberti, who encouraged sympathisers with the *volgare* to compete for a prize by submitting vernacular works on the classical theme of *amicitia*. The Certame, modelled on ancient poetic contests, and presided over by a humanist jury which was to award a silver laurel wreath to the winner, was another Alberti enterprise aimed at ennobling the vernacular: Alberti's own composition was even written in classical hexameters (*Opere*, II, p. 45). One of the participants, Niccolò di Francesco della Luna, offered a new element in rejecting Bruni's thesis about Latin. He pointed out that all languages in their origins were weak and undeveloped, that Latin had eventually 'annihilated' all the other languages of Italy including early Tuscan or Etruscan, but that now Tuscan would be enriched ('amplificata') by this sort of literary contest, which had benefited Latin so much in the past.[5] The Latinate name of the Certame symbolised that the enterprise was a new defence of the vernacular, not by writers from a superseded

5 See Gorni, 'Storia del Certame', p. 178.

tradition like Domenico da Prato or Rinuccini, but from inside the humanist camp itself, and the notion of Tuscan being a revived form of Etruscan
was a sop to Bruni who had made much of the continuities between
ancient Etruscan and contemporary Florentine civilisation in his *History
of the Florentine People* (1415–44). Nevertheless the project failed in that
the humanist jury refused to award the silver laurel wreath, which thus
became an equally powerful symbol of Alberti's failure to win over the
more intransigent humanists. Alberti himself probably wrote the anonymous 'Protesta' which accused the detractors of the *volgare* of approving
only what was ancient, but in so doing they were transgressing against
the sympathy shown by the ancients themselves towards Latin in its early
stages, and towards the early Latin writers who were 'perhaps clever, but
wrote with little art' (Gorni, 'Storia', p. 172). The Certame, like Alberti's
other attempts to rehabilitate the vernacular, was an original initiative
which ignored the preceding Trecento tradition and worked along strictly
humanist lines; but like his other initiatives, it ended, if not in defeat, at
least in stalemate.

Unlike Gherardi, Palmieri and Bruni, Alberti, in the proem to the
third book of *Della famiglia*, defends the vernacular on purely linguistic
grounds, without reference to the Tre Corone. He subscribes to Biondo's
thesis, that the *volgare* was a natural language that arose from the adulter-
ation of Latin by the barbarian invaders of Italy, and therefore a language
still in the process of developing, and he claims that the vernacular has
as many 'ornamenti' as Latin and that it too will become 'refined and
polished' if the learned will only use it as a literary medium (*Opere*, I,
pp. 155–6). This strictly linguistic defence, ignoring the literary achievements of the Tre Corone, is paralleled by Alberti's own Tuscan prose, with
its Latinate syntax and lexis which owes nothing to the prose of Dante or
Boccaccio. But in the generation after Alberti, when defence of the vernacular will pass into attack, in theorists like Landino and practitioners
of prose and verse like Lorenzo and Poliziano, the literary models of the
Tre Corone will regain influence. The stalemate in the debate between
Bruni and Biondo in 1435 is emblematic of the wider impasse reached in
the status of the two languages as a whole in the 1430s.

Thus, after the Certame Coronario, in the 1450s, Gianozzo Manetti
(1396–1459) departed from the example of Bruni's vernacular *Vite di
Dante e del Petrarca* to write the biographies of the Tre Corone in Latin,
since, he claims, humanists would ignore lives written in the *volgare*
(*Le vite*, ed. Solerti, p. 112). What is needed to resolve the impasse is
a theorist who is both a competent humanist but also someone aware of
the impossibility of developing the vernacular along the unnaturally Latinate lines proposed by Alberti, and therefore of the desirability of a return
to the naturalness of the language of Dante, Petrarch and Boccaccio.

The key decade in this final phase is the 1470s, though there are some significant contributions to the debate before then. The situation in Ferrara in the 1450s is indicative of the oscillations in the evaluation of the Tuscan literary tradition: Angelo Decembrio's *Politia literaria* (1462), drawing up the ideal library for Leonello d'Este, clearly relegated the Tre Corone to the section of medieval barbarism which housed texts like Walter of Châtillon, Cassiodorus and Isidore (cit. by Tavoni, *Latino*, p. 227); yet in 1459 Ludovico Carbone could urge Borso d'Este to read the *Commedia* since its vernacular language is so polished and its content so profound that it is as worthy as if it had been composed in Latin (cit. by Vitale, *La questione della lingua*, p. 34).

However, the most important formulation of the new status of the vernacular came from inside Florence. Cristoforo Landino (1424–1504), who in his youthful Latin love elegies, *Xandra* (1459), had experimented in treating themes from the vernacular Petrarchan tradition in the style of the Latin elegists, later in life reversed the process and elaborated a programme of *trasferimento* of the riches of classical literature into the *volgare*.[6] Regarding himself as Alberti's pupil, he took up his call to utilise the vernacular in a series of critical writings and translations. In his *Prolusione petrarchesca* (1467) he clearly echoed Alberti's defence of the language, attacking the humanist detractors who found the *volgare* 'neither copious nor ornate', urging his pupils to use the language in order to polish what was still unrefined, and claiming that its achievements to date, with so few practitioners, proved that it possessed 'an innate copiousness' (*Scritti*, I, p. 33). Like Biondo, he made extensive use of Cicero's *Brutus* to demonstrate the evolutionary nature of the development of Latin literature, a dynamic model which the vernacular should follow, since its weaknesses are due not to intrinsic demerits but to the lack of writers who have used the medium. But although Landino coined the famous maxim that 'a good Tuscan writer must also be a good Latinist' (I, p. 38), and elaborated a theory of *trasferimento* of lexis and stylistic embellishment from Latin to the *volgare*, nevertheless he seems to imply a critique of Alberti's Latinate prose when he urges that the *contaminatio* between the two languages should take place 'but not going against the nature of the language' (I, p. 38). The work ends on a cautious note, admitting that Tuscan did not yet possess many elegant turns of phrase (I, p. 39), and that consequently the Tuscans should imitate the Romans by enriching their tongue with Latin lexis in the same way as the Latin writers had exploited the lexical riches of Greek.

---

[6] For Landino's incorporation of Petrarchan elements in the *Xandra*, see Cardini, *La critica del Landino*, pp. 1–65; and for his programme of *trasferimento*, see pp. 113–232.

Landino's translations into the vernacular are now rightly regarded as forming part of his programme of *trasferimento*: the translation of the Elder Pliny (1476) and of Giovanni Simonetta's *Sforziade* (1490), dedicated respectively to Ferrante of Naples and to Ludovico il Moro, deliberately stressed the prestige of Florentine over other vernaculars in works addressed to the rulers of Naples and Milan. Both works claimed that Tuscan was common to the whole of Italy and quite familiar to many other nations (*Scritti*, I, pp. 83, 190), and even Landino's *Formulario di epistole* (a guide to writing epistles in the vernacular, dated to 1485) can be seen as part of the same campaign of annexing new areas of the rhetorical tradition for the *volgare*.

In the course of the 1470s Landino turned, under the influence of the Platonism of Marsilio Ficino (1433–99), to Dante's *Commedia* rather than to Petrarch's poems, as the exemplary vernacular text. In his *Disputationes camaldulenses* (1474) he suggests that Dante's poem is a legitimate reworking of Virgil's *Aeneid* in line with humanist notions of *imitatio*, and he displays none of the anxieties exhibited by Petrarch and Boccaccio a century earlier in linking this vernacular poem with the Latin tradition. Landino's influential Neoplatonic commentary on the *Commedia* (1481) was instrumental not just in reclaiming Dante for Florentine culture, but also in elevating him to the status of a classical author, by providing the first Quattrocento commentary on a single vernacular text and by exploiting to good effect the new technology of printing and Botticelli's woodcuts. In the important proem to the commentary he also aligns Petrarch with the classical tradition, seeing his vernacular *rime* not as stemming from the Provençal or *stilnovo* matrix, but as a modern equivalent of Alcaeus, Ovid or Propertius (*Scritti*, I, pp. 137–8). As for Dante, Landino actually claims that he deserves greater praise than Homer or Virgil since the ancient poets had been preceded by others who had to some extent developed Greek and Latin, whereas Dante had nothing before him but 'the babbling infancy' of the language (I, p. 137). Dante is seen now not only in the old formula as being the first to revive poetry, but in specifically Landinian terms as the first to carry out that process of *trasferimento* from the Latin to the vernacular which was the sole guarantor of a literature which could stand comparison with that of Antiquity. Dante thus demonstrated that the Tuscan language was capable of dealing with and embellishing any subject (I, p. 137). This section of Landino's proem ends with a reconsideration of the new state of the *volgare*, which has none of the hesitancy of the earlier formulation in the *Prolusione petrarchesca*: by 1481 Landino believes that thanks to writers such as the Tre Corone, Alberti and Lorenzo, the language is in a state of continuous, dynamic improvement, is already 'copious and elegant, and will become even more so every day, if scholars apply themselves to using it' (I, p. 139). A key factor behind this positive estimate is that whereas for Dante and Bruni the *volgare* had been the language of nature and Latin the language of art, for Landino both Latin and the vernacular are products of *natura* which must be enhanced by *arte*.

Similarly positive attitudes were adopted in the same period, though with slightly different emphasis, by both Angelo Poliziano (1454–94) and by Lorenzo de' Medici (1449–92). The *Raccolta aragonese* (1476), a collection of Tuscan poetry from its origins down to Lorenzo's time, sent by Lorenzo to the Neapolitan king, also represents an aggressive affirmation of Tuscan literary achievements. The introductory letter, probably by Poliziano,[7] outlines a series of sometimes far-fetched parallels between the vernacular and classical traditions. As many Greek and Latin writers were lost in the Middle Ages, so ('similmente') – Poliziano claims rather vaguely – many early Tuscan poems were neglected. The gathering together of these *rime* in the *Raccolta* is compared to Pisistratus collecting the *disjecta membra* of the Homeric poems, suggesting once again that the vernacular is undergoing a renaissance analogous to the revival of Greek and Latin. On the linguistic front the letter endorses Alberti's and Landino's claims that the language was 'neither poor . . . nor crude, but copious and highly polished' and capable of expressing any sentiment in any of the three styles. The parallels with Antiquity continue with the restatement of Petrarch's (unfounded) contention (*Fam.* 1.1.6) that vernacular *rime* were nothing less than a renaissance of ancient Latin Saturnian or rhymed poetry. Thus before settling down to providing a stylistic portrait of the individual poets in the anthology, Poliziano enhances the general prestige of poetry in the *volgare* by a series of more or less tenuous links with the decline and rebirth of classical literatures.

The high point of this exaltation of Tuscan is reached with Lorenzo de' Medici's *Comento de' miei sonetti* (c. 1491). In his introduction he responds to the criticism that the *volgare* is not capable of dealing with serious topics by pointing to the variety of subjects and styles in the writings of the Tre Corone and of Guido Cavalcanti, concluding that the reader of these works will agree that no vernacular other than Tuscan is more suited to dealing with these matters (*Opere*, I, pp. 18–21). Lorenzo here is merely endorsing Landino's and Poliziano's claims for the all-round versatility of the language, but like Bruni before him he has a less blinkered view of the prestige of Latin because he also brings in the question of Greek, which was now accurately seen to be more copious than Latin, and which also had a number of dialects, like the Italian vernacular. Lorenzo also reworks the claims of the proem to Landino's Dante commentary when he sees the development of the *volgare* in terms of dynamic growth:

---

7 The letter is printed in Lorenzo de' Medici, *Opere*, I, pp. 3–8. In what follows, references in the text to Lorenzo's works are to this edition. For the letter's attribution to Poliziano, see Santoro, 'Poliziano o il Magnifico?'.

what he adds, though, is the political dimension of linking the spread of Tuscan to the extent of Florentine rule: 'The phase that has lasted until now could be called the adolescence of our language, because every minute it becomes more and more elegant and graceful. And it could easily in its mature, adult age develop into greater perfection, particularly if Florentine rule meets with success and increases . . .' (*Opere*, I, p. 21). Here Lorenzo is returning to those links between language, literature and empire which had fascinated humanists of the previous generation such as Bruni, Alberti and Valla; but whereas the latter looked backwards to the decline of the Roman Empire and the corruption of Latin, Lorenzo is looking forward with confidence to a positive future for the Tuscan vernacular.[8]

Yet Lorenzo's optimism was to prove unfounded in political and literary if not in linguistic terms. The eclectic vitality of the literature of the Medicean age was, in the light of the new century, to be considered as an undisciplined confusion of literary models and linguistic tones, a poetic licence that was in need of the ordered purism imposed by Pietro Bembo (1470–1547). In his influential *Prose della volgar lingua* (1525) Bembo will defend the vernacular on his own terms, ignoring the Quattrocento defences of the language from Alberti to Lorenzo. Instead he will apply to the *volgare* the rigid Ciceronianism embraced by himself and other humanists in their Latin works: just as for the Latin Ciceronianists the only two acceptable literary models were Cicero for prose and Virgil for verse, so in the vernacular Bembo restricts the literary and linguistic models available to vernacular writers to just two: Petrarch for poetry and Boccaccio for prose. The *contaminatio* of Latin and vernacular advocated by Alberti and Landino, and the mixture of learned and popular registers practised by Poliziano and Lorenzo will be seen as symptoms of chaotic decline rather than youthful vitality. Where the Medicean age had optimistically compared its vernacular achievements with humanist progress in Latin and had discerned only the model of birth, development and maturity in the *volgare* from the time of Dante to the period of Lorenzo and Poliziano, Bembo will superimpose a different tripartite perspective, also parallel to the vicissitudes of Latin, but now seeing the Tre-, Quattro- and Cinquecento respectively as Golden Age, Decadence and Revival.

From the age of Dante to that of Lorenzo enormous strides were made in the humanist understanding of Latin: where Dante had believed that Latin was an immutable, artificial language which had not changed from Antiquity to his own day, the Quattrocento humanists perceived that Latin too was a natural language with its own history, and were eventually as interested in its archaic and decadent periods as in its Ciceronian

---

[8] See Garin's edition of Valla's proems to the *Elegantiae* in *Prosatori latini*, pp. 594–600.

heyday. But although Latin always retained its prestige as the language of scholarship, these perceptions also allowed intellectuals to see the vernacular in a similarly evolutionary perspective. Once humanists had learned how to produce an exact copy not just of Cicero's Latin but also of Plautine, Apuleian and Tacitean styles,[9] there was no room for further development in Renaissance Latin. By the time of Bembo, the question is no longer which language should be used, but which vernacular.

Although we have examined the stages by which the vernacular eventually regained parity with Latin, it must be remembered that the defence of the *volgare* in the Quattrocento was proclaimed by only a few lone voices in a generally hostile environment. It should also be noted that in the century from the death of Petrarch to the age of Lorenzo, and particularly in the wake of the disenchantment aroused by the *Africa*, the importance of verse was eclipsed in both languages – so much so that the phrase 'il secolo senza poesia' was coined to refer to the absence of serious poetry in both Latin and the *volgare*. Already by 1379 Salutati, in claiming Petrarch's superiority over Cicero and Virgil, based his argument on the pre-eminence of prose over poetry (*Ep.* I, p. 338). Italian intellectuals followed Petrarch's lead not only by channelling their creative energies into Latin rather than the vernacular, but also by writing their major works not in verse but in a polished prose that effectively recreated the patina of classical Latin.[10]

This shift is reflected in the development of the humanist myth of the rebirth of Antiquity, since there is a clear progression from Boccaccio's formulation of it as a revival of poetry under Dante and Petrarch to a more scholarly recovery of classical texts and Ciceronian prose style.[11] It was not that later humanists were not interested in criticism relating to poetry; on the contrary, they were forced to elaborate a series of defences of poetry which refined the arguments advanced by Boccaccio and Petrarch. But the humanist interpretation of poetry in the Quattrocento impinged little on criticism relating to prose, not least because the former dealt largely with the question of consumption of literature, while the latter concerned itself with the production of Latin prose. For these reasons poetic and prose criticism will be examined separately in the two chapters that follow, and they will be concerned largely with Latin rather than vernacular compositions.

[9] On the humanist cult of Apuleian Latin see Dionisotti, *Gli umanisti e il volgare*, pp. 78–130; D'Amico, 'Renaissance Latin Prose', and McLaughlin, *Literary Imitation*, pp. 216–25, 276–7.
[10] See Holmes, *The Florentine Enlightenment*, pp. 100–2, for this shift from Latin poetry to prose; similarly Valla explicitly states that his aim in the *Elegantiae* is not so much the pursuit of poetic licence as the usage of orators (*Opera*, I, p. 22).
[11] On the changing notions of the revival of Antiquity, see McLaughlin, 'Humanist Concepts', and Fubini, 'L'umanista', p. 458.

24

Humanist views on the study of Italian poetry in the early Italian Renaissance

David Robey

This chapter is concerned with the arguments put forward by Italian humanists in the fourteenth and fifteenth centuries as to how and why poetry should be read, and therefore with one of the central themes of literary criticism, or more exactly literary theory, in the early Italian Renaissance.[1] (The date from which the Renaissance starts is a matter over which opinions legitimately differ; here, as far as Italy is concerned, I am using the expression 'early Renaissance' to cover the fourteenth and fifteenth centuries.) The study and imitation of the classical poets was, of course, a major humanist interest, and poetry occupied an important place in the new curriculum of secondary education. But of all the subjects with which the humanists were concerned it was also the most contentious. In the fourteenth and fifteenth centuries Italian humanists were attacked from a number of quarters because of their poetic interests. The attack came from theologians, monks and the clergy, as well as from members of the established professions of law and medicine. Its main substance was the argument that classical poetry distracted men's minds from better things with stories that were not only pagan and therefore mendacious, but also lascivious and immoral. Moreover, they had been condemned both by classical figures such as Plato and Boethius and by Fathers of the church; 'the songs of the poets are the food of devils', St Jerome wrote for instance (*Epist.* 21.13 [*CSEL* 54]; see also Plato, *Rep.* 2.376-3, 403 and Boethius, *De cons. phil.* 1 met. 1).

The humanist answer to this attack was for the most part formulated by Petrarch and Boccaccio in the mid-fourteenth century, following a line of defence adopted a few decades earlier by the Paduan poet and scholar Albertino Mussato, which in its turn drew on a long and influential tradition of literary interpretation that has figured largely in earlier sections of this volume.[2] With variations of tone and emphasis – Petrarch's views in particular changed somewhat across the years – Petrarch's and Boccaccio's

---

[1] For the definition of 'humanism' and 'humanist', see Kristeller, 'The Humanist Movement'.
[2] Mussato, *Opera*; excerpts in Garin (ed.), *Il pensiero pedagogico*, pp. 2–19.

arguments on the subject of poetry were substantially identical.[3] Their main contention was that the classical poets, far from being mendacious and lascivious, communicated important truths under the veil of allegory, truths of three kinds, moral, natural and historical. The poets either tell us how we should live our lives, or describe phenomena in the natural world, or commemorate the deeds of great men in the past. They do this under the veil of allegory in order to hide these truths from vulgar minds – the *vulgus* – and to give the learned pleasure through the difficulty of deciphering them. Thus the seeming immorality and paganism of much of the material of classical poetry is an appearance that should not deceive us. In reality the poets were the first theologians of the ancients, as Aristotle said in his *Metaphysics*; they were the first to write about divine things, and they did so as believers in one God, not as polytheists, although their knowledge of divinity extended only as far as the limits of human reason. With this last qualification, that the poets were restricted by the limits of human reason, Petrarch and Boccaccio both insisted that classical poetry, when properly understood in its allegorical sense, was (apart from a few exceptions) wholly in agreement with the teachings of the Bible. Moreover, poetry and the Bible had in common not only their content but their form as well, since the Bible also made extensive use of allegorical modes of expression; what we call *figura* or *parabola* in the Bible, Boccaccio argued, we call *fabula* or *fictio* in poetry (*Genealogia deorum gentilium* 14.9).

The terms *fabula* and *fictio*, and the emphasis on the limits of human reason, all make it clear that Petrarch's and Boccaccio's conception of allegory corresponds to Dante's 'allegory of the poets', not to his 'allegory of the theologians', although the distinction between the two types is not so rigidly maintained. At the same time the status which Petrarch and Boccaccio assign to the classical poets is a very elevated one. Allegorical interpretation is associated by both with the Ciceronian topos of divine inspiration (see *Pro Archia* 8.18), and with the idea of the rarity of poets in the world. It is also associated with an ascetic, world-denying ethic and the ideal of the solitary life; the true poet turns his back on urban society and the pursuit of power and wealth, and cultivates his studies amidst the fields and forests. Both writers at the same time insisted on the poet's usefulness to his fellow-men, though neither went so far as to argue that poetry was an indispensable subject of study; poets inspire men to virtue, particularly by perpetuating the memory of great deeds. Thus Petrarch and Boccaccio both rejected the argument that poets were condemned by

---

[3] See Petrarch, *Le familiari*, II, pp. 301–10, *Lettere senili*, II, pp. 438–42, *Invective contra medicum* and *Collatio laureationis*; Boccaccio, *Trattatello in laude di Dante*, and Books 14 and 15 of the *Genealogia deorum gentilium*.

Plato, Boethius and the church Fathers. Plato's and Boethius' rejection related not to poetry in general, they argued, but only to the 'scenic' or 'comic' poets – an ill-defined group which apparently did not include the major writers of comedies and tragedies; and the Fathers not only on occasion defended the poets, but themselves quoted extensively from their works.

At the end of his *Genealogia deorum gentilium* Boccaccio puts forward a further argument in defence of his poetic interests that was to play an important role in the educational thinking of his humanist successors. As different men are endowed by nature with different aptitudes, so each should follow the calling to which he is by nature best suited, and in his case that calling was poetry: 'Being, then, bred, born and nourished for different pursuits, it is enough that we follow to the full our own natural calling, and not stray into another' (15.10). Originating in classical thought, this principle is developed by some humanist educational theorists of the following century to form the basis of a curriculum very different from that of classical pedagogy, in which pupils' choice of specialisation is dictated entirely by their natural disposition. We shall return to this principle briefly in due course, but its significance for our topic is limited, since it concerns general issues of education and has no special relevance to the study of poetry.

Now, there is no doubt that to a very large extent Petrarch's and Boccaccio's arguments determined the views on poetry expressed by Italian humanists for the rest of the fourteenth century and in most of the fifteenth century as well. Boccaccio's *Genealogia deorum gentilium* (which he was still writing in 1371, towards the end of his life, and which contains the fullest expression of his and Petrarch's poetic theory) remained an immensely influential work throughout the Renaissance. In the rest of this discussion, however, we shall pay special attention to the ways in which views on poetry can be said to have changed, after the deaths of Petrarch and Boccaccio in the 1370s, and with the dramatic development of humanism in the first half of the following century. At the end of the fourteenth century humanism was for the most part still the private pursuit of enthusiastic amateurs. The period that followed saw not only an enormous expansion and development of classical studies, most notably the introduction of the systematic study of Greek, but also their institutionalisation as the main component of secondary education, at least in the most prestigious schools; it saw the widespread occupation by humanists of positions of influence in public affairs as well as in teaching, and the extensive diffusion of classically inspired ideas of a radically novel kind, particularly in the spheres of moral and educational thought. By the middle of the Quattrocento the classical revival was in most respects complete, and the humanist movement had established itself as the dominant feature of Italian cultural and social life.[4] It is thus natural to look for changes in humanist writings on poetry corresponding to these changes in the humanist movement as a whole. We shall see that such changes are greater and more interesting than has usually been acknowledged by historians of humanism, who have tended very much to stress the continuity between Petrarch's and Boccaccio's arguments and those of their successors.[5]

Before we consider these changes, some general observations are in order. In the first place the writings in question relate only to the consumption, not to the production of poetry, to literary or critical theory rather than to poetics. They are mainly concerned with issues of education – a fact we shall have to consider further in due course – and in the humanist curriculum reading poetry played an important part but writing it on the whole did not. While the humanists themselves did frequently compose Latin verses, their verses corresponded only in a limited way to the views on poetry expressed in their prose writings – which makes the interpretation of these views particularly difficult. It is only well into the sixteenth century that the theory and practice of poetry can be said to agree consistently with one another. Petrarch's *Trionfi* are a very evident instance of personification allegory; his classical epic, the *Africa*, is not allegorical, nor are most of the verses written by his successors in the fifteenth century. Second, humanist views on poetry in this as in the fourteenth century were not generally concerned with writing in Italian. With some notable exceptions, as we have seen in the preceding chapter, most fifteenth-century humanists avoided the vernacular, and though there was a continuing debate on its merits, especially towards the end of the Quattrocento, this debate was purely marginal to discussions of the general nature and function of poetry. Vernacular classicism is of course, as far as Italy was concerned, almost entirely a sixteenth-century phenomenon. Finally, although interesting changes occurred in humanist approaches to poetry in the first half of the fifteenth century, these were not changes of a strictly theoretical nature. While one may reasonably say that Petrarch and Boccaccio possessed a theory of poetry, one cannot say that this theory was significantly extended or modified or questioned at the level of ideas in the course of the next hundred years or so. It is only with the Neoplatonism of the later fifteenth century – the finishing-point of the

4 Guarino da Verona, *Epistolario*, II, pp. 581–4. See also Grendler, *Schooling in Renaissance Italy*.
5 Seznec, *The Survival of the Pagan Gods*, pp. 103ff.; Sabbadini, *Storia del ciceronianismo*, pp. 92–9, 103–11; Vossler, *Poetische Theorien*; Buck, *Italienische Dichtungslehre*, pp. 54–116; Garin, *L'educazione in Europa*, pp. 81ff., 96ff., and also 'Le favole antiche'; Vasoli, 'L'estetica dell'Umanesimo'; Trinkaus, 'In Our Image and Likeness', II, pp. 683–721; Greenfield, *Poetics*; Kallendorf, 'The Rhetorical Criticism of Literature'.

present discussion – and then with the Aristotelianism of the sixteenth, that new ideas enter the humanist discussion of poetry in any significant way.

What we shall be concerned with, then, are mainly changes of attitude and emphasis concerning the study of the classical poets, changes we may legitimately see as signs of a shifting awareness, however little claim they may have to theoretical status – though there must always be a considerable measure of doubt as to how far we can take humanists' assertions on any subject as evidence of what they actually thought or felt. In describing these changes it is important to distinguish between two different stages of development. The first stage can be seen in the work of two humanists of the generation after Petrarch and Boccaccio: Coluccio Salutati, who was born in 1331, served as chancellor of Florence from 1375 until his death in 1406, and was the most influential humanist of the later Trecento; and the papal secretary Francesco da Fiano, who was born some two decades later. The second stage was effected by the generation of humanists born in the 1370s, together with their immediate successors – the generation of the humanist 'avant-garde'.

Salutati wrote a number of defences of poetry in the form of letters, as well as a large unfinished treatise on poetic myth, the *De laboribus Herculis.*[6] These texts are in large part a reiteration of the position of Petrarch and Boccaccio; like theirs, Salutati's argument centres on the difference between the literal and the hidden meaning of classical poetry, the 'shell' (*cortex*) and the 'kernel' (*medulla*), drawing on the three traditional modes of interpreting the allegory of the poets, as Dante termed it: the physical, the moral, and the historical or euhemeristic. However, in certain respects Salutati carries the argument further than his predecessors. Petrarch and Boccaccio had argued that the poets were secret monotheists, but had tended to the belief that their knowledge of divinity extended only as far as the limits of human reason (see, for instance, *Genealogia deorum gentilium* 14.13); the theme of divine inspiration thus related to the natural wisdom of the poets and to their skills as writers, rather than to any special revelation from above. On the other hand, in his earlier letters, as well as in the *De laboribus Herculis*, Salutati argues that the allegorical content of the poets' writings can include elements of specifically Christian revelation, that the doctrine of the Trinity, for instance, can be found in Virgil; for like Petrarch, Salutati believed that the interpretation of poetry did not have to depend on what its historical author consciously intended (Salutati, *Epistolario*, I, pp. 302–3. Compare

---

[6] Salutati, *Epistolario*, especially I, pp. 298–307, 321–9; III, pp. 289–95, 539–43; IV, pp. 170–240. See also, particularly on changes in Salutati's view of poetry, Witt, 'Coluccio Salutati' and *Hercules at the Crossroads*; Craven, 'Coluccio Salutati's Defence of Poetry'.

De laboribus Herculis 2.2; Petrarch, *Lettere senili*, I, pp. 240ff.). Moreover, Salutati insisted rather more than Petrarch and Boccaccio on the substantial identity of the modes of expression employed by poetry and Scripture, that Scripture was in its essence and of necessity poetic. Poetry, he argued, is to be defined not as a versified discourse, but as that form of locution which 'either through things or through words means something other than that which it shows'; and such a form of locution is necessarily used also by Scripture, since it is only possible to speak of the divine in figurative or metaphorical, and therefore poetic, terms – a point also made by St Thomas Aquinas, though with far stronger reservations on the subject of the value of poetry.[7]

With this even more radical assimilation of poetry to Scripture, clearly, Salutati assigns to poetry an even higher position in the scale of knowledge than it had for Petrarch and Boccaccio. However, his arguments in this respect are far from unqualified. He reiterates the traditional distinction made by Dante between theological or scriptural and poetic allegory, that in the former the literal meaning is true, whereas in the latter it is not; and while insisting that poetry is superior to all other secular arts and sciences, following Petrarch and Boccaccio he concedes without reservation that Scripture and theology are of greater importance for human life (*Epistolario*, I, p. 323; III, p. 292 and *De laboribus Herculis* 1.3). Salutati never doubted that poetry, like all forms of purely human knowledge, should only be treated as a means to a higher goal, a *via* rather than a *terminus* (*Epistolario*, IV; pp. 186–7). In contrast, such qualifications are notably absent from the defence that Francesco da Fiano wrote in Rome between 1399 and 1404, against the 'ridiculous slanderers and rancorous detractors of the poets'.[8] This reiterates most of the main arguments of Petrarch, Boccaccio and Salutati in favour of poetry but omits their reservations, including those concerning the differences between poetry and Scripture; if one takes the argument literally, it appears to insist that the two kinds of text are in all essential respects the same. As a result, signs of an extreme classicism, even of paganising tendencies, have been seen in the text, an interpretation to which we shall shortly return.[9]

So far we have considered ways in which Salutati and, even more, Francesco da Fiano pursue to further extremes the line of argument of Petrarch and Boccaccio. But although much the greater part of Salutati's defence of poetry is aimed in this direction, in certain important respects his writings mark a new orientation in the debate, and anticipate some

---

[7] Salutati, *Epistolario*, IV, pp. 176–7; Curtius, *European Literature*, pp. 217–19.
[8] Baron, *Crisis of the Early Italian Renaissance*, pp. 295–314; Francesco da Fiano, *Contra ridiculos oblocutores et fellitos detractores poetarum*.
[9] Baron, *Crisis of the Early Italian Renaissance*, pp. 295–300.

of the developments that occur in the course of the first half of the fifteenth century. What distinguishes Salutati's theory above all from those of Petrarch, Boccaccio, and also Francesco da Fiano, is that it is a theory of education as well. Petrarch and Boccaccio were concerned to defend the status of the classical poets and their own private interest in poetry, but were not interested in the question of the kind of texts that children should be taught in school; it is well known that Petrarch despised school-teaching as an ungrateful occupation (*Le familiari*, III, pp. 20–1). On the other hand Salutati's last letter in particular was a long answer, interrupted by his death in 1406, to the *Lucula noctis* of the Florentine Dominican Giovanni Dominici, a polemical treatise that conceded 'with gritted teeth', it has been said, that classical literature might be read by mature men of firm faith, but insisted with a lengthy array of arguments that it should be wholly excluded from the schooling of the young.[10] The theme of Salutati's reply was that all the liberal arts are essential to education and that the highest of all these arts is poetry.

In a loose sense this view of poetry is not only educational but civic. Unlike Francesco da Fiano, Salutati abandons the Petrarchan idea of the poet as a solitary sage living amidst the woods and fields, and assumes that the study of poetry is normally pursued by those engaged in the life of the world in towns (*Epistolario*, III, pp. 539–43). This assumption is associated with a rather greater stress on the capacity of poetry to move and convince, a capacity which results, in Salutati's view, from its appeal to the faculty of imagination or fantasy, and which seems to be a major reason for the high status he assigns to the art (see for example, *De laboribus Herculis*, pp. 20ff.; Salutati, *Epistolario*, IV, p. 230). There are also signs, though it is still a relatively minor point, of the special association of poetry and rhetoric which, as we shall see, features so prominently in the views of the next generations of humanists. For Salutati rather more than for Petrarch and Boccaccio, poetry is an important aid in the acquisition of eloquence; the poet is 'closely related to the orator, rather more restricted as regards rhythm, but freer in his licence with words' (*Epistolario*, IV, pp. 202; also I, p. 298). These arguments are related, clearly, to Salutati's frequent insistence on the superiority of the will over the intellect and to his conclusion that the highest kind of life is the *vita activa et civilis*, the Aristotelian life of political activity. But he was equally capable on occasion of arguing exactly the opposite,[11] and there is no evidence of his associating education in general and the study of poetry

---

[10] See Salutati, *Epistolario*, IV, pp. 205ff.; Garin, *L'educazione in Europa*, pp. 88ff.; Da Prati, *Giovanni Dominici*; Denley, 'Giovanni Dominici's Opposition to Humanism'; Ronconi, 'Dominici'.

[11] See for instance Salutati, *De nobilitate legum*; *De seculo et religione*.

in particular specifically with a career in public affairs. For Salutati the aims of education are broadly social rather than narrowly political.

Thus in the views of the most influential humanist at the turn of the century we can see new developments that indicate the increasing strength of the classical revival, and we can also see the persistent dominance of a traditional approach, the allegorical mode of interpretation, the effect of which can only be seen as a substantial disavowal of the real novelty of the new movement's interests. This dual character of Salutati's attitude to poetry needs to be underlined, because of the tendency in the last few decades to place the greater emphasis on the innovative elements in his work and in the Trecento defences as a whole. There is no doubt a good measure of truth in the assertion that for the humanists from Petrarch onwards classical poetry is 'human poetry'; it 'consecrates worldly things projecting them into a divine atmosphere', that it was 'under the sign of great poetry that men found themselves once again',[12] or in the suggestion that Francesco da Fiano's polemic and up to a point Salutati's later writings as well betray an extreme classicism, even 'paganising tendencies'.[13] These points, together with the observations that have been made on the importance of the theme of inventiveness (*invenire*) in Boccaccio's view of poetry, and on the celebration of the 'myth of the life of strong and glorious men' in the *De laboribus Herculis*,[14] all help to account for the evident differences between the Trecento defences and medieval allegorisations of Virgil and Ovid. But it is equally important to acknowledge, in the continued dominance of allegorical interpretation, a major limiting factor on the classicism of these defences. Whatever their novelty, they still offered a reading of ancient poetry that was essentially recuperative and reductive, that suppressed in large part its real historical properties by projecting onto it the conventional knowledge of the time: commonplaces of Christian morality, simple notions of medieval science, historical events of mainly imaginary origins. How far did the next generation of humanists alter this approach?

The first signs of a new attitude appear at the very end of the Trecento, shortly before the classes of the Byzantine scholar Manuel Chrysoloras, which introduced the Florentine humanists to the serious study of Greek, and some years before the death of Salutati in 1406. In 1397 there occurred an event – or at least there was widespread report of an event – that had a considerable impact on the humanist world. The *condottiere* Carlo Malatesta had entered the city of Mantua after a battle nearby, and ordered to be destroyed a statue of Virgil that had stood in the city for centuries. The outrage caused by the report of this event gave rise to three new

---

[12] Garin, 'Le favole antiche', pp. 72, 74; *L'educazione in Europa*, p. 81.
[13] Baron, *The Crisis of the Early Italian Renaissance*, pp. 295–314.
[14] Buck, *Italienische Dichtungslehre*, p. 83; Garin, 'Le favole antiche', p. 76.

defences of poetry in general and Virgil in particular, one of them anonymous, one by Salutati, and one by Pier Paolo Vergerio, a young protégé of Salutati's who was born in 1370 and lived for the most part in Padua, around the turn of the century, but had close connections with the group of Florentine humanists of whom Salutati was leader. The anonymous defence merely reiterates and expands Boccaccio's arguments.[15] Salutati pursues the line of argument that characterises most of his writings on the subject, though it may be, as has been suggested, that this was the first occasion on which he developed the radical point concerning the 'equal need of both poetry and religion to employ figurative speech'.[16] Vergerio's defence, on the other hand, seems to be fundamentally different from the other two. Whereas both of these centre on the issue of allegorical interpretation, allegorical interpretation is not even mentioned by Vergerio. He simply emphasises the role of poets and writers in general in perpetuating the memory of the great deeds of the past and in inciting men's minds to virtue; the *ratio* of poets, especially heroic poets, is to 'praise virtue and blame vice and turpitude' (compare Petrarch, *Africa* 2, ll. 450ff.).

It would be wrong to suggest here that Vergerio consciously and deliberately rejects the principle of allegorical interpretation, or that there is anything particularly novel about the arguments he does put forward. His point that poetry records the deeds of the past, praises virtue, and blames vice, is not in the least incompatible with this principle, and in the course of his letter he refers to the *fabula* and *figmenta* of the poets, to their divine inspiration and their rarity – all of these being notions closely associated with the allegorical defences we have been considering. It may be that Vergerio merely felt that the idea of allegorical interpretation was unnecessary in that particular context, since his main subject was the highly moral Virgil rather than a more ethically questionable poet such as Ovid; he says, in fact, that it is not his intention to say what the function (*vis*) of poetry is. Nevertheless, in its marked contrast with all the other defences, Vergerio's silence on the subject of allegory is striking, especially since it is continued later in his major work, the *De ingenuis moribus*, the first and most influential of all the humanist treatises on education. This text, written in 1402 or 1403, deals with the study of all the liberal arts, but in a very different way, for instance, from Salutati's letter to Dominici written a few years later. As we saw, a major concern of Salutati's letter was to justify secular studies as consistent with and conducive to the faith, and the allegorical interpretation of poetry plays a prominent part in his

[15] Robey, 'Virgil's Statue'; Salutati, *Epistolario*, III, pp. 285–95 and p. 285, n. 1; Vergerio, *Epistolario*, pp. 189–202, xi ff.; Zabughin, *Vergilio nel Rinascimento*, pp. 112ff.; Dominici, *Lucula*, ed. Coulon, pp. xxxvi ff.; Robey, 'P. P. Vergerio the Elder'. See also Fisher, 'Three Meditations on the Destruction of Virgil's Statue'.
[16] Baron, *The Crisis of the Early Italian Renaissance*, p. 298.

argument. Vergerio's *De ingenuis moribus*, in contrast, is celebratory rather than justificatory; there is no trace of an attempt to relate classical studies to the teachings of the church, and the subject of poetry is dealt with in two brief (and not particularly novel) assertions: that (much as Boccaccio argued in *Genealogia deorum gentilium* 15.10) some children are particularly suited to poetic study by their natural disposition; and that poetry is closely connected to rhetoric – the subject to which he gives most attention – but 'although it can contribute much to our lives and to our powers of eloquence, it seems more suited to purposes of enjoyment'. Is Vergerio's silence on the subject of allegory representative of a general tendency in the generations after Salutati's?

It must be said straightaway that the allegorical interpretation of the poets by no means disappears in the course of the fifteenth century. On the contrary, between the death of Salutati and the end of the century when, as we shall see, the Florentine Neoplatonists gave a new impetus and to some extent a new direction to the practice of allegorisation, a number of humanist texts reiterate with little or no modification the poetic theories of Petrarch, Boccaccio and Salutati. In a letter of 1423 the antiquarian Ciriaco d'Ancona wrote a defence of poetry centring on the theme of Virgil's secret monotheism, and on the notion that Christian mysteries are hidden under the surface of his works ('But what did this divine poet not know about the divine mysteries?').[17] Four years later, in a letter of 1427 to the same Ciriaco, the well-known scholar Francesco Filelfo reiterated Salutati's interpretation of the first six books of the *Aeneid* as an allegorical representation of the six ages of the life of man – in confutation of what he called the common opinion of schoolmasters, that Virgil only wrote his poem in order to imitate Homer and praise Augustus (*Epistolarum familarum libri XXXVII*, fols. 2r–3r). In the second book of his history of the Latin writers, published in 1437 and the first modern history of literature, the Paduan humanist Sicco Polenton discusses the origins and function of poetry in terms strongly reminiscent of Petrarch's and Boccaccio's (*Scriptorum illustrium latinae linguae libri XVIII*, pp. viii ff., 42ff.). And, in his *Politia literaria libri septem*, a book on matters of literary taste published in 1462, Angelo Decembrio offers, among a vast number of dialogues on literary and linguistic questions, a brief defence of poetry through the mouths of Guarino da Verona and his pupil Leonello d'Este (*Politiae literariae* 5.63). The cultivated discussions of Decembrio's humanist characters are interrupted by a monk, Augustine, who accuses the classical poets of paganism and immorality, and criticises the company for devoting its time to them. The accusation and criticism are rapidly, politely and blandly dealt with by Guarino and Leonello by means of the

---

[17] Morici, 'Dante e Ciriaco d'Ancona'.

traditional euhemeristic explanation and the argument of the poets' hidden monotheism. At the end of the debate the monk leaves shaking his head, and the humanists resume their literary conversation without troubling their consciences further.

I shall return shortly to Guarino's views on poetry, when I consider more distinctive treatments of the subject from the Quattrocento. But we should first note a group of texts whose arguments are equally unoriginal, but which are more interesting than those just described, because they document the spread of the defence of poetry outside the strictly humanist sphere. The best known of these is the *Concordantiae poetarum philosophorum et theologorum* by the Venetian doctor and natural philosopher Giovanni Caldiera. This work was written by Caldiera to encourage his religious-minded daughter to take an interest in classical literature;[18] it can be dated between 1447 and 1455, during the Pontificate of the humanist Nicholas V who, it will be seen, seems to have inspired a number of defences or celebrations of classical poetry and classical studies. As his title indicates, Caldiera's purpose is to show how classical poetry, more exactly the mythical content of classical poetry, is, when properly interpreted, in full agreement with the teachings of moral and natural philosophers and also with those of the Bible. He proceeds typically by recounting a myth, allegorising it in euhemeristic, moral and physical terms, and then adding a *spiritualis expositio* that points to a hidden meaning of a specifically Christian kind. The work is interesting, it has been observed, as a mid-fifteenth-century example of a genre not to be found in the Quattrocento, that of mythographic repertories like the *Genealogia deorum gentilium* and the *De laboribus Herculis*. It might be added that in spite of its scant theoretical content – it offers only the briefest general discussion of poetry – it is also remarkable for the extent to which it pursues the specifically Christian interpretation of classical myths, an interpretation which, we have noted, was generally absent from the works of Petrarch and Boccaccio.

Caldiera was not professionally concerned with the humanistic disciplines (the *studia humanitatis*), but he was a scholar with strong humanist interests. On the other hand, two earlier fifteenth-century defences have virtually nothing about them that is humanistic, apart from their general purpose. Their form is wholly unclassical, and they show no interest whatever in the specifically literary properties of texts. The first, which seems to belong to the first decades of the century, is a treatise by the Florentine professor of medicine, Giovanni Baldo di Faenza, the purpose of which is to show that 'no science of the gentiles is contrary to the Catholic faith' (*Tractatus*, fol. 1r). Following the author's professional

---

[18] See Trinkaus, *'In Our Image and Likeness'*, II, pp. 704–12.

interests the argument centres mainly on classical natural philosophy, but on occasion the usual allegorical interpretation of the poets is reiterated, no doubt reflecting the views of Salutati (for example, fols. 14v, 17r, 26r). A more striking and substantial work is the *De consonantia nature et gratie* of the Dominican theologian and Inquisitor Raffaele di Pornassio, also written during the Pontificate of Nicholas V, and dedicated to him.[19] The text of this consists of the synthesised version or *harmonia* of the Four Gospels by Ammonius Alexandrinus, which the author glosses with citations from or references to the works of the classical philosophers, poets and historians, adding comments of his own in order to point out the agreement thus indicated between the teachings of grace and those of human reason. The main emphasis here, once again following the author's professional interest, is on moral philosophy. The classical poets feature fairly prominently in this bulky and awkward volume, but their treatment is remarkably simplistic. Raffaele does not even draw on the allegorical tradition, but contents himself with the mere demonstration that, taken at the letter, the poets and the Gospels are in agreement. The work is of interest, then, merely as an expression of faith in this principle from a rather unexpected source.

When we turn from these conventional exercises in harmonistics to the humanist writings on education, a very different picture of the study of poetry presents itself. The views of two contemporaries of Vergerio's, Guarino da Verona and Florentine Chancellor Leonardo Bruni, seem to be particularly close; that is, the more theoretical points that Bruni makes in his *De studiis et litteris*, written in the 1420s in Florence and addressed to a woman, correspond substantially, as far as poetry is concerned, to our main source of information about Guarino's teaching practice, the *De ordine docendi* of his son Battista, written in 1459.[20] For both Bruni and Guarino poetry was an essential part of a liberal education, especially for Bruni, who argued that it is the subject to which we are most inclined by nature, and that there is nothing that delights our minds as much as harmony and rhythm; elsewhere, in a letter, Bruni resuscitated the Platonic notion of the divine *furor* of poets, a notion, we shall see, which came into much greater prominence later in the century (*Epistolarum libri VIII*, II, pp. 36–40; compare Plato, *Phaedrus* 245).

Guarino perhaps did not wholly share this enthusiasm, which echoes that of the earlier defences; for him, as for other fifteenth-century educators, poetry had an important but clearly circumscribed position in the curriculum, falling under the heading of grammar, as in Quintilian's

---

[19] The text refers (fol. 2v) to the recent election of the pope (in 1447).
[20] In Garin (ed.), *Il pensiero pedagogico*, pp. 146–69 and 434–71; tr. into English in Woodward, *Vittorino da Feltre*, pp. 119–33, 161–78.

Institutio oratoria, and taught at the earlier stages of schooling. Unlike Vergerio, both Bruni and Guarino advocated allegorical interpretation, but with what seems a major difference of emphasis from the earlier defences.[21] Allegory is now no longer the central consideration. In Bruni's text in particular it is mentioned only in connection with the immoral, or apparently immoral elements in the poets, elements which Bruni argues are relatively infrequent. Instead he insists on what the letter of poems can teach about life in the world and nature, the usefulness (*utilitas*) and knowledge (*multarum rerum cognitio*) that can be derived from them; and equally on their formal properties, their elegance and beauty of style (*elegantia, concinnitas*). Similarly, in his account of his father's teaching Battista Guarino lays considerable stress on the information about the classical world contained in the poets, the *sententiae* 'useful both to life and to everyday speech',[22] the correctness (*proprietas*) and elegance of their language and its value for the acquisition of eloquence. This sort of formal consideration in particular had featured only to a small extent in the earlier humanist defences.

Just as Vergerio had associated poetry mainly with enjoyment, so there are signs in Bruni and Battista Guarino of the beginnings of a specifically aesthetic appreciation of the poet's art, an attitude valuing artistic ability for its own sake as well as for its use in the acquisition of eloquence. This can be seen in Bruni's argument on the outwardly immoral passages in the *Aeneid*: 'When I read about Dido's loves in Virgil, I am accustomed to admire the poet's genius [*ingenium*], but to pay no attention at all to the matter itself, because I know it to be false'; and much the same point is made by Battista Guarino.[23] But this is aestheticism of a very inchoate sort, and is not pursued further either by Bruni and Battista or by any of their Quattrocento successors. There is little explicit evidence for the assertion that in the Quattrocento classical mythology constituted 'only an object of aesthetic contemplation'.[24]

However, Bruni's words do express a principle which features quite prominently in the work of some fifteenth-century writers, including Guarino: the principle of selective reading, that children and men should appreciate and benefit from the useful parts of classical poetry, and simply ignore those that are immoral or lascivious. This principle belongs to fifteenth-century educational thought much more than to the fourteenth-century defences, which, apart from ill-defined references to the 'scenic' writers, insisted without discrimination on the allegorical truth of everything that the poets wrote. It derives particularly from St Basil's homily

[21] See also Guarino da Verona, *Epistolario*, III, pp. 419ff.
[22] Garin (ed.), *Il pensiero pedagogico*, p. 456.   [23] Garin, pp. 166, 464.
[24] Ronconi, *Le origini*, pp. 150–1.

on reading gentile literature, a text translated from the Greek by Bruni at the beginning of the century, and destined to become one of the most widely read educational works in the Renaissance.[25] This text offered the humanists a view of classical literature that paid little attention, if any, to the question of allegory, but at the same time insisted on literature's moral and spiritual utility to Christians who were able to discriminate. St Basil's image of the bee that flies from flower to flower, selecting what is good and ignoring what is bad, was to become one of the commonplaces of subsequent humanist writing.

The shift of attention to the literal level of poetry becomes even more apparent when we turn to the other great humanist schoolmaster, Vittorino da Feltre. Vittorino himself wrote scarcely anything at all, and our knowledge about his teaching is almost entirely derived from his four biographers, whose accounts vary greatly in their scope.[26] But for him as for Guarino it is clear that the study of poetry played an important role in the early part of the curriculum under the general heading of grammar. Virgil was studied almost from the beginning of a child's education, followed by a remarkably wide range of Latin and Greek poets, all of them subjected to the process of close analytical reading which was an essential part of Guarino's method as well. The range included Ovid (whom Vittorino called 'lascivum et amabilem'), Terence and Plautus among the Latin writers, though he recognised that these might be morally dangerous for some; Juvenal, on the other hand, was excluded, 'because he spoke too openly and obscenely'.[27] Yet nowhere does any one of the four biographers mention the topic of allegorical interpretation. To judge from their accounts, Vittorino's emphasis was all on the moral precepts to be derived from the literal content of the poets, their judgement (*gravitas sententiarum*), together with their 'abundance of words', their linguistic propriety and their eloquence. This is one of a number of signs of the strikingly secular and practical character of Vittorino's teaching, in spite of the unanimous emphasis of all his biographers on his personal piety and high moral standards.

If we consider the educational writings of the next generation of humanists, the treatises of Maffeo Vegio and Aeneas Sylvius (Enea Silvio Piccolomini, the future Pius II) and Leon Battista Alberti's dialogue on family life, we find what seems a substantially similar view of the study of poetry in the latter two, though a somewhat divergent one in the first (Matteo Palmieri's *Della vita civile* does not deal with the subject specifically, but no doubt assumes its inclusion under the heading of grammar). Vegio

---

[25] St Basil's *De legendis gentilium libris* survives in innumerable Latin manuscripts and editions, often together with the treatise of Vergerio; for example, the first edition of the latter (Venice, C. Valdarfer, *c.* 1471) (Copinger 5984).
[26] In Garin (ed.), *Il pensiero pedagogico*, pp. 504–713.   [27] Garin (ed.), p. 686.

was the most religious-minded of the humanist educators of the fifteenth century, and this is reflected in the dominant concern of his treatise (written in 1444) with moral training, in its relative lack of interest in the formal properties of poetry, and in the prominence it gives to allegorical interpretation; nevertheless the classical poets, with the exception of those of doubtful moral influence, play an important part in his programme of studies (*De educatione liberorum et eorum claris moribus* 2.18; excerpts in Garin (ed.), *Il pensiero pedagogico*, pp. 171–9). On the other hand, allegorical interpretation does not feature at all in Alberti's dialogue (1432–4) or in Aeneas Sylvius' two major educational writings, both of them in the form of letters addressed to future rulers, and written in 1443 and 1450 respectively.[28] The emphasis here is all on the linguistic and oratorical skills that can be learnt from classical poetry, together with the moral teaching and the worldly knowledge that it conveys at a purely literal level.

As descriptions of real or ideal programmes of education rather than defences of poetry, the texts just considered are not entirely comparable, evidently, with the earlier writings of Petrarch, Boccaccio, Salutati and Francesco da Fiano. But we also have a number of works from the middle of the fifteenth century that are specifically concerned with the defence of poetry or classical literature in general, and that treat their topic in a more original way than the other more or less contemporary defences considered earlier. The best known of these are two letters written in 1450 and 1453 respectively by Guarino and Aeneas Sylvius, the first in reply to an attack on the classics by a friar, Giovanni da Prato, the second in defence of the author's poetic interests against criticisms from Viennese scholars whom he met at the imperial court (*Epistolario*, II, pp. 519–32; Wolkan (ed.), *Fontes* 68, pp. 315–47). In neither of the two defences is allegorical interpretation in any way a major factor. If Guarino seems to have used it in his teaching, here he only refers in passing to the allegorical meaning of the *Aeneid*, and Aeneas Sylvius simply mentions the euhemeristic explanation of the pagan gods. Instead both authors' arguments centre on the authority and example of the church Fathers, on the moral lessons to be derived from a literal reading of the classics (for instance the *exempla* and precepts in Terence and Juvenal), on the principle of selective reading and St Basil's image of the bee, and on the point that the description of immoral deeds (of which the Bible is also full, as Aeneas Sylvius points out) is not in itself corrupting. The religious element in both texts is worth noting, in the repeated reference to the Fathers and in the emphasis on the Christian use of the classics. Guarino's, in fact, is the more religious

---

[28] In Wolkan (ed.), *Fontes* 61, pp. 222–36, and 67, pp. 103–58; the second and larger of these texts is the *De liberorum educatione*.

of the two (although Aeneas Sylvius was then a bishop and writing to a cardinal); his starting-point is the proposition that theology is the queen of the sciences, and the other disciplines her servants. It is odd that in both texts the relationship of poetry to eloquence is scarcely mentioned; this is however a theme of an earlier defence of poetry by Aeneas Sylvius, written in 1444, where the civic benefits of oratory and poetry, and the need of the former for the latter, are particularly stressed (Wolkan (ed.), *Fontes* 61, pp. 326–31).

We have two further defences from the 1450s, both of them rather less well known and still available only in manuscript, and both connected with the city of Verona. The first is a dialogue by the Augustinian canon Timoteo Maffei, a Veronese pupil of Guarino's, on the question whether both sacred and worldly studies should be pursued by monks. It was written between 1450 and 1454 and is a defence, yet again dedicated to Nicholas V, against the criticisms of rigorous monastics, who had maintained that a monk's duty was to cultivate *sancta rusticitas*, and not to concern himself with any kind of learning.[29] Maffei's dialogue was not, in fact, the first humanistic discussion of monastic studies; one was written by a layman and friend of Vergerio's, Ognibene della Scola, in about 1415, and another by the Benedictine Girolamo Agliotti in Arezzo in 1442 (*De vita religiosa et monastica* and *De monachis erudiendis* respectively). Agliotti's discussion (also a dialogue, the protagonist of which is another and more famous humanist monk, Ambrogio Traversari) need not concern us particularly here, since it discusses classical studies for the most part in very general terms, and has scarcely anything to say on the subject of poetry. In Ognibene's treatise, on the other hand, poetry is the first subject considered under the heading of secular letters, and is a leading consideration in the discussion, the conclusion of which is that all branches of learning are necessary to the study of theology and should therefore be actively pursued by monks. His position seems in fact quite close to that of Guarino and Aeneas Sylvius, though he is writing some decades earlier; there is no explicit discussion of allegory (but it could be assumed as a factor in poetry), and the emphasis is all on the moral lessons that can be learnt from the poets, apparently through a literal reading, and on the importance of selecting, like St Basil's bee, the good elements from the bad. Maffei's defence reiterates much the same arguments, but is evidently more remarkable as the work of a monk rather than a layman. In his rather brief discussion of the poets there is again no mention of allegorical interpretation; he merely insists that even the comic and satirical poets, although there is much in them that is immoral, can still act as the

---

[29] Maffei, *In sanctam rusticitatem litteras impugnantem*; Zippel, 'Le vite di Paolo II', pp. 8–9; Guarino da Verona, *Epistolario*, III, pp. 427–31.

servants of theology, and that monks should learn, again like the bee, to turn them to the purposes of good living by selecting the good from the bad. The argument is buttressed with the usual citations from the Bible and the church Fathers.

Ognibene's and Maffei's texts therefore mark a significant difference from the position of Salutati, who assumed, as we saw, that the poets and other classical writers should be studied by laymen but certainly not by monks. This seems to be quite striking evidence of the spread of the impact of humanism in the first decades of the fifteenth century. The second Veronese defence, on the other hand, is concerned not with monastic studies in particular, but with the general utility of classical literature for Christians, especially for the young. It is a set of three orations on oratory and poetry by a pupil of Vittorino's, Antonio Beccaria, delivered probably in 1454 or 1455 in front of the humanist bishop of Verona, Ermolao Barbaro.[30] (Ermolao Barbaro was the author of an attack on the poets, written shortly after Beccaria's defence, though not aimed at it. The ground of the attack is not religious at all, but lay and civic; it concerns the education of the young to be good citizens, a goal which poetry supposedly compromises.)[31] As a well-known humanist and more recently a priest, Beccaria set out to confute the view of certain Veronese ecclesiastics, a view which he claims he had thought already extinct, that the orators, poets and other classical writers should not be read by Christians. His orations constitute, in a verbose, disorganised and repetitive form, probably the most extensive collection of arguments against this view produced in the fifteenth century, though they add nothing new to the debate. The third oration, which deals entirely with poetry, centres on the three traditional views – moral, physical and euhemeristic – of poetic allegory, a fact which confirms that even in fairly advanced humanist circles the fourteenth-century view of poetry continued to flourish. At the same time Beccaria's defence distinguishes itself quite clearly from those of the previous century by its emphasis on the use of poetry for the acquisition of eloquence, and by a general absence of the insistent subordination of poetry to religion, the *via non terminus* argument, that played such an important part in the work of Salutati and his predecessors; for all his lack of novelty, Beccaria's spirit is very different from theirs. As the mid-century defence closest in purpose and scope to Salutati's last writings on poetry, the orations may provide the best indication of the development of humanist attitudes to the art in the intervening fifty years.

---

[30] Beccaria, *Orationes defensoriae*; Ronconi, 'Il grammatico Antonio Beccaria'.
[31] Ermolao Barbaro il Vecchio, *Orationes contra poetas*.

Let us now return to our earlier question: how far is Vergerio's silence on the subject of allegory representative of a general tendency in the generations after Salutati's? It will now be clear that, while the idea and practice of allegorisation certainly did not disappear, they are strikingly absent from a number of humanist writings on poetry, and where they do feature it is generally in a much reduced role, alongside a stronger association of poetry with the acquisition of eloquence. Since much of the work we have considered concerns questions of education, this recession of allegorisation must in part be attributable to reasons of a practical pedagogical nature. What we know of the importance of systematic analytical reading and memorisation in humanist teaching, together with the more recent argument that humanist schools may have achieved a far lower level of literary competence than their spokesmen claimed, both tend to suggest that schoolchildren and their teachers were usually occupied with more concrete and elementary matters than the search for hidden meanings. Nevertheless, in view of the enormous prominence of allegorisation in the preceding discussions of poetry, it is difficult not to see the silence of Vergerio and others on the subject as a choice, a deliberate suspension of the traditional mode of interpretation.

This silence also seems to be evidence of a much more confident, tolerant and realistic approach to the classics than that of the polemical apologies of the century before. It has been common in Renaissance studies of the last few decades to use the term 'civic' in connection with the attitudes of humanists of the first half of the fifteenth century, such as Vergerio, Bruni and Guarino, and the term can help to explain their apparent abandonment, partial or total, of the practice of allegorisation. A concern with living a full life in the world might well produce a greater willingness to take classical literature at its face value, without recourse to hidden meanings. But while the generations after Salutati were probably more concerned than he was with the usefulness of poetry and the other *studia humanitatis* as a preparation for a life of political activity, it needs to be stressed that this kind of life was by no means the only concern of fifteenth-century writings on poetry and education in general; some, like Aeneas Sylvius' letters, were mainly directed towards it, while others, like Vergerio's, Vegio's and Battista Guarino's treatises and the dialogue of Timoteo Maffei, were not. Although it may well be true that the actual historical function of humanism was to serve as a programme for the ruling class, the *studia humanitatis* were not generally viewed in anything like such narrow terms by most of their major exponents. What is common to most, though not all, of Salutati's successors is that, like him, they viewed poetry in the context of an active, social life, and that, unlike him, they expressed little concern to subordinate the study of poetry to the demands of religion. One may therefore describe their conception of poetry as a worldly one in most senses of the word, or as the affirmation of 'truly human' rather than religious values.[32] Only in some cases can we say that this conception was a civic one in strict Aristotelian terms.

Suspension of allegorisation does not, however, mean open rejection, of which there is scarcely any evidence in humanist writings. The most substantial instance during the period we have been considering is in a manuscript version of the *De avaritia* of Poggio Bracciolini, one of Salutati's humanist successors as chancellor of Florence.[33] In the course of Poggio's dialogue on avarice one of the participants contests the allegorical interpretation of the classical Harpies as standing for this vice, and the contestation becomes a general condemnation of the allegorical view of mythology. Poggio writes of the 'ridiculous and inept' interpretation 'unworthy of a scholar' that sees in such fables anything other than a 'desire to delight the listeners' ear': 'What is more vain . . . than to suppose that the stories of Plautus or Terence and others signify something more hidden or more obscure under the guise of other persons?' But the context is a polemical one, and the author's main concern is not with the study of poetry. It is therefore difficult to take the passage as in any way representative of contemporary views – a point made also by Seznec about a similar criticism of allegorisation by Rabelais in the following century.[34]

It is not hard to see why we should have no evidence, apart from Poggio's text, of humanists explicitly rejecting allegorisation, for the function it performed was clearly too valuable – a conclusion we can draw from its continued, indeed increased, use at the end of the fifteenth century and beyond. No better theory was available to Poggio and his contemporaries in the first half of the Quattrocento for reconciling their literary interests with their duties as Christians, duties which, it is well known, scarcely any humanist ever called seriously into question. Whatever they may personally have felt about it, allegorical interpretation must have represented for them a vital instrument of last resort for justifying their professional concerns. Besides, reflection on the process of interpretation should bring home to us some of the parallels between medieval and Renaissance allegorisation and the kind of academic literary criticism commonly practised today, since all of them involve the extraction of general propositions from the specific details of narrative. What, after all, are the 'themes' that modern interpretation looks for in texts, if not a 'hidden' level of meaning? The difference between such practice and that of the type we have been considering has been neatly put by Todorov, through the distinction between

---

[32] Ronconi, *Le origini*, p. 149. [33] See Garin, *La cultura filosofica*, pp. 36–7.
[34] Seznec, *The Survival of the Pagan Gods*, pp. 95–6.

readings constrained by the text of departure – that of the author – and those constrained by a particular text of arrival, religious, philosophical or whatever.[35] The idea of an allegorisation constrained by the text of departure, obviously a determining factor in modern scholarly practice, was simply not a part of the humanists' intellectual equipment; their allegorical readings – but not, of course, their more philological studies – were entirely dominated by the texts of arrival referred to earlier, the commonplaces of Christian morality, simple notions of medieval science, and so on. Nevertheless there is a sufficient similarity between our modes of reading and theirs for us to take seriously their use of allegorisation, and not to dismiss it too readily as a mere weapon for polemic.

There are, evidently, a number of reasons why the humanists should have failed to develop a new and more adequate theory of poetry. A lack of interest in and knowledge of Greek poetic theory must have had some part to play, though whether as cause or effect is not clear. The absence of a powerful opposition was also clearly an important factor; in the first half of the Quattrocento, it has been observed, there was no one to continue Dominici's attack.[36] And thirdly, the academic and pedagogical nature of the humanists' interest in poetry must have limited the stimulus to theoretical innovation; the poetics of the sixteenth century obviously owe much to later humanists' interest in vernacular writing. But it is significant that this failure in the matter of poetic theory is part of a broader theoretical deficiency. The humanists of the earlier fifteenth century were concerned with literature, with rhetoric and with education, and not, except in a limited way, with philosophy. They adopted positions of a quite radical kind in contrast with Christian teaching, but their tendency, as a recent historian has argued, was 'not to quarrel with traditional Christian ideas but to bypass them'; they 'glorified some aspects of pagan philosophy but avoided following through its implications'.[37]

This notion seems the best framework for understanding the silence of Vergerio and some of his successors on the subject of allegorical interpretation. On the one hand this silence must indicate a considerable degree of dissatisfaction with the traditional theory of poetry and consequently a much greater tolerance of its literal content, however much this conflicted with traditional moral views – feelings which one can easily see as reflections of the greater confidence and energy of the humanist movement in the first half of the fifteenth century. Yet on the other hand the same silence indicates not a revision but a temporary suspension of the theoretical discussion. An acceptance of poetry's literal content is tacitly

[35] Todorov, *Symbolisme et interprétation*, pp. 159–61; *Symbolism and Interpretation*, pp. 166–8.
[36] Holmes, *The Florentine Enlightenment*, p. 120.   [37] Holmes, pp. 63, 136.

acknowledged, but the implications of this acceptance are simply not pursued. As in other areas of their activity, Vergerio and others seem simply to have taken for granted that intellectual interests of a profoundly worldly kind could safely coexist with a traditional Christian faith.

In the later part of the Quattrocento, at all events, allegorisation returns with a vengeance, in parallel with the move from worldly to metaphysical interests which many have seen in the development of humanism in the course of the century. Ficino's translations of, and commentaries on, Plato and Plotinus encouraged the direct and systematic exploitation of ideas on art and poetry that had figured only indirectly and occasionally in the work of his predecessors, and proposed a new philosophical content – a new text of arrival – as the goal of allegorical interpretation. The work of Cristoforo Landino is the most substantial expression of the new, Platonic, approach to the study of poetry. Written in 1472, the third and fourth books of his *Disputationes camaldulenses*[38] contain, in support of an argument in favour of contemplative life, an allegorical interpretation of Virgil's *Aeneid*, which according to its author constitutes the first systematic philosophical commentary on the poem (pp. 116–17). Virgil is seen as a follower of Platonic doctrine, embodying in Aeneas man's search for the supreme good of contemplation (Italy), which he finally achieves after overcoming the attractions of sensual and material things (Troy, the Harpies, etc.), and involvement in the active civic life (Dido and Carthage). The commentary on the *Commedia*, written immediately afterwards and referred to in earlier sections of this volume, is similarly claimed by Landino to be the first systematic allegorical interpretation of the poem and enrols Dante as well in the ranks of the Platonists.[39] Both commentaries start from the Platonic notion, rehearsed in a famous letter of Ficino's written a few years earlier, of the *furor divinus* of the poets, who evoke through the harmony of their verses the divine and celestial harmonies that each soul contemplates directly before the birth of the body.[40] As we have seen, this notion had figured in the work of Bruni, and is present in that of Salutati as well, but in both cases in the context of a view of poetry that is predominantly worldly and can only be described in a very general way as Neoplatonic (Bruni, *Epistolarum libri VIII*, II, pp. 36–40; compare Salutati, *De laboribus Herculis* 1.5–9).

However, an extended treatment of Florentine Platonism is scarcely in order in a volume devoted to medieval criticism. The work we have been dealing with up to this point can legitimately be seen as the last stage in

---

[38] For the dating, see Landino, *Disputationes camaldulenses*, pp. xxx–xxxiii.

[39] Landino, *Scritti critici*, particularly I, p. 172. For the date see Cardini, *La critica del Landino*, p. 17.

[40] *Disputationes camaldulenses*, pp. 111–14; *Scritti critici*, I, pp. 143–5. The Ficino letter is that to Peregrino Agli of 1457, in Ficino, *Opera*, I, ii, pp. 612–15.

the history of medieval modes of interpretation, in spite of belonging to an age for which, in Italy, the term 'medieval' is never used. In contrast the Platonism of the later Quattrocento marks the beginning of a new and more distinctly Renaissance phase in the study of poetry, with its use of new classical sources in the context of a new view of the world and man. Yet even here the element of continuity remains very strong. Despite Landino's claim to have written a new, philosophical, commentary on Virgil, and despite the undoubted novelty in the content of his interpretation, the method is still very substantially that of his medieval and humanist predecessors.

25

Humanist criticism of Latin and vernacular prose

Martin McLaughlin

Chapter 23 documented the manner in which the humanist revolution initiated by Petrarch diverted intellectual energy away from the *volgare* into the study and writing of Latin. Consequently prose literary criticism in this period is, as we shall see, largely dominated by the increasing sensitivity displayed by Italian humanists towards developing a classical prose style in Latin. Only towards the end of the fifteenth century do critics take the first steps towards an analysis of vernacular prose. This section will thus be mostly concerned with the development of Latin prose criticism, a development which comprises four major phases. First there is Petrarch's discovery of the distance that separated medieval Latin *dictamen* from Cicero's Latin; then Bruni achieves an almost exact replica of classical prose; subsequently Valla inaugurates a more rigorous and practical guide to acceptable lexis and syntax; and lastly, the second half of the Quattrocento witnesses the emergence of both a rigid Ciceronianism, championed by Cortese and later Bembo, and an eclectic anti-Ciceronianism, promoted by Poliziano.

If the Petrarchan revolution forced Boccaccio and his successors to question Dante's wisdom in using the *volgare*, the same upheaval also caused a reappraisal of Dante's Latin works. In the first half of the Trecento the consensus on Dante's greatness had been universal. In the 1340s Giovanni Villani, in the first brief biographical note on Dante, was prepared to criticise his fellow-citizen's *mores*, but was unable to find fault with his Latin works. In particular he praised the 'robust and elegant Latin' of the *De vulgari eloquentia*, as well as Dante's epistles which were composed 'in the high style, with excellent *sententiae* and quotations from ancient authors, and were highly praised by learned connoisseurs' (*Cronica* 9.136). Villani, ignorant of Latin, has only words of praise for Dante's works in the learned language, though he has to rely on the opinion of those who knew Latin.

But in 1345, around the time when Villani was writing this chapter on Dante, Petrarch discovered in the cathedral library at Verona Cicero's *Letters to Atticus*, a find which was to transform Petrarch's views both on Cicero the man and on the correct style for writing Latin epistles. The discovery led him to attack the 'medieval' plural form of address ('vos') and replace it with the 'tu' used by Cicero, rightly claiming that he was the first to reinstate this more sound classical usage (*Familiares* 23.14.1). In general terms he attacked the Latin used in the millennium from the end of the classical period to his own times as beneath even the lowest of the three styles used in ancient times (*Fam.* 13.5.12), and claimed that the Latin of curial and legal circles was inferior to his own (*Fam.* 13.5; 14.2.3). Outside Italy Petrarch's clear, less ornate lexis impressed his contemporaries: Jan že Streda, working in the imperial chancery, was particularly struck by the stylistic gulf between his own artificial *dictamen* and Petrarch's more 'humane' style.[1]

Petrarch's ideals in Latin prose could be summed up as an embryonic but unslavish Ciceronianism. In a late letter (*Seniles* 16.1) he charts his obsession with Cicero back to his schooldays when he would sit charmed by the 'mere sweetness and sonority of Cicero's words' while his class-mates were studying traditional medieval school-texts (*Opera*, p. 946). This was reinforced by his discovery of the *Pro Archia* (1333) and the *Letters to Atticus*, as well as his close reading of the *Tusculan Disputa-tions* and the existing portions of the *Orator* and the *De oratore*. Yet his adulation of Cicero was different from the servile Ciceronianism advocated by later humanists: from Quintilian (*Institutio oratoria* 10.2) he learned to abhor exclusive imitation of one author or verbatim imitation (*Fam.* 1.8; 22.2; 23.19) and he was prepared to be critical of Cicero not only for his political involvement (*Fam.* 24.2, 24.3), but even on literary grounds, objecting to the ephemeral content of his letters (*Fam.* 1.1.29), circumscribing his literary supremacy to the field of Latin prose (*Fam.* 21.15.24), and stressing the inadequacy of his verse (*Fam.* 24.4.5).

As for other Latin authors, Petrarch's canon is more coherent than that of his predecessors. Dante had regarded Latin as static (*Convivio* 1.5.8) and had advocated for vernacular poets an indiscriminate imita-tion of eight Latin authors, including (bizarrely) even lesser prose-writers such as Frontinus and Orosius (*De vulgari eloquentia* 2.6.7). Petrarch, devising a similar list of eight authors (*Fam.* 23.19.11), could establish a more rigorous distinction between major writers in the different genres (Virgil, Horace, Boethius, Cicero) and their respective minor equivalents (Ennius, Plautus, Martianus Capella, Apuleius). Petrarch thus exercised a critical sense regarding classical Latin which was completely new, and which allowed him, for instance, to confirm that the recently discovered portions of the *Academica* were in Cicero's inimitable style (*Seniles* 16.1; *Opera*, p. 948), and to reject as bogus Latin an Austrian forgery, purport-ing to be a tax exemption for the Austrians drawn up by Julius Caesar himself (*Seniles* 16.5; *Opera*, pp. 955–6). Nevertheless Petrarch lacked that

[1] See S. Rizzo, 'Il latino del Petrarca', pp. 41–2.

sensitivity to the chronology of the decline of Latin which was to become a feature of Quattrocento humanism. Certainly he felt that the peak had been reached in Cicero's time (*Fam.* 13.5.17), but he was capable of imitating Plautus and the Elder Pliny in his letters as well as more predictable epistolary models such as Cicero and Seneca. He still regarded Priscian as 'the prince of grammarians' (*Fam.* 23.19.8), described Florus as a 'most elegant writer', and in general failed to distinguish between prosaic and poetic diction, using poetic lexis in his Latin prose and versifying Livy's words in the *Africa*.[2]

The impact of Petrarch's message was most strongly felt by Boccaccio. As a young man Boccaccio had at first been fascinated by the ornate *dictamen* of Dante's letters: at an early stage he transcribed three of them (Dante, *Ep.* 3, 11, 12) and imitated two of them in his own juvenile efforts in the genre (Boccaccio, *Ep.* 1, 2). But after his reading of Petrarch's very different Latin epistles, Boccaccio tried to disavow his own early epistolary enthusiasms by removing his name from the sole manuscript which contained them (Florence, Laurenziana MS 29.8), and by writing Latin epistles modelled more closely on his new master, Petrarch (Boccaccio, *Ep.* 9, 10, 11, etc.).[3] Petrarch's criticism of Dante's Latin in *Familiares* 21.15, determined by his own revulsion at contemporary traditions of epistolography, the *ars dictaminis*, also caused other modifications in the second redaction of Boccaccio's *Trattatello in laude di Dante*: having spoken warmly of Dante's letters in the first version, now Boccaccio makes no mention of them at all, and he also downgrades the importance of his other Latin prose works, the *Monarchia* and the *De vulgari eloquentia* (2.133, 134, 138).

Coluccio Salutati (1331–1406) embraced Petrarch's legacy in writing Latin, seeing his use of 'tu' instead of 'vos' as a key aspect of the *renovatio* worked by his predecessor, and campaigning against other aspects of scholastic Latin such as exotic, unclassical lexis and the excessive use of the *cursus*. In 1383 he criticised the 'pedestrian' Latin of Benvenuto da Imola's commentary on Dante, castigating his deployment of the *cursus* and homoioteleuton as 'scholastic and puerile'.[4] Salutati was aware that such frivolities belonged to post-classical Latin and were condemned by Cicero (*Ad Herennium* 4.20.27) and Gellius (*Noctes atticae* 1.10.4). Such sensitivity is not surprising in view of Salutati's innovative survey of the evolution of Latin in a letter of 1395 (*Epistolario*, III, pp. 76–91). This letter predictably places Cicero at the peak of Latin literature, but

[2] Martellotti, 'Latinità del Petrarca'.
[3] See Billanovich, *Restauri boccacceschi*, pp. 49–78.
[4] Salutati, *Epistolario*, II, pp. 76–8. Salutati was no doubt thinking of Benvenuto's rhyming praise of Dante's 'profunditas admirabilis', 'utilitas desiderabilis' and 'fertilitas ineffabilis' (Benvenuto, *Comentum*, I, p. 7).

more originally outlines the subsequent development of Latin. Salutati discusses a second period, from Seneca to Cassiodorus, in which writers kept Ciceronian eloquence alive; but the following epoch, comprising authors such as Ivo and Bernard of Chartres, Peter of Blois, Abelard and John of Salisbury, is dismissed as 'even more remote from the previous two ages in style than in time' (*Epistolario*, III, pp. 83–4).

However, Salutati's condemnation of medieval Latin was accompanied by a zeal for the Tre Corone that seemed contradictory to the younger generation of humanists. After Petrarch's death in 1374, the Florentine chancellor had made exaggerated claims about Petrarch's *Invective* outdoing even Cicero's *Verrine Speeches*, and ranked his *De viris illustribus* and other treatises on a par with the Roman orator's philosophical works (*Epistolario*, I, p. 180). But he was forced to moderate these claims: by 1405 he conceded that the *De viris* is inferior to the histories of Livy or Sallust (*Epistolario*, IV, p. 140), and in his last letter he agreed that Petrarch's invectives and treatises were inferior to Cicero's (*Epistolario*, IV, p. 166). The fact that Salutati as well as Cino Rinuccini, in his *Invettiva*, single out for defence Petrarch's *De viris illustribus*, suggests that the younger humanists regarded it as belonging to a superseded mode of historiography, compared with the new models favoured by Bruni and Poggio, such as Livy, Sallust and Plutarch.

Dante's status also came under close scrutiny as the Trecento drew to a close. Boccaccio had claimed that Dante's motives for writing the *Commedia* in the vernacular were positive, because he wanted the poem to be accessible to his fellow-countrymen, and because the princes to whom such works were normally dedicated could not understand Latin (*Trattatello* 1.191–2; 2.128–30). But Benvenuto's commentary on the poem first records the criticism that Dante wrote in the *volgare* because his Latin could not cope with such an arduous theme (*Comentum* I, p. 79). Although Benvenuto rejects this slur, Filippo Villani in his *De . . . famosis civibus* (1382–95) and his commentary on *Inferno* (c. 1405) concedes that Dante turned to the vernacular because he was more adept at the latter, and that his Latin, compared to those of the classical poets, was like 'sackcloth beside purple silk'.[5] By the time Leonardo Bruni (1369–1444) writes his *Vita di Dante* in 1436, it can be openly admitted, even in this eulogistic biography, that Dante himself recognised that he was more suited to the vernacular than Latin (*Vite di Dante e del Petrarca*, p. 550).

---

[5] *De . . . famosis civibus*, p. 357; and *Expositio*, p. 77. Villani's formulation of this shift of language ('Cumque se potentiorem ea vulgari eloquentia sentiret, . . . se ad componendum vulgarem famosissimam comoediam convertit'), may have been influenced by Salutati's mention in a similar context of Virgil's shift from prose to poetry ('ex quo de rethoricis ad poeticam se convertit'; *Epistolario*, I, p. 181). Certainly it is echoed by Domenico Bandini: 'sed quum nosceret stylo suo non aequare Maronem, nec alios poetas celebres superare, se ad maternum idioma convertit' (*Le vite di Dante, Petrarca e Boccaccio*, ed. Solerti, p. 92).

Although Bruni agreed with Salutati over details such as the orthography of 'michi' and 'nichil' (Bruni, *Epistule*, II, pp. 107–8), in more fundamental literary questions the younger man differed widely from his predecessor in the Florentine Chancery. Salutati in his last years accused the younger humanists, Bruni, Poggio and Niccoli, of an uncritical acceptance of Antiquity's superiority over the present (*Epistolario*, IV, pp. 126–45), which is probably reflected in the attack on contemporary culture in Book 1 of Bruni's *Dialogi ad Petrum Paulum Histrum* (1401–6). In particular, Salutati attacked Bruni's slavish imitation of Cicero's formulas for opening Latin letters (*Epistolario*, IV, pp. 147–58), though Bruni showed that Salutati's medieval form was both ungrammatical and ambiguous (*Epistolario*, IV, pp. 375–8).

However, it was Bruni's *Dialogi* that marked the real watershed as the new century began. Bruni's Latin here, free of unclassical lexis, syntax and *cursus*, comes much closer to the Latin of a Ciceronian dialogue than even the illustrious attempt in the genre by Petrarch in the *Secretum*. Even Salutati's Latin now seems to be more than a generation removed from Bruni's. The key to Bruni's almost perfect replica of classical Latin lay in his sensitivity to lexis and his well-documented interest in prose rhythm (Bruni, *Opere letterarie*, pp. 162–70, 252–8). Although Bruni's concern for *numerus* originally came from his reading of Aristotle's *Rhetoric*, this sensitivity was no doubt enhanced by the discovery of the full version of Cicero's *Orator* at Lodi in 1421. It is not surprising, then, that in the aftermath of the Lodi discovery Bruni in the *De studiis et litteris* (1422–9) should devote such attention to prose rhythm.

Although the substance of the *Dialogi* ends on a note of compromise, with Niccoli retracting his attacks on the Tre Corone, the Latin style of the work is so unlike the Latin of the Trecento as to subvert that compromise and to constitute a manifesto of the new generation, the new century and the new language. If Easter 1300 was the dramatic date of Dante's vernacular *Commedia*, Easter 1401 was an equally symbolic setting for Bruni's Latin dialogue, ushering in a century in which the major attention of Italian intellectuals would be devoted to reproducing classical Latin prose. The criticisms in Book 1, of Dante's lack of 'Latinitas' in his epistles, caused by reading the 'quodlibeta fratrum', and of the Latin of Petrarch's *Invective*, the genre in which Salutati had claimed he outdid Cicero, are never directly refuted – indeed the *Invective* are significantly not mentioned in Book 2. There is a similar lack of conviction about the defence of Boccaccio's erudition in the second book, and even Salutati is implicitly criticised in the attacks on two of his favourite authors, Cassiodorus and 'Alcidus' (*Opere letterarie*, p. 92). In the later *Vite di Dante e del Petrarca* (p. 552), Bruni again attacks Dante's Latin as being written 'in the monkish, scholastic fashion', particularly the *Monarchia*, which is written 'inelegantly, without any graceful style' (*Vite*, p. 52). Similarly Petrarch's Latin, though it marks an improvement in trying to attain a Ciceronian style, is now regarded as imperfect. Bruni does not mention any of Petrarch's Latin works, for his achievement is seen to reside not in his writings, but in his 'opening up the road of humanist studies' by discovering and studying ancient texts (*Vita del Petrarca*; *Opere letterarie*, p. 556). Boccaccio is felt never to have mastered Latin properly, a common accusation, mentioned also in Rinuccini's invective, and Bruni also considers both Boccaccio's and Salutati's definition of *poeta* as inaccurate. Indeed Bruni's chief motivation for writing Dante's biography was the inadequacy of Boccaccio's *Trattatello*: it was as 'full of tears and sighs' as the *Fiammetta* or *Decameron*, whereas Bruni ignores entirely Dante's love lyrics and concentrates on his civic involvement and his moral poetry.

By the 1430s, then, there is a consensus about Dante's and Boccaccio's deficiencies in Latin prose, and a sense that Petrarch's achievement lies not so much in his Latin writings as in his initiating humanist scholarship. Bruni proceeds beyond Salutati's level of literary analysis, his exploitation of the Senecan topos about writers being proficient in only one genre (*Controversiae* 3, Pref. 8), and his generic statements about outdoing Antiquity, to reach a more precise assessment of the achievements and limitations of the Tre Corone. Bruni continued Petrarch's legacy in being prepared to criticise even established *auctores*: he wrote new, critical biographies of Cicero and Aristotle as well as of Dante and Petrarch. His biographies of the vernacular writers are modelled on Plutarch's *Lives* (some of which Bruni had translated into Latin) both in their structure and in the comparison between the two authors at the end.

But more than Plutarch, it was the 1421 discovery at Lodi of major rhetorical works by Cicero that was the most significant influence on prose literary criticism in the Quattrocento. The manuscript containing the complete texts of the *De oratore*, *Orator* and the hitherto unknown *Brutus* was deciphered and transcribed by Gasparino Barzizza (1359–1431) and Flavio Biondo (1392–1463), allowing even minor humanists like Antonio da Rho (1395–1447) and Sicco Polenton (1375/6–1447), pupils of Barzizza, to measure the distance that separated Petrarch's and Salutati's Latin from the Ciceronian norm.[6] Polenton's *Scriptorum illustrium latinae linguae libri XVIII* (1437) is a survey by genre of the major Latin writers of Antiquity, with occasional remarks about more recent authors. Although there is no critical depth in Polenton's analysis,

---

[6] Antonio da Rho acknowledges in his *Apologia* (1428) that Petrarch's Latin is inferior to that of Antonio's generation, and that his true excellence lay not in Latin prose, but in his vernacular poetry (*Apologia*, ed. Lombardi, pp. 80–2). He also criticises Salutati's and Petrarch's abuse of the *cursus velox* (in his unpublished *De numero oratorio*, in Milan, Biblioteca Ambrosiana, MS B.124 Sup., fol. 149r).

occasionally the feeling of a new age breaks through, as when he notes the importance of the Lodi discovery or when he alludes to contemporary dissatisfaction with Petrarch's achievement.[7]

The impact on Biondo was even greater. In his first work, the *De verbis romanae locutionis* (1435), he challenged Bruni's view that there were two distinct languages used in ancient Rome and made telling use of the evidence he found in the *Orator* and *Brutus*. By 1450, when he wrote the *Italia illustrata*, Biondo could reverse Filippo Villani's praise of Salutati as 'another Cicero' (Salutati, *Ep.* 4.492), pointing out that his Latin was un-Ciceronian, and impute Petrarch's deficiencies in the language to his failure to possess the complete texts of Quintilian (discovered by Poggio in 1416) and of Cicero's rhetorical works found at Lodi (*De Roma triumphante libri X*, pp. 304, 346). The Lodi texts, since they dealt primarily with rhetoric and literary history, provided the humanists of the Quattrocento with both the urge and the critical terminology to conduct a more rigorous examination of contemporary and recent humanist writings.

By 1450, Aeneas Sylvius (Enea Silvio Piccolomini), the future Pius II, could proclaim that Guarino, Bruni and Poggio were as worthy of imitation as classical authors, and the claim would have encountered almost universal consensus (*Opera omnia*, p. 984). But, as we shall see, there were criticisms voiced against all three. Guarino da Verona (1374–1460) had emerged as the great humanist educator of the early part of the century. He followed Petrarch and Salutati in championing the clarity of Ciceronian Latin against the obscurities of medieval *dictamen* (Guarino, *Epistolario*, I, pp. 84–6). Late in life, in 1452, he traced his own development as a Latinist from his early efforts in *dictamen* to the new clarity of diction and style ushered in by the discovery of Cicero's works and the teaching of Manuel Chrysoloras (*Ep.* II, pp. 582–3). But in the 1430s Guarino's Latin came under fire from George of Trebizond (1395–1484). In Book 5 of his *Rhetorica* Trebizond attacked and rewrote part of Guarino's Latin eulogy for the *condottiere* Francesco Conte di Carmagnola (1428), criticising its lexis, syntax and its lack of periodic sentences.[8] This critique prefigured the more rigorous Ciceronianism which would emerge in the second half of the century. The criticism of Bruni and Poggio came from an even more influential voice: Lorenzo Valla (1407–57).

In the first half of the Quattrocento Bruni had met with almost unanimous acclaim, but as the century progressed his Latin came under fire. Although Bruni's translations of Aristotle were criticised by Alonso da

---

[7] Polenton uncritically sees as equally responsible for the revival of poetry Albertino Mussato and Dante (*Scriptorum illustrium*, pp. 123–4). His mention of criticism of Petrarch is on p. 139. On Polenton's limitations see G. Ferraù's introduction to Paolo Cortese, *De hominibus doctis*, pp. 17–18.

[8] See the analysis in Baxandall, *Giotto and the Orators*, pp. 138–9.

Cartagena, Ambrogio Traversari and P. C. Decembrio, the most explicit criticism of his Latin came from Bruni's younger contemporary, Valla. Already in 1435 he considered the style of Bruni's *Laudatio* 'loose, disorganised and weak, lacking in dignity and intelligence, and in many places not even Latin but almost a corruption of Latin' (Valla, *Epistole*, p. 163); and shortly after Bruni's death, in a letter of 1446, Valla claimed to have found over 400 errors in Bruni's translation of Aristotle's *Politics* (*Epistole*, pp. 288–9).

Valla was the most critical spirit of his generation: his first work, the lost *Comparatio Ciceronis Quintilianique* (1426), shocked the humanist establishment by claiming that Quintilian was superior to Cicero. His letter to Giovanni Serra (1440) represents his literary credo, rejecting the medieval Latin of such authors as Hugutio of Pisa, Accursius, Albert the Great and Ockham, and defending his right to criticise even Priscian, since he provides rules which are often at odds with the 'maximi auctores' (*Epistole*, pp. 193–203). Valla's acumen was based on a sharp sensitivity to periods of Latinity. His disputes with Poggio, Facio and Antonio da Rho demonstrate his superiority over the previous generation of humanists, who had embraced a notional Ciceronianism which Valla was able to prove was too lax to become a useful norm for the future. Valla was interested not only in the precise significance of individual Latin terms, but also in establishing acceptable Latin syntax. This he did both in his polemics and in his major work, the *Elegantiae linguae latinae* (1449). Here he carefully distinguished between various periods of Latin, and departed from the loose eclecticism of previous humanists from Petrarch to Poggio by limiting acceptability to the Latin of the ages of Cicero and Quintilian, and by finding fault even with established school authors such as Priscian, Servius and Donatus.

Although Valla was not himself a Ciceronian, nevertheless he was aware of what words and constructions were used by each author and it was this formidable knowledge which allowed him to castigate his eminent contemporaries. In an age devoid of concordances Valla still knew, for instance, that in Cicero only 'affectio' not 'affectus' is found, that 'quatenus' is never used for 'quoniam', and so on (*Opera omnia*, I, pp. 277, 421). Thus when Poggio attacked him for using un-Ciceronian terms such as 'leguleius' and 'architectari', Valla was able to show that both words occurred in the Roman orator (I, p. 295), whereas Poggio's 'disturbium' (I, p. 285), 'passio' (I, p. 317) and 'bursa' (I, p. 320) are totally unclassical. In terms of lexis Valla was more broad-minded than others, admitting contemporary neologisms and late-antique words for the sake of clarity, but in syntax he rejected the usage of writers such as Macrobius, Gellius and Apuleius, when they conflicted with Cicero and Quintilian. Yet despite possessing the rigour to be a strict Ciceronian, Valla never became one.

On the contrary, he is prepared to use and defend Latin neologisms, both for place-names ('Florentia' not the ancient 'Fluentia', 'Ferraria' not 'Forum Appii') and for technological inventions such as cannons, clocks and glasses (Valla, *Gesta Ferdinandi*, pp. 11, 194–204). Attacked by Bartolomeo Facio (1400–57) for using words such as 'Maomettani', 'bombarda' and 'prophetare', Valla is able to show that the classical alternatives proposed by Facio ('Afri Hispaniae incolae', 'tormentum', 'divinare') are too imprecise (*Antidotum in Facium*, pp. 100, 106, 128).

In the second half of the Quattrocento Italian humanism seemed to undergo a tripartite specialisation: Florence was dominated by Marsilio Ficino (1433–99) and Angelo Poliziano (1454–94), with their respective interests in Platonic philosophy and textual philology, while Rome became the centre of the Ciceronianist movement. Before looking at the first of these three strands of humanism, it is worth recalling the background to the whole question of the relations between philosophy and rhetoric.

Bruni had provided humanist Latin translations of Aristotle's *Ethics* (*c.* 1417) and *Politics* (*c.* 1435) to replace the 'barbaric' medieval versions. He attacked his predecessors for retaining Greek words (such as 'eutrapelia') when they could have chosen from a host of classical synonyms ('urbanitas', 'festivitas', 'comitas' or 'iucunditas'). Bruni himself had gone to Cicero, Seneca and the church Fathers for his Latin, whereas the medieval translator had derived his unclassical terms such as 'delectatio', 'tristitia' and 'malitia', from the uneducated masses – Bruni instead had used 'voluptas', 'dolor' and 'vitium', following the translation of Cicero himself (*De finibus* 2.4.13; 3.12.40; compare Bruni, *Schriften*, pp. 76–81). But Bruni's enterprise was not universally approved. In 1435 Alonso de Cartagena claimed that the medieval 'bonum per se' was more accurate than Bruni's Ciceronian 'summum bonum', since it respected Aristotle's 'simplicity of concept and specific verbal propriety' (Seigel, *Rhetoric and Philosophy*, p. 128, n. 65). In 1438 Pier Candido Decembrio criticised Bruni's 'optimorum civium potestatem' as a translation of 'aristocratia', agreeing with Alonso against Bruni that some technical terms ought to remain in Greek (Hankins, *Plato in the Italian Renaissance*, II, pp. 581–2).

Valla was more comprehensive than Bruni in attacking barbaric Latin, condemning the language not only of the philosophers but also of the medieval grammarians, jurists and theologians. He censured both scholastic terminology such as 'ens', 'entitas' and 'quidditas', and also any trace of vernacular influence (*Opera*, II, p. 350). Bruni's and Valla's attitudes would have found a broad consensus amongst fellow humanists in the first half of the fifteenth century. Opposition only came from logicians, churchmen like Alonso de Cartagena, or ideological antagonists like Bruni's

counterpart in Milan, Decembrio. But in the second half of the Quattrocento there are a number of voices within the humanist camp itself which
re-evaluate the status of philosophical and legal language.

There is an interesting letter by Ficino in 1454 which seems to attest to
this transition in Florence from a rhetorical to a philosophical humanism.
He tells his correspondent, Antonio Serafico, that they should dispense
with the old style of epistolography, adopted by garrulous humanists, full
of lengthy introductions, periphrases and excessive verbiage; instead they
should write 'in the philosophical style, attending more to the weighty
thought than to the words' (Hankins, I, p. 270). Also in the 1450s, Lorenzo
Pisano in his *Dialogi quinque* contrasted the simplicity of Christian
wisdom with inflated classical eloquence, and in his *De amore* pointed to
two distinct philosophical styles, the pleasant Platonic-Ciceronian mode,
now out of favour with contemporary philosophers, and the Aristotelian
style: 'terse, dry, crafty, and full of thorny qualifications' (Field, *Origins of
the Platonic Academy*, pp. 137, 169 n. 149). In 1462–3 Benedetto Accolti
(1415–66), in his *Dialogus de praestantia virorum sui aevi*, also adopts the
view opposite to Bruni and Valla, maintaining that the language in which
philosophy and legal texts are written is immaterial. What counts is the
substance, and therefore on these grounds the medieval philosophers, theologians and jurists (Aquinas, Albert the Great, Accursius, even Giovanni
Dominici are mentioned) are superior to the ancients (Accolti, *Dialogus*,
pp. 122–3). Ten years later in 1473, Alamanno Rinuccini (1426–1504) can
claim that dialectic and philosophy have never suffered decline, and that
recently John Argyropoulos (1410–90) has brought them to new heights
in Florence (*Lettere ed orazioni*, p. 107).

The debate reached a climax when in 1485 Pico della Mirandola
(1463–94) engaged in a famous dispute with Ermolao Barbaro (1454–93)
over the proper style for philosophical discourse. Barbaro had adopted the
conventional humanist stance, deriving from Petrarch, Bruni and Valla,
that the medieval philosophers had been 'sordid, crude, uncouth, barbaric'
(Barbaro, *Epistulae*, I, p. 86). But Pico defends their ineloquent style on
the grounds that philosophy and eloquence are incompatible. Pico claims
that there is a kind of majesty in the squalid Latin of the scholastics and
that philosophers need to employ a brief, meditative style: therefore it
may not be elegant to use a verb like 'causari' for 'produci', but it is more
consistent with logical discourse (*Prosatori*, p. 818). The authoritative
voices of Ficino, Poliziano and Pico helped to establish not only a sympathy for philosophical studies, but also a generally more tolerant stylistic
atmosphere in Medicean Florence. However, one of the major critics of
this period, Cristoforo Landino (1424–1504), evinces no sympathy for
the scholastic style; a pupil of Poggio, who openly admitted that he had
no philosophical skills, Landino rejected the new scholastic enthusiasms
of Rinuccini and Argyropoulos.

Landino began his career as the heir to the rhetorical tradition of Bruni and Poggio: primarily interested in poetry and rhetoric, only in the 1470s did he develop links with Ficino and Neoplatonism. In 1458 he proclaimed his distance from Argyropoulos, when in his introductory lecture to Cicero's *Tusculan Disputations* he criticised the tortuous Latin of scholastic philosophers (*Scritti*, I, p. 14). But Landino also rejected the legacy of Valla's 'scientific philology', spurning as minutiae, in 1465, Valla's interest in the historical details of a text such as Cicero's *Letters to Atticus*, and proclaiming the pre-eminence of the rhetorical aspects (Cardini, *La critica del Landino*, pp. 44–65). His major critical contributions reside in his introductory lecture to his course on Petrarch (1467) and the proem to his great commentary on Dante (1481).

In the *Prolusione petrarchesca* Landino begins with a general sketch of the development of Latin literature which is largely indebted for its concepts and terminology to Cicero's *Brutus* (*Scritti*, I, pp. 33–40; II, pp. 40–51). When it comes to his assessment of vernacular prose, he mentions just five names: Boccaccio, Bruni, Alberti, Palmieri and Bonaccorso da Montemagno. His judgement on Boccaccio's vernacular works is more positive than Bruni's, though not without some qualification: 'Boccaccio made a great contribution to Florentine eloquence, but that contribution would have been greater if he had worked harder and had not tended to rely on his natural talents to such an extent that he was rather negligent in the rules of eloquence' (I, p. 35). Apart from Ciceronian terminology, the mainstays of Landino's critical vocabulary are these Horatian oppositions of natural talent (*natura, ingegno*) versus discipline (*arte, precetti retorici*). Although there is a hint of censure of Alberti's Latinate prose (I, p. 38), the whole thrust of the passage is eulogistic rather than critical. On Alberti and Palmieri Landino merely recycles some of the traditional divisions of rhetoric (*elegantia, compositio, dignitas*), and adds his own notion of *trasferimento*: 'note with how much industry Alberti has managed to transfer to our language all the elements of elegance, composition, and dignity of speech available in Latin writers' (I, p. 36).

In the 1470s Landino abandons this early rhetorical criticism for a Neoplatonic allegorical critique, which finds its fullest expression in his commentary on Dante. In the proem to his *Comento sopra la 'Comedia'* (1481) Landino provides a list of Florentines famous in *eloquenza*, which is merely an updated and vernacular version of Filippo Villani's *De . . . famosis civibus*. The intent is largely encomiastic: he has no criticisms to offer on Salutati's Latin, and what he says about other writers of Latin prose, Bruni, Poggio, Traversari, Dati and Alberti, is not particularly incisive.

The most original literary critic in either Latin or the vernacular in the second half of the century was Poliziano. The introductory lecture to his first academic course in the Florentine Studio (1480–1) constitutes his literary manifesto: rejecting the major models of Cicero and Virgil, Poliziano chooses and justifies his choice of Quintilian and Statius. He claims that minor authors are useful models for young students; and he makes the important point, derived from a 'new' source, Tacitus' *Dialogus*, that what is different from classical Latin is not necessarily inferior, and that it is essential to have more than one literary model: Cicero himself adopts a range of different styles ranging from the Attic to the Asian; therefore the whole enterprise of a monolithic Ciceronianism was theoretically misguided.[9]

In his major work of scholarship, the *Miscellanea* (1489), Poliziano deliberately cultivated the *varietas* of writers such as Aulus Gellius rather than the *ordo* of Cicero. His *Lamia*, or introduction to Aristotle's *Prior Analytics* (1492), is a similar virtuoso display of varieties of Latin, influenced again by his interest in disciplines such as philosophy, law, medicine and dialectic. In his introductory letter to his collected *Epistulae*, he explicitly acknowledges that his epistles are un-Ciceronian, and justifies this style by quoting a series of late Latin authors who claimed that Cicero should not be followed in epistolography (*Opera omnia*, pp. 1–2). Poliziano's closest correspondents, Barbaro, Pico and Filippo Beroaldo, all belonged to the anti-Ciceronian school in varying degrees, whereas men such as Paolo Cortese (1465–1510) and Bartolomeo Scala (1430–97) attacked Poliziano's Latin from a Ciceronian standpoint.

The dispute with Cortese, which proved to have greater resonance than the disagreement with Scala, occurred in 1485 when Poliziano criticised a collection of Latin letters sent to him by Cortese for his approval. Poliziano condemns them because they are unoriginal imitations of Cicero, whereas eloquence should have the variety stressed by later authors such as Quintilian and Seneca; his key point is that Ciceronianism prevents writers from expressing themselves (*Prosatori*, pp. 902–4). Cortese's reply shows that he is not an extreme Ciceronian: he acknowledges the variety of eloquence and its different styles, but he feels that the self-expression advocated by his opponent is an unattainable ideal since the imitative principle is innate in all human creativity, according to Aristotle. What Cortese is attacking is a reliance on self-expression and eclectic imitation which in the end produces an uneven Latin style (*Prosatori*, pp. 904–10).

Cortese's major dialogue, the *De hominibus doctis* (c. 1490), has traditionally been regarded as the first coherent work of literary criticism in the Quattrocento. It certainly is a comprehensive survey, examining the

---

[9] There is an edition of the lecture in *Prosatori latini*, pp. 870–84. Poliziano's 'Neque autem statim deterius dixerimus quod diversum sit' (p. 878) is derived clearly from Tacitus: 'nec statim deterius esse quod diversum est' (*Dialogus* 18.3).

progress of humanist writers from 1400 to 1480. The fact that the only living writers mentioned, Giorgio Merula, Ermolao Barbaro, Pomponio Leto and Giovanni Pontano, were all rivals to the Florentine humanist hegemony, suggests that the work offers a tacit criticism of the twin trends of contemporary Florentine humanism, Ficino's Neoplatonism and Poliziano's philology. Cortese's account marks a notable advance over those of his predecessors: Polenton had seen mostly continuity between the writers of Antiquity and the humanist era, and Filippo Villani and Landino had restricted themselves to an encomiastic account of the Florentine contribution to the revival of letters. Cortese, however, provides a coherent, historical and critical assessment, from a Ciceronian perspective, of the achievements and limitations of Quattrocento humanism. Both the structure and terminology of the work derive from the *Brutus*, so not only is everything seen within a perspective of progress, but occasionally Cortese lifts whole sentences from his model to describe the Latin of, say, Valla or Pius II. Thus the critical terms and adjectives are authentically Ciceronian, but the judgements remain largely abstract and opaque.[10]

The Tre Corone, accorded a position of honour in Landino's account, are here relegated to a parenthesis, since Cortese considers only their Latin works. In this perspective, even Salutati's letters are no longer worth reading (p. 116). Cortese agrees with Landino in his estimate of Bruni as the first to attain a classical tone in his Latin; but he is more specific than Landino, who vaguely mentions Bruni's 'ornamenti', while Cortese notes his sensitivity to prose rhythm. Against the consensus of the first half of the century, Cortese is prepared to state that Bruni is not so much a Cicero, more a Livy in the timbre of his Latin. He is equally harsh on the others who had been too easily accorded the title of Ciceronian: Poggio's is seen to be a notional Ciceronianism, while Guarino's Latin is noted as inelegant in both lexis and syntax (p. 135). Even Valla is criticised, since although his individual words are chosen carefully on the basis of Valla's great lexical expertise, his overall style lacks harmony of composition (p. 145). The prose writers who emerge with most credit are Pontano, whose Latin is an instance of the correct kind of imitation (p. 152), and Teodoro Gaza, who in his translations from the Greek is the first to realise the humanist ideal of combining eloquence with philosophy (p. 166). Although the scheme and language of the dialogue come from the *Brutus*, the interest in prose rhythm derives from the *Orator*, while the union of eloquence and philosophy and the concern for imitation are the key topics of the *De oratore*. Thus the texts discovered in 1421 continued to shape the best literary criticism of the second half of the Quattrocento. Cortese's silence on contemporary Florentine humanists suggests that he sees the

---

[10] See Ferraù's introduction to his edition of Cortese, *De hominibus doctis*.

future of humanism in the Ciceronianism he had learned in Rome rather than the philosophy and philology prevailing in Florence under Ficino and Poliziano.

Around the same time Marcantonio Sabellico (1436–1506) wrote another Latin history of Quattrocento literature. The *De latinae linguae reparatione* (*c.* 1490) also reviews the humanist writers of the century from a critical perspective, though Sabellico owes as much to Quintilian as to Cicero for his critical terminology, and tends to stress more positively the achievements of Veneto humanists such as Vergerio and Barzizza. He also differs from Cortese in being less critical of Valla, and devoting even less space to the Tre Corone. Indeed there is a more explicit anti-Tuscan bias in his account, since he finds Ficino's translations from the Greek inferior to Barbaro's, and castigates Landino for his careless commentaries on Virgil and Horace, and for his decision to translate Pliny into the vernacular. The dialogue lacks the chronological rigour of Cortese's work, but it includes an epilogue praising the writers of recent commentaries on classical authors: Perotti, Calderini and Poliziano.

The last great humanist critic of the century is Giovanni Pontano (1429–1503). He begins in the early *De aspiratione* (published 1481) by following the example of his master Valla: he distinguishes between the great models, Cicero, Caesar and Sallust, and writers of 'sordidae locutionis' such as Macrobius; and he castigates Bruni for justifying his spelling of 'michi' and 'nichil' on the evidence of the Tre Corone and Salutati – according to Pontano these men could not write either 'latine' or 'grammatice' (*Dialoghi*, p. liii). But in subsequent works Pontano moves away from such concerns to broader interests.

The opening of his early dialogue, *Charon* (1467–71, published 1491), satirises the polemics of Valla and Poggio and their concerns with whether Gaul was divided into 'tris' or 'tres partes', whether one should say 'dixisse oportet' or 'dicere oportuit' and so on (*Dialoghi*, pp. 34–5). Similarly the opening of the *Antonius* (1481, published 1491) mocks Valla's approval of neologisms such as 'horologium' and 'campana' (p. 57). That Valla is the target is confirmed when the new wave of scholars is criticised for championing Quintilian against Cicero, not realising that the two writers are mostly in agreement: Pontano's aim is to save Cicero from the rabid attacks of contemporary 'grammatici' (pp. 58, 66). The main topic of this dialogue is an attack on Gellius' claim that Virgil was inferior to Claudian and Pindar in his description of the eruption of Etna. The overall thrust of Pontano in this work is to counteract the new fashion for castigating the major models, Cicero and Virgil, but at the same time to display Pontano's ability to write un-Ciceronian Latin if necessary. The opening of his major critical work, *Actius* (1495–1501, published 1507), mocks the contemporary interest in archaic legal terms. Although the dialogue's main purpose is to provide that treatise on the writing of Latin history which Cortese's *De hominibus doctis* had noted was the most serious gap in ancient and contemporary humanist writings, it also deals with other topics of relevance. Pontano considers, for instance, the importance of alliteration in prose and poetry, the novelty of his discussion being underlined by his neologism 'allitteratio' (p. 181). As for historiography, his first counsel is that history should be written without rhetorical frills. He illustrates how sensitive Livy is to rhythm, so that no rewriting of one of his famous periods could produce a more rhythmic effect (pp. 202–3). He also provides clear examples of *brevitas* and *celeritas*, cardinal virtues in historiography, noting that Sallust is best at swift descriptions, but too harsh and laconic in set speeches; while Livy possesses a slightly richer, less spare style than Sallust in descriptions (pp. 211–12). He reaffirms the importance for the attainment of *brevitas* of using clear diction and avoiding the contemporary cult of 'stale and obsolete words' (p. 213). As in all his works, Pontano here is more interested in where an area of Latin prose, in this case historiography, overlaps with poetry than in the inhibitions imposed on composition by grammatical quibbles, and he makes an original contribution in stressing the importance of rhythm and alliteration. But Pontano remains, for all his openness about Latin, far from the Florentine sympathy for the style of recent philosophical works: in the *Aegidius* (c. 1501, published 1507; pp. 280–4) he criticises the medieval translations of Aristotle for their poor Latin, and complains that contemporary students of eloquence are as uninterested in philosophy as philosophers in eloquence.

By 1500, then, humanists were in no doubt about the progress that had been made in Latin prose from the middle of the Trecento: they were now capable of reproducing almost exact copies of the Ciceronian or, at the other extreme, Apuleian style, while the Latin of Dante, Petrarch and even Salutati clearly belonged to the past. But to complete this discussion, we must look at the criticism of vernacular prose authors in this period. Boccaccio, who even in his own lifetime had repudiated his works in the *volgare*, rarely escapes criticism in the fifteenth century. Filippo Villani talks vaguely of him 'straying rather too freely because of his youthfully lascivious genius' (*De . . . famosis civibus*, p. 376). Palmieri is more explicit, condemning his works for being 'full of much lasciviousness and instances of dissolute love affairs' (*Della vita civile*, p. 6). Landino, as we have seen, is more concerned with the questions of native genius as opposed to discipline, and blames Boccaccio for relying too much on the former (*Scritti*, I, p. 35). Lorenzo de' Medici is the first critic who has nothing negative to say about Boccaccio, even though he discusses mostly the content of the *Decameron*. For him, Boccaccio's masterpiece demonstrates the capacity of the vernacular to express the complete range of human emotions and vicissitudes; for this reason, Lorenzo argues, one can only admire both Boccaccio's 'invenzione', and his 'copia ed eloquenzia' (*Opere*, I, pp. 20–1). But Lorenzo's account goes no deeper than this, since his aim is not so much a critical analysis of Boccaccio's prose as a propagandistic flourish on behalf of Tuscan achievements in the *volgare*.

The first steps towards a more discerning approach to Boccaccio appear in Paolo Cortese and Vincenzo Calmeta (1460–1508). Cortese, in his *De cardinalatu* (1510), makes a tripartite distinction between the florid style of Boccaccio's minor works, the low style of Giovanni Villani's *Cronica*, and the middle style of the *Decameron* (Dionisotti, *Gli umanisti*, p. 66). This perception was shared by Calmeta, who around the same time warns that the *Filocolo* and *Fiammetta*, though popular around 1500, are inferior to the *Decameron* since the minor works are more affected and decorative in style, compared with the less obtrusive artistry of his masterpiece (*Prose e lettere*, p. 21). Calmeta, like Landino, insists on the importance of *ars* alongside *ingenium*, campaigning against the Neoplatonic notion that simple poetic *furor* is sufficient to provide great literature. For Calmeta, there is a major distinction to be made between occasional adornments and frills ('fuchi, ornamenti e calamistri', terms from Cicero) on the one hand, and on the other the serious consistency ('continuazione', also from Cicero) which characterises great literature (pp. 7–13).

There is an extraordinary parallelism in the development of the vernacular and Latin in the fifteenth century. The first half of the Quattrocento sees humanists engaging with the 'nuts and bolts' of acquiring classical Latin lexis and syntax in the same way that Alberti and Palmieri try to create a vernacular prose style from scratch, using the lexis and syntax of Latin. After 1450 Latin humanists can achieve an authentic Ciceronian fluency at the same time as Lorenzo and, to a lesser extent, Landino and Pico discover the naturalness of Trecento vernacular prose. But once Ciceronianism becomes a restrictive rather than expansive ideal, the wide-ranging eclecticism of Poliziano's Latin becomes an almost predictable reaction. This eclecticism gives way in the last decade of the Quattrocento and the first years of the Cinquecento to an exclusive cult of archaic or late-antique Latin, typified by writers such as Filippo Beroaldo (1453–1505) and G. B. Pio (*c.* 1480–1542). Their exotic Latin is paralleled in the vernacular by the Latinate, 'Apuleian' language of Francesco Colonna's *Hypnerotomachia Poliphili* (1499). This exuberance in both languages is what leads to the Ciceronian reaction which will triumph in the sixteenth century, first of all in Latin and then in the vernacular. Pietro Bembo (1470–1547) will be the authoritative figure who will ignore the achievements of Laurentian Florence, and champion the Ciceronianist cause, first in Latin in his 1512 dispute with Giovan Francesco Pico (1470–1533), and then in the vernacular in his *Prose della volgar lingua* (1525). The first major prose work of the new century will be Bembo's *Asolani* (1505), in which Boccaccio's language will constitute the sole model.

The turning-points in the development of humanist prose criticism are, then, clearly observable. The revolution begins with Petrarch's discovery of the divergence between Cicero's letters and contemporary traditions of *dictamen*. But if Petrarch and Salutati begin to eliminate medieval lexis and the *cursus*, it is Bruni who inaugurates a totally classical sensibility to lexis and prose rhythm. This last element becomes a key topic after the discovery of the Ciceronian texts at Lodi in 1421, and it surfaces in the works of Cortese and Pontano. The next stage is Valla's rigorous classification of periods of Latinity and the beginning of a practical rather than notional Ciceronianism. The second half of the century is characterised both by Ciceronian zeal, and by anti-Ciceronianism. The latter movement evolves in three phases, beginning with a revaluation of the language of scholastic philosophy and law in Florence; then Poliziano extends this to embrace the Latinity of all the minor writers of Antiquity; finally eclecticism turns into an exclusive cult of archaic and late Latin which becomes as rigid as Ciceronianism itself.

Progress is clearly made in critical terminology, which became more sophisticated in the fifteenth century compared with the rather primitive Trecento statements about outdoing Antiquity. Similarly the comprehensive critical surveys of a century of humanism by Cortese and Sabellico, despite their abstract language, represent more ambitious critical projects compared with the isolated *ad hominem* polemics of their predecessors. Humanist critical vocabulary derived from Cicero, Quintilian, Horace and Plato, and found ready vernacular equivalents in the language of Landino and Calmeta. But attention was largely confined to lexis, with only Trebizonda, Valla and Pontano considering in practical detail questions of syntax and composition. Nevertheless the critical spirit that lay at the heart of Italian humanism ensured that each successive generation was keen to establish the limitations of its masters and to progress beyond them.

This survey ends with 1500, not only because of the convenience of the date, but particularly since the sixteenth century in Italy marks the beginning of a new critical world. It may be symbolic that in 1500 Beroaldo's great commentary on Apuleius is published, with the commentator flaunting his enthusiasm for Apuleian Latin. But in 1501 and 1502 Aldus Manutius will publish Bembo's editions of Petrarch and Dante, devoid of commentary, with Bembo concentrating on establishing the correct philology of these key vernacular texts. Beroaldo's enormous commentary on the subject-matter and style of the bizarre Latin author belongs to the past; the future in Italy will be concerned with the correct language to be adopted when writing in the *volgare*. Bembo's editions look forward to his *Prose della volgar lingua* (1525), since that dialogue has a fictional date of 1502 and is concerned exclusively with stylistic and linguistic questions. Even when dealing with Boccaccio, we are entering that new critical world, where language and style, not content, are the ultimate criteria. From the time of Petrarch and Salutati content, particularly moral, Christian content, had been considered more important than stylistic adornment, so Boccaccio's vernacular works had been consigned to critical oblivion or obloquy; but in the new century Bembo is prepared to champion Boccaccio as the sole model for vernacular prose and to defend him on exclusively stylistic grounds. He boldly maintains that even those parts of the *Decameron* which lack judgement, are written 'with a good, elegant style'; Bembo's revolutionary principle is that 'the subject-matter is certainly what makes or at least can make a poem either grand, lowly or medium in style, but never what makes it good or bad in itself' (*Prose*, pp. 175–6).

Part VII

Byzantine literary theory and criticism

26

Byzantine criticism and the uses of literature

Thomas M. Conley

A year or so before his death in 1332, at the end of a distinguished career as a scholar and public servant in the imperial court, Theodore Metochites composed his *Epistasia kai Krisis*, a critical comparison between two pre-eminent orators in the Greek rhetorical tradition, Aristides and Demosthenes. After setting out their respective stylistic merits at some length and discussing their effectiveness, the profit to be gained from reading their discourses, and the different political circumstances in which they wrote, Metochites announces his verdict. Demosthenes was indeed eloquence incarnate – an opinion shared by the vast majority of his critical predecessors – but it is Aristides who should be awarded the palm. He is, Metochites writes, the more 'useful' of the two (§31.14–23). Like himself and the readers of this *epistasia*, Aristides lived under a monarchy and composed a sort of rhetoric appropriate to that political setting.

Metochites' 'essay' has been variously praised by scholars as a masterpiece of humanist criticism and condemned for not being literary criticism at all, but the work of an astute politician – which Metochites was. To readers persuaded that 'literature' can be set apart from other 'modes' of discourse, Metochites' observations may indeed seem odd, perhaps confused or disingenuous, since they appear to confound literary principles and political aims. But Metochites' essay, though by no means a paradigm of Byzantine criticism, is far from atypical. It exhibits a number of presumptions that are more or less constant in the large body of critical literature that extends over six centuries, from Photios in the ninth century to the Fall of Constantinople in 1453. There is in this corpus no recognition of 'literature' as a separate category of discourse, for instance; and there is consequently no independent method or vocabulary for dealing with it critically. Further, the 'overlap' one can observe in Metochites of 'aesthetic' with 'rhetorical' and 'political' concerns, even at the level of style, is consistent with the persistent interest one finds in Byzantine critics in the relations between word choice, composition and *êthos* ('moral character'). Hence, the cast of previous critics he exploits in his argument (Hermogenes, Dionysius of Halicarnassus, and other late-classical authorities) is typical – as is the fact that he very rarely acknowledges them explicitly. Even Metochites' political stance, sensitive as it is to broad considerations of status and identity while responsive as well to the narrower interests of the 'scholarly community', is one often detected in earlier Byzantine writers from Photios onwards. Yet it cannot be said that Metochites simply applies a set of rigid and inflexible rules in his assessments of the orators he writes about. His selection of Aristides, after all, was a marked departure from the conventional view, taken by critics since Hermogenes, of Demosthenes as the paragon of eloquence.

We shall have occasion to look at Metochites more carefully in due course. Here at the outset, we might suggest that the blend of timeliness and timelessness we see in his *Epistasia* can be taken to be generally the case with Byzantine 'literary' criticism viewed broadly: Metochites is a late chapter, so to speak, in a long story of permanence and change.

1. Grounds and aims of criticism

'Criticism' was understood by a Byzantine reader or writer to have its feet in grammar, its head in rhetoric, and its eyes on moral utility. The basis of the *kriseis* of a Photios or a Eustathios or a Metochites was to be found in that last and best part of the 'grammatical' art, the assessment of literary productions (*krisis tôn poiêmatôn*), the criteria and ends of which were matters of consensus in educational and literary settings – as is evident, for instance, from the scholiastic tradition that grew around the second-century *Technê grammatikê* of Dionysius Thrax between the ninth and the thirteenth centuries. Strictly speaking, grammar, a subject taught to only a few, was concerned at the elementary level with the precise understanding of syntax and usage, rules of prosody, and how to identify and construe tropes with a view towards developing in the student the ability to read (aloud) intelligently what was inscribed 'in the letters'. At a higher level, those skills were to be turned to establishing the authenticity of the text, without particular regard for whether it was well written (*kalôs gegraptai*) or not (as in *Scholia in Dionysii Thracis*, pp. 170.2–5, 303.27–34.8, 586.14–31). That task was a different one, as it involved the corollary issues of whether the poet or writer was himself good or bad and to what good (*ôpheleion, chrêsimon*) the work might be put. Treatment of questions of moral character (*êthos*) and its formation and effect (*telos*) belonged to the 'art of speaking well' (*eu legein, kalôs legein*), rhetoric. Judgements of those issues were therefore distinguished from grammatical concerns, but not separated, as it was impossible to sustain those judgements independently of the grammatical preliminaries.

The standards by which Byzantine critics judged *êthos* and *telos* were mostly ones they had inherited from classical and late-classical antecedents – to speak of 'sources' or 'influences' begs the question – who provided the critical vocabularies and canons that could be, but were not always, used as guidelines. Since these authors were taught to almost everyone in the grammar and rhetoric curricula in school, they provided a standard frame of reference within which texts could be discussed. The most frequently cited of those authors is Hermogenes, or works thought to be by Hermogenes, along with Dionysius of Halicarnassus, 'Demetrius' and 'Longinus',[1] whose works were in circulation after the tenth century. The references we find to them are as often as not derived at second or third hand and not always with their intentions clearly in mind. This may be in part because Byzantine readers were confused by apparent disagreements among the authorities (for example the different critical vocabularies used by Dionysius and Hermogenes) or simply because they did not have the actual texts at hand. But if there is 'deviation', it is frequently due not to ignorance but to the fact that the critical intentions of Photios (ninth century) or Psellos (eleventh) or Chortasmenos (fourteenth–fifteenth) were different from, and took precedence over, those of the authorities they cited to render their judgements 'normal' and therefore persuasive. Like their counterparts in the West, and as we do today, Byzantine critics used the past to help make sense of their present; and for that end, their antecedents provided resources, rather than merely imposing limitations.

Byzantine 'literary criticism', then, is a complex of textual, technical and practical concerns. While it is clear that Byzantine critics worked within a fairly stable frame of reference, it is not nearly as clear that all of them – or even many of them – tacitly adhered to a set of abstract, unchanging 'rules' from which they and the writers they studied could depart only at great risk. We must keep our eyes on the antecedents of Byzantine critical writing. But we must be careful not to assume a priori that those antecedents determined subsequent critical judgements – as though, for instance, it might be possible to read Hermogenes' *Peri ideôn* ('On Types of Style') or Menander Rhetor on epideictic, and then Josephus or Gregory of Nazianzus,[2] and be able to predict what Photios or Psellos might say about them. The study of Byzantine criticism would, if we could do that,

---

[1] Hermogenes of Tarsus (*fl.* CE 180) was the leading authority on rhetoric in the Greek East. Dionysius of Halicarnassus (*fl. c.* 30 BCE) was the author of an influential *On Composition* and a collection of critical essays on the canonical Attic orators. Demetrius (*fl.* first century CE) composed an important *Peri hermeneias* ('On Expression'); and his contemporary, 'Longinus', is famous for his *Peri hypsous* ('On the Sublime').

[2] Two handbooks outlining the conventions of epideictic oratory are traditionally attributed to Menander Rhetor (late third century CE). Flavius Josephus (d. CE 95) wrote *Jewish Antiquities*, which was important to Byzantine chronographers and admired by Byzantine readers for its lucid style. Gregory of Nazianzus (late fourth century CE) was a prominent church Father, renowned for his eloquence.

be very boring indeed, and redundant. Byzantine critical concerns and the methods used in addressing them were in fact rather more 'locally' defined – sometimes, indeed, by very particular political circumstances – than their apparently formalistic procedures might suggest. Just as Byzantine literary production has in recent years been discovered to be far less mindlessly imitative, 'ohne Geschichte',[3] and theory-driven than the last generation of scholars thought it was, it may be time to recognise that Byzantine criticism is a far richer field of study than is commonly thought.

2. The first Byzantine 'humanist': Photios

The latter half of the ninth century, during the reigns of Theophilus, Michael III and Basil I, witnessed a cultural revival. The leading figure in this revival was Photios, sometime diplomat, once head of the college of imperial secretaries (*prôtoasekretis*), twice patriarch, and author of a collection of critical notices on almost 400 writers that came later to be known as the *Myriobiblôn*, 'Of Ten Thousand Books', and still later as the *Bibliotheca*. In histories of criticism, Photios' *Bibliotheca* is a landmark in Byzantine literary history. For Photios' successors, it was something less than that, as for a long time it was not widely in circulation. Yet it is important nonetheless for what it tells us of prevailing norms at his time. And it is interesting in the present instance as much for what it does not do as for what it does.[4]

The most noticeable omission from the *Bibliotheca* is of any substantial mention of classical authors aside from the 'canonical' Attic orators (Demosthenes, Isocrates *et al.*, treated more or less *en bloc*) and some passing references to Herodotus, Ctesias and Theopompus. Aside from an entry on the hexameters of Eudocia (*Bibl.* codd. 183–4, 127b4–129a11), Photios has nothing at all to say about poetry – indeed, 'poetic' composition is generally seen as a fault, not only because it is inappropriate in the composition of prose but also because it is 'hard on the ears'. It is unlikely that this material was left out because Photios' readers were already familiar with it, so it is important that we get some idea of the general criteria that guided Photios' selection as well as his judgements of the works he does discuss. What is strikingly absent there is any uniform literary theory systematically applied to the texts he discusses. This

---

[3] See the observations in van Dieten, 'Byzantinische Literatur'.
[4] The 280 'critical notices' that comprise the *Bibliotheca* are traditionally called 'codices', as though each one corresponded to a volume in Photius' library. Citations are, accordingly, to 'codex' and page numbers in the Henry edition. On the reception history, see Diller, 'Photius' *Bibliotheca*'.

is not to say there are no guiding principles, but that the principles are less 'literary' than they are practical.

Thus, despite the fact that he will from time to time take note of the 'beauty' of an author's style (e.g. cod. 269, 497b36–41, on the *kallonê* of Hesychios), Photios does not approach his subjects armed with the received canons of any 'Literarästhetik', much less a theory of literature. (Photius' use of 'kata tên logikên theôrian' at the end of cod. 280, 545b14ff. implies nothing like 'literary theory'.) In fact, he is generally suspicious of 'elegant speaking' (*kalliepeia*). What Photios means by *kallonê* may perhaps be hinted at in a comment he makes about its apparent opposite, as he puts it in his remarks on the style of the theological tracts of Eunomios: '[it] is so forced, compacted, indeed welded together that a reader must beat the air with his lips if he wants to read out clearly what Eunomios has jerry-built by squeezing and interpolating and mutilating' (cod. 138, 97b42–98a5). This observation may also be an example of Photios' independence of mind, as it contrasts sharply with the assessment of Eunomios by Gregory of Nyssa (PG 45, 400A), for instance. He also seems able to separate considerations of style from content, as when he allows that the diction and composition of Achilles Tatius is altogether distinguished and pleasing to the ear despite the unseemly subjects of which he writes. But these, in the end, repel the reader (cod. 87, 66a17–24). So, too, with the historian Zosimos: although himself impious and frequently among those 'who bark at the pious', his language is distinct and pure (*eukrines te kai katharos*) (cod. 98, 84b6).

In the final analysis, however, the excellences of style cannot stand on their own. Photios' general view might better be summarised as 'A man is what he writes' than 'quot homines, tot genera dicendi'. Like some of his learned predecessors, none of whom ever saw 'virtues' of style as a function of purely verbal configurations, Photios perceived a profound and decisive connection between style and character. The lack of stylistic 'charm' (*hêdys*) and 'brilliance' (*lamprotês*) in Eusebius, for instance, shows him to be correspondingly lacking in 'insight' (*ankhinoia*) and 'firmness' (*statheron*) and consequently incapable of precision (*akribeia*) in his discussions of dogma (cod. 13, 4b1–5). This compares interestingly with his description of St Paul the Apostle's style, the product of 'an inborn beauty [*kallos*] of speech' (*Epist.* 165, 2.25–7). The voice of Dio of Prusa is 'sweet' (*glykys*) and poised, but the pungency (*drimytês*) one senses in his writings is that of the man himself (cod. 209, 165b1–16). To perceive the *katharotês*, *lamprotês* and *glykytês* of Basil's style (cod. 141, 98b10–16) is to perceive 'the character of the man himself' (cod. 143, 98b30–3). The ornate (*poikilê*) yet clear (*saphes*) style of Sopatros, on the other side, is what makes reading his works so useful, as they lead the reader to virtue and nobility (cod. 161, 105a5–14). Photios may on some occasions condemn an author's moral integrity quite apart from any consideration of his style (as in the cases of Philoponus [cod. 55, 15a 30–15b5] and Hegesias [cod. 250, 446a16–28], both of whom Photios dismisses pretty much out of hand as mad or vulgar); but style seems always to hold the key. The 'prolixity and digressions' of Theodorus of Antioch, which 'shed no little darkness [*zophos*] over his writings' (cod. 177, 123a37), are not just stylistic faults but moral infirmities; and, similarly, the stylistic failings of Damaskios Diadochos' *Mirabilia* (cod. 130, 96a2–5) are made all the more inexcusable for his 'dozing amidst the deep darkness of idolatry'.

The sorts of judgements Photios makes in these passages and elsewhere are not of course uniquely his, but often rehearse the judgements of his predecessors. Sometimes he is open about his use of available critical material. For instance, he credits the historians Duris of Samos and Kleochares of Smyrlea in his discussion of Theopompus (cod. 176, 121a41–121b9, 121b9–16); and he quotes Caecilius of Calacte in his notes on Antiphon (cod. 259, 485b9–486a11). Usually he is not so open, as in his observations on Aristides, which owe much to scholia available to him, and as in his comments on Isaeus, which apparently derive from Pseudo-Plutarch (cod. 263, 490a11–31). The most conspicuous 'authority' is, of course, Hermogenes, whose *Peri ideôn* was for him a sort of critical benchmark. Photios was clearly very familiar with this work, a fact made abundantly evident, for example, from the close correspondence in thought as well as vocabulary between his critique of Isocrates in cod. 159 and points made by Hermogenes at *Peri ideôn* 2.11 (pp. 395–8). As we can see from the passages cited before, the vocabulary of Hermogenes' treatment of qualities of style (*ideai*) is almost ubiquitous in Photios' evaluations. Significantly, not all of that vocabulary seems to have been appropriate for Photios' purposes – indeed, Photios simply omits more of Hermogenes' 'ideas' than he uses. Thus, it is important not to overestimate the importance of Hermogenean lore, as a system of criticism, in the *Bibliotheca*. Photios uses the entire range of available authoritative critical materials, including perhaps many whose actual origins were unknown to him; but he uses them not for his predecessors' purposes, but for his own.

Those purposes were, above all, practical in two different but related ways. First, the 280 notices in the *Bibliotheca* provide Photios' readers with enormous quantities of information on everything from obscure but acceptable lexical items (as at codd. 145–58) to outstanding turns of phrase (241, 242) or bibliographic and biographical data (as in the codices on the canonical Attic orators). Such information would be useful to the writer aspiring to the mastery of proper rhetorical expression that would be required of anyone holding public office. In this connection, we should recall that Photios had held the office of head of the

college of imperial secretaries (*prôtoasekretis*). The second sort of usefulness is suggested by his frequent references to the utility of good style in
denouncing heresy (cod. 85, 65a38–65b1), for instance, and in his recommendations of the works and authors most likely to lead to moral and
spiritual improvement. In this respect, it can be said that, however important the resources found, for example, in Dionysius of Halicarnassus or
Hermogenes or Pseudo-Plutarch were to Photios' project, the agenda of
the *Bibliotheca* was defined not by those non-Christian authorities, but by
such Christian works as the 'Letter to the Youths' of St Basil, a work that
enjoyed considerable popularity in Photios' day and after. The overriding
theme of the *Bibliotheca*, then, is 'usefulness' (*to chrêsimon*) in the formation of the literary foundation necessary for both professional success
and the maintenance of orthodox morality.

As we have remarked, Photios was writing in an age of cultural revival
not limited to parochial concerns of the court in Constantinople but with
a substantial international dimension as well. Photios' career as govern-
ment official and patriarch involved not only the administration of affairs
in the capital but political and ecclesiastical relations with the West, the
evangelisation of the Slavs, and, in the East, diplomatic relations with
Baghdad. It also involved him in the bitter disputes of the age, particularly
the iconoclastic controversy and the theological and political manoeu-
vring that went with it. In the midst of all this, Photios continued to
assemble the literary heritage he thought needed to be preserved, sorted,
evaluated and passed on. It is perhaps the particular climate of dispute
in which the *Bibliotheca* was composed that may explain the fact that,
while the oldest extant manuscript copy was produced close to Photios'
lifetime (now Venice, Biblioteca Nazionale Marciana, MS gr. 450) early
in the tenth century, the next oldest (Marciana MS gr. 451) dates from the
twelfth. Photios' ideas about the usefulness of familiarity with writings
from the past were not shared by all his contemporaries, as is clear from
the decidedly partisan and negative judgement we find in an aside in the
Life of the Patriarch Ignatius, Photios' bitter rival, by Niketas David ('The
Paphlagonian'): 'It is on shifting foundations of sand, on worldly learning
and the vanity of erudition not ruled by Christ, that he set his mind and
heart . . . and this schooled him in every kind of wickedness and every
cause for scandal' (PG 105, 509). The 'revival of learning', in short, was
not one that exhibited undiluted enthusiasm for the literary past.

3. Arethas to Doxapatres

This same Niketas David figures in a literary/political controversy that
flared up in the first decade of the tenth century. Niketas' own literary

production seems to have been devoted mainly to commentaries on Scripture (notably, on the psalms) and eulogies of saints. One of those eulogies, the *Encomium* on Gregory of Nazianzus, provoked a scathing critical response from a former colleague, Arethas of Caesaraea (*c.* 860–*c.* 935). Niketas, he charges, had done little more than ape Gregory's eulogy of St Basil. The result was not only an instance of slavish imitation ('deinos gar ho mômos . . .'; I, p. 267.8–10), but 'useless' (p. 268.5), 'out of control' (pp. 268.29–269.4), 'frigid' (p. 269.8ff.) and 'obscure' (p. 269.25ff.). Niketas' failure to produce anything original stemmed in part from his dullness and in part from his inability to understand 'the valuable advice of Hermogenes' (p. 269.26–28).

This sort of critical invective is far from rare in the opening decades of the tenth century. There is another letter by Arethas in which he attacks Leo Choirosphaktes for his literary pretensions and resulting obscurity, for instance (I, pp. 202.20–203.6); and there is also a response written by Arethas to an unknown critic who had charged him with 'obscurity' (I, pp. 186–91). In the latter, Arethas asserts the ignorance of his critic, noting that sometimes obscurity lies in the eye of the beholder. If any conclusions can be drawn from Arethas' extant speeches and the many scholia attributed to him, Arethas' style was not generally obscure; but, ironically, his defence against that charge is itself not a very good example of stylistic clarity, crammed as his sentences are with internal references and allusions to a multitude of authorities on the subject. What does emerge from these letters, however, is the important notion that awkward, obscure style resulting from ignorance of classical letters could be a fatal objection against anyone holding high public office, not to mention a position as a teacher.

Arethas' chief importance in Byzantine literary history is as an editor and commentator on secular and religious works. His own prodigious accomplishments in establishing and elucidating texts from the past came early in a century notable for a proliferation of manuscripts reflecting a wide-scale effort to collect, sort out, and comment on materials bearing on every field of learning. This century has been called an Age of Encyclopaedism, and for good reason. One of the fields that scholars of the age attempted to consolidate was, of course, rhetoric, as is evident from the relatively large number of anthologies and collections of rhetorical texts and commentaries produced from the time of Arethas down through the middle of the next century.

Notable among those manuscripts are Vatican, Biblioteca Vaticana, MS gr. 99 (tenth century), which contains a number of speeches by Dio of Prusa in the same order as the ones discussed by Photios in the *Bibliotheca*; numerous manuscripts of Aristides (e.g. Vatican, Biblioteca Vaticana, MS Urb.gr. 122; Paris, Bibliothèque nationale de France, MS Coisl. 345

[tenth century], which contains, among other things, a 'Collection of Useful Readings [*lexeôn chrêsimôn*] from Lucian' [fols. 178v–86r], attributed by some to Arethas), the important 'editions' of the works of Hermogenes, along with commentary, in Paris, Bibliothèque nationale de France, MSS gr. 1983 and 3032, and finally, the important Bibliothèque nationale de France, MS gr. 1741, which contains the earliest known versions of a number of works, including the *Rhetoric* of Aristotle. Such manuscripts, in turn, provided scholars with an enormous fund of information which they sought to integrate and clarify, as seems to be the case, for instance, in the commentary on Aphthonius' *Progymnasmata* by John of Sardis. Scholia and commentaries produced during the tenth and early eleventh centuries continue to assimilate 'new' material, much of it reflecting deep and troubled awareness of the problems of rationalising or, indeed, establishing literary standards from the past for the present.

Thus, we find in the commentary by John Sikeliotes on Hermogenes' *On Ideas* a number of assorted observations that display an acute awareness of the problems caused by the new material. Sikeliotes is, for instance, frustrated by previous attempts to sort out the 'ideas' of style as they are explained by Hermogenes (*RG*, VI, p. 282.18–27) and by the difficulty of reconciling Hermogenes' 'ideas' with the 'characters' of style explicated by 'Demetrius' (VI, p. 62.15–25; VI, pp. 71.6–72.12). He attempts to assimilate to Hermogenean doctrine the lessons of the treatise on the composition of words by Dionysius of Halicarnassus (VI, pp. 226.7–20, 242.5–10); he also discusses the relations between style and moral character, citing Dionysius' *On Demosthenes* (see VI, pp. 63.4–64.9, 68.15–21), and cites with interest the favourable notice of the style of Moses by 'Longinus' (VI, p. 211.10–15). Poetry, he says, has little to offer in the way of spiritual utility (*chreia psyches*; VI, p. 61.11); he notes that the Hermogenean 'idea' of *trachytês* ('ruggedness') is absent in 'our theologians' (VI, p. 152.9–12); and allows that, as Demosthenes 'seems childlike by comparison', the model of eloquence is to be seen rather in Gregory of Nazianzus (VI, pp. 99.12, 341.10–15). In general, Sikeliotes is not afraid to depart from received wisdom (e.g. at VI, p. 282.14–27), speaking frankly to his reader, sometimes even bringing in his own experiences as evidence (VI, pp. 447.14–448.15).

Similar concerns are evident in a body of literature which corresponds to, shares origins with, and treats roughly the same topics as, the *accessus ad auctores* in the West (see above, Chapters 5, 6 and 14): the anonymous prolegomena to Hermogenes found in several manuscripts from the late tenth/early eleventh century), where we find observations on, for instance, the differences between rhetoric and poetry (*PS*, p. 38.10–13). In his extensive remarks, John Doxapatres goes even further afield than his predecessor Sikeliotes in finding material in works by obscure authors that could be assimilated into the Hermogenean tradition (for example, at *PS*, p. 82.5–12, where he claims to have read their books). Neither is he afraid to be critical of 'the ancients': for instance, he observes (*PS*, p. 103.10–21) that Aristotle's definition of rhetoric is at once too broad, in that it fails to distinguish it adequately from dialectic, and too narrow, in that it says nothing of 'speaking well'. Doxapatres has some definite ideas on the nature of the connection between thought and expression (*PS*, pp. 122.6–123.16), and is quite clear on the goal of rhetoric: it is 'to turn people to the good [*ta kala*]' (*PS*, p. 85.20–27).

4. Critic as careerist: Michael Psellos

The attempts by scholars after Arethas to consolidate the tradition echo in many ways the concerns of Photios, on the one hand, and set the stage, on the other, for a subsequent body of critical literature during the eleventh century, particularly the critical 'essays' of Michael Psellos. Psellos (1018–78?), who held a succession of offices in the imperial court in Constantinople, was one of the outstanding scholars of his day, and did not hesitate to let his contemporaries know it. His omnivorous reading, enormously broad range of interests, and inclinations to take on a role as cultural arbiter are everywhere apparent in his writings, especially perhaps in those that might be classed as instances of literary criticism.

Among his *opuscula* we count several synoptic 'treatises' on rhetoric (one in verse), none of which was intended to be particularly original or adventurous. Two of them, in fact, are quite derivative without being completely candid about their sources: the *Peri rhêtorikês* found in (among others) Milan, Biblioteca Ambrosiana, MS gr. 530, which incorporates extensive material from an 'Art' attributed to Longinus) and his *Peri synthêkês tôn tou logou merôn*, most of which is a pastiche of passages from a work of roughly the same title by Dionysius of Halicarnassus. There can be little doubt that Psellos meant these to be taken as, if not original contributions, his own best thoughts on the subjects they treat.

Psellos also composed two 'literary' *synkriseis* ('comparisons'), one between the poetry of Euripides and that of George of Pisidia (*fl.* 630) and the other a comparison of the romances by Achilles Tatius and Heliodorus. It is not clear which of the former he justified a preference for (the last page is badly damaged in the best manuscript). In fact, it may be that he awarded the prize to neither[5] – if only because the criteria he appears to be using are either too vague ('tragic quality') or too specific (use of various metrical feet, but without citations to explain what he means).

---

[5] Ljubarskij, 'Antičnaia Ritorika', p. 118.

The purpose of the latter essay is, he says, to defend Heliodorus against charges of obscurity (levelled in a putative debate in which Psellos assigns himself a part) and poor character delineation in the case of Chariclea in his *Aethiopica*. Neither defence is very tenacious or effective: Psellos ends by arguing that, whatever problems Heliodorus might have, he is still preferable to Achilles Tatius, whose subject-matter is quite obscene. On the other hand, Psellos allows, the diction of Achilles Tatius exhibits stylistic qualities of *glykytês* and *saphêneia*, and it is certainly permissible to 'pluck flowers from the garden' of his style. In neither essay, therefore, do we see much more than praise and blame cast in a variety of terms that leave most of the actual deciding to the reader.

Psellos' *Logos* on the character of the style of the famed theologian and orator Gregory of Nazianzus is much longer than the preceding *synkriseis* and promises fuller and more definitive treatment. Here Psellos brings to bear an almost unbelievable array of authorities, citing as models everyone from Demosthenes and Isocrates to Polemon and Aeschines Socraticus in a florid display of erudition he probably did not in fact possess. Gregory is a model of stylistic virtue as well as a great teacher of Christian doctrine. In fact, Psellos explains that he often reads Gregory's prose not for what he might learn, but for its literary charms, 'spending time among the spring blossoms of his diction' (ll. 49–50), admiring 'the precious stones and pearls' that ornament his style (ll. 69–72), and getting carried away by the beautiful harmonies. If there is a 'character' to Gregory's style, it is one that has never been seen in any other author, and can consequently be specified only by a sort of critical *via negativa* (ll. 126–34). Psellos finds it hard, he says, to identify the sources of his excellence (ll. 187–9, 203–6), as it has a certain *je ne sais quoi* that transcends all *technê* (ll. 254ff.). This is high praise indeed.

It is not praise that Psellos consistently reserved for Gregory, however. In an essay on the stylistic 'characters' of the Fathers, *Charaktêres paterôn*, Psellos works through a four-part *synkrisis* comparing the styles of Gregory of Nazianzus, Gregory of Nyssa and his brother Basil (the Great), and John Chrysostom. Nazianzus embodies the virtues of Aristides (p. 126.18–23), Lysias (p. 127.2–7) and the other great Attic writers, particularly as regards their 'solemnity' (*semnotês*). Out of many *charaktêres*, representing the three traditional levels of style, Nazianzus fashions a single stylistic idea – the contours of which are barely visible, one might add, to Psellos' reader. Basil's eloquence, by contrast, lies not in his mastery of the 'methods' of *deinotês* ('rhetorical virtuosity') but in a certain 'unstudied' quality (*atechnôs*, p. 129.8); and if Basil's eloquence is, in effect, the converse of Nazianzus', his brother's has features in common with both. Chrysostom combines all the *ideai* (p. 130.11ff.); but that fact does not explain his eloquence, as he did not achieve his by speaking according to the canons of the art but was, rather, himself a canon for it (p. 130.15–18). Thus, in the final analysis, Chrysostom's style is incomparable in its grace and power. 'Incomparability' arrived at by way of a critical *via negativa* seems to be for Psellos a rather flexible critical strategy, in short.

Psellos' use of this *via negativa* may, in fact, be an indication of his perception that the old categories, whether taken from Dionysius or 'Demetrius' or Hermogenes, simply do not provide a vocabulary adequate to the job of evaluating Christian eloquence. Thus, on the one hand, it may be said that the 'noble works' of Symeon the Metaphrast are instances of the imitation of fine style (*ta kallista*) and the best models for the formation of character (*êthos*), as Psellos observes in his encomium on Symeon (*Scripta minora*, I, p. 101.14–20). But strictly speaking, there is no comparison between the pagan greats (e.g. Demosthenes) and Symeon, for they aimed at the short-term benefit (*to ôpheloun*) to their listeners, which is 'small and feeble' (*brachy te kai asthenes*), whereas Symeon aims at the refinement of virtue and spiritual salvation (p. 106.7–14).

The motives for Psellos' critical pronouncements were, at best, mixed. His amazing displays of erudition suggest a measure of conscious self-promotion, but the limits he sets on the application of ancient standards to Christian authors are consistent with a desire to place those authors in the forefront as models not only of style but of moral character, thereby benefiting his readers. Psellos is insistent in maintaining that his views were not determined by those of 'Longinus', Sopatros, or even those of Hermogenes (*Scripta minora* I, pp. 361.10–16, 370.5–18); and while in his *Encomium to Mauropous* he praises the style of his friend as comparing with the best of Demosthenes, the better comparison would, he says, be with Nazianzus, in both literary and spiritual terms (*MB* V, pp. 149.29–150.28). As frustrating as his critical pronouncements might be at times, Psellos remains an interesting mixture of *érudit*, exhibitionist and spokesman for the politically and theologically orthodox order. Given his position in the courts of a succession of Byzantine rulers as functionary, eulogist and, eventually, 'Head Philosopher' (*hypatos tôn philosophôn*), one could hardly expect otherwise.

5. The Comnenian era (1081–1204)

If Arethas and Psellos can be taken as representative, such examples of literary criticism as we see in Byzantine sources probably ought not to be viewed as instantiations of some set of theoretical rules, but read against a shifting background of debate and the tricky questions about political status with which those debates were involved. Those critics were, moreover, not faceless literary bureaucrats but strong personalities, and the elite to which they belonged was far from homogeneous. The same was true, but to a much greater degree, of the critics we know from the period extending from the accession of Alexios I Comnenos to the sack of Constantinople by Venetian crusaders in 1204.

Literary criticism in the Comnenian era is a staggeringly complex affair, arising in a variety of scenarios involving many different venues. We hear from insiders and outsiders alike, those holding official positions and those not. In both groups we find scholars and writers striking out in new directions even as they bear witness to traditional literary values in both their theoretical pronouncements and their rhetorical practice – speeches, poems, commentaries and polemics – all of which were part of their struggles to obtain aristocratic or even imperial patronage and thus to survive as *littérateurs*.[6]

The struggles for literary survival that seem to characterise this era might be explained as direct and indirect results of a concentration of literary as well as political authority which gave rise to what might be termed an administrative aesthetic. This is evident in the creation in the late-eleventh century of such positions as that of *maïstôr tôn rhêtorôn*, the official court orator, for instance, which resulted in a remarkable mixture of conservatism and innovation in rhetorical conventions handed down therefrom. Clear evidence for this can be seen in the account of conflicts among rhetoricians given by Nikephoros Basilakes (d. *c.* 1180) in his autobiographical 'Prologue' (ed. Garzya, pp. 7.14–22, 8.26–28, 9.14–17) as well as in a number of speeches delivered on both public and private occasions during the first half of the century. On the conservative side, the results of such of an aesthetic dictated 'from the top' are evident in the acts of censorship committed by emperors and church officials alike, of which in a literary context the condemnation by the Patriarch Mouzalon of a Life of St Paraskeve on the grounds that its style was excessively vulgar (*Reg. patr.* 1.3, no. 1032) is a noteworthy (albeit possibly unique) example. On the other side, there is a large body of literature produced on commission for high-ranking personages, meeting the demands of a new literary marketplace. There is also evidence of a considerable increase in literary activity outside the boundaries of conventional genres – even outside of court circles. This cultural development was noted by Theodore Prodromos and complained about by John Tzetzes in his *Chiliades* (Book 8, ll. 517–24). The increasing popularity of erotic romance and of works composed in the so-called 'political verse' form, along with some unprecedented intrusions of the vernacular, or demotic, Greek of the day into the

---

[6] On the literary strife so evident in this period, see Garzya, 'Polemiken'; on patterns of patronage, see Mullett, 'Aristocracy' and E. Jeffreys, 'Eirene'.

normally 'Atticising' literary language, resulted in renewed debates about the decay of poetry and challenges to accepted literary standards, and about the proper role of writers and the relevance of their audiences (e.g. Tzetzes, *Iambi*, p. 38.121–30; Michael Choniates, *Sôzomena* I, pp. 6–20, 21.6–22).

We possess a very large number of ceremonial speeches from the twelfth century. If they can be taken to reflect literary concerns, they suggest that, although Hermogenes and the canonical Attic orators continued to be important in the schools, their status as models for public discourse waned significantly during the Comnenian era. This is hinted at in the funeral eulogies of that extraordinary public figure under John II and Manuel I Comnenos, Alexios Aristenos. These speeches, one by Nikephoros Basilakes (pp. 10–25) and three by Theodore Prodromos (pp. 525–9, 552–8, 561–5), are uniform in their praise for Aristenos' eloquence precisely on the grounds that he did not restrict himself to the prescriptions of the old authorities but mixed wisdom and eloquence in ways appropriate to the social needs of his day, thus greatly benefiting the state (Basilakes, pp. 18.19–19.2, 21.15–23; Prodromos at, for example, p. 533.9–16). Praise of eloquence is a standard topic in *enkômia* and *epitaphioi* throughout the period, but the praise given by orators is more frequently cast in terms that are almost poetic[7] rather than in terms of comparisons with Demosthenes or Isocrates. Hermogenean critical vocabulary is conspicuously absent. Even in the many *basilikoi logoi* (i.e. imperial court orations) extant from this period we see a marked and self-conscious shift away from classical models over to the style of the Old Testament prophets, particularly to that of the prophet-king-poet, David. The psalms begin to exercise an enormous influence on court rhetoric from the time of Alexios down to the accession of the Angeloi late in the twelfth century. Long passages of recombined verses from psalms appear both in the occasional court poetry composed by Theodore Prodromos, as in, for example, his Poem 17 (edited by Hörandner), and even in eulogies delivered before the emperors as court orators sought to speak 'Davidically' in praising them.[8] The only classical author quoted or alluded to nearly as often as David is Homer, most frequently of course in descriptions of military feats. The criteria of excellence in these speeches, then, seem to be contemporary rhetorical criteria of 'usefulness' and decorum (*to prepon*), not the degree to which they conform to 'rules' laid down by late-classical authorities.

---

[7] See for example: imagery of fire (Basilakes to Aristenos, p. 23.24–9; Niketas Eugenianos, *Monody*, 452.16–19); light (Eugenianos 454.6); general descriptions in poetic terms (K. Manasses, *Oratio*, ll. 290–315).

[8] See for example Basilakes to John II Comnenos, p. 71.3–26; Skizenos, *FRB*, 363.25–64.10; Euthymios Malakes, *Enc.* I, pp. 541.2–42.6.

If it is true that, to the contrary, the letters and speeches of Michael Italikos, for instance, seem to represent a continued respect for the 'traditional' authorities (see, for instance, 60.23–32, 158.20–3), we need to bear in mind that he was constrained by literary standards not of his own, but of the preceding generation. This comes out clearly in his apologetic letter to Gregory Kamateros (pp. 136–8) defending a composition that had not been well received by that old student of Theophylaktos of Ohrid. Likewise, it is clear that for Gregory of Corinth (*fl.* 1140) it was necessary that students have 'archetypes' to imitate; yet when we look closely at the list of authors he recommends, we see that most of them are not classical but post-classical and patristic; and that among them are some rather more recent than that – namely, Symeon Metaphrastes and Michael Psellos.[9] Imitation of classical authors, in other words, seems not to have been taken for granted as an unmistakeable mark of literary virtue.

The same gradual shift away from classical authorities to criteria of rhetorical appropriateness is evident in the criticism found in commentaries composed in the Comnenian era, not the least because many of the commentators not only held office in the courts of the emperors but were also the very orators who spoke in praise of them. Thus, the commentary on the psalms by Euthymios Zigabenos (contained in PG 128), a prominent theologian in the court of Alexios I, contains hundreds of observations on David's style, explaining apparent oddities in the style of the psalms by reference not only to the '*idiôma* of the Ancient Prophets' but also to its rhetorical aims (for example, 'to soften the hearts of his hearers'), sketching, in the process, the dimensions of a peculiarly 'Davidic' style that seems to have reappeared later in *basilikoi logoi* composed for delivery in the court. That Zigabenos makes no reference whatsoever to Hermogenes or any other of the old rhetoricians may be a recognition of the constraints of piety, but we recall that Photios had no compunction about using Hermogenean vocabulary in his discussions of Paul's style, for instance.

The standards applied to literature by Eustathios (*c.* 1115–96) in his commentaries and elsewhere seem likewise not to be concerned with conformity to abstract rules of genre or expression handed down from Antiquity. It is true that his scholia on Homer are full of Hermogenean terminology, but the role that the terminology plays in his critical observations is almost incidental. Thus, he can point out that Achilles' speech to Agamemnon in *Iliad* A could be said according to Hermogenes to exhibit a particular stylistic idea in its combination of *lexis, methodos*

---

[9] See the excerpt printed by Kominis, *Pardo,* pp. 127–9, from the end of Gregory's *Peri syntaxeôs.*

and *ennoia* (style, stance and thought) but to say that is only to point out features of the speech to students in terms with which they are already familiar. The principal criterion for deciding whether a speech by Achilles or Thersites is well expressed or not is a matter of *kairos*, appropriateness to the rhetorical situation, as is the case with the Thersites episode in *Iliad* B (see Eustathios' comments at *Scholia* 1.303.7–15, 312.26–30, 319.4–12). Eustathios' interest in points of argument, his sensitivity to speakers' intentions and awareness of audience reaction are all recorded in the service of his goal of showing how Homer, 'in a pleasant way', provides useful lessons in manners, feelings and action and 'in thousands of other areas', he claims (Prol. 3.12–22) to his readers.[10] Eustathios applies the same criterion of *to chrêsimon*, we might add, to tragedy and comedy (*Opusc.* 88.69–77), to Pindar (in spite of his habitual obscurity [*asapheia*]; Prooim. p. 288.10–13), and to his own work, as he states at the end of the preface to his account of the siege of Thessalonike (p. 4.3–12, and see p. 158.3–18).

In arguing for the useful as the criterion for judging literature, Eustathios is not simply repeating a standard that everyone took for granted. It is clear from his preface to the scholia on the *Iliad* that he saw himself as asserting that principle as a more sensible one than others applied to the explanation of the text, chiefly, it seems, the tendency to allegorise Homer (see for example 2.13–20; p. 4.11–17). The method of allegorising 'profane' authors in order to justify reading them was, of course, both old and widespread. In Eustathios' own day, Philagathos, bishop of Rossano in Sicily (*fl. c.* 1135), used allegory to defend Heliodorus against his detractors, arguing that the story of Charicleia was an allegory of the soul's salvation (*Comment.*, p. 369, ll. 64–110); and John Tzetzes had produced allegories (with which Eustathios was undoubtedly familiar) to explain Hesiod and Homer alike.

It may, in fact, be Tzetzes' allegories that Eustathios had in mind. They were contemporaries, and there are strong suggestions that Eustathios borrowed from Tzetzes without crediting him: for example, Eustathios, *Scholia* 1.607.8, seems to be verbatim from Tzetzes' notes on Lycophron; and 200.46–201.7 would seem to come from Tzetzes *ad Plutum* 415. Tzetzes was no doubt a difficult character, by turns vain (see for example his *Scholia in Aristophanem* 4.3; p. 1048.7–12), nasty (4.1; pp. 43.21–44.2), and very competitive (4.3; p. 837.3–5). But his complaints about people stealing his material, as in *Epistle* 42 (pp. 60–3), may have had some foundation.

Tzetzes' critical allegiances were, by his own account, with the 'ancients' rather than the 'moderns', as is clear from the reasons he gives for

---

[10] On Homer as *euchrêstos poiêtês* ('a useful poet'), see *Scholia* 1.10–16, 2.34–38, 5.31–6.3.

considering himself more erudite and orthodox than his detractors (e.g. at *Scholia* 4.2; pp. 835.9–36.3 and *Ep.* 64; p. 92). His strictures on prosody are rigidly conservative – perhaps he shared the view of his predecessor, Mauropous (Poem 34, ed. De Lagarde), that the decline of knowledge of metres was a sure sign of the decay of civilisation (as various notes on Aristophanes attest: *Scholia* 4.1, 98.22–99.19, 105.12–25; 123.16-124-11, etc.); and he places enormous emphasis on the traditional stylistic virtue of *saphêneia* ('clarity') and on precise diction sanctioned by ancient authorities (*akribeia*).

What is interesting about the latter pronouncements is the frequency with which they appear in his *Allegories* (e.g. *Iliad*, ll.171, 250, 479, etc.; *Odyssey*, ll. 40–56 [p. 254]; *Theogony*, ll.43–9 [p. 26] and paraphrases, such as the paraphrase of Hermogenes (*AGrO* IV, e.g. pp. 2.21, 86.10–26, 125.5–27 [citing Doxapatres and Sikeliotes], 129.7–19). These allegories and paraphrases, in turn, were composed in the fifteen-syllable verses of 'political verse' which, even if it did have its origins in the distant past, was hardly a classical form. We are thus faced with something of a paradox: a learned scholar asserting traditional rules for proper expression in a form itself not authorised by any classical, post-classical or patristic precedent. The justification seems to be that these compositions, like the 'political verses' of Prodromos, were composed on commission for half-educated members of prestigious families – in the case of the *Theogony* allegories, for Manuel I Comnenos' sister-in-law, the *sebastokratorissa* Irene. In composing those allegories, it would therefore seem, Tzetzes was at once ingratiating himself with the sources of literary and political patronage and assuring his audience(s) that there was much of worth in those old pagan poems, and in composing such paraphrases as that of Hermogenes, that he was solidly in support of traditional literary values: clarity of style and usefulness. Tzetzes' assurances on these points were, unfortunately for him, less than successful. He seems never to have attained the status in the court that Basilakes and Prodromos did, despite his remarkable output. The competition was tough. Indeed, his complaints about poverty may well have been more than mere literary commonplaces.[11]

Other signs of change in literary tastes and standards can be seen in the lively interest among twelfth-century readers and writers in the erotic romance and satire and in the appearance of literary compositions in 'demotic' Greek. Byzantine critics were, traditionally, rather ambivalent about the novels of Achilles Tatius and Heliodorus, as we have seen. Yet a succession of writers found audiences for romances composed along the

---

[11] M. Jeffreys, p. 154; compare *Ep.* 49; pp. 69–70 (ed. Leone) and *Ep.* 80; pp. 119–20. But see Beaton, 'Poverty', pp. 3–8.

lines of those late-classical authors. Prodromos composed his *Rhodanthe and Dosikles* and his student Eugenianos *Drosilla and Charikles*. Konstantinos Manasses composed his *Aristandros and Kallithea* about 1160 in political verse; and Eustathios Makrembolites in the 1180s produced his *Ismene and Ismenias*.[12] All of these show, aside from the fact that their authors were capable of writing in a variety of literary 'registers', creative forays beyond the limits of both stylistic and, in some cases, moralising conventions. Likewise, satires composed by Prodromos and others reveal 'a talent to abuse' (to use Baldwin's term) not evident in the extant literature from preceding centuries. We find 'demotic' Greek used in the 'beggar poetry' sometimes attributed to Prodromos (the '*Ptôchoprodromika*') and in a poem, 'From his Jail Cell', addressed by Michael Glykas to Manuel I Comnenos. It is true that the use of the vernacular may have been 'proper' only in 'beggar poetry', and that Glykas was, in spite of his pleas, blinded and kept in prison anyway. But the appearance of such verses in the vernacular, the circulation of satiric prose and verse, and the innovative handling of the novel form all suggest that, in practice, there was in the twelfth century a much wider range of acceptance of non-canonical literature than ever before – some of it composed by writers who, on other occasions, saw fit to invoke the very canons they transgressed when they took up the critical cudgels against their contemporaries.

The complexity of the literary scene during the twelfth century, in short, was of a different order of magnitude, so far as we can see from the evidence left us, from that of earlier periods in Byzantine literary history. Literary criticism was motivated by far more than an interest in preserving traditional standards; literary production, while sometimes judged by those standards by those who could gain from doing so, went well beyond the formal constraints of archaising pronouncements.

6. Recovery and decline

After a half century of being displaced from Constantinople as a result of the sack of the city in 1204 by crusaders from the West, Palaiologan rulers called on the talents and learning of writers and scholars in their attempts to reconstitute the Hellenic heritage that set the Byzantines apart from the barbarous 'Latins'. Nikephoros Blemmydes (1197–1272) and scholars like him had valiantly tried to preserve the records of authentic Byzantine culture during the so-called Nicaean Exile; and they did that with some success. Upon the restoration of the emperor to the throne in Constantinople in 1261, the patriarchal and imperial schools were

[12] See Beaton, *Medieval Greek Romance*, pp. 67–86. The dates are much debated.

reopened, libraries were reassembled, and new texts of old works were produced to fill them. This task was taken on by a generation of scholars and members of the imperial family – Maximos Planudes, Manuel Moschopoulos, Thomas Magister, Demetrios Triklinios and Theodora Raoulaina, niece of Michael VIII Palaiologos – who set about restoring, re-editing and putting into circulation a large number of improved texts of both classical and ecclesiastical authors. We get a hint of the difficulty of their task from a marginal note in a manuscript of Plutarch's *Moralia* (Paris, Bibliothèque nationale de France, MS gr. 1671) in which Planudes complains of the difficulty of restoring words that time had erased from the old copies he worked with.

This period of intense grammatical activity, motivated as it was by Hellenic self-consciousness (a recurrent theme in many letters and poems from the period),[13] gave rise to vigorous attempts to reclaim the past and consequently to literary debates in abundance. We see, above all, renewed conflict between 'ancients' and 'moderns'. We see also the familiar split between those men of letters who were politically well placed (Metochites, for much of his life) and those who were not, but aspired to be (Nikephoros Choumnos and Manuel Philes, for example). As in earlier periods of Byzantine history, mastery of the arts of eloquence was a necessary qualification for high public office.[14] There are signs, however, of an increasing isolation of intellectuals skilled in traditional eloquence and some continuing attempts to forge a new literary idiom closer to the vernacular than to any putative Attic ideal. Balancing the strong pull exercised by the certainties of the past, there is in this period an erosion of those certainties that in the end proved to be almost complete.

The authority of the past was clearly the reward in the attempts (which go back to Blemmydes) to resuscitate the old *enkyklios paideia* in all its parts, including the arts of the quadrivium. In their paraphrases, synopses and collections of scholia, scholars like Georgios Pachymeres, Joseph Rhakendytes and Planudes sought both to reconstitute the rhetoric curriculum and rectify it. Thus, we see all the familiar names and works and exemplars – chiefly Hermogenes and Demosthenes – but resituated in a new analytic and more comprehensive framework. Planudes, in particular, sought to organise the disparate lessons of various rhetorical traditions by dividing and distributing terms in definitions he formulated, in a manner reminiscent of methods used by Aristotle, in an obvious attempt to present

---

[13] Manuel II Palaiologos, who came to the throne in 1391, writes (*Ep.* 52; p. 150) that he felt compelled to promote literary studies among his subjects 'so that as they mingle so much with barbarians, they might not themselves become barbarians'.

[14] See for example Metochites, Poem 4.36–56 (ed. Ševčenko and Featherstone); Georgios Lapithes (*fl. c.* 1340), 'Stichoi politikoi', ll. 176–87; Nikephoros Gregoras, *Phlorentios*, p. 508.11–19.

a new synthesis of traditional lore (see for instance *RG* V, pp. 214.15–24, 218.4–11).

One forceful advocate of strict adherence to the traditions handed down by the ancients was Nikephoros Choumnos (1260–1327), a student of George of Cyprus. In an essay on criticism, *Peri logôn kriseôs kai ergasias* (*AGr.* III, pp. 356–64), Choumnos lays out standards by which one can distinguish good expression from bad according to the teachings of the ancients. Choumnos counsels strict adherence to Attic diction (p. 360.28–30), avoidance of excessive length and unnecessary digressions, and, above all, of obscurity in diction and composition (pp. 357.20–25, 363.4–8). One's style should exhibit *êthos* and *kallos* 'so as to enchant and fascinate the listener' (p. 362.15–20); and one's composition (*diathesis*, 359.3–8) should be 'organic' (citing Plato's *Phaedrus*), not like the modern sort which 'like a dancing camel gets all twisted up in itself' (p. 362.9–11).

Choumnos composed another essay, his *Pros tous dyscherainontas* (*AGr.* III, pp. 395–91), an attack on bad rhetoric and faulty astronomy. The best rhetoric, he says, is based on the definitions and rules arising from exact knowledge (*epistêmê*) derived from the orators and leaders of old – Plato and Demosthenes – not Thucydides, for example, or other obscure writers whose stylistic antics remind us of the fitful motions of apes and frogs (p. 373.9–13). As for the study of astronomy, why should anyone take seriously one who goes about 'beating the air' about the motions of the planets and phases of the moon, merely echoing the obscurities and errors of Aristotle (pp. 375.19–376.21)? On both subjects, let us recognise the authority not of the ignorant and uneducated 'modern' writers but that of the ancients, who were 'brimming with exact knowledge'.

It is not immediately evident whom Choumnos had in his sights in this essay, but by the middle it is clear that his target is Theodore Metochites. Metochites replied in kind in two essays deriding Choumnos' claims to expertise in either rhetoric or astronomy.[15] Not only does Choumnos fail to understand the nature of true eloquence, Metochites sarcastically observes; he fails to use his sources rightly. What Choumnos sees as obscure is due not to stylistic failings but to his own ignorance. Indeed, Hermogenes himself – not as commonly understood (*kata tous pollous*), but correctly – endorses all the qualities of style Choumnos calls 'obscure', including that of the admirable Thucydides (*Logos* 13.14–18; pp. 201–11). It is, in short, Metochites who is most in accord with ancient criteria, not his opponent. As for astronomy, Choumnos has never written anything on the subject that qualifies

---

[15] Ševčenko, *Etudes*, *Logoi* 13 (pp. 189–217) and 14 (pp. 219–65), both with facing French translations.

him to speak about it, Metochites complains; and his ignorance of Aristotle is proof of his lack of both taste and erudition (*Logos* 14.21–2; pp. 245–7).

This attack by Choumnos and the responses by Metochites are not just quarrels about abstract literary or scientific questions. The issue here was political as well, as Choumnos' attack was mounted in the wake of his unsuccessful attempt to work his way into the circle of *literati* close to the emperor Andronikos II about 1325. Metochites was himself to fall from grace some three years later, when Andronikos was forced to abdicate. But in the meantime he sought to protect his station by fending off his detractors – hence the sharp and derisive tones and strident declarations of literary orthodoxy by both. Choumnos seems to have been consistent in his conservatism; Metochites, by contrast, seems to have been rather less so. It is interesting, for instance, that he could cite Aristotle as he does (14.21), quoting the *Metaphysics* in his response to Choumnos, if only because he had, some years before, complained in his *Miscellanies* (3, pp. 23–34; 21, pp. 155–9) that Aristotle's obscurity was the result of perverse envy of Plato and a desire to conceal the fact that he 'knew naught of which he wrote'. Thus we see both using 'the past' as a weapon, with each claiming to be its authentic representative.

Within a year after the death of Choumnos in 1327, Metochites was forced to retire from public life. While residing in the monastery of the Chora, where he occupied himself still with literary matters, he composed the *epistasia* comparing Demosthenes and Aristides. It is clear that, like the *Logoi* ('orations') he composed against Choumnos, this essay is as political as it is literary. Here, too, we find Metochites using Hermogenes and Dionysius of Halicarnassus and the rest as his authorities. But it is not those who provide the final criterion by which the two are judged. Demosthenes' ultimate failure, Metochites writes, lay in his devotion to democratic politics, which required that he speak according to the expectations of his audience. By the same token, however, Aristides spoke in a way suited to the monarchy under which he lived; and that makes him, not his Athenian predecessor, the truly useful and appropriate model for writers and speakers working in the setting of the Palaiologan court.

Metochites' judgement in favour of Aristides is in some ways peculiar, for we do not see such frankly political considerations playing so decisive a role in previous criticism. His choice makes sense, however, when it is viewed against the background of the sorts of social and political tensions that had begun to trouble the empire since the restoration of 1261 and would continue to until the final collapse in the next century. Metochites remembered well that Michael VIII Palaiologos himself had been excommunicated by the Patriarch Arsenios, an action that resulted in decades of conflict. He had seen the early phases of the Palamite controversy and taken part in the debates over relations between the Orthodox church and the papacy in Rome. In all of these loomed the spectres of *ataxia* ('disorder'), and political disaster. These in turn were detected in any deviation from absolute imperial authority, particularly if that deviation took a turn towards '*dêmokratia*', which Metochites had years before condemned as the work of the devil (*Misc.* 96, 607.12). Critics long before Metochites had perceived the 'democratic' dimension of Demosthenes' eloquence; but in 1332 that political character had taken on a rather more sinister significance – to the point where it outweighed any literary or rhetorical 'excellence' one might care to admit in his works. What we see in the *Epistasia*, then, is an example of how political preoccupations could redirect traditional literary premises assumed by those claiming to base their verdicts on traditional standards.

Metochites' essay seems to foreshadow a perception, which became prominent in the work of his successors, connecting 'bad' writing with political decay.[16] All these writers accordingly held tenaciously to traditional (Attic) standards, sometimes indulging in archaism to the point of absurdity (as in Kydones, *Monody*, cols. 644D-45B) regardless of what other issues (e.g. anti- or pro-Union with Rome) might have divided them. As it happened, of course, 'good' writing, which the countless apologetics, memoirs and tendentious histories of this age were meant to embody, was not enough to hold the centre together. Adherence to high literary standards could do nothing to prevent earthquakes, eclipses and plagues such as those that occurred in mid-century. Nor could Gregoras' explanations of those phenomena (*History*, II, p. 624), Joseph Bryennios' tract 'On the Causes of Our Sufferings', or the apocalyptic literature that appears on the scene calm the panic at the news of the blockade of the city by the Turks and the appearance on the horizon of Mongol hordes as the fourteenth century drew to a close.

The succession of critical judgements one sees over the course of the last decades of the fourteenth century describes a downward curve, as it were, on a scale of relevance. Despite all protestations to the contrary, the literature sanctioned by tradition and those who produced it became increasingly detached from reality. However, it was not only natural disasters and external threats that contributed to the demise of traditional canons of literature in this final waning phase of Byzantine criticism. The appearance of 'simplified' versions of Anna Comnena's *Alexiad* and Blemmydes' *Basilikos Andrias* in the first half of the fourteenth century suggests

---

[16] See for example Demetrios Kydones in his *Apologia*, p. 370, ll. 24–35; John Chortasmenos, Letters 10 and 19, pp. 160ff., 168–70, and Gennadius Scholarios (IV, p. 406.22–32).

that there was a significant segment of the reading public with less than refined tastes, some of it perhaps incapable of reading the elevated style of the originals. It might also be argued that the literary interests of the very figures the educated elite were trying to preserve in their positions of authority were also partly responsible. The circulation in court circles of the 'demotic' erotic romance *Kallimachos and Chrysorrhoé*, composed early in the century by the nephew of Michael VIII Palaiologos, Andronikos, must have ratified, if it did not initiate, a new trend towards writing in a Greek closer to that used by the common folk than to the archaising Greek in which Byzantine literature was mostly composed. At first, these romances were composed exclusively by and for the highest strata of Byzantine society – as indeed such works had been in the twelfth century. By the end of the century, we see evidence that such works were composed for the entertainment of the literate members of lower classes, outside court circles. This sort of 'democratisation' of literary media may have given birth to modern Greek literature; but it marked also the death of the ancient, in Constantinople and its provinces at least. The resurrection of the ancient would take place – was already taking place, in fact – far to the West, in Italy.

Conclusion

Even in an account as broad as the present one, a few persistent features of Byzantine literary criticism emerge. They are not, however, the features ordinarily associated with the literary activity of the era from the ninth-century revival of learning to the last gasp of the Empire. Instead of slavish imitation and millennial stasis, abstract judgements devoid of any individuality, and predictable homogeneity, we find abundant instances of disagreement among the experts, canonical authority bent to fit contemporary circumstance, variety, and even innovation. As intimately familiar with the literary standards of late Antiquity as Byzantine scholars were, they clearly saw the past as a resource, not as a limitation. Broadly political considerations and ethical concerns turn out to dominate aesthetic, sometimes even theological, ones. 'Universal' standards of judgement are regularly used by Byzantine critics to warrant assertions of utility and worth bearing on particular situations as those situations dictate and depending on who it is that is making the claims. This suggests a need for the reassessment of the commonplace which depicts any sort of individualism or topicality as a deviation from, or rebellion against, some set of norms presumed to apply everywhere and always.[17] It is tempting, in characterising

[17] See especially the arguments advanced by Kazhdan, *Studies*, pp. 188–95, and Beck, *Schaffen*.

Byzantine literary practice, to draw parallels not with the medieval Latin West, but with the literary/political quarrels of sixteenth-century Italy or France, or seventeenth-century England, or indeed of twentieth-century Europe and the Americas, where appeals to 'permanent' truths are so often seen in debates about changing issues of legitimacy and political direction. Such parallels need not be drawn here, however, for us to see that rumours of Byzantine stagnation are, when it comes to the criticism of letters, greatly exaggerated.

Bibliography

Introduction

Accessus ad auctores, ed. R. B. C. Huygens (Berchem and Brussels, 1954).

Adams, Hazard (ed.), *Critical Theory since Plato* (New York, 1971).

Allen, Judson Boyce, *The Ethical Poetic of the Later Middle Ages: A Decorum of Convenient Distinction* (Toronto, 1982).

— *The Friar as Critic: Literary Attitudes in the Later Middle Ages* (Nashville TN, 1971).

Andersen, Elisabeth *et al.* (eds.), *Autor und Autorschaft im Mittelalter: Kolloquium Meissen 1995* (Tübingen, 1998).

Atkins, John W. H., *English Literary Criticism: The Medieval Phase* (1943; rpt. London, 1952).

Auerbach, Erich, *Literary Language and its Public in Late Latin Antiquity and in the Middle Ages*, tr. R. Manheim (New York, 1965).

Bareiss, Karl-Heinz, *Comoedia: Die Entwicklung der Komödiendiskussion von Aristoteles bis Ben Jonson* (Frankfurt a. M., 1982).

Barry, Peter, *Beginning Theory: An Introduction to Literary and Cultural Theory* (Manchester, 1995).

Baswell, Christopher, *Virgil in Medieval England: Figuring the 'Aeneid' from the Twelfth Century to Chaucer* (Cambridge, 1995).

Bernard Silvester (?), *Commentary on Martianus Capella's 'De nuptiis Philologiae et Mercurii'*, ed. H. J. Westra (Toronto, 1986).

Bersuire, Pierre, *Reductorium morale, lib. XV: Ovidius moralizatus, cap. 1: De formis figurisque deorum, Textus e codice Brux., Bibl. Reg. 863–9 critice editus*, ed. J. Engels, Werkmateriaal 3 (Utrecht, 1966).

Black, Robert, *Humanism and Education in Medieval and Renaissance Italy: Tradition and Innovation in Latin Schools from the Twelfth to the Fifteenth Century* (Cambridge, 2001).

Bolgar, R. R. (ed.), *Classical Influences on European Culture, A.D. 500–1500* (Cambridge, 1971).

Boccaccio, Giovanni, tr. C. G. Osgood, *Boccaccio on Poetry: Being the Preface and the Fourteenth and Fifteenth Books of Boccaccio's 'Genealogia deorum gentilium' in an English Version with Introductory Essay and Commentary* (Princeton NJ, 1930).

Brooks, Nicholas (ed.), *Latin and the Vernacular Languages in Early Medieval Britain* (Leicester, 1982).

Brown-Grant, Rosalind, *Christine de Pizan and the Moral Defence of Women* (Cambridge, 1999).

Camargo, Martin, *Medieval Rhetoric of Prose Composition: Five English 'Artes dictandi' and their Tradition* (Binghamton NY, 1995).

Carruthers, Mary, *The Book of Memory: A Study of Memory in Medieval Culture* (Cambridge, 1990).

The Craft of Thought: Meditation, Rhetoric, and the Making of Images, 400–1200 (Cambridge, 2000).

Conley, Thomas M., *Rhetoric in the European Tradition* (Chicago and London, 1990).

Conrad of Hirsau, *Dialogus super auctores*, ed. R. B. C. Huygens (Berchem and Brussels, 1955).

Copeland, Rita, *Pedagogy, Intellectuals, and Dissent in the Later Middle Ages: Lollardy and Ideas of Learning* (Cambridge, 2001).

Rhetoric, Hermeneutics, and Translation in the Middle Ages: Academic Traditions and Vernacular Texts (Cambridge, 1991).

Coulson, Frank T., and Roy, Bruno, *Incipitarium Ovidianum: A Finding Guide for Texts related to the Study of Ovid in the Middle Ages and Renaissance* (Turnhout, 2000).

Curtius, Ernst R., *Europäische Literatur und lateinisches Mittelalter* (2nd edn, Bern, 1948). English tr. of the first edition under the title *European Literature and the Latin Middle Ages*, by W. R. Trask (London, 1953).

Dagenais, John, *The Ethics of Reading in Manuscript Culture: Glossing the 'Libro de buen amor'* (Princeton NJ, 1994).

Dahan, Gilbert, 'Notes et textes sur la poétique au Moyen Âge', *AHDLMA*, 47 (1980), 171–239.

De Bruyne, Edgar, *Études d'esthétique médiévale* (3 vols., Bruges, 1946); abridged and tr. E. B. Hennessy as *The Esthetics of the Middle Ages* (New York, 1969).

Demats, Paule, *Fabula: Trois études de mythographie antique et médiévale* (Geneva, 1973).

Dronke, Peter, *Fabula: Explorations into the Uses of Myth in Medieval Platonism* (Leiden, 1974).

Gehl, Paul L., *A Moral Art: Grammar, Society and Culture in Trecento Florence* (Ithaca NY, 1993).

Ghosh, Kantik, *The Wycliffite Heresy: Authority and the Interpretation of Texts* (Cambridge, 2002).

Gómez Redondo, Fernando, *Artes poéticas medievales*, Colección arcadia des las letras, 1 (Madrid, 2000).

Greenfield, Concetta Carestia, *Humanist and Scholastic Poetics, 1250–1500* (Lewisburg PA, 1981).

Hardison, O. B., 'Towards a History of Medieval Literary Criticism', *M&H*, 7 (1976), 1–12.

Harland, Richard (ed.), *Literary Theory from Plato to Barthes* (London, 1999).

Haug, Walter, *Literaturtheorie im deutschen Mittelalter* (2nd rev. edn, Darmstadt, 1985); tr. J. M. Catling as *Vernacular Literary Theory in the Middle Ages: The German Tradition, 800–1300, in its European Context* (Cambridge, 1997).

Hexter, Ralph J., *Ovid and Medieval Schooling: Studies in Medieval School Commentaries on Ovid's 'Ars amatoria', 'Epistulae ex Ponto', and 'Epistulae heroidum'* (Munich, 1986).

Hudson, Anne, *Lollards and their Books* (London and Ronceverte WV, 1985).

Hunt, R. W., 'The Introductions to the *Artes* in the Twelfth Century', in *Studia medievalia in honorem admodum Reverendi Patris Raymundi Josephi Martin* (Bruges, 1948), pp. 85–112; rpt. in Hunt's *Collected Papers on the History of Grammar in the Middle Ages*, ed. G. L. Bursill-Hall (Amsterdam, 1980), pp. 117–44.

Hunt, Tony, *Teaching and Learning Latin in Thirteenth-Century England* (3 vols., Cambridge, 1991).

Irvine, Martin, *The Making of Textual Culture: 'Grammatica' and Literary Theory* (Cambridge, 1994).

Kelly, Henry Ansgar, *Chaucerian Tragedy* (Woodbridge, 1997).

Ideas and Forms of Tragedy from Aristotle to the Middle Ages (Cambridge, 1993).

Tragedy and Comedy from Dante to Pseudo-Dante, University of California Publications in Modern Philology, 121 (Berkeley CA, 1989).

Kindermann, Udo, *Satyra: Die Theorie der Satire im Mittellateinischen: Vorstudie zu einer Gattungsgeschichte*, Erlanger Beiträge zur Sprach- und Kunstwissenschaft, 58 (Nuremberg, 1978).

Kristeller, Paul Oskar (editor in chief), *Catalogus translationum et commentariorum: Mediaeval and Renaissance Latin Translations and Commentaries* (Washington DC, 1960–).

Lubac, Henri de, *Exégèse médiévale: Les quatre sens de l'écriture* (4 vols., Paris, 1959–64).

McKeon, Richard, 'Rhetoric in the Middle Ages', rpt. in R. S. Crane (ed.), *Critics and Criticism: Ancient and Modern* (Chicago, 1952), pp. 260–96.

Minnis, Alastair J., *Medieval Theory of Authorship: Scholastic Literary Attitudes in the Later Middle Ages* (1984; 2nd edn, Aldershot, 1988).

and Scott, A. B., with Wallace, David (eds.), *Medieval Literary Theory and Criticism, c. 1100 – c. 1375: The Commentary-Tradition* (1988; rev. edn, Oxford, 1991; rpt. 2001).

Munk Olsen, Birger *I classici nel canone scolastico altomedievale* (Spoleto, 1991).

Murphy, J. J., *Rhetoric in the Middle Ages* (Berkeley CA, 1974).

Olson, Glending, *Literature as Recreation in the Later Middle Ages* (Ithaca NY, 1982).

Patterson, Lee, *Negotiating the Past: The Historical Understanding of Medieval Literature* (Madison WI, 1987).

Preminger, Alex, Hardison, O. B., and Kerrane, Kevin (eds.), *Classical and Medieval Literary Criticism: Translations and Interpretations* (New York, 1974).

Przychocki, G., 'Accessus Ovidiani', *Rozprawy Akademii Umiejętności, Wydział filologiczny*, serya 3, tom. 4 (1911), 65–126.

Quain, E. A., 'The Medieval *Accessus ad auctores*', *Traditio*, 3 (1945), 215–64.

Reynolds, Suzanne, *Medieval Reading: Grammar, Rhetoric and the Classical Text* (Cambridge, 1996).

Robertson, D. W., Jr., *A Preface to Chaucer: Studies in Medieval Perspectives* (Princeton NJ, 1969).

Saintsbury, George, *History of Criticism and Literary Taste in Europe* (2nd edn, 3 vols., London, 1902–4).

Sandkühler, Bruno, *Die frühen Dantekommentare und ihr Verhältnis zur mittel-alterlichen Kommentartradition* (Munich, 1967).

Smalley, Beryl, *The Study of the Bible in the Middle Ages* (3rd edn, Oxford, 1984).

Southern, R. W., *Medieval Humanism and Other Studies* (New York, 1970).

Scholastic Humanism and the Unification of Europe (2 vols., Oxford, 1994–2000).

Stock, Brian, *Augustine the Reader: Meditation, Self-knowledge, and the Ethics of Interpretation* (Cambridge MA, 1996).

The Implications of Literacy: Written Language and Models of Interpretation in the Eleventh and Twelfth Centuries (Princeton NJ, 1983).

Listening for the Text: On the Uses of the Past (Baltimore MD, 1990).

Myth and Science in the Twelfth Century: A Study of Bernard Silvester (Princeton NJ, 1972).

Trinkaus, Charles E., *In Our Image and Likeness: Humanity and Divinity in Italian Humanist Thought* (Notre Dame IN, 1995).

Renaissance Transformations of Late Medieval Thought (Aldershot, 1999).

Trinkaus, Charles E., and Oberman, H. O. (eds.), *The Pursuit of Holiness in Late Medieval and Renaissance Religion* (Leiden, 1974).

Ullmann, Walter, *Medieval Foundations of Renaissance Humanism* (London, 1977).

Ward, John O., *Ciceronian Rhetoric in Treatise, Scholion and Commentary* (Turnhout, 1995).

Weiss, Julian, *The Poet's Art: Literary Theory in Castile c. 1400–60*, Medium Ævum Monographs, n.s. 14 (Oxford, 1990).

Wetherbee, Winthrop, *Platonism and Poetry in the Twelfth Century: The Literary Influence of the School of Chartres* (Princeton NJ, 1972).

Wheatley, Edward, *Mastering Aesop: Medieval Education, Chaucer and his Followers* (Gainsville FA, 2000).

Whitman, Jon (ed.), *Interpretation and Allegory: Antiquity to the Modern Period* (Leiden, 2000).

Wimsatt, W. K., and Brooks, C., *Literary Criticism: A Short History* (London, 1957).

Witt, Ronald G., *In the Footsteps of the Ancients: The Origins of Humanism from Lovato to Bruni* (Leiden, 2000).

Wogan-Browne, Jocelyn, *et al.* (eds.), *The Idea of the Vernacular: An Anthology of Middle English Literary Theory, 1280–1520* (Exeter and University Park PA, 1999).

Zimmerman, M. (ed.), *'Auctor' et 'auctoritas': invention et conformisme dans l'écriture médiévale, actes du colloque à l'Université de Saint-Quentin-en-Yvelines (14–16 juin 1999)* (Geneva, 2001).

The liberal arts and the arts of Latin textuality

Primary sources

Abbo of Fleury (Abbo Floriacensis), *Quaestiones grammaticales, Apologeticus, Epistulae*, PL 139, 417–578.

Quaestiones grammaticales, ed. A. Guerreau-Jalabert (Paris, 1982).

Abelard, Peter, *Dialectica: First Complete Edition of the Parisian Manuscript*, ed. L. M. de Rijk (2nd edn, Assen, 1956).

Glosses on Aristotle's *Peri Hermeneias*, ed. B. Geyer, *Peter Abaelards Philosophische Schriften*, 1. 2, *Die Glossen zu Peri Hermeneias*, BGPM, Texte und Untersuchungen, 21, 3 (Münster i.W., 1927); tr. in H. Arens, *Aristotle's Theory of Language and its Tradition: Texts from 500–1750* (Amsterdam, 1984), pp. 231–302.

Ad habendam materiam, ed. Servus of Sint Anthonis Gieben, O.F.M.Cap., 'Preaching in the Thirteenth Century: A Note on Ms. Gonville and Caius 439', *Collectanea franciscana*, 32 (1962), 310–24.

Adalbert of Samaria, *Praecepta dictaminum*, ed. F.-J. Schmale, MGH, Quellen zur Geistesgeschichte des Mittelalters, 3 (Weimar, 1961).

Ælfric, *Aelfrics Grammatik und Glossar*, ed. J. Zupitza, 2nd edn intro. H. Gneuss (Berlin, 1966).

Aimeric, *Ars lectoria*, ed. H. F. Reijnders, *Vivarium*, 9 (1971), 119–37; 10 (1972), 41–101, 124–76.

Alan of Lille, *Anticlaudianus*, ed. R. Bossuat (Paris, 1955); tr. J. J. Sheridan (Toronto, 1973).

Liber parabolarum (seu *Parvum doctrinale*), PL 210, 81–94.

De planctu naturae, ed. N. M. Häring, *Studi medievali*, 3rd ser. 19 (1978), 797–879; tr. J. J. Sheridan (Toronto, 1980).

Alberic of Monte Cassino, *Flores rhetorici*, ed. D. M. Inguanez and H. M. Willard, *Miscellanea cassinese*, 14 (Montecassino, 1938); tr. J. N. Miller in Miller, Prosser and Benson (eds.), *Readings in Medieval Rhetoric*, pp. 132–61.

Restauri Albericiani, ed. G. C. Alessio, *Medioevo romanzo*, 2 (1975), 321–44.

De rithmis, ed. H. H. Davis, *MS*, 28 (1966), 198–227.

Alcok, Simon, *De modo dividendi themata*, ed. M. F. Boynton, 'Simon Alcok on Expanding the Sermon', *HTR*, 34 (1941), 201–16.

Alcuin, *De dialectica*, PL 101, 949–76.

Disputatio Pippini regalis et nobilissimi iuvenis cum Albino scholastico, PL 101, 975–80.

De grammatica, PL 101, 849–902.

Orthographia, ed. H. Keil, *GL*, 7, 295–312; also ed. A. Marsili (Pisa, 1952).

De rhetorica, ed. W. S. Howell, *The Rhetoric of Alcuin and Charlemagne* (1941; rpt. New York, 1965); also ed. G. Halm, *Rhetores latini minores*, pp. 523–50, and PL 101, 919–46.

Alcuin (?) and Charlemagne, 'De litteris colendis', MGH, *Leges, Sect. II, Capitularia Regum Francorum*, no. 29, p. 79; also ed. L. Wallach, in *Alcuin and Charlemagne: Studies in Carolingian History and Literature* (Ithaca NY, 1959), pp. 202–4.

Aldhelm, *Opera*, ed. R. Ehwald, MGH, AA 15 (3 vols., 1913–19; rpt. Berlin, 1961).

The Prose Works, tr. M. Lapidge and M. Herren (Cambridge, 1979).

Alexander of Villa Dei, *Doctrinale*, ed. D. Reichling, Monumenta germaniae paedagogica, 12 (Berlin, 1893).

Ecclesiale, ed. L. R. Lind (Lawrence KS, 1958).

Alexander Nequam, *Corrogationes Promethei*. Oxford, Bodleian Library, MS Bodley 550, fols. 1r–100r; MS Bodley 760, fols. 99r–171v; Auct. F.5.23, fols. 7r–86r.

Alfonso d'Alprao, *Ars praedicandi*, ed. A. G. Hauf, 'El *Ars Praedicandi* de Fr. Alfonso d'Alprao, O.F.M.: Aportación al estudio de la teoría de la predicación en la Península Ibérica', *AFH*, 72 (1979), 233–329.

Anonymous of Bologna, *Rationes dictandi*, in Rockinger (ed.), *Briefsteller und Formelbücher*, pp. 9–28; tr. J. J. Murphy in Murphy (ed.), *Three Medieval Rhetorical Arts*, pp. 5–25.

Anselm, *De grammatico*, ed. D. P. Henry (Notre Dame IN, 1964).

Antonio da Tempo, *Summa artis rithmici vulgaris dictaminis*, ed. R. Andrews, Collezione di opere inedite o rare, 136 (Bologna, 1977).

Aristotle, *De arte poetica*, tr. William of Moerbeke, ed. E. Valgimigli, Aristoteles Latinus, 33 (Bruges, 1953).

Arnaud de Mareuil, *Les Saluts d'amour*, ed. P. Bec (Toulouse, 1961).

Ars dictandi aurelianensis, in Rockinger (ed.), *Briefsteller und Formelbücher*, pp. 103–14.

Arsegino, *Quadriga* and *Proverbi*, ed. P. Marangon, *Quaderni per la storia dell'Università di Padova*, 9–10 (1976–7), 1–44.

Augustine, *Contra academicos; De beata vita; De ordine; De magistro; De libero arbitrio*, ed. W. M. Green and K.-D. Daur, CCSL 29 (Turnhout, 1970).

De dialectica, ed. J. Pinborg and tr. B. D. Jackson (Dordrecht and Boston MA, 1975).

De doctrina christiana, ed. J. Martin, CCSL 32 (Turnhout, 1962); tr. D. W. Robertson Jr. (New York, 1958).

Averroes, *Three Short Commentaries on Aristotle's 'Topics', 'Rhetoric', and 'Poetics'*, ed. and tr. C. E. Butterworth (New York, 1977).

Bacon, Roger, *Bachonis grammatica graeca: The Greek Grammar of Roger Bacon and a Fragment of his Hebrew Grammar*, ed. E. Nolan and S. A. Hirsch (Cambridge, 1902).

Summa gramatica Magistri Rogeri Bacon necnon Sumule dialectices, ed. R. Steele, in Opera hactenus inedita Rogeri Baconi, 15 (Oxford, 1940).

Baldwin, *Liber dictaminum*, ed. S. Dursza, *Quadrivium*, 13 (1972), 5–24.

Baldwin of Viktring, *Ars dictaminis*, ed. D. Schaller, *Deutsches Archiv für Erforschung des Mittelalters*, 35 (1979), 127–37.

Bede, *Libri II de arte metrica et de schematibus et tropis: The Art of Poetry and Rhetoric*, ed. and tr. C. B. Kendall (Saarbrücken, 1991).

Bene of Florence, *Candelabrum*, ed. G. C. Alessio (Padua, 1983).

Bernard, Pseudo-, *Cartula (De contemptu mundi)*, PL 184, 1307–14.

Bernard Silvester, (?) *Commentum super sex libros Eneidos Virgilii*, ed. J. W. and E. F. Jones (Lincoln NE and London, 1977); tr. E. G. Schreiber and T. E. Maresca, *Commentary on the First Six Books of Vergil's 'Aeneid'* (Lincoln NE and London, 1979).

Dictamen, ed. M. Brini Savorelli, *Rivista critica di storia della filosofia*, 20 (1965), 201–30.

Bernold of Kaisersheim (Kaisheim), *Summula dictaminis*, in Rockinger (ed.), *Briefsteller und Formelbücher*, pp. 845–924.

Bichilino da Spello, *Pomerium rethorice*, ed. V. Licitra, *Quaderni del Centro per il collegamento degli studi medievali e umanistici nell'Università di Perugia*, 5 (Florence, 1979).

Boethius, *Anicii Manlii Severini Boetii commentarii in librum Aristotelis 'Peri hermeneias'*, ed. G. Meiser (Leipzig, 1887); tr. in H. Arens, *Aristotle's Theory of Language and its Tradition: Texts from 500–1750* (Amsterdam, 1984), pp. 159–204.

Boethius of Dacia, *Modi significandi sive quaestiones super Priscianum maiorem*, ed. J. Pinborg and H. Roos, Corpus philosophorum danicorum medii ævi, 4 (Copenhagen, 1969).

Bonaventure, St, *Sermones dominicales*, ed. J. G. Bougerol, Bibliotheca franciscana scholastica medii ævi, 27 (Grottaferrata, 1977).

Bonaventure, Pseudo-, *Ars concionandi*, ed. Patres Collegii a S. Bonaventura, Bonaventure, *Opera omnia* (15 vols., Quaracchi, 1882–1902), IX, pp. 8–21; tr. H. C. Hazel Jr., Ph.D. diss., Washington State University, 1972; summarised in Hazel, 'The Bonaventuran *Ars concionandi*', *Western Speech*, 36 (1972), 241–50.

Boncompagno da Signa, *Cedrus*, in Rockinger (ed.), *Briefsteller und Formelbücher*, pp. 121–7.

Palma, in S. Carl (ed.), *Aus Leben und Schriften des Magisters Boncompagno* (Freiburg-im-Breisgau and Leipzig, 1894), pp. 105–27.

Rhetorica novissima, ed. A.Gaudenzi, *Scripta anecdota antiquissimorum glossatorum*, Bibliotheca iuridica medii ævi, ed. G. Palmerio (Bologna, 1892), II, pp. 249–97.

Rota Veneris: A Facsimile Reproduction of the Strassburg Incunabulum with Introduction, Translation, and Notes, ed. J. Purkart (Delmar NY, 1975).

Bondi, John, of Aquilegia, *Practica sive usus dictaminis*, in Rockinger (ed.), *Briefsteller und Formelbücher*, pp. 956–66.

Bono da Lucca, *Cedrus libanus*, ed. G. Vecchi, Istituto di filologia romanza dell'Università di Roma, Testi e manuali, 46 (Modena, 1963).

Briggis, John, *Compilacio de arte dictandi*, in Camargo (ed.), *Rhetorics of Prose Composition*, pp. 88–104.

Brinton, Thomas, *Sermones*, ed. M. A. Devlin, *The Sermons of Thomas Brinton, Bishop of Rochester (1373–1389)*, Camden Third Series, 85–6 (2 vols., London, 1954).

Camargo, Martin (ed.), *Medieval Rhetorics of Prose Composition: Five English 'Artes Dictandi' and Their Tradition*, Medieval and Renaissance Texts and Studies, 115 (Binghamton NY, 1995).

Cartula (*De contemptu mundi*). See: Bernard, Pseudo-

Cassiodorus, *Expositio psalmorum*, ed. M. Adriaen, CCSL 97–8 (2 vols., Turnhout, 1958).

Institutiones, ed. R. A. B. Mynors (Oxford, 1937); tr. L. W. Jones, *An Introduction to Divine and Human Readings by Cassiodorus Senator* (New York, 1946).

Charland, T.-M. (ed.), *Artes praedicandi: contribution à l'histoire de la rhétorique au Moyen Âge* (Paris, 1936).

Chaucer, Geoffrey, *The Riverside Chaucer*, gen. ed. L. D. Benson (Boston MA, 1987).

Christine de Pizan, *The Epistle of Othea, translated from the French Text of Christine de Pisan by Stephen Scrope*, ed. G. L. Bühler, EETS OS 264 (London, 1937).

Cola di Rienzo, *Briefwechsel des Cola di Rienzo*, ed. K. Burdach and P. Piur, Vom Mittelalter zur Reformation: Forschungen zur Geschichte der deutschen Bildung, 2.4 (Berlin, 1912).

Compendium rhetoricae venustatis, ed. S. Dursza, *Filológiai közlöny*, 20 (1974), 299–305.

Dati, Agostino, *Senensis clarissimi oratoris atque philosophi de elegantia et de conficiendis epistolis* (Paris, 1508).

Deschamps, Eustache, *L'Art de dictier*, in *Œuvres complètes*, VII, ed. Marquis de Queux de Saint-Hilaire and C. Raynaud, SATF (Paris, 1891), pp. 266–92.

Diomedes, *Ars grammatica*, ed. H. Keil, *GL*, 4, 299–529.

Dominicus Dominici of Viseu, *Summa dictaminis secundum quod notarii episcoporum et archyepiscoporum debeant officium exercere*, in Rockinger (ed.), *Briefsteller und Formelbücher*, pp. 524–92.

Donatus, Aelius, *Ars grammatica (Ars minor, Ars maior)*, ed. L. Holtz, *Donat et la tradition de l'enseignement grammatical* (Paris, 1981); also ed. H. Keil, *GL*, 4, 353–402.

Les Douze dames de rhétorique, ed. and tr. C. Brown, *Allegorica*, 16 (1995), 73–105.

Dû bist mîn, ih bin dîn: Die lateinischen Liebes-(und Freundschafts-) Briefe des clm 19411: Abbildungen, Text und Übersetzung, ed. J. Kühnel, Litterae: Göppinger Beiträge zur Textgeschichte, 52 (Göppingen, 1977).

Dursza, S. (ed.), 'L'*ars dictaminis* di un maestro italiano del secolo XII', *Acta literaria academiae scientiarum Hungaricae* [Budapest], 12 (1970), 159–73.

Dybinus, Nicolaus, *Declaratorio oracionis de beata Dorothea*, ed. S. P. Jaffe, Beiträge zur Literatur des XV. bis XVIII. Jahrhunderts, 5 (Wiesbaden, 1974).

An Early Commentary on the 'Poetria nova' of Geoffrey of Vinsauf, ed. M. C. Woods (New York, 1985).

Eberhard the German (Everardus Alemannus), in Faral (ed.), *Les Arts poétiques*, pp. 336–77.

Évrard of Béthune, *Graecismus*, ed. J. Wrobel, Corpus grammaticorum medii ævi, 1 (Breslau, 1887).

Facetus (incipit: 'Cum nihil utilius'), in *Der deutsche Facetus*, ed. C. Schroeder, Palaestra 86 (Berlin, 1911).

Guido Faba, *Dictamina rhetorica*, ed. A. Gaudenzi, *Propugnatore*, n.s. 25 (1892), 1:86–129, 2:58–109.

Doctrina ad inveniendas incipiendas et formandas materias et ad ea que circa huiusmodi requiruntur, in Rockinger (ed.), *Briefsteller und Formelbücher*, pp. 185–96.

Epistole, ed. A. Gaudenzi, *Propugnatore*, n.s. 26 (1893), 1:359–90, 2:373–89.

Summa de vitiis et virtutibus, ed. V. Pini, *Quadrivium*, 1 (1956), 97–152.

Summa dictaminis, ed. A. Gaudenzi, *Propugnatore*, n.s. 3, 1 (1890), 287–328; 2 (1890), 345–93.

'Un trattato inedito di Guido Fava', ed. L. Chirico, *Biblion: Rivista di bibliofilia e di erudizione varia*, 1 (1946–7), 227–34.

Faral, Edmond (ed.), *Les Arts poétiques du XIIe et du XIIIe siècle*, Bibliothèque de l'École des hautes études, 238 (1923; rpt. Geneva, 1982).

The First Grammatical Treatise [Icelandic], ed. H. Benediktsson, University of Iceland Publications in Linguistics, 1 (Reykjavik, 1972).

Formularius de modo prosandi, in Rockinger (ed.), *Briefsteller und Formelbücher*, pp. 725–838.

Francigena, Henry, 'Die Briefmuster des Henricus Francigena', ed. B. Odebrecht, *Archiv für Urkundenforschung*, 14 (1936), 231–61.

Fulgentius, *Opera*, ed. R. Helm (Leipzig, 1898); tr. L. G. Whitbread, *Fulgentius the Mythographer* (Columbus OH, 1971).

Geoffrey of Vinsauf, *Documentum de modo et arte dictandi et versificandi*, ed. Faral, *Les Arts poétiques*, pp. 265–320; tr. R. P. Parr (Milwaukee WI, 1968), pp. 265–320.

Poetria nova, ed. Faral, *Les Arts poétiques*, pp. 15–93; tr. M. F. Nims (Toronto, 1967); also J. B. Kopp in Murphy (ed.), *Three Medieval Rhetorical Arts*, pp. 32–108; ed. and tr. E. Gallo, *The 'Poetria Nova' and its Sources in Early Rhetorical Doctrine* (The Hague, 1971).

Summa de arte dictandi, ed. V. Licitra, *Studi medievali*, 3rd ser. 7 (1966), 866–913.

Geraldus (or Girardus) de Piscario, *Ars faciendi sermones*, ed. F. M. Delorme, 'L'*Ars faciendi sermones* de Géraud du Pescher', *Antonianum*, 19 (1944), 169–98.

Gervase of Melkley, *Ars versificaria*, ed. H.-J. Gräbener as *Gervais von Melkley: Ars poetica*, Forschungen zur romanischen Philologie, 17 (Münster, 1965); tr. C. Yodice, 'Gervais of Melkley's Treatise on the Art of Versifying and the Method of Composing in Prose', Ph.D. diss., Rutgers University, 1973.

Giovanni del Virgilio, *Ars dictaminis*, ed. P. O. Kristeller, *Italia medioevale e umanistica*, 4 (1961), 181–200.

Giovanni di Bonandrea, *Ars dictaminis*, in J. Banker, 'Giovanni di Bonandrea's *Ars dictaminis* Treatise and the Doctrine of Invention in the Italian Rhetorical Tradition of the Thirteenth and Early Fourteenth Centuries', Ph.D. diss., University of Rochester, 1972.

Gundissalinus, Dominicus, *De divisione philosophiae*, ed. L. Baur, BGPM, Texte und Untersuchungen, 4, 2–3 (Munich, 1903).

Henri d'Andeli, *La Bataille des VII ars*, ed. and tr. L. J. Paetow, in *Two Medieval Satires on the University of Paris: 'La Bataille des VII ars' of Henri d'Andeli and the 'Morale scolarium' of John of Garland* (Berkeley CA, 1914), pp. 37–60.

Higden, Ralph, *Ars componendi sermones*, ed. M. Jennings, *The 'Ars componendi sermones' of Ranulph Higden, O.S.B.* (Leiden, 1991).

Honorius 'of Autun', *De animae exsilio et patria, alias de artibus*, PL 172, 1241–6.

De imagine mundi, PL 172, 115–88.

Philosophia mundi, PL 172, 39–102.

Hugh of Bologna, *Rationes dictandi prosaice*, in Rockinger (ed.), *Briefsteller und Formelbücher*, pp. 53–94.

Hugh of St Victor, *Didascalicon*, ed. G. H. Buttimer (Washington DC, 1939); tr. J. Taylor (New York, 1961).

De grammatica and *Epitome Dindimi in philosophiam*, ed. R. Baron, *Hugonis de Sancto Victore opera propaedeutica* (Notre Dame IN, 1966).

Hugutio of Pisa, *Magnae derivationes*. London, British Library, MS Add. 18380; Paris, Bibliothèque nationale de France, MS Lat. 15462. For excerpts see Riessner, *Die Magnae derivationes*.

Humbert of Romans, *De eruditione praedicatorum*, ed. J. J. Berthier, *B. Humberti de Romanis, De vita regulari* (Rome, 1888–9), II, pp. 373–484; tr. S. Tugwell, *Treatise on the Formation of Preachers*, in Tugwell (ed.), *Early Dominicans: Selected Writings* (Ramsey NJ and London, 1982), pp. 81–370.

Isidore of Seville, *Etymologiae sive origines*, ed. W. M. Lindsay (2 vols., Oxford, 1911).

Opera, PL 81–4.

Jacques of Dinant, *Summa dictaminis*, ed. E. Polak, Études de philologie et d'historie, 28 (Geneva, 1975).

John Balbus of Genoa, *Catholicon* (1460; rpt. Westmead, Hants., 1971).

John of Dacia, *Summa grammatica*, in *Johannis Daci opera*, ed. A. Otto, Corpus philosophorum danicorum medii ævi, 1 (Copenhagen, 1955).

John of Bologna, *Summa notarie*, in Rockinger (ed.), *Briefsteller und Formelbücher*, pp. 599–712.

John of Garland, *Clavis compendii* and *Compendium grammatice*. Cambridge, Gonville and Gaius College, MSS 385/605, 593/453, 136/76; Bruges, Bibliothèque publique, MS 546.

Compendium gramatice, ed. T. Haye (Cologne, 1995).

Dictionarius, pr. in facs. and tr. B. B. Rubin (Lawrence KA, 1981).

Integumenta on Ovid's *Metamorphoses*, ed. L. K. Born, Ph.D. diss., University of Chicago, 1927; also ed. F. Ghisalberti, *Integumenta Ovidii: poematto inedito de seculo XII* (Messina, 1933).

Multo[rum] vocabulo[rum] equiuoco[rum] interpretatio (London, [1514]).

Parisiana poetria, ed. and tr. T. Lawler (New Haven CT and London, 1974).

Synonyma (London, [1502]).

John of La Rochelle, *Processus negociandi themata sermonum*, ed. G. Cantini, 'Processus negociandi themata sermonum di Giovanni della Rochella O.F.M.', *Antonianum*, 26 (1951), 247–70.

John of Limoges, *Libellus de dictamine et dictatorio syllogismorum*, ed. C. Horváth, *Johannis lemovicensis opera omnia* (3 vols., Veszprém, 1932), I, pp. 1–69.

John of Salisbury, *Metalogicon*, ed. G. G. J. Webb (Oxford, 1929); tr. D. D. McGarry (Berkeley CA, 1955).

Policraticus, ed. G. G. J. Webb (Oxford, 1909); tr. in part by C. J. Nederman (Cambridge, 1990).

Juan Gil de Zamora, *Dictaminis epithalamium*, ed. C. Faulhaber, Biblioteca degli studi mediolatini e volgari, n.s. 2 (Pisa, 1978).

Julian of Toledo, *Ars grammatica*, ed. M. A. H. Maestra Yenes (Toledo, 1973).

Kilwardby, Robert, *De ortu scientiarum*, ed. A. G. Judy (Oxford, 1976).

Tractatus super Priscianum maiorem. Selections ed. by K. M. Fredborg *et al.*, 'The Commentary on *Priscianus Maior* ascribed to Robert Kilwardby', *CIMAGL*, 15 (Copenhagen, 1975).

Konrad of Mure, *Summa de arte prosandi*, in Rockinger (ed.), *Briefsteller und Formelbücher*, pp. 417–82.

Landino, Cristoforo, *Formulario di epistole volgare, missive, e responsive e altri fiori di ornati parliamenti* (Milan, 1500).

Las Leys d'Amors, ed. J. Anglade (4 vols., Toulouse, 1919–20).

Latini, Brunetto, *Li Livres dou tresor*, ed. F. J. Carmody, University of California Publications in Modern Philology, 22 (Berkeley CA, 1948).

Il Tesoro, ed. P. Chabaille (4 vols., Bologna, 1878).

Laurence of Aquilegia, *Practica dictaminis*, ed. S. Capdevila, *Analecta sacra tarraconensia*, 6 (1930), 207–29.

Lipsius, Justus, *Conscribendis latine epistolis* (Magdeburg, 1594).

Ludolf of Hildesheim, *Summa dictaminum*, in Rockinger (ed.), *Briefsteller und Formelbücher*, pp. 359–400.

Maccagnolo, Enzo (ed.), *Il Divino e il megacosmo: Testi filosofici e scientifici della scuola di Chartres: Teodorico di Chartres, Guglielmo di Conches, Bernardo Silvestre* (Milan, 1980).

Marbod of Rennes, *De ornamentis verborum*, PL 171, 1687–92; also ed. R. Leotta (Florence, 1998).

Martianus Capella, *De nuptiis Philologiae et Mercurii*, ed. J. Willis (Leipzig, 1983); tr. W. H. Stahl *et al.*, *Martianus Capella and the Seven Liberal Arts* (2 vols., New York, 1971–7).

Martin of Cordova, *Ars praedicandi*, ed. F. Rubio, '*Ars praedicandi* de Fray Martin de Cordoba', *La Ciudad de Dios*, 172 (1959), 327–48.

Martin of Dacia, *Opera*, ed. H. Roos, Corpus philosophorum danicorum medii ævi, 2 (Copenhagen, 1961).

Matthew of Vendôme, *Ars versificatoria*, in Faral (ed.), *Les Arts poétiques*, pp. 109–93; also in *Opera*, ed. F. Munari (3 vols., Rome 1977–88), III. Tr. A. E. Galyon (Ames IA, 1980); also tr. R. P. Parr (Milwaukee WI, 1981).

In Tobiam paraphrasis metrica, in *Opera*, ed. Munari, II, pp. 159–255.

Merke, Thomas, *Formula moderni et usitati dictaminis*, in Camargo (ed.), *Rhetorics of Prose Composition*, pp. 122–47.

Middle English Sermons, ed. W. O. Ross, EETS OS 209 (London, 1940).

Miller, J. M., Prosser, M. H., and Benson, T. W. (eds.), *Readings in Medieval Rhetoric* (Bloomington IN and London, 1973).

Murphy, J. J. (ed.), *Three Medieval Rhetorical Arts* (Berkeley CA, 1971).

Onulf of Speyer, *Colores rhetorici*, ed. W. Wattenbach, 'Magister Onulf von Speier', *Sitzungsberichte der königlichen preussischen Akademie der Wissenschaften zu Berlin*, 20 (1894), 361–86.

Pantin, William A. (ed.), 'A Medieval Treatise on Letter-writing with Examples from the Rylands Latin MS 394', *Bulletin of the John Rylands Library*, 13 (1929), 326–82.

Papias, *Ars grammatica*, ed. R. Cervani (Bologna, 1998).

Vocabulista (Elementarium) (Venice, 1469; rpt. Turin, 1966).

Patience, ed. J. J. Anderson (Manchester, 1969).

The 'Pearl' Poems: An Omnibus Edition, ed. W. Vantuono (2 vols., New York, 1984).

Paul of Camadoli, *Introductiones dictandi*, ed. V. Sivo, Studi e ricerche dell'Istituto di Latino, 3 (Genoa, 1980), pp. 69–100.

Perottus, Nicolaus, *Rudimenta grammatices* (Rome, 1473).

Peter Helias, *Summa super Priscianum*, ed. J. E. Tolson, intro. M. Gibson, *CIMAGL*, 27–8 (Copenhagen, 1978), 1–210; also ed. L. Reilly (2 vols., Turnhout, 1993).

[Peter of Blois], *Libellus de arte dictandi rhetorice*, in Camargo (ed.), *Rhetorics of Prose Composition*, pp. 45–87.

Pons of Provence, in C. Fierville, *Une Grammaire latine inédite du XIIIe siècle* (Paris, 1886).

Precepta prosaici dictaminis secundum Tullium, ed. F.-J. Schmale (Bonn, 1950).

Priscian, *Institutio de nomine et pronomine et verbo*, ed. M. Passalacqua, Testi grammaticali latini, 2 (Urbino, 1992).

Institutiones grammaticae, ed. M. Hertz in H. Keil, *GL*, 2, 1–597, and 3, pp. 1–384.

Opuscula, ed. M. Passalacqua (2 vols., Rome, 1987–99).

Quintilian, *Institutio oratoria*, ed. and tr. as *The Orator's Education* by D. A. Russell (5 vols., Cambridge, MA and London, 2001).

Rabanus Maurus, *De clericorum institutione*, PL 107, 297–420.

Raimbaut d'Aurenga, *The Life and Works of the Troubadour Raimbaut d'Orange*, ed. W. T. Pattison (Minneapolis MN, 1952).

Ralph of Beauvais, *Glose super Donatum*, ed. C. H. Kneepkens (Nijmegen, 1982).

Regina sedens rhetorica, in Camargo (ed.), *Rhetorics of Prose Composition*, pp. 176–219.

Remigius of Auxerre, *Commentarius in Boetii consolationem philosophiae* (extracts), ed. E. T. Silk, Papers and Monographs of the American Academy in Rome, 9 (Rome, 1935), pp. 312–43.

Commentarius in Disticha Catonis, ed. A. Mancini, Rendiconti della Reale Accademia dei Lincei, 5th ser. 11 (1902), 175–98, 369–82.

Commentarius in Phocam, ed. M. Manitius, *Didaskaleion*, 2 (1913), 74–88.

Commentarius in Prisciani institutionem de nomine, ed. M. de Marco, *Aevum*, 26 (1952), 503–17.

Commentum in Donati artem maiorem, ed. H. Hagen, *GL* Suppl. (vol. 8), pp. 219–66, and J. P. Elder, 'The Missing Portions of the *Commentum Einsidlense* on Donatus's Ars Grammatica', *Harvard Studies in Classical Philology*, 56 (1947), 129–60.

Commentum in Donati artem minorem, ed. W. Fox (Leipzig, 1902).

Commentum in Martianum Capellam, Libri I–II, ed. C. E. Lutz (Leiden, 1962).

Glosses on Bede, *De arte metrica*, ed. M. H. King, *Bedae opera didascalica*, CCSL 123A (Turnhout, 1975), pp. 82–171.

Glosses on Prudentius, ed. J. M. Burnam, *Commentaire anonyme sur Prudence d'après le manuscrit 413 de Valenciennes* (Paris, 1910).

Glosses on Sedulius, *Carmen paschale*, in Sedulius, *Opera omnia*, ed. Huemer, pp. 316–59.

Richard of Pophis, ed. E. Batzer, 'Zur Kenntnis der Formularsammlung des Richard von Pofi', *Heidelberger Abhandlungen zur mittleren und neueren Geschichte*, 28 (1910), 1–149.

Richard of Thetford, *Ars dilatandi sermones*, ed. and tr. G. J. Engelhardt, 'A Treatise on the Eight Modes of Dilatation', *Allegorica*, 3 (1978), 77–160.

Robert of Basevorn, *Forma praedicandi*, ed. Charland, *Artes praedicandi*, pp. 233–323; tr. L. Krul in Murphy, *Three Medieval Rhetorical Arts*, pp. 114–215.

Rockinger, Ludwig (ed.), *Briefsteller und Formelbücher des 11. bis 14. Jahrhunderts*, Quellen und Erörterungen zur bayerischen und deutschen Geschichte, 9 (2 vols., 1863; rpt. New York, 1961).

Ruiz, Juan, *Libro de buen amor*, ed. G. B. Gybbon-Monypenny (Madrid, 1988).

Sampson, Thomas, *Modus dictandi*, in Camargo (ed.), *Rhetorics of Prose Composition*, pp. 154–68.

Sedulius, *Opera omnia*, ed. J. Huemer, CSEL 10 (Vienna, 1885).

Sedulius Scottus, *In Donati Artem Maiorem*, ed. B. Löfstedt, CCCM (Turnhout, 1977).

Sergius, *In Artem Donati*, ed. H. Keil, GL, 4, 475–565.

Servius, *In Artem Donati*, ed. H. Keil, GL, 4, 404–48.

In Vergilii carmina commentarii, ed. G. Thilo and H. Hagen (2 vols., Leipzig, 1923).

Siger of Courtrai, *Summa modorum significandi*, ed. J. Pinborg (Amsterdam, 1977).

Siguinus, Magister, *Ars lectoria*, ed. J. Engels, C. H. Kneepkens and H. F. Reijnders (Leiden, 1979).

Simon, Master, *Notabilia super summa de arte dictandi*, in Rockinger (ed.), *Briefsteller und Formelbücher*, pp. 973–84.

Simon of Dacia, *Opera*, ed. A. Otto, Corpus philosophorum danicorum medii ævi, 3 (Copenhagen, 1963).

Le Stile et manière de composer, dicter, et escrire toute sorte d'epistres, ou lettres missives, tant par réponse que autrement, avec epitome de la poinctuation françoise (Lyon, 1555?).

Summa de arte prosandi, in Rockinger (ed.), *Briefsteller und Formelbücher*, pp. 209–346.

Summa de ordine et processu iudicii spiritualis, in Rockinger (ed.), *Briefsteller und Formelbücher*, pp. 993–1026.

A Thirteenth-Century Anthology of Rhetorical Poems: Glasgow MS Hunterian V.8.14, ed. B. Harbert (Toronto, 1975).

Thobiadis. See: Matthew of Vendôme

Thomas of Capua, *Ars dictandi*, ed. E. Heller, Sitzungsberichte der Heidelberger Akademie der Wissenschaften, philosophisch-historische Klasse, 1928–9, 4 (Heidelberg, 1929).

Thomas of Chobham, *Summa de arte praedicandi*, ed. F. Morenzoni, CCCM 82 (Turnhout, 1988).

Thomas of Erfurt, *Grammatica speculativa*, ed. and tr. G. L. Bursill-Hall (London, 1972).

Thomson, Ian, and Perraud, Louis (tr.), *Ten Latin Schooltexts of the Later Middle Ages* (Lewiston ME and Queenston, 1990).

Three Middle English Sermons from the Worcester Chapter Manuscript F.10, ed. D. M. Grisdale (Leeds, 1939).

Tommasino of Armannino, *Microcosmus*, ed. G. Bertoni, *Archivum romanicum*, 5 (1921), 19–28.

Transmundus, *Introductiones dictandi*, ed. A. Dalzell (Toronto, 1995).

Il Trattatello di colori rettorici, ed. A. Scolari, 'Un volgarizzamento trecentesco della *Rhetorica ad Herennium*', *Medioevo romanzo*, 9 (1984), 215–266.

I trattati medievali di ritmica latina, ed. G. Mari, *Memorie del reale Istituto lombardo di science e lettere*, 20 (Milan, 1899).

Ventura da Bergamo, *Brevis doctrina dictaminis*, ed. D. Thomson and J. J. Murphy, *Studi medievali*, 3rd ser. 23 (1982), 361–86.

Vergilius Maro Grammaticus, *Epitomi ed Epistole*, ed. G. Polara (Naples, 1979).

Victorinus, Marius, *Ars grammatica*, ed. H. Keil, *GL*, 6, 3–184.

Victorinus, Maximus, *Ars grammatica*, ed. H. Keil, *GL*, 6, 187–242.

Vincent of Beauvais, *Speculum quadruplex sive Speculum maius* (1624; rpt. Graz, 1965).

Waleys, Thomas, *De modo componendi sermones*, ed. Charland, *Artes praedicandi*, pp. 327–403; tr. D. E. Grosser, M.A. diss., Cornell University, 1949.

William of Auvergne, *Ars praedicandi*, ed. A. de Poorter, 'Un manuel de prédication médiévale: Le ms. 97 de Bruges', *Revue néo-scolastique de philosophie*, 25 (1923), 192–209.

William of Conches, *Glose super Priscianum*. Paris, Bibliothèque nationale de France, MS Lat. 15130; Florence, Medicea-Laurenziana, MS San Marco 310.

William of Ockham, *Summa Logicae, pars prima, pars secunda, tertiae prima*, ed. P. Boehner (2 vols., St Bonaventure NY, 1951–4); partially tr. M. J. Loux, *Ockham's Theory of Terms: Part I of the 'Summa logicae'* (Notre Dame IN, 1974).

Zöllner, Walter (ed.), 'Die Halberstädter *Ars Dictandi* aus den Jahren 1193–94', *Wissenschaftliche Zeitschrift der Halberstadter Universität*, 13 (1964), 159–73.

Secondary sources

Alessio, Gian Carlo, 'Brunetto Latini e Cicerone (e i dettatori)', *Italia medioevale e umanistica*, 22 (1979), 123–63.

Alford, John A., 'The Grammatical Metaphor: A Survey of its Use in the Middle Ages', *Speculum*, 57 (1982), 728–60.

'The Role of the Quotations in *Piers Plowman*', *Speculum*, 52 (1977), 80–99.

Allen, Judson B., *The Ethical Poetic of the Later Middle Ages: A Decorum of Convenient Distinction* (Toronto, 1982).

The Friar as Critic (Nashville TN, 1971).

Anderson, J. J., 'The Prologue of *Patience*', *MP*, 63 (1966), 283–7.

Anhorn, Judy Schaaf, '*Sermo Poematis*: Homiletic Tradition of *Purity* and *Piers Plowman*', Ph.D. diss., Yale University, 1976.

Arbusow, Leonid, *Colores rhetorici: Eine Auswahl rhetorischer Figuren und Gemeinplätze als Hilfsmittel für akademische übungen an mittelalterlichen Texten* (Göttingen, 1948).

Arts libéraux et philosophie au Moyen Âge: Actes du quatrième congrès international de philosophie médiévale (Montreal, 1969).

Astell, Ann, 'Cassiodorus' *Commentary on the Psalms* as an *Ars rhetorica*', *Rhetorica*, 17 (1999), 37–75.

Auvray, Lucien, 'Documents orléanais du XIIe et du XIIIe siècle: Extraits du formulaire de Bernard de Meung', *Mémoires de la société archéologique et historique de l'Orléanais*, 23 (1892), 393–413.

Baerwald, Herman, *Das Baumgartenberger Formelbuch: Eine Quelle zur Geschichte des XIII. Jahrhunderts vornehmlich der Zeiten Rudolfs von Habsburg*, Fontes rerum austriacarum, Abt. 2, 25 (Vienna, 1866).

Bagliani, Agostino Paravicini, 'Eine Briefsammlung für Rektoren des Kirchenstaates (1250–1320)', *Deutsches Archiv für Erforschung des Mittelalters*, 35 (1979), 138–208.

Bagni, Paolo, *La costituzione della poesia nelle artes del XII–XIII secolo*, Università degli Studi di Bologna facolta di lettere e filosofia: Studi e ricerche, n.s. 20 (Bologna, 1968).

Baldwin, John W., *Masters, Princes, and Merchants: The Social Views of Peter the Chanter and his Circle* (2 vols., Princeton NJ, 1970).

Bataillon, Louis Jacques, 'De la *lectio* à la *predicatio*: Commentaires bibliques et sermons au XIIIe siècle', *Revue des sciences philosophiques et théologiques*, 70 (1986), 559–75.

Benson, Robert L., et al. (eds.), *Renaissance and Renewal in the Twelfth Century* (Cambridge MA, 1982).

Bériou, Nicole,'La Prédication au béguinage de Paris pendant l'année liturgique 1272–1273', *Recherches augustiniennes*, 13(1978), 105–229.

Beyer, Heinz-Jurgen, 'Die Frühphase der *ars dictandi*', *Studi medievali*, 3rd ser. 18 (1977), 19–43.

Bloomfield, Morton W., '*Patience* and the *Mashal*', in J. B. Bessinger Jr. and R. R. Raymo (eds.), *Medieval Studies in Honor of L. H. Hornstein* (New York, 1976), pp. 41–9.

Bonaventure, Brother, 'The Teaching of Latin in Later Medieval England', *MS*, 23 (1961), 1–20.

Brearley, Denis G., 'A Bibliography of Recent Publications Concerning the History of Grammar During the Carolingian Renaissance', *Studi medievali*, 3rd ser. 21 (1980), 917–23.

Bremond, C., LeGoff, J., and Schmitt, J.-C., *L'Exemplum*, Typologie des sources du Moyen Âge occidental, 40 (Turnhout, 1982).

Bresslau, Harry, *Handbuch der Urkundenlehre für Deutschland und Italien* (4th edn, 2 vols., Berlin, 1968–9).

Briscoe, Marianne G., *Artes praedicandi*, Typologie des sources du Moyen Âge occidental, 61 (Turnhout, 1992).

'Preaching and Medieval English Drama', in M. G. Briscoe and J. C. Coldewey (eds.), *Contexts for Early English Drama* (Bloomington IN, 1989), pp. 150–72.

Brown, C., 'Du nouveau sur la "mystere" des *Douze Dames de Rhetorique*: Le role de Georges Chastellain', *Bulletin de la Commission Royale d'Histoire*, 153 (1987), 181–225.

Brown, Carleton (ed.), *The Pardoner's Tale* (Oxford, 1935).

Bultot, Robert, '*Grammatica, Ethica* et *Contemptus mundi* aux XIIe et XIIIe siècles', in *Arts libéraux*, pp. 815–27.

Burke, James F., 'The *Libro del cavallero Zifar* and the Medieval Sermon', *Viator*, 1 (1970), 207–21.

Bursill-Hall, G. L., 'Johannes de Garlandia – Forgotten Grammarian and the Manuscript Tradition', *Hist. Ling.*, 3 (1976), 155–77.

'Medieval Donatus Commentaries', in *Hist. Ling.*, 8 (1981), 69–97.

Speculative Grammars of the Middle Ages (The Hague, 1971).

'Teaching Grammars of the Middle Ages: Notes on the Manuscript Tradition', *Hist. Ling.*, 4 (1977), 1–29.

'The Middle Ages', *Current Trends in Linguistics*, 13 (1975), 179–230.

'Towards a History of Linguistics in the Middle Ages, 1100–1450', in D. Hymes (ed.), *Studies in the History of Linguistics* (Bloomington IN, 1972), pp. 77–92.

Camargo, Martin, *Ars dictaminis, ars dictandi*, Typologie des sources du Moyen Âge occidental, 60 (Turnhout, 1991).

The Middle English Verse Love Epistle, Studien zur englischen Philologie, n.F. 28 (Tübingen, 1991).

'Toward a Comprehensive Art of Written Discourse: Geoffrey of Vinsauf and the *Ars dictaminis*', *Rhetorica*, 6 (1988), 167–94.

'*Tria sunt*: The Long and the Short of Geoffrey of Vinsauf's *Documentum de modo et arte dictandi et versificandi*', *Speculum*, 74 (1999), 935–55.

Caplan, Harry, 'Classical Rhetoric and the Mediaeval Theory of Preaching', *CP*, 28 (1933), 73–96.

'The Four Senses of Scriptural Interpretation and the Mediaeval Theory of Preaching', *Speculum*, 4 (1929), 282–90.

'A Late-Mediaeval Tractate on Preaching', in *Studies in Rhetoric and Public Speaking in Honor of James A. Winans* (New York, 1925), pp. 61–90.

Mediaeval 'artes praedicandi': A Hand-List, Cornell Studies in Classical Philology, 24 (Ithaca NY, 1934).

Mediaeval 'artes praedicandi': A Supplementary Hand-List, Cornell Studies in Classical Philology, 25 (Ithaca NY, 1936).

Of Eloquence: Studies in Ancient and Mediaeval Rhetoric, ed. A. King and H. North (Ithaca NY, 1970). [A collection of the essays listed here as published 1927–33.]

'Rhetorical Invention in Some Mediaeval Tractates on Preaching', *Speculum*, 2 (1927), 284–95.

Capua, Francesco di, *Fonti ed esempi per lo studio dello 'stilus curiae romanae' medioevale*, Testi medievali, 3 (Rome, 1941).

Scritti minori (2 vols., Rome, 1959).

Cartellieri, Alexander, *Ein Donaueschinger Briefsteller: Lateinische Stilübungen des XII. Jahrhunderts aus der Orléans'schen Schule* (Innsbruck, 1898).

Chance, Jane, 'Allegory and Structure in *Pearl*: The Four Senses of the *ars praedi-candi* and Fourteenth-Century Homiletic Poetry', in R. J. Blanch, M. Y. Miller and J. N. Wasserman (eds.), *Text and Matter: New Critical Perspectives of the Pearl-Poet* (Troy NY, 1991), pp. 33–59.

Chapman, C. O., 'Chaucer on Preachers and Preaching', *PMLA*, 44 (1928), 178–85.

'The Pardoner's Tale: A Medieval Sermon', *MLN*, 41 (1926), 506–9.

'The Parson's Tale: A Medieval Sermon', *MLN*, 42 (1927), 229–34.

Chapman, Janet A., 'Juan Ruiz's "Learned Sermon"', in Gybbon-Monypenny (ed.), *'Libro de buen amor' Studies*, pp. 29–51.

Chenu, M.-D., 'Auctor, actor, autor', *Archivum latinitatis medii ævi (Bulletin du Cange)*, 3 (1927), 81–6.

'Grammaire et théologie au XIIe et XIII siècles', *AHDLMA*, 10–11 (1935–6), 5–28; rpt. in Chenu, *Théologie au douzieme siècle*, pp. 90–107.

La Théologie au douzieme siècle (Paris, 1957).

Clark, Albert C., *The Cursus in Mediaeval and Vulgar Latin* (Oxford, 1910).

Fontes prosae numerosae (Oxford, 1909).

Prose Rhythm in English (Oxford, 1913).

Clark, Donald L., *John Milton at St Paul's School* (New York, 1948).

Clogan, Paul M., 'Literary Genres in a Medieval Textbook', *M&H*, n.s. 11 (1982), 199–209.

Colish, Marcia L., *The Mirror of Knowledge: A Study in the Medieval Theory of Knowledge* (rev. edn, Lincoln NA, 1983).

Constable, Giles, *Letters and Letter-Collections*, Typologie des sources du Moyen Âge occidental, 17 (Turnhout, 1976).

Coulter, Cornelia G., 'Boccaccio's Knowledge of Quintilian', *Speculum*, 33 (1958), 490–6.

Covington, M. A., *Syntactic Theory in the High Middle Ages: Modistic Models of Sentence Structure* (Cambridge, 1984).

d'Alverny, Marie-Thérèse, 'La Sagesse et ses sept filles: Recherches sur les allégories de la philosophie et des arts libéraux du IXe au XIIe siècle', in *Mélanges dédiées à la mémoire de Félix Grat* (2 vols., Paris, 1946–9), I, pp. 245–78.

Dalzell, Ann, 'The *Forma dictandi* attributed to Alberto of Morra and Related Texts', *MS*, 39 (1977), 440–65.

Davy, M. M., *Les Sermons universitaires parisiens de 1230–1231: Contribution à l'histoire de la prédication médiévale*, Études de philosophie médiévale, 15 (Paris, 1931).

De Rijk, L. M., *Logica modernorum: A Contribution to the History of Early Terminist Logic* (2 vols., Assen, 1962–7).

Delcorno, Carlo, 'Origini della predicazione francescana', in *Francesco d'Assisi e Francescanesimo dal 1216 al 1226: Atti del IV Convegno Internazionale, Assisi 1976* (Assisi, 1977), pp. 127–60.

'Rassegna di studi sulla predicazione medievale e umanistica (1970–1980)', *Lettere italiane*, 33 (1981), 235–76.

Delhaye, Philippe, '"Grammatica" et "Ethica" au XIIe siècle', *RTAM*, 25 (1958), 59–110.

'L'Organisation scolaire au XIIe siècle', *Traditio*, 5 (1947), 211–68.

Delisle, Léopold, 'Le Formulaire de Tréguier et les écoliers bretons des écoles d'Orléans au commencement du XIVe siècle', *Mémoires de la société archéologique et historique de l'Orléans*, 23 (1892), 41–64.

'Des Recueils épistolaires de Bérard de Naples', *Notices et extraits*, 27 (1879), 87–149.

'Notice sur une *Summa dictaminis* jadis conservée à Beauvais', *Notices et extraits*, 36 (1899), 171–205.

Denholm-Young, Noel, 'The *Cursus* in England', in Denholm-Young, *Collected Papers* (Cardiff, 1969), pp. 42–73.

Deyermond, Alan D., 'The Sermon and its Use in Medieval Castilian Literature', *La Corónica*, 8 (1980), 127–45.

'Some Aspects of Parody in the *Libro de buen amor*', in Gybbon-Monypenny (ed.), '*Libro de buen amor*' *Studies*, pp. 53–78.

Dörrie, Heinrich, *Der heroische Brief: Bestandsaufnahme, Geschichte, Kritik einer humanistisch-barocken Literaturgattung* (Berlin, 1968).

Erdmann, Carl, '*Leonitas*: Zur mittelalterlichen Lehre von Kursus, Rhythmus und Reim', in *Corona quernea: Festgabe Karl Strecker zum 80. Geburtstage darge-bracht*, Schriften des Reichsinstituts für ältere deutsche Geschichtskunde, MGH, 6 (1941; rpt. Stuttgart, 1952).

Evans, G. R., *Alan of Lille: The Frontiers of Theology in the Later Twelfth Century* (Cambridge, 1983).

'The Place of Peter the Chanter's *De tropis loquendi*', *Analecta cisterciensia*, 39 (1983), 231–53.

'St. Anselm's Technical Terms of Grammar', *Latomus*, 38 (1979), 413–21.

Faulhaber, Charles B., 'Las retóricas clásicas y medievales en bibliotecas castel-lanas', *Abaco*, 4 (1973), 151–300.

'Las retóricas hispanolatinas medievales siglos XII–XIII', in *Repertorio de his-toria de las ciencias eclesiásticas en España*, 7 (1979), 11–94.

Fisher, John H., 'Chancery Standard and Modern Written English', *Journal of the Society of Archivists*, 6 (1979), 136–44.

Fleming, John V., 'Hoccleve's "Letter of Cupid" and the "Quarrel" over the *Roman de la Rose*', *MÆ*, 40 (1971), 21–40.

Fletcher, Alan J., 'The Preaching of the Pardoner', *SAC*, 11 (1989), 15–35.

Forti, Fiorenzo, 'La *transumptio* nei dettatori bolognesi e in Dante', in *Dante e Bologna nei tempi di Dante* (Bologna, 1967), pp. 127–49.

Fredborg, K. M., 'The Commentaries on Cicero's *De inventione* and *Rhetorica ad Herennium* by William of Champeaux', *CIMAGL*, 17 (1976), 1–69.

'The Commentary of Thierry of Chartres on Cicero's *De inventione*', *CIMAGL*, 7 (1971), 225–60.

'The Dependence of Petrus Helias' *Summa Super Priscianum* on William of Conches' *Glose super Priscianum*', *CIMAGL*, 11 (1973), 1–57.

'Petrus Helias on Rhetoric', *CIMAGL*, 13 (1974), 31–41.

'Some Notes on the Grammar of William of Conches', *CIMAGL*, 37 (1981), 21–44.

'*Tractatus Glosarum Prisciani* in MS Vat. Lat. 1486', *CIMAGL*, 21 (1977), 21–44.

'Universal Grammar according to some Twelfth-Century Grammarians', in K. Koerner, H.-J. Niederehe and R. H. Robins (eds.), *Studies in Medieval Linguistic Thought Dedicated to G. L. Bursill-Hall* (Amsterdam, 1980), pp. 69–84.

Friis-Jensen, Karsten, 'The *Ars poetriae* in Twelfth-Century France: The Horace of Matthew of Vendôme, Geoffrey of Vinsauf, and John of Garland', *CIMAGL*, 60 (1990), 319–88.

Gallick, Susan, '*Artes Praedicandi*: Early Printed Editions', *MS*, 39 (1977), 477–89.

'The Continuity of the Rhetorical Tradition: Manuscript to incunabulum', *Manuscripta*, 23 (1979), 31–47.

'A Look at Chaucer and his Preachers', *Speculum*, 50 (1975), 456–76.

Gaudenzi, Augusto, 'Sulla cronologia delle opere dei dettatori Bolognesi da Buoncompagno a Bene di Lucca', *Bullettino dell'Istituto storico italiano*, 14 (1895), 85–174.

Gehl, Paul F., 'From Monastic Rhetoric to *Ars dictaminis*: Traditionalism and Innovation in the Schools of Twelfth-Century Italy', *The American Benedictine Review*, 34 (1983), 33–47.

A Moral Art: Grammar, Society and Culture in Trecento Florence (Ithaca NY, 1993).

Ghellinck, Joseph de, *L'Essor de la littérature latine au XIIe siècle* (2 vols., Brussels and Paris, 1946).

Gibson, Margaret, 'The Collected Works of Priscian: The Printed Editions, 1470–1859', *Studi medievali*, 3rd ser. 18 (1977), 249–60.

'The Early Scholastic *Glosule* to Priscian, *Institutiones grammaticae*: The Text and its Influence', *Studi medievali*, 3rd ser. 20 (1979), 235–54.

Gilson, Étienne, 'Michel Menot et la technique du sermon médiéval', in *Les idées et les lettres* (Paris, 1932), pp. 93–154.

Glauche, Günter, *Schullektüre im Mittelalter: Entstehung und Wandlungen des Lektürekanons bis 1200 nach den Quellen dargestellt*, Münchener Beiträge zur Mediävistik und Renaissance-Forschung, 5 (Munich, 1970).

Grabmann, M., *Die Geschichte der scholastischen Methode* (2 vols., Basel, 1961).

'Die Kommentar des seligen Jordanus von Sachsen zum *Priscianus minor*', in *Mittelalterliches Geistesleben* III (Munich, 1959), pp. 232–42.

Grondeux, Anne, *Le 'Graecismus' d'Évrard de Béthune à travers ses gloses: entre grammaire positive et grammaire spéculative du XIIIe au XVe siècle*, Studia artistarum: Études sur la Faculté des arts dans les universités médiévales, 8 (Turnhout, 2000).

Gybbon-Monypenny, G. B. (ed.), '*Libro de buen amor*' *Studies* (London, 1970).

Haskins, Charles H., 'Early Bolognese Formulary', in *Mélanges d'historie offerts à Henri Pirenne* (Brussels, 1926), pp. 201–10.

'Italian Master Bernard', in H. W. C. Davis (ed.), *Essays in History Presented to Reginald Lane Poole* (Oxford, 1927), pp. 21–6.

'The Life of Medieval Students as Illustrated by Their Letters', in Haskins, *Studies in Mediaeval Culture*, pp. 1–35.

Studies in Mediaeval Culture (Oxford, 1929).

Hendley, Brian P., 'John of Salisbury's Defense of the Trivium', in *Arts libéraux*, pp. 753–62.

Herman, Gerald, 'Henri d'Andeli's Epic Parody: *La bataille des sept ars*', *Annuale medievale*, 18 (1977), 54–64.

Hilary, Christine Ryan, Notes on the *Pardoner's Tale*, in *The Riverside Chaucer*, gen. ed. L. D. Benson (Boston MA, 1987), pp. 901–10.

Hilke, Alfons, 'Die anglonormannische Kompilation didaktisch-epischen Inhalts der Hs. Bibl. nat. nouv. acq. fr. 7517', *Zeitschrift für französische Sprache und Literatur*, 47 (1925), 423–54.

Hill, Ordelle G., 'The Audience of *Patience*', MP, 66 (1968), 103–9.

Holtz, Louis, *Donat et la tradition de l'enseignement grammatical: Étude sur l'Ars Donati et sa diffusion, IVe–IXe siècles, et édition critique* (Paris, 1981).

'Irish Grammarians and the Continent in the Seventh Century', in *Columbanus and Merovingian Monasticism*, ed. H. B. Clarke and M. Brennan (Oxford, 1981), pp. 135–52.

Holtzmann, Walther, 'Eine oberitalienische *Ars dictandi* und die Briefsammlung des Priors Peter von St. Jean in Sens', *Neues Archiv*, 46 (1926), 34–52.

Hunt, R. W., *The History of Grammar in the Middle Ages: Collected Papers*, ed. G. L. Bursill-Hall (Amsterdam, 1980).

'The Introductions to the *Artes* in the Twelfth Century', *Studia mediaevalia in honorem admodum Reverendi Patris Raymundi Josephi Martin* (Bruges, 1948), pp. 85–112; rpt. in Hunt, *History of Grammar*, pp. 117–44.

'Oxford Grammar Masters in the Middle Ages', in *Oxford Studies Presented to Daniel Callus*, Oxford Historical Society, n.s. 16 (Oxford, 1964), pp. 163–93; rpt. in Hunt, *History of Grammar*, pp. 167–97.

The Schools and the Cloister: The Life and Writings of Alexander Nequam (1157–1217), ed. and rev. M. Gibson (Oxford, 1984).

'Studies on Priscian in the Eleventh and Twelfth Centuries, 1: Petrus Helias and his Predecessors', *Medieval and Renaissance Studies*, 1 (1941–3), 194–231; rpt. in Hunt, *History of Grammar*, pp. 1–38.

'Studies on Priscian in the Twelfth Century, II: The School of Ralph of Beauvais', *Medieval and Renaissance Studies* 2 (1950), 1–56; rpt. in Hunt, *History of Grammar*, pp. 39–94.

Hunt, Tony, *Teaching and Learning Latin in Thirteenth-Century England* (3 vols., Cambridge, 1991).

Huntsman, Jeffrey F., 'Grammar', in D. L. Wagner (ed.), *The Seven Liberal Arts in the Middle Ages* (Bloomington IN, 1983), pp. 58–95.

Irvine, Martin, 'Bede the Grammarian and the Scope of Grammatical Studies in Eighth-Century Northumbria', *Anglo-Saxon England*, 15 (1986), 15–44.

'A Guide to the Sources of the Medieval Theories of Interpretation, Signs, and the Arts of Discourse: Aristotle to Ockham', *Semiotica*, 63 (1987), 89–108.

'Interpretation and the Semiotics of Allegory in the Works of Clement of Alexandria, Origen, and Augustine', *Semiotica*, 63 (1987), 33–71.

The Making of Textual Culture: 'Grammatica' and Literary Theory (Cambridge, 1994).

'Medieval Grammatical Theory and Chaucer's *House of Fame*', *Speculum*, 60 (1985), 850–76.

Janson, Tore, *Prose Rhythm in Medieval Latin from the Ninth to the Thirteenth Century*, Acta Universitatis Stockholmiensis, Studia Latina Stockholmiensia, 20 (Stockholm, 1975).

Jeauneau, Édouard, 'Deux Rédactions des gloses de Guillaume de Conches sur Priscian', *RTAM*, 27 (1960), 211–47; rpt. in *Lectio philosophorum*, pp. 335–70.

Lectio philosophorum: Recherches sur l'École de Chartres (Amsterdam, 1973).

Jennings, Margaret, '*Rhetor redivivus*? Cicero in the *artes praedicandi*', *AHDLMA*, 61 (1989), 91–122.

Jolivet, Jean, *Arts du langage et théologie chez Abélard*, Études de philosophie médiévale, 57 (Paris, 1969).

'Comparaison des théories du langage chez Abélard et chez les nominalistes du XIVe siècle', in E. M. Buytaert (ed.), *Peter Abelard: Proceedings of the International Conference*, Medievalia Lovaniensia, 1st ser. pt. 2 (Leuven, 1974), pp. 163–78.

'L'Enjeu de la grammaire pour Godescalc', in *Jean Scot Érigène et l'histoire de la philosophie*, Actes du colloques internationaux, 561 (Paris, 1977), pp. 79–87.

Kantorowicz, Ernst H., 'Anonymi *Aurea Gemma*', *M&H*, 1 (1943), 41–57.

'Petrus de Vinea in England', *Mitteilungen des Österreichischen Instituts für Geschichtsforschung*, 51 (1937), 43–88.

Kelly, Douglas, *The Arts of Poetry and Prose*, Typologie des sources du Moyen Âge occidental, 59 (Turnhout, 1991).

'The Scope of the Treatment of Composition in the Twelfth- and Thirteenth-Century Arts of Poetry', *Speculum*, 41 (1966), 261–78.

Kemmler, Fritz, '*Exempla*' in Context: A Historical and Critical Study of Robert Mannyng of Brunne's '*Handling Synne*' (Tübingen, 1984).

Kennedy, George A., *Classical Rhetoric and its Christian and Secular Tradition from Ancient to Modern Times* (Chapel Hill NC, 1980).

New Testament Interpretation through Rhetorical Criticism (Chapel Hill NC, 1984).

Kindrick, Robert L., 'Henryson and the *ars praedicandi*', in Kindrick, *Henryson and the Medieval Arts of Rhetoric* (New York, 1993), pp. 189–271.

Kittendorf, Doris E., '*Cleanness* and the Fourteenth-Century *artes praedicandi*', *Michigan Academician*, 11 (1979), 319–30.

Klopsch, Paul, *Einführung in die Dichtungslehren des lateinischen Mittelalters* (Darmstadt, 1980).

Koch, J. (ed.), *Artes liberales: Von der antiken Bildung zur Wissenschaft des Mittelalters*, Studien und Texte zur Geistesgeschichte des Mittelalters, 5 (Leiden, 1959).

Kretzman, Norman, 'The Culmination of the Old Logic in Peter Abelard', in Benson (ed.), *Renaissance and Renewal*, pp. 488–511.

Kretzman, Norman, Kenny, Anthony, and Pinborg, Jan (eds.), *The Cambridge History of Later Medieval Philosophy* (Cambridge, 1982).

Kristeller, Paul O., 'Matteo de Libri, Bolognese Notary of the Thirteenth Century and his *Artes dictaminis*', in *Miscellanea Giovanni Galbiati, Fontes ambrosiani*, 26 (Milan, 1951), II, pp. 225–50.

Ladner, Gerhart, 'Formularbehelfe in der Kanzlei Kaiser Friedrichs II. und die Briefe des Petrus de Vinea', *Mitteilungen des Österreichischen Institut für Geschichtsforschung, Ergänzungsband*, 12.1 (1932), 92–198.

Laistner, M. L. W., *Thought and Letters in Western Europe, A.D. 500 to 900* (2nd edn, Ithaca NY, 1957).

Langkabel, Hermann, *Die Staatsbriefe Coluccio Salutatis* (Vienna, 1981).

Langlois, Charles V., 'Formulaires de lettres du XIIe du XIIIe, et du XIV siècles', *Notices et extraits*, 34.1 (1891), 1–32, 305–22; 34.2 (1895), 1–18, 19–29; 35.2 (1897), 409–34, 793–830.

Lausberg, Heinrich, *Handbuch der literarischen Rhetorik* (2 vols., 1960; 2nd edn, Munich, 1973); tr. M. T. Bliss, A. Jansen and D. E. Orton, ed. D. E. Orton and R. Dean, as *A Handbook of Literary Rhetoric: A Foundation for Literary Study* (Leiden, 1998).

Law, Vivien, 'Anglo-Saxon England: Ælfric's *Excerptiones de arte grammatica anglice*', *Histoire epistémologie langage*, 9 (1987), 47–71.

The Insular Latin Grammarians (Woodbridge, 1982).

'Late Latin Grammars in the Early Middle Ages: A Typological History', *Hist. Ling.*, 13 (1986), 365–80.

'Linguistics in the Early Middle Ages: The Insular and Carolingian Grammarians', *Transactions of the Philological Society* (1985), 171–93.

'Originality in the Medieval Normative Tradition', in T. Bynon and F. R. Palmer (eds.), *Studies in the History of Western Linguistics in Honor of R. H. Robins* (Cambridge, 1986), pp. 43–55.

Lawton, David A., 'Gaytryge's Sermon, *Dictamen*, and Middle English Alliterative Verse', *MP*, 76 (1979), 329–43.

Le Saulnier de Saint-Jouan, Henri-Georges, 'Pons le Provençal maître en "Dictamen" (XIIIe siècle)', diss., École nationale des chartes (2 vols., Paris, 1957).

Leach, Arthur F. (ed. and tr.), *Educational Charters and Documents* (Cambridge, 1911).

Leclercq, Jean, 'Le Genre épistolaire au Moyen Âge', *Revue du moyen âge latin*, 2 (1946), 63–70.

The Love of Learning and the Desire for God, tr. K. Misrahi (New York, 1974).

'Smaragde et la grammaire chrétienne', *Revue du moyen âge latin*, 4 (1948), 15–22.

Lecoy, Félix, *Recherches sur le 'Libro de buen amor' de Juan Ruiz, Archiprêtre de Hita* (Paris, 1938).

Lehmann, Paul, *Erforschung des Mittelalters* (4 vols., Leipzig, 1941–60).

Mittelalterliche Bibliothekskataloge Deutschlands und der Schweiz (Munich, 1918–).

Lerner, R. E., 'A Collection of Sermons Given in Paris c. 1267, including a New Text by Saint Bonaventura on the Life of Saint Francis', *Speculum*, 49 (1974), 466–98.

Letson, D. R., 'The Form of the Old English Homily', *ABR*, 30 (1979), 399–431.

Licitra, Vincenzo, 'La *Summa de arte dictandi* di Maestro Goffredo', *Studi medievali*, 3rd ser. 7 (1966), 865–913.

Lindholm, Gudrun, *Studien zum mittellateinischen Prosarythmus: Seine Entwicklung und sein Abklingen in der Briefliteratur Italiens*, Studia latina stockholmiensia, 10 (Stockholm and Uppsala, 1963).

Löfstedt, Bengt, and Lanham, Carol D., 'Zu den neugefundenen Salzburger Formelbüchern und Briefen', *Eranos*, 73 (1975), 69–100.

Longère, Jean, *Œuvres oratoires de maîtres parisiens au XIIe siècle: Étude historique et doctrinale* (2 vols., Paris, 1975).

La Prédication médiévale (Paris, 1983).

Loserth, J., 'Formularbücher der Grazer Universitätsbibliothek', *Neues Archiv*, 21 (1895–6), 307–11; 22 (1896–7), 299–307; 23 (1897–8), 751–61.

Luscombe, D. E., *The School of Peter Abelard: The Influence of Abelard's Thought in the Early Scholastic Period* (Cambridge, 1969).

Lutz, Eckard Conrad, *Rhetorica divina: Mittelhochdeutsches Prologgebete und die rhetorische Kultur des Mittelalters*, Quellen and Forschungen zur Sprach- und Kulturgeschichte der germanischen Volker, n.F. 82 (206) (Berlin, 1984).

Manitius, M., *Geschichte der lateinischen Literatur des Mittelalters* (3 vols., Munich, 1911–31).

Matonis, Ann T. E., 'The Welsh Bardic Grammars and the Western Grammatical Tradition', *MP*, 79 (1981), 121–45.

McKeon, Richard, 'Rhetoric in the Middle Ages', *Speculum*, 17 (1940), 1–32; rpt. in R. S. Crane (ed.), *Critics and Criticism* (Chicago, 1952), pp. 260–96.

Means, Michael H., 'The Homiletic Structure of *Cleanness*', *SMC*, 5 (1975), 165–72.

Meisenzahl, J., 'Die Bedeutung des Bernhard von Meung für das mittelalterliche Notariats- und Schulwesen', Ph. D. diss., Würzburg, 1960.

Melli, Elio, 'I *salut* e l'epistolografia medievale', *Convivium*, 30 (1962), 385–98.

Meredith, Peter, '*Nolo Mortem* and the *Ludus Coventriae* Play of the *Woman Taken in Adultery*', *MÆ*, 38 (1969), 38–54.

Merrix, Robert P., 'Sermon Structure in the *Pardoner's Tale*', *ChR*, 17 (1983), 235–49.

Meyer, Paul, 'Notice sur les *Corregationes Promethei* d'Alexandre Neckham', *Notices et extraits*, 35 (1897), 641–82.

Minnis, Alastair J., 'Chaucer's Pardoner and the "Office of Preacher"', in P. Boitani and A. Torti (eds.), *Intellectuals and Writers in Fourteenth-Century Europe* (Tübingen, 1986), pp. 88–119.

Mroczkowski, Przemyslaw, '*The Friar's Tale* and its Pulpit Background', in *English Studies Today, Second Series*, ed. G. A. Bonnard (Bern, 1961), pp. 107–20.

Murphy, James J., 'The Arts of Discourse, 1050–1400', *MS*, 23 (1961), 194–205.

'The Discourse of the Future: Towards an Understanding of Medieval Literary Theory', in K. Busby and N. J. Lacy (eds.), *Conjunctures: Medieval Studies in Honor of Douglas Kelly* (Amsterdam, 1994), pp. 359–73.

Medieval Rhetoric: A Select Bibliography (2nd edn, Toronto, 1989).

'The Middle Ages', in Winifred Bryan Horner (ed.), *The Present State of Scholarship in Historical and Contemporary Rhetoric* (Columbia MO, 1983), pp. 40–74.

Rhetoric in the Middle Ages: A History of Rhetorical Theory from Saint Augustine to the Renaissance (Berkeley CA, 1974).

'The Teaching of Latin as a Second Language in the Twelfth Century', *Hist. Ling.*, 7 (1980), 159–75.

(ed.), *Medieval Eloquence: Studies in the Theory and Practice of Medieval Rhetoric* (Berkeley CA, 1978).

Myers, Doris E. T., 'The *Artes Praedicandi* and Chaucer's Canterbury Preachers', Ph.D. diss., University of Nebraska, 1967.

Nicolau, Mathieu G., *L'Origine du 'cursus' rhythmique et les débuts de l'accent d'intensité en latin* (Paris, 1930).

Nims, Margaret F., '*Translatio*: "Difficult Statement" in Medieval Poetic Theory', *University of Toronto Quarterly*, 43 (1974), 215–30.

Norden, Eduard, *Die antike Kunstprosa vom VI. Jahrhundert v. Chr. bis in die Zeit der Renaissance* (5th edn, 2 vols., Stuttgart, 1958).

Ó Cuilleanáin, Cormac, *Religion and the Clergy in Boccaccio's 'Decameron'* (Rome, 1984).

O'Donnell, James J., *Cassiodorus* (Berkeley CA, 1979).

Olsson, Kurt, 'Grammar, Manhood, and Tears: The Curiosity of Chaucer's Monk', *MP*, 76 (1978–9), 1–12.

Orme, Nicholas, *English Schools in the Later Middle Ages* (London, 1973).

Owen, Nancy H., 'The Pardoner's Introduction, Prologue, and Tale: Sermon and Fabliau', *JEGP*, 66 (1967), 541–9.

Paetow, Louis J., *The Arts Course at Medieval Universities with Special Reference to Grammar and Rhetoric* (Champaign IL, 1910).

Paret, G., Brunet, A., and Tremblay, P., *La Renaissance du XIIe siècle: Les écoles et l'enseignement* (Paris, 1933).

Parkes, M. B., 'The Contribution of Insular Scribes of the Seventh and Eighth Centuries to the "Grammar of Legibility"', in A. Maierù (ed.), *Grafia e interpunzione del latino nel medioevo* (Rome, 1985), pp. 15–30.

'The Literacy of the Laity', in D. Daiches and A. K. Thorlby (eds.), *Literature and Western Civilization* (London, 1973), pp. 555–77.

Pause and Effect: An Introduction to the History of Punctuation in the West (Aldershot, 1992).

'Punctuation, or Pause and Effect', in Murphy (ed.), *Medieval Eloquence*, pp. 127–42.

Scribes, Scripts and Readers: Studies in the Communication, Presentation, and Dissemination of Medieval Texts (London, 1991).

Parodi, Ernesto G., 'Osservazioni sul *cursus* nelle opere latine e volgari del Boccaccio', *Miscellanea storica della Valdelsa*, 21 (1913), 232–45.

Passalacqua, Marina, *I Codici di Prisciano* (Rome, 1978).

Patt, William D., 'Early *Ars dictaminis* as Response to a Changing Society', *Viator*, 9 (1978), 135–55.

Patterson, Warner F., *Three Centuries of French Poetic Theory: A Critical History of the Chief Arts of Poetry in France (1328–1630)*, University of Michigan Publications in Language and Literature, 14–15 (2 vols., Ann Arbor MI, 1935).

Pearsall, Derek, *The Life of Geoffrey Chaucer: A Critical Biography* (1992; rpt. Oxford, 1994).

Peek, George S., 'Sermon Themes and Sermon Structure in *Everyman*', *South Central Bulletin*, 40 (1983), 159–60.

Percival, W. K., 'The Grammatical Tradition and the Rise of the Vernaculars', *Current Trends in Linguistics*, 13 (1975), 231–75.

Pfander, Homer G., *The Popular Sermon of the Medieval Friar in England* (New York, 1937).

Pinborg, Jan, *Die Entwicklung der Sprachtheorie im Mittelalter* (Münster, 1967). *Logik und Semantik im Mittelalter: Ein Überblick* (Stuttgart-Bad Cannstatt, 1972).

'Speculative Grammar', in Kretzman *et al.* (eds.), *Cambridge History of Late Medieval Philosophy*, pp. 254–69.

Plechl, Hellmut, 'Studien zur Tegernseer Briefsammlung des 12. Jahrhunderts', *Deutsches Archiv für Erforschung des Mittelalters*, 11 (1955), 422–61; 12 (1956), 73–113, 388–452; 13 (1957), 35–114, 394–481.

Plezia, Marian, 'L'Origine de la théorie du *cursus* rythmique au XIIe siècle', *Archivum latinitatis medii ævi*, 32 (1972), 5–22.

Polak, Emil, 'Dictamen', in J. R. Stayer (ed.), *A Dictionary of the Middle Ages* (10 vols., New York, 1982), IV, pp. 173–7.

Medieval and Renaissance Letter Treatises and Form Letters: A Census of Manuscripts Found in Eastern Europe and the Former U.S.S.R., Davis (Cal.) Medieval Texts and Studies, 8 (Leiden and New York, 1993).

Medieval and Renaissance Letter Treatises and Form Letters: A Census of Manuscripts Found in Part of Western Europe, Japan, and the United States of America, Davis (Cal.) Medieval Texts and Studies, 9 (Leiden and New York, 1994).

Polheim, Karl, *Die lateinische Reimprosa* (Berlin, 1963).

Poole, Reginald L., *Lectures on the History of the Papal Chancery down to the Time of Innocent III* (Cambridge, 1915).

Pratt, Robert A., 'Chaucer and the Hand that Fed Him', *Speculum*, 41 (1966), 619–42.

Purcell, William M., *'Ars poetriae': Rhetorical and Grammatical Invention at the Margin of Literacy* (Columbia SC, 1996).

Quadlbauer, Franz, *Die antike Theorie der Genera dicendi im lateinischen Mittelalter*, Österreichische Akademie der Wissenschaften, philosophisch-historische Klasse, Sitzungsberichte 241, 2 (Vienna, 1962).

'Zur Theorie der Komposition in der mittelalterlichen Rhetorik und Poetik', in B. Vickers (ed.), *Rhetoric Revalued: Papers from the International Society for the History of Rhetoric* (Binghamton NY, 1982), pp. 115–31.

Quilligan, Maureen, 'Allegory, Allegoresis, and the Deallegorization of Language: The *Roman de la Rose*, the *De planctu naturae*, and the *Parlement of Foules*', in M. Bloomfield (ed.), *Allegory, Myth, and Symbol, Harvard English Studies*, 9 (1981), 163–86.

'Words and Sex: The Language of Allegory in the *De planctu naturae*, the *Roman de la Rose*, and Book III of *The Faerie Queen*', *Allegorica*, 2 (1977), 195–216.

Reinsma, Luke, 'The Middle Ages', in W. B. Horner (ed.), *Historical Rhetoric: An Annotated Bibliography of Sources in English* (Boston MA, 1980), pp. 45–108.

Richardson, Henry Gerald, 'Business Training in Medieval Oxford', *American Historical Review*, 46 (1941), 259–80.

Rickert, Edith, 'Chaucer at School', *MP*, 29 (1932), 257–74.

Rico, Francisco, *Predicación y literatura en la España medieval* (Cadiz, 1977).

Riessner, C., *Die 'Magnae derivationes' des Uguccione da Pisa und ihre Bedeutung für die romanische Philologie* (Rome, 1965).

Roberts, Phyllis Barzillay, *Stephanus de Lingua-Tonante: Studies in the Sermons of Stephen Langton* (Toronto, 1968).

Robins, R. H., *Ancient and Medieval Grammatical Theory in Europe* (London, 1951).

A Short History of Linguistics (2nd edn, London, 1979).

Robson, C. A., *Maurice of Sully and the Medieval Vernacular Homily* (Oxford, 1952).

Rollinson, Philip, *Classical Theories of Allegory and Christian Culture* (Pittsburg PA, 1980).

Roos, Heinrich, 'Die Stellung der Grammatik im Lehrbetrieb des 13. Jahrhunderts', in Koch (ed.), *Artes liberales*, pp. 94–106.

'Le Trivium à XIIIe siècle', *Arts libéraux*, pp. 193–7.

Rosier, I., *La Grammaire spéculative des modistes* (Lille, 1983).

Rosier-Catach, I., 'Roger Bacon: Grammar', in J. Hackett (ed.), *Roger Bacon and the Sciences: Commemorative Essays*, Studien und Texte zur Geistesgeschichte des Mittelalters, 57 (Leiden, 1997), pp. 67–102.

Ross, W. O., 'A Brief *Forma predicandi*', *MP*, 34 (1936–7), 337–44.

Roth, Dorothea, *Die mittelalterliche Predigttheorie und das 'Manuale curatorum' des Johann Ulrich Surgant* (Basel, 1956).

Ruhe, Ernstpeter, *De amasio ad amasiam: Zur Gattungsgeschichte des mittelalterlichen Liebesbriefes*, Beiträge zur romanischen Philologie des Mittelalters, 10 (Munich, 1975).

Samaran, Charles, 'Une *Summa grammaticalis* du XIIIe siècle avec gloses provençales', *Archivum latinitatis medii aevi (Bulletin du Cange)*, 31 (1961), 157–224.

Sambin, Paolo, 'Un certame dettatorio tra due notai pontifici (1260): Lettere inedite di Giordano da Terracina e di Giovanni da Capua', *Note e discussioni erudite*, 5 (Rome, 1955), 21–49.

Scaglione, Aldo, '*Ars grammatica*': A Bibliographic Survey, Two Essays on the Grammar of the Latin and Italian Subjunctive, and A Note on the Ablative Absolute*, Janua linguarum, series minor, 77 (The Hague, 1970).

The Classical Theory of Composition from its Origins to the Present: A Historical Survey, University of North Carolina Studies in Comparative Literature, 53 (Chapel Hill NC, 1972).

Schalk, Fritz, 'Zur Entwicklung der Artes in Frankreich und Italien', in Koch (ed.), *Artes liberales*, pp. 137–48.

Schaller, Dieter, 'Probleme der Überlieferung und Verfasserschaft lateinischer Liebesbriefe des hohen Mittelalters', *Mittellateinisches Jahrbuch*, 3 (1966), 25–36.

Schaller, Hans Martin, '*Ars dictaminis, Ars dictandi*', *Lexikon des Mittelalters*, 1 (Munich, 1980), 1034–9.

'Dichtungslehren und Briefsteller', in P. Weimar (ed.), *Die Renaissance der Wissenschaften im 12. Jahrhundert* (Zurich, 1981), pp. 249–71.

'Zur Entstehung der sogenannten Briefsammlung des Petrus de Vinea', *Archiv*, 12 (1956), 114–59.

'Die Kanzlei Kaiser Friedrichs II: Ihr Personal und ihr Sprachstil. 1. Teil: Das Personal der Kanzlei', *Archiv für Diplomatik, Schriftgeschichte, Siegel- und Wappenkunde*, 4 (1958), 264–327.

'Studien zur Briefsammlung des Kardinals Thomas von Capua', *Deutsches Archiv*, 21 (1965), 371–518.

Schiaffini, Alfredo, *Tradizione e poesia nella prosa d'arte italiana dalla latinità medievale al Boccaccio* (2nd edn, 1943; rpt. Rome, 1969).

Schmale, Franz-Josef, 'Die Bologneser Schule der *Ars dictandi*', *Deutsches Archiv für Erforschung des Mittelalters*, 13 (1957), 16–34.

'Der Briefsteller Bernhards von Meung', *Mitteilungen des Österreichischen Instituts für Geschichtsforschung*, 66 (1958), 1–28.

Schmitt, Wolfgang O., 'Die Ianua (Donatus): Ein Beitrag zur lateinischen Schulgrammatik des Mittelalters und der Renaissance', *Beiträge zur Inkunabelkunde*, 3.4 (1969), 43–80.

Schneyer, Johannes Baptist, 'Eine Sermonesliste des Nicolaus de Byard OFM', *AFH*, 60 (1967), pp. 3–41.

Geschichte der katholischen Predigt (Freiburg i. Br., 1969).

Sedgwick, Walter B., 'The Style and Vocabulary of the Latin Arts of Poetry of the Twelfth and Thirteenth Centuries', *Speculum*, 3 (1928), 349–81.

Shain, C. E., 'Pulpit Rhetoric in Three Canterbury Tales', *MLN*, 70 (1955), 235–45.

Smalley, Beryl, *English Friars and Antiquity in the Early Fourteenth Century* (Oxford, 1960).

'Oxford University Sermons 1290–1293', in J. J. G. Alexander and M. T. Gibson (eds.), *Medieval Learning and Literature: Essays Presented to R. W. Hunt* (Oxford, 1976), pp. 307–27.

Southern, R. W., *Medieval Humanism and Other Studies* (New York, 1970).

'From Schools to University', in J. I. Catto (ed.), *The History of the University of Oxford, I: The Early Oxford Schools* (Oxford, 1984), pp. 1–36.

Spallone, Mario, 'La trasmissione della *Rhetorica ad Herennium* nell' Italia meridionale tra il'XI e il XII secolo', *Bolletino del comitato par la preparazione dell'edizione nazionale dei classici greci e latini*, 1 (1980), 158–90.

Spearing, A. C., 'The Art of Preaching and *Piers Plowman*', in Spearing, *Criticism and Medieval Poetry* (London, 1964), pp. 68–95; (2nd edn, New York, 1972), pp. 107–34.

Stobbe, Otto, '*Summa curiae regis*: Ein Formelbuch aus der Zeit König Rudolf's I und Albrechts I', *Archiv für ältere deutsche Geschichtskunde*, 32 (1907; rpt. 1984), 424–56.

Stock, Brian, *The Implications of Literacy: Written Language and Models of Interpretation in the Eleventh and Twelfth Centuries* (Princeton NJ, 1983).

Stockton, Eric W., 'The Deadliest Sin in *The Pardoner's Tale*', *TSL*, 6 (1961), 47–59.

Szarmach, Paul E., and Huppé, Bernard F. (eds.), *The Old English Homily and its Backgrounds* (Albany NY, 1978).

Szklenar, Hans, *Magister Nicolaus de Dybin, Vorstudien zu einer Edition seiner Schriften: Ein Beitrag zur Geschichte der literarischen Rhetorik im späteren Mittelalter* (Munich, 1981).

Taylor, John, 'Letters and Letter-Collections in England, 1300–1420', *Nottingham Medieval Studies*, 28 (1980), 57–70.

Thiry, Claude, 'Rhétorique et genres littéraires au XVe siècle', in M. Wilmet (ed.), *Sémantique lexicale et sémantique grammaticale en moyen français: Colloque organisé par le Centre d'études linguistiques et littéraires de la Vrije Universiteit Brussel (28–29 Septembre, 1978)* (Brussels, 1980).

Thomson, David, *A Descriptive Catalogue of Middle English Grammatical Texts* (New York, 1979).

An Edition of Middle English Grammatical Texts (New York, 1984).

'The Oxford Grammar Masters Revisited', *MS*, 45 (1983), 298–310.

Thomson, David, and Murphy, J. J., 'Dictamen as a Developed Genre: The Fourteenth-Century *Brevis doctrina dictaminis* of Ventura da Bergamo', *Studi medievali*, 3rd ser. 23 (1982), 361–86.

Thomson, S. Harrison, 'Robert Kilwardby's Commentaries *In Priscianum* and *In Barbarismum Donati*', *New Scholasticism*, 12 (1938), 52–65.

Thurot, Charles, 'Notices et extraits de divers manuscrits latins pour servir à l'histoire des doctrines grammaticales au Moyen Âge', *Notices et extraits*, 22 (1869; rpt. 1964).

Tibber, P., 'The Origins of the Scholastic Sermon, c. 1130–1210', D. Phil. diss., Oxford University, 1983.

Tilliette, Jean-Yves, *Des Mots à la parole: Une lecture de la 'Poetria nova' de Geoffroy de Vinsauf* (Geneva, 2000).

Travis, Peter W., 'Chaucer's Trivial Fox Chase and the Peasant's Revolt', *Journal of Medieval and Renaissance Studies*, 18 (1988), 195–220.

'Reading Chaucer *ab ovo*: Mock-exemplum in the *Nun's Priest's Tale*', in J. J. Paxson, L. M. Clopper and S. Tomasch (eds.), *The Performance of Middle English Culture: Essays on Chaucer and the Drama in Honor of Martin Stevens* (Cambridge, 1998), 161–81.

Tunberg, Terence O., 'What is Boncompagno's "Newest Rhetoric"?', *Traditio*, 42 (1986), 299–334.

Ullman, Pierre L., 'Juan Ruiz's Prologue', *MLN*, 82 (1967), 149–70.

Usher, Jonathan, 'Frate Cipolla's *ars praedicandi* or a "récit du discours" in Boccaccio', *MLR*, 88 (1993), 321–36.

Valois, Noël, *De arte scribendi epistolas apud Gallicos medii aevi scriptores rhetoresve* (Paris, 1880).

Vantuono, William, 'The Structure and Sources of *Patience*', *MS*, 34 (1972), 401–21.

Vecchi, Giuseppe, *Il magistero delle 'Artes' latine a Bologna nel medioevo*, Publicazioni della Facoltà di Magistero Università di Bologna, 2 (Bologna, 1958).

'Il "proverbio" nella pratica letteraria dei dettatori della scuola di Bologna', *Studi mediolatini e volgari*, 2 (1954), 283–302.

Vinaver, Eugene, *Études sur le 'Tristan' en prose: les sources, les manuscripts, bibliographie critique* (Paris, 1925).

Voigts, Linda E., 'A Letter from a Middle English Dictaminal Formulary in Harvard Law Library MS 43', *Speculum*, 56 (1981), 575–81.

Wagner, David (ed.), *The Seven Liberal Arts in the Middle Ages* (Bloomington IN, 1983).

Ward, John O., *Ciceronian Rhetoric in Treatise, Scholion and Commentary* (Turnhout, 1995).

Wendehorst, Alfred, *Tabula formarum curie episcope: Das Formularbuch der Würzburger Bischofskanzlei von ca. 1324*, Quellen und Forschungen zur Geschichte des Bistums und Hochstifts Würzburg, 13 (Würzburg, 1957).

Wenzel, Siegfried, 'Academic Sermons at Oxford in the Early Fifteenth Century', *Speculum*, 70 (1995), 305–29.

'Chaucer and the Language of Contemporary Preaching', *SP*, 73 (1976), 138–61.

'The Joyous Art of Preaching; or, the Preacher and the Fabliau', *Anglia*, 97 (1979), 304–25.

Macaronic Sermons: Bilingualism and Preaching in Late-Medieval England (Ann Arbor MI, 1994).

'Medieval Sermons', in John A. Alford (ed.), *A Companion to Piers Plowman* (Berkeley CA, 1988), pp. 155–72.

'Medieval Sermons and the Study of Literature', in P. Boitani and A. Torti (eds.), *Medieval and Pseudo-Medieval Literature* (Tübingen, 1984), pp. 19–32.

'Notes on the *Parson's Tale*', *ChR*, 16 (1982), 237–56.

Preachers, Poets, and the Early English Lyric (Princeton NJ, 1986).

'A Sermon in Praise of Philosophy', *Traditio*, 50 (1995), 249–59.

Verses in Sermons: 'Fasciculus Morum' and its Middle English Poems (Cambridge MA, 1978).

Wieruszowski, Helen, 'Arezzo as a Center of Learning and Letters in the Thirteenth Century', *Traditio*, 9 (1953), 321–91.

'*Ars dictaminis* in the Time of Dante', *M&H*, 1 (1943), 95–108.

'Rhetoric and the Classics in Italian Education of the Thirteenth Century', *Studia graziana*, 11 (1967), 169–208.

'A Twelfth-Century *Ars dictaminis* in the Barberini Collection of the Vatican Library', in Wieruszowski, *Politics and Culture in Medieval Spain and Italy* (Rome, 1971), pp. 336–45.

Williams, David, 'The Point of *Patience*', *MP*, 68 (1970–71), 127–36.

Wilson, Edward, *The Gawain-Poet* (Leiden, 1976).

Witt, Ronald, 'Boncompagno and the Defense of Rhetoric', *Journal of Medieval and Renaissance Studies*, 16 (1986), 1–31.

'Medieval *Ars dictaminis* and the Beginnings of Humanism: A New Construction of the Problem', *Renaissance Quarterly*, 35 (1982), 1–35.

'Medieval Italian Culture and the Origins of Humanism as a Stylistic Ideal', in A. Rabil, Jr. (ed.), *Renaissance Humanism: Foundations, Forms, and Legacy* (2 vols., Philadelphia PA, 1988), I, pp. 29–70.

'On Bene of Florence's Conception of the French and Roman *Cursus*', *Rhetorica*, 3 (1985), 77–98.

Worstbrock, Franz Josef, 'Die Antikenrezeption in der mittelalterlichen und der humanistischen *Ars dictandi*' in A. Buck (ed.), *Die Rezeption der Antike: zum Problem der Kontinuität zwischen Mittelalter und Renaissance*, Wolfenbütteler Abhandlungen zur Renaissance-Forschung, 1 (Hamburg, 1981), pp. 187–207.

Repertorium der 'Artes dictandi' des Mittelalters, 1: Von den Anfängen bis um 1200, Münstersche Mittelalter-Schriften, 66 (Munich, 1992).

Wright, Roger, 'Late Latin and Early Romance: Alcuin's *De orthographia* and the Council of Tours (813 A.D.)', *Papers of the Liverpool Latin Seminar*, 3 (1981), 343–61.

Late Latin and Early Romance in Spain and Carolingian France (Liverpool, 1982).

Zaccagnini, Guido, 'Lettere ed orazioni dei grammatici dei secc. XIII e XIV', *Archivum romanicum*, 7 (1923), 517–34.

La vita dei maestri e degli scholari nello studio di Bologna nei secoli XIII e XIV, Biblioteca dell'Archivum romanicum, 1st ser. 5 (Geneva, 1926).

Zafarana, Zelina, 'La predicazione francescana', in *Atti dell' VIII Congresso della Società internazionale de studi francescani, 1980* (Assisi, 1981), pp. 203–50.

Zink, Michel, *La prédication en langue romane avant 1300* (Paris, 1976).

Ziolkowski, Jan, *Alan of Lille's Grammar of Sex: The Meaning of Grammar to a Twelfth-Century Intellectual* (Cambridge MA, 1985).

Zöllner, Walter, 'Eine neue Bearbeitung der *Flores dictaminum* des Bernhard von Meung', *Wissenschaftliche Zeitschrift der Martin-Luther Universität Halle-Wittenberg*, gesellschafts- und sprachwissenschaftliche Reihe 13, 5 (1964), pp. 335–42.

The study of classical authors

Primary sources

Accessus ad auctores, ed. R. B. C. Huygens, *Latomus*, 12 (1953), 296–311, 460–86; re-ed. Huygens, *Accessus ad Auctores; Bernard d'Utrecht; Conrad d'Hirsau, Dialogus super Auctores* (Leiden, 1970), pp. 19–54.

'*Accessus ad auctores*: Twelfth-Century Introductions to Ovid', tr. A. G. Elliott, *Allegorica*, 5 (1980), 6–48.

Acro, Pseudo-, *Scholia in Horatium vetustiora*, ed. O. Keller (2 vols., Leipzig, 1902–4).

Aimeric, *Ars lectoria*, ed. H. F. Reijnders, *Vivarium*, 9 (1971), 119–37; 10 (1972), 41–101, 124–76.

Alan of Lille, *Anticlaudianus*, ed. R. Bossuat (Paris, 1955); tr. J. J. Sheridan (Toronto, 1973).

Liber parabolarum (or *Parvum doctrinale*), PL 210, 81–94.

De planctu naturae, ed. N. M. Häring, *Studi medievali*, 3rd ser. 19 (1978), pp. 797–879; tr. J. J. Sheridan (Toronto, 1980).

Alberic of London (?), *Poetria* [i.e. 'Mythographus Tertius'], 'Prologus', ed. C. F. W. Jacobs and F. A. Ukert, *Beiträge zur älteren Literatur der Herzogl. öffentlichen Bibliothek zu Gotha* (Leipzig, 1835), I.2., pp. 202–4.

Alcuin, *The Bishops, Kings and Saints of York*, ed. P. Godman (Oxford, 1982).

Aldhelm, *De metris* and *De pedum regulis*, tr. N. Wright in *Poetic Works*, pp. 183–219.

Opera, ed. R. Ehwald, MGH AA15 (Berlin, 1919).

The Poetic Works, tr. M. Lapidge and J. L. Rosier (Cambridge, 1985).

The Prose Works, tr. M. Lapidge and M. Herren (Cambridge, 1979).

Alexander of Villa Dei, *Doctrinale*, ed. D. Reichling, Monumenta germaniae paedagogica, 12 (Berlin, 1893).

Alighieri, Jacopo, *Chiose alla cantica dell'Inferno*, ed. Jarro [G. Piccini] (Florence, 1915).

Antiovidianus, ed. K. Kienast in *Aus Petrarcas ältesten deutschen Schülerkreisen: Vom Mittelalter zur Reformation*, ed. K. Burdach, 4 (Berlin, 1929), pp. 81–111.

Arnulf of Orléans, *Allegoriae super Metamorphosin*, ed. F. Ghisalberti, 'Arnolfo d'Orléans, un cultore di Ovidio nel secolo XII', *Memorie del reale Istituto lombardo di scienze e lettere, casse di littere*, 24.4 (1932), 157–229.

Glosule super Lucanum, ed. B. M. Marti, American Academy in Rome, Papers and Monographs, 18 (Rome, 1958).

Averroes' Middle Commentary on Aristotle's 'Poetics', tr. C. E. Butterworth (Princeton, 1986).

Avianus, *Fables*, ed. and tr. F. Gaide, Collection des universités de France (Paris, 1980).

Bacon, Roger, *Moralis philosophia*, ed. E. Massa (Zurich, 1953).

Opus maius, ed. J. H. Bridges (London, 1900).

Opera quaedam hactenus inedita, ed. J. S. Brewer, Rolls Series, 15 (London, 1859).

Baudri of Bourgueil, *Carmina*, ed. K. Hilbert (Heidelberg, 1979).

Carmina, ed. and tr. J.-Y. Tilliette (Paris, 1998).

Bede, *Libri II de arte metrica et de schematibus et tropis: The Art of Poetry and Rhetoric*, ed. and tr. C. B. Kendall (Saarbrücken, 1991).

Bernard, Pseudo-, *Cartula* (*De contemptu mundi*), PL 184, 1307–14.

Bernard of Chartres, *Glosae super Platonem*, ed. P. E. Dutton (Toronto, 1991).

Bernard of Cluny, *De contemptu mundi*, ed. H. C. Hoskier (London, 1929).

Bernard of Utrecht, *Commentum in Theodulum*, ed. R. B. C. Huygens, Biblioteca degli Studi Medievali, 8 (Spoleto, 1977). Dedication and *accessus* ed. Huygens, *Accessus, etc.* (1970), pp. 55–69.

Bernard Silvester, *Cosmographia*, ed. P. Dronke (Leiden, 1978); tr. W. Wetherbee (New York, 1973).

(?) *Commentary on Martianus Capella*, ed. H. Westra, Pontifical Institute of Mediaeval Studies, Texts and Studies, 80 (Toronto, 1986).

(?) *Commentum super sex libros Eneidos Virgilii*, ed. J. W. and E. F. Jones (Lincoln NE and London, 1977); tr. E. G. Schreiber and T. E. Maresca (Lincoln NE and London, 1979).

Bersuire, Pierre, *Reductorium morale, lib. XV: Ovidius moralizatus, cap. 1: De formis figurisque deorum, Textus e codice Brux., Bibl. Reg. 863–9 critice editus*, ed. J. Engels, Werkmateriaal 3 (Utrecht, 1966).

'Selections from *De Formis Figurisque Deorum*', tr. W. Reynolds, *Allegorica*, 2 (1978), 58–89.

Boethius, Pseudo-, *De disciplina scholarium*, ed. O. Weijers, Studien und Texte zur Geistesgeschichte des Mittelalters, 12 (1976).

Calcidius, *Timaeus a Calcidio translatus commentarioque instructus*, ed. J. H. Waszink, Plato latinus, 4 (London and Leiden, 1975).

Chaucer, Geoffrey, *The Riverside Chaucer*, gen. ed. L. D. Benson (Boston MA, 1987).

Cicero, *Brutus*, ed. and tr. G. L. Hendrickson (London, 1971).

Claudian, *De raptu Proserpinae*, ed. J. B. Hall, Cambridge Classical Texts and Commentaries, 11 (Cambridge, 1969).

Commedie latine del XII e XIII secolo, ed. F. Bertini, Publicazioni dell'Istituto di filologia classica e medievale, 48, 61, 68, 79, 95 (Genoa, 1976–86; in progress).

Conrad of Hirsau, *Dialogus super auctores*, ed. R. B. C. Huygens, Collection Latomus, 17 (Brussels, 1955); re-ed. Huygens, *Accessus ad Auctores, etc.* (1970), pp. 71–131.

Dares Phrygius, *De excidio Troiae historia*, ed. F. Meister (1877; rpt. Leipzig, 1991).

Le Débat sur le 'Roman de la Rose', ed. E. Hicks (Paris, 1977).

Disticha Catonis, ed. M. Boas and H. J. Botschuyver (Amsterdam, 1952).

Donatus, Aelius, 'Vita Vergilii', ed. J. Brummer, *Vitae Vergilianae* (Leipzig, 1912), pp. 1–19.

Dunchad, *Glossae in Martianum*, ed. C. E. Lutz (Lancaster PA, 1944).

Facetus (incipit: 'Cum nihil utilius'), in *Der deutsche Facetus*, ed. C. Schroeder, Palaestra 86 (Berlin, 1911).

Facetus (incipit: 'Moribus et vita'), ed. A Morel-Fatio, *Romania*, 15 (1886), 224–35.

Le facet en françoys: edition critique des cinq traductions des deux Facetus latins, ed. J. Morawski (Poznan, 1923).

Faral, Edmond (ed.), *Les Arts poétiques du XIIe et du XIIIe siècle*, Bibliothèque de l'École des hautes études, 238 (1923; rpt. Geneva, 1982).

Fortunatus, Venantius, *Opera poetica*, ed. F. Leo, MGH AA 4.1 (Berlin, 1961).

Fulgentius, *Expositio Virgilianae continentiae*, ed. T. Agozzino and F. Zanlucchi (Padua, 1972).

Opera, ed. R. Helm (Leipzig, 1898); tr. L. G. Whitbread, *Fulgentius the Mythographer* (Columbus OH, 1971).

Gundissalinus, Dominicus, *De divisione philosophiae*, ed. L. Baur, BGPM, 4, 2–3 (Münster, 1903).

De scientiis, ed. P. M. Alonso Alonso (Madrid, 1954).

Heiric of Auxerre, *Collectanea*, ed. R. Quadri, Spicilegium Friburgense, 11 (Fribourg, 1966).

(?), *Scholia in Horatium*, ed. H. J. Botschuyver (Amsterdam, 1942).

Henri d'Andeli, *La Bataille des VII ars*, ed. L. J. Paetow, Memoirs of the University of California, 4.1 (Berkeley CA, 1914).

Hermannus Alemannus, *De arte poetica cum Averrois expositione*, ed. L. Minio-Paluello, Corpus philosophorum medii ævi, Aristoteles latinus, 33 (2nd edn, Brussels, 1968).

Hisperica Famina I: The A-Text, ed. M. W. Herren (Toronto, 1974).

Hugo von Trimberg, *Registrum multorum auctorum*, ed. K. Langosch, Germanische Studien, 235 (Berlin, 1942).

Ilias latina, ed. M. Scaffai (Bologna, 1982).

Isidore of Seville, 'De diis gentium' (*Etymologiae* 8.11), ed. and tr. K. N. MacFarlane, *Isidore of Seville on the Pagan Gods*, Transactions of the American Philosophical Society, 70.3 (Philadelphia PA, 1980).

Etymologiae, ed. W. M. Lindsay (2 vols., Oxford, 1911).

Isopets, Recueil général des, ed. J. Bastin and P. Ruelle, SATF (4 vols., 1929–84).

Jean de Hautfuney, *Tabula super Speculum historiale fratris Vincentii*, ed. Monique Paulmier[-Foucart], *Spicae: Cahiers de l'Atelier Vincent de Beauvais*, 2–3 (1980–1).

John of Garland, *Integumenta Ovidii*, ed. F. Ghisalberti (Messina and Milan, 1933).

Morale scolarium, ed. L. J. Paetow, Memoirs of the University of California, 4.2 (Berkeley CA, 1927).

Parisiana poetria, ed. and tr. T. Lawler (New Haven CT and London, 1974).

De triumphis ecclesiae, ed. T. Wright, Roxburghe Club (London, 1856).

John of Hanville (Johannes de Hauvilla), *Architrenius*, ed. P. G. Schmidt (Munich, 1974); also ed. and tr. W. Wetherbee (Cambridge, 1994).

John of Salisbury, *Metalogicon*, ed. C. C. J. Webb (Oxford, 1929).

John Scotus Eriugena, *Annotationes in Marcianum*, ed. C. E. Lutz (Cambridge MA, 1939).

Expositiones super hierarchiam caelestem, ed. J. Barbet, CCCM 31 (Turnhout, 1975).

Joseph of Exeter, *Iliad*, ed. L. Gompf, *Josephus Iscanus: Werke und Briefe* (Leiden, 1970); tr. G. Roberts (Cape Town, 1970).

Juvenal, *Saturarum libri V cum scholiis antiquis*, ed. O. Jahn (Berlin, 1851).

Juvencus, Caius Vettius Aquilinus, *Evangeliorum libri quattuor*, ed. J. Huemer, CSEL 24 (Vienna, 1891).

Vier Juvenal-Kommentare aus dem 12. Jh., ed. B. Löfstedt (Amsterdam, 1995).

Lactantius Placidus (?), *Commentarius in Statii Thebaiden*, ed. R. Jahnke (Leipzig, 1898).

(?) *Metamorphoseon narrationes*, ed. D. A. Slater, *Towards a Text of the 'Metamorphosis' of Ovid* (Oxford, 1927), unpaginated.

Macrobius, Ambrosius Theodosius, *Commentary on the Dream of Scipio*, tr. W. H. Stahl (New York, 1952).

Opera, ed. J. Willis, (2nd edn, 2 vols., Stuttgart, 1970). I: *Saturnalia*. II: *Commentarii in Somnium Scipionis*.

Saturnalia, tr. P. V. Davies (New York, 1969).

Marbod of Rennes, *De ornamentis verborum* and *Liber decem capitulorum*, ed. R. Leotta (Florence, 1998).

Martianus Capella, *De nuptiis Philologiae et Mercurii*, ed. J. Willis (Leipzig, 1983); tr. W. H. Stahl and R. Johnson (2 vols., New York, 1971–7).

Matthew of Vendôme, *Ars versificatoria*, in Faral (ed.), *Les Arts poétiques*, pp. 109–93; also in *Opera*, ed. F. Munari (3 vols., Rome 1977–88), III. Tr. A. E. Galyon (Ames IA, 1980); also tr. R. P. Parr (Milwaukee WI, 1981).

In Tobiam paraphrasis metrica, in *Opera*, II, pp. 159–255.

Matthias of Linköping, '*Poetria*' et '*Testa nucis*', ed. S. Sawicki, *Samlaren*, n.s. 17 (1936), 109–52.

Testa nucis and *Poetria*, ed. and tr. B. Bergh, Samlingar utgivna av Svenska fornskriftsällskapet, 2nd ser. Latinska skrifter 9.2 (Arlöv, 1996).

Maximian, *Elegies*, ed. E. Baehrens, Poetae latini minores, 5 (Leipzig 1883), pp. 313–48.

Mussato, Albertino, *Argumenta tragaediarum Senecae; Commentarii in L. A. Senecae tragaedias fragmenta nuper reperta*, ed. A. C. Megas (Thessaloniki, 1969).

Opera (Venice, 1630), rpt. in J. Georg Graevius (ed.), *Thesaurus antiquitatem et historiarum Italiae* (Leiden, 1722), VI.2, cols. 34–62.

Nequam, Alexander, *De naturis rerum in Ecclesiasten*, Books I–II, ed. T. Wright, Rolls Series, 34 (London, 1863).

(?), *Sacerdos ad altare*, ed. Hunt, *Teaching Latin*, I, pp. 250–73.

Notker Labeo, *Die Schriften Notkers und seiner Schule*, ed. P. Piper (3 vols., Freiburg and Tübingen, 1882).

Ovid, Pseudo-, *De Vetula*, ed. D. M. Robathan (Amsterdam, 1968); also ed. P. Klopsch, Mittellateinische Studien und Texte, 2 (Leiden and Cologne, 1967).

Ovide moralisé, ed. C. de Boer, Publications de l'Académie royale néerlandaise (5 vols., Amsterdam, 1915–38).

Ovide moralisé en prose (texte du quinzième siècle), ed. C. de Boer (Amsterdam, 1954).

Pamphilus, ed. F. G. Becker, *Mittellateinisches Jahrbuch*, 9 (Düsseldorf, 1972).

Persius, *Satirarum liber cum scholiis antiquis*, ed. O. Jahn (Leipzig, 1843).

Prudentius, Aurelius Clemens, *Carmina*, ed. M. P. Cunningham, CCSL 126 (Turnhout, 1966).

Contra Symmachum, ed. G. Garuti (L'Aquila, Rome, 1996).

La Querelle de la Rose: Letters and Documents, tr. J. L. Baird and J. R. Kane, North Carolina Studies in the Romance Languages and Literatures, 199 (Chapel Hill NC, 1978).

La Queste del Saint Graal, ed. A. Pauphilet (1923; rpt. Paris, 1984).

Rabanus Maurus, *In honorem sanctae crucis*, ed. M. Perrin, CCCM 100 (Turnhout, 1997).

Opera omnia, PL 107–112.

Ralph of Longchamp (=Radulphus de Longo Campo), *In Anticlaudianum Alani commentum*, ed. J. Sułowski (Warsaw, 1972).

The Register of Congregation 1448–1463, ed. W. A. Pantin and W. T. Mitchell, Oxford Historical Society, n.s. 22 (Oxford, 1972).

Remigius of Auxerre, Commentary on Boethius, *De consolatione philosophiae* (excerpts), ed. H. F. Stewart, 'A Commentary by Remigius Autissiodorensis on the *De consolatione philosophiae* of Boethius', *Journal of Theological Studies*, 17 (1915–16), 22–42; version ed. E. T. Silk, *Saeculi noni auctoris in Boetii Consolationem Philosophiae commentarius*, American Academy in Rome, Papers and Monographs, 9 (1935), pp. 305–43.

Commentum in Martianum Capellam, Libri I–II, ed. C. E. Lutz (Leiden, 1962).

Sacerdos ad altare [by Alexander Nequam?], ed. T. Hunt in *Teaching and Learning Latin in Thirteenth-Century England* (3 vols., Cambridge, 1991), I, pp. 250–73.

Salutati, Colluccio, *De laboribus Herculis*, ed. B. L. Ullmann (Turin, 1951).

Scholia Terentiana, ed. F. Schlee (Leipzig, 1893).

Scholia Vindobonensia ad Horatii artem poeticam, ed. J. Zechmeister (Vienna, 1877).

Sedulius, *Opera omnia*, ed. J. Huemer, CSEL 10 (Vienna, 1885).

Sedulius Scottus, *Collectaneum in Apostolum*, ed. H. J. Frede and H. Stanjek (2 vols., Freiburg, 1996–7).

Collectaneum miscellaneum; supplementum, ed. D. Simpson and F. Dolbeau, CCCM 67 (Turnhout, 1990).

Servius, *In Vergili carmina commentarii*, ed. G. Thilo and H. Hagen (3 vols. in 4, Leipzig, 1881–1902).

Statius, *Achilleis*, ed. O. A. W. Dilke (Cambridge, 1954); also ed. P. M. Clogan, *The Medieval Achilleid* (Leiden, 1968).

Thebais, ed. A. Klotz and T. C. Klinnert (Leipzig, 1973).

Statuta antiqua universitatis Oxoniensis, ed. S. Gibson (Oxford, 1931).

Super Thebaiden, in Fulgentius, *Opera*, ed. R. Helm (Leipzig, 1898), pp. 180–6.

'Theodulus', *Ecloga*, ed. R. P. H. Green, *Seven Versions of Carolingian Pastoral* (Reading, 1980).

Trevet, Nicholas, *Il Commento . . . al Tieste di Seneca*, ed. E. Franceschini, Orbis Romanus, 11 (Milan, 1938).

'Vatican Mythographers', ed. G. H. Bode, *Scriptores rerum mythicarum latini tres Romae nuper repertae* (2 vols., 1834; rpt. Hildesheim, 1996).

Le Premier Mythographe du Vatican, ed. N. Zorzetti (Paris, 1995).

Vincent of Beauvais, *De eruditione filiorum nobilium*, ed. A. Steiner (Cambridge MA, 1938).

Speculum maius (Douai, 1624) [the so-called Vulgate version].

Speculum maius, Apologia totius operis, ed. A.-D. von den Brincken, 'Geschichtsbetrachtung bei Vincenz von Beauvais', *Deutsches Archiv für Erforschung des Mittelalters*, 34 (1978), 409–99.

The 'Vulgate' Commentary on Ovid's 'Metamorphoses': The Creation Myth and the Story of Orpheus, ed. F. T. Coulson, Toronto Medieval Latin Texts, 20 (Toronto, 1991).

Walsingham, Thomas, *De archana deorum*, ed. R. J. van Kluyve (Durham NC, 1968).
Historia anglicana, ed. H. T. Riley, Rolls Series, 28 (2 vols., London, 1863–4).
Walter of Châtillon, *Alexandreis*, ed. M. L. Colker (Padua, 1978).
'Walter of England', *Fables*, ed. A. E. Wright (Toronto, 1997).
Walter of Speyer, *Libellus scholasticus*, ed. P. Vossen (Berlin, 1962).
William of Conches, *Glosae in Iuvenalem*, ed. B. Wilson, Textes philosophiques du Moyen Âge, 18 (Paris, 1980).
Glosae super Boetium, ed. L. Nauta, CCCM 158 (Turnhout, 1999).
Glosae super Platonem, ed. É. Jeauneau (Paris, 1965).
William de Montibus, *Poeniteas cito*, ed. Goering, *William de Montibus*, pp. 107–38 [see under Goering, J. W., in the following section].
William of Saint-Thierry, *Commentary on the Song of Songs*, ed. M. M. Davy, Bibliothèque des textes philosophiques (Paris, 1958).

Secondary sources

Allen, Judson B., 'Commentary as Criticism: Formal Cause, Discursive Form and the Late Medieval *Accessus*', in J. Ijsewijn and E. Kessler (eds.), *Acta Conventus Neo-Latini Lovaniensis* (Munich, 1973), pp. 29–48.
The Ethical Poetic of the Later Middle Ages: A Decorum of Convenient Distinction (Toronto, 1980).
The Friar as Critic: Literary Attitudes in the Later Middle Ages (Nashville TN, 1971).
'Hermann the German's Averroistic Aristotle and Medieval Poetic Theory', *Mosaic*, 9 (1976), 67–81.
Alton, E. H., 'The Medieval Commentators on Ovid's *Fasti*', *Hermathena*, 44 (1926), 119–51.
Alton, E. H., and Wormell, D. E. W., 'Ovid in the Medieval Schoolroom', *Hermathena*, 94 (1960), 21–38; 95 (1961), 67–82.
Anderson, David, *Before 'The Knight's Tale': Imitation of Classical Epic in Boccaccio's 'Teseida'* (Philadelphia PA, 1988).
Anderson, Harald, '*Accessus* to Statius', Ph.D. diss., Ohio State University, Columbus, 1997.
'The Manuscripts of Statius', Licence of Mediaeval Studies diss., Pontifical Institute of Mediaeval Studies, University of Toronto, 1999.
Anderson, William S., 'The Marston Manuscript of Juvenal', *Traditio*, 13 (1957), 407–14.
Atelier Vincent de Beauvais, *Bibliographie des travaux*: www.univ-nancy2.fr/RECHERCHE/MOYENAGE/Vincentdebeauvais/Vdbbib.html
Barnes, Timothy D., *Tertullian: A Historical and Literary Study* (Oxford, 1971).
Baswell, Christopher, 'Latinitas', in Wallace (ed.), *Cambridge History of Medieval English Literature*, pp. 122–51.
'The Medieval Allegorization of the *Aeneid*: MS Cambridge, Peterhouse 158', *Traditio*, 41 (1985), 181–237.

Virgil in Medieval England: Figuring the 'Aeneid' from the Twelfth Century to Chaucer (Cambridge, 1995).

Berchem, Denis van, 'Poètes et grammairiens: Recherches sur la tradition scolaire d'explication des auteurs', *Museum helveticum*, 9 (1952), 79–87.

Bergh, Birger, 'Critical Notes on Magister Matthias' *Poetria*', *Eranos*, 76 (1978), 129–43.

Binkley, Peter, 'Medieval Latin Poetic Anthologies (VI): The Cotton Anthology of Henry of Avranches (BL Cotton Vespasian D. V. fols 151–184)', *MS*, 52 (1990), 221–54.

Bischoff, Bernhard, 'Die Bibliothek im Dienste der Schule', in *La Scuola nell'Occidente Latino nell'Alto Medioevo*, Settimane di Studio, 19 (2 vols., Spoleto, 1972), pp. 385–415; rpt. in Bischoff, *Mittelalterliche Studien*, III, pp. 213–33.

'Hadoardus and the Manuscripts of Classical Authors from Corbie', in *Didascaliae: Studies in Honor of A. M. Albareda*, ed. S. Prete (New York, 1961), pp. 39–57.

'Die Hofbibliothek Karls der Grossen', in *Karl der Grosse: Lebenswerk und Nachleben*, ed. W. Braunfels (5 vols., 1965–6), II, *Geistiges Leben*, ed. B. Bischoff, pp. 42–62.

'Living with the Satirists', in *Classical Influences on European Culture A.D. 500–1500*, ed. R. R. Bolgar (Cambridge, 1971), pp. 81–92; rpt. in Bischoff, *Mittelalterliche Studien*, III, pp. 260–70.

'Eine mittelalterliche Ovid-Legende', *Historisches Jahrbuch*, 71 (1952), pp. 268–73; rpt. in Bischoff, *Mittelalterliche Studien: Ausgewählte Aufsätze zur Schriftkunde und Literhaturgeschichte* (3 vols., Stuttgart, 1966–81), I, pp. 144–50.

Mittelalterliche Studien: Ausgewählte Aufsätze zur Schriftkunde und Literaturgeschichte (3 vols., Stuttgart, 1966–81).

'Paläographie und frühmittelalterliche Klassiküberlieferung', in *La cultura antica nell'occidente latino dal VII al'XI secolo*, Settimane di Studio, 22 (2 vols., Spoleto, 1975), I, pp. 59–85; rpt. in Bischoff, *Mittelalterliche Studien*, III, pp. 55–71.

'Wendepunkt in der Geschichte der lateinischen Exegese im Frühmittelalter', *Sacris erudiri*, 6 (1955), pp. 189–281; rpt. in Bischoff, *Mittelalterliche Studien*, I, 205–74.

Black, Deborah L., 'The "Imaginative Syllogism" in Arabic Philosophy: A Medieval Contribution to the Philosophical Study of Metaphor', *MS*, 51 (1989), 242–67.

Black, Robert, *Humanism and Education in Medieval and Renaissance Italy: Tradition and Innovation in Latin Schools from the Twelfth to the Fifteenth Century* (Cambridge, 2001).

Bloch, Herbert, 'The Pagan Revival in the West at the End of the Fourth Century', in A. Momigliano (ed.), *The Conflict between Paganism and Christianity in the Fourth Century* (Oxford, 1963), pp. 193–218.

Boas, M., 'De librorum Catoniarum historia atque compositione', *Mnemosyne*, n.s. 42 (1944), 17–46.

Boggess, William F., 'Aristotle's Poetics in the Fourteenth Century', *SP*, 67 (1970), 278–94.

'Hermannus Alemannus and Catharsis in the Medieval Latin *Poetics*', *Classical World*, 62 (1969), 212–14.

Bolgar, R. R. (ed.), *Classical Influences on European Culture A.D. 500–1500* (Cambridge, 1971).

The Classical Heritage and its Beneficiaries (1954; rpt. Cambridge, 1973).

Bolton, Diane K., 'Remigian Commentaries on the "Consolation of Philosophy" and their Sources', *Traditio*, 33 (1977), 381–94.

Bonaventure, Brother, 'The Teaching of Latin in Later Medieval England', *MS*, 23 (1961), 1–20.

Bond, Gerald, 'Composing Yourself: Ovid's *Heroides*, Baudri of Bourgueil and the Problem of Persona', *Mediaevalia*, 13 (1989 for 1987), 83–117.

'*Iocus amoris*: The Poetry of Baudri of Bourgueil and the Formation of the Ovidian Subculture', *Traditio*, 42 (1986), 143–93.

Bourgain, Pascale, 'Virgile et la poésie latine du bas Moyen Âge', in *Lectures médiévales de Virgile*, pp. 167–87.

Brinkmann, Hennig, *Mittelalterliche Hermeneutik* (Darmstadt, 1980).

Brown, Alison Goddard, 'The *Facetus* [Moribus et vita]: or, The Art of Courtly Living', *Allegorica*, 2 (1978), 27–57.

Brown, George H., 'The Preservation and Transmission of Northumbrian Culture on the Continent: Alcuin's Debt to Bede', in P. E. Szarmach and J. T. Rosenthal (eds.), *The Preservation and Transmission of Anglo-Saxon Culture* (Kalamazoo MI, 1997), pp. 159–75.

Brown, T. J., 'An Historical Introduction to the Use of Classical Latin Authors in the British Isles from the Fifth to the Eleventh Century', in *La cultura antica nell'occidente latino dal VII al'XI secolo*, Settimane di Studio, 22 (2 vols., Spoleto, 1975), I, pp. 237–99.

Brugnoli, Giorgio, 'Donato, Elio', *Enciclopedia Virgiliana* (5 vols. in 6, Rome, 1984–91), II, pp. 125–7.

'Servio', *Enciclopedia Virgiliana* (5 vols. in 6, Rome, 1984–91), IV, pp. 805–13.

Brunhölzl, Franz, 'Der Bildungsauftrag der Hofschule', in *Karl der Grosse. Lebenswerk und Nachleben*, ed. W. Braunfels (5 vols., 1965–6), II, *Geistiges Leben*, ed. B. Bischoff, pp. 28–41.

Bühler, Winfried, 'Die Pariser Horazscholien – eine neue Quelle der Mythographi Vaticani 1 und 2', *Philologus*, 105 (1961), 123–35.

'Theodulus' *Ecloga* and *Mythographus Vaticanus I*', *California Studies in Classical Antiquity*, 1 (1968), 65–71.

Bultot, R., 'La *Chartula* et l'enseignement du mépris du monde dans les écoles et les universités médiévales', *Studi medievali*, 3rd ser. 8 (1967), 787–834.

Burnett, Charles, 'A Note on the Origins of the Third Vatican Mythographer', *Journal of the Warburg and Courtauld Institutes*, 44 (1981), 160–6.

Burrow, J. A., *The Ages of Man: A Study in Medieval Writing and Thought* (Oxford, 1986).

Burton, Rosemary, *Classical Poets in the 'Florilegium Gallicum'*, Lateinische Sprache und Literatur des Mittelalters, 14 (Frankfurt, 1983).

Butzer, P. L., Kerner, M., and Oberschelp, W. (eds.), *Karl der Grosse und sein Nachwirken: 1200 Jahre Kultur und Wissenschaft in Europa* (Turnhout, 1997).

Calabrese, Michael, *Chaucer's Ovidian Arts of Love* (Gainesville FL, 1994).

Callus, Daniel A., 'Robert Grosseteste as Scholar', in D. A. Callus (ed.), *Robert Grosseteste, Scholar and Bishop* (Oxford, 1955), pp. 1–69.

Cameron, Alan, 'The Date and Identity of Macrobius', *Journal of Roman Studies*, 56 (1966), 25–38.

Chavannes-Mazel, Claudine A., and Smith, Margaret M. (eds.), *Medieval Manuscripts of the Latin Classics: Production and Use* (Los Altos CA, 1996).

Chenu, M. D., 'Grammaire et théologie aux XIIe et XIIIe siècles', *AHDLMA*, 10 (1936), 5–28.

Cinquino, J., 'Coluccio Salutati, Defender of Poetry', *Italica*, 26 (1953), 131–5.

Clarke, A. K., and Levy, H. L., 'Claudius Claudianus', in Kristeller (ed.), *Catalogus*, III, pp. 141–71.

Clogan, Paul M., *Medieval Achilleid*. See Statius, *Achilleis*.

Codoñer, C., 'The Poetry of Eugenius of Toledo', *Papers of the Liverpool Latin Society*, 3 (1981), 323–42.

Contreni, John J., 'A propos de quelques manuscrits de l'école de Laon au XIe siècle: découvertes et problèmes', *Le Moyen Âge*, 78 (1972), 5–39.

The Cathedral School of Laon from 850 to 930: Its Manuscripts and Masters, Münchener Beiträge zur Mediävistik und Renaissance-Forschung, 29 (Munich, 1978).

'John Scottus, Martin Hiberniensis, the Liberal Arts, and Teaching', in M. W. Herren (ed.), *Insular Latin Studies*, Papers in Medieval Studies, 1 (Toronto, 1981), pp. 23–44.

'The Pursuit of Knowledge in Carolingian Europe', in Sullivan (ed.), *'Gentle Voices of Teachers'*, pp. 106–41.

'Three Carolingian Texts Attributed to Laon: Reconsiderations', *Studi medievali*, 3rd ser. 17 (1976), 797–813.

Copeland, Rita, 'Rhetoric and Vernacular Translation in the Middle Ages', *SAC*, 9 (1987), 41–75.

Rhetoric, Hermeneutics, and Translation in the Middle Ages: Academic Traditions and Vernacular Texts (Cambridge, 1991).

Copeland, Rita (ed.), *Criticism and Dissent in the Middle Ages* (Cambridge, 1996).

Copeland, Rita, and Melville, Stephen, 'Allegory and Allegoresis, Rhetoric and Hermeneutics', *Exemplaria*, 3 (1991), 159–87.

Coulson, Frank T., 'A Checklist of Newly Discovered Manuscripts of the *Allegoriae* of Giovanni del Virgilio', *Studi medievalia*, 37 (1996), 443–53.

'Hitherto Unedited Medieval and Renaissance Lives of Ovid (1)', *MS*, 49 (1987), 152–207.

'MSS of the Vulgate Commentary on Ovid's *Metamorphoses*: A Checklist', *Scriptorium*, 39 (1985), 118–29.

'New Manuscript Evidence for Sources of the *Accessus* of Arnoul d'Orléans to the *Metamorphoses* of Ovid', *Manuscripta*, 30 (1986), 103–7.

'A Study of the "Vulgate" Commentary on the *Metamorphoses* of Ovid and a Critical Edition of the Glosses to Book 1', Ph.D. diss., University of Toronto, 1982.

'The "Vulgate" Commentary on Ovid's *Metamorphoses*', *Mediaevalia*, 13 (1989 for 1987), 29–61.

Coulson, Frank T., and Molyviati-Toptsis, U., 'Vaticanus latinus 2877: A Hitherto Unedited Allegorization of Ovid's *Metamorphoses*', *Journal of Medieval Latin*, 2 (1992), 134–202.

Coulson, Frank T., and Roy, Bruno, *Incipitarium Ovidianum: A Finding Guide for Texts Related to the Study of Ovid in the Middle Ages and Renaissance* (Turnhout, 2000).

Coulter, James A., *The Literary Microcosm: Theories of Interpretation of the Later Neoplatonists*, Columbia Studies in the Classical Tradition, 2 (Leiden, 1976).

Courcelle, Pierre, *La Consolation de Philosophie dans la tradition littéraire: Antécédents et postérité de Boèce* (Paris, 1967).

'Les Exégèses chrétiennes de la quatrième Eglogue', *Revue des études anciennes*, 59 (1957), 294–319.

Late Latin Writers and their Greek Sources, tr. H. E. Wedeck (Cambridge MA, 1969).

Lecteurs païens et lecteurs chrétiens de l'Énéide, Mémoires de l'Académie des inscriptions et belles-lettres, n.s. 4 (2 vols., Paris, 1984).

'Les Pères de l'Église devant les enfers virgiliens', *AHDLMA*, 22 (1955), 5–74.

Curtius, Ernst R., *Europäische Literatur und lateinisches Mittelalter* (2nd edn, Bern, 1948). English tr. of the first edition under the title *European Literature and the Latin Middle Ages*, by W. R. Trask (London, 1953).

Daintree, David, 'The Virgil Commentary of Aelius Donatus – Black Hole or "Éminence grise"?', *Greece and Rome*, 37 (1990), 65–79.

d'Alverny, Marie-Thérèse, 'La Sagesse et ses sept filles: Recherches sur les allégories de la Philosophie et des arts libéraux du XIe au XIIe siècle', in *Mélanges dédiées à la mémoire de Félix Grat* (2 vols., Paris, 1946–9), I, pp. 245–78.

'Variations sur un thème de Virgile dans un sermon d'Alain de Lille', in *Melanges d'Archéologie et d'Histoire offerts à André Piganiol*, ed. R. Chevallier (3 vols., Paris, 1966), III, pp. 1517–28.

Dane, Joseph A., '*Integumentum* as Interpretation: Note on William of Conches's Commentary on Macrobius (I, 2, 10–11)', *Classical Folia*, 32 (1978), 201–15.

D'Avray, David, *Preaching of the Friars: Sermons Diffused from Paris before 1300* (Oxford, 1985).

de Angelis, Violetta, 'I commenti medievali alla Tebaide di Stazio: Anselmo di Laon, Goffredo Babione, Ilario d'Orléans', in Mann and Olsen (eds.), *Medieval and Renaissance Scholarship*, pp. 75–136.

' . . . e l'ultimo Lucano', in A. A. Iannucci (ed.), *Dante e la 'bella scola' della poesia: autorità e sfida poetica* (Ravenna, 1993), pp. 145–203.

Davies, Martin, and Goldfinch, John (eds.), *Vergil: A Census of Printed Editions 1469–1500*, Occasional Papers of the Bibliographical Society, 7 (London, 1992).

De Bruyne, Edgar, *Études d'esthétique médiévale* (3 vols., Bruges, 1946); abridged and tr. E. B. Hennessy as *The Esthetics of the Middle Ages* (New York, 1969).

Delhaye, P., 'L'Enseignement de la philosophie morale au XIIe siècle', *MS*, 11 (1949), 77–99.

'"Grammatica" et "Ethica" au XIIe siècle', *RTAM*, 25 (1958), 59–110.

Demats, Paule, *Fabula: Trois études de mythographie antique et médiévale* (Geneva, 1973).

Desmond, Marilynn R. (ed.), *Ovid in Medieval Culture*, Mediaevalia, 13 (1989 for 1987).

Reading Dido: Gender, Textuality and the Medieval 'Aeneid' (Minneapolis MN, 1994).

Di Cesare, M., 'Cristoforo Landino on the Name and Nature of Poetry: The Critic as Hero', *ChR*, 21 (1986), 155–81.

Dinkova-Bruun, G., 'Medieval Latin Poetic Anthologies (VII)', *MS*, 64 (2002), 61–109.

Dronke, Peter, 'Bernardo Silvestre', in *Enciclopedia Virgiliana* (Rome, 1984), I, cols. 59–65.

Fabula: Explorations into the Uses of Myth in Medieval Platonism, Mittellateinische Studien und Texte, 9 (Leiden, 1974).

'Integumenta Virgilii', in *Lectures médiévales de Virgile*, Collection de l'École française de Rome, 80 (Rome, 1985), pp. 313–29.

Medieval Latin and the Rise of European Love-Lyric (2nd edn, 2 vols., Oxford, 1968).

The Medieval Poet and his World, Storia e Letteratura, Raccolta di studi e testi, 164 (Rome, 1984).

'Pseudo-Ovid, Facetus and the Arts of Love', *Mittellateinisches Jahrbuch*, 11 (1976), 126–31.

Dürr, Julius, 'Das Leben Juvenals', *Wissenschaftliche Beilage zum Programm des Königlichen Gymnasiums in Ulm* (Ulm, 1888), pp. 2–28.

Dutton, Paul E., 'Evidence that Dubthach's Priscian Codex Once Belonged to Eriugena', in H. J. Westra (ed.), *From Athens to Chartres: Neoplatonism and Medieval Thought: Studies in Honour of Edouard Jeauneau* (Leiden, 1992), pp. 15–45.

'The Uncovering of the *Glosae super Platonem* of Bernard of Chartres', *MS*, 44 (1984), 192–221.

Edwards, M. C., 'A Study of Six Characters in Chaucer's *Legend of Good Women* with Reference to Medieval Scholia on Ovid's *Heroides*', B. Litt. thesis, Oxford University, 1970.

Elder, J. P., 'A Medieval Cornutus on Persius', *Speculum*, 22 (1947), 240–8.

Elliott, Kathleen O., and Elder, J. P., 'A Critical Edition of the Vatican Mythographers', *TAPA*, 78 (1947), 189–207.

Enciclopedia Virgiliana (5 vols. in 6, Rome, 1984–91).

Engels, J., 'L'Édition critique de *l'Ovidius moralizatus* de Bersuire', *Vivarium*, 9 (1971), 19–48.

Fichtenau, Heinrich, *The Carolingian Empire*, tr. P. Munz (Oxford, 1957).

Fontaine, Jacques, 'L'Apport de la tradition poétique romaine à la formation de l'hymnodie latine chrétienne', *Revue des études latines*, 52 (1974), 318–55.

Isidore de Seville et la culture classique dans l'Espagne wisigothique (2 vols., Paris, 1959).

'Isidoro', *Enciclopedia Virgiliana* (5 vols. in 6, Rome, 1984–91), III, pp. 26–8.

Fredborg, K. M., ' "Difficile est propria communia dicere" (Horats A. P. 128). Horatsfortolkningens bidrag til middelalderens poetik', *Museum Tusculanum*, 40–3 (Copenhagen, 1980), 583–97.

Friis-Jensen, Karsten, 'The *Ars Poetica* in Twelfth-Century France: The Horace of Matthew of Vendôme, Geoffrey of Vinsauf and John of Garland', *CIMAGL*, 60 (1990), 319–88.

'The *Ars Poetica* in Twelfth-Century France: Addenda and Corrigenda', *CIMAGL*, 61 (1991), 184.

'Horace and the Early Writers of Arts of Poetry' in S. Ebbesen (ed.), *Sprachtheorien in Spätantike und Mittelalter* (Tübingen, 1995), pp. 360–401.

'*Horatius liricus et ethicus*: Two Twelfth-Century School Texts on Horace's Poems', *CIMAGL*, 57 (1988), 81–147.

'Medieval Commentaries on Horace', in Mann and Olsen (eds.), *Medieval and Renaissance Scholarship*, pp. 51–73.

'The Medieval Horace and his Lyrics', in *Horace: L'Œuvre et les imitations: Un siècle d'interprétation* (Geneva, 1993), pp. 257–303.

Friis-Jensen, Karsten, and Olsen, B. Munk, and Smith, O. L., 'Bibliography of Classical Scholarship in the Middle Ages and the Early Renaissance (9th to 15th Centuries)', in N. Mann and B. Munk Olsen (eds.), *Medieval and Renaissance Scholarship*, Mittellateinische Studien und Texte, 21 (Leiden, 1997), pp. 197–252.

Funaioli, Gino, *Esegesi Virgiliana antica* (Milan, 1930).

Ganz, Peter, '*Archani celestis non ignorans*: Ein unbekannter Ovid-Kommentar', in *Verbum et Signum* [Friedrich Ohly Festschrift] (2 vols., Munich, 1975), I, pp. 195–208.

Gersh, Stephen, *Middle Platonism and Neoplatonism* (2 vols., Notre Dame IN, 1986).

Geymonat, Mario, 'Filargirio', *Enciclopedia Virgiliana* (5 vols. in 6, Rome, 1984–91), II, pp. 520–21.

Ghisalberti, Fausto, 'Giovanni del Virgilio espositore delle *Metamorfosi*', *Giornale dantesco*, 34 (1933), 1–110.

'Medieval Biographies of Ovid', *Journal of the Warburg and Courtauld Institutes*, 9 (1946), 10–59.

Gibson, Margaret, 'The Study of the *Timaeus* in the Eleventh and Twelfth Centuries', *Pensamiento*, 25 (1969), 183–94.

Ginsberg, Warren, '*Ovidius ethicus*? Ovid and the Medieval Commentary Tradition', in J. J. Paxson and C. A. Gravlee (eds.), *Desiring Discourse: The Literature of Love, Ovid through Chaucer* (Selinsgrove PA and London, 1998), pp. 62–86.

Glauche, Günter, 'Die Rolle der Schulautoren im Unterricht von 800 bis 1100', in *La Scuola nell'Occidente Latino nell'Alto Medioevo*, Settimane di Studio, 19 (2 vols., Spoleto, 1972), pp. 617–36.

Schullektüre im Mittelalter: Entstehung und Wandlungen des Lektürekanons bis 1200 nach den Quellen dargestellt, Münchener Beiträge zur Mediävistik und Renaissance-Forschung, 5 (Munich, 1970).

Gneuss, Helmut, *Hymnar und Hymnen im englischen Mittelalter*, Buchreiche der Anglia Zeitschrift für englische Philologie, 12 (Tübingen, 1968).

Godman, Peter (ed.), *Poetry of the Carolingian Renaissance* (Norman OK, 1985).

Godman, Peter, and Murray, Oswyn (eds.), *Latin Poetry and the Classical Tradition: Essays in Medieval and Renaissance Literature*, Oxford-Warburg Studies (Oxford, 1990).

Goering, J. W., *William de Montibus (c. 1140–1213): The Schools and the Literature of Pastoral Care* (Toronto, 1992).

Gössmann, Elisabeth, *Antiqui und Moderni im Mittelalter: Eine geschichtliche Standortsbestimmung* (Munich and Vienna, 1974).

Gotoff, Harold C., *The Transmission of the Text of Lucan in the Ninth Century* (Cambridge MA, 1971).

Green, R. H., 'Dante's Allegory of Poets and the Medieval Theory of Poetic Fiction', *Comparative Literature*, 9 (1957), 118–28.

Green, R. P. H., 'The Genesis of a Medieval Textbook: The Models and Sources of the *Ecloga Theoduli*', *Viator*, 13 (1982), 49–106.

Green, R. P. H. (ed.), *Seven Versions of Carolingian Pastoral* (Reading, 1980).

Greenfield, Concetta Carestia, *Humanist and Scholastic Poetics, 1250–1500* (Lewisburg PA, 1981).

Gregory, Tullio, *Giovanni Scoto Eriugena: Tre studi* (Florence, 1963).

Platonismo medievale: studi e ricerche (Rome, 1958).

Hagendahl, H., *Augustine and the Latin Classics*, Studia graeca et latina Gothoburgensia, 20 (Gothenburg, 1967).

Hall, F. W., *A Companion to Classical Texts* (Oxford, 1913).

Halliwell, Stephen, *Aristotle's Poetics* (London, 1986).

'Aristotle's Poetics', in Kennedy (ed.), *Cambridge History of Literary Criticism* 1, pp. 149–83.

Hamesse, Jacqueline (ed.), *Les Prologues médiévaux: Actes du colloque internationale organisé par l'Academia belgica et l'École française de Rome (Rome, 26–8 mars 1998)* (Turnhout, 2000).

Hamilton, G. L., 'Theodolus: A Medieval Textbook', *MP*, 7 (1909), 169–85.

Hardison, O. B., 'The Place of Averroes' Commentary on the *Poetics* in the History of Medieval Criticism', *Medieval and Renaissance Studies* [Durham NC], 4 (1970 for 1968), 57–81.

Häring, N. M., 'Commentary and Hermeneutics', in R. L. Benson and G. Constable (eds.), *Renaissance and Renewal in the Twelfth Century* (Oxford, 1982), pp. 173–200.

Haye, Thomas, *Oratio: Mittelalterliche Redekunst in lateinischer Sprache*, Mittellateinische Studien und Texte, 27 (Leiden, 1999).

Hazleton, R., 'The Christianisation of "Cato": The *Disticha Catonis* in the Light of Late Medieval Commentaries', *MS*, 19 (1957), 157–73.

Henkel, Nikolaus, 'Die Ecloga Theoduli und ihre literarischen Gegenkonzeptionen', *Mittellateinisches Jahrbuch*, 24–5 (1989–90), 151–62.

Herren, Michael, 'Classical and Secular Learning among the Irish before the Carolingian Renaissance', *Florilegium*, 3 (1981), 118–57.

'The Humanism of John Scottus', in Leonardi (ed.), *Umanesimi medievali*, pp. 191–9.

Hexter, Ralph, 'The *Allegari* of Pierre Bersuire: Interpretation and the *Reductorium Morale*', *Allegorica*, 10 (1989), 51–84.

'Medieval Articulations of Ovid's *Metamorphoses*: From Lactantian Segmentation to Arnulfian Allegory', *Mediaevalia*, 13 (1987), 63–82.

'The Metamorphosis of Sodom: The Ps-Cyprian *De Sodoma* as an Ovidian Episode', *Traditio*, 44 (1988), 1–35.

Ovid and Medieval Schooling: Studies in Medieval School Commentaries on Ovid's 'Ars amatoria', 'Epistulae ex Ponto', and 'Epistulae heroidum' (Munich, 1986).

'Ovid's Body', in J. I. Porter (ed.), *Constructions of the Classical Body* (Ann Arbor MI, 1999), pp. 327–54.

Holtz, Louis, 'À l'École de Donat, de saint Augustin à Bède', *Latomus*, 36 (1977), 522–38.

Donat et la tradition de l'enseignement grammatical (Paris, 1981).

'L'Humanisme de Loup de Ferrières', in Leonardi (ed.), *Umanesimi medievali*, pp. 201–13.

'Les Nouvelles Tendances de la pédagogie grammaticale au Xe siècle', *Mittellateinisches Jahrbuch*, 24–5 (1989–90), 163–73.

'La Redécouverte de Virgile aux VIIIe et IXe siècles d'après les manuscrits conservés', in *Lectures médiévales de Virgile*, Collection de l'École française de Rome, 80 (Rome, 1985), pp. 9–30.

'La Survie de Virgile dans le haut Moyen Âge', in R. Chevallier (ed.), *Présence de Vergile: Actes du Colloque des 9, 11, et 12 Décembre 1976 (Paris E.N.S., Tours)* (Paris, 1978), pp. 209–22.

Hunt, R. W., *Collected Papers on the History of Grammar in the Middle Ages*, ed. G. L. Bursill-Hall, Studies in the History of Linguistics, 5 (Amsterdam, 1980).

'English Learning in the Late Twelfth Century', in *Essays in Medieval History*, ed. Southern, pp. 106–28.

'The Introductions to the *Artes* in the Twelfth Century', in *Studia medievalia in honorem admodum Reverendi Patris Raymundi Josephi Martin* (Bruges, 1948), pp. 85–112; rpt. in Hunt, *Collected Papers*, pp. 117–44.

The Schools and the Cloister: The Life and Writings of Alexander Nequam (1157–1217) (Oxford, 1984).

'Studies on Priscian in the Twelfth Century, II: The School of Ralph of Beauvais', *Medieval and Renaissance Studies*, 2 (1950), 1–56; rpt. in Hunt, *Collected Papers*, pp. 39–94.

Hunt, Tony, 'Chrestien and Macrobius', *Classica et medievalia*, 33 (1981–82), 211–27.

'*Prodesse et Delectare*: Metaphors of Pleasure and Instruction in Old French', *Neuphilologische Mitteilungen*, 80 (1979), 17–35.

'Redating Chrestien de Troyes', *Bulletin bibliographique de la Société Internationale Arthurienne*, 30 (1978), 209–37.

Teaching and Learning Latin in Thirteenth-Century England (3 vols., Cambridge, 1991).

Hunter Blair, Peter, *The World of Bede* (London, 1970); rev. edn by M. Lapidge (Cambridge, 1990).

Huygens, R. B. C., 'Notes sur le *Dialogus super auctores* de Conrad de Hirsau et le commentaire sur Théodule de Bernard d'Utrecht', *Latomus*, 13 (1954). 420–8.

Irvine, Martin, *The Making of Textual Culture: 'Grammatica' and Literary Theory, 350–1100* (Cambridge, 1994).

Jeauneau, Édouard, 'Berkeley, University of California, Bancroft Library MS 2 (Notes de Lecture)', *MS*, 50 (1988), 438–56.

'Jean Scot Érigène et le grec', *Archivum latinitatis medii ævi (Bulletin du Cange)*, 41 (1979), 5–50.

'Notes sur l'École de Chartres', *Studi medievali*, 3rd ser. 5 (1964), 821–65; rpt. in his *Lectio philosophorum*, pp. 5–49.

Quatre Thèmes erigéniens [Conférence Albert-le-Grand 1974] (Montreal and Paris, 1978).

'L'Usage de la notion d'integumentum à travers les gloses de Guillaume de Conches', *AHDLMA*, 24 (1957), 35–100; rpt. in his *Lectio philosophorum: Recherches sur l'école de Chartres* (Amsterdam, 1973), pp. 127–92.

Jenaro-MacLennan, L., *The Trecento Commentaries on the 'Divina Commedia' and the 'Epistle to Cangrande'* (Oxford, 1974).

Jeudy, Colette, '*Accessus* aux œuvres d'Horace', *Revue d'histoire des textes*, 1 (1971), 211.

Jeudy, Colette, and Riou, Yves-François, 'L'Achilléide de Stace au Moyen Âge: Abrégés et arguments', *Revue d'histoire des textes*, 4 (1974), 143–80.

Jolivet, Jean, 'Quelques Cas de 'platonisme grammatical' du VIIe au XIIe siècle', in P. Gallais and Y.-F. Riou (ed.), *Mélanges offerts à René Crozet* (2 vols., Poitiers, 1966), I, pp. 93–9.

Jones, J. W., 'Allegorical Interpretation in Servius', *Classical Journal*, 56 (1961), 217–26.

'The So-Called Silvestris Commentary on the *Aeneid* and Two Other Interpretations', *Speculum*, 64 (1989), 838–48.

Kaster, Robert A., 'The Grammarian's Authority', *Classical Philology*, 75 (1980), 216–41.

Guardians of Language: The Grammarian and Society in Late Antiquity (Berkeley CA, 1988).

'Macrobius and Servius: *Verecundia* and the Grammarian's Function', *Harvard Studies in Classical Philology*, 84 (1980), 219–62.

Kelly, Henry Ansgar, 'Aristotle-Averroës-Allemanus on Tragedy: The Influence of the *Poetics* on the Latin Middle Ages', *Viator*, 10 (1979), 161–209.

Chaucerian Tragedy (Woodbridge, 1997).

Ideas and Forms of Tragedy from Aristotle to the Middle Ages (Cambridge, 1993).

Tragedy and Comedy from Dante to Pseudo-Dante, University of California Publications in Modern Philology, 121 (Berkeley CA, 1989).

Kemal, S., *The Poetics of Alfarabi and Avicenna* (Leiden, 1991).

Kennedy, George A. (ed.), *The Cambridge History of Literary Criticism, I: Classical Criticism* (Cambridge, 1989).

Kennedy, William, *Authorizing Petrarch* (Ithaca NY, 1994).

Kindermann, Udo, *Satyra: Die Theorie der Satire im Mittellateinischen. Vorstudie zu einer Gattungsgeschichte*, Erlanger Beiträge zur Sprach- und Kunstwissenschaft, 58 (1978).

Klinck, Hroswitha, *Die lateinische Etymologie des Mittelalters*, Medium ævum, 17 (Munich, 1970).

Kretzmann, Norman, Kenny, Anthony, Pinborg, Jan, and Stump, Eleanor (eds.), *The Cambridge History of Later Medieval Philosophy* (Cambridge, 1982).

Kristeller, P. O., *et al.* (eds.), *Catalogus translationum et commentariorum: Medieval and Renaissance Latin Translations and Commentaries* (Washington DC, 1960–).

Medieval Aspects of Renaissance Learning (Durham NC, 1974).

Laistner, M. L. W., *The Intellectual Heritage of the Early Middle Ages*, ed. C. G. Starr (Ithaca NY, 1957).

Thought and Letters in Western Europe, 500–900 (2nd edn, Ithaca NY, 1957).

Lamberton, Robert, *Homer the Theologian: Neoplatonist Allegorical Reading and the Growth of the Epic Tradition* (Berkeley CA, 1986).

Landgraf, A., *Écrits théologiques de l'école d'Abelard*, Spicilegium sacrum Lovaniense, 14 (1934).

Lapidge, Michael, *Anglo-Latin Literature, 600–899* (London, 1996).

'The Authorship of the Adonic Verses "Ad Fidolium" Attributed to Columbanus', *Studi medievali*, 3rd ser. 18 (1977), 249–314.

Lapidge, Michael, and Page, R. I., 'The Study of Latin Texts in late Anglo-Saxon England. [1] The Evidence of Latin Glosses. [2] The Evidence of English Glosses', in N. Brooks (ed.), *Latin and the Vernacular Languages in Early Medieval Britain* (Leicester, 1982), pp. 99–165.

Leader, Damian, 'Grammar in Late Medieval Oxford and Cambridge', *History of Education*, 12 (1983), 9–14.

Leclercq, Jean, *The Love of Learning and the Desire for God*, tr. C. Misrahi (New York, 1961).

Monks and Love in Twelfth-Century France (Oxford, 1979).

Lectures médiévales de Virgile, Collection de l'école française de Rome, 80 (Rome, 1985).

Lehmann, Paul, *Die Parodie im Mittelalter* (Stuttgart, 1963).

Lemoine, Fanny, *Martianus Capella: A Literary Re-evaluation*, Münchener Beiträge zur Mediävistik und Renaissance-Forschung, 10 (Munich, 1972).

Leonardi, Claudio, 'I codici di Marziano Capella', *Aevum*, 33 (1959), 443–89; 34 (1960), 1–99, 411–524. Rpt. as one vol. (Milan, 1961?).

'I commenti altomedievali ai classici pagani: da Severino Boezio a Remigio d'Auxerre', *La cultura antica nell'occidente latino dal VII all'XI secolo*, Settimane di studio, 22 (2 vols., Spoleto, 1975), I, pp. 459–508.

'Nuove voci poetiche tra secolo IX e XI', *Studi medievali*, 3rd ser. 2 (1961), 139–68.

'Remigio d'Auxerre e l'eredità della scuola carolingia', in *I classici nel medioevo e nell'umanesimo: miscellanea filologica* (Genoa, 1975), pp. 271–88.

Leonardi, Claudio (ed.), *Gli umanesimi medievali* (Florence, 1998).

Lepschy, Giulio (ed.), *History of Linguistics, II: Classical and Medieval Linguistics* (London, 1994).

Levine, Philip, 'The Continuity and Preservation of the Latin Tradition', in L. White, Jr. (ed.), *The Transformation of the Roman World* (Berkeley and Los Angeles CA, 1966), pp. 206–31.

Levine, Robert, 'Exploiting Ovid: Medieval Allegorizations of the Metamorphoses', *Medioevo romanzo*, 14 (1989), 197–213.

Lohr, C. H., 'Medieval Latin Aristotle Commentaries', *Traditio*, 23 (1967) 313–413 [A–F]; 24 (1968) 149–245 [G–I]; 26 (1970) 135–216 [Jacobus–Johannes Juff]; 27 (1971) 251–351 [Johannes de Kanthi–M]; 28 (1972) 281–392 [N–Richardus]; 29 (1973) 93–197, 393–6 [Robertus–W]; 30 (1972) 119–44 [supplement] (Florence, 1988–95).

Lusignan, Serge, *Préface au 'Speculum maius' de Vincent de Beauvais: Réfraction et diffraction*, Cahiers d'études médiévales, 5 (Montreal and Paris, 1979).

Lusignan, Serge, and Paulmier-Foucart, Monique (eds.), *Lector et compilator: Vincent de Beauvais, frère prêcheur; un intellectuel et son milieu au XIIIe siècle* (Grâne, 1997).

Malcovati, Enrica, *M. Anneo Lucano* (Milan, 1940).

Mancini, Augusto, 'Sul commento oraziano del codice della Bibliotheca Publica di Lucca N. 1433', *Congresso internazionale di scienze storiche, atti* 2 (Rome, 1905), pp. 243–8.

Mann, Jill, 'Satiric Subject and Satiric Object in Goliardic Literature', *Mittellateinisches Jahrbuch*, 15 (1980), 63–86.

Mann, Nicholas, and Olsen, Birger Munk (eds.), *Medieval and Renaissance Scholarship: Proceedings of the Second European Science Foundation Workshop on the Classical Tradition in the Middle Ages and the Renaissance (London, the Warburg Institute, 27–28 November 1992)* (Leiden, 1997).

Marchesi, C., 'Gli scoliasti di Persio', *Rivista di Filologia*, 39 (1911), 564–85; 40 (1912), 1–35.

Mariani, Ferminia, 'Persio nella scuola d'Auxerre e l'adnotatio secundum Remigium', *Giornale italiano di filologia*, 18 (1965), 145–61.

Marinone, Nino, 'Elio Donato, Macrobio e Servio commentatori di Virgilio', in his *Analecta graecolatina* (Bologna, 1990), pp. 193–264.

Marshall, P. K., Martin, Janet, and Rouse, Richard H., 'Clare College MS 26 and the Circulation of Aulus Gellius in Medieval England and France', *MS*, 42 (1980), 353–94.

Marti, Berthe M., 'Literary Criticism in Medieval Commentaries on Lucan', *TAPA*, 72 (1941), 245–54.

Massa, Eugenio, 'Ruggero Bacone e la "Poetica" di Aristotele', *Giornale Critico della filosofia Italiana*, 32 (1953), 457–73.

Ruggero Bacone: etica e poetica nella storia dell 'Opus maius', Uomini e dottrine, 3 (Rome 1955).

McEvoy, James, *The Philosophy of Robert Grosseteste* (Oxford, 1982).

McKenzie, Donald F., *Bibliography and the Sociology of the Text* (Cambridge, 1999).

McKinley, Kathryn L., *Reading the Ovidian Heroine: 'Metamorphoses' Commentaries, 1100–1618* (Leiden, 2001).

McKitterick, Rosamund, *The Frankish Kings and Culture in the Early Middle Ages* (Aldershot, 1995).

Megas, C., *The Pre-Humanist Circle of Padua (Lovato Lovati – Albertino Mussato) and the Tragedies of L. A. Seneca* (Thessaloniki, 1967).

Mehtonen, Päivi, *Old Concepts and New Poetics: Historia, Argumentum, and Fabula in the Twelfth- and Early Thirteenth-Century Latin Poetics of Fiction*, Finnish Society of Sciences and Letters, Commentationes humanarum litterarum, 108 (Helsinki, 1996).

Meiser, C., 'Ueber einen Commentar zu den Metamorphosen des Ovid', *Sitzungsberichte der Königlichen bayerischen Akademie der Wissenschaften, philosophisch-philologisch-und historische Classe* (1885), 47–89.

Menocal, Maria R., *The Arabic Role in Medieval Literary History* (Philadelphia PA, 1987).

Miller, Paul, 'John Gower, Satiric Poet', in *Gower's 'Confessio Amantis': Responses and Reassessments*, ed. A. J. Minnis (Woodbridge, 1983), pp. 79–105.

Minnis, Alastair J., 'The Influence of Academic Prologues on the Prologues and Literary Attitudes of Late-Medieval English Writers', *MS*, 43 (1981), 342–83.

'Late-Medieval Discussions of *Compilatio* and the Role of the *Compilator*', *BPP*, 101 (1979), 385–421.

Magister amoris: The 'Roman de la Rose' and Vernacular Hermeneutics (Oxford, 2001).

Medieval Theory of Authorship: Scholastic Literary Attitudes in the Later Middle Ages (1984; 2nd edn, Aldershot, 1988).

Minnis, Alastair J. (ed.), *Chaucer's 'Boece' and the Medieval Tradition of Boethius* (Woodbridge, 1993).

The Medieval Boethius: Studies in the Vernacular Translations of 'De consolatione philosophiae' (Cambridge, 1987).

Minnis, Alastair J., and Scott, A. B., with Wallace, David (eds.), *Medieval Literary Theory and Criticism, c. 1100–c. 1375: The Commentary-Tradition* (1988; rev. edn, Oxford, 1991; rpt. 2001).

Moos, Peter von, 'Lucans *tragedia* im Hochmittelalter: Pessimismus, *contemptus mundi* und Gegenwartserfahrung (Otto von Freising *Vita Henrici IV*, Johann von Salisbury)', *Mittellateinisches Jahrbuch*, 14 (1979), 127–86.

'*Poeta* und *historicus* im Mittelalter: Zum Mimesis-Problem am Beispiel einiger Urteile über Lucan', *PBB*, 98 (1976), 93–130.

Moss, Ann, *Latin Commentaries on Ovid from the Renaissance* (Summertown TN, 1998).

Ovid in Renaissance France: A Survey of the Latin Editions of Ovid and Commentaries Printed in France before 1600, Warburg Institute Surveys, 8 (London, 1982).

Most, G. W. (ed.), *Commentaries - Kommentare* (Göttingen, 1999).

Munari, Franco, *Ovid im Mittelalter* (Geneva, 1960).

Munk Olsen, Birger, *I classici nel canone scolastico altomedievale*, Quaderni di cultura mediolatina, 1 (Spoleto, 1991).

'Les Classiques au Xe siècle', *Mittellateinisches Jahrbuch*, 24–5 (1989–90), 341–7.

'Les Classiques latins dans les florilèges médiévaux antérieurs au xiiie siècle', *Revue d'histoire des textes*, 9 (1979), 47–121; 10 (1980), 23–72.

'L'édition des textes antiques au Moyen Âge', in M. Børch, A. Haarder and J. McGrew (eds.), *The Medieval Text: Editors and Critics* (Odense, 1990), pp. 83–100.

L'Étude des auteurs classiques latins aux XIe et XIIe siècles (3 vols. in 4, Paris, 1982–9).

'L'Étude des textes littéraires classiques dans les écoles pendant le haut Moyen Âge', in O. Pecere (ed.), *Itinerari dei testi antichi*, Saggi di Storia Antica, 3 (Rome, 1991), pp. 105–14.

'Les Florilèges d'auteurs classiques', in *Les genres littéraires dans les sources théologiques et philosophiques médiévales: définition, critique et exploitation* (Leuven, 1982), pp. 151–63.

'Ovide au Moyen Âge (du IXe au XIIe siècle)', in G. Cavillo (ed.), *Le strade del testo* (Rome, 1987), pp. 67–96.

'La Popularité des textes classiques entre le IXe et le XIIe siècle', *Revue d'histoire des textes*, 14–15 (1984–5), 169–81.

Murrin, Michael, *The Allegorical Epic: Essays in Its Rise and Decline* (Chicago, 1980).

Nogara, B., 'Di alcune vite e commenti medioevali di Ovidio', *Miscellanea Ceriani* (Milan, 1910), 413–31.

O'Donnell, James J., *Cassiodorus* (Berkeley and Los Angeles CA, 1979).

O'Donnell, J. Reginald, 'Coluccio Salutati on the Poet-Teacher', *MS*, 22 (1960), 240–56.

Olson, Glending, *Literature as Recreation in the Later Middle Ages* (Ithaca NY, 1982).

Ong, Walter, 'The Writer's Audience is Always a Fiction', *PMLA*, 90 (1975), 9–21.

Orbán, Árpád Peter, 'Anonymi Teutonici commentum in Theoduli eglogam e codice Utrecht, U. B. 292 editum', *Vivarium*, 11 (1973), 1–42; 12 (1974), 133–45; 13 (1975), 77–88; 14 (1976), 50–61; 15 (1977), 143–58; 17 (1979), 116–33; 19 (1981), 56–69 [incomplete].

Orchard, Andy, 'After Aldhelm: The Teaching and Transmission of the Anglo-Latin Hexameter', *Journal of Medieval Latin*, 2 (1992), 96–133.

The Poetic Art of Aldhelm (Cambridge, 1994).

Orme, Nicholas, *English Schools in the Middle Ages* (London, 1973).

Otis, Brooks, 'The *Argumenta* of the So-Called Lactantius', *Harvard Studies in Classical Philology*, 47 (1936), 131–63.

Paetow, L. J. (ed.), *Two Medieval Satires on the University of Paris: 'La bataille des VII ars' of Henri d'Andeli and the 'Morale scolarium' of John of Garland*, Memoirs of the University of California, 4. 1–2 (Berkeley CA, 1927).

Parkes, M. B., 'The Influence of the Concepts of *Ordinatio* and *Compilatio* on the Development of the Book', in J. J. G. Alexander and M. T. Gibson (eds.), *Medieval Learning and Literature: Essays Presented to R. W. Hunt* (Oxford, 1975), pp. 115–41.

Pastore-Scocchi, Manlio, 'Un Chapitre d'histoire littéraire aux XIVe et XVe siècles: "Seneca poeta tragicus"', in J. Jacquot (ed.), *Les tragédies de Sénèque et le théâtre de la renaissance* (Paris, 1964), pp. 11–36.

Paulmier, Monique, 'Les *flores* d'auteurs antiques et médiévaux dans le *Speculum historiale*', *Spicae: Cahiers de l'Atelier Vincent de Beauvais*, 1 (1978), 31–70.

Pellegrin, Elizabeth, 'Les Manuscrits de Loup de Ferrières. A propos du ms. Orleans 162 (139) corrigé de sa main', *Bibliothèque de l'école des chartes*, 115 (1957), pp. 5–31.

'Notes sur un commentaire médiéval des *Sententiae* de Publilius Syrus', *Revue d'histoire des textes*, 6 (1976), 305–22.

'Les *Remedia Amoris* d'Ovide, texte scolaire médiéval', *Bibliothèque de l' école des chartes*, 115 (1957), 172–9.

Petitmengin, Pierre, and Munk Olsen, Birger, 'Bibliographie de la réception de la littérature classique du IXe au XVe siècle', in C. Leonardi and B. Munk Olsen (eds.), *The Classical Tradition in the Middle Ages and Renaissance*, Biblioteca di medioevo latino, 15 (Spoleto, 1995), pp. 199–274.

Pfeiffer, Rudolph, *A History of Classical Scholarship from 1300 to 1850* (Oxford, 1976).

Pittalunga, Stefano, 'Ovidio "Ethicus" fra satira e parodia nella commedia latina medievale', in I. Gallo and L. Nicastri (eds.), *Aetates ovidianae: lettori di Ovidio dell'antiche al rinascimento*, Publicazioni dell'Università degli Studi di Salerno, 43 (Naples, 1995), pp. 209–22.

Préaux, Jean, 'Jean Scot et Martin de Laon en face du *De nuptiis* de Martianus Capella', in *Jean Scot Érigène et l'histoire de la philosophie* (Paris, 1977), pp. 161–70.

Preminger, Alex, Hardison, O. B., and Kerrane, Kevin (eds.), *Classical and Medieval Literary Criticism: Translations and Interpretations* (New York, 1974).

Przychocki, G., 'Accessus Ovidiani', *Rozprawy Akademii Umiejetności*, Wydział filologiczny, serya 3, tom. 4 (1911), 65–126.

Quadri, Riccardo, *I Collectanea di Eirico de Auxerre*, Spicilegium Friburgense, 11 (Fribourg, 1966).

Quain, E. A., 'The Medieval *Accessus ad auctores*', *Traditio*, 3 (1945), 215–64.

Quinn, Betty Nye, 'Ps. Theodulus', in Kristeller (ed.), *Catalogus*, II, pp. 383–408.

Rand, E. K., 'The Classics in the Thirteenth Century', *Speculum*, 4 (1929), 249–69.

'Early Medieval Commentaries on Terence', *Classical Philology*, 4 (1909), 359–79.

'A *Vade Mecum* of Liberal Culture in a Ms. of Fleury', *Philological Quarterly*, 1 (1922), 258–77.

Rauner-Hafner, Gabriele, 'Die Vergilinterpretation des Fulgentius', *Mittellateinisches Jahrbuch*, 13 (1978), 7–49.

Raynaud de Lage, Guy, *Alain de Lille, poète du XIIe siècle* (Montreal, 1951).

Reeve, M. D., 'Statius', in L. D. Reynolds (ed.), *Texts and Transmission: A Survey of the Latin Classics* (Oxford, 1983), pp. 394–9.

Reeve, M. D., and Rouse, Richard H., 'New Light on the Transmission of Donatus's "Commentum Terentii"', *Viator*, 9 (1978), 235–49.

Reynolds, L. D., *The Medieval Tradition of Seneca's Letters* (Oxford, 1965).

Reynolds, L. D. (ed.), *Texts and Transmission: A Survey of the Latin Classics* (Oxford, 1983).

Reynolds, L. D. and Wilson, N. G., *Scribes and Scholars: A Guide to the Transmission of Greek and Latin Literature* (2nd edn, Oxford, 1974).

Reynolds, Suzanne, 'Inventing Authority', in Felicity Riddy (ed.), *Prestige, Authority and Power in Late Medieval Manuscripts and Texts* (Cambridge, 2000), pp. 7–16.

Medieval Reading: Grammar, Rhetoric and the Classical Text (Cambridge, 1996).

Riché, Pierre, *The Carolingians: A Family Who Forged Europe*, tr. M. I. Allen (Philadelphia PA, 1993).

Education and Culture in the Barbarian West, tr. J. J. Contreni (Columbia SC, 1976).

Rigg, A. G., *A History of Anglo-Latin Literature 1066–1422* (Cambridge, 1992).

'Medieval Latin Poetic Anthologies (I–V)', *MS*, 39 (1977), 281–336; 40 (1978), 387–407; 41 (1979), 257–74; 43 (1981), 472–97; (with David Townsend) 49 (1987), 352–90.

Riou, Yves-François, 'Les Commentaires médiévaux de Térence', in Mann and Olsen (eds.), *Medieval and Renaissance Scholarship*, pp. 33–49.

'Essai sur la tradition manuscrite du *Commentum Brunsianum* des Comédies de Térence', *Revue d'histoire des textes*, 3 (1973), 79–113.

'Quelques Aspects de la tradition manuscrite des *Carmina* d'Eugène de Tolède: Du *Liber Catonianus* aux *Auctores Octo Morales*', *Revue d'histoire des textes*, 2 (1972), 11–44.

Robathan, Dorothy, and Cranz, F. Edward, 'Persius', in Kristeller (ed.), *Catalogus*, III, pp. 201–312.

Robey, David, 'Humanist Views on the Study of Poetry in the Early Italian Renaissance', *History of Education*, 13 (1984), 7–25.

Robinson, Fred C., 'Syntactical Glosses in Latin Manuscripts of Anglo-Saxon Provenance', *Speculum*, 48 (1973), 443–75.

Robson, Alan, 'Dante's Reading of the Latin Poets and the Structure of the *Commedia*', in C. Grayson (ed.), *The World of Dante: Essays on Dante and his Times* (Oxford, 1980), pp. 81–121.

Roos, Paolo, *Sentenzia e proverbio nell'Antichità e il 'Distici di Catone'* (Brescia, 1984).

Rosa, L., 'Su alcuni commenti inediti alle Opere di Ovidio', *Annali di Lettere e Filosofia* [Universita di Napoli], 5 (1955), 191–231.

Rouse, Richard H., 'The *A* Text of Seneca's Tragedies in the Thirteenth Century', *Revue d'histoire des textes*, 1 (1971), 93–121.

'*Florilegia* and Latin Classical Authors in Twelfth- and Thirteenth-Century Orléans', *Viator*, 10 (1979), 131–60.

Rouse, Richard H., and Rouse, Mary A., *Preachers, Florilegia and Sermons: Studies on the 'Manipulus Florum' of Thomas of Ireland*, Pontifical Institute of Medieval Studies, Studies and Texts, 47 (Toronto, 1979).

Sabbadini, Remigio, 'Biografi e commentatori de Terenzio', *Studi italiani di filologia classica*, 5 (1897), 289–327.

Salman, Phillips, 'Instruction and Delight in Medieval and Renaissance Literary Criticism', *Renaissance Quarterly*, 32 (1979), 303–32.

Salmon, P. B., 'The "Three Voices" of Poetry in Mediaeval Literary Theory', *MÆ*, 30 (1961), 1–18.

Sanford, Eva M., 'Giovanni Tortelli's Commentary on Juvenal', *TAPA*, 52 (1951), 207–18.

'Juvenal', in Kristeller (ed.), *Catalogus*, I, pp. 175–238.

'Lucan and his Roman Critics', *Classical Philology*, 26 (1931), 233–57.

'The Use of Classical Authors in the *Libri Manuales*', *TAPA*, 55 (1924), 190–248.

Schetter, W., *Studien zur Überlieferung und Kritik des Elegikers Maximian*, Klassisch-philologische Studien, 36 (Wiesbaden, 1970).

Schindel, U., *Die lateinischen Figurenlehren des 5. bis 7. Jahrhunderts und Donats Vergilkommentar* (Göttingen, 1974).

Schmidt, P. L., 'Rezeption und Überliefung der Tragödien Senecas bis zum Ausgang des Mittelalters', in E. Lefèvre (ed.), *Der Einfluss Senecas auf das europäische Drama* (Darmstadt, 1978), pp. 12–73.

Schotter, Anne Harland, 'The Transformation of Ovid in the Twelfth-Century *Pamphilus*', in J. J. Paxson and C. A. Gravlee (eds.), *Desiring Discourse: The Literature of Love, Ovid through Chaucer* (Selinsgrove PA and London, 1998), pp. 72–86.

Schwarz, Alexander, 'Glossen als Texte', *PBB*, 99 (1977), 25–36.

Setaioli, Aldo, 'Évidence et évidenciation: le message de Virgile et son explication par Servius (*ad Aeneidem*, 6, 703)', in C. Levy and L. Pernot (eds.), *Dire l'évidence: philosophie et rhétorique antiques* (Paris, 1997), pp. 59–73.

Severus, P. E. von, *Lupus von Ferrières, Gestalt und Werk eines Vermittlers antiken Geistesgutes im 9. Jahrhundert* (Munster, 1940).

Sharpe, Richard, *A Handlist of Latin Writers of Great Britain and Ireland before 1540*, Publications of the Journal of Medieval Latin, 1 (1997), with supplement.

Shooner, Hugues-V., 'Les *Bursarii Ovidianorum* de Guillaume d'Orléans', *MS*, 43 (1981), 405–24.

Siewert, Klaus, 'Vernacular Glosses and Classical Authors', in Mann and Olsen (eds.), *Medieval and Renaissance Scholarship*, pp. 137–52.

Silvestre, Hubert, 'Le Schéma "moderne" des *accessus*', *Latomus*, 16 (1957), 684–9.

Smalley, Beryl, *English Friars and Antiquity in the Early Fourteenth Century* (Oxford, 1960).

Smits, E. R., 'Helinand de Froidmont and the A-Text of Seneca's Tragedies', *Mnemosyne*, 36 (1983), 324–58.

Southern, R. W., *Medieval Humanism and Other Studies* (Oxford, 1970).

Platonism, Scholastic Method, and the School of Chartres, The Stenton Lecture 1978 (Reading, 1979).

Southern, R. W. (ed.), *Essays in Medieval History* (London, 1968).

Spaltenstein, François, *Commentaire des élégies de Maximian*, Bibliotheca helvetica romana, 20 (Rome, 1983).

Stadter, P., 'Planudes, Plutarch and Pace of Ferrara', *Italia medioevale e umanistica*, 16 (1973), 137–62.

Stock, Brian, *After Augustine: The Meditative Reader and the Text* (Philadelphia PA, 2001).

Augustine the Reader: Meditation, Self-Knowledge, and the Ethics of Interpretation (Cambridge MA, 1996).

The Implications of Literacy: Written Language and Models of Interpretation in the Eleventh and Twelfth Centuries (Princeton NJ, 1983).

'A Note on *Thebaid* Commentaries: Paris, B.N. 3012', *Traditio*, 27 (1971), 468–71.

Stroh, W., *Ovid im Urteil der Nachwelt* (Darmstadt, 1969).

Sullivan, Richard E. (ed.), *'The Gentle Voices of Teachers': Aspects of Learning in the Carolingian Age* (Columbus OH, 1995).

Swanson, Jenny, *John of Wales: A Study of the Works and Ideas of a Thirteenth-Century Friar* (Cambridge, 1989).

Sweeney, Robert D., *Prolegomena to an Edition of the Scholia to Statius*, Mnemosyne, Suppl. 8 (Leiden, 1969).

Tarrant, Richard J., 'Ovid', in L. D. Reynolds (ed.), *Texts and Transmission: A Survey of the Latin Classics* (Oxford, 1983), pp. 257–84.

Thomson, David, 'The Oxford Grammar Masters Revisited', *MS*, 45 (1983), 298–310.

Thorndike, Lynn, *University Records and Life in the Middle Ages*, Records of Civilisation: Sources and Studies, 38 (New York, 1944).

Thurot, Charles, 'Documents relatifs à l'histoire de la grammaire au Moyen Âge', *Comptes rendus de l'Académie des Inscriptions et Belles-Lettres*, n.s. 6 (1870), 242–51.

Tigerstedt, E. N., 'Observations on the Reception of the Aristotelian *Poetics* in the Latin West', *Studies in the Renaissance*, 15 (1968), 7–24.

Trapp, J. B., 'The Poet Laureate: Rome, *Renovatio* and *Translatio Imperii*', in P. A. Ramsey (ed.), *Rome in the Renaissance: The City and the Myth*, Medieval and Renaissance Texts and Studies, 18 (Binghamton NY, 1982), pp. 93–130.

Trimpi, Wesley, *Muses of One Mind: The Literary Analysis of Experience and its Continuity* (Princeton NJ, 1983).

Trinkaus, Charles, 'A Humanist's Image of Humanism: The Inaugural Orations of Bartolommeo della Fonte', *Studies in the Renaissance*, 7 (1960), 90–129.

The Poet as Philosopher: Petrarch and the Formation of Renaissance Consciousness (New Haven CT, 1979).

'The Unknown Quattrocento Poetics of Bartolommeo della Fonte', *Studies in the Renaissance*, 13 (1966), 40–122.

Troncarelli, Fabio, 'Per una ricerca sui commenti altomedievali al *De consolatione* di Boezio', *Miscellanea in memoria di Giorgio Cencetti* (Turin, 1973), pp. 363–80.

Tradizioni Perdute: la 'Consolatio philosophiae' nell'alto medioevo, Medioevo e umanesimo, 42 (Padua, 1981).

Tunberg, Terence O., 'Conrad of Hirsau and his Approach to the *Auctores*', *M&H*, n.s. 15 (1987), 65–94.

Uitti, Karl, 'À propos de philologie', *Littérature*, 41 (1981), 30–46.

Viarre, Simone, *La survie d'Ovide dans la littérature scientifique des XIIe et XIIIe siècles* (Poitiers, 1966).

Villa, Claudia, *La 'lectura Terentii', I: Da Ildemaro a Francesco Petrarca*, Studi sul Petrarca, 17 (Padua, 1984).

'I manoscritti di Orazio I', *Aevum*, 66 (1992), 95–135.

'Tra *fabula* e *historia*: Manegoldo di Lautenbach e il "maestro di Orazio"', *Aevum*, 70 (1996), 245–56.

'Per una tipologia del commento mediolatino: l'Ars Poetica di Orazio', in O. Besconi and C. Caruso (eds.), *Il Commento ai Testi* (Basle, 1992).

Vinchesi, Maria Assunta, 'La fortuna di Lucano fra tarda antichità e medioevo' I, *Cultura e scuola*, 20.77 (1981), 62–72; II, *Cultura e scuola*, 20.78 (1981), 66–75.

Wallace, David (ed.), *The Cambridge History of Medieval English Literature* (Cambridge, 1999).

Wallach, Liutpold, *Alcuin and Charlemagne: Studies in Carolingian History and Literature* (2nd edn, Ithaca NY, 1968).

Weinberg, B., *A History of Literary Criticism in the Italian Renaissance* (2 vols., Chicago, 1961).

Westra, Haijo, 'The Allegorical Interpretation of Myth: Its Origins, Justification and Effect', in A.Welkenhuyser, H. Braet and W. Verbeke (eds.), *Mediaeval Antiquity* (Leuven, 1995), pp. 277–91.

Wetherbee, Winthrop, 'Philosophy, Commentary, and Mythic Narrative in Twelfth-Century France', in J. Whitman (ed.), *Interpretation and Allegory: Antiquity to the Modern Period* (Leiden, 2000), pp. 211–29.

'Philosophy, Cosmology, and the Twelfth-Century Renaissance', in P. Dronke (ed.), *A History of Twelfth-Century Western Philosophy* (Cambridge, 1988), pp. 21–53.

Platonism and Poetry in the Twelfth Century (Princeton NJ, 1972).

Wheatley, Edward, *Mastering Aesop: Medieval Education, Chaucer, and his Followers* (Gainesville FA, 2000).

Whitbread, L. G., 'Conrad of Hirsau as a Literary Critic', *Speculum*, 47 (1972), 142–68.

Wieland, Gernot, *The Latin Glosses on Arator and Prudentius in Cambridge University Library MS GG.5.35*, Studies and Texts, 61 (Toronto, 1983).

Wieruszowski, Helen, 'Rhetoric and Classics in Italian Education of the Thirteenth Century', *Studia Gratiana*, 11 (1967), 171–207.

Wilson, Evelyn Faye, 'The *Georgica spiritualia* of John of Garland', *Speculum*, 8 (1933), 358–77.

'Pastoral and Epithalamium in Latin Literature', *Speculum*, 23 (1948), 35–57.

Witt, Ronald G., 'Coluccio Salutati and the Conception of the *Poeta Theologus* in the Fourteenth Century', *Renaissance Quarterly*, 30 (1977), 538–63.

Wittig, Joseph S., 'King Alfred's *Boethius* and its Latin Sources: A Reconsideration', *Anglo-Saxon England*, 11 (1983), 157–98.

Woods, Marjorie Curry, 'A Medieval Rhetoric Goes to School – and to University: The Commentaries on the *Poetria Nova*', *Rhetorica*, 9 (1991), 55–65.

'Rape and the Pedagogical Rhetoric of Sexual Violence', in Copeland (ed.) *Criticism and Dissent*, pp. 56–86.

Woods, Marjorie Curry (ed.), *An Early Commentary on the 'Poetria Nova' of Geoffrey de Vinsauf* (New York and London, 1984).

Woods, Marjorie Curry, and Copeland, Rita, 'Classroom and Confession', in Wallace (ed.), *Cambridge History of Medieval English Literature*, pp. 376–406.

Wright, Neil, 'Bede and Vergil', *Romanobarbarica*, 6 (1981), 361–79.

Zeeman, Nicolette, 'The Schools Give a License to Poets', in Copeland (ed.) *Criticism and Dissent*, pp. 151–80.

Zetzel, James E. G., 'On the History of Latin Scholia II: The *Commentum Cornuti* in the Ninth Century', *M&H*, n.s. 10 (1981), 19–31.

Textual psychologies: imagination, memory, pleasure

Primary sources

Alfonso of Jaén, *Epistola solitarii ad reges*, in A. Jönsson, *Alfonso of Jaén, His Life and Works* (Lund, 1989), pp. 115–71.

Alighieri, Dante, *The Divine Comedy*, ed. and tr. Charles S. Singleton (6 vols., Princeton, 1971–5).

Literary Criticism of Dante Alighieri, tr. R. S. Haller (Lincoln NE, 1973).

La Vita Nova, tr. B. Reynolds (Harmondsworth, 1969).

Angela of Foligno, *Complete Works*, tr. P. Lachance (New York, 1993).

Aquinas, Thomas, St, *Commentary on the Nicomachean Ethics*, tr. C. I. Litzinger (2 vols., Chicago, 1964).

The Disputed Questions on Truth, tr. R. W. Mulligan (3 vols., Chicago, 1963).

Summa theologiae, Blackfriars edn (60 vols., London and New York, 1964–76).

Aristotle, *Aristotle's 'De Anima' in the Version of William of Moerbeke and the Commentary of St Thomas Aquinas*, tr. K. Foster and S. Humphries (London, 1951).

Augustine, *The Literal Meaning of Genesis*, tr. J. H. Taylor (2 vols., New York, 1982).

Works, vol. 6: *Letters*, vol. 1, tr. J. G. Cunningham (Edinburgh, 1872).

Auriol, Peter, *Compendium sensus litteralis totius divinae scripturae*, ed. P. Deeboeck (Quaracchi, 1896).

Avicenna, *Commentary on the 'Poetics' of Aristotle*, ed. I. M. Dahiyat (Leiden, 1974).

Barnabas of Reggio, *De conservanda sanitate*. Paris, Bibliothèque nationale de France, MS nouv. acq. lat. 1430, fols. 1r–10v.

Bartholomew the Englishman [Bartolomaeus Anglicus], *De proprietatibus rerum* (1601; rpt. Frankfurt, 1964); tr. John Trevisa (1398), *On the Properties of Things*, ed. M. C. Seymour et al. (2 vols., Oxford, 1975).

Bernard de Gordon, *Lilium medicinae* (Lyon, 1574).

Boccaccio, Giovanni, tr. Charles G. Osgood, *Boccaccio on Poetry: Being the Preface and the Fourteenth and Fifteenth Books of Boccaccio's 'Genealogia deorum gentilium' in an English Version with Introductory Essay and Commentary* (Princeton NJ, 1930).

   Decameron, ed. V. Branca (Florence, 1965).

Boethius of Dacia, *Boethii Daci opera: Opuscula de aeternitate mundi, de summo bono, de somniis*, ed. N. G. Green-Pedersen, Corpus philosophorum danicorum medii ævi, 6.2 (Copenhagen, 1976); tr. J. F. Wippel, *On the Supreme Good, On the Eternity of the World, On Dreams* (Toronto, 1987).

Bonaventure, Pseudo- [= Johannes de Caulibus?], *Meditations on the Life of Christ: An Illustrated Manuscript of the Fourteenth Century (Paris, Bib. Nat., MS Ital. 115)*, tr. I. Ragusa and R. B. Green (Princeton NJ, 1961).

Bonet, Honoré, *The Tree of Battles*, tr. G. W. Coopland (Liverpool, 1949).

Bridget of Sweden, *Life and Selected Revelations*, tr. A. R. Kezel (New York, 1990).

Buridan, John, *Questiones super decem libros ethicorum* (1513; rpt. Frankfurt, 1968).

The Chastising of God's Children, ed. J. Bazire and E. Colledge (Oxford, 1957).

Chaucer, Geoffrey, *The Riverside Chaucer*, gen. ed. L. D. Benson (Boston MA, 1987).

The Cloud of Unknowing and Related Treatises on Contemplative Prayer, ed. P. Hodgson, Analecta Cartusiana, 3 (Salzburg, 1982).

Coleridge, Samuel Taylor, *Biographia literaria, or Biographical Sketches of My Literary Life and Opinions*, ed. G. Watson (1975; rpt. London, 1977).

Croniques et conquestes de Charlemaine, ed. R. Guiette (2 vols. in 3, Brussels, 1940–51).

De Deguileville, Guillaume, *Le Pèlerinage de vie humaine*, ed. J. J. Stürzinger (London, 1893); tr. E. Clasby (New York and London, 1992).

Deschamps, Eustache, *L'Art de dictier*, ed. and tr. D. M. Sinnreich-Levi (East Lansing MI, 1994).

Disticha Catonis, ed. M. Boas (Amsterdam, 1952); tr. W. J. Chase, *The Distichs of Cato: A Famous Medieval Textbook*, University of Wisconsin Studies in the Social Sciences and History, 8 (Madison WI, 1922).

Dives et Pauper, ed. P. H. Barnum, EETS OS 275, 280 (2 vols., Oxford, 1976–80).

Evrart de Conty, *Le Livre des Eschez amoureux moralisés*, ed. F. Guichard-Tesson and B. Roy, Bibliothèque du moyen français, 2 (Montreal and Paris, 1994).

Froissart, Jean, *Chroniques*, ed. K. de Lettenhove (28 vols., Brussels, 1867–77).

Gertrude of Helfta, *The Herald of Divine Love*, tr. and ed. M. Winkworth (New York, 1993).

Gottfried von Strassburg, *Tristan*, ed. R. Bechstein and P. Ganz (2 vols., Wiesbaden, 1978).

Grosseteste, Robert, 'Robert Grosseteste's Commentary on the "Celestial Hierarchy" of Pseudo-Dionysius the Areopagite: An Edition, Translation and Introduction to his Text and Commentary', by J. S. McQuade, Ph.D. diss., Queen's University of Belfast, 1961. [Quade's work covers only Chapters 1–9 of Grosseteste's commentary; the project was completed by J. J. McEvoy, 'Robert Grosseteste on the "Celestial Hierarchy" of Pseudo-Dionysius: An Edition and Translation of his Commentary, chapters 10–15', M.A. diss., Queen's University of Belfast, 1967.]

Guido delle Colonne, *Historia destructionis Troiae*, ed. N. E. Griffin (Cambridge MA, 1936); tr. M. E. Meek (Bloomington IN and London, 1974).

Henryson, Robert, *Poems*, ed. D. Fox (Oxford, 1981).

Higden, Ralph, *Polychronicon, with the English Translations of John Trevisa and of an Unknown Writer of the Fifteenth Century*, ed. C. Babington and J. R. Lumby, Rolls Series, 41 (9 vols., London, 1865–86).

Hilton, Walter, *De adoracione ymaginum*, in Hilton, *Latin Writings*, ed. J. P. H. Clark and C. Taylor, Analecta Cartusiana, 124 (2 vols., Salzburg, 1987), I, pp. 175–214.

Hugh of St Victor, *De tribus maximis circumstantiis gestorum*, ed. W. M. Green, *Speculum*, 18 (1943), 484–93.

Didascalicon, tr. J. Taylor (New York, 1961).

Italian Renaissance Tales, tr. J. L. Smarr (Rochester MI, 1983).

Jacques de Vitry, *The Life of Marie d'Oignies*, tr. M. H. King (rev. edn, Toronto, 1993).

Jean de Meun and Guillaume de Lorris, *Le Roman de la Rose*, ed. F. Lecoy (3 vols., Paris, 1965–70); tr. C. Dahlberg (1971, rpt Hanover NH and London, 1983); also tr. F. Horgan (Oxford, 1994).

Johannes de Caulibus. See: Bonaventure, Pseudo-

John of Salisbury, *Policraticus*, ed. and tr. C. J. Nederman (Cambridge, 1990).

John of San Gimignano, *Summa de exemplis ac similitudinibus rerum* (Venice, 1497).

John of Wales, *Florilegium de vita et dictis illustrium philosophorum* (Rome, 1655).

Las Leys d'Amors, ed. J. Anglade (4 vols., Toulouse, 1919–20).

The Life of Juliana of Mont-Cornillon, tr. B. Newman (Toronto, [1988]).

The Life of Saint Thomas Aquinas: Biographical Documents, ed. and tr. K. Foster (London and Baltimore, 1959).

Love, Nicholas, *Mirror of the Blessed Life of Jesus Christ*, ed. M. G. Sargent (New York and London, 1992).

Lydgate, John, *The Minor Poems of Lydgate*, pt. 1, ed. H. N. MacCracken, EETS ES 107 (Oxford, 1911).

Macrobius, *Commentary on 'The Dream of Scipio'*, tr. W. H. Stahl (1952; rpt. New York, 1990).

Matthew of Linköping, *Poetria*, in *'Testa nucis' and 'Poetria'*, ed. B. Bergh, Samlingar utgivna av Svenska Fornskriftsällskapet, ser. 2, Latinska skrifter, Band
9.2 (Berlings, 1996), pp. 44–89.

Monumens de la littérature romane, ed. A. F. Gatien-Arnoult (3 vols., Toulouse,
1841–2).

Oresme, Nicole, *De causis mirabilium*, ed. and tr. B. Hansen, *Nicole Oresme and
the Marvels of Nature* (Toronto, 1985).

Le Livre de éthiques d'Aristote, ed. A. D. Menut (New York, 1940).

Pecock, Reginald, *Pecock's Repressor*, ed. C. Babington, Rolls Series, 19 (2 vols.,
London, 1860).

Pico della Mirandola, Giovan Francesco, *On the Imagination*, ed. and tr.
H. Caplan (New Haven and London, 1930).

Richard de Fournival, *Li Bestiaires d'amours* and *Li Response du bestiaire*, ed.
C. Segre (Milan and Naples, 1957).

Richard of St Victor, *Selected Writings on Contemplation*, tr. C. Kirchberger
(London, 1957).

Roman de la Rose, ed. F. Lecoy (3 vols., Paris, 1965–70); tr. C. Dahlberg
(1971; rpt. Hanover NH and London, 1983); also tr. F. Horgan (Oxford,
1994).

Stephen of Bourbon, *Anecdotes historiques, legendes et apologues tirés du recueil
inédit d'Étienne de Bourbon*, ed. A. Lecoy de la Marche (Paris, 1877).

Thomas of Chobham, *Summa confessorum*, ed. F. Broomfield (Leuven, 1968).

Summa de arte praedicandi, ed. F. Morenzoni, CCCM 82 (Turnhout, 1988).

Tretise of Miraclis Pleyinge, ed. C. Davidson (Kalamazoo MI, 1993).

Vincent of Beauvais, *Speculum maius, Apologia totius operis*, ed. A.-D. von
den Brincken, 'Geschichtsbetrachtung bei Vincenz von Beauvais', *Deutsches
Archiv für Erforschung des Mittelalters*, 34 (1978), 409–99.

Speculum quadruplex sive Speculum maius (1624; rpt. Graz, 1965).

Waleys, Thomas, *De modo componendi sermones*, ed. T.-M. Charland, *Artes
praedicandi: contribution à l'histoire de la rhétorique au Moyen Âge* (Paris,
1936), pp. 327–403.

Secondary sources

Abrams, M. H., *The Mirror and the Lamp* (1953; rpt. New York, 1958).

Allen, Judson Boyce, *The Ethical Poetic of the Later Middle Ages: A Decorum of
Convenient Distinction* (Toronto, 1982).

Aston, Margaret, *England's Iconoclasts, 1: Laws against Images* (Oxford, 1988).

Lollards and Reformers: Images and Literacy in Late Medieval Religion
(London, 1984).

Balogh, Josef, '*Voces paginarum*: Beiträge zur Geschichte des lauten Lessens und
Schreibens', *Philologus*, 82 (1927), 84–109, 202–40.

Barish, Jonas, *The Antitheatrical Prejudice* (Berkeley and Los Angeles CA, 1981).

Bond, Gerald A., '*Iocus amoris*: The Poetry of Baudri of Bourgueil and the
Formation of the Ovidian Subculture', *Traditio*, 42 (1986), 143–93.

Bundy, M. W., *The Theory of Imagination in Classical and Mediaeval Thought*
(Urbana IL, 1927).

Camille, Michael, *The Gothic Idol: Ideology and Image-Making in Medieval Art* (New York, 1989).

Carruthers, Mary, *The Book of Memory: A Study of Memory in Medieval Culture* (Cambridge, 1990).

The Craft of Thought: Meditation, Rhetoric, and the Making of Images, 400–1200 (Cambridge, 1998).

Chambers, E. K., *The Mediaeval Stage* (2 vols., 1903; rpt. London, 1967).

Chenu, M.-D., '*Imaginatio*: Note de lexicographie philosophique médiévale', *Studi e testi*, 122 (1946), 593–602.

'Le *De spiritu imaginativo* de R. Kilwardby, O. P. (d. 1279)', *Revue des sciences philosophiques et théologiques*, 15 (1926), 507–17.

Clanchy, M. T., *From Memory to Written Record, England 1066–1307* (London and Cambridge MA, 1979).

Clark, David L., 'Optics for Preachers: The *De oculo morali* by Peter of Limoges', *The Michigan Academician*, 9 (1977), 329–43.

Clements, Robert J., and Gibaldi, Joseph, *Anatomy of the Novella* (New York, 1977).

Clopper, Lawrence M., '*Miracula* and *The Tretise of Miraclis Pleyinge*', *Speculum*, 65 (1990), 878–905.

Coleman, Janet, *Ancient and Medieval Memories: Studies in the Reconstruction of the Past* (Cambridge, 1992).

Davis, Nicholas, 'The *Tretise of Myraclis Pleyinge*: On Milieu and Authorship', *Medieval English Theatre*, 12 (1990), 124–51.

de Gandillac, Maurice, 'Encyclopédies pré-médiévales et médiévales', *Cahiers d'histoire mondiale*, 9 (1966), 483–518.

Dieter, Otto A., '*Arbor picta*: The Medieval Tree of Preaching', *Quarterly Journal of Speech*, 51 (1965), 123–44.

DiLorenzo, Raymond, 'Imagination as the First Way to Contemplation in Richard of St Victor's *Benjamin Minor*', *M&H*, n.s. 11 (1982), 77–98.

Faral, Edmond, *Les Jongleurs en France au Moyen Âge* (1910; rpt. New York, 1970).

Foulet, L., 'Études sur le vocabulaire abstrait de Froissart: *Imaginer*', *Romania*, 68 (1945), 257–72.

Gougaud, L., 'Muta predicatio', *Revue bénédictine*, 42 (1930), 168–71.

Green, Richard Firth, *Poets and Princepleasers: Literature and the English Court in the Late Middle Ages* (Toronto, 1980).

Gründel, J., *Das 'Speculum Universale' des Radulphus Ardens* (Munich, 1961).

Hagen, Susan K., 'The Pilgrimage of the Life of Man: A Medieval Theory of Vision and Remembrance', Ph.D. diss., University of Virginia, 1976.

Hamburger, Jeffrey, 'The Visual and the Visionary: The Image in Late Medieval Monastic Devotions', *Viator*, 20 (1989), 161–205.

Hartung, Wolfgang, *Die spielleute* (Wiesbaden, 1982).

Harvey, E. Ruth, *The Inward Wits: Psychological Theory in the Middle Ages and the Renaissance*, Warburg Institute Surveys, 6 (London, 1975).

Hassall, W. O., 'Plays at Clerkenwell', *MLR*, 33 (1938), 564–7.

Hirsch, E. D., Jr., 'Two Traditions of Literary Evaluation', in J. P. Strelka (ed.), *Literary Theory and Criticism* (2 vols., New York, 1985), I, pp. 283–98.

Hissette, R., *Enquête sur les 219 articles condamnés à Paris le 7 mars 1277* (Leuven and Paris, 1977).

Hortis, Attilio, *Studi sulle opere latine del Boccaccio* (Trieste, 1879).

Kaulbach, Ernest, *Imaginative Prophecy in the B-Text of 'Piers Plowman'* (Cambridge, 1993).

Kelly, Douglas, *Medieval Imagination: Rhetoric and the Poetry of Courtly Love* (Madison WI, 1978).

Kemp, Martin, 'From "Mimesis" to "Fantasia": The Quattrocento Vocabulary of Creation, Inspiration and Genius in the Visual Arts', *Viator*, 8 (1977), 347–98.

Kolve, V. A., *Chaucer and the Imagery of Narrative* (London, 1984).

Kruger, Steven, *Dreaming in the Middle Ages* (Cambridge, 1992).

La Charité, Raymond C., 'Rabelais: The Book as Therapy', in E. R. Peschel (ed.), *Medicine and Literature* (New York, 1980), pp. 11–17.

Lain Entralgo, Pedro, *The Therapy of the Word in Classical Antiquity*, ed. and tr. L. J. Rather and J. M. Sharp (New Haven CT, 1970).

Lindberg, David C., 'Alhazen's Theory of Vision and its Reception in the West', *Isis*, 58 (1967), 321–41.

Lönnroth, Lars, *Njáls saga: A Critical Introduction* (Berkeley CA, 1976).

McKitterick, Rosamund, 'Text and Image in the Carolingian World', in R. McKitterick (ed.), *The Uses of Literacy in Early Medieval Europe* (Cambridge, 1990), pp. 297–318.

Minnis, Alastair J., 'Affection and Imagination in *The Cloud of Unknowing* and Walter Hilton's *Scale of Perfection*', *Traditio*, 39 (1983), 323–66.

'"Figures of olde werk": Chaucer's Poetic Sculptures', in P. Lindley and T. Frangenberg (eds.), *Secular Sculpture 1350–1550* (Stamford, 2000), pp. 124–43.

'Langland's Ymaginatif and Late-Medieval Theories of Imagination', *Comparative Criticism*, 3 (1981), 71–103.

Medieval Theory of Authorship: Scholastic Literary Attitudes in the Later Middle Ages (1984; 2nd edn, Aldershot, 1988).

Minnis, Alastair J. and Scott, A. B., with Wallace, D. (eds.), *Medieval Literary Theory and Criticism, c. 1100 – c. 1375: The Commentary-Tradition* (1988; rev. edn, Oxford, 1991; rpt. 2001).

Montgomery, Robert L., *The Reader's Eye: Studies in Didactic Literary Theory from Dante to Tasso* (Berkeley and Los Angeles CA, 1979).

Ogilvy, J. D. A., '*Mimi, scurrae, histriones*: Entertainers of the Early Middle Ages', *Speculum*, 38 (1963), 603–19.

Olson, Glending, *Literature as Recreation in the Later Middle Ages* (Ithaca NY, 1982).

'The Medieval Fortunes of *Theatrica*', *Traditio*, 42 (1986), 265–86.

'Plays as Play: A Medieval Ethical Theory of Performance and the Intellectual Context of the *Tretise of Miraclis Pleyinge*', *Viator*, 26 (1995), 195–221.

'Toward a Poetics of the Late Medieval Court Lyric', in L. Ebin (ed.), *Vernacular Poetics in the Middle Ages* (Kalamazoo MI, 1984), pp. 227–48.

Onians, John, 'Abstraction and Imagination in Late Antiquity', *Art History*, 3 (1980), 1–24.

Pack, R. A., 'An *Ars Memorativa* from the Late Middle Ages', *AHDLMA*, 46 (1979), 221–65.

Palmer, Nigel, '*Antiquitus depingebatur*: The Roman Pictures of Death and Misfortune in the *Ackermann aus Böhman* and *Tkadleček*, and in the Writings of the English Classicizing Friars', *Deutsche Vierteljahrsschrift für Literaturwissenschaft und Geistesgeschichte*, 57 (1983), 171–239.

Pantin, W. A., 'The Letters of John Mason: A Fourteenth-Century Formulary from St. Augustine's, Canterbury', in T. A. Sandquist and M. R. Powicke (eds.), *Essays in Medieval History Presented to Bertie Wilkinson* (Toronto, 1969), pp. 192–219.

Parkes, M. B., 'The Influence of the Concepts of *Ordinatio* and *Compilatio* on the Development of the Book', in J. J. G. Alexander and M. T. Gibson (eds.), *Medieval Learning and Literature: Essays Presented to R. W. Hunt* (Oxford, 1975), pp. 115–41.

Picoche, J., *Le Vocabulaire psychologique dans les Chroniques de Froissart* (Paris, 1976).

Preminger, Alex, Hardison, O. B., and Kerrane, Kevin (eds.), *Classical and Medieval Literary Criticism: Translations and Interpretations* (New York, 1974).

Ringborn, S., 'Devotional Images and Imaginative Devotions: Notes on the Place of Art in Late Medieval Piety', *Gazette des Beaux-Arts*, 6th ser. 73 (1969), 159–70.

Rivers, Kimberly, 'Memory and Medieval Preaching: Mnemonic Advice in the *Ars praedicandi* of Francesc Eiximenis (ca. 1327–1409)', *Viator*, 30 (1999), 253–84.

Robertson, D. W., Jr., *A Preface to Chaucer* (Princeton NJ, 1962).

Rouse, Richard H., and Mary A., *Preachers, Florilegia and Sermons: Studies on the 'Manipulus florum' of Thomas of Ireland* (Toronto, 1979) [includes an edition of the Preface].

'*Statim invenire*: Schools, Preachers, and New Attitudes to the Page', in R. Benson and G. Constable (eds.), *Renaissance and Renewal in the Twelfth Century* (Cambridge MA, 1982), pp. 201–35.

Salman, Phillips, 'Instruction and Delight in Medieval and Renaissance Literary Criticism', *Renaissance Quarterly*, 32 (1979), 303–32.

Smalley, B., *English Friars and Antiquity in the Early Fourteenth Century* (Oxford, 1960).

Spence, Jonathan D., *The Memory Palace of Matteo Ricci* (New York, 1984).

Suchomski, Joachim, '*Delectatio*' und '*utilitas*': Ein Beitrag zum Verständnis mittelalterlicher komischer Literatur (Bern, 1975).

Trimpi, Wesley, 'The Quality of Fiction: The Rhetorical Transmission of Literary Theory', *Traditio*, 30 (1974), 1–118.

Welter, J. T., *L'Exemplum dans la littérature religieuse et didactique du Moyen Âge* (Paris and Toulouse, 1927).

West, Philip J., 'Rumination in Bede's Account of Caedmon', *Monastic Studies*, 12 (1976), 217–26.

Yates, Francis A., *The Art of Memory* (1966; rpt. Harmondsworth, 1969).

Zinn, Grover A., 'Hugh of St Victor and the Art of Memory', *Viator*, 5 (1974), 211–34.

Medieval Irish literary theory and criticism

Primary sources

Acallamh na Senórach, ed. W. Stokes (Leipzig, 1900).
'Airbertach mac Cosse's Poem on the Psalter', ed. P. Ó Néill, *Éigse*, 17 (1977–9), 19–46.
Airec menman Uraird maic Coisse, ed. M. E. Byrne, in *Anecdota from Irish Manuscripts*, ed. O. J. Bergin *et al.* (5 vols., Halle and Dublin, 1908), II, pp. 42–76.
The Annals of Tigernach, tr. W. Stokes (Lampeter, 1993).
Auraicept na n-Éces, ed. G. Calder (Edinburgh, 1917).
The Banquet of Dun na nGedh and the Battle of Magh Rath, ed. J. O'Donovan (Dublin, 1842).
Bethada Naém nÉrenn, ed. C. Plummer (2 vols., Oxford, 1922).
'The Caldron of Poesy', ed. L. Breatnach, *Ériu*, 32 (1981), 45–93.
The Celtic Poets: Songs and Tales from Early Ireland and Wales, tr. P. K. Ford (Belmont MA, 1999).
The Codex Palatino-Vaticanus No. 830, ed. B. MacCarthy (Dublin, 1892) [includes antiquated translation of parts of the Metrical Tracts].
'The Colloquy of the Two Sages', ed. and tr. W. Stokes, *Revue celtique*, 26 (1905), 4–64, 284–5.
Dooley, Ann, and Roe, Harry (tr.), *Tales of the Elders of Ireland* (Oxford, 1999).
Hibernica Minora, being a Fragment of an Old-Irish Treatise on the Psalter, ed. K. Meyer (Oxford, 1894).
Immram Curaig Máele Dúin. See: *The Voyage of Máel Dúin*
'[Irish Grammatical Tracts] V. Metrical Faults', ed. O. J. Bergin, *Ériu*, 17 (1955), 259–93.
The Irish Liber Hymnorum, ed. J. H. Bernard and R. Atkinson (2 vols., London, 1898).
Keating, Geoffrey, *Foras feasa ar Éirinn: The History of Ireland*, ed. and tr. D. Comyn and P. S. Dinneen (4 vols., London, 1902–4).
Meyer, Kuno, 'Addenda to the *Echtra Nerai*', *Revue celtique*, 11 (1890), 210.
Miscellanea Hibernica, ed. K. Meyer, University of Illinois Studies in Language and Literature, 2.4 (Urbana IL, 1916), pp. 18–24.
'Mittelirische Verslehren' and 'Zu den mittelirischen Verslehren', ed. R. Thurneysen in *Gesammelte Schriften* (3 vols., Tübingen, 1991–5), II, pp. 340–521, 644–75.
Ó Dálaigh, Gofraidh Fionn, 'A Poem by Gofraidh Fionn Ó Dálaigh', ed. and tr. L. McKenna in S. Pender (ed.), *Essays and Studies Presented to Professor Tadhg Ua Donnchadha* (Cork, 1947), pp. 66–76.
'An Old-Irish Tract on the Privileges and Responsibilities of Poets', ed. E. J. Gwynn, *Ériu*, 13 (1940–2), 1–60, 220–36.
'Pflichten und Gebühren des *ollam*', ed. K. Meyer, *Zeitschrift für celtische Philologie*, 12 (1918), 295–6.

Scéla Mucce Meic Dathó, ed. R. Thurneysen (Dublin, 1975).

Sedulius Scottus, *In Donati artem maiorem*, ed. B. Löfstedt, CCCM (Turnhout, 1977).

Serglige Con Culainn, ed. M. Dillon (Dublin, 1953).

Táin Bó Cúalnge from the Book of Leinster, ed. C. O'Rahilly (Dublin, 1970).

Uraicecht na Ríar: The Poetic Grades in Early Irish Law, ed. L. Breatnach (Dublin, 1987).

The Voyage of Máel Dúin, ed. H. P. A. Oskamp (Groningen, 1970).

Secondary sources

Baumgarten, Rolf, 'Etymological Aetiology in Irish Tradition', *Ériu*, 41 (1990), 115–22.

Bergin, Osborn (ed.), *Irish Bardic Poetry* (Dublin, 1970).

Breatnach, Caoimhín, 'The Religious Significance of *Oidheadh Chloinne Lir*', *Ériu*, 50 (1999), 1–40.

Breatnach, Liam, 'Poets and Poetry', in McCone and Simms (eds.), *Progress in Medieval Irish Studies*, pp. 65–77.

Breatnach, Pádraig A., 'Bernhard Bischoff (d. 1991), The Munich School of Medieval Latin Philology, and Irish Medieval Studies', *Cambrian Medieval Celtic Studies*, 26 (1993), 1–14.

'The Chief's Poet', *Proceedings of the Royal Irish Academy*, 83, sect. C (1983), 37–79.

'The Metres of Citations in the Irish Grammatical Tracts', *Éigse*, 32 (2000), 7–22.

Byrne, Francis John, '*Senchas*: The Nature of Gaelic Historical Tradition', *Historical Studies*, 9 (1974), 137–59.

Carey, John, 'The Three Things Required of a Poet', *Ériu*, 48 (1997), 40–58.

Chadwin, Tom, 'The *remscéla Tána Bó Cualngi*', *Cambrian Medieval Celtic Studies*, 34 (1997), 67–75.

Corthals, Johan, 'Early Irish *Retoirics* and their Late Antique Background', *Cambrian Medieval Celtic Studies*, 31 (Summer, 1996), 17–36.

Davies, Morgan Thomas, 'Protocols of Reading in Early Irish Literature: Notes on some Notes to *Orgain Denna Ríg* and *Amra Coluim Cille*', *Cambrian Medieval Celtic Studies*, 32 (1996), 1–23.

Dumville, David, 'Ulster Heroes in the Early Irish Annals: A Caveat', *Éigse*, 17.1 (1977), 47–54.

Ford, Patrick K., 'The Blind, the Dumb, and the Ugly: Aspects of Poets and their Craft in Early Ireland and Wales', *Cambridge Medieval Celtic Studies*, 19 (1990), 27–40.

Greenwood, Eamon M., 'Characterisation and Narrative Intent in the Book of Leinster Version of *Táin Bó Cúailnge*', in H. L. C. Tristram (ed.), *Medieval Insular Literature between the Oral and the Written, II* (Tübingen, 1997), pp. 81–116.

Henry, P. L., 'A Celtic-English Prosodic Feature', *Zeitschrift für celtische Philologie*, 29 (1962–4), 91–9.

Herbert, Máire, '*Cathréim Cellaig*: Some Literary and Historical Considerations', *Zeitschrift für celtische Philologie*, 49–50 (1997), 320–32.

'The Preface to *Amra Coluim Cille*', in D. Ó Corráin *et al.* (eds.), *Sages, Saints and Storytellers* (Maynooth, 1989), pp. 67–75.

'The World, the Text, and the Critic of Early Irish Heroic Narrative', *Text and Context* (1988), 1–9.

Hollo, Kaarina, 'Metrical Irregularity in Old and Middle Irish Syllabic Verse', in A. Ahlqvist *et al.* (ed.), *Celtica Helsingiensia* (Helsinki, 1996), pp. 47–56.

Kelleher, John V., 'The Táin and the Annals', *Ériu*, 22 (1971), 107–27.

Kelly, Fergus, *A Guide to Early Irish Law* (Dublin, 1988).

Kelly, Patricia, 'The *Táin* as Literature', in J. P. Mallory (ed.), *Aspects of the Táin* (Belfast, 1992), pp. 69–102.

Kidd, I. G., *Posidonius*, II, *The Commentary* (2 vols., Cambridge, 1988).

Law, Vivien, *Wisdom, Authority and Grammar in the Seventh Century: Decoding Virgilius Maro Grammaticus* (Cambridge, 1995).

Mac Cana, Proinsias, *The Learned Tales of Medieval Ireland* (Dublin, 1980).

'Placenames and Mythology in Irish Tradition: Places, Pilgrimages and Things', in G. W. MacLennan (ed.), *Proceedings of the First North American Congress of Celtic Studies* (Ottawa, 1988), pp. 319–41.

MacNeill, Eoin 'Ancient Irish Law: The Law of Status or Franchise', *Proceedings of the Royal Irish Academy*, 36, sect. C (1923), 265–316.

McCone, Kim, *Pagan Past and Christian Present in Early Irish Literature* (Maynooth, 1990).

McCone, Kim, and Simms, Katharine (eds.), *Progress in Medieval Irish Studies* (Maynooth, 1996).

McManus, Damian, 'Classical Modern Irish', in McCone and Simms (eds.), *Progress in Medieval Irish Studies*, pp. 165–87.

Review of Tristram (ed.), *Metrik und Medienwechsel*, in *Éigse*, 28 (1994–5), 173–83.

'*Úaim do rinn*: Linking Alliteration or a Lost *dúnad*?', *Ériu*, 46 (1995), 59–63.

Murphy, Gerard, 'Bards and filidh', *Éigse*, 2 (1940), 200–7.

Early Irish Metrics (Dublin, 1961).

Murray, Kevin, 'The Finality of the *Táin*', *Cambrian Medieval Celtic Studies* 41 (Summer, 2001), 17–23.

Nagy, Joseph Falaky, *Conversing with Angels and Ancients: Literary Myths of Medieval Ireland* (Ithaca NY and London, 1997).

Ní Chonghaile, Nóirín, and Tristram, H. L. C., 'Die mittelirischen Sagenlisten zwischen Mündlichkeit und Schriftlichkeit', in H. L. C. Tristram (ed.), *Deutsche, Kelten und Iren: 150 Jahre deutsche Keltologie* (Hamburg, 1990), pp. 249–68.

Ó Corráin, Donnchadh, 'Historical Need and Literary Narrative', in D. Ellis Evans *et al.* (eds.), *Proceedings of the Seventh International Congress of Celtic Studies* (Oxford, 1986), pp. 141–58.

'Legend as Critic', in T. Dunne (ed.), *The Writer as Witness: Literature as Historical Evidence* (Cork, 1987), pp. 23–38.

Ó Cuív, Brian, 'The Concepts of "Correct" and "Faulty" in Medieval Irish Bardic Tradition', in R. Bielmeier and R. Stempel (eds.), *Indogermanica et Caucasica* (Berlin, 1994), pp. 395–406.

'Scél: arramainte: stair', *Éigse*, 11 (1964–6), 18.

'Some Developments in Irish Metrics', *Éigse*, 12 (1967–8), 273–90.

Ó hAodha, Donncha, 'The First Middle Irish Metrical Tract', in Tristram (ed.), *Metrik und Medienwechsel*, pp. 207–44.

Ó hUiginn, Ruairí, 'The Background and Development of *Taín Bó Cúailnge*', in J. P. Mallory (ed.), *Aspects of the Táin* (Belfast, 1992), pp. 29–67.

Ó Macháin, Pádraig, 'The Early Modern Irish Prosodic Tracts and the Editing of "Bardic Verse"', in Tristram (ed.), *Metrik und Medienwechsel*, pp. 273–87.

Ó Néill, Pádraig, 'The Latin Colophon to the *Táin Bó Cúailnge* in the Book of Leinster: A Critical View of Old Irish Literature', *Celtica*, 23 (1999), 269–75.

'The Old-Irish Treatise on the Psalter and its Hiberno-Latin Background', *Ériu*, 30 (1979), 148–64.

Ó Riain, Pádraig, 'Der Schein, der trügt: Die irische Heldensage als kirchenpolitische Aussage', in H. L. C. Tristram (ed.), *New Methods in the Research of Epic* (Tübingen, 1998), pp. 143–51.

O'Sullivan, William, 'Notes on the Scripts and Make-up of the Book of Leinster', *Celtica*, 7 (1966), 1–31.

Poppe, Erich, '*Grammatica, grammatic*, Augustine, and the *Táin*', in J. Carey *et al.* (eds.), *Ildánach Ildírech: A Festschrift for Proinsias Mac Cana* (Andover and Aberystwyth, 1999), pp. 203–10.

'Reconstructing Medieval Irish Literary Theory: The Lesson of *Airec menman Uraird maic Coise*', *Cambrian Medieval Celtic Studies*, 37 (1999), 33–54.

Richter, Michael, *The Formation of the Medieval West* (Blackrock, 1994).

Scowcroft, R. Mark, 'Abstract Narrative in Ireland', *Ériu*, 46 (1995), 121–58.

Simms, Katharine, 'Literacy and the Irish Bards', in H. Pryce (ed.), *Literacy in Medieval Celtic Societies* (Cambridge, 1998), pp. 238–58.

Sims-Williams, Patrick, 'The Medieval World of Robin Flower', in M. de Mórdha (ed.), *Bláithín: Flower* (An Daingean, 1998), pp. 73–96.

'Person-switching in Celtic Panegyric: Figure or Fault?', *Celtic Studies Association of North America Yearbook*, 3/4 (2004), 315–26.

Thurneysen, Rudolf, *Die irische Helden- und Königsage bis zum 17. Jahrhundert* (Halle, 1921), pp. 252–3.

Toner, Gregory, 'Reconstructing the Earliest Irish Tale Lists', *Éigse*, 32 (2000), 88–120.

'The Ulster Cycle: Historiography or Fiction?', *Cambrian Medieval Celtic Studies*, 40 (Winter, 2000), 1–20.

Tranter, Stephen N., *Clavis Metrica: Háttatal, Háttalykill and the Irish Metrical Tracts* (Basel and Frankfurt, 1997).

'Divided and Scattered, Trussed and Supported: Stanzaic Form in Irish and Old Norse Tracts', in Tristram (ed.), *Metrik und Medienwechsel*, pp. 245–72.

'Metrikwandel – Weltbildwandel: Die irische Metrik im Sog der Christianisierung', in H. L. C. Tristram (ed.), *New Methods in the Research of Epic* (Tübingen, 1998), pp. 38–49.

Tristram, Hildegard L. C. (ed.), *Metrik und Medienwechsel: Metrics and Media* (Tübingen, 1991).

'Warum Cenn Faelad sein "Gehirn des Vergessens" verlor – Wort und Schrift in der älteren irischen Literatur', in H. L. C. Tristram (ed.), *Deutsche, Kelten und Iren: 150 Jahre deutsche Keltologie* (Hamburg, 1990), pp. 207–48.

Watkins, Calvert, *How to Kill a Dragon: Aspects of Indo-European Poetics* (Oxford, 1995).
'Indo-European Metrics and Archaic Irish Verse', *Celtica*, 6 (1963), 194–249.

Anglo-Saxon textual attitudes

Primary sources

Ælfric, *Grammatik und Glossar*, ed. J. Zupitza (Berlin, 1880).
Ælfric, *Lives of Saints*, ed. W. W. Skeat, EETS OS 76, 82, 94, 114 (rpt. as 2 vols., London, 1966).
Ælfric, *Catholic Homilies, The First Series: Text*, ed. P. A. M. Clemoes, EETS SS 17 (London, 1997).
Alfred, *King Alfred's Old English Version of Boethius De Consolatione philosophiae*, ed. W. J. Sedgefield (Oxford, 1899).
King Alfred's Version of St. Augustine's 'Soliloquies', ed. T. A. Carnicelli (Cambridge MA, 1969).
King Alfred's West-Saxon Version of Gregory's 'Pastoral Care', ed. H. Sweet, EETS OS 45 (London, 1958).
The Anglo-Saxon Poetic Records, ed. G. P. Krapp and E. V. K. Dobbie (6 vols., New York, 1931–42).
Anglo-Saxon Poetry, ed. and tr. S. A. J. Bradley (London, 1995).
Anglo-Saxon Prose, tr. M. Swanton (London, 1975).
Bede, *Historia ecclesiastica*, ed. and tr. B. Colgrave and R. A. B. Mynors, *Bede's Ecclesiastical History of the English People* (Oxford, 1991).
'Beowulf' and 'The Fight at Finnsburg', ed. F. Klaeber (3rd edn, Boston MA, 1950).
Beowulf, tr. Seamus Heaney (London, 1999).
'Beowulf': A Student Edition, ed. G. Jack (Oxford, 1994).
Byrhtferth, *Enchiridion*, ed. P. S. Baker and M. Lapidge, EETS SS 15 (London, 1995).
Heliand und Genesis, ed. O. Behaghel, Altdeutsche Textbibliothek, 4, 10th edn, rev. B. Taeger (Tübingen, 1996).
Isidore of Seville, *Etymologiae*, ed. W. L. Lindsay (2 vols., 1911; rpt. Oxford, 1985).
The Old English 'Apollonius of Tyre', ed. P. Goolden (Oxford, 1953).
The Old English Orosius, ed. J. Bately, EETS SS 6 (London, 1980).
Percy, Thomas, *Reliques of Ancient English Poetry* (London, 1765).

Secondary sources

Bäuml, Franz, 'Medieval Texts and the Two Theories of Oral Performance: A Proposal for a Third Theory', *New Literary History*, 16 (1984–5), 31–49.
'Varieties and Consequences of Medieval Literacy and Illiteracy', *Speculum*, 55 (1980), 237–65.
Bliss, Alan, *An Introduction to Old English Metre* (Oxford, 1962).

Chase, Colin (ed.), *The Dating of Beowulf* (Toronto, 1981).

Clanchy, M. T., *From Memory to Written Record: England 1066–1307* (2nd edn, Oxford, 1993).

Coleman, Joyce, *Public Reading and the Reading Public in Late Medieval England and France* (Cambridge, 1996).

Foley, John Miles, *The Singer of Tales in Performance* (Bloomington and Indianapolis IN, 1995).

Frantzen, Allen J., *The Desire for Origins: New Language, Old English and Teaching the Tradition* (New Brunswick NJ, 1990).

Fry, Donald K., 'Cædmon as a Formulaic Poet', in J. J. Duggan (ed.), *Oral Literature: Seven Essays* (New York, 1975), pp. 41–61.

Godden, Malcolm, and Lapidge, Michael (eds.), *The Cambridge Companion to Old English Literature* (Cambridge, 1991).

Gretsch, Mechthild, *The Intellectual Foundations of the English Benedictine Reform* (Cambridge, 1999).

Hainsworth, J. B., and Hatto, A. T. (eds.), *Traditions of Epic and Heroic Poetry* (2 vols., London, 1989).

Hill, J., 'Reform and Resistance: Preaching Styles in Late Anglo-Saxon England', in J. Hamesse and X. Hermand (eds.), *De l'Homélie au sermon: histoire de la prédication médiévale: actes du colloque international de Louvain-la-Neuve (9–11 juillet 1992)* (Louvain-la-Neuve, 1993), pp. 15–46.

Jabbour, Alan, 'Memorial Transmission in Old English Poetry', *ChR*, 3 (1969), 174–90.

Jager, Eric, 'Speech and the Chest in Old English Poetry: Orality or Pectorality?', *Speculum*, 65 (1990), 845–59.

Jauss, Hans Robert, *Question and Answer: On the Forms of Dialogic Understanding*, tr. M. Hays (Minneapolis MN, 1989).

Lapidge, Michael, *Anglo-Latin Literature, 600–899* (London, 1996).

Anglo-Latin Literature, 900–1066 (London, 1993).

Lord, Albert Bates, *The Singer of Tales* (Cambridge MA, 1960).

Momma, H., *The Composition of Old English Poetry* (Cambridge, 1997).

O'Brien O'Keeffe, Katherine, *Visible Song: Transitional Literacy in Old English Verse* (Cambridge, 1990).

Opland, Jeff, 'The Words for Poets and Poetry', in his *Anglo-Saxon Oral Poetry: A Study of the Traditions* (New Haven CT and London, 1980), pp. 230–56.

Orchard, Andy, 'Crying Wolf: Oral Style and the *Sermones Lupi*', *Anglo-Saxon England*, 21 (1993), 239–64.

'Oral Tradition', in K. O'Brien O'Keeffe (ed.), *Reading Old English Texts* (Cambridge, 1997), pp. 101–24.

Page, R. I., *Runes and Runic Inscriptions* (Woodbridge, 1995).

Pasternack, Carol Braun, *The Textuality of Old English Poetry* (Cambridge, 1995).

Koselleck, Reinhart, *Futures Past: On the Semantics of Historical Time*, tr. K. Tribe (Cambridge MA and London, 1985).

Reynolds, Susan, 'What Do We Mean by "Anglo-Saxon" and "Anglo-Saxons"?', *Journal of British Studies*, 24 (1985), 395–414.

Schaefer, Ursula, 'Hearing from Books: The Rise of Fictionality in Old English Poetry', in A. N. Doane and C. B. Pasternack (eds.), *Vox intexta: Orality and Textuality in the Middle Ages* (Madison WI, 1991), pp. 117–36.

Scragg, Donald G., and Weinberg, Lois (eds.), *Literary Appropriations of the Anglo-Saxons from the Thirteenth to the Twentieth Century* (Cambridge, 2000).

Stanley, E. G., *Imagining the Anglo-Saxon Past* (Woodbridge, 2000).

Toon, Thomas E., 'Old English Dialects', in R. M. Hogg (ed.), *The Cambridge History of the English Language, I: The Beginnings to 1066* (Cambridge, 1992), pp. 409–51.

Wormald, Patrick, 'Bede, the Bretwaldas and the Origins of the *Gens Anglorum*', in P. Wormald (ed.), *Ideal and Reality in Frankish and Anglo-Saxon Society: Studies Presented to J. M. Wallace-Hadrill* (Oxford, 1983), pp. 99–130.

Zumthor, Paul, *La Lettre et la voix: de la 'littérature' médiévale* (Paris, 1987).

Literary theory and practice in early-medieval Germany

Primary sources

The shorter OHG texts mentioned – including the *Lay of Hildebrand*, the *Wessobrunn Creation and Prayer*, *Muspilli* and *Ludwigslied* – are most readily found in collections such as: Braune, W., and Ebbinghaus, E. A. (eds.), *Althochdeutsches Lesebuch* (17th edn, Tübingen, 1994), and Schlosser, H. D. (ed.), *Althochdeutsche Literatur: Eine Textauswahl mit Übertragungen* (Berlin, 1998).

Einhard, *Vita Karoli Magni*, ed. O. Holder-Egger (1911; rpt. Hanover, 1965).

Epistolae Karolini aevi, IV, ed. E. Dümmler and E. Perels, MGH (1902–25; rpt. Munich, 1978).

Heliand und Genesis, ed. O. Behaghel, Altdeutsche Textbibliothek, 4, 10th edn, rev. B. Taeger (Tübingen, 1996).

Isidore, *Der althochdeutsche Isidor*, ed. G. A. Hench, Quellen und Forschungen zur Sprach- und Culturgeschichte der germanischen Völker, 72 (Strassburg, 1893).

Notker, *Notkers des Deutschen Werke*, ed. E. H. Sehrt and T. Starck.
    Vol. 1, 1–3: Boethius, *De consolatione philosophiae*, Altdeutsche Textbibliothek, 32–4 (3 vols., Tübingen, 1933–4).
    Vol. 2: Marcianus Capella, *De nuptiis Philologiae et Mercurii*, Altdeutsche Textbibliothek, 37 (Tübingen, 1935).
    Vol. 3, 1–3: *Der Psalter*, Altdeutsche Textbibliothek, 40, 42, 43 (3 vols., Tübingen, 1952–5).
    Die Werke Notkers des Deutschen, ed. J. C. King and P. W. Tax, Neue Ausgabe (Tübingen, 1972–).

Otfrid of Weißenburg, *Otfrids Evangelienbuch*, ed. O. Erdmann and L. Wolff, Altdeutsche Textbibliothek, 49 (6th edn, Tübingen, 1973).

Tatian, *Die lateinisch-althochdeutsche Tatianbilingue Stiftsbibliothek St. Gallen Cod. 56*, ed. A. Masser, Studien zum Althochdeutschen, 25 (Göttingen, 1994).

Tatian: lateinisch und deutsch, ed. E. Sievers, Bibliothek der ältesten deutschen Literatur-Denkmäler, 5 (2nd edn, 1892; rpt. Paderborn, 1966).

Secondary sources

Backes, Herbert, *Die Hochzeit Merkurs und der Philologie: Studien zu Notkers Martian-Übersetzung* (Sigmaringen, 1982).

Bergmann, R., Tiefenbach, H., and Voetz, L. (eds.), *Althochdeutsch* (2 vols., Heidelberg, 1987).

Bliss, Alan, *An Introduction to Old English Metre* (Oxford, 1962).

Bostock, J. K., *A Handbook on Old High German Literature*, 2nd edn, rev. by K. C. King and D. R. McLintock (Oxford, 1976).

Curtius, Ernst R., *Europäische Literatur und lateinisches Mittelalter* (2nd edn, Bern, 1948). English tr. of the first edition under the title *European Literature and the Latin Middle Ages*, by W. R. Trask (London, 1953).

de Smet, G., 'Die Winileod in Karls Edikt von 789', in *Studien zur deutschen Sprache und Literatur des Mittelalters: Festschrift für Hugo Moser*, ed. W. Besch *et al.* (Berlin, 1974), pp. 1–7.

Edwards, Cyril, *The Beginnings of German Literature: Comparative and Interdisciplinary Approaches to Old High German* (Rochester NY, 2002).

'German Vernacular Literature: A Survey', in R. McKitterick (ed.), *Carolingian Culture: Emulation and Innovation* (Cambridge, 1993), pp. 141–70.

'Winileodos? Zu Nonnen, Zensur und den Spuren der althochdeutschen Liebeslyrik', in W. Haubrichs *et al.* (eds.), *Theodisca: Beiträge zur althochdeutschen und altniederdeutschen Sprache und Literatur in der Kultur des frühen Mittelalters* (Berlin, 2000), pp. 189–206.

Engel, Werner, 'Die dichtungstheoretischen Bezeichnungen im *Liber evangeliorum* Otfrids von Weißenburg', doctoral diss., Frankfurt, 1969.

Ernst, Ulrich, *Der Liber Evangeliorum Otfrids von Weißenburg, Literarästhetik und Verstechnik im Lichte der Tradition*, Kölner Germanistische Studien, 11 (Cologne and Vienna, 1975).

Ernst, U., and Neuser, P. E. (eds.), *Die Genese der europäischen Endreimdichtung*, Wege der Forschung, 444 (Darmstadt, 1977).

Foerste, W., 'Otfrids literarisches Verhältnis zum Heliand', in J. Eichhoff and I. Rauch (eds.), *Der Heliand*, Wege der Forschung, 321 (Darmstadt, 1973), pp. 93–131.

Gantert, Klaus, *Akkommodation und eingeschriebener Kommentar: Untersuchungen zur Übertragungsstrategie des Helianddichters*, ScriptOralia, 111 (Tübingen, 1998).

Georgi, Anette, *Das lateinische und deutsche Preisgedicht des Mittelalters*, Philologische Studien und Quellen, 48 (Berlin 1969).

Groseclose, J. S., and Murdoch, B. O., *Die althochdeutschen poetischen Denkmäler*, Sammlung Metzler, 140 (Stuttgart, 1976).

Gürich, Günther, 'Otfrids Evangelienbuch als Kreuzfigur', *Zeitschrift für deutsches Altertum*, 95 (1966), 267–70.

Haubrichs, Wolfgang, *Geschichte der deutschen Literatur von den Anfängen bis zum Beginn der Neuzeit*, vol. I: *Von den Anfängen bis zum hohen Mittelalter*, pt. 1: *Die Anfänge: Versuche volkssprachiger Schriftlichkeit im frühen Mittelalter (ca. 700–1050/60)*, ed. J. Heinzle (Frankfurt, 1988).

Haug, Walter, *Literaturtheorie im deutschen Mittelalter* (2nd rev. edn, Darmstadt, 1985); tr. J. M. Catling as *Vernacular Literary Theory in the Middle Ages: The German Tradition, 800–1300, in its European Context* (Cambridge, 1997).

Hellgardt, Ernst, 'Notkers des Deutschen Brief an Bischof Hugo von Sitten', in K. Grubmüller *et al.* (eds.), *Befund und Deutung: Zum Verhältnis von Empirie und Interpretation in Sprach- und Literaturwissenschaft* (Tübingen, 1979), pp. 169–92.

Henrotte, Gale A., 'The Sound of Otfried's Germanic Verse', in A. Classen (ed.), *Von Otfried von Weißenburg bis zum 15. Jahrhundert: Proceedings from the 24th International Congress on Medieval Studies, May 4–7 1989*, Göppinger Arbeiten zur Germanistik, 539 (Göppingen, 1991), pp. 1–11.

Hoffmann, Werner, *Altdeutsche Metrik*, Sammlung Metzler, 64 (2nd and rev. edn, Stuttgart, 1981).

Kartschoke, Dieter, *Bibeldichtung: Studien zur Geschichte der epischen Bibelparaphrase von Juvencus bis Otfrid von Weißenburg* (Munich, 1975).

Kleiber, Wolfgang, *Otfrid von Weißenburg: Untersuchungen zur handschriftlichen Überlieferung und Studien zum Aufbau des Evangelienbuches*, Bibliotheca germanica, 14 (Bern and Munich, 1971).

Lehmann, W. P., *The Alliteration of Old Saxon Poetry*, Norsk Tidskrift for Sprogvidenskap, Suppl. 3 (Oslo, 1953); rpt. in J. Eichhoff and I. Rauch (eds.), *Der Heliand*, Wege der Forschung, 321 (Darmstadt, 1973), pp. 144–76.

Langosch, Karl, *Profile des lateinischen Mittelalters* (Darmstadt, 1965).

Magoun, Francis P., Jr., 'Otfrids Ad Liutbertum', *PMLA*, 58 (1943), 869–90.

Matzel, Klaus, *Untersuchungen zur Verfasserschaft, Sprache und Herkunft der althochdeutschen Übersetzungen der Isidor-Sippe*, Rheinisches Archiv, 75 (Bonn, 1970).

McKitterick, Rosamund, *The Carolingians and the Written Word* (Cambridge, 1989).

Meissburger, Gerhard, 'Zum sogenannten Heldenliederbuch Karls des Großen', *Germanisch-romanische Monatsschrift*, 44 (1963), 105–19.

Meyer, Heinz and Suntrup, Rudolf, *Lexikon der mittelalterlichen Zahlenbedeutungen*, Münstersche Mittelalter-Schriften, 56 (Munich, 1987).

Much, R., *Die Germania des Tacitus*, 3rd edn, rev. W. Lange (Heidelberg, 1967).

Murdoch, B. O., *Old High German Literature* (Boston MA, 1983).

Patzlaff, Rainer, *Otfrid von Weißenburg und die mittelalterliche versus-Tradition: Untersuchungen zur formgeschichtlichen Stellung der Otfridstrophe*, Hermaea, n.F. 35 (Tübingen, 1975).

Rathofer, Johannes, *Der Heliand: Theologischer Sinn als tektonische Form*, Niederdeutsche Studien, 9 (Cologne and Graz, 1962).

Schulz, Klaus, *Art und Herkunft des variierenden Stils in Otfrids Evangeliendichtung*, Medium ævum, Philologische Studien, 15 (Munich, 1968).

Schwarz, Hans, 'Ahd. liod und sein sprachliches Feld', *PBB*, 75 (Halle, 1953), 321–65.

See, Klaus von, *Germanische Verskunst*, Sammlung Metzler, 67 (Stuttgart, 1967). 'Stabreim und Endreim', *PBB*, 102 (1980), 399–417.

Sonderegger, Stefan, 'Notker der Deutsche als Meister einer volkssprachigen Stilistik', in Bergmann, Tiefenbach and Voetz (eds.), *Althochdeutsch*, I, pp. 839–71.

Stutz, Elfriede, 'Spiegelungen volkssprachlicher Verspraxis bei Otfrid', in Bergmann, Tiefenbach and Voetz (eds.), *Althochdeutsch*, I, pp. 772–94.

Taeger, Burkhard, *Zahlensymbolik bei Hraban, bei Hincmar und im 'Heliand'? Studien zur Zahlensymbolik im Frühmittelalter*, Münchener Texte und Untersuchungen zur deutschen Literatur des Mittelalters, 30 (Munich, 1970).

Urmoneit, Erika, *Der Wortschatz des Ludwigsliedes im Umkreis der althochdeutschen Literatur*, Münstersche Mittelalter-Schriften, 11 (Munich, 1973).

Vollmann-Profe, Gisela, *Kommentar zu Otfrids Evangelienbuch, Teil I* (Bonn, 1976).

Werlich, E., 'Der westgermanische Skop', *Zeitschrift für deutsche Philologie*, 86 (1967), 352–75.

Werner, J., 'Leier und Harfe im germanischen Frühmittelalter', in *Aus Verfassungs- und Landesgeschichte: Festschrift Theodor Mayer*, ed. H. Büttner *et al.* (Lindau and Konstanz, 1954), pp. 9–15.

Zanni, Roland, *Heliand, Genesis und das Altenglische: Die altsächsische Stabreimdichtung zwischen germanischer Oraltradition und altenglischer Bibelepik*, Quellen und Forschungen zur Sprach- und Kulturgeschichte der germanischen Völker, n.F. 76 (Berlin and New York, 1980).

Literary criticism in Welsh before *c.* 1300

Primary sources

Armes Prydein, ed. I. Williams, English version by R. Bromwich (Dublin, 1972).

'The Black Book of Carmarthen "Stanzas of the Graves"', ed. T. Jones, *Proceedings of the British Academy*, 53 (1967), 97–137.

Blodeugerdd Barddas o Ganu Crefyddol Cynnar, ed. M. Haycock (Swansea, 1994).

Book of Taliesin, Facsimile and Text, ed. J. G. Evans (Llanbedrog, 1910).

Breudwyt Ronabwy, ed. M. Richards (Cardiff, 1948).

The Cambridge Juvencus Manuscript Glossed in Latin, Old Welsh, and Old Irish, ed. H. McKee (Aberystwyth, 2000).

Canu Aneirin, ed. I. Williams (Cardiff, 1938).

Cyfres Beirdd y Tywysogion, ed. R. G. Gruffydd (7 vols., Cardiff, 1991–6) [references are to vol., poem and line].

Early Welsh Saga Poetry: A Study and Edition of the Englynion, ed. J. Rowland (Cambridge, 1990).

Geoffrey of Monmouth, *The History of the Kings of Britain*, tr. L. Thorpe (Harmondsworth, 1966).

Vita Merlini: The Life of Merlin, ed. and tr. B. Clarke (Cardiff, 1973).

Gerald of Wales, *'The Journey through Wales' and 'The Description of Wales'*, tr. L. Thorpe (Harmondsworth, 1978).

Gildas, *De excidio Britanniae*, ed. and tr. M. Winterbottom (London and Chichester, 1978).

The Gododdin of Aneirin: Text and Context from Dark-Age North Britain, ed. J. T. Koch (Cardiff, 1997).

Gramadegau'r Penceirddiaid, ed. G. J. Williams and E. J. Jones (Cardiff, 1934).

Historia Brittonum. See *Nennius: British History and the Welsh Annals*, ed. and tr. J. Morris, History from the Sources 8 (London and Chichester, 1980).

Iolo Goch, *Gwaith Iolo Goch*, ed. D. R. Johnston (Cardiff, 1988).

'The Juvencus Poems', ed. and tr. I. Williams, rpt. in Williams, *Beginnings of Welsh Poetry*, pp. 89–121.

Llyfr Du Caerfyrddin, ed. A. O. H. Jarman (Cardiff, 1982).

Llyfr Gwyn Rhydderch: Y Chwedlau a'r Rhamantau, ed. J. G. Evans (1907; rpt. Cardiff, 1973).

'An Old Welsh Verse [= 'St Padarn's Staff']', ed. I. Williams, rpt. in Williams, *Beginnings of Welsh Poetry*, pp. 181–9.

Pedeir Keinc y Mabinogi, ed. I. Williams (Cardiff, 1930).

The Poems of Taliesin, ed. I. Williams, English version by J. E. C. Williams (Dublin, 1968).

The Poetry in the Red Book of Hergest, ed. J. G. Evans (Llanbedrog, 1911).

Trioedd Ynys Prydein, ed. R. Bromwich (2nd edn, Cardiff, 1978).

'Two Poems from the Book of Taliesin: (i) The Praise of Tenby (ii) An Early Anglesey Poem', ed. I. Williams, rpt. in Williams, *Beginnings of Welsh Poetry*, pp. 155–80.

'A Welsh "Dark Age" Court Poem', ed. and tr. R. G. Gruffydd, in *Ildánach Ildírech*, ed. J. Carey *et al.* (Andover MA and Aberystwyth, 1999), pp. 39–48.

Williams, Ifor, *The Beginnings of Welsh Poetry*, ed. R. Bromwich (2nd edn, Cardiff, 1980).

Secondary sources

Bosco, Sister (N. G. Costigan), 'Awen y Cynfeirdd a'r Gogynfeirdd', in Roberts and Owen (eds.), *Beirdd a Thywysogion*, pp. 14–38.

Breeze, Andrew, 'Llyfr durgrys', *Bulletin of the Board of Celtic Studies*, 33 (1986), 145.

Davies, Sioned, *Crefft y Cyfarwydd* (Cardiff, 1996).

'Written Text as Performance: The Implications for Middle Welsh Prose Narratives', in Pryce (ed.), *Literacy in Medieval Celtic Societies*, pp. 133–48.

Dumville, David N., 'The Historical Value of the *Historia Brittonum*', rpt. in Dumville, *Histories and Pseudo-histories of the Insular Middle Ages* (Aldershot, 1990), Ch. 7.

Evans, Dylan Foster, *Goganwr am Gig Ynyd: The Poet as Satirist in Medieval Wales* (Aberystwth, 1996).

Ford, Patrick K., 'The Death of Aneirin', *Bulletin of the Board of Celtic Studies*, 34 (1987), 41–50.

'The Poet as *Cyfarwydd* in Early Welsh Tradition', *Studia Celtica*, 10–11 (1975–6), 152–62.

Gruffydd, R. Geraint, 'The *Englynion* of Llyfr Aneirin', in K. A. Klar, E. E. Sweetser and C. Thomas (eds.), *A Celtic Florilegium: Studies in Memory of Brendan O Hehir* (Andover MA, 1996), pp. 32–42.

Haycock, Marged, 'Taliesin's Questions', *Cambrian Medieval Celtic Studies*, 33 (Summer, 1997), 19–80.

Huws, Daniel, *Llyfr Aneirin: A Facsimile* (Cardiff and Aberystwyth, 1989). *Medieval Welsh Manuscripts* (Cardiff, 2000).

James, Christine, '"Llwyr wybodau, llên a llyfrau": Hopcyn ap Tomas a'r Traddodiad Llenyddol Cymraeg', in H. T. Edwards (ed.), *Cwm Tawe* (Llandysul, 1994), pp. 4–44.

Jenkins, Dafydd, 'Bardd Teulu and Pencerdd', in T. M. Charles-Edwards, M. E. Owen and P. Russell (eds.), *The Welsh King and his Court* (Cardiff, 2000), pp. 142–66.

Jones, Nerys Ann, 'Y Gogynfeirdd a'r Englyn', in Roberts and Owen (eds.), *Beirdd a Thywysogion*, pp. 288–301.

Klar, Kathryn A., 'What are the *Gwarchanau*?', in Roberts (ed.), *Early Welsh Poetry*, pp. 97–137.

Lewis, Henry, 'Credo Athanasius Sant', *Bulletin of the Board of Celtic Studies*, 5 (1929–31), 193–203.

Lloyd-Jones, John, *Geirfa Barddoniaeth Gynnar Gymraeg* (Cardiff, 1931–63) [this dictionary ran from A–H, as far as *Heilic*].

Lloyd-Morgan, Ceridwen, 'French Texts, Welsh Translators', in R. Ellis (ed.), *The Medieval Translator 2* (Cambridge, 1991), pp. 45–63.

'More Written about than Writing? Welsh Women and the Written Word', in Pryce (ed.), *Literacy in Medieval Celtic Societies*, pp. 149–65.

'Rhai Agweddau ar Gyfieithu yng Nghymru'r Oesoedd Canol', *Ysgrifau Beirniadol*, 13 (1985), 134–45.

Mac Cana, Proinsias, *The Learned Tales of Medieval Ireland* (Dublin, 1980), Appendix A 'The Welsh *cyfarwydd*', pp. 132–41.

'Prosimetrum in Insular Celtic Literature', in J. Harris and K. Reichl (eds.), *Prosimetrum: Crosscultural Perspectives on Narrative in Prose and Verse* (Woodbridge, 1997), pp. 99–130.

McKee, Helen, 'Scribes and Glosses from Dark Age Wales: The Cambridge Juvencus Manuscript', *Cambrian Medieval Celtic Studies*, 39 (Summer, 2000), 1–22.

McKenna, Catherine, 'Bygwth a Dychan mewn Barddoniaeth Llys Gymraeg', in Roberts and Owen (eds.), *Beirdd a Thywysogion*, pp. 108–21.

Owen, Ann Parry, 'Canu Arwyrain Beirdd y Tywysogion', *Ysgrifau Beirniadol*, 24 (1998), 44–59.

Owen, Morfydd E., 'Chwedl a Hanes: y Cynfeirdd yng Ngwaith y Gogynfeirdd', *Ysgrifau Beirniadol*, 19 (1993), 13–28.

'Noddwyr a Beirdd', in Roberts and Owen (eds.), *Beirdd a Thywysogion*, pp. 75–107.

Pryce, Huw (ed.), *Literacy in Medieval Celtic Societies* (Cambridge, 1998).

Roberts, Brynley F. (ed.), *Early Welsh Poetry: Studies in the Book of Aneirin* (Aberystwyth, 1988).

'Where were the Four Branches of the Mabinogi Written?' in J. F. Nagy (ed.), *The Individual in Celtic Literatures*, CSANA Yearbook 1 (Dublin, 2001), pp. 61–73.

'*Ystoria*', *Bulletin of the Board of Celtic Studies*, 26 (1974), 13–20.

Roberts, Brynley F., and Owen, Morfydd E. (eds.), *Beirdd a Thywysogion: Barddoniaeth Llys yng Nghymru, Iwerddon a'r Alban* (Cardiff, 1996).

Rowland, Jenny, 'Genres', in Roberts (ed.), *Early Welsh Poetry* (Aberystwyth, 1988), pp. 179–208.

'The Prose Setting of the Early Welsh *Englynion Chwedlonol*', *Ériu*, 36 (1985), 29–43.

Russell, Paul, *Celtic Word Formation: The Velar Suffixes* (Dublin, 1990).

Sims-Williams, Patrick, 'Gildas and Vernacular Poetry', in M. Lapidge and D. Dumville (eds.), *Gildas: New Approaches* (Woodbridge, 1984), pp. 169–92.

'Some Functions of Origin Stories in Early Medieval Wales', in T. Nyberg *et al.* (eds.), *History and Heroic Tale: A Symposium* (Odense, 1985), pp. 97–132.

Skene, W. F., *The Four Ancient Books of Wales* (Edinburgh, 1868).

Slotkin, Edgar M., 'The Fabula, Story, and Text of *Breuddwyd Rhonabwy*', *Cambridge Medieval Celtic Studies*, 18 (Winter, 1989), 89–111.

Thomas, R. J., Bevan, Gareth J., and Donovan, Patrick J. (eds.), *Geiriadur Prifysgol Cymru, A Dictionary of the Welsh Language* (Cardiff, 1950–).

Tristram, H. L. C., 'Early Modes of Insular Expression', in L. Breatnach, K. McCone and D. Ó Corráin (eds.), *Sages, Saints and Storytellers: Celtic Studies in Honour of Professor James Carney* (Maynooth, 1989), pp. 427–48.

Watkins, Calvert, *How to Kill a Dragon: Aspects of Indo-European Poetics* (Oxford, 1995).

Williams, Glanmor, *The Welsh Church from Conquest to Reformation* (Cardiff, 1962).

Williams, J. E. Caerwyn, 'Bardus gallice cantor appellatur . . .', in Roberts and Owen (eds.), *Beirdd a Thywysogion*, pp. 1–13.

'Gildas, Maelgwn and the Bards', in R. R. Davies *et al.* (eds.), *Welsh Society and Nationhood: Historical Essays Presented to Glanmor Williams* (Cardiff, 1984), pp. 19–34.

'Yr Arglwydd Rhys ac "Eisteddfod" Aberteifi 1176', in N. A. Jones and H. Pryce (eds.), *Yr Arglwydd Rhys* (Cardiff, 1996), pp. 94–128.

Criticism and literary theory in Old Norse-Icelandic

Primary sources

Egils saga Skallagrímssonar, ed. S. Nordal, Íslenzk Fornrit, 2 (Reykjavik, 1933).

The First Grammatical Treatise, ed. H. Benediktsson, University of Iceland Publications in Linguistics, 1 (Reykjavik, 1972).

Jón Guðmundsson lærði, *Eddurit . . . I: Þættir úr fræðasögu 17. aldar; II: Texti*, ed. E. G. Pétursson, Rit Stofnunar Árna Magnússonar á Íslandi, 46 (2 vols., Reykjavik, 1998).

Rǫgnvaldr, Earl of Orkney. See: Þórarinsson, Hallr.

[*The Second Grammatical Treatise*], *The So-Called Second Grammatical Treatise*, ed. F. Raschellà (Florence, 1982).

Snorrason, Oddr, *Saga Óláfs Tryggvasonar af Oddr Snorrason munk*, ed. F. Jónsson (Copenhagen, 1932).

Sturluson, Snorri, *Edda*, tr. A. Faulkes (London and Melbourne, 1987).

Edda: Háttatal, ed. A. Faulkes, University College London, Viking Society for Northern Research (1991; rpt. London, 1999).

Edda: Prologue and Gylfaginning, ed. A. Faulkes, University College London, Viking Society for Northern Research (1982; rpt. London, 1988).

Edda: Skáldskaparmál, ed. A. Faulkes, University College London, Viking Society for Northern Research (2 vols., London, 1998).

Edda Snorra Sturlusonar, ed. F. Jónsson (Copenhagen, 1931).

Two Versions of Snorra Edda from the Seventeenth Century, ed. A. Faulkes, Rit Stofnunar Árna Magnússonar á Íslandi, 13, 14 (2 vols., Reykjavik, 1977–9). I: *Edda Magnúsar Ólafssonar (Laufás Edda)*; II: *Edda Islandorum: Völuspá, Hávamál* [P. H. Resen's edition of 1665].

Þórarinsson, Hallr, and Rǫgnvaldr, Earl of Orkney, *Háttalykill enn forni*, ed. J. Helgason and A. Holtsmark, Bibliotheca Arnamagnæana, 1 (Copenhagen, 1941).

Þorgils saga ok Hafliða, ed. U. Brown (London, 1952).

Þórðarson, Óláfr, hvítaskáld, *Dritte Grammatische Abhandlung*, ed. and tr. T. Krömmelbein (Oslo, 1998).

'The Foundation of Grammar: An Edition of the First Section of Ólafr Þórðarson's Grammatical Treatise', ed. T. Wills, Ph.D. diss., University of Sydney, 2001 [available electronically at http://www.arts.usyd.edu.au/~tarwills/thesis/].

Þórðarson, Óláfr, hvítaskáld, *et al.* [*Third and Fourth Grammatical Treatises*], *Den tredje og fjærde grammatiske afhandling i Snorres Edda Tilligemed de Grammatiske Afhandlingers Prolog og To Andre Tillæg*, ed. B. M. Ólsen, Samfund til udgivelse af gammel nordisk litteratur, 12; Islands grammatiske litteratur i middelalderen, 2 (Copenhagen, 1884).

Secondary sources

Almqvist, Bo, *Norrön niddiktning: Traditionshistoriska studier i versmagi*, Nordiska texter och undersökningar, 21, 23 (2 vols., Uppsala and Stockholm, 1965–74). I: *Nid mot furstar*; II.1–2: *Nid mot missionärer: Senmedeltida nidtraditioner*.

Amory, Frederic, 'Second Thoughts on *Skáldskaparmál*', *Scandinavian Studies*, 63 (1990), 331–9.

'Things Greek and the *Riddarasögur*', *Speculum*, 59 (1984), 509–23.

Clover, Carol, 'Skaldic Sensibility', *Arkiv för nordisk filologi*, 93 (1978), 68–81.

Clunies Ross, Margaret (ed.), *Old Icelandic Literature and Society* (Cambridge, 2000).

Prolonged Echoes: Old Norse Myths in Medieval Northern Society, I: The Myths, The Viking Collection, 7 (Odense, 1994).

'The Skald Sagas as a Genre: Definitions and Typical Features', in R. Poole (ed.), *Skaldsagas: Text, Vocation and Desire in the Icelandic Sagas of Poets*, Reallexikon der germanischen Altertumskunde, Ergänzungsband 27 (Berlin and New York, 2001), pp. 25–49.

Skáldskaparmál: Snorri Sturluson's 'Ars Poetica' and Medieval Theories of Language, The Viking Collection, 4 (Odense, 1987).

Collings, Lucy G., 'The *Málskrúðsfræði* and the Latin Tradition in Iceland', M.A. diss., Cornell University, 1967.

Faulkes, Anthony, 'Edda', *Gripla*, 2 (1977), 32–9.

'The Sources of *Skáldskaparmál*: Snorri's Intellectual Background', in A. Wolf (ed.), *Snorri Sturluson: Kolloquium anläßlich der 750. Wiederkehr seines Todestages* (Tübingen, 1993), pp. 59–76.

Foote, Peter, 'Latin Rhetoric and Icelandic Poetry: Some Contacts', in *Aurvandilstá: Norse Studies*, The Viking Collection, 2 (Odense, 1984), pp. 249–70. [Originally published in *Saga och sed* (1982), 107–27]

Frank, Roberta, 'Skaldic Poetry', in C. J. Clover and J. Lindow (eds.), *Old Norse-Icelandic Literature: A Critical Guide*, Islandica, 45 (Ithaca NY and London, 1985), pp. 157–96.

'Snorri and the Mead of Poetry', in U. Dronke *et al.* (eds.), *Specvlvm Norrœnvm: Norse Studies in Memory of Gabriel Turville-Petre* (Odense, 1981), pp. 155–70.

Harris, Joseph, 'Eddic Poetry', in C. J. Clover and J. Lindow (eds.), *Old Norse-Icelandic Literature: A Critical Guide*, Islandica, 45 (Ithaca NY and London, 1985), pp. 68–156.

Heusler, Andreas, *Die altgermanische Dichtung* (1943; rpt. Darmstadt, 1957).

Holtsmark, Anne, *Studier i Snorres mytologi*, Skrifter utg. av det norske Videnskaps-Akademi i Oslo, II Hist.-filos. Klasse, n.s. 4 (Oslo, 1964).

Johansson, Karl Gunnar, *Studier i Codex Wormianus: Skrifttradition och avskriftsverksamhet vid ett isländskt skriptorium under 1300-talet*, Nordistica Gothoburgensia, 20; Acta Universitatis Gothoburgensis (Gothenburg, 1997).

Klingenberg, Heinz, 'Types of Eddic Mythological Poetry', in R. J. Glendinning and H. Bessason (eds.), *Edda: A Collection of Essays*, University of Manitoba Icelandic Studies, 4 (Winnipeg, 1983), pp. 134–64.

Kreutzer, Gerd, *Die Dichtungslehre der Skalden* (2nd edn, Meisenheim-am-Glan, 1977).

Krömmelbein, Thomas, 'Creative Compilers: Observations on the Manuscript Tradition of *Snorra Edda*', in Ú. Bragason (ed.), *Snorrastefna* (Reykjavik, 1992), pp. 113–29.

Lehmann, W. P., *The Development of Germanic Verse Form* (Austin TX, 1956).

Lönnroth, Lars, 'Den muntliga kulturens genrer: Diskursformer i Snorre Sturlassons Edda', in D. Hedman and J. Svedjedal (eds.), *Fictionens förvandlingar: En vänbok till Bo Bennich-Björkman* (Uppsala, 1996), pp. 182–93.

Marold, Edith, 'Die Poetik von *Háttatal* und *Skáldskaparmál*', in H. Fix (ed.), *Quantitätsproblematik und Metrik: Greifswalder Symposium zur germanischen Grammatik*, Amsterdamer Beiträge zur älteren Germanistik, 42 (Amsterdam, 1995), pp. 103–24.

Meulengracht Sørensen, Preben, *Fortælling og ære: Studier i islændingesagaerne* (Aarhus, 1993).

The Unmanly Man: Concepts of Sexual Defamation in Early Northern Society, tr. J. Turville-Petre, The Viking Collection, 1 (Odense, 1983).

Micillo, Valeria, 'Classical Tradition and Norse Tradition in the *Third Grammatical Treatise*', *Arkiv för nordisk filologi*, 108 (1993), 68–79.

'Die grammatische Tradition des insularen Mittelalters in Island: Spuren insularer Einflüsse im *Dritten Grammatischen Traktat*', in E. Poppe and H. Tristram (eds.), *Übersetzung, Adaptation und Akkulturation im insularen Mittelalter* (Münster, 1999), pp. 215–29.

Nordal, Guðrún, *Tools of Literacy: The Role of Skaldic Verse in Icelandic Textual Culture of the Twelfth and Thirteenth Centuries* (Toronto, 2001).

Quinn, Judy, 'The Naming of Eddic Mythological Poems in Medieval Manuscripts', in G. Barnes *et al.* (eds.), *Medieval Icelandic Fiction and Folktale, Parergon*, n.s. 8 (1990), 97–115.

Raschellà, Fabrizio, 'Die altisländische grammatische Literatur: Forschungsstand und Perspektiven zukünftiger Untersuchungen', *Göttingische Gelehrte Anzeigen*, 235 (1983), 271–315.

'Grammatical Treatises', in P. Pulsiano and K. Wolf (eds.), *Medieval Scandinavia: An Encyclopedia* (New York and London, 1993), pp. 235–7.

Steblin-Kamenskij, M. I., 'On the Etymology of the Word *skáld*', in J. Benediktsson *et al.* (eds.), *Afmælisrit Jóns Helgasonar 30. júní 1969* (Reykjavik, 1969), pp. 421–30.

Tómasson, Sverrir, *Formálar íslenskra sagnaritara á miðöldum*, Rit Stofnunar Árna Magnússonar á Íslandi, 33 (Reykjavik, 1988).

Tranter, Stephen, *Clavis Metrica: Háttatal, Háttalykill and the Irish Metrical Tracts*, Beiträge zur nordischen Philologie, 25 (Basel and Frankfurt, 1997).

'Medieval Icelandic *Artes Poeticae*', in Clunies Ross (ed.), *Old Icelandic Literature*, pp. 140–60.

Whaley, Diana, 'A Useful Past: Historical Writing in Medieval Iceland', in Clunies Ross (ed.), *Old Icelandic Literature*, pp. 161–202.

Latin commentary tradition and vernacular literature

Primary sources

'Aȝens hem þat seyn þat hooli wryt schulde not or may not be drawen into Engliche', ed. C. F. Bühler, *MÆ*, 7 (1938), 167–83; also ed. Deanesly, *Lollard Bible*, pp. 437–45.

Alegre, Francesc, *Los quinze libres de transformacions del poeta Ovidi* [translation and gloss by Francesc Alegre] (Barcelona, 1494).

Alfonso X, *General estoria*, ed. A. G. Solalinde, L. A. Kasten and V. R. B. Oelschlager (Madrid, 1930–).

Alfred, *King Alfred's Old English Version of Boethius, 'De consolatione philosophiae'*, ed. W. J. Sedgefield (Oxford, 1899).

Algezira, Alfonso de. See: Nicholas of Lyre

Alighieri, Dante, *Il Convivio*, ed. C. Vasoli and D. De Robertis, in Dante, *Opere minori*, I.2 (2 vols., Milan and Naples, 1979–88).

Vita Nova, ed. D. De Robertis (Milan and Naples, 1980).

De vulgari eloquentia, ed. and tr. S. Botterill (Cambridge, 1996).

[Alighieri, Pietro], *La exposiçion sobre . . . la Comedia de Dante . . . conpuesta de mosen Pedro su fijo* [anonymous translation]. Madrid, Biblioteca Nacional, MS 10207.

L'Art d'amours: Traduction et commentaire de l''Ars amatoria' d'Ovide, ed. B. Roy (Leiden, 1974).

[Benvenuto da Imola], *La glosa sobre Dante en latin tornada en romançe* [anonymous partial translation; *Inferno*, cantos 1–7]. Madrid, Biblioteca Nacional, MS 10208.

La glosa del sagrado poeta . . . Dante [*Purgatorio* only], tr. Martín González de Lucena. Madrid, Biblioteca Nacional, MS 10196.

Bernard of Cluny, *De contemptu mundi*, ed. H. C. Hoskier (London, 1929).

Bersuire, Pierre, *Reductorium morale* (Venice, 1583).

Text and Concordance of 'Morales de Ovidio': A Fifteenth-Century Castilian Translation of the 'Ovidius moralizatus' (Pierre Bercuire), Madrid, Biblioteca Nacional, MS 10144, ed. D. C. Carr, Madison WI, Hispanic Seminary of Medieval Studies, 1992.

Bible, *The Holy Bible. . . . Made from the Latin Vulgate by John Wycliffe and his Followers*, ed. J. Forshall and D. Madden (4 vols., Oxford, 1850).

Biblia de Osuna. Madrid, Biblioteca Nacional, MS 10232.

Boccaccio, Giovanni, *De casibus virorum illustrium*, ed. P. G. Ricci and V. Zaccaria in *Opere*, ed. V. Branca *et al.*, 9 (Milan, 1983).

Decameron, ed. V. Branca (Florence, 1965).

[*Genealogia deorum gentilium*], *La genealogia de los dioses segund Juan Bocacio de Cercaldo*, Books 1–13, tr. Martín de Avila. Madrid, Biblioteca Nacional, MSS 10062 and 10221, and Fundación Lázaro Galdiano, MS 657.

[Boethius, *De consolatione philosophiae*], ed. R. Schroth, *Eine altfranzösische Übersetzung der 'Consolatio philosophiae' des Boethius (Handschrift Troyes Nr. 898)* (Bern and Frankfurt, 1976).

Liber Boecij de [con]solatione philosophie in textu latina alemanica[que] lingua refertus ac translat[us] vna cu[m] apparatu & expositione beati Thome de aquino ordinis predicatorum (Nuremberg, 1473).

Libro de Boecio de Consolacion [anonymous interpolated version]. Madrid, Biblioteca Nacional, MS 17814, fols. 1r–59r, and Library of the late D. Antonio Rodríguez-Moñino, MS V-6-75, fols. 1r–45r.

[tr. Pero López de Ayala (?)], *Libro de la consolaçion natural de Boecio romano*. Madrid, Biblioteca Nacional, MS 10220.

Bokenham, Osbern, *Legendys of Hooly Wummen*, ed. M. S. Serjeantson, EETS OS 206 (Oxford, 1938).

Butler, William, 'Determinatio contra translationem anglicanam', ed. Deanesly, *Lollard Bible*, pp. 399–418 [see under Deanesly, Margaret, in the following section].

Caxton, William, *Aesop*, ed. R. T. Lenaghan (Cambridge MA, 1967).

Chaucer, Geoffrey, *Boece*, in *The Riverside Chaucer*, pp. 395–469.

Monk's Tale, in *The Riverside Chaucer*, pp. 240–52.

The Riverside Chaucer, gen. ed. L. D. Benson (Boston MA, 1987).

Treatise on the Astrolabe, in *The Riverside Chaucer*, pp. 661–83.

Christine de Pizan, *The Epistle of Othea, translated by Stephen Scrope*, ed. C. F. Bühler, EETS OS 264 (Oxford, 1970).

The Court of Sapience: Spätmittelenglisches allegorisch-didaktisches Visionsgedicht, ed. R. Spindler, Beiträge zur englischen Philologie, 6 (Leipzig, 1927). [The later edition, by R. Harvey (Toronto and London, 1984), does not include the Latin apparatus.]

Le Débat sur le Roman de la Rose, ed. E. Hicks (Paris, 1977).

Dionysius de Burgo, *Commentarii in Valerium Maximum* (Strassburg, *c.* 1470).

[*Disticha Catonis*], *Castigos exemplos de Caton* [anonymous verse translation] (Lisbon, 1521).

Douglas, Gavin, *Virgil's 'Aeneid' translated into Scottish Verse*, ed. D. F. C. Coldwell, Scottish Text Society, 3rd ser. 25, 27, 28, 30 (4 vols., Edinburgh, 1957–64).

Evrart de Conty, *Le Livre des Eschez amoureux moralisés*, ed. F. Guichard-Tesson and B. Roy, Bibliothèque du moyen français, 2 (Montreal and Paris, 1993).

Eschez amoureux, ed. C. Kraft, *Die Liebesgarten-Allegorie der 'Echecs amoureux': Kritische Ausgabe und Kommentar* (Frankfurt and Bern, 1977).

Li Fet des Romains, ed. L.-F. Flutre and K. Sneyders de Vogel (Geneva, 1977).

Francesco da Barberino, *I Documenti d'Amore*, ed. F. Egidi (4 vols., Rome, 1905–27).

García, Martín, *La traslation del muy excellente doctor Chaton llamado fecha por un egregio maestro Martin Garcia nombrado* (1467) (Saragossa, 1485?).

García de Santa María, Gonzalo, *El Caton en latin e en romance* (Saragossa, 1493).

González de Lucena, Martín. See: Benvenuto da Imola

Gower, John, *Works*, ed. G. C. Macaulay (4 vols., Oxford, 1899–1902).

Guillaume de Lorris. See: Jean de Meun.

Henryson, Robert, *Poems*, ed. D. Fox (Oxford, 1981).

Hermannus Alemannus, *De arte poetica cum Averrois expositione*, ed. L. Minio-Paluello, Corpus philosophorum medii ævi, Aristoteles latinus, 33 (2nd edn, Brussels, 1968).

Higden, Ralph, *Polychronicon, with the English Translations of John Trevisa and of an Unknown Writer of the Fifteenth Century*, ed. C. Babington and J. R. Lumby, Rolls Series, 41 (9 vols., London, 1865–6).

Hudson, Anne (ed.), *Selections from English Wycliffite Writings* (1978; rpt. Cambridge, 1997).

Hugutio of Pisa, *Magnae derivationes*. Oxford, Bodleian Library, MS Bodley 376.

Jacob van Maerlant, *Alexanders geesten*, ed. J. Franck (Groningen, 1882).

Jean de Meun, *Li Livres de confort*, ed. V. L. Dedeck-Héry, 'Boethius' *De consolatione* by Jean de Meun', *MS*, 14 (1952), 165–275.

Jean de Meun and Guillaume de Lorris, *Le Roman de la Rose*, ed. F. Lecoy (3 vols., Paris, 1965–70); tr. C. Dahlberg (1971; rpt. Hanover NH and London, 1983); also tr. F. Horgan (Oxford, 1994).

John Balbus of Genoa, *Catholicon* (1460; rpt. Westmead, Hants., 1971).

John of Garland, *Morale scolarium*, ed. L. J. Paetow, Memoirs of the University of California, 4.2 (Berkeley CA, 1927).

Parisiana poetria, ed. and tr. T. Lawler (New Haven CT and London, 1974).

Langland, William, *Piers Plowman, B-Text*, ed. A. V. C. Schmidt (London, 1995).

Latini, Brunetto, *Li Livres dou Tresor*, ed. F. J. Carmody (Berkeley CA, 1948).

[Lucan, *Pharsalia*], *Libro que fizo Lucano de las batallas de los emperadores*. Madrid, Biblioteca Nacional, MS 10805.

Lumière as lais, ed. G. Hasketh, ANTS (3 vols., London, 1996–9).

Macrobius, Ambrosius Theodosius, *Commentary on the Dream of Scipio*, tr. W. H. Stahl (New York, 1952).

Madrigal, Alfonso de (El Tostado), *Comento de Eusebio* (5 vols., Salamanca, 1506–7).

In Eusebium. Madrid, Biblioteca Nacional, MS 1796.

La interpretacion o traslacion del libro de las cronicas o tiempos de Eusebio Cesariense. Madrid, Biblioteca Nacional, MS 10811.

Martín de Avila. See: Boccaccio, *Genealogia*

Mechthild von Magdeburg, *Das fliessende Licht der Gottheit*, ed. H. Neumann and G. Vollman-Profe, Münchener Texte und Untersuchungen (Munich, 1990).

Mum and the Sothsegger, ed. H. Barr, in *The 'Piers Plowman' Tradition* (London, 1993), pp. 137–202.

Murphy, J. J. (ed.), *Three Medieval Rhetorical Arts* (Berkeley CA, 1971).

Nicholas of Lyre, *Postilla litteralis in totam Bibliam*, in *Biblia latina* (4 vols., Lyon, c. 1488).

La suma sobre et Viejo e Nuevo Testamento sacada e copilada por el muy exsçelente fray Nicolao de Lira; tr. Alfonso de Algezira. Madrid, Biblioteca Nacional, MSS 10282–10287.

Notker, *Notkers des Deutschen Werke*, ed. E. H. Sehrt and T. Starck, vol. 1, 1–3: Boethius, *De consolatione philosophiae*, Altdeutsche Textbibliothek, 32–4 (3 vols., Tübingen, 1933–4).

Oresme, Nicole, *Le Livre de éthiques d'Aristote*, ed. A. D. Menut (New York, 1940).

Le Livre de politiques d'Aristote, ed. A. D. Menut, Transactions of the American Philosophical Society, n.s. 60, pt. 6 (Philadelphia, 1970).

Ovide moralisé, ed. C. de Boer (5 vols., Amsterdam, 1915–38).

Palmer, Thomas, 'De translatione sacrae scripturae in linguam anglicanam', ed. Deanesly, *Lollard Bible*, pp. 418–37 [see under Deanesly, Margaret, in the following section].

La Querelle de la Rose: Letters and Documents, tr. J. L. Baird and J. R. Kane, North Carolina Studies in the Romance Languages and Literatures, 199 (Chapel Hill NC, 1978).

Reynaerts historie: Reynke de vos: Gegenüberstellung einer Auswahl aus den niederländischen Fassungen und des niederdeutschen Textes von 1498, ed. J. Goossens (Darmstadt, 1983).

Ruiz, Juan, *Libro de buen amor*, ed. G. B. Gybbon-Monypenny (Madrid, 1988).

Servius, *In Vergilii carmina commentarii*, ed. G. Thilo and H. Hagen (3 vols. in 4, Leipzig, 1881–1902).

Thomasin von Zerklaere, *Der welsche Gast*, ed. F. W. Von Kries (4 vols., Göppingen, 1984–5).

[Trevet, Nicholas], *Libro de Boeçio Severino . . . e es llamado este libro de consolaçion e fue declarado por . . . frey Nicolas Trebet* [anonymous translation]. Madrid, Biblioteca Nacional, MS 9160.

Trevisa, John, *On the Properties of Things*, ed. M. C. Seymour *et al.* (2 vols., Oxford, 1975). [Tr. of Bartholomew the Englishman (Bartholomaeus Anglicus), *De proprietatibus rerum*.]

Ullerston, Richard, 'Tractatus de translacione sacre scripture in vulgare'. Vienna, Österr. Nationalbibl., MS Pal. Lat. 4133, fols. 195r–207v.

Usk, Thomas, *The Testament of Love*, in *Chaucerian and Other Pieces*, ed. W. W. Skeat (Oxford, 1897), pp. 1–145; also ed. R. A. Shoaf (Kalamazoo MI, 1998).

Villena, Enrique de, *Los doze trabajos de Hercules*, ed. M. Morreale (Madrid, 1958).

Obras completas, ed. P. M. Cátedra (3 vols., Madrid, 1994–2000).

La primera versión castellana de 'La Eneida' de Virgilio: los libros I-III traducidos y comentados por Enrique de Villena, ed. R. Santiago Lacuesta (Madrid, 1979).

La traduccion de la 'Divina Commedia' atribuida a D. Enrique de Aragon: estudio y edicion del Infierno, ed. J. A. Pascual (Salamanca, 1974).

Vincent of Beauvais, *Speculum maius, Apologia totius operis*, ed. A.-D. von den Brincken, 'Geschichtsbetrachtung bei Vincenz von Beauvais', *Deutsches Archiv für Erforschung des Mittelalters*, 34 (1978), 409–99.

Walter of Châtillon, *Moralisch-satirische Gedichte*, ed. K. Strecker (Heidelberg, 1929).

Walton, John, *Boethius de consolatione philosophiae*, ed. M. Science, EETS OS 170 (London, 1927).

The Boke of comfort called in laten Boetius de Consolatione philosophiae, translated in to englesse tonge by J. Walton (Tavistock, 1525).

William of Conches, *Glosae super Boetium*, ed. L. Nauta, CCCM 158 (Turnhout, 1999).

Wireker, Nigel ('de Longchamps'), *Speculum stultorum*, ed. J. H. Mozley and R. R. Raymo (Berkeley CA, 1960).

Wyclif, John [works attributed to], *The English Works of Wyclif Hitherto Unprinted*, ed. F. D. Matthew, EETS OS 72 (2nd edn, London. 1902).

Wycliffite tracts on translation. Cambridge, University Library, MS Ii.vi.26, fols. 1r–58v.

Secondary sources

Allen, H. E., 'The *Manuel des pechiez* and the Scholastic Prologue', *RR*, 8 (1917), 434–62.

Alvar, Carlos, and Lucía Megías, José Manuel, *Diccionario filológico de literatura medieval española: textos y transmisión* (Madrid, 2002).

Anderson, David, *Before 'The Knight's Tale': Imitation of Classical Epic in Boccaccio's 'Teseida'* (Philadelphia PA, 1988).

Atkinson, J. Keith, 'A Fourteenth-Century Picard Translation-Commentary of the *Consolatio philosophiae*', in Minnis (ed.), *Medieval Boethius*, pp. 32–62.

Badel, P.-Y., *Le 'Roman de la Rose' au XIVe siècle: Étude de la réception de l'œuvre* (Geneva, 1980).

Berger, Samuel, 'Les Bibles castillanes', *Romania*, 28 (1899), 360–408, 508–67.

Bolton, D. K., 'Remigian Commentaries on the *Consolation of Philosophy* and their Sources', *Traditio*, 33 (1977), 381–94.

'The Study of the *Consolation of Philosophy* in Anglo-Saxon England', *AHDLMA*, 44 (1977), 33–78.

Brown-Grant, Rosalind, *Christine de Pizan and the Moral Defence of Women* (Cambridge, 1999).

Copeland, Rita, *Rhetoric, Hermeneutics, and Translation in the Middle Ages: Academic Traditions and Vernacular Texts* (Cambridge, 1991).

Crespo, Roberto, 'Il prologo alla traduzione della *Consolatio philosophiae* di Jean de Meun e il commento di Guglielmo d'Aragonia', in W. den Boer *et al.* (eds.), *Romanitas et christianitas: Studia I. H. Waszink oblata* (Amsterdam and London, 1973), pp. 55–70.

Cropp, Glynnis, '*Le Livre de Boece de consolacion*: From Translation to Glossed Text', in Minnis (ed.), *Medieval Boethius*, pp. 63–88.

'The Medieval French Tradition', in Hoenen and Nauta (eds.), *Boethius*, pp. 243–65.

'Le Prologue de Jean de Meun et *Le Livre de Boece de consolacion*', *Romania*, 103 (1982), 278–98.

Deanesly, Margaret, *The Lollard Bible and Other Medieval Bible Versions* (Cambridge, 1920).

Dembowski, Peter, 'Scientific Translation and Translators' Glossing in Four Medieval French Translators', in J. Beer (ed.), *Translation Theory and Practice in the Middle Ages* (Kalamazoo MI, 1997), pp. 113–34.

Donaghey, Brian, 'Nicholas Trevet's Use of King Alfred's Translation of Boethius', in Minnis (ed.), *Medieval Boethius*, pp. 1–31.

Donaghey, Brian, and Taavitsainen, Irma, 'Walton's Boethius: From Manuscript to Print', *English Studies*, 80 (1999), 398–407.

Dwyer, Richard A., *Boethian Fictions: Narratives in the Medieval French Versions of the 'Consolatio philosophiae'* (Cambridge MA, 1976).

Edwards, M. C., 'A Study of Six Characters in Chaucer's *Legend of Good Women* with Reference to Medieval Scholia on Ovid's *Heroides*', B. Litt. diss., Oxford University, 1970.

Engels, Joseph, *Études sur l'Ovide moralisé* (Groningen, 1945).

Fowler, Alastair, *Kinds of Literature: An Introduction to the Theory of Genres and Modes* (Oxford, 1982).

Ghisalberti, F., 'Giovanni del Virgilio espositore delle *Metamorfosi*', *Giornale dantesco*, 34 (1933), 1–110.

Gibson, M. T. (ed.), *Boethius: His Life, Thought and Influence* (Oxford, 1981).

Goldin, Daniela, 'Testo e immagine nei *Documenti d'Amore* di Francesco da Barberino', *Quaderni d'italianistica*, 1 (1980), 125–38.

Goris, Mariken, *Boethius in het Nederlands: Studie naar en tekstuitgave van de Gentse Boethius (1485), boek II* (Hilversum, 2000).

Goris, Mariken, and Wissink, Wilma, 'The Medieval Dutch Tradition of Boethius' *Consolatio philosophiae*', in J. F. M. Maarten and L. Nauta (eds.), *Boethius in the Middle Ages: Latin and Vernacular Traditions of the 'Consolatio Philosophiae'* (Leiden, 1977), pp. 121–65

Guichard-Tesson, F., 'Evrart de Conty, auteur de la *Glose des Echecs amoureux*', *Le Moyen français*, 8–9 (1981), 111–48.

'La *Glose des Echecs amoureux*: Un savoir à tendance laïque: comment l'interpréter?', *Fifteenth-Century Studies*, 10 (1984), 229–60.

'Le Métier de traducteur et de commentateur au XIVe siècle d'après Evrart de Conty', *Le Moyen français*, 24–5 (1990), 131–67.

Hanna, Ralph, 'The Difficulty of Ricardian Prose Translation: The Case of the Lollards', *MLQ*, 51 (1990), 319–40.

Henkel, Nikolaus, *Deutsche Übersetzungen lateinischer Schultexte: Ihre Verbreitung und Funktion im Mittelalter und in der frühen Neuzeit*, Münchener Texte und Untersuchungen, 90 (Munich, 1988).

Herrero Llorente, Victor José, 'Influencia de Lucano en la obra de Alfonso el Sabio: Una traducción anónima e inédita', *Revista de Archivos, Bibliotecas y Museos*, 67 (1959), 697–715.

Hoenen, Maarten J. F. M., and Nauta, Lodi (eds.), *Boethius in the Middle Ages: Latin and Vernacular Traditions of the 'Consolatio philosophiae'* (Leiden and New York, 1997).

Hollander, Robert, 'The Validity of Boccaccio's Self-Exegesis in his *Teseida*', *M&H*, n.s. 8 (1977), 163–83.

Hudson, Anne, 'The Debate on Bible Translation, Oxford, 1401', in Hudson, *Lollards and their Books* (London, 1985), pp. 67–84.

Hunt, Richard, 'The Lost Preface to the *Liber derivationum* of Osbern of Gloucester', in Hunt, *The History of Grammar in the Middle Ages: Collected Papers*, ed. G. L. Bursill-Hall, Amsterdam Studies in the Theory and History of Linguistic Science, 3rd ser. 5 (Amsterdam, 1980), pp. 151–66.

Hunt, Tony, 'Aristotle, Dialectic and Courtly Literature', *Viator*, 10 (1979), 95–129.

'Les Paraboles Maistre Alain', *Forum for Modern Language Studies*, 21 (1985), 362–75.

'Une Traduction partielle des *Parabolae* d'Alain de Lille', *Le Moyen Âge*, 87 (1981), 45–56.

Teaching and Learning Latin in Thirteenth-Century England (3 vols., Cambridge, 1991).

'Vernacular Glosses in Medieval Manuscripts', *Cultura neolatina*, 39 (1979), 9–37.

Johnson, Ian, '*Auctricitas*? Holy Women and their Middle English Texts', in R. Voaden (ed.), *Prophets Abroad: The Reception of Continental Holy Women in Late-Medieval England* (Cambridge, 1996), pp. 177–97.

'New Evidence for the Authorship of Walton's Boethius', *Notes and Queries*, n.s. 43 (1996), 19–21.

'Placing Walton's Boethius', in Hoenen and Nauta (eds.), *Boethius*, pp. 217–42.

'Tales of a True Translator: Anecdote, Autobiography and Medieval Literary Theory in Osbern Bokenham's *Legendys of Hooly Wummen*', in R. Ellis and R. Evans (eds.), *The Medieval Translator* 4 (Exeter, 1994), pp. 104–24.

'Vernacular Valorising: Functions and Fashionings of Literary Theory in Middle English Translation of Authority', in J. Beer (ed.), *Translation Theory and Practice in the Middle Ages* (Kalamazoo MI, 1997), pp. 239–54.

'Walton's Sapient Orpheus', in Minnis (ed.), *Medieval Boethius*, pp. 139–68.

Jones, Joan Morton, '*The Chess of Love* [Old French Text with Translation and Commentary]', Ph.D. diss., University of Nebraska, 1968.

Keightley, R. G., 'Alfonso de Madrigal and the *Chronici canones* of Eusebius', *Journal of Medieval and Renaissance Studies*, 7 (1977), 225–48.

'Boethius in Spain: A Classified Checklist of Early Translations', in Minnis (ed.), *Medieval Boethius*, pp. 169–87.

'Boethius, Villena and Juan de Mena', *Bulletin of Hispanic Studies*, 55 (1978), 189–202.

Kelly, H. A., *Chaucerian Tragedy* (Woodbridge, 1997).

Ideas and Forms of Tragedy from Aristotle to the Middle Ages (Cambridge, 1993).

'The Non-Tragedy of Arthur', in G. Kratzmann and J. Simpson (eds.), *Medieval English Religious and Ethical Literature: Essays in Honour of G. H. Russell* (Cambridge, 1986), pp. 92–114.

Tragedy and Comedy from Dante to Pseudo-Dante, University of California Publications in Modern Philology, 121 (Berkeley CA, 1989).

Kneepkens, C. H. J. M., and van Oostrom, F. P., 'Maerlants *Alexanders geesten* en de *Alexandreis*: een terreinverkenning', *De nieuwe taalgids*, 69 (1976), 483–500.

Machan, T. W., 'Glosses in the Manuscripts of Chaucer's *Boece*', in Minnis (ed.), *Medieval Boethius*, pp. 125–38.

Marti, B. M., 'Arnulfus and the *Faits des Romains*', *MLQ*, 2 (1941), 3–23.

Menéndez Pelayo, Marcelino, *Bibliografía hispano-latina clásica*, ed. E. Sánchez Reyes, Edición nacional de las obras completas de Menéndez Pelayo, 44–53 (10 vols., Santander, 1950–3).

Meuvaert, P., 'John Erghome and the *Vaticinium Roberti Bridlington*', *Speculum*, 41 (1966), 656–64.

Miller, Paul, 'John Gower, Satiric Poet', in Minnis (ed.), *Gower's 'Confessio amantis'*, pp. 79–105.

Minnis, Alastair J., '*Amor* and *Auctoritas* in the Self-Commentary of Dante and Francesco da Barberino', *Poetica* [Tokyo], 32 (1990), 25–42.

'Aspects of the Medieval French and English Traditions of Boethius' *De Consolatione Philosophiae*', in Gibson (ed.), *Boethius*, pp. 312–61.

'"Authorial Intention" and "Literal Sense" in the Exegetical Theories of Richard FitzRalph and John Wyclif', *Proceedings of the Royal Irish Academy*, 75, sect. C, 1 (Dublin, 1975).

'Chaucer's Commentator: Nicholas Trevet and the *Boece*', in Minnis (ed.), *Chaucer's 'Boece'*, pp. 83–166.

'"Glosynge is a glorious thing": Chaucer at Work on the *Boece*', in Minnis (ed.), *Medieval Boethius*, pp. 106–24.

'"Moral Gower" and Medieval Literary Theory', in Minnis (ed.), *Gower's 'Confessio amantis'*, pp. 50–78.

Minnis, Alastair J. (ed.), *Chaucer's 'Boece' and the Medieval Tradition of Boethius* (Woodbridge, 1993).

Gower's 'Confessio amantis': Responses and Reassessments (Cambridge, 1983).

The Medieval Boethius: Studies in the Vernacular Translations of 'De consolatione philosophiae' (Woodbridge, 1987).

Morreale, Margherita, 'La *Biblia moralizada* latino-castellana de la Biblioteca Nacional de Madrid (MS 10232)', *Spanische Forschungen der Görresgesellschaft*, 29 (1975), 437–56.

Ouy, Gilbert, 'Humanism and Nationalism in France at the Turn of the Fifteenth Century', in B. P. McGuire (ed.), *The Birth of Identities: Denmark and Europe in the Middle Ages* (Copenhagen, 1996), pp. 107–25.

Palmer, Nigel, 'The German Boethius Translation Printed in 1473 in Its Historical Context', in Hoenen and Nauta (eds.), *Boethius*, pp. 287–302.

'Latin and Vernacular in the Northern European Tradition of the *De consolatione philosophiae*', in Gibson (ed.), *Boethius*, pp. 362–409.

Piccus, Jules, 'El traductor español de *De genealogia deorum*', *Homenaje a Rodríguez-Moñino* (2 vols., Madrid, 1966), II, pp. 59–72.

Recio, Roxana (ed.), *La traducción en España ss. XIV-XVI* (León, 1995).

Rico, Francisco, *Alfonso el Sabio y la 'General estoria'* (2nd edn, Barcelona, 1984).

Russell, P. E., *Traducciones y traductores en la Península Ibérica, 1400–1550* (Bellaterra, 1985).

Sherman, C. R., *Imaging Aristotle: Verbal and Visual Representation in Fourteenth-Century France* (Berkeley CA, 1995).

Stackmann, Karl, 'Heinrich von Mügeln', in *Die deutsche Literatur des Mittelalters: Verfasserlexikon*, 2nd edn ed. K. Ruh *et al.*, vol. 3 (Berlin and New York 1981), cols. 815–27.

Thomas, Antoine, *Francesco da Barberino: Littérature provençale en Italie au Moyen Âge* (Paris, 1883).

Watson, Nicholas, 'Censorship and Cultural Change in Late-Medieval England: Vernacular Theology, the Oxford Translation Debate and Arundel's Constitutions of 1409', *Speculum*, 70 (1996), 822–64.

Wheatley, Edward, *Mastering Aesop: Medieval Education, Chaucer and his Followers* (Gainesville FA, 2000).

Willard, C. C., 'Raoul de Presles's Translation of Saint Augustine's *De civitate Dei*', in J. Beer (ed.), *Medieval Translators and their Craft* (Kalamazoo MI, 1989), pp. 329–46.

Wittig, Joseph, 'King Alfred's Boethius and its Latin Sources: A Reconsideration', *Anglo-Saxon England*, 11 (1983), 157–98.

Vernacular literary consciousness *c.* 1100–*c.* 1500: French, German and English evidence

Primary sources

Adenet le Roi, *Œuvres*, ed. A. Henry (5 vols. in 6, Bruges, 1951–71).

Angier, 'La Vie de Saint Grégoire le Grand [de Jean le Diacre] traduite du latin par Frère Angier, religieux de Sainte-Frideswide', ed. P. Meyer, *Romania*, 12 (1883), 145–208.

Aucassin et Nicolette, ed. F. W. Bourdillon (Manchester and London, 1930).

Benedeit, *Le Voyage de Saint Brandan*, ed. B. Merrilees (Paris, 1984).

Benoît de Sainte-Maure, *Le Roman de Troie*, ed. L. Constans, SATF (6 vols., Paris, 1904–12).

Béroul, *Le Roman de Tristan*, ed. E. Muret, 4th edn rev. L. M. Defourques (Paris, 1979).

Bertran de Bar-sur-Aube, *Aymeri de Narbonne*, ed. L. Demaison, SATF (Paris, 1887).

Girart de Vienne, ed. W. van Emden, SATF (Paris, 1977).

Bevis of Southampton, ed. A. Stimming (5 vols., Dresden, 1911–20).

Boccaccio, Giovanni, *Decameron*, tr. G. H. McWilliam (2nd edn, London, 1995).

Bodel, Jean, *La Chanson des Saisnes*, ed. A. Brasseur (2 vols., Geneva, 1989).

The Book of Courtesy, ed. F. J. Furnivall, EETS ES 3 (London, 1868).

The Book of Margery Kempe, ed. S. B. Meech, EETS OS 212 (London, 1940).

The Book of Privy Counselling, in *The Cloud of Unknowing, etc.*, ed. Hodgson, pp. 75–99.

Caxton, William, *The History of Reynard the Fox*, ed. N. F. Blake, EETS OS 263 (London, 1970).

Preface to *Le Morte Darthur*, in Malory, *Works*, ed. E. Vinaver (2nd edn, Oxford, 1977).

La Chanson d'Antioche, ed. S. Duparc-Quioc (Paris, 1976).

La Chanson de Roland, ed. J. Dufournet (Paris, 1993).

Chaucer, Geoffrey, *The Canterbury Tales*, in *The Riverside Chaucer*, pp. 1–328.

House of Fame, in *The Riverside Chaucer*, pp. 347–73.

Legend of Good Women, in *The Riverside Chaucer*, pp. 587–630.

The Parliament of Fowls, in *The Riverside Chaucer*, pp. 383–94.

The Riverside Chaucer, gen. ed. L. D. Benson (Boston MA, 1987).

Troilus and Criseyde, in *The Riverside Chaucer*, pp. 471–585.

La Chevalerie de Judas Machabée, ed. J. R. Smeets (Assen, 1955).

La chevalerie Ogier de Danemarche, ed. J. Barrois, Romans des douze pairs de France, 8–9 (2 vols., Paris, 1842).

'*Le Chevalier au cygne*' and '*La Fin d'Elias*', ed. J. A. Nelson (University AL, 1985).

Chrétien de Troyes, *Romans*, ed. M. Roques, A. Micha and F. Lecoy (6 vols., Paris, 1952–75).

Christine de Pizan, *Cent ballades d'amant et de dame*, ed. J. Cerquiglini (Paris, 1982).

Le Chemin de longue étude, ed. Andrea Tarnowski (Paris, 2000).

'*Epistre au Dieu d'Amours*' *and '*Dit de la Rose*'*; *Thomas Hoccleve's '*The Letter of Cupid*', ed. T. S. Fenster and M. C. Erler (Leiden and New York, 1990).

Le Livre de la cité des dames, ed. M. C. Curnow, Ph.D diss., Vanderbilt University, 1975.

Le Livre de l'Advision Cristine, ed. C. Reno and L. Dulac (Paris, 2001).

Le Livre de trois vertus, ed. C. C. Willard with E. Hicks (Paris, 1989).

Cleanness, in *The Poems of the 'Pearl' Manuscript*, ed. M. Andrew and R. Waldron (London, 1978).

'*The Cloud of Unknowing*' *and Related Treatises on Contemplative Prayer*, ed. P. Hodgson, Analecta Cartusiana, 3 (Salzburg, 1982).

Denis Piramus, *La Vie seint Edmund le Rei*, ed. H. Kjellman (Gothenburg, 1935).

Deschamps, Eustache, *L'Art de dictier*, ed. and tr. D. M. Sinnreich-Levi (East Lansing MI, 1994).

Œuvres complètes, ed. Le Marquis de Queux de Saint-Hilaire, SATF (11 vols., Paris, 1878–1903).

Deschaux, Robert (ed.), *Les Œuvres de Pierre Chastellain et de Vaillant: Poètes du XVe siècle* (Geneva, 1982).

La destructioun de Rome, ed. L. Formisano, ANTS Plain Texts (London, 1990).

Dictys Cretensis, *Ephemeridos belli Troiani libri*, ed. W. Eisenhut (Leipzig, 1973).

Durmart le Gallois, ed. J. Gildea (2 vols., Villanova PA, 1965–6).

'*Ecbasis cuiusdam captivi per tropologiam*': *An Eleventh-Century Latin Beast Epic*, ed. and tr. E. H. Zeydel (Chapel Hill NC, 1964).

Eilhart von Oberge, *Tristrant*, ed. D. Buschinger (Göppingen, 1976).

Eructavit: An Old French Metrical Paraphrase of Psalm XLIV, ed. T. Atkinson Jenkins (Dresden, 1909).

Évangile de L'Enfance, ed. M. B. McCann (Toronto, 1984).

La Fin d'Elias. See: *Le Chevalier au cygne*

Froissart, Jean, *Le Joli Buisson de Jonece*, ed. A. Fourrier (Geneva, 1975).

Méliador, ed. A. Longnon (3 vols., Paris, 1895–9).

Œuvres complètes, ed. Le Marquis de Queux de Saint Hilaire and G. Raynaud, SATF (11 vols., Paris, 1878–1903).

Gaimar, Geoffroy, *L'Estoire des Engleis*, ed. A. Bell, ANTS (Oxford, 1960).

Gautier de Coinci, *Les Miracles de Nostre Dame*, ed. V. F. Koenig (4 vols., Geneva, 1955–70).

Gerbert de Montreuil, *Le Roman de la Violette ou de Gerart de Nevers*, ed. D. L. Buffum, SATF (Paris, 1928).

Gervaise, *Bestiaire*, ed. P. Meyer, *Romania*, 1 (1872), 410–43.

Gottfried von Strassburg, *Tristan und Isold*, ed. F. Ranke (4th edn, Dublin and Zurich, 1959).

Gower, John, *Confessio amantis*, in *The English Works of John Gower*, ed. G. C. Macaulay, EETS ES 81, 82 (2 vols., Oxford, 1900–1).

Guido delle Colonne, *Historia destructionis Troiae*, ed. N. E. Griffin (Cambridge MA, 1936); tr. M. E. Meek (Bloomington IN and London, 1974).

Hartmann von Aue, *Der arme Heinrich*, ed. H. Paul (1882; rpt. Tübingen, 2001).

Gregorius, ed. H. Paul (1873; rpt. Tübingen, 1992).

Heinrich von Freiberg, *Dichtungen*, ed. A. Bernt (Hildesheim and New York, 1978).

Heinrich von Morungen: included in *Des Minnesangs Frühling* [MF]; see p. 781 below.

Heinrich von Mügeln, *Der meide kranz*, ed. K. Stackmann with M. Stolz, *Die kleineren Dichtungen Heinrichs von Mügeln*, Deutsche Texte des Mittelalters, 84 (2nd edn, Berlin, 2003), pp. 47–203.

Henryson, Robert, *Fables*, in *Poems*, ed. D. Fox (Oxford, 1981), pp. 3–110.

Herbort von Fritzlar, *Liet von Troye*, ed. G. K. Frommann (Quedlinburg and Leipzig, 1837).

Hérenc, Baudet, *Doctrinal de la seconde retorique*, ed. Langlois, *Recueil*, III.

Histoire de Philippe-Auguste, Prologue, ed. P. Meyer, *Romania*, 6 (1877), 417–18.

Hoccleve, Thomas, *Dialogue with a Friend*, in *Hoccleve's Works, 1: The Minor Poems*, ed. F. J. Furnivall, EETS ES 61 (London, 1892), pp. 110–39.

Regement of Princes, ed. F. J. Furnivall, EETS ES 72 (London, 1897).

Hue de Rotelande, *Ipomedon*, ed. A. J. Holden (Paris, 1979).

Hunbaut, ed. J. Stürzinger (Dresden, 1914).

Instructif de la seconde rhétorique, in *Le Jardin de plaisance*, ed. Droz and Piaget, II, pp. 44–50.

Isidore of Seville, *Etymologiae sive origines*, ed. W. M. Lindsay (2 vols., Oxford, 1911).

Isopet de Lyon. See: *Isopets*

Isopets, Recueil général des, ed. J. Bastin and P. Ruelle, SATF (4 vols., 1929–84).

James I, King of Scotland, *The Kingis Quair*, ed. J. Norton-Smith (Leiden, 1981).

Le Jardin de plaisance et fleur de rhétorique, ed. E. Droz and A. Piaget (2 vols., Paris, 1910–25).

Jean de Meun and Guillaume de Lorris, *Le Roman de la Rose*, ed. F. Lecoy (3 vols., Paris, 1965–70); tr. C. Dahlberg (1971; rpt. Hanover NH and London, 1983); also tr. F. Horgan (Oxford, 1994).

Johannes von Tepl, *Der Ackermann: Mittelhochdeutsch/Neuhochdeutsch*, Reclams Universal-Bibliothek, 18075 (2nd edn, Stuttgart, 2002).

Julian of Norwich, *A Book of Showings to the Anchoress Julian of Norwich*, ed. E. Colledge and J. Walsh (2 vols., Toronto, 1978).

Konrad von Würzburg, *Partonopier und Meliur, Turnei von Nantheiz, Saint Nicolaus, Lieder und Sprüche*, ed. K. Bartsch (Vienna, 1871).

Der trojanische Krieg, ed. A. von Keller (Stuttgart, 1858).

Lamprecht der Pfaffe, *Alexanderlied*, ed. I. Ruttmann (Darmstadt, 1974).

Langland, William, *The Vision of Piers Plowman: A Complete Edition of the B-Text*, ed. A. V. C. Schmidt (2nd edn, London, 1987).

Langlois, E. (ed.), *Recueil d'arts de seconde rhétorique* (6 vols., Paris, 1902).

Latini, Brunetto, *Li Livres dou tresor*, ed. F. J. Carmody (Berkeley CA, 1948).

Legrand, Jacques, *Archiloge Sophie: Livre de bonnes meurs*, ed. E. Beltran (Geneva and Paris, 1986).

Lucidarius, 1: Kritischer Text, ed. D. Gottschall and G. Steer (Tübingen, 1994).

Lydgate, John, *The Fall of Princes*, ed. H. Bergen, EETS ES 121, 122, 123, 124 (4 vols., London, 1924–7).

The Pilgrimage of the Life of Man, ed. F. J. Furnivall, EETS ES 77, 83, 92 (3 vols., London, 1899–1904).

Siege of Thebes, ed. A. Erdmann, EETS ES 108, 125 (2 vols., London, 1911–30).

Troy Book, ed. H. Bergen, EETS ES 97, 103 (2 vols., London, 1906–8).

Machaut, Guillaume de, *La Fonteinne amoureuse*, ed. J. Cerquiglini-Toulet (Paris, 1993); also ed. and tr. R. Barton Palmer (New York and London, 1993).

Le Jugement du roy de Behaigne and *Remede de fortune*, ed. J. I. Wimsatt and W. W. Kibler (Athens GA, 1988).

Le Jugement dou roy de Navarre, ed. and tr. R. Barton Palmer (New York and London, 1988).

Le Livre dou voir dit, ed. P. Imbs and J. Cerguiglini-Toulet (Paris, 1999).

Œuvres, ed. E. Hoepffner (3 vols., Paris, 1908–21).

Mannyng, Robert (of Brunne), *Handlyng Synne*, ed. I. Sullens (New York, 1983).

The Story of England, pt. 1, ed. F. J. Furnivall (London, 1887).

Mauritius von Craûn, ed. H. Reinitzer, Altdeutsche Textbibliothek, 113 (Tübingen, 2000).

Des Minnesangs Frühling, I: Texte, 38th rev. edn ed. H. Moser and H. Tervooren (Stuttgart, 1988). [For MF references.]

Molinet, Jean, *Art de rhétorique*, ed. Langlois, *Recueil*, V.

La Mort Aymeri de Narbonne, ed. J. Couraye du Parc, SATF (Paris, 1884).

Mum and the Sothsegger, ed. M. Day and R. Steel, EETS OS 199 (London, 1936).

Neidhart, *Lieder*, ed. E. Wiessner *et al.*, Altdeutsche Textbibliothek, 47 (5th edn, Tübingen, 1999). [For WL (= Winterlieder) references.]

Das Nibelungenlied, ed. U. Schulze (Stuttgart, 1997).

The Owl and the Nightingale, ed. E. G. Stanley (Manchester, 1972).

Partonope of Blois, in *The Middle English Versions of Partonope of Blois*, ed. A. T. Bödtker, EETS ES 109 (London, 1912).

Partonopeu de Blois, ed. J. Gildea (3 parts in 2 vols., Villanova PA, 1967–70).

Passion poem (from Oxford, Jesus College, MS 29), ed. R. Morris in *An Old English Miscellany*, EETS OS 49 (London, 1872), pp. 37–57.

Pecock, Reginald, *The Reule of Crysten Religioun*, ed. W. C. Greet, EETS OS 171 (London, 1927).

Philippe de Rémi, sire de Beaumanoir, *Œuvres poétiques*, ed. H. Suchier, SATF (2 vols., Paris, 1884–5).

Pierce the Ploughman's Crede, ed. H. Barr in *The 'Piers Plowman' Tradition* (London, 1993), pp. 61–97.

Pierre de Beauvais, *Le Bestiaire*, ed. G. R. Mermier (Paris, 1977).

Pierre de la Cépède, *Paris et Vienne*, ed. R. Kaltenbacher (Erlangen, 1904).

Le Poème moral: traité de vie chrétienne écrit dans la région wallone vers l'an 1200, ed. A. Bayot (Brussels, 1929).

La Prise d'Orange, ed. C. Régnier (Paris, 1970).

Puttenham, George, *Arte of English Poesie*, in *Elizabethan Critical Essays*, ed. G. Gregory Smith (2 vols., 1904; rpt. Oxford, 1950), II, pp. 1–193.

Les Quinze Signes du jugement dernier, ed. E. Kraemer (Helsinki, 1966).

Raoul de Houdenc, *Meraugis von Portlesguez*, ed. M. Friedwagner (Halle, 1897).

Règles de la seconde rhétorique, ed. Langlois, *Recueil*, II.

Reinbot von Durne, *Der heilige Georg*, ed. C. von Kraus (Heidelberg, 1907).

Renart, Jean, *L'Escoufle*, ed. F. Sweetser (Geneva, 1974).

Roman de la Rose ou de Guillaume de Dôle, ed. F. Lecoy (Paris, 1962).

René d'Anjou, *Le Livre du cœur d'amour épris*, ed. F. Bouchet (Paris, 2003).

Reynke de Vos: nach der Lübecker Ausgabe von 1498, ed. H. J. Gernentz (Neumünster, 1987).

Richars li Biaus, ed. A. J. Holden (Paris, 1983).

Robert de Blois, *Sämmtliche Werke*, ed. J. Ulrich (3 vols., Berlin, 1889–95).

Le Roman d'Alexandre, II: Version of Alexandre de Paris, ed. E. C. Armstrong et al. (Princeton NJ, 1937).

Le Roman de Renart, ed. E. Martin (4 vols., Strassburg, 1882–7).

Le Roman de Thèbes, ed. L. Constans (2 vols., Paris, 1890).

The Romance of Yder, ed. and tr. A. Adams (Cambridge, 1983).

Li Romans de Durmart le Galois, ed. E. Stengel (1873; rpt. Amsterdam, 1969).

Rudolf von Ems, *Barlaam und Josaphat*, ed. F. Pfeiffer (Leipzig, 1843).

Ruodlieb. See: *Waltharius*

Sampson, Rodney (ed.), *Early Romance Texts: An Anthology* (Cambridge, 1980).

Sidney, Sir Philip, *An Apology for Poetry*, ed. G. Shepherd (Manchester, 1973).

Skelton, John, *The Garlande of Laurell*, in *The Complete English Poems*, ed. J. Scattergood (Harmondsworth, 1983), pp. 312–57.

A Stanzaic Life of Christ, ed. F. A. Foster, EETS OS 166 (London, 1926).

Thomas, *Roman de Tristan*, ed. B. H. Wind, Textes littéraires français, 92 (Geneva, 1960).

Thomasin von Zerklaere, *Der welsche Gast*, ed. F. W. von Kries (4 vols., Göppingen, 1984–5).

Traité de l'art de rhétorique, ed. Langlois, *Recueil*, IV.

Traité de rhétorique, ed. Langlois, *Recueil*, VI.

Trevisa, John, *Dialogus inter dominum et clericum*, ed. R. Waldron, in E. D. Kennedy, R. Waldron and J. S. Wittig (eds.), *Medieval English Studies Presented to George Kane* (Woodbridge, 1988), pp. 285–99.

Polychronicon, with the English Translations of John Trevisa and of an Unknown Writer of the Fifteenth Century, ed. C. Babington and J. R. Lumby, Rolls Series, 41 (9 vols., London, 1865–6).

Turpin, Pseudo-, *The Old French Johannes Translation of the 'Pseudo-Turpin Chronicle'*, ed. R. N. Walpole (Berkeley CA, 1976).

Ulrich von Eschenbach [Etzenbach], *Alexander*, ed. W. Toischer (Stuttgart, 1888).

Ulrich von Lichtenstein, *Werke*, ed. K. Lachmann (Berlin, 1841).

Usk, Thomas, *The Testament of Love*, in *Chaucerian and Other Pieces*, ed. W. W. Skeat (Oxford, 1897), pp. 1–145; also ed. R. A. Shoaf (Kalamazoo MI, 1998).

La Vie de Saint Alexis, ed. C. Storey (Oxford, 1946).

'La Vie de Saint Grégoire le Grand [de Jean le Diacre] traduite du latin par Frère Angier, religieux de Sainte-Frideswide', ed. P. Meyer, *Romania*, 12 (1883), 145–208.

Vie des pères, extract ed. P. Meyer, *Histoire littéraire de la France* (1906), 293.

Wace, *Le Roman de Rou*, ed. A. J. Holden (3 vols., Paris, 1970–3).

'*Waltharius*' and '*Ruodlieb*', ed. and tr. D. M. Kratz (New York, 1984).

Walther von der Vogelweide, *Leich, Lieder, Sangsprüche*, ed. K. Lachmann, rev. C. Cormeau with T. Bein and H. Brunner (14th edn, Berlin and New York, 1998).

Walton, John, *Boethius de consolatione philosophiae*, ed. M. Science, EETS OS 170 (London, 1927).

The Wars of Alexander, ed. W. W. Skeat, EETS ES 47 (London, 1886).

Winner and Waster, ed. T. Turville-Petre, in B. Ford (ed.), *Medieval Literature, I: Chaucer and the Alliterative Tradition* (Harmondsworth, Middlesex, 1982), pp. 398–415.

Wolfram von Eschenbach, *Parzival: Studienausgabe*, based on the 6th edn of K. Lachmann, tr. P. Knecht, intro. B. Shirok (Berlin and New York, 1998).

Secondary sources

Brewer, Derek (ed.), *Chaucer: The Critical Heritage* (2 vols., London, 1978).

Brownlee, Kevin, 'Guillaume de Machaut's *Remede de Fortune*: The Lyric Anthology as Narrative Progression', in D. Fenoaltea and D. L. Rubin (eds.), *The Ladder of High Designs: Structure and Interpretation of the French Lyric Sequence* (Charlottesville VA, 1991), pp. 1–25.

Poetic Individuality in Guillaume de Machaut (Madison WI, 1984).

Burrow, J. A. (ed.), *Geoffrey Chaucer: A Critical Anthology* (1969; rpt. Harmondsworth, 1982).

'The Poet as Petitioner', *SAC*, 3 (1981), 61–75.

Butterfield, Ardis, *Poetry and Music in Medieval France from Jean Renart to Guillaume de Machaut* (Cambridge, 2002).

Cerquiglini, Jacqueline, '*Un engin si soutil*': Guillaume de Machaut et l'écriture au XIVe siècle (Paris, 1985).

Chaytor, H. J., *From Script to Print* (Cambridge, 1945).

Clanchy, M. T., *From Memory to Written Record: England 1066–1307* (2nd edn, Oxford, 1993).

Dragonetti, Roger, '"La Poesie . . . ceste musique naturelle": Essai d'exégèse d'un passage de *l'Art de dictier* d'Eustache Deschamps', in G. de Poerck *et al.* (eds.), *Mélanges . . . Robert Guiette* (Antwerp, 1961), pp. 49–64.

Earp, Lawrence, *Guillaume de Machaut: A Guide to Research* (New York, 1995).

'Lyrics for Reading and Lyrics for Singing in Late Medieval France: The Development of the Dance Lyric from Adam de la Halle to Guillaume de Machaut', in R. A. Baltzer, T. Cable and J. I. Wimsatt (eds.), *The Union of Words and Music in Medieval Poetry* (Austin TX, 1991), pp. 101–31.

Green, D. H., 'Oral Poetry and Written Composition', in D. H. Green and L. P. Johnson, *Approaches to Wolfram von Eschenbach: Five Essays* (Bern, 1978), pp. 163–272.

Green, Richard F., *Poets and Princepleasers: Literature and the English Court in the Late Middle Ages* (Toronto, 1980).

Grosse, Max, *Das Buch im Roman: Studien zu Buchverweis und Autoritätszitat in altfranzösischen Texten* (Munich, 1994).

Gruber, Jörn, *Die Dialektik des Trobar: Untersuchungen zur Struktur und Entwicklung des occitanischen und französischen Minnesangs des 12. Jahrhunderts* (Tübingen, 1983).

Howlett, D. R., *The English Origins of Old French Literature* (Blackrock, Co. Dublin, 1996).

Hunt, Tony, 'The Tragedy of Roland: An Aristotelian View', *MLR*, 74 (1979), 791–805.

Kelly, Douglas, *The Arts of Poetry and Prose* (Turnhout, 1991).

'*En uni dire* (*Tristan* Douce 839) and the Composition of Thomas's *Tristan*', *MP*, 67 (1969–70), 9–17.

Medieval Imagination: Rhetoric and the Poetry of Courtly Love (Madison WI, 1978).

Kindermann, U., *Satyra: Die Theorie der Satire in Mittellateinischen: Vorstudie*, Erlanger Beiträge zur Sprach- und Kunst-wissenschaft, 58 (Nuremberg, 1978).

Laing, Margaret, *Catalogue of Sources for a Linguistic Atlas of Early Medieval English* (Cambridge, 1993).

Lusignan, Serge, *Parler vulgairement: Les intellectuels et la langue française aux XIIIe et XIVe siècles* (Paris and Montreal, 1987).

Méchoulan, Éric, 'Les Arts de rhétorique du XVe siècle: La théorie, masque de la *theoria?*', in M.-L. Ollier (ed.), *Masques et déguisements dans la littérature médiévale* (Montreal and Paris, 1988), pp. 213–22.

Mühlethaler, Jean-Claude, 'Un Poète face à sa postérité: Lecture des deux ballades de Deschamps pour la mort de Machaut', *Studi francesi*, 33 (1989), 387–410.

Mühlethaler, Jean-Claude, and Cerquiglini-Toulet, Jacqueline 'Poétique en transition: *L'Instruction de la seconde réthorique*, balises pour un chantier', *Études de lettres*, 4 (2002), 9–22.

Meyer, P., 'Les Manuscrits français de Cambridge', *Romania*, 15 (1886), 236–357.

Middleton, Anne, 'The Idea of Public Poetry in the Reign of Richard II', *Speculum*, 53 (1978), 94–114.

Olson, Glending, *Literature as Recreation in the Later Middle Ages* (Ithaca NY and London, 1982).

Page, Christopher, 'Machaut's Pupil Deschamps on the Performance of Music: Voices or Instruments in the Fourteenth-Century *Chanson*', *Early Music*, 5 (1977), 484–91.

Paris, Gaston, *Les Plus Anciens Monuments de la langue française (IXe, Xe siècle)*, SATF (Paris, 1875).

Patterson, Warner F., *Three Centuries of French Poetic Theory: A Critical History of the Chief Arts of Poetry in France (1328–1630)* (2 vols., Ann Arbor MI, 1935).

Poirion, Daniel, 'Jacques Legrand: une poétique de la fiction', *Littérales*, 4 (1988), 227–49.

Schnell, R., 'Prosaauflösung und Geschichtsschreibung im deutschen Spätmittelalter', in L. Grenzmann and K. Stackmann (eds.), *Literatur und Laienbildung im Spätmittelalter und in der Reformationzeit, Symposion Wolfenbüttel 1981* (Stuttgart and Tübingen, 1984), pp. 214–48.

Schwietering, J., 'Die Demutsformel mittelhochdeutscher Dichter', rpt. in Schwietering, *Philologische Schriften* (Munich, 1969), pp. 140–215.

Simpson, James, 'Dante's "Astripetam Aquilam" and the Theme of Poetic Discretion in the *House of Fame*', *Essays and Studies* (1986), 1–18.

Spearing, A. C., *Medieval to Renaissance in English Poetry* (Cambridge, 1985).

Stengel, Edmund, *Die ältesten französischen Sprachdenkmäler: Genauer Abdruck und Bibliographie*, Ausgaben und Abhandlungen aus dem Gebiete der romanischen Philologie, 11 (Marburg, 1884).

Stock, Brian, *The Implications of Literacy* (Princeton NJ, 1983).

Thiry, Claude, 'Rhétorique et genres littéraires au XVe siècle', in M. Wilmet (ed.), *Sémantique lexicale et sémantique grammaticale en moyen français* (Brussels, 1978), pp. 23–50.

Tuve, Rosemond, *Allegorical Imagery: Some Medieval Books and their Posterity* (Princeton NJ, 1966).

Wachinger, Burghart, *Erzählen für die Gesundheit: Diätetik und Literatur im Mittelalter: vorgetragen am 25 November 2000* (Heidelberg, 2001).

Zink, Michel, *La Subjectivité littéraire autour du siècle de saint Louis* (Paris, 1985).

Zumthor, Paul, *La Lettre et la voix: de la 'littérature' médiévale* (Paris, 1987).

Toward a Medieval Poetics, tr. P. Bennett (Minneapolis MN, 1992).

Occitan grammars and the art of troubadour poetry

Primary sources

Arnaut Daniel, *Canzoni*, ed. G. Toja (Florence, 1960).

Berenguer de Noya, *Mirall de trobar*, ed. P. Palumbo (Palermo, 1955).

Bernart de Ventadorn, *Lieder mit Einleitung und Glossar*, ed. C. Appel (Halle, 1915).

Bernart Marti, *Edizione critica*, ed. F. Beggiato (Modena, 1984).

Biographies des troubadours, ed. J. Boutière and A. H. Schutz (2nd edn, Paris, 1964).

Catalan treatise on troubadour genres (Barcelona, Archiva de la Corona de Aragón, Ripoll MS 129), in Raimon Vidal, *Razos*, ed. Marshall, pp. 101–3.

Cercamon, *Edizione critica*, ed. V. Tortoreto (Modena, 1981).

Cerveri de Girona, *Lirica*, ed. J. Coromines (2 vols., Barcelona, 1988).

Chrétien de Troyes, *Chansons courtoises*, ed. M.-C. Zai (Bern, 1974).

Doctrina de compondre dictats, in Raimon Vidal, *Razos*, ed. Marshall, pp. 93–8.

Giraut de Borneil, *Cansos and Sirventes*, ed. R. V. Sharman (Cambridge, 1988).

Guilhem IX, *Guglielmo d'Aquitania: poésie*, ed. N. Pasero (Modena, 1973).

Guilhem Ademar, *Poésies*, ed. K. Almqvist (Uppsala, 1961).

Jaufre Rudel, *Canzoniere*, ed. G. Chiarini (Rome, 1985).

Jaume March, *Diccionari de Rims*, ed. A. Griera (Barcelona, 1921).

Joan de Castellnou, *Obres en Prosa*, ed. J. M. Casas Homs (2 vols., Barcelona, 1969). I: *Compendi*. II: *Glosari, with Raimon de Cornet, Doctrinal*.

Jofre de Foixà, *Regles de trobar*, in Raimon Vidal, *Razos*, ed. Marshall, pp. 55–91.

John of Garland, *Parisiana poetria*, ed. and tr. T. Lawler (New Haven CT and London, 1974).

Leys d'Amors: Monumens de la Littérature Romane, vols. I-III, ed. A. F. Gatien-Arnoult (Toulouse, 1841–3); *Las Leys d'Amors*, ed. J. Anglade (4 vols., Toulouse and Paris, 1919–20); *Las Flors del Gay Saber*, ed. J. Anglade (Barcelona, 1926).

Luis de Averçó, *Torcimany*, ed. J. M. Casas Homs (2 vols., Barcelona, 1956).

Marcabru, *A Critical Edition*, ed. S. Gaunt, R. Harvey and L. Paterson (Cambridge, 2000).

Monk of Montaudon, *Les Poésies du Moine de Montaudon*, ed. M. J. Routledge (Montpellier, 1977).

Peire d'Alvernhe, *Poesie*, ed. A. Fratta (Rome, 1996).

Peirol, *Peirol: Troubadour of Auvergne*, ed. S. C. Aston (Cambridge, 1953).

Raimbaut d'Aurenga, *The Life and Works of the Troubadour Raimbaut d'Orange*, ed. W. T. Pattison (Minneapolis MN, 1952).

Raimbaut de Vaqueiras, *Poems*, ed. J. Linskill (The Hague, 1964).

Raimon de Cornet, *Doctrinal de trobar*, ed. J.-B. Noulet and C. Chabaneau in *Deux Manuscrits provençaux du XIVe siècle contenant des poésies de Raimon de Cornet, de Peire de Ladils, et d'autres poètes de l'école toulousaine* (Montpellier and Paris, 1888), pp. 199–215.

Raimon de Miraval, *Poésies*, ed. L. T. Topsfield (Paris, 1971).

Raimon Vidal, 'Abrils issia' in *Obra poètica*, ed. H. Field (2 vols., Barcelona, 1989).

The 'Razos de trobar' and Associated Texts, ed. J. H. Marshall (Oxford, 1972).

Terramagnino da Pisa, *Doctrina d'Acort*, in Raimon Vidal, *Razos*, ed. Marshall, pp. 27–53.

Uc Faidit, *The Donatz Proensals*, ed. J. H. Marshall (Oxford, 1969).

Vidas and *razos*. See: *Biographies des troubadours*

Secondary sources

Bec, Pierre, 'Le Problème des genres chez les premiers troubadours', *Cahiers de civilisation médiévale*, 25 (1982), 31–47.

Beltrami, Pietro G., and Vatteroni, Sergio, *Rimario trobadorico provenzale* (2 vols. to date; Pisa, 1988–94).

Billy, Dominique, *L'Architecture lyrique médiévale* (Montpellier, 1989).

Bossy, Michel-André, 'The *trobar clus* of Raimbaut d'Aurenga, Giraut de Bornelh and Arnaut Daniel', *Medievalia*, 19 (1996), 203–19.

Burgwinkle, William E., *Love for Sale: Materialist Readings of the Troubadour Razo Corpus* (New York and London, 1997).

'The *chansonniers* as Books', in Gaunt and Kay (eds.), *The Troubadours*, pp. 246–62.

Chailly, Jacques, 'Les Premiers Troubadours et les *versus* de l'École d'Aquitaine', *Romania*, 76 (1955), 212–39.

Chambers, Frank M., 'Imitation of Form in the Old Provençal Lyric', *RP*, 6 (1952–3), 104–20.

An Introduction to Old Provença Versification (Philadelphia PA, 1985).

Egan, Margarita, 'Commentary, *vitae poetae* and *vida*: Latin and Old Provençal "Lives of Poets"', *RP*, 37 (1983–4), 36–48.

Frank, Istvan, *Répertoire métrique de la poésie des troubadours* (2 vols., Paris, 1953–7).

Gaunt, Simon, 'Orality and Writing: The Text of the Troubadour Poem', in Gaunt and Kay (eds.), *The Troubadours*, pp. 228–45.

Troubadours and Irony (Cambridge, 1989).

Gaunt, Simon, and Kay, Sarah (eds.), *The Troubadours: An Introduction* (Cambridge, 1999).

Gaunt, Simon, and Paterson, Linda M. (eds.), *The Troubadours and the Epic: Essays in Memory of W. Mary Hackett* (Warwick, 1987).

Gennrich, Friedrich, *Die Kontrafaktur im Liedschaffen des Mittelalters* (Langen-bei-Frankfurt, 1965).

Girolamo, Costanzo di, *I trovatori* (Turin, 1990).

Gruber, Jörn, *Die Dialektik des Trobar* (Tübingen, 1983).

Harvey, Ruth E., *The Troubadour Marcabru and Love* (London, 1989).

Jeanroy, Alfred, 'Les *Leys d'Amors*', *Histoire littéraire de la France*, 38 (1949), 139–233.

Kay, Sarah, 'Continuation as Criticism: The Case of Jaufre Rudel', *MÆ*, 56 (1987), 46–64.

'Derivation, Derived Rhyme and the *Trobairitz*', in W. D. Paden Jr. (ed.), *The Voice of the Trobairitz: Perspectives on the Women Troubadours* (Philadelphia PA, 1989), pp. 157–82.

'Rhetoric and Subjectivity in the Troubadour Lyric', in Gaunt and Paterson (eds.), *The Troubadours and the Epic*, pp. 102–42.

Subjectivity in Troubadour Poetry (Cambridge, 1990).

Köhler, Erich, 'Marcabru und die beiden Schulen', *Cultura neolatina*, 30 (1970), 300–14.

Trobadorlyrik und höfischer Roman (Berlin, 1962).

Law, Vivien, 'Originality in the Medieval Normative Tradition', in T. Bynon and F. R. Palmer (eds.), *Studies in the History of Western Linguistics* (Cambridge, 1986), pp. 43–55.

Léglu, Catherine, *Between Sequence and Sirventes: Aspects of Parody in the Troubadour Lyric* (Oxford, 2000).

'Moral and Satirical Poetry', in Gaunt and Kay (eds.), *The Troubadours*, pp. 47–65.

Lejeune, Rita, 'Thèmes communs de troubadours et vie de société', in *Littérature et société occitanes au Moyen Âge* (Liège, 1979), pp. 287–98.

Makin, Peter, 'Pound and Troubadour Word Arts', in Gaunt and Paterson (eds.), *The Troubadours and the Epic*, pp. 1–36.

Marshall, John H., 'Imitation of Metrical Form in Peire Cardenal', *RP*, 32 (1978–9), 18–48.

'Observations on the Sources of the Treatment of Rhetoric in the *Leys d'Amors*', *MLR*, 64 (1969), 39–52.

'Pour l'Étude des *contrafacta* dans la poésie des troubadours', *Romania*, 101 (1980), 289–335.

'Le *vers* au XIIe siècle: genre poétique?', *Revue de langue et littérature d'Oc*, 12–13 (1962–3), 55–63.

'Une Versification lyrique popularisante en ancien provençal', in P. T. Ricketts (ed.), *Actes du premier congrès international de l'AIEO* (London, 1987), pp. 35–66.

Meneghetti, Maria Luisa, 'Intertextuality and Dialogism in the Troubadours', in Gaunt and Kay (eds.), *The Troubadours*, pp. 181–96.

Il pubblico dei trovatori (Modena, 1984).

'Uno stornello nunziante: Fonti, significato e datazione dei due vers dell' *Estornel* di Marcabru', in L. Rossi (ed.), *Cantarem d'aquestz trobadors: Studi occitanici in onore de Giuseppe Tavani* (Alessandria, 1995), pp. 47–63.

Milone, Luigi, 'Retorica del potere e poetica dell'oscuro da Guglielmo IX a Raimbaut d'Aurenga', *Quaderni del circolo filologico-linguistico padovano*, 10 (1979), 149–77.

Mölk, Ulrich, *Trobar clus, trobar leu* (Munich, 1968).

Monson, Don A., 'Jaufré Rudel et l'amour lointain: les origines d'une légende', *Romania*, 106 (1985), 36–56.

Page, Christopher, *Voices and Instruments of the Middle Ages* (London, 1987).

Paterson, Linda M., *Troubadours and Eloquence* (Oxford, 1975).

Pollmann, Leo, *Trobar clus* (Münster, 1965).

Rieger, Dietmar, *Gattungen und Gattungsbezeichnungen der Trobadorlyrik: Untersuchungen zum altprovenzalischen Sirventes* (Tübingen, 1976).

Roncaglia, Aurelio, 'Carestia', *Cultura neolatina*, 18 (1958), 123–37.

'Riflessi di posizioni cistercensi nella poesia del XII secolo: discussione sui fondamenti religiosi del "trobar naturau" di Marcabruno', in *I cistercensi e il lazio* (Rome, 1978), pp. 11–22.

'Trobar clus: discussione aperta', *Cultura neolatina*, 29 (1969), 5–55.

Rossi, Luciano, 'Chrétien de Troyes e i trovatori: *Tristan, Linhaura, Carestia*', *Vox romanica*, 46 (1987), 26–62.

Routledge, Michael, 'The Later Troubadours', in Gaunt and Kay (eds.), *The Troubadours*, pp. 99–112.

Shapiro, Marianne, '*Entrebescar los motz*: Word-Weaving and Divine Rhetoric', *Zeitschrift für romanische Philologie*, 100 (1984), 355–83.

Spence, Sarah, 'Rhetoric and Hermeneutics', in Gaunt and Kay (eds.), *The Troubadours*, pp. 164–80.

Sutherland, Dorothy R., 'L'Élément théâtral dans la *canso* chez les troubadours de l'époque classique', *Revue de langue et de littérature d'Oc*, 12–13 (1962–3), 95–101.

Switten, Margaret, 'Music and Versification: *fetz Marcabrus los motz e l so*', in Gaunt and Kay (eds.), *The Troubadours*, pp. 141–63.

Topsfield, Leslie T., *Troubadours and Love* (Cambridge, 1975).

Van Vleck, Amelia, *Memory and Re-Creation in Troubadour Lyric* (Berkeley CA, 1991).

Literary theory and polemic in Castile, *c.* 1200–*c.* 1500

Primary sources

Alfonso X, el Sabio, *Complete Works*, ed. L. Kasten and J. Nitti (Madison WI, 1986).

General estoria: primera parte, ed. A. G. Solalinde (Madrid, 1930).

General estoria: segunda parte, ed. A. G. Solalinde, L. A. Kasten and V. R. B. Oelschläger (2 vols., Madrid, 1957–61).

Cancioneiro da Biblioteca Nacional, 'L'Art de trouver du chansonnier Colocci-Brancuti', ed. J. M. d'Heur, *Arquivos do Centro Cultural Português*, 9 (1975), 321–98.

Baena, Juan Alfonso de, *Cancionero*, ed. J. M. Azáceta, Clásicos Hispánicos (3 vols., Madrid, 1966).

Boccaccio, Giovanni, *Genealogie deorum gentilium libri*, ed. V. Romano (Bari, 1951); in part tr. C. G. Osgood, *Boccaccio on Poetry: Being the Preface and the Fourteenth and Fifteenth Books of Boccaccio's 'Genealogia deorum gentilium' in an English Version with Introductory Essay and Commentary* (Princeton NJ, 1930).

Cantigas d'escarnho e de mal dizer dos cancioneiros medievais galego-portugueses, ed. M. Rodrigues Lapa (1965; 2nd edn, Vigo, 1970).

Cartagena, Alonso de, *Un tratado de Alonso de Cartagena sobre la educación y los estudios literarios*, ed. J. N. H. Lawrance (Barcelona, 1979).

Geoffrey of Vinsauf, *Poetria nova*, ed. F. Faral in *Les Arts poétiques du XIIe et du XIIIe siècle*, Bibliothèque de l'École des hautes études, 238 (1923; rpt. Geneva, 1982), pp. 194–262.

Ibn'Ezra, Moses, *Kitab al-muhadara wal-mudakara*, Spanish tr. M. A. Mas (Madrid, 1986).

Imperial, Micer Francisco, *'El dezir a las syete virtudes' y otros poemas*, ed. C. I. Nepaulsingh (Madrid, 1977).

Juan Gil de Zamora, *Dictaminis epithalamium*, ed. C. Faulhaber, Biblioteca degli studi mediolatini e volgari, n.s. 2 (Pisa, 1978).

Juan Manuel, *El conde Lucanor*, ed. J. M. Blecua (Madrid, 1985).

Libro de los estados, ed. R. B. Tate and I. R. Macpherson (Oxford, 1974).

López de Mendoza, Íñigo, Marqués de Santillana, *Obras completas*, ed. A. Gómez Moreno and M. P. A. M. Kerkhof (Barcelona, 1988).

Madrigal, Alfonso de (El Tostado), *Comento de Eusebio* (5 vols., Salamanca, 1506–7).

In Eusebium. Madrid, Biblioteca Nacional, MS 1796.

La interpretacion o traslacion del libro de las cronicas o tienpos de Eusebio Cesariensse. Madrid, Biblioteca Nacional, MS 10811.

Mena, Juan de, *La coronación del marqués de Santillana*, in *Obras completas*, ed. M. A. Pérez Priego (Madrid, 1989), pp. 105–208.

El laberinto de Fortuna, and anon. commentary. Madrid, Biblioteca de Bartolomé March, MS 20-5-6, fols. 39r–68v [*Cancionero de Barrantes* fragment].

El laberinto de Fortuna, and anon. commentary. Paris, Bibliothèque nationale de France, fonds espagnol MS 229, fols. 2r–76v.

Murphy, J. J. (ed.), *Three Medieval Rhetorical Arts* (Berkeley CA, 1971).

Nebrija, Elio Antonio de, *Gramática de la lengua castellana*, ed. A. Quilis (Madrid, 1980).

De vi ac potestate litterarum, ed. A. Quilis and P. Usábel (Madrid, 1987).

Núñez, Hernán, *Las trezientas del famosíssimo poeta Juan de Mena con glosa* (Seville, 1499; 2nd edn, Granada, 1505).

Ovid, Pseudo-, *De Vetula*, ed. D. M. Robathan (Amsterdam, 1968); also ed. P. Klopsch, Mittellateinische Studien und Texte, 2 (Leiden and Cologne, 1967).

Pamphilus, ed. F. G. Becker, Mittellateinisches Jahrbuch, 9 (Düsseldorf, 1972).

Las poéticas castellanas de la Edad Media, ed. F. López Estrada (Madrid, 1985).

Riquier, Guiraut, 'La supplica di Guiraut Riquier e la risposta di Alfonso X di Castiglia', ed. V. Bertolucci-Pizzorusso, *Studi mediolatini e volgari*, 14 (1966), 10–135.

Ruiz, Juan, *Libro de buen amor*, ed. G. B. Gybbon-Monypenny (Madrid, 1988).

Santillana, Marqués de.   See: López de Mendoza, Íñigo

Segovia, Pero Guillén de, *La gaya ciencia*, ed. J. M. Casas Homs (Madrid, 1962).

Villena, Enrique de, 'El *Arte de trovar* de don Enrique de Villena', ed. F. J. Sánchez Cantón, *Revista de Filología Española*, 6 (1919), 158–80.

Traducción y glosas de la 'Eneida', ed. P. M. Cátedra (3 vols., Salamanca, 1989).

Secondary sources

Aguirre, Elvira de, *Die 'Arte de trovar' von Enrique de Villena* (Cologne, 1968).

Asís, María Dolores de, *Hernán Núñez en la historia de los estudios clásicos* (Madrid, 1977).

Balaguer, Joaquín, 'Las ideas de Nebrija acerca de la versificación castellana', in his *Apuntes para una historia prosódica de la métrica castellana* (Madrid, 1964), pp. 9–24.

Beltrán, Vicente, 'Los trovadores en la corte de Castilla y León (II): Alfonso X, Guiraut Riquier y Pero da Ponte', *Romania*, 107 (1986), 486–503.

Birkenmajer, A., 'Der Streit des Alonso von Cartagena mit Leonardo Bruni Aretino', BGPM, 20 (1917–22), Heft 5 (1922), pp. 129–210, 226–35.

Brann, Ross, *The Compunctious Poet: Cultural Ambiguity and Hebrew Poetry in Muslim Spain* (Baltimore MD, 1991).

Brown, Catherine, *Contrary Things: Exegesis, Dialectic, and the Poetics of Didacticism* (Stanford CA, 1998).

Brownlee, Marina Scordilis, *The Status of the Reading Subject in the 'Libro de buen amor'* (Chapel Hill NC, 1985).

Cátedra, Pedro M., 'Enrique de Villena y algunos humanistas', in *Nebrija y la introducción*, pp. 187–203.

Exégesis-ciencia-literatura: la exposición del salmo 'Quoniam videbo' de Enrique de Villena (Madrid, 1985).

Cherchi, Paolo, '*Brevedad, oscuredad*, synchysis in *El Conde Lucanor* (parts II–IV)', *Medioevo romanzo*, 9 (1984), 361–74.

Clarke, Dorothy Clotelle, 'Juan del Encina's *Una arte de poesía castellana*', *RP*, 4 (1953), 254–9.

d'Heur, Jean-Marie, *Troubadours d'Oc et troubadours galiciens-portugais: Recherches sur quelques échanges dans la littérature de l'Europe au Moyen Âge* (Paris, 1973).

Dagenais, John, *The Ethics of Reading in Manuscript Culture: Glossing the 'Libro de buen amor'* (Princeton NJ, 1994).

'A Further Source for the Literary Ideas in Juan Ruiz's Prologue', *Journal of Hispanic Philology*, 11 (1986–7), 23–52.

Di Camillo, Ottavio, *El humanismo castellano del siglo XV* (Valencia, 1976).

Faulhaber, Charles, *Latin Rhetorical Theory in Thirteenth and Fourteenth Century Castile* (Berkeley CA, 1972).

Retóricas clásicas y medievales en bibliotecas castellanas, Ábaco, 4 (Madrid, 1973), 151–300.

'Las retóricas hispanolatinas medievales (siglos XIII–XV)', *Repertorio de historia de las ciencias eclesiásticas en España*, 7 (1979), 11–65.

Fraker, Charles, *Studies on the 'Cancionero de Baena'* (Chapel Hill NC, 1966).

García de la Concha, Víctor, 'La impostación religiosa de la reforma humanística en España: Nebrija y los poetas cristianos', in *Nebrija y la introducción*, pp. 123–43.

(ed.), *Nebrija y la introducción del Renacimiento en España: Actas de la III Academia Literaria Renacentista* (Salamanca, 1983).

Gerli, E. Michael, '*Recta voluntas est bonus amor*: St Augustine and the Didactic Structure of the *Libro de buen amor*', *RP*, 35 (1981–2), 500–8.

Gómez Moreno, Ángel, 'Clerecía', in C. Alvar and Á. Gómez Moreno, *La poesía épica y de clerecía medievales* (Madrid, 1988), pp. 71–98.

El 'Proemio e carta' del marqués de Santillana y la teoría poética del siglo XV (Barcelona, 1990).

'La teoría poética en los estudios de literatura medieval española', in C. Alvar and A. Gómez Moreno, *La poesía lírica medieval* (Madrid, 1987), pp. 125–40.

Gómez Redondo, F., *Aires poéticas medievales* (Madrid, 2000).

Joset, Jacques, *Nuevas investigaciones sobre 'El libro de buen amor'* (Madrid, 1988).

Johnston, Mark D., 'Literary Tradition and the Idea of Language in the *Artes de trobar*', *Dispositio*, 2 (1977), 208–18.

'Poetry and Courtliness in Baena's Prologue', *La Corónica*, 25:1 (Fall, 1996), 93–105.

'The Translation of the Troubadour Tradition in the *Torcimany* of Lluis d'Averçó', *SP*, 78 (1981), 151–67.

Keightley, Ronald G., 'Alfonso de Madrigal and the *Chronici canones* of Eusebius', *Journal of Medieval and Renaissance Studies*, 7 (1977), 225–48.

'Enrique de Villena's *Los doze trabajos de Hércules*: A Reappraisal', *Journal of Hispanic Philology*, 3 (1978–79), 49–68.

Kohut, Karl, 'Der Beitrag der Theologie zum Literaturbegriff in der Zeit Juans II von Kastilien: Alonso de Cartagena (1384–1456) und Alonso de Madrigal, genannt el Tostado (1400?–55)', *Romanische Forschungen*, 89 (1977), 183–226.

'La posición de la literatura en los sistemas científicos del siglo XV', *Iberoro-mania*, n.s. 7 (1978), 67–87.

'La teoría de la poesía cortesana en el *Prólogo* de Juan Alfonso de Baena', in W. Hempel and D. Briesemeister (eds.), *Actas del coloquio hispano-alemán Ramón Menéndez Pidal* (Tübingen, 1982), pp. 120–37.

Las teorías literarias en España y Portugal durante los siglos XV y XVI: estado de la investigación y problemática (Madrid, 1973).

Lawrance, Jeremy N. H., 'Humanism in the Iberian Peninsula', in A. Goodman and A. MacKay (eds.), *The Impact of Humanism on Western Europe* (London, 1990), pp. 220–58.

'The Spread of Lay Literacy in Late Medieval Castile', *Bulletin of Hispanic Studies*, 62 (1985), 79–94.

'La Traduction espagnole du *De libris gentilium legendis* de Saint Basile, dédiée au Marquis de Santillane (Paris, BN Ms esp. 458)', *Atalaya*, 1 (1991), 81–116.

Lomax, Derek W., 'Notes sur un métier: les jongleurs castillans en 1316', in *Les Espagnes médiévales, aspects économiques et sociaux: mélanges offerts à Jean Gautier Dalché* (Nice, 1983), pp. 229–36.

López Estrada, Francisco, '*El arte de poesía castellana* de Juan del Encina (1496)', in A. Redondo (ed.), *L'Humanisme dans les lettres espagnoles: XIXe colloque internationale d'études humanistes* (Paris, 1979), pp. 151–68.

Macpherson, Ian, 'Don Juan Manuel: The Literary Process', *SP*, 70 (1973), 1–18.

Menéndez Pidal, Ramón, *Poesía juglaresca y orígines de las literaturas románicas: problemas de historia literaria y cultural* (Madrid, 1957).

Miguel Prendes, Sol, *El espejo y el piélago: la 'Eneida' castellana de Enrique de Villena* (Kassel, 1998).

Nader, Helen, '"The Greek Commander" Hernán Núñez de Toledo, Spanish Humanist and Civic Leader', *Renaissance Quarterly*, 31 (1978), 463–85.

Nalle, Sara T., 'Literacy and Culture in Early Modern Castile', *Past and Present*, 125 (1989), 65–96.

Niederehe, Hans-J., *Alfonso el Sabio y la lingüística de su tiempo* (Madrid, 1987); tr. from the 1975 German edn.

Palafox, Eloísa, *Las éticas del 'Exemplum': Los 'Castigos del rey don Sancho IV', 'El conde Lucanor', y el 'Libro de buen amor'* (Mexico City, 1998).

Pérez Priego, Miguel Ángel, 'De Dante a Juan de Mena: sobre el género literario de *comedia', 1616'. Anuario de la Sociedad Española de Literatura General y Comparada*, 1 (1978), 151–8.

Potvin, Claudine, *Illusion et pouvoir: La poétique du 'Cancionero de Baena'*, Cahiers d'études médiévales, 9 (Montreal, 1989).

Recio, Roxana, 'Alfonso de Madrigal (El Tostado): la traducción como teoría entre lo medieval y lo renacentista', *La Corónica*, 19:2 (Spring, 1991), 112–31.

Recio, Roxana (ed.), *La traducción en España, ss. XIV–XVI* (León, 1995).

Rico, Francisco, *Alfonso el Sabio y la 'General estoria'* (2nd edn, Barcelona, 1984).

'Crítica de texto y modelos de cultura en el Prólogo general de don Juan Manuel', *Studia in honorem prof. M. de Riquer* (4 vols., Barcelona, 1986), I, pp. 409–23.

Nebrija frente a los bárbaros (Salamanca, 1978).

Round, Nicholas G., 'Renaissance Culture and its Opponents in Fifteenth-Century Castile', *MLR*, 57 (1962), 204–15.

Russell, P. E., 'Las armas contra las letras: para una definición del humanismo español del siglo XV', in *Temas de la 'Celestina' y otros estudios: del 'Cid' al 'Quijote'* (Barcelona, 1978), pp. 207–39.

Traducciones y traductores en la Península Ibérica (1400–1550) (Bellaterra and Barcelona, 1985).

Sáenz-Badillos, Ángel, and Borrás, Judit Targona, *Gramáticos hebreos de Al-Andalús (siglos X–XII): filología y biblia* (Cordova, 1988).

Santiago Lacuesta, Ramón, 'Sobre "el primer ensayo de una prosodia y ortografía castellanas": el *Arte de trovar* de Enrique de Villena', *Miscellanea barcelonensia*, 42 (1975), 35–52.

Schiff, Mario, *La Bibliothèque du Marquis de Santillane* (1905; rpt. Amsterdam, 1970).

Seidenspinner-Núñez, Dayle, 'On "Dios y el mundo": Author and Reader Response in Juan Ruiz and Juan Manuel', *RP*, 42 (1988–9), 251–66.

'Readers, Response, and Repertoires: *Rezeptionstheorie* and the Archpriest's Text', *La Corónica*, 19:1 (Fall, 1990), 96–111.

Street, Florence, 'Hernán Núñez and the Earliest Printed Editions of Mena's *Laberinto de Fortuna*', *MLR*, 61 (1966), 51–63.

Tavani, Giuseppe, 'La satira morale e letteraria', *Grundriss der romanische Literaturen des Mittelalters*, 6 (1968), 272–4, 309–13.

Taylor, Barry, 'Don Jaime de Jérica y el público de *El Conde Lucanor*', *Revista de Filología Española*, 66 (1986), 39–58.

'Juan Manuel's Cipher in the *Libro de los estados*', *La Corónica*, 12 (1983–4), 32–44.

Thomas, Antoine, *Jean de Gerson et l'éducation des dauphins de France* (Paris, 1930).

Valle Rodríguez, Carlos del, *El diván poético de Dunash del Labrat: la introducción de la métrica árabe* (Madrid, 1988).

Walsh, J. K., 'Juan Ruiz and the *mester de clerezía*: Lost Context and Lost Parody', *RP*, 33 (1979), 62–86.

Review of Brownlee, *Reading Subject*, in *La Corónica*, 14 (1985–86), 321–6.

Weiss, Julian, 'Las "fermosas e peregrinas ystorias": sobre la glosa ornamental cuatrocentista', *Revista de Literatura Medieval*, 2 (1990), 103–12.

'Juan de Mena's *Coronación*: satire or *sátira*?', *Journal of Hispanic Philology*, 6 (1981–2), 113–38.

'Medieval Poetics and the Social Meaning of Form', *Atalaya*, 8 (1997 [1998]), 171–86.

'On the Conventionality of the *Cantigas d'amor*', *La Corónica*, 26:1 (Fall, 1997), 63–83; rpt. in W. D. Paden (ed.), *Medieval Lyric: Genres in Historical Context* (Urbana IL, 2000), pp. 126–45.

The Poet's Art: Literary Theory in Castile c. 1400–60, Medium Ævum Monographs, n.s. 14 (Oxford, 1990).
'Political Commentary: Hernán Núñez's *Glosa a "Las trescientas"* ', in A. Deyermond and J. Lawrance (eds.), *Letters and Society in Fifteenth-Century Spain: Studies Presented to P. E. Russell on his Eightieth Birthday* (Llangrannog, 1993), pp. 205–16.
'Tiempo y materia en la poética de Juan del Encina', in J. Guijarro Ceballos (ed.), *Humanismo y literatura en tiempos de Juan del Encina* (Salamanca, 1999), pp. 241–57.

Literary criticism in Middle High German literature

Primary sources

Abelard, Peter, *Historia calamitatum*, ed. J. Monfrin (4th edn, Paris, 1978).
Allra kappa kvæði, ed. G. Cederschiöld, *Arkiv for nordisk filologi*, 1 (1883), 62–80.
Eberhard the German (Everardus Alemannus), in Faral (ed.), *Les Arts poétiques*, pp. 336–77.
Faral, Edmond (ed.), *Les arts poétiques du XIIe et du XIIIe siècle*, Bibliothèque de l'École des hautes études, 238 (1923; rpt. Geneva, 1982).
Geoffrey of Vinsauf, *Poetria nova*, in Faral (ed.), *Les Arts poétiques*, pp. 194–262.
Gottfried von Strassburg, *Tristan*, ed. R. Bechstein, rev. P. Ganz, Deutsche Klassiker des Mittelalters, n.F. 4 (Wiesbaden, 1978).
Tristan und Isold, ed. F. Ranke (4th edn, Dublin and Zurich, 1959).
Hartmann von Aue, *Iwein*, ed. G. F. Benecke and K. Lachmann, 7th rev. edn by L. Wolff (Berlin, 1968).
Heinrich von dem Türlin, *Die Krone (Verse 1–12281). Nach der Handschrift 2779 der Österreichischen Nationalbibliothek*, ed. F. P. Knapp and M. N. Niesner, Altdeutsche Textbibliothek, 112 (Tübingen, 1999).
Heinrich von Veldeke, *Eneasroman. Mhd. / Nhd.*, rev. and tr. D. Kartschoke, Reclams Universalbibliothek, 8303 (2nd rev. edn, Stuttgart, 1997).
Herman Dâmen: Untersuchung und Neuausgabe seiner Gedichte, ed. P. Schlupkoten, diss. Marburg (Breslau, 1913).
Hugo von Trimberg, *Registrum multorum auctorum*, ed. K. Langosch (1942; rpt. Nendeln, 1969).
Der Renner, ed. G. Ehrismann, StLV 247, 248, 252, 256 (1908–11; rpt. Berlin, 1970).
Lucan [= M. Annaeus Lucanus], *De bello civili libri decem* [= *Pharsalia*], ed. A. E. Housman (Oxford, 1926).
Matthew of Vendôme, *Ars versificatoria*, in Faral (ed.), *Les arts poétiques*, pp. 106–93; also in *Opera*, ed. F. Munari (3 vols., Rome 1977–88), III. Tr. A. E. Galyon (Ames IA, 1980); also tr. R. P. Parr (Milwaukee WI, 1981).
Peire d'Alvernha, *Liriche: Testo, traduzione e note*, ed. A. Del Monte, Collezione di filologia romanza, 1 (Turin, 1955).
Pütrich, Jakob, von Reichertshausen, *Ehrenbrief*, ed. M. Mueller, diss., City University of New York, 1985.

Rudolf von Ems, *Alexander*, ed. V. Junk, *StLV* 172, 174 (1928–9; rpt. Darmstadt, 1965).

Willehalm von Orlens, ed. V. Junk, Deutsche Texte des Mittelalters, 2 (1905; rpt. Dublin and Zurich, 1967).

Schweikle, Günther (ed.), *Dichter über Dichter in mittelhochdeutscher Literatur* (Tübingen, 1970).

Walther von der Vogelweide, *Leich, Lieder, Sangsprüche*, ed. K. Lachmann, rev. C. Cormeau with T. Bein and H. Brunner (14th edn, Berlin and New York, 1996).

Wolfram von Eschenbach, *Parzival: Studienausgabe*, based on the 6th edn of K. Lachmann, tr. P. Knecht, intro. B. Schirok (Berlin and New York, 1998).

Willehalm, Nach der Handschrift 857 der Stiftsbibliothek St. Gallen, ed. Joachim Heinzle, Bibliothek des Mittelalters, 9 (Frankfurt, 1991).

Secondary sources

Chinca, Mark, *Gottfried von Strassburg: Tristan* (Cambridge, 1997).

History, Fiction, Verisimilitude: Studies in the Poetics of Gottfried's 'Tristan', Texts and Dissertations 35; Bithell Series of Dissertations 18 (London, 1993).

Chinca, Mark, and Young, Christopher, 'Literary Theory and the German Romance in the Literary Field *c.* 1200', in U. Peters (ed.), *Text und Kultur: Mittelalterliche Literatur 1150–1450* (Stuttgart and Weimar, 2001), pp. 612–44.

Cormeau, Christoph, *'Wigalois' und 'Diu Crône': Zwei Kapitel zur Gattungsgeschichte des nachklassischen Aventiureromans*, Münchener Texte und Untersuchungen, 57 (Munich, 1977).

Coxon, Sebastian, *The Presentation of Authorship in Medieval German Narrative Literature 1220–1290* (Oxford, 2001).

De Bruyne, Edgar, *Études d'esthétique médiévale* (3 vols., Bruges, 1946); abridged and tr. E. B. Hennessy as *The Esthetics of the Middle Ages* (New York, 1969).

Draesner, Ulrike, *Wege durch erzählte Welten: Intertextuelle Verweise als Mittel der Bedeutungskonstitution in Wolframs 'Parzival'*, Mikrokosmos, 36 (Frankfurt, 1993).

Fromm, Hans, 'Gottfried von Straßburg und Abaelard', *PBB*, 95, *Sonderheft: Festschrift für Ingeborg Schröbler* (1973), 196–216.

'Tristans Schwertleite', *Deutsche Vierteljahrsschrift*, 41 (1967), 333–50.

Gaunt, Simon, *Troubadours and Irony* (Cambridge, 1989).

Green, Dennis H., *Medieval Listening and Reading* (Cambridge, 1994).

'On the Primary Reception of Narrative Literature in Medieval Germany', *Forum for Modern Language Studies*, 20 (1984), 289–308.

'Zur primären Rezeption von Wolframs *Parzival*', in K. Gärtner and J. Heinzle (eds.), *Studien zu Wolfram von Eschenbach: Festschrift für Werner Schröder zum 75. Geburtstag* (Tübingen, 1989), pp. 271–88.

Grubmüller, K., *et al.* (eds.), *Befund und Deutung: Zum Verhälntis von Empirie und Interpretation in Sprach- und Literaturwissenschaft* (Tübingen, 1979).

Grundlehner, Philip, 'Gottfried von Strassburg and the Crisis of Language', in W. C. McDonald (ed.), *Spectrum medii aevi: Essays in Early German Literature in Honor of George F. Jones*, Göppinger Arbeiten zur Germanistik, 362 (Göppingen, 1983), pp. 139–55.

Hahn, Ingrid, 'Zu Gottfrieds von Straßburg Literaturschau', *Zeitschrift für deutsches Altertum*, 96 (1967), 218–36; rpt. in Wolf, *Gottfried von Straßburg*, pp. 424–52.

Haug, Walter, '*Der aventiure meine*', in *Würzburger Prosastudien II: Untersuchungen zur Literatur und Sprache des Mittelalters: Festschrift Kurt Ruh*, Medium ævum, 31 (Munich, 1975), pp. 93–111.

Literaturtheorie im deutschen Mittelalter (2nd rev. edn, Darmstadt, 1985); tr. J. M. Catling as *Vernacular Literary Theory in the Middle Ages: The German Tradition, 800–1300, in its European Context* (Cambridge, 1997).

Heinzle, Joachim, *Wandlungen und Neuansätze im 13. Jahrhundert (1220/ 30–1280/90)*, Geschichte der deutschen Literatur von den Anfängen bis zum Beginn der Neuzeit, 2.2 (1984; rpt. Tübingen, 1988).

Hoffmann, Werner, 'Die *vindaere wilder maere*', *Euphorion*, 89 (1995), 129–50.

Huber, Christoph, 'Bibliographie zum *Tristan* Gottfrieds von Straßburg (seit 1984)', in '*Encomia–Deutsch': Höfische Literatur und Klerikerkultur; Wissen–Bildung–Gesellschaft*, Sonderheft der Deutschen Sektion der International Courtly Literature Society (Tübingen, 2000), pp. 80–128.

Gottfried von Straßburg: Tristan, Klassiker-Lektüren, 3 (2nd rev. edn, Berlin, 2001).

'Wort-Ding-Entsprechungen. Zur Sprach- und Stiltheorie Gottfrieds von Straßburg', in Grubmüller (ed.), *Befund und Deutung*, pp. 268–302.

Jackson, W. T. H., 'The Literary Views of Gottfried von Straßburg', *PMLA*, 85 (1970), 992–1001.

Kellner, Beate, 'Autorität und Gedächtnis. Strategien der Legitimierung volkssprachlichen Erzählens im Mittelalter am Beispiel von Gottfrieds von Straßburg "Tristan"', in J. Fohrmann, I. Kasten and E. Neuland (eds.), *Autorität der/in Sprache, Literatur, neuen Medien: Vorträge des Bonner Germanistentags 1997* (Bielefeld, 1999), II, pp. 484–508.

Kolb, Herbert, 'Der ware Elicon: Zu Gottfrieds Tristan vv. 4862–4907', *Deutsche Vierteljahrsschrift*, 41 (1967), 1–26; rpt. in Wolf (ed.), *Gottfried von Straßburg*, pp. 453–88.

Krohn, Rüdiger, *Gottfried von Straßburg: Tristan, III: Kommentar, Nachwort und Register*, Reclams Universal-Bibliothek, 4473 (Stuttgart, 1980).

Minis, Cola, *Er inpfete das erste rîs* (Groningen, 1963).

Müller, Karl Friedrich, *Die literarische Kritik in der mittelhochdeutschen Dichtung und ihr Wesen* (1933; rpt. Darmstadt, 1967).

Müller-Kleimann, Sigrid, *Gottfrieds Urteil über den zeitgenössischen deutschen Roman: Ein Kommentar zu den Tristanversen 4619–4748*, Helfant Studien, 6 (Stuttgart, 1990).

Nellmann, Eberhard, 'Wolfram und Kyot als Vindære wilder mære: Überlegungen zu "Tristan" 4619–88 und "Parzival" 4531–17', *Zeitschrift für deutsches Altertum und deutsche Literatur*, 117 (1988), 31–67.

Ohly, Friedrich, 'Vom geistigen Sinn des Wortes im Mittelalter', *Zeitschrift für deutsches Altertum und deutsche Literatur*, 89 (1958), 1–23; rpt. in Ohly,

Schriften zur mittelalterlichen Bedeutungsforschung (Darmstadt, 1977), pp. 1–31.

Okken, Lambertus, *Kommentar zum Tristan-Roman Gottfrieds von Straßburg*, Amsterdamer Publikationen zur Sprache und Literatur, 57, 58 (2nd edn, 2 vols., Amsterdam and Atlanta GA, 1998).

Pattison, Walter T., 'The Background of Peire d'Alvernhe's *Chantarai d'aqest trobadors*', *MP*, 31 (1933), 19–34.

Sawicki, Stanislaw, *Gottfried von Straßburg und die Poetik des Mittelalters* (Berlin, 1932).

Schulze, Ursula, 'Literarkritische Äußerungen im Tristan Gottfrieds von Straßburg', *PBB*, 88 (1967), 489–517; rpt. in Wolf, *Gottfried von Straßburg*, pp. 489–517.

Stein, Peter K., 'Tristans Schwertleite: Zur Einschätzung ritterlich-höfischer Dichtung durch Gottfried von Straßburg', *Deutsche Vierteljahrsschrift*, 51 (1977), 300–50.

Steinhoff, Hans-Hugo, *Bibliographie zu Gottfried von Straßburg*, Bibliographien zur deutschen Literatur, 5 (Berlin, 1971); II: *Berichtszeitraum 1970–1983*, Bibliographien zur deutschen Literatur, 9 (Berlin, 1986).

Winkelman, Johan H., 'Die Baummetapher im literarischen Exkurs Gottfrieds von Straßburg', *Amsterdamer Beiträge zur älteren Germanistik*, 8 (1975), 85–112.

Wolf, Alois (ed.), *Gottfried von Straßburg*, Wege der Forschung, 320 (Darmstadt, 1973).

Worstbrock, Franz Josef, 'Ein Lucanzitat bei Abaelard und Gotfrid', *PBB*, 98 (1976), 351–6.

Later literary criticism in Wales

Primary sources

Cywyddau Iolo Goch ac Eraill, ed. H. Lewis, T. Roberts and I. Williams (Cardiff, 1937).

Gramadegau'r Penceirddiaid, ed. G. J. Williams and E. J. Jones (Cardiff, 1934).

Gwaith Dafydd ap Gwilym, ed. T. Parry (Cardiff, 1952).

Gwaith Einion Offeiriad a Dafydd Ddu o Hiraddug, ed. R. G. Gruffydd and Rh. Ifans (Aberystwyth, 1997).

Secondary sources

Breeze, Andrew, 'Llyfr durgrys', *Bulletin of the Board of Celtic Studies*, 33 (1986), 145.

Bromwich, Rachel, *Aspects of the Poetry of Dafydd ap Gwilym* (Cardiff, 1986).

Bryant-Quinn, M. P. '"Trugaredd Mawr Trwy Gariad": Golwg ar Ganu Siôn Cent', *Llên Cymru*, 27 (2004), 71–85.

Finegan, Jack, *Handbook of Biblical Chronology* (Princeton, 1964).

Gruffydd, R. Geraint, 'Wales's Second Grammarian: Dafydd Ddu of Hiraddug', *Proceedings of the British Academy*, 90 (1996), 1–28.

Jones, Bobi, 'Pwnc Mawr Beirniadaeth Lenyddol Gymraeg', in J. E. Caerwyn Williams (ed.), *Ysgrifau Beirniadol*, 3 (Denbigh, 1967), 253–88.

Jones, J. T., 'Gramadeg Einion Offeiriad', *Bulletin of the Board of Celtic Studies*, 2 (1925), 184–200.

Lewis, Ceri W., 'Einion Offeiriad and the Bardic Grammar', in A. O. H. Jarman and G. Rees Hughes (eds.), *A Guide to Welsh Literature, II: 1280 – c. 1500* (Swansea, 1979), pp. 58–87. Rev. edn by D. Johnston (Cardiff, 1997).

Lewis, Saunders, *Braslun o Hanes Llenyddiaeth Gymraeg* (Cardiff, 1932). *Gramadegau'r Penceirddiaid* (Cardiff, 1967).

Matonis, A. T. E., 'A Case Study: Historical and Textual Aspects of the Welsh Bardic Grammar', *Cambrian Medieval Celtic Studies*, 41 (Summer, 2001), 24–36.

'The Concept of Poetry in the Middle Ages: The Welsh Evidence from the Bardic Grammars', *Bulletin of the Board of Celtic Studies*, 36 (1989), 1–12.

'Later Medieval Poetics and Some Welsh Bardic Debates', *Bulletin of the Board of Celtic Studies*, 29 (1980–2), 635–65.

'Literary Taxonomies and Genre in the Welsh Bardic Grammars', *Zeitschrift für Celtische Philologie*, 47 (1995), 211–34.

'Problems Relating to the Composition of the Welsh Bardic Grammars', in A. T. E. Matonis and D. F. Melia (eds.), *Celtic Language, Celtic Culture: A Festschrift for Eric P. Hamp* (Van Nuys CA, 1990), pp. 273–9.

'The Welsh Bardic Grammars and the Western Grammatical Tradition', *MP*, 79 (1981), 121–45.

Parry, Thomas, 'Statud Gruffudd ap Cynan', *Bulletin of the Board of Celtic Studies*, 5 (1929–31), 25–33.

'The Welsh Metrical Treatise Attributed to Einion Offeiriad', *Proceedings of the British Academy*, 47 (1961), 177–95.

Poppe, Erich, 'The Figures of Speech in *Gramadegau'r Penceirddiaid*', *Bulletin of the Board of Celtic Studies*, 38 (1991), 102–4.

'Latin Grammatical Categories in the Vernacular: The Case of Declension in Welsh', *Historiographia linguistica*, 18 (1991), 269–80.

'Tense and Mood in Welsh Grammars, c. 1400 to 1621', *National Library of Wales Journal*, 29 (1995–6), 17–38.

Russell, Paul, '*Gwr gwynn y law*: Figures of Speech in *Gramadegau'r Penceirddiaid* and Latin Grammarians', *Cambrian Medieval Celtic Studies*, 32 (Winter, 1996), 95–104.

Smith, J. Beverley, 'Einion Offeiriad', *Bulletin of the Board of Celtic Studies*, 20 (1962–4), 339–47.

Williams, G. J., 'Gramadeg Gutun Owain', *Bulletin of the Board of Celtic Studies*, 4 (1927–9), 207–21.

Latin and vernacular in Italian literary theory

Primary sources

Accolti, Benedetto, *Dialogus de praestantia virorum sui aevi*, in Filippo Villani, *De origine civitatis Florentie et de eiusdem famosis civibus*, ed. G. C. Galletti (Florence, 1847), pp. 105–28.

Aeneas Silvius. See: Piccolomini, Enea Silvio (Pius II)

Agliotti, Girolamo, *De monachis erudiendis*, in *Hieronymi Aliotti Arretini epistolae et opuscula* (2 vols., Arezzo, 1769), II, pp. 176–292.

Alan of Lille, *Anticlaudianus*, ed. R. Bossuat (Paris, 1955); tr. J. J. Sheridan (Toronto, 1973).

Alberti, Leon Battista, *Della famiglia*, in *Opere volgari*, I, pp. 3–341.

Opere volgari, ed. C. Grayson (3 vols., Bari, 1960–73).

Della pittura, in *Opere volgari*, III, pp. 7–107.

La prima grammatica della lingua volgare: La Grammatichetta Vaticana Cal. Vat. Reg. 1370, ed. C. Grayson (Bologna, 1964).

Rime, in *Opere volgari*, II, pp. 1–51.

Alighieri, Dante, *La Commedia secondo l'antica vulgata*, ed. G. Petrocchi (2nd edn, 4 vols., Florence, 1994).

Il Convivio, ed. C. Vasoli and D. De Robertis, in Dante Alighieri, *Opere minori*, I.2 (2 vols., Milan and Naples, 1979–88).

Le Egloghe, ed. G. Brugnoli and R. Scarcia (Milan and Naples, 1980).

Epistola XIII, ed. G. Brugnoli, in *Opere minori*, II, pp. 598–643.

Epistole, ed. A. Frugoni, in *Opere minori*, II, pp. 522–97.

Monarchia, ed. P. Shaw (Cambridge, 1995).

Rime della maturità e dell'esilio, ed. M. Barbi and V. Pernicone (Florence, 1969).

Rime della 'Vita Nuova' e della giovinezza, ed. M. Barbi and F. Maggini (Florence, 1956).

De vulgari eloquentia, ed. P. V. Mengaldo, in *Opere minori*, II, pp. 1–237.

Alighieri, Jacopo, *Chiose all' 'Inferno'*, ed. S. Bellomo (Padua, 1990).

Alighieri, Pietro, *Il 'Commentarium' di Pietro Alighieri nelle redazioni Ashburnhamiana e Ottoboniana*, ed. R. della Vedova and M. T. Silvotti (Florence, 1978) [Pietro I, II and III].

'Anonimo Fiorentino', *Commento alla 'Divina Commedia' d'Anonimo Fiorentino del secolo XIV*, ed. P. Fanfani (3 vols., Bologna, 1866–74).

'Anonimo Latino', *Anonymous Latin Commentary on Dante's 'Commedia': Reconstructed Text*, ed. V. Cioffari (Spoleto, 1989).

Antonio da Rho, *Apologia, Orazioni*, ed. G. Lombardi (Rome, 1982).

De numero oratorio. Milan, Biblioteca Ambrosiana, MS B.124 Sup.

Bambaglioli, Graziolo de', *Commento all''Inferno' di Dante*, ed. L. C. Rossi (Pisa, 1998).

Il commento dantesco di Graziolo de' Bambaglioli, ed. A. Fiammazzo (Savona, 1915).

Barbaro, Ermolao, *Epistulae, orationes et carmina*, ed. V. Branca (2 vols., Florence, 1943).

Barbaro, Ermolao il Vecchio, *Orationes contra poetas*, ed. G. Ronconi (Florence, 1972).

Barzizza [delli Bargigi], Guiniforte, *Lo 'Inferno' della 'Commedia' di Dante Alighieri col comento di Guiniforte delli Bargigi*, ed. G. Zacheroni (Marseilles and Florence, 1838).

Beccaria, A., *Orationes defensoriae*. Vatican Library, MS Capp. 3, fols. 38r–94r.

Bembo, Pietro, *Gli asolani*, ed. G. Dilemmi (Florence, 1991).

Prose della volgar lingua, in *Prose e rime*, ed. C. Dionisotti (Turin, 1960), pp. 73–309.

Bembo, Pietro, and Pico della Mirandola, Giovan Francesco, *Le epistole 'De Imitatione'*, ed. G. Santangelo (Florence, 1954).

Bene of Florence, *Candelabrum*, ed. G. C. Alessio (Padua, 1983).

Benvenuto de Rambaldis da Imola, *Comentum super Dantis Aldigherij... Comoediam*, ed. J. P. Lacaita (5 vols., Florence, 1887).

Biondo, Flavio, *Italia illustrata*, in Biondo, *De Roma triumphante libri X*, pp. 293–422.

De Roma triumphante libri X (Basel, 1531).

De verbis romanae locutionis, in Tavoni, *Latino, grammatica, volgare*, pp. 197–215.

Boccaccio, Giovanni, *Epistule*, ed. G. Auzzas, in *Opere*, ed. Branca, V.1 (Milan, 1992), pp. 493–856.

Esposizioni sopra la 'Comedia' di Dante, ed. G. Padoan (Verona, 1965).

Genealogie deorum gentilium libri, ed. V. Romano (Bari, 1951); in part tr. C. G. Osgood, *Boccaccio on Poetry: Being the Preface and the Fourteenth and Fifteenth Books of Boccaccio's 'Genealogia deorum gentilium' in an English Version with Introductory Essay and Commentary* (Princeton NJ, 1930).

Opere, ed. V. Branca *et al.* (12 vols., Milan, 1964–92).

Rime, ed. V. Branca, in *Opere*, ed. Branca, V.1 (Milan, 1992), pp. 3–374.

Trattatello in laude di Dante, ed. P. G. Ricci, in *Opere*, ed. Branca, III (Milan, 1974), pp. 437–538.

Bracciolini, Poggio, *De avaritia (Dialogus contra avaritiam)*, ed. G. Germano and A. Nardi (Livorno, 1994).

Bruni, Leonardo, *Dialogi ad Petrum Paulum Histrum*, in Bruni, *Opere letterarie e politiche*, pp. 78–143.

Epistolarum libri VIII, ed. L. Mehus (2 vols., Florence, 1741).

Historiarum Florentini populi libri XII, ed. E. Santini and C. Di Pierro, in *Rerum italicarum scriptores*, 19.3 (Città di Castello, 1914).

Humanistich-Philosophische Schriften, ed. H. Baron (Leipzig and Berlin, 1928).

Laudatio Florentine urbis, ed. S. U. Baldassarri (Tavarnuzze [Florence], 2000).

Opere letterarie e politiche, ed. P. Viti (Turin, 1996).

De studiis et litteris, in Garin (ed.), *Il pensiero pedagogico*, pp. 146–69.

Le vite di Dante e del Petrarca, in Bruni, *Opere letterarie e politiche*, pp. 531–60.

Caldiera, Giovanni, *Concordantiae poetarum philosophorum et theologorum* (Venice, 1547).

Calmeta, Vincenzo, *Prose e lettere edite ed inedite (con due appendici di altri inediti)*, ed. C. Grayson (Bologna, 1959).

Le Chiose Ambrosiane alla 'Commedia', ed. L. C. Rossi (Pisa, 1990).

Le Chiose Cagliaritane scelte e annotate, ed. E. Carrara (Città di Castello, 1902).

['*Chiose Cassinesi*']: *Il codice cassinese della 'Divina Commedia'* (Montecassino, 1865).

['*Chiose Marciane*']: *Le antiche chiose anonime all' 'Inferno' di Dante secondo il testo Marciano*, ed. G. Avalle (Città di Castello, 1900).

['*Chiose Selmiane*']: *Chiose anonime alla prima Cantica della 'Divina Commedia'*, ed. F. Selmi (Turin, 1865).

Colonna, Francesco, *Hypnerotomachia Poliphili*, ed. G. Pozzi and L. A. Ciapponi (2 vols., Padua, 1964).

Cortese, Paolo, *De Cardinalatu* (Castro Cortesio, 1510).

Epistle to Poliziano, in *Prosatori latini del Quattrocento*, pp. 904–10.

De hominibus doctis, ed. G. Ferraù (Palermo, 1979).

Decembrio, Angelo, *Politiae literariae libri septem* (Basel, 1562).

Dino del Garbo, [Commentary on 'Donna mi prega'], in *Guido Cavalcanti: 'Rime'*, ed. G. Favati (Milan and Naples, 1957), pp. 347–78.

Dominici, Giovanni, *Lucula noctis*, ed. R. Coulon (Paris 1908); also ed. E. Hunt (Notre Dame IN, 1940).

'Falso Boccaccio', *Chiose sopra Dante* (Florence, 1846).

Ficino, Marsilio, *Opera* (1576; rpt. Turin, 1959).

Filelfo, Francesco, *Epistolarum familiarum libri XXXVII* (Venice, 1502).

Francesco da Barberino, *I Documenti d'amore*, ed. F. Egidi (4 vols., Rome, 1905–27).

Francesco da Fiano, *Contra ridiculos oblocutores et fellitos detractores poetarum*, ed. M.-L. Plaisant, *Rinascimento*, s. II.2 (1961), 119–62; also ed. I. Taù, *Archivio italiano per la storia della pietà*, 4 (1965), 253–350.

Garin, E. (ed.), *Il pensiero pedagogico dello umanesimo* (Florence, 1958).

George of Trebizond, *Rhetoricorum libri V* (Venice, 1523).

Gherardi da Prato, Giovanni, *Il Paradiso degli Alberti*, ed. A. Lanza (Rome, 1975).

Giovanni Baldo di Faenza, *Tractatus*. Florence, Biblioteca Laurenziana, MS Plut. XIX, 30, fols. 1r–30r.

Graziolo de' Bambaglioli.   See: Bambaglioli, Graziolo de'.

Guarino da Verona, *Epistolario*, ed. R. Sabbadini (3 vols., Venice, 1915–19).

Guarino, Battista, *De ordine docendi*, in Garin (ed.), *Il pensiero pedagogico*, pp. 434–71.

Guido da Pisa, *Expositiones et glose super Comediam Dantis*, ed. V. Cioffari (Albany NY, 1974).

Jacopo della Lana, *Comedia di Dante degli Allaghieri col Commento di Jacopo della Lana*, ed. L. Scarabelli (3 vols., Bologna, 1866).

John of Garland, *Parisiana poetria*, ed. and tr. T. Lawler (New Haven CT and London, 1974).

Landino, Cristoforo, *La 'Commedia' di Dante Alighieri* [with commentary] (Venice, 1491).

Disputationes camaldulenses, ed. P. Lohe (Florence, 1980).

Formulario di epistole, Proemio, in *Scritti critici e teorici*, I, pp. 181–2.

Proemio al comento dantesco, in *Scritti critici e teorici*, I, pp. 100–64.

Prolusione petrarchesca, in *Scritti critici e teorici*, I, pp. 33–40.

Scritti critici e teorici, ed. R. Cardini (2 vols., Rome, 1974).

Translation of the Elder Pliny, Proemio, in *Scritti critici e teorici*, I, pp. 81–93.

Translation of Giovanni Simonetta's *Sforziade*, Proemio, in *Scritti critici e teorici*, I, pp. 187–91.

Xandra, in *Carmina omnia*, ed. A. Perosa (Florence, 1939), pp. 1–152.

Lanza, A. (ed.), *Polemiche e berte letterarie nella Firenze del primo Quattrocento* (1971; 2nd edn, Rome, 1989).

Lorenzo de' Medici, *Opere*, ed. A. Simioni (2 vols., Bari, 1913).

Maffei, Timoteo, *In sanctam rusticitatem litteras impugnantem*. Vatican Library, MS Vat. lat. 5076, fols. 1r–87r; Venice, Biblioteca Nazionale Marciana, MS Lat. XI 64 (4358); Florence, Biblioteca Laurenziana, MS Plut. 90 sup. 48, fols. 88r–125v.

Manetti, Giannozzo, *De vita et moribus trium illustrium poetarum Florentinorum*, in *Le vite di Dante, Petrarca e Boccaccio*, ed. A. Solerti (Milan, 1904), pp. 108–51.

Maramauro, Guglielmo, *Expositione sopra l' 'Inferno' di Dante Alligieri*, ed. P. G. Pisoni and S. Bellomo (Padua, 1998).

Matthew of Vendôme, *Ars versificatoria*, in E. Faral (ed.), *Les arts poétiques du XIIe et du XIIIe siècle*, Bibliothèque de l'École des hautes études, 238 (1923; rpt. Geneva, 1982), pp. 109–93; also in *Opera*, ed. F. Munari (3 vols., Rome 1977–88), III. Tr. A. E. Galyon (Ames IA, 1980); also tr. R. P. Parr (Milwaukee WI, 1981).

Mussato, Albertino, *Opera* (Venice, 1630) rpt. in J. Georg Graevius (ed.), *Thesaurus antiquitatem et historiarum Italiae* (Leiden, 1722), VI.2, cols. 34–62.

Ognibene della Scola, *De vita religiosa et monastica*. Vatican Library, MS Vat. lat. 4271.

Ottimo I: L''Ottimo commento' *della 'Divina Commedia': testo inedito d'un contemporaneo di Dante*, ed. A. Torri (3 vols., Pisa, 1827–9).

Ottimo III: extracts ed. G. Vandelli, 'Una nuova redazione dell'*Ottimo*', *Studi danteschi*, 14 (1930), 93–174.

Palmieri, Matteo, *Della vita civile*, ed. G. Belloni (Florence, 1982).

Petrarch, Francis, *Africa*, ed. N. Festa, Edizione nazionale, 1 (Florence, 1926).

Le familiari, ed. V. Rossi and U. Bosco (4 vols., Florence, 1933–42).

Invective contra medicum and *Collatio laureationis*, in *Opere latine* (2 vols., Turin, 1975), II, pp. 817–1023, 1255–83.

Lettere senili, tr. G. Fracasetti (2 vols., Florence, 1869–92).

Opera omnia (Basel, 1581).

Secretum, in *Opere latine*, ed. A. Bufano (2 vols., Turin, 1975), I, pp. 44–259.

Seniles, in *Opera omnia*, pp. 735–968.

Seniles V.2, ed. M. Berté (Florence, 1998).

Trionfi, ed. G. Bezzola (Milan, 1984).

De viris illustribus, ed. G. Martellotti, Edizione nazionale, 2 (Florence, 1964).

Piccolomini, Enea Silvio (Pius II), *Der Briefwechsel des Eneas Silvius Piccolomini*, ed. R. Wolkan, Fontes rerum austriacarum, 2 Abt., 61 (1909), 67 (1912), 68 (1918).

Epistola ad Ladislaum posthumum, in *Der Briefwechsel*, ed. Wolkan, Fontes rerum austriacarum, 2 Abt., 67 (1912), no. 40.

De liberorum educatione, ed. and tr. J. S. Nelson (Washington DC, 1940).

Opera omnia (Basel, 1551).

Pico della Mirandola, Giovan Francesco. See: Bembo, Pietro

Pico della Mirandola, Giovanni, *Epistle to Ermolao Barbaro*, in *Prosatori latini del Quattrocento*, pp. 804–22.

Pius II. See: Piccolomini, Enea Silvio

Polenton, Sicco, *Scriptorum illustrium latinae linguae libri XVIII*, ed. B. L. Ullman (Rome, 1928).

Poliziano, Angelo, *Lamia: Praelectio in Priora Aristotelis analytica*, ed. A. Wesseling (Leiden, 1986).

Miscellanea: Miscellaneorum centuria secunda, ed. V. Branca and M. P. Stocchi (4 vols., Florence, 1972).

Opera quae quidem extitere hactenus omnia (Basel, 1553).

'Oratio super Fabio Quintiliano et Statii *Sylvis*', in *Prosatori latini del quattrocento*, pp. 870–84.

Pontano, Giovanni, *De aspiratione* (Naples, 1481).

I dialoghi, ed. C. Previtera (Florence, 1943).

Prosatori latini del Quattrocento, ed. E. Garin (Milan and Naples, 1952).

Raffaele di Pornassio, *De consonantia nature et gratie*. Venice, Biblioteca Nazionale Marciana, MS Lat. III, 115 (2476).

Rinuccini, Alamanno, *Lettere ed orazioni*, ed. V. R. Giustiniani (Florence, 1953).

Rinuccini, Cino, *Invettiva*, in Lanza (ed.), *Polemiche* (1971) pp. 261–7.

Sabellico, Marcantonio, *De latinae linguae reparatione*, ed. G. Bottari (Messina, 1999).

Salutati, Coluccio, *Epistolario*, ed. F. Novati (4 vols., Rome, 1891–1905).

De fato et fortuna, ed. C. Bianca (Florence, 1985).

De laboribus Herculis, ed. B. L. Ullman (Zurich, 1951).

De nobilitate legum et medicinae, ed. E. Garin (Florence, 1947).

De seculo et religione, ed. B. L. Ullman (Florence, 1957).

Seriacopi, Massimo, 'Un commento inedito di fine Trecento ai canti 2–5 dell'*Inferno*', *Dante Studies*, 117 (1999), 199–244.

Serravalle, Giovanni Bertoldi da, *Translatio et comentum totius libri Dantis Aldigherii*, ed. M. da Civezza and T. Domenichelli (Prato, 1891).

'Talice da Ricaldone, Stefano', *La 'Commedia' di Dante Alighieri col commento inedito di Stefano Talice da Ricaldone*, ed. V. Promis and C. Negroni (3 vols., Milan, 1888).

Valla, Lorenzo, *Antidotum in Facium*, ed. A. Wesseling (Amsterdam, 1978).

Epistole, ed. O. Besomi and M. Regoliosi (Padua, 1984).

Gesta Ferdinandi Regis Aragonum, ed. O. Besomi (Padua, 1973).

Opera omnia (Basel, 1540), rpt. with intro. by E. Garin (2 vols., Turin, 1962).

Proems to *Elegantiarum linguae latinae libri VI*, in *Prosatori latini del Quattrocento*, pp. 594–630.

Vegio, Maffeo, *De educatione liberorum et eorum claris moribus*, ed. M. W. Fanning and A. S. Sullivan (2 vols., Washington DC, 1933–6).

Vergerio, Pier Paolo, *De ingenuis moribus*, ed. A. Gnesotto, *Atti e memorie della R. Accademia di scienze, lettere ed arti di Padova*, 34 (1917), 94–154.

Epistolario, ed. L. Smith (Rome 1934).

Villani, Filippo, *Expositio seu comentum super 'Comedia' Dantis Allegherii*, ed. S. Bellomo (Florence, 1989).

De origine civitatis Florentie et de eiusdem famosis civibus, ed. G. Tanturli (Padua, 1997).

Villani, Giovanni, *Cronica: con le continuazioni di Matteo e Filippo*, ed. G. Aquilecchia (Turin, 1979).

Le vite di Dante, Petrarca e Boccaccio scritte fino al secolo decimosesto, ed. A. Solerti (Milan, 1905).

Woodward, W. H., *Vittorino da Feltre and Other Humanist Educators* (Cambridge, 1897).

Secondary sources

Allen, Judson Boyce, *The Ethical Poetic of the Later Middle Ages: A Decorum of Convenient Distinction* (Toronto, 1982).

Ascoli, Albert R., 'Access to Authority: Dante in the Epistle to Cangrande', in Z. G. Barański (ed.), *Seminario dantesco internazionale / International Dante Seminar I* (Florence, 1997), pp. 309–52.

Azzetta, Luca, 'Le chiose alla *Commedia* di Andrea Lancia, l'*Epistola a Cangrande* e altre questioni dantesche', *L'Alighieri*, n. s. 21 (2003), 5–75.

Barański, Zygmunt G., *'Chiosar con altro testo': Leggere Dante nel Trecento* (Fiesole, 2001).

'*Comedía*: Notes on Dante, the Epistle to Cangrande, and Medieval Comedy', *Lectura Dantis*, 8 (1991), 26–55; rev. in Barański, *'Chiosar'*, pp. 41–76.

'Il *Convivio* e la poesia: problemi di definizione', in F. Tateo and D. M. Pegorari (eds.), *Contesti della 'Commedia': Lectura Dantis Fridericiana 2002–2003* (Bari, 2004), pp. 9–64.

Dante e i segni: Saggi per una storia intellettuale di Dante Alighieri (Naples, 2000).

'The Poetics of Meter: "terza rima", *canto*, *canzon*, *cantica*', in T. J. Cachey, Jr. (ed.), *Dante Now* (South Bend IN and London, 1994), pp. 3–41.

'*Sole nuovo, luce nuova': Saggi sul rinnovamento culturale in Dante* (Turin, 1996).

Barański, Zygmunt G. (ed.) *'Libri poetarum in quattuor species dividuntur': Essays on Dante and 'Genre'*, suppl. 2, *The Italianist*, 15 (1995).

Barberi Squarotti, G., 'Le poetiche del Trecento in Italia', in *Momenti e problemi di storia dell'estetica*, Problemi ed orientamenti critici di lingua e di letteratura italiana, 5 (4 vols., Milan, 1959–61), I, pp. 255–324.

Barbi, Michele, 'Benvenuto da Imola e non Stefano Talice da Ricaldone', in *Problemi di critica dantesca: prima serie* (Florence, 1934), pp. 429–53.

'La lettura di Benvenuto da Imola e i suoi rapporti con altri commenti', in *Problemi di critica dantesca: seconda serie* (Florence, 1941), pp. 435–70.

Bareiss, Karl-Heinz, *Comoedia: Die Entwicklung der Komödiendiskussion von Aristotles bis Ben Jonson* (Frankfurt, 1982).

Bargagli Stoffi-Mühlethaler, B., '"Poeta", "poetare" e sinonimi: studio semantico su Dante e la poesia duecentesca', *Studi di lessicografia italiana*, 8 (1986), 5–299.

Barolini, Teodolinda, *Dante's Poets* (Princeton NJ, 1984).

The Undivine Comedy: Detheologizing Dante (Princeton NJ, 1993).

Baron, Hans, *The Crisis of the Early Italian Renaissance* (2nd edn, Princeton NJ, 1966).

Baroni, G., and Pettinelli, R. A., *Storia della critica letteraria in Italia* (Turin, 1997).

Baxandall, Michael, *Giotto and the Orators: Humanist Observers of Painting in Italy and the Discovery of Pictorial Composition* (Oxford, 1971).

Bellomo, Saverio, 'Primi appunti sull'*Ottimo Commento* dantesco', *Giornale storico della letteratura italiana*, 157 (1980), 533–40.

Berisso, Marco, 'Per una definizione di prosopopea: Dante, *Convivio*, III.ix.2', *Lingua e stile*, 26 (1991), 121–32.

Billanovich, G., 'Giovanni del Virgilio, Pietro da Moglio, Francesco da Fiano', *Italia medievale e umanistica*, 6 (1963), 208–23.

Restauri boccacceschi (Rome, 1945).

Bolgar, R. R., *The Classical Heritage and its Beneficiaries* (1954; rpt. Cambridge, 1973).

Boli, Todd, 'Boccaccio's *Trattatello in laude di Dante* or *Dante Resartus*', *Renaissance Quarterly*, 41 (1988), 389–412.

Borghi, L., 'La dottrina morale di Coluccio Salutati', *Annali della Scuola Normale di Pisa*, s. 2, 3 (1934), 75–102.

Botterill, Steven, '"Quae non licet homini loqui": The Ineffability of Mystical Experience in *Paradiso* 1 and the Epistle to Can Grande', *MLR*, 83 (1988), 332–41.

Brugnoli, Giorgio, 'Epistole: Introduzione', in Dante Alighieri, *Opere minori* (2 vols., Milan and Naples, 1979–1988), II, 512–21.

Buck, August, *Italienische Dichtungslehre vom Mittelalter bis zum Ausgang der Renaissance*, Beihefte zur Zeitschrift für Romanische Philologie, 94 (Tübingen, 1952).

Buck, August (ed.), *Die italienische Literatur im Zeitalter Dantes und am Übergang vom Mittelalter zur Renaissance*, Grundriß der romanischen Literaturen des Mittelalters, 10.1 (Heidelberg, 1987), pp. 166–208.

Cardini, Roberto, *La critica del Landino* (Florence, 1973).

Cavallari, Elisabetta, *La fortuna di Dante nel Trecento* (Florence, 1921).

Cecchini, Enzo, 'Introduzione', in Dante Alighieri, *Epistola a Cangrande* (Florence, 1995), pp. v–li.

Cloetta, Wilhelm, *Komödie und Tragödie im Mittelalter* (Halle, 1890).

Contini, Gianfranco, *Un'idea di Dante* (Turin, 1976).

Varianti e altra linguistica (Turin, 1970).

Craven, W. G., 'Coluccio Salutati's Defence of Poetry', *Renaissance Studies*, 10 (1996), 1–30.

Curtius, Ernst Robert, 'Dante und das lateinische Mittelalter', *Romanische Forschungen*, 57 (1943), 153–85.

Europäische Literatur und lateinisches Mittelalter (2nd edn, Bern, 1948). English tr. of the first edition under the title *European Literature and the Latin Middle Ages*, by W. R. Trask (London, 1953).

D'Amico, J., 'The Progress of Renaissance Latin Prose: The Case of Apuleianism', *Renaissance Quarterly*, 37 (1984), 351–92.

Da Prati, P., *Giovanni Dominici e l'umanesimo* (Naples 1965).

Denley, Peter, 'Giovanni Dominici's Opposition to Humanism', *Religion and Humanism*, Studies in Church History, 17 (Oxford 1982), pp. 103–14.

Dionisotti, Carlo, *Gli umanisti e il volgare fra Quattro e Cinquecento* (Florence, 1968).

Douglas, R. M., 'Talent and Vocation in Humanist and Protestant Thought', in T. K. Rabb and J. E. Seigel (eds.), *Action and Conviction in Early Modern Europe* (Princeton NJ, 1969), pp. 261–98.

Dronke, Peter, *Dante and Medieval Latin Traditions* (Cambridge, 1986).

Emerton, E., *Humanism and Tyranny* (Cambridge MA, 1925).

Enciclopedia dantesca (6 vols., Rome, 1970–9).

Field, Arthur, *The Origins of the Platonic Academy of Florence* (Princeton NJ, 1988).

Fisher, A., 'Three Meditations on the Destruction of Virgil's Statue: The Early Humanist Theory of Poetry', *Renaissance Quarterly*, 40 (1987), 607–35.

Fubini, R., *L'umanesimo italiano e i suoi storici: Origini rinascimentali – critica moderna* (Milan, 2001).

'L'umanista: ritorno di un paradigma? Saggio per un profilo storico dal Petrarca ad Erasmo', *Archivio storico italiano*, 147 (1989), 435–508.

Garin, E., *La cultura filosofica del Rinascimento italiano* (Florence, 1961).

L'educazione in Europa (1400–1600) (Bari, 1957).

'Le favole antiche', in Garin, *Medioevo e Rinascimento*, pp. 63–84.

Medioevo e Rinascimento (Bari, 1976).

L'umanesimo italiano (Bari, 1964); tr. by P. Munz as *Italian Humanism* (Oxford, 1965).

Gilson, Simon, *Dante and Renaissance Florence* (Cambridge, 2005).

Giustiniani, V. R., 'Il Filelfo: L'interpretazione allegorica di Virgilio e la tripartizione platonica dell'animo', in V. Branca *et al.* (eds.), *Umanesimo e Rinascimento: Studi offerti a P. O. Kristeller* (Florence, 1980), pp. 33–44.

Gorni, Guglielmo, 'Le forme primarie del testo poetico', in A. Asor Rosa (ed.), *Letteratura italiana* (9 vols., Turin, 1982–2000), III.i, pp. 439–518.

'Storia del Certame Coronario', *Rinascimento*, 12 (1972), 135–81.

Grafton, A. T., 'Renaissance Readers and Ancient Texts: Comments on some Commentaries', *Renaissance Quarterly*, 38 (1985), 615–49.

Grafton, A. T., and Jardine, L., 'Humanism and the School of Guarino: A Problem of Evaluation', *Past and Present*, 66 (1982), 78–9.

Greenfield, Concetta Carestia, *Humanist and Scholastic Poetics, 1250–1500* (Lewisburg PA, 1981).

Grendler, Paul F., *Schooling in Renaissance Italy: Literacy and Learning 1300–1600* (Baltimore MD and London, 1989).

Guthmüller, B., 'Lateinisch und volksprachliche Kommentare zu Ovids Metamorphosen', in A. Buck and O. Herding (eds.), *Der Kommentar in der Renaissance*, Kommission für Humanismusforschung, Mitteilung 1 (Boppard, 1975).

Hall, Ralph G., and Sowell, Madison U., '*Cursus* in the Can Grande Epistle: A Forger Shows His Hand?', *Lectura Dantis*, 5 (1989), 89–104.

Hankins, James, *Plato in the Italian Renaissance* (2 vols., Leiden and New York, 1990).

Hardie, Colin, 'The Epistle to Cangrande Again', *Deutsches Dante-Jahrbuch*, 38 (1960), 51–74.

Hollander, Robert, *Allegory in Dante's 'Commedia'* (Princeton NJ, 1969).

Dante's 'Epistle to Cangrande' (Ann Arbor MI, 1993).

Holmes, G., *The Florentine Enlightenment 1400–1450* (Oxford, 1992).

Iannucci, Amilcare A. (ed.), *Dante e la 'bella scola' della poesia: Autorità e sfida poetica* (Ravenna, 1993).

'Dante's Theory of Genres', *Dante Studies*, 91 (1975), 1–25.

Jenaro-MacLennan, L., 'The Dating of Guido da Pisa's Commentary on the *Inferno*', *Italian Studies*, 23 (1968), 19–54.

The Trecento Commentaries on the 'Divina Commedia' and the 'Epistle to Cangrande' (Oxford, 1974).

Kallendorf, C., 'Cristoforo Landino's *Aeneid* and the Humanist Critical Tradition', *Renaissance Quarterly*, 36 (1983), 519–46.

'The Rhetorical Criticism of Literature in Early Italian Humanism from Boccaccio to Landino', *Rhetorica*, 2 (1983), 33–59.

Kelly, Henry A., *Tragedy and Comedy from Dante to Pseudo-Dante*, University of California Publications in Modern Philology, 121 (Berkeley CA, 1989).

Kristeller, P. O., 'The Humanist Movement', in Kristeller, *The Classics and Renaissance Thought* (Cambridge MA, 1955), pp. 2–23.

La Favia, Louis Marcello, *Benvenuto Rambaldi da Imola: dantista* (Madrid, 1977).

Lindhardt, J., *Rhetor, Poeta, Historicus: Studien über rhetorische Erkenntnis und Lebensanschauung im italienischen Renaissancehumanismus* (Leiden, 1979).

Mancini, Augusto, 'Nuovi dubbi ed ipotesi sulla Epistola a Cangrande', *Atti della R. Accademia d'Italia, rendiconti: classe di scienze morali, storiche e filologiche*, ser. 7, 4 (1943), 227–42.

Martellotti, G., 'Latinità del Petrarca', *Studi petrarcheschi*, 7 (1961), 219–30.

Martin, Alfred W. O. von, *Coluccio Salutati und das humanistische Lebensideal*, Beiträge zur Kulturgeschichte des Mittelalters und der Renaissance, 23 (Leipzig, 1916).

Martinelli, Bruno, 'La dottrina dell'Empireo nell'Epistola a Cangrande (capp. 24–37)', *Studi danteschi*, 57 (1985), 49–143.

Martines, L., *Power and Imagination* (London, 1979).

McLaughlin, M. L., 'Humanist Concepts of Renaissance and Middle Ages in the Tre- and Quattrocento', *Renaissance Studies*, 2 (1988), 131–42.

Literary Imitation in the Italian Renaissance: The Theory and Practice of Literary Imitation in Italy from Dante to Bembo (Oxford, 1995).

Mazzoni, Francesco, 'La critica dantesca del secolo XIV', *Cultura e scuola*, 13–14 (1965), 285–97.

'L'Epistola a Cangrande', *Atti della Accademia Nazionale dei Lincei: classe di scienze morali, storiche e filologiche*, ser. 8, 10 (1955), 157–98.

'Guido da Pisa interprete di Dante e la sua fortuna presso il Boccaccio', *Studi danteschi*, 35 (1958), 20–128.

'Jacopo della Lana e la crisi nell'interpretazione della *Divina Commedia*', in *Dante e Bologna nei tempi di Dante*, VII centenario della nascita di Dante, 11 (Bologna, 1967), pp. 265–306.

'Per la storia della critica dantesca, I: Jacopo Alighieri e Graziolo Bambaglioli (1322–24)', *Studi danteschi*, 30 (1951), 157–202.

'Pietro Alighieri interprete di Dante', *Studi danteschi*, 40 (1963), 279–360.

Mengaldo, Pier Vincenzo, 'Dante come critico', *La parola del testo*, 1 (1997), 36–54.

Linguistica e retorica di Dante (Pisa, 1978).

Michel, K., *Der liber de consonancia nature et gracie des Raphael von Pornaxio*, BGPM, 18.1 (Münster, 1915).

Minnis, Alastair J., *Medieval Theory of Authorship: Scholastic Literary Attitudes in the Later Middle Ages* (1984; 2nd edn, Aldershot, 1988).

Minnis, Alastair J., and Scott, A. B., with Wallace, David (eds.), *Medieval Literary Theory and Criticism, c. 1100–c. 1375: The Commentary-Tradition* (1988; rev. edn, Oxford, 1991; rpt. 2001).

Montgomery, R., *The Reader's Eye* (Berkeley CA, 1979).

Moore, Edward, 'The Genuineness of the Dedicatory Epistle to Can Grande', in *Studies on Dante: Third Series*, ed. C. Hardie (Oxford, 1968), pp. 284–369.

Morici, M., 'Dante e Ciriaco d'Ancona', *Giornale dantesco*, 7 (1899), 70–7.

Müller, Gregor, *Mensch und Bildung im italienischen Renaissance-Humanismus. Vittorino da Feltre und die humanistischen Erziehungsdenker* (Baden-Baden, 1984).

Nardi, Bruno, 'Osservazioni sul medievale *accessus ad auctores* in rapporto all'Epistola a Cangrande', in *Studi e problemi di critica testuale: Convengno di studi di filologia italiana nel centenario della Commissione per I testi di lingua, 7–9 aprile 1960* (Bologna, 1961), pp. 273–305.

Il punto sull'Epistola a Cangrande (Florence, 1960).

Nasti, Paola, 'Autorità, *topos* e modello: Salomone nei commenti trecenteschi alla *Commedia*', *The Italianist*, 19 (1999), 5–49.

'La memoria del *Cantico* nella *Vita Nuova*: una nota preliminare', *The Italianist*, 18 (1998), 14–27.

Orvieto, E., 'Guido da Pisa e il commento inedito all'*Inferno* dantesco: Le chiose al trentatreesimo canto', *Italica*, 46 (1969), 17–32.

Padoan, Giorgio, 'La "mirabile visione" di Dante e l'Epistola a Cangrande', in Padoan, *Il pio Enea, l'empio Ulisse* (Ravenna, 1977), pp. 30–63.

L'ultima opera di Giovanni Boccaccio: le 'Esposizioni sopra il Dante' (Padua, 1959).

Paolazzi, Carlo, *Dante e la 'Comedia' nel Trecento* (Milan, 1989).

'Petrarca, Boccaccio e il *Trattatello in laude di Dante*', *Studi danteschi*, 55 (1983), 165–249.

Paratore, Ettore, *Tradizione e struttura in Dante* (Florence, 1968).

Parker, Deborah, *Commentary and Ideology: Dante in the Renaissance* (Durham NC and London, 1993).

Pépin, Jean, *Dante et la tradition de l'allégorie* (Montreal and Paris, 1971).

Pertile, Lino, 'Canto-cantica-Comedía e l'Epistola a Cangrande', Lectura Dantis, 9 (1991), 105–23.

Picone, Michelangelo, 'Baratteria e stile comico in Dante (Inferno XXI–XXIII)', in G. C. Alessio and R. Hollander (eds.), Saggi danteschi americani (Milan, 1989), pp. 63–86.

'Dante e la tradizione arturiana', Romanische Forschungen, 94 (1982), 1–18.

'Paradiso IX: Folchetto e la diaspora trobadorica', Medioevo romanzo, 8 (1981–3), 47–89.

'Vita Nuova' e tradizione romanza (Padua, 1979).

Picone, Michelangelo (ed.) Dante e le forme dell'allegoresi (Ravenna, 1987).

Picone, Michelangelo, and Crivelli, Tatiana (eds.), Dante: Mito e poesia (Florence, 1999).

Pisoni, Pier Giacomo, 'Guglielmo Maramauro commentatore di Dante e amico del Petrarca', Studi petrarcheschi, 1 (1984), 253–5.

Procaccioli, Paolo, Filologia ed esegesi dantesca nel Quattrocento: l''Inferno' nel 'Comento sopra La comedia' di Cristoforo Landino (Florence, 1989).

Quadlbauer, Franz, Die antike Theorie der 'Genera dicendi' im lateinischen Mittelalter, Österreichische Akademie der Wissenschaften, philosophisch-historische Klasse, Sitzungsberichte 241, 2 (Vienna, 1962).

Quint, D., 'Humanism and Modernity: A Reconsideration of Bruni's Dialogus', Renaissance Quarterly, 38 (1985), 423–45.

Ricklin, Thomas (ed.), Das Schreiben an Cangrande della Scala (Hamburg, 1993).

Rizzo, S., 'Il latino del Petrarca nelle Familiari', in A. C. Dionisotti, A. Grafton and J. Kraye (eds.), The Uses of Greek and Latin (London, 1988), pp. 41–56.

'Petrarca, il latino e il volgare', Quaderni petrarcheschi, 7 (1990), 7–40.

Ricerche sul latino umanistico (Rome, 2002).

Robey, David, 'Humanism and Education in the Early Quattrocento: The De ingenuis moribus of P. P. Vergerio', Bibliothèque d'Humanisme et Renaissance, 42 (1980), 27–58.

'P. P. Vergerio the Elder: Republicanism and Civic Values in the Work of an Early Humanist', Past and Present, 58 (1973), 3–37.

'Studia Humanitatis, the Humanities, Modern Languages', in C. E. J. Griffiths and R. Hastings (eds.), The Cultural Heritage of the Italian Renaissance (Lewiston NY, 1993), pp. 78–109.

'Virgil's Statue at Mantua and the Defence of Poetry: An Unpublished Letter of 1397', Rinascimento, 20 (1969), 183–203.

'Vittorino da Feltre e Vergerio', in N. Giannetto (ed.), Vittorino e la sua scuola (Florence, 1981), pp. 241–53.

Rocca, Luigi, Di alcuni commenti della 'Divina Commedia' composti nei primi vent'anni dopo la morte di Dante (Florence, 1891).

Ronconi, G., s.v. 'Dominici', in Dizionario critico della letteratura italiana (3 vols., Turin, 1973), II, pp. 11–17.

'Il grammatico Antonio Beccaria difensore della poesia e la sua "Oratio in Terentium"', in *Medioeveo e Rinascimento Veneto (in onore di L. Lazzarini)* (2 vols., Padua, 1979), I, pp. 397–426.

Le origini delle dispute umanistiche sulla poesia (Rome, 1976).

Rüben, H., *Der Humanist und Regularkanoniker Timoteo Maffei aus Verona (c. 1415–70)* (Aachen, 1975).

Sabbadini, R., *Storia del ciceronianismo* (Turin, 1885).

Sandkühler, Bruno, *Die frühen Dantekommentare und ihr Verhältnis zur mittelalterlichen Kommentartradition* (Munich, 1967).

Santoro, M., 'Poliziano o il Magnifico?', *Giornale italiano di filologia*, 1 (1948), 139–49.

Seigel, Jerrold E., '"Civic Humanism" or Ciceronian Rhetoric?', *Past and Present*, 34 (1966), 3–48.

Rhetoric and Philosophy in Renaissance Humanism: The Union of Eloquence and Wisdom, Petrarch to Valla (Princeton, 1968).

Seznec, J., *La Survivance des dieux antiques* (London, 1940); tr. B. F. Sessions as *The Survival of the Pagan Gods* (New York, 1953).

Tateo, Francesco, *Questioni di poetica dantesca* (Bari, 1972).

'Retorica' e 'poetica' fra Medioevo e Rinascimento (Bari, 1960).

Tavoni, Mirko, *Latino, grammatica, volgare: storia di una questione umanistica* (Padua, 1984).

Todorov, Tzvetan, *Symbolisme et interprétation* (Paris, 1978); tr. by C. Porter as *Symbolism and Interpretation* (London, 1983).

Trabalza, C., *La critica letteraria (Dai primordi dell'Umanesimo all'Età nostra)*, vol. II (Milan, 1915) [= O. Bacci and C. Trabalza, *La critica letteraria*, II].

Trinkaus, C., *'In Our Image and Likeness': Humanity and Divinity in Italian Humanist Thought* (2 vols., London, 1970).

Trovato, Mario, 'Il primo trattato del *Convivio* visto alla luce dell'*accessus ad auctores*', *Misure critiche*, 6 (1976), 5–14.

Ullman, B. L., *The Humanism of Coluccio Salutati* (Padua, 1963).

Vallone, Aldo, *Storia della critica dantesca dal XIV al XX secolo* (2 vols., Padua, 1981).

Vasoli, C., 'L'estetica dell'Umanesimo e del Rinascimento', in *Momenti e problemi di storia dell'estetica*, Problemi ed orientament critici di lingua e di letteratura italiana, 5 (4 vols., Milan, 1959–61), I, pp. 325–43.

Villa, Claudia, *La 'Lectura Terentii'* (Padua, 1984).

Vitale, Maurizio, *La questione della lingua* (Palermo, 1978).

Vossler, K., *Poetische Theorien in der Italienischen Frührenaissance*, Literaturhistorische Forschungen, 12 (Berlin, 1900).

Witt, Ronald G., 'Coluccio Salutati and the Conception of the *Poeta Theologus* in the Fourteenth Century', *Renaissance Quarterly*, 30 (1977), 53–70.

Hercules at the Crossroads: The Life, Works and Thought of Coluccio Salutati (Durham NC, 1983).

Zabughin, V., *Vergilio nel Rinascimento italiano* (2 vols., Bologna, 1921–3).

Zippel, G. (ed.), 'Le vite di Paolo II di Gaspare di Verona e Michele Canensi', *Rerum italicarum scriptores*, 3.16 (2nd edn, Città di Castello, 1904).

Byzantine literary theory and criticism

Primary sources

Anecdota graeca, ed. J. Boissonade (4 vols., Paris, 1829–32).

Anecdota graeca oxoniensia, ed. J. Cramer (4 vols., Oxford, 1835–7).

Arethas, *Arethae scripta minora* (2 vols., ed. L. Westerink, Leipzig, 1968–72).

Basilakes, Nikephoros, *Orationes et epistolae*, ed. A. Garzya (Leipzig, 1984).

Bryennios, Joseph, ['On the Causes of Our Sufferings'], in L. Oikonomos (ed.), 'L'état intellectuel et moral des byzantins vers le milieu du XIVe siècle d'après une page de Joseph Bryennios', *Mélanges Charles Diehl* (2 vols., Paris, 1930), I, pp. 225–33.

Choniates, Michael, *Ta sôzomena*, ed. S. Lambros (2 vols., 1879–80; rpt. Groningen, 1968).

Chortasmenos, John, *Briefe, Gedichte, und kleine Schriften*, ed. H. Hunger, Wiener Byzantische Studien, 7 (Vienna, 1969).

Choumnos, Nikephoros, *Peri logôn kai kriseôs*, AGr, III, pp. 356–64.

Pros tous dycheraintas, AGr, III, pp. 365–91.

Demetrius, *Peri hermeneias* [On Style], ed. L. Radermacher (1901; rpt. Stuttgart., 1967).

Dionysius of Halicarnassus, *Dionysii Halicarnasei quae extant*, vols. 5 and 6, ed. H. Usener and L. Radermacher (Leipzig, 1899–1929).

Eustathios, *Commentarii ad Homeri Iliadem*, ed. M. van der Valk (4 vols., Leiden, 1971–6).

Opuscula, ed. L. Tafel (Nuremberg, 1832).

Scholia vetera in Pindari carmina, Prooimion, ed. A. Drachmann (3 vols., 1927; rpt. Amsterdam, 1969), III, pp. 285–306.

'Siege of Thessalonike', ed. S. Kyriakides, *Espugnazione di Tessalonica*, Testi e monumenti, 5 (Palermo, 1961).

Fontes rerum byzantinarum, ed. V. Regel and N. Novasadskij (1892–1917; rpt. Leipzig, 1982).

Gennadios Scholarios, *Œuvres*, ed. L. Petit *et al.* (8 vols., Paris, 1928–36).

Glykas, Michael, ['Poem from his Jail Cell'], ed. E. Legrand in his *Bibliothèque greque vulgaire* (9 vols., 1880–1902), I, pp. 18–37.

Gregory of Nazianzus, *Sermones*, PG 35 and 36.

Gregoras, Nikephoros, *Historia*, ed. L. Schoepen (3 vols., Bonn, 1829–55).

Phlorentios, ed. A. Jahn, *Neue Jahrbücher für Philologie und Pädagogik*, Suppl. Bd., 10 (1844), 485–536.

Hermogenes, *Opera*, ed. H. Rabe (1913; rpt. Stuttgart, 1969).

['On Types of Style'], tr. C.W. Wooten (Chapel Hill NC, 1987).

John Doxapatres, *Prolegomena*, in PS, pp. 80–155, 304–18, 360–74, 420–9.

John Mauropous, *Opera quae in codice Vaticano graeco 676 supersunt*, ed. P. de Lagarde, *Abhandlungen der Göttinger Gesellschaft der Wissenschaften*, 28 (1881), 1–228.

John Sardianus, *Scholia ad Aphthonium*, ed. H. Rabe (Leipzig, 1928).

John Sikeliotes, *Scholia ad Hermogenis Ideas*, in RG, VI, pp. 56–504.

Josephus, Flavius, *Opera omnia*, ed. B. Niese (7 vols., Berlin, 1887–94).

Kydones, Demetrios, *Apologia*, in G. Mercati (ed.), *Notizie di Procoro e Demetrio Cidone, Manuele Caleca e Teodoro Meletiniota ad altri appunti per la storia della teologia e della letteratura bizantina del secolo XIV* (Vatican City, 1931), pp. 359–435.

['Monody for the Dead of Thessalonike'], PG 109, 639–52.

Lapithes, Georgios, 'Stichoi politikoi', ed. J. Boissonade, *Notices et extraits des manuscrits de la Bibliothèque Nationale*, 12.2 (Paris, 1831), 15–69.

Longinus, *Peri hypseôs* [On the Sublime], ed. D. A. Russell (Oxford, 1964).

Malakes, Euthymios, ['Encomium to Manuel'], ed. K. Bonis, [*Theologika*], 19 (1949), 524–50.

Manasses, Konstantinos, *Oratio ad Manuelem*, ed. K. Horna, *Wiener Studien*, 28 (1906), 173–84.

Menander of Laodicea, *Treatises* and *Testimonia*, ed. and tr. D. A. Russell and N. G. Wilson (Oxford, 1981).

Mesaiônikê bibliothekê, ed. K. Sathas (7 vols., Venice, 1872–94).

Metochites, Theodoros, *Epistasia*, ed. M. Gigante in his *Saggio critico su Demostene e Aristide* (Milan, 1969), pp. 47–83.

Logoi, ed. I. Ševčenko in his *Études sur la polémique entre Théodore Métochite et Nicéphore Choumnos* (Brussels, 1962), pp. 189–265.

Miscellanea, ed. C. Müller (1821; rpt. Amsterdam, 1966).

[Poems], ed. I. Ševčenko and J. Featherstone, 'Two Poems by Theodore Metochites', *Greek Orthodox Theological Review*, 26 (1981), 1–45.

Michael Italikos, *Lettres et discours*, ed. P. Gautier (Paris, 1972).

Niketas David, *The Encomium of Gregory Nazianzen*, ed. J. Rizzo, Subsidia hagiographica, 58 (Brussels, 1976).

Niketas Eugenianos, [*Monody for Theodore Prodromos*], ed. L. Petit, 'Monodie de Nicétas Eugénianos sur Théodore Prodrome', [*Vizantijskij vremennik*], 9 (1907), 452–63.

Palaiologos, Andronikos, *Le Roman de Callimaque et de Chrysorrhoé: texte établie et traduit*, ed. M. Pichard (Paris, 1956).

Palaiologos, Manuel, *The Letters of Manuel II Palaeologus*, ed. G. T. Dennis, CFHB, 8 (Washington DC, 1977).

Philagathos of Rossano, *Commentatio in Charicleam*, in *Heliodori Aethiopica*, ed. A. Colonna (Rome, 1938), pp. 366–70.

Photios, *Epistulae et Amphilochia*, ed. B. Laourdas and L. Westerink (6 vols. in 7, Leipzig, 1983–88).

Bibliotheca, ed. R. Henry (9 vols., Paris, 1959–91).

Planudes, Maximos, *Epistulae*, ed. M. Treu (1890; rpt. Amsterdam, 1960).

Scholia ad Hermogenem, RG, V, pp. 212–576.

Prolegomenôn syllogê, ed. H. Rabe (Leipzig, 1935).

Psellos, Michael, *Charaktêres paterôn*, ed. J. Boissonade, [Michael Psellus], *De operatione daemonum* (Nuremburg, 1838), pp. 124–30.

['Encomium to J. Mauropous'], MB, V, pp. 142–67.

Essays on Euripides and George of Pisidia and on Heliodorus and on Achilles Tatius, ed. A. R. Dyck, Byzantina vindobonensia, 16 (Vienna, 1986).

['On the Rhetorical Character of Gregory Nazianzus'], ed. A. Mayer, *Byzantinische Zeitschrift*, 20 (1911), 48–60.

Peri rhêtorikês, ed. P. Gautier, 'Michel Psellos et la rhétorique de Longin', *Prometheus*, 3 (1977), 193–203.

Peri synthekês, ed. G. Aujac, 'Michel Psellos et Denys d'Halicarnasse: le traité "Sur la composition des éléments du langage"', *Revue des études byzantines*, 33 (1975), 257–75.

Scripta minora, ed. E. Kurtz and F. Drexl (2 vols., Milan, 1936–41).

Les regestes des actes du patriarchat de Constantinople, I: Les actes des patriarches, ed. V. Grumel (Paris, 1932–47).

Rhetores graeci, ed. C. Walz (9 vols., Stuttgart and London, 1832–6).

Scholia in Dionysii Thracis artem grammaticam, ed. A. Hilgard (Leipzig, 1901).

Theodore Prodromos, *Encomia to Aristenos*, ed. F. J. G. de La Porte du Theil, *Notices et extraits des manuscrits de la Bibliothèque nationale*, 6 (1801), 525–9, 552–8, 561–5.

[Poems], ed. W. Hörandner, *Theodorus Prodromos: historische Gedichte*, Wiener Byzantinische Studien, 11 (Vienna, 1974).

[Satires], ed. G. Podestà, 'Le Satire lucianesche di Teodoro Prodromo', *Aevum*, 19 (1945), 239–52; 21 (1947), 3–25.

Tzetzes, John, ['Allegories on the *Iliad*'], ed. J. Boissonade, *Tzetzae Allegoriae Iliadis* (Paris, 1851).

['Allegories on the *Odyssey*'], ed. H. Hunger, 'Johannes Tzetzes, Allegorien zur Odyssee, Buch 1–12', *Byzantinische Zeitschrift*, 49 (1956), 249–310.

['Allegories on the *Theogony*'], ed. C. Wendel, 'Das unbekannte Schlußstück der Theogonie des Tzetzes', *Byzantinische Zeitschrift*, 40 (1940), 24–6.

[*Chiliades*], ed. P. A. M. Leone, *Ioannis Tzetzae Historiae* (Naples, 1968).

Epistulae, ed. P. A. M. Leone (Leipzig, 1972).

Iambi, ed. P. A. M. Leone, *Rivista di studi bizantini e neoellenici*, 6–7 (1969–70), 127–56.

['Paraphrase of Hermogenes'], ed. J. Cramer, *AGrO*, IV, pp. 1–148.

Scholia in Aristophanem, pars 4, ed. L. Massa Positano, D. Holwerda and W. J. W. Koster (4 vols., Groningen and Amsterdam, 1960–4).

Zigabenos, Euthymios, *Commentaria in psalmos*, PG 128, 41–1326.

Secondary sources

Alexiou, Margaret, 'A Critical Reappraisal of Eustathios Makrembolites' *Hysmine and Hysminias*', *Byzantine and Modern Greek Studies*, 3 (1977), 23–43.

Aujac, Germaine, 'Michel Psellos et Denys d'Halicarnasse: le traité "Sur la composition des elements du langage"', *Revue des études byzantines*, 33 (1975), 257–75.

Baldwin, Barry, 'Photius and Poetry', *Byzantine and Modern Greek Studies*, 4 (1978), 9–14.

'A Talent to Abuse: Some Aspects of Byzantine Satire', *Byzantinische Forschungen*, 8 (1982), 19–28.

Bateman, John, 'The Critique of Isocrates' Style in Photius' *Bibliotheca*', *Illinois Classical Studies*, 6 (1981), 182–96.

Beaton, Roderick, *The Medieval Greek Romance* (1989; rev. edn, London, 1996).

'The Rhetoric of Poverty: The Lives and Opinions of Theodore Prodromos', *Byzantine and Modern Greek Studies*, 11 (1987), 1–28.

Beck, Hans-Georg, *Das literarische Schaffen der Byzantiner*, Sitzungsberichte der Österreichischen Akadamie der Wissenschaften, philosophisch-historische Klasse, 294.4 (Vienna, 1974).

Browning, R., 'The Patriarchal Schools of Constantinople', *Byzantion*, 32 (1962), 167–202; 33 (1963), 11–40.

Buchwald, Wolfgang, Hohlweg, Armin, and Prinz, Otto, *Tusculum-Lexicon griechischer und lateinischer Autoren des Altertums und des Mittelalters* (3rd edn, Munich, 1982).

Cesaretti, Paolo, 'Bisanzio allegorica (XI–XII secolo)', *Strumenti critici*, n.s. 5 (1990), 23–44.

Conley, Thomas M., 'Late Classical and Medieval Greek Rhetorics', in his *Rhetoric in the European Tradition* (Chicago and London, 1990), pp. 53–71.

'Practice to Theory: Byzantine "Poetrics"', in J. Abbenes, S. Slings and I. Sluiter (eds.), *Greek Literary Theory after Aristotle* (Amsterdam, 1995), pp. 310–20.

de Vries van der Velden, Eva, *Théodore Métochite: une réévaluation* (Amsterdam, 1987).

Diller, Aubrey, 'Photius' *Bibliotheca* in Byzantine Literature', *Dumbarton Oaks Papers*, 16 (1962), 389–96.

Dostálova, Ruzena, 'Zur Entwicklung der Literarästhetik in Byzanz von Gregorios von Nazianz zu Eustathios', in V. Vavrínek (ed.), *Beiträge zur byzantinischen Geschichte im 9. – 11. Jahrhundert* (Prague, 1978), pp. 143–77.

Garzya, Antonio, 'Literarische und rhetorische Polemiken der Komnenenzeit', *Byzantinoslavica*, 34 (1973), 1–14.

'Topik und Tendenz in der byzantinischen Literatur', *Anzeiger der Österreichischen Akadamie der Wissenschaften, Philosophisch-historische Klasse*, 113 (1976), 301–19; Italian tr. in Garzya, *Il mandarino e il quotidiano: saggi sulla letteratura tardoantica e bizantina* (Naples, 1983), pp. 11–34.

Hunger, Herbert, *Anonyme Metaphrase zu Anna Komnene, Alexias XI –XII*, Wiener Byzantinische Studien, 15 (1981).

'Die byzantinische Literatur der Komnenenzeit: Versuch einer Neubewertung', *Anzeiger der Österreichischen Akadamie der Wissenschaften, Philosophisch-historische Klasse*, 105 (1968), 59–76.

Die hochsprachliche profane Literatur der Byzantiner (2 vols., Munich, 1978).

Johannes Chortasmenos: Briefe, Gedichte, und kleine Schriften, Wiener Byzantinische Studien, 7 (Vienna, 1969).

'Johannes Tzetzes, Allegorien zur Odyssee, Buch 1–12', *Byzantinische Zeitschrift*, 49 (1956), 249–310.

'Zeitgeschichte in der Rhetorik des sterbenden Byzanz', *Wiener Archiv für Slawentums und Osteuropas*, 3 (1959), 152–61.

Hunger, Herbert, and Ševčenko, Ihor, *Des Nikephoros Blemmydes [Basilikos Andrias] und dessen Metaphrase von Georgios Galesiotes und Georgios Oinaiotes*, Wiener Byzantinische Studien, 18 (Vienna, 1986).

Jeffreys, Elizabeth, 'The Sevastokratorissa Eirene as Literary Patroness: The Monk Iakovos', *Jahrbuch der Österreichischen Byzantinistik*, 32 (1982), 63–71.

Jeffreys, Michael, 'The Nature and Origins of the Political Verse', *Dumbarton Oaks Papers*, 28 (1974), 141–95.

Kazhdan, Alexander, *Studies on Byzantine Literature of the Eleventh and Twelfth Centuries* (Cambridge, 1984).

Kennedy, George, *Greek Rhetoric under Christian Emperors* (Princeton NJ, 1963).

Knös, Börje, 'Qui est l'auteur de Callimaque et Chrysorrhoé?', *[Hellenika]*, 17 (1962), 274–95.

Kominis, Athanasios, *Gregorio Pardo* (Rome and Athens, 1960).

Kustas, George, 'The Function and Evolution of Byzantine Rhetoric', *Viator*, 1 (1970), pp. 53–73.

'The Literary Criticism of Photius: A Christian Definition of Style', *[Hellenika]*, 17 (1962), 132–69.

Studies in Byzantine Rhetoric [Analekta Vlatadon], 17 (Thessaloniki, 1973).

Lemerle, Paul, *Le Premier humanisme byzantin* (Paris, 1971); tr. H. Lindsay and A. Moffatt as *Byzantine Humanism* (Canberra, 1986).

Lindberg, Gertrud, *Studies in Hermogenes and Eustathios* (Lund, 1977).

'Eustathius on Homer: Some of his Approaches to the Text, Exemplified from his Comments on the First Book of the *Iliad*', *Eranos*, 83 (1985), 125–40.

Ljubarskij, Iakov, 'Antičnaia Ritorika v Vizantijskoje Kultur', in L. Freiberg (ed.), *[Antičnost i Vizantija]* (Moscow, 1975).

Mercati, Giovanni, *Notizie di Procoro e Demetrio Cidone, Manuele Caleca e Teodoro Meletiniota ad altri appunti per la storia della teologia e della letteratura bizantina del secolo XIV* (Vatican City, 1931).

Monfasani, J., *George of Trebizond: A Biography and a Study of his Rhetoric and Logic* (Leiden, 1976).

Mullett, Margaret, 'Aristocracy and Patronage in the Literary Circles of Comnenian Constantinople', in M. Angold (ed.), *The Byzantine Aristocracy: IX–XIII Centuries*, British Archaeological Reports, 221 (Oxford, 1984), pp. 173–201.

Pertusi, Agostino, *Fine di Bisanzio e fine del mondo: significato e ruolo storico delle profezie sulla caduta di Costantinopoli in oriente e in occidente* (Rome, 1988).

Ruether, R., *Gregory of Nazianzus: Rhetor and Philosopher* (Oxford, 1969).

Ševčenko, Ihor, *Études sur la polémique entre Théodore Métochite et Nicéphore Choumnos* (Brussels, 1952).

'Levels of Style in Byzantine Literature', *Jahrbuch der Österreichischen Byzantinistik*, 31 (1981), 289–312.

'A Shadow Outline of Virtue: The Classical Heritage of Greek Christianity', in K. Weitzmann (ed.), *Age of Spirituality: A Symposium* (New York, 1980), pp. 53–75.

Treadgold, W. T., *The Byzantine Revival: 780–832* (Stanford CA, 1988).

van Dieten, Jan-Louis, 'Die byzantinische Literatur – eine Literatur ohne Geschichte?', *Historische Zeitschrift*, 231 (1980), 101–9.

Wendel, Carl, 'Das unbekannte Schlußstück der Theogonie des Tzetzes', *Byzantinische Zeitschrift*, 40 (1940), 23–6.

Wilson, Nigel, *Basil the Great on the Value of Greek Literature* (London, 1975).

Scholars of Byzantium (London, 1983).

Index

841